# Collins
# Spanish
Dictionary

**HarperCollins**
Westerhill Road
Bishopbriggs
Glasgow
G64 2QT
Great Britain

www.collins.co.uk

Fourth Edition 2007

Reprint 10 9 8 7 6 5 4 3 2 1 0

© HarperCollins Publishers 1998, 2001, 2005, 2007
© Collins Bartholomew 2007

ISBN 978-0-00-725350-0

Collins® and Bank of English® are registered trademarks of HarperCollins Publishers Limited

A catalogue record for this book is available from the British Library

Art direction by Mark Thomson
Designed by Wolfgang Homola
Typeset by Davidson's Pre-Press, Glasgow

Printed in Italy by Rotolito Lombarda S.p.A.

**Acknowledgements**
We would like to thank those authors and publishers who kindly gave permission for copyright material to be used in the Collins Word Web. We would also like to thank Times Newspapers Ltd for providing valuable data.

MANAGING EDITOR
Maree Airlie

EDITORIAL COORDINATION
Joyce Littlejohn, Susie Beattie

EDITORS
Teresa Álvarez, Jeremy Butterfield, Cordelia Lilly, Fernando León Solís, Gerry Breslin, Malihé Forghani-Nowbari, Jane Horwood, Anna Jené Palat, Lesley Johnston, Victoria Ordóñez Diví, Carol Styles, Eduardo Vallejo, José María Ruiz Vaca

TECHNICAL SUPPORT
Thomas Callan

SERIES EDITOR
Lorna Knight

Our thanks to the following for their help in researching the project:
Maree Airlie, Teresa Álvarez, Phyllis Gautier, Janet Gough, Sharon Hunter, Mary James, Cordelia Lilly, Carol MacLeod, Jill McNair, Janet Chalmers

William Collins' dream of knowledge for all began with the publication of his first book in 1819. A self-educated mill worker, he not only enriched millions of lives, but also founded a flourishing publishing house. Today, staying true to this spirit, Collins books are packed with inspiration, innovation, and practical expertise. They place you at the centre of a world of possibility and give you exactly what you need to explore it.

Language is the key to this exploration, and at the heart of Collins Dictionaries is language as it is really used. New words, phrases, and meanings spring up every day, and all of them are captured and analysed by the Collins Word Web. Constantly updated, and with over 2.5 billion entries, this living language resource is unique to our dictionaries.

Words are tools for life. And a Collins Dictionary makes them work for you.

**Collins. Do more.**

# Contents

# Introduction

*Collins Easy Learning Spanish Dictionary* is an innovative dictionary designed specifically for anyone starting to learn Spanish. We are grateful to all those teachers who have contributed to its development by advising us on how to tailor it to the needs of their students. We also gratefully acknowledge the help of the examining boards, whom we have consulted throughout this project, and whose word lists and exam papers we carefully studied when compiling this dictionary.

Free downloadable resources are now available for teachers and learners of Spanish at **www.collinsdictionaries.com/easyresources**.

### Note on trademarks

Entered words which we have reason to believe constitute trademarks have been designated as such. However, neither the presence nor the absence of such designation should be regarded as affecting the legal status of any trademark.

# Dictionary skills

Using a dictionary is a skill you can improve with practice and by following some basic guidelines. This section gives you a detailed explanation of how to use this dictionary to ensure you get the most out of it.

The answers to the questions in this section are on page 16.

## Make sure you look on the right side of the dictionary

The Spanish – English side comes first, followed by the English – Spanish. At the side of the page, you will see a tab with either **Spanish – English** or **English – Spanish**, so you know immediately if you're looking up the side you want.

1 **Which side of the dictionary would you look up to translate 'la bicicleta'?**

## Finding the word you want

When looking for a word, for example **feliz**, look at the first letter – **f** – and find the **F** section in the Spanish – English side. At the top of each page, you'll find the first and last words on that page. When you find the page with the words starting with **fe**, scan down the page until you find the word you want. Remember that even if a word has an accent on it, for example **fórmula**, it makes no difference to the alphabetical order. The exception to this rule is ñ (*n tilde*), which is treated as a separate letter in Spanish, so that *leña* follows *lento*.

2 **On which page will you find the word – 'hermana'?**
3 **Which comes first – 'francesa' or 'francés'?**

To help you expand your vocabulary, we have also suggested possible alternatives in the WORD POWER features at the most common adjectives in English – try looking up **big** on page 24 and learning some of the words you could use.

## Make sure you look at the right entry

An entry is made up of a **word**, its translations, and, often, example phrases to show you how to use the translations. If there is more than one entry for the same word, then there is a note to tell you so. Look at the following example entries:

**flat** ADJECTIVE
▷ *see also* **flat** NOUN
llano (FEM llana)
□ a flat surface  una superficie llana
■ **flat shoes** zapatos bajos
■ **I've got a flat tyre.** Tengo una rueda desinflada.

**flat** NOUN
▷ *see also* **flat** ADJECTIVE
el piso  (el apartamento *Latin America*)

4 **Which of the two entries above will help you translate the phrase *'My car has a flat tyre'*? Look for the two clues which are there to help you:**
> **an example similar to what you want to say**
> **the word** ADJECTIVE

**Look out for information notes which have this symbol on the left-hand side. They will give you guidance on grammatical points, and tell you about differences between Spanish and British life.**

## Choosing the right translation

The main translation of a word is shown on a new line and is underlined to make it stand out from the rest of the entry. If there is more than one main translation for a word, each one is numbered. On the English – Spanish side, Latin American equivalents are shown in brackets after the main translation, and are labelled *Latin America*.

Often you will see phrases in light blue, preceded by a white square □. These help you to choose the translation you want because they show how the translation they follow can be used.

**5 Use the phrases given at the entry *'hard'* to help you translate: *'This bread is hard'*.**

Words often have more than one meaning and more than one translation. For example, a **pool** can be a puddle, a pond or a swimming pool; **pool** can also be a game. When you are translating from English into Spanish, be careful to choose the Spanish word that has the particular meaning you want. The dictionary offers you a lot of help with this. Look at the following entry:

**pool** NOUN
1 el estanque *(pond)*
2 la piscina *(swimming pool)*
3 el billar americano *(game)*
   ▪ **a pool table** una mesa de billar
   ▪ **the pools** las quinielas ▫ I do the pools every week. Juego a las quinielas todas las semanas.

The underlining highlights all the main translations, the numbers tell you that there is more than one possible translation and the words in brackets in *italics* after the translations help you choose the translation you want.

**6 How would you translate *'I like playing pool'*?**

**Never take the first translation you see without looking at the others. Always look to see if there is more than one translation underlined.**

Phrases in **bold type** preceded by a blue or black square ▪/▪ are phrases which are particularly common or important. Sometimes these phrases have a completely different translation from the main translation; sometimes the translation is the same. For example:

el **acuerdo** NOUN
agreement
   ▫ llegar a un acuerdo to reach an agreement
   ▪ **estar de acuerdo con alguien** to agree with somebody
   ▪ **ponerse de acuerdo** to agree ▫ Al final no nos pusimos de acuerdo. In the end we couldn't agree. ▫ Nos pusimos de acuerdo para prepararle una bienvenida. We agreed to organize a welcome for him.
   ▪ **¡De acuerdo!** All right!

When you look up a word, make sure you look beyond the main translations to see if the entry includes any **bold phrases**.

7  **Look up 'ir' to help you translate the sentence 'Voy a casa mañana'?**

## Making use of the phrases in the dictionary

Sometimes when you look up a word you will find not only the word, but the exact phrase you want. For example, you might want to say '*What's the date today?*'. Look up **date** and you will find that exact phrase and its translation.

Sometimes you have to adapt what you find in the dictionary. If you want to say '*I ate a sandwich*' and look up **eat** you will find:

to **eat** VERB
comer
□ Would you like something to eat?
¿Quieres comer algo?

You have to substitute **comí** for the infinitive form **comer**. You will often have to adapt the infinitive in this way, adding the correct ending and choosing the present, future or past form. For help with this, look at the verb tables. On the **Spanish – English** side of the dictionary, you will notice that verbs are followed by a number in square brackets, which correspond to verb tables on pages 19-30 in the middle section of this dictionary. **Estudiar** is a verb ending in –ar so it follows the same pattern as verb number [25] **hablar**, which is set out in full on page 24.

8  **How would you say '*I don't eat meat*'?**

Phrases containing nouns and adjectives also need to be adapted. You may need to make the noun plural, or the adjective feminine or plural. Remember that some Spanish nouns and adjectives change their spelling in the feminine or plural and that this is shown in the entry.

9  **How would you say '*The boys are Spanish*'?**

## Don't overuse the dictionary

It takes time to look up words so try to avoid using the dictionary unnecessarily, especially in exams. Think carefully about what you want to say and see if you can put it another way, using words you already know. To rephrase things you can:

> Use a word with a similar meaning. This is particularly easy with adjectives, as there are a lot of words which mean *good, bad, big* etc and you're sure to know at least one.

> Use negatives: if the cake you made was a total disaster, you could just say it wasn't very good.

> Use particular examples instead of general terms. If you are asked to describe the sports *facilities* in your area, and time is short, you could say something like *'In our town there is a swimming pool and a football ground.'*

**10** **How could you say *'Argentina is huge'* without looking up the word *'huge'*?**

You can also often guess the meaning of a Spanish word by using others to give you a clue. If you see the sentence *'María lee un buen libro'*, you may not know the meaning of the word **lee**, but you know it's a verb because it's preceded by **María**. Therefore it must be something you can do to a book: **read**. So the translation is: *María is reading a good book.*

**11** **Try NOT to use your dictionary to work out the meaning of the sentence 'La chica escribe una carta a su amiga en español'.**

# Parts of speech

If you look up the word **flat**, you will see that there are two entries for this word as it can be a noun or an adjective. It helps to choose correctly between entries if you know how to recognize these different types of words.

## Nouns and pronouns

Nouns often appear with words like *a, the, this, that, my, your* and *his.* They can be singular (abbreviated to SING in the dictionary):

*his* **dog**      *her* **cat**      *a* **street**

or plural (abbreviated to PL in the dictionary):

*the* **facts**      *those* **people**      *his* **shoes**      *our* **holidays**

They can be the subject of a verb:

**Vegetables** *are good for you*

or the object of a verb:

*I play* **tennis**

Words like *I, me, you, he, she, him, her* and *they* are pronouns. They can be used instead of nouns. You can refer to a person as *he* or *she* or to a thing as *it.*

**I bought my mother a box of chocolates.**

**12  Which three words in this sentence are nouns?**

**13  Which of the nouns is plural?**

**14  Which word is a pronoun?**

Spanish nouns are either masculine or feminine (abbreviated to MASC and FEM). Masculine nouns are shown by **el**:

**el** *hombre*      **el** *gato*      **el** *fútbol*

Feminine nouns are shown by **la**:

**la** *mujer*      **la** *economía*      **la** *fábrica*

The plural forms of **el** and **la** are **los** and **las**. The plural of most Spanish nouns is made by adding **s** if the word ends in a vowel, or **es** if it ends in a consonant:

*los gatos*        *las mujeres*

## Adjectives

**Flat** can be an adjective as well as a noun. Adjectives describe nouns: your tyre can be **flat**, you can have a pair of **flat** shoes.

**15** **In which sentence is *'dark'* an adjective?**
   *I'm afraid of the dark.*
   *The girl has dark hair.*

Spanish adjectives can be masculine or feminine, singular or plural, depending on the noun they describe:

un chico **guapo** (MASC SING)
una chica **guapa** (FEM SING: replace -**o** of masculine with -**a**)
unos chicos **guapos** (MASC PL = masculine singular + **s**)
unas chicas **guapas** (FEM PL = feminine singular + **s**)

The masculine and feminine singular forms of regular adjectives are shown on both sides of the dictionary. So if you want to find out what kind of houses **unas casas viejas** are, look under **viejo**.

There are separate masculine and feminine, singular and plural forms for irregular adjectives of nationality, and those ending in -**án**, -**ín**, -**ón**, eg **español** MASCULINE SINGULAR, **española**, FEMININE SINGULAR, **españoles** MASCULINE PLURAL, **españolas** FEMININE PLURAL.

Adjectives ending in -**or** also follow the above pattern unless they are comparatives. The feminine is shown in the dictionary for adjectives of this type.

**hablador** (FEM **habladora**) ADJECTIVE        **talkative** ADJECTIVE
**1** chatty                                        hablador (FEM habladora)
**2** gossipy

Other adjectives ending in a consonant do not have a separate feminine form, but do change in the plural, eg **azul** MASCULINE and FEMININE SINGULAR, **azul<u>es</u>** MASCULINE and FEMININE PLURAL.

**feliz** (FEM **feliz**, PL **felices**) ADJECTIVE
<u>happy</u>
□ Se la ve muy feliz.  She looks very happy.
■ **¡Feliz cumpleaños!**  Happy birthday!
■ **¡Feliz Año Nuevo!**  Happy New Year!
■ **¡Felices Navidades!**  Happy Christmas!

**happy** ADJECTIVE
<u>feliz</u> (FEM feliz, PL felices)
□ Janet looks happy.  Janet parece feliz.
■ **to be happy with something**  estar contento con algo  □ I'm very happy with your work.  Estoy muy contento con tu trabajo.
■ **Happy birthday!**  ¡Feliz cumpleaños!
■ **a happy ending**  un final feliz

If the masculine form of an adjective ends in -**e** or -**a**, the feminine form is the same, and both the masculine and feminine plurals are formed by adding -**s** to the masculine, eg **verde** MASCULINE and FEMININE SINGULAR, **verde<u>s</u>** MASCULINE and FEMININE PLURAL. Some adjectives remain the same whether they're masculine, feminine or plural. This is also shown in the dictionary:

el **rosa**  ADJECTIVE, NOUN
<u>pink</u>
□ Va vestida de rosa.  She's wearing pink.
■ **Llevaba unos calcetines rosa.**  He was wearing pink socks.

# Verbs

*She's going to record the programme for me.*
*His time in the race was a new world record.*

**Record** is a verb in the first sentence. In the second, it is a noun.

One way to recognize a verb is that it frequently comes with a pronoun such as **I**, **you** or **she**, or with somebody's name. Verbs can relate to the present, the past or the future. They have a number of different forms to show this: **I'm going** (present), **he will go** (future), and **Nicola went by herself** (past). Often verbs appear with **to**: **they promised to go**. This basic form of the verb is called the infinitive.

In this dictionary, verbs are preceded by 'to', so you can identify them at a glance. No matter which of the four previous examples you want to translate, you should look up 'to **go**', not '**going**' or '**went**'. If you want to translate '**I thought**', look up 'to **think**'.

**16** **What would you look up to translate the verbs in these phrases?**

*I came*    *she's crying*    *they've done it*    *he's out*

Verbs have different endings in Spanish, depending on whether you are talking about **yo**, **tú**, **nosotros** etc: **yo hablo**, **tú hablas**, **nosotros hablamos** etc. They also have different forms for the present, future, past etc. **Hablamos** (*we speak* = present), **hemos hablado** (*we spoke* = past), **hablaremos** (*we will speak* = future). **Hablar** is the infinitive and is the form that appears in the dictionary.

Sometimes the verb changes completely between the infinitive form and the **yo**, **tú**, **él** etc form. For example, *to give* is **dar**, but *I give* is **doy**, and **digo** comes from **decir** (*to say*).

On pages 24-30 of the middle section of this dictionary, you will find 7 of the most important regular and irregular Spanish verbs shown in full. On pages 19-23, you will find a list of the main forms of other key Spanish verbs. On the **Spanish – English** side of the dictionary, each Spanish verb has a number beside it – if you look this number up in the verb table section on pages 19-30 you will find the verb forms for that type of verb. Irregular Spanish verbs are marked in the dictionary with an asterisk.

to **fulfil** VERB
realizar*
□ He fulfilled his dream to visit China. Realizó su sueño de viajar a China.
■ **to fulfil a promise** cumplir una promesa

**ir\*** VERBO [27]
**1** to go
□ Anoche fuimos al cine. We went to the cinema last night. □ ¿A qué colegio vas? What school do you go to?
■ **ir de vacaciones** to go on holiday
■ **ir a por** to go and get

**17** **Which verb pattern does the verb estudiar follow?**

## Adverbs

An adverb is a word that describes a verb or an adjective:

*Write **soon**.*                     *Check your work **carefully**.*

*The film was **very** good.*

In the sentence *'The swimming pool is open daily'*, **daily** is an adverb describing the adjective **open**. In the phrase *'my daily routine'*, **daily** is an adjective describing the noun **routine**. We use the same word in English for both adjective and adverb forms, but to get the right Spanish translation, it is important to know if it's being used as an adjective or an adverb. When you look up **daily** you find:

**daily** ADJECTIVE, ADVERB
1 diario
   □ daily life  la vida diaria   □ It's part of my daily
   routine.  Forma parte de mi rutina diaria.
   ■ **a daily paper**  un periódico
2 todos los días
   □ The pool is open daily.  La piscina abre todos
   los días.

The examples show you **daily** being used as an adjective and as an adverb and will help you choose the right Spanish translation.

**Take the sentence *'The menu changes daily'*.**
18 **Is *'daily'* an adverb or an adjective here?**

## Prepositions

Prepositions are words like **for**, **with** and **across**, which are followed by nouns or pronouns:

*I've got a present **for** David.    Come **with** me.    He ran **across** the road.*

*The party's **over**.*
*The shop's just **over** the road.*

19 **Which sentence shows a preposition followed by a noun?**

# Answers

1 the Spanish side
2 on page 159
3 **francés** comes first
4 the first (ADJECTIVE) entry
5 **Este pan está duro.**
6 **Me gusta jugar al billar americano.**
7 **I'm going home tomorrow.**
8 **No como carne.**
9 **Los niños son españoles.**
10 **Argentina es muy grande.**
11 **The girl is writing a letter to her friend in Spanish.**
12 **mother**, **box** and **chocolates** are nouns
13 **chocolates** is plural
14 **I** is a pronoun
15 in the second sentence
16 to **come**, to **cry**, to **do**, to **be**
17 **hablar**, number [25]
18 daily is an **adverb**
19 the second sentence

# Aa

**a** *(a + el = al)* PREPOSITION
1 to
□ Fueron a Madrid. They went to Madrid.
■ **Me caí al río.** I fell into the river.
■ **Se subieron al tejado.** They climbed onto the roof.
■ **Marta llegó a la oficina.** Marta arrived at the office.
■ **Está a 15 km de aquí.** It's 15 km from here.
2 at
□ a las 10 at 10 o'clock □ a medianoche at midnight □ a los 24 años at the age of 24 □ Íbamos a más de 90 km por hora. We were going at over 90 km an hour.
■ **Estamos a 9 de julio.** It's the 9th of July.
■ **Los huevos están a 1,50 euros la docena.** Eggs are 1.50 euros a dozen.
■ **una vez a la semana** once a week □ Voy a verle. I'm going to see him. □ Vine a decírtelo. I came to tell you. □ Me obligaban a comer. They forced me to eat.
■ **Al verlo, lo reconocí inmediatamente.** When I saw him, I recognized him immediately.
■ **Nos cruzamos al salir.** We bumped into each other as we were going out. □ Se lo di a Ana. I gave it to Ana. □ Le enseñé a Pablo el libro que me dejaste. I showed Pablo the book you lent me.
■ **Se lo compré a él.** I bought it from him.
■ **Vi a Juan.** I saw Juan.
■ **Llamé al médico.** I called the doctor.
■ **Gira a la derecha.** Turn right.
■ **Me voy a casa.** I'm going home.
■ **¡A comer!** Lunch is ready!

la **abadía** NOUN
abbey (PL abbeys)

**abajo** ADVERB
1 below
□ Los platos y las tazas están abajo. The plates and cups are below. □ La montaña no parece tan alta desde abajo. The mountain doesn't seem so high from below.
■ **Mete las cervezas abajo del todo.** Put the beers at the bottom.
■ **El estante de abajo.** The bottom shelf.
■ **La parte de abajo del contenedor.** The bottom of the container.
2 downstairs
□ Abajo están la cocina y el salón. The kitchen and lounge are downstairs. □ Hay una fiesta en el piso de abajo. There's a party in the flat downstairs.
■ **más abajo** further down
■ **ir calle abajo** to go down the street
■ **Todos los bolsos son de 50 euros para abajo.** All the bags are 50 euros or under.
■ **abajo de** *(Latin America)* under

**abandonado** (FEM abandonada) ADJECTIVE
■ **un pueblo abandonado** a deserted village

**abandonar** VERB [25]
1 to leave
□ Decidieron abandonar el país. They decided to leave the country.
■ **Abandonó a su familia.** He deserted his family.
■ **Mucha gente abandona a sus perros en Navidad.** A lot of people abandon their dogs at Christmas.
2 to give up
□ Tuve que abandonar la idea de comprarme otro coche. I had to give up the idea of buying another car.

el **abanico** NOUN
fan

**abarrotado** (FEM abarrotada) ADJECTIVE
packed
□ abarrotado de gente packed with people

la **abarrotería** NOUN *(Mexico)*
grocer's (PL grocers' shops)

los **abarrotes** NOUN *(Mexico, Chile)*
groceries

**abastecer\*** VERB [12]
■ **abastecer de algo a alguien** to supply somebody with something
■ **Nos abastecimos bien de comida para el viaje.** We stocked up with food for the trip.

el **abdomen** NOUN
stomach

los **abdominales** NOUN
sit-ups
□ hacer abdominales to do sit-ups
el **abecedario** NOUN
alphabet
la **abeja** NOUN
bee
el **abeto** NOUN
fir
**abierto** VERB
▷ see also **abierto** ADJECTIVE ▷ see **abrir**
**abierto** (FEM **abierta**) ADJECTIVE
▷ see also **abierto** VERB
1 open
□ ¿Están abiertas las tiendas? Are the shops open?
2 on
□ No dejes el gas abierto. Don't leave the gas on.
el **abogado**, la **abogada** NOUN
lawyer
**abolir** VERB
to abolish
**abollar** VERB [25]
to dent
□ Me han abollado el coche. Someone has dented my car.
■ **abollarse** to get dented
**abombarse** VERB [25] (Latin America)
to go bad
**abonar** VERB [25]
1 to pay
□ abonar dinero en una cuenta to pay money into an account
2 to fertilize
□ Hay que abonar el terreno antes de sembrar. The land has to be fertilized before sowing.
■ **abonarse a 1** to take out a subscription to **2** to join
el **abono** NOUN
1 fertilizer
2 season ticket
**abortar** VERB [25]
1 to have an abortion
2 to miscarry
el **aborto** NOUN
1 abortion
2 miscarriage
**abrasar** VERB [25]
to burn
□ El fuego le abrasó las manos. The fire burned his hands.
■ **abrasarse** to be burned □ Mucha gente se abrasó viva en el incendio. A lot of people were burned alive in the fire.
**abrazar*** VERB [13]
to hug

□ Al verme me abrazó. He hugged me when he saw me.
■ **¡Abrázame fuerte!** Give me a big hug!
■ **abrazarse** to hug □ Se abrazaron y se besaron. They hugged and kissed.
el **abrazo** NOUN
hug
□ ¡Dame un abrazo! Give me a hug!
■ **Siempre están dándose besos y abrazos.** They're always hugging and kissing.
■ **'un abrazo'** 'with best wishes'
el **abrebotellas** (PL los **abrebotellas**) NOUN
bottle opener
el **abrelatas** (PL los **abrelatas**) NOUN
tin opener
la **abreviatura** NOUN
abbreviation
el **abridor** NOUN
1 bottle opener
2 tin opener
**abrigar*** VERB [37]
■ **Esta chaqueta abriga mucho.** This jacket's great for keeping warm.
■ **Ponte algo que te abrigue.** Put something warm on.
■ **Abriga bien al niño, que hace frío.** Wrap the baby up well – it's cold.
■ **abrigarse** to wrap up well
el **abrigo** NOUN
coat
□ un abrigo de pieles a fur coat
■ **ropa de abrigo** warm clothing
**abril** MASC NOUN
April
□ en abril in April □ Nació el 20 de abril. He was born on 20 April.
**abrir*** VERB [58]
1 to open
□ Las tiendas abren a las diez. The shops open at ten o'clock. □ Abre la ventana. Open the window.
■ **¡Abre, soy yo!** Open the door, it's me!
2 to turn on
□ ¿Has abierto el gas? Have you turned the gas on?
■ **abrirse** to open □ De repente se abrió la puerta. Suddenly the door opened.
**abrocharse** VERB [25]
to do up
□ Abróchate la camisa. Do your shirt up.
■ **Abróchense los cinturones.** Please fasten your seatbelts.
**absoluto** (FEM **absoluta**) ADJECTIVE
absolute
□ Nos dio garantía absoluta. He gave us an absolute guarantee.
■ **La operación fue un éxito absoluto.**

The operation was a complete success.

■ **en absoluto** at all □ ¿Te molesta que fume? — En absoluto. Do you mind if I smoke? — Not at all. □ nada en absoluto nothing at all

**absorber** VERB [8]
to absorb

**abstemio** (FEM **abstemia**) ADJECTIVE
teetotal

□ Soy abstemio. I'm teetotal.

la **abstención** (PL las **abstenciones**) NOUN
abstention

**abstenerse\*** VERB [53]
to abstain

□ Yo me abstengo. I'm abstaining.

■ **abstenerse de hacer algo** to refrain from doing something

**abstracto** (FEM **abstracta**) ADJECTIVE
abstract

**absurdo** (FEM **absurda**) ADJECTIVE
absurd

■ **lo absurdo es que** ... the absurd thing is that ...

la **abuela** NOUN
grandmother

□ mi abuela my grandmother

■ ¿Dónde está la abuela? Where's Gran?

el **abuelo** NOUN
grandfather

□ mi abuelo my grandfather

■ ¿Dónde está el abuelo? Where's Grandad?

■ **mis abuelos** my grandparents

**abultado** (FEM **abultada**) ADJECTIVE
bulky

**abultar** VERB [25]
to be bulky

□ No abulta mucho. It isn't very bulky.

■ **Tus cosas apenas abultan.** Your things hardly take up any space at all.

**abundante** (FEM **abundante**) ADJECTIVE
1 plenty of

□ Habrá comida y bebida abundante. There'll be plenty of food and drink.

2 enormous

□ El año pasado tuvimos abundantes pérdidas. We had enormous losses last year.

**aburrido** (FEM **aburrida**) ADJECTIVE
1 bored

□ Estaba aburrida y me marché. I was bored so I left.

2 boring

□ una película muy aburrida a very boring film □ No seas aburrida y vente al cine. Don't be boring and come to the film.

3 tired

□ Estaba aburrido de esperarte, así que me

fui. I was tired of waiting for you, so I left.

el **aburrimiento** NOUN

■ ¡Qué aburrimiento! What a bore this is!

■ **Estoy muerto de aburrimiento.** I'm bored stiff.

**aburrirse** VERB [58]
to get bored

□ Me aburro viendo la tele. I get bored watching television.

**abusar** VERB [25]

■ **abusar de alguien 1** to take advantage of somebody **2** to abuse somebody

■ **Está bien beber de vez en cuando pero sin abusar.** Drinking every so often is fine as long as you don't overdo it.

■ **No conviene abusar del aceite en las comidas.** You shouldn't use too much oil in food.

■ **Abusó de nuestra hospitalidad.** He abused our hospitality.

el **abuso** NOUN
abuse

□ el abuso de las drogas drug abuse

■ **los abusos sexuales** sexual abuse sing

■ **Lo que han hecho me parece un abuso.** I think what they've done is outrageous.

**acá** ADVERB
here

□ ¡Vente para acá! Come over here!

■ **Hay que ponerlo más acá.** You'll have to bring it closer.

**acabar** VERB [25]
to finish

□ Cuando acabe esta cerveza me voy. When I've finished this beer I'm going. □ Ayer acabé de pintar la valla. Yesterday I finished painting the fence.

■ **acabar con 1** to put an end to □ Hay que acabar con tanto desorden. We must put an end to all this confusion. **2** to finish

□ Hemos acabado con todas las provisiones. We've finished all our provisions.

■ **Acabo de ver a tu padre.** I've just seen your father. □ Acababa de entrar cuando sonó el teléfono. I had just come in when the phone rang.

■ **acabarse** to run out □ La impresora te avisa cuando se acaba el papel. The printer tells you when the paper runs out. □ Se me acabó el tabaco. I ran out of cigarettes.

la **academia** NOUN
school

□ una academia de idiomas a language school

■ **una academia militar** a military academy

**académico** (FEM **académica**) ADJECTIVE
academic

□ el curso académico the academic year

la **acampada** NOUN
■ ir de acampada to go camping

**acampar** VERB [25]
to camp

el **acantilado** NOUN
cliff

**acariciar** VERB [25]
1 to stroke
2 to caress

**acaso** ADVERB
■ ¿Acaso tengo yo la culpa? Is it MY fault?
■ por si acaso just in case
■ No necesito nada; si acaso, un poco de leche. I don't need anything; well maybe a little milk.
■ Si acaso lo vieras, dile que me llame. If you should see him, tell him to call me.

**acatarrarse** VERB [25]
to catch cold

**acceder** VERB [8]
■ acceder a 1 to agree to □ Al final accedió a venir. In the end he agreed to come. 2 to gain access to

**accesible** (FEM accesible) ADJECTIVE
1 accessible
□ Es un lugar sólo accesible por barco. The place is only accessible by boat.
2 approachable
□ Es una persona muy accesible. He's very approachable.

el **acceso** NOUN
access
□ La casa tiene acceso por delante y por detrás. Access to the house is from the front and from the rear. □ Tiene acceso a información confidencial. He has access to confidential information.
■ Quieren mejorar los accesos al aeropuerto. They want to improve access to the airport.
■ las pruebas de acceso a la universidad university entrance exams

el **accesorio** NOUN
accessories
□ accesorios para el automóvil car accessories

**accidentado** (FEM accidentada) ADJECTIVE
1 rough
2 eventful

el **accidente** NOUN
accident
□ los accidentes de trabajo accidents in the workplace
■ Han tenido un accidente. They've had a car accident.

la **acción** (PL las acciones) NOUN
1 action

□ una película llena de acción an action-packed film
■ entrar en acción to go into action
2 share
□ comprar acciones de una empresa to buy shares in a company

el/la **accionista** NOUN
shareholder

el **aceite** NOUN
oil
■ el aceite de girasol sunflower oil
■ el aceite de oliva olive oil

**aceitoso** (FEM aceitosa) ADJECTIVE
oily

la **aceituna** NOUN
olive
□ aceitunas rellenas stuffed olives

el **acelerador** NOUN
accelerator

**acelerar** VERB [25]
to accelerate
□ Aceleré para adelantarlos. I accelerated to overtake them.
■ ¡Acelera, que no llegamos! Speed up or we'll never get there!
■ acelerar el paso to walk faster

las **acelgas** NOUN
spinach beet sing

el **acento** NOUN
1 accent
□ 'Té' lleva acento cuando significa 'bebida'. 'Té' has an accent when it means 'drink'. □ Tiene un acento cerrado del sur. He has a strong southern accent.
2 stress
□ ¿Qué sílaba lleva el acento en 'microphone'? Which syllable is the stress on in 'microphone'?

**acentuarse\*** VERB [1]
to have an accent
□ No se acentúa. It doesn't have an accent.

**aceptable** (FEM aceptable) ADJECTIVE
acceptable

**aceptar** VERB [25]
to accept
□ Acepté su invitación. I accepted his invitation. □ Cuesta aceptar la derrota. It's hard to accept defeat.
■ aceptar hacer algo to agree to do something

la **acequia** NOUN
irrigation channel

la **acera** NOUN
pavement

**acerca** ADVERB
■ acerca de about □ un documental acerca de la fauna africana a documentary about African wildlife

**acercar\*** VERB [48]
1 to pass
□ ¿Me acercas los alicates? Could you pass me the pliers?
2 to bring over
□ Acerca la silla. Bring your chair over here.
■ ¿Acerco más la cama a la ventana? Shall I put the bed nearer the window?
■ Nos acercaron al aeropuerto. They gave us a lift to the airport.
■ acercarse 1 to come closer □ Acércate, que te vea. Come closer so that I can see you. 2 to go over □ Me acerqué a la ventana. I went over to the window.
□ Acércate a la tienda y trae una botella de agua. Go over to the shop and get a bottle of water.
■ Ya se acerca la Navidad. Christmas is getting near.

el **acero** NOUN
steel
□ acero inoxidable stainless steel

**acertar\*** VERB [39]
1 to get...right
□ He acertado todas las respuestas. I got all the answers right.
■ No acerté. I got it wrong.
■ Creo que hemos acertado con estas cortinas. I think these curtains were a good choice.
2 to guess
□ Si aciertas cuántos caramelos hay, te los regalo todos. If you guess how many sweets there are, I'll give you them all.
■ Acerté en el blanco. I hit the target.

**ácido** (FEM **ácida**) ADJECTIVE
acid

el **ácido** NOUN
acid

**acierto** VERB ▷ see **acertar**
el **acierto** NOUN
1 right answer
□ Tuve más aciertos que fallos en el examen. I got more right answers than wrong ones in the exam.
2 good idea
□ Fue un acierto ir de vacaciones a la montaña. Going to the mountains on holiday was a good idea.

**aclarar** VERB [25]
1 to rinse
□ Aclara la ropa antes de tenderla. Rinse the washing before hanging it out.
2 to clear up
□ Necesito que me aclares unas dudas. I need you to clear up some doubts for me.
□ No me iré hasta que no se aclare este asunto. I shan't go until this business is

cleared up.
■ Con tantos números no me aclaro. There are so many numbers that I can't get it straight.

el **acné** NOUN
acne

**acobardarse** VERB [25]
■ No se acobarda por nada. He isn't frightened by anything.

**acogedor** (FEM **acogedora**) ADJECTIVE
cosy
□ un cuarto muy acogedor a very cosy room

**acoger\*** VERB [7]
to receive
□ La ciudad acoge todos los años a miles de visitantes. The city receives thousands of visitors every year.
■ Me acogieron muy bien en Estados Unidos. I was made very welcome in the United States.

la **acogida** NOUN
reception
□ una fría acogida a cold reception
■ una calurosa acogida a warm welcome
■ tener buena acogida to be well received

**acomodado** (FEM **acomodada**) ADJECTIVE
well-off

el **acomodador** NOUN
usher

la **acomodadora** NOUN
usherette

**acompañar** VERB [25]
1 to come with
□ Si vas al centro te acompaño. If you're going to the centre of town I'll come with you.
2 to go with
□ Me pidió que la acompañara a la estación. She asked me to go to the station with her.
■ ¿Quieres que te acompañe a casa? Would you like me to see you home?
3 to stay with
□ Me acompañó hasta que llegó el autobús. He stayed with me until the bus arrived.

**aconsejar** VERB [25]
1 to advise
■ aconsejar a alguien que haga algo to advise somebody to do something
■ Te aconsejo que lo hagas. I'd advise you to do it.
2 to recommend
□ Debe de ser bueno cuando lo aconseja el médico. It must be good if the doctor recommends it.

el **acontecimiento** NOUN
event

**acordar\*** VERB [11]
to agree on

5

□ Acordamos un precio y unas condiciones. We agreed on a price and terms.
■ **acordar hacer algo** to agree to do something

**acordarse\*** VERB [11]
to remember

□ Ahora mismo no me acuerdo. Right now I can't remember.
■ **acordarse de** to remember □ ¿Te acuerdas de mí? Do you remember me?
□ Acuérdate de cerrar la puerta con llave. Remember to lock the door.
■ **acordarse de haber hecho algo** to remember doing something

el **acordeón** (PL los **acordeones**) NOUN
accordion

**acostado** (FEM **acostada**) ADJECTIVE
■ **estar acostado** to be in bed

**acostarse\*** VERB [11]
1 to lie down
2 to go to bed
■ **acostarse con alguien** to go to bed with somebody

**acostumbrarse** VERB [25]
■ **acostumbrarse a** to get used to □ No me acostumbro a la vida en la ciudad. I can't get used to city life.
■ **acostumbrarse a hacer algo** to get used to doing something □ Ya me he acostumbrado a trabajar de noche. I've got used to working at night now.

el/la **acróbata** NOUN
acrobat

la **actitud** NOUN
attitude

la **actividad** NOUN
activity (PL activities)

**activo** (FEM **activa**) ADJECTIVE
active

□ Es una mujer muy activa. She's a very active woman.

el **acto** NOUN
1 act
□ Romper el carnet fue un acto de rebeldía. Tearing his ID card up was an act of rebellion.
2 ceremony (PL ceremonies)
□ Grandes personalidades acudieron al acto. There were some important people at the ceremony.
■ **acto seguido** immediately afterwards
□ Acto seguido la gente echó a correr. Immediately afterwards people began running.
■ **en el acto** instantly
■ **Te arreglan tus zapatos en el acto.** They will repair your shoes while you wait.

el **actor** NOUN

actor

la **actriz** (PL las **actrices**) NOUN
actress (PL actresses)

la **actuación** (PL las **actuaciones**) NOUN
1 performance
□ Fue una actuación muy buena. It was a very good performance.
2 gig
□ Esta noche tenemos una actuación en el Café del Jazz. Tonight we're doing a gig at the Café del Jazz.

**actual** (FEM **actual**) ADJECTIVE
present
□ la situación actual del país the country's present situation
■ **uno de los mejores pintores del arte actual** one of the greatest painters of today

**LANGUAGE TIP** Be careful! The Spanish word **actual** does not mean **actual**.

la **actualidad** NOUN
■ **un repaso a la actualidad nacional** a round-up of the national news
■ **un tema de gran actualidad** a very topical issue
■ **en la actualidad** 1 currently □ Hay en la actualidad más de 2 millones de parados. There are currently over 2 million unemployed. 2 nowadays □ Eso ya no ocurre en la actualidad. That doesn't happen nowadays.

**actualmente** ADVERB
1 nowadays
□ Actualmente apenas se utilizan las máquinas de escribir. Typewriters are hardly used nowadays.
2 currently
□ Soy geólogo, pero actualmente estoy en paro. I'm a geologist but I'm currently out of work.

**LANGUAGE TIP** Be careful! **actualmente** does not mean **actually**.

**actuar\*** VERB [1]
1 to act
□ Es difícil actuar con naturalidad delante de las cámaras. It's hard to act naturally in front of the cameras.
■ **Hay que actuar con cautela.** We'll have to be cautious.
■ **No comprendo tu forma de actuar.** I can't understand your behaviour.
■ **No actuó en esa película.** He wasn't in that film.
2 to perform
□ Hoy actúan en el Café del Jazz. Today they'll be performing at the Café del Jazz.

la **acuarela** NOUN
watercolour

el **acuario** NOUN
aquarium

**Acuario** MASC NOUN
Aquarius

■ **Soy acuario.** I'm Aquarius.

**acuático** (FEM **acuática**) ADJECTIVE
■ **esquí acuático** water skiing
■ **aves acuáticas** waterfowl *pl*

**acudir** VERB [58]
1 to go
  □ Acudieron en su ayuda. They went to her
  aid. □ Acudió a un amigo en busca de
  consejo. He went to a friend for advice.
  ■ **No tengo a quien acudir.** I have no one
  to turn to.
  ■ **acudir a una cita** to keep an
  appointment
2 to come
  □ El perro acude cuando lo llamo. The dog
  comes when I call.

**acuerdo** VERB ▷ *see* acordar

el **acuerdo** NOUN
agreement
  □ llegar a un acuerdo to reach an
  agreement
  ■ **estar de acuerdo con alguien** to agree
  with somebody
  ■ **ponerse de acuerdo** to agree □ Al final
  no nos pusimos de acuerdo. In the end we
  couldn't agree. □ Nos pusimos de acuerdo
  para prepararle una bienvenida. We agreed
  to organize a welcome for him.
  ■ **¡De acuerdo!** All right!

la **acupuntura** NOUN
acupuncture

**acurrucarse*** VERB [25]
to curl up

**acusar** VERB [25]
1 to accuse
  □ Su novia lo acusaba de mentiroso. His
  girlfriend accused him of being a liar.
  ■ **Los otros te acusan a ti de haber roto el
  jarrón.** The others say it was you who broke
  the vase.
2 to charge
  □ Me acusan de homicidio. They're
  charging me with homicide.

**acústico** (FEM **acústica**) ADJECTIVE
acoustic
  □ una guitarra acústica an acoustic guitar

**adaptar** VERB [25]
to adapt
  □ Es la misma receta pero adaptada. It's the
  same recipe, but I've adapted it.
  ■ **adaptarse** to adapt □ No consigo
  adaptarme a la vida en el campo. I can't
  seem to adapt to country life.

**adecuado** (FEM **adecuada**) ADJECTIVE

1 suitable
  □ No es la ropa más adecuada para ir de
  boda. They aren't the most suitable clothes
  to wear to a wedding.
2 right
  □ Has entrado en el momento adecuado.
  You've arrived at just the right moment.
  □ el hombre adecuado para el puesto the
  right man for the job
**a. de J.C.** ABBREVIATION (= *antes de Jesucristo*)
  B.C. (= *before Christ*)

**adelantado** (FEM **adelantada**) ADJECTIVE
1 advanced
  □ Suecia es un país muy adelantado.
  Sweden is a very advanced country.
  ■ **los niños más adelantados de la clase**
  the children who are doing best in the class
2 fast
  □ Este reloj va adelantado. This watch is
  fast.
  ■ **pagar por adelantado** to pay in advance

**adelantar** VERB [25]
1 to bring...forward
  □ Tuvimos que adelantar la boda. We had to
  bring the wedding forward.
2 to overtake
  □ Adelanta a ese camión cuando puedas.
  Overtake that lorry when you can.
3 to put...forward
  □ El domingo hay que adelantar los relojes
  una hora. On Sunday we'll have to put the
  clocks forward an hour.
  ■ **Así no adelantas nada.** You won't get
  anywhere that way.
  ■ **Tu reloj adelanta.** Your watch gains.

**adelantarse** VERB
to go on ahead
  □ Me adelanté para coger asiento. I went on
  ahead to get a seat.
  ■ **adelantarse a alguien** to get ahead of
  somebody □ Se nos adelantaron los de la
  competencia. The competition got ahead of
  us.

**adelante** ADVERB
  ▷ *see also* **adelante** EXCLAMATION
  forward
  □ Se inclinó hacia adelante. He leant
  forward.
  ■ **¿Nos vamos adelante para ver mejor?**
  Shall we sit near the front to get a better
  view?
  ■ **más adelante 1** further on □ El pueblo
  está más adelante. The village is further on.
  **2** later □ Más adelante hablaremos de los
  resultados. Later we'll discuss the results.
  ■ **adelante de** (*Latin America*) in front of
  ■ **Hay que seguir adelante.** We must go
  on.

**a**

■ **de ahora en adelante** from now on
**adelante** EXCLAMATION
▷ *see also* **adelante** ADVERB
1 come on!
2 come in!
el **adelanto** NOUN
advance
□ los adelantos de la ciencia the advances in science □ Le pidió un adelanto a su jefe. He asked his boss for an advance.
**adelgazar\*** VERB [13]
to lose weight
□ ¡Cómo has adelgazado! What a lot of weight you've lost!
■ **He adelgazado cinco kilos.** I've lost five kilos.
**además** ADVERB
1 as well
□ Es profesor y además carpintero. He's a teacher and a carpenter as well.
2 what's more
□ El baño es demasiado pequeño y, además, no tiene ventana. The bathroom's too small and, what's more, it hasn't got a window.
3 besides
□ Además, no tienes nada que perder. Besides, you've got nothing to lose.
■ **además de** as well as □ El ordenador es, además de rápido, eficaz. The computer is efficient as well as fast.
**adentro** ADVERB
inside
□ Empezó a llover y se metieron adentro. It began to rain so they went inside.
■ **tierra adentro** inland
■ **adentro de** *(Latin America)* inside
□ desde adentro de la casa from inside the house
**adhesivo** (FEM **adhesiva**) ADJECTIVE
sticky
□ cinta adhesiva sticky tape
el **adhesivo** NOUN
sticker
la **adicción** (PL las **adicciones**) NOUN
addiction
la **adición** (PL las **adiciones**) NOUN
*(River Plate)*
bill
**adicto** (FEM **adicta**) ADJECTIVE
addicted
□ Es adicto a la cafeína. He is addicted to caffeine.
el **adicto**, la **adicta** NOUN
addict
□ un adicto a las drogas a drug addict
**adinerado** (FEM **adinerada**) ADJECTIVE
wealthy
**adiós** EXCLAMATION

1 goodbye!
■ **decir adiós a alguien** to say goodbye to somebody
2 hello!
el **aditivo** NOUN
additive
la **adivinanza** NOUN
guess (PL guesses)
**adivinar** VERB [25]
to guess
□ Adivina quién viene. Guess who's coming.
■ **adivinar el pensamiento a alguien** to read somebody's mind
■ **adivinar el futuro** to see into the future
el **adjetivo** NOUN
adjective
**adjunto** (FEM **adjunta**) ADJECTIVE
1 enclosed
2 attached
3 deputy
□ el director adjunto the deputy head
la **administración** (PL las **administraciones**) NOUN
1 administration
□ Master de Administración de Empresas Master of Business Administration
2 civil service
□ Carmen trabaja en la administración. Carmen works for the civil service.
el **administrador de Web**, la **administradora de Web** NOUN
webmaster
**administrativo** (FEM **administrativa**) ADJECTIVE
administrative
□ gastos administrativos administrative expenses
■ **trabajo administrativo** clerical work
el **administrativo**, la **administrativa** NOUN
clerk
la **admiración** NOUN
1 admiration
□ Siento profunda admiración por él. I have great admiration for him.
2 amazement
□ para admiración de todos to everyone's amazement
■ **Su franqueza causó admiración entre los presentes.** His frankness amazed everyone there.
■ **signo de admiración** exclamation mark
**admirar** VERB [25]
to admire
□ Todos la admiran. Everyone admires her.
■ **Me admira lo poco que gastas en ropa.** I'm amazed at how little you spend on clothes.

**admitir** VERB [58]
1 to admit
□ Admite que estabas equivocado. Admit you were wrong.
2 to accept
□ La máquina no admite monedas de dos euros. The machine doesn't accept two-euro coins.
■ **Espero que me admitan a la universidad.** I hope I'll get a place at university.
3 to allow in
□ Aquí no admiten perros. Dogs aren't allowed in here.

**el/la adolescente** NOUN
teenager

**adonde** CONJUNCTION
where
■ **la ciudad adonde nos dirigimos** the city we're going to

**adónde** ADVERB
where
□ ¿Adónde ibas? Where were you going?

**la adopción** (PL las **adopciones**) NOUN
adoption

**adoptar** VERB [25]
to adopt

**adoptivo** (FEM **adoptiva**) ADJECTIVE
■ **un hijo adoptivo** an adopted child
■ **mis padres adoptivos** my adoptive parents

**adorar** VERB [25]
1 to adore
□ Adora a sus hijos. He adores his children.
2 to worship
□ adorar a Dios to worship God

**adornar** VERB [25]
to decorate

**el adorno** NOUN
1 ornament
□ Quitó los adornos de la estantería para limpiarla. He took the ornaments off the shelf to clean it.
2 decoration
□ Habían puesto adornos en las calles. Decorations had been put up in the streets.
□ Es sólo de adorno. It's only for decoration.

**adosado** (FEM **adosada**) ADJECTIVE
■ **un chalet adosado** a terraced house

**adquirir\*** VERB [2]
to acquire
□ adquirir conocimientos de algo to acquire a knowledge of something
■ **adquirir velocidad** to gain speed
■ **adquirir fama** to achieve fame
■ **adquirir una vivienda** to purchase a property
■ **adquirir importancia** to become important

■ **Lo podrá adquirir en tiendas especializadas.** You'll be able to get it from specialist shops.

**adrede** ADVERB
on purpose

**la aduana** NOUN
customs *sing*

**el aduanero**, la **aduanera** NOUN
customs officer

**el adulto** NOUN
adult
■ **educación de adultos** adult education

**el adverbio** NOUN
adverb

**el adversario**, la **adversaria** NOUN
opponent

**la advertencia** NOUN
warning

**advertir\*** VERB [51]
1 to warn
□ Ya te advertí que no intervinieras. I warned you not to get involved.
■ **advertir a alguien de algo** to warn somebody about something
■ **Te advierto que no va a ser nada fácil.** I must warn you that it won't be at all easy.
2 to notice
□ No advertí nada extraño en su comportamiento. I didn't notice anything strange about his behaviour.

**aéreo** (FEM **aérea**) ADJECTIVE
air
□ un ataque aéreo an air raid
■ **por vía aérea** by air mail
■ **una fotografía aérea** an aerial photograph

**el aerobic** NOUN
aerobics *sing*

**el aeromozo**, la **aeromoza** NOUN
*(Latin America)*
flight attendant

**el aeropuerto** NOUN
airport

**el aerosol** NOUN
aerosol

**el afán** (PL los **afanes**) NOUN
1 ambition
□ Todo su afán era ser pintora. Her great ambition was to be a painter.
2 effort
■ **Trabajan con mucho afán.** They put a lot of effort into their work.

**afectado** (FEM **afectada**) ADJECTIVE
upset
□ Está muy afectado por la noticia. He's very upset at the news.

**afectar** VERB [25]

**to affect**

□ Esto a ti no te afecta. This doesn't affect you.

■ **Me afectó mucho la noticia.** The news upset me terribly.

**afectivo** (FEM **afectiva**) ADJECTIVE
emotional

□ problemas afectivos emotional problems

el **afecto** NOUN
affection

□ Me cuesta demostrar afecto. I find it difficult to show affection.

■ **tener afecto a alguien** to be fond of somebody

**afectuoso** (FEM **afectuosa**) ADJECTIVE
affectionate

□ Es un chico muy afectuoso. He's a very affectionate boy.

■ **'Un saludo afectuoso'** 'With best wishes'

**afeitar** VERB [25]
to shave

■ **afeitarse** to shave □ Voy a afeitarme. I'm going to shave.

■ **Me afeité la barba.** I shaved off my beard.

**Afganistán** MASC NOUN
Afghanistan

el **afiche** NOUN (Latin America)
poster

la **afición** (PL las **aficiones**) NOUN
1 hobby (PL hobbies)

□ Mi afición es la filatelia. My hobby is stamp collecting. □ por afición as a hobby

■ **Tengo mucha afición por el ciclismo.** I'm very keen on cycling.

■ **En este país hay poca afición al teatro.** In this country people aren't very interested in the theatre.

2 fans pl

□ la afición del Athletic the Athletic fans

**aficionado** (FEM **aficionada**) ADJECTIVE
1 keen

□ Es muy aficionada a la pintura. She's very keen on painting.

2 amateur

□ un equipo de fútbol aficionado an amateur football team

el **aficionado**, la **aficionada** NOUN
1 enthusiast

□ un libro para los aficionados al bricolaje a book for DIY enthusiasts

2 lover

□ los aficionados al teatro theatre lovers

3 amateur

□ un partido para aficionados a game for amateurs

**aficionarse** VERB [25]

■ **aficionarse a algo 1** to take up

something □ Raúl se aficionó al billar. Raúl took up billiards. **2** to become interested in something □ Me he aficionado al teatro. I've become interested in the theatre.

■ **Me he aficionado al chocolate suizo.** I've developed a taste for Swiss chocolate.

**afilado** (FEM **afilada**) ADJECTIVE
sharp

**afilar** VERB [25]
to sharpen

**afiliarse** VERB [25]

■ **afiliarse a algo** to join something

**afinar** VERB [25]
to tune

□ afinar un violín to tune a violin

**afirmar** VERB [25]

■ **afirmar que ...** to say that ... □ Afirmaba que no la conocía. He said that he didn't know her.

■ **Afirma haberla visto aquella noche.** He says that he saw her that night.

**afirmativo** (FEM **afirmativa**) ADJECTIVE
affirmative

**aflojar** VERB [25]
to loosen

■ **Tengo que aflojarme la corbata.** I must loosen my tie.

■ **aflojarse** to come loose □ Se ha aflojado un tornillo. A screw has come loose.

el **afluente** NOUN
tributary (PL tributaries)

**afónico** (FEM **afónica**) ADJECTIVE

■ **Estoy afónico.** I've lost my voice.

el **aforo** NOUN
capacity (PL capacities)

□ El teatro tiene un aforo de 2.000 personas. The theatre has a capacity of 2000 people.

**afortunadamente** ADVERB
fortunately

**afortunado** (FEM **afortunada**) ADJECTIVE
lucky

□ Es un tipo afortunado. He's a lucky guy.

**África** FEM NOUN
Africa

el **africano** (FEM la **africana**) ADJECTIVE, NOUN
African

**afrontar** VERB [25]
to face up to

□ afrontar un problema to face up to a problem

**afuera** ADVERB
outside

□ Vámonos afuera. Let's go outside.

■ **afuera de** (Latin America) outside

las **afueras** NOUN
outskirts

□ en las afueras de Barcelona on the outskirts of Barcelona

■ **un barrio a las afueras de Londres** a London suburb

**agacharse** VERB [25]
1 to crouch down
2 to bend down

la **agarradera** NOUN *(Latin America)*
handle

**agarrado** (FEM **agarrada**) ADJECTIVE
stingy

**agarrar** VERB [25]
1 to grab
□ Agarró al niño por el hombro. He grabbed the child by the shoulder.
2 to hold
□ Agarra bien la sartén. Hold the frying pan firmly.
3 to catch
□ Ya han agarrado al ladrón. They've already caught the thief. □ He agarrado un buen resfriado. I've caught an awful cold.
4 to take *(Latin America)*
□ Agarré otro pedazo de pastel. I took another piece of cake.
■ **agarrarse** to hold on □ Agárrate a la barandilla. Hold on to the rail.

la **agencia** NOUN
agency (PL agencies)
□ una agencia de noticias a news agency
□ una agencia de publicidad an advertising agency
■ **una agencia inmobiliaria** an estate agent's
■ **una agencia de viajes** a travel agent's

la **agenda** NOUN
1 diary (PL diaries)
2 address book

> **LANGUAGE TIP** Be careful! The Spanish word **agenda** does not mean **agenda**.

el/la **agente** NOUN
agent
■ **un agente de bolsa** a stockbroker
■ **un agente de seguros** an insurance broker
■ **un agente de policía** a police officer

**ágil** (FEM **ágil**) ADJECTIVE
agile

**agitado** (FEM **agitada**) ADJECTIVE
hectic

**agitar** VERB [25]
1 to stir
□ Agitaba su café con una cucharilla. He was stirring his coffee with a teaspoon.
2 to shake
□ Agítese antes de usar. Shake before use.
3 to wave
□ La gente agitaba los pañuelos. People were waving their handkerchiefs.

**aglomerarse** VERB [25]
■ **La gente se aglomeraba a la entrada.** People were crowding around the entrance.

**agobiante** (FEM **agobiante**) ADJECTIVE
1 stifling
2 overwhelming
3 exhausting

**agobiar** VERB [25]
■ **Le agobian sus problemas.** His problems are getting on top of him.
■ **agobiarse** to worry □ No te agobies; ya encontraremos una solución. Don't worry, we'll find a solution.

**agosto** MASC NOUN
August
□ en agosto in August □ Nació el 8 de agosto. He was born on 8 August.

**agotado** (FEM **agotada**) ADJECTIVE
1 exhausted
□ Estoy agotado. I'm exhausted.
2 sold out
□ Ese modelo en concreto está agotado. That particular model is sold out.

**agotador** (FEM **agotadora**) ADJECTIVE
exhausting

**agotar** VERB [25]
1 to use up
□ Agotamos todas nuestras reservas de combustible. We used up all our fuel supplies.
2 to tire out
□ Me agota tanto ejercicio. All this exercise is tiring me out.
■ **agotarse** to run out □ Se está agotando la leña. The firewood's running out.
■ **Se agotaron todas las entradas.** The tickets sold out.

**agradable** (FEM **agradable**) ADJECTIVE
nice

**agradar** VERB [25]
■ **Esto no me agrada.** I don't like this.

**agradecer*** VERB [12]
■ **agradecer algo a alguien** to thank somebody for something
■ **Te agradezco tu interés.** Thank you for your interest.
■ **Le agradecería me enviara ...** I should be grateful if you would send me ...

**agradecido** (FEM **agradecida**) ADJECTIVE
■ **estar agradecido a alguien por algo** to be grateful to somebody for something

el **agrado** NOUN
■ **no fue de mi agrado** it was not to my liking

**agrario** (FEM **agraria**) ADJECTIVE
agricultural
□ la política agraria agricultural policy

**agredir** VERB [58]

to attack

**la agresión** (PL las **agresiones**) NOUN
1 attack

□ una brutal agresión de dos jóvenes a brutal attack on two young people
2 aggression

□ un acto de agresión an act of aggression

**agresivo** (FEM **agresiva**) ADJECTIVE
aggressive

**agrícola** (FEM **agrícola**) ADJECTIVE
agricultural

el **agricultor**, la **agricultora** NOUN
farmer

la **agricultura** NOUN
farming

**agridulce** (FEM **agridulce**) ADJECTIVE
sweet-and-sour

□ salsa agridulce sweet-and-sour sauce

**agrio** (FEM **agria**) ADJECTIVE
1 sour
2 tart

la **agrupación** (PL las **agrupaciones**) NOUN
group

**agrupar** VERB [25]
1 to group

□ agrupados en distintas categorías grouped into different categories □ Los insectos se agrupan en varias categorías. Insects can be grouped into several categories.
2 to bring together

□ una organización que agrupa a varios países an organization which brings several countries together

■ **Los ecologistas se han agrupado en varios partidos.** The ecologists have formed several parties.

■ **Se agruparon en torno a su jefe.** They gathered round their boss.

el **agua** FEM NOUN
water

■ **agua corriente** running water
■ **agua potable** drinking water
■ **agua dulce** fresh water
■ **agua salada** salt water
■ **agua de colonia** cologne
■ **agua oxigenada** peroxide

el **aguacate** NOUN
avocado (PL avocados)

el/la **aguafiestas** (PL los/las **aguafiestas**) NOUN
spoilsport

la **aguanieve** NOUN
sleet

**aguantar** VERB [25]
1 to stand

□ No aguanto la ópera. I can't stand opera. □ Su vecina no la aguanta. Her neighbour

can't stand her.
2 to take

□ La estantería no va a aguantar el peso. The shelf won't take the weight. □ ¡No aguanto más! I can't take any more!
3 to hold

□ Aguántame el martillo un momento. Can you hold the hammer for me for a moment? □ Aguanta la respiración. Hold your breath.
4 to last

□ Este abrigo ya no aguanta otro invierno. This coat won't last another winter.

■ **No pude aguantar la risa.** I couldn't help laughing.

■ **Últimamente estás que no hay quien te aguante.** You've been unbearable lately.

■ **¿Puedes aguantarte hasta que lleguemos a casa?** Can you hold out until we get home?

■ **Si no puede venir, que se aguante.** If he can't come, he'll just have to lump it.

el **aguante** NOUN

■ **tener aguante 1** to be patient **2** to have stamina

**aguardar** VERB [25]
to wait for

**agudo** (FEM **aguda**) ADJECTIVE
1 sharp
2 high-pitched
3 acute
4 witty

el **aguijón** (PL los **aguijones**) NOUN
sting

el **águila** FEM NOUN
eagle

la **aguja** NOUN
needle

■ **las agujas del reloj** the hands of the clock

el **agujero** NOUN
1 hole

■ **hacer un agujero** to make a hole
2 pocket

la **agujeta** NOUN (Mexico)
shoe lace

las **agujetas** NOUN

■ **tener agujetas** to be stiff

**ahí** ADVERB
there

□ ¡Ahí están! There they are! □ Ahí llega el tren. There's the train.

■ **Ahí está el problema.** That's the problem.

■ **ahí arriba** up there
■ **Están ahí dentro.** They're in there.
■ **Lo tienes ahí mismo.** You've got it right there.
■ **de ahí que** that's why

**por ahí 1** over there □ Tú busca por ahí.
You look over there. **2** somewhere □ Nos
iremos por ahí a celebrarlo. We'll go out
somewhere to celebrate.
**¿Las tijeras? Andarán por ahí.** The
scissors? They must be somewhere around.
**3** thereabouts □ 200 o por ahí **200** or
thereabouts
**ahogarse\*** VERB [37]
**1** to drown
□ Se ahogó en el río. He drowned in the
river.
**2** to suffocate
□ Se ahogaron por falta de aire. They
suffocated for lack of air.
**3** to get breathless
□ Me ahogo subiendo las cuestas. I get
breathless going uphill.
**ahora** ADVERB
now
□ ¿Dónde vamos ahora? Where are we
going now?
**Ahora te lo digo.** I'll tell you in a
moment.
**ahora mismo** right now □ Ahora mismo
está de viaje. He's away on a trip right now.
**Ahora mismo voy.** I'm just coming.
**de ahora en adelante** from now on
**hasta ahora 1** so far □ Hasta ahora nadie
se ha quejado. Nobody has complained so
far. **2** till now □ Hasta ahora nadie se había
quejado. Nobody had complained till now.
**¡Hasta ahora!** See you shortly!
**ahora bien** however □ Aceptó las
condiciones. Ahora bien, hace falta que las
cumpla. He accepted the conditions.
However, he now needs to comply with
them.
**por ahora** for the moment □ Por ahora
no cambies nada. Don't change anything
for the moment.
**ahorcar\*** VERB [48]
to hang
**ahorcarse** to hang oneself
**ahorita** ADVERB (Latin America)
now
**ahorrar** VERB [25]
to save
los **ahorros** NOUN
savings
**ahumado** (FEM **ahumada**) ADJECTIVE
smoked
el **aire** NOUN
**1** air
□ Necesitamos aire para respirar. We need
air to breathe.
**aire acondicionado** air conditioning
**tomar el aire** to get some fresh air

**2** wind
□ El aire se le llevó el sombrero. The wind
blew his hat off.
**Hace mucho aire.** It's very windy.
**al aire libre 1** outdoors □ Comimos al
aire libre. We had lunch outdoors.
**2** outdoor □ una fiesta al aire libre an
outdoor party
**aislado** (FEM **aislada**) ADJECTIVE
isolated
□ Es un caso aislado. It's an isolated case.
**El pueblo estaba aislado por la nieve.**
The village was cut off by the snow.
el **ajedrez** (PL los **ajedreces**) NOUN
**1** chess
□ jugar al ajedrez to play chess
**2** chess set
□ Tráete el ajedrez y echamos una partida.
Get the chess set and we'll have a game.
**ajeno** (FEM **ajena**) ADJECTIVE
**No respeta la opinión ajena.** He doesn't
respect other people's opinions.
**por razones ajenas a nuestra voluntad**
for reasons beyond our control
**ajetreado** (FEM **ajetreada**) ADJECTIVE
busy
□ Ha sido un día muy ajetreado. It has been
a very busy day.
el **ají** NOUN (River Plate)
chili sauce
el **ajo** NOUN
garlic
**ajustado** (FEM **ajustada**) ADJECTIVE
tight
□ Lleva ropa muy ajustada. He wears very
tight clothes. □ La falda me queda un poco
ajustada. The skirt's a bit tight on me.
**ajustar** VERB [25]
**1** to adjust
□ Hay que ajustar los frenos. The brakes
need adjusting.
**2** to tighten
□ Ajusté bien todas las tuercas. I tightened
up all the nuts.
**3** to fit
□ Esta puerta no ajusta bien. This door
doesn't fit very well.
**ajustarse a 1** to fit in with □ Tendremos
que ajustarnos al horario previsto. We'll
have to fit in with the programme. □ Tu
versión no se ajusta a la realidad. Your
version doesn't fit in with the facts. **2** to
keep to □ Nos ajustaremos al presupuesto.
We'll keep to the budget.
**al** PREPOSITION ▷ see **a**
el **ala** FEM NOUN
**1** wing
**2** brim

13

**Spanish-English**

**a**

**alabar** VERB [25]
to praise
la **alambrada** NOUN
fence
□ una alambrada eléctrica an electric fence
el **alambre** NOUN
wire
el **álamo** NOUN
poplar
**alardear** VERB
■ alardear de algo to boast about
something
el **alargador** NOUN
extension lead
**alargar*** VERB [37]
1 to lengthen
□ Hay que alargar un poco las mangas.
We'll need to lengthen the sleeves a little.
2 to extend
□ Van a alargar esta línea de metro. This
underground line is going to be extended.
□ Decidieron alargar las vacaciones. They
decided to extend their holidays.
3 to stretch out
□ Alargué el brazo para apagar la luz. I
stretched out my arm to put out the light.
4 to pass
□ ¿Me alargas la llave inglesa? Will you pass
me the wrench?
■ alargarse 1 to get longer □ Ya van
alargándose los días. The days are getting
longer. 2 to go on □ La fiesta se alargó
hasta el amanecer. The party went on into
the early hours.
la **alarma** NOUN
alarm
□ Saltó la alarma. The alarm went off.
■ dar la voz de alarma to raise the alarm
■ alarma de incendios fire alarm
el **alba** FEM NOUN
dawn
■ al alba at dawn
el/la **albañil** NOUN
1 builder
2 bricklayer
el **albaricoque** NOUN
apricot
la **alberca** NOUN (Latin America)
swimming pool
el **albergue** NOUN
1 mountain refuge
2 hostel
■ un albergue juvenil a youth hostel
las **albóndigas** NOUN
meatballs
el **albornoz** (PL los **albornoces**) NOUN
bathrobe
14  el **alboroto** NOUN

racket
□ ¡Vaya alboroto que estaban montando los
niños! What a racket the kids were making!
el **álbum** (PL los **álbumes**) NOUN
album
la **alcachofa** NOUN
1 artichoke
2 shower head
3 rose
el **alcalde**, la **alcaldesa** NOUN
mayor
el **alcance** NOUN
1 range
□ misiles de largo alcance long-range
missiles
2 scale
□ Se desconoce el alcance de la catástrofe.
The scale of the disaster isn't yet known.
■ Está al alcance de todos. It's within
everybody's reach.
la **alcantarilla** NOUN
1 sewer
2 drain
■ una boca de alcantarilla a manhole
**alcanzar*** VERB [13]
1 to catch up with
□ La alcancé cuando salía por la puerta.
I caught up with her just as she was going
out of the door.
2 to reach
□ alcanzar la cima de la montaña to reach
the top of the mountain
3 to find
□ alcanzar la fama to find fame
4 to pass
□ ¿Me alcanzas las tijeras? Could you pass
me the scissors?
■ Con dos botellas alcanzará para todos.
Two bottles will be enough for all of us.
el **alcaucil** NOUN (River Plate)
artichoke
la **alcoba** NOUN
bedroom
  **LANGUAGE TIP** Be careful! alcoba does
  not mean **alcove**.
el **alcohol** NOUN
alcohol
■ cerveza sin alcohol non-alcoholic beer
**alcohólico** (FEM **alcohólica**) ADJECTIVE
alcoholic
la **aldea** NOUN
village
el **aldeano**, la **aldeana** NOUN
villager
**alegrar** VERB [25]
to cheer up
□ Intenté alegrarlos con unos chistes. I tried
to cheer them up with a few jokes.

■ **Me alegra que hayas venido.** I'm glad you've come.

■ **alegrarse** to be glad □ ¿Te gusta? Me alegro. You like it? I'm glad.

■ **alegrarse de algo** to be glad about something □ Me alegro de tu ascenso. I'm glad about your promotion.

■ **Me alegro de oír que estás bien.** I'm glad to hear that you're well.

■ **alegrarse por alguien** to be happy for somebody □ Me alegro por ti. I'm happy for you.

**alegre** (FEM **alegre**) ADJECTIVE
cheerful

■ **Estoy muy alegre.** I'm feeling very happy.

la **alegría** NOUN

■ **Sentí una gran alegría.** I was really happy.

■ **¡Qué alegría!** How lovely!

**alejarse** VERB [25]
to move away
□ Aléjate un poco del fuego. Move a bit further away from the fire.

■ **El barco se iba alejando de la costa.** The boat was getting further and further away from the coast.

el **alemán** (FEM la **alemana**) ADJECTIVE, NOUN
German

el **alemán** NOUN
German

**Alemania** FEM NOUN
Germany

**alentador** ADJECTIVE (FEM **alentadora**)
encouraging

la **alergia** NOUN
allergy (PL allergies)

■ **la alergia al polen** hay fever

la **alerta** ADJECTIVE, NOUN, ADVERB
alert

■ **dar la alerta** to give the alert

■ **estar alerta** to be alert

la **aleta** NOUN
1 fin
2 flipper
3 wing

el **alfabeto** NOUN
alphabet

la **alfarería** NOUN
pottery (PL potteries)

el **alfarero**, la **alfarera** NOUN
potter

el **alféizar** NOUN
sill

el **alfil** NOUN
bishop

el **alfiler** NOUN
pin

la **alfombra** NOUN

1 rug
2 carpet

la **alfombrilla** NOUN
mat

las **algas** NOUN
seaweed *sing*

**algo** PRONOUN
▷ see also **algo** ADVERB
1 something
□ Algo se está quemando. Something is burning. □ ¿Quieres algo de comer? Would you like something to eat? □ ¿Te pasa algo? Is something the matter?

■ **Aún queda algo de café.** There's still some coffee left.

2 anything
□ ¿Algo más? Anything else? □ ¿Has visto algo que te guste? Have you seen anything you like?

■ **algo así como** a bit like □ Es algo así como una nave espacial. It's a bit like a spaceship.

■ **o algo así** or something of the sort

■ **Por algo será.** There must be a reason for it.

**algo** ADVERB
▷ see also **algo** PRONOUN
rather
□ La falda te está algo corta, pero puede valer. The skirt's rather short on you, but it may be all right.

el **algodón** (PL los **algodones**) NOUN
cotton
□ ropa de algodón cotton clothes

■ **Me puse algodones en los oídos.** I put cotton wool in my ears.

**alguien** PRONOUN
1 somebody
□ Alguien llama a la puerta. There's somebody knocking at the door. □ ¿Necesitas que te ayude alguien? Do you need somebody to help you?

2 anybody
□ ¿Conoces a alguien aquí? Do you know anybody here?

**algún** ADJECTIVE (FEM **alguna**, MASC PL **algunos**)
1 some
□ Algún día iré. I'll go there some day.

2 any
□ ¿Compraste algún cuadro? Did you buy any pictures?

■ **¿Quieres alguna cosa más?** Was there anything else?

■ **algún que otro ...** the odd ... □ He leído algún que otro libro sobre el tema. I've read the odd book on the subject.

**alguno** PRONOUN (FEM **alguna**)
1 somebody

□ Siempre hay alguno que se queja. There's always somebody who complains.

■ **Algunos piensan que no ocurrió así.** Some people think that it didn't happen like that.

**2** one

□ Tiene que haber sido alguno de ellos. It must have been one of them. □ Tiene que estar en alguna de estas cajas. It must be in one of these boxes.

**3** some

□ Son tantas maletas que alguna siempre se pierde. There are so many suitcases that some inevitably get lost.

■ **Sólo conozco a algunos de los vecinos.** I only know some of the neighbours.

**4** any

□ Necesito una aspirina. ¿Te queda alguna? I need an aspirin. Have you got any left?

□ Si alguno quiere irse que se vaya. If any of them want to leave, fine. □ ¿Lo sabe alguno de vosotros? Do any of you know?

el **aliado**, la **aliada** NOUN
ally (PL allies)

la **alianza** NOUN

**1** alliance

□ formar una alianza to form an alliance

**2** wedding ring

**aliarse*** VERB [21]

■ **aliarse con alguien** to form an alliance with somebody

los **alicates** NOUN
pliers

el **aliento** NOUN
breath

□ Tengo mal aliento. I've got bad breath.

■ **Llegué sin aliento.** I arrived out of breath.

**aligerar** VERB [25]
to make...lighter

□ aligerar la carga del barco to make the cargo lighter

■ **¡Aligera o llegaremos tarde!** Hurry up or we'll be late!

la **alimentación** NOUN
diet

□ Hay que cuidar la alimentación. You need to be sensible about your diet.

■ **una tienda de alimentación** a grocer's shop

**alimentar** VERB [25]
to feed

□ alimentar a un niño to feed a child

■ **Esto no alimenta.** That's not very nutritious.

■ **alimentarse de algo** to live on something

el **alimento** NOUN

food

■ **alimentos congelados** frozen food sing

■ **Las legumbres tienen mucho alimento.** Pulses are very nutritious.

la **alineación** (PL las **alineaciones**) NOUN
line-up

**aliñar** VERB [25]
to season

el **aliño** NOUN
dressing

**aliviar** VERB [25]
to make...better

□ El jarabe te aliviará la tos. The syrup will make your cough better. □ Estas pastillas te aliviarán. These pills will make you better.

el **alivio** NOUN
relief

■ **¡Qué alivio!** What a relief!

**allá** ADVERB
there

□ allá arriba up there

■ **más allá** further on

■ **Échate un poco más allá.** Move over that way a bit.

■ **más allá de** beyond

■ **¡Allá tú!** That's up to you!

■ **el más allá** the next world

**allanar** VERB [25]
to level

**allí** ADVERB
there

□ Allí está. There it is.

■ **Allí viene tu hermana.** Here comes your sister.

■ **allí abajo** down there

■ **allí mismo** right there

■ **Marta es de por allí.** Marta comes from somewhere around there.

el **alma** FEM NOUN
soul

■ **Lo siento en el alma.** I'm really sorry.

el **almacén** (PL los **almacenes**) NOUN
store

■ **unos grandes almacenes** a department store

**almacenar** VERB [25]
to store

la **almeja** NOUN
clam

la **almendra** NOUN
almond

el **almíbar** NOUN
syrup

■ **en almíbar** in syrup

el **almirante** NOUN
admiral

la **almohada** NOUN
pillow

la **almohadilla** NOUN
cushion

**almorzar\*** VERB [3]
to have lunch
□ No he almorzado todavía. I haven't had
lunch yet.
■ ¿Qué has almorzado? What did you have
for lunch?

**almuerzo** VERB ▷ see **almorzar**

el **almuerzo** NOUN
lunch (PL lunches)

**aló** EXCLAMATION (Latin America)
hello!

**alocado** (FEM **alocada**) ADJECTIVE
crazy
□ una decisión alocada a crazy decision
■ una chica un poco alocada a rather silly
girl

el **alojamiento** NOUN
accommodation

**alojarse** VERB [25]
to stay
□ ¿Dónde os alojáis? Where are you staying?

la **alpargata** NOUN
espadrille

los **Alpes** NOUN
the Alps

el **alpinismo** NOUN
mountaineering

el/la **alpinista** NOUN
mountaineer

**alquilar** VERB [25]
1 to rent
□ Alquilaremos un apartamento en la playa.
We'll rent an apartment near the beach.
2 to let
□ Alquilan habitaciones a estudiantes. They
let rooms to students.
■ 'se alquila' 'to let'
3 to hire
□ Alquilamos un coche. We hired a car.

el **alquiler** NOUN
rent
□ pagar el alquiler to pay the rent
■ un piso de alquiler a rented flat
■ un coche de alquiler a hire car
■ alquiler de automóviles car-hire

**alrededor** ADVERB
■ alrededor de 1 around □ El satélite gira
alrededor de la Tierra. The satellite goes
around the Earth. □ A su alrededor todos
gritaban. Everybody around him was
shouting. 2 about □ Deben de ser alrededor
de las dos. It must be about two o'clock.

los **alrededores** NOUN
■ Ocurrió en los alrededores de Madrid.
It happened near Madrid.
■ Hay muchas tiendas en los alrededores

del museo. There are a lot of shops in the
area around the museum.

el **alta** FEM NOUN
■ dar de alta a alguien to discharge
somebody
■ darse de alta to join

el **altar** NOUN
altar

el **altavoz** (PL los **altavoces**) NOUN
loudspeaker

**alterar** VERB [25]
to change
□ Alteraron el orden. They changed the
order.
■ alterar el orden público to cause a
breach of the peace
■ alterarse to get upset □ ¡No te alteres!
Don't get upset!

**alternar** VERB [25]
■ alternar algo con algo to alternate
something with something
■ Alterna con gente del teatro. He mixes
with people from the theatre.

la **alternativa** NOUN
alternative
■ No tenemos otra alternativa. We have
no alternative.

**alterno** (FEM **alterna**) ADJECTIVE
alternate
□ en días alternos on alternate days
■ corriente alterna alternating current

los **altibajos** NOUN
ups and downs
□ tener altibajos to have ups and downs

la **altitud** NOUN
altitude

**alto** (FEM **alta**) ADJECTIVE
▷ see also **alto** ADVERB, EXCLAMATION
1 tall
□ Es un chico muy alto. He's a very tall boy.
□ un edificio muy alto a very tall building
2 high
□ El Everest es la montaña más alta del
mundo. Everest is the highest mountain in
the world. □ Sacó notas altas en todos los
exámenes. He got high marks in all his
exams.
3 loud
□ La música está demasiado alta. The
music's too loud.
■ a altas horas de la noche in the middle
of the night
■ Celebraron la victoria por todo lo alto.
They celebrated the victory in style.
■ alta fidelidad hi-fi
■ una familia de clase alta an upper-class
family

**alto** ADVERB

17

**Spanish-English**

**a**

▷ *see also* **alto** ADJECTIVE, EXCLAMATION
high
□ subir muy alto to go up very high
■ **Pepe habla muy alto.** Pepe has got a
very loud voice.
■ **¡Más alto, por favor!** Speak up, please!
■ **Pon el volumen más alto.** Turn the
volume up.

**alto** EXCLAMATION
▷ *see also* **alto** ADJECTIVE, ADVERB
stop!

el **alto** NOUN
■ **La pared tiene dos metros de alto.**
The wall is two metres high.
■ **en lo alto de** at the top of
■ **hacer un alto** to stop □ A las dos
haremos un alto para comer. We'll stop to
have lunch at two o'clock.
■ **pasar algo por alto** to overlook
something
■ **el alto el fuego** ceasefire

el **altoparlante** NOUN *(Latin America)*
loudspeaker

la **altura** NOUN
height
□ Volamos a una altura de 15.000 pies.
We're flying at a height of 15,000 feet.
■ **La pared tiene dos metros de altura.**
The wall's two metres high.
■ **cuando llegues a la altura del hospital**
when you reach the hospital
■ **a estas alturas** at this stage □ A estas
alturas no podemos hacer nada. There's
nothing we can do at this stage.

las **alubias** NOUN
beans

**alucinar** VERB [25]
to be amazed
□ Alucino con las cosas que haces. I'm
amazed at the things you do.

el **alud** NOUN
avalanche

**aludir** VERB [58]
to refer
□ No aludió a lo del otro día. He didn't refer
to that business the other day.
■ **No se dio por aludida.** She didn't take
the hint.

el **aluminio** NOUN
aluminium

el **alumno**, la **alumna** NOUN
pupil

la **alusión** (PL las **alusiones**) NOUN
■ **hacer alusión a** to refer to

la **alverja** NOUN *(Latin America)*
pea

el **alza** FEM NOUN
rise

□ un alza de los precios a rise in prices
■ **El balonmano es un deporte en alza.**
Handball is becoming increasingly popular.

**alzar*** VERB [13]
to raise
□ alzar la voz to raise one's voice
■ **alzarse** to rise □ Se alzó el telón. The
curtain rose.
■ **alzarse en armas** to take up arms

el **ama** FEM NOUN
owner
■ **ama de casa** housewife
⊙ **LANGUAGE TIP** Word for word, **ama de
casa** means 'owner of house'.
■ **ama de llaves** housekeeper
⊙ **LANGUAGE TIP** Word for word, **ama de
llaves** means 'owner of keys'.

**amable** (FEM **amable**) ADJECTIVE
kind
■ **Es usted muy amable.** You're very kind.

**amamantar** VERB [25]
1 to breast-feed
2 to suckle

**amanecer*** VERB [12]
1 to get light
□ Amanece a las siete. It gets light at seven.
2 to wake up
□ El niño amaneció con fiebre. The boy
woke up with a temperature.

el **amanecer** NOUN
dawn

el/la **amante** NOUN
lover
■ **amantes del cine** cinema lovers

la **amapola** NOUN
poppy (PL poppies)

**amar** VERB [25]
to love

**amargado** (FEM **amargada**) ADJECTIVE
bitter
■ **estar amargado por algo** to be bitter
about something

**amargar*** VERB [37]
to spoil
□ Ya me habéis amargado la tarde. You've
spoilt my evening.
■ **amargar la vida a alguien** to make
somebody's life a misery
■ **amargarse** to get upset □ No te
amargues por tan poca cosa. It's not worth
getting upset about such a little thing.

**amargo** (FEM **amarga**) ADJECTIVE
bitter

el **amarillo** ADJECTIVE, NOUN
yellow
■ **la prensa amarilla** the gutter press

**amarrar** VERB [25]
1 to moor

**2** to tie up
**3** to do up *(Latin America)*
▫ Se amarró los zapatos. He did up his shoes.

el/la **amateur** (PL los/las **amateurs**) ADJECTIVE, NOUN
amateur

el **Amazonas** NOUN
the Amazon

el **ámbar** NOUN
amber

la **ambición** (PL las **ambiciones**) NOUN
ambition

**ambicioso** (FEM **ambiciosa**) ADJECTIVE
ambitious

el **ambientador** NOUN
air freshener

el **ambiente** NOUN
atmosphere
▫ Se respira un ambiente tenso. There's a tense atmosphere.
■ Había un ambiente muy cargado en la habitación. It was very stuffy in the room.
■ Necesito cambiar de ambiente. I need a change of scene.
■ el medio ambiente the environment

**ambiguo** (FEM **ambigua**) ADJECTIVE
ambiguous

el **ámbito** NOUN
scope

**ambos** (FEM **ambas**) PRONOUN
both
▫ Vinieron ambos. They both came.
▫ Ambos tenéis los ojos azules. You've both got blue eyes.

la **ambulancia** NOUN
ambulance

el **ambulatorio** NOUN
out-patients' department

**amén** EXCLAMATION
amen

**amenace** VERB ▷see amenazar

la **amenaza** NOUN
threat

**amenazar*** VERB [13]
to threaten
■ amenazar a alguien con hacer algo to threaten to do something ▫ Le amenazó con decírselo al profesor. He threatened to tell the teacher.

**ameno** (FEM **amena**) ADJECTIVE
enjoyable

**América** FEM NOUN
the Americas
■ América Central Central America
■ América Latina Latin America
■ América del Sur South America
■ el español de América Latin American

Spanish

la **americana** NOUN
**1** jacket
**2** American

el **americano** ADJECTIVE, NOUN
American

la **ametralladora** NOUN
machine gun

las **amígdalas** NOUN
tonsils

el **amigo**, la **amiga** NOUN
friend
■ hacerse amigos to become friends
■ ser muy amigos to be good friends

la **amistad** NOUN
friendship
■ hacer amistad con alguien to make friends with somebody
■ las amistades friends

**amistoso** (FEM **amistosa**) ADJECTIVE
friendly

el **amo** NOUN
owner
▫ el amo del perro the dog's owner

**amontonar** VERB [25]
to pile up
■ Se me amontona el trabajo. My work's piling up.

el **amor** NOUN
love
■ hacer el amor to make love
■ amor propio self-esteem

**amoratado** (FEM **amoratada**) ADJECTIVE
**1** blue
**2** black and blue

**amortiguar*** VERB
**1** to cushion
**2** to muffle

**ampliar*** VERB [21]
**1** to expand
**2** to enlarge
**3** to extend

el **amplificador** NOUN
amplifier

**amplio** (FEM **amplia**) ADJECTIVE
**1** wide
▫ una calle muy amplia a very wide street
**2** spacious
▫ una habitación amplia a spacious room
**3** loose
▫ ropa amplia loose clothing

la **ampolla** NOUN
blister

**amputar** VERB [25]
to amputate

**amueblar** VERB [25]
to furnish
▫ un piso amueblado a furnished flat

**a**

■ **un piso sin amueblar** an unfurnished flat
**analfabeto** (FEM **analfabeta**) ADJECTIVE
illiterate
el **analgésico** NOUN
painkiller
el **análisis** (PL los **análisis**) NOUN
1 analysis (PL analyses)
 □ un análisis de la situación an analysis of
 the situation
2 test
 □ un análisis de sangre a blood test
**analizar*** VERB [1 3]
to analyse
la **anarquía** NOUN
anarchy
la **anatomía** NOUN
anatomy
**ancho** (FEM **ancha**) ADJECTIVE
1 wide
 □ una calle ancha a wide street
2 loose
 □ Le gusta llevar ropa ancha. He likes to
 wear loose clothing.
 ■ **Me está ancho el vestido.** The dress is
 too big for me.
 ■ **Es ancho de espaldas.** He's broad-
 shouldered.
el **ancho** NOUN
width
 □ el ancho de la tela the width of the cloth
 ■ **¿Cuánto mide de ancho?** How wide is it?
 ■ **Mide tres metros de ancho.** It's three
 metres wide.
 ■ **Le hice un corte a lo ancho.** I cut it
 crossways.
la **anchoa** NOUN
anchovy
la **anchura** NOUN
width
 □ Midió la anchura de la mesa. He
 measured the width of the table.
 ■ **¿Qué anchura tiene?** How wide is it?
 ■ **Tiene tres metros de anchura.** It's three
 metres wide.
la **anciana** NOUN
elderly woman
**anciano** (FEM **anciana**) ADJECTIVE
elderly
el **anciano** NOUN
elderly man
 ■ **los ancianos** the elderly
el **ancla** FEM NOUN
anchor
**anda** EXCLAMATION
1 well I never!
 □ ¡Anda, un billete de 50 euros! Well I never,
 a 50-euro note!
2 come on

□ ¡Anda, ponte el abrigo y vámonos! Come
on, put your coat on and let's go!
 ■ **¡Anda ya!** You're not serious!
**Andalucía** FEM NOUN
Andalusia
el **andaluz** (FEM la **andaluza**, MASC PL
**andaluces**) ADJECTIVE, NOUN
Andalusian
el **andamio** NOUN
scaffolding
 □ Ya han quitado los andamios. They've
 taken the scaffolding down now.
**andar*** VERB [4]
1 to walk
 □ Anduvimos varios kilómetros. We walked
 several kilometres.
 ■ **Iremos andando a la estación.** We'll
 walk to the station.
2 to be
 □ Últimamente ando muy liado. I've been
 very busy lately. □ No sé por dónde anda.
 I don't know where he is. □ ¿Qué tal andas?
 How are you? □ Ando buscando un socio.
 I'm looking for a partner.
 ■ **andar mal de dinero** to be short of
 money
 ■ **Anda por los cuarenta.** He's about forty.
 ■ **Siempre andan a gritos.** They're always
 shouting.
3 to go
 □ Este reloj anda muy bien. This watch goes
 very well.
 ■ **¡No andes ahí!** Keep away from there!
 ■ **Ándate con cuidado.** Take care.
el **andén** (PL los **andenes**) NOUN
platform
los **Andes** NOUN
the Andes
**anduve** VERB ▷ see **andar**
la **anécdota** NOUN
anecdote
la **anemia** NOUN
anaemia
la **anestesia** NOUN
anaesthetic
 ■ **poner anestesia a alguien** to give
 somebody an anaesthetic
el **anfiteatro** NOUN
1 amphitheatre
2 lecture theatre
el **ángel** NOUN
angel
las **anginas** NOUN
 ■ **tener anginas** to have tonsillitis
el **anglosajón** (FEM la **anglosajona**, MASC PL
los **anglosajones**) ADJECTIVE, NOUN
Anglo-Saxon
el **anglosajón** NOUN

Anglo-Saxon

el **ángulo** NOUN
angle

■ **en ángulo recto** at right angles

el **anillo** NOUN
ring

■ **un anillo de boda** a wedding ring

**animado** (FEM **animada**) ADJECTIVE
1 cheerful
  □ Últimamente parece que está más animada. She has seemed more cheerful lately.
2 lively
  □ Fue una fiesta muy animada. It was a very lively party.

■ **dibujos animados** cartoons

el **animador**, la **animadora** NOUN
1 entertainments officer
2 animator

el **animal** NOUN
animal

■ **los animales domésticos** pets

**animar** VERB [25]
1 to cheer up
  □ Lo ha pasado muy mal y necesita que la animen. She has had a rough time and needs cheering up.
2 to cheer on
  □ Estuvimos animando al equipo. We were cheering the team on.
3 to liven up
  □ Sus chistes animaron la fiesta. His jokes livened up the party.

■ **animar a alguien a que haga algo** to encourage somebody to do something
■ **animarse** to cheer up □ ¡Vamos, anímate hombre! Come on, cheer up mate!
■ **animarse a hacer algo** to make up one's mind to do something

el **ánimo** NOUN
■ **Está muy mal de ánimo.** He's in very low spirits.
■ **dar ánimos a alguien 1** to cheer somebody up **2** to give somebody moral support
■ **tener ánimos para hacer algo** to feel like doing something

**ánimo** EXCLAMATION
cheer up!
  □ ¡Ánimo, chaval, que no es el fin del mundo! Cheer up mate, it's not the end of the world!

el **anís** (PL los **anises**) NOUN
anisette

el **aniversario** NOUN
anniversary (PL anniversaries)
  □ su aniversario de boda their wedding anniversary

**anoche** ADVERB
last night

■ **antes de anoche** the night before last

**anochecer*** VERB [12]
to get dark
  □ En invierno anochece muy temprano. It gets dark very early in winter.

**anónimo** (FEM **anónima**) ADJECTIVE
anonymous

el **anónimo** NOUN
anonymous threat

el **anorak** (PL los **anoraks**) NOUN
anorak

**anormal** (FEM **anormal**) ADJECTIVE
odd
  □ Yo no noté nada anormal en su comportamiento. I didn't notice anything odd about his behaviour.
■ **¡Soy anormal!** What a fool I am!

**anotar** VERB [25]
1 to take a note of
  □ Anota mi dirección. Take a note of my address.
2 to score
  □ Jones anotó 34 puntos. Jones scored 34 points.

la **ansiedad** NOUN
anxiety

**ansioso** (FEM **ansiosa**) ADJECTIVE
■ **estar ansioso por hacer algo** to be eager to do something

el **Antártico** NOUN
the Antarctic

**ante** PREPOSITION
1 before
  □ Le da vergüenza aparecer ante tanta gente. She's shy about appearing before so many people.
2 in the face of
  □ Mantuvo la calma ante el peligro. He remained calm in the face of danger.

el **ante** NOUN
suede

**anteanoche** ADVERB
the night before last

**anteayer** ADVERB
the day before yesterday

los **antecedentes** NOUN
■ **antecedentes penales** criminal record sing

la **antelación** NOUN
■ **hacer una reserva con antelación** to make an advance booking
■ **Deben avisarte con un mes de antelación.** They must give you a month's notice.

**antemano** ADVERB
■ **de antemano** in advance □ Yo lo sabía de

antemano. I knew in advance.

la **antena** NOUN
aerial
■ **una antena parabólica** a satellite dish

los **anteojos** NOUN (Latin America)
glasses
■ **los anteojos de sol** sunglasses

los **antepasados** NOUN
ancestors

**anterior** (FEM **anterior**) ADJECTIVE
1 before
□ La semana anterior llovió mucho. It rained a lot the week before. □ Su boda fue anterior a la nuestra. Their wedding was before ours.
2 front
□ las extremidades anteriores the front limbs

**anteriormente** ADVERB
previously

**antes** ADVERB
1 before
□ Esta película ya la he visto antes. I've seen this film before. □ Él estaba aquí antes que yo. He was here before me. □ la noche antes the night before
■ **El supermercado está justo antes del semáforo.** The supermarket is just before the lights.
■ **antes de** before □ antes de la cena before dinner □ antes de ir al teatro before going to the theatre □ antes de que te vayas before you go
2 first
□ Nosotros llegamos antes. We arrived first.
■ **Antes no había tanto desempleo.** There didn't use to be so much unemployment.
■ **cuanto antes mejor** the sooner the better
■ **lo antes posible** as soon as possible
■ **antes de nada** first and foremost
■ **Antes que verle prefiero esperar aquí.** I'd rather wait here than see him.

el **antibiótico** NOUN
antibiotic

**anticipado** (FEM **anticipada**) ADJECTIVE
early
□ convocar elecciones anticipadas to call early elections
■ **por anticipado** in advance □ pagar por anticipado to pay in advance

**anticipar** VERB [25]
1 to foresee
□ Es imposible anticipar lo que va a ocurrir. It's impossible to foresee what will happen.
2 to bring...forward
□ Habrá que anticipar la reunión. We'll have to bring the meeting forward.

3 to pay...in advance
□ Tuvimos que anticipar el alquiler de dos meses. We had to pay two months' rent in advance.
■ **anticiparse a alguien** to get in before somebody □ Se me anticipó y pagó la cuenta. He got in before me and paid the bill.
■ **Se anticipó a su tiempo.** He was ahead of his time.

el **anticipo** NOUN
advance
□ pedir un anticipo to ask for an advance
■ **ser un anticipo de algo** to be a foretaste of something

el **anticonceptivo** ADJECTIVE, NOUN
contraceptive

**anticuado** (FEM **anticuada**) ADJECTIVE
outdated
■ **quedarse anticuado** to become outdated

la **anticuaria** NOUN
antique dealer

el **anticuario** NOUN
1 antique shop
2 antique dealer

el **antifaz** (PL los **antifaces**) NOUN
mask

**antiguamente** ADVERB
1 in the past
□ Antiguamente no se gastaba tanto. In the past people didn't spend so much money.
2 formerly
□ Antiguamente tenía el nombre de Sociedad de Naciones. Formerly it was called the Society of Nations.

la **antigüedad** NOUN
■ **Es un monumento de gran antigüedad.** It's a very old monument.
■ **en la antigüedad** in ancient times
■ **las antigüedades** antiques
■ **una tienda de antigüedades** an antique shop

**antiguo** (FEM **antigua**) ADJECTIVE
1 old
□ Este reloj es muy antiguo. This clock is very old.
2 ancient
□ Estudia historia antigua. He studies ancient history.
3 former
□ el antiguo secretario general del partido the former general secretary of the party

las **Antillas** NOUN
the West Indies

**antipático** (FEM **antipática**) ADJECTIVE
unfriendly

**antirrobo** (PL **antirrobo**) ADJECTIVE

anti-theft
□ un sistema antirrobo an anti-theft system
el **antiséptico** ADJECTIVE, NOUN
antiseptic
**antojarse** VERB [25]
to feel like
■ **Siempre hace lo que se le antoja.** He always does what he feels like.
■ **Se me ha antojado un helado.** I really fancy an ice-cream.
la **antorcha** NOUN
torch (PL torches)
la **antropología** NOUN
anthropology
**anual** (FEM **anual**) ADJECTIVE
annual
**anular** VERB [25]
1 to call off
□ Anularon el partido por la lluvia. The match was called off owing to the rain.
2 to disallow
□ El árbitro anuló el gol. The referee disallowed the goal.
3 to overturn
□ El Tribunal Supremo anuló la sentencia. The Supreme Court overturned the sentence.
el **anular** NOUN
ring finger
**anunciar** VERB [25]
1 to advertise
□ anunciar detergente to advertise washing powder
2 to announce
□ anunciar una decisión to announce a decision
el **anuncio** NOUN
1 advertisement
□ Pusieron un anuncio en el periódico. They put an advertisement in the paper.
■ **anuncios por palabras** small ads
2 announcement
□ Tengo que hacer un anuncio importante. I have an important announcement to make.
el **anzuelo** NOUN
hook
la **añadidura** NOUN
■ **por añadidura** in addition
**añadir** VERB [58]
to add
los **añicos** NOUN
■ **hacer algo añicos** to smash something to pieces
■ **hacerse añicos** to smash to pieces
el **año** NOUN
year
□ Estuve allí el año pasado. I was there last

year.
■ **el año que viene** next year
■ **el año escolar** the school year
■ **¡Feliz Año Nuevo!** Happy New Year!
■ **los años 80** the 80s
■ **¿Cuántos años tiene?** How old is he?
■ **Tiene 15 años.** He's 15.
**apagado** (FEM **apagada**) ADJECTIVE
switched off
□ La tele estaba apagada. The TV was switched off.
**apagar*** VERB [37]
1 to switch off
□ Apaga la tele. Switch the TV off. □ No apagues la luz. Don't switch the light off.
2 to put out
□ Por favor, apaguen sus cigarrillos. Please put your cigarettes out.
■ **apagar el fuego** to put the fire out
el **apagón** (PL los **apagones**) NOUN
power cut
**apañado** (FEM **apañada**) ADJECTIVE
resourceful
□ ¡Qué apañada eres! How resourceful you are!
**apañarse** VERB [25]
to manage
□ ¿Podrás hacerlo solo? — Ya me apañaré. Can you do it on your own? — I'll manage.
■ **apañarse con algo** to make do with something □ Nos apañaremos con la comida que sobró. We can make do with the leftovers.
el **aparador** NOUN
1 sideboard
2 shop window (Mexico)
el **aparato** NOUN
■ **No sé manejar este aparato.** I don't know how to operate this.
■ **un aparato de televisión** a television
■ **los aparatos de gimnasia** the apparatus
■ **Fabrican aparatos electrónicos.** They make electronic equipment.
■ **un aparato electrodoméstico** an electrical appliance
el **aparcamiento** NOUN
1 car park
□ un aparcamiento subterráneo an underground car park
2 parking place
□ buscar aparcamiento to look for a parking place
**aparcar*** VERB [48]
to park
■ **'prohibido aparcar'** 'no parking'
**aparecer*** VERB [12]
1 to appear
□ De repente apareció la policía. Suddenly

the police appeared.

**2** to turn up

☐ Aparecieron casi una hora tarde. They turned up nearly an hour late. ☐ ¿Han aparecido ya las tijeras? Have the scissors turned up yet?

**3** to come out

☐ Su nueva novela aparecerá el mes próximo. His latest novel will come out next month.

**aparentar** VERB [25]
to appear

☐ Aparentaba no enterarse. He appeared not to understand.

■ **Aparenta más edad de la que tiene.** He looks older than he is.

**aparente** (FEM **aparente**) ADJECTIVE
apparent

**aparentemente** ADVERB
apparently

la **apariencia** NOUN

■ **Tiene la apariencia de un profesor de universidad.** He looks like a university lecturer.

■ **En apariencia nada ha cambiado.** On the surface, nothing had changed.

■ **guardar las apariencias** to keep up appearances

**apartado** (FEM **apartada**) ADJECTIVE
isolated

☐ un lugar apartado an isolated place

■ **Vive apartado de todos.** He lives a secluded life.

el **apartado** NOUN
section

☐ en el siguiente apartado in the following section

■ **apartado de correos** PO box

el **apartamento** NOUN
apartment

**apartar** VERB [25]

**1** to remove

☐ Lo apartaron del equipo. They removed him from the team.

**2** to move out of the way

☐ Aparta todas las sillas. Move all the chairs out of the way.

■ **¡Aparta!** Stand back!

**3** to set aside

☐ Hay que apartar algo del sueldo para las vacaciones. You'll have to set aside some of your pay for the holidays.

■ **apartarse** to stand back ☐ Apártense de la puerta. Stand back from the door.

**aparte** ADVERB

▷ see also **aparte** ADJECTIVE
separately

☐ Cada caso será tratado aparte. Each case

will be dealt with separately.

■ **La ropa que no valga ponla aparte.** Put the clothes that aren't any use on one side.

■ **aparte de 1** apart from ☐ Nadie protestó aparte de ella. Nobody complained apart from her. **2** as well as ☐ Aparte de los patines, también quería una bici. I'd like a bike as well as the skates.

■ **punto y aparte** full stop, new paragraph

**aparte** (FEM **aparte**) ADJECTIVE

▷ see also **aparte** ADVERB
separate

☐ El tuyo es un caso aparte. You're a separate case.

**apasionante** (FEM **apasionante**) ADJECTIVE
exciting

**apasionar** VERB [25]

■ **Le apasiona el fútbol.** He's crazy about football.

**apdo.** ABBREVIATION (= apartado de correos)
PO box (= Post Office box)

**apearse** VERB [25]

■ **apearse de** to get off

el **apego** NOUN

■ **tener apego a algo** to be attached to something

**apellidarse** VERB [25]

■ **Se apellida Pérez.** His surname is Pérez.

el **apellido** NOUN
surname

**apenado** (FEM **apenada**) ADJECTIVE

**1** sad

**2** embarrassed (Latin America)

**apenas** ADVERB, CONJUNCTION

**1** hardly

☐ No tenemos apenas nada de comer. We've got hardly anything to eat. ☐ Apenas podía levantarse. He could hardly stand up.

**2** hardly ever

☐ Apenas voy al cine. I hardly ever go to the cinema.

**3** barely

☐ Hace apenas 10 minutos que hablé con ella. I spoke to her barely 10 minutes ago.

■ **Terminé en apenas dos horas.** It only took me two hours to finish.

**4** as soon as

☐ Apenas me vio, se puso a llorar. As soon as he saw me he began to cry.

la **apendicitis** NOUN
appendicitis

el **aperitivo** NOUN
aperitif

la **apertura** NOUN
opening

☐ el acto de apertura the opening ceremony

**apestar** VERB [25]
to stink

□ Te apestan los pies. Your feet stink.
■ **apestar a** to stink of

**apetecer\*** VERB [12]
■ **¿Te apetece una tortilla?** Do you fancy an omelette?
■ **No, gracias, ahora no me apetece.** No, thanks, I don't feel like it just now.

el **apetito** NOUN
appetite
□ Eso te va a quitar el apetito. You won't have any appetite left.
■ **No tengo apetito.** I'm not hungry.

**apetitoso** (FEM **apetitosa**) ADJECTIVE
1 tasty
2 tempting

el **apio** NOUN
celery

**aplastante** (FEM **aplastante**) ADJECTIVE
overwhelming

**aplastar** VERB [25]
to squash
□ Me senté encima del regalo y lo aplasté. I sat on the present and squashed it.

**aplaudir** VERB [58]
to clap
□ Todos aplaudían. Everyone clapped.

el **aplauso** NOUN
applause
■ **Los aplausos duraron varios minutos.** The applause lasted for several minutes.

**aplazar\*** VERB [13]
to postpone

la **aplicación** (PL las **aplicaciones**) NOUN
application
□ un producto con muchas aplicaciones a product with a lot of applications

**aplicado** (FEM **aplicada**) ADJECTIVE
hard-working
□ un alumno aplicado a hard-working pupil

**aplicar\*** VERB [48]
1 to apply
□ Aplíquese sobre la zona afectada. Apply to the affected area.
2 to enforce
□ No se aplicaron las normas. The rules weren't enforced.

**apoderarse** VERB [25]
■ **apoderarse de un lugar** to take over a place
■ **Se apoderaron de las joyas.** They went off with the jewels.

el **apodo** NOUN
nickname

el **apogeo** NOUN
height
□ en el apogeo de su poder at the height of his power
■ **La fiesta estaba en su apogeo.** The party

was in full swing.

**aportar** VERB [25]
to provide

**aposta** ADVERB
on purpose

**apostar\*** VERB [11]
to bet
■ **apostar por algo** to bet on something
■ **¿Qué te apuestas a que ...?** What's the betting that ...?

el **apóstrofo** NOUN
apostrophe

**apoyar** VERB [25]
1 to lean
□ Apoya el espejo contra la pared. Lean the mirror against the wall.
2 to rest
□ Apoya la espalda en este cojín. Rest your back against this cushion.
3 to support
□ Todos mis compañeros me apoyan. All my colleagues support me.
■ **apoyarse** to lean □ No te apoyes en la mesa. Don't lean on the table.

el **apoyo** NOUN
support

**apreciar** VERB [25]
■ **apreciar a alguien** to be fond of somebody □ Lo apreciábamos mucho. We were very fond of him.
■ **Aprecio mucho mi tiempo libre.** I really value my free time.

el **aprecio** NOUN
■ **tener aprecio a alguien** to be fond of somebody

**aprender** VERB [8]
to learn
□ Ya me he aprendido los verbos irregulares. I've already learnt the irregular verbs.
■ **aprender a hacer algo** to learn to do something
■ **aprender algo de memoria** to learn something by heart

el **aprendiz**, la **aprendiza** (MASC PL los **aprendices**) NOUN
trainee
□ Es aprendiz de mecánico. He's a trainee mechanic.
■ **estar de aprendiz** to be doing an apprenticeship

el **aprendizaje** NOUN
learning
□ dificultades de aprendizaje learning difficulties

**aprensivo** (FEM **aprensiva**) ADJECTIVE
overanxious

**apresurado** (FEM **apresurada**) ADJECTIVE
hasty

**apresurarse** VERB [25]
- **No nos apresuremos.** Let's not be hasty.
- **Me apresuré a sugerir que ...** I hastily suggested that ...

**apretado** (FEM **apretada**) ADJECTIVE
1 tight
  - □ Estos pantalones me están muy apretados. These trousers are very tight on me. □ Tenemos un programa muy apretado. We've got a very tight programme.
2 cramped
  - □ Íbamos muy apretados en el autobús. We were very cramped on the bus.

**apretar\*** VERB [39]
1 to tighten
  - □ Aprieta bien los tornillos. Tighten up the screws.
2 to press
  - □ Aprieta este botón. Press this button.
  - **apretar el gatillo** to press the trigger
  - **Me aprietan los zapatos.** My shoes are too tight.
  - **La apretó contra su pecho.** He clasped her to his bosom.
  - **Apretaos un poco para que me siente yo también.** Move up a bit so I can sit down too.
  - **apretarse el cinturón** to tighten one's belt

el **aprieto** NOUN
  - **estar en un aprieto** to be in a tight spot

**aprisa** ADVERB
fast
  - □ No vayas tan aprisa. Don't go so fast.
  - **¡Aprisa!** Hurry up!

**aprobar\*** VERB [11]
1 to pass
  - □ aprobar un examen to pass an exam
  - **Han aprobado una ley antitabaco.** They've passed an anti-smoking law.
  - **aprobar por los pelos** to scrape through
2 to approve
  - □ La decisión fue aprobada por mayoría. The decision was approved by a majority.
3 to approve of
  - □ No apruebo esa conducta. I don't approve of that sort of behaviour.

**apropiado** (FEM **apropiada**) ADJECTIVE
suitable

**aprovechar** VERB [25]
1 to make good use of
  - □ No aprovecha el tiempo. He doesn't make good use of his time. □ Mi madre aprovecha toda la comida que sobra. My mother makes good use of any leftovers.
2 to use
  - □ Aprovecharé los ratos libres para estudiar.

I'll use the free time to study.
  - **aprovecho la ocasión para decirles ...** I'd like to take this opportunity to tell you ...
  - **Aprovecharé ahora que estoy solo para llamarle.** I'll call him now while I'm on my own.
  - **¡Que aproveche!** Enjoy your meal!
  - **aprovecharse de** to take advantage of
  - □ Me aproveché de la situación. I took advantage of the situation. □ Todos se aprovechan del pobre chico. Everyone takes advantage of the poor boy.

**aproximadamente** ADVERB
about

**aproximado** (FEM **aproximada**) ADJECTIVE
approximate

**aproximarse** VERB [25]
to approach
  - □ Se aproximaba un barco. A boat was approaching.

**apruebo** VERB ▷ see **aprobar**

la **aptitud** NOUN
1 suitability
2 aptitude

**apto** (FEM **apta**) ADJECTIVE
  - **ser apto para algo** to be suitable for something □ No es apta para el puesto. She isn't suitable for the job.
  - **una película no apta para niños** an unsuitable film for children

la **apuesta** NOUN
bet
  - □ Hicimos una apuesta. We had a bet.

**apuesto** VERB ▷ see **apostar**

**apuntar** VERB [25]
1 to write down
  - □ Apúntalo o se te olvidará. Write it down or you'll forget.
  - **Apunta mis datos.** Can you take a note of my details?
2 to point
  - □ Apuntó el arma hacia nosotros. He pointed the gun at us.
  - **Me apuntó con el dedo.** He pointed at me.
  - **Luis me apuntó en el examen.** Luis gave me the answers in the exam.
  - **apuntarse** to put one's name down
  - □ Nos hemos apuntado para el viaje a Marruecos. We've put our names down for the trip to Morocco.
  - **apuntarse a un curso** to enrol on a course
  - **¡Yo me apunto!** Count me in!
  - **LANGUAGE TIP** Be careful! **apuntar** does not mean **to appoint**.

los **apuntes** NOUN
notes

■ **tomar apuntes** to take notes
**apuñalar** VERB [25]
to stab
**apurado** (FEM **apurada**) ADJECTIVE
difficult
□ Estábamos en una situación bastante apurada. We were in rather a difficult situation.
■ **Si estás apurado de dinero, dímelo.** If you're short of money, tell me.
■ **estar apurado** to feel embarrassed
**apurar** VERB [25]
to finish up
□ Apura la cerveza que nos vamos. Finish up your beer and let's go.
■ **apurarse 1** to hurry up □ ¡Apúrate! Hurry up! **2** to worry □ Yo me encargo; no te apures por nada. I'll deal with it – don't you worry about anything.
el **apuro** NOUN
fix
□ El dinero de la herencia los sacó del apuro. The money they inherited got them out of the fix.
■ **Pasé muchos apuros para salir del agua.** I had a lot of trouble getting out of the water.
■ **Me da mucho apuro no llevar ningún regalo.** I feel very embarrassed about not taking a present.
■ **estar en apuros** to be in trouble
**aquel** (FEM **aquella**) ADJECTIVE
that
□ Me gusta más aquella mesa. I prefer that table.
**aquél** (FEM **aquélla**) PRONOUN
that one
□ Éste no, aquél. Not this one, that one.
■ **Aquél no era el que yo quería.** That wasn't the one I wanted.
**aquello** PRONOUN
■ **aquello que hay allí** that thing over there
■ **Me fui; aquello era insoportable.** I left. It was just unbearable.
■ **¿Qué fue de aquello del viaje alrededor del mundo?** What ever happened to that round-the-world trip idea?
**aquellos** (FEM **aquellas**) PL ADJECTIVE
those
□ ¿Ves aquellas montañas? Can you see those mountains?
**aquéllos** (FEM **aquéllas**) PL PRONOUN
those ones
□ Aquéllos de allí son mejores. Those ones over there are better.
■ **Aquéllos no eran los que vimos ayer.** Those aren't the ones we saw yesterday.
**aquí** ADVERB

**1** here
□ Aquí está el informe que me pediste. Here's the report you asked me for.
■ **aquí abajo** down here
■ **aquí arriba** up here
■ **aquí mismo** right here
■ **por aquí 1** around here □ Lo tenía por aquí en alguna parte. I had it around here somewhere. **2** this way □ Pasen por aquí, si son tan amables. Please come this way.
**2** now
■ **de aquí en adelante** from now on
■ **de aquí a siete días** a week from now
■ **hasta aquí 1** up to here □ Hasta aquí el camino es cuesta abajo. Up to here the path goes downhill. **2** up to now □ Hasta aquí todos han ido pagando. Up to now everyone has paid.
el/la **árabe** ADJECTIVE, NOUN
Arab
el **árabe** NOUN
Arabic
**Arabia** FEM NOUN
■ **Arabia Saudí** Saudi Arabia
el **arado** NOUN
plough
la **araña** NOUN
spider
**arañar** VERB [25]
to scratch
□ Me arañó el gato. The cat scratched me.
□ Me arañé la cara con las zarzas. I scratched my face on the brambles.
■ **Pedro se arañó las rodillas al caer.** Pedro grazed his knees when he fell over.
el **arañazo** NOUN
scratch (PL scratches)
**arar** VERB [25]
to plough
el **árbitro**, la **árbitra** NOUN
referee
el **árbol** NOUN
tree
□ un árbol frutal a fruit tree
■ **el árbol de Navidad** the Christmas tree
■ **un árbol genealógico** a family tree
el **arbusto** NOUN
**1** bush (PL bushes)
**2** shrub
el **arca** FEM NOUN
chest
■ **el Arca de Noé** Noah's Ark
las **arcadas** NOUN
■ **Me dieron arcadas con el olor.** The smell made me retch.
el **arcén** (PL los **arcenes**) NOUN
hard shoulder
el **archivador** NOUN

**1** filing cabinet
**2** file
**archivar** VERB [25]
to file
el **archivo** NOUN
**1** archive
**2** file
■ **los archivos policiales** police files
la **arcilla** NOUN
clay
el **arco** NOUN
**1** bow
**2** arch (PL arches)
■ **el arco iris** the rainbow
⚬ LANGUAGE TIP Word for word, **arco iris** means 'iris arch'.
**arder** VERB [8]
to burn
▢ Ese tronco no va a arder. That log won't burn.
■ **¡La sopa está ardiendo!** The soup's boiling hot!
■ **El jefe está que arde.** The boss is seething.
la **ardilla** NOUN
squirrel
el **ardor** NOUN
passion
■ **Defiende sus ideas con ardor.** He defends his ideas passionately.
■ **tener ardor de estómago** to have heartburn
el **área** FEM NOUN
**1** area
▢ el área del triángulo the area of the triangle ▢ en áreas muy pobladas in heavily populated areas
■ **en distintas áreas del país** in different parts of the country
■ **un área de descanso** a lay-by
■ **un área de servicios** a service area
**2** penalty area
▢ una falta al borde del área a foul on the edge of the penalty area
la **arena** NOUN
sand
■ **arenas movedizas** quicksand *sing*
⚬ LANGUAGE TIP Word for word, **arenas movedizas** means 'moving sands'.
el **arenque** NOUN
herring
■ **arenques ahumados** kippers
**Argelia** FEM NOUN
Algeria
el **argelino** (FEM la **argelina**) ADJECTIVE, NOUN
Algerian
**Argentina** FEM NOUN
Argentina

el **argentino** (FEM la **argentina**) ADJECTIVE, NOUN
Argentinian
la **argolla** NOUN
ring
el **argot** (PL los **argots**) NOUN
**1** slang
**2** jargon
el **argumento** NOUN
**1** argument
▢ los argumentos a favor del desarme the arguments in favour of disarmament
**2** plot
▢ el argumento de la película the plot of the film
**árido** (FEM **árida**) ADJECTIVE
arid
**Aries** MASC NOUN
Aries
■ **Soy aries.** I'm Aries.
el/la **aristócrata** NOUN
aristocrat
el **arma** FEM NOUN
**1** weapon
▢ Los guerrilleros entregaron las armas. The guerrillas handed over their weapons. ▢ Se prohibió el uso de armas químicas. The use of chemical weapons was banned.
■ **un fabricante de armas** an arms manufacturer
**2** gun
▢ Nos apuntaba con un arma. He pointed a gun at us.
■ **un arma de fuego** a firearm
la **armada** NOUN
navy (PL navies)
la **armadura** NOUN
armour
■ **una armadura medieval** a medieval suit of armour
el **armamento** NOUN
arms *pl*
▢ negociaciones para la limitación de armamento talks on arms control
**armar** VERB [25]
**1** to arm
▢ No iban armados. They weren't armed.
**2** to assemble
▢ El armario viene desmontado y luego tú lo armas. The cupboard comes in pieces and you assemble it.
**3** to make
▢ Los vecinos de arriba arman mucho jaleo. Our upstairs neighbours make a lot of noise.
■ **Si no aceptan voy a armar un escándalo.** If they don't agree I'm going to make a fuss.
■ **armarse un lío** to get in a muddle

■ **armarse de paciencia** to be patient

■ **armarse de valor** to summon up one's courage

■ **Se armó la gorda.** *(colloquial)* All hell broke loose.

el **armario** NOUN

1 cupboard

■ **un armario de cocina** a kitchen cupboard

2 wardrobe

■ **un armario empotrado** a built-in wardrobe

el **armazón** (PL los **armazones**) NOUN frame

la **armonía** NOUN harmony

la **armónica** NOUN mouth organ

el **aro** NOUN

1 ring

□ los aros olímpicos the Olympic rings

2 hoop

el **aroma** NOUN aroma

la **aromaterapia** NOUN aromatherapy

el **arpa** FEM NOUN harp

la **arqueóloga** NOUN archaeologist

la **arqueología** NOUN archaeology

el **arqueólogo** NOUN archaeologist

el **arquero**, la **arquera** NOUN *(Latin America)* goalkeeper

el **arquitecto**, la **arquitecta** NOUN architect

la **arquitectura** NOUN architecture

**arrancar*** VERB [48]

1 to pull up

□ Estaba arrancando malas hierbas. I was pulling up weeds.

■ **El viento arrancó varios árboles.** Several trees were uprooted by the wind.

■ **arrancar algo de raíz** to pull something up by the roots

2 to pull out

□ Le arranqué una espina del dedo. I pulled a thorn out of his finger.

3 to tear out

□ Arrancó una hoja del cuaderno. He tore a page out of the exercise book.

4 to pull off

□ Me arranqué la tirita. I pulled off the sticking plaster.

5 to snatch

□ Me lo arrancaron de las manos. They snatched it from me.

■ **Arranca y vámonos.** Start the engine and let's get going.

■ **arrancarle información a alguien** to drag information out of somebody

**arrasar** VERB [25]

1 to sweep away

□ El pueblo fue arrasado por las inundaciones. The village was swept away by the floods.

2 to destroy

□ El fuego arrasó la cosecha. The harvest was destroyed by fire.

■ **Los socialistas arrasaron en las elecciones.** The socialists swept the board in the elections.

**arrastrar** VERB [25]

1 to drag

□ Arrastraba una enorme maleta. He was dragging an enormous suitcase.

2 to sweep along

□ El aire nos arrastraba. The wind swept us along.

3 to trail on the ground

□ Las cortinas arrastran un poco. The curtains trail on the ground slightly.

□ Llevas la falda arrastrando. Your skirt's trailing on the ground.

■ **arrastrarse** to crawl □ Llegaron hasta la valla arrastrándose. They crawled up to the fence.

**arrebatar** VERB [25]

snatch

□ Me lo arrebató de las manos. He snatched it from me.

el **arrecife** NOUN reef

■ **los arrecifes de coral** coral reefs

**arreglar** VERB [25]

1 to fix

□ ¿Sabrás arreglarme el grifo? Could you fix the tap for me?

■ **Están arreglando las aceras.** The pavements are being repaired.

2 to do up

□ Este verano hemos arreglado la cocina. This summer we did up the kitchen.

3 to sort out

□ Si tienes algún problema, él te lo arregla. If you have any problems, he'll sort them out for you.

■ **Deja tu cuarto arreglado antes de salir.** Leave your room tidy before going out.

■ **arreglarse 1** to get ready □ Se arregló para salir. She got ready to go out. **2** to work out □ Ya verás como todo se arregla. It'll all work out, you'll see. **3** to manage □ ¿Qué tal te arreglas sin coche? How are you managing without a car?

■ **arreglarse el pelo** to do one's hair

■ **arreglárselas para hacer algo** to manage to do something

el **arreglo** NOUN

**1** repair

□ El tostador sólo necesita un pequeño arreglo. The toaster only needs a minor repair.

■ **Esta tele no tiene arreglo.** This TV is unrepairable.

■ **Este problema no tiene arreglo.** There's no solution to this problem.

**2** compromise

□ Llegamos a un arreglo. We reached a compromise.

■ **con arreglo a** in accordance with

**arrepentirse\*** VERB [51]

■ **arrepentirse de algo** to regret something

■ **arrepentirse de haber hecho algo** to regret doing something

**arrestar** VERB [25]

to arrest

el **arresto** NOUN

arrest

□ un arresto domiciliario house arrest

**arriba** ADVERB

above

□ Los platos y las tazas están arriba. The plates and mugs are above. □ Visto desde arriba parece más pequeño. Seen from above it looks smaller.

■ **Pon esos libros arriba del todo.** Put those books on top.

■ **la parte de arriba del biquini** the bikini top □ Arriba están los dormitorios. The bedrooms are upstairs. □ los vecinos de arriba our upstairs neighbours

■ **allí arriba** up there

■ **más arriba** further up

■ **ir calle arriba** to go up the street

■ **Tenemos bolsos de 20 euros para arriba.** We've got bags from 20 euros upwards.

■ **arriba de 1** (Latin America) on top of □ Lo dejé arriba del refrigerador. I left it on top of the fridge. **2** (Latin America) above □ Viven en el departamento arriba del mío. They live in the flat above mine.

■ **mirar a alguien de arriba abajo** to look somebody up and down

**arriesgado** (FEM **arriesgada**) ADJECTIVE

risky

**arriesgar\*** VERB [37]

to risk

□ Carlos arriesgó su vida para salvar a su perro. Carlos risked his life to save his dog.

■ **arriesgarse** to take a risk □ Se arriesgó pero salió ganando. He took a risk but he came out on top.

■ **arriesgarse a hacer algo** to risk doing something □ Me arriesgo a perderlo todo. I risk losing everything.

**arrimar** VERB [25]

to bring...closer

□ Arrima tu silla a la mía. Bring your chair closer to mine.

■ **Vamos a arrimar la mesa a la pared.** Let's put the table by the wall.

■ **arrimarse** to get close □ Al aparcar procura arrimarte a la acera. Try to get close to the pavement when parking.

■ **Arrímate a mí.** Come closer.

**arrodillarse** VERB [25]

to kneel down

**arrogante** (FEM **arrogante**) ADJECTIVE

arrogant

**arrojar** VERB [25]

**1** to throw

□ Arrojaban piedras y palos. They were throwing sticks and stones.

■ **arrojar a alguien de un sitio** to throw somebody out of a place

**2** to dump

□ 'Prohibido arrojar basuras' 'No dumping'

■ **arrojarse** to throw oneself □ Un hincha se arrojó al campo. A fan threw himself onto the pitch.

**arropar** VERB [25]

**1** to tuck in

□ Voy a arropar al niño. I'll go and tuck the baby in.

**2** to wrap up

□ Arrópala bien. Wrap her up well.

■ **arrópate bien 1** tuck yourself up warmly **2** wrap up well

el **arroyo** NOUN

stream

el **arroz** (PL los **arroces**) NOUN

rice

■ **arroz blanco** white rice

■ **arroz con leche** rice pudding

◯ **LANGUAGE TIP** Word for word, **arroz con leche** means 'rice with milk'.

la **arruga** NOUN

**1** wrinkle

**2** crease

**arrugarse\*** VERB [37]

**1** to get wrinkled

□ La piel se va arrugando. Skin gets increasingly wrinkled.

**2** to get creased

□ Se me han arrugado los pantalones.

My trousers have got creased. □ Procura que no se arrugue el sobre. Try not to let the envelope get creased.

**arruinar** VERB [25]
to ruin

□ Esto arruinó mis planes. That ruined my plans.

■ **arruinarse** to be ruined □ Con aquel negocio se arruinó. He was ruined thanks to that deal.

el **arte** (PL las **artes**) NOUN
1 art

□ el arte del Renacimiento Renaissance art

■ **el arte abstracto** abstract art
■ **el arte dramático** drama
■ **las artes plásticas** plastic arts
2 flair

□ Tiene arte para la cocina. She has a flair for cooking.

■ **por arte de magia** by magic

el **artefacto** NOUN
device

□ un artefacto explosivo an explosive device

la **arteria** NOUN
artery (PL arteries)

la **artesana** NOUN
craftswoman (PL craftswomen)

la **artesanía** NOUN
■ **la artesanía local** local crafts
■ **objetos de artesanía** hand-crafted goods

el **artesano** NOUN
craftsman (PL craftsmen)

**ártico** (FEM **ártica**) ADJECTIVE
arctic

la **articulación** (PL las **articulaciones**) NOUN
joint

el **artículo** NOUN
article

□ el artículo determinado the definite article □ el artículo indeterminado the indefinite article

■ **artículos de lujo** luxury goods
■ **artículos de escritorio** stationery
■ **artículos de tocador** toiletries

**artificial** (FEM **artificial**) ADJECTIVE
artificial

el/la **artista** NOUN
artist

■ **un artista** actor
■ **una artista** actress

la **arveja** NOUN (Latin America)
pea

el **arzobispo** NOUN
archbishop

el **as** NOUN
ace

□ el as de picas the ace of spades

■ **ser un as de la cocina** to be a wizard at cooking

el **asa** FEM NOUN
handle

**asado** (FEM **asada**) ADJECTIVE
roast

□ pollo asado roast chicken

el **asado** NOUN
1 roast
2 barbecue (Latin America)

**asaltar** VERB [25]
1 to storm

□ Los rebeldes asaltaron la embajada. The rebels stormed the embassy.
2 to raid

□ Asaltaron un banco. They raided a bank.
3 to mug

□ Me asaltaron a la salida del banco. I was mugged coming out of the bank.

el **asalto** NOUN
1 raid

□ un asalto a una gasolinera a raid on a petrol station

■ **durante el asalto al parlamento** during the storming of parliament
2 round

la **asamblea** NOUN
1 meeting

□ organizar una asamblea to organize a meeting
2 assembly

□ una asamblea legislativa a legislative assembly

**asar** VERB [25]
to roast

■ **asar algo a la parrilla** to grill something
■ **Me aso de calor.** I'm boiling.
■ **Aquí se asa uno.** It's boiling in here.

**ascender*** VERB [20]
1 to rise

□ El globo comenzó a ascender. The balloon began to rise.
2 to be promoted

□ Ascendió a teniente. He was promoted to lieutenant.

■ **ascender a primera división** to go up to the first division

el **ascenso** NOUN
promotion

el **ascensor** NOUN
lift

**asciendo** VERB ▷see ascender

el **asco** NOUN
■ **El ajo me da asco.** I think garlic's revolting.
■ **¡Puaj! ¡Qué asco!** Yuk! How revolting!
■ **La casa está hecha un asco.** The house

is filthy.

**asegurar** VERB [25]

**1** to insure

□ Hemos asegurado la casa. We've insured the house.

**2** to assure

□ Te aseguro que es verdad. I assure you it's true.

■ **No he sido yo. Te lo aseguro.** It wasn't me, I assure you.

■ **Ella asegura que no lo conoce.** She says that she doesn't know him.

**3** to fasten securely

□ Asegura bien la cuerda. Fasten the rope securely.

■ **asegurarse de** to make sure □ Asegúrate de que los grifos están cerrados. Make sure the taps are turned off.

el **aseo** NOUN

■ **el cuarto de aseo** the toilet

LANGUAGE TIP Word for word, **cuarto de aseo** means 'room of cleanliness'.

■ **el aseo personal** personal hygiene

■ **los aseos** the toilets

**asequible** (FEM **asequible**) ADJECTIVE

**1** affordable

□ un precio asequible an affordable price

**2** achievable

□ una meta asequible an achievable goal

la **asesina** NOUN

murderer

**asesinar** VERB [25]

to murder

el **asesinato** NOUN

murder

el **asesino** NOUN

murderer

el **asesor**, la **asesora** NOUN

consultant

■ **asesor fiscal** tax consultant

■ **asesor de imagen** public relations consultant

el **asfalto** NOUN

tarmac

la **asfixia** NOUN

suffocation

**asfixiarse** VERB [25]

to suffocate

□ Me asfixio de calor. I'm suffocating in this heat.

**así** ADVERB

**1** like this

□ Se hace así. You do it like this.

**2** like that

□ Es así: como lo hace Jorge. It's like that: the way Jorge is doing it. □ ¿Ves aquel abrigo? Quiero algo así. Do you see that coat? I'd like something like that.

■ **un tomate así de grande** a tomato this big

■ **Así es la vida.** That's life.

■ **así, así** so-so □ ¿Te gusta? — Así, así. Do you like it? — So-so.

■ **así es** that's right □ ¿Y ocurrió todo en un día? — Así es. And it all happened the same day? — That's right.

■ **¿No es así?** Isn't that so?

■ **así que ...** so ... □ No me gusta, así que lo tiraré. I don't like it, so I'll throw it away.

■ **... o así** ... or thereabouts □ quince euros o así fifteen euros or thereabouts

■ **y así sucesivamente** and so on

**Asia** FEM NOUN

Asia

el **asiático** (FEM la **asiática**) ADJECTIVE, NOUN

Asian

el **asiento** NOUN

seat

■ **el asiento delantero** the front seat

■ **el asiento trasero** the back seat

la **asignatura** NOUN

subject

■ **Tiene dos asignaturas pendientes.** He's got two subjects to retake.

el **asilo** NOUN

**1** home

■ **un asilo de ancianos** an old people's home

■ **un asilo de pobres** a hostel for the poor

**2** asylum

□ asilo político political asylum

**asimilar** VERB [25]

to assimilate

□ Hay que asimilar lo aprendido. You have to assimilate what you've learnt.

■ **El cambio es grande y cuesta asimilarlo.** It's a big change and it takes getting used to.

la **asistencia** NOUN

■ **asistencia médica 1** medical attention □ Tuvieron que recibir asistencia médica. They needed medical attention. **2** medical care □ El seguro cubre la asistencia médica. The insurance covers medical care.

■ **asistencia técnica** technical support

la **asistenta** NOUN

cleaner

el/la **asistente** NOUN

assistant

■ **asistente social** social worker

■ **los asistentes al acto** those present at the ceremony

**asistir** VERB [58]

**1** to go

□ No asistieron a la ceremonia. They didn't go to the ceremony.

**2** to treat

□ Le asistió un médico que había de guardia. He was treated by a duty doctor.

el **asma** FEM NOUN
asthma

la **asociación** (PL las **asociaciones**) NOUN
association

□ por asociación de ideas by an association of ideas

**asociar** VERB [25]
to associate

□ Asocio la lluvia con Londres. I associate rain with London.

■ **asociarse** to go into partnership □ Los dos empresarios decidieron asociarse. The two businessmen decided to go into partnership.

**asolearse** VERB [25] (Latin America)
to sunbathe

**asomar** VERB [25]

■ **Te asoma el pañuelo por el bolsillo.** Your handkerchief's sticking out of your pocket.

■ **No asomes la cabeza por la ventanilla.** Don't lean out of the window.

■ **Me asomé a la terraza a ver quién gritaba.** I went out onto the balcony to see who was shouting.

■ **Asómate a la ventana.** Look out of the window.

**asombrar** VERB [25]
to amaze

□ Me asombra que no lo sepas. I'm amazed you don't know.

■ **Intentaba asombrarnos con sus conocimientos.** He was trying to stun us with his knowledge.

■ **asombrarse** to be amazed □ Se asombró de lo tarde que era. He was amazed at how late it was.

el **asombro** NOUN
amazement

□ La gente la observaba con asombro. People were looking at her in amazement.

**asombroso** (FEM **asombrosa**) ADJECTIVE
amazing

el **aspecto** NOUN

**1** appearance

□ A ver si cuidas más tu aspecto. Try taking a bit more trouble with your appearance.

**2** aspect

□ Nos interesa mucho el aspecto económico. We are very interested in the financial aspect.

■ **tener buen aspecto 1** to look well **2** to look good

**áspero** (FEM **áspera**) ADJECTIVE

**1** rough

**2** harsh

la **aspiradora** NOUN
vacuum cleaner

**aspirar** VERB [25]

**1** to breathe in

■ **Aspire profundamente.** Take a deep breath.

■ **aspirar a hacer algo** to hope to do something

**2** to hoover (Latin America)

la **aspirina** NOUN
aspirin

**asqueroso** (FEM **asquerosa**) ADJECTIVE

**1** disgusting

**2** filthy

□ Esta cocina está asquerosa. This kitchen is filthy.

**3** horrible

□ Esta gente es asquerosa. They're horrible people.

la **astilla** NOUN
splinter

el **astro** NOUN
star

la **astrología** NOUN
astrology

el/la **astronauta** NOUN
astronaut

la **astronomía** NOUN
astronomy

**astuto** (FEM **astuta**) ADJECTIVE
clever

**asumir** VERB [58]
to accept

□ Ya he asumido que no voy a ganar. I've already accepted that I'm not going to win.

■ **Asumo toda la responsabilidad.** I take full responsibility.

■ **No estoy dispuesta a asumir ese riesgo.** I'm not prepared to take that risk.

el **asunto** NOUN
matter

□ Es un asunto muy delicado. It's a very delicate matter.

■ **el ministro de asuntos exteriores** the minister for foreign affairs

■ **No me gusta que se metan en mis asuntos.** I don't like anyone meddling in my affairs.

■ **¡Eso no es asunto tuyo!** That's none of your business!

**asustar** VERB [25]

**1** to frighten

□ No me asustan los fantasmas. I'm not frightened of ghosts.

**2** to startle

□ ¡Huy! Me has asustado. Goodness! You startled me.

■ **asustarse** to get frightened □ Se asusta por nada. He gets frightened over nothing.
■ **No te asustes.** Don't be frightened.

**atacar\*** VERB [48]
to attack

el **atado** NOUN *(River Plate)*
■ **un atado de cigarrillos** a packet of cigarettes

el **atajo** NOUN
short cut
□ Cogeremos un atajo. We'll take a short cut.

el **ataque** NOUN
attack
□ un ataque contra alguien an attack on somebody
■ **un ataque cardíaco** a heart attack
■ **Le dio un ataque de risa.** He burst out laughing.
■ **un ataque de nervios** a fit of panic

**atar** VERB [25]
to tie
□ Ata al perro a la farola. Tie the dog to the lamppost.
■ **Átate los cordones.** Tie your shoelaces up.

**atardecer\*** VERB [12]
to get dark
□ Está atardeciendo. It's getting dark.

el **atardecer** NOUN
dusk
■ **al atardecer** at dusk

**atareado** (FEM **atareada**) ADJECTIVE
busy

el **atasco** NOUN
traffic jam

el **ataúd** NOUN
coffin

**Atenas** FEM NOUN
Athens

la **atención** (PL las **atenciones**) NOUN
■ **Hay que poner más atención.** You should pay more attention.
■ **Escucha con atención.** He listens attentively.
■ **Me llamó la atención lo grande que era la casa.** I was struck by how big the house was.
■ **El director del colegio le llamó la atención.** The headmaster gave him a talking-to.
■ **Estás llamando la atención con ese sombrero.** You're attracting attention in that hat.

**atención** EXCLAMATION
Attention!
■ **¡Atención, por favor!** May I have your attention please?

■ **'¡Atención!'** 'Danger!'

**atender\*** VERB [20]
1 to serve
□ ¿Le atienden? Are you being served?
2 to attend to
□ Tengo que atender a un par de clientes. I've got a couple of clients to attend to.
3 to look after
□ atender a los enfermos to look after the sick
4 to pay attention to
□ Todos en clase atendían al profesor. Everyone in the class was paying attention to the teacher.
■ **atender los consejos de alguien** to listen to somebody's advice
■ **La recepcionista atiende al teléfono.** The receptionist answers the telephone.
■ **No atendieron nuestra petición.** They didn't take any notice of our petition.

el **atentado** NOUN
attack
□ un atentado terrorista a terrorist attack
□ un atentado suicida a suicide attack

**atentamente** ADVERB
1 Yours sincerely
2 Yours faithfully

**atento** (FEM **atenta**) ADJECTIVE
thoughtful
□ Es un chico muy atento. He's a very thoughtful boy.
■ **Estaban atentos a las explicaciones del instructor.** They were listening attentively to the instructor's explanations.

el **aterrizaje** NOUN
landing
■ **un aterrizaje forzoso** an emergency landing

**aterrizar\*** VERB [13]
to land

**atestado** (FEM **atestada**) ADJECTIVE
packed
□ El local estaba atestado de gente. The place was packed with people.

**atiborrarse** VERB [25]
to stuff oneself
□ Se atiborró de pasteles. He stuffed himself with cakes.

el **ático** NOUN
top-floor flat
■ **un ático de lujo** a luxurious penthouse

**atiendo** VERB ▷ see **atender**

**atlántico** (FEM **atlántica**) ADJECTIVE
Atlantic
■ **el océano Atlántico** the Atlantic Ocean

el **atlas** (PL los **atlas**) NOUN
atlas (PL atlases)

el/la **atleta** NOUN

athlete

el **atletismo** NOUN
athletics

la **atmósfera** NOUN
atmosphere

**atolondrado** (FEM **atolondrada**) ADJECTIVE
scatterbrained

**atómico** (FEM **atómica**) ADJECTIVE
atomic

el **átomo** NOUN
the atom

**atónito** (FEM **atónita**) ADJECTIVE
amazed

■ **quedarse atónito** to be amazed

el **atracador**, la **atracadora** NOUN
1 robber
□ un atracador de bancos a bank robber
2 mugger
□ Unos atracadores le robaron el bolso. She had her bag stolen by muggers.

**atracar**\* VERB [48]
1 to hold up
□ atracar un banco to hold up a bank
2 to mug
□ La atracaron en la plaza. She was mugged in the square.

la **atracción** (PL las **atracciones**) NOUN
attraction
□ una atracción turística a tourist attraction
■ **sentir atracción por algo** to be attracted to something □ Sentía atracción por él. I was attracted to him.

el **atraco** NOUN
1 hold-up
□ un atraco a un banco a hold-up at a bank
2 mugging
□ un atraco en plena calle a mugging in broad daylight

**atractivo** (FEM **atractiva**) ADJECTIVE
attractive
□ un hombre muy atractivo a very attractive man

el **atractivo** NOUN
attraction
■ **Es una chica con un atractivo especial.** She's a really charming girl.

**atraer**\* VERB [54]
to attract
□ Si bajamos los precios atraeremos a más clientes. If we put our prices down we'll attract more customers.
■ **Esa chica me atrae mucho.** I find that girl very attractive.
■ **No me atrae mucho lo del viaje a Turquía.** That Turkey trip doesn't appeal to me much.

**atrapar** VERB [25]
to catch

**atrás** ADVERB
□ Los niños viajan siempre atrás. The children always travel in the back.
■ **la parte de atrás** the back
■ **el asiento de atrás** the back seat □ Mirar hacia atrás. To look back. □ Está más atrás. It's further back.
■ **Ir para atrás.** To go backwards. □ El coche de atrás va a adelantarnos. The car behind is going to overtake us. □ Yo me quedé atrás porque iba muy cansado. I stayed behind because I was very tired.
■ **años atrás** years ago

**atrasado** (FEM **atrasada**) ADJECTIVE
1 backward
□ Es un país muy atrasado. It's a very backward country.
2 back
□ números atrasados de una revista back numbers of a magazine □ pagos atrasados back payments
3 behind
□ Va bastante atrasado en la escuela. He's rather behind at school.
■ **Tengo mucho trabajo atrasado.** I'm very behind with my work.
■ **El reloj está atrasado.** The clock's slow.
4 late (Latin America)
□ Siempre llega atrasada al trabajo. She's always late for work.

**atrasar** VERB [25]
1 to delay
□ Tuvimos que atrasar nuestra salida. We had to delay our departure.
2 to put back
□ Acordaos de atrasar una hora vuestros relojes. Remember to put your watches back one hour.
■ **atrasarse** to be late □ El tren se atrasó. The train was late.

**atravesar**\* VERB [39]
1 to cross
□ Atravesamos el río. We crossed the river.
2 to go through
□ La navaja le atravesó el hígado. The blade went through his liver. □ Atravesamos un mal momento. We're going through a bad patch.

**atravieso** VERB ▷ see atravesar

**atreverse** VERB [8]
to dare
□ No me atreví a decírselo. I didn't dare tell him.
■ **No me atrevo.** I daren't.
■ **La gente no se atreve a salir de noche.** People are afraid to go out at night.

**atrevido** (FEM **atrevida**) ADJECTIVE
1 daring

□ El periodista le hizo preguntas muy atrevidas. The reporter asked him some very daring questions. □ un escote muy atrevido a very daring neckline

**2** cheeky

□ No seas tan atrevido con el jefe. Don't be so cheeky to the boss.

**atropellar** VERB [25]
to run over

□ Un coche atropelló al perro. The dog was run over by a car.

**el/la ATS** ABBREVIATION *(= Ayudante Técnico Sanitario)*
Registered Nurse

**el atún** (PL los **atunes**) NOUN
tuna (PL tuna *o* tunas)

**audaz** (FEM **audaz**, PL **audaces**) ADJECTIVE
daring

**la audiencia** NOUN
audience

□ Su programa tiene mucha audiencia. His programme has a large audience.

**audiovisual** (FEM **audiovisual**) ADJECTIVE
audiovisual

**el auditorio** NOUN
**1** auditorium

□ El auditorio estaba lleno. The auditorium was full.

**2** audience

□ Todo el auditorio aplaudió a la orquesta. The whole audience applauded the orchestra.

**el aula** FEM NOUN
classroom

**aumentar** VERB [25]
to increase

□ El gobierno ha aumentado el presupuesto de educación. The government has increased the education budget.

■ **aumentar de peso** to put on weight

**el aumento** NOUN
increase

□ Se ha producido un aumento de la productividad. There has been an increase in productivity.

■ **Los precios van en aumento.** Prices are going up.

**aun** ADVERB
even

□ Aun sentado me duele la pierna. Even when I'm sitting down, my leg hurts.

■ **aun así** even so

■ **aun cuando** even if

**aún** ADVERB
**1** still

□ Aún me queda un poco para terminar. I've still got a little bit left to finish. □ ¿Aún te duele? Is it still hurting?

**2** yet

□ Aún no han llegado los periódicos de hoy. Today's papers haven't arrived yet. □ ¿No ha venido aún? Hasn't he got here yet? □ Y aún no me has devuelto el libro. You still haven't given me the book back.

**3** even

□ La película es aún más aburrida de lo que creía. The film's even more boring than I thought it would be. □ Aquello nos unió aún más. That brought us even closer together.

**aunque** CONJUNCTION
**1** although

□ Me gusta el francés, aunque prefiero el alemán. I like French, although I prefer German. □ Estoy pensando en ir, aunque no sé cuándo. I'm thinking of going, though I don't know when.

**2** even though

□ Seguí andando, aunque me dolía mucho la pierna. I went on walking, even though my leg was hurting badly.

■ **No te lo daré, aunque protestes.** I won't give it to you however much you complain.

**3** even if

□ Pienso irme, aunque tenga que salir por la ventana. I shall leave, even if I have to climb out of the window.

**el auricular** NOUN
receiver

■ **los auriculares** headphones

**la ausencia** NOUN
absence

**ausente** (FEM **ausente**) ADJECTIVE
absent

**Australia** FEM NOUN
Australia

**el australiano** (FEM la **australiana**) ADJECTIVE, NOUN
Australian

**Austria** FEM NOUN
Austria

**el austriaco** (FEM la **austriaca**) ADJECTIVE, NOUN
Austrian

**auténtico** (FEM **auténtica**) ADJECTIVE
**1** real

□ Es de cuero auténtico. It's real leather.

**2** genuine

□ El cuadro era auténtico. The painting was genuine.

■ **Es un auténtico campeón.** He's a real champion.

**el auto** NOUN
car

**la autobiografía** NOUN
autobiography (PL autobiographies)

**el autobús** (PL los **autobuses**) NOUN

bus (PL buses)

■ **en autobús** by bus

■ **un autobús de línea** a coach

el **autocar** NOUN
coach (PL coaches)

la **autoedición** NOUN
desktop publishing

la **autoescuela** NOUN
driving school

el **autógrafo** NOUN
autograph

**automático** (FEM **automática**) ADJECTIVE
automatic

el **automóvil** NOUN
car

el/la **automovilista** NOUN
motorist

la **autonomía** NOUN

1 autonomy
□ un estatuto de autonomía a statute of autonomy □ Tengo mucha autonomía en mi trabajo. I have a lot of autonomy in my work.

2 autonomous region
□ Andalucía es una de las autonomías más extensas. Andalusia is one of the biggest autonomous ones.

**autonómico** (FEM **autonómica**) ADJECTIVE
regional

**autónomo** (FEM **autónoma**) ADJECTIVE

1 autonomous
□ las comunidades autónomas the autonomous regions

2 self-employed
□ Ser autónomo tiene sus ventajas. Being self-employed has its advantages.

la **autopista** NOUN
motorway

■ **autopista de peaje** toll motorway

el **autor**, la **autora** NOUN
author
□ el autor de la novela the author of the novel

■ **el autor del cuadro** the painter

■ **los presuntos autores del crimen** the suspected killers

la **autoridad** NOUN
authority

**autorizado** (FEM **autorizada**) ADJECTIVE
authorized

**autorizar\*** VERB [13]
to authorize
□ No le han autorizado la entrada al país. His entry into the country hasn't been authorized.

■ **Eso no te autoriza a tratarlo así.** That doesn't give you the right to treat him this way.

el **autoservicio** NOUN

1 supermarket
□ Sale más económico comprar en el autoservicio. It's cheaper to shop at the supermarket.

2 self-service restaurant
□ Comimos en un autoservicio. We ate at a self-service restaurant.

el **autostop** NOUN
hitch-hiking

■ **hacer autostop** to hitch-hike

el/la **autostopista** NOUN
hitch-hiker

la **autovía** NOUN
dual carriageway

el **auxilio** NOUN
help
□ una llamada de auxilio a call for help

■ **los primeros auxilios** first aid

**auxilio** EXCLAMATION
help!

**avanzar\*** VERB [13]
to make progress
□ Isabel avanzó mucho el pasado trimestre. Isabel made a lot of progress last term.

■ **¿Qué tal avanza el proyecto?** How's the project coming on?

**avaricioso** (FEM **avariciosa**) ADJECTIVE
greedy

**avaro** (FEM **avara**) ADJECTIVE
miserly

**Avda.** ABBREVIATION (= Avenida)
Ave. (= Avenue)

el **AVE** ABBREVIATION (= Alta Velocidad Española)
high-speed train

el **ave** FEM NOUN
bird

■ **un ave de rapiña** a bird of prey

■ **aves de corral** poultry sing

la **avellana** NOUN
hazelnut

la **avena** NOUN
oats pl

la **avenida** NOUN
avenue

**aventajar** VERB [25]

■ **El Salamanca aventaja en tres puntos al Córdoba.** Salamanca has a three-point lead over Córdoba.

**aventar\*** VERB [39] (Mexico)
to throw

el **aventón** (PL los **aventones**) NOUN
(Mexico)
lift
□ Le di un aventón. I gave him a lift.

la **aventura** NOUN

1 adventure

□ Te contaré nuestras aventuras en África.
I'll tell you about our adventures in Africa.
**2** affair
□ Tuvo una aventura con su vecino. She had
an affair with her neighbour.

**avergonzar*** VERB [13]
to embarrass
□ Me avergonzaste delante de todos.
You embarrassed me in front of everyone.
■ **Me avergüenzan estas situaciones.**
I find this sort of situation embarrassing.
■ **No me avergüenza nuestra relación.**
I'm not ashamed of our relationship.
■ **avergonzarse de algo** to be ashamed
of something □ No hay de qué
avergonzarse. There's nothing to be
ashamed of.
■ **Me avergüenzo de haberme portado
tan mal.** I'm ashamed of myself for
behaving so badly.

**la avería** NOUN
■ **El coche tiene una avería.** The car has
broken down.

**averiarse*** VERB [21]
to break down

**averiguar*** VERB
to find out
□ La policía no ha conseguido averiguar
dónde se escondió el arma. The police
haven't managed to find out where the
weapon was hidden.

**el avestruz** (PL los **avestruces**) NOUN
ostrich (PL ostriches)

**la aviación** (PL las **aviaciones**) NOUN
**1** aviation
□ aviación civil civil aviation
**2** air force
□ Es oficial de aviación. He's an officer in
the air force.

**aviento** VERB ▷ see **aventar**

**el avión** (PL los **aviones**) NOUN
plane
■ **ir en avión** to fly

**la avioneta** NOUN
light aircraft

**avisar** VERB [25]
**1** to warn
□ Ya nos avisaron de que había nieve en la
carretera. They had warned us that there
was snow on the roads.
**2** to let...know
□ Avísanos si hay alguna novedad. Let us
know if there's any news.
**3** to call
□ avisar al médico to call the doctor
□ Avisaron a una ambulancia. They called
an ambulance.

38 **el aviso** NOUN

**1** warning
□ El árbitro le dio un aviso. The referee gave
him a warning.
**2** notice
□ Había un aviso en la puerta. There was a
notice on the door.
■ **hasta nuevo aviso** until further notice

**la avispa** NOUN
wasp

**ay** EXCLAMATION
**1** ow!
□ ¡Ay! ¡Me has pisado! Ow! You've trodden
on my toe!
**2** oh no!
□ ¡Ay! ¡Creo que nos han engañado! Oh no!
I think they've cheated us!

**ayer** ADVERB
yesterday
■ **antes de ayer** the day before yesterday
■ **ayer por la mañana** yesterday morning
■ **ayer por la tarde 1** yesterday afternoon
**2** yesterday evening
■ **ayer por la noche** last night

**la ayuda** NOUN
help
■ **la ayuda humanitaria** humanitarian aid

**el/la ayudante** NOUN
assistant

**ayudar** VERB [25]
to help
□ ¿Me ayudas con los ejercicios? Could you
help me with these exercises?
■ **ayudar a alguien a hacer algo** to help
somebody do something

**el ayuntamiento** NOUN
**1** council
□ El ayuntamiento recauda sus propios
impuestos. The council collects its own
taxes.
**2** town hall
□ ¿Dónde está el ayuntamiento? Where's
the town hall?
**3** city hall
□ ¿Dónde está el ayuntamiento? Where's
the city hall?

**la azafata** NOUN
air-hostess
■ **una azafata de congresos** a conference
hostess

**el azar** NOUN
chance
□ Nos encontramos por azar. We met by
chance.
■ **al azar** at random □ Escoge uno al azar.
Pick one at random.

**azotar** VERB [25]
to whip

**la azotea** NOUN

roof

el/la **azteca** ADJECTIVE, NOUN
Aztec

el **azúcar** NOUN
sugar

▪ **azúcar moreno** brown sugar
▪ **un caramelo sin azúcar** a sugar-free
sweet

el **azul** ADJECTIVE, NOUN
blue

▫ una puerta azul a blue door ▫ Yo iba de
azul. I was dressed in blue.

▪ **azul celeste** sky blue
▪ **azul marino** navy blue

el **azulejo** NOUN
tile

# Bb

el **babero** NOUN
bib

el **babi** NOUN
smock

la **baca** NOUN
roof rack

el **bacalao** NOUN
cod

el **bache** NOUN
1 pothole
2 bump

el **Bachillerato** NOUN

> **DID YOU KNOW...?**
> The **Bachillerato** is a two-year
> secondary school course leading to
> university.

la **bacteria** NOUN
bacterium (PL bacteria)

el **bafle** NOUN
loudspeaker

la **bahía** NOUN
bay (PL bays)

**bailar** VERB [25]
to dance

■ **sacar a bailar a alguien** to ask someone
to dance

el **bailarín**, la **bailarina** NOUN (MASC PL los
**bailarines**
dancer

el **baile** NOUN
dance

□ Me han invitado a un baile. I have been
invited to a dance.

la **baja** NOUN

■ **darse de baja** to leave □ Se dieron de
baja en el club. They left the club.

■ **estar de baja** to be on sick leave

la **bajada** NOUN
drop

□ Hubo una bajada de las temperaturas.
There was a drop in temperature.

■ **Me caí en la bajada de la montaña.** I fell
going down the mountain.

■ **La bajada hasta la playa es muy
pronunciada.** The road down to the beach
is very steep.

**bajar** VERB [25]
1 to go down

□ Bajó la escalera muy despacio. He went
down the stairs very slowly.

2 to come down

□ Baja y ayúdame. Come down and help
me. □ Han bajado los precios. Prices have
come down.

■ **Los coches han bajado de precio.** Cars
have come down in price.

3 to take down

□ ¿Has bajado la basura? Have you taken
the rubbish down?

4 to bring down

□ ¿Me bajas el abrigo? Hace frío aquí fuera.
Could you bring my coat down, it's cold out
here.

5 to get down

□ ¿Me bajas la maleta del armario? Could
you get me the suitcase down from the
wardrobe?

6 to put down

□ ¿Bajo la persiana? Shall I put the blind
down? □ Los comercios han bajado los
precios. Businesses have put their prices
down.

■ **¡Baja la voz, que no estoy sordo!** Keep
your voice down, I'm not deaf!

7 to turn down

□ Baja la radio que no oigo nada. Turn the
radio down, I can't hear a thing.

8 to download

■ **bajarse de 1** to get off □ Se bajó del
autobús antes que yo. He got off the bus
before me. **2** to get out of □ ¡Bájate del
coche! Get out of the car! **3** to get down
from □ ¡Bájate de ahí! Get down from there!

**bajo** (FEM **baja**) ADJECTIVE

▷ see also **bajo** PREPOSITION, ADVERB

1 low

□ una silla muy baja a very low chair

■ **la temporada baja** the low season

2 short

□ Mi hermano es muy bajo. My brother is
very short.

■ **Viven en la planta baja.** They live on the

ground floor.

■ **Hablaban en voz baja.** They spoke quietly.

**bajo** PREPOSITION

▷ *see also* **bajo** ADJECTIVE, ADVERB
under

□ bajo el título de … under the title of …

□ Juan llevaba un libro bajo el brazo. Juan was carrying a book under his arm.

■ **bajo tierra** underground

**bajo** ADVERB

▷ *see also* **bajo** ADJECTIVE, PREPOSITION

1 low

□ El avión volaba muy bajo. The plane was flying very low.

2 quietly

□ ¡Habla bajo! Speak quietly!

el **bajo** NOUN

1 bass (PL basses)

□ Elena toca el bajo en un grupo. Elena plays bass in a group.

2 ground floor

□ Vivo en un bajo. I live on the ground floor.

el **bakalao** NOUN
techno

la **bala** NOUN
bullet

el **balcón** (PL los **balcones**) NOUN
balcony (PL balconies)

la **baldosa** NOUN
tile

el **baldosín** (PL los **baldosines**) NOUN
tile

**balear** (FEM **balear**) ADJECTIVE
Balearic

**Baleares** FEM PL NOUN
the Balearic Islands

la **ballena** NOUN
whale

el **ballet** (PL los **ballets**) NOUN
ballet

el **balneario** NOUN
spa

el **balón** (PL los **balones**) NOUN
ball

el **baloncesto** NOUN
basketball

el **balonmano** NOUN
handball

el **balonvolea** NOUN
volleyball

la **balsa** NOUN
raft

la **banana** NOUN *(Latin America)*
banana

**bancario** (FEM **bancaria**) ADJECTIVE
bank

el **banco** NOUN

1 bank

2 bench (PL benches)

3 pew

la **banda** NOUN

1 band

□ Toca la trompeta en la banda del pueblo. He plays the trumpet in the village band.

2 gang

□ La policía ha cogido a toda la banda. The police have caught the whole gang.

3 sash (PL sashes)

□ Las autoridades llevaban una banda azul. The dignitaries were wearing blue sashes.

■ **la banda ancha** broadband

■ **la banda sonora** the soundtrack

**LANGUAGE TIP** Word for word, **banda sonora** means 'sound band'.

la **bandeja** NOUN
tray (PL trays)

la **bandera** NOUN
flag

■ **la bandera blanca** the white flag

el **bandido** NOUN
bandit

el **bando** NOUN
side

□ Un bando está a favor y el otro en contra. One side is in favour and the other is against.

la **banqueta** NOUN

1 stool

2 pavement *(Mexico)*

el **banquete** NOUN
banquet

■ **el banquete de bodas** the wedding reception

el **banquillo** NOUN
bench (PL benches)

□ El entrenador está en el banquillo. The trainer is sitting on the bench.

■ **el banquillo de los acusados** the dock

el **bañador** NOUN

1 swimming trunks *pl*

2 swimming costume

**bañarse** VERB [25]

1 to have a bath

□ Me gusta más bañarme que ducharme. I prefer having a bath to having a shower.

2 to go for a swim

□ Estuve en la playa pero no me bañé. I was on the beach but I didn't go for a swim.

la **bañera** NOUN
bath

el **baño** NOUN
bathroom

□ ¿Dónde está el baño, por favor? Where is the bathroom, please?

■ **darse un baño 1** to have a bath **2** to go

for a swim

el **bar** NOUN
bar

la **baraja** NOUN
pack of cards

la **barandilla** NOUN
1 banisters pl
2 railing

la **barata** NOUN (Mexico)
sale

**barato** (FEM **barata**) ADJECTIVE
▷ see also **barato** ADVERB
cheap
□ Esta marca es más barata que aquélla. This brand is cheaper than that one.

**barato** ADVERB
▷ see also **barato** ADJECTIVE
cheaply
□ Aquí se come muy barato. You can eat really cheaply here.

la **barba** NOUN
beard
■ **dejarse barba** to grow a beard

la **barbacoa** NOUN
barbecue

la **barbaridad** NOUN
atrocity (PL atrocities)
□ Hicieron barbaridades en la guerra. They committed atrocities during the war.
■ **Pablo come una barbaridad.** Pablo eats an awful lot.
■ **decir barbaridades** to talk nonsense
■ **¡Qué barbaridad!** Good grief!

la **barbilla** NOUN
chin

la **barca** NOUN
boat

el **barco** NOUN
1 ship
■ **un barco de guerra** a warship
2 boat
■ **un barco de vela** a sailing boat

la **barda** NOUN (Mexico)
fence

el **barniz** (PL los **barnices**) NOUN
varnish (PL varnishes)

**barnizar\*** VERB [13]
to varnish

la **barra** NOUN
bar
□ una barra metálica a metal bar □ Me tomé un café en la barra. I had a coffee at the bar.
■ **una barra de pan** a French loaf
■ **una barra de labios** lipstick
■ **las barras paralelas** the parallel bars

la **barraca** NOUN
small farmhouse

■ **una barraca de feria** a fairground stall

el **barranco** NOUN
ravine

**barrer** VERB [8]
to sweep

la **barrera** NOUN
barrier
■ **una barrera de seguridad** a safety barrier

la **barriga** NOUN
belly (PL bellies)
□ Estás echando barriga. You're getting a bit of a belly.
■ **Me duele la barriga.** I have a sore stomach.

el **barril** NOUN
barrel

el **barrilete** NOUN (River Plate)
kite

el **barrio** NOUN
area
□ Ese chico no es del barrio. That boy's not from this area.
■ **la pescadería del barrio** the local fishmonger's
■ **el barrio chino** the red-light district

el **barro** NOUN
1 mud
□ Me llené los zapatos de barro. My shoes got covered in mud.
2 clay
□ una vasija de barro a clay pot

el **barrote** NOUN
bar
□ los barrotes de la ventana the bars on the window

el **barullo** NOUN
1 racket
■ **armar barullo** to make a racket
2 mess
□ Esta habitación está hecha un barullo. This room is a mess.

**basarse** VERB [25]
■ **Mi conclusión se basa en los datos.** My conclusion is based on the facts.
■ **¿En qué te basas para decir eso?** What grounds have you got for saying that?
■ **Para la novela me basé en la vida de mi abuela.** I based the novel on the life of my grandmother.

la **báscula** NOUN
scales pl

la **base** NOUN
1 base
□ la base de la columna the base of the column
2 basis (PL bases)
□ El esfuerzo es la base del éxito. Effort is

the basis for success.

■ **las bases del concurso** the rules of the competition

■ **Lo consiguió a base de mucho trabajo.** She managed it through hard work.

■ **una base militar** a military base

■ **una base de datos** a database

**básico** (FEM **básica**) ADJECTIVE
basic

**bastante** (FEM **bastante**) ADJECTIVE, PRONOUN
▷ *see also* **bastante** ADVERB

1 enough

□ No tengo bastante dinero. I haven't enough money. □ Ya hay bastantes libros en casa. There are enough books in the house. □ ¿Hay bastante? Is there enough?

2 quite a lot of

□ Vino bastante gente. Quite a lot of people came.

■ **Se tarda bastante tiempo en llegar.** It takes quite a while to get there.

■ **Voy a tardar bastante.** I'm going to take quite a while.

**bastante** ADVERB
▷ *see also* **bastante** ADJECTIVE, PRONOUN

1 quite

□ Son bastante ricos. They are quite rich. □ Juegas bastante bien. You play quite well.

2 quite a lot

□ Sus padres ganan bastante. Their parents earn quite a lot.

**bastar** VERB [25]
to be enough

□ Con esto basta. That's enough. □ ¡Basta ya de tonterías! That's enough of your nonsense!

■ **¡Basta!** That's enough!

■ **bastarse** to manage □ Yo me basto solo. I can manage on my own.

**basto** (FEM **basta**) ADJECTIVE
coarse

□ Esta tela es muy basta. It's a very coarse material.

■ **¡Qué basto eres!** You've got no manners!

**el bastón** (PL los **bastones**) NOUN
stick

■ **un bastón de esquí** a ski stick

**los bastos** NOUN
clubs

**DID YOU KNOW...?**
**Bastos** are clubs, one of the suits in the Spanish card deck.

**la basura** NOUN

1 rubbish

□ Eso es basura. That's rubbish.

■ **tirar algo a la basura** to put something in the bin

2 litter

□ Hay mucha basura en la calle. There's a lot of litter in the street.

**el basurero** NOUN

1 dustman (PL dustmen)

2 rubbish dump

3 rubbish bin (Chile, Mexico)

**la bata** NOUN

1 dressing gown

2 lab coat

**la batalla** NOUN
battle

**la batería** NOUN

1 battery (PL batteries)

□ Se ha agotado la batería. The battery is flat.

2 drums pl

□ ¿Tocas la batería? Do you play the drums?

■ **aparcar en batería** to park at an angle to the kerb

■ **una batería de cocina** a set of kitchen equipment

3 drummer

□ La batería del grupo se llama Amanda. The group's drummer is called Amanda.

**el batería** NOUN
drummer

□ El batería del grupo se llama Juan. The group's drummer is called Juan.

**el batido** NOUN
milkshake

□ un batido de fresa a strawberry milkshake

**la batidora** NOUN
mixer

**batir** VERB [58]

1 to beat

2 to whip

3 to break

**el baúl** NOUN

1 chest

2 trunk

3 boot (River Plate)

**el bautizo** NOUN
christening

**la bayeta** NOUN
cloth

■ **¿Has pasado la bayeta por la mesa?** Have you wiped the table?

**el bebe**, la **beba** NOUN (River Plate)
baby (PL babies)

**el bebé** (PL los **bebés**) NOUN
baby (PL babies)

**el bebedero** NOUN (Chile, Mexico)
drinking fountain

**beber** VERB [8]
to drink

■ **Se bebió la leche de un trago.** He drank the milk in one gulp.

**la bebida** NOUN

drink

■ **bebidas alcohólicas** alcoholic drinks

**bebido** (FEM **bebida**) ADJECTIVE
drunk

■ **estar bebido** to be drunk

la **beca** NOUN
1 grant
2 scholarship

el **béisbol** NOUN
baseball

el **belén** (PL los **belenes**) NOUN
crib

el/la **belga** ADJECTIVE, NOUN
Belgian

**Bélgica** FEM NOUN
Belgium

la **belleza** NOUN
beauty (PL beauties)

**bello** (FEM **bella**) ADJECTIVE
beautiful

■ **bellas artes** fine art *sing*

**bendecir\*** VERB [15]
to bless

la **bendición** (PL las **bendiciones**) NOUN
blessing

**beneficiar** VERB [25]
to benefit

■ **beneficiarse de algo** to benefit from
something

el **beneficio** NOUN
profit

□ Obtuvieron un beneficio de un millón
de euros. They made a profit of a million
euros.

■ **No han tenido beneficios este año.**
They didn't make any profit this year.

■ **sacar beneficio de algo** to benefit from
something □ Seguro que espera sacar algún
beneficio. He definitely expects to benefit
from it.

■ **a beneficio de** in aid of □ un concierto a
beneficio de las víctimas del terremoto a
concert in aid of the earthquake victims

**benéfico** (FEM **benéfica**) ADJECTIVE
charity (PL charities)

□ un concierto benéfico a charity concert

el **berberecho** NOUN
cockle

la **berenjena** NOUN
aubergine

las **bermudas** NOUN
Bermuda shorts

■ **unas bermudas** a pair of Bermuda
shorts

la **berza** NOUN
cabbage

**besar** VERB [25]
to kiss

■ **Ana y Pepe se besaron.** Ana and Pepe
kissed each other.

el **beso** NOUN
kiss (PL kisses)

■ **dar un beso a alguien** to give somebody
a kiss

la **bestia** NOUN
beast

**bestia** (FEM **bestia**) ADJECTIVE
■ **¡Qué bestia eres!** You're so rough!
■ **Tiró de él a lo bestia.** He pulled him
roughly.

el **besugo** NOUN
sea bream

el **betún** NOUN
shoe polish

el **biberón** (PL los **biberones**) NOUN
baby's bottle

■ **Voy a dar el biberón al niño.** I'm going to
give the baby his bottle.

la **Biblia** NOUN
Bible

la **biblioteca** NOUN
library (PL libraries)

el **bicarbonato** NOUN
bicarbonate

el **bicho** NOUN
insect

□ Me ha picado un bicho. I've been bitten
by an insect.

■ **un bicho raro** *(colloquial)* an oddball

la **bici** NOUN
bike

la **bicicleta** NOUN
bicycle

■ **una bicicleta de montaña** a mountain
bike

el **bidé** (PL los **bidés**) NOUN
bidet

el **bidón** (PL los **bidones**) NOUN
drum

el **bien** NOUN
good

□ Lo digo por tu bien. I'm telling you for
your own good.

■ **los bienes** possessions □ todos los
bienes de la familia all the family's
possessions

**bien** ADVERB
1 well
□ Habla bien el español. He speaks Spanish
well. □ El traje me está bien. The suit fits
me well.
2 good
□ Huele bien. It smells good. □ Sabe bien.
It tastes good.
■ **Has contestado bien.** You gave the right
answer.

■ **Lo pasamos muy bien.** We had a very good time.

**3** very

□ un café **bien** caliente a very hot coffee

■ **¿Estás bien?** Are you OK?

■ **¡Está bien! Lo haré.** OK! I'll do it.

■ **Ese libro está muy bien.** That's a very good book.

■ **Está muy bien que ahorres dinero.** It's good that you're saving.

■ **¡Eso no está bien!** That's not very nice!

■ **Hiciste bien en decírselo.** You were right to tell him.

■ **¡Ya está bien!** That's enough!

■ **¡Qué bien!** Excellent!

el **bienestar** NOUN
well-being

la **bienvenida** NOUN

■ **dar la bienvenida a alguien** to welcome somebody

■ **una fiesta de bienvenida** a welcome party

**bienvenido** (FEM **bienvenida**) ADJECTIVE

▷ see also **bienvenido** EXCLAMATION
welcome

□ Siempre serás bienvenido aquí. You will always be welcome here.

**bienvenido** EXCLAMATION

▷ see also **bienvenido** ADJECTIVE
welcome!

el **bife** NOUN (Chile, River Plate)
steak

la **bifurcación** (PL las **bifurcaciones**) NOUN
fork

el **bigote** NOUN
moustache

el **bikini** NOUN
bikini

**bilingüe** (FEM **bilingüe**) ADJECTIVE
bilingual

el **billar** NOUN
billiards sing

■ **el billar americano** pool

el **billete** NOUN

**1** ticket

□ un billete de metro an underground ticket

■ **sacar un billete** to buy a ticket

■ **un billete de ida y vuelta** a return ticket

LANGUAGE TIP Word for word, **billete de ida y vuelta** means 'ticket for going and coming back'.

■ **un billete electrónico** an e-ticket

**2** note

□ un billete de veinte euros a twenty-euro note

el **billón** (PL los **billones**) NOUN

■ **un billón** a million millions

DID YOU KNOW...?
La palabra **billion** equivale a mil millones.

el **bingo** NOUN

**1** bingo

□ jugar al bingo to play bingo

**2** bingo hall

□ Van a abrir un bingo aquí. They're opening a bingo hall here.

**biodegradable** (FEM **biodegradable**) ADJECTIVE
biodegradable

la **biografía** NOUN
biography (PL biographies)

la **biología** NOUN
biology

**biológico** (FEM **biológica**) ADJECTIVE

**1** organic

**2** biological

el **biombo** NOUN
folding screen

el **biquini** NOUN
bikini (PL bikinis)

la **birome** NOUN (River Plate)
ballpoint pen

la **birria** NOUN

■ **ser una birria** (colloquial) to be rubbish

la **bisabuela** NOUN
great-grandmother

el **bisabuelo** NOUN
great-grandfather

■ **mis bisabuelos** my great-grandparents

la **bisagra** NOUN
hinge

**bisiesto** (FEM **bisiesta**) ADJECTIVE

■ **un año bisiesto** a leap year

la **bisnieta** NOUN
great-granddaughter

el **bisnieto** NOUN
great-grandson

■ **tus bisnietos** your great-grandchildren

el **bistec** (PL los **bistecs**) NOUN
steak

la **bisutería** NOUN
costume jewellery

■ **Son de bisutería.** They're costume jewellery.

**bizco** (FEM **bizca**) ADJECTIVE
cross-eyed

el **bizcocho** NOUN
sponge cake

**blanco** (FEM **blanca**) ADJECTIVE
white

□ un vestido blanco a white dress

el **blanco** NOUN
white

□ Me gusta el blanco. I like white.

■ **dar en el blanco** to hit the target

**b**

■ **dejar algo en blanco** to leave something blank

■ **Cuando iba a responder me quedé en blanco.** Just as I was about to reply my mind went blank.

**blando** (FEM **blanda**) ADJECTIVE
1 soft
　□ Este colchón es muy blando. This mattress is very soft.
2 easy
　□ Es muy blando con sus alumnos. He's very easy on his pupils.

el **bloc** (PL los **blocs**) NOUN
　writing pad
　■ un bloc de dibujo a drawing pad

el **blog** NOUN
　blog

el **bloque** NOUN
　block
　■ un bloque de pisos a block of flats

**bloquear** VERB [25]
　to block
　□ La nieve bloqueó las carreteras. The snow blocked the roads.

el **Bluetooth®** NOUN
　Bluetooth®

la **blusa** NOUN
　blouse

la **bobada** NOUN
　■ hacer bobadas to do stupid things
　■ Este programa es una bobada. This programme is stupid.
　■ decir bobadas to talk nonsense

la **bobina** NOUN
　reel

**bobo** (FEM **boba**) ADJECTIVE
　silly

la **boca** NOUN
　mouth
　□ No debes hablar con la boca llena. You shouldn't talk with your mouth full. □ No abrió la boca en toda la tarde. He didn't open his mouth all afternoon.
　■ boca abajo face down
　■ boca arriba face up
　■ Me quedé con la boca abierta. I was dumbfounded.
　■ la boca del metro the entrance to the underground

la **bocacalle** NOUN
　■ Es una bocacalle del Paseo Central. It's a side street off the Paseo Central.
　■ La primera bocacalle a la derecha. The first road on the right.

el **bocadillo** NOUN
　■ Ya me he comido el bocadillo. I've already had my roll.
　■ un bocadillo de queso a cheese baguette

el **bocado** NOUN
1 bite
　□ Dame un bocado de tu bocadillo. Let me have a bite of your sandwich.
　■ No he probado bocado desde ayer. I haven't had a bite to eat since yesterday.
2 mouthful
　□ Intentaba hablar entre bocado y bocado. I was trying to talk between mouthfuls.

el **bocata** NOUN = bocadillo

el **bochorno** NOUN
　■ Hace bochorno. It's muggy.

la **bocina** NOUN
1 horn
2 receiver (Chile, River Plate)

la **boda** NOUN
　wedding
　■ las bodas de oro golden wedding sing
　■ las bodas de plata silver wedding sing

la **bodega** NOUN
1 cellar
2 wine cellar
3 wine shop
4 hold

la **bofetada** NOUN
　slap
　□ dar una bofetada a alguien to give somebody a slap

el **boicot** (PL los **boicots**) NOUN
　boycott
　■ hacer el boicot a algo to boycott something

la **boina** NOUN
　beret

la **bola** NOUN
　ball
　■ una bola de nieve a snowball

la **bolera** NOUN
　bowling alley

la **boletería** NOUN (Latin America)
　ticket office

el **boletín** (PL los **boletines**) NOUN
　bulletin
　■ un boletín informativo a news bulletin

el **boleto** NOUN
　ticket
　□ un boleto de lotería a lottery ticket
　■ un boleto de quinielas a pools coupon
　■ un boleto electrónico an e-ticket

el **boli** NOUN
　pen

el **bolígrafo** NOUN
　pen

el **bolillo** NOUN (Mexico)
　bun

**Bolivia** FEM NOUN
　Bolivia

el **boliviano** (FEM la **boliviana**) ADJECTIVE,

NOUN
Bolivian

la **bollería** NOUN
pastries pl

el **bollo** NOUN
1 bun
□ Me he comido un bollo para desayunar. I had a bun for breakfast.
2 dent
□ Tengo el coche lleno de bollos. My car is full of dents.

los **bolos** NOUN
1 bowls sing
2 tenpin bowling sing

la **bolsa** NOUN
1 bag
□ una bolsa de plástico a plastic bag
■ una bolsa de deportes a sports bag
■ una bolsa de viaje a travel bag
2 handbag (Mexico)
■ la Bolsa the Stock Exchange

el **bolsillo** NOUN
pocket
□ Sacó las llaves del bolsillo. He took the keys out of his pocket.
■ un libro de bolsillo a paperback
LANGUAGE TIP Word for word, **libro de bolsillo** means 'book for the pocket'.

el **bolso** NOUN
bag

la **bomba** NOUN
1 bomb
□ la bomba atómica the atomic bomb
2 pump
□ una bomba de agua a water pump
■ pasarlo bomba to have a brilliant time

la **bombacha** NOUN (River Plate)
panties pl

**bombardear** VERB [25]
to bombard
■ bombardear a alguien a preguntas to bombard somebody with questions

el **bombero** NOUN
fireman (PL firemen)
■ llamar a los bomberos to call the fire brigade

la **bombilla** NOUN
lightbulb

la **bombita** NOUN (River Plate)
lightbulb

el **bombo** NOUN
bass drum

el **bombón** (PL los **bombones**) NOUN
chocolate

la **bombona** NOUN
gas cylinder

la **bondad** NOUN
kindness

□ un acto de bondad an act of kindness
■ ¿Tendría la bondad de ...? Would you be so kind as to ...?

el **boniato** NOUN
sweet potato (PL sweet potatoes)

**bonito** (FEM **bonita**) ADJECTIVE
pretty
□ una casa muy bonita a very pretty house

el **bonito** NOUN
tuna (PL tuna o tunas)

el **bonobús** (PL los **bonobuses**) NOUN
bus pass (PL bus passes)

el **boquerón** (PL los **boquerones**) NOUN
anchovy (PL anchovies)

el **boquete** NOUN
hole
□ Abrieron un boquete en el muro. They made a hole in the wall.

la **borda** NOUN
■ echar algo por la borda to throw something overboard

**bordar** VERB [25]
to embroider

el **borde** NOUN
edge
□ al borde de la mesa at the edge of the table
■ estar al borde de algo to be on the verge of something

**borde** (FEM **borde**) ADJECTIVE
■ ¡No seas borde! Don't be so horrible!

el **bordillo** NOUN
kerb
□ Los coches no pueden subirse al bordillo. Cars are not allowed onto the kerb.

**bordo** MASC NOUN
■ subir a bordo to get on board

la **borrachera** NOUN
■ coger una borrachera to get drunk

**borracho** (FEM **borracha**) ADJECTIVE
drunk
□ Estás borracho. You're drunk.

el **borrador** NOUN
1 rough draft
□ Escribe primero un borrador. First write a rough draft.
2 duster
□ Usó un trapo como borrador. He used a rag as a duster.

**borrar** VERB [25]
1 to rub out
□ Borra toda la palabra. Rub out the whole word.
2 to clean
□ Borra la pizarra. Clean the blackboard.
3 to wipe
□ No borres esa cinta. Don't wipe that tape.
■ borrarse de 1 to take one's name off

47

□ Voy a borrarme de la lista. I'm going to take my name off the list. **2** to leave □ Se borró del club. He left the club.

la **borrasca** NOUN
■ Viene una borrasca por el Atlántico. There's low pressure over the Atlantic.

el **borrón** (PL los **borrones**) NOUN
stain

**borroso** (FEM **borrosa**) ADJECTIVE
blurred
□ Lo veo muy borroso. It looks very blurred.

**Bosnia** FEM NOUN
Bosnia

el **bosnio** (FEM la **bosnia**) ADJECTIVE, NOUN
Bosnian

el **bosque** NOUN
**1** wood
**2** forest

**bostezar*** VERB [13]
to yawn

la **bota** NOUN
boot
■ unas botas de agua a pair of wellingtons
LANGUAGE TIP Word for word, **botas de agua** means 'boots of water'.
■ una bota de vino a wineskin

la **botana** NOUN (Mexico)
snack

la **botánica** NOUN
botany

**botánico** (FEM **botánica**) ADJECTIVE
botanical

**botar** VERB [25]
**1** to bounce
□ Esta pelota no bota. This ball isn't bouncing.
**2** to jump
□ Botar de alegría. To jump with joy.
**3** to throw out (Latin America)
□ Boté los libros. I threw the books out.

el **bote** NOUN
**1** can
**2** tin
**3** jar
**4** boat
■ un bote salvavidas a lifeboat
■ pegar un bote to jump

la **botella** NOUN
bottle

el **botellín** (PL los **botellines**) NOUN
bottle
□ un botellín de cerveza a bottle of beer

el **botijo** NOUN
DID YOU KNOW...?
A **botijo** is an earthenware water container with spouts.

el **botín** (PL los **botines**) NOUN
**1** ankle boot

**2** haul

el **botiquín** (PL los **botiquines**) NOUN
**1** medicine cupboard
**2** first-aid kit
**3** sick bay

el **botón** (PL los **botones**) NOUN
button
□ He perdido un botón de la camisa. I've lost a button off my shirt.
■ pulsar un botón to press a button

la **bóveda** NOUN
vault

el **boxeador**, la **boxeadora** NOUN
boxer

**boxear** VERB [25]
to box

el **boxeo** NOUN
boxing

el **bozal** NOUN
muzzle

las **bragas** NOUN
knickers
■ unas bragas a pair of knickers

la **bragueta** NOUN
fly (PL flies)

la **brasa** NOUN
■ carne a la brasa barbecued meat
■ las brasas the embers

el **brasier** NOUN (Mexico)
bra

**Brasil** MASC NOUN
Brazil

el **brasileño** (FEM la **brasileña**) ADJECTIVE, NOUN
Brazilian

el **brasilero** (FEM la **brasilera**) ADJECTIVE, NOUN (Latin America) = **brasileño**

**bravo** (FEM **brava**) ADJECTIVE
▷ see also **bravo** EXCLAMATION
■ un toro bravo a fighting bull

**bravo** EXCLAMATION
▷ see also **bravo** ADJECTIVE
well done!

la **braza** NOUN
breaststroke
■ nadar a braza to do the breaststroke

el **brazalete** NOUN
bracelet

el **brazo** NOUN
arm
□ Me duele el brazo. My arm hurts.
□ Estaba sentada con los brazos cruzados. She was sitting with her arms folded.
■ ir del brazo to walk arm-in-arm
■ un brazo de gitano a swiss roll

la **brecha** NOUN
opening
■ Me he hecho una brecha en la cabeza.

I've split my head open.

**breve** (FEM **breve**) ADJECTIVE
1 brief
▫ por breves momentos for a few brief moments ▫ Para no aburrirlos seré breve. To avoid boring you I will be brief.
2 short
▫ un relato breve a short story
■ **en breve** shortly

el **bricolaje** NOUN
DIY
▫ una tienda de bricolaje a DIY shop

**brillante** (FEM **brillante**) ADJECTIVE
1 shiny
▫ Tenía el pelo brillante. Her hair was shiny.
■ **El coche estaba brillante.** The car was shining.
■ **blanco brillante** brilliant white
2 outstanding
▫ un alumno brillante an outstanding student

el **brillante** NOUN
diamond

**brillar** VERB [25]
1 to shine
▫ Hoy brilla el sol. The sun is shining today.
2 to sparkle

el **brillo** NOUN
1 shine
2 sparkle
■ **La pantalla tiene mucho brillo.** The screen is too bright.
■ **sacar brillo a algo** to polish something

**brincar\*** VERB [48]
to jump up and down
▫ ¡Deja de brincar! Stop jumping up and down!
■ **brincar de alegría** to jump for joy

el **brinco** NOUN
■ **pegar un brinco** to jump
■ **Bajé tres escalones de un brinco.** I jumped down three steps.

**brindar** VERB [25]
■ **brindar por** to drink a toast to
■ **brindarse a hacer algo** to offer to do something ▫ Se brindó a ayudarme. He offered to help me.

el **brindis** (PL los **brindis**) NOUN
toast
■ **hacer un brindis** to make a toast

la **brisa** NOUN
breeze

**británico** (FEM **británica**) ADJECTIVE
British

el **británico**, la **británica** NOUN
British person
■ **los británicos** the British

la **brocha** NOUN
1 paintbrush (PL paintbrushes)

2 shaving brush (PL shaving brushes)

el **broche** NOUN
1 brooch (PL brooches)
2 clasp

la **broma** NOUN
joke
■ **gastar una broma a alguien** to play a joke on someone
■ **decir algo en broma** to say something as a joke
■ **una broma pesada** a practical joke

**bromear** VERB [25]
to joke

el/la **bromista** NOUN
joker

la **bronca** NOUN
1 row
▫ Tuvieron una bronca muy gorda. They had a huge row.
■ **echar una bronca a alguien** to tell somebody off
2 fuss
■ **armar una bronca** to kick up a fuss

el **bronce** NOUN
bronze

**bronceado** (FEM **bronceada**) ADJECTIVE
tanned

el **bronceado** NOUN
suntan

el **bronceador** NOUN
suntan lotion

la **bronquitis** NOUN
bronchitis

**brotar** VERB [25]
to sprout

**bruces** ADVERB
■ **Me caí de bruces.** I fell flat on my face.

la **bruja** NOUN
witch (PL witches)

el **brujo** NOUN
wizard

la **brújula** NOUN
compass (PL compasses)

la **bruma** NOUN
mist

**brusco** (FEM **brusca**) ADJECTIVE
1 sudden
▫ un movimiento brusco a sudden movement
2 abrupt
▫ una persona brusca an abrupt person

**bruto** (FEM **bruta**) ADJECTIVE
gross
▫ el salario bruto gross salary
■ **¡No seas bruto!** Don't be so rough!
■ **un diamante en bruto** a rough diamond

**bucear** VERB [25]
to dive

## buen – butano

**buen** ADJECTIVE = **bueno**
**bueno** (FEM **buena**) ADJECTIVE
good
- □ Es un buen libro. It's a good book.
- □ Hace buen tiempo. The weather's good.
- □ Tiene buena voz. She has a good voice.
- □ Es buena persona. He's a good person.
- □ un buen trozo a good slice □ Le eché un buen rapapolvo. I gave him a good telling-off.
- ■ **ser bueno para** to be good for □ Esta bebida es buena para la salud. This drink is good for your health.
- ■ **Está muy bueno este bizcocho.** This sponge cake is lovely.
- ■ **Lo bueno fue que ni siquiera quiso venir.** The best thing was that he didn't even want to come.
- ■ **¡Bueno! 1** OK! **2** (Mexico) Hello!
- ■ **Bueno. ¿Y qué?** Well?
- ■ **¡Buenas!** Hello!
- ■ **Irás por las buenas o por las malas.** You'll go whether you like it or not.

**el buey** NOUN
ox (PL oxen)

**la bufanda** NOUN
scarf (PL scarves)

**el bufete** NOUN
- ■ **un bufete de abogados** a legal practice

**el buffet** (PL los **buffets**) NOUN
buffet
- ■ **buffet libre** free buffet

**la buhardilla** NOUN
attic

**el búho** NOUN
owl

**el buitre** NOUN
vulture

**la bujía** NOUN
spark plug

**Bulgaria** FEM NOUN
Bulgaria

**el búlgaro** (FEM la **búlgara**) ADJECTIVE, NOUN
Bulgarian

**el búlgaro** NOUN
Bulgarian

**el bulto** NOUN
**1** lump
- □ Tengo un bulto en la frente. I have a lump on my forehead.
**2** figure
- □ Sólo vi un bulto. I only saw a figure.
- ■ **Llevábamos muchos bultos.** We were carrying a lot of bags.

**el buñuelo** NOUN
doughnut

**BUP** MASC NOUN (= Bachillerato Unificado Polivalente)

**DID YOU KNOW…?**
The **BUP** was a three-year secondary course leading to university.

**el buque** NOUN
ship
- ■ **un buque de guerra** a warship

**la burbuja** NOUN
bubble
- ■ **un refresco sin burbujas** a still drink
- ■ **un refresco con burbujas** a fizzy drink

**la burla** NOUN
- ■ **hacer burla de alguien** to make fun of someone

**burlarse** VERB [25]
- ■ **burlarse de alguien** to make fun of someone

**el buró** (PL los **burós**) NOUN (Mexico)
bedside table

**la burocracia** NOUN
bureaucracy (PL bureaucracies)

**la burrada** NOUN (colloquial)
- ■ **hacer burradas** to do stupid things
- □ No hagas burradas con el coche. Don't do anything stupid with the car.

**el burro** NOUN
**1** donkey (PL donkeys)
**2** idiot
- □ Eres un burro. You're an idiot.

**burro** (FEM **burra**) ADJECTIVE
**1** thick
**2** rough

**la busca** NOUN
- ■ **en busca de** in search of

**el busca** NOUN
bleeper

**el buscador** NOUN
search engine

**buscar*** VERB [48]
to look for
- □ Estoy buscando las gafas. I'm looking for my glasses. □ Ana busca trabajo. Ana's looking for work.
- ■ **Te voy a buscar a la estación.** I'll come and get you at the station.
- ■ **Mi madre siempre me viene a buscar al colegio en coche.** My mother always picks me up from school in the car.
- ■ **buscar una palabra en el diccionario** to look up a word in the dictionary
- ■ **Él se lo ha buscado.** He was asking for it.

**la búsqueda** NOUN
search (PL searches)

**la butaca** NOUN
**1** armchair
**2** seat

**el butano** NOUN
bottled gas
- ■ **color butano** bright orange

el **buzo** NOUN
  diver

el **buzón** (PL los **buzones**) NOUN
1  letterbox (PL letterboxes)
2  postbox (PL postboxes)

■ **echar una carta al buzón** to post a
letter
■ **buzón de voz** voice mail
  ◌ **LANGUAGE TIP** Word for word, **buzón
  de voz** means 'box of voice'.

# Cc

**C/** ABBREVIATION (= *calle*)
St (= *Street*)

el **caballero** NOUN
gentleman (PL gentlemen)
□ damas y caballeros ladies and gentlemen
■ **¿Dónde está la sección de caballeros?**
Where is the men's department?
■ **'Caballeros'** 'Gents'

el **caballo** NOUN
1 horse
■ **¿Te gusta montar a caballo?** Do you like
riding?
■ **un caballo de carreras** a racehorse
2 knight

la **cabaña** NOUN
hut

el **cabello** NOUN
hair

**caber\*** VERB
to fit
□ No cabe en mi armario. It won't fit in my
cupboard.
■ **En mi coche caben dos maletas más.**
There's room for two more suitcases in my
car.
■ **No cabe nadie más.** There's no room for
anyone else.

la **cabeza** NOUN
head
□ Se rascó la cabeza. He scratched his head.
■ **Al oírlos volví la cabeza.** When I heard
them I looked round.
■ **Se tiró al agua de cabeza.** He dived
headfirst into the water.
■ **estar a la cabeza de la clasificación** to
be at the top of the league

la **cabina** NOUN
1 phone box (PL phone boxes)
2 booth (PL booths)
3 cockpit
4 cubicle

el **cable** NOUN
cable

el **cabo** NOUN
1 cape
■ **Cabo Cañaveral** Cape Canaveral

2 corporal
■ **al cabo de dos días** after two days
■ **llevar algo a cabo** to carry something out

la **cabra** NOUN
goat
■ **¡Estás como una cabra!** *(colloquial)*
You're crazy!

**cabrá** VERB ▷*see* **caber**

**cabreado** (FEM **cabreada**) ADJECTIVE
annoyed

**cabrear** VERB
■ **Lo que más me cabrea es que me**
**mientas.** What really annoys me is when
you lie to me.
■ **cabrearse** to get annoyed

la **caca** NOUN
■ **hacer caca 1** to do a poo **2** to go to the
loo

el **cacahuate** NOUN *(Mexico)*
peanut

el **cacahuete** NOUN
peanut

el **cacao** NOUN
1 cocoa
2 lipsalve

la **cacerola** NOUN
saucepan

el **cacharro** NOUN
■ **los cacharros** the pots and pans

el **cachondeo** NOUN
■ **Las clases eran un cachondeo.**
*(colloquial)* The classes were a joke.
■ **No le hagas caso, está de cachondeo.**
*(colloquial)* Don't pay any attention to him,
he's having you on.

el **cachorro**, la **cachorra** NOUN
1 puppy (PL puppies)
2 cub

el **cactus** (PL los **cactus**) NOUN
cactus (PL cacti)

**cada** (FEM **cada**) ADJECTIVE
1 each
□ Cada libro es de un color distinto. Each
book is a different colour.
■ **cada uno** each one
2 every

□ **cada año** every year □ **cada vez que la veo** every time I see her □ **uno de cada diez** one out of every ten

■ **Viene cada vez más gente.** More and more people are coming.

■ **Viene cada vez menos.** He comes less and less often.

■ **Cada vez hace más frío.** It's getting colder and colder.

■ **¿Cada cuánto vas al dentista?** How often do you go to the dentist?

el **cadáver** NOUN
corpse

la **cadena** NOUN
1 chain
□ **una cadena de oro** a gold chain
■ **una reacción en cadena** a chain reaction
■ **tirar de la cadena del wáter** to flush the toilet
■ **la cadena de montaje** the assembly line
2 channel
□ **Por la cadena 3 ponen una película.** There's a film on channel 3.
■ **cadena perpetua** life imprisonment

la **cadera** NOUN
hip

**caducar*** VERB [48]
to expire
■ **Esta leche está caducada.** This milk is past its sell-by date.

**caer*** VERB [5]
to fall
□ **Me hice daño al caer.** I fell and hurt myself.
■ **El avión cayó al mar.** The plane came down in the sea.
■ **Su cumpleaños cae en viernes.** Her birthday falls on a Friday.
■ **caerse** to fall □ **Tropecé y me caí.** I tripped and fell.
■ **El niño se cayó de la cama.** The child fell out of bed.
■ **No te vayas a caer del caballo.** Be careful not to fall off the horse.
■ **Se cayó por la ventana.** He fell out of the window.
■ **Se me cayeron las monedas.** I dropped the coins.
■ **¡No caigo!** I don't get it!
■ **Su hermano me cae muy bien.** I really like his brother.

el **café** (PL los **cafés**) NOUN
1 coffee
■ **un café con leche** a white coffee
■ **un café solo** a black coffee

**LANGUAGE TIP** Word for word, **café solo** means 'cafe alone'.

2 café

**DID YOU KNOW...?**
En Gran Bretaña no se venden bebidas alcohólicas en los cafés y éstos cierran, por lo general, a las 5.30 p.m.

la **cafetera** NOUN
coffee pot

la **cafetería** NOUN
café

**cagar*** VERB
to have a crap (vulgar)

la **caída** NOUN
fall

**caigo** VERB ▷ see **caer**

el **caimán** (PL los **caimanes**) NOUN
alligator

la **caja** NOUN
1 box (PL boxes)
□ **una caja de zapatos** a shoe box
2 case
3 crate
4 checkout
5 till
6 cash desk
■ **la caja de ahorros** the savings bank
■ **la caja de cambios** the gearbox
■ **la caja fuerte** the safe

el **cajero** NOUN
■ **un cajero automático** a cash dispenser

el **cajero**, la **cajera** NOUN
■ **Trabajo de cajera en un supermercado.** I work on the checkout in a supermarket.

el **cajón** (PL los **cajones**) NOUN
1 drawer
2 crate
3 coffin (Latin America)

la **cajuela** NOUN (Mexico)
boot

la **cala** NOUN
cove

el **calabacín** (PL los **calabacines**) NOUN
courgette

la **calabacita** NOUN (Mexico)
courgette

la **calabaza** NOUN
pumpkin

**calado** (FEM **calada**) ADJECTIVE
soaked
□ **Estaba calado hasta los huesos.** He was soaked to the skin.

el **calamar** NOUN
squid
■ **calamares a la romana** squid fried in batter

el **calambre** NOUN
1 cramp
□ **Tengo un calambre en la pierna.** I've got cramp in my leg.

**2** electric shock

□ Si tocas el cable te dará calambre. If you touch the cable you'll get an electric shock.

**calar** VERB [25]
to soak

□ La lluvia me caló hasta los huesos. I got soaked to the skin in the rain.

■ **Se le caló el coche.** He stalled the car.

la **calavera** NOUN
skull

**calcar\*** VERB [48]
to trace

■ **Es calcado a su abuelo.** He's the spitting image of his grandfather.

el **calcetín** (PL los **calcetines**) NOUN
sock

el **calcio** NOUN
calcium

la **calculadora** NOUN
calculator

**calcular** VERB [25]
to calculate

□ Calculé lo que nos costaría. I calculated what it would cost us.

■ **Calculo que nos llevará unos tres días.** I reckon that it will take us around three days.

el **cálculo** NOUN
calculation

■ **según mis cálculos** according to my calculations

el **caldo** NOUN
broth

□ Yo tomaré el caldo de verduras. I'll take the vegetable broth.

■ **una pastilla de caldo** a stock cube

la **calefacción** NOUN
heating

□ calefacción central central heating

el **calendario** NOUN
calendar

el **calentador** NOUN
heater

el **calentamiento** NOUN

■ **el calentamiento del planeta** global warming

■ **ejercicios de calentamiento** warm-up exercises

**calentar\*** VERB [39]

**1** to heat up

□ ¿Quieres que te caliente la leche? Do you want me to heat up the milk for you?

**2** to warm up

■ **calentarse 1** to heat up □ Espera a que se caliente el agua. Wait for the water to heat up. **2** to warm up □ Deja que se caliente el motor. Let the engine warm up.

la **calentura** NOUN

**1** temperature

□ Tiene un poco de calentura. He's got a bit of a temperature.

**2** cold sore

la **calidad** NOUN
quality (PL qualities)

□ Lo que importa es la calidad. What matters is quality.

**caliente** VERB
▷ see also **caliente** ADJECTIVE ▷ see **calentar**

**caliente** (FEM **caliente**) ADJECTIVE
▷ see also **caliente** VERB

**1** hot

□ Esta sopa está muy caliente. This soup is very hot.

**2** warm

□ ¡Esta cerveza está caliente! This beer is warm!

■ **Mi habitación está calentita.** My room is nice and warm.

la **calificación** (PL las **calificaciones**) NOUN
mark

□ Obtuvo buenas calificaciones. He got good marks.

■ **boletín de calificaciones** school report

**calificar\*** VERB [48]
to mark

□ El profesor califica los ejercicios. The teacher marks the exercises.

■ **Me calificó con sobresaliente.** He gave me an A.

**callado** (FEM **callada**) ADJECTIVE
quiet

□ Estuvo callado bastante rato. He was quiet for quite a while. □ una persona muy callada a very quiet person

**callar** VERB [25]
to be quiet

□ Calla, que no me dejas concentrarme. Be quiet, I can't concentrate.

■ **callarse 1** to keep quiet □ Prefirió callarse. He preferred to keep quiet. **2** to stop talking □ Al entrar el profesor todos se callaron. When the teacher came in, everyone stopped talking.

■ **¡Cállate!** *(colloquial)* Shut up!

la **calle** NOUN

**1** street

□ Viven en la calle Peñalver, 13. They live at number 13, Peñalver Street.

■ **Hoy no he salido a la calle.** I haven't been out today.

■ **una calle peatonal** a pedestrian precinct

**2** lane

el **callejero** NOUN
street map

el **callejón** (PL los **callejones**) NOUN
alley (PL alleys)

el **callo** NOUN

**1** corn
**2** callus (PL calluses)
- **callos** tripe *sing*

la **calma** NOUN
  calm
- **Todo estaba en calma.** Everything was calm.
- **Logró mantener la calma.** He managed to keep calm.
- **Piénsalo con calma.** Think about it calmly.
- **Tómatelo con calma.** Take it easy.

el **calmante** NOUN
**1** painkiller
**2** tranquillizer

**calmar** VERB [25]
**1** to calm down
  □ Intenté calmarla un poco. I tried to calm her down a little. □ ¡Cálmate! Calm down!
**2** to relieve

el **calor** NOUN
  heat
  □ No se puede trabajar con este calor. It's impossible to work in this heat.
- **Hace calor.** It's hot.
- **Tengo calor.** I'm hot.
- **entrar en calor** to get warm

la **caloría** NOUN
  calorie

**caluroso** (FEM **calurosa**) ADJECTIVE
  hot

**calvo** (FEM **calva**) ADJECTIVE
  bald
- **Se está quedando calvo.** He's going bald.

el **calzado** NOUN
  footwear

los **calzoncillos** NOUN
  underpants
- **unos calzoncillos** a pair of underpants

los **calzones** NOUN *(Chile)*
  panties

la **cama** NOUN
  bed
- **hacer la cama** to make the bed
- **Está en la cama.** He's in bed.
- **meterse en la cama** to get into bed

la **cámara** NOUN
**1** camera
- **una cámara digital** a digital camera
- **a cámara lenta** in slow motion
**2** inner tube
- **la cámara de comercio** the Chamber of Commerce
- **música de cámara** chamber music

la **camarera** NOUN
**1** waitress (PL waitresses)
**2** maid

el **camarero** NOUN
**1** waiter
**2** bellboy

el **camarote** NOUN
  cabin

**cambiar** VERB [25]
**1** to change
  □ No has cambiado nada. You haven't changed a bit.
- **Quiero cambiar este abrigo por uno más grande.** I want to change this coat for a larger size.
- **Tenemos que cambiar de tren en París.** We have to change trains in Paris.
- **He cambiado de idea.** I've changed my mind.
**2** to swap
  □ Te cambio mi bolígrafo por tu goma. I'll swap my ballpoint for your rubber.
- **Me gusta el tuyo, te lo cambio.** I like yours, let's swap.
- **cambiarse** to get changed □ Voy a cambiarme. I'm going to get changed.
- **Se han cambiado de coche.** They have changed car.
- **cambiarse de sitio** to move
- **cambiarse de casa** to move house

el **cambio** NOUN
**1** change
  □ un cambio brusco de temperatura a sudden change in temperature □ ¿Tiene cambio de veinte euros? Have you got change of twenty euros? □ ¿Te han dado bien el cambio? Have they given you the right change?
**2** small change
  □ Necesito cambio. I need small change.
**3** exchange
  □ ¿A cómo está el cambio? What's the exchange rate?
- **Me lo regaló a cambio del favor que le hice.** He gave it to me in return for the favour I did him.
- **en cambio** on the other hand

el **camello** NOUN
**1** camel
**2** drug pusher

la **camilla** NOUN
**1** stretcher
**2** couch (PL couches)

**caminar** VERB [25]
  to walk

la **caminata** NOUN
  long walk

el **camino** NOUN
**1** path
- **un camino de montaña** a mountain track

**2** way

□ ¿Sabes el camino a su casa? Do you know the way to his house?

■ **A medio camino paramos a comer.** Half-way there, we stopped to eat.

■ **La farmacia me queda de camino.** The chemist's is on my way.

el **camión** (PL los **camiones**) NOUN

**1** lorry (PL lorries)

■ **un camión cisterna** a tanker

■ **el camión de la basura** the dustcart

**2** bus (PL buses) *(Mexico)*

el **camionero**, la **camionera** NOUN
lorry driver

la **camioneta** NOUN
van

la **camisa** NOUN
shirt

la **camiseta** NOUN

**1** T-shirt

**2** vest

**3** shirt

el **camisón** (PL los **camisones**) NOUN
nightdress (PL nightdresses)

el **camote** NOUN *(Mexico)*
sweet potato (PL sweet potatoes)

el **campamento** NOUN
camp

□ un campamento de verano a summer camp

la **campana** NOUN
bell

la **campaña** NOUN
campaign

■ **la campaña electoral** the election campaign

■ **una campaña publicitaria** an advertising campaign

el **campeón**, la **campeona** NOUN
champion

el **campeonato** NOUN
championship

el **campesino**, la **campesina** NOUN

**1** country person (PL country people)

**2** peasant

el **camping** (PL los **campings**) NOUN

**1** camping

□ ir de camping to go camping

**2** campsite

□ Estamos en un camping. We're at a campsite.

el **campo** NOUN

**1** country

□ Prefiero vivir en el campo. I prefer living in the country.

**2** countryside

□ El campo se pone verde en primavera. The countryside turns green in springtime.

■ **Corrían campo a través.** They were running cross-country.

■ **el trabajo del campo** farm work

■ **Ya no se ven bueyes en el campo.** You don't see oxen in the fields any more.

**3** pitch (PL pitches)

■ **un campo de deportes** a sports ground

■ **un campo de golf** a golf course

■ **un campo de concentración** a concentration camp

la **cana** NOUN
grey hair

■ **Tiene canas.** He's got grey hair.

■ **Le están saliendo canas.** He's going grey.

**Canadá** MASC NOUN
Canada

el/la **canadiense** ADJECTIVE, NOUN
Canadian

el **canal** NOUN

**1** channel

□ Por el canal 2 ponen una película. They're showing a film on channel 2.

■ **el Canal de la Mancha** the English Channel

**2** canal

□ un canal de riego an irrigation canal

■ **el Canal de Panamá** the Panama Canal

el **canapé** (PL los **canapés**) NOUN
canapé

**Canarias** FEM PL NOUN
the Canaries

■ **las Islas Canarias** the Canary Islands

el **canario** NOUN
canary (PL canaries)

la **canasta** NOUN
basket

**cancelar** VERB [25]
to cancel

**Cáncer** MASC NOUN
Cancer

■ **Soy cáncer.** I'm Cancer.

el **cáncer** NOUN
cancer

□ cáncer de mama breast cancer

la **cancha** NOUN

**1** court

**2** pitch (PL pitches) *(Latin America)*

la **canción** (PL las **canciones**) NOUN
song

■ **una canción de cuna** a lullaby

el **candado** NOUN
padlock

■ **Estaba cerrado con candado.** It was padlocked.

el **candidato**, la **candidata** NOUN
candidate

■ **presentarse como candidato a la**

la **canela** NOUN
cinnamon

los **canelones** NOUN
cannelloni *sing*

el **cangrejo** NOUN
1 crab
2 crayfish (PL crayfish)

el **canguro** NOUN
kangaroo

el/la **canguro** NOUN
baby-sitter
■ **hacer de canguro** to baby-sit

la **canica** NOUN
marble
■ **jugar a las canicas** to play marbles

la **canilla** NOUN *(River Plate)*
tap

la **canoa** NOUN
canoe

**cansado** (FEM **cansada**) ADJECTIVE
1 tired
□ Estoy muy cansado. I'm very tired.
■ **Estoy cansado de hacer lo mismo todos los días.** I'm tired of doing the same thing every day.
2 tiring
□ Es un trabajo muy cansado. It's a very tiring job.

el **cansancio** NOUN
■ **¡Qué cansancio!** I'm so tired!

**cansar** VERB [25]
■ **Es un viaje que cansa.** It's a tiring journey.
■ **cansarse** to get tired □ Está muy débil y enseguida se cansa. He is very weak and gets tired quickly.
■ **Me cansé de esperarlo y me marché.** I got tired of waiting for him and I left.

el/la **cantante** NOUN
singer

**cantar** VERB [25]
to sing

la **cantidad** NOUN
1 amount
□ una cierta cantidad de dinero a certain amount of money
2 quantity (PL quantities)
□ La calidad es más importante que la cantidad. Quality is more important than quantity.
■ **¡Qué cantidad de gente!** What a lot of people!
■ **Había cantidad de turistas.** There were loads of tourists.

la **cantimplora** NOUN
water bottle

el **canto** NOUN
1 edge
2 singing
□ Mi hermana estudia canto. My sister is studying singing.
3 song

la **caña** NOUN
cane
■ **caña de azúcar** sugar cane
■ **Me tomé dos cañas.** I had two beers.
■ **una caña de pescar** a fishing rod

la **cañería** NOUN
pipe

el **caos** NOUN
chaos
□ Aquello fue un verdadero caos. That was absolute chaos.

la **capa** NOUN
1 layer
■ **la capa de ozono** the ozone layer
2 cloak

la **capacidad** NOUN
1 ability (PL abilities)
□ Nadie duda de tu capacidad. No one doubts your ability.
2 capacity (PL capacities)
□ El teatro tiene capacidad para mil espectadores. The theatre has a seating capacity of a thousand.

**capaz** (FEM **capaz**, PL **capaces**) ADJECTIVE
capable
□ Es capaz de olvidarse el pasaporte. He's quite capable of forgetting his passport.
■ **Por ella sería capaz de cualquier cosa.** He would do anything for her.

la **capilla** NOUN
chapel

la **capital** NOUN
capital

el **capitán**, la **capitana** NOUN
captain

el **capítulo** NOUN
1 chapter
2 episode

el **capricho** NOUN
whim
□ Hacer un crucero fue un puro capricho. Going on a cruise was just a whim.
■ **Lo compré por capricho.** I bought it on a whim.
■ **Decidí viajar en primera para darme un capricho.** I decided to travel first class to give myself a treat.

**Capricornio** MASC NOUN
Capricorn
■ **Soy capricornio.** I'm Capricorn.

**capturar** VERB [25]
to capture

la **capucha** NOUN

# caqui – cariño

1 hood
2 top

**caqui** (PL **caqui**) ADJECTIVE
khaki

la **cara** NOUN
1 face
   □ Tiene la cara alargada. He has a long face.
   ■ **Tienes mala cara.** You don't look well.
   ■ **Tenía cara de pocos amigos.** He looked very unfriendly.
   ■ **No pongas esa cara.** Don't look like that.
2 cheek
   □ ¡Qué cara! What a cheek!
3 side
   □ un folio escrito por las dos caras a sheet written on both sides
   ■ **¿Cara o cruz?** Heads or tails?
   ⊙ LANGUAGE TIP Word for word, **¿Cara o cruz?** means 'Face or cross?'
   ■ **Lo echamos a cara o cruz.** We tossed for it.

el **caracol** NOUN
1 snail
2 winkle

el **carácter** (PL los **caracteres**) NOUN
nature
   □ Tiene el carácter de su padre. He has his father's nature.
   ■ **tener buen carácter** to be good-natured
   ■ **tener mal carácter** to be bad-tempered
   ■ **La chica tiene mucho carácter.** The girl has a strong personality.

la **característica** NOUN
characteristic

**caramba** EXCLAMATION
goodness!

el **caramelo** NOUN
sweet

la **caravana** NOUN
caravan
   ■ **Había una caravana de dos kilómetros.** There was a two kilometre tailback.

el **carbón** NOUN
coal
   ■ **carbón de leña** charcoal

la **carcajada** NOUN
   ■ **soltar una carcajada** to burst out laughing
   ■ **reírse a carcajadas** to roar with laughter

la **cárcel** NOUN
prison
   □ Todavía está en la cárcel. He's still in prison.

el **cardenal** NOUN
1 bruise
2 cardinal

**cardiaco** (FEM **cardiaca**) ADJECTIVE
cardiac

   □ ataque cardiaco cardiac arrest

la **careta** NOUN
mask

la **carga** NOUN
1 load
   □ carga máxima maximum load
2 burden
   □ No quiero ser una carga para ellos. I don't want to be a burden to them.
3 refill

**cargado** (FEM **cargada**) ADJECTIVE
1 loaded
2 stuffy
3 strong
   ■ **Venía cargada de paquetes.** She was laden with parcels.

el **cargamento** NOUN
1 cargo (PL cargoes)
2 load

**cargar\*** VERB [37]
1 to load
   □ Cargaron el coche de maletas. They loaded the car with suitcases.
2 to fill
3 to charge
   ■ **Tuve que cargar con todo.** I had to take responsibility for everything.
   ■ **cargarse algo** (colloquial) to break something □ Te vas a cargar el vídeo. You're going to break the video.

el **cargo** NOUN
post
   □ un cargo de mucha responsabilidad a very responsible post
   ■ **Está a cargo de la contabilidad.** He's in charge of keeping the books.

el **Caribe** NOUN
the Caribbean

el **caribeño** (FEM la **caribeña**) ADJECTIVE, NOUN
Caribbean

la **caricatura** NOUN
caricature

la **caricia** NOUN
caress (PL caresses)
   ■ **Le hacía caricias al bebé.** She was caressing the baby.

la **caridad** NOUN
charity (PL charities)

la **caries** (PL las **caries**) NOUN
1 tooth decay
   □ Es importante prevenir la caries dental. It's important to prevent tooth decay.
2 cavity (PL cavities)

el **cariño** NOUN
affection
   □ Lo recuerdo con cariño. I remember him with affection.
   ■ **Les tengo mucho cariño.** I'm very fond

C

of them.

■ **Le ha tomado cariño al gato.** He has become fond of the cat.

■ **Ven aquí, cariño.** Come here, darling.

**cariñoso** (FEM **cariñosa**) ADJECTIVE
affectionate

□ Es muy cariñosa con los niños. She is very affectionate towards the children.

el **carnaval** NOUN
carnival

> **DID YOU KNOW...?**
> The **carnaval** is the traditional period of celebrating prior to the start of Lent.

la **carne** NOUN
meat

□ No como carne. I don't eat meat.

■ **carne de cerdo** pork

■ **carne de puerco** *(Mexico)* pork

■ **carne de cordero** lamb

■ **carne molida** *(Latin America)* mince

■ **carne picada** mince

■ **carne de ternera** veal

■ **carne de vaca** beef

■ **carne de res** *(Mexico)* beef

el **carnet** (PL los **carnets**) NOUN
card

■ **el carnet de identidad** identity card

■ **un carnet de conducir** a driving licence

la **carnicería** NOUN
butcher's (PL butchers' shops)

□ Lo compré en la carnicería. I bought it at the butcher's.

el **carnicero**, la **carnicera** NOUN
butcher

**caro** (FEM **cara**) ADJECTIVE, ADVERB
expensive

□ Las entradas me costaron muy caras. The tickets were very expensive. □ Aquí todo lo venden tan caro. Everything is so expensive here.

la **carpeta** NOUN
folder

la **carpintería** NOUN
1 carpenter's shop
2 carpentry

el **carpintero**, la **carpintera** NOUN
carpenter

la **carrera** NOUN
1 race

□ una carrera de caballos a horse race

■ **Me di una carrera para alcanzar el autobús.** I had to run to catch the bus.

2 degree

□ Está haciendo la carrera de derecho. He's doing a law degree.

3 career

□ Estaba en el mejor momento de su

carrera. He was at the height of his career.

4 ladder

□ Tienes una carrera en las medias. You've got a ladder in your tights.

el **carrete** NOUN
1 film
2 reel

la **carretera** NOUN
road

■ **una carretera nacional** an A-road

■ **una carretera de circunvalación** a bypass

la **carretilla** NOUN
wheelbarrow

el **carril** NOUN
1 lane
2 rail

el **carril-bici** NOUN (PL los **carriles-bici**)
cycle lane

el **carrito** NOUN
trolley (PL trolleys)

el **carro** NOUN
1 cart
2 trolley (PL trolleys)
3 car *(Latin America)*

■ **un carro de combate** a tank

la **carroza** NOUN
1 coach (PL coaches)
2 float

la **carta** NOUN
1 letter

□ Le he escrito una carta a Juan. I've written Juan a letter.

■ **echar una carta** to post a letter

2 card

□ jugar a las cartas to play cards

3 menu

□ El camarero nos trajo la carta. The waiter brought us the menu.

■ **la carta de vinos** the wine list

el **cartel** NOUN
1 poster
2 sign

□ Un cartel que pone 'prohibida la entrada'. A sign which says 'no entry'.

la **cartelera** NOUN
1 billboard
2 listings *pl*

■ **Estuvo tres años en la cartelera.** It ran for three years.

la **cartera** NOUN
1 wallet
2 briefcase
3 satchel
4 handbag *(Latin America)*
5 postwoman (PL postwomen)

el **cartero** NOUN
postman (PL postmen)

el **cartón** (PL los **cartones**) NOUN
1 cardboard
  □ una caja de cartón  a cardboard box
2 carton

el **cartucho** NOUN
  cartridge

la **cartulina** NOUN
  card

la **casa** NOUN
1 house
  □ una casa de dos plantas  a two-storey house
2 home
  □ Estábamos en casa.  We were at home.
  □ Le dolía la cabeza y se fue a casa.  She had a headache so she went home.
  ■ **Estábamos en casa de Juan.**  We were at Juan's.
  ■ **una casa de discos**  a record company

**casado** (FEM **casada**) ADJECTIVE
  married
  □ una mujer casada  a married woman
  ■ **Está casado con una francesa.**  He's married to a French woman.

**casarse** VERB [25]
  to get married
  □ Quieren casarse.  They want to get married.
  ■ **Se casó con una periodista.**  He married a journalist.

el **cascabel** NOUN
  small bell

la **cascada** NOUN
  waterfall

**cascar*** VERB [48]
  to crack

la **cáscara** NOUN
1 shell
2 skin

el **casco** NOUN
  helmet
  □ El ciclista llevaba casco.  The cyclist was wearing a helmet.
  ■ **el casco antiguo de la ciudad**  the old part of the town
  ■ **el casco urbano**  the town centre
  ■ **los cascos**  headphones

**casero** (FEM **casera**) ADJECTIVE
  homemade
  □ mermelada casera  homemade jam

la **caseta** NOUN
1 kennel
2 bathing hut
3 stall

el **casete** NOUN
1 cassette player
2 cassette

la **casete** NOUN
  cassette

**casi** ADVERB
  almost
  □ Casi me ahogo.  I almost drowned.  □ Son casi las cinco.  It's almost five o'clock.  □ Casi me ahogo.  I nearly drowned.  □ Casi no comí.  I hardly ate.  □ No queda casi nada en la nevera.  There's hardly anything left in the refrigerator.  □ Casi nunca se equivoca.  He hardly ever makes a mistake.

la **casilla** NOUN
1 box (PL boxes)
2 square
  ■ **Casilla de Correos** (River Plate)  post-office box number

el **casino** NOUN
  casino (PL casinos)

el **caso** NOUN
  case
  □ En casos así es mejor callarse.  In such cases it's better to keep quiet.
  ■ **en ese caso**  in that case
  ■ **En caso de que llueva, iremos en autobús.**  If it rains, we'll go by bus.
  ■ **El caso es que no me queda dinero.**  The thing is, I haven't got any money left.
  ■ **No le hagas caso.**  Don't take any notice of him.
  ■ **Hazle caso que ella tiene más experiencia.**  Listen to her, she has more experience.

la **caspa** NOUN
  dandruff

la **cassette** = casete

el **cassette** = casete

la **castaña** NOUN
  chestnut

**castaño** (FEM **castaña**) ADJECTIVE
  chestnut
  □ Mi hermana tiene el pelo castaño.  My sister has chestnut hair.

las **castañuelas** NOUN
  castanets

el **castellano** (FEM la **castellana**) ADJECTIVE, NOUN
  Castilian

el **castellano** NOUN
  Spanish

**castigar*** VERB [37]
  to punish
  □ Mi padre me castigó por contestarle.  My father punished me for answering him back.

el **castigo** NOUN
  punishment
  □ Tuve que escribirlo diez veces, como castigo.  I had to write it out ten times, as punishment.

**Castilla** FEM NOUN

Castile

el **castillo** NOUN
castle

la **casualidad** NOUN
coincidence

■ **¡Qué casualidad!** What a coincidence!
■ **Nos encontramos por casualidad.** We met by chance.
■ **Da la casualidad que nacimos el mismo día.** It so happens that we were born on the same day.

el **catalán** (FEM la **catalana**, MASC PL los **catalanes**) ADJECTIVE, NOUN
Catalan

el **catalán** NOUN
Catalan

el **catálogo** NOUN
catalogue

**Cataluña** FEM NOUN
Catalonia

la **catarata** NOUN
waterfall

■ **las cataratas del Niágara** Niagara Falls

el **catarro** NOUN
cold

□ Vas a pillar un catarro. You're going to catch a cold.

la **catástrofe** NOUN
catastrophe

la **catedral** NOUN
cathedral

el **catedrático**, la **catedrática** NOUN
1 professor
2 principal teacher

la **categoría** NOUN
category (PL categories)

□ Cada grupo está dividido en tres categorías. Each group is divided into three categories.
■ **un hotel de primera categoría** a first-class hotel
■ **un puesto de poca categoría** a low-ranking position

el **católico** (FEM la **católica**) ADJECTIVE, NOUN
Catholic

□ Soy católico. I am a Catholic.

**catorce** (FEM catorce) ADJECTIVE, PRONOUN
fourteen

■ **el catorce de enero** the fourteenth of January

el **caucho** NOUN
rubber

la **causa** NOUN
cause

□ No se sabe la causa del accidente. The cause of the accident is unknown.
■ **a causa de** because of

**causar** VERB [25]
to cause

□ La lluvia causó muchos daños. The rain caused a lot of damage.
■ **Su visita me causó mucha alegría.** His visit made me very happy.
■ **Rosa me causó buena impresión.** Rosa made a good impression on me.

**cavar** VERB [25]
to dig

□ cavar un hoyo to dig a hole

la **caverna** NOUN
cave

**cayendo** VERB ▷ see caer

la **caza** NOUN
1 hunting
2 shooting

el **cazador** NOUN
hunter

la **cazadora** NOUN
1 jacket
2 hunter

**cazar*** VERB [13]
1 to hunt

□ Salieron a cazar ciervos. They went deer-hunting.
2 to shoot

□ Cazaron muchas codornices. They shot a lot of quail.

el **cazo** NOUN
1 saucepan
2 ladle

la **cazuela** NOUN
pot

el **CD** (PL los **CDs**) NOUN
CD

el **CD-ROM** (PL los **CD-ROMs**) NOUN
CD-ROM

la **CE** ABBREVIATION (= Comunidad Europea)
EC (= European Community)

el **cebo** NOUN
bait

la **cebolla** NOUN
onion

la **cebolleta** NOUN
1 spring onion
2 pickled onion

la **cebra** NOUN
zebra

■ **un paso de cebra** a zebra crossing

**ceder** VERB [8]
1 to give in

□ Al final tuve que ceder. Finally I had to give in.
2 to give way

□ La estantería cedió por el peso de los libros. The shelves gave way under the weight of the books.
■ **'Ceda el paso'** 'Give way'

**Spanish-English**

la **ceguera** NOUN
blindness

la **ceja** NOUN
eyebrow

la **celda** NOUN
cell

la **celebración** (PL las **celebraciones**) NOUN
celebration

**celebrar** VERB [25]
1 to celebrate
 ■ **En octubre se celebra el día de la Hispanidad.** Columbus Day is in October.
2 to hold

**célebre** (FEM **célebre**) ADJECTIVE
famous

el **celo** NOUN
Sellotape®

el **celofán** NOUN
cellophane

los **celos** NOUN
jealousy *sing*
 □ Lo hizo por celos. He did it out of jealousy.
 ■ **Tiene celos de su mejor amiga.** She's jealous of her best friend.
 ■ **Lo hace para darle celos.** He does it to make her jealous.

**celoso** (FEM **celosa**) ADJECTIVE
jealous
 □ Está celoso de su hermano. He's jealous of his brother.

la **célula** NOUN
cell

la **celulitis** NOUN
cellulite

el **cementerio** NOUN
cemetery (PL cemeteries)
 ■ **un cementerio de coches** a scrapyard

el **cemento** NOUN
1 cement
 ■ **el cemento armado** reinforced concrete
2 glue (*Latin America*)

la **cena** NOUN
dinner
 □ La cena es a las nueve. Dinner is at nine o'clock.

**cenar** VERB [25]
to have dinner
 □ No he cenado. I haven't had dinner.
 ■ **¿Qué quieres cenar?** What do you want for dinner?

el **cenicero** NOUN
ashtray (PL ashtrays)

la **ceniza** NOUN
ash (PL ashes)

la **censura** NOUN
censorship

el **centavo** NOUN
cent

la **centésima** NOUN
 ■ **una centésima de segundo** a hundredth of a second

**centígrado** (FEM **centígrada**) ADJECTIVE
centigrade
 □ veinte grados centígrados twenty degrees centigrade

el **centímetro** NOUN
centimetre

el **céntimo** NOUN
cent

**central** (FEM **central**) ADJECTIVE
central

la **central** NOUN
head office
 ■ **una central eléctrica** a power-station
 ■ **una central nuclear** a nuclear power-station

la **centralita** NOUN
switchboard

**céntrico** (FEM **céntrica**) ADJECTIVE
central
 □ Está en un barrio céntrico. It's in a central area.
 ■ **Es un piso céntrico.** The flat is in the centre of town.

el **centro** NOUN
centre
 □ en pleno centro de la ciudad right in the town centre
 ■ **Fui al centro a hacer unas compras.** I went into town to do some shopping.
 ■ **un centro comercial** a shopping centre
 ■ **un centro de deportes** a sports centre
 ■ **un centro médico** a hospital

el **centroamericano** (FEM la **centroamericana**) ADJECTIVE, NOUN
Central American

**ceñido** (FEM **ceñida**) ADJECTIVE
tight
 ■ **Esta falda me queda muy ceñida.** This skirt's too tight for me.

**cepillar** VERB [25]
to brush
 ■ **Se está cepillando los dientes.** He's brushing his teeth.

el **cepillo** NOUN
brush (PL brushes)
 ■ **un cepillo de dientes** a toothbrush

la **cera** NOUN
wax

la **cerámica** NOUN
pottery
 □ Me gusta la cerámica. I like pottery.
 ■ **una cerámica** a piece of pottery

**cerca** ADVERB
near
 □ El colegio está muy cerca. The school is

very near.

■ **¿Hay algún banco por aquí cerca?** Is there a bank nearby?

■ **cerca de la iglesia** near the church

■ **cerca de dos horas** nearly two hours

■ **Quería verlo de cerca.** I wanted to see it close up.

**cercano** (FEM **cercana**) ADJECTIVE
nearby

□ Viven en un pueblo cercano. They live in a nearby village.

■ **una de las calles cercanas a la catedral** one of the streets close to the cathedral

■ **el Cercano Oriente** the Near East

el **cerdo** NOUN

1 pig

□ Tienen cerdos. They keep pigs.

2 pork

□ No comemos cerdo. We don't eat pork.

el **cereal** NOUN
cereal

■ **Los niños desayunan cereales.** The children have cereal for breakfast.

el **cerebro** NOUN
brain

la **ceremonia** NOUN
ceremony (PL ceremonies)

la **cereza** NOUN
cherry (PL cherries)

la **cerilla** NOUN
match (PL matches)

□ una caja de cerillas a box of matches

el **cerillo** NOUN (Mexico)
match (PL matches)

el **cero** NOUN
zero (PL zeros o zeroes)

■ **Estamos a cinco grados bajo cero.** It's five degrees below zero.

■ **cero coma tres** zero point three

■ **Van dos a cero.** The score is two-nil.

■ **Empataron a cero.** It was a no-score draw.

■ **quince a cero** fifteen-love

■ **Tuve que empezar desde cero.** I had to start from scratch.

el **cerquillo** NOUN (Latin America)
fringe

**cerrado** (FEM **cerrada**) ADJECTIVE
closed

□ Las tiendas están cerradas. The shops are closed.

■ **una curva muy cerrada** a very sharp bend

la **cerradura** NOUN
lock

**cerrar*** VERB [39]

1 to close

□ No cierran al mediodía. They don't close

at noon. □ Cerró el libro. He closed the book. □ No puedo cerrar la maleta. I can't shut this suitcase.

2 to turn off

□ Cierra el grifo. Turn off the tap.

■ **Cerré la puerta con llave.** I locked the door.

■ **La puerta se cerró de golpe.** The door slammed shut.

■ **Se me cierran los ojos.** I can't keep my eyes open.

el **cerrojo** NOUN
bolt

■ **echar el cerrojo** to bolt the door

**certificado** (FEM **certificada**) ADJECTIVE
registered

■ **Mandé el paquete certificado.** I sent the parcel by registered post.

el **certificado** NOUN
certificate

la **cervecería** NOUN
bar

la **cerveza** NOUN
beer

□ Fuimos a tomar unas cervezas. We went to have a few beers.

■ **la cerveza de barril** draught beer

**cesar** VERB [25]
to stop

■ **No cesa de hablar.** He never stops talking.

■ **No cesaba de repetirlo.** He kept repeating it.

el **césped** NOUN
grass

□ 'no pisar el césped' 'keep off the grass'

la **cesta** NOUN
basket

■ **una cesta de Navidad** a Christmas hamper

el **cesto** NOUN
basket

el **chabacano** NOUN (Mexico)
apricot

la **chabola** NOUN
shack

■ **un barrio de chabolas** a shantytown

el **chaleco** NOUN
waistcoat

■ **un chaleco salvavidas** a life-jacket

el **chalet** (PL los **chalets**) NOUN

1 cottage

2 villa

3 house

el **champán** (PL los **champanes**) NOUN
champagne

el **champiñón** (PL los **champiñones**) NOUN
mushroom

**c**

el **champú** (PL los **champús**) NOUN
shampoo (PL shampoos)

el **chancho**, la **chancha** NOUN (River
Plate)
pig

la **chancleta** NOUN
flip-flop
■ **unas chancletas** a pair of flip-flops

el **chándal** (PL los **chándals**) NOUN
tracksuit

el **chantaje** NOUN
blackmail
■ **hacer chantaje a alguien** to blackmail
somebody

la **chapa** NOUN
1 badge
2 top
3 sheet
4 panel
5 number plate (Latin America)

**chapado** (FEM **chapada**) ADJECTIVE
■ **chapado en oro** gold-plated

el **chaparrón** (PL los **chaparrones**) NOUN
■ **Anoche cayó un buen chaparrón.** There
was a real downpour last night.
■ **Es sólo un chaparrón.** It's just a shower.

**chapotear** VERB
to splash around

la **chapuza** NOUN
botched job
■ **hacer chapuzas** to do odd jobs

el **chapuzón** (PL los **chapuzones**) NOUN
■ **darse un chapuzón** to go for a dip

la **chaqueta** NOUN
1 cardigan
2 jacket

la **charca** NOUN
pond

el **charco** NOUN
puddle

la **charcutería** NOUN
delicatessen

la **charla** NOUN
1 chat
□ Estuvimos de charla. We had a chat.
2 talk
□ Dio una charla sobre teatro clásico.
He gave a talk on classical theatre.

**charlar** VERB [25]
to chat

el **chasco** NOUN
■ **llevarse un chasco** to be disappointed

el **chat** NOUN
chatroom

la **chatarra** NOUN
scrap metal

la **chava** NOUN (Mexico)
girl

el **chavo** NOUN (Mexico)
boy

**checar*** VERB [48] (Mexico)
to check

el **checo** (FEM la **checa**) ADJECTIVE, NOUN
Czech
■ **la República Checa** the Czech Republic

el **checo** NOUN
Czech

el **chef** (PL los **chefs**) NOUN
chef (PL chefs)

el **cheque** NOUN
cheque
■ **los cheques de viaje** traveller's cheques

el **chequeo** NOUN
check-up (PL check-ups)
□ hacerse un chequeo to have a check-up

**chévere** (FEM **chévere**) ADJECTIVE, ADVERB
(Latin America)
great

la **chica** NOUN
girl

el **chícharo** NOUN (Mexico)
pea

el **chichón** (PL los **chichones**) NOUN
bump
□ Me ha salido un chichón en la frente.
I've got a bump on my forehead.

el **chicle** NOUN
chewing gum

**chico** (FEM **chica**) ADJECTIVE
small

el **chico** NOUN
1 boy
□ los chicos de la clase the boys in the class
2 guy
□ Me parece un chico muy guapo. I think
he's a cute guy.

**Chile** MASC NOUN
Chile

el **chileno** (FEM la **chilena**) ADJECTIVE, NOUN
Chilean

**chillar** VERB [25]
1 to scream
2 to squeak
3 to squeal
4 to screech

la **chimenea** NOUN
1 chimney (PL chimneys)
□ Salía humo de la chimenea. There was
smoke coming out of the chimney.
2 fireplace
□ sentado frente a la chimenea sitting in
front of the fireplace
■ **Enciende la chimenea.** Light the fire.

el **chimpancé** (PL los **chimpancés**) NOUN
chimpanzee

**China** FEM NOUN

China
la **china** NOUN
1 Chinese woman
2 stone
□ Se me ha metido una china en el zapato.
I've got a stone in my shoe.
la **chinche** NOUN *(Mexico, River Plate)*
drawing pin
la **chincheta** NOUN
drawing pin
**chino** (FEM **china**) ADJECTIVE
Chinese
el **chino** NOUN
1 Chinese man
■ **los chinos** the Chinese
2 Chinese
**Chipre** MASC NOUN
Cyprus
la **chirimoya** NOUN
custard apple
**chirriar*** VERB [21]
to squeak
el **chisme** NOUN
1 thing
2 piece of gossip
**chismorrear** VERB [25]
to gossip
**chismoso** (FEM **chismosa**) ADJECTIVE
■ **¡No seas chismoso!** Don't be such a
gossip!
el **chiste** NOUN
1 joke
□ contar un chiste to tell a joke
■ **un chiste verde** a dirty joke
⋯ LANGUAGE TIP Word for word, **chiste**
⋯ **verde** means 'green joke'.
2 cartoon
□ el chiste del periódico the newspaper
cartoon
**chocar*** VERB [48]
■ **chocar contra 1** to hit □ El coche chocó
contra un árbol. The car hit a tree. **2** to
bump into □ Me choqué contra una farola. I
bumped into a lamppost.
■ **chocar con algo** to crash into something
■ **Los trenes chocaron de frente.** The
trains crashed head-on.
■ **Me choca que no sepas nada.** I'm
shocked that you don't know anything
about it.
el **chocolate** NOUN
chocolate
□ chocolate con leche milk chocolate
■ **Nos tomamos un chocolate.** We had a
cup of hot chocolate.
la **chocolatina** NOUN
chocolate bar
el/la **chófer** NOUN

1 driver
2 chauffeur
el **chopo** NOUN
black poplar
el **choque** NOUN
1 crash (PL crashes)
2 clash (PL clashes)
el **chorizo** NOUN
⋯ **DID YOU KNOW...?**
⋯ **Chorizo** is a kind of spicy sausage.
el **chorrito** NOUN
dash
□ Échame un chorrito de leche. Just a dash
of milk, please.
el **chorro** NOUN
■ **salir a chorros** to gush out
la **choza** NOUN
hut
el **chubasco** NOUN
heavy shower
el **chubasquero** NOUN
cagoule
la **chuleta** NOUN
chop
□ una chuleta de cerdo a pork chop
**chulo** (FEM **chula**) ADJECTIVE
1 cocky *(colloquial)*
■ **ponerse chulo con alguien** to get cocky
with someone
2 neat *(colloquial)*
□ ¡Qué mochila más chula! What a neat
rucksack!
**chupar** VERB [25]
to suck
□ Se chupaba el dedo. He was sucking his
thumb.
el **chupete** NOUN
dummy (PL dummies)
el **churro** NOUN
⋯ **DID YOU KNOW...?**
⋯ A **Churro** is a type of fritter typically
⋯ served with a cup of hot chocolate at
⋯ cafés or **churrerías** (churro stalls/
⋯ shops).
el **cíber** ABBREVIATION *(= cibercafé)*
Internet café
el **cibercafé** NOUN
Internet café
el **ciberespacio** NOUN
cyberspace
la **cicatriz** (PL las **cicatrices**) NOUN
scar
□ Me quedó una cicatriz en la cara. I was left
with a scar on my face.
el **ciclismo** NOUN
cycling
■ **Mi hermano hace ciclismo.** My brother
is a cyclist.

el/la **ciclista** NOUN
cyclist

el **ciclo** NOUN
cycle

la **ciega** NOUN
blind woman (PL blind women)
■ **Avanzábamos a ciegas.** We couldn't see where we were going.
■ **Tomaron la decisión a ciegas.** They took the decision blindly.

**ciego** (FEM **ciega**) ADJECTIVE
blind
■ **quedarse ciego** to go blind

el **ciego** NOUN
blind man
■ **los ciegos** the blind

el **cielo** NOUN
1 sky (PL skies)
□ No había ni una nube en el cielo. There wasn't a single cloud in the sky.
2 heaven
□ ir al cielo to go to heaven

**cien** (FEM **cien**) ADJECTIVE, PRONOUN
a hundred
□ Había unos cien invitados en la boda. There were about a hundred guests at the wedding. □ cien mil a hundred thousand
■ **cien por cien** a hundred percent □ Es cien por cien algodón. It's a hundred percent cotton.

la **ciencia** NOUN
science
□ Me gustan mucho las ciencias. I really enjoy science. □ ciencias sociales social sciences
■ **ciencias empresariales** business studies

la **ciencia-ficción** NOUN
science fiction
□ novelas de ciencia-ficción science fiction novels

la **científica** NOUN
scientist

**científico** (FEM **científica**) ADJECTIVE
scientific

el **científico** NOUN
scientist

**ciento** (FEM **ciento**) ADJECTIVE, PRONOUN
a hundred
■ **ciento cuarenta y dos libras** a hundred and forty two pounds
■ **Recibimos cientos de cartas.** We received hundreds of letters.
■ **el diez por ciento de la población** ten percent of the population

el **cierre** NOUN
1 clasp
2 closing-down
■ **un cierre relámpago** (River Plate) a zip

**cierro** VERB ▷ see **cerrar**

**cierto** (FEM **cierta**) ADJECTIVE
1 true
□ No, eso no es cierto. No, that's not true.
2 certain
□ Viene ciertos días a la semana. He comes certain days of the week.
■ **por cierto** by the way

el **ciervo** NOUN
deer (PL deer)

la **cifra** NOUN
figure
□ un número de cuatro cifras a four-figure number

el **cigarrillo** NOUN
cigarette

el **cigarro** NOUN
cigarette

la **cigüeña** NOUN
stork

la **cima** NOUN
top
□ Quiere llegar a la cima. He wants to get to the top.

los **cimientos** NOUN
foundations

**cinco** (FEM **cinco**) ADJECTIVE, PRONOUN
five
■ **Son las cinco.** It's five o'clock.
■ **el cinco de enero** the fifth of January

**cincuenta** (FEM **cincuenta**) ADJECTIVE, PRONOUN
fifty
□ Tiene cincuenta años. He's fifty.
■ **el cincuenta aniversario** the fiftieth anniversary

el **cine** NOUN
cinema
■ **ir al cine** to go to the cinema
■ **una actriz de cine** a film actress

**cínico** (FEM **cínica**) ADJECTIVE
cynical

la **cinta** NOUN
1 ribbon
2 tape
■ **una cinta de vídeo** a videotape
■ **cinta aislante** insulating tape
■ **una cinta transportadora** a conveyor belt

la **cintura** NOUN
waist
□ ¿Cuánto mides de cintura? What's your waist size?

el **cinturón** (PL los **cinturones**) NOUN
belt
■ **el cinturón de seguridad** the safety belt

el **ciprés** (PL los **cipreses**) NOUN
cypress

el **circo** NOUN
circus (PL circuses)

el **circuito** NOUN
1 track
 ▫ El corredor dio cuatro vueltas al circuito.
 The runner ran four laps of the track.
2 circuit
 ■ circuito cerrado de televisión closed-circuit television

la **circulación** NOUN
1 traffic
 ▫ un accidente de circulación a traffic accident
2 circulation

**circular** VERB [25]
1 to drive
 ▫ En Australia se circula por la derecha. In Australia they drive on the left.
 ■ ¡Circulen! Move along please!
2 to circulate
3 to go round
 ▫ Circula el rumor de que se van casar. There's a rumour going round that they're getting married.

el **círculo** NOUN
circle
 ▫ Las sillas estaban puestas en círculo. The chairs were set out in a circle.

la **circunferencia** NOUN
circumference

la **circunstancia** NOUN
circumstance

la **ciruela** NOUN
plum
 ■ una ciruela pasa a prune

la **cirugía** NOUN
surgery (PL surgeries)
 ■ hacerse la cirugía plástica to have plastic surgery

el **cirujano**, la **cirujana** NOUN
surgeon

el **cisne** NOUN
swan

la **cisterna** NOUN
cistern

la **cita** NOUN
1 appointment
 ▫ Tengo cita con el Sr. Pérez. I've got an appointment with Mr. Pérez.
2 date
 ▫ No llegues tarde a la cita. Don't be late for your date.
3 quotation
 ▫ una cita de Quevedo a quotation from Quevedo

**citar** VERB [25]
1 to quote
 ▫ Siempre está citando a los clásicos. He's always quoting the classics.
2 to mention
 ▫ Citó el caso que ocurrió el otro día. He mentioned as an example what happened the other day.
 ■ Nos han citado a las diez. We've been given an appointment for ten o'clock.
 ■ Me he citado con Elena. I've arranged to meet Elena.

la **ciudad** NOUN
1 city (PL cities)
 ▫ una ciudad como Salamanca a city like Salamanca
2 town
 ▫ una pequeña ciudad al norte de Londres a small town north of London
 ■ la ciudad universitaria the university campus

el **ciudadano**, la **ciudadana** NOUN
citizen
 ▫ ser ciudadano español to be a Spanish citizen

**civil** (FEM civil) ADJECTIVE
civil
 ▫ la guerra civil the Civil War

la **civilización** (PL las **civilizaciones**) NOUN
civilization

**civilizado** (FEM civilizada) ADJECTIVE
civilized

la **clara** NOUN
white

el **clarinete** NOUN
clarinet

**claro** (FEM clara) ADJECTIVE
▷ see also **claro** ADVERB
1 clear
 ▫ Lo quiero mañana. ¿Está claro? I want it tomorrow. Is that clear?
 ■ Está claro que esconden algo. It's obvious that they are hiding something.
 ■ No tengo muy claro lo que quiero hacer. I'm not very sure about what I want to do.
2 light
 ▫ una camisa azul claro a light blue shirt

**claro** ADVERB
▷ see also **claro** ADJECTIVE
clearly
 ▫ Lo oí muy claro. I heard it very clearly.
 ■ Quiero que me hables claro. I want you to be frank with me.
 ■ No he sacado nada en claro de la reunión. I'm none the wiser after that meeting.
 ■ ¡Claro! 1 Sure! ▫ ¿Te gusta el fútbol? — ¡Claro! Do you like football? — Sure! 2 Of course! ▫ ¿Te oyó? — ¡Claro que me oyó! Did he hear you? — Of course he heard me!

la **clase** NOUN
1 class (PL classes)
  □ A las diez tengo clase de física. I have a physics class at ten.
  ■ **Mi hermana da clases de inglés.** My sister teaches English.
  ■ **Hoy no hay clase.** There's no school today.
  ■ **clases de conducir** driving lessons
  ■ **clases particulares** private classes
2 classroom
3 kind
  □ Había juguetes de todas clases. There were all kinds of toys.
  ■ **la clase media** the middle class

**clásico** (FEM **clásica**) ADJECTIVE
1 classical
  □ Me gusta la música clásica. I like classical music.
2 classic
  □ Es el clásico ejemplo de malnutrición. It's the classic case of malnutrition.

la **clasificación** (PL las **clasificaciones**) NOUN
classification
  ■ **estar a la cabeza de la clasificación** to be at the top of the table

**clasificar*** VERB [48]
to classify
  ■ **Esperan clasificarse para la final.** They hope to qualify for the final.
  ■ **Se clasificaron en tercer lugar.** They came third.

**clavar** VERB [25]
  ■ **clavar una punta en algo** to hammer a nail into something
  ■ **Las tablas están mal clavadas.** The boards aren't properly nailed down.
  ■ **Me he clavado una espina en el dedo.** I got a thorn in my finger.
  ■ **Aquí te clavan.** You get ripped off in this place.

la **clave** NOUN
1 code
  ■ **un mensaje en clave** a coded message
2 key
  □ la clave del éxito the key to success
  ■ **la clave de sol** the treble clef

el **clavel** NOUN
carnation

la **clavícula** NOUN
collar bone

el **clavo** NOUN
nail

el **clic** NOUN
click
  ■ **hacer clic en** to click on

el **cliente**, la **clienta** NOUN

1 customer
2 client
3 guest

el **clima** NOUN
climate
  □ Es un país de clima tropical. It's a country with a tropical climate.

**climatizado** (FEM **climatizada**) ADJECTIVE
1 air-conditioned
2 heated

la **clínica** NOUN
hospital

**clínico** (FEM **clínica**) ADJECTIVE
clinical

el **clip** (PL los **clips**) NOUN
1 paper clip
2 clip

la **cloaca** NOUN
sewer

el **cloro** NOUN
chlorine

el **club** (PL los **clubs**) NOUN
club
  □ el club de tenis the tennis club

**cobarde** (FEM **cobarde**) ADJECTIVE
cowardly
  □ una actitud cobarde a cowardly attitude
  ■ **¡No seas cobarde!** Don't be such a coward!

el/la **cobarde** NOUN
coward

la **cobaya** NOUN
guinea-pig

la **cobija** NOUN *(Latin America)*
blanket

**cobrar** VERB [25]
to charge
  □ Me cobró treinta euros por la reparación. He charged me thirty euros for the repair.
  ■ **cuando cobre el sueldo de este mes** when I get my wages this month
  ■ **¿Me cobra los cafés?** How much do I owe for the coffees?
  ■ **¡Cóbrese, por favor!** Can I pay, please?
  ■ **cobrar un cheque** to cash a cheque

el **cobre** NOUN
copper

el **cobro** NOUN
  ■ **llamar a cobro revertido** to reverse the charges

la **Coca-Cola®** (PL las **Coca-Colas**) NOUN
Coke®

la **cocaína** NOUN
cocaine

**cocer*** VERB [6]
1 to boil
  □ Cocer las verduras durante tres minutos. Boil the vegetables for three minutes.

**2** to cook
  □ Las zanahorias no están cocidas todavía. The carrots aren't properly cooked yet.
  ■ **Tarda diez minutos en cocerse.** It takes ten minutes to cook.

el **coche** NOUN

**1** car
  □ Fuimos a Sevilla en coche. We went to Seville by car.
  ■ **un coche de carreras** a racing car
  ■ **los coches de choque** the bumper cars

**2** pram

**3** carriage
  ■ **Fuimos en coche cama.** We took the sleeper.
  ■ **un coche de bomberos** a fire engine

**cochino** (FEM **cochina**) ADJECTIVE
  filthy

el **cochino** NOUN
  pig

el **cocido** NOUN
  stew

> **DID YOU KNOW...?**
> The **cocido madrileño** is a stew of chickpeas, vegetables and meat.

la **cocina** NOUN

**1** kitchen
  □ Comemos en la cocina. We eat in the kitchen.

**2** cooker
  □ una cocina de gas a gas cooker
  ■ **la cocina vasca** Basque cuisine
  ■ **un libro de cocina** a cookery book

**cocinar** VERB [25]
  to cook
  □ No sabe cocinar. He can't cook.
  ■ **Cocinas muy bien.** You're a very good cook.

el **cocinero**, la **cocinera** NOUN
  cook
  □ Soy cocinero. I'm a cook.

el **coco** NOUN
  coconut

el **cocodrilo** NOUN
  crocodile

el **código** NOUN
  code
  ■ **el código de la circulación** the highway code
  ■ **el código postal** the postcode

el **codo** NOUN
  elbow

la **codorniz** (PL las **codornices**) NOUN
  quail

**coger\*** VERB [7]

**1** to take
  □ Coge el que más te guste. Take the one which you like best. □ Coja la primera calle a

la derecha. Take the first street on the right.

**2** to catch
  □ ¡Coge la pelota! Catch the ball! □ La cogieron robando. They caught her stealing.
  ■ **coger un resfriado** to catch a cold

**3** to pick up
  □ Coge al niño, que está llorando. Pick up the baby, he's crying.

**4** to get
  □ ¿Nos coges dos entradas? Would you get us two tickets?

**5** to borrow
  □ ¿Te puedo coger el bolígrafo? Can I borrow your pen?
  ■ **Voy a coger el autobús.** I'm going to get the bus.
  ■ **Le cogió cariño al gato.** He took a liking to the cat.
  ■ **Iban cogidos de la mano.** They were walking hand in hand.

el **cohete** NOUN
  rocket
  ■ **un cohete espacial** a rocket

**cohibido** (FEM **cohibida**) ADJECTIVE
  inhibited
  ■ **sentirse cohibido** to feel inhibited

la **coincidencia** NOUN
  coincidence
  ■ **¡Qué coincidencia!** What a coincidence!

**coincidir** VERB [58]
  to match
  □ Las huellas dactilares coinciden. The fingerprints match.
  ■ **Coincidimos en el tren.** We happened to meet on the train.
  ■ **Es que esas fechas coinciden con mi viaje.** The problem is, those dates clash with my trip.

**cojear** VERB [25]

**1** to limp
  □ Todavía cojea un poco. He's still limping a little.

**2** to be lame
  ■ **Cojea del pie izquierdo.** He's lame in his left leg.

**3** to wobble

el **cojín** (PL los **cojines**) NOUN
  cushion

**cojo** VERB
  ▷ see also **cojo** ADJECTIVE ▷ see **coger**

**cojo** (FEM **coja**) ADJECTIVE
  ▷ see also **cojo** VERB

**1** lame
  ■ **Está cojo.** He's lame.
  ■ **Vas un poco cojo.** You're limping a bit.

**2** wobbly

la **col** NOUN
  cabbage

■ **las coles de Bruselas** Brussels sprouts
la **cola** NOUN
1 tail
2 queue
  □ Había mucha cola para el baño. There was a long queue for the toilets.
  ■ **hacer cola** to queue
3 glue
**colaborar** VERB [25]
  ■ **Todo el pueblo colaboró.** Everyone in the village joined in.
  ■ **Se negó a colaborar con nosotros.** He refused to cooperate with us.
el **colador** NOUN
1 strainer
2 sieve
**colar** VERB [11]
  to strain
  ■ **colarse** (colloquial) to push in □ No te cueles. Don't push in.
  ■ **Nos colamos en el cine.** We sneaked into the cinema without paying.
la **colcha** NOUN
  bedspread
el **colchón** (PL los **colchones**) NOUN
  mattress (PL mattresses)
  ■ **un colchón de aire** an airbed
la **colchoneta** NOUN
1 mat
2 air bed
la **colección** (PL las **colecciones**) NOUN
  collection
**coleccionar** VERB [25]
  to collect
la **colecta** NOUN
  collection
  ■ **Hicieron una colecta para comprarle el billete.** They had a collection to buy him the ticket.
el **colectivo** NOUN (River Plate)
  bus (PL buses)
el/la **colega** NOUN
1 colleague
2 mate (colloquial)
el **colegio** NOUN
  school
  □ Voy al colegio en bicicleta. I cycle to school. □ ¿Todavía vas al colegio? Are you still at school? □ Mi hermano estaba en el colegio. My brother was at school.
  ■ **un colegio de curas** a Catholic boys' school
  ■ **un colegio de monjas** a convent school
  ■ **un colegio público** a state school
  ■ **un colegio mayor** a hall of residence
el **colesterol** NOUN
  cholesterol
la **coleta** NOUN

ponytail
  ■ **La niña llevaba coletas.** The girl wore her hair in bunches.
**colgado** (FEM **colgada**) ADJECTIVE
  hanging
  □ Había varios cuadros colgados en la pared. There were several pictures hanging on the wall.
  ■ **Debe de tener el teléfono mal colgado.** He must have the telephone off the hook.
el **colgante** NOUN
  pendant
**colgar\*** VERB
  to hang
  □ Colgamos un cuadro en la pared. We hung a picture on the wall.
  ■ **¡No dejes la chaqueta en la silla, cuélgala!** Don't leave your jacket on the chair, hang it up!
  ■ **Me colgó el teléfono.** He hung up on me.
  ■ **¡Cuelga, por favor, que quiero hacer una llamada!** Hang up, please. I want to use the phone!
  ■ **No cuelgue, por favor.** Please hold.
la **coliflor** NOUN
  cauliflower
la **colilla** NOUN
  cigarette end
la **colina** NOUN
  hill
la **colisión** NOUN
  collision
el **collar** NOUN
1 necklace
2 collar
la **colmena** NOUN
  beehive
el **colmillo** NOUN
1 canine tooth
2 fang
3 tusk
el **colmo** NOUN
  ■ **¡Esto ya es el colmo!** This really is the last straw!
  ■ **Para colmo de males, empezó a llover.** To make matters worse, it started to rain.
**colocar\*** VERB [48]
1 to put
  □ Colocamos la mesa en medio del comedor. We put the table in the middle of the dining room.
2 to arrange
  □ He colocado los libros por temas. I've arranged the books by subject.
  ■ **colocarse 1** to get a job □ Se colocó de aprendiz en un taller. He got a job as an apprentice in a workshop. **2** (colloquial) to

get plastered **3** *(colloquial)* to get high
■ **¡Colocaos en fila!** Get into a line!
■ **El equipo se ha colocado en quinto lugar.** The team are now in fifth place.

**Colombia** FEM NOUN
Colombia

el **colombiano** (FEM la **colombiana**)
ADJECTIVE, NOUN
Colombian

la **colonia** NOUN
1 perfume
2 colony (PL colonies)
3 district *(Mexico)*
■ **una colonia de verano** a summer camp

**colonizar\*** VERB [13]
to colonize

**coloquial** (FEM **coloquial**) ADJECTIVE
colloquial

el **color** NOUN
colour
□ ¿De qué color son? What colour are they?
■ **un vestido de color azul** a blue dress
■ **una televisión en color** a colour television

**colorado** (FEM **colorada**) ADJECTIVE
red
■ **ponerse colorado** to blush

la **columna** NOUN
column
■ **la columna vertebral** the spine

el **columpio** NOUN
swing

la **coma** NOUN
comma
□ palabras separadas por comas words separated by commas
■ **cero coma ocho** zero point eight

el **coma** NOUN
coma
■ **estar en coma** to be in a coma

la **comadrona** NOUN
midwife (PL midwives)

el/la **comandante** NOUN
major
■ **el comandante en jefe** the commander in chief

la **comba** NOUN
skipping rope
■ **saltar a la comba** to skip

el **combate** NOUN
battle
□ entrar en combate to go into battle
■ **un piloto de combate** a fighter pilot
■ **un combate de boxeo** a boxing match

**combinar** VERB [25]
1 to combine
□ Combina los estudios con el trabajo. He combines his studies with work.

2 to match
□ colores que combinan con el azul colours which match with blue

el **combustible** NOUN
fuel

la **comedia** NOUN
comedy (PL comedies)

el **comedor** NOUN
1 dining room
2 refectory (PL refectories)
3 canteen

**comentar** VERB [25]
1 to say
□ Comentó que le había parecido muy joven. He said that she had seemed very young.
2 to discuss
□ Comentamos el tema en clase. We discussed the subject in class.
■ **Me han comentado que es una película muy buena.** I've been told that is a very good film.

el **comentario** NOUN
comment
□ No hizo ningún comentario. He made no comment.
■ **Fue un comentario desagradable.** It was an unpleasant remark.

el/la **comentarista** NOUN
commentator

**comenzar\*** VERB [19]
to begin
■ **Comenzó a llover.** It began to rain.

**comer** VERB [8]
1 to eat
□ ¿Quieres comer algo? Do you want something to eat?
■ **Me comí una manzana.** I had an apple.
2 to have lunch
□ Comimos en el hotel. We had lunch in the hotel.
■ **Hemos comido paella.** We had paella for lunch.
■ **¿Qué hay para comer?** What is there for lunch?
3 to have dinner *(Latin America)*
■ **Le estaba dando de comer a su hijo.** She was feeding her son.
■ **No te comas el coco por eso.** *(colloquial)* Don't worry too much about it.

**comercial** (FEM **comercial**) ADJECTIVE
1 business
2 trade
3 commercial
□ una película muy comercial a very commercial film

el/la **comerciante** NOUN
shopkeeper

71

el **comercio** NOUN
1 trade
  □ el comercio exterior foreign trade
  ■ **el comercio electrónico** e-commerce
2 shop
  □ ¿A qué hora cierran los comercios? What time do the shops close?

el **cometa** NOUN
  comet

la **cometa** NOUN
  kite

**cometer** VERB [8]
1 to commit
2 to make

el **cómic** (PL los **cómics**) NOUN
  comic
  □ un cómic nuevo a new comic
  ■ **un personaje de cómic** a comic-book character

**cómico** (FEM **cómica**) ADJECTIVE
1 comical
  □ Fue muy cómico. It was very comical.
2 comic
  □ un actor cómico a comic actor

la **comida** NOUN
1 food
  □ La comida es muy buena en el hotel. The food in the hotel is very good.
2 lunch (PL lunches)
  □ La comida es a la una y media. Lunch is at half past one.
3 supper (*Latin America*)
4 meal
  □ Es la comida más importante del día. It's the most important meal of the day.

**comienzo** VERB ▷ see **comenzar**

las **comillas** NOUN
  quotation marks
  ■ **entre comillas** in quotation marks

la **comisaría** NOUN
  police station

la **comisión** (PL las **comisiones**) NOUN
1 commission
  □ una comisión del 20% a 20% commission
2 committee
  □ La comisión organizadora del festival. The festival organizing committee.

el **comité** (PL los **comités**) NOUN
  committee

**como** ADVERB, CONJUNCTION
1 like
  □ Tienen un perro como el nuestro. They've got a dog like ours.  □ Se portó como un imbécil. He behaved like an idiot.
  ■ **Sabe como a cebolla.** It tastes a bit like onion.
2 as

□ Lo hice como me habían enseñado. I did it as I had been taught.  □ Lo usé como cuchara. I used it as a spoon.  □ blanco como la nieve as white as snow  □ Como ella no llegaba, me fui. As she didn't arrive, I left.
  ■ **Hazlo como te dijo ella.** Do it the way she told you.
  ■ **Es tan alto como tú.** He is as tall as you.
  ■ **tal como lo había planeado** just as I had planned it
  ■ **como si** as if  □ Siguió leyendo, como si no hubiera oído nada. He kept on reading, as if he had heard nothing.
3 if
  □ Como lo vuelvas a hacer se lo digo a tu madre. If you do it again I'll tell your mother.
4 about
  □ Vinieron como unas diez personas. About ten people came.  □ Llegó como a las cuatro. He arrived about four o'clock.

**cómo** ADVERB
  how
  □ ¿Cómo se dice en inglés? How do you say it in English?  □ ¿Cómo están tus padres? How are your parents?  □ No sé cómo voy a explicárselo. I don't know how I'm going to explain it to him.
  ■ **¿A cómo están las manzanas?** How much are the apples?
  ■ **¿Cómo es de grande?** How big is it?
  ■ **¿Cómo es su novio? 1** What's her boyfriend like? **2** What does her boyfriend look like?
  ■ **Perdón, ¿cómo has dicho?** Sorry, what did you say?
  ■ **¡Cómo! ¿Mañana?** What? Tomorrow?
  ■ **¡Cómo corría!** Boy, was he running!

la **cómoda** NOUN
  chest of drawers (PL chests of drawers)

la **comodidad** NOUN
1 comfort
  □ Sólo le interesa su propia comodidad. He's only interested in his own comfort.
2 convenience
  □ la comodidad de vivir en el centro the convenience of living in the centre

**cómodo** (FEM **cómoda**) ADJECTIVE
1 comfortable
  □ un sillón cómodo a comfortable chair
  □ Me siento cómodo en tu casa. I feel comfortable in your house.
2 convenient
  □ Tener un coche es muy cómodo. Having a car is very convenient.

el **compact disc** (PL los **compact discs**) NOUN
1 compact disc

**2** compact disc player

**compadecer*** VERB [12]
to feel sorry for
□ Te compadezco. I feel sorry for you.

el **compañero**, la **compañera** NOUN
**1** classmate
**2** workmate
**3** partner
■ un compañero de piso a flatmate

la **compañía** NOUN
company (PL companies)
□ una compañía de seguros an insurance company
■ **El chico andaba en malas compañías.** The boy was keeping bad company.
■ **Ana vino a hacerme compañía.** Ana came to keep me company.
■ **una compañía aérea** an airline

la **comparación** (PL las **comparaciones**) NOUN
comparison
■ **Mi coche no tiene comparación con el tuyo.** There's no comparison between my car and yours.
■ **Mi cuarto es pequeñísimo en comparación con el tuyo.** My room is tiny compared to yours.

**comparar** VERB [25]
to compare
□ Siempre me comparan con mi hermana. I'm always being compared to my sister.

**compartir** VERB [58]
to share

el **compás** (PL los **compases**) NOUN
compass (PL compasses)
■ **bailar al compás de la música** to dance in time to the music

**compatible** (FEM **compatible**) ADJECTIVE
compatible

**compensar** VERB [25]
**1** to make up for
□ Intentan compensar la falta de medios con la imaginación. What they lack in resources they try to make up for in imagination.
**2** to compensate
□ Compensarán a los agricultores por las pérdidas. The farmers will be compensated for their losses.
■ **No me compensa con el sueldo que pagan.** It's not worth my while for the salary they pay.
■ **No compensa viajar tan lejos por tan poco tiempo.** It's not worth travelling that far for such a short time.
■ **No sé si compensa.** I don't know if it's worth it.

la **competencia** NOUN

**1** rivalry
□ la competencia entre dos hermanos the rivalry between two brothers
**2** competition
□ Una campaña para desacreditar a la competencia. A campaign to discredit the competition.
■ **una competencia deportiva** (Latin America) a sports competition
■ **No quiere hacerle la competencia a su mejor amigo.** He doesn't want to compete with his best friend.

**competente** (FEM **competente**) ADJECTIVE
competent

la **competición** (PL las **competiciones**) NOUN
competition

**competir*** VERB [38]
to compete
■ **Van a competir contra los mejores del mundo.** They're going to compete against the best in the world.
■ **competir por un título** to compete for a title

**complacer*** VERB
to please

el **complejo** NOUN
complex (PL complexes)
■ **Tiene complejo porque es gordo.** He's got a complex about being fat.
■ **un complejo deportivo** a sports complex

**completar** VERB [25]
to complete

**completo** (FEM **completa**) ADJECTIVE
**1** complete
□ las obras completas de Lorca the complete works of Lorca
**2** full
□ Los hoteles estaban completos. The hotels were full.
■ **Me olvidé por completo.** I completely forgot.

**complicado** (FEM **complicada**) ADJECTIVE
complicated

**complicar*** VERB [48]
to complicate
■ **complicarse** to get complicated □ La situación se fue complicando cada día más. The situation was getting more complicated by the day.
■ **No quiero complicarme la vida.** I don't want to make life more difficult for myself.

el/la **cómplice** NOUN
accomplice

**componer*** VERB [41]
to compose
□ Él compuso la música. He composed the music. □ El comité se compone de seis

miembros. The committee is made up of six members.

el **comportamiento** NOUN
behaviour

**comportarse** VERB [25]
to behave

la **compra** NOUN
shopping
- **hacer la compra** to do the shopping
- **Hice unas compras en el centro.** I did some shopping in the centre.
- **ir de compras** to go shopping

**comprar** VERB [25]
to buy
▫ Les compré un helado a los niños. I bought an ice-cream for the children.
- **Le compré el coche a mi amigo.** I bought my friend's car.
- **Quiero comprarme unos zapatos.** I want to buy a pair of shoes.

**comprender** VERB [8]
to understand
▫ ¡No lo comprendo! I don't understand it!

**comprensivo** (FEM **comprensiva**) ADJECTIVE
understanding

la **compresa** NOUN
sanitary towel

el **comprimido** NOUN
pill

el **comprobante** NOUN
receipt

**comprobar\*** VERB [11]
to check

**comprometerse** VERB [8]
▫ Me he comprometido a ayudarlos. I have promised to help them.
- **No quiero comprometerme por si después no puedo ir.** I don't want to commit myself in case I can't go.

el **compromiso** NOUN
engagement
▫ El ministro canceló sus compromisos. The minister cancelled his engagements.
▫ Se iban a casar pero rompieron el compromiso. They were going to get married but they broke off their engagement.
- **Puede probarlo sin ningún compromiso.** You can try it with no obligation.
- **Iba a ir pero sólo por compromiso.** I was going to go but only out of duty.
- **poner a alguien en un compromiso** to put someone in a difficult situation

**compruebo** VERB ▷ see **comprobar**

**compuesto** VERB ▷ see **componer**

**compuesto** (FEM **compuesta**) ADJECTIVE
- **un jurado compuesto de seis miembros**

a jury made up of six members

el **computador**, la **computadora**
NOUN (Latin America)
computer
- **un computador portátil** a laptop

**común** (FEM **común**) ADJECTIVE
common
▫ un apellido muy común a very common surname
- **No tenemos nada en común.** We have nothing in common.
- **Hicimos el trabajo en común.** We did the work between us.
- **las zonas de uso común** the communal areas

la **comunicación** (PL las **comunicaciones**)
NOUN
communication
- **Se ha cortado la comunicación.** We've been cut off.

**comunicar\*** VERB [48]
to be engaged
▫ Siempre está comunicando. The line is always engaged.
- **comunicarse** to communicate ▫ Le cuesta comunicarse con los demás. He finds it hard to communicate with others.
- **Los dos despachos se comunican.** The two offices are connected.

la **comunidad** NOUN
community (PL communities)
- **la Comunidad Europea** the European Community
- **una comunidad autónoma** an autonomous region

la **comunión** (PL las **comuniones**) NOUN
communion
- **Voy a hacer la primera comunión.** I'm going to make my first communion.

el/la **comunista** (ADJECTIVE, NOUN
communist

**con** PREPOSITION
with
▫ Vivo con mis padres. I live with my parents. ▫ ¿Con quién vas a ir? Who are you going with?
- **Lo he escrito con bolígrafo.** I wrote it in pen.
- **Voy a hablar con Luis.** I'll talk to Luis.
- **café con leche** white coffee
- **Ábrelo con cuidado.** Open it carefully.
- **Con estudiar un poco apruebas.** With a bit of studying you should pass.
- **Con que me digas tu teléfono basta.** If you just give me your phone number that'll be enough.
- **con tal de que no llegues tarde** as long as you don't arrive late

**Spanish-English**

el **concejal**, la **concejala** NOUN
town councillor

**concentrarse** VERB [25]
1 to concentrate
□ Me cuesta concentrarme. I find it hard to concentrate.
■ **Concéntrate en lo que estás haciendo.** Concentrate on what you're doing.
2 to gather
□ Los manifestantes se concentraron en la plaza. The demonstrators gathered in the square.

**concertar*** VERB [39]
to arrange

la **concha** NOUN
shell

la **conciencia** NOUN
conscience
□ Tengo la conciencia tranquila. My conscience is clear.
■ **Le remuerde la conciencia.** His conscience is pricking him.
■ **Lo han estudiado a conciencia.** They've studied it thoroughly.

el **concierto** NOUN
1 concert
□ Van a dar varios conciertos en Madrid. They're going to give several concerts in Madrid.
2 concerto (PL concertos)
□ un concierto para violín a violin concerto

la **conclusión** (PL las **conclusiones**) NOUN
conclusion
□ Llegamos a la conclusión de que no valía la pena. We reached the conclusion that it wasn't worthwhile.

**concreto** (FEM **concreta**) ADJECTIVE
1 specific
□ por poner un ejemplo concreto to take a specific example
■ **No hablo de personas concretas.** I don't mean anyone in particular.
2 definite
□ Todavía no hay fechas concretas. There are no definite dates yet.
■ **este modelo en concreto** this particular model
■ **No me refiero a nadie en concreto.** I don't mean anyone in particular.
■ **Todavía no hemos decidido nada en concreto.** We still haven't decided anything definite.

**concurrido** (FEM **concurrida**) ADJECTIVE
busy

el/la **concursante** NOUN
competitor

el **concurso** NOUN
1 game show
2 competition
□ un concurso de poesía a poetry competition
■ **un concurso de belleza** a beauty contest

el **conde** NOUN
count

la **condecoración** (PL las **condecoraciones**) NOUN
decoration

la **condena** NOUN
sentence
■ **cumplir una condena** to serve a sentence

**condenar** VERB [25]
to sentence
□ Lo condenaron a tres años de cárcel. He was sentenced to three years in prison.

la **condesa** NOUN
countess

la **condición** (PL las **condiciones**) NOUN
condition
■ **a condición de que apruebes** on condition that you pass
■ **El piso está en muy malas condiciones.** The flat is in a very bad state.
■ **No está en condiciones de viajar.** He's not fit to travel.

el **condón** (PL los **condones**) NOUN
condom

**conducir*** VERB [9]
1 to drive
■ **No sé conducir.** I can't drive.
2 to ride
■ **Enfadarse no conduce a nada.** Getting angry won't get you anywhere.

la **conducta** NOUN
behaviour

el **conductor**, la **conductora** NOUN
driver

**conduzco** VERB ▷ see **conducir**

**conectar** VERB [25]
to connect
□ conectar dos cables to connect two cables
■ **Vamos a conectar ahora con el estadio.** Now we go over to the stadium.
■ **Le cuesta conectar con la gente.** He has trouble relating to people.

el **conejillo** NOUN
■ **un conejillo de Indias** a guinea-pig

el **conejo** NOUN
rabbit

la **conexión** (PL las **conexiones**) NOUN
connection

la **conferencia** NOUN
1 lecture
2 conference
3 long-distance call

**c**

**confesar\*** VERB [39]
1 to confess to
□ confesar un crimen to confess to a crime
2 to admit
□ Confesó que había sido él. He admitted that it had been him.
■ **confesarse** to go to confession □ Se confiesa todos los domingos. He goes to confession every Sunday.

el **confeti** NOUN
confetti

la **confianza** NOUN
trust
□ Han puesto toda su confianza en él. They have put all their trust in him.
■ **Tengo confianza en ti.** I trust you.
■ **No tiene confianza en sí mismo.** He has no self-confidence.
■ **un empleado de confianza** a trusted employee
■ **Se lo dije porque tenemos mucha confianza.** I told her about it because we're very close.
■ **Los alumnos se toman muchas confianzas con él.** The pupils take too many liberties with him.

**confiar\*** VERB [21]
to trust
□ No confío en ella. I don't trust her.
■ **Confiaba en que su familia le ayudaría.** He was confident that his family would help him.
■ **No hay que confiarse demasiado.** You mustn't be over-confident.

**confidencial** (FEM **confidencial**) ADJECTIVE
confidential

**confieso** VERB ▷ see confesar

**confirmar** VERB [25]
to confirm

la **confitería** NOUN
cake shop

el **conflicto** NOUN
conflict

**conformarse** VERB [25]
■ **conformarse con** to be satisfied with
□ Tengo que conformarme con lo que tengo. I have to be satisfied with what I've got.
■ **Se conforman con poco.** They're easily satisfied.
■ **Tendrás que conformarte con uno más barato.** You'll have to make do with a cheaper one.

**conforme** (FEM **conforme**) ADJECTIVE
satisfied
□ No se quedó muy conforme con esa explicación. He wasn't very satisfied with that explanation.

■ **estar conforme** to agree □ ¿Estáis todos conformes? Do you all agree?

**confortable** (FEM **confortable**) ADJECTIVE
comfortable

**confundir** VERB [58]
1 to mistake
□ confundir la sal con el azúcar to mistake the salt for the sugar □ La gente me confunde con mi hermana. People mistake me for my sister.
2 to confuse
□ Su explicación me confundió todavía más. His explanation confused me even more.
■ **Confundí las fechas.** I got the dates mixed up.
■ **¡Vaya! ¡Me he confundido!** Oh! I've made a mistake!
■ **Me confundí de piso.** I got the wrong flat.

la **confusión** (PL las **confusiones**) NOUN
confusion

**confuso** (FEM **confusa**) ADJECTIVE
confused

**congelado** (FEM **congelada**) ADJECTIVE
frozen

el **congelador** NOUN
freezer

**congelar** VERB [25]
to freeze
■ **Me estoy congelando.** I'm freezing.

**congestionado** (FEM **congestionada**) ADJECTIVE
1 blocked
2 congested

el **congreso** NOUN
conference
■ **un congreso médico** a medical conference
■ **el Congreso de los Diputados** The Lower Chamber of the Spanish Parliament.

la **conjunción** (PL las **conjunciones**) NOUN
conjunction

el **conjunto** NOUN
1 collection
□ El libro es un conjunto de poemas de amor. The book is a collection of love poems.
2 group
□ un conjunto de música pop a pop group
■ **un conjunto de falda y blusa** a matching skirt and blouse
■ **Hay que estudiar esos países en conjunto.** You have to study these countries as a whole.

**conmemorar** VERB [25]
to commemorate

**conmigo** PRONOUN
with me

□ **¿Por qué no vienes conmigo?** Why don't you come with me?

■ **Rosa quiere hablar conmigo.** Rosa wants to talk to me.

■ **No estoy satisfecho conmigo mismo.** I'm not proud of myself.

**conmovedor** (FEM **conmovedora**) ADJECTIVE
moving

**conmover*** VERB [33]
to move

el **cono** NOUN
cone

■ **el Cono Sur** the Southern Cone

**conocer*** VERB [12]
1 to know
□ **Conozco a todos sus hermanos.** I know all his brothers. □ **Conozco un buen restaurante.** I know a good restaurant.
■ **Nos conocemos desde el colegio.** We know each other from school.
■ **Me encantaría conocer China.** I would love to visit China.
2 to meet
□ **La conocí en una fiesta.** I met her at a party. □ **¿Dónde os conocisteis?** Where did you first meet?

la **conocida** NOUN
acquaintance
□ **Es una conocida mía.** She's an acquaintance of mine.

**conocido** (FEM **conocida**) ADJECTIVE
well-known
□ **un actor muy conocido** a well-known actor

el **conocido** NOUN
acquaintance
□ **Son conocidos nuestros.** They are acquaintances of ours.

el **conocimiento** NOUN
consciousness
■ **perder el conocimiento** to lose consciousness
■ **Tengo algunos conocimientos de francés.** I have some knowledge of French.

**conozco** VERB ▷ see **conocer**

**conque** CONJUNCTION
so
□ **Hemos terminado, conque podéis iros.** We've finished, so you may leave now.

**conquistar** VERB [25]
1 to conquer
□ **los países conquistados por los romanos** the countries conquered by the Romans
2 to win...over
□ **La conquistó con su sonrisa.** He won her over with his smile.

**consciente** (FEM **consciente**) ADJECTIVE
conscious

□ **El enfermo no estaba consciente.** The patient wasn't conscious.
■ **Es plenamente consciente de sus limitaciones.** He's fully aware of his shortcomings.

la **consecuencia** NOUN
consequence
□ **Todo es una consecuencia de su falta de disciplina.** Everything is a consequence of his lack of discipline.
■ **Perdió el conocimiento a consecuencia del golpe.** He lost consciousness as a result of the blow.

**consecutivo** (FEM **consecutiva**) ADJECTIVE
consecutive
□ **tres semanas consecutivas** three consecutive weeks

**conseguir*** VERB [50]
1 to get
□ **Él me consiguió el trabajo.** He got me the job.
2 to achieve
□ **Consiguió las mejores calificaciones de la clase.** He achieved the best results in the class.
■ **Nuestro equipo consiguió el triunfo.** Our team won.
■ **Después de muchos intentos, al final lo consiguió.** After many attempts, he finally succeeded.
■ **Finalmente conseguí convencerla.** I finally managed to convince her.
■ **No conseguí que se lo comiera.** I couldn't get him to eat it.

el **consejo** NOUN
advice
□ **Fui a pedirle consejo.** I went to ask him for advice.
■ **¿Quieres que te dé un consejo?** Would you like me to give you some advice?

**consentir*** VERB [51]
1 to allow
□ **No consiento que me faltes al respeto.** I won't allow you to be disrespectful to me.
2 to spoil
□ **Su abuela lo consiente demasiado.** His grandmother spoils him too much.

el/la **conserje** NOUN
1 caretaker
2 janitor
3 porter

la **conserva** NOUN
■ **No comemos muchas conservas.** We don't eat much tinned food.
■ **atún en conserva** tinned tuna

**conservador** (FEM **conservadora**) ADJECTIVE
conservative

el **conservante** NOUN

77

preservative

**conservar** VERB [25]
1 to keep
□ Debe conservarse en la nevera. It should be kept in the fridge. □ conservar las amistades to keep friends
2 to preserve
□ El frío conserva mejor los alimentos. The cold preserves food better.
■ **Enrique se conserva joven.** Enrique looks good for his age.

el **conservatorio** NOUN
music school

**considerable** (FEM **considerable**) ADJECTIVE
considerable

**considerado** (FEM **considerada**) ADJECTIVE
considerate
□ Es muy considerado con su madre. He's very considerate towards his mother.
■ **Está muy bien considerada entre los profesores.** She's very highly regarded among the teachers.

**considerar** VERB [25]
to consider
□ Lo considero una pérdida de tiempo. I consider it a waste of time.

**consiento** VERB ▷ see **consentir**

la **consigna** NOUN
left-luggage office

**consigo** VERB
▷ see also **consigo** PRONOUN ▷ see **conseguir**

**consigo** PRONOUN
▷ see also **consigo** VERB
1 with him
2 with her
3 with you
■ **No está satisfecho consigo mismo.** He is not proud of himself.

**consiguiendo** VERB ▷ see **conseguir**

**consiguiente** (FEM **consiguiente**) ADJECTIVE
consequent
■ **por consiguiente** therefore

**consintiendo** VERB ▷ see **consentir**

**consistir** VERB [58]
■ **El menú consiste en tres platos.** The menu consists of three courses.
■ **¿En qué consiste el trabajo?** What does the job involve?
■ **En eso consiste el secreto.** That's the secret.

la **consola** NOUN
console
■ **consola de videojuegos** games console

**consolar*** VERB [11]
to console
□ No pudimos consolarla. We were unable to console her.
■ **Para consolarme me compré un**

helado. I bought an ice cream to cheer myself up.

la **consonante** NOUN
consonant

**constante** (FEM **constante**) ADJECTIVE
constant
□ el ruido constante de los coches the constant noise of the cars
■ **Tienes que ser más constante.** You should keep working at it.

**constantemente** ADVERB
constantly

**constar** VERB [25]
■ **La obra consta de siete relatos.** The work consists of seven stories.
■ **¡Que conste que yo pagué mi parte!** Don't forget that I paid my share!

**constipado** (FEM **constipada**) ADJECTIVE
■ **estar constipado** to have a cold
  🛈 **LANGUAGE TIP** Be careful! **constipado** does not mean **constipated**.

el **constipado** NOUN
cold
□ coger un constipado to catch a cold

la **constitución** (PL las **constituciones**) NOUN
constitution

la **construcción** (PL las **construcciones**) NOUN
construction
□ un edificio en construcción a building under construction
■ **Trabajan en la construcción.** They work in the building industry.

el **constructor**, la **constructora** NOUN
builder
□ Es constructor. He's a builder.

**construir*** VERB [10]
to build

**consuelo** VERB ▷ see **consolar**

el **consuelo** NOUN
consolation

el/la **cónsul** NOUN
consul

el **consulado** NOUN
consulate

la **consulta** NOUN
surgery (PL surgeries)
□ La doctora no tiene consulta los martes. The doctor doesn't hold a surgery on Tuesdays.
■ **horas de consulta** surgery hours
■ **un libro de consulta** a reference book

**consultar** VERB [25]
to consult
□ consultar a un médico to consult a doctor
■ **Tengo que consultarlo con mi familia.** I must discuss it with my family.

**consultorio** NOUN
1  surgery
2  problem page
3  phone-in
la **consumición** (PL las **consumiciones**)
    NOUN
    drink
    □ Con la entrada tienes una consumición.
    The admission price includes a drink.
**consumir** VERB [58]
1  to use
    □ Mi coche consume mucha gasolina.
    My car uses a lot of petrol.
2  to drink
    ■ No podemos estar en el bar sin
    consumir. We can't stay in the pub without
    buying a drink.
    ■ Sólo piensan en consumir. Spending
    money is all they think about.
el **consumo** NOUN
    consumption
    □ el consumo de bebidas alcohólicas
    alcohol consumption
    ■ una charla sobre el consumo de drogas
    a talk on drug use
    ■ la sociedad de consumo the consumer
    society
la **contabilidad** NOUN
    accountancy
    □ Estudia contabilidad. He's studying
    accountancy.
    ■ Mi madre lleva la contabilidad. My
    mother keeps the books.
el/la **contable** NOUN
    accountant
**contactar** VERB [25]
    ■ contactar con alguien to contact
    someone
el **contacto** NOUN
1  contact
    □ el contacto físico physical contact
2  touch
    □ Nos mantenemos en contacto por
    teléfono. We keep in touch by phone. □ Me
    puse en contacto con su familia. I got in
    touch with her family.
**contado**
    ■ al contado ADVERB
    ■ Lo pagué al contado. I paid cash for it.
el **contador** NOUN
    meter
    □ el contador de la luz the electricity meter
el **contador**, la **contadora** NOUN (Latin
    America)
    accountant
**contagiar** VERB [25]
    ■ No quiero contagiarte. I don't want to
    give it to you.

■ Tiene la gripe y no quiere que los niños
se contagien. He has the flu and doesn't
want the children to catch it.
**contagioso** (FEM **contagiosa**) ADJECTIVE
    infectious
la **contaminación** NOUN
    pollution
    □ la contaminación del aire  air pollution
**contaminar** VERB [25]
    to pollute
    □ El humo contamina la atmósfera. Smoke
    pollutes the atmosphere.
**contar*** VERB [11]
1  to count
    □ Sabe contar hasta diez. He can count to
    ten.
2  to tell
    □ Les conté un cuento a los niños. I told the
    children a story. □ Cuéntame lo que pasó.
    Tell me what happened.
    ■ Cuento contigo. I'm counting on you.
    ■ ¿Qué te cuentas? (colloquial) How's
    things?
**contendrá** VERB ▷ see contener
**contener*** VERB [53]
    to contain
    □ La caja contenía monedas antiguas. The
    box contained old coins.
    ■ contenerse to control oneself
el **contenido** NOUN
    contents pl
    □ el contenido de la maleta  the contents of
    the suitcase
**contentarse** VERB [25]
    ■ Se contenta con cualquier juguete.
    She is happy with any toy.
    ■ Tuve que contentarme con el segundo
    premio. I had to be satisfied with second
    prize.
**contento** (FEM **contenta**) ADJECTIVE
    happy
    □ Estaba contento porque era su
    cumpleaños. He was happy because it was
    his birthday.
    ■ estar contento con algo to be pleased
    with something
la **contestación** (PL las **contestaciones**)
    NOUN
    reply (PL replies)
    ■ No me des esas contestaciones.
    Don't answer back.
el **contestador** NOUN
    ■ el contestador automático the
    answering machine
**contestar** VERB [25]
    to answer
    □ Contesté a todas las preguntas.
    I answered all the questions.

■ **Les he llamado varias veces y no contestan.** I've phoned them several times and there's no answer.
■ **Me escribieron y tengo que contestarles.** They wrote to me and I have to reply to them.

**contigo** PRONOUN
with you
□ Quiero ir contigo. I want to go with you.
■ **Necesito hablar contigo.** I need to talk to you.

el **continente** NOUN
continent

**continuamente** ADVERB
constantly

**continuar\*** VERB [1]
to continue
□ Continuaremos la reunión por la tarde. We will continue the meeting in the afternoon. □ Si continúa así habrá que llevarlo al hospital. If he continues like this, he'll have to be taken to hospital.
■ **Continuó estudiando toda la noche.** He carried on studying right through the night.

**continuo** (FEM **continua**) ADJECTIVE
1 constant
2 continuous

**contra** PREPOSITION
against
□ Eran dos contra uno. They were two against one. □ El domingo jugamos contra el Málaga. We play against Malaga on Sunday.
■ **Me choqué contra una farola.** I bumped into a lamppost.
■ **Estoy en contra de la pena de muerte.** I'm against the death penalty.

el **contrabajo** NOUN
double bass (PL double basses)

el **contrabando** NOUN
smuggling
□ el contrabando de drogas drug smuggling
■ **Lo trajeron al país de contrabando.** They smuggled it into the country.

**contradecir\*** VERB [15]
to contradict

la **contradicción** (PL las **contradicciones**) NOUN
contradiction

**contradicho** VERB ▷ see **contradecir**
**contradigo** VERB ▷ see **contradecir**
**contradije** VERB ▷ see **contradecir**
**contradiré** VERB ▷ see **contradecir**
**contraer\*** VERB
1 to tense
2 to contract
■ **contraerse** to contract

la **contraria** NOUN

■ **llevar la contraria a alguien** 1 to contradict somebody 2 to do the opposite of what somebody wants

**contrario** (FEM **contraria**) ADJECTIVE
1 opposing
2 opposite
□ Los dos coches iban en dirección contraria. The two cars were travelling in opposite directions.
■ **Ella opina lo contrario.** She thinks the opposite.
■ **Al contrario, me gusta mucho.** On the contrary, I like it a lot.
■ **De lo contrario, tendré que castigarte.** Otherwise, I will have to punish you.

la **contraseña** NOUN
password

**contrastar** VERB [25]
to contrast
□ El rojo contrasta con el negro. Red contrasts with black.

el **contraste** NOUN
contrast

**contratar** VERB [25]
1 to hire
2 to sign up

el **contrato** NOUN
contract

la **contribución** (PL las **contribuciones**) NOUN
1 contribution
□ Le agradecemos su contribución. Thank you for your contribution.
2 tax (PL taxes)
□ la contribución municipal local tax

**contribuir\*** VERB [10]
to contribute
□ Todos contribuyeron al éxito de la fiesta. Everyone contributed to the success of the party. □ Cada uno contribuyó con diez euros para el regalo. Each person contributed ten euros towards the present.

el/la **contribuyente** NOUN
taxpayer

el/la **contrincante** NOUN
opponent

el **control** NOUN
1 control
□ Nunca pierde el control. He never loses control.
2 road-block
□ Hay un control a 3 kilómetros. There's a road-block 3 kilometres further on.
■ **el control de pasaportes** passport control

**controlar** VERB [25]
to control
■ **Tuve que controlarme para no pegarle.**

I had to control myself, otherwise I would have hit him.

■ **No te preocupes, todo está controlado.** Don't worry, everything is under control.

**convencer\*** VERB [12]

1 to convince

□ Su argumento me convenció. His argument convinced me. □ La convencí de que era necesario. I convinced her that it was necessary.

■ **No me convence nada la idea.** I'm not convinced by the idea.

2 to persuade

□ La convencimos para que nos acompañara. We persuaded her to go with us.

**convencional** (FEM **convencional**) ADJECTIVE
conventional

**conveniente** (FEM **conveniente**) ADJECTIVE
convenient

□ Cuando te sea más conveniente. Whenever is more convenient for you.

■ **Sería conveniente que se lo dijeras.** It would be advisable to tell him.

**convenir\*** VERB [56]

to suit

□ el método que más le convenga the method that suits you best

■ **Te conviene descansar un poco.** You ought to get some rest.

■ **Quizá convenga recordar que ...** It might be appropriate to recall that ...

**la conversación** (PL las **conversaciones**) NOUN
conversation

□ Necesito clases de conversación. I need conversation classes.

■ **las conversaciones de paz** peace talks

**convertir\*** VERB [51]

to turn

□ Convirtieron la casa en colegio. They turned the house into a school.

■ **convertirse** to convert □ Se convirtió al cristianismo. He converted to Christianity.

■ **convertirse en 1** to become □ Se convirtió en un hombre rico. He became a rich man. □ El convento se convirtió en hotel. The convent became a hotel. **2** to turn into □ Se convirtió en una pesadilla. It turned into a nightmare. □ La oruga se convierte en mariposa. The caterpillar turns into a butterfly.

**convocar\*** VERB [48]

to call

□ Nos convocaron a una reunión. They called us to a meeting.

**el coñac** (PL los **coñacs**) NOUN

brandy (PL brandies)

**la cooperación** NOUN
cooperation

**cooperar** VERB [25]

to cooperate

□ Cooperaron con la policía en el caso. They cooperated with the police on the case.

**la copa** NOUN

1 glass (PL glasses)

□ Sólo tomé una copa de champán. I only had one glass of champagne.

2 drink

■ **Fuimos a tomar unas copas.** We went for a few drinks.

3 top

■ **copas**

DID YOU KNOW...?

**copas** are goblets, one of the suits in the Spanish card deck.

**la copia** NOUN

copy (PL copies)

□ hacer una copia to make a copy

■ **una copia impresa** a printout

**copiar** VERB [25]

to copy

■ **to copy and paste** copiar y pegar

**el copo** NOUN

■ **un copo de nieve** a snowflake

■ **copos de avena** rolled oats

**el corazón** (PL los **corazones**) NOUN

heart

□ Está mal del corazón. He has heart trouble.

■ **Tiene muy buen corazón.** He is very kind-hearted.

**la corbata** NOUN
tie

**el corcho** NOUN
cork

■ **un tapón de corcho** a cork

**el cordel** NOUN
cord

**el cordero** NOUN
lamb

□ Comimos chuletas de cordero. We had lamb chops.

**el cordón** (PL los **cordones**) NOUN

1 shoelace

2 cable

**la corneta** NOUN
bugle

**el coro** NOUN

1 choir

2 chorus

**la corona** NOUN
crown

■ **una corona de flores** a garland

**el coronel** NOUN

colonel
**corporal** (FEM **corporal**) ADJECTIVE
1 body
2 corporal
3 personal
el **corral** NOUN
1 farmyard
2 playpen
la **correa** NOUN
1 belt
2 lead
3 strap
**correcto** (FEM **correcta**) ADJECTIVE
correct
□ Las respuestas eran correctas. The answers were correct.
el **corredor**, la **corredora** NOUN
runner
**corregir**\* VERB [18]
1 to correct
□ Corrígeme si me equivoco. Correct me if I get it wrong.
2 to mark
□ Tengo que corregir los exámenes. I have to mark the exams.
el **correo** NOUN
post
□ Me lo mandó por correo. He sent it to me by post.
■ **Correos** post office □ Fui a Correos a comprar sellos. I went to the post office to buy stamps.
■ **el servicio de correos** the postal service
■ **correo electrónico** email
**correr** VERB [8]
1 to run
□ Tuve que correr para coger el autobús. I had to run to catch the bus.
■ **El ladrón echó a correr.** The thief started to run.
2 to hurry
□ Corre que llegamos tarde. Hurry or we'll be late.
■ **No corras que te equivocarás.** Don't rush or you'll make a mistake.
3 to go fast
□ No corras tanto, que hay hielo en la carretera. Don't go so fast, the road's icy.
4 to move
□ Corre un poco la silla para allá. Move the chair that way a little. □ Córrete un poco hacia la izquierda. Move a bit to the left.
■ **¿Quieres que corra la cortina?** Do you want me to draw the curtains?
la **correspondencia** NOUN
■ **un curso por correspondencia** a correspondence course
**corresponder** VERB [8]

■ **Me pagó lo que me correspondía.** He paid me my share.
■ **Estas fotos corresponden a otro álbum.** These photos belong to another album.
■ **No me corresponde a mí hacerlo.** It's not for to me to do it.
**correspondiente** (FEM **correspondiente**) ADJECTIVE
relevant
□ toda la documentación correspondiente all the relevant documentation
■ **los datos correspondientes al año pasado** the figures for last year
el/la **corresponsal** NOUN
correspondent
la **corrida** NOUN
bullfight
**corriente** (FEM **corriente**) ADJECTIVE
common
□ Pérez es un apellido muy corriente. Pérez is a very common surname.
■ **Es un caso poco corriente.** It's an unusual case.
■ **Tengo que ponerle al corriente de lo que ha pasado.** I have to let him know what has happened.
la **corriente** NOUN
1 current
■ **Te va a dar corriente.** You'll get an electric shock.
2 draught
■ **Si está de mal humor es mejor seguirle la corriente.** If he's in a bad mood it's best just to humour him.
**corrijo** VERB ▷ see **corregir**
el **corro** NOUN
ring
□ Los niños hicieron un corro. The children formed a ring.
la **corrupción** NOUN
corruption
**cortado** (FEM **cortada**) ADJECTIVE
1 sour
2 chapped
3 closed
■ **Juan estaba muy cortado con mis padres.** Juan was very shy with my parents.
el **cortado** NOUN

**DID YOU KNOW...?**
A **cortado** is a small white coffee with only a little milk.

**cortar** VERB [25]
1 to cut
□ Corta la manzana por la mitad. Cut the apple in half. □ Me corté el dedo con un cristal. I cut my finger on a piece of broken glass.
■ **Te vas a cortar.** You're going to cut

yourself.
- **Estas tijeras no cortan.** These scissors are blunt.

2 to cut off
  □ **Han cortado el gas.** The gas has been cut off.

3 to close
- **Fui a cortarme el pelo.** I went to get my hair cut.
- **De repente se cortó la comunicación.** Suddenly we were cut off.

el **cortaúñas** (PL los **cortaúñas**) NOUN
nail clippers pl

el **corte** NOUN
cut
  □ **Tenía un corte en la frente.** He had a cut on his forehead.
- **un corte de pelo** a haircut
- **Me da corte pedírselo.** I'm embarrassed to ask him.

**cortés** (FEM **cortésa**, MASC PL **corteses**)
ADJECTIVE
polite

la **cortesía** NOUN
courtesy
- **por cortesía** as a courtesy

la **corteza** NOUN
1 crust
2 rind
3 bark

la **cortina** NOUN
curtain

**corto** (FEM **corta**) ADJECTIVE
short
  □ **Susana tiene el pelo corto.** Susana has short hair.
- **Las mangas me están cortas.** The sleeves are too short for me.
- **ser corto de vista** to be short-sighted
- **¡Carlos es más corto ...!** (colloquial) Carlos is so dim!

el **corto** ABBREVIATION (= cortometraje)
short film

el **cortocircuito** NOUN
short-circuit

la **cosa** NOUN
thing
  □ **¿Qué es esa cosa redonda?** What's that round thing? □ **Cogí mis cosas y me fui.** I picked up my things and left.
- **cualquier cosa** anything
- **¿Me puedes decir una cosa?** Can you tell me something?
- **¡Qué cosa más rara!** How strange!
- **Son cosas de la edad.** It's just old age.

la **cosecha** NOUN
harvest

**cosechar** VERB [25]
to harvest

**coser** VERB [8]
to sew
  □ **Me estaba cosiendo un botón.** I was sewing on a button.

el **cosmético** NOUN
cosmetic

las **cosquillas** NOUN
- **hacer cosquillas a alguien** to tickle someone
- **Tiene muchas cosquillas.** He's very ticklish.

la **costa** NOUN
coast
  □ **Pasamos el verano en la costa.** We spend the summer on the coast.
- **Vive a costa de los demás.** He lives at the expense of others.

el **costado** NOUN
side
- **Estaba tumbado de costado.** He was lying on his side.

**costar*** VERB [11]
to cost
  □ **Cuesta mucho dinero.** It costs a lot of money. □ **¿Cuánto cuesta?** How much does it cost? □ **Me costó diez euros.** It cost me ten euros.
- **Las matemáticas le cuestan mucho.** He finds maths very difficult.
- **Me cuesta hablarle.** I find it hard to talk to him.

**Costa Rica** FEM NOUN
Costa Rica

el/la **costarricense** (ADJECTIVE, NOUN
Costa Rican

el **costarriqueño** (FEM la **costarriqueña**)
ADJECTIVE, NOUN
Costa Rican

el **coste** NOUN
cost
  □ **el coste de la vida** the cost of living

la **costilla** NOUN
rib

el **costo** NOUN
cost

**costoso** (FEM **costosa**) ADJECTIVE
expensive

la **costra** NOUN
1 scab
2 crust

la **costumbre** NOUN
1 habit
  □ **Tiene la mala costumbre de mentir.** He has the bad habit of lying.
2 custom
  □ **una costumbre británica** a British custom
- **Se le olvidó, como de costumbre.** He

forgot, as usual.
■ **Nos sentamos en el sitio de costumbre.**
We sat in our usual place.

la **costura** NOUN
1 seam
□ Se te ha descosido la costura de la falda.
Your skirt has come apart at the seam.
2 sewing
□ No me gusta la costura. I don't like
sewing.

**cotidiano** (FEM **cotidiana**) ADJECTIVE
everyday
□ la vida cotidiana everyday life

el/la **cotilla** NOUN
gossip

**cotillear** VERB [25]
to gossip

el **cotilleo** NOUN
gossip

**COU** ABBREVIATION (= *Curso de Orientación
Universitaria*)

> **DID YOU KNOW…?**
> This is the former term for the final
> year at school before university.

el **cráneo** NOUN
skull

la **creación** (PL las **creaciones**) NOUN
creation

**crear** VERB [25]
to create
■ **No quiero crearme problemas.** I don't
want to create problems for myself.
■ **crearse enemigos** to make enemies

**creativo** (FEM **creativa**) ADJECTIVE
creative

**crecer*** VERB [12]
1 to grow
□ Me crece mucho el pelo. My hair grows
very fast. □ ¡Cómo has crecido! Haven't you
grown!
2 to grow up
□ Crecí en Sevilla. I grew up in Seville.

el **crecimiento** NOUN
growth

el **crédito** NOUN
1 loan
□ Pedí un crédito al banco. I asked the bank
for a loan.
2 credit
□ comprar algo a crédito to buy something
on credit

la **creencia** NOUN
belief

**creer*** VERB [30]
1 to believe
□ ¿Crees en los fantasmas? Do you believe
in ghosts? □ Nadie me cree. Nobody
believes me.

■ **Eso no se lo cree nadie.** No one will
believe that.
2 to think
□ No creo que pueda ir. I don't think I'll be
able to go.
■ **Se cree muy lista.** She thinks she's pretty
clever.
■ **Creo que sí.** I think so.
■ **Creo que no.** I don't think so.

**creído** (FEM **creída**) ADJECTIVE
■ **Es muy creído.** He's so full of himself.

la **crema** NOUN
cream
□ Me pongo crema en las manos. I put
cream on my hands.
■ **la crema de afeitar** shaving cream
■ **crema de champiñones** cream of
mushroom soup
■ **una blusa de color crema** a cream-
coloured blouse

la **cremallera** NOUN
zip
□ Súbete la cremallera. Pull up your zip.

el **crematorio** NOUN
crematorium (PL crematoria)

**creyendo** VERB ▷ see **creer**

el/la **creyente** NOUN
believer

**crezco** VERB ▷ see **crecer**

la **cría** NOUN
1 baby
■ **una cría de cebra** a baby zebra
■ **La leona tuvo dos crías.** The lioness had
two cubs.
■ **La hembra es muy protectora de sus
crías.** The female is very protective of her
young.
2 girl

la **criada** NOUN
maid

el **criado** NOUN
servant

**criar*** VERB [21]
1 to raise
2 to breed
3 to bring up
□ Me criaron mis abuelos. My grandparents
brought me up.
■ **Me crié en Sevilla.** I grew up in Seville.

el **crimen** (PL los **crímenes**) NOUN
1 murder
□ cometer un crimen to commit murder
2 crime
□ los crímenes de guerra war crimes

el/la **criminal** NOUN
criminal

el **crío** NOUN
1 baby

■ **¡No seas crío!** Don't be such a baby!

2 boy

■ **los críos** the children

la **crisis** (PL las **crisis**) NOUN
crisis (PL crises)

□ una crisis política  a political crisis

■ **una crisis nerviosa** a nervous breakdown

el **cristal** NOUN

1 glass (PL glasses)

□ una botella de cristal  a glass bottle

■ **Me corté con un cristal.** I cut myself on a piece of broken glass.

■ **En el suelo había cristales rotos.** There was some broken glass on the floor.

2 window pane

□ Los niños rompieron el cristal.  The children broke the window pane.

■ **limpiar los cristales** to clean the windows

3 crystal

□ una estatuilla de cristal  a crystal statuette

el **cristiano** (FEM la **cristiana**) ADJECTIVE, NOUN
Christian

**Cristo** MASC NOUN
Christ

la **crítica** NOUN

1 criticism

■ **No hagas caso de sus críticas.** Pay no attention to his criticism.

2 review

□ La película ha tenido muy buenas críticas. The film got very good reviews.

3 critic

□ Es crítica de cine.  She's a film critic.

**criticar\*** VERB [48]
to criticize

□ Siempre me está criticando.  He's always criticizing me.

**crítico** (FEM **crítica**) ADJECTIVE
critical

□ Llegó en un momento crítico.  He arrived at a critical moment.

el **crítico** NOUN
critic

□ Es crítico de cine.  He's a film critic.

el **croissant** (PL los **croissants**) NOUN
croissant

el **cromo** NOUN
picture card

**crónico** (FEM **crónica**) ADJECTIVE
chronic

**cronometrar** VERB [25]
to time

el **cronómetro** NOUN
stopwatch (PL stopwatches)

la **croqueta** NOUN
croquette

□ croquetas de pollo  chicken croquettes

el **cruce** NOUN
crossroads

□ En el cruce hay un semáforo.  There are traffic lights at the crossroads.

■ **un cruce de peatones** a pedestrian crossing

**crucial** (FEM **crucial**) ADJECTIVE
crucial

el **crucifijo** NOUN
crucifix (PL crucifixes)

el **crucigrama** NOUN
crossword

**crudo** (FEM **cruda**) ADJECTIVE

1 raw

□ las zanahorias crudas  raw carrots

2 underdone

□ El filete estaba crudo.  The fillet was underdone.

**cruel** (FEM **cruel**) ADJECTIVE
cruel

la **crueldad** NOUN
cruelty

**crujiente** (FEM **crujiente**) ADJECTIVE

1 crunchy

2 crusty

**crujir** VERB [58]

1 to rustle

2 to creak

3 to crunch

la **cruz** (PL las **cruces**) NOUN
cross (PL crosses)

■ **la Cruz Roja** the Red Cross

**cruzado** (FEM **cruzada**) ADJECTIVE

■ **Había un tronco cruzado en la carretera.** There was a tree trunk lying across the road.

**cruzar\*** VERB [13]

1 to cross

2 to fold

■ **Nos cruzamos en la calle.** We passed each other in the street.

el **cuaderno** NOUN
notebook

■ **un cuaderno de ejercicios** an exercise book

la **cuadra** NOUN

1 stable

2 block (Latin America)

□ Está a dos cuadras de aquí.  It's two blocks from here.

el **cuadrado** ADJECTIVE, NOUN
square

■ **dos metros cuadrados** two square metres

**cuadrar** VERB [25]
to tally

□ Las cuentas no cuadran.  The accounts

don't tally.
■ **Eso no cuadra con lo que ella nos contó.** That doesn't fit in with what she told us.
**cuadriculado** (FEM **cuadriculada**) ADJECTIVE
■ **papel cuadriculado** squared paper
el **cuadro** NOUN
1 painting
□ un cuadro de Picasso a painting by Picasso □ ¿Quién pintó ese cuadro? Who did that painting?
2 picture
□ Hay varios cuadros en la pared. There are several pictures on the wall.
■ **un mantel a cuadros** a checked tablecloth
**cuajar** VERB [25]
1 to set
2 to lie
■ **cuajarse** to curdle
**cual** PRONOUN (PL **cuales**)
1 who
□ el primo del cual te estuve hablando the cousin who I was speaking to you about
2 which
□ la ventana desde la cual nos observaban the window from which they were watching us
■ **lo cual** which □ Se ofendió, lo cual es comprensible. He took offence, which is understandable.
■ **con lo cual** with the result that
■ **sea cual sea la razón** whatever the reason may be
**cuál** PRONOUN (PL **cuáles**)
1 what
□ ¿Cuál es la solución? What is the solution? □ No sé cuál es la solución. I don't know what the solution is.
2 which one
□ ¿Cuál te gusta más? Which one do you like best? □ ¿Cuáles quieres? Which ones do you want?
la **cualidad** NOUN
quality (PL qualities)
**cualquier** ADJECTIVE ▷ see **cualquiera**
**cualquiera** (FEM **cualquiera**) ADJECTIVE
▷ see also **cualquiera** PRONOUN
any
□ en cualquier ciudad española in any Spanish town □ Puedes usar un bolígrafo cualquiera. You can use any pen.
■ **No es un empleo cualquiera.** It's not just any job.
■ **cualquier cosa** anything
■ **cualquier persona** anyone
■ **en cualquier sitio** anywhere
**cualquiera** PRONOUN
▷ see also **cualquiera** ADJECTIVE

1 anyone
□ Cualquiera puede hacer eso. Anyone can do that.
■ **cualquiera que le conozca** anyone who knows him
2 any one
□ Me da igual, cualquiera. It doesn't matter, any one.
■ **en cualquiera de las habitaciones** in any one of the rooms
■ **cualquiera que elijas** whichever one you choose
3 either
□ ¿Cuál de los dos prefieres? — Cualquiera. Which of the two do you prefer? — Either.
**cuando** CONJUNCTION
when
□ cuando vienen a vernos when they come to see us □ Lo haré cuando tenga tiempo. I'll do it when I have time.
■ **Puedes venir cuando quieras.** You can come whenever you like.
**cuándo** ADVERB
when
□ ¿Cuándo te va mejor? When suits you? □ No sabe cuándo ocurrió. He doesn't know when it happened.
■ **¿Desde cuándo trabajas aquí?** Since when have you worked here?
**cuanto** (FEM **cuanta**) ADJECTIVE, PRONOUN
■ **Termínalo cuanto antes.** Finish it as soon as possible.
■ **Cuanto más lo pienso menos lo entiendo.** The more I think about it, the less I understand it.
■ **Cuantas menos personas haya mejor.** The fewer people the better.
■ **En cuanto oí su voz me eché a llorar.** As soon as I heard his voice I began to cry.
■ **Había sólo unos cuantos invitados.** There were only a few guests.
■ **en cuanto a** as for
**cuánto** (FEM **cuánta**) ADJECTIVE, PRONOUN
1 how much
□ ¿Cuánto dinero? How much money? □ ¿Cuánto le debo? How much do I owe you? □ Me dijo cuánto costaba. He told me how much it was.
2 how many
□ ¿Cuántas sillas? How many chairs? □ No sé cuántos necesito. I don't know how many I need.
■ **¿A cuántos estamos?** What's the date?
■ **¡Cuánta gente!** What a lot of people!
■ **¿Cuánto hay de aquí a Bilbao?** How far is it from here to Bilbao?
■ **¿Cuánto tiempo llevas estudiando inglés?** How long have you been studying

English?

**cuarenta** (FEM **cuarenta**) ADJECTIVE, PRONOUN
forty
▫ Tiene cuarenta años. He's forty.
■ **el cuarenta aniversario** the fortieth
anniversary

el **cuartel** NOUN
barracks (PL barracks)
■ **el cuartel general** the headquarters

**cuarto** (FEM **cuarta**) ADJECTIVE, PRONOUN
fourth
▫ Vivo en el cuarto piso. I live on the fourth
floor.

el **cuarto** NOUN
**1** room
▫ Los niños jugaban en su cuarto. The
children were playing in their room.
■ **el cuarto de estar** the living room
■ **el cuarto de baño** the bathroom
**2** quarter
▫ un cuarto de hora a quarter of an hour
■ **Son las once y cuarto.** It's a quarter past
eleven.
■ **A las diez menos cuarto.** At a quarter to
ten.
■ **Es un cuarto para las diez.** (*Latin
America*) It's a quarter to ten.

el **cuate** NOUN (*Mexico*)
**1** twin brother
**2** guy

**cuatro** (FEM **cuatro**) ADJECTIVE, PRONOUN
four
■ **Son las cuatro.** It's four o'clock.
■ **el cuatro de julio** the fourth of July

**cuatrocientos** (FEM **cuatrocientas**)
ADJECTIVE, PRONOUN
four hundred

**Cuba** FEM NOUN
Cuba

el **cubano** (FEM la **cubana**) ADJECTIVE, NOUN
Cuban

la **cubertería** NOUN
cutlery

**cúbico** (FEM **cúbica**) ADJECTIVE
cubic
▫ tres metros cúbicos three cubic metres

la **cubierta** NOUN
**1** cover
**2** tyre
**3** deck

**cubierto** VERB ▷ *see* **cubrir**

**cubierto** (FEM **cubierta**) ADJECTIVE
covered
▫ Estaba todo cubierto de nieve. Everything
was covered in snow.
■ **una piscina cubierta** an indoor
swimming pool

los **cubiertos** NOUN

cutlery *sing*

el **cubito de hielo** NOUN
ice-cube

el **cubo** NOUN
bucket
■ **el cubo de la basura** the dustbin
■ **tres elevado al cubo** three cubed

**cubrir*** VERB
to cover
▫ Son capaces de cubrir grandes distancias.
They can cover great distances.
■ **Las mujeres se cubren la cara con un
velo.** The women cover their face with a
veil.
■ **El agua casi me cubría.** I was almost out
of my depth.

la **cucaracha** NOUN
cockroach

la **cuchara** NOUN
spoon

la **cucharada** NOUN
spoonful
▫ una cucharada de jarabe a spoonful of
syrup

la **cucharilla** NOUN
teaspoon

el **cucharón** (PL los **cucharones**) NOUN
ladle

**cuchichear** VERB [25]
to whisper

la **cuchilla** NOUN
blade
■ **una cuchilla de afeitar** a razor blade

el **cuchillo** NOUN
knife (PL knives)

**cuclillas**
■ **en cuclillas** ADVERB squatting
■ **ponerse en cuclillas** to squat down

el **cucurucho** NOUN
cone

**cuelgo** VERB ▷ *see* **colgar**

el **cuello** NOUN
**1** neck
**2** collar

la **cuenta** NOUN
**1** bill
▫ El camarero nos trajo la cuenta. The
waiter brought us the bill.
**2** account
■ **una cuenta corriente** a current account
■ **Ahora trabaja por su cuenta.** He's self-
employed now.
■ **una cuenta de correo** an email account
■ **darse cuenta 1** to realize ▫ Perdona, no
me daba cuenta de que eras vegetariano.
Sorry, I didn't realize you were a vegetarian.
**2** to notice ▫ ¿Te has dado cuenta de que
han cortado el árbol? Did you notice they've

C

cut down that tree?

■ **tener algo en cuenta** to bear something in mind □ También hay que tener en cuenta su edad. You must also bear in mind her age.

**cuento** VERB ▷ see **contar**

el **cuento** NOUN
story (PL stories)
□ La abuela nos contaba cuentos. Grandma used to tell us stories.
■ **un cuento de hadas** a fairy-tale

la **cuerda** NOUN
1 rope
□ Le ataron las manos con una cuerda. They tied his hands together with a rope.
2 string
□ Necesito una cuerda para atar este paquete. I need some string to tie up this parcel. □ La guitarra tiene ocho cuerdas. The guitar has eight strings.
■ **la cuerda floja** the tightrope
■ **dar cuerda a un reloj** to wind up a watch

el **cuerno** NOUN
horn

el **cuero** NOUN
leather
□ una chaqueta de cuero a leather jacket

el **cuerpo** NOUN
body (PL bodies)
□ el cuerpo humano the human body
■ **el cuerpo de bomberos** the fire-brigade

el **cuervo** NOUN
raven

**cuesta** VERB ▷ see **costar**

la **cuesta** NOUN
slope
□ una cuesta muy empinada a very steep slope
■ **ir cuesta abajo** to go downhill
■ **ir cuesta arriba** to go uphill
■ **Llevaba la caja a cuestas.** He was carrying the box on his back.

la **cuestión** (PL las **cuestiones**) NOUN
matter
□ Eso es otra cuestión. That's another matter.
■ **Llegaron en cuestión de minutos.** They arrived in a matter of minutes.

la **cueva** NOUN
cave

**cuezo** VERB ▷ see **cocer**

el **cuidado** NOUN
care
□ Pone mucho cuidado en su trabajo. He takes great care over his work.
■ **Conducía con cuidado.** He was driving carefully.

■ **Debes tener mucho cuidado al cruzar la calle.** You must be very careful crossing the street.
■ **¡Cuidado!** Careful!
■ **Carlos está al cuidado de los niños.** Carlos looks after the children.
■ **cuidados intensivos** intensive care sing

**cuidadoso** (FEM **cuidadosa**) ADJECTIVE
careful

**cuidar** VERB [25]
to look after
□ Ella cuida de los niños. She looks after the children.
■ **cuidarse** to look after oneself □ Tienes que cuidarte. Make sure you look after yourself.
■ **¡Cuídate!** Take care!

la **culebra** NOUN
snake

el **culebrón** NOUN (PL los **culebrones**)
soap(-opera) (colloquial)

el **culo** NOUN
bum (colloquial)

la **culpa** NOUN
fault
□ La culpa es mía. It's my fault.
■ **Tú tienes la culpa de todo.** It's all your fault.
■ **Siempre me echan la culpa a mí.** They're always blaming me.
■ **por culpa del mal tiempo** because of the bad weather

**culpable** (FEM **culpable**) ADJECTIVE
guilty
□ Yo no soy culpable. I'm not guilty.
□ Se siente culpable de lo que ha pasado. He feels guilty about what has happened.

el/la **culpable** NOUN
culprit
■ **Ella es la culpable de todo.** She is to blame for everything.

**cultivar** VERB [25]
1 to grow
2 to farm

**culto** (FEM **culta**) ADJECTIVE
1 cultured
2 formal

la **cultura** NOUN
culture

el **culturismo** NOUN
body-building

la **cumbre** NOUN
summit

el **cumpleaños** (PL los **cumpleaños**) NOUN
birthday (PL birthdays)
□ Mañana es mi cumpleaños. It's my birthday tomorrow.
■ **¡Feliz cumpleaños!** Happy birthday!

**cumplir** VERB [58]
1 to carry out
2 to keep
3 to observe
4 to serve

■ **Sólo he cumplido con mi deber.** I have only done my duty.
■ **Mañana cumplo dieciséis años.** I'll be sixteen tomorrow.
■ **El viernes se cumple el plazo para entregar las solicitudes.** Friday is the deadline for handing in applications.

la **cuna** NOUN
cradle

la **cuneta** NOUN
ditch (PL ditches)

la **cuñada** NOUN
sister-in-law (PL sisters-in-law)

el **cuñado** NOUN
brother-in-law (PL brothers-in-law)

la **cuota** NOUN
fee
□ La cuota de socio son veinte euros al mes. The membership fee is 20 euros per year.

**cupo** VERB ▷ *see* caber

el **cupón** (PL los cupones) NOUN
1 voucher
2 ticket

la **cura** NOUN
1 cure
□ No tiene cura. There is no cure for it.
2 therapy (PL therapies)
□ una cura de reposo rest therapy

el **cura** NOUN
priest

**curar** VERB [25]
1 to cure
2 to treat
■ **Espero que te cures pronto.** I hope that you get better soon.
■ **Ya se le ha curado la herida.** His wound has already healed.

la **curiosidad** NOUN
curiosity

■ **Lo pregunté por curiosidad.** I asked out of curiosity.
■ **Tengo curiosidad por saber cuánto gana.** I'm curious to know how much he earns.

**curioso** (FEM **curiosa**) ADJECTIVE
1 curious
□ Tiene una forma muy curiosa. It's a very curious shape.
■ **¡Qué curioso!** How odd!
2 nosy
□ No seas curioso. Don't be nosy.

la **curita** NOUN *(Latin America)*
sticking plaster

**cursi** (FEM **cursi**) ADJECTIVE
1 affected
2 twee

el **cursillo** NOUN
course
□ un cursillo de cocina a cookery course
■ **hacer un cursillo de natación** to have swimming lessons

el **curso** NOUN
1 year
□ un chico de mi curso a boy in my year
□ Hago segundo curso. I'm in the second year.
■ **el curso académico** the academic year
2 course
□ Hice un curso de alemán. I did a German course.

la **curva** NOUN
1 bend
□ Hay algunas curvas muy cerradas. There are some very sharp bends.
2 curve
□ dibujar una curva to draw a curve

**cuyo** (FEM **cuya**) ADJECTIVE
whose
□ El marido, cuyo nombre era Ricardo, estaba jubilado. The husband, whose name was Ricardo, was retired. □ La señora en cuya casa me hospedé. The lady whose house I stayed in.

# Dd

el **dado** NOUN
dice (PL dice)
■ **jugar a los dados** to play dice

la **dama** NOUN
lady (PL ladies)
□ Damas y caballeros ... Ladies and
gentlemen ...
■ **las damas** draughts □ jugar a las damas
to play draughts

el **damasco** NOUN (Latin America)
apricot

**danés** (FEM **danesa**, MASC PL **daneses**)
ADJECTIVE
Danish

el **danés**, la **danesa** (MASC PL los **daneses**)
NOUN
Dane

el **danés** NOUN
Danish

**dañar** VERB [25]
1 to damage
2 to hurt
■ **Se dañó la pierna.** She hurt her leg.

el **daño** NOUN
damage
□ El daño producido no es muy grave.
The damage isn't very serious.
■ **ocasionar daños** to cause damage
□ La sequía ha ocasionado graves daños.
The drought has caused a lot of damage.
■ **hacer daño a alguien** to hurt somebody
■ **hacerse daño** to hurt oneself

**dar\*** VERB [14]
1 to give
□ Le dio un bocadillo a su hijo. He gave his
son a sandwich. □ Se lo di a Teresa. I gave it
to Teresa.
■ **Me dio mucha alegría verla.** I was very
pleased to see her.
■ **Déme 2 kilos.** 2 kilos please.
2 to strike
□ El reloj dio las 6. The clock struck 6.
■ **dar a** to look out onto □ Mi ventana da al
jardín. My window looks out onto the
garden.
■ **dar con** to find □ Dimos con él dos horas

más tarde. We found him two hours later.
■ **Al final di con la solución.** I finally came
up with the answer.
■ **El sol me da en la cara.** The sun's shining
in my face.
■ **¿Qué más te da?** What does it matter to
you?
■ **Se han dado muchos casos.** There have
been a lot of cases.
■ **Se me dan bien las ciencias.** I'm good at
science.
■ **darse un baño** to have a bath
■ **darse por vencido** to give up

el **dátil** NOUN
date

el **dato** NOUN
■ **Ése es un dato importante.** That's an
important piece of information.
■ **Necesito más datos para poder juzgar.**
I need more information to be able to judge.
■ **reunir datos para un proyecto de
investigación** to gather data for a research
project
■ **los datos personales** personal details

**de** (de + el = del) PREPOSITION
1 of
□ un paquete de caramelos a packet of
sweets
■ **una copa de vino** 1 a glass of wine 2 a
wine glass
■ **la casa de Isabel** Isabel's house
■ **las clases de inglés** English classes
■ **un anillo de oro** a gold ring
■ **una máquina de coser** a sewing
machine
■ **es de ellos** it's theirs
■ **a las 8 de la mañana** at 8 o'clock in the
morning
2 from
□ Soy de Gijón. I'm from Gijón.
■ **salir del cine** to leave the cinema
3 than
□ Es más difícil de lo que creía. It's more
difficult than I thought it would be.
■ **más de 500 personas** over 500 people
■ **De haberlo sabido ...** If I'd known ...

**dé** VERB ▷ see **dar**

**debajo** ADVERB
underneath
□ Levanta la maceta, la llave está debajo.
Lift up the flowerpot, the key's underneath.
■ **debajo de** under □ debajo de la mesa
under the table

el **debate** NOUN
debate

**debatir** VERB [58]
to debate

el **deber** NOUN
duty (PL duties)
□ Sólo cumplí con mi deber. I simply did my
duty.
■ **los deberes** homework *sing*

**deber** VERB [8]
**1** must
□ Debo intentar verla. I must try to see her.
□ No debes preocuparte. You mustn't
worry.
■ **Debería dejar de fumar.** I should stop
smoking.
■ **No deberías haberla dejado sola.**
You shouldn't have left her alone.
■ **como debe ser** as it should be
■ **deber de** must □ Debe de ser
canadiense. He must be Canadian.
■ **No debe de tener mucho dinero.**
He can't have much money.
**2** to owe
□ ¿Cuánto le debo? How much do I owe
you?
■ **deberse a** to be due to □ El retraso se
debió a una huelga. The delay was due to a
strike.

**debido** (FEM **debida**) ADJECTIVE
■ **debido a** owing to □ Debido al mal
tiempo, el vuelo se suspendió. Owing to the
bad weather, the flight was cancelled.
■ **Habla como es debido.** Speak properly.

**débil** (FEM **débil**) ADJECTIVE
weak

la **debilidad** NOUN
weakness (PL weaknesses)
■ **tener debilidad por algo** to have a
weakness for something
■ **tener debilidad por alguien** to have a
soft spot for somebody

**debilitar** VERB [25]
to weaken

la **década** NOUN
decade

la **decena** NOUN
ten
□ decenas de miles de tens of thousands of
■ **Habrá una decena de libros.** There must
be about ten books.

**decente** (FEM **decente**) ADJECTIVE
decent
□ Exigen un sueldo decente. They are
demanding a decent wage.

la **decepción** (PL las **decepciones**) NOUN
disappointment

> **LANGUAGE TIP** Be careful! **decepción**
> does not mean **deception**.

**decepcionar** VERB [25]
to disappoint
□ Me has decepcionado de nuevo. You've
disappointed me again.
■ **La película me decepcionó.** The film
was disappointing.

**decidido** (FEM **decidida**) ADJECTIVE
determined
□ Estoy decidido a hacerlo. I'm determined
to do it. □ Julia es una mujer muy decidida.
Julia is a very determined woman.

**decidir** VERB [58]
to decide
□ Tú decides. You decide.
■ **decidirse a hacer algo** to decide to do
something
■ **decidirse por algo** to decide on
something
■ **¡Decídete!** Make up your mind!

el **decimal** ADJECTIVE, NOUN
decimal

**décimo** (FEM **décima**) ADJECTIVE, PRONOUN
tenth
■ **Vivo en el décimo.** I live on the tenth
floor.

el **décimo** NOUN
■ **un décimo de lotería** a tenth part of a
lottery ticket

> **DID YOU KNOW...?**
> In Spain's National Lottery, whole
> tickets are very expensive so smaller
> shares such as **décimos** are also sold.

**decir\*** VERB [15]
**1** to say
□ ¿Qué dijo? What did he say? □ ¿Cómo se
dice 'casa' en inglés? How do you say 'casa'
in English?
■ **es decir** that's to say
■ **es un decir** it's a manner of speaking
■ **¡Diga?** Hello?
**2** to tell
□ Me dijo que no vendría. He told me that
he wouldn't come.
■ **decirle a alguien que haga algo** to tell
somebody to do something □ Me dijo que
esperara fuera. He told me to wait outside.
■ **¡No me digas!** Really?
■ **querer decir** to mean □ No sé lo que
quiere decir. I don't know what it means.

la **decisión** (PL las **decisiones**) NOUN

decision

□ tomar una decisión to take a decision

**decisivo** (FEM **decisiva**) ADJECTIVE
decisive

la **declaración** (PL las **declaraciones**) NOUN
1 statement

□ El ministro no quiso hacer ninguna declaración. The minister didn't want to make a statement.

2 evidence

□ Prestó declaración ante el juez. He gave evidence before the judge.

■ **una declaración de amor** a declaration of love

■ **la declaración de la renta** the income tax return

**declarar** VERB [25]
1 to declare

□ ¿Algo que declarar? Anything to declare?
□ El presidente declaró que apoyaría el proyecto. The president declared his support for the project.

2 to give evidence

□ declarar en un juicio to give evidence at a trial

■ **declarar culpable a alguien** to find somebody guilty

■ **declararse 1** to declare oneself □ Se declaró partidario de hacerlo. He declared himself in favour of doing it. **2** to break out □ Se declaró un incendio en el bosque. A fire broke out in the forest.

■ **declararse a alguien** to propose to somebody

el **decorador**, la **decoradora** NOUN
interior decorator

**decorar** VERB [25]
to decorate

el **decreto** NOUN
decree

el **dedal** NOUN
thimble

**dedicar*** VERB [48]
1 to devote

□ Dedicó su vida a los demás. He devoted his life to others.

2 to dedicate

□ Dedicó el poema a su padre. He dedicated the poem to his father.

■ **¿A qué se dedica?** What does he do for a living?

■ **Ayer me dediqué a arreglar los armarios.** I spent yesterday tidying the cupboards.

la **dedicatoria** NOUN
dedication

el **dedo** NOUN
1 finger

□ Lleva un anillo en el dedo meñique. She wears a ring on her little finger.

■ **hacer dedo** to hitch a lift

■ **no mover un dedo** not to lift a finger

2 toe

■ **el dedo gordo 1** the thumb **2** the big toe

**deducir*** VERB [9]
to deduce

□ Deduje que había mentido. I deduced that he'd lied.

el **defecto** NOUN
1 defect

□ El jarrón tiene un pequeño defecto. The vase has a small defect.

2 fault

□ Le encuentra defectos a todo. He finds fault with everything.

**defender*** VERB [20]
to defend

□ Defendió a su amigo de las críticas. He defended his friend against criticisms.

■ **defenderse** to defend oneself

□ Tenemos que defendernos del enemigo. We have got to defend ourselves against the enemy.

■ **Me defiendo en inglés.** I can get by in English.

la **defensa** NOUN
defence

■ **salir en defensa de alguien** to come to somebody's defence

■ **en defensa propia** in self-defence

el **defensor**, la **defensora** NOUN
defender

**deficiente** (FEM **deficiente**) ADJECTIVE
poor

□ Su trabajo es muy deficiente. His work is very poor.

la **definición** (PL las **definiciones**) NOUN
definition

**definir** VERB [58]
to define

**definitivo** (FEM **definitiva**) ADJECTIVE
definitive

□ Esta solución no es definitiva. This is not a definitive solution.

■ **en definitiva** in short

**deformar** VERB
1 to deform

■ **No cuelgues el jersey así que lo deformarás.** Don't hang the jersey up like that or you'll pull it out of shape.

2 to distort

■ **deformarse** to become deformed

■ **Si lo lavas en la lavadora, se deformará.** If you wash it in the washing machine, it'll lose its shape.

**defraudar** VERB [25]

**1** to disappoint
□ Su comportamiento la defraudó. His behaviour disappointed her.
**2** to defraud
□ Defraudar dinero a Hacienda es delito. It's an offence to defraud the Treasury of money.

**dejar** VERB [25]
**1** to leave
□ He dejado las llaves en la mesa. I've left the keys on the table. □ Su novio la ha dejado. Her fiancé has left her. □ Déjame tranquilo. Leave me alone. □ Dejó todo su dinero a sus hijos. He left all his money to his children.
■ ¡Déjalo ya! Don't worry about it!
■ Deja mucho que desear. It leaves a lot to be desired.
**2** to let
□ Mis padres no me dejan salir de noche. My parents won't let me go out at night.
■ dejar caer to drop □ Dejó caer la bandeja. She dropped the tray.
**3** to lend
□ Le dejé mi libro de matemáticas. I lent him my maths book.
**4** to give up
□ Dejó el esquí después del accidente. He gave up skiing after the accident.
■ dejar de to stop □ dejar de fumar to stop smoking
■ dejarse to leave □ Se dejó el bolso en un taxi. She left her bag in a taxi.

**del** PREPOSITION (= *de* + *el*) ▷ see de
**el delantal** NOUN
apron

**delante** ADVERB
in front
□ Siéntate delante. You sit in front.
■ de delante front □ la rueda de delante the front wheel
■ la parte de delante the front
■ delante de **1** in front of □ No digas nada delante de los niños. Don't say anything in front of the children. **2** opposite □ Mi casa está delante de la escuela. My house is opposite the school.
■ pasar por delante de to go past □ Ayer pasé por delante de tu casa. I went past your house yesterday.
■ hacia delante forward □ Se inclinó hacia delante. He leaned forward.

**delantero** (FEM **delantera**) ADJECTIVE
front
□ los asientos delanteros the front seats
■ la parte delantera del coche the front of the car

**delatar** VERB

**1** to inform on
□ el hombre que los delató the man who informed on them
■ Los delató a la policía. He tipped the police off about them.
**2** to give away
□ Tu sonrisa te delata. Your smile gives you away.

**la delegación** (PL las **delegaciones**) NOUN
*(Mexico)*
police station

**el delegado**, la **delegada** NOUN
delegate
■ el delegado de clase the class representative

**deletrear** VERB [25]
to spell out

**el delfín** (PL los **delfines**) NOUN
dolphin

**delgado** (FEM **delgada**) ADJECTIVE
**1** slim
□ Todas las modelos están delgadas. All models are slim.
**2** thin
□ Esta tela es demasiado delgada. This material is too thin.

**delicado** (FEM **delicada**) ADJECTIVE
**1** delicate
□ Estas copas son muy delicadas. These glasses are very delicate. □ Se trata de un asunto muy delicado. It's a very delicate subject.
**2** thoughtful
□ Enviarte flores ha sido un gesto muy delicado. Sending you flowers was a very thoughtful gesture.

**la delicia** NOUN
delight
□ ¡Qué delicia! What a delight!
■ Este guiso es una delicia. This stew is delicious.

**delicioso** (FEM **deliciosa**) ADJECTIVE
delicious

**el/la delincuente** NOUN
criminal
□ Es uno de los delincuentes más buscados. He's one of the most wanted criminals.
■ un delincuente juvenil a juvenile delinquent

**el delito** NOUN
crime

**la demanda** NOUN
demand
□ la oferta y la demanda supply and demand
■ Se manifestaron en demanda de un aumento salarial. They demonstrated for a wage increase.

■ **presentar una demanda contra alguien** to sue somebody

**demás** (FEM **demás**) ADJECTIVE
▷ see also **demás** PRONOUN
other
□ los demás niños  the other children

**demás** PRONOUN
▷ see also **demás** ADJECTIVE
■ **los demás**  the others
■ **lo demás**  the rest  □ Yo limpio las ventanas y lo demás lo limpias tú.  I'll clean the windows and you clean the rest.
■ **todo lo demás**  everything else

**demasiado** (FEM **demasiada**) ADJECTIVE
▷ see also **demasiado** ADVERB
too much (PL too many)
□ demasiado vino  too much wine
□ demasiados libros  too many books

**demasiado** ADVERB
▷ see also **demasiado** ADJECTIVE
**1** too
□ Es demasiado pesado para levantarlo.  It's too heavy to lift.  □ Caminas demasiado deprisa.  You walk too quickly.
**2** too much
□ Hablas demasiado.  You talk too much.

la **democracia** NOUN
democracy (PL democracies)

**democrático** (FEM **democrática**) ADJECTIVE
democratic

el **demonio** NOUN
devil
■ ¡Jaime es un auténtico demonio! Jaime's a real devil!
■ ¡Demonios! Hell! (colloquial)
■ ¿Qué demonios será? (colloquial) What the devil can it be?

la **demostración** (PL las **demostraciones**) NOUN
**1** demonstration
**2** proof

**demostrar\*** VERB [11]
**1** to demonstrate
**2** to prove
□ Tendrá que demostrar su inocencia.  He will have to prove his innocence.
■ Así sólo demuestras tu ignorancia. That way you only show how ignorant you are.

la **densidad** NOUN
density
□ la densidad de población  population density

**denso** (FEM **densa**) ADJECTIVE
**1** thick
**2** heavy

la **dentadura** NOUN
teeth pl
■ la dentadura postiza  false teeth pl

el **dentífrico** NOUN
toothpaste

el/la **dentista** NOUN
dentist

**dentro** ADVERB
inside
□ ¿Qué hay dentro?  What's inside?
■ **por dentro**  inside  □ Mira bien por dentro. Have a good look inside.
■ **Está aquí dentro.**  It's in here.
■ **dentro de**  in  □ Mételo dentro del sobre. Put it in the envelope.  □ dentro de tres meses  in three months
■ **dentro de poco**  soon
■ **dentro de lo que cabe**  as far as it goes

la **denuncia** NOUN
■ **Voy a ponerle una denuncia por hacer tanto ruido.**  I'm going to report him for making so much noise.
■ **Le pusieron una denuncia por verter residuos en el río.**  He was reported to the authorities for tipping waste into the river.

**denunciar** VERB [25]
to report

el **departamento** NOUN
**1** department
**2** compartment
**3** flat (Latin America)

**depender** VERB [8]
■ **depender de**  to depend on  □ El precio depende de la calidad.  The price depends on the quality.
■ **Depende.**  It depends.
■ **No depende de mí.**  It's not up to me.

el **dependiente**, la **dependienta** NOUN
sales assistant

el **deporte** NOUN
sport
□ No hago mucho deporte.  I don't do much sport.  □ los deportes de invierno  winter sports

**deportista** (FEM **deportista**) ADJECTIVE
sporty
□ Alicia es poco deportista.  Alicia is not very sporty.

el **deportista** NOUN
sportsman (PL sportsmen)

la **deportista** NOUN
sportswoman (PL sportswomen)

**deportivo** (FEM **deportiva**) ADJECTIVE
**1** sports
□ un club deportivo  a sports club
**2** sporting

el **depósito** NOUN
**1** tank
**2** deposit

la **depresión** (PL las **depresiones**) NOUN

**1** depression
■ **tener una depresión** to be suffering from depression
**2** hollow

**deprimido** (FEM **deprimida**) ADJECTIVE
depressed

**deprimir** VERB [58]
to depress
■ **deprimirse por algo** to get depressed about something

**deprisa** ADVERB
quickly
▢ Acabaron muy deprisa. They finished very quickly.
■ **¡Deprisa!** Hurry up!
■ **Lo hacen todo deprisa y corriendo.** They do everything in a rush.

la **derecha** NOUN
**1** right hand
▢ Escribo con la derecha. I write with my right hand.
**2** right
▢ doblar a la derecha to turn right ▢ La derecha ganó las elecciones. The elections were won by the right.
■ **ser de derechas** to be right-wing ▢ un partido de derechas a right-wing party
■ **a la derecha** on the right ▢ la segunda calle a la derecha the second turning on the right
■ **a la derecha del castillo** to the right of the castle
■ **conducir por la derecha** to drive on the right

**derecho** (FEM **derecha**) ADJECTIVE
▷ see also **derecho** ADVERB, NOUN
**1** right
▢ Me duele el ojo derecho. I've got a pain in my right eye. ▢ Escribo con la mano derecha. I write with my right hand.
■ **a mano derecha** on the right-hand side
**2** straight
▢ ¡Ponte derecho! Stand up straight!

**derecho** ADVERB
▷ see also **derecho** ADJECTIVE, NOUN
straight
▢ Vino derecho hacia mí. He came straight towards me. ▢ Siga derecho. Carry straight on.

el **derecho** NOUN
▷ see also **derecho** ADVERB, ADJECTIVE
**1** right
▢ tener derecho a hacer algo to have the right to do something ▢ No tienes derecho a decir eso. You have no right to say that. ▢ los derechos humanos human rights
■ **¡No hay derecho!** It's not fair!
**2** law

▢ Estudio derecho. I'm studying law.
■ **Ponte la camiseta del derecho.** Put your T-shirt on the right way out.

**derramar** VERB [25]
to spill
▢ Derramó vino sobre el mantel. He spilt wine on the tablecloth.

**derrapar** VERB [25]
to skid

**derretir*** VERB [38]
to melt
■ **derretirse** to melt ▢ El queso se ha derretido. The cheese has melted. ▢ El hielo se está derritiendo. The ice is melting.
■ **derretirse de calor** to be melting

**derribar** VERB [25]
**1** to demolish
**2** to shoot down
**3** to overthrow

la **derrota** NOUN
defeat
▢ sufrir una derrota to suffer a defeat

**derrotar** VERB [25]
to defeat

**derrumbar** VERB [25]
to pull down
▢ Han derrumbado el cine. The cinema has been pulled down.
■ **derrumbarse** to collapse ▢ El edificio se derrumbó. The building collapsed.

**desabrochar** VERB [25]
to undo
■ **desabrocharse 1** to undo ▢ Me desabroché la blusa. I undid my blouse.
**2** to come undone ▢ Se te ha desabrochado la cremallera. Your zip has come undone.

el **desacuerdo** NOUN
disagreement

**desafiar*** VERB [21]
to challenge
▢ Mi hermano me desafió a una carrera. My brother challenged me to a race.

**desafinar** VERB
to go out of tune

el **desafío** NOUN
challenge

**desafortunado** (FEM **desafortunada**)
ADJECTIVE
unfortunate

**desagradable** (FEM **desagradable**)
ADJECTIVE
unpleasant
▢ un olor muy desagradable a very unpleasant smell
■ **ser desagradable con alguien** to be unpleasant to somebody

**desagradecido** (FEM **desagradecida**)
ADJECTIVE

ungrateful

**el desagüe** NOUN
1 wastepipe
2 drain

**desahogarse\*** VERB [37]
■ **Se desahogó conmigo.** He poured out his heart to me.
■ **Lloraba para desahogarse.** He was crying to let off steam.

**desalojar** VERB [25]
to clear
□ La policía desalojó a los manifestantes. The police cleared the demonstrators. □ Los bomberos desalojaron el edificio. The firemen cleared the building.

**desanimado** (FEM **desanimada**) ADJECTIVE
1 downhearted
2 dull

**desanimar** VERB [25]
to discourage
□ Me desanimó su falta de interés. His lack of interest discouraged me.
■ **desanimarse** to lose heart

**desaparecer\*** VERB [12]
to disappear
□ Me han desaparecido las gafas. My glasses have disappeared. □ La mancha ha desaparecido. The stain has disappeared.
■ **¡Desaparece de mi vista!** Get out of my sight!

la **desaparición** (PL las **desapariciones**) NOUN
disappearance

**desapercibido** (FEM **desapercibida**) ADJECTIVE
■ **pasar desapercibido** to go unnoticed

**desaprovechar** VERB [25]
to waste
□ Han desaprovechado una gran oportunidad. They've wasted a great opportunity.

el **desarme** NOUN
disarmament
□ el desarme nuclear nuclear disarmament

**desarrollar** VERB [25]
to develop
□ El estudio desarrolla la mente. Study develops the mind.
■ **La UNICEF desarrolla una labor importante.** UNICEF carries out important work.
■ **desarrollarse 1** to develop □ La empresa se desarrolla rápidamente. The business is developing rapidly. **2** to take place □ La reunión se desarrolló sin incidentes. The meeting took place without incident.

el **desarrollo** NOUN
development

□ Es importante para el desarrollo del niño. It's important for a child's development.
■ **La industria está en pleno desarrollo.** The industry is expanding steadily.
■ **un país en vías de desarrollo** a developing country

el **desastre** NOUN
disaster
□ un gran desastre económico a major economic disaster □ La función fue un desastre. The show was a disaster.
■ **Soy un desastre para la gimnasia.** I'm hopeless at gymnastics.
■ **Siempre va hecho un desastre.** He always looks a mess.

**desastroso** (FEM **desastrosa**) ADJECTIVE
disastrous

**desatar** VERB [25]
1 to undo
2 to untie
■ **desatarse 1** to come undone **2** to get loose **3** to break

**desayunar** VERB [25]
1 to have breakfast
□ Nunca desayuno. I never have breakfast.
2 to have...for breakfast
□ Desayuné café con leche y un bollo. I had coffee and a roll for breakfast.

el **desayuno** NOUN
breakfast

**descalzarse\*** VERB [13]
to take one's shoes off

**descalzo** (FEM **descalza**) ADJECTIVE
barefoot
□ Paseaban descalzos por la playa. They walked barefoot along the beach.
■ **No entres en la cocina descalzo.** Don't come into the kitchen in bare feet.

el **descampado** NOUN
open space

**descansar** VERB [25]
1 to rest
□ Tienes que descansar. You must rest.
■ **descanse en paz** may he rest in peace
2 to sleep
□ ¡Que descanses! Sleep well!

el **descansillo** NOUN
landing

el **descanso** NOUN
1 rest
□ He caminado mucho, necesito un descanso. I've done a lot of walking, I need a rest.
2 break
□ Cada dos horas me tomo un descanso. I have a break every two hours.
3 relief
□ ¡Qué descanso! What a relief!

**4** interval
**5** half time
■ **tomarse unos días de descanso** to take a few days off

el **descapotable** NOUN
convertible

**descarado** (FEM **descarada**) ADJECTIVE
cheeky
□ ¡No seas descarado! Don't be cheeky!

la **descarga** NOUN
**1** unloading
**2** discharge

**descargar*** VERB [37]
**1** to unload
□ Me ayudó a descargar los muebles de la camioneta. He helped me unload the furniture from the van.
**2** to take out
□ Descarga su mal humor sobre mí. He takes his bad moods out on me.
**3** to download
■ **descargarse** to go flat

el **descaro** NOUN
nerve
□ ¡Qué descaro! What a nerve!

**descender*** VERB [20]
to go down
□ Descendieron por la escalinata. They went down the staircase. □ Ha descendido el nivel del pantano. The level of the reservoir has gone down.
■ **descender de** to be descended from
□ Desciende de una familia noble. He is descended from a noble family.
■ **Mi equipo ha descendido de categoría.** My team has been relegated.

el/la **descendiente** NOUN
descendant

el **descenso** NOUN
**1** drop
□ Va a haber un descenso de las temperaturas. There's going to be a drop in temperature.
**2** descent
□ Los ciclistas iniciaron el descenso del puerto. The cyclists began the descent from the mountain pass.
**3** relegation
□ el descenso a segunda división relegation to the second division

**descolgar*** VERB
**1** to take down
□ Descolgó las cortinas para lavarlas. He took down the curtains to wash them.
**2** to pick up the phone
□ Descolgó y marcó el número. He picked up the phone and dialled the number.
■ **descolgar el teléfono** to pick up the phone

■ **descolgarse por una pared** to lower oneself down a wall

**descomponerse*** VERB [41] (*Latin America*)
to break down

**desconcertar*** VERB [39]
to disconcert
■ **desconcertarse** to be disconcerted
□ Se desconcertó al verla allí. He was disconcerted to see her there.

**desconectar** VERB [25]
**1** to unplug
**2** to disconnect

**desconfiado** (FEM **desconfiada**) ADJECTIVE
distrustful

la **desconfianza** NOUN
distrust

**desconfiar*** VERB [21]
■ **Desconfío de él.** I don't trust him.
■ **Desconfía siempre de las apariencias.** Always beware of appearances.

**descongelar** VERB [25]
to defrost
■ **descongelarse** to defrost

el **desconocido**, la **desconocida** NOUN
stranger

**desconocido** (FEM **desconocida**) ADJECTIVE
unknown
□ un actor desconocido an unknown actor
■ **Está desconocido.** He's unrecognizable.

**descontar*** VERB [11]
to deduct
□ Me descuentan un parte del sueldo. Part of my salary is deducted.
■ **Descuentan el 5% si se paga en metálico.** They give a 5% discount if you pay cash.
■ **Descontaron cinco euros del precio marcado.** They took five euros off the marked price.

**descontento** (FEM **descontenta**) ADJECTIVE
unhappy
□ Están descontentos de mis notas. They're unhappy with my marks.

**descoser** VERB [8]
to unpick
■ **descoserse** to come apart at the seams

**descremado** (FEM **descremada**) ADJECTIVE
skimmed

**describir*** VERB
to describe

la **descripción** (PL las **descripciones**) NOUN
description

el **descubierto** NOUN
overdraft

el **descubrimiento** NOUN

## descubrir – desengaño

discovery (PL discoveries)

**descubrir\*** VERB

1 to discover

□ Colón descubrió América en 1492. Columbus discovered America in 1492.

2 to find out

□ ¡Me has descubierto! You've found me out!

el **descuento** NOUN

discount

□ Me hicieron un descuento del 3%. They gave me a 3% discount.

■ **con descuento** at a discount

**descuidado** (FEM **descuidada**) ADJECTIVE

1 careless

□ Es muy descuidada con sus juguetes. She's very careless with her toys.

2 neglected

□ El jardín estaba descuidado. The garden was neglected.

**descuidar** VERB [25]

to neglect

□ Descuidó su negocio. He neglected his business.

■ **Descuida, que yo lo haré.** Don't worry, I'll do it.

■ **descuidarse** to let one's attention wander □ Se descuidó un segundo y el niño cruzó la calle. He let his attention wander for a second and the child crossed the road.

el **descuido** NOUN

oversight

□ Me olvidé de invitarla, fue un descuido. I forgot to invite her, it was an oversight.

**desde** PREPOSITION

1 from

□ Desde Burgos hasta mi casa hay 30 km. It's 30km from Burgos to my house. □ Te llamaré desde la oficina. I'll ring you from the office.

2 since

□ Desde que llegó no ha salido. He hasn't been out since he arrived. □ La conozco desde niño. I've known her since I was a child. □ desde entonces since then

■ **¿Desde cuándo vives aquí?** How long have you been living here?

■ **desde hace tres años** for three years

■ **desde ahora en adelante** from now on

■ **desde luego** of course

**desdichado** (FEM **desdichada**) ADJECTIVE

1 ill-fated

2 unlucky

**desdoblar** VERB [25]

to unfold

□ Desdobló el plano. He unfolded the map.

**desear** VERB [25]

to wish

□ Te deseo mucha suerte. I wish you lots of luck.

■ **Estoy deseando que esto termine.** I'm longing for this to finish.

■ **¿Qué desea?** What can I do for you?

■ **dejar mucho que desear** to leave a lot to be desired

**desechable** (FEM **desechable**) ADJECTIVE

disposable

los **desechos** NOUN

waste sing

□ los desechos nucleares nuclear waste

**desembarcar\*** VERB [48]

1 to disembark

□ Fue el primero en desembarcar. He was the first to disembark.

2 to unload

□ Han desembarcado la mercancía. They've unloaded the goods.

el **desembarco** NOUN

landing

**desembocar\*** VERB [48]

■ **desembocar en 1** to flow into □ El Ebro desemboca en el Mediterráneo. The Ebro flows into the Mediterranean. **2** to lead into □ Este callejón desemboca en la Avenida Pablo Casals. This alley leads into Avenida Pablo Casals.

**desempacar\*** VERB [48] (Latin America)

to unpack

el **desempate** NOUN

play-off

■ **el partido de desempate** the deciding match

■ **En el minuto veinte llegó el gol del desempate.** The goal which broke the deadlock came in the twentieth minute.

el **desempleado**, la **desempleada** NOUN

unemployed person

■ **los desempleados** the unemployed

el **desempleo** NOUN

unemployment

**desenchufar** VERB [25]

to unplug

**desengañar** VERB [25]

■ **Su traición la desengañó.** His betrayal opened her eyes.

■ **¡Desengáñate! No está interesada en ti.** Stop fooling yourself! She isn't interested in you.

el **desengaño** NOUN

disappointment

□ ¡Qué desengaño! What a disappointment!

■ **llevarse un desengaño** to be disappointed

■ **sufrir un desengaño amoroso** to be disappointed in love

**desenredar** VERB [25]
1 to untangle
2 to resolve
**desenrollar** VERB [25]
1 to unwind
2 to unroll
**desenroscar*** VERB [48]
to unscrew
**desenvolver*** VERB [59]
to unwrap
□ Desenvolvió todos los paquetes. He unwrapped all the parcels.
■ **desenvolverse** to cope □ Se desenvuelve bien en este tipo de situaciones. He copes well in this sort of situation.
■ **desenvolverse bien** to do well
el **deseo** NOUN
wish (PL wishes)
□ Pide un deseo. Make a wish.
**desequilibrado** (FEM **desequilibrada**)
ADJECTIVE
unbalanced
**desértico** (FEM **desértica**) ADJECTIVE
desert
□ una región desértica a desert region
**desesperado** (FEM **desesperada**) ADJECTIVE
desperate
el **desesperado**, la **desesperada**
NOUN
■ Corría como un desesperado. He was running like mad.
**desesperante** (FEM **desesperante**)
ADJECTIVE
infuriating
**desesperar** VERB [25]
1 to drive...mad
□ Los atascos me desesperan. Traffic jams drive me mad.
2 to despair
□ No desesperes y sigue intentándolo. Don't despair, just keep trying.
■ **desesperarse** to get exasperated
**desfavorable** (FEM **desfavorable**) ADJECTIVE
unfavourable
el **desfiladero** NOUN
gorge
**desfilar** VERB [25]
to parade
el **desfile** NOUN
parade
■ un desfile de modas a fashion show
la **desgana** NOUN
1 loss of appetite
2 reluctance
■ hacer algo con desgana to do something reluctantly
**desganado** (FEM **desganada**) ADJECTIVE
■ estar desganado 1 to have little appetite

2 to be lethargic
**desgarrar** VERB [25]
to tear up
□ Desgarró la sábana para hacer trapos. He tore up the sheet to make rags.
■ **desgarrarse** to rip □ La cortina se desgarró. The curtain ripped.
el **desgarrón** (PL los **desgarrones**) NOUN
rip
**desgastar** VERB [25]
1 to wear out
2 to wear away
■ **desgastarse** to get worn out
el **desgaste** NOUN
1 wear and tear
2 erosion
la **desgracia** NOUN
tragedy (PL tragedies)
□ Su muerte fue una auténtica desgracia. His death was an absolute tragedy.
■ Ha tenido una vida llena de desgracias. He's had a lot of misfortune in his life.
■ por desgracia 1 sadly □ Por desgracia no se salvó nadie. Sadly there were no survivors. 2 unfortunately □ Por desgracia he vuelto a suspender. Unfortunately I've failed again.
■ tener la desgracia de to be unfortunate enough to □ Tuvo la desgracia de perder a su hijo. He was unfortunate enough to lose his son.
■ No hubo desgracias personales. There were no casualties.
**desgraciado** (FEM **desgraciada**) ADJECTIVE
1 unhappy
□ Desde que Ana le dejó ha sido muy desgraciado. He has been very unhappy since Ana left him.
2 tragic
□ Murió en un desgraciado accidente. He died in a tragic accident.
**deshabitado** (FEM **deshabitada**) ADJECTIVE
1 uninhabited
2 unoccupied
**deshacer*** VERB [26]
1 to untie
2 to unpack
3 to melt
4 to unpick
■ deshacerse 1 to come undone 2 to melt
■ deshacerse de algo to get rid of something
**deshecho** (FEM **deshecha**) ADJECTIVE
1 undone
2 unmade
3 broken
4 melted
■ Estoy deshecho. 1 I'm shattered. 2 I'm

devastated.

**deshidratarse** VERB
to become dehydrated

el **deshielo** NOUN
thaw

**deshinchar** VERB [25]
to let down

■ **deshincharse 1** to go down **2** to go flat

**desierto** (FEM **desierta**) ADJECTIVE
deserted

□ El pueblo parecía desierto. The village seemed deserted.

el **desierto** NOUN
desert

**desigual** (FEM **desigual**) ADJECTIVE
1 different
2 uneven
3 unequal

la **desilusión** (PL las **desilusiones**) NOUN
disappointment

□ ¡Qué desilusión! What a disappointment!

■ **llevarse una desilusión** to be disappointed

**desilusionar** VERB [25]
to disappoint

□ No quiero desilusionarte, pero ... I don't want to disappoint you, but ...

■ **Su conferencia me desilusionó.** His lecture was disappointing.

■ **desilusionarse** to be disappointed

el **desinfectante** NOUN
disinfectant

**desinfectar** VERB [25]
to disinfect

**desinflar** VERB [25]
to let down

□ Alguien me ha desinflado los neumáticos. Somebody has let my tyres down.

el **desinterés** NOUN
lack of interest

□ Muestra un total desinterés por sus estudios. He shows a total lack of interest in his studies.

**deslizarse*** VERB [13]
to slide

□ El trineo se deslizaba por la nieve. The sledge slid over the snow.

**deslumbrar** VERB [25]
to dazzle

□ Las luces del coche me deslumbraron. The car headlights dazzled me. □ Tanta riqueza la deslumbró. She was dazzled by so much wealth.

**desmayarse** VERB [25]
to faint

el **desmayo** NOUN
faint

■ **sufrir un desmayo** to faint

**desmemoriado** (FEM **desmemoriada**)
ADJECTIVE
forgetful

**desmontar** VERB [25]
1 to take apart
2 to take down
3 to strip down
4 to dismount

**desnatado** (FEM **desnatada**) ADJECTIVE
1 skimmed
2 low-fat

**desnudar** VERB [25]
to undress

■ **desnudarse** to get undressed

**desnudo** (FEM **desnuda**) ADJECTIVE
1 naked

□ una escultura de un hombre desnudo a sculpture of a naked man

■ **Duerme desnudo.** He sleeps in the nude.
2 bare

□ Sin los cuadros la pared parece desnuda. The wall looks bare without the paintings.

**desobedecer*** VERB [12]
to disobey

**desobediente** (FEM **desobediente**)
ADJECTIVE
disobedient

el **desodorante** NOUN
deodorant

el **desorden** (PL los **desórdenes**) NOUN
mess

□ Hay mucha desorden en esta casa. This whole house is in a mess.

■ **los desórdenes callejeros** street disturbances

**desordenado** (FEM **desordenada**) ADJECTIVE
untidy

**desordenar** VERB [25]
to mess up

□ Los niños han desordenado la habitación. The children have messed up the room.

la **desorganización** NOUN
disorganization

**desorientar** VERB [25]
to confuse

□ Tus consejos me desorientan más. Your advice confuses me more.

■ **desorientarse** to lose one's way □ Se desorientó al salir del metro. He lost his way when he came out of the underground.

**despachar** VERB [25]
1 to sell

□ También despachamos sellos. We also sell stamps.
2 to serve

□ Me despachó un dependiente muy educado. I was served by a very polite sales assistant.

**3** to dismiss
  □ Me despachó sin ninguna explicación. He dismissed me without any explanation.

**el despacho** NOUN
**1** office
  ■ **los muebles de despacho** office furniture
  ■ **una mesa de despacho** a desk
**2** study (PL studies)
  □ Está trabajando en su despacho. He's working in his study.
  ■ **un despacho de billetes** a booking office

**despacio** ADVERB
  slowly
  □ Conduce despacio. Drive slowly.
  ■ **¡Despacio!** Take it easy!

**despectivo** (FEM **despectiva**) ADJECTIVE
**1** contemptuous
  □ Me habló en un tono muy despectivo. He spoke to me in a very contemptuous tone.
**2** pejorative
  □ 'Mujerzuela' es una palabra despectiva. 'Mujerzuela' is a pejorative term.

**la despedida** NOUN
  ■ **Le hicimos una buena despedida a Marta.** We gave Marta a good send-off.
  ■ **una fiesta de despedida** a farewell party
  ■ **una despedida de soltero** a stag party
  ■ **una despedida de soltera** a hen party

**despedir\*** VERB [38]
**1** to say goodbye to
  □ Salí a la calle a despedirla. I went out into the street to say goodbye to her.
  ■ **Fueron a despedirlo al aeropuerto.** They went to the airport to see him off.
**2** to dismiss
  □ Lo despidieron por llegar tarde. He was dismissed for being late.
  ■ **despedirse** to say goodbye □ Se despidieron en la estación. They said goodbye at the station. □ despedirse de alguien to say goodbye to somebody

**despegar\*** VERB [37]
  to take off
  □ Despegó la etiqueta del precio. He took the price label off. □ El avión despegó con retraso. The plane took off late.
  ■ **despegarse** to come unstuck

**el despegue** NOUN
  takeoff

**despeinar** VERB [25]
  ■ **despeinar a alguien** to mess somebody's hair up
  ■ **No me toques el pelo, que me despeinas.** Don't touch my hair, you'll mess it up.
  ■ **Se despeinó al vestirse.** She messed up her hair getting dressed.

**despejado** (FEM **despejada**) ADJECTIVE
  clear
  □ El cielo estaba despejado. The sky was clear.
  ■ **Por las mañanas tengo la mente más despejada.** My head's clearer in the mornings.

**despejar** VERB [25]
  to clear
  □ La policía ha despejado la zona. The police have cleared the area. □ El aire fresco te despejará. The fresh air will clear your head.
  ■ **¡Despejen!** Move along!
  ■ **Tomaré un café para despejarme.** I'll have a coffee to wake myself up.

**despellejar** VERB [25]
  to skin

**la despensa** NOUN
  larder

**desperdiciar** VERB [25]
**1** to waste
  □ Está mal desperdiciar la comida. It's wrong to waste food.
**2** to throw away
  □ Desperdició la oportunidad de hacerse rico. He threw away the chance to get rich.

**el desperdicio** NOUN
  waste
  □ Tirar toda esta comida es un desperdicio. It's a waste to throw away all this food.
  ■ **los desperdicios** scraps □ Le dimos los desperdicios al perro. We gave the dog the scraps.
  ■ **El libro no tiene desperdicio.** It's an excellent book from beginning to end.

**desperezarse\*** VERB [13]
  to stretch

**el desperfecto** NOUN
  flaw
  ■ **El pantalón tenía un pequeño desperfecto.** There was a slight flaw in the trousers.
  ■ **sufrir desperfectos** to get damaged

**el despertador** NOUN
  alarm clock

**despertar\*** VERB [39]
**1** to wake up
  □ No me despiertes hasta las once. Don't wake me up until eleven o'clock.
**2** to arouse
  □ El debate despertó un gran interés. The debate aroused a lot of interest.
  ■ **despertarse** to wake up

**el despido** NOUN
  dismissal

**despierto** (FEM **despierta**) ADJECTIVE
**1** awake
  □ A las siete ya estaba despierto. He was

already awake by seven o'clock.

**2** bright

□ Es un niño muy despierto. He's a very bright boy.

el **despistado**, la **despistada** NOUN
scatterbrain

□ Eres un despistado. You're a scatterbrain.

**despistado** (FEM **despistada**) ADJECTIVE
absent-minded

□ Es tan despistado que siempre se olvida las llaves. He's so absent-minded that he's always forgetting his keys.

**despistar** VERB [25]

**1** to shake off

□ Despistaron al coche que los seguía. They managed to shake off the car that was following them.

**2** to be misleading

□ Estas instrucciones, más que ayudar, despistan. These instructions are more misleading than helpful.

■ **Me despisté y salí de la autopista demasiado tarde.** I wasn't concentrating and I turned off the motorway too late.

el **despiste** NOUN
absent-mindedness

□ Su despiste es conocido por todos. His absent-mindedness is notorious.

■ **¡Vaya despiste que tienes!** How absent-minded can you get!

**desplazar** VERB [13]

**1** to move

**2** to take the place of

■ **desplazarse** to commute

**desplegar\*** VERB [34]

**1** to unfold

□ Desplegó el mapa. He unfolded the map.

**2** to spread

□ El águila desplegó las alas. The eagle spread its wings.

■ **desplegarse** to be deployed □ El ejército se desplegó por la ciudad. The army was deployed throughout the city.

**desplomarse** VERB [25]
to collapse

□ Se ha desplomado el techo. The roof has collapsed.

**despreciar** VERB [25]
to despise

el **desprecio** NOUN
contempt

■ **Habló de ellos con desprecio.** He spoke of them contemptuously.

■ **Le hicieron el desprecio de no acudir.** They snubbed him by not turning up.

**desprender** VERB
to give off

■ **desprenderse** to fall off □ Se desprendió

una baldosa. A tile fell off.

■ **desprenderse de algo** to give something up □ No quería desprenderse de la casa. He didn't want to give the house up.

**despreocuparse** VERB [25]
to stop worrying

□ Despreocúpate porque ya no tiene remedio. Stop worrying because there's nothing we can do about it now.

■ **despreocuparse de todo** to show no concern for anything

**desprevenido** (FEM **desprevenida**)
ADJECTIVE

■ **pillar a alguien desprevenido** to catch somebody unawares

**después** ADVERB

**1** afterwards

□ Después todos estábamos muy cansados. Afterwards we were all very tired.

■ **Primero cenaré y después saldré.** I'll have dinner first and go out after that.

**2** later

□ Ellos llegaron después. They arrived later.
□ un año después a year later

**3** next

□ ¿Qué viene después? What comes next?

■ **después de** after □ Tu nombre está después del mío. Your name comes after mine. □ Después de comer fuimos de paseo. After lunch we went for a walk.

■ **después de todo** after all

■ **después de que** after □ después de que te acostaras after you had gone to bed

**destacar\*** VERB [48]

**1** to stress

□ Me gustaría destacar la importancia de esto. I'd like to stress the importance of this.

**2** to stand out

□ Isabel destacaba por su generosidad. Isabel's generosity made her stand out.

el **destapador** NOUN (Latin America)
bottle opener

**destapar** VERB [25]

**1** to open

**2** to take the lid off

■ **destaparse** to get uncovered □ El niño se destapa por las noches. The child gets uncovered at night.

**desteñir\*** VERB [45]

**1** to run

□ Estos pantalones destiñen. These trousers run.

**2** to fade

□ El sol ha desteñido las cortinas. The sun has faded the curtains.

■ **desteñirse** to fade □ Se ha desteñido el jersey. This jumper has faded.

**desternillarse** VERB [25]
- **desternillarse de risa** *(colloquial)* to split one's sides laughing

**destinar** VERB [25]
1 to post
  □ Lo han destinado a Madrid. He has been posted to Madrid.
2 to earmark
  □ Destinaron los fondos a una ONG. The funds were earmarked for an NGO.
- **El libro está destinado al público infantil.** The book is aimed at children.

el **destinatario**, la **destinataria** NOUN
addressee

el **destino** NOUN
1 destination
  □ Por fin llegamos a nuestro destino. We finally arrived at our destination.
- **el tren con destino a Valencia** the train to Valencia
- **salir con destino a** to leave for
2 posting
  □ Cada dos años me cambian de destino. They give me a new posting every two years.
3 use
  □ Quiero saber qué destino tendrá este dinero. I want to know what use will be made of this money.

el **destornillador** NOUN
screwdriver

**destornillar** VERB [25]
to unscrew

la **destreza** NOUN
skill

**destrozar*** VERB [13]
to wreck
  □ Tu perro ha destrozado la silla. Your dog has wrecked the chair.
- **La noticia le destrozó el corazón.** The news broke his heart.

los **destrozos** NOUN
damage *sing*
  □ La lluvia ocasionó grandes destrozos. The rain caused a lot of damage.

la **destrucción** NOUN
destruction

**destruir*** VERB [10]
1 to destroy
  □ Los huracanes destruyen edificios enteros. Hurricanes can destroy whole buildings.
2 to ruin
  □ Aquello destruyó su carrera. That business ruined his career.
3 to demolish
  □ Con cuatro palabras destruyó todos mis argumentos. He demolished all my arguments with a few words.

**desvalijar** VERB [25]
1 to burgle
2 to rob

el **desván** (PL los **desvanes**) NOUN
attic

**desvelar** VERB
1 to keep...awake
  □ El café me desvela. Coffee keeps me awake.
2 to reveal
  □ Nos desveló todos sus secretos. He revealed all his secrets to us.
- **Se desvelan por sus hijos.** They're devoted to their children.

la **desventaja** NOUN
disadvantage
- **estar en desventaja** to be at a disadvantage

**desviar*** VERB [21]
to divert
  □ Desviaron la circulación. Traffic was diverted.
- **Quería desviar mi atención.** He wanted to divert my attention.
- **desviar la mirada** to look away
- **desviarse** to turn off  □ No debes desviarte de la carretera principal. You mustn't turn off the main road.  □ Nos estamos desviando del tema. We're getting off the point.

el **desvío** NOUN
1 turning
  □ Coge el primer desvío a la derecha. Take the first turning on the right.
2 diversion
  □ Hay un desvío por obras. There's a diversion due to roadworks.

el **detalle** NOUN
detail
  □ No recuerdo todos los detalles. I don't remember all the details.
- **No pierde detalle.** He doesn't miss a trick.
- **Quiero comprarte un detalle.** I want to buy you a little something.
- **tener un detalle con alguien** to be considerate towards somebody
- **¡Qué detalle!** How thoughtful!
- **vender al detalle** to sell retail

**detectar** VERB [25]
to detect

el/la **detective** NOUN
detective
  □ un detective privado a private detective

**detener*** VERB [53]
1 to stop
  □ ¡Detenlos! Stop them!
2 to arrest

□ Han detenido a los ladrones. They've arrested the thieves.

■ **detenerse** to stop □ Nos detuvimos en el semáforo. We stopped at the lights.

■ **¡Deténgase!** Stop!

el **detergente** NOUN
detergent

**deteriorar** VERB [25]
to damage

□ La lluvia ha deteriorado el tejado. The rain has damaged the roof.

■ **deteriorarse** to deteriorate □ Su salud se ha deteriorado. His health has deteriorated.

la **determinación** NOUN
determination

□ Luchó contra su enfermedad con gran determinación. He fought his illness with great determination.

■ **tomar una determinación** to take a decision

**determinado** (FEM **determinada**) ADJECTIVE

1 certain

□ En determinadas ocasiones es mejor callarse. There are certain occasions when it's better to say nothing.

■ **No hemos quedado a una hora determinada.** We haven't fixed a definite time.

2 particular

□ ¿Buscas algún libro determinado? Are you looking for a particular book?

**determinar** VERB [25]

1 to determine

□ Trataron de determinar la causa del accidente. They tried to determine the cause of the accident.

2 to fix

□ determinar la fecha de una reunión to fix the date of a meeting

3 to bring about

□ Aquello determinó la caída del gobierno. That brought about the fall of the government.

4 to state

□ El reglamento determina que ... The rules state that ...

**detestar** VERB [25]
to detest

**detrás** ADVERB
behind

□ El resto de los niños vienen detrás. The rest of the children are coming on behind.

■ **detrás de** behind □ Se escondió detrás de un árbol. He hid behind a tree.

■ **uno detrás de otro** one after another

■ **La critican por detrás.** They criticize her behind her back.

la **deuda** NOUN

debt

■ **contraer deudas** to get into debt

■ **estar en deuda con alguien** to be in somebody's debt

la **devolución** (PL las **devoluciones**) NOUN

1 return

2 repayment

■ **No se admiten devoluciones.** Goods cannot be returned.

**devolver*** VERB [59]

1 to give back

□ ¿Me puedes devolver la cinta que te presté? Could you give me back the tape I lent you?

■ **Me devolvieron mal el cambio.** They gave me the wrong change.

■ **Te devolveré el favor cuando pueda.** I'll return the favour when I can.

2 to take back

□ Devolví la falda porque me iba pequeña. I took the skirt back as it was too small for me.

3 to throw up (colloquial)

□ Devolvió toda la cena. He threw up his dinner.

**devorar** VERB [25]
to devour

□ Los leones devoraron un ciervo. The lions devoured a deer.

■ **devorar un bocadillo** to wolf down a sandwich

**di** VERB ▷ see decir

el **día** NOUN
day (PL days)

□ Pasaré dos días en la playa. I'll spend a couple of days at the beach. □ Duerme de día y trabaja de noche. He sleeps during the day and works at night.

■ **Es de día.** It's daylight.

■ **¿Qué día es hoy? 1** What's the date today? **2** What day is it today?

■ **el día de mañana** tomorrow

■ **al día siguiente** the following day

■ **todos los días** every day

■ **un día de estos** one of these days

■ **un día sí y otro no** every other day

■ **¡Buenos días!** Good morning!

■ **un día de fiesta** a public holiday

■ **un día feriado** (Latin America) a public holiday

■ **un día laborable** a working day

■ **pan del día** fresh bread

el **diablo** NOUN
devil

□ No creo en el diablo. I don't believe in the devil. □ Juanito es un verdadero diablo. Juanito's a real little devil.

■ **¿Cómo diablos lo has hecho?** (colloquial)

How the devil did you do it?
■ **Hace un frío de mil diablos.** *(colloquial)*
It's hellishly cold.

el **diagnóstico** NOUN
diagnosis (PL diagnoses)

la **diagonal** ADJECTIVE, NOUN
diagonal
■ **en diagonal** diagonally

el **dialecto** NOUN
dialect

**dialogar*** VERB [37]
■ **dialogar con alguien** to hold talks with
somebody □ El ministro dialogará con los
sindicatos. The minister will hold talks with
the unions.

el **diálogo** NOUN
conversation
□ Fue un diálogo interesante. It was an
interesting conversation.
■ **No hay diálogo entre los dos bandos.**
There's no dialogue between the two sides.

el **diamante** NOUN
diamond
■ **diamantes** diamonds

el **diámetro** NOUN
diameter

la **diana** NOUN
1 bull's-eye
□ dar en la diana to get a bull's-eye
2 dartboard
□ En el bar hay una diana y dardos. There's
a dartboard and darts in the bar.

la **diapositiva** NOUN
slide

**diario** ADJECTIVE
daily
□ la rutina diaria the daily routine
■ **la ropa de diario** everyday clothes
■ **a diario** every day □ Va al gimnasio a
diario. He goes to the gym every day.

el **diario** NOUN
1 newspaper
2 diary (PL diaries)

la **diarrea** NOUN
diarrhoea

el/la **dibujante** NOUN
1 artist
2 cartoonist
3 draughtsman (PL draughtsmen)

**dibujar** VERB [25]
to draw
□ No sé dibujar. I can't draw. □ Dibujó un
árbol en la pizarra. He drew a tree on the
blackboard.

el **dibujo** NOUN
drawing
□ el dibujo técnico technical drawing
■ **los dibujos animados** cartoons

el **diccionario** NOUN
dictionary (PL dictionaries)

**dicho** VERB
▷ see also **dicho** ADJECTIVE, NOUN ▷ see **decir**

**dicho** (FEM **dicha**) ADJECTIVE
▷ see also **dicho** VERB, NOUN
■ **en dichos países** in the countries
mentioned above
■ **mejor dicho** or rather □ Vendré el lunes,
mejor dicho, el martes. I'll come on
Monday, or rather, on Tuesday.
■ **dicho y hecho** no sooner said than done

el **dicho** NOUN
▷ see also **dicho** VERB, ADJECTIVE
saying

**dichoso** (FEM **dichosa**) ADJECTIVE
1 happy
2 lucky
■ **¡Dichoso ruido!** Damned noise!
*(colloquial)*

**diciembre** MASC NOUN
December
□ en diciembre in December □ Llegaron
el 6 de diciembre. They arrived on
6 December.

**diciendo** VERB ▷ see **decir**

el **dictado** NOUN
dictation
□ La maestra nos hizo un dictado.
The teacher gave us a dictation.

el **dictador**, la **dictadora** NOUN
dictator

la **dictadura** NOUN
dictatorship

**dictar** VERB [25]
to dictate
□ El maestro nos dictó un párrafo del libro.
The teacher dictated a paragraph of the
book to us.
■ **dictar sentencia** to pass sentence

**diecinueve** (FEM **diecinueve**) ADJECTIVE,
PRONOUN
nineteen
□ Tengo diecinueve años. I'm nineteen.
■ **el diecinueve de julio** the nineteenth of
July
■ **en el siglo diecinueve** in the nineteenth
century

**dieciocho** (FEM **dieciocho**) ADJECTIVE,
PRONOUN
eighteen
□ Tengo dieciocho años. I'm eighteen.
■ **el dieciocho de abril** the eighteenth of
April
■ **en el siglo dieciocho** in the eighteenth
century

**dieciséis** (FEM **dieciséis**) ADJECTIVE, PRONOUN
sixteen

□ Tengo dieciséis años. I'm sixteen.
■ **el dieciséis de febrero** the sixteenth of February
■ **en el siglo dieciséis** in the sixteenth century

**diecisiete** (FEM **diecisiete**) ADJECTIVE, PRONOUN
seventeen

□ Tengo diecisiete años. I'm seventeen.
■ **el diecisiete de enero** the seventeenth of January
■ **en el siglo diecisiete** in the seventeenth century

el **diente** NOUN
tooth (PL teeth)

□ lavarse los dientes to clean one's teeth
■ **un diente de leche** a milk tooth
■ **un diente de ajo** a clove of garlic

la **dieta** NOUN
diet

□ una dieta vegetariana a vegetarian diet
■ **estar a dieta** to be on a diet
■ **ponerse a dieta** to go on a diet
■ **dietas** expenses

**diez** (FEM **diez**) ADJECTIVE, PRONOUN
ten

□ Tengo diez años. I'm ten.
■ **Son las diez.** It's ten o'clock.
■ **el diez de agosto** the tenth of August
■ **el siglo diez** the tenth century

la **diferencia** NOUN
difference

■ **a diferencia de** unlike □ A diferencia de su hermana, a ella le encanta viajar. Unlike her sister, she loves travelling.

**diferenciar** VERB [25]
■ **¿En qué se diferencian?** What's the difference between them?
■ **Sólo se diferencian en el tamaño.** The only difference between them is their size.
■ **Se diferencia de los demás por su bondad.** His kindness sets him apart from the rest.
■ **No diferencia el color rojo del verde.** He can't tell the difference between red and green.

**diferente** (FEM **diferente**) ADJECTIVE
different

**difícil** (FEM **difícil**) ADJECTIVE
difficult

□ Es un problema difícil de entender. It's a difficult problem to understand. □ Resulta difícil concentrarse. It's difficult to concentrate. □ Es un hombre difícil. He's a difficult man.

la **dificultad** NOUN
difficulty (PL difficulties)

□ con dificultad with difficulty

■ **tener dificultades para hacer algo** to have difficulty doing something
■ **Nos pusieron muchas dificultades para obtener el visado.** They made it very difficult for us to get a visa.

**dificultar** VERB [25]
to make...difficult

□ La niebla dificultaba la visibilidad. The fog made visibility difficult.

**digerir*** VERB [51]
to digest

la **digestión** NOUN
digestion

■ **hacer la digestión** to digest

**digestivo** (FEM **digestiva**) ADJECTIVE
digestive

**digital** (FEM **digital**) ADJECTIVE
digital

□ un reloj digital a digital watch
■ **una huella digital** a fingerprint

la **dignidad** NOUN
dignity

□ Se comportó con gran dignidad. He behaved with great dignity.

**digno** (FEM **digna**) ADJECTIVE
1 decent
2 honourable

■ **digno de mención** worth mentioning
■ **digno de verse** worth seeing

**digo** VERB ▷ see **decir**
**dije** VERB ▷ see **decir**

**diluir*** VERB [10]
to dilute

**diluviar** VERB [25]
■ **Está diluviando.** It's pouring with rain.

el **diluvio** NOUN
downpour

□ Cayó un diluvio. There was a downpour.
■ **un diluvio de cartas** a flood of letters

la **dimensión** (PL las **dimensiones**) NOUN
dimension

□ en tres dimensiones in three dimensions
■ **un cine de grandes dimensiones** a huge cinema

el **diminutivo** NOUN
diminutive

**diminuto** (FEM **diminuta**) ADJECTIVE
tiny

la **dimisión** (PL las **dimisiones**) NOUN
resignation

□ presentar la dimisión to hand in one's resignation

**dimitir** VERB [58]
to resign

□ Ha dimitido de su cargo. He has resigned from his post.

**Dinamarca** FEM NOUN
Denmark

**dinámico** (FEM **dinámica**) ADJECTIVE
dynamic

el **dinero** NOUN
money
□ No tengo más dinero. I haven't got any more money.
■ **una familia de dinero** a wealthy family
■ **andar mal de dinero** to be short of money
■ **dinero suelto** loose change

el **dinosaurio** NOUN
dinosaur

**dio** VERB ▷ see **dar**

**Dios** MASC NOUN
God
□ ¡Gracias a Dios! Thank God! □ ¡Dios mío! My God!
■ **¡Por Dios!** For God's sake!
■ **¡Si Dios quiere!** God willing!
■ **No vino ni Dios.** (colloquial) Nobody turned up.

el **dios** (PL los **dioses**) NOUN
god

la **diosa** NOUN
goddess (PL goddesses)

el **diploma** NOUN
diploma

la **diplomacia** NOUN
diplomacy

**diplomático** (FEM **diplomática**) ADJECTIVE
diplomatic

el **diplomático**, la **diplomática** NOUN
diplomat

el **diptongo** NOUN
dipthong

el **diputado**, la **diputada** NOUN
Member of Parliament

**dirá** VERB ▷ see **decir**

la **dirección** (PL las **direcciones**) NOUN
1 direction
□ Íbamos en dirección equivocada. We were going in the wrong direction.
■ **Tienes que ir en esta dirección.** You have to go this way.
■ **una calle de dirección única** a one-way street
■ **'dirección prohibida'** 'no entry'
■ **'todas direcciones'** 'all routes'
2 address (PL addresses)
□ Apúntame tu dirección aquí. Can you write your address down here for me?
3 management
□ la dirección de la empresa the management of the company □ Ha tomado la dirección del proyecto. He's taken over the management of the project.

**directo** (FEM **directa**) ADJECTIVE
1 direct

□ Hay un tren directo a Valencia. There's a direct train to Valencia. □ una pregunta directa a direct question
2 straight
□ Se fue directa a casa. She went straight home.
■ **transmitir en directo** to broadcast live

el **director**, la **directora** NOUN
1 manager
2 headteacher
3 director
4 conductor
5 editor

el **directorio** NOUN
1 directory (PL directories)
2 phone book (Latin America)
3 directory

el/la **dirigente** NOUN
1 leader
2 manager

**dirigir\*** VERB [16]
1 to manage
□ Dirige la empresa desde hace diez años. He has been managing the company for ten years.
2 to lead
□ Dirigirá la expedición. He'll be leading the expedition.
3 to aim at
□ Este anuncio va dirigido a los niños. This advertisement is aimed at children.
■ **no dirigir la palabra a alguien** not to speak to somebody
4 to direct
5 to conduct
■ **dirigirse a 1** to address □ El Rey se dirigió a la nación. The King addressed the nation. **2** to write to □ Me dirijo a ustedes para pedirles más información I am writing to you to ask you for more information. **3** to make one's way to □ Se dirigió a la terminal del aeropuerto. He made his way to the airport terminal.

**discapacitado** (FEM **discapacitada**) ADJECTIVE
disabled

**discar\*** VERB [48] (Latin America)
to dial

la **disciplina** NOUN
discipline

el **disco** NOUN
1 record
2 light
3 discus
■ **un disco compacto** a compact disc
■ **el disco duro** the hard disk

la **discoteca** NOUN
discotheque

107

la **discreción** NOUN
discretion
■ **Ha actuado con mucha discreción.**
He was very discreet.
**discreto** (FEM **discreta**) ADJECTIVE
discreet
□ No dirá nada porque es muy discreto.
He won't say anything because he's very
discreet.
■ **un color discreto** a sober colour
■ **un sueldo discreto** a modest salary
la **discriminación** NOUN
□ la discriminación racial racial
discrimination
la **disculpa** NOUN
■ **pedir disculpas a alguien por algo** to
apologize to somebody for something
**disculpar** VERB [25]
to excuse
□ Disculpa ¿me dejas pasar? Excuse me,
can I go past?
■ **disculparse** to apologize □ Se disculpó
por llegar tarde. He apologized for being
late.
el **discurso** NOUN
speech (PL speeches)
□ pronunciar un discurso to make a speech
la **discusión** (PL las **discusiones**) NOUN
discussion
□ El tema fue sometido a discusión. The
subject came up for discussion.
■ **tener una discusión con alguien** to have
an argument with somebody
**discutir** VERB [58]
1 to quarrel
□ Siempre discuten por dinero. They're
always quarrelling about money. □ He
discutido con mi hermana. I've quarrelled
with my sister.
■ **Discutió con su madre.** He had an
argument with his mother.
2 to discuss
□ Tenemos que discutir el nuevo proyecto.
We've got to discuss the new project.
**diseñar** VERB [25]
to design
el **diseño** NOUN
1 design
2 drawing (arte)
el **disfraz** (PL los **disfraces**) NOUN
1 disguise
□ Llevaba un disfraz para que no lo
reconocieran. He wore a disguise so as not
to be recognized.
2 costume
□ un disfraz de vaquero a cowboy costume
■ **una fiesta de disfraces** a fancy-dress
party

**disfrazarse*** VERB [13]
■ **disfrazarse de 1** to disguise oneself as
□ Se disfrazó de mujer para escapar. He
disguised himself as a woman in order to
escape. **2** to dress up as □ Su hija se
disfrazó de hada. His daughter dressed up
as a fairy.
**disfrutar** VERB [25]
to enjoy oneself
□ Disfruté mucho en la fiesta. I really
enjoyed myself at the party.
■ **Disfruto leyendo.** I enjoy reading.
■ **disfrutar de buena salud** to enjoy good
health
**disgustado** (FEM **disgustada**) ADJECTIVE
upset
**LANGUAGE TIP** Be careful! **disgustado**
does not mean **disgusted**.
**disgustar** VERB [25]
to upset
□ Me disgustó su tono. His tone upset me.
■ **disgustarse** to get upset □ Me disgusté
cuando descubrí que mentía. I got upset
when I found out he was lying.
■ **disgustarse con alguien** to fall out with
somebody
el **disgusto** NOUN
■ **dar un disgusto a alguien** to upset
somebody
■ **llevarse un disgusto** to get upset
■ **hacer algo a disgusto** to do something
unwillingly
■ **estar a disgusto** to be ill at ease
**disimular** VERB [25]
to hide
□ Intentó disimular su enfado. He tried to
hide his annoyance.
■ **No disimules, sé que has sido tú.** Don't
bother pretending, I know it was you.
la **disminución** (PL las **disminuciones**)
NOUN
fall
□ una disminución d en el número de robos
a fall in the number of thefts
el **disminuido**, la **disminuida** NOUN
■ **un disminuido mental** a mentally
handicapped person
■ **un disminuido físico** a physically
handicapped person
**disminuir*** VERB [10]
to fall
□ Ha disminuido el número de accidentes.
The number of accidents has fallen.
**disolver*** VERB [33]
1 to dissolve
2 to break up
■ **disolverse** to break up
**disparar** VERB [25]

to shoot

□ Le dispararon en la pierna. They shot him in the leg.

■ **disparar a alguien** to shoot at somebody

■ **Disparó dos tiros.** He fired two shots.

■ **dispararse 1** to go off **2** to shoot up

el **disparate** NOUN

silly thing

□ He hecho muchos disparates en mi vida. I've done a lot of silly things in my life.

■ **decir disparates** to talk nonsense

■ **¡Qué disparate!** How absurd!

el **disparo** NOUN

shot

**disponer*** VERB [41]

to arrange

□ Dispusieron las sillas en un círculo. They arranged the chairs in a circle.

■ **disponer de** to have □ Disponéis de diez minutos para leer las preguntas. You have ten minutes to read the questions.

■ **disponerse a hacer algo** to get ready to do something

**disponible** (FEM **disponible**) ADJECTIVE

available

□ El director no estará disponible hasta las 4. The manager won't be available until 4 o'clock.

**dispuesto** (FEM **dispuesta**) ADJECTIVE

**1** prepared

□ estar dispuesto a hacer algo to be prepared to do something

**2** ready

□ Todo está dispuesto para la fiesta. Everything's ready for the party.

la **disputa** NOUN

dispute

el **disquete** NOUN

diskette

la **distancia** NOUN

distance

■ **mantenerse a distancia** to keep at a distance

■ **¿Qué distancia hay entre Madrid y Barcelona?** How far is Madrid from Barcelona?

■ **¿A qué distancia está la estación?** How far's the station?

■ **a 20 kilómetros de distancia** 20 kilometres away

la **distinción** (PL las **distinciones**) NOUN

distinction

□ hacer una distinción entre ... to make a distinction between ...

■ **No hace distinciones entre sus alumnos.** He treats all his pupils the same.

**distinguido** (FEM **distinguida**) ADJECTIVE

distinguished

**distinguir*** VERB

**1** to distinguish

□ Resulta difícil distinguir el macho de la hembra. It's difficult to distinguish the male from the female.

■ **No distingue entre el rojo y el verde.** He can't tell the difference between red and green.

■ **No sé distinguir entre un coche u otro.** I can't tell one car from another.

■ **Se parecen tanto que no los distingo.** They're so alike that I can't tell them apart.

**2** to make out

□ No pude distinguirla entre tanta gente. I couldn't make her out amongst so many people.

■ **distinguirse** to stand out □ No le gusta distinguirse de los demás. He doesn't like to stand out.

**distinto** (FEM **distinta**) ADJECTIVE

different

□ Carlos es distinto a los demás. Carlos is different from other people.

■ **distintos** several □ distintas clases de coches several types of car

la **distracción** (PL las **distracciones**) NOUN

pastime

□ Coser es mi distracción favorita. My favourite pastime is sewing.

■ **En el pueblo hay pocas distracciones.** There isn't much to do in the village.

**distraer*** VERB [54]

**1** to keep...entertained

□ Les pondré un vídeo para distraerlos. I'll put a video on to keep them entertained.

**2** to distract

□ No me distraigas, que tengo trabajo. Don't distract me. I've got work to do.

■ **Me distrae mucho escuchar música.** I really enjoy listening to music.

■ **Me distraje un momento y me pasé de parada.** I let my mind wander for a minute and missed my stop.

**distraído** (FEM **distraída**) ADJECTIVE

absent-minded

□ Mi padre es muy distraído. My father is very absent-minded.

■ **Perdona, estaba distraído.** Sorry, I wasn't concentrating.

la **distribución** (PL las **distribuciones**) NOUN

**1** layout

□ la distribución de las habitaciones the layout of the rooms

**2** distribution

□ la distribución de la riqueza the distribution of wealth

**distribuir*** VERB [10]

**d**

to distribute
□ Ellos distribuyen nuestros productos en el extranjero. They distribute our products abroad.

**distribuyendo** VERB ▷ see **distribuir**

el **distrito** NOUN
district
□ un distrito postal a postal district
■ **un distrito electoral** a constituency

la **diversión** (PL las **diversiones**) NOUN
entertainment

◌ **LANGUAGE TIP** Be careful! **diversión** does not mean **diversion**.

**diverso** (FEM **diversa**) ADJECTIVE
different
□ Dieron explicaciones muy diversas del incidente. They gave very different explanations for the incident.
■ **diversos** various □ diversos libros various books

**divertido** (FEM **divertida**) ADJECTIVE
1 funny
2 enjoyable
■ **Fue muy divertido.** It was great fun.

**divertir*** VERB [51]
to entertain
□ Nos divirtió con sus anécdotas. He entertained us with his stories.
■ **divertirse** to have a good time

**dividir** VERB [58]
to divide
□ El libro está dividido en dos partes. The book is divided into two parts. □ Dividió sus tierras entre sus tres hijas. He divided his land between his three daughters. □ Divide cuatro entre dos. Divide four by two.
■ **dividirse 1** to divide □ Nos dividimos el trabajo entre los tres. We divided the work between the three of us. **2** to share □ Se dividieron el dinero de la lotería. They shared the lottery money.

**divierto** VERB ▷ see **divertir**

**divino** (FEM **divina**) ADJECTIVE
divine

la **división** (PL las **divisiones**) NOUN
division
□ en primera división in the first division
□ Ya sabe hacer divisiones. He already knows how to do division.

**divorciarse** VERB [25]
to get divorced
■ **Se ha divorciado de su mujer.** He has got divorced from his wife.

el **divorcio** NOUN
divorce

**divulgar*** VERB [37]
to spread
□ divulgar rumores to spread rumours

el **DNI** ABBREVIATION (= Documento Nacional de Identidad)
ID card

**doblar** VERB [25]
1 to double
□ Le han doblado el sueldo. They've doubled his salary.
2 to fold
□ Dobla los pañuelos y guárdalos. Fold the handkerchiefs and put them away.
3 to turn
□ Cuando llegues al cruce, dobla a la derecha. When you reach the junction, turn right.
4 to dub
□ Doblan todas las películas extranjeras. All foreign films are dubbed.
5 to toll
□ Las campanas de la iglesia estaban doblando. The church bells were tolling.

**doble** (FEM **doble**) ADJECTIVE
double
□ una frase con doble sentido an expression with a double meaning □ una habitación doble a double room

el **doble** NOUN
twice as much
□ Su sueldo es el doble del mío. His salary's twice as much as mine. □ Comes el doble que yo. You eat twice as much as I do.
■ **Trabaja el doble que tú.** He works twice as hard as you do.
■ **jugar un partido de dobles** to play doubles

**doce** (FEM **doce**) ADJECTIVE, PRONOUN
twelve
□ Tengo doce años. I'm twelve.
■ **Son las doce.** It's twelve o'clock.
■ **el siglo doce** the twelfth century

la **docena** NOUN
dozen

el **doctor**, la **doctora** NOUN
doctor

la **doctrina** NOUN
doctrine

el **documental** NOUN
documentary (PL documentaries)

el **documento** NOUN
document
□ un documento oficial an official document
■ **el documento nacional de identidad** the identity card
■ **un documento adjunto** an attachment

el **dólar** NOUN
dollar

**doler*** VERB [33]
to hurt

□ Me duele el brazo. My arm hurts. □ Esta inyección no duele. This injection won't hurt. □ Me dolió que me mintiera. I was hurt that he lied to me.
- **Me duele la cabeza.** I've got a headache.
- **Me duele el pecho.** I've got a pain in my chest.
- **Me duele la garganta.** I've got a sore throat.

el **dolor** NOUN
pain
□ Gritó de dolor. He cried out in pain.
- **Tengo dolor de cabeza.** I've got a headache.
- **Tengo dolor de estómago.** I've got stomach ache.
- **Tengo dolor de muelas.** I've got toothache.
- **Tengo dolor de oídos.** I've got earache.
- **Tengo dolor de garganta.** I've got a sore throat.

**doméstico** (FEM **doméstica**) ADJECTIVE
domestic
□ para uso doméstico for domestic use
- **las tareas domésticas** the housework
- **un animal doméstico** a pet

el **domicilio** NOUN
residence
□ su domicilio particular their private residence
- **servicio a domicilio** home delivery

**dominar** VERB [25]
1 to dominate
□ El padre dominaba totalmente a los hijos. The father totally dominated his children.
- **tener dominado a alguien** to have somebody at one's mercy
2 to control
□ No pudo dominar su mal genio. He couldn't control his temper.
3 to be fluent in
□ Mi hermana domina el inglés. My sister is fluent in English.
4 to bring under control
□ Los bomberos tardaron en dominar el incendio. The fire brigade took a long time to bring the fire under control.
- **dominarse** to control oneself

el **domingo** NOUN
Sunday
□ La vi el domingo. I saw her on Sunday. □ todos los domingos every Sunday □ el domingo pasado last Sunday □ el domingo que viene next Sunday □ Jugamos los domingos. We play on Sundays.

el **dominicano** (FEM la **dominicana**)
ADJECTIVE, NOUN
Dominican

el **dominio** NOUN
1 command
□ Tiene un gran dominio del inglés. He has a good command of English.
2 rule
□ Francia estuvo bajo el dominio romano. France was under Roman rule.
3 control
□ Ejerce un dominio absoluto sobre sus seguidores. He exercises absolute control over his followers.
- **dominio de sí mismo** self-control
- **ser del dominio público** to be public knowledge

el **dominó** NOUN
1 domino
2 dominoes *sing*
□ jugar al dominó to play dominoes

el **don** NOUN
gift
□ Tiene un don para la música. He has a gift for music.
- **tener don de gentes** to be good with people
- **don Juan Gómez** Mr Juan Gómez

　 DID YOU KNOW...?
　 cuando **don** va seguido sólo del nombre de pila, se traduce por **Mr** más el apellido.
- **Es un don nadie.** He's a nobody.

la **dona** NOUN *(Mexico)*
doughnut

el/la **donante** NOUN
donor
□ un donante de órganos an organ donor

el **donativo** NOUN
donation

**donde** ADVERB
where
□ La nota está donde la dejaste. The note's where you left it.

**dónde** ADVERB
where
□ ¿Dónde vas? Where are you going? □ Le pregunté dónde estaba la catedral. I asked him where the cathedral was. □ ¿Sabes dónde está? Do you know where he is?
- **¿De dónde eres?** Where are you from?
- **¿Por dónde se va al cine?** How do you get to the cinema?

la **doña** NOUN
- **doña Marta García** Mrs Marta García

　 DID YOU KNOW...?
　 cuando **doña** va seguido sólo del nombre de pila, se traduce por **Mrs** más el apellido.

**dorado** (FEM **dorada**) ADJECTIVE
golden

**d**

111

## dormir – duradero

**dormir\*** VERB [17]
to sleep
□ Antonio durmió 10 horas. Antonio slept for 10 hours.
■ **Se me ha dormido el brazo.** My arm has gone to sleep.
■ **dormir la siesta** to have a nap
■ **dormir como un tronco** to sleep like a log
■ **estar medio dormido** to be half asleep
■ **dormirse** to fall asleep

el **dormitorio** NOUN
1 bedroom
2 dormitory (PL dormitories)

el **dorso** NOUN
back
□ Se apuntó el teléfono en el dorso de la mano. He wrote the telephone number on the back of his hand.
■ **'véase al dorso'** 'see over'

**dos** ADJECTIVE, PRONOUN
1 two
□ ¿Tienes los dos libros que te dejé? Have you got the two books I lent you? □ Tiene dos años. He's two.
■ **Son las dos.** It's two o'clock.
■ **de dos en dos** in twos
■ **el dos de enero** the second of January
■ **cada dos por tres** every five minutes
2 both
□ Al final vinieron los dos. In the end they both came. □ Nos han suspendido a los dos. We have both failed. □ Mis dos hijos han emigrado. Both of my sons have emigrated. □ Los hemos invitado a los dos. We've invited both of them.

**doscientos** (FEM **doscientas**) ADJECTIVE, PRONOUN
two hundred
□ doscientos cincuenta two hundred and fifty

la **dosis** (PL las **dosis**) NOUN
dose

**doy** VERB ▷ see **dar**

el **dragón** (PL los **dragones**) NOUN
dragon

el **drama** NOUN
drama

**dramático** (FEM **dramática**) ADJECTIVE
dramatic

la **droga** NOUN
drug
□ las drogas blandas soft drugs □ las drogas duras hard drugs □ el problema de la droga the drug problem

el **drogadicto**, la **drogadicta** NOUN
drug addict

**drogar\*** VERB [37]

to drug
■ **drogarse** to take drugs

la **droguería** NOUN
DID YOU KNOW...?
This is a shop selling cleaning materials, paint and toiletries.

la **ducha** NOUN
shower
□ darse una ducha to have a shower

**ducharse** VERB [25]
to have a shower

la **duda** NOUN
doubt
■ **Tengo mis dudas.** I have my doubts.
■ **sin duda** no doubt
■ **sin duda alguna** without a doubt
■ **no cabe duda** there's no doubt about it
■ **Tengo una duda.** I have a query.
■ **poner algo en duda** to call something into question
■ **¿Alguna duda?** Any questions?

**dudar** VERB [25]
to doubt
□ Lo dudo. I doubt it.
■ **Dudo que sea cierto.** I doubt if it's true.
■ **Dudó si comprarlo o no.** He wasn't sure whether to buy it or not.

**dudoso** (FEM **dudosa**) ADJECTIVE
1 doubtful
□ Es dudoso que vengan. It's doubtful whether they'll come.
2 dubious
□ un chiste de dudoso gusto a joke in dubious taste

**duelo** VERB ▷ see **doler**

el **dueño**, la **dueña** NOUN
owner
■ **ser dueño de sí mismo** to have self-control

**duermo** VERB ▷ see **dormir**

el **Duero** NOUN
the Douro

**dulce** (FEM **dulce**) ADJECTIVE
1 sweet
2 gentle

el **dulce** NOUN
sweet

el **dúo** NOUN
duet
■ **cantar a dúo** to sing a duet

la **duración** NOUN
length
□ Depende de la duración de la película. It depends on the length of the film.
■ **una pila de larga duración** a long-life battery

**duradero** (FEM **duradera**) ADJECTIVE
1 lasting

**2** hard-wearing
**durante** ADVERB
during
□ Tuve que trabajar durante las vacaciones. He had to work during the holidays.
■ **durante toda la noche** all night long
■ **Habló durante una hora.** He spoke for an hour.
**durar** VERB [25]
to last
□ La película dura dos horas. The film lasts two hours. □ Sólo duró dos meses como director. He only lasted two months as manager. □ Todavía le dura el enfado. He's still angry.
el **durazno** NOUN (Latin America)
peach (PL peaches)
la **dureza** NOUN
**1** hardness
□ la dureza del acero the hardness of steel
**2** harshness
□ la dureza de sus palabras the harshness of his words
**3** callus (PL calluses)
□ Tiene una dureza en la planta del pie. He has a callus on the sole of his foot.

**durmiendo** VERB ▷ see **dormir**
**duro** (FEM **dura**) ADJECTIVE
▷ see also **duro** ADVERB, NOUN
**1** hard
□ Los diamantes son muy duros. Diamonds are very hard.
**2** tough
□ Esta carne está dura. This meat's tough.
**3** harsh
□ El clima es muy duro. The climate is very harsh.
■ **a duras penas** with great difficulty
■ **ser duro con alguien** to be hard on somebody
■ **ser duro de oído** to be hard of hearing
**duro** ADVERB
▷ see also **duro** ADJECTIVE, NOUN
hard
□ trabajar duro to work hard
el **duro** NOUN
▷ see also **duro** ADJECTIVE, ADVERB
five-peseta coin
■ **estar sin un duro** to be broke (colloquial)
el **DVD** ABBREVIATION (= Disco de Vídeo Digital)
DVD

# Ee

**e** CONJUNCTION

> **LANGUAGE TIP** e is used instead of **y** in front of words beginning with **i** and **hi**, but not **hie**.

and
□ Pablo e Inés. Pablo and Inés.

**echar** VERB [25]

1 to throw
□ Échame las llaves. Throw me the keys over.
■ **Eché la carta en el buzón.** I posted the letter.

2 to put
□ Tengo que echar gasolina. I need to put petrol in the car.
■ **¿Te echo más whisky?** Shall I pour you some more whisky?

3 to throw out
□ Me echó de su casa. He threw me out of the house.

4 to expel
□ Lo han echado del colegio. He's been expelled from school.
■ **La echaron del trabajo.** They sacked her.
■ **La chimenea echa humo.** Smoke is coming out of the chimney.
■ **¿Qué echan hoy en la tele?** What's on TV today?
■ **echar de menos a alguien** to miss somebody □ Echo de menos a mi familia. I miss my family.
■ **¿Cuántos años me echas?** How old do you think I am?
■ **echar una ojeada (a)** to browse
■ **echarse 1** to lie down □ Me eché en el sofá y me dormí. I lay down on the sofa and slept. **2** to jump □ Los niños se echaron al agua. The children jumped into the water.

**el eco** NOUN
echo (PL echoes)

**la ecología** NOUN
ecology

**ecológico** (FEM **ecológica**) ADJECTIVE
ecological
□ un desastre ecológico an ecological disaster

■ **un producto ecológico** an environmentally friendly product

**ecologista** (FEM **ecologista**) ADJECTIVE
environmental
□ un grupo ecologista an environmental group

**el/la ecologista** NOUN
environmentalist

**la economía** NOUN

1 economy (PL economies)
□ Un país de economía capitalista.
A country with a capitalist economy.

2 economics sing
□ Quiero estudiar economía. I want to study economics.

**económico** (FEM **económica**) ADJECTIVE

1 economic
□ una profunda crisis económica a deep economic crisis

2 economical
■ **un motor económico** an economical engine

3 inexpensive
□ Ese restaurante es muy económico.
That restaurant's very inexpensive.

**el/la economista** NOUN
economist

**economizar*** VERB [13]
to economize
□ Economiza en la comida para gastarlo en joyas. She economizes on food to spend money on jewels.

**Ecuador** MASC NOUN
Ecuador

**el ecuatoriano** (FEM la **ecuatoriana**)
ADJECTIVE, NOUN
Ecuadorean

**la edad** NOUN
age
□ Tenemos la misma edad. We're the same age.
■ **¿Qué edad tienen?** How old are they?
■ **No tiene edad para votar.** She isn't old enough to vote.
■ **Está en la edad del pavo.** She's at that difficult age.

la **edición** (PL las **ediciones**) NOUN
edition
□ una edición de bolsillo a pocket edition
**edificar*** VERB [48]
to build
□ Están edificando un centro deportivo.
They're building a sports centre.
el **edificio** NOUN
building
**Edimburgo** MASC NOUN
Edinburgh
**editar** VERB [25]
to publish
el **editor**, la **editora** NOUN
publisher
la **editorial** NOUN
publisher
el **edredón** (PL los **edredones**) NOUN
1 eiderdown
2 duvet
la **educación** NOUN
1 education
□ Han aumentado el presupuesto de
educación. They've increased the education
budget.
■ **educación física** PE
2 upbringing
□ Rosa recibió una educación muy estricta.
Rosa had a very strict upbringing.
■ **Señalar es de mala educación.** It's rude
to point.
■ **Se lo pedí con educación.** I asked her
politely.
■ **Es una falta de educación hablar con la
boca llena.** It's bad manners to speak with
your mouth full.
**educado** (FEM **educada**) ADJECTIVE
polite
■ **Me contestó de forma educada.** He
answered me politely.
■ **Es un chico bien educado.** He's a well-
mannered boy.
**educar*** VERB [48]
1 to educate
□ Se educó en un colegio alemán. He was
educated at a German school.
2 to bring up
□ Educaron a sus hijos de una manera muy
estricta. They brought their children up very
strictly.
**educativo** (FEM **educativa**) ADJECTIVE
educational
**EE.UU.** ABBREVIATION (= *Estados Unidos*)
USA
**efectivamente** ADVERB
□ Efectivamente, estaba donde tú decías.
You were right, he was where you said.
□ Entonces, ¿Es usted su padre? —

Efectivamente. So, are you his father? —
That's right.
**efectivo** (FEM **efectiva**) ADJECTIVE
effective
□ un medicamento muy efectivo a very
effective medicine
■ **pagar en efectivo** to pay in cash
el **efecto** NOUN
effect
■ **efectos especiales** special effects
■ **hacer efecto** to take effect □ La aspirina
enseguida me hizo efecto. The aspirin took
effect on me immediately.
■ **en efecto** indeed □ En efecto, fue como
tú dijiste. Indeed, it was just as you said.
■ **Devolvió la pelota con efecto.** He put
some spin on the ball.
**efectuar*** VERB [1]
to carry out
**eficaz** (FEM **eficaz**) ADJECTIVE
1 effective
□ un remedio eficaz an effective remedy
2 efficient
□ un funcionario eficaz an efficient civil
servant
**eficiente** (FEM **eficiente**) ADJECTIVE
efficient
el **egipcio** (FEM la **egipcia**) ADJECTIVE, NOUN
Egyptian
**Egipto** MASC NOUN
Egypt
el **egoísmo** NOUN
selfishness
**egoísta** (FEM **egoísta**) ADJECTIVE
selfish
el/la **egoísta** NOUN
□ María es una egoísta. Maria's very selfish.
**Eire** MASC NOUN
Eire
el **eje** NOUN
1 axle
2 axis
la **ejecución** (PL las **ejecuciones**) NOUN
execution
**ejecutar** VERB [25]
1 to carry out
□ Ejecutaron el proyecto según lo previsto.
They carried out the project according to
plan.
2 to execute
□ La ejecutaron al amanecer. They executed
her at dawn.
el **ejecutivo**, la **ejecutiva** NOUN
executive
el **ejemplar** NOUN
copy (PL copies)
el **ejemplo** NOUN
example

□ ¿Puedes ponerme un ejemplo? Can you give me an example?
■ **por ejemplo** for example
■ **Debes dar ejemplo a tu hermano pequeño.** You must set your younger brother an example.

**ejercer\*** VERB
■ **Ejerce de abogado.** He's a practising lawyer.
■ **Ejerce mucha influencia sobre sus hermanos.** He has a lot of influence on his brothers.

el **ejercicio** NOUN
exercise
□ La maestra nos puso varios ejercicios. The teacher gave us several exercises to do.
■ **hacer ejercicio** to exercise

el **ejército** NOUN
army (PL armies)

el **ejote** NOUN *(Mexico)*
green bean

**el** (FEM SING **la**, MASC PL **los**, FEM PL **las**) ARTICLE
the
□ Perdí el autobús. I missed the bus.
■ **el del sombrero rojo** the one with the red hat
■ **Yo fui el que lo encontró.** I was the one who found it. □ Ayer me lavé la cabeza. I washed my hair yesterday. □ Me puse el abrigo. I put my coat on. □ Tiene un coche bonito, pero prefiero el de Juan. He's got a nice car, but I prefer Juan's. □ No me gusta el pescado. I don't like fish. □ Vendrá el lunes que viene. He's coming next Monday. □ Ha llamado el Sr. Sendra. Mr Sendra called.

**él** PRONOUN
1 he
□ Me lo dijo él. He told me.
2 him
□ Se lo di a él. I gave it to him. □ Su mujer es más alta que él. His wife is taller than him.
■ **él mismo** himself □ No lo sabe ni él mismo. He doesn't even know himself.
■ **de él** his □ El coche es de él. The car's his.

**elaborar** VERB [25]
to produce

**elástico** (FEM **elástica**) ADJECTIVE
■ **un tejido elástico** a stretchy material
■ **una goma elástica** an elastic band

la **elección** (PL las **elecciones**) NOUN
1 election
□ Han convocado elecciones generales. General elections have been called.
2 choice
□ Ésa es una buena elección. That's a good choice. □ No tuve elección. I had no choice.

**electoral** (FEM **electoral**) ADJECTIVE
■ **la campaña electoral** the election campaign

la **electricidad** NOUN
electricity

el/la **electricista** NOUN
electrician
□ Mi primo es electricista. My cousin's an electrician.

**eléctrico** (FEM **eléctrica**) ADJECTIVE
1 electric
□ una guitarra eléctrica an electric guitar
2 electrical
□ a causa de un fallo eléctrico due to an electrical fault

el **electrodoméstico** NOUN
domestic appliance

la **electrónica** NOUN
electronics *sing*

**electrónico** (FEM **electrónica**) ADJECTIVE
electronic
■ **el correo electrónico** email

el **elefante** NOUN
elephant

**elegante** (FEM **elegante**) ADJECTIVE
smart

**elegir\*** VERB [18]
1 to choose
□ No sabía qué color elegir. I didn't know what colour to choose.
■ **Te dan a elegir entre dos modelos.** You're given a choice of two models.
2 to elect
□ Me eligieron delegado de curso. I was elected class representative.

el **elemento** NOUN
element

**elevado** (FEM **elevada**) ADJECTIVE
high

**elevar** VERB [25]
to raise

**eligiendo** VERB ▷ *see* **elegir**

**elijo** VERB ▷ *see* **elegir**

**eliminar** VERB [25]
1 to remove
□ un detergente que elimina las manchas a washing powder that removes the stains
2 to eliminate
□ Fueron eliminados de la competición. They were eliminated from the competition.

el **elixir bucal** NOUN
mouthwash

**ella** PRONOUN
1 she
□ Ella no estaba en casa. She was not at home.
2 her

□ El regalo es para ella. The present's for her. □ Él estaba más nervioso que ella. He was more nervous than her.

■ **ella misma** herself □ Me lo dijo ella misma. She told me herself.

■ **de ella** hers □ Este abrigo es de ella. This coat's hers.

**ellos** (FEM **ellas**) PL PRONOUN

**1** they
□ Ellos todavía no lo saben. They don't know yet.

**2** them
□ Yo me iré con ellas. I'll leave with them. □ Somos mejores que ellos. We're better than them.

■ **ellos mismos** themselves □ Me lo dijeron ellos mismos. They told me themselves.

■ **de ellos** theirs □ El coche era de ellos. The car was theirs.

**elogiar** VERB [25]
to praise

el **elote** NOUN (Mexico)

**1** corncob

**2** sweetcorn

**e-mail** NOUN

**1** email

**2** email address (PL email addresses)

la **embajada** NOUN
embassy (PL embassies)

el **embajador**, la **embajadora** NOUN
ambassador

**embalar** VERB [25]
to pack

el **embalse** NOUN
reservoir

**embarazada** (FEM **embarazada**) ADJECTIVE
pregnant
□ Estaba embarazada de cuatro meses. She was four months pregnant.

■ **quedarse embarazada** to get pregnant

　LANGUAGE TIP Be careful!
　**embarazada** does not mean
　embarrassed.

**embarazoso** (FEM **embarazosa**) ADJECTIVE
embarrassing

**embarcar*** VERB [48]
to board
□ Los pasajeros ya estaban embarcando. The passengers were already boarding.

el **embargo** NOUN
embargo

■ **sin embargo** nevertheless

**embobado** (FEM **embobada**) ADJECTIVE

■ **Se quedaron mirándola embobados.** They watched her in fascination.

■ **Está embobado con su novia.** His girlfriend has got him under her spell.

**emborracharse** VERB [25]

to get drunk

**embotellado** (FEM **embotellada**) ADJECTIVE
bottled

el **embotellamiento** NOUN
traffic jam

el **embrague** NOUN
clutch

**embrollarse** VERB [25]

**1** to get tangled up
□ Las cuerdas se embrollaron. The ropes got tangled up.

**2** to get muddled up
□ Me embrollé con tanta información. With so much information, I got muddled up.

el **embrollo** NOUN
tangle

**embrujado** (FEM **embrujada**) ADJECTIVE
haunted
□ una casa embrujada a haunted house

el **embudo** NOUN
spout

el **embustero**, la **embustera** NOUN
fibber

el **embutido** NOUN
cold meats
□ No comemos mucho embutido. We don't eat a lot of cold meats.

la **emergencia** NOUN
emergency (PL emergencies)

■ **la salida de emergencia** the emergency exit

■ **en caso de emergencia** in case of emergency

**emigrar** VERB [25]

**1** to emigrate

**2** to migrate

la **emisión** (PL las **emisiones**) NOUN

**1** broadcast

**2** emission

**emitir** VERB [58]

**1** to broadcast

**2** to give off

la **emoción** (PL las **emociones**) NOUN
emotion
□ Me temblaba la voz de emoción. My voice was trembling with emotion.

■ **Su carta me produjo gran emoción.** I was very moved by his letter.

■ **¡Qué emoción!** How exciting!

**emocionado** (FEM **emocionada**) ADJECTIVE

**1** moved

**2** excited

**emocionante** (FEM **emocionante**)
ADJECTIVE

**1** moving
□ La despedida fue muy emocionante. The farewell was very moving.

**2** exciting

□ El partido fue muy emocionante. The match was very exciting.

**emocionarse** VERB

to be moved

□ Me emocioné mucho con la película. I was very moved by the film.

■ **Se emocionó al volver a ver a su padre.** She got emotional when she saw her father again.

**emotivo** (FEM **emotiva**) ADJECTIVE

1 moving

2 emotional

□ La vuelta a casa fue muy emotiva. It was a very emotional homecoming.

**empacharse** VERB [25]

to get a tummy upset

□ Me empaché por comer tanto chocolate. I got a tummy upset through eating so much chocolate.

**empalagoso** (FEM **empalagosa**) ADJECTIVE

sickly

**empalmar** VERB [25]

1 to connect

□ Empalma los dos cables. Connect the two wires.

2 to join

□ Esta carretera empalma con la autopista. This road joins the motorway.

la **empanada** NOUN

pasty (PL pasties)

**empañarse** VERB [25]

to get steamed up

□ Se me empañaron las gafas al entrar en el museo. My glasses got steamed up when I went into the museum.

■ **Los cristales del dormitorio estaban empañados.** There was condensation on the bedroom windows.

**empapar** VERB [25]

to soak

□ Cierra la ducha que me estás empapando. Can you turn the shower off, you're soaking me.

■ **Se me empaparon los calcetines.** My socks got soaked.

■ **estar empapado hasta los huesos** to be soaked to the skin

**empapelar** VERB [25]

to paper

**empaquetar** VERB [25]

to pack

□ Empaqueta todos tus libros. Pack all your books.

el **emparedado** NOUN (Latin America)

sandwich (PL sandwiches)

**emparejar** VERB [25]

to pair up (objetos, personas)

**empastar** VERB [25]

■ **Me han empastado dos muelas.** I've had two fillings.

el **empaste** NOUN

filling

**empatar** VERB [25]

to draw

□ Empatamos a uno. We drew one-all.

□ Los dos candidatos empataron en la votación. The two candidates got the same number of votes.

el **empate** NOUN

1 draw

□ un empate a cero a goalless draw

2 tie

**empedernido** (FEM **empedernida**) ADJECTIVE

■ **un fumador empedernido** a chronic smoker

■ **Es un lector empedernido.** He's a compulsive reader.

**empeñado** (FEM **empeñada**) ADJECTIVE

determined

□ Está empeñado en aprobar el curso. He's determined to get through the course.

■ **Está empeñada en que yo soy mayor que ella.** She insists that I'm older than she is.

**empeñarse** VERB [25]

■ **empeñarse en hacer algo** 1 to be determined to do something □ Se había empeñado en irse con él. She was determined to go with him. 2 to insist on doing something □ Se empeñó en que nos quedáramos a cenar. He insisted that we should stay for dinner.

**empeorar** VERB [25]

1 to get worse

□ Empeoró tras la operación. He got worse after the operation.

2 to make...worse

□ Tu comentario sólo emperorará las cosas. Your comment will only make matters worse.

**empezar*** VERB [19]

to start

□ Las vacaciones empiezan el día 1. The holidays start on the first.

■ **empezar a hacer algo** to start doing something □ Ha empezado a nevar. It's started snowing.

■ **volver a empezar** to start again

**empinado** (FEM **empinada**) ADJECTIVE

steep

el **empleado**, la **empleada** NOUN

1 employee

2 shop assistant (Latin America)

■ **una empleada del hogar** a servant

**emplear** VERB [25]

**1** to use
□ Puedes emplear cualquier jabón. You can use any soap.

**2** to employ
□ La fábrica emplea a veinte trabajadores. The factory employs twenty workers.
■ **Le está bien empleado.** It serves her right.

**el empleo** NOUN
job
□ Ha encontrado empleo en un restaurante. He has found a job in a restaurant.
■ **estar sin empleo** to be unemployed
■ **'modo de empleo'** 'how to use'

**empollar** VERB [25]
to swot
□ Me pasé la noche empollando. I spent the whole night swotting.

**el empollón** la **empollona** (MASC PL los **empollones** NOUN
swot

**la empresa** NOUN
firm
□ Trabaja en una empresa de informática. He works in a computer firm.

**la empresaria** NOUN
businesswoman (PL businesswomen)

**el empresario** NOUN
businessman (PL businessmen)

**empujar** VERB [25]
to push
□ Tuvimos que empujarle al coche. We had to push the car.

**el empujón** (PL los **empujones** NOUN
□ Me dieron un empujón y me caí. They pushed me and I fell.
■ **abrirse paso a empujones** to shove one's way through

**en** PREPOSITION

**1** in
□ en el armario in the wardrobe □ Viven en Granada. They live in Granada. □ Nació en invierno. He was born in winter. □ Lo hice en dos días. I did it in two days. □ Hablamos en inglés. We speak in English. □ Está en el hospital. She's in hospital.

**2** into
□ Entré en el banco. I went into the bank. □ Me metí en la cama a las diez. I got into bed at ten o'clock.

**3** on
□ Las llaves están en la mesa. The keys are on the table. □ Lo encontré tirado en el suelo. I found it lying on the floor. □ La librería está en la calle Pelayo. The bookshop is on Pelayo street. □ La oficina está en el quinto piso. The office is on the fifth floor.

■ **Mi cumpleaños cae en viernes.** My birthday falls on a Friday.

**4** at
□ Yo estaba en casa. I was at home. □ Te veo en el cine. See you at the cinema. □ Vivía en el número 17. I was living at number 17. □ en ese momento at that moment □ en Navidades at Christmas

**5** by
□ Vinimos en avión. We came by plane.
■ **ser el primero en llegar** to be the first to arrive

**enamorado** (FEM **enamorada** ADJECTIVE
■ **estar enamorado de alguien** to be in love with somebody

**enamorarse** VERB [25]
to fall in love
□ Se ha enamorado de Yolanda. He's fallen in love with Yolanda. □ Se enamoraron nada más verse. They fell in love at first sight.

**el enano** la **enana** NOUN
dwarf (PL dwarves)

**encabezar*** VERB [13]
to head
□ El Betis encabeza la clasificación de la liga. Betis are heading the League. □ la cita que encabeza el artículo the quote heading the article

**encajar** VERB

**1** to fit
□ Las piezas no encajan. The pieces don't fit.

**2** to cope with
□ Ha encajado muy bien la muerte de su madre. She's coped very well with her mother's death.

**encaminarse** VERB [25]
■ **Nos encaminamos hacia el pueblo.** We headed towards the village.

**encantado** (FEM **encantada** ADJECTIVE

**1** delighted
□ Está encantada con su nuevo coche. She's delighted with her new car.

**2** enchanted
□ un castillo encantado an enchanted castle
■ **¡Encantado de conocerle!** Pleased to meet you!

**encantador** (FEM **encantadora** ADJECTIVE
charming

**encantar** VERB [25]
to love
□ Me encantan los animales. I love animals. □ Les encanta esquiar. They love skiing. □ Me encantaría que vinieras. I'd love you to come.

**el encanto** NOUN
charm

■ **Eugenia es un encanto.** Eugenia is charming.

**encarcelar** VERB [25]
to imprison

el **encargado**, la **encargada** NOUN
manager
□ Quiero hablar con el encargado. I'd like to talk to the manager.

**encargar*** VERB [37]
1 to order
□ Encargamos dos pizzas. We ordered two pizzas.
2 to ask
□ Le encargó que le recogiera los documentos. She asked him to fetch the documents for her.
■ **Yo me encargaré de avisar a los demás.** I'll take care of letting the others know.
■ **Estoy encargada de vender las entradas.** I'm in charge of selling the tickets.

**encariñarse** VERB [25]
■ **encariñarse con** to grow fond of

el **encendedor** NOUN
lighter

**encender*** VERB [20]
1 to light
2 to switch on

**encendido** (FEM **encendida**) ADJECTIVE
1 on
□ La tele estaba encendida. The telly was on.
2 lit
□ El cigarro no está bien encendido. Your cigarette isn't properly lit.

el **encerado** NOUN
blackboard

**encerrar*** VERB [39]
1 to shut up
□ Encerré el gato en la cocina. I shut the cat up in the kitchen. □ Me encerré en mi cuarto para estudiar. I shut myself up in my room to study.
2 to lock up
□ Lo encerraron en un calabozo. They locked him up in a cell.
■ **Los manifestantes se encerraron en el ayuntamiento.** The demonstrators held a sit-in in the town hall.

la **enchilada** NOUN (Mexico)
stuffed tortilla

el **enchufado**, la **enchufada** NOUN
■ **Amelia es la enchufada del profesor.** (colloquial) Amelia's the teacher's pet.

**enchufar** VERB [25]
to plug in
□ Enchufa la tele. Plug the TV in.

el **enchufe** NOUN

1 plug
2 socket
■ **Consiguió ese puesto por enchufe.** He got that job through pulling strings.

la **encía** NOUN
gum

la **enciclopedia** NOUN
encyclopaedia

**enciendo** VERB ▷ see **encender**

**encierro** VERB ▷ see **encerrar**

**encima** ADVERB
on
□ Pon el cenicero aquí encima. Put the ashtray on there. □ No llevo dinero encima. I haven't got any money on me.
■ **encima de 1** on □ Ponlo encima de la mesa. Put it on the table. **2** on top of □ Mi maleta está encima del armario. My case is on top of the wardrobe.
■ **Lo leí por encima.** I glanced at it.
■ **por encima de 1** above □ Los helicópteros volaban por encima de nuestras cabezas. The helicopters were flying above our heads. □ Las temperaturas han subido por encima de lo normal. Temperatures have been above average. **2** over □ Tuve que saltar por encima de la mesa. I had to jump over the table.
■ **¡Y encima no te da ni las gracias!** And on top of it he doesn't even thank you!

la **encina** NOUN
oak tree

**encoger*** VERB [7]
to shrink
□ Este jersey ha encogido. This jumper has shrunk.
■ **Antonio se encogió de hombros.** Antonio shrugged his shoulders.

**encontrar*** VERB [11]
to find
□ Mi hermano ha encontrado trabajo. My brother has found a job. □ Lo encuentro un poco arrogante. I find him a bit arrogant.
■ **No encuentro las llaves.** I can't find the keys.
■ **encontrarse 1** to feel □ Ahora se encuentra mejor. Now she's feeling better. **2** to meet □ Nos encontramos en el cine. We met at the cinema.
■ **Me encontré con Manolo en la calle.** I bumped into Manolo in the street.

el **encuentro** NOUN
1 meeting
■ **punto de encuentro** meeting point
2 match (PL matches)

la **encuesta** NOUN
survey

**enderezar*** VERB [13]

to straigthen

**endulzar\*** VERB [13]
to sweeten

**endurecer\*** VERB [12]
to tone up

el **enemigo** (FEM la **enemiga**) ADJECTIVE, NOUN
enemy (PL enemies)
□ el ejército enemigo the enemy army

**enemistarse** VERB [25]
to fall out
□ Se enemistó con sus primos. He fell out
with his cousins.

la **energía** NOUN
energy
□ ahorrar energía to save energy
■ **la energía solar** solar power
■ **la energía eléctrica** electricity

**enérgico** (FEM **enérgica**) ADJECTIVE
energetic
□ Es una persona muy enérgica. She's very
energetic.

**enero** MASC NOUN
January
□ en enero in January □ Nació el 6 de enero.
He was born on 6 January.

**enfadado** (FEM **enfadada**) ADJECTIVE
angry
□ Mi padre estaba muy enfadado conmigo.
My father was very angry with me.
■ **Ana y su novio están enfadados.** Ana
and her boyfriend have fallen out.

**enfadarse** VERB [25]
to be angry
□ Papá se va a enfadar mucho contigo. Dad
will be very angry with you.
■ **Mi hermana y su novio se han
enfadado.** My brother and his girlfriend
have fallen out.

el **enfado** NOUN
■ **Ya se le ha pasado el enfado.** He isn't
angry anymore.

**enfermarse** VERB [25] (*Latin America*)
to fall ill

la **enfermedad** NOUN
1 illness (PL illnesses)
□ Adelgazó mucho durante su enfermedad.
He lost a lot of weight during his illness.
2 disease
□ Tiene una enfermedad contagiosa. He's
got an infectious disease.

la **enfermería** NOUN
sick bay

el **enfermero**, la **enfermera** NOUN
nurse
□ Mi madre es enfermera. My mother's a
nurse.

**enfermo** (FEM **enferma**) ADJECTIVE
ill

□ He estado enferma toda la semana. I've
been ill all week.
■ **¿Cuándo te pusiste enfermo?** When did
you get ill?
■ **¡Me pones enfermo!** You make me sick!

el **enfermo**, la **enferma** NOUN
patient
■ **Los enfermos deben tomar
precauciones especiales.** Sick people
need to take special precautions.

**enfocar\*** VERB [48]
1 to focus on
□ El fotógrafo enfocó el ciervo. The
photographer focussed on the deer.
2 to approach
□ Depende de cómo enfoques el problema.
It depends on how you approach the
problem.

**enfrentarse** VERB [25]
■ **enfrentarse a algo** to face something
□ Tienes que enfrentarte al problema. You
have to face the problem.

**enfrente** ADVERB
opposite
□ Luisa estaba sentada enfrente. Luisa was
sitting opposite.
■ **La panadería está enfrente.** The baker's
is across the street.
■ **de enfrente** opposite □ la casa de
enfrente the house opposite
■ **enfrente de** opposite □ Mi casa está
enfrente del colegio. My house is opposite
the school.

**enfriarse\*** VERB [21]
1 to get cold
□ La sopa se ha enfriado. The soup has got
cold.
2 to cool down
□ Hay que dejar que se enfríe el motor. We
must let the engine cool down.
3 to catch cold
□ Ponte el abrigo que te vas a enfriar. Put
your coat on or you'll catch cold.

**enganchar** VERB [25]
to hook
□ Enganché la correa al collar del perro.
I hooked the lead onto the dog's collar.
■ **engancharse** to get caught □ Se me
enganchó el jersey en la valla. My jumper
got caught on a rosebush.

**engañar** VERB [25]
1 to cheat
□ Te han engañado: no es de oro. You've
been cheated. It's not gold.
2 to lie
□ No me engañes y dime quién lo hizo.
Don't lie to me and tell me who did it.
3 to cheat on

□ Su novio la engaña. Her boyfriend is cheating on her.

■ **Las apariencias engañan.** Appearances can be deceptive.

el **engaño** NOUN

**1** con

□ Fue un engaño. It was a con.

**2** deception

□ Carmen siguió manteniendo el engaño. Carmen continued to keep up the deception.

**engordar** VERB [25]

**1** to put on weight

□ No quiero engordar. I don't want to put on weight.

■ **He engordado dos kilos.** I've put on two kilos.

**2** to be fattening

□ Los caramelos engordan mucho. Sweets are very fattening.

**engreído** (FEM **engreída** ADJECTIVE

conceited

la **enhorabuena** NOUN

■ **¡Enhorabuena!** Congratulations!

■ **Me dieron la enhorabuena por el premio.** They congratulated me on winning the prize.

el **enlace** NOUN

**1** connection

■ **Perdí el enlace con Buenos Aires.** I missed the connecting flight to Buenos Aires.

**2** link

**enlatado** (FEM **enlatada** ADJECTIVE

tinned

**enlazar*** VERB [13]

to connect

□ Este vuelo enlaza con el de Moscú. This flight connects with the Moscow flight.

**enloquecer*** VERB

to be crazy about

□ Le enloquecen las motos. He's crazy about motorbikes.

**enmarcar*** VERB [48]

to frame

**enmoquetado** (FEM **enmoquetada** ADJECTIVE

carpeted

**enojado** (FEM **enojada** ADJECTIVE

angry

□ Mi padre estaba muy enojado conmigo. My father was very angry with me.

■ **Ana y su novio están enojados.** Ana and her boyfriend have fallen out.

**enojarse** VERB

to be angry

□ Mi madre se va a enojar. My mother will be angry. □ Manolo y Luis se han enojado. Manolo and Luis have fallen out.

**enorme** (FEM **enorme** ADJECTIVE

enormous

□ Tienen una casa enorme. They have an enormous house.

la **enredadera** NOUN

creeper

**enredarse** VERB [25]

**1** to get tangled up

□ Se me ha enredado el pelo. My hair's got all tangled up.

**2** to get into a tangle

□ Me enredé haciendo las cuentas. I got into a tangle with the accounts.

**enrevesado** (FEM **enrevesada** ADJECTIVE

difficult

**enriquecerse*** VERB [12]

to get rich

□ Se enriquecieron tratando con armas. They got rich dealing in arms.

**enrollar** VERB [25]

to roll up

□ No dobles el póster, enróllalo. Don't fold the poster, roll it up. □ Enrolla la cuerda en este palo. Roll the rope round the stick.

■ **Se enrolló con Juan en la discoteca.** (colloquial) She got off with Juan in the disco.

**enroscar*** VERB [48]

**1** to screw in

■ **Enrosca bien la tapa.** Screw the top on tight.

**2** to coil

□ La manguera se le enroscó en la pierna. The hose coiled round his leg.

la **ensalada** NOUN

salad

la **ensaladilla** NOUN

■ **una ensaladilla rusa** a Russian salad

**ensanchar** VERB [25]

to widen

□ Están ensanchando la carretera. They're widening the road.

■ **ensancharse** to stretch □ Mi jersey se ha ensanchado. My jumper has stretched.

**ensayar** VERB [25]

to rehearse

el **ensayo** NOUN

rehearsal

□ Esta tarde tenemos ensayo. We've got a rehearsal this afternoon.

**enseguida** ADVERB

straight away

□ La ambulancia llegó enseguida. The ambulance arrived straight away.

■ **Enseguida te atiendo.** I'll be with you in a minute.

la **enseñanza** NOUN

**1** teaching

□ la enseñanza de lenguas extranjeras the teaching of foreign languages

**2** education

□ Debería invertirse más dinero en la enseñanza. More money should be invested in education.

■ **la enseñanza primaria** primary education

**enseñar** VERB [25]

**1** to teach

□ Ricardo enseña inglés en un colegio. Ricardo teaches English in a school. □ Mi padre me enseñó a nadar. My father taught me to swim.

**2** to show

□ Ana me enseñó todos sus videojuegos. Ana showed me all her video games.

■ **Les enseñé el colegio.** I showed them round the school.

**ensuciar** VERB [25]

to get...dirty

□ Vas a ensuciar el sofá. You'll get the sofa dirty.

■ **ensuciarse** to get dirty □ No toques la pintura que te vas a ensuciar. Don't touch the paint or you'll get dirty. □ Me he ensuciado las manos. I've got my hands dirty.

■ **Te has ensuciado de barro los pantalones.** You've got mud on your trousers.

**entender*** VERB [20]

to understand

□ No entiendo el francés. I don't understand French. □ ¿Lo entiendes? Do you understand?

■ **¿Entiendes lo que quiero decir?** Do you know what I mean?

■ **Creo que lo he entendido mal.** I think I've misunderstood.

■ **Mi primo entiende mucho de coches.** My cousin knows a lot about cars.

■ **entenderse 1** to get on □ Mi hermana y yo no nos entendemos. My sister and I don't get on. **2** to communicate □ Se entienden por gestos. They communicate through sign language.

■ **Dio a entender que no le gustaba.** He implied that he didn't like it.

el **entendido**, la **entendida** NOUN

expert

□ No soy un entendido en el tema. I'm not an expert on the subject.

**enterarse** VERB [25]

**1** to find out

□ Me enteré por Manolo. I found out from Manolo. □ Entérate bien de todos los detalles. Make sure you find out about all

the details.

■ **Se enteraron del accidente por la tele.** They heard about the accident on the TV.

■ **Me sacaron una muela y ni me enteré.** They took out a tooth and I didn't notice a thing.

**2** to understand

□ No me hables en francés que no me entero. Don't talk to me in French – I won't understand.

**entero** (FEM **entera**) ADJECTIVE

whole

□ Se comió el paquete entero de galletas. He ate the whole packet of biscuits. □ Se pasó la noche entera estudiando. He spent the whole night studying.

■ **la leche entera** full-cream milk

**enterrar*** VERB [39]

to bury

**entiendo** VERB ▷ see **entender**

**entierro** VERB ▷ see **enterrar**

el **entierro** NOUN

funeral

**entonces** ADVERB

**1** then

□ Si no es tu padre, ¿entonces quién es? If he isn't your father, then who is he? □ Me recogió y entonces fuimos al cine. He picked me up and then we went to the cinema. □ Iban andando porque entonces no tenían coche. They would walk because they didn't have a car then.

**2** so

□ ¿Entonces, vienes o te quedas? So, are you coming or staying?

■ **desde entonces** since then

■ **para entonces** by then

el **entorno** NOUN

surroundings pl

la **entrada** NOUN

**1** entrance

□ Nos vemos en la entrada. I'll see you at the entrance.

■ **'entrada libre'** 'free admission'

**2** ticket

□ Tengo entradas para el teatro. I've got tickets for the theatre.

**3** entry (PL entries)

□ la entrada de España en el conflicto Spain's entry into the conflict

■ **'prohibida la entrada'** 'no entry'

**4** deposit

□ Dimos una entrada de diez mil euros. We paid a ten-thousand-euro deposit.

el **entrante** NOUN

starter

**entrar** VERB [25]

**1** to go in

## entre – envase

□ **Abrí la puerta y entré.** I opened the door and went in. □ **Mi amiga entró al banco.** My friend went into the bank.

■ **Pedro entra a trabajar a las 8.** Pedro starts work at 8 o'clock.

■ **No me dejaron entrar por ser menor de 16 años.** They wouldn't let me in because I was under 16.

**2** to come in
□ **¿Se puede? — Sí, entra.** May I? — Yes, come in. □ **Entraron en mi cuarto mientras yo dormía.** They came into my room while I was asleep.

**3** to fit
□ **Estos zapatos no me entran.** These shoes don't fit me. □ **La maleta no entra en el maletero.** The case won't fit in the boot.

■ **El vino no entra en el precio.** The wine is not included in the price.

■ **Le entraron ganas de reír.** She wanted to laugh.

■ **De repente le entró sueño.** He suddenly felt sleepy.

■ **Me ha entrado hambre al verte comer.** Watching you eat has made me hungry.

**entre** PREPOSITION

**1** between
□ **Lo terminamos entre los dos.** Between the two of us we finished it. □ **Vendrá entre las diez y las once.** He'll be coming between ten and eleven.

**2** among
□ **Había un baúl entre las maletas.** There was a trunk in among the cases. □ **Las mujeres hablaban entre sí.** The women were talking among themselves.

■ **Le compraremos un regalo entre todos.** We'll buy her a present between all of us.

**3** by
□ **15 dividido entre 3 es 5.** 15 divided by 3 is 5.

**entreabierto** (FEM **entreabierta**) ADJECTIVE
ajar

**entregar*** VERB [37]

**1** to hand in
□ **Marta entregó el examen.** Marta handed her exam paper in.

**2** to deliver
□ **El cartero entregó el paquete.** The postman delivered the parcel.

**3** to present with
□ **El director le entregó la medalla.** The director presented him with the medal.

■ **El ladrón se entregó a la policía.** The thief gave himself up.

**los entremeses** NOUN
appetizers

**el entrenador**, **la entrenadora** NOUN

coach (PL coaches)

**el entrenamiento** NOUN
training

**entretanto** ADVERB
meanwhile

**entrenarse** VERB [25]
to train

**entretener*** VERB [53]

**1** to entertain
■ **La tele entretiene mucho.** TV is very entertaining.

**2** to keep
□ **Una vecina me entretuvo hablando en las escaleras.** A neighbour kept me talking on the stairs.

■ **entretenerse** to amuse oneself □ **Se entretienen viendo los dibujos animados.** They amuse themselves by watching cartoons.

■ **No os entretengáis jugando.** Don't hang about playing.

**entretenido** (FEM **entretenida**) ADJECTIVE
entertaining
□ **La película es muy entretenida.** The film is very entertaining.

**la entrevista** NOUN
interview
■ **hacer una entrevista a alguien** to interview somebody □ **Le hicieron una entrevista por la radio.** They interviewed her on the radio.

**el entrevistador**, **la entrevistadora**
NOUN
interviewer

**entrevistar** VERB [25]
to interview

**entrometerse** VERB [8]
to meddle
□ **No te entrometas en mis asuntos.** Don't meddle in my affairs.

**entusiasmado** (FEM **entusiasmada**)
ADJECTIVE
excited
□ **Estaba entusiasmado con su fiesta de cumpleaños.** He was excited about his birthday party.

**entusiasmarse** VERB [25]
to get excited
□ **Se entusiasmó con la idea de hacer una fiesta.** He got very excited about the idea of having a party.

**el entusiasmo** NOUN
enthusiasm
■ **con entusiasmo** enthusiastically

**enumerar** VERB [25]
to list

**el envase** NOUN
container

□ Viene en envases de plástico. It comes in a plastic container.
■ **'envase no retornable'** 'non-returnable bottle'

**envejecer*** VERB [12]
to age
□ Sus padres han envejecido mucho. His parents have aged a lot.

**enviar*** VERB [21]
to send
□ Envíame las fotos. Send me the photos.
■ **Juan me envió el regalo por correo.** Juan posted me the present.

la **envidia** NOUN
envy
■ **¡Qué envidia!** I'm so jealous!
■ **Le tiene envidia a Ana.** She's jealous of Ana.
■ **Le da envidia que mi coche sea mejor.** He's jealous that my car is better.

**envidiar** VERB [25]
to envy
□ ¡No te envidio! I don't envy you!

**envidioso** (FEM **envidiosa**) ADJECTIVE
envious

**envolver*** VERB [59]
to wrap up
□ Llevaba al niño envuelto en una manta. She carried the baby wrapped up in a blanket.
■ **¿Desea que se lo envuelva para regalo?** Would you like it gift-wrapped?

**envuelto** VERB ▷ see **envolver**

la **epidemia** NOUN
epidemic

el **episodio** NOUN
episode

la **época** NOUN
time
□ En aquella época vivíamos en Alicante. At that time we were living in Alicante. □ en esta época del año at this time of year

**equilibrado** (FEM **equilibrada**) ADJECTIVE
balanced

el **equilibrio** NOUN
balance
□ Perdí el equilibrio y me caí. I lost my balance and fell over. □ Luis podía mantener el equilibrio en la cuerda floja. Luis managed to keep his balance on the tightrope.

el **equipaje** NOUN
luggage
■ **equipaje de mano** hand luggage

el **equipo** NOUN
1 team
□ un equipo de baloncesto a basketball team

2 equipment
□ Me robaron todo el equipo de esquí. They stole all my skiing equipment.
■ **el equipo de música** the stereo
○ **LANGUAGE TIP** Word for word, **equipo de música** means 'music equipment'.

la **equitación** NOUN
riding

**equivaler*** VERB [55]
■ **equivaler a algo** to be equivalent to something

la **equivocación** (PL las **equivocaciones**) NOUN
mistake
■ **He marcado otro número por equivocación.** I dialled another number by mistake.

**equivocado** (FEM **equivocada**) ADJECTIVE
wrong
□ Estás equivocada. You're wrong. □ Elena me dio el número equivocado. Elena gave me the wrong number.

**equivocarse*** VERB [48]
1 to make a mistake
□ Me equivoqué muchas veces en el examen. I made a lot of mistakes in the exam.
2 to be wrong
□ Si crees que voy a dejarte ir, te equivocas. If you think I'm going to let you go, you're wrong.
■ **Perdone, me he equivocado de número.** Sorry, wrong number.
■ **Se equivocaron de tren.** They caught the wrong train.

**era** VERB ▷ see **ser**

**eres** VERB ▷ see **ser**

el **erizo** NOUN
hedgehog
■ **un erizo de mar** a sea urchin

el **error** NOUN
mistake
□ Fue un error contárselo a Luisa. Telling Luisa about it was a mistake. □ Cometí muchos errores en el examen. I made a lot of mistakes in the exam.

**eructar** VERB [25]
to burp

el **eructo** NOUN
burp

**es** VERB ▷ see **ser**

**esa** ADJECTIVE ▷ see **ese**

**ésa** PRONOUN ▷ see **ése**

**esbelto** (FEM **esbelta**) ADJECTIVE
slender

**escabullirse*** VERB
1 to slip away
□ Se escabulló de la fiesta. He managed to

e

slip away from the party.
**2** to wriggle out of
□ No debes escabullirte de tus obligaciones. You mustn't try to wriggle out of your responsibilities.

la **escala** NOUN
**1** scale
□ a escala nacional on a national scale
**2** stopover
□ Tenemos una escala de tres horas en Bruselas. We've got a three-hour stopover in Brussels.
■ **Hicimos escala en Roma.** We stopped over in Rome.

**escalar** VERB [25]
to climb

la **escalera** NOUN
stairs *pl*
□ bajar las escaleras to go down the stairs
■ **una escalera de mármol** a marble staircase
■ **una escalera de mano** a ladder

> LANGUAGE TIP Word for word, **escalera de mano** means 'hand stairs'.

■ **la escalera de incendios** the fire escape
■ **una escalera mecánica** an escalator

el **escalofrío** NOUN
■ **Tengo escalofríos.** I'm shivering.
■ **La escena te produce escalofríos.** The scene makes you shudder.

el **escalón** (PL los **escalones**) NOUN
step

la **escama** NOUN
scale

**escandalizarse\*** VERB [13]
to shock
□ Mi abuela se escandalizó. My grandmother was shocked.

el **escándalo** NOUN
**1** scandal
■ **La boda produjo un gran escándalo.** The wedding caused a huge scandal.
**2** racket
□ ¿Qué escándalo es éste? What's all this racket?

**escandaloso** (FEM **escandalosa**) ADJECTIVE
noisy

el **escandinavo** ADJECTIVE, NOUN
Scandinavian
■ **un escandinavo** a Scandinavian
■ **una escandinava** a Scandinavian
■ **los escandinavos** the Scandinavians

el **escáner** NOUN
**1** scanner
**2** scan
□ hacerse un escáner to have a scan

**escapar** VERB [25]

to escape
□ Conseguí escapar de la fiesta. I managed to escape from the party.
■ **No quiero dejar escapar esta oportunidad.** I don't want to let this opportunity slip.
■ **escaparse** to escape □ El ladrón se escapó de la cárcel. The thief escaped from prison. □ El calor se escapa por esta rendija. The heat escapes through this grill.
■ **Se me escapó un eructo.** I let out a burp.

el **escaparate** NOUN
shop window
■ **ir de escaparates** to go window-shopping

el **escape** NOUN
leak
□ Había un escape de gas. There was a gas leak.

**escaquearse** VERB [25]
■ **escaquearse de clase** to skip school

el **escarabajo** NOUN
beetle

**escarbar** VERB [25]
to dig
□ Los niños escarbaban en la arena. The children were digging in the sand.

la **escarcha** NOUN
frost

la **escasez** NOUN
shortage
□ Hay escasez de agua. There is a shortage of water.

**escaso** (FEM **escasa**) ADJECTIVE
scarce
□ Los alimentos eran muy escasos. Food was scarce.
■ **Habrá escasa visibilidad en las carreteras.** Visibility on the roads will be poor.
■ **Duró una hora escasa.** It lasted barely an hour.

la **escayola** NOUN
plaster
□ Mañana me quitan la escayola. I'm getting my plaster taken off tomorrow.

**escayolar** VERB [25]
■ **Le escayolaron la pierna.** They put his leg in plaster.

la **escena** NOUN
scene

el **escenario** NOUN
stage

**escéptico** (FEM **escéptica**) ADJECTIVE
sceptical

el **esclavo**, la **esclava** NOUN
slave

la **escoba** NOUN

broom
**escocer\*** VERB [6]
to sting
□ Me escuecen los ojos. My eyes are
stinging.
**escocés** (FEM **escocesa**, MASC PL **escoceses**)
ADJECTIVE
Scottish
■ **el whisky escocés** Scotch whisky
■ **una falda escocesa** a kilt
el **escocés** (PL los **escoceses**) NOUN
Scotsman (PL Scotsmen)
□ los escoceses Scottish people
la **escocesa** NOUN
Scotswoman (PL Scotswomen)
**Escocia** FEM NOUN
Scotland
**escoger\*** VERB [7]
to choose
□ Yo escogí el azul. I chose the blue one.
**escolar** (FEM **escolar**) ADJECTIVE
school
□ el uniforme escolar school uniform
los **escombros** NOUN
rubble *sing*
**esconder** VERB [8]
to hide
□ Lo escondí en el cajón. I hid it in the box.
■ **Me escondí debajo de la cama.** I hid
under the bed.
las **escondidas** NOUN
■ **jugar a las escondidas** *(Latin America)* to
play hide-and-seek
■ **a escondidas** in secret □ Fuman a
escondidas. They smoke in secret.
el **escondite** NOUN
■ **jugar al escondite** to play hide-and-seek
la **escopeta** NOUN
shotgun
**Escorpio** MASC NOUN
Scorpio
■ **Soy escorpio.** I'm Scorpio.
el **escorpión** (PL los **escorpiones**) NOUN
scorpion
**escribir\*** VERB [0]
to write
□ Les escribí una carta. I wrote them a
letter. □ Escribe pronto. Write soon.
■ **Nos escribimos de vez en cuando.** We
write to each other from time to time.
■ **¿Cómo se escribe tu nombre?** How do
you spell your name?
■ **escribir a máquina** to type
**escrito** (FEM **escrita**) ADJECTIVE
written
□ un examen escrito a written exam
el **escritor**, la **escritora** NOUN
writer

□ Pablo es escritor. Pablo's a writer.
el **escritorio** NOUN
**1** desk
**2** office *(Latin America)*
la **escritura** NOUN
writing
**escrupuloso** (FEM **escrupulosa**) ADJECTIVE
fussy
□ Es muy escrupuloso con la comida. He's
very fussy about food.
**escuchar** VERB [25]
to listen
□ Juan escuchaba con atención. Juan was
listening attentively. □ Escucha el consejo
de tus padres. Listen to your parents'
advice. □ Me gusta escuchar música. I like
listening to music.
el **escudo** NOUN
**1** shield
**2** badge
la **escuela** NOUN
school
□ Hoy no tengo que ir a la escuela. I don't
have to go to school today.
■ **la escuela primaria** primary school
■ **Escuela Oficial de Idiomas**

> **DID YOU KNOW...?**
> The **Escuelas Oficiales** are state-run
> language schools where you can
> study a wide range of foreign
> languages. The qualification obtained
> is highly regarded.

**esculcar\*** VERB *(Mexico)*
to search
la **escultura** NOUN
sculpture
**escupir** VERB [58]
to spit
**escurridizo** (FEM **escurridiza**) ADJECTIVE
slippery
el **escurridor** NOUN
**1** colander
**2** plate rack
**escurrir** VERB [58]
**1** to wring
**2** to drain
**ese** (FEM **esa**) ADJECTIVE
that
□ Dame ese libro. Give me that book.
■ **A partir de ese momento empezó a
mejorar.** From then on it began to get
better.
**ése** (FEM **ésa**) PRONOUN
that one
□ Prefiero ésa. I prefer that one.
■ **¿Quién es ése?** Who's that?
**esencial** (FEM **esencial**) ADJECTIVE
essential

**Spanish-English**

**e**

■ **He entendido lo esencial de la conversación.** I understood the main points of the conversation.

**esforzarse\*** VERB
to make an effort
□ Tienes que esforzarte si quieres ganar. You have to make an effort if you want to win.
■ **Se esforzó todo lo que pudo por aprobar el examen.** He did all he could to pass the exam.

el **esfuerzo** NOUN
effort
□ Tuve que hacer un esfuerzo para comer. I had to make an effort to eat.

**esfumarse** VERB [25]
to vanish

la **esgrima** NOUN
fencing

el **esguince** NOUN
sprain
■ **Me hice un esguince en el tobillo.** I've sprained my ankle.

el **esmalte** NOUN
■ **el esmalte de uñas** nail varnish

**esmerarse** VERB
■ **Se esmeró para que todo saliera bien.** He did his best so that everything came out right.
■ **No necesitas esmerarte tanto en la presentación.** You don't need to make such an effort with the presentation.

**esnob** (FEM **esnob**, PL **esnobs**) ADJECTIVE
snobbish

la **ESO** ABBREVIATION (= Enseñanza Secundaria obligatoria)

> **DID YOU KNOW...?**
> ESO is the compulsory secondary education course done by 12 to 16 year-olds.

**eso** PRONOUN
that
□ Eso es mentira. That's a lie. □ ¡Eso es! That's it!
■ **a eso de las cinco** at about five
■ **En eso llamaron a la puerta.** Just then there was a ring at the door.
■ **Por eso te lo dije.** That's why I told you.
■ **¡Y eso que estaba lloviendo!** And it was raining and everything!

**esos** (FEM **esas**) PL ADJECTIVE
those
□ Trae esas sillas aquí. Bring those chairs over here.

**ésos** (FEM **ésas**) PL PRONOUN
those ones
□ Ésos de ahí son mejores. Those ones over there are better.

■ **Ésos no son los que vimos ayer.** Those aren't the ones we saw yesterday.

**espabilar** VERB [25] = **despabilar**

el **espacio** NOUN
1 room
□ No hay espacio para tantas sillas. There isn't room for so many chairs. □ El piano ocupa mucho espacio. The piano takes up a lot of room.
2 space
□ Deja más espacio entre las líneas. Leave more space between the lines.
■ **un espacio en blanco** a gap
■ **viajar por el espacio** to travel in space

la **espada** NOUN
sword
■ **espadas**

> **DID YOU KNOW...?**
> Espadas are swords, one of the suits in the Spanish card deck.
> **LANGUAGE TIP** Be careful! espada does not mean spade.

los **espaguetis** NOUN
spaghetti sing

la **espalda** NOUN
back
□ Me duele la espalda. My back aches.
■ **Estaba tumbada de espaldas.** She was lying on her back.
■ **Ana estaba de espaldas a mí.** Ana had her back to me.
■ **Le dispararon por la espalda.** They shot him from behind.
■ **Me encanta nadar a espalda.** I love swimming backstroke.

el **espantapájaros** (PL los **espantapájaros**) NOUN
scarecrow

**espantar** VERB [25]
1 to frighten
2 to frighten off
3 to horrify
□ Me espantan los zapatos de tacón. I hate high heels.
■ **espantarse** to get frightened

**espantoso** (FEM **espantosa**) ADJECTIVE
awful
□ un monstruo espantoso an awful monster □ Los niños hacían un ruido espantoso. The children were making an awful noise.
■ **Hacía un frío espantoso.** It was awfully cold.

**España** FEM NOUN
Spain

**español** (FEM **española**) ADJECTIVE
Spanish

el **español**, la **española** NOUN

Spaniard
- **los españoles** the Spanish

el **español** NOUN
Spanish

el **esparadrapo** NOUN
plaster
□ Me puse un esparadrapo en la herida.
I put a plaster on the wound.

el **espárrago** NOUN
asparagus
□ ¿Te gustan los espárragos? Do you like asparagus?
- **La mandé a freir espárragos.** I told her to buzz off.

la **especia** NOUN
spice

**especial** (FEM **especial**) ADJECTIVE
special
□ Fue un día muy especial. It was a very special day.
- **en especial** particularly □ ¿Desea ver a alguien en especial? Is there anybody you particularly want to see?

la **especialidad** NOUN
speciality (PL specialities)
□ la especialidad de la casa the speciality of the house

el/la **especialista** NOUN
specialist

**especializarse*** VERB [13]
- **Rosario se especializó en pediatría.** Rosario specialized in paediatrics.

**especialmente** ADVERB
1 especially
□ Me gusta mucho el pan, especialmente el integral. I love bread, especially wholemeal bread.
2 specially
□ un vestido diseñado especialmente para ella a dress designed specially for her

la **especie** NOUN
species

**específico** (FEM **específica**) ADJECTIVE
specific

**espectacular** (FEM **espectacular**) ADJECTIVE
spectacular

el **espectáculo** NOUN
performance
□ El espectáculo empieza a las ocho. The performance starts at eight.
- **Dio el espectáculo delante de todo el mundo.** He made a spectacle of himself in front of everyone.

el **espectador**, la **espectadora** NOUN
spectator
- **los espectadores** the audience

el **espejo** NOUN
mirror
□ Me miré en el espejo. I looked at myself in the mirror.
- **el espejo retrovisor** rearview mirror

**espeluznante** (FEM **espeluznante**)
ADJECTIVE
hair-raising

la **espera** NOUN
wait
□ tras una espera de tres horas after a three-hour wait
- **estar a la espera de algo** to be expecting something

la **esperanza** NOUN
hope
- **No tengo esperanzas de aprobar.** I have no hope of passing.
- **No pierdas las esperanzas.** Don't give up hope.

**esperar** VERB [25]
1 to wait
□ Espera en la puerta, ahora mismo voy. Wait at the door. I'm just coming.
- **Espera un momento, por favor.** Hang on a moment, please.
2 to wait for
□ No me esperéis. Don't wait for me.
- **Me hizo esperar una hora.** He kept me waiting for an hour.
3 to expect
□ Llegaron antes de lo que yo esperaba. They arrived sooner than I expected.
□ Esperaban que Juan les pidiera perdón. They were expecting Juan to apologize.
□ Llamará cuando menos lo esperes. He'll call when you're least expecting it. □ No esperes que venga a ayudarte. Don't expect him to come and help you.
- **esperar un bebé** to be expecting a baby
- **Me espera un largo día de trabajo.** I've got a long day of work ahead of me.
- **Era de esperar que no viniera.** He was bound not to come.
4 to hope
□ Espero que no sea nada grave. I hope it isn't anything serious.
- **¿Vendrás a la fiesta? — Espero que sí.** Are you coming to the party? — I hope so.
- **¿Crees que Carmen se enfadará? — Espero que no.** Do you think Carmen will be angry? — I hope not.
- **Fuimos a esperarla a la estación.** We went to the station to meet her.

**espeso** (FEM **espesa**) ADJECTIVE
thick

el/la **espía** NOUN
spy (PL spies)

**espiar*** VERB [21]

e

129

to spy on
□ Los vecinos nos espiaban. The neighbours were spying on us.

la **espina** NOUN
1 thorn
2 bone
■ **espina dorsal** backbone

la **espinaca** NOUN
spinach
□ No me gustan las espinacas. I don't like spinach.

la **espinilla** NOUN
1 shin
2 blackhead

el **espionaje** NOUN
spying
■ **una novela de espionaje** a spy story

**espirar** VERB
to breathe out

el **espíritu** NOUN
spirit

**espiritual** (FEM **espiritual**) ADJECTIVE
spiritual

**espléndido** (FEM **espléndida**) ADJECTIVE
splendid

la **esponja** NOUN
sponge

**esponjoso** (FEM **esponjosa**) ADJECTIVE
spongy

**espontáneo** (FEM **espontánea**) ADJECTIVE
spontaneous
□ Fue una reacción espontánea. It was a spontaneous reaction.
■ **de manera espontánea** spontaneously

la **esposa** NOUN
wife (PL wives)
■ **las esposas** handcuffs

el **esposo** NOUN
husband

la **espuma** NOUN
1 foam
2 head
■ **la espuma de afeitar** shaving cream

**espumoso** (FEM **espumosa**) ADJECTIVE
■ **vino espumoso** sparkling wine

el **esqueleto** NOUN
skeleton

el **esquema** NOUN
1 outline
2 diagram

el **esquí** (PL los **esquís**) NOUN
1 skiing
□ Me gusta mucho el esquí. I enjoy skiing a lot.
■ **el esquí acuático** water skiing
■ **una pista de esquí** a ski slope
2 ski (PL skis)

**esquiar\*** VERB [21]

to ski
□ ¿Sabes esquiar? Can you ski?

el/la **esquimal** ADJECTIVE, NOUN
Inuit (PL Inuit)

la **esquina** NOUN
corner
■ **doblar la esquina** to turn the corner

**esquivar** VERB [25]
to dodge

**esta** (FEM **esta**) ADJECTIVE ▷ see **este**

**ésta** PRONOUN ▷ see **ésta**

**está** VERB ▷ see **estar**

**estable** (FEM **estable**) ADJECTIVE
stable

**establecer\*** VERB [12]
to establish
□ Se ha establecido una buena relación entre los dos países. A good relationship has been established between the two countries.
■ **Han logrado establecer contacto con el barco.** They've managed to make contact with the boat.
■ **La familia se estableció en Madrid.** The family settled in Madrid.

el **establecimiento** NOUN
establishment
■ **un establecimiento comercial** a commercial establishment

el **establo** NOUN
stable

la **estación** (PL las **estaciones**) NOUN
1 station
□ la estación de autobuses the bus station
□ la estación de ferrocarril the railway station
2 season
□ las cuatro estaciones del año the four seasons of the year
■ **una estación de esquí** a ski resort
■ **una estación de servicio** a service station

**estacionar** VERB [25]
to park

**estacionarse** VERB [25] (Chile, River Plate, Mexico)
to park

la **estadía** NOUN (Latin America)
stay

el **estadio** NOUN
stadium

el **estado** NOUN
state
□ La carretera está en mal estado. The road is in a bad state.
■ **El Estado Español** The Spanish State
■ **estado civil** marital status
■ **María está en estado.** María is

los **Estados Unidos** NOUN
the United States
□ en Estados Unidos in the United States

el/la **estadounidense** ADJECTIVE, NOUN
American

**estafar** VERB [25]
to swindle
□ Les estafaron mil euros. They swindled a thousand euros out of them.

**estallar** VERB [25]
1 to explode
2 to burst
3 to break out

la **estampilla** NOUN *(Latin America)*
stamp

**estancado** (FEM **estancada**) ADJECTIVE
stagnant

la **estancia** NOUN
1 stay
2 ranch (PL ranches)

el **estanco** NOUN
tobacconist's

**estándar** (FEM **estándar**) ADJECTIVE
standard
□ Éstos son los modelos estándar. These are the standard models.

el **estanque** NOUN
pond

el **estante** NOUN
shelf (PL shelves)
□ Puse los libros en el estante. I put the books on the shelf.

la **estantería** NOUN
1 shelves *pl*
□ la estantería de la cocina the kitchen shelves
2 bookshelves *pl*
3 shelf unit

el **estaño** NOUN
tin

**estar*** VERB [22]
1 to be
□ En la cama se está muy bien. It's nice being in bed. □ ¿Dónde estabas? Where were you? □ Madrid está en el centro de España. Madrid is in the centre of Spain.
■ ¿Está Mónica? Is Mónica there? □ ¿Cómo estás? How are you? □ Estoy muy cansada. I'm very tired. □ ¿Estás casado o soltero? Are you married or single? □ Estamos de vacaciones. We're on holiday.
■ Hoy no estoy para bromas. I'm not in the mood for jokes today.
2 to look
□ ¡Qué guapa estás esta noche! You look really pretty tonight! □ Ese vestido te está muy bien. That dress looks very good on

you. □ ¿A cuánto está el kilo de naranjas? What price are oranges per kilo? □ Estamos a 30 de enero. It's 30 January. □ Estábamos a 30°C. The temperature was 30°C.
□ Estamos esperando a Manolo. We're waiting for Manolo. □ María estaba sentada en la arena. María was sitting on the sand.
□ La radio está rota. The radio's broken.
■ ¡Ya está! Ya sé lo que podemos hacer. That's it! I know what we can do.
■ estarse to be □ ¡Estáte quieto! Keep still!

**estas** PL ADJECTIVE ▷ see **estos**

**éstas** PL PRONOUN ▷ see **éstos**

**estatal** (FEM **estatal**) ADJECTIVE
state
□ un colegio estatal a state school

la **estatua** NOUN
statue

la **estatura** NOUN
height
□ ¿Cuál es tu estatura? What height are you? □ Tiene casi dos metros de estatura. He's over six and half feet tall.

el **este** NOUN, ADJECTIVE
east
□ el este del país the east of the country □ en la costa este on the east coast □ en el este de España in the East of Spain
■ vientos del este easterly winds
■ los países del Este the Eastern bloc countries

**este** (FEM **esta**) ADJECTIVE
this
□ este libro this book

**éste** (FEM **ésta**) PRONOUN
this one
□ Ésta me gusta más. I prefer this one.
■ Éste no es el que vi ayer. This is not the one I saw yesterday.

**esté** VERB ▷ see **estar**

la **estera** NOUN
mat

el **estéreo** (PL los **estéreos**) NOUN
stereo (PL stereos)

**esterlina** (FEM **esterlina**) ADJECTIVE
■ diez libras esterlinas ten pounds sterling

**estético** (FEM **estética**) ADJECTIVE
■ Se ha hecho la cirugía estética. He's had plastic surgery.

el **estiércol** NOUN
manure

el **estilo** NOUN
style
□ Ese no es mi estilo. That's not my style.
■ un estilo de vida similar al nuestro a similar lifestyle to ours
■ Tiene mucho estilo vistiendo. He dresses very stylishly.

e

131

la **estima** NOUN
■ **Lo tengo en gran estima.** I think very highly of him.
**estimado** (FEM **estimada**) ADJECTIVE
■ **Estimado señor Pérez** Dear Mr Pérez
**estimulante** (FEM **estimulante**) ADJECTIVE
stimulating
**estimular** VERB [25]
1 to encourage
□ Es una forma de estimular a los jugadores. It's a way of encouraging the players.
2 to stimulate
**estirar** VERB [25]
to stretch
□ Voy a salir a estirar las piernas. I'm going to go out and stretch my legs.
**esto** PRONOUN
this
□ ¿Para qué es esto? What's this for?
■ **En esto llegó Juan.** Just then Juan arrived.
el **estofado** NOUN
stew
el **estómago** NOUN
stomach
□ Me dolía el estómago. I had stomach ache.
**estorbar** VERB [25]
to be in the way
□ Las maletas estorban aquí. The cases are in the way here.
**estornudar** VERB [25]
to sneeze
**estos** (FEM **estas**) PL ADJECTIVE
these
■ **estas maletas** these cases
**éstos** (FEM **éstas**) PL PRONOUN
these ones
□ Éstos son los míos. These ones are mine.
■ **Éstos no son los que vimos ayer.** These are not the ones we saw yesterday.
■ **un día de éstos** one of these days
**estoy** VERB ▷ see **estar**
**estrafalario** (FEM **estrafalaria**) ADJECTIVE
1 eccentric
2 outlandish
**estrangular** VERB [25]
to strangle
**estratégico** (FEM **estratégica**) ADJECTIVE
strategic
**estrechar** VERB [25]
to take in
□ ¿Me puedes estrechar esta falda? Can you take in this skirt for me?
■ **La carretera se estrecha en el puente.** The road gets narrower over the bridge.
■ **Se estrecharon la mano.** They shook hands.

**estrecho** (FEM **estrecha**) ADJECTIVE

1 narrow
2 tight
□ La falda me va muy estrecha. The skirt is very tight on me.
el **estrecho** NOUN
strait
■ **el estrecho de Gibraltar** the straits of Gibraltar
la **estrella** NOUN
star
■ **una estrella de cine** a film star
■ **una estrella de mar** a starfish
LANGUAGE TIP Word for word, **estrella de mar** means 'sea star'.
**estrellarse** VERB [25]
to smash
□ El camión se estrelló contra un árbol. The lorry smashed into a tree.
**estrenar** VERB [25]
to premiere
□ La película se estrenó en junio. The film was premiered in June.
■ **Mañana estrenaré el vestido.** I'll wear the dress for the first time tomorrow.
el **estreno** NOUN
premiere
**estreñido** (FEM **estreñida**) ADJECTIVE
constipated
el **estrés** NOUN
stress
**estricto** (FEM **estricta**) ADJECTIVE
strict
**estridente** (FEM **estridente**) ADJECTIVE
loud
el **estropajo** NOUN
scourer
**estropeado** (FEM **estropeada**) ADJECTIVE
1 broken
2 broken down
**estropear** VERB [25]
1 to break
2 to ruin
□ Ese jabón me estropeó la ropa. That soap ruined my clothes. □ La lluvia nos estropeó las vacaciones. The rain ruined our holidays.
■ **estropearse** to break □ Se nos ha estropeado la tele. The TV's broken.
■ **Se me estropeó el coche en la autopista.** My car broke down on the motorway.
■ **La fruta se está estropeando con este calor.** The fruit's going off in this heat.
la **estructura** NOUN
structure
**estrujar** VERB [25]
1 to squeeze
2 to wring
el **estuche** NOUN

case
el/la **estudiante** NOUN
  student
**estudiar** VERB [25]
1 to study
  □ Quiere estudiar medicina. She wants to study medicine.
2 to learn
  □ Tengo que estudiar cuatro lecciones para el examen. I have to learn four lessons for the exam.
el **estudio** NOUN
1 studio
2 studio flat
  ■ **Ha dejado los estudios.** He's given up his studies.
**estudioso** (FEM **estudiosa**) ADJECTIVE
  studious
la **estufa** NOUN
1 heater
  □ una estufa de gas a gas heater □ una estufa eléctrica an electric heater
2 stove (Mexico)
**estupendamente** ADVERB
  ■ **Me encuentro estupendamente.** I feel great.
  ■ **Nos lo pasamos estupendamente.** We had a great time.
**estupendo** (FEM **estupenda**) ADJECTIVE
  great
  □ Pasamos unas Navidades estupendas. We had a great Christmas.
  ■ **¡Estupendo!** Great!
la **estupidez** (PL las **estupideces**) NOUN
  ■ **No dice más que estupideces.** He just talks rubbish.
  ■ **Lo que hizo fue una estupidez.** What he did was stupid.
**estúpido** (FEM **estúpida**) ADJECTIVE
  stupid
el **estúpido**, la **estúpida** NOUN
  idiot
  □ Ese tío es un estúpido. That guy's an idiot.
**estuve** VERB ▷ see **estar**
la **etapa** NOUN
  stage
  □ Lo hicimos por etapas. We did it in stages.
**etc.** ABBREVIATION (= etcétera)
  etc.
**eterno** (FEM **eterna**) ADJECTIVE
  eternal
la **ética** NOUN
1 ethics
2 ethics pl
**ético** (FEM **ética**) ADJECTIVE
  ethical
**Etiopía** FEM NOUN
  Ethiopia

la **etiqueta** NOUN
  label
  ■ **traje de etiqueta** formal dress
**étnico** (FEM **étnica**) ADJECTIVE
  ethnic
**ETT** ABBREVIATION (= Empresa de Trabajo Temporal)
  temp agency
**eufórico** (FEM **eufórica**) ADJECTIVE
  ecstatic
el **euro** NOUN
  euro
**Europa** FEM NOUN
  Europe
el **europeo** (FEM la **europea**) ADJECTIVE, NOUN
  European
**Euskadi** NOUN
  the Basque Country
el **euskera** NOUN
  Basque

> **DID YOU KNOW...?**
> Basque is one of Spain's four official languages, and there is Basque-language radio and television. It is not from the same family of languages as Spanish.

**evacuar\*** VERB [25]
  to evacuate
**evadir** VERB [58]
1 to avoid
2 to evade
la **evaluación** (PL las **evaluaciones**) NOUN
  assessment
  □ evaluación continua continuous assessment
**evaluar\*** VERB [1]
  to assess
el **evangelio** NOUN
  gospel
**evaporarse** VERB [25]
  to evaporate
**evasivo** (FEM **evasiva**) ADJECTIVE
  evasive
**eventual** (FEM **eventual**) ADJECTIVE
  ■ **un trabajo eventual** a temporary job
la **evidencia** NOUN
  evidence
  ■ **Ante la evidencia de las hechos, se confesó culpable.** Faced with the evidence, he pleaded guilty.
  ■ **Carlos la puso en evidencia delante de todos.** Carlos showed her up in front of everyone.
**evidente** (FEM **evidente**) ADJECTIVE
  obvious
  ■ **Era evidente que estaba agotada.** She was obviously exhausted.
**evidentemente** ADVERB

e

obviously

**evitar** VERB [25]
1 to avoid
▫ Quiero evitar ese riesgo. I want to avoid that risk. ▫ Intento evitar a Luisa. I'm trying to avoid Luisa.
■ **No pude evitarlo.** I couldn't help it.
2 to save
▫ Esto nos evitará muchos problemas. This will save us a lot of problems.

la **evolución** (PL las **evoluciones**) NOUN
progress
▫ Seguimos de cerca la evolución del paciente. We are keeping a close watch on the patient's progress.
■ **la teoría de la evolución** the theory of evolution

**evolucionar** VERB [25]
1 to develop
▫ Este país no ha evolucionado en la última década. This country hasn't developed in the last decade.
■ **El enfermo evoluciona favorablemente.** The patient is making good progress.
2 to evolve

**ex** PREFIX
ex
■ **su ex-marido** her ex-husband

**exactamente** ADVERB
exactly

la **exactitud** NOUN
■ **No lo sabemos con exactitud.** We don't know exactly.

**exacto** (FEM **exacta**) ADJECTIVE
1 exact
▫ el precio exacto the exact price
■ **El tren salió a la hora exacta.** The train left bang on time.
2 accurate
▫ Tus conclusiones no son muy exactas. Your conclusions aren't very accurate.
■ **Tenemos que defender nuestros derechos. — ¡Exacto!** We have to stand up for our rights. — Exactly!

la **exageración** (PL las **exageraciones**) NOUN
exaggeration

**exagerado** (FEM **exagerada**) ADJECTIVE
exaggerated
■ **¡No seas exagerada, no era tan alto!** Don't exaggerate! He wasn't that tall.
■ **El precio me parece exagerado.** I think the price is excessive.

**exagerar** VERB [25]
to exaggerate

el **examen** (PL los **exámenes**) NOUN
exam
■ **el examen de conducir** driving test

**examinar** VERB [25]
to examine
▫ El médico la examinó. The doctor examined her. ▫ Nos examinaron dos profesores. We were examined by two teachers.
■ **Mañana me examino de inglés.** Tomorrow I've got an English exam.

la **excavadora** NOUN
digger

**excavar** VERB [25]
to dig
▫ Los niños estaban excavando en la arena. The children were digging in the sand. ▫ Están excavando un túnel. They're digging a tunnel.

**excelente** (FEM **excelente**) ADJECTIVE
excellent

**excéntrico** (FEM **excéntrica**) ADJECTIVE
eccentric

la **excepción** (PL las **excepciones**) NOUN
exception
■ **a excepción de** except for

**excepcional** (FEM **excepcional**) ADJECTIVE
exceptional

**excepto** PREPOSITION
except for
▫ todos, excepto Juan everyone, except for Juan

**excesivo** (FEM **excesiva**) ADJECTIVE
excessive

el **exceso** NOUN
■ **Anoche bebí en exceso.** Last night I drank to excess.
■ **exceso de equipaje** excess luggage
■ **Me multaron por exceso de velocidad.** They fined me for speeding.

**excitarse** VERB [25]
▫ Se excitó mucho en la discusión. He got very worked up in the argument.

**exclamar** VERB [25]
to exclaim

**excluir*** VERB [10]
to exclude
▫ Me excluyeron de la lista. They excluded me from the list.

**exclusivo** (FEM **exclusiva**) ADJECTIVE
exclusive

**excluyendo** VERB ▷see **excluir**

la **excursión** (PL las **excursiones**) NOUN
trip
▫ Mañana vamos de excursión con el colegio. Tomorrow we're going on a school trip.

la **excusa** NOUN
excuse

la **exhibición** (PL las **exhibiciones**) NOUN
exhibition

**exhibir** VERB [58]
to exhibit
■ **Le gusta mucho exhibirse.** He likes drawing attention to himself.

**exigente** (FEM **exigente**) ADJECTIVE
demanding
□ El jefe es muy exigente con nosotros. The boss is very demanding with us.

**exigir\*** VERB [16]
**1** to demand
□ Exigió hablar con el encargado. He demanded to speak to the manager.
■ **La maestra nos exige demasiado.** Our teacher is too demanding.
**2** to require
□ Ese puesto exige mucha paciencia. This job requires a lot of patience.
■ **Exigen tres años de experiencia para el puesto.** They're asking for three years' experience for the job.

el **exiliado**, la **exiliada** NOUN
exile

**existir** VERB [58]
to exist
□ ¿Existen los fantasmas? Do ghosts exist?
■ **Existen dos maneras de hacerlo.** There are two ways of doing it.

el **éxito** NOUN
success (PL successes)
□ Esa novela será un gran éxito. That novel will be a great success.
■ **Su película tuvo mucho éxito.** His film was very successful.
■ **Acabaron con éxito el proyecto.** They completed the project successfully.
◌ **LANGUAGE TIP** Be careful! **éxito** does not mean **exit**.

**exótico** (FEM **exótica**) ADJECTIVE
exotic

la **expansión** (PL las **expansiones**) NOUN
expansion

la **expedición** (PL las **expediciones**) NOUN
expedition

el **expediente** NOUN
file
■ **expediente académico** student record
■ **Le han abierto expediente por mala conducta.** He has been disciplined for bad behaviour.

el **expendio** NOUN (Latin America)
shop

**expensas** FEM PL NOUN
■ **a expensas de su salud** at the cost of her health
■ **vivir a expensas de alguien** to live at somebody's expense

la **experiencia** NOUN
experience

□ 'Se requiere experiencia laboral' 'Work experience required'
■ **con experiencia** experienced
■ **sin experiencia** inexperienced

**experimental** (FEM **experimental**) ADJECTIVE
experimental

**experimentar** VERB [25]
**1** to experiment
□ experimentar con animales to experiment on animals
**2** to experience

el **experimento** NOUN
experiment

el **experto**, la **experta** NOUN
expert
■ **Es un experto en informática.** He's a computer expert.

la **explanada** NOUN
open area

la **explicación** (PL las **explicaciones**) NOUN
explanation

**explicar\*** VERB [48]
to explain
□ Le expliqué cómo se hacía una paella. I explained to her how to make a paella.
■ **Antonio se explica muy bien.** Antonio is very good at expressing himself.
■ **¿Me explico?** Do I make myself clear?
■ **No me lo explico.** I can't understand it.

el **explorador**, la **exploradora** NOUN
explorer

**explorar** VERB [25]
to explore

la **explosión** (PL las **explosiones**) NOUN
explosion
■ **El artefacto hizo explosión.** The device exploded.

el **explosivo** NOUN
explosive

la **explotación** (PL las **explotaciones**) NOUN
exploitation

**explotar** VERB [25]
**1** to exploit
□ Sabe explotar sus posibilidades. He knows how to exploit his potential.
**2** to explode
□ La caldera explotó. The boiler exploded.

**exponer\*** VERB [41]
**1** to display
**2** to present

la **exportación** (PL las **exportaciones**) NOUN
export

**exportar** VERB [25]
to export

la **exposición** (PL las **exposiciones**) NOUN

exhibition
□ montar una exposición to put on an exhibition

**expresamente** ADVERB
1 specifically
□ Mencioné expresamente tu nombre. I specifically mentioned your name.
2 specially
□ Fui expresamente a devolvérselo. I went specially to give it back to him.

**expresar** VERB [25]
to express
□ No sabe expresarse. He doesn't know how to express himself.

la **expresión** (PL las **expresiones**) NOUN
expression

**expresivo** (FEM **expresiva**) ADJECTIVE
expressive

el **expreso** NOUN
1 express
2 espresso

**exprimir** VERB [58]
to squeeze

**expuesto** VERB ▷ see **exponer**

**expulsar** VERB [25]
1 to expel
□ La expulsaron del colegio. They expelled her from school.
2 to send off
□ El árbitro lo expulsó del campo. The referee sent him off the pitch.

la **expulsión** (PL las **expulsiones**) NOUN
expulsion
■ **La expulsión del jugador fue injusta.** Sending the player off was unfair.

**exquisito** (FEM **exquisita**) ADJECTIVE
delicious
□ El postre estaba exquisito. The dessert was delicious.

el **éxtasis** NOUN
ecstasy

**extender*** VERB [20]
to spread
□ Extendí la toalla sobre la arena. I spread the towel out on the sand. □ El fuego se extendió rápidamente. The fire spread quickly.
■ **extender los brazos** to stretch one's arms out

**extendido** (FEM **extendida**) ADJECTIVE
oustretched

la **extensión** (PL las **extensiones**) NOUN
area
□ una enorme extensión de tierra an enormous area of land
■ **¿Me pone con la extensión 212, por favor?** Can you put me through to extension 212, please?

**extenso** (FEM **extensa**) ADJECTIVE
extensive

**exterior** (FEM **exterior**) ADJECTIVE
1 outside
2 foreign

el **exterior** NOUN
outside
■ **Salimos al exterior para ver qué pasaba.** We went outside to see what was going on.

**externo** (FEM **externa**) ADJECTIVE
1 outside
2 outer

**extiendo** VERB ▷ see **extender**

la **extinción** NOUN
putting out
■ **una especie en vías de extinción** an endangered species

el **extinguidor** NOUN (Latin America)
fire extinguisher

**extinguir*** VERB
to put out
■ **extinguirse** to become extinct
■ **El fuego se fue extinguiendo lentamente.** The fire was slowly going out.

**extinto** (FEM **extinta**) ADJECTIVE
extinct

el **extintor** NOUN
fire extinguisher

**extra** (FEM **extra**) ADJECTIVE
extra
□ una manta extra an extra blanket
■ **chocolate de calidad extra** top quality chocolate

el/la **extra** NOUN
extra

el **extractor** NOUN
extractor fan
□ un extractor de humos a smoke extractor

**extraer*** VERB [54]
1 to extract
□ El dentista me ha extraído la muela. The dentist has extracted my tooth.
2 to draw

**extraescolar** (FEM **extraescolara**) ADJECTIVE
■ **actividades extraescolares** extracurricular activities

**extraigo** VERB ▷ see **extraer**

**extranjero** (FEM **extranjera**) ADJECTIVE
foreign

el **extranjero**, la **extranjera** NOUN
foreigner
■ **vivir en el extranjero** to live abroad
■ **viajar al extranjero** to travel abroad

**extrañar** VERB [25]
to miss
□ Extraña mucho a sus padres. He misses his parents a lot.

■ **Me extraña que no haya llegado.** I'm surprised he hasn't arrived.

■ **¡Ya me extrañaba a mí!** I thought it was strange!

■ **extrañarse de algo** to be surprised at something ▫ Se extrañó de vernos juntos. He was surprised to see us together.

la **extrañeza** NOUN

■ **Nos miró con extrañeza.** He looked at us in surprise.

**extraño** (FEM **extraña** ADJECTIVE
strange

■ **¡Qué extraño!** How strange!

**extraordinario** (FEM **extraordinaria** ADJECTIVE
extraordinary

**extravagante** (FEM **extravagante** ADJECTIVE
extravagant

**extraviado** (FEM **extraviada** ADJECTIVE
1 lost
2 missing

**extraviar*** VERB
to mislay

▫ Me extraviaron el equipaje en el aeropuerto. They mislaid my luggage at the airport.

el/la **extremista** ADJECTIVE, NOUN
extremist

**extremo** (FEM **extrema** ADJECTIVE
extreme

▫ Ése es un caso extremo. That's an extreme case.

■ **la extrema derecha** the far Right

■ **extremo derecho** right winger

■ **el Extremo Oriente** the Far East

el **extremo** NOUN
end

▫ Cogí la cuerda por un extremo. I took hold of one end of the rope.

■ **pasar de un extremo a otro** to go from one extreme to the other

■ **en último extremo** as a last resort

**extrovertido** (FEM **extrovertida** ADJECTIVE
outgoing

▫ José es muy extrovertido. José is very outgoing.

**exuberante** (FEM **exuberante** ADJECTIVE
lush

e

# Ff

la **fábrica** NOUN
factory (PL factories)
■ **una fábrica de cerveza** a brewery
  ⟡ LANGUAGE TIP Be careful! **fábrica** does not mean **fabric**.

el/la **fabricante** NOUN
manufacturer

**fabricar*** VERB [48]
to make
■ **'fabricado en China'** 'made in China'

la **fachada** NOUN
■ **la fachada del edificio** the front of the building

**fácil** (FEM **fácil**) ADJECTIVE
easy
□ El examen fue muy fácil. The exam was very easy.
■ **Es fácil de entender.** It's easy to understand.
■ **Es fácil que se le haya perdido.** He may have lost it.

la **facilidad** NOUN
■ **Se me rompen las uñas con facilidad.** My nails break easily.
■ **Pepe tiene facilidad para los idiomas.** Pepe has a gift for languages.
■ **Te dan facilidades de pago.** They offer credit facilities.

**facilitar** VERB [25]
to make...easier
□ Un ordenador facilita mucho el trabajo. A computer makes work much easier.
■ **El banco me facilitó la información.** The bank provided me with the information.

el **factor** NOUN
factor
□ La edad del paciente es un factor importante. The age of the patient is an important factor.

la **factura** NOUN
bill
□ la factura del gas the gas bill

**facturar** VERB [25]
to check in

la **facultad** NOUN
1 faculty (PL faculties)

□ Mi abuela está perdiendo facultades. My grandmother is losing her faculties.
■ **la Facultad de Derecho** the Law Faculty
2 university
■ **ir a la facultad** to go to university

la **faena** NOUN
work
■ **las faenas domésticas** the housework

la **falda** NOUN
skirt

**fallar** VERB [25]
to fail
□ Le falla la memoria. His memory is failing.
■ **Fallé el tiro.** I missed.

**fallecer*** VERB [12]
to die

el **fallo** NOUN
1 fault
□ un pequeño fallo eléctrico a small electrical fault
2 failure
□ debido a un fallo de motor due to engine failure
3 mistake
□ ¡Qué fallo! What a stupid mistake!
■ **Fue un fallo humano.** It was human error.

**falsificar*** VERB [48]
to forge

**falso** (FEM **falsa**) ADJECTIVE
1 false
2 forged
■ **Los diamantes eran falsos.** The diamonds were fakes.
■ **Eso es falso.** That's not true.

la **falta** NOUN
1 lack
□ la falta de dinero lack of money
2 foul
□ Ha sido falta. It was a foul.
■ **Tiene cinco faltas de asistencia.** He has been absent five times.
■ **Eso es una falta de educación.** That's bad manners.
■ **una falta de ortografía** a spelling mistake

■ **Me hace falta un ordenador.** I need a computer.

■ **No hace falta que vengáis.** You don't need to come.

**faltar** VERB [25]
to be missing
□ Me falta un bolígrafo. One of my pens is missing.

■ **Faltan varios libros del estante.** There are several books missing from the shelf.

■ **No podemos irnos. Falta Manolo.** We can't go. Manolo isn't here yet.

■ **A la sopa le falta sal.** There isn't enough salt in the soup.

■ **Falta media hora para comer.** There's half an hour to go before lunch.

■ **¿Te falta mucho?** Will you be long?

■ **faltar al colegio** to miss school

la **fama** NOUN
fame
■ **llegar a la fama** to become famous
■ **tener mala fama** to have a bad reputation
■ **Tiene fama de mujeriego.** He has a reputation for being a womanizer.

la **familia** NOUN
family (PL families)
■ **una familia numerosa** a large family

**familiar** (FEM **familiar**) ADJECTIVE
1 family
□ la vida familiar family life
2 familiar
□ Su cara me es familiar. Your face is familiar.

el/la **familiar** NOUN
relative
□ un familiar mío a relative of mine

**famoso** (FEM **famosa**) ADJECTIVE
famous

el/la **fan** (PL los **fans**) NOUN
fan

la **fantasía** NOUN
fantasy (PL fantasies)
□ un mundo de fantasía a fantasy world
□ Son fantasías infantiles. They're just children's fantasies.
■ **las joyas de fantasía** costume jewellery
*sing*

el **fantasma** NOUN
ghost

**fantástico** (FEM **fantástica**) ADJECTIVE
fantastic

el **farmacéutico**, la **farmacéutica**
NOUN
chemist

la **farmacia** NOUN
chemist's (PL chemists' shops)
□ Lo compré en la farmacia. I bought it at

the chemist's.
■ **una farmacia de guardia** a duty chemist's

el **faro** NOUN
1 lighthouse
2 headlight
3 lamp
■ **los faros antiniebla** foglamps

el **farol** NOUN
1 streetlamp
2 lantern

la **farola** NOUN
1 streetlamp
□ a la luz de la farola by the light of the streetlamp
2 lamppost
□ El coche chocó contra una farola. The car hit a lamppost.

el **fascículo** NOUN
part
□ el primer fascículo del libro the first part of the book

**fascinante** (FEM **fascinante**) ADJECTIVE
fascinating

el/la **fascista** ADJECTIVE, NOUN
fascist

la **fase** NOUN
phase

**fastidiar** VERB [25]
1 to annoy
□ Lo que más me fastidia es tener que decírselo. What annoys me most is having to tell him.
■ **Esa actitud me fastidia mucho.** I find this attitude very annoying.
2 to pester
□ ¡Deja ya de fastidiarme! Will you stop pestering me!
3 to spoil
□ El accidente nos fastidió las vacaciones. The accident spoilt our holidays.

el **fastidio** NOUN
■ **¡Qué fastidio!** What a nuisance!

**fatal** (FEM **fatal**) ADJECTIVE
▷ *see also* **fatal** ADVERB
awful
□ Nos hizo un tiempo fatal. We had awful weather. □ Me siento fatal. I feel awful.
□ La obra estuvo fatal. The play was awful.
■ **Me parece fatal que le trates así.** I think it's rotten of you to treat him like that.

**fatal** ADVERB
▷ *see also* **fatal** ADJECTIVE
■ **Lo pasé fatal.** I had an awful time.
■ **Lo hice fatal.** I made a mess of it.

el **favor** NOUN
favour
□ ¿Puedes hacerme un favor? Can you do

f

me a favour?
- **por favor** please
- **¡Haced el favor de callaros!** Will you please be quiet!
- **estar a favor de algo** to be in favour of something

**favorecer\*** VERB [12]
to suit
□ Esa chaqueta te favorece mucho. That jacket really suits you.

**favorito** (FEM **favorita**) ADJECTIVE
favourite
□ ¿Cuál es tu color favorito? What's your favourite colour?

el **fax** (PL los **fax**) NOUN
fax (PL faxes)
- **mandar algo por fax** to fax something

la **fe** NOUN
faith
- **tener fe en algo** to have faith in something

**febrero** MASC NOUN
February
□ en febrero in February □ Ella nació el 28 de febrero. She was born on 28 February.

la **fecha** NOUN
date
□ ¿En qué fecha estamos? What's the date today?
- **La carta tiene fecha del 21 de enero.** The letter is dated the 21st of January.
- **la fecha de caducidad** the use-by date
- **la fecha límite** the closing date
- **la fecha tope** the deadline
- **su fecha de nacimiento** his date of birth

la **felicidad** NOUN
happiness
□ Carmen lloraba de felicidad. Carmen was crying with happiness.
- **¡Felicidades! 1** Happy birthday! **2** Congratulations!

la **felicitación** (PL las **felicitaciones**) NOUN
congratulations *pl*
□ Mi felicitación al ganador. My congratulations to the winner.
- **He recibido muchas felicitaciones.** Lots of people have congratulated me.

**felicitar** VERB [25]
to congratulate
□ La felicité por sus notas. I congratulated her on her exam results.
- **¡Te felicito!** Congratulations!
- **felicitar a alguien por su cumpleaños** to wish somebody a happy birthday

**feliz** (FEM **feliz**, PL **felices**) ADJECTIVE
happy
□ Se la ve muy feliz. She looks very happy.
- **¡Feliz cumpleaños!** Happy birthday!

- **¡Feliz Año Nuevo!** Happy New Year!
- **¡Felices Navidades!** Happy Christmas!

el **felpudo** NOUN
doormat

**femenino** (FEM **femenina**) ADJECTIVE
1 feminine
□ una chica muy femenina a very feminine girl
2 female
□ el sexo femenino the female sex
3 women's
□ el tenis femenino women's tennis

el **femenino** NOUN
feminine
□ El femenino de 'lobo' es 'loba'. The feminine of 'lobo' is 'loba'.

**fenomenal** (FEM **fenomenal**) ADJECTIVE, ADVERB
great
□ Nos hizo un tiempo fenomenal. We had great weather.
- **Lo pasé fenomenal.** I had a great time.

**feo** (FEM **fea**) ADJECTIVE
ugly
□ un edificio muy feo a very ugly building

el **féretro** NOUN
coffin

la **feria** NOUN
1 fair
- **una feria de muestras** a trade fair
2 small change (*Mexico*)
3 street market (*Chile, River Plate*)

la **ferretería** NOUN
ironmonger's (PL ironmongers' shops)
□ Lo compré en la ferretería. I bought it at the ironmonger's.

el **ferrocarril** NOUN
railway

**fértil** (FEM **fértil**) ADJECTIVE
fertile

el **fertilizante** NOUN
fertilizer

**festejar** VERB [25] (*Latin America*)
to celebrate

el **festival** NOUN
festival

**festivo** (FEM **festiva**) ADJECTIVE
festive
- **un día festivo** a holiday

el **feto** NOUN
foetus (PL foetuses)

**fiable** (FEM **fiable**) ADJECTIVE
reliable

los **fiambres** NOUN
cold meats

la **fianza** NOUN
deposit
□ Dejé una fianza de 20 euros. I left a

20-euro deposit.

**fiar\*** VERB [21]

■ **Es un hombre de fiar.** He's completely trustworthy.

■ **fiarse de alguien** to trust somebody
□ No me fío de él. I don't trust him.

la **fibra** NOUN
fibre
□ fibras artificiales man-made fibres

la **ficha** NOUN
1 index card
2 counter
■ **una ficha de dominó** a domino (PL dominoes)

**fichar** VERB [25]
1 to clock in
2 to clock out
3 to sign up

el **fichero** NOUN
1 filing cabinet
2 card index
3 file

los **fideos** NOUN
1 noodles
2 pasta *sing (River Plate)*

la **fiebre** NOUN
1 temperature
□ Le bajó la fiebre. His temperature came down.
■ **tener fiebre** to have a temperature
2 fever
□ la fiebre amarilla yellow fever

**fiel** (FEM **fiel**) ADJECTIVE
faithful
■ **ser fiel a alguien** to be faithful to somebody

la **fiera** NOUN
wild animal

la **fiesta** NOUN
1 party (PL parties)
□ Voy a dar una fiesta para celebrarlo. I'm going to have a party to celebrate.
■ **una fiesta de cumpleaños** a birthday party
2 holiday
□ El lunes es fiesta. Monday is a holiday.
■ **El pueblo está en fiestas.** There's a fiesta on in the town.

la **figura** NOUN
figure
□ una figura de porcelana a porcelain figure

**figurar** VERB [25]
to appear
□ Su nombre no figura en la lista. His name doesn't appear on the list.
■ **figurarse** to imagine □ Figúrate lo que debió sufrir. Just imagine how he must have suffered.

■ **¡Ya me lo figuraba!** I thought as much!

**fijar** VERB [25]
to fix
□ Tienes que fijar la fecha. You must fix the date.
■ **fijarse 1** to pay attention □ Tienes que fijarte más en lo que haces. You must pay more attention to what you're doing. **2** to notice □ No me fijé en la ropa que llevaba. I didn't notice what she was wearing.
■ **¡Fíjate en esos dos!** Just look at those two!

**fijo** (FEM **fija**) ADJECTIVE
1 fixed
□ Gano un sueldo fijo. I earn a fixed salary.
2 permanent
■ **Está fija en la empresa.** She's got a permanent job in the company.

la **fila** NOUN
1 row
□ Estábamos sentados en segunda fila. We were sitting in the second row.
2 line
□ Los niños se pusieron en fila. The children got into line.

el **filete** NOUN
1 steak
□ un filete con patatas fritas steak and chips
2 fillet
□ un filete de merluza a hake fillet

**Filipinas** FEM PL NOUN
the Philippines

**filmar** VERB [25]
to film
□ Mi hermano filmó nuestra boda. My brother filmed our wedding.
■ **filmar una película** to shoot a film

el **filo** NOUN
■ **Tiene poco filo.** It isn't very sharp.

**filoso** (FEM **filosa**) ADJECTIVE *(Latin America)*
sharp

la **filosofía** NOUN
philosophy

**filtrar** VERB [25]
to filter
□ Hay que filtrar el agua. The water needs filtering.
■ **filtrarse 1** to seep □ El agua se filtraba por las paredes. Water was seeping in through the walls. **2** to filter □ La luz se filtraba por las rendijas. Light was filtering in through the cracks.

el **filtro** NOUN
filter

el **fin** NOUN
end
□ el fin de una era the end of an era
■ **a fines de** at the end of □ a fines de abril

141

**Spanish-English**

at the end of April

■ **al fin** finally □ Al fin llegaron a un acuerdo. They finally reached an agreement.

■ **al fin y al cabo** after all

■ **En fin, ¡qué le vamos a hacer!** Oh well, what can we do about it!

■ **por fin** at last □ ¡Por fin hemos llegado! We've got here at last!

■ **el fin de año** New Year's Eve

■ **el fin de semana** the weekend

**final** (FEM **final**) ADJECTIVE
final
□ el resultado final the final result

el **final** NOUN
end
□ Al final de la calle hay un colegio. At the end of the street there's a school.

■ **a finales de mayo** at the end of May

■ **al final** in the end □ Al final tuve que darle la razón. In the end I had to admit that he was right.

■ **un final feliz** a happy ending

la **final** NOUN
final
□ la final de la copa the cup final

la **finca** NOUN
country house

**fingir*** VERB [16]
to pretend
□ Fingió no haberme oído. He pretended not to have heard me.

**finlandés** (FEM **finlandesa**, MASC PL **finlandeses**) ADJECTIVE
Finnish

el **finlandés**, la **finlandesa** (MASC PL los **finlandeses**) NOUN
Finn

el **finlandés** NOUN
Finnish

**Finlandia** FEM NOUN
Finland

**fino** (FEM **fina**) ADJECTIVE
1 thin
2 fine
3 slender

la **firma** NOUN
signature

**firmar** VERB [25]
to sign

**firme** (FEM **firme**) ADJECTIVE
1 steady
□ Mantén la escalera firme. Can you hold the ladder steady?
2 firm
□ Se mostró muy firme con ella. He was very firm with her.

el/la **fiscal** NOUN

public prosecutor

**fisgar*** VERB [37]
to snoop
□ La encontré fisgando en mi bolso. I found her snooping in my bag.

la **física** NOUN
1 physics *sing*
2 physicist

**físico** (FEM **física**) ADJECTIVE
physical

el **físico** NOUN
physicist

**flaco** (FEM **flaca**) ADJECTIVE
thin

la **flama** NOUN (*Mexico*)
flame

el **flamenco** NOUN
flamenco

el **flan** NOUN
crème caramel

el **flash** (PL los **flashes**) NOUN
flash (PL flashes)

la **flauta** NOUN
1 recorder
2 flute

la **flecha** NOUN
arrow

el **flechazo** NOUN
■ **Fue un flechazo.** It was love at first sight.

los **flecos** NOUN
fringe *sing*
□ los flecos de la cortina the curtain fringe

el **flequillo** NOUN
fringe

**flexible** (FEM **flexible**) ADJECTIVE
flexible

**flojo** (FEM **floja**) ADJECTIVE
1 loose
2 slack
3 weak
4 lazy (*Latin America*)
■ **Todavía tengo las piernas muy flojas.** My legs are still very weak.
■ **Está flojo en matemáticas.** He's weak at maths.

la **flor** NOUN
flower
□ un ramo de flores a bunch of flowers

el **florero** NOUN
vase

la **floristería** NOUN
florist's (PL florists' shops)
□ Las compré en la floristería. I bought them at the florist's.

el **flotador** NOUN
1 rubber ring
2 armband

**flotar** VERB [25]

to float
**flote** ADVERB
■ **a flote** afloat □ La barca se mantuvo a flote. The boat stayed afloat.
**fluir\*** VERB [10]
to flow
**fluorescente** (FEM **fluorescente)** ADJECTIVE
fluorescent
**fluyendo** VERB ▷ see **fluir**
la **foca** NOUN
seal
el **foco** NOUN
1 spotlight
2 floodlight
3 headlight (Latin America)
4 light bulb (Mexico)
■ **el foco de atención** the focus of attention
el **folio** NOUN
sheet of paper (PL sheets of paper)
■ **un documento de 20 folios** a 20-page document
■ **un sobre de tamaño folio** an A4-size envelope
el **folklore** NOUN
folklore
el **folleto** NOUN
1 brochure
2 leaflet
**fomentar** VERB [25]
to promote
la **fonda** NOUN
1 boarding house
2 restaurant
el **fondo** NOUN
1 bottom
□ el fondo de la cazuela the bottom of the pan
■ **en el fondo del mar** at the bottom of the sea
2 end
□ Mi habitación está al fondo del pasillo. My room's at the end of the corridor.
■ **estudiar una materia a fondo** to study a subject in depth
■ **un corredor de fondo** a long-distance runner
■ **en el fondo** deep down
■ **recaudar fondos** to raise funds
el **fontanero**, la **fontanera** NOUN
plumber
el **footing** NOUN
jogging
□ Hago footing todas las mañanas. I go jogging every morning.
**forestal** (FEM **forestal)** ADJECTIVE
forest
□ un incendio forestal a forest fire

la **forma** NOUN
1 shape
□ Me gusta la forma de esa mesa. I like the shape of that table.
■ **en forma de pera** pear-shaped
2 way
□ Me miraba de una forma extraña. She was looking at me in a strange way.
■ **de todas formas** anyway
■ **estar en forma** to be fit
la **formación** (PL las **formaciones)** NOUN
training
■ **formación profesional** vocational training
**formal** (FEM **formal)** ADJECTIVE
responsible
□ un chico muy formal a very responsible boy
■ **Sé formal y pórtate bien.** Be good and behave yourself.
**formar** VERB [25]
to start
□ Quieren formar una orquesta. They want to start an orchestra.
■ **Se formó una cola enorme en la puerta.** A huge queue formed at the door.
■ **estar formado por** to be made up of
■ **formar parte de algo** to be part of something
**formidable** (FEM **formidable)** ADJECTIVE
fantastic
□ Pedro tiene un coche formidable. Pedro has got a fantastic car. □ Desde aquí hay una vista formidable. There's a fantastic view from here.
la **fórmula** NOUN
formula
□ una fórmula mágica a magic formula
■ **coches de Fórmula 1** Formula 1 cars
el **formulario** NOUN
form
□ Hay que rellenar un formulario. You have to fill in a form.
**forrar** VERB [25]
1 to line
2 to cover
el **forro** NOUN
1 lining
2 cover
la **fortuna** NOUN
fortune
□ Vale una fortuna. It's worth a fortune.
■ **por fortuna** luckily
**forzar\*** VERB
to force
■ **Estás forzando la vista.** You're straining your eyes.
la **fosa** NOUN

**1** ditch (PL ditches)
**2** grave
el **fósforo** NOUN
match
la **foto** NOUN
photo (PL photos)
□ Les hice una foto a los niños. I took a photo of the children.
la **fotocopia** NOUN
photocopy (PL photocopies)
□ Hice dos fotocopias del recibo. I made two photocopies of the receipt.
la **fotocopiadora** NOUN
photocopier
**fotocopiar** VERB [25]
to photocopy
la **fotógrafa** NOUN
photographer
la **fotografía** NOUN
**1** photograph
□ una fotografía de mis padres a photograph of my parents
**2** photography
□ un curso de fotografía a photography course
el **fotógrafo** NOUN
photographer
**fracasar** VERB [25]
to fail
el **fracaso** NOUN
failure
la **fracción** (PL las fracciones) NOUN
fraction
la **fractura** NOUN
fracture
**frágil** (FEM frágil) ADJECTIVE
fragile
el **fraile** NOUN
friar
la **frambuesa** NOUN
raspberry (PL raspberries)
**francés** (FEM francesa, MASC PL franceses) ADJECTIVE
French
el **francés** (PL los franceses) NOUN
**1** Frenchman (PL Frenchmen)
■ los franceses the French
**2** French
la **francesa** NOUN
Frenchwoman (PL Frenchwomen)
**Francia** FEM NOUN
France
**franco** (FEM franca) ADJECTIVE
frank
■ para serte franco ... to be frank with you

el **franco** NOUN
franc

el **franqueo** NOUN
postage
el **frasco** NOUN
bottle
□ un frasco de perfume a bottle of perfume
la **frase** NOUN
sentence
■ una frase hecha a set phrase
el **fraude** NOUN
fraud
la **frazada** NOUN (Latin America)
blanket
la **frecuencia** NOUN
frequency (PL frequencies)
□ ¿En qué frecuencia está? What frequency is it on?
■ Nos vemos con frecuencia. We often see each other.
■ ¿Con qué frecuencia tienen estos síntomas? How often do they get these symptoms?
**frecuente** (FEM frecuente) ADJECTIVE
**1** common
□ un error bastante frecuente a fairly common mistake
**2** frequent
□ sus frecuentes viajes al extranjero his frequent trips abroad
el **fregadero** NOUN
sink
**fregar*** VERB [34]
to wash
□ Tengo que fregar la cazuela. I've got to wash the pan.
■ fregar los platos to wash the dishes
■ Yo estaba en la cocina fregando. I was in the kitchen washing the dishes.
■ fregar el suelo to mop the floor
la **fregona** NOUN
mop
**freír*** VERB [23]
to fry
□ No sabe ni freír un huevo. He can't even fry an egg.
**frenar** VERB [25]
to brake
el **frenazo** NOUN
■ Tuve que dar un frenazo. I had to brake suddenly.
el **freno** NOUN
brake
□ Me quedé sin frenos. My brakes failed.
■ el freno de mano the handbrake
la **frente** NOUN
forehead
□ Tiene una cicatriz en la frente. He has a scar on his forehead.
el **frente** NOUN

front
  □ un frente frío a cold front  □ un frente común a united front
  ■ **frente a** opposite  □ Frente al hotel hay un banco. There's a bank opposite the hotel.
  ■ **Los coches chocaron de frente.** The cars collided head on.
  ■ **Viene un coche de frente.** There's a car coming straight for us.
  ■ **hacer frente a algo** to face up to something

la **fresa** NOUN
  strawberry (PL strawberries)

**fresco** (FEM **fresca**) ADJECTIVE
  1 cool
  2 fresh
  ■ **hace fresco** 1 it's chilly  2 it's cool

el **fresco** NOUN
  ■ **Hace fresco.** It's a bit chilly.

**friego** VERB ▷ see **fregar**

el **frigorífico** NOUN
  fridge

el **frijol** NOUN (Latin America)
  bean

**frío** VERB
  ▷ see also **frío** ADJECTIVE, NOUN ▷ see **freír**

**frío** (FEM **fría**) ADJECTIVE
  ▷ see also **frío** VERB, NOUN
  cold
  □ Tengo las manos frías. My hands are cold.
  ■ **Estuvo muy frío conmigo.** He was very cold towards me.

el **frío** NOUN
  ▷ see also **frío** VERB, ADJECTIVE
  ■ **Hace frío.** It's cold.
  ■ **Tengo mucho frío.** I'm very cold.

**frito** VERB
  ▷ see also **frito** VERB ▷ see **freír**

**frito** (FEM **frita**) ADJECTIVE
  ▷ see also **frito** ADJECTIVE
  fried
  □ huevos fritos fried eggs

la **frontera** NOUN
  border
  □ Nos pararon en la frontera. We were stopped at the border.

el **frontón** (PL los **frontones**) NOUN
  1 pelota court
  2 pelota

**frotar** VERB [25]
  to rub
  □ ¿Te froto la espalda? Shall I rub your back for you?
  ■ **El niño se frotaba las manos para calentarse.** The child was rubbing his hands to get warm.

**fruncir\*** VERB

  ■ **fruncir el ceño** to frown

**frustrado** (FEM **frustrada**) ADJECTIVE
  frustrated
  □ Se siente frustrado. He feels frustrated.

la **fruta** NOUN
  fruit
  □ La fruta está muy cara. Fruit is very expensive.

la **frutería** NOUN
  greengrocer's (PL greengrocers' shops)
  □ Lo compré en la frutería. I bought it at the greengrocer's.

la **frutilla** NOUN (River Plate)
  strawberry (PL strawberries)

el **fruto** NOUN
  fruit
  □ el fruto de nuestro trabajo the fruit of our labours
  ■ **los frutos secos** nuts

**fue** VERB ▷ see **ir**, **ser**

el **fuego** NOUN
  fire
  □ encender el fuego to light the fire
  ■ **prender fuego a algo** to set fire to something
  ■ **Puse la cazuela al fuego.** I put the pot on to heat.
  ■ **cocinar algo a fuego lento** to cook something on a low heat
  ■ **¿Tiene fuego, por favor?** Have you got a light, please?
  ■ **fuegos artificiales** fireworks
  
  **LANGUAGE TIP** Word for word, **fuegos artificiales** means 'artificial fires'.

la **fuente** NOUN
  1 fountain
  2 dish (PL dishes)

**fuera** VERB
  ▷ see also **fuera** ADVERB ▷ see **ir**, **ser**

**fuera** ADVERB
  ▷ see also **fuera** VERB
  1 outside
  □ Los niños estaban jugando fuera. The children were playing outside.  □ Por fuera es blanco. It is white on the outside.
  ■ **¡Estamos aquí fuera!** We are out here!
  ■ **Hoy vamos a cenar fuera.** We're going out for dinner tonight.
  2 away
  □ Mis padres llevan varios días fuera. My parents have been away for several days.
  ■ **El enfermo está fuera de peligro.** The patient is out of danger.
  ■ **fuera de mi casa** outside my house

**fuerte** (FEM **fuerte**) ADJECTIVE
  ▷ see also **fuerte** ADVERB
  1 strong
  2 loud

**3** hard
**4** bad
■ **'un beso muy fuerte'** 'lots of love'
**fuerte** ADVERB
▷ *see also* **fuerte** ADJECTIVE
loudly
□ Hablaba fuerte. He was talking loudly.
■ **Agárrate fuerte.** Hold on tight.
■ **No le pegues tan fuerte.** Don't hit him so hard.
la **fuerza** NOUN
strength
□ No le quedaban fuerzas. He had no strength left.
■ **tener mucha fuerza** to be very strong
■ **Sólo lo conseguirás a fuerza de practicar.** You'll only manage it by practising.
■ **No te lo comas a la fuerza.** Don't force yourself to eat it.
■ **la fuerza de gravedad** the force of gravity
■ **la fuerza de voluntad** willpower
**fuerzo** VERB ▷ *see* **forzar**
**fugarse\*** VERB [25]
to escape
**fui** VERB ▷ *see* **ir, ser**
el **fumador**, la **fumadora** NOUN
smoker
■ **sección para no fumadores** non-smoking section
**fumar** VERB [25]
to smoke
□ Quiero dejar de fumar. I want to give up smoking.
la **función** (PL las **funciones**) NOUN
**1** function
□ Los insectos desempeñan una función muy importante. Insects perform a very useful function.
**2** role
□ la función de la policía en la sociedad the role of the police in society
**3** show
□ Los niños representan una función en el colegio. The children are putting on a show at school.
**funcionar** VERB [25]
to work
□ El ascensor no funciona. The lift isn't working.
■ **'No funciona.'** 'Out of order.'
■ **Funciona con pilas.** It runs on batteries.
el **funcionario**, la **funcionaria** NOUN
civil servant

la **funda** NOUN
cover
■ **una funda de almohada** a pillowcase
**fundamental** (FEM **fundamental**)
ADJECTIVE
basic
□ Hay dos tipos fundamentales de personas. There are two basic types of people.
■ **Es fundamental que entendamos el problema.** It is essential that we understand the problem.
**fundar** VERB [25]
to found
**fundirse** VERB [58]
to melt
□ La nieve se está fundiendo. The snow's melting.
■ **Se han fundido los fusibles.** The fuses have blown.
el **funeral** NOUN
funeral
la **funeraria** NOUN
undertaker's
la **furgoneta** NOUN
van
la **furia** NOUN
fury
**furioso** (FEM **furiosa**) ADJECTIVE
furious
□ Mi padre estaba furioso conmigo. My father was furious with me.
**furtivo** (FEM **furtiva**) ADJECTIVE
■ **la pesca furtiva** poaching
■ **un cazador furtivo** a poacher
el **fusible** NOUN
fuse
□ Han saltado los fusibles. The fuses have blown.
el **fusil** NOUN
rifle
el **fútbol** NOUN
football
□ jugar al fútbol to play football
el **futbolín** (PL los **futbolines**) NOUN
table football
el/la **futbolista** NOUN
footballer
□ Quiere ser futbolista. He wants to be a footballer.
el **futuro** ADJECTIVE, NOUN
future
□ su futuro marido your future husband
■ **El futuro de 'comes' es 'comerás'.** The future of 'comes' is 'comerás'.
■ **la futura madre** the mother-to-be

# Gg

la **gabardina** NOUN
raincoat

el **gabinete** NOUN
1 office
  ■ **el gabinete de prensa** press office
2 cabinet

las **gafas** NOUN
1 glasses
  □ Tengo que llevar gafas. I have to wear glasses.
  ■ **Había unas gafas encima de la mesa.** There was a pair of glasses on the table.
2 goggles
  ■ **las gafas de sol** sunglasses

la **gaita** NOUN
bagpipes pl
  □ tocar la gaita to play the bagpipes
  ■ **¡Menuda gaita!** What a pain!

los **gajes** NOUN
  ■ **Son gajes del oficio.** They're occupational hazards.

el **gajo** NOUN
segment

la **galaxia** NOUN
galaxy (PL galaxies)

la **galería** NOUN
gallery (PL galleries)
  □ una galería de arte an art gallery
  ■ **una galería comercial** a shopping centre

**Gales** MASC NOUN
Wales
  ■ **el País de Gales** Wales

**galés** (FEM **galesa**, MASC PL **galeses** ADJECTIVE
Welsh

el **galés** (PL los **galeses** NOUN
1 Welshman (PL Welshmen)
  □ los galeses the Welsh
2 Welsh

la **galesa** NOUN
Welshwoman (PL Welshwomen)

el **galgo** NOUN
greyhound
  □ una carrera de galgos a greyhound race

**Galicia** FEM NOUN
Galicia

el **gallego** (FEM la **gallega** ADJECTIVE, NOUN
Galician

el **gallego** NOUN
Galician

la **galleta** NOUN
biscuit
  ■ **una galleta salada** a cracker

la **gallina** NOUN
hen
  ■ **Sólo pensarlo me pone la carne de gallina.** It gives me goosepimples just thinking about it.
  ■ **jugar a la gallinita ciega** to play blind man's buff

el/la **gallina** NOUN
  ■ **¡Eres un gallina!** (colloquial) You're chicken!

el **gallinero** NOUN
1 henhouse
2 madhouse (colloquial)
  □ La clase era un gallinero. The class was a madhouse.

el **gallo** NOUN
cock
  ■ **en menos que canta un gallo** in an instant
  ⏺ LANGUAGE TIP Word for word, **en menos que canta un gallo** means 'in less than a cock crows'.

**galopar** VERB [25]
to gallop

la **gama** NOUN
range
  □ una amplia gama de ordenadores a wide range of computers

la **gamba** NOUN
prawn

el **gamberro**, la **gamberra** NOUN
hooligan

la **gana** NOUN
  ■ **Me visto como me da la gana.** I dress the way I want to.
  ■ **¡No me da la gana!** I don't want to!
  ■ **Hazlo como te dé la gana.** Do it however you like.
  ■ **hacer algo de mala gana** to do something reluctantly

g

■ **tener ganas de hacer algo** to feel like doing something
■ **Tengo ganas de que llegue el sábado.** I'm looking forward to Saturday.

la **ganadería** NOUN
■ **Se dedican a la ganadería.** They raise cattle.

el **ganado** NOUN
livestock
□ alimento para el ganado livestock feed
■ **el ganado vacuno** cattle

**ganador** (FEM **ganadora**) ADJECTIVE
winning
□ el equipo ganador the winning team

el **ganador**, la **ganadora** NOUN
winner

la **ganancia** NOUN
profit
□ las pérdidas y las ganancias profits and losses

**ganar** VERB [25]
1 to earn
□ Gana un buen sueldo. He earns a good wage.
■ **ganarse la vida** to earn a living
2 to win
□ ¿Quién ganó la carrera? Who won the race? □ Lo importante no es ganar. Winning isn't the most important thing.
3 to beat
□ Ganamos al Olimpic tres a cero. We beat Olimpic three-nil.
■ **Con eso no ganas nada.** You won't achieve anything by doing that.
■ **ganar tiempo** to save time
■ **¡Te lo has ganado!** You deserve it!
■ **salir ganando** to do well □ Salí ganando con la venta del coche. I did well out of the sale of the car.

el **ganchillo** NOUN
crochet
□ una aguja de ganchillo a crochet hook
■ **hacer ganchillo** to crochet

el **gancho** NOUN
1 hook
□ Colgué el abrigo de un gancho. I hung the coat on a hook.
■ **Maradona tiene gancho.** Maradona is a crowd-puller.
2 hanger (Latin America)

**gandul** (FEM **gandula**) ADJECTIVE
lazy

el **gandul**, la **gandula** NOUN
good-for-nothing
□ Su marido es un gandul. Her husband is a good-for-nothing.

la **ganga** NOUN
bargain

□ A ese precio es una ganga. It's a real bargain at that price.

el **gángster** (PL los **gángsters**) NOUN
gangster

el **ganso**, la **gansa** NOUN
goose (PL geese)

el **garabato** NOUN
1 doodle
□ una página llena de garabatos a page full of doodles
■ **Me pasé la clase haciendo garabatos.** I spent the whole class doodling.
2 scribble
□ Los garabatos eran ininteligibles. The scribbles were unintelligible.
■ **Mientras pensaba iba haciendo garabatos en una libreta.** As I was thinking I scribbled away in my notebook.

el **garaje** NOUN
garage
□ Metí el coche en el garaje. I put the car in the garage.
■ **una plaza de garaje** a parking space

la **garantía** NOUN
guarantee
□ La lavadora está todavía en garantía. The washing machine is still under guarantee.

**garantizar*** VERB [13]
to guarantee
□ No te lo puedo garantizar. I can't guarantee it.

el **garbanzo** NOUN
chick pea

la **garganta** NOUN
throat
□ Me duele la garganta. I've got a sore throat.

la **gargantilla** NOUN
necklace

las **gárgaras** NOUN
■ **hacer gárgaras** to gargle

la **garita** NOUN
sentry box (PL sentry boxes)

la **garra** NOUN
1 claw
2 talon

la **garrafa** NOUN
carafe

**DID YOU KNOW...?**
A **garrafa** is also a large bottle with handles.

■ **vino de garrafa** cheap wine

la **garúa** NOUN (Latin America)
drizzle

el **gas** (PL los **gases**) NOUN
gas
□ ¿No hueles a gas? Can you smell gas?
■ **agua mineral sin gas** still mineral water

- **una bebida sin gas** a still drink
- **agua mineral con gas** sparkling mineral water
- **los gases del tubo de escape** exhaust fumes
- **gases lacrimógenos** tear gas *sing*
- **El niño tiene muchos gases.** The baby's got a lot of wind.
- **Pasó una moto a todo gas.** A motorbike shot past at full speed.

la **gasa** NOUN
gauze

la **gaseosa** NOUN

> **DID YOU KNOW...?**
> A **gaseosa** is a drink of sweet fizzy water.

el **gasoil** NOUN
diesel oil

el **gasóleo** NOUN
diesel oil

la **gasolina** NOUN
petrol
□ Tengo que echar gasolina. I have to fill up with petrol.
- **gasolina súper** four-star petrol
- **gasolina sin plomo** unleaded petrol

la **gasolinera** NOUN
petrol station

**gastado** (FEM **gastada**) ADJECTIVE
worn
□ La moqueta está muy gastada. The carpet is very worn.

**gastar** VERB [25]
1 to spend
- **Javier gasta mucho en ropa.** Javier spends a lot of money on clothes.
2 to use
□ Gastamos mucha agua. We use a lot of water.
- **Gasté toda una caja de cerillas.** I used up a whole box of matches.
- **¿Qué numero de zapato gastas?** What size shoes do you take?
- **Le gastamos una broma a Juan.** We played a joke on Juan.
- **Se han gastado las pilas.** The batteries have run out.
- **Se me han gastado las suelas.** The soles of my shoes have worn out.

el **gasto** NOUN
expense
□ Es un gasto tremendo. It's a horrendous expense. □ Este año hemos tenido muchos gastos. We've had a lot of expenses this year.
- **gastos de envío** postage and packing *sing*
  > **LANGUAGE TIP** Word for word, **gastos de envío** means 'sending expenses'.

- **el gasto público** public spending

la **gata** NOUN
cat
- **andar a gatas** to crawl □ El niño todavía anda a gatas. The baby is still crawling.
- **Tienes que subir las escaleras a gatas.** You have to go up the stairs on all fours.

**gatear** VERB [25]
to crawl

el **gato** NOUN
1 cat
2 jack

la **gaviota** NOUN
seagull

el **gay** (PL los **gays**) ADJECTIVE, NOUN
gay

el **gazpacho** NOUN

> **DID YOU KNOW...?**
> **Gazpacho** is a refreshing soup made from tomatoes, cucumber, garlic, peppers, oil and vinegar and served cold.

el **gel** NOUN
gel
□ gel de baño bath gel

la **gelatina** NOUN
jelly (PL jellies)

el **gemelo** (FEM la **gemela**) ADJECTIVE, NOUN
identical twin
□ Son gemelos. They're identical twins.
□ mi hermano gemelo my identical twin

los **gemelos** NOUN
1 binoculars
2 cufflinks

**Géminis** MASC NOUN
Gemini
- **Soy géminis.** I'm Gemini.

el **gen** NOUN
gene

la **generación** (PL las **generaciones**) NOUN
generation

**general** (FEM **general**) ADJECTIVE
general
□ medicina general general medicine
- **en general** in general
- **por lo general** generally □ Por lo general me acuesto temprano. I generally go to bed early.

el/la **general** NOUN
general

**generalizar*** VERB [13]
to generalize
□ No se puede generalizar. You can't generalize.

**generalmente** ADVERB
generally

**generar** VERB [25]
to generate

## género – giro

**el género** NOUN
1 gender
2 kind
  □ ¿Qué género de música prefieres? What kind of music do you prefer?
3 material
  □ Para las cortinas necesitamos un género más grueso. We need a thicker material for the curtains.
  ■ **el género humano** the human race

**la generosidad** NOUN
generosity

**generoso** (FEM **generosa**) ADJECTIVE
generous

**genial** (FEM **genial**) ADJECTIVE
brilliant
  □ Antonio tuvo una idea genial. Antonio had a brilliant idea.  □ El concierto estuvo genial. It was a brilliant concert.

**el genio** NOUN
1 temper
  □ ¡Menudo genio tiene tu padre! Your father has got such a temper!
  ■ **tener mal genio** to have a bad temper
2 genius (PL geniuses)
  □ ¡Eres un genio! You're a genius!
3 genie

**los genitales** NOUN
genitals

**el genoma** NOUN
genome

**la gente** NOUN
people
  □ Había poca gente en la sala. There were few people in the room.  □ La gente está cansada de promesas. People are tired of promises.
  ■ **Son buena gente.** They're good people.
  ■ **Óscar es buena gente.** Óscar's a good sort.
  ■ **la gente de la calle** the people in the street

**la geografía** NOUN
geography

**la geología** NOUN
geology

**la geometría** NOUN
geometry

**el geranio** NOUN
geranium

**el/la gerente** NOUN
manager
  □ Isabel es gerente de ventas. Isabel is a sales manager.

**el germen** (PL los **gérmenes**) NOUN
germ

**germinar** VERB [25]
to germinate

**el gesto** NOUN
  ■ **Hizo un gesto de alivio.** He looked relieved.
  ■ **Me hizo un gesto para que me sentara.** He made a sign for me to sit down.

**la gestoría** NOUN
  **DID YOU KNOW...?**
  A **gestoría** is a private agency which deals with government departments on behalf of its clients.

**Gibraltar** MASC NOUN
Gibraltar

**el gibraltareño** (FEM la **gibraltareña**) ADJECTIVE, NOUN
Gibraltarian

**el/la gigante** NOUN
giant

**gigantesco** (FEM **gigantesca**) ADJECTIVE
gigantic

**la gimnasia** NOUN
gymnastics sing
  □ Después del recreo tenemos gimnasia. After break we have gymnastics.
  ■ **Mi madre hace gimnasia todas las mañanas.** My mother does exercises every morning.

**el gimnasio** NOUN
gym

**el/la gimnasta** NOUN
gymnast

**la ginebra** NOUN
gin

**el ginecólogo, la ginecóloga** NOUN
gynaecologist
  □ Soy ginecóloga. I'm a gynaecologist.

**la gira** NOUN
tour
  □ Hicimos una gira por toda Europa. We did a tour all round Europe.
  ■ **estar de gira** to be on tour

**girar** VERB [25]
1 to turn
  □ Al llegar al semáforo gira a la derecha. When you get to the lights turn right.  □ Giré la cabeza para ver quién era. I turned my head to see who it was.
2 to rotate
  □ La Tierra gira alrededor de su eje. The Earth rotates on its axis.
  ■ **La Luna gira alrededor de la Tierra.** The moon revolves around the Earth.

**el girasol** NOUN
sunflower

**el giro** NOUN
1 turn
  □ El avión dio un giro de 90 grados. The plane did a 90 degree turn.
2 postal order

g

□ Voy a mandarte un giro de 100 euros.
I'll send you a 100-euro postal order.

el **gitano** la **gitana** NOUN
gypsy (PL gypsies)

la **glándula** NOUN
gland

**global** (FEM **global**) ADJECTIVE
global
□ una solución global a global solution

el **globo** NOUN
balloon
▪ **un globo terráqueo** a globe

la **glorieta** NOUN
roundabout

**glotón** (FEM **glotona**, MASC PL **glotones**)
ADJECTIVE
greedy

**gobernar** * VERB [39]
to govern

el **gobierno** NOUN
government

el **gol** NOUN
goal
▪ **meter un gol** to score a goal

el **golf** NOUN
golf
▪ **jugar al golf** to play golf

el **golfo** NOUN
gulf
□ el Golfo pérsico the Persian Gulf

la **golondrina** NOUN
swallow

la **golosina** NOUN
sweet

**goloso** (FEM **golosa**) ADJECTIVE
▪ **ser goloso** to have a sweet tooth □ Soy
muy golosa. I've got a very sweet tooth.

el **golpe** NOUN
▪ **Me he dado un golpe en el codo.**
I banged my elbow.
▪ **Se dio un golpe contra la pared.** He hit
the wall.
▪ **El coche de atrás nos dio un golpe.**
The car behind ran into us.
knock
□ Oímos un golpe en la puerta. We heard a
knock at the door.
▪ **Di unos golpecitos a la puerta antes de
entrar.** I tapped on the door before going
in.
▪ **de golpe** suddenly □ De golpe decidió
dejar el trabajo. He suddenly decided to give
up work.
▪ **La puerta se cerró de golpe.** The door
slammed shut.
▪ **no dar golpe** to be bone idle

**golpear** VERB [25]
1 to hit

□ Me golpeó en la cara con su raqueta.
He hit me in the face with his racquet.
2 to bang
□ El maestro golpeó el pupitre con la mano.
The teacher banged the desk with his hand.
▪ **Me golpeé la cabeza contra el armario.**
I banged my head on the cupboard.

la **goma** NOUN
1 eraser
□ ¿Me prestas la goma? Can you lend me
your eraser?
▪ **una goma de borrar** an eraser □ unos
guantes de goma a pair of rubber gloves
2 elastic band
□ Necesito una goma para el pelo. I need an
elastic band for my hair.

**gordo** (FEM **gorda**) ADJECTIVE
1 fat
□ Estoy muy gordo. I'm very fat.
2 thick
3 big
□ Debe de ser algo bastante gordo. It must
be something pretty big.
▪ **Su mujer me cae gorda.** I can't stand his
wife.

el **gorila** NOUN
gorilla

la **gorra** NOUN
cap
▪ **de gorra** for free □ Entramos de gorra.
We got in for free.

el **gorrión** (PL **los gorriones**) NOUN
sparrow

el **gorro** NOUN
hat
□ Llevaba un gorro de lana. He wore a
woollen hat.
▪ **un gorro de baño** a swimming cap
▪ **Ya estoy hasta el gorro.** I'm absolutely
fed up.

el **gorrón** la **gorrona** (MASC PL **los
gorrones**) NOUN
scrounger

la **gota** NOUN
drop
□ Sólo bebí una gota de vino. I only had a
drop of wine.
▪ **Están cayendo cuatro gotas.** It's
spitting.

**gotear** VERB [25]
1 to drip
2 to leak

la **gotera** NOUN
leak
□ Tenemos goteras en la cocina. We've got
some leaks in the kitchen.

**gozar** * VERB [13]
▪ **gozar de algo** to enjoy something

□ Quiere gozar de la vida. He wants to enjoy life. □ Mis abuelos gozan de buena salud. My grandparents enjoy good health.

la **grabación** (PL las **grabaciones**) NOUN
recording

la **grabadora** NOUN
recorder

**grabar** VERB [25]

**1** to tape
□ Quiero grabar esta película. I want to tape this film.

**2** to record
□ Lo grabaron en vivo. It was recorded live.

**3** to engrave
□ Grabó sus iniciales en la medalla. He engraved his initials on the medal.
■ **Lo tengo grabado en la memoria.** It's etched on my memory.

la **gracia** NOUN
■ **tener gracia** to be funny □ Sus chistes tienen mucha gracia. His jokes are very funny.
■ **Yo no le veo la gracia.** I don't see what's so funny.
■ **Me hizo mucha gracia.** It was so funny.
■ **No me hace gracia tener que salir con este tiempo.** I'm not too pleased about having to go out in this weather.
■ **¡Muchas gracias!** Thanks very much!
■ **dar las gracias a alguien por algo** to thank somebody for something □ Vino a darme las gracias por las flores. He came to thank me for the flowers.
■ **Ni siquiera me dio las gracias.** He didn't even say thank you.
■ **gracias a** thanks to □ Gracias a él me encuentro con vida. Thanks to him I'm still alive.

**gracioso** (FEM **graciosa**) ADJECTIVE
funny
□ ¡Qué gracioso! How funny!

las **gradas** NOUN
terraces

el **grado** NOUN
degree
□ Estaban a diez grados bajo cero. It was ten degrees below zero. □ quemaduras de primer grado first-degree burns

**graduado** (FEM **graduada**) ADJECTIVE
■ **gafas graduadas** prescription glasses

**gradual** (FEM **gradual**) ADJECTIVE
gradual

**graduar\*** VERB [1]
to adjust
■ **Tengo que graduarme la vista.** I've got to have my eyes tested.
■ **Se graduó en Medicina hace dos años.** He graduated in Medicine two years ago.

la **gráfica** NOUN
graph

**gráfico** (FEM **gráfica**) ADJECTIVE
graphic

el **gráfico** NOUN
table

la **gramática** NOUN
grammar
□ un libro de gramática inglesa a book on English grammar

el **gramo** NOUN
gram

> **DID YOU KNOW…?**
> En los países anglosajones el peso a menudo se expresa en onzas **ounces**. Una onza equivale a 28.35 gramos.

**gran** ADJECTIVE ▷ see **grande**

la **granada** NOUN
pomegranate
■ **una granada de mano** a hand grenade

**granate** (FEM **granate**) ADJECTIVE
maroon
□ una bufanda granate a maroon scarf

**Gran Bretaña** FEM NOUN
Great Britain

**grande** (FEM **grande**) ADJECTIVE

**1** big
□ Viven en una casa muy grande. They live in a very big house.
■ **¿Cómo es de grande?** How big is it?
■ **La camisa me está grande.** The shirt is too big for me.

**2** large
□ un gran número de visitantes a large number of visitors □ grandes sumas de dinero large sums of money

**3** great
□ un gran pintor a great painter □ Es una ventaja muy grande. It's a great advantage.
■ **Me llevé una alegría muy grande.** I felt very happy.
■ **Lo pasamos en grande.** We had a great time.
■ **unos grandes almacenes** a department store

> **LANGUAGE TIP** Word for word, **grandes almacenes** means 'big warehouses'.

**granel** ADVERB
■ **a granel** in bulk □ Venden las aceitunas a granel. They sell olives in bulk.

el **granero** NOUN
barn

el **granizado** NOUN

> **DID YOU KNOW…?**
> A **granizado** is a crushed ice drink.

**granizar\*** VERB [13]
to hail
□ Está granizando. It's hailing.

el **granizo** NOUN
hail

la **granja** NOUN
farm
■ una granja avícola a poultry farm

el **granjero**, la **granjera** NOUN
farmer

el **grano** NOUN
1 grain
2 bean
3 spot
□ Me ha salido un grano en la frente. I've got a spot on my forehead.
■ ir al grano to get to the point

la **grapa** NOUN
staple

la **grapadora** NOUN
stapler

la **grasa** NOUN
1 fat
□ No me va bien tanta grasa. So much fat isn't good for me.
2 grease
■ La cocina está llena de grasa. The cooker's really greasy.

**grasiento** (FEM grasienta) ADJECTIVE
greasy

**graso** (FEM grasa) ADJECTIVE
greasy
□ Tengo el cutis graso. I've got greasy skin.

**gratis** (PL gratis) ADJECTIVE, ADVERB
1 free
□ La entrada es gratis. Entry is free.
2 for free
□ Te lo arreglan gratis. They'll fix it for free.

**gratuito** (FEM gratuita) ADJECTIVE
free

la **grava** NOUN
gravel

**grave** (FEM grave) ADJECTIVE
1 serious
□ Tenemos un problema grave. We've got a serious problem.
■ Su padre está grave. His father is seriously ill.
2 low

la **gravedad** NOUN
gravity
□ la ley de la gravedad the law of gravity
■ estar herido de gravedad to be seriously injured

**gravemente** ADVERB
seriously
■ estar gravemente enfermo to be seriously ill

**Grecia** FEM NOUN
Greece

el **griego** (FEM la griega) ADJECTIVE, NOUN
Greek

el **griego** NOUN
Greek

la **grieta** NOUN
crack

el **grifo** NOUN
tap
□ abrir el grifo to turn on the tap □ cerrar el grifo to turn off the tap

el **grillo** NOUN
cricket

la **gripe** NOUN
flu
□ tener la gripe to have the flu

el **gris** ADJECTIVE, NOUN
grey
□ una puerta gris a grey door

**gritar** VERB [25]
1 to shout
■ El público le gritaba al árbitro. The crowd were shouting at the referee.
■ Niños, no gritéis tanto. Children, stop shouting so much.
2 to scream
□ El enfermo no podía dejar de gritar. The patient couldn't stop screaming.

el **grito** NOUN
1 shout
□ gritos de protesta shouts of protest
■ ¡No des esos gritos! Stop shouting like that!
2 scream
□ Oímos un grito en la calle. We heard a scream outside.
■ dando gritos a viva voz screaming at the top of his voice
■ Es el último grito. It's all the rage.

la **grosella** NOUN
redcurrant

**grosero** (FEM grosera) ADJECTIVE
rude

el **grosor** NOUN
thickness
■ La pared tiene 30cm de grosor. The wall is 30cm thick.

la **grúa** NOUN
crane
■ La grúa se ha llevado el coche. My car was towed away.

**grueso** (FEM gruesa) ADJECTIVE
1 thick
2 stout

el **grumo** NOUN
lump

**gruñir**\* VERB
to grumble
□ El abuelo siempre está gruñendo. Grandad is always grumbling.

## grupo – guitarra

**el grupo** NOUN

1 group
□ Se dividieron en grupos. They divided into groups.
■ **el grupo sanguíneo** blood group
■ **Los alumnos trabajan en grupo.** The students work in groups.

2 band
□ un grupo de rock a rock band

**el guacho**, la **guacha** NOUN (Andes, River Plate)
homeless child

**el guajolote** NOUN (Mexico)
turkey

**el guante** NOUN
glove
□ Uso guantes de goma. I use rubber gloves.
■ **unos guantes** a pair of gloves

**la guantera** NOUN
glove compartment

**guapo** (FEM **guapa**) ADJECTIVE

1 handsome
2 pretty
3 beautiful
■ **¡Ven, guapo!** Come here, love!

**el/la guarda** NOUN
keeper
■ **guarda jurado** armed security guard

**el guardabarros** (PL los **guardabarros**) NOUN
mudguard

**el/la guardaespaldas** (MASC PL los/las **guardaespaldas**) NOUN
bodyguard

**guardar** VERB [25]

1 to put away
□ Los niños guardaron los juguetes. The children put away their toys. □ Guardé los documentos en el cajón. I put the documents away in the drawer.
■ **Raúl se guardó el pañuelo en el bolsillo.** Raúl put the handkerchief in his pocket.

2 to keep
□ Guarda el recibo. Keep the receipt. □ No sabe guardar un secreto. He can't keep a secret.
■ **No les guardo rencor.** I don't bear them a grudge.
■ **guardar las apariencias** to keep up appearances
■ **guardar un fichero** to save a file

**el guardarropa** NOUN
cloakroom

**la guardería** NOUN
nursery (PL nurseries)

**la guardia** NOUN
■ **de guardia** on duty □ Me atendió el médico de guardia. I was seen by the doctor on duty. □ Estoy de guardia. I'm on duty.
■ **la Guardia Civil** the Civil Guard

**el/la guardia** NOUN
police officer

**el guarro**, la **guarra** NOUN (colloquial)
■ **¡Eres un guarro!** You're disgusting!

**guay** (FEM **guay**) ADJECTIVE
cool (colloquial)
□ ¡Qué moto más guay! What a cool bike!

**güero** (FEM **güera**) ADJECTIVE (Mexico)
blonde

**la guerra** NOUN
war
□ la Segunda Guerra Mundial the Second World War
■ **declarar la guerra a un país** to declare war on a country
■ **estar en guerra** to be at war

**el/la guía** NOUN
guide
□ El guía vino a recogernos al aeropuerto. The guide came to pick us up at the airport.

**la guía** NOUN
guidebook
□ Compré una guía turística de Londres. I bought a tourist guidebook of London.
■ **una guía de hoteles** a hotel guide
■ **una guía telefónica** a telephone directory

**guiar*** VERB [21]
to guide
□ Mi amigo nos guió a la estación. My friend guided us to the station.
■ **Nos guiamos por un mapa que teníamos.** We found our way using a map that we had.

**el guijarro** NOUN
pebble

**la guinda** NOUN
cherry (PL cherries)

**la guindilla** NOUN
chilli pepper

**guiñar** VERB [25]
to wink
■ **Me guiñó el ojo.** He winked at me.

**el guión** (PL los **guiones**) NOUN

1 hyphen
■ **La palabra 'self-defence' lleva guión.** The word 'self-defence' is hyphenated.
2 dash
3 script

**el guisante** NOUN
pea

**guisar** VERB [25]
to cook

**la guitarra** NOUN
guitar

el **gusano** NOUN
1 worm
   - **un gusano de seda** a silk worm
2 maggot
3 caterpillar

**gustar** VERB [25]
   - **Me gustan las uvas.** I like grapes.
   - **¿Te gusta viajar?** Do you like travelling?
   - **Me gustó como hablaba.** I liked the way he spoke.
   - **Me gustaría conocerla.** I would like to meet her.
   - **Me gusta su hermana.** I fancy his sister.
   - **Le gusta más llevar pantalones.** She prefers to wear trousers.

el **gusto** NOUN
   taste
   □ No tiene gusto para vestirse. He has no taste in clothes. □ He decorado la habitación a mi gusto. I've decorated the room to my taste.
   - **un comentario de mal gusto** a tasteless remark
   - **Le noto un gusto a almendras.** It tastes of almonds.
   - **¡Con mucho gusto!** With pleasure!
   - **¡Mucho gusto en conocerle!** I'm very pleased to meet you!
   - **sentirse a gusto** to feel at ease

g

# Hh

**ha** VERB ▷*see* **haber**
el **haba** NOUN
broad bean
**Habana** NOUN
■ **La Habana** Havana
**haber\*** VERB [24]
to have
□ He comido. I've eaten. □ Hemos comido. We've eaten. □ Había comido. I'd eaten.
□ Se ha sentado. She's sat down.
■ **De haberlo sabido, habría ido.** If I'd known, I would have gone.
■ **¡Haberlo dicho antes!** You should have said so before!
■ **hay**
□ Hay una iglesia en la esquina. There's a church on the corner. □ Hubo una guerra. There was a war. □ Hay treinta alumnos en mi clase. There are thirty pupils in my class. □ ¿Hay entradas? Are there any tickets?
■ **¡No hay de qué!** Don't mention it!
■ **¿Qué hay?** *(colloquial)* How are things?
■ **¿Qué hubo?** *(Mexico: colloquial)* How are things?
■ **hay que ...**
■ **Hay que ser respetuoso.** You must be respectful.
■ **¡Habrá que decírselo!** We'll have to tell him!
**hábil** (FEM **hábil**) ADJECTIVE
skilful
□ Es un jugador muy hábil. He's a very skilful player.
■ **Es muy hábil con las manos.** He's very good with his hands.
■ **Es muy hábil para los negocios.** He's a very able businessman.
la **habilidad** NOUN
skill
□ Ha demostrado una gran habilidad para los negocios. He's shown great business skill.
■ **Tiene mucha habilidad para los idiomas.** She's very good at languages.
la **habitación** (PL las **habitaciones**) NOUN
1 bedroom

2 room
■ **una habitación doble** a double room
■ **una habitación individual** a single room
el/la **habitante** NOUN
inhabitant
■ **los habitantes de la zona** people living in the area
**habitar** VERB [25]
to live in
□ los que habitaban en la zona those who lived in the area
■ **La casa está todavía sin habitar.** The house is still unoccupied.
el **hábito** NOUN
habit
□ Fumar es un mal hábito. Smoking is a bad habit.
**habitual** (FEM **habitual**) ADJECTIVE
usual
□ No es habitual verlos juntos. It's not usual to see them together.
■ **un cliente habitual** a regular customer
el **habla** NOUN
speech
■ **Ha perdido el habla.** He's lost the power of speech.
■ **países de habla inglesa** English-speaking countries
■ **¿Señor López? — Al habla.** Señor López? — Speaking.
**hablador** (FEM **habladora**) ADJECTIVE
1 chatty
2 gossipy
las **habladurías** NOUN
gossip *sing*
el/la **hablante** NOUN
speaker
**hablar** VERB [25]
1 to speak
□ ¿Hablas español? Do you speak Spanish?
■ **¿Quién habla?** Who's calling?
2 to talk
□ Estuvimos hablando toda la tarde. We were talking all afternoon.
■ **hablar con alguien 1** to speak to someone □ ¿Has hablado ya con el

profesor? Have you spoken to the teacher yet? **2** to talk to someone □ Necesito hablar contigo. I need to talk to you.

■ **hablar de algo** to talk about something
■ **¿Vas a ayudarle en la mudanza? — ¡Ni hablar!** Are you going to help him with the move? — No way!

**habré** VERB ▷ see **haber**

**hacer\*** VERB [26]

**1** to make
□ Tengo que hacer la cama. I've got to make the bed. □ Voy a hacer una tortilla. I'm going to make an omelette. □ Están haciendo mucho ruido. They're making a lot of noise.

**2** to do
□ ¿Qué haces? What are you doing? □ Estoy haciendo los deberes. I'm doing my homework. □ Hago mucho deporte. I do a lot of sport. □ ¿Qué hace tu padre? What does your father do?

**3** to be
□ Hace calor. It's hot. □ Ojalá haga buen tiempo. I hope the weather's nice. □ Hizo dos grados bajo cero. It was two degrees below zero.

■ **hace ... 1** ago □ Terminé hace una hora. I finished an hour ago. □ Ha estado aquí hasta hace poco. He was here a few minutes ago. **2** for □ Hace un mes que voy. I've been going for a month.

■ **¿Hace mucho que esperas?** Have you been waiting long?

■ **hacer hacer algo** to have something done □ Hicieron pintar la fachada del colegio. They had the front of the school painted.

■ **hacer a alguien hacer algo** to make someone do something □ Hace estudiar a los alumnos. He makes the pupils study.

■ **hacer clic en** to click on

■ **hacerse** to become □ Quiere hacerse famoso. He wants to become famous. □ Se hicieron amigos. They became friends.

■ **Ya se está haciendo viejo.** He's getting old now.

el **hacha** FEM NOUN
axe

**hacia** PREPOSITION

**1** towards
□ Venía hacia mí. He was coming towards me. □ su actitud hacia sus padres his attitude towards his parents

**2** at about
□ Volveremos hacia las tres. We'll be back at about three.

■ **hacia adelante** forwards
■ **hacia atrás** backwards
■ **hacia dentro** inside
■ **hacia fuera** outside
■ **hacia abajo** down
■ **hacia arriba** up

el **hada** NOUN
fairy (PL fairies)

■ **un hada madrina** a fairy godmother
■ **un cuento de hadas** a fairy tale

**hago** VERB ▷ see **hacer**

**hala** EXCLAMATION
come on!

**halagar\*** VERB [37]
to flatter

**hallar** VERB [25]
to find

■ **hallarse** to be □ Se halla fuera del país. He's out of the country.

la **hamaca** NOUN

**1** hammock
**2** deckchair
**3** swing (River Plate)

el **hambre** NOUN
hunger

■ **tener hambre** to be hungry □ Tengo mucha hambre. I'm very hungry.

la **hamburguesa** NOUN
hamburger

el **hámster** (PL los **hámsters**) NOUN
hamster

el **hardware** NOUN
hardware

**haré** VERB ▷ see **hacer**

la **harina** NOUN
flour

■ **harina de trigo** wheat flour

**hartar** VERB [25]

■ **hartarse** to get fed up □ Me harté de estudiar. I got fed up with studying.

■ **Me harté de pasteles.** I stuffed myself with cakes.

■ **¡Me estás hartando!** You're getting on my nerves!

**harto** (FEM **harta**) ADJECTIVE
▷ see also **harto** ADVERB

**1** fed up

■ **estar harto de algo** to be fed up with something □ Estábamos hartos de repetirlo. We were fed up with repeating it. □ ¡Me tienes harto! I'm fed up with you!

**2** a lot of (Latin America)
□ Había harta comida. There was a lot of food.

**harto** ADVERB
▷ see also **harto** ADJECTIVE (Latin America)

**1** very
□ Es un idioma harto difícil. It's a very difficult language.

**2** a lot

157

□ Tenemos harto que estudiar. We've got a lot to study.

**hasta** ADVERB

▷ *see also* **hasta** PREPOSITION, CONJUNCTION

even

□ Estudia hasta cuando está de vacaciones. He even studies when he's on holiday.

**hasta** PREPOSITION, CONJUNCTION

▷ *see also* **hasta** ADVERB

1 till

□ Está abierto hasta las cuatro. It's open till four o'clock.

■ **¿Hasta cuándo?** How long? □ ¿Hasta cuándo te quedas? — Hasta la semana que viene. How long are you staying? — Till next week.

■ **Hasta ahora no ha llamado nadie.** No one has called up to now.

■ **hasta que** until □ Espera aquí hasta que te llamen. Wait here until you're called.

2 up to

□ Caminamos hasta la puerta. We walked up to the door.

3 as far as

□ Desde aquí se ve hasta el pueblo de al lado. From here you can see as far as the next town.

■ **¡Hasta luego!** See you!

■ **¡Hasta el sábado!** See you on Saturday!

**hay** VERB ▷ *see* **haber**

**haz** VERB ▷ *see* **hacer**

**he** VERB

▷ *see also* **he** ADVERB ▷ *see* **haber**

**he** ADVERB

▷ *see also* **he** VERB

■ **He aquí un ejemplo.** Here's an example.

■ **He aquí unos ejemplos.** Here are some examples.

■ **he aquí por qué ...** that's why ...

la **hebilla** NOUN

buckle

el **hebreo** (FEM la **hebrea**) ADJECTIVE, NOUN

Hebrew

el **hebreo** NOUN

Hebrew

el **hechizo** NOUN

spell

**hecho** VERB

▷ *see also* **hecho** ADJECTIVE, NOUN ▷ *see* **hacer**

**hecho** (FEM **hecha**) ADJECTIVE

▷ *see also* **hecho** VERB, NOUN

made

□ ¿De qué está hecho? What's it made of?

■ **hecho a mano** handmade

■ **hecho a máquina** machine-made

■ **Me gusta la carne bien hecha.** I like my meat well done.

■ **un filete poco hecho** a rare steak

■ **¡Bien hecho!** Well done!

■ **un hombre hecho y derecho** a fully grown man

el **hecho** NOUN ADJECTIVE, VERB

1 fact

□ el hecho de que ... the fact that ...

■ **el hecho es que ...** the fact is that ...

2 event

□ un hecho histórico an historic event

■ **de hecho** in fact

la **helada** NOUN

frost

la **heladera** NOUN *(River Plate)*

refrigerator

la **heladería** NOUN

ice-cream parlour

**helado** (FEM **helada**) ADJECTIVE

1 frozen

□ El lago está helado. The lake's frozen over.

2 freezing

□ Este cuarto está helado. This room's freezing. □ ¡Estoy helado! I'm freezing!

el **helado** NOUN

ice cream

□ un helado de chocolate a chocolate ice cream

**helar\*** VERB [39]

to freeze

□ El frío ha helado las tuberías. The cold has frozen the pipes. □ Esta noche va a helar. It's going to freeze tonight.

■ **helarse** to freeze □ Me estoy helando. I'm freezing.

■ **Anoche heló.** There was a frost last night.

el **helecho** NOUN

fern

el **helicóptero** NOUN

helicopter

la **hembra** ADJECTIVE, NOUN

female

□ un elefante hembra a female elephant

**hemos** VERB ▷ *see* **haber**

**heredar** VERB [25]

to inherit

la **heredera** NOUN

heiress (PL heiresses)

el **heredero** NOUN

heir

la **herencia** NOUN

inheritance

la **herida** NOUN

1 wound

□ una herida de bala a bullet wound □ una herida de cuchillo a stab wound

2 injury (PL injuries)

□ Murió a causa de las heridas del accidente. He died from injuries received in the accident.

**herido** (FEM **herida**) ADJECTIVE
1 wounded
2 injured
**herir*** VERB [51]
1 to wound
  □ Lo hirieron en el pecho. He was wounded in the chest.
2 to injure
  □ Resultó gravemente herido en la caída. He was seriously injured in the fall.
la **hermana** NOUN
  sister
la **hermanastra** NOUN
  stepsister
el **hermanastro** NOUN
  stepbrother
  ■ **mis hermanastros 1** my stepbrothers **2** my stepbrothers and sisters
el **hermano** NOUN
  brother
  ■ **mis hermanos 1** my brothers **2** my brothers and sisters
**hermético** (FEM **hermética**) ADJECTIVE
  airtight
**hermoso** (FEM **hermosa**) ADJECTIVE
  beautiful
la **hermosura** NOUN
  beauty
  □ el secreto de su hermosura the secret of her beauty
  ■ **¡Qué hermosura de paisaje!** What a beautiful landscape!
el **héroe** NOUN
  hero (PL heroes)
la **heroína** NOUN
  heroine
el **heroinómano**, la **heroinómana** NOUN
  heroin addict
la **herradura** NOUN
  horseshoe
la **herramienta** NOUN
  tool
el **herrero** NOUN
  blacksmith
**hervir*** VERB [51]
  to boil
  □ El agua está hirviendo. The water's boiling.
  ■ **hervir agua** to boil water
el/la **heterosexual** ADJECTIVE, NOUN
  heterosexual
**hice** VERB ▷see hacer
**hielo** VERB ▷see helar
el **hielo** NOUN
  ice
la **hierba** NOUN
1 grass

2 herb
  ■ **una mala hierba** a weed
  ○ **LANGUAGE TIP** Word for word, **mala hierba** means 'bad grass'.
la **hierbabuena** NOUN
  mint
el **hierbajo** NOUN
  weed
el **hierro** NOUN
  iron
  □ una caja de hierro an iron box
el **hígado** NOUN
  liver
la **higiene** NOUN
  hygiene
**higiénico** (FEM **higiénica**) ADJECTIVE
  hygienic
  ■ **poco higiénico** unhygienic
el **higo** NOUN
  fig
  ■ **un higo chumbo** a prickly pear
la **higuera** NOUN
  fig tree
la **hija** NOUN
  daughter
  ■ **Soy hija única.** I'm an only child.
  ■ **Sí, hija mía, tienes razón.** Yes, my dear, you're right.
la **hijastra** NOUN
  stepdaughter
el **hijastro** NOUN
  stepson
  ■ **mis hijastros 1** my stepsons **2** my stepchildren
el **hijo** NOUN
  son
  □ su hijo mayor his oldest son
  ■ **mis hijos 1** my sons **2** my children
  ■ **Soy hijo único.** I'm an only child.
la **hilera** NOUN
1 row
  □ una hilera de casas a row of houses
2 line
  □ ponerse en hilera to get into a line
el **hilo** NOUN
1 thread
  □ hilo de coser sewing thread
2 linen
  □ un traje de hilo a linen suit
  ■ **los hilos del teléfono** the telephone wires
el **himno** NOUN
  hymn
  ■ **el himno nacional** the national anthem
el/la **hincha** NOUN
  fan
  □ los hinchas del fútbol football fans
**hinchado** (FEM **hinchada**) ADJECTIVE

Spanish-English

swollen

el **hipermercado** NOUN
hypermarket

el **hipo** NOUN
hiccups
□ Tengo hipo. I've got hiccups. □ Me ha dado hipo. It's given me hiccups.

**hipócrita** (FEM **hipócrita**) ADJECTIVE
hypocritical
■ ¡No seas hipócrita! Don't be such a hypocrite!

el/la **hipócrita** NOUN
hypocrite

el **hipódromo** NOUN
racecourse

el **hipopótamo** NOUN
hippo (PL hippos)

la **hipoteca** NOUN
mortgage

**hiriendo** VERB ▷ see herir

**hirviendo** VERB ▷ see hervir

**hispanohablante** (FEM **hispanohablante**) ADJECTIVE
Spanish-speaking
□ los países hispanohablantes Spanish-speaking countries

el/la **hispanohablante** NOUN
Spanish-speaker

la **historia** NOUN
1 history
□ la historia de España Spanish history
2 story (PL stories)
□ El libro cuenta la historia de dos niños. The book tells the story of two children.
■ la misma historia de siempre the same old story

el **historial** NOUN
record

**histórico** (FEM **histórica**) ADJECTIVE
1 historic
□ una ciudad histórica a historic city
2 historical
□ un personaje histórico a historical character

la **historieta** NOUN
comic strip

**hizo** VERB ▷ see hacer

el **hobby** NOUN
hobby (PL hobbies)
■ Lo hago por hobby. I do it as a hobby.

el **hockey** NOUN
hockey
■ el hockey sobre hielo ice hockey

el **hogar** NOUN
home
□ en todos los hogares españoles in every Spanish home
■ productos para el hogar household

products

la **hoguera** NOUN
bonfire

la **hoja** NOUN
1 leaf (PL leaves)
2 sheet
□ una hoja de papel a sheet of paper
■ una hoja de cálculo a spreadsheet
■ una hoja de solicitud an application form
3 page
□ las hojas de un libro the pages of a book
■ una hoja de afeitar a razor blade

el **hojaldre** NOUN
puff pastry

**hojear** VERB [25]
to leaf through

**hola** EXCLAMATION
hello!

**Holanda** FEM NOUN
Holland

**holandés** (FEM **holandesa**, MASC PL **holandeses**) ADJECTIVE
Dutch

el **holandés** (PL los **holandeses**) NOUN
1 Dutchman (PL Dutchmen)
■ los holandeses the Dutch
2 Dutch

la **holandesa** NOUN
Dutchwoman (PL Dutchwomen)

**holgazán** (FEM **holgazana**, MASC PL **holgazanes**) ADJECTIVE
lazy

el **hollín** NOUN
soot

el **hombre** NOUN
man (PL men)
■ un hombre de negocios a businessman
■ la historia del hombre sobre la tierra the history of mankind on earth

el **hombro** NOUN
shoulder
■ encogerse de hombros to shrug one's shoulders

el **homenaje** NOUN
tribute
■ en homenaje a in honour of

el/la **homosexual** ADJECTIVE, NOUN
homosexual

**hondo** (FEM **honda**) ADJECTIVE
deep
□ un pozo muy hondo a very deep well □ Se ha tirado por la parte honda de la piscina. He dived into the deep end of the pool.

**Honduras** FEM NOUN
Honduras

el **hondureño** (FEM la **hondureña**) ADJECTIVE, NOUN

Honduran

la **honestidad** NOUN
1 honesty
2 decency

**honesto** (FEM **honesta**) ADJECTIVE
honest
□ un vendedor honesto an honest salesman

el **hongo** NOUN
1 fungus
2 mushroom *(Latin America)*

el **honor** NOUN
honour

la **honradez** NOUN
honesty

**honrado** (FEM **honrada**) ADJECTIVE
honest
□ Es una persona muy honrada. He's a very honest person.

la **hora** NOUN
1 hour
□ El viaje dura una hora. The journey lasts an hour.
2 time
□ ¿Qué hora es? What's the time? □ ¿Tienes hora? Have you got the time?
■ **¿A qué hora llega?** What time is he arriving?
■ **llegar a la hora** to arrive on time
■ **la hora de cenar** dinner time
■ **a última hora** at the last minute
3 period
■ **Después de inglés tenemos una hora libre.** After English we have a free period.
4 appointment
□ Tengo hora para el dentista. I've got an appointment at the dentist's.
■ **horas extras** overtime *sing*
■ **en mis horas libres** in my spare time

el **horario** NOUN
timetable
■ **el horario de trenes** the train timetable
■ **horario de visitas** visiting hours *pl*

la **horchata** NOUN

> **DID YOU KNOW...?**
> **Horchata** is a milky looking drink made from tiger nuts and served with ice.

**horizontal** (FEM **horizontal**) ADJECTIVE
horizontal

el **horizonte** NOUN
horizon
□ en el horizonte on the horizon

la **hormiga** NOUN
ant

el **hormigón** NOUN
concrete

el **hormigueo** NOUN
pins and needles

□ Tengo hormigueo en la pierna. I've got pins and needles in my leg.

el **horno** NOUN
oven
□ ¡Este lugar es un horno! This place is like an oven!
■ **pescado al horno** baked fish
■ **pollo al horno** roast chicken
■ **un horno microondas** a microwave oven

el **horóscopo** NOUN
horoscope

la **horquilla** NOUN
hairgrip

**horrible** (FEM **horrible**) ADJECTIVE
awful
□ El tiempo ha estado horrible. The weather has been awful.

el **horror** NOUN
horror
□ los horrores de la guerra the horrors of war
■ **tener horror a algo** to be terrified of something □ Les tengo horror a las arañas. I'm terrified of spiders.
■ **¡Qué horror!** How awful!

**horroroso** (FEM **horrorosa**) ADJECTIVE
1 horrific
□ un accidente horroroso a horrific accident
2 hideous
□ ¡Qué camisa mas horrorosa! What a hideous shirt!

la **hortaliza** NOUN
vegetable

**hortera** (FEM **hortera**) ADJECTIVE
naff *(colloquial)*
□ Tiene un gusto muy hortera. He's got really naff taste.

**hospedarse** VERB [25]
to stay
□ Se hospedaron en un hotel. They stayed in a hotel.

el **hospital** NOUN
hospital
□ La tuvieron que llevar al hospital. She had to be taken to hospital.

la **hospitalidad** NOUN
hospitality

el **hostal** NOUN
small hotel

la **hostia** NOUN
host

el **hotel** NOUN
hotel

**hoy** ADVERB
today
□ Hoy no tenemos clases. We haven't got any classes today. □ el periódico de hoy today's paper □ los jóvenes de hoy young

people today
- **desde hoy en adelante** from now on
- **hoy en día** nowadays
- **hoy por la mañana** this morning

el **hoyo** NOUN
hole

**hube** VERB ▷ see **haber**

la **hucha** NOUN
moneybox

**hueco** (FEM **hueca**) ADJECTIVE
hollow

el **hueco** NOUN
1 space
  □ Deja un hueco para la respuesta. Leave a space for the answer.
  - **Hazme un hueco para sentarme.** Make a bit of room so that I can sit down.
2 free period
  □ Los lunes tengo un hueco entre clase y clase. I have a free period between classes on Mondays.
  - **Entró por un hueco que había en la valla.** He got in through a gap in the fence.

la **huelga** NOUN
strike
  □ una huelga general a general strike
  - **estar en huelga** to be on strike
  - **declararse en huelga** to go on strike

el/la **huelguista** NOUN
striker

la **huella** NOUN
footprint
  - **huellas** tracks
  - **Desapareció sin dejar huella.** He disappeared without trace.
  - **huella digital** fingerprint

**huelo** VERB ▷ see **oler**

**huérfano** (FEM **huérfana**) ADJECTIVE
  - **un niño huérfano** an orphan
  - **ser huérfano** to be an orphan
  - **es huérfano de padre** he's lost his father
  - **quedarse huérfano** to be orphaned

el **huérfano**, la **huérfana** NOUN
orphan

la **huerta** NOUN
1 vegetable garden
2 orchard

el **huerto** NOUN
1 kitchen garden
2 orchard

el **hueso** NOUN
1 bone
2 stone
  - **aceitunas sin hueso** pitted olives
  - **La profesora de francés es un hueso.** *(colloquial)* The French teacher's a real dragon.

162 el/la **huésped** NOUN

guest

el **huevo** NOUN
egg
  - **un huevo duro** a hard-boiled egg
  - **un huevo escalfado** a poached egg
  - **un huevo frito** a fried egg
  - **huevos revueltos** scrambled eggs
  - **un huevo pasado por agua** a soft-boiled egg

la **huida** NOUN
escape

**huir\*** VERB [10]
to escape
  □ Huyó de la cárcel. He escaped from prison.
  - **Huyeron del país.** They fled the country.
  - **salir huyendo** to run away

el **hule** NOUN
1 oilcloth
2 rubber *(Mexico)*
  □ una liga de hule a rubber band

la **humanidad** NOUN
humanity

**humano** (FEM **humana**) ADJECTIVE
human
  □ el cuerpo humano the human body
  - **los seres humanos** human beings

el **humano** NOUN
human being

la **humareda** NOUN
cloud of smoke

la **humedad** NOUN
1 dampness
2 humidity

**húmedo** (FEM **húmeda**) ADJECTIVE
1 damp
  □ La ropa está húmeda todavía. The clothes are still damp.
2 humid
  □ El día estaba muy húmedo. It was a very humid day.

**humilde** (FEM **humilde**) ADJECTIVE
humble
  □ Era de familia humilde. She was from a humble background.

el **humo** NOUN
smoke
  □ El humo de la chimenea. The smoke from the chimney.
  - **darse humos** to brag
  - **bajar los humos a alguien** to take someone down a peg or two
  - **Estaba que echaba humo.** She was absolutely fuming.

el **humor** NOUN
mood
  □ No está de humor para bromas. He's not in the mood for jokes.

■ **estar de buen humor** to be in a good mood
■ **estar de mal humor** to be in a bad mood
■ **Tiene un gran sentido del humor.** He has got a good sense of humour.
■ **humor negro** black humour

**hundirse** VERB [58]

1 to sink
  □ El barco se hundió durante la tormenta. The boat sank during the storm.
2 to collapse
  □ El techo se hundió con el peso. The ceiling collapsed under the weight.

el **húngaro** (FEM la **húngara**) ADJECTIVE, NOUN
  Hungarian

el **húngaro** NOUN
  Hungarian

**Hungría** FEM NOUN
  Hungary

el **huracán** NOUN
  hurricane

**hurgar\*** VERB [37]
  to rummage
  □ La encontré hurgando en los cajones. I found her rummaging through the drawers. □ Hurgó en sus bolsillos buscando las llaves. He rummaged in his pockets for the keys.
  ■ **hurgarse la nariz** to pick one's nose

**huyendo** VERB ▷ see **huir**

h

# Ii

**I.B.** ABBREVIATION (= *Instituto de Bachillerato*)

> DID YOU KNOW...?
> In Spain the **Institutos de Bachillerato** are state secondary schools for 12- to 18-year-olds.

**iba** VERB ▷ see **ir**

el **iberoamericano** (FEM la **iberoamericana**) ADJECTIVE, NOUN
Latin American

el **iceberg** (PL los **icebergs**) NOUN
iceberg

el **icono** NOUN
icon

la **ictericia** NOUN
jaundice

la **ida** NOUN
single
□ ¿Cuánto cuesta la ida? How much does a single cost?
■ **¿Me da uno de ida y vuelta para Londres, por favor?** A return to London please.
■ **un billete de ida y vuelta** a return ticket
■ **un boleto de ida y vuelta** (*Latin America*) a return ticket
■ **a la ida** on the way there
■ **El viaje de ida duró dos horas.** The journey there took two hours.

la **idea** NOUN
idea
□ ¡Qué buena idea! What a good idea! □ No tengo ni idea. I haven't the faintest idea.
■ **Mi idea era que nos juntáramos en mi casa.** I thought that we could meet at my house.
■ **Ya me voy haciendo a la idea.** I'm beginning to get used to the idea.
■ **cambiar de idea** to change one's mind □ He cambiado de idea. I've changed my mind.

**ideal** (FEM **ideal**) ADJECTIVE
ideal
□ el lugar ideal para las vacaciones the ideal place for the holidays

el **ideal** NOUN
ideal

□ los ideales democráticos democratic ideals □ Mi ideal sería trabajar cuatro horas diarias. My ideal would be to work four hours a day.

**idear** VERB [25]
to devise
□ Idearon un nuevo sistema. They devised a new system.

**idéntico** (FEM **idéntica**) ADJECTIVE
identical
□ Tiene una falda idéntica a la mía. She has an identical skirt to mine.
■ **Es idéntica a su padre.** She's the spitting image of her father.

**identificar\*** VERB [48]
to identify
□ Ya han identificado a la víctima. They've already identified the victim.
■ **identificarse con alguien** to identify with somebody

el **idioma** NOUN
language
□ Habla tres idiomas a la perfección. He speaks three languages perfectly.

**idiota** (FEM **idiota**) ADJECTIVE
stupid
□ ¡No seas tan idiota! Don't be so stupid!

el/la **idiota** NOUN
idiot

la **idiotez** (PL las **idioteces**) NOUN
■ **Deja de decir idioteces.** Stop talking nonsense.

el **ídolo** NOUN
idol

la **iglesia** NOUN
church (PL churches)
□ Voy a la iglesia todos los domingos. I go to church every Sunday.
■ **la Iglesia católica** the Catholic Church

**ignorante** (FEM **ignorante**) ADJECTIVE
ignorant

**ignorar** VERB [25]
1 not to know
□ Ignoramos su paradero. We don't know his whereabouts.
2 to ignore

□ Es mejor ignorarla. It's best to ignore her.

**igual** (FEM **igual**) ADJECTIVE

▷ see also **igual** ADVERB

1 equal

□ Se repartieron el dinero en partes iguales. They divided the money into equal shares.

■ **X es igual a Y.** X is equal to Y.

2 the same

□ Todas las casas son iguales. All the houses are the same.

■ **Es igual a su madre. 1** She looks just like her mother. **2** She's just like her mother.

■ **Tengo una falda igual que la tuya.** I've got a skirt just like yours.

■ **ir iguales** to be even

■ **Van quince iguales.** It's fifteen all.

■ **Es igual hoy que mañana.** Today or tomorrow, it doesn't matter.

■ **Me da igual.** I don't mind.

**igual** ADVERB

▷ see also **igual** ADJECTIVE

1 the same

□ Se visten igual. They dress the same.

2 maybe

□ Igual no lo saben todavía. Maybe they don't know yet.

3 anyway

□ No hizo nada pero la castigaron igual. She didn't do anything but they punished her anyway.

**la igualdad** NOUN

equality

□ la igualdad racial racial equality

■ **la igualdad de oportunidades** equal opportunities

**igualmente** ADVERB

the same to you

□ ¡Feliz Navidad! — Gracias, igualmente. Happy Christmas! — Thanks, the same to you.

**ilegal** (FEM **ilegal**) ADJECTIVE

illegal

**ilegible** (FEM **ilegible**) ADJECTIVE

illegible

□ Tiene una letra ilegible. His handwriting's illegible.

**ileso** (FEM **ilesa**) ADJECTIVE

unhurt

□ Salió ileso del accidente. He escaped unhurt from the accident.

■ **Todos resultaron ilesos.** No one was hurt.

**la iluminación** NOUN

lighting

□ La iluminación de las calles es insuficiente. The street lighting is poor.

■ **Se cortó la iluminación del estadio.** The stadium floodlighting went out.

**iluminar** VERB [25]

to light

□ las farolas que iluminan la calle the streetlamps that light the street □ Unas velas iluminaban la habitación. The room was lit by candles.

■ **El flash le iluminó el rostro.** The flash lit up his face.

■ **Esta lámpara ilumina muy poco.** This lamp gives out very little light.

■ **Se le iluminó la cara.** His face lit up.

**la ilusión** (PL las **ilusiones**) NOUN

1 hope

□ Llegó aquí con muchísima ilusión. He arrived here full of hope. □ No te hagas muchas ilusiones. Don't build your hopes up.

2 dream

□ Mi mayor ilusión es llegar a ser médico. My dream is to become a doctor.

3 illusion

□ una ilusión óptica an optical illusion

■ **Le hace mucha ilusión que vengas.** He's really looking forward to you coming.

■ **Tu regalo me hizo mucha ilusión.** I was delighted to get your present.

■ **¡Qué ilusión!** How wonderful!

**ilusionado** (FEM **ilusionada**) ADJECTIVE

excited

**ilusionar** VERB [25]

■ **Me ilusiona mucho la idea.** I'm really excited about the idea.

■ **ilusionarse** to build up one's hopes □ No te ilusiones demasiado. Don't build up your hopes too much.

■ **ilusionarse con algo** to get really excited about something

**la ilustración** (PL las **ilustraciones**) NOUN

illustration

**la imagen** (PL las **imágenes**) NOUN

1 image

□ Han decidido cambiar de imagen. They've decided to change their image.

■ **ser la viva imagen de alguien** to be the spitting image of somebody

2 picture

□ Las películas dan una imagen falsa de América. Films give a false picture of America.

**la imaginación** (PL las **imaginaciones**) NOUN

imagination

□ Tiene mucha imaginación. He has a vivid imagination.

■ **Esas son imaginaciones tuyas.** You're imagining things.

■ **Ni se me pasó por la imaginación.** It never even occurred to me.

# imaginarse – importancia

**imaginarse** VERB [25]
to imagine
  □ No te imaginas lo mal que me sentí. You can't imagine how bad I felt. □ Me imagino que seguirá en Madrid. I imagine that he's still in Madrid.
  ■ **Me imagino que sí.** I imagine so.
  ■ **Me imagino que no.** I wouldn't think so.
  ■ **¿Se enfadó mucho? — ¡Imagínate!** Was he very angry? — What do you think!

el **imán** (PL los **imanes**) NOUN
magnet

**imbécil** (FEM **imbécil**) ADJECTIVE
stupid
  □ ¡No seas imbécil! Don't be stupid!

la **imitación** (PL las **imitaciones**) NOUN
1 impression
  □ Es muy buena haciendo imitaciones. She's very good at doing impressions.
2 imitation
  □ Aprendemos a hablar por imitación. We learn to speak by imitation. □ los diamantes de imitación imitation diamonds □ Es imitación de cuero. It's imitation leather.

**imitar** VERB [25]
to copy
  □ Imita todo lo que hace su hermano. He copies everything his brother does.
  ■ **imitar a alguien** to do an impression of somebody □ Imita muy bien a la directora. She does a very good impression of the headmistress.
  ■ **imitar un acento** to imitate an accent

**impaciente** (FEM **impaciente**) ADJECTIVE
impatient
  □ Se estaba empezando a poner impaciente. He was beginning to get impatient.
  □ Estarás impaciente por saberlo. You'll be impatient to know.

**impar** (FEM **impar**) ADJECTIVE
odd
  □ un número impar an odd number

el **impar** NOUN
odd number

**imparcial** (FEM **imparcial**) ADJECTIVE
impartial

**impecable** (FEM **impecable**) ADJECTIVE
impeccable
  □ Su comportamiento siempre ha sido impecable. His behaviour has always been impeccable.
  ■ **Siempre va impecable.** He is always impeccably dressed.

**impedir*** VERB [38]
1 to prevent
  □ Trataron de impedir la huida de los presos. They tried to prevent the prisoners' escape.
  □ impedir que alguien haga algo to prevent

somebody from doing something
2 to stop
  □ A mí nadie me lo va a impedir. Nobody is going to stop me.
3 to block
  □ Un camión nos impedía el paso. A lorry was blocking our way.

el **imperdible** NOUN
safety pin

el **imperio** NOUN
empire

**impermeable** (FEM **impermeable**)
ADJECTIVE
waterproof
  □ una tela impermeable waterproof material

el **impermeable** NOUN
raincoat

**impersonal** (FEM **impersonal**) ADJECTIVE
impersonal

**impertinente** (FEM **impertinente**)
ADJECTIVE
impertinent

**impidiendo** VERB ▷ see **impedir**
**impido** VERB ▷ see **impedir**
**imponer*** VERB [41]
to impose
  □ Le impusieron una multa de 50 euros. They imposed a 50-euro fine on him.
  ■ **imponerse 1** to triumph □ El corredor nigeriano se impuso en la segunda carrera. The Nigerian runner triumphed in the second race. **2** to assert oneself □ Sabe imponerse. He knows how to assert himself.

la **importación** (PL las **importaciones**)
NOUN
import
  □ una empresa de importación/exportación an import-export business
  ■ **los artículos de importación** imported goods
  ■ **Está prohibida su importación.** There's a ban on importing it.

la **importancia** NOUN
importance
  □ un asunto de suma importancia a matter of great importance
  ■ **dar importancia a algo** to attach importance to something □ Les da demasiada importancia a los detalles. He attaches too much importance to details.
  ■ **darse importancia** to give oneself airs
  ■ **La educación tiene mucha importancia.** Education is very important.
  ■ **¡Me he olvidado tu libro! — No tiene importancia.** I've forgotten your book! — It doesn't matter.

■ **cuestiones sin importancia**
unimportant matters
**importante** (FEM **importante**) ADJECTIVE
important
■ **lo importante** the important thing □ Lo
importante es que vengas. The important
thing is that you come.
**importar** VERB [25]
1 to import
□ Importa especias de la India. He imports
spices from India.
2 to matter
□ ¿Y eso qué importa? And what does that
matter?
■ **no importa 1** it doesn't matter □ No
importa lo que piensen los demás. It
doesn't matter what other people think.
**2** never mind □ No importa, podemos
hacerlo mañana. Never mind, we can do it
tomorrow.
■ **No me importa levantarme temprano.**
I don't mind getting up early. □ ¿Le importa
que fume? Do you mind if I smoke?
■ **¿Y a ti qué te importa?** What's it to you?
■ **Me importan mucho mis estudios.** My
studies are very important to me.
■ **Me importa un bledo.** I couldn't care less.
**imposible** (FEM **imposible**) ADJECTIVE
impossible
□ Es imposible predecir quién ganará. It's
impossible to predict who will win. □ Es
imposible de saber por anticipado. It's
impossible to predict. □ El abuelo está
imposible hoy. Granddad is being
impossible today.
■ **Me es imposible comprenderla.** I can't
understand her.
■ **Es imposible que lo sepan.** They can't
possibly know.
el **impostor**, la **impostora** NOUN
impostor
**imprescindible** (FEM **imprescindible**)
ADJECTIVE
essential
la **impresión** (PL las **impresiones**) NOUN
impression
□ Le causó muy buena impresión a mis
padres. He made a very good impression on
my parents.
■ **Tengo la impresión de que no va a
venir.** I have a feeling that he won't come.
■ **Me dio mucha impresión verlo tan
delgado.** I was shocked to see him looking
so thin.
**impresionante** (FEM **impresionante**)
ADJECTIVE
1 impressive
□ una colección de sellos impresionante an

impressive stamp collection
2 amazing
□ una cantidad impresionante de coches an
amazing number of cars
3 striking
□ El parecido es impresionante. The
likeness is striking.
■ **paisajes de una belleza impresionante**
strikingly beautiful landscapes
**impresionar** VERB [25]
1 to shock
□ Me impresionó mucho su palidez. I was
really shocked at how pale he was.
2 to impress
□ Unos poemas me impresionaron más que
otros. Some poems impressed me more
than others.
■ **Impresiona lo rápido que es.** His speed
is impressive.
■ **impresionarse** to be impressed □ Se
impresiona con facilidad. He's easily
impressed.
el **impreso** NOUN
form
□ un impreso de solicitud an application
form
la **impresora** NOUN
printer
□ una impresora láser a laser printer
**imprevisible** (FEM **imprevisible**) ADJECTIVE
1 unforeseeable
□ acontecimientos imprevisibles
unforeseeable events
2 unpredictable
□ Sus reacciones son imprevisibles. His
reactions are unpredictable.
**imprevisto** (FEM **imprevista**) ADJECTIVE
unexpected
el **imprevisto** NOUN
■ **si no surge algún imprevisto** if nothing
unexpected comes up
**imprimir*** VERB [58]
to print
**improvisar** VERB [25]
to improvise
la **imprudencia** NOUN
■ **Saltar la tapia fue una imprudencia.**
It was unwise to jump over the wall.
■ **El accidente fue debido a una
imprudencia del conductor.** The accident
was caused by reckless driving.
**imprudente** (FEM **imprudente**) ADJECTIVE
unwise
□ Sería imprudente nadar aquí. It would be
unwise to go swimming here.
■ **conductores imprudentes** reckless
drivers
**impuesto** VERB ▷ see **imponer**

167

**Spanish-English**

el **impuesto** NOUN
tax (PL taxes)
- **el impuesto sobre la renta** income tax
- **el impuesto sobre el valor añadido** value-added tax
- **el impuesto sobre el valor agregado** (*Latin America*) value-added tax
- **libre de impuestos** duty-free □ Lo compré en la tienda libre de impuestos. I bought it at the duty-free shop.

**impulsar** VERB [25]
to drive
□ Está impulsado por un motor eléctrico. It's driven by an electric motor. □ La ambición la impulsó a mentir. Ambition drove her to lie.
- **una política destinada a impulsar el comercio** a policy designed to boost trade

el **impulso** NOUN
impulse
□ Actué por impulso. I acted on impulse.
- **Mi primer impulso fue salir corriendo.** My first instinct was to run away.
- **Tomó impulso antes de saltar.** He took a run up before jumping.

**inaceptable** (FEM **inaceptable**) ADJECTIVE
unacceptable

**inadecuado** (FEM **inadecuada**) ADJECTIVE
unsuitable

**inadvertido** (FEM **inadvertida**) ADJECTIVE
- **pasar inadvertido** to go unnoticed □ Tu ausencia no pasó inadvertida. Your absence didn't go unnoticed.

**inapropiado** (FEM **inapropiada**) ADJECTIVE
unsuitable
□ Esos zapatos son inapropiados para ir al campo. Those shoes are unsuitable for the country.

la **inauguración** (PL las **inauguraciones**) NOUN
opening
□ Había mucha gente en la inauguración. There were a lot of people at the opening. □ la ceremonia de inauguración the opening ceremony

**inaugurar** VERB [25]
to open
□ Mañana inauguran el nuevo hospital. The new hospital is being opened tomorrow.

el/la **inca** ADJECTIVE, NOUN
Inca

la **incapacidad** NOUN
inability
□ debido a su incapacidad para concentrarse owing to his inability to concentrate
- **la incapacidad física** physical disability
- **la incapacidad mental** mental disability

**incapaz** (FEM **incapaz**, PL **incapaces**)
ADJECTIVE
incapable
□ Es incapaz de estarse callado. He is incapable of keeping quiet.
- **Hoy soy incapaz de concentrarme.** I can't concentrate today.

**incendiarse** VERB [25]
to catch fire
□ Se le incendió el coche. His car caught fire.

el **incendio** NOUN
fire
□ Se declaró un incendio en el hotel. A fire broke out in the hotel.

el **incentivo** NOUN
incentive
□ No tengo incentivo para estudiar. I have no incentive to study.

el **incidente** NOUN
incident
□ La reunión transcurrió sin incidentes. The meeting passed off without incident.

**incierto** (FEM **incierta**) ADJECTIVE
uncertain
□ un porvenir incierto an uncertain future

**inclinar** VERB [25]
to tilt
□ Inclina un poco más la sombrilla. Can you tilt the sun umbrella a bit more?
- **inclinar la cabeza** to nod
- **inclinarse 1** to bend down □ Se inclinó para besarlo. She bent down to kiss him. **2** to lean □ inclinarse sobre algo to lean over something □ inclinarse hacia delante to lean forward □ inclinarse hacia atrás to lean back **3** to bow □ inclinarse ante alguien to bow to somebody

**incluido** (FEM **incluida**) ADJECTIVE
included
□ El servicio no está incluido en el precio. Service is not included.

**incluir*** VERB [10]
to include
□ El precio incluye las comidas. The price includes meals.
- **El examen no incluye este tema.** This topic doesn't come into the exam.

**inclusive** ADVERB
**1** inclusive
□ Está abierto de lunes a sábado inclusive. It's open from Monday to Saturday inclusive.
**2** including
□ hasta el capítulo diez inclusive up to and including chapter ten

**incluso** ADVERB
even
□ He tenido que estudiar incluso los domingos. I've even had to study on Sundays.

**incluyendo** VERB ▷ see **incluir**

**incómodo** (FEM **incómoda)** ADJECTIVE
uncomfortable
□ Este asiento es muy incómodo. This seat
is very uncomfortable. □ Se siente muy
incómoda cuando está con él. She feels very
uncomfortable with him.

**incompetente** (FEM **incompetente)**
ADJECTIVE
incompetent

**incompleto** (FEM **incompleta)** ADJECTIVE
incomplete

**incomprensible** (FEM **incomprensible)**
ADJECTIVE
incomprehensible

**inconsciente** (FEM **inconsciente)** ADJECTIVE
1 unconscious
□ estar inconsciente to be unconscious
□ Quedó inconsciente con el golpe. The
force of the blow left him unconscious.
□ un deseo inconsciente an unconscious
desire
2 thoughtless
□ ¡Qué inconsciente eres! How thoughtless
you are!

**inconveniente** (FEM **inconveniente)**
ADJECTIVE
inconvenient
□ a una hora inconveniente at an
inconvenient time

el **inconveniente** NOUN
1 problem
□ Ha surgido un inconveniente. A problem
has come up.
2 drawback
□ El plan tiene sus inconvenientes. The plan
has its drawbacks.
■ **No tengo ningún inconveniente.** I have
no objection.
■ **No tengo inconveniente en**
**preguntárselo.** I don't mind asking him.
■ **¿Tienes algún inconveniente en que le**
**dé tu teléfono?** Do you mind if I give him
your telephone number?

**incorrecto** (FEM **incorrecta)** ADJECTIVE
1 incorrect
□ una respuesta incorrecta an incorrect
answer
2 impolite
□ Has estado muy incorrecto. You were very
impolite.

**increíble** (FEM **increíble)** ADJECTIVE
incredible

**inculto** (FEM **inculta)** ADJECTIVE
ignorant

**incurable** (FEM **incurable)** ADJECTIVE
incurable

**indeciso** (FEM **indecisa)** ADJECTIVE

indecisive
□ Es una persona muy indecisa. She's very
indecisive.
■ **Estoy indecisa, no sé cuál comprar.**
I can't make up my mind, I don't know
which to buy.

**indefenso** (FEM **indefensa)** ADJECTIVE
defenceless

la **indemnización** (PL las
**indemnizaciones)** NOUN
compensation
□ Recibieron mil dólares de indemnización.
They received a thousand dollars
compensation.
■ **la indemnización por daños y perjuicios**
damages *pl*

**indemnizar*** VERB [13]
to compensate
□ El gobierno indemnizará a las víctimas. The
government will compensate the victims.
■ **Nos tienen que indemnizar.** They've got
to pay us compensation.

la **independencia** NOUN
independence

**independiente** (FEM **independiente)**
ADJECTIVE
1 independent
□ Es una chica muy independiente. She's a
very independent girl.
2 self-contained
□ Son apartamentos independientes. They
are self-contained flats.

**independientemente** ADVERB
independently
□ Los dos motores funcionan
independientemente. The two engines
work independently.
■ **Iremos, independientemente de lo que**
**hayan decidido.** We'll go, regardless of
what they have decided.

**independizarse*** VERB [13]
to become independent
□ Quiero independizarme. I want to
become independent.

la **india** NOUN
Indian

**India** FEM NOUN
■ **La India** India

la **indicación** (PL las **indicaciones)** NOUN
sign
■ **Nos hizo una indicación para que**
**siguiéramos.** He signalled to us to go on.
■ **indicaciones 1** instructions □ Hay que
seguir las indicaciones del manual. You'll
need to follow the instructions in the
manual. **2** directions □ Me dio indicaciones
de cómo llegar. He gave me directions for
getting there.

i

**indicar\*** VERB [48]
**1** to indicate
  □ El termómetro indicaba treinta grados. The thermometer indicated thirty degrees. □ Todo indica que ... Everything indicates that ...
**2** to tell
  □ ¿Puede indicarme dónde hay una gasolinera? Please can you tell where there's a petrol station? □ Un guardia me indicó el camino. A policeman told me the way.
**3** to advise
  □ El médico me indicó que no fumara. The doctor advised me not to smoke.

el **índice** NOUN
**1** index (PL indexes o indices)
  □ un índice alfabético an alphabetical index
  ■ **el índice de materias** the table of contents
  ■ **el índice de natalidad** the birth rate
**2** index finger

la **indiferencia** NOUN
  indifference

**indiferente** (FEM **indiferente**) ADJECTIVE
  indifferent
  □ Parece indiferente al cariño. She seems indifferent to affection.
  ■ **Es indiferente que viva en Glasgow o Edimburgo.** It makes no difference whether he lives in Glasgow or Edinburgh.
  ■ **Me es indiferente hacerlo hoy o mañana.** I don't mind whether I do it today or tomorrow.

**indígena** (FEM **indígena**) ADJECTIVE
  indigenous
  □ la población indígena the indigenous population

el/la **indígena** NOUN
  native

la **indigestión** NOUN
  indigestion

**indignado** (FEM **indignada**) ADJECTIVE
  angry
  □ Están muy indignados con ella. They're very angry with her.

**indignar** VERB [25]
  to infuriate
  □ Su comportamiento los indignó. His behaviour infuriated them.
  ■ **indignarse por algo** to get angry about something
  ■ **indignarse con alguien** to be furious with somebody

el **indio** ADJECTIVE, NOUN
  Indian

la **indirecta** NOUN
  hint

□ lanzar una indirecta to drop a hint

**indirecto** (FEM **indirecta**) ADJECTIVE
  indirect

**indispensable** (FEM **indispensable**) ADJECTIVE
  essential
  □ Es indispensable saber inglés. It's essential to know English.
  ■ **Llevaba sólo lo indispensable.** He was carrying only the essentials.

**individual** (FEM **individual**) ADJECTIVE
**1** individual
  □ Los venden en paquetes individuales. They're sold in individual packets.
**2** single
  □ Quisiera una habitación individual. I'd like a single room.

el **individual** NOUN
  singles pl
  □ la final del individual femenino the ladies' singles final

el **individuo** NOUN
  individual

la **industria** NOUN
  industry (PL industries)
  □ la industria pesada heavy industry □ la industria petrolífera the oil industry

**industrial** (FEM **industrial**) ADJECTIVE
  industrial

el/la **industrial** NOUN
  industrialist

**ineficiente** (FEM **ineficiente**) ADJECTIVE
  inefficient

**inesperado** (FEM **inesperada**) ADJECTIVE
  unexpected
  □ una visita inesperada an unexpected visit

**inestable** (FEM **inestable**) ADJECTIVE
**1** unsteady
**2** changeable

**inevitable** (FEM **inevitable**) ADJECTIVE
  inevitable

**inexacto** (FEM **inexacta**) ADJECTIVE
  inaccurate
  □ La biografía contiene muchos datos inexactos. The biography contains a lot of inaccurate details.

**inexperto** (FEM **inexperta**) ADJECTIVE
  inexperienced

**inexplicable** (FEM **inexplicable**) ADJECTIVE
  inexplicable

**infantil** (FEM **infantil**) ADJECTIVE
**1** children's
  □ un programa infantil a children's programme
**2** childish
  □ ¡No seas tan infantil! Don't be so childish!

el **infarto** NOUN
  heart attack

□ Le dio un infarto. He had a heart attack.

la **infección** (PL las **infecciones**) NOUN
infection

□ tener una infección to have an infection
□ Tiene una infección de oídos. He has got
an ear infection.

**infeliz** (FEM **infeliz**, PL **infelices**) ADJECTIVE
unhappy

**inferior** (FEM **inferior**) ADJECTIVE

1 lower

□ Tenía el labio inferior hinchado. His lower
lip was swollen. □ Las temperaturas han
sido inferiores a lo normal. Temperatures
have been lower than normal.

2 inferior

□ de calidad inferior of inferior quality
■ **un número inferior a nueve** a number
below nine

el **infiernillo** NOUN
stove

el **infierno** NOUN
hell

el **infinitivo** NOUN
infinitive

**inflable** (FEM **inflable**) ADJECTIVE
inflatable

la **inflación** NOUN
inflation

□ Hay que reducir la inflación. Inflation has
to be reduced.

**inflamable** (FEM **inflamable**) ADJECTIVE
inflammable

**inflar** VERB [25]

1 to blow up
2 to inflate

la **influencia** NOUN
influence

□ Mi abuelo tuvo una gran influencia en mí.
My grandfather had a great influence on me.

**influenciar** VERB [25]
to influence

**influir\*** VERB [10]

■ **dos hombres que influyeron en su vida**
two men who influenced his life
■ **Mis padres influyeron mucho en mí.** My
parents had a great influence on me.
■ **El cansancio ha influido en su
rendimiento.** Tiredness has affected his
work.

la **información** (PL las **informaciones**)
NOUN

1 information

□ Quisiera información sobre los cursos de
inglés. I'd like some information on English
courses.
■ **una información muy importante** a
very important piece of information

2 news sing

□ Este canal tiene mucha información
deportiva. There's a lot of sports news on
this channel.

3 directory enquiries

□ Llama a información y pide que te den el
número. Call directory enquiries and ask
them for the number.
■ **Pregunta en información de dónde sale
el tren.** Ask at the information desk which
platform the train leaves from.

**informal** (FEM **informal**) ADJECTIVE

1 informal

□ un ambiente muy informal a very
informal atmosphere
■ **Prefiero la ropa informal.** I prefer casual
clothes.

2 unreliable

□ Es una persona muy informal. He's a very
unreliable person.

**informar** VERB [25]
to inform

□ Nos informaron de que venía con retraso.
They informed us that it was going to be late.
■ **Les han informado mal.** You've been
misinformed.
■ **¿Me podría informar sobre los cursos
de inglés?** Could you give me some
information about English courses?
■ **informarse de algo** to find out about
something

la **informática** NOUN
computing

□ los avances de la informática advances in
computing
■ **Quiere estudiar informática.** He wants
to study computer science.

**informático** (FEM **informática**) ADJECTIVE
computer

□ un programa informático a computer
program

el **informático** NOUN
computer expert

el **informe** NOUN
report

□ Presentó un informe detallado sobre lo
ocurrido. He gave a detailed report about
what had happened.
■ **según mis informes** according to my
information
■ **pedir informes** to ask for references

la **infusión** (PL las **infusiones**) NOUN
herbal tea

■ **una infusión de manzanilla** a camomile
tea

**ingeniar** VERB [25]
to devise

□ Habían ingeniado un sistema para evadir
impuestos. They had devised a system for

171

evading taxes.

■ **ingeniárselas** to manage □ No sé cómo se las ingenió para conseguir el dinero. I don't know how he managed to get the money.

la **ingeniera** NOUN
engineer
□ Quiere ser ingeniera. She wants to be an engineer.

la **ingeniería** NOUN
engineering

el **ingeniero** NOUN
engineer
□ Quiere ser ingeniero. He wants to be an engineer.
■ **un ingeniero agrónomo** an agriculturist

el **ingenio** NOUN
1 ingenuity
2 wit
■ **un ingenio azucarero** *(Latin America)* a sugar refinery

**ingenioso** (FEM **ingeniosa**) ADJECTIVE
1 ingenious
□ ¡Qué idea más ingeniosa! What an ingenious idea!
2 witty
□ un comentario ingenioso a witty comment

**ingenuo** (FEM **ingenua**) ADJECTIVE
naïve

**Inglaterra** FEM NOUN
England

**inglés** (FEM **inglesa**, MASC PL **ingleses**)
ADJECTIVE
English
□ la comida inglesa English food

el **inglés** (PL los **ingleses**) NOUN
1 Englishman (PL Englishmen)
■ **los ingleses** the English
2 English
□ El inglés le resulta difícil. He finds English difficult.

la **inglesa** NOUN
Englishwoman (PL Englishwomen)

el **ingrediente** NOUN
ingredient

**ingresar** VERB [25]
to pay in
□ ingresar un cheque en una cuenta to pay a cheque into an account
■ **ingresar en el hospital** to go into hospital
■ **Han vuelto a ingresar a mi abuela.** They've taken my grandmother into hospital again.
■ **ingresar en un club** to join a club

el **ingreso** NOUN
admission
■ **un examen de ingreso** an entrance exam

■ **los ingresos** income *sing* □ Tiene unos ingresos muy bajos. He has a very low income.

la **inicial** NOUN
initial

la **iniciativa** NOUN
initiative
□ Lo hizo por iniciativa propia. He did it on his own initiative.

la **injusticia** NOUN
injustice
□ Lucharon contra las injusticias sociales. They fought against social injustices.
■ **Es una injusticia que lo hayan expulsado.** It was unfair of them to expel him.

**injusto** (FEM **injusta**) ADJECTIVE
unfair

**inmaduro** (FEM **inmadura**) ADJECTIVE
1 immature
2 unripe

**inmediatamente** ADVERB
immediately

**inmediato** (FEM **inmediata**) ADJECTIVE
immediate
■ **inmediato a algo** next to something □ en el edificio inmediato a la embajada in the building next to the embassy
■ **de inmediato** immediately

**inmenso** (FEM **inmensa**) ADJECTIVE
immense
■ **la inmensa mayoría** the vast majority

la **inmigración** NOUN
immigration

el/la **inmigrante** NOUN
immigrant

**inmoral** (FEM **inmoral**) ADJECTIVE
immoral

**inmortal** (FEM **inmortal**) ADJECTIVE
immortal

**inmóvil** (FEM **inmóvil**) ADJECTIVE
motionless
□ Se quedó inmóvil. He remained motionless.

**innecesario** (FEM **innecesaria**) ADJECTIVE
unnecessary

**inocente** (FEM **inocente**) ADJECTIVE
innocent
□ Es inocente. He's innocent.
■ **El jurado la declaró inocente.** The jury found her not guilty.

**inofensivo** (FEM **inofensiva**) ADJECTIVE
harmless

**inolvidable** (FEM **inolvidable**) ADJECTIVE
unforgettable

**inquietante** (FEM **inquietante**) ADJECTIVE
worrying

**inquietar** VERB [25]

to worry
- **inquietarse** to worry □ ¡No te inquietes! Don't worry!

**inquieto** (FEM **inquieta**) ADJECTIVE
1 worried
□ Estaba inquieta porque su hijo no había llegado. She was worried because her son hadn't come home.
2 restless
□ Es un niño muy inquieto y le cuesta dormirse. He's a very restless boy and finds it hard to get to sleep.

el **inquilino**, la **inquilina** NOUN
1 tenant
2 lodger

**insatisfecho** (FEM **insatisfecha**) ADJECTIVE
dissatisfied

**inscribirse*** VERB
to enrol
□ Se inscribió en un curso de idiomas. He enrolled on a language course.

la **inscripción** (PL las **inscripciones**) NOUN
1 enrolment
□ Mañana se cierra la inscripción. Tomorrow is the last day for enrollment.
2 inscription
□ Sobre la puerta hay una inscripción con el año. Above the door there's an inscription with the year on it.

**inscrito** VERB ▷ see **inscribirse**

el **insecto** NOUN
insect

la **inseguridad** NOUN
insecurity
□ la inseguridad en el trabajo  job insecurity
- **la inseguridad ciudadana** the lack of safety on the streets

**inseguro** (FEM **insegura**) ADJECTIVE
1 insecure
2 unsafe

**insensato** (FEM **insensata**) ADJECTIVE
foolish

**insensible** (FEM **insensible**) ADJECTIVE
insensitive
□ Se han vuelto insensibles al frío. They have become insensitive to the cold.
- **Es insensible al sufrimiento ajeno.** He is blind to the suffering of others.

la **insignia** NOUN
badge

**insignificante** (FEM **insignificante**) ADJECTIVE
insignificant

**insinuar*** VERB [1]
to hint at
□ No lo dijo pero lo insinuó. He didn't say it but he hinted at it.
- **¿Insinúas que miento?** Are you insinuating that I'm lying?

**insípido** (FEM **insípida**) ADJECTIVE
insipid

**insistir** VERB [58]
to insist
□ insistir en hacer algo  to insist on doing something □ Insiste en que vea a un médico. He's insisting that I see a doctor.

la **insolación** NOUN
sunstroke

**insolente** (FEM **insolente**) ADJECTIVE
insolent

**insoportable** (FEM **insoportable**) ADJECTIVE
unbearable

el **inspector**, la **inspectora** NOUN
inspector

las **instalaciones** NOUN
facilities
□ El hotel tiene unas estupendas instalaciones deportivas. The hotel has excellent sports facilities.

**instalar** VERB [25]
1 to install
□ Instaló una alarma en el coche. He installed an alarm in the car.
2 to set up
□ Aquí van a instalar unas oficinas. They're going to set up offices here.
- **instalarse** to settle □ Decidieron instalarse en el centro. They decided to settle in the town centre.

**instantáneo** (FEM **instantánea**) ADJECTIVE
instantaneous
- **el café instantáneo** instant coffee

el **instante** NOUN
moment
□ por un instante  for a moment
- **A cada instante suena el teléfono.** The phone rings all the time.
- **al instante** right away

el **instinto** NOUN
instinct

la **institución** (PL las **instituciones**) NOUN
institution

el **instituto** NOUN
institute
□ el Instituto Británico  the British Institute
- **un instituto de enseñanza secundaria** a secondary school

las **instrucciones** NOUN
instructions

**instructivo** (FEM **instructiva**) ADJECTIVE
educational

el **instructor**, la **instructora** NOUN
instructor
□ un instructor de esquí  a ski instructor
□ un instructor de autoescuela  a driving instructor

el **instrumento** NOUN
instrument

**insuficiente** (FEM **insuficiente**) ADJECTIVE
insufficient
□ una cantidad insuficiente de dinero  an insufficient amount of money

el **insuficiente** NOUN
■ Sacó un insuficiente en francés. He got an F in French.

la **insulina** NOUN
insulin

**insultar** VERB [25]
to insult

el **insulto** NOUN
insult

el/la **intelectual** ADJECTIVE, NOUN
intellectual

la **inteligencia** NOUN
intelligence

**inteligente** (FEM **inteligente**) ADJECTIVE
intelligent

la **intención** (PL las **intenciones**) NOUN
intention
□ No tengo la más mínima intención de hacerlo. I haven't got the slightest intention of doing it.
■ tener intención de hacer algo to intend to do something □ Tenía intención de descansar un rato. He intended to rest for a while.
■ Lo que cuenta es la intención. It's the thought that counts.

**intencionado** (FEM **intencionada**)
ADJECTIVE
deliberate
□ La patada fue intencionada. It was a deliberate kick.
■ bien intencionado well-meaning
■ mal intencionado malicious

**intensivo** (FEM **intensiva**) ADJECTIVE
intensive
□ un curso intensivo de inglés  an intensive English course

**intenso** (FEM **intensa**) ADJECTIVE
intense

**intentar** VERB [25]
to try
□ ¿Por qué no lo intentas otra vez? Why don't you try again? □ intentar hacer algo to try to do something

el **intento** NOUN
attempt
□ Aprobó al primer intento. He passed at the first attempt.

**intercambiar** VERB [25]
1 to exchange
2 to swap

el **intercambio** NOUN

exchange

el **interés** (PL los **intereses**) NOUN
interest
□ Tienes que poner más interés en tus estudios. You must take more of an interest in your studies. □ El banco da un interés del 5%. The bank gives 5% interest.
■ tener interés en hacer algo to be keen to do something
■ Todo lo hace por interés. Everything he does is out of self-interest.

**interesante** (FEM **interesante**) ADJECTIVE
interesting

**interesar** VERB [25]
to interest
□ Eso es algo que siempre me ha interesado. That's something that has always interested me.
■ Me interesa mucho la física. I'm very interested in physics.
■ interesarse por algo to ask about something

el **interfono** NOUN
intercom

**interior** (FEM **interior**) ADJECTIVE
1 inside
2 inner

el **interior** NOUN
■ El tren se detuvo en el interior del túnel. The train stopped inside the tunnel.

el/la **interiorista** NOUN
interior designer

**intermedio** (FEM **intermedia**) ADJECTIVE
1 intermediate
2 medium

el **intermedio** NOUN
interval

**interminable** (FEM **interminable**) ADJECTIVE
endless

**intermitente** (FEM **intermitente**) ADJECTIVE
1 intermittent
2 flashing

el **intermitente** NOUN
indicator

**internacional** (FEM **internacional**)
ADJECTIVE
international

el **internado** NOUN
boarding school

el/la **internauta** NOUN
internet user

el/la **Internet** NOUN
the internet
□ en Internet on the internet

**interno** (FEM **interna**) ADJECTIVE
■ estar interno en un colegio to be a boarder at a school

el **interno**, la **interna** NOUN

**1** boarder
**2** houseman (PL housemen)

la **interpretación** (PL las **interpretaciones**) NOUN
interpretation

■ **la interpretación simultánea** simultaneous interpreting
■ **Todo fue producto de una mala interpretación.** It was all the result of a misunderstanding.

**interpretar** VERB [25]
**1** to interpret
□ Sabe interpretar los sueños. He knows how to interpret dreams.
**2** to play
□ Interpreta el papel de Victoria. She plays the part of Victoria.
**3** to perform
□ Interpretó una pieza de Mozart. He performed a piece by Mozart.
■ **No me interpretes mal.** Don't misunderstand me.

el/la **intérprete** NOUN
interpreter
□ Quiere ser intérprete. She wants to be an interpreter.

**interrogar\*** VERB [37]
to question
□ Fue interrogado por la policía. He was questioned by the police.

**interrumpir** VERB [58]
**1** to interrupt
**2** to cut short
**3** to block
□ Estás interrumpiendo el paso. You're blocking the way.

la **interrupción** (PL las **interrupciones**) NOUN
interruption

el **interruptor** NOUN
switch (PL switches)

**interurbano** (FEM **interurbana**) ADJECTIVE
long-distance

el **intervalo** NOUN
interval

**intervenir\*** VERB [56]
**1** to take part
□ No intervino en el debate. He did not take part in the debate.
**2** to intervene
□ La policía intervino para separarlos. The police intervened to separate them.

la **intimidad** NOUN
**1** private life
□ Protege mucho su intimidad. He's very protective of his private life.
**2** privacy
□ En esta casa no tengo ninguna intimidad.

I have no privacy in this house.
■ **La boda se celebró en la intimidad.** It was a private wedding.

**intimidar** VERB [25]
to intimidate

**íntimo** (FEM **íntima**) ADJECTIVE
intimate
□ mis secretos íntimos my intimate secrets
■ **Es un amigo íntimo.** He's a close friend.

la **introducción** (PL las **introducciones**) NOUN
introduction

**introducir\*** VERB [9]
**1** to insert
□ Introdujo la moneda en la ranura. He inserted the coin in the slot.
**2** to bring in
□ Quieren introducir un nuevo sistema de trabajo. They want to bring in new working methods.
■ **Han introducido cambios en el horario.** They've made changes to the timetable.

**introvertido** (FEM **introvertida**) ADJECTIVE
introverted

el **intruso**, la **intrusa** NOUN
intruder

la **intuición** NOUN
intuition
□ la intuición femenina feminine intuition
■ **por intuición** intuitively

la **inundación** (PL las **inundaciones**) NOUN
flood

**inundar** VERB [25]
to flood
□ El río inundó el pueblo. The river flooded the village.
■ **inundarse** to be flooded □ Se nos inundó el baño. Our bathroom was flooded.

**inútil** (FEM **inútil**) ADJECTIVE
useless
□ La oficina está llena de trastos inútiles. The office is full of useless rubbish. □ Es inútil tratar de hacerle entender. It's useless trying to make him understand.
■ **Es inútil que esperes.** There's no point in your waiting.

el/la **inútil** (PL los/las **inútiles**) NOUN
■ **¡Es un inútil!** He's useless!

**invadir** VERB [58]
to invade

la **inválida** NOUN
disabled woman (PL disabled women)

**inválido** (FEM **inválida**) ADJECTIVE
disabled
□ Quedó inválida después del accidente. She was left disabled following the accident.

el **inválido** NOUN
disabled man (PL disabled men)

■ **los inválidos** the disabled

la **invasión** (PL las **invasiones**) NOUN
invasion

**inventar** VERB [25]
1 to invent
□ Inventaron un nuevo sistema. They invented a new system.
2 to make up
□ Inventó toda la historia. He made up the whole story.

el **invento** NOUN
invention

el **inventor**, la **inventora** NOUN
inventor

el **invernadero** NOUN
greenhouse
■ **el efecto invernadero** the greenhouse effect

**invernar** VERB [39]
to hibernate

**inverosímil** (FEM **inverosímil**) ADJECTIVE
unlikely

la **inversión** (PL las **inversiones**) NOUN
investment

**inverso** (FEM **inversa**) ADJECTIVE
reverse
□ en orden inverso in reverse order
■ **a la inversa** the other way round

**invertir*** VERB [51]
1 to invest
□ He invertido mucho dinero en esto. I've invested a lot of money in this.
2 to spend
□ Hemos invertido muchas horas en el proyecto. We've spent a lot of time on this project.
3 to reverse

la **investigación** (PL las **investigaciones**) NOUN
1 research
□ Está haciendo una investigación sobre Internet. He's doing some research on the Internet.
2 investigation
3 inquiry (PL inquiries)
□ Se hará una investigación pública. There will be a public inquiry.

el **invierno** NOUN
winter
□ en invierno in winter □ el invierno pasado last winter

**invisible** (FEM **invisible**) ADJECTIVE
invisible

la **invitación** (PL las **invitaciones**) NOUN
invitation

el **invitado**, la **invitada** NOUN
guest
□ Es el invitado de honor. He's the guest of

honour.

**invitar** VERB [25]
to invite
□ Me invitó a una fiesta. He invited me to a party. □ Me gustaría invitarla a cenar. I'd like to invite her to dinner.
■ **Te invito a un café.** I'll buy you a coffee.
■ **Esta vez invito yo.** This time it's on me.

la **inyección** (PL las **inyecciones**) NOUN
injection
□ ponerle una inyección a alguien to give someone an injection

**inyectar** VERB [25]
■ **Le tuvieron que inyectar insulina.** They had to give him insulin injections.
■ **inyectarse algo** to inject oneself with something □ Se había inyectado heroína. He had injected himself with heroin.

**ir*** VERB [27]
1 to go
□ Anoche fuimos al cine. We went to the cinema last night. □ ¿A qué colegio vas? What school do you go to?
■ **ir de vacaciones** to go on holiday
■ **ir a por** to go and get □ Voy a por el paraguas. I'll go and get the umbrella. □ Ha ido a por el médico. She has gone to get the doctor.
■ **Voy a hacerlo mañana.** I'm going to do it tomorrow.
■ **vamos** let's go □ Vamos a casa. Let's go home.
■ **¡Vamos!** Come on! □ ¡Vamos! ¡Di algo! Come on! Say something!
■ **¡Vamos a ver!** Let's see!
2 to be
□ Iba muy bien vestido. He was very well dressed. □ Iba con su madre. He was with his mother. □ como iba diciendo as I was saying □ Va a ser difícil. It will be difficult.
3 to come
□ ¡Ahora voy! I'm just coming!
■ **¿Puedo ir contigo?** Can I come with you?
■ **ir a pie** to walk
■ **ir en avión** to fly
■ **¿Cómo te va?** How are things?
■ **¿Cómo te va en los estudios?** How are you getting on with your studies?
■ **¡Que te vaya bien!** Take care of yourself!
■ **¡Qué va!** What are you talking about!
■ **¡Vaya! ¿Qué haces tú por aquí?** Well, what a surprise! What are you doing here?
■ **¡Vaya coche!** What a car!
■ **irse 1** to leave □ Acaba de irse. He has just left. **2** to go out □ Se ha ido la luz. The lights have gone out.
■ **¡Vámonos!** Let's go!
■ **¡Vete!** Go away!

■ **Vete a hacer los deberes.** Go and do your homework.

**Irak** MASC NOUN
Iraq

**Irán** MASC NOUN
Iran

el/la **iraní** (PL los/las **iraníes**) ADJECTIVE, NOUN
Iranian

el/la **iraquí** (PL los/las **iraquíes**) ADJECTIVE, NOUN
Iraqui

**Irlanda** FEM NOUN
Ireland
□ Irlanda del Norte  Northern Ireland

**irlandés** (FEM **irlandesa**, MASC PL **irlandeses**) ADJECTIVE
Irish
□ un café irlandés  an Irish coffee

el **irlandés** (PL los **irlandeses**) NOUN
1 Irishman (PL Irishmen)
■ **los irlandeses** the Irish
2 Irish

la **irlandesa** NOUN
Irishwoman (PL Irishwomen)

**irónico** (FEM **irónica**) ADJECTIVE
ironic

**irracional** (FEM **irracional**) ADJECTIVE
irrational

**irrelevante** (FEM **irrelevante**) ADJECTIVE
irrelevant

**irresistible** (FEM **irresistible**) ADJECTIVE
irresistible

**irresponsable** (FEM **irresponsable**) ADJECTIVE
irresponsible

**irritante** (FEM **irritante**) ADJECTIVE
irritating

**irritar** VERB [25]
to irritate

**irrompible** (FEM **irrompible**) ADJECTIVE
unbreakable

la **isla** NOUN
island
□ una isla desierta  a desert island
■ **la Isla de Pascua** Easter Island

el **Islam** NOUN
Islam

**islámico** (FEM **islámica**) ADJECTIVE
Islamic

**islandés** (FEM **islandesa**, MASC PL **islandeses**) ADJECTIVE
Icelandic

el **islandés**, la **islandesa** (MASC PL los **islandeses**) NOUN
Icelander

el **islandés** NOUN
Icelandic

**Islandia** FEM NOUN
Iceland

el **isleño** NOUN
islander

**Israel** MASC NOUN
Israel

el/la **israelí** (PL los/las **israelíes**) ADJECTIVE, NOUN
Israeli

**Italia** FEM NOUN
Italy

el **italiano** (FEM la **italiana**) ADJECTIVE, NOUN
Italian

el **italiano** NOUN
Italian

el **itinerario** NOUN
1 route
□ Hicimos el itinerario de costumbre. We took the usual route.
2 itinerary (PL itineraries)
□ Me gustaría incluir Roma en el itinerario. I'd like to include Rome on our itinerary.

el **IVA** ABBREVIATION
▷ see also **IVA** ABBREVIATION (= Impuesto sobre el Valor Añadido)
VAT (= Value Added Tax)

el **IVA** ABBREVIATION
▷ see also **IVA** ABBREVIATION (= Impuesto sobre el Valor Agregado) (Latin America)
VAT (= Value Added Tax)

**izar**\* VERB [13]
to hoist
□ Izaron la bandera a media asta. They hoisted the flag to half mast.

la **izquierda** NOUN
1 left hand
■ **Escribo con la izquierda.** I write with my left hand.
2 left
□ doblar a la izquierda to turn left □ La izquierda ganó las elecciones. The elections were won by the left.
■ **ser de izquierdas** to be left-wing □ un partido de izquierdas a left-wing party
■ **a la izquierda** on the left □ la segunda calle a la izquierda the second turning on the left
■ **a la izquierda del edificio** to the left of the building
■ **conducir por la izquierda** to drive on the left

**izquierdo** (FEM **izquierda**) ADJECTIVE
left
□ Levanta la mano izquierda. Raise your left hand.
■ **Escribo con la mano izquierda.** I write with my left hand.
■ **el lado izquierdo** the left side
■ **a mano izquierda** on the left-hand side

# Jj

**el jabón** (PL los **jabones**) NOUN
soap

**la jaiba** NOUN (Latin America)
crab

**jalar** VERB [25] (Latin America)
1 to pull
□ No le jales el pelo. Don't pull his hair.
2 to take
□ Jaló un folleto de la mesa. He took a leaflet from the table.

**jamás** ADVERB
never
□ Jamás he visto nada parecido. I've never seen anything like it.

**el jamón** (PL los **jamones**) NOUN
ham
□ un bocadillo de jamón  a ham sandwich
■ **jamón serrano** cured ham
■ **jamón de York** boiled ham

**Japón** MASC NOUN
Japan

**el japonés** (FEM la **japonesa**, MASC PL los **japoneses**) ADJECTIVE, NOUN
Japanese

**el japonés** NOUN
Japanese

**el jarabe** NOUN
syrup
■ **jarabe para la tos** cough syrup

**el jardín** (PL los **jardines**) NOUN
garden
■ **el jardín de infancia** nursery school

**la jardinera** NOUN
1 gardener
2 window box

**la jardinería** NOUN
gardening

**el jardinero** NOUN
gardener

**la jarra** NOUN
1 jug
2 beer glass

**el jarro** NOUN
jug

**el jarrón** (PL los **jarrones**) NOUN
vase

**la jaula** NOUN
cage

**el jefe**, la **jefa** NOUN
1 boss (PL bosses)
□ Carlos es mi jefe. Carlos is my boss.
2 head
□ El jefe de la empresa dimitió. The head of the company resigned.
■ **el jefe del departamento** the head of department
■ **jefe de estado** head of state
■ **el jefe del grupo guerrillero** the leader of the guerrilla group

**el jerez** NOUN
sherry

**la jeringuilla** NOUN
syringe

**el jersey** (PL los **jerséis**) NOUN
jumper

**Jesús** EXCLAMATION
1 Bless you!
2 Good God!

**el jinete** NOUN
jockey (PL jockeys)

**la jirafa** NOUN
giraffe

**el jitomate** NOUN (Mexico)
tomato (PL tomatoes)

**la jornada** NOUN
■ **jornada de trabajo** working day
■ **trabajar a jornada completa** to work full-time
■ **trabajar a media jornada** to work part-time

**joven** (FEM **joven**, PL **jóvenes**) ADJECTIVE
young
□ un chico joven  a young boy

**el/la joven** (PL los/las **jóvenes**) NOUN
■ **un joven** a young man
■ **una joven** a young woman
■ **los jóvenes** young people

**la joya** NOUN
jewel
■ **Me han robado mis joyas.** My jewellery has been stolen.

**la joyera** NOUN

jeweller

**la joyería** NOUN
jeweller's

**el joyero** NOUN
1 jeweller
2 jewellery box

**la jubilación** (PL las **jubilaciones**) NOUN
1 retirement
□ La edad de jubilación es a los 65 años.
The retirement age is 65.
2 pension
□ cobrar la jubilación to get one's pension

**jubilado** (FEM **jubilada**) ADJECTIVE
retired
■ **estar jubilado** to be retired

**el jubilado, la jubilada** NOUN
pensioner

**jubilarse** VERB [25]
to retire

**la judía** NOUN
Jew
■ **judía blanca** haricot bean
■ **judía verde** green bean

**judío** (FEM **judía**) ADJECTIVE
Jewish

**el judío** NOUN
Jew

**el judo** NOUN
judo

**juego** VERB ▷ see **jugar**

**el juego** NOUN
1 game
□ un juego de ordenador a computer game
■ **juegos de cartas** card games
■ **juegos de mesa** board games
2 gambling
□ Lo perdió todo en el juego. He lost
everything through gambling.
3 set
□ un juego de café a coffee set
■ **Las cortinas hacen juego con el sofá.**
The curtains go with the sofa.

**la juerga** NOUN
■ **irse de juerga** to go out on the town

**el jueves** (PL los **jueves**) NOUN
Thursday
□ La vi el jueves. I saw her on Thursday.
□ todos los jueves every Thursday □ el
jueves pasado last Thursday □ el jueves que
viene next Thursday □ Jugamos los jueves.
We play on Thursdays.

**el juez, la jueza** (MASC PL los **jueces**) NOUN
judge
■ **juez de línea** linesman (PL linesmen)

**el jugador, la jugadora** NOUN
player

**jugar\*** VERB [28]
1 to play

□ ¿Jugamos una partida de dominó? Shall
we have a game of dominoes?
■ **jugar al fútbol** to play football
2 to gamble
□ Perdió un dineral jugando en el casino.
He lost a fortune gambling at the casino.
■ **jugar a la lotería** to do the lottery

**el jugo** NOUN
1 juice
2 gravy

**el juguete** NOUN
toy (PL toys)
■ **un avión de juguete** a toy plane

**la juguetería** NOUN
toy shop

**el juicio** NOUN
trial
□ El juicio empieza mañana. The trial starts
tomorrow.
■ **llevar a alguien a juicio** to take someone
to court

**julio** MASC NOUN
July
□ en julio in July □ Nació el 4 de julio.
He was born on 4 July.

**la jungla** NOUN
jungle

**junio** MASC NOUN
June
□ en junio in June □ Nací el 20 de junio.
I was born on 20 June.

**la junta** NOUN
committee
■ **La junta directiva tiene la última
palabra.** The board of management has the
final say.

**juntar** VERB [25]
1 to put together
□ Vamos a juntar los pupitres. Let's put the
desks together.
2 to gather together
□ Consiguieron juntar a mil personas. They
managed to gather together one thousand
people.
■ **juntarse 1** to move closer together □ Si
os juntáis más, cabremos todos. If you
move closer together we'll all fit in. **2** to
meet up □ Nos juntamos los domingos para
comer. We meet up for dinner on Sundays.

**junto** (FEM **junta**) ADJECTIVE
▷ see also **junto** ADVERB
1 close together
□ Los muebles están demasiado juntos. The
furniture is too close together.
2 together
□ Cuando estamos juntos apenas hablamos.
We hardly talk when we're together.
■ **todo junto** all together □ Ponlo todo

junto en una sola bolsa.  Put it all together in one bag.

**junto** ADVERB
  ▷ *see also* **junto** ADJECTIVE
  ■ **junto a** by □ Hay una mesa junto a la ventana.  There's a table by the window.
  ■ **junto con** together with
  ■ **Mi apellido se escribe todo junto.** My surname is all in one word.

el **jurado** NOUN
**1** jury (PL juries)
**2** panel

**jurar** VERB [25]
  to swear

la **justicia** NOUN
  justice

**justificar\*** VERB [48]
  to justify

**justo** (FEM **justa**) ADJECTIVE
  ▷ *see also* **justo** ADVERB
**1** fair
  □ Tuvo un juicio justo.  He had a fair trial.
**2** right
  ■ **Este reloj siempre da la hora justa.** This watch always tells the right time.
  □ Apareció en el momento justo.  He appeared at the right time.
**3** tight
  □ Me están muy justos estos pantalones. These trousers are tight on me.

**4** just enough
  □ Tengo el dinero justo para el billete.  I have just enough money for the ticket.

**justo** ADVERB
  ▷ *see also* **justo** ADJECTIVE
  just
  □ El supermercado está justo al doblar la esquina.  The supermarket is just round the corner.  □ La vi justo cuando entrábamos. I saw her just as we came in.
  ■ **Me dio un puñetazo justo en la nariz.** He punched me right on the nose.

**juvenil** (FEM **juvenil**) ADJECTIVE
**1** youth
**2** junior
  ■ **la literatura juvenil** young people's literature

la **juventud** NOUN
**1** youth
  □ Fue soldado en su juventud.  He was a soldier in his youth.
**2** youngsters *pl*
  □ La juventud viene aquí a divertirse. Youngsters come here to have fun.

el **juzgado** NOUN
  court

**juzgar\*** VERB [37]
  to try
  □ Lo juzgaron por un delito menor.  He was tried on a minor charge.

# Kk

el **kárate** NOUN
karate

el **kilo** NOUN
kilo
□ un kilo de tomates a kilo of tomatoes

el **kilogramo** NOUN
kilogramme

el **kilómetro** NOUN
kilometre
□ Está a tres kilómetros de aquí. It's three kilometres from here. □ a 90 kilómetros por hora at 90 kilometres per hour
■ ¡Caminamos kilómetros y kilómetros! We walked for miles!

el **kiosco** NOUN
news stand

# Ll

**la** ARTICLE
▷ *see also* **la** PRONOUN
the
  □ la pared the wall
  ■ **la del sombrero rojo** the girl in the red hat
  ■ **Yo fui la que te despertó.** It was I who woke you up.
  ■ **Ayer me lavé la cabeza.** I washed my hair yesterday.
  ■ **Abróchate la camisa.** Do your shirt up.
  ■ **Tiene una casa bonita, pero prefiero la de Juan.** He's got a lovely house, but I prefer Juan's.
  ■ **No me gusta la fruta.** I don't like fruit.
  ■ **Vendrá la semana que viene.** He'll come next week.
  ■ **Me he encontrado a la Sra. Sendra.** I met Mrs Sendra.

**la** PRONOUN
▷ *see also* **la** ARTICLE
**1** her
  □ La quiero. I love her.
  ■ **La han despedido.** She has been sacked.
**2** you
  □ La acompaño hasta la puerta. I'll see you out.
**3** it
  □ No la toques. Don't touch it.

el **labio** NOUN
lip

la **labor** NOUN
work
  □ Mi labor consiste en regar las plantas. My work is watering the plants.
  ■ **las labores domésticas** the housework

**laborable** (FEM **laborable**) ADJECTIVE
  ■ **día laborable** working day

**laboral** (FEM **laboral**) ADJECTIVE
**1** working
**2** labour
**3** industrial

el **laboratorio** NOUN
laboratory (PL laboratories)

la **laca** NOUN
**1** hairspray

**2** lacquer
  ■ **la laca de uñas** nail varnish

**lácteo** (FEM **láctea**) ADJECTIVE
  ■ **los productos lácteos** dairy products

la **ladera** NOUN
hillside

el **lado** NOUN
side
  □ a los dos lados de la carretera on both sides of the road  □ Hay gente por todos lados. There are people everywhere.
  □ Tiene que estar en otro lado. It must be somewhere else.
  ■ **Mi casa está aquí al lado.** My house is right nearby.
  ■ **la mesa de al lado** the next table
  ■ **al lado de** beside  □ La silla que está al lado del armario. The chair beside the wardrobe.
  ■ **Felipe se sentó a mi lado.** Felipe sat beside me.
  ■ **por un lado ..., por otro lado ...** on the one hand ..., on the other hand ...

**ladrar** VERB [25]
to bark
  □ El perro les ladró. The dog barked at them.

el **ladrillo** NOUN
brick

el **ladrón**, la **ladrona** NOUN
**1** thief (PL thieves)
  □ Un ladrón me quitó el bolso. A thief took my bag.
**2** burglar
  □ Los ladrones entraron en la casa. The burglars broke into the house.
**3** robber
  □ Tres ladrones atracaron el banco. Three robbers raided the bank.

el **lagarto** NOUN
lizard

el **lago** NOUN
lake

la **lágrima** NOUN
tear

la **laguna** NOUN
lake

**lamentar** VERB [25]
■ **Lamento lo ocurrido.** I am sorry about what happened.
■ **lamentarse** to complain □ De nada vale lamentarse. There's no use complaining.

**lamer** VERB [8]
to lick

la **lámina** NOUN
1 sheet
2 plate

la **lámpara** NOUN
lamp

la **lana** NOUN
wool
■ **una bufanda de lana** a woollen scarf

la **lancha** NOUN
motorboat
■ **una lancha de salvamento** a lifeboat

la **langosta** NOUN
1 lobster
2 locust

el **langostino** NOUN
king prawn

**lanzar\*** VERB [13]
1 to throw
□ Lanzó una piedra al río. He threw a stone into the river.
2 to launch
□ Han lanzado dos satélites al espacio. They have launched two satellites into space.
■ **lanzarse** to dive □ Los niños se lanzaron a la piscina. The children dived into the swimming pool.

el **lapicero** NOUN
pencil

la **lápida** NOUN
gravestone

el **lápiz** (PL los **lápices**) NOUN
pencil
□ Escribió mi dirección a lápiz. He wrote my address in pencil.
■ **los lápices de colores** crayons
■ **un lápiz de labios** lipstick
■ **un lápiz de ojos** an eyeliner

**largo** (FEM **larga**) ADJECTIVE
long
□ Fue una conferencia muy larga. It was a very long conference. □ Esta cuerda es demasiado larga. This piece of string is too long.

el **largo** NOUN
length
□ Nadé cuatro largos de la piscina. I swam four lengths of the pool.
■ **¿Cuánto mide de largo?** How long is it?
■ **Tiene nueve metros de largo.** It's nine metres long.
■ **a lo largo del río** along the river

■ **a lo largo de la semana** throughout the week
■ **Pasó de largo sin saludar.** He passed by without saying hello.

💭 **LANGUAGE TIP** Be careful! **largo** does not mean **large**.

**las** ARTICLE
▷ see also **las** PRONOUN
the
□ las paredes the walls
■ **las del estante de arriba** the ones on the top shelf
■ **Me duelen las piernas.** My legs hurt.
■ **Poneos las bufandas.** Put on your scarves.
■ **Estas fotos son bonitas, pero prefiero las de Pedro.** These photos are nice, but I prefer Pedro's.
■ **No me gustan las arañas.** I don't like spiders.
■ **Vino a las seis de la tarde.** He came at six in the evening.

**las** PRONOUN
▷ see also **las** ARTICLE
1 them
□ Las vi por la calle. I saw them in the street.
■ **Las han despedido.** They've been sacked.
2 you
□ Las acompañaré hasta la puerta, señoras. I'll see you out, ladies.

el **láser** NOUN
laser

la **lástima** NOUN
■ **Me da lástima de ella.** I feel sorry for her.
■ **Es una lástima que no puedas venir.** It's a shame you can't come.
■ **¡Qué lástima!** What a shame!

la **lata** NOUN
1 tin
2 can
■ **Deja de dar la lata.** Stop being a pain.

**lateral** (FEM **lateral**) ADJECTIVE
side
□ la puerta lateral the side door

el **latido** NOUN
beat

el **látigo** NOUN
whip

el **latín** NOUN
Latin

**Latinoamérica** FEM NOUN
Latin America

el **latinoamericano** (FEM la **latinoamericana**) ADJECTIVE, NOUN
Latin American

**latir** VERB [58]
to beat

183

el **laurel** NOUN
laurel
- **una hoja de laurel** a bay leaf

el **lavabo** NOUN
1 sink
  □ Llené el lavabo de agua. I filled the sink with water.
2 toilet
  □ Voy al lavabo. I'm going to the toilet.

el **lavado** NOUN
wash
- **el lavado en seco** dry cleaning

la **lavadora** NOUN
washing machine

la **lavandería** NOUN
launderette

el **lavaplatos** (PL los **lavaplatos**) NOUN
1 dishwasher
2 sink (Mexico)

**lavar** VERB [25]
to wash
  □ Lava estos vasos. Wash these glasses.
- **lavar la ropa** to do the washing
- **lavarse** to wash □ Me lavo todos los días. I wash every day.
- **Ayer me lavé la cabeza.** I washed my hair yesterday.
- **Lávate los dientes.** Brush your teeth.

el **lavarropas** (PL los **lavarropas**) NOUN (Mexico)
washing machine

el **lavavajillas** (PL los **lavavajillas**) NOUN
1 dishwasher
2 washing-up liquid

el **lazo** NOUN
1 bow
2 ribbon

**le** PRONOUN
1 him
  □ Le mandé una carta. I sent him a letter.
  □ Le miré con atención. I watched him carefully.
- **Le abrí la puerta.** I opened the door for him.
2 her
  □ Le mandé una carta. I sent her a letter.
- **No le hablé de ti.** I didn't speak to her about you.
- **Le busqué el libro.** I looked out the book for her.
3 you
  □ Le presento a la Señora Gutiérrez. Let me introduce you to Mrs. Gutiérrez.
- **Le he arreglado el ordenador.** I've fixed the computer for you. □ Le huelen los pies. His feet smell. □ Le arrastra la falda. Her skirt is trailing on the floor.

184  la **lealtad** NOUN

loyalty (PL loyalties)

la **lección** (PL las **lecciones**) NOUN
lesson

la **leche** NOUN
milk
- **la leche desnatada** skimmed milk
- **la leche en polvo** powdered milk

la **lechuga** NOUN
lettuce

la **lechuza** NOUN
owl

el **lector**, la **lectora** NOUN
1 reader
  □ Varios lectores se quejaron del artículo. Several readers complained about the article.
2 language assistant
  □ Es la lectora de francés. She's the French language assistant.

el **lector** NOUN
- **un lector de CD** a CD player

la **lectura** NOUN
reading
  □ Me encanta la lectura. I love reading.

**leer\*** VERB [30]
to read

**legal** (FEM legal) ADJECTIVE
legal

la **legaña** NOUN
- **tener legañas** to have sleep in one's eyes

la **legumbre** NOUN
pulse

**lejano** (FEM lejana) ADJECTIVE
distant
  □ un sitio muy lejano a very distant place

la **lejía** NOUN
bleach

**lejos** ADVERB
far
  □ ¿Está lejos? Is it far? □ No está lejos de aquí. It's not far from here.
- **De lejos parecía un avión.** From a distance it looked like a plane.

la **lencería** NOUN
lingerie

la **lengua** NOUN
1 tongue
  □ Me he mordido la lengua. I've bitten my tongue.
2 language
  □ Habla varias lenguas. He speaks several languages.
- **mi lengua materna** my mother tongue

el **lenguado** NOUN
sole

el **lenguaje** NOUN
language

la **lente** NOUN

lense
- **las lentes de contacto** contact lenses

la **lenteja** NOUN
lentil

los **lentes** NOUN *(Latin America)*
glasses
- **los lentes de sol** sunglasses

la **lentilla** NOUN
contact lens

**lento** (FEM **lenta**) ADJECTIVE
▷ *see also* **lento** ADVERB
slow
□ un proceso lento a slow progress

**lento** ADVERB
▷ *see also* **lento** ADJECTIVE
slowly
□ Vas un poco lento. You're going a bit
slowly.

la **leña** NOUN
firewood

**Leo** MASC NOUN
Leo
- **Soy leo.** I'm Leo.

el **león** (PL los **leones**) NOUN
lion

la **leona** NOUN
lioness (PL lionesses)

el **leopardo** NOUN
leopard

los **leotardos** NOUN
woolly tights

**les** PRONOUN
1 them
□ Les mandé una carta. I sent them a letter.
□ Les miré con atención. I watched them
carefully.
- **Les abrí la puerta.** I opened the door for
them.
- **Les eché de comer a los gatos.** I gave
the cats something to eat.
2 you
□ Les presento a la Señora Gutiérrez. Let me
introduce you to Mrs. Gutiérrez.
- **Les he arreglado el ordenador.** I've fixed
the computer for you. □ Les huelen los pies.
Their feet smell. □ Les arrastraban los
abrigos. Their coats were trailing on the
floor.

la **lesbiana** NOUN
lesbian

la **lesión** (PL las **lesiones**) NOUN
injury (PL injuries)

**lesionado** (FEM **lesionada**) ADJECTIVE
injured
□ Está lesionado. He's injured.

la **letra** NOUN
1 letter
□ la letra 'a' the letter 'a'

2 handwriting
□ Tengo muy mala letra. My handwriting's
very poor.
3 lyrics *pl*
□ Él escribe la letra de sus canciones. He
writes the lyrics for his songs.

el **letrero** NOUN
sign

**levantar** VERB [25]
to lift
□ Levanta la tapa. Lift the lid.
- **Levantad la mano si tenéis alguna
duda.** Raise your hand if you are unclear.
- **levantarse** to get up □ Hoy me he
levantado temprano. I got up early this
morning. □ Me levanté y seguí caminando.
I got up and carried on walking.

**leve** (FEM **leve**) ADJECTIVE
minor
□ Sólo tiene heridas leves. He only has
minor injuries. □ Cometió una falta leve.
He committed a minor mistake.

la **ley** (PL las **leyes**) NOUN
law
□ la ley de la gravedad the law of gravity

**leyendo** VERB ▷ *see* **leer**

**liar*** VERB [21]
1 to tie up
□ Lía este paquete con una cuerda. Tie up
this parcel with some string.
2 to confuse
□ Me liaron con tantas explicaciones. They
confused me with all their explanations.
- **A mí no me líes en esto.** Don't get me
mixed up in this.
- **liarse** to get muddled up □ Me estoy
liando, empezaré otra vez. I'm getting
muddled up, I'll start again.
- **Se lió a tortas con su hermano.** He got
into a fight with his brother.
- **Nos liamos a hablar y se nos pasó la
hora.** We got talking and we forgot the
time.

**Líbano** MASC NOUN
Lebanon

el/la **liberal** ADJECTIVE, NOUN
liberal

**liberar** VERB [25]
to free

la **libertad** NOUN
freedom
□ libertad de expresión freedom of
expression
- **No tengo libertad para hacer lo que
quiera.** I'm not free to do what I want.
- **El rehén está en libertad.** The hostage is
free.
- **poner a alguien en libertad** to release

somebody

la **libra** NOUN
pound

> **DID YOU KNOW...?**
> En los países anglosajones el peso a
> menudo se expresa en libras **pounds**.
> Un kilogramo equivale a 2.2 libras
> aproximadamente.

■ **libra esterlina** pound sterling

**Libra** MASC NOUN
Libra

■ **Soy libra.** I'm Libra.

**librarse** VERB

■ **librarse de 1** to get out of □ ¡No te librar
a librarás de fregar los platos! You're not
going to get out of doing the washing-up!
**2** to get rid of □ Logré librarme de mi
hermana. I managed to get rid of my sister.
■ **Se libró del castigo por pura suerte.**
He got away with it by pure good luck.

**libre** (FEM **libre**) ADJECTIVE
free
□ ¿Está libre este asiento? Is this seat free?
□ El martes estoy libre, así que podemos
quedar. I'm free on Tuesday so we can meet
up.
■ **los 100 metros libres** the 100 metres
freestyle

la **librería** NOUN
**1** bookshop
**2** bookshelf (PL bookshelves)

> **LANGUAGE TIP** Be careful! librería
> does not mean **library**.

el **librero** NOUN (Chile, Mexico)
bookcase

la **libreta** NOUN
notebook
■ **una libreta de ahorros** a savings book

el **libro** NOUN
book
■ **un libro de bolsillo** a paperback
■ **un libro de texto** a text book

la **licencia** NOUN
licence
□ una licencia de armas a gun licence
■ **la licencia de obras** planning permission
■ **estar de licencia** (Latin America) to be on
leave

el **licenciado**, la **licenciada** NOUN
graduate
□ un licenciado en historia a history
graduate

la **licenciatura** NOUN
degree

el **licor** NOUN
liqueur
□ un licor de pera a pear liqueur
■ **Bebimos cerveza y licores.** We drank

beer and spirits.

el/la **líder** NOUN
leader

la **liebre** NOUN
hare

la **liga** NOUN
**1** league
**2** garter

**ligar*** VERB [37]
■ **Ayer ligué con una chica.** (colloquial) I
got off with a girl yesterday.

**ligero** (FEM **ligera**) ADJECTIVE
**1** light
□ Me gusta llevar ropa ligera. I like to wear
light clothing. □ Comimos algo ligero. We
ate something light.
**2** slight
□ Tengo un ligero dolor de cabeza. I have a
slight headache.
■ **Andaba a paso ligero.** He walked quickly.

la **lila** NOUN
lilac

la **lima** NOUN
**1** file
□ una lima de uñas a nail file
**2** lime

**limitar** VERB [25]
to limit
□ Limitaron el tiempo del examen a dos
horas. The exam time was limited to two
hours.
■ **España limita con Francia.** Spain has a
border with France.
■ **Yo me limité a observar.** I just watched.

el **límite** NOUN
**1** limit
□ el límite de velocidad the speed limit
■ **fecha límite** deadline
**2** boundary (PL boundaries)
□ Está dentro de los límites de la finca.
It's within the boundaries of the estate.

el **limón** (PL los **limones**) NOUN
lemon

la **limonada** NOUN
lemonade

la **limosna** NOUN
■ **pedir limosna** to beg

el **limpiaparabrisas** (PL los
**limpiaparabrisas**) NOUN
windscreen-wiper

**limpiar** VERB [25]
**1** to clean
□ El sábado voy a limpiar la casa. I'm going
to clean the house on Saturday.
**2** to wipe
□ ¿Has limpiado la mesa? Have you wiped
the table? □ Límpiate la nariz. Wipe your
nose.

la **limpieza** NOUN
  cleaning
    □ Yo hago la limpieza los sábados. I do the cleaning on Saturdays.
    ■ **limpieza en seco** dry cleaning

**limpio** (FEM **limpia**) ADJECTIVE
  clean
    □ El baño está muy limpio. The bathroom's very clean.
    ■ **Voy a pasar esto a limpio.** I'm going to write this out neat.

**lindo** (FEM **linda**) ADJECTIVE
1 pretty
    □ sus lindos ojos her pretty eyes
2 nice (Latin America)
    □ un día muy lindo a very nice day

la **línea** NOUN
  line
    □ Dibujó una línea recta. He drew a straight line.
    ■ **Vaya en línea recta.** Go straight ahead.
    ■ **una línea aérea** an airline
    ■ **en línea** online

el **lino** NOUN
  linen

la **linterna** NOUN
  torch (PL torches)

el **lío** NOUN
    ■ **En mi mesa hay un lío enorme de papeles.** My desk is in a real muddle with all these papers.
    ■ **hacerse un lío** to get muddled up □ Se hizo un lío con tantos nombres. He got muddled up with all the names.
    ■ **Esta ecuación es un lío.** This equation is a real headache.
    ■ **Si sigues así te vas a meter en un lío.** If you carry on like that you'll get yourself into a real mess.

la **liquidación** NOUN
  sale

el **líquido** ADJECTIVE, NOUN
  liquid

**Lisboa** FEM NOUN
  Lisbon

**liso** (FEM **lisa**) ADJECTIVE
1 smooth
2 straight
3 plain

la **lista** NOUN
  list
    □ la lista de espera the waiting list
    ■ **pasar lista** to call the register
    ■ **la lista de correo** mailing list

**listo** (FEM **lista**) ADJECTIVE
1 clever
    □ Es una chica muy lista. She's a very clever girl.

2 ready
    □ ¿Estás listo? Are you ready?

la **litera** NOUN
1 bunk bed
2 berth

la **literatura** NOUN
  literature

el **litro** NOUN
  litre

**liviano** (FEM **liviana**) ADJECTIVE
  light

la **llaga** NOUN
  sore

la **llama** NOUN
  flame

la **llamada** NOUN
  call
    ■ **hacer una llamada telefónica** to make a phone call

**llamar** VERB [25]
1 to call
    □ Me llamaron mentiroso. They called me a liar. □ llamar a la policía to call the police
2 to ring
3 to knock
    ■ **llamar por teléfono a alguien** to phone somebody
    ■ **¿Cómo te llamas?** What's your name?
    ■ **Me llamo Adela.** My name's Adela.

**llano** (FEM **llana**) ADJECTIVE
  flat

la **llanta** NOUN
1 wheel rim
2 tyre (Latin America)

la **llave** NOUN
1 key
    □ las llaves del coche the car keys
    ■ **Echa la llave de la puerta cuando salgas.** Lock the door when you go out.
    ■ **una llave inglesa** a spanner
    **LANGUAGE TIP** Word for word, **llave inglesa** means 'English key'.
2 tap (Latin America)

el **llavero** NOUN
  keyring

la **llegada** NOUN
1 arrival
2 finish

**llegar**\* VERB [37]
1 to get to
    □ Estaba lloviendo cuando llegamos a Granada. It was raining when we got to Granada.
    ■ **¿A qué hora llegaste a casa?** What time did you get home?
2 to arrive
    □ Carmen no ha llegado todavía. Carmen hasn't arrived yet.

■ **No llegues tarde.** Don't be late.

■ **Con tres euros no me llega.** Three euros isn't enough.

**3** to reach

□ No llego al estante de arriba. I can't reach the top shelf.

■ **El agua me llegaba hasta las rodillas.** The water came up to my knees.

■ **llegar a ser** to become

**llenar** VERB [25]

to fill

□ Llena la jarra de agua. Fill the jug with water.

**lleno** (FEM **llena**) ADJECTIVE

full

□ Todos los hoteles están llenos. All the hotels are full. □ El restaurante estaba lleno de gente. The restaurant was full of people.

**llevar** VERB [25]

**1** to take

□ ¿Llevas los vasos a la cocina? Can you take the glasses to the kitchen? □ No llevará mucho tiempo. It won't take long.

**2** to wear

□ María llevaba un abrigo muy bonito. María was wearing a nice coat.

**3** to give a lift

□ Sofía nos llevó a casa. Sofía gave us a lift home.

**4** to carry

□ Yo te llevo la maleta. I'll carry your case.

■ **Sólo llevo diez euros.** I've only got ten euros on me.

■ **¿Cuánto tiempo llevas aquí?** How long have you been here?

■ **Llevo horas esperando aquí.** I've been waiting here for hours.

■ **Mi hermana mayor me lleva ocho años.** My elder sister is eight years older than me.

■ **llevarse algo** to take something

□ Llévatelo. Take it with you. □ ¿Le gusta? — Sí, me lo llevo. Do you like it? — Yes, I'll take it!

■ **Me llevo bien con mi hermano.** I get on well with my brother.

■ **Nos llevamos muy mal.** We get on very badly.

**llorar** VERB [25]

to cry

**llover\*** VERB [31]

to rain

■ **llover a cántaros** to pour down

**lloviznar** VERB [25]

to drizzle

**llueve** VERB ▷ see **llover**

la **lluvia** NOUN

rain

□ bajo la lluvia in the rain

■ **la lluvia ácida** acid rain

**lluvioso** (FEM **lluviosa**) ADJECTIVE

rainy

**lo** ARTICLE

▷ see also **lo** PRONOUN

■ **Lo peor fue que no pudimos entrar.** The worst thing was we couldn't get in.

■ **No me gusta lo picante.** I don't like spicy things.

■ **Pon en mi habitación lo de Pedro.** Put Pedro's things in my room.

■ **Lo mío son las matemáticas.** Maths is my thing.

■ **Lo de vender la casa no me parece bien.** I don't like this idea of selling the house.

■ **Olvida lo de ayer.** Forget what happened yesterday.

■ **¡No sabes lo aburrido que es!** You don't know how boring he is!

■ **lo que 1** what □ Lo que más me gusta es nadar. What I like most is swimming.

**2** whatever □ Ponte lo que quieras. Wear whatever you like.

■ **más de lo que** more than □ Cuesta más de lo que crees. It costs more than you think.

**lo** PRONOUN

▷ see also **lo** ARTICLE

**1** him

□ No lo conozco. I don't know him.

■ **Lo han despedido.** He's been sacked.

**2** you

□ Yo a usted lo conozco. I know you.

**3** it

□ No lo veo. I can't see it. □ Voy a pensarlo. I'll think about it.

■ **No lo sabía.** I didn't know.

■ **No parece lista pero lo es.** She doesn't seem clever but she is.

el **lobo** NOUN

wolf (PL wolves)

la **loca** NOUN

madwoman (PL madwomen)

**local** (FEM **local**) ADJECTIVE

local

□ un producto local a local product

el **local** NOUN

premises pl

□ Lo echaron del local. They threw him off the premises.

■ **Ensayan en un local cerca de aquí.** They rehearse in a place near here.

la **localidad** NOUN

**1** town

□ una localidad al sur de Madrid a town south of Madrid

**2** seat

□ Reserve sus localidades con antelación.

Book your seats in advance.

**localizar\*** VERB [13]

**1** to reach

□ Me puedes localizar en este teléfono. You can reach me at this number.

**2** to locate

□ No han conseguido localizar a las víctimas. They have been unable to locate the victims.

**la loción** (PL las **lociones**) NOUN

lotion

**loco** (FEM **loca**) ADJECTIVE

**1** mad

□ volverse loco to go mad

■ **volver loco a alguien** to drive somebody mad

**2** crazy

□ ¿Estás loco? Are you crazy? □ Está loco con su moto nueva. He's crazy about his new motorbike.

■ **Me vuelve loco el marisco.** I'm crazy about seafood.

**el loco** NOUN

madman (PL madmen)

**la locura** NOUN

madness

□ Es una locura ir solo. It's madness to go on your own.

**el locutor**, **la locutora** NOUN

newsreader

**lógico** (FEM **lógica**) ADJECTIVE

**1** logical

□ No es un razonamiento lógico. It's not logical reasoning.

**2** natural

□ Es una reacción lógica. It's a natural reaction.

■ **Es lógico que no quiera venir.** It's only natural he doesn't want to come.

**lograr** VERB [25]

**1** to get

□ Lograron lo que se proponían. They got what they wanted.

**2** to manage

□ Logré que me concediera una entrevista. I managed to get an interview with him.

**la lombriz** (PL las **lombrices**) NOUN

worm

**el lomo** NOUN

**1** back

**2** loin

**3** spine

**la lona** NOUN

canvas (PL canvases)

**la loncha** NOUN

slice

**Londres** MASC NOUN

London

**la longitud** NOUN

length

■ **Tiene tres metros de longitud.** It's three metres long.

**el loro** NOUN

parrot

**los** ARTICLE

▷ see also **los** PRONOUN

the

□ los barcos the boats

■ **los de las bufandas rojas** the people in the red scarves

■ **Se lavaron los pies en el río.** They washed their feet in the river.

■ **Abrochaos los abrigos.** Button your coats.

■ **Me gustan sus cuadros, pero prefiero los de Ana.** I like his paintings, but I prefer Ana's.

■ **No me gustan los melocotones.** I don't like peaches.

■ **Sólo vienen los lunes.** They only come on Mondays.

**los** PRONOUN

▷ see also **los** ARTICLE

**1** them

□ Los vi por la calle. I saw them in the street.

■ **Los han despedido.** They've been sacked.

**2** you

□ Los acompaño hasta la puerta, señores. I'll see you to the door, gentlemen.

**la lotería** NOUN

lottery (PL lotteries)

□ Le tocó la lotería. He won the lottery.

**la lucha** NOUN

fight

■ **lucha libre** wrestling

⋯ **LANGUAGE TIP** Word for word, **lucha libre** means 'free fight'.

**luchar** VERB [25]

to fight

**lucir\*** VERB

to shine

□ Lucían las estrellas. The stars were shining.

■ **Carlos se lució en el examen.** Carlos performed brilliantly in the exam.

**luego** ADVERB

▷ see also **luego** CONJUNCTION

**1** then

□ Primero se puso de pie y luego habló. First he stood up and then he spoke.

**2** later

□ Mi mujer viene luego. My wife's coming later.

■ **desde luego** of course □ ¡Desde luego que me gusta! Of course I like it!

■ **¡Hasta luego!** See you!

**3** soon *(Chile, Mexico)*
□ Vuelvo luego. I'll be back soon.
**luego** CONJUNCTION
▷ *see also* **luego** ADVERB
therefore
□ Yo he pagado, luego tengo derecho a verlo. I have paid, therefore I have a right to see it.
el **lugar** NOUN
place
□ Este lugar es muy bonito. This is a lovely place.
■ **Llegó en último lugar.** He came last.
■ **en lugar de** instead of
■ **tener lugar** to take place
el **lujo** NOUN
luxury (PL luxuries)
■ **un coche de lujo** a luxury car
**lujoso** (FEM **lujosa**) ADJECTIVE
luxurious
la **luna** NOUN
**1** moon
**2** window pane
**3** window
■ **la luna de miel** honeymoon

el **lunar** NOUN
mole
■ **una corbata de lunares** a spotted tie
el **lunes** (PL los **lunes**) NOUN
Monday
□ La vi el lunes. I saw her on Monday.
□ todos los lunes every Monday □ el lunes pasado last Monday □ el lunes que viene next Monday □ Jugamos los lunes. We play on Mondays.
la **lupa** NOUN
magnifying glass
el **luto** NOUN
■ **estar de luto por alguien** to be in mourning for somebody
**Luxemburgo** MASC NOUN
Luxembourg
la **luz** (PL las **luces**) NOUN
**1** light
□ Enciende la luz, por favor. Put on the light please.
**2** electricity
□ No hay luz en todo el edificio. There's no electricity in the whole building.
■ **dar a luz** to give birth

# Mm

los **macarrones** NOUN
macaroni *sing*
□ Me gustan los macarrones. I like macaroni.

la **macedonia** NOUN
fruit salad

la **maceta** NOUN
flowerpot

**machacar\*** VERB [48]
1 to crush
□ Machacó los ajos en el mortero. He crushed the garlic in the mortar.
2 to thrash
□ El equipo visitante los machacó. The visiting team thrashed them.

el **macho** ADJECTIVE, NOUN
male
□ un conejo macho a male rabbit

la **madera** NOUN
wood
□ Está hecho de madera. It's made of wood.
■ un juguete de madera a wooden toy
■ Dame esa madera. Give me that piece of wood.
■ Tiene madera de profesor. He's got the makings of a teacher.

la **madrastra** NOUN
stepmother

la **madre** NOUN
mother
■ ¡Madre mía! Goodness!

**Madrid** MASC NOUN
Madrid

**madrileño** (FEM **madrileña**) ADJECTIVE
from Madrid
□ Soy madrileño. I'm from Madrid.

la **madrina** NOUN
1 godmother
2 matron of honour (PL matrons of honour)

la **madrugada** NOUN
early morning
■ levantarse de madrugada 1 to get up early 2 to get up at daybreak
■ a las 4 de la madrugada at 4 o'clock in the morning

**madrugar\*** VERB [37]
to get up early

**maduro** (FEM **madura**) ADJECTIVE
1 mature
2 ripe

el **maestro**, la **maestra** NOUN
teacher
□ Mi tía es maestra. My aunt's a teacher.
■ un maestro de escuela a schoolteacher

la **magia** NOUN
magic

**mágico** (FEM **mágica**) ADJECTIVE
magic
□ una varita mágica a magic wand

el **magisterio** NOUN
■ Estudia magisterio. He's training to be a teacher.

**magnífico** (FEM **magnífica**) ADJECTIVE
splendid

el **mago**, la **maga** NOUN
magician
■ los Reyes Magos the Three Wise Men

el **maíz** (PL los **maíces**) NOUN
1 maize
2 sweetcorn
■ una mazorca de maíz a corn cob

la **majestad** NOUN
■ Su Majestad 1 His Majesty 2 Her Majesty

**majo** (FEM **maja**) ADJECTIVE
1 nice
2 pretty

**mal** ADJECTIVE
▷ see also **mal** ADVERB, NOUN = **malo**

**mal** ADVERB
▷ see also **mal** ADJECTIVE, NOUN
1 badly
□ Toca la guitarra muy mal. He plays the guitar very badly. □ un trabajo mal pagado a badly paid job
■ Esta habitación huele mal. This room smells bad.
■ Lo pasé muy mal. I had a very bad time.
■ Me entendió mal. He misunderstood me.
■ hablar mal de alguien to speak ill of someone
2 wrong

□ Han escrito mal mi apellido. They've spelt my surname wrong. □ Está mal mentir. It's wrong to tell lies.

el **mal** NOUN ADJECTIVE, NOUN
evil
□ el bien y el mal good and evil

la **mala** NOUN
■ **la mala de la película** the villain in the film

**malcriado** (FEM **malcriada**) ADJECTIVE
badly brought up

**maldito** (FEM **maldita**) ADJECTIVE
damned
□ ¡Malditos vecinos! Damned neighbours!
■ **¡Malditas las ganas que tengo de verle!** I really don't feel like seeing him!
■ **¡Maldita sea!** Damn it!

**maleducado** (FEM **maleducada**) ADJECTIVE
bad-mannered

el **malentendido** NOUN
misunderstanding

el **malestar** NOUN
discomfort

la **maleta** NOUN
suitcase
■ **hacer la maleta** to pack

el **maletero** NOUN
boot

el **maletín** (PL los **maletines**) NOUN
briefcase

**malgastar** VERB [25]
to waste

**malhumorado** (FEM **malhumorada**) ADJECTIVE
bad-tempered
■ **Hoy parece malhumorado.** He appears to be in a bad mood today.

la **malicia** NOUN
1 malice
2 mischief

**malicioso** (FEM **maliciosa**) ADJECTIVE
malicious

la **malla** NOUN
1 mesh
2 leotard
■ **una malla de baño** (River Plate) a swimsuit
■ **mallas** 1 tights 2 leggings

**Mallorca** FEM NOUN
Majorca

el **malo** NOUN
■ **el malo de la película** the villain in the film

**malo** (FEM **mala**) ADJECTIVE
1 bad
□ un mal día a bad day □ Este programa es muy malo. This is a very bad programme.
□ Soy muy mala para las matemáticas.

I'm very bad at maths.
■ **Hace malo.** The weather's bad.
■ **Lo malo es que ...** the trouble is that ...
2 naughty
□ ¿Por qué eres tan malo? Why are you so naughty?
3 off
□ Esta carne está mala. This meat's off.
4 ill
□ Mi hija está mala. My daughter's ill. □ Se puso malo después de comer. He started to feel ill after lunch.

**maltratar** VERB [25]
to ill-treat
□ Maltrata a su perro. He ill-treats his dog.
■ **los niños maltratados** abused children

**malvado** (FEM **malvada**) ADJECTIVE
evil

la **mama** NOUN
1 breast
2 mum

la **mamá** (PL las **mamás**) NOUN
mum
□ tu mamá your mum □ ¡Hola, mamá! Hi Mum!

**mamar** VERB
to suckle
□ El cordero aún mama. The lamb is still suckling.
■ **El bebé mama cada cuatro horas.** The baby has a feed every four hours.
■ **dar de mamar** to breastfeed

el **mamífero** NOUN
mammal

el **manantial** NOUN
spring

la **mancha** NOUN
stain

**manchar** VERB [25]
to stain
□ La cerveza no mancha. Beer doesn't stain.
■ **mancharse** to get dirty □ No te manches la camisa. Don't get your shirt dirty.
■ **Me he manchado el vestido de tinta.** I've got ink stains on my dress.

**mandar** VERB [25]
1 to order
□ El sargento le mandó barrer el patio. The sergeant ordered him to sweep the yard.
■ **Nos mandó callar.** He told us to be quiet.
■ **Aquí mando yo.** I'm the boss here.
2 to send
□ Se lo mandaremos por correo. We'll send it to you by post. □ Me mandaron a hacer un recado. They sent me on an errand.
■ **mandar llamar a alguien** (Latin America) to send for someone
■ **mandar a arreglar algo** (Latin America)

to have something repaired
- **¿Mande?** *(Mexico)* Pardon?
- **El médico me mandó un jarabe.** The doctor gave me a prescription for syrup.

la **mandarina** NOUN
tangerine

la **mandíbula** NOUN
jaw

el **mando** NOUN
- **un alto mando** a high-ranking officer
- **Está al mando del proyecto.** He's in charge of the project.
- **el mando a distancia** the remote control
- **los mandos** the controls

la **manecilla** NOUN
hand
□ las manecillas del reloj the hands of the clock

**manejable** (FEM **manejable**) ADJECTIVE
1 manoeuvrable
□ un coche muy manejable a very manoeuvrable car
2 easy to use
□ Este taladro es muy manejable. This drill is very easy to use.

**manejar** VERB [25]
1 to operate
2 to manage
3 to drive *(Latin America)*
- **un examen de manejar** *(Latin America)* a driving test

la **manera** NOUN
way
□ Lo hice a mi manera. I did it my way.
- **de todas maneras** anyway
- **No hay manera de convencerla.** There's nothing one can do to convince her.
- **de manera que** 1 so □ No has hecho los deberes, de manera que no hay tele. You haven't done your homework so there's no TV. 2 so that □ Lo puse de manera que pudieran verlo. I put it so that they could see it.
- **¡De ninguna manera!** Certainly not!

la **manga** NOUN
sleeve
□ Súbete las mangas. Roll your sleeves up.
- **de manga corta** short-sleeved
- **de manga larga** long-sleeved

el **mango** NOUN
1 handle
2 mango

la **manguera** NOUN
hose

la **manía** NOUN
- **Tiene la manía de repetir todo lo que digo.** He has an irritating habit of repeating everything I say.

- **El profesor me tiene manía.** *(colloquial)* The teacher has it in for me.

**maniático** (FEM **maniática**) ADJECTIVE
- **Es muy maniático para comer.** He's very fussy about eating.
- **Es una maniática del orden.** She's obsessed with keeping things tidy.

la **manifestación** (PL las **manifestaciones**) NOUN
demonstration
□ Convocaron una manifestación contra el terrorismo. They held a demonstration against terrorism.

el/la **manifestante** NOUN
demonstrator

**manifestarse*** VERB [39]
to demonstrate

el **manillar** NOUN
handlebars *pl*

la **maniobra** NOUN
manoeuvre
□ una maniobra política a political manoeuvre
- **hacer maniobras** to manoeuvre

**manipular** VERB [25]
1 to handle
□ La higiene es imprescindible para manipular alimentos. Hygiene is essential when handling food.
2 to manipulate
□ La publicidad manipula a la opinión pública. Advertising manipulates public opinion.

el/la **maniquí** (PL los/las **maniquíes**) NOUN
model

el **maniquí** (PL los **maniquíes**) NOUN
dummy (PL dummies)

la **manivela** NOUN
crank

la **mano** NOUN
hand
□ Dame la mano. Give me your hand.
- **tener algo a mano** to have something to hand
- **hecho a mano** handmade
- **de segunda mano** secondhand
- **echar una mano** to lend a hand
- **estrechar la mano a alguien** to shake somebody's hand
- **la mano de obra** labour

  LANGUAGE TIP Word for word, **mano de obra** means 'hand of work'.
- **una mano de pintura** a coat of paint

el **manojo** NOUN
bunch (PL bunches)
□ un manojo de llaves a bunch of keys

la **manopla** NOUN
mitten

□ El niño llevaba manoplas. The child was wearing mittens.

■ **una manopla de cocina** an oven-glove

**manso** (FEM **mansa**) ADJECTIVE
tame

la **manta** NOUN
blanket

la **manteca** NOUN
butter *(River Plate)*

■ **manteca de cerdo** lard

el **mantel** NOUN
tablecloth

**mantener\*** VERB [53]

1 to keep
□ Les mantendremos informados. We'll keep you informed. □ mantener la calma to keep calm

2 to support
□ Mantiene a su familia. He supports his family.

■ **mantener una conversación** to have a conversation

■ **mantenerse** to support oneself

■ **mantenerse en forma** to keep fit

■ **mantenerse en pie** to remain standing

el **mantenimiento** NOUN
maintenance
□ el encargado de mantenimiento the person in charge of maintenance

■ **ejercicios de mantenimiento** keep-fit exercises

la **mantequilla** NOUN
butter

**mantuve** VERB ▷ *see* **mantener**

el **manual** ADJECTIVE, NOUN
manual

el **manubrio** NOUN *(Latin America)*
handlebars *pl*

el **manuscrito** NOUN
manuscript

la **manzana** NOUN

1 apple

2 block

el **manzano** NOUN
apple tree

la **maña** NOUN

■ **Tiene mucha maña para hacer arreglos caseros.** She's a dab hand at mending things around the house.

la **mañana** NOUN
morning
□ Llegó a las nueve de la mañana. He arrived at nine o'clock in the morning.

■ **Por la mañana voy al gimnasio.** In the mornings I go to the gym.

■ **a media mañana** mid-morning

**mañana** ADVERB
tomorrow

□ ¡Hasta mañana! See you tomorrow!

■ **pasado mañana** the day after tomorrow

■ **mañana por la mañana** tomorrow morning

■ **mañana por la noche** tomorrow night

el **mapa** NOUN
map
□ El pueblo no está en el mapa. The village isn't on the map. □ un mapa de carreteras a road map

la **maqueta** NOUN
model

el **maquillaje** NOUN
make-up *sing*

**maquillarse** VERB [25]
to put one's make-up on

la **máquina** NOUN
machine
□ una máquina de coser a sewing machine □ una máquina expendedora a vending machine □ una máquina tragaperras a fruit machine

■ **una máquina de afeitar** an electric razor

■ **una máquina de escribir** a typewriter

■ **escrito a máquina** typed

■ **una máquina fotográfica** a camera

la **maquinilla** NOUN
razor
□ una maquinilla eléctrica an electric razor

el **mar** NOUN
sea

■ **por mar** by sea

■ **en alta mar** on the high seas

■ **Lo hizo la mar de bien.** He did it really well.

el **maratón** (PL los **maratones**) NOUN
marathon

la **maravilla** NOUN

■ **¡Qué maravilla de casa!** What a wonderful house!

■ **ser una maravilla** to be wonderful

■ **Se llevan de maravilla.** They get on wonderfully well together.

**maravilloso** (FEM **maravillosa**) ADJECTIVE
marvellous

la **marca** NOUN

1 mark
□ Había marcas de neumático en la arena. There were tyre marks in the sand.

2 make
□ ¿De qué marca es tu coche? What make's your car?

3 brand
□ una conocida marca de cigarrillos a well-known brand of cigarettes

■ **la ropa de marca** designer clothes

el **marcador** NOUN

1 scoreboard

**2** bookmark

**marcar\*** VERB [48]
**1** to mark
**2** to brand
**3** to dial
**4** to score
**5** to set
■ **Mi reloj marca las 2.** It's 2 o'clock according to my watch.
■ **marcar algo con una equis** to put a cross on something

la **marcha** NOUN
**1** departure
□ Su marcha les dejó muy tristes. His departure left them feeling very sad.
**2** gear
□ cambiar de marcha to change gear
■ **salir de marcha** to go out on the town
■ **a toda marcha** at full speed
■ **estar en marcha 1** to be running **2** to be underway
■ **dar marcha atrás** to reverse
■ **No te subas nunca a un tren en marcha.** Never get onto a moving train.

**marcharse** VERB [25]
to leave

el **marco** NOUN
frame

la **marea** NOUN
tide
■ **una marea negra** an oil slick
○ LANGUAGE TIP Word for word, **marea negra** means 'black tide'.

**mareado** (FEM **mareada**) ADJECTIVE
■ **Estoy mareado. 1** I feel dizzy. **2** I feel sick.

**marear** VERB [25]
to make...feel sick
□ Ese olor me marea. That smell makes me feel sick.
■ **marearse 1** to get dizzy □ Te marearás si das tantas vueltas. You'll get dizzy going round and round like that. **2** to get seasick □ ¿Te mareas cuando vas en barco? Do you get seasick when you travel by boat? **3** to get carsick □ Siempre me mareo en coche. I always get carsick.
■ **¡No me marees!** Stop going on at me!

el **mareo** NOUN
**1** sea sickness
**2** car sickness
■ **Le dio un mareo a causa del calor.** The heat made her feel ill.

el **marfil** NOUN
ivory

la **margarina** NOUN
margarine

la **margarita** NOUN
daisy (PL daisies)

el **margen** (PL los **márgenes**) NOUN
margin
□ Escribe las notas al margen. Write your notes in the margin.

el **marido** NOUN
husband

el **marinero** NOUN
sailor

la **mariposa** NOUN
butterfly (PL butterflies)

el **marisco** NOUN
shellfish (PL shellfish)
□ No me gusta el marisco. I don't like shellfish.

el **mármol** NOUN
marble

**marrón** (FEM **marrón**, PL **marrones**) ADJECTIVE
brown
□ un traje marrón a brown suit

**Marruecos** MASC NOUN
Morocco

el **martes** (PL los **martes**) NOUN
Tuesday
□ La vi el martes. I saw her on Tuesday.
□ todos los martes every Tuesday □ el martes pasado last Tuesday □ el martes que viene next Tuesday □ Jugamos los martes. We play on Tuesdays.

el **martillo** NOUN
hammer

**marzo** MASC NOUN
March
□ en marzo in March □ Nací el 17 de marzo. I was born on 17 March.

**más** ADJECTIVE, ADVERB
more
□ Ahora salgo más. I go out more these days.
■ **Últimamente nos vemos más.** We've been seeing more of each other lately.
■ **¿Quieres más?** Would you like some more?
■ **No tengo más dinero.** I haven't any more money. □ barato – más barato cheap – cheaper □ joven – más joven young – younger □ largo – más largo long – longer □ grande – más grande big – bigger □ contento – más contento happy – happier □ rápido – más rápido fast – faster □ temprano – más temprano early – earlier
■ **lejos – más lejos** far – further □ hermoso – más hermoso beautiful – more beautiful □ guapo – más guapo handsome – more handsome □ deprisa – más deprisa quickly – more quickly □ Es más grande que el tuyo. It's bigger than yours. □ Corre más rápido que yo. He runs faster than I do.
■ **Trabaja más que yo.** He works harder than I do.

■ **más de mil libros** more than a thousand books

■ **No tiene más de dieciséis años.** He isn't more than sixteen.

■ **más de lo que yo creía** more than I thought □ el bolígrafo más barato the cheapest pen □ el niño más joven the youngest child □ el coche más grande the biggest car □ la persona más feliz the happiest person □ el más inteligente de todos the most intelligent of all of them

■ **su película más innovadora** his most innovative film

■ **Paco es el que come más.** Paco's the one who eats the most.

■ **Fue el que más trabajó.** He was the one who worked the hardest.

■ **el punto más lejano** the furthest point

■ **¿Qué más?** What else?

■ **¡Qué perro más sucio!** What a filthy dog!

■ **Tenemos uno de más.** We have one too many.

■ **Por más que estudio no apruebo.** However hard I study I don't pass.

■ **más o menos** more or less

■ **2 más 2 son 4** 2 and 2 are 4

■ **14 más 20 menos 12 es igual a 22** 14 plus 20 minus 12 equals 22

la **masa** NOUN
1 dough
□ la masa de pan bread dough
2 mass (PL masses)
■ **las masas** the masses
■ **en masa 1** mass □ la producción en masa mass production **2** en masse □ Fueron en masa a recibir al futbolista. They went en masse to greet the footballer.

el **masaje** NOUN
massage

la **máscara** NOUN
mask

**masculino** (FEM **masculina**) ADJECTIVE
1 male
□ el sexo masculino the male sex
2 men's
□ la ropa masculina men's clothing
3 masculine
□ el pronombre masculino 'él' the masculine pronoun 'él'

**masticar\*** VERB [48]
to chew

**matar** VERB
to kill
□ El jefe me va a matar. The boss will kill me.
■ **matarse** to be killed □ Se mataron en un accidente de coche. They were killed in a car accident.

196 el **matasellos** (PL los **matasellos**) NOUN

postmark

**mate** (FEM **mate**) ADJECTIVE
matt

el **mate** NOUN
1 checkmate
2 maté

las **matemáticas** NOUN
mathematics *sing*

la **materia** NOUN
1 matter
□ materia orgánica organic matter
2 material
□ la materia prima raw material
3 subject
□ Es un experto en la materia. He's an expert on the subject.
■ **entrar en materia** to get to the point

el **material** ADJECTIVE, NOUN
material
□ los materiales de desecho waste material

**materno** (FEM **materna**) ADJECTIVE
maternal
□ mi abuela materna my maternal grandmother
■ **mi lengua materna** my mother tongue

el **matiz** (PL los **matices**) NOUN
shade

el **matorral** NOUN
bushes *pl*

la **matrícula** NOUN
registration
■ **la matrícula del coche 1** the registration number of the car **2** the number plate of the car

**matricular** VERB
to register
■ **matricularse** to enrol

el **matrimonio** NOUN
1 marriage
□ El matrimonio se celebró en la iglesia del pueblo. The marriage took place in the village church.
2 couple
□ Eran un matrimonio feliz. They were a happy couple.

**maullar** VERB
to miaow

**máximo** (FEM **máxima**) ADJECTIVE
maximum
□ la velocidad máxima the maximum speed

el **máximo** NOUN
maximum
□ un máximo de 50 euros a maximum of 50 euros
■ **como máximo 1** at the most □ Te costará 5.000 libras como máximo. It'll cost you £5,000 at the most. **2** at the latest □ Llegaré a las diez como máximo. I'll be

there by ten o'clock at the latest.

**mayo** MASC NOUN
May
□ en mayo in May □ Nací el 28 de mayo. I was born on 28 May.

la **mayonesa** NOUN
mayonnaise

**mayor** (FEM **mayor**) ADJECTIVE, PRONOUN
1 older
□ Paco es mayor que Nacho. Paco is older than Nacho. □ Es tres años mayor que yo. He is three years older than me.
■ **el hermano mayor 1** the older brother **2** the oldest brother
■ **Soy el mayor. 1** I'm the older. **2** I'm the oldest.
■ **Nuestros hijos ya son mayores.** Our children are grown-up now.
■ **la gente mayor** the elderly
2 bigger
□ Necesitamos una casa mayor. We need a bigger house.
■ **la mayor iglesia del mundo.** the biggest church in the world

el/la **mayor** NOUN
■ **un mayor de edad** an adult
■ **los mayores** grown-ups

la **mayoría** NOUN
majority (PL majorities)
■ **Somos mayoría.** We are in the majority.
■ **La mayoría de los estudiantes son pobres.** Most students are poor.
■ **la mayoría de nosotros** most of us

la **mayúscula** NOUN
capital letter
□ Empieza cada frase con mayúscula. Start each sentence with a capital letter.
■ **Escríbelo con mayúsculas.** Write it in capitals.
■ **una M mayúscula** a capital M

el **mazapán** (PL los **mazapanes**) NOUN
marzipan

**me** PRONOUN
1 me
□ Me quiere. He loves me. □ Me regaló una pulsera. He gave me a bracelet.
■ **Me lo dio.** He gave it to me.
■ **¿Me echas esta carta?** Will you post this letter for me?
2 myself
□ No me hice daño. I didn't hurt myself.
■ **me dije a mí mismo** I said to myself
□ Me duelen los pies. My feet hurt. □ Me puse el abrigo. I put my coat on.

**mear** VERB
to piss (vulgar)
■ **mearse** to wet oneself
■ **mearse de risa** (vulgar) to piss oneself

laughing

la **mecánica** NOUN
1 mechanic
□ Quiere ser mecánica. She wants to be a mechanic.
2 mechanics sing

**mecánico** (FEM **mecánica**) ADJECTIVE
mechanical

el **mecánico** NOUN
mechanic
□ Es mecánico. He's a mechanic.

el **mecanismo** NOUN
mechanism

la **mecanografía** NOUN
typing

la **mecha** NOUN
1 wick
2 fuse

el **mechero** NOUN
cigarette lighter

la **medalla** NOUN
medal

la **media** NOUN
1 average
□ Trabajo una media de seis horas diarias. I work an average of six hours a day.
2 sock (Latin America)
■ **medias 1** stockings **2** tights
■ **medias bombachas** (River Plate) tights
■ **a las cuatro y media** at half past four

**mediados** PL NOUN
■ **a mediados de** around the middle of

**mediano** (FEM **mediana**) ADJECTIVE
medium
□ de mediana estatura of medium height
■ **de tamaño mediano** medium-sized
■ **el hijo mediano** the middle son

la **medianoche** NOUN
midnight
□ a medianoche at midnight

**mediante** PREPOSITION
■ **Izaron las cajas mediante una polea.** They lifted the crates using a pulley.

**mediático** (FEM **mediática**) ADJECTIVE
media

el **medicamento** NOUN
medicine

la **medicina** NOUN
medicine
□ Estudia medicina en la universidad. He's studying medicine at university. □ ¿Te has tomado ya la medicina? Have you taken your medicine yet?

el **médico**, la **médica** NOUN
doctor
□ Quiere ser médica. She wants to be a doctor. □ el médico de cabecera the family doctor

■ **ir al médico** to go to the doctor's
la **medida** NOUN
measure
□ medidas de seguridad security measures
□ tomar medidas contra la inflación to take
measures against inflation
■ **El sastre le tomó las medidas.** The tailor
took his measurements.
■ **un traje a medida** a made-to-measure
suit
■ **a medida que ...** as ... □ Saludaba a los
invitados a medida que iban llegando. He
greeted the guests as they arrived.
**medio** (FEM **media**) ADJECTIVE
▷ see also **medio** ADVERB, NOUN
1 half
□ medio litro half a litre □ Nos queda media
botella de leche. We've got half a bottle of
milk left. □ media hora half an hour □ una
hora y media an hour and a half
■ **Son las ocho y media.** It's half past eight.
2 average
□ la temperatura media the average
temperature
**medio** ADVERB
▷ see also **medio** ADJECTIVE, NOUN
half
□ Estaba medio dormido. He was half
asleep. □ una manzana a medio comer a
half eaten apple
el **medio** NOUN
▷ see also **medio** ADJECTIVE, ADVERB
1 middle
□ Está en el medio. It's in the middle.
■ **en medio de** in the middle of
2 means
□ un medio de transporte a means of
transport
■ **por medio de** by means of
■ **medios** means □ por medios pacíficos
by peaceful means
■ **los medios de comunicación** the media
■ **el medio ambiente** the environment
el **mediodía** NOUN
■ **al mediodía 1** at midday **2** at lunchtime
**medir\*** VERB [38]
to measure
□ ¿Has medido la ventana? Have you
measured the window?
■ **¿Cuánto mides? — Mido 1.50 m.** How
tall are you? — I'm 1.5 m tall.
■ **¿Cuánto mide esta habitación? — Mide
3 m por 4.** How big is this room? — It
measures 3 m by 4.
el **Mediterráneo** NOUN
the Mediterranean
**mediterráneo** (FEM **mediterránea**)
ADJECTIVE

Mediterranean
la **medusa** NOUN
jellyfish (PL jellyfish)
la **mejilla** NOUN
cheek
el **mejillón** (PL los **mejillones**) NOUN
mussel
**mejor** (FEM **mejor**) ADJECTIVE
1 better
□ Éste es mejor que el otro. This one is
better than the other one.
■ **Es el mejor de los dos.** He's the better of
the two.
2 best
□ mi mejor amiga my best friend □ el mejor
de la clase the best in the class □ Es el
mejor de todos. He's the best of the lot.
**mejor** ADVERB
1 better
□ La conozco mejor que tú. I know her
better than you do.
2 best
□ ¿Quién lo hace mejor? Who does it best?
■ **a lo mejor** probably
■ **Mejor nos vamos.** We had better go.
la **mejora** NOUN
improvement
**mejorar** VERB [25]
to improve
□ El tiempo está mejorando. The weather's
improving. □ Han mejorado el servicio.
They have improved the service.
■ **¡Que te mejores!** Get well soon!
la **mejoría** NOUN
improvement
la **melena** NOUN
1 long hair
□ Lleva una melena rubia. She has long
blond hair.
2 mane
el **mellizo** (FEM la **melliza**) ADJECTIVE, NOUN
twin
□ Son mellizos. They're twins.
el **melocotón** (PL los **melocotones**) NOUN
peach (PL peaches)
la **melodía** NOUN
tune
□ tararear una melodía to hum a tune
el **melón** (PL los **melones**) NOUN
melon
la **memoria** NOUN
memory (PL memories)
□ tener mala memoria to have a bad
memory
■ **aprender algo de memoria** to learn
something by heart
**memorizar\*** VERB
to memorize

**mencionar** VERB [25]
to mention

el **mendigo**, la **mendiga** NOUN
beggar

**menor** (FEM **menor**) ADJECTIVE, PRONOUN
1 younger
▫ Es tres años menor que yo. He's three years younger than me. ▫ Juanito es menor que Pepe. Juanito is younger than Pepe.
■ **el hermano menor 1** the younger brother **2** the youngest brother
■ **Yo soy el menor. 1** I'm the younger. **2** I'm the youngest.
2 smaller
▫ una talla menor a smaller size
■ **No tiene la menor importancia.** It's not in the least important.

el/la **menor** NOUN
■ **un menor de edad** a minor
■ **los menores** the under-18s

**Menorca** FEM NOUN
Minorca

**menos** ADJECTIVE, ADVERB
1 less
▫ Fernando está menos deprimido. Fernando is less depressed. ▫ Ahora salgo menos. I go out less these days.
■ **Últimamente nos vemos menos.** We've been seeing less of each other recently.
▫ menos harina less flour ▫ menos gatos fewer cats ▫ menos gente fewer people
■ **menos...que** less...than ▫ Me gusta menos que el otro. I like it less than the other one. ▫ Lo hizo menos cuidadosamente que ayer. He did it less carefully than yesterday.
■ **Trabaja menos que yo.** He doesn't work as hard as I do.
■ **menos de 50 cajas** fewer than 50 boxes
■ **Tiene menos de dieciocho años.** He's under eighteen.
2 least
▫ el chico menos desobediente de la clase the least disobedient boy in the class
■ **Fue el que menos trabajó.** He was the one who worked the least hard. ▫ el método que lleva menos tiempo the method which takes the least time ▫ el examen con menos errores the exam paper with the fewest mistakes
■ **No quiero verle y menos visitarle.** I don't want to see him, let alone visit him.
■ **¡Menos mal!** Thank goodness!
■ **al menos** at least
■ **por lo menos** at least
■ **¡Ni mucho menos!** No way!

**menos** PREPOSITION
except

▫ todos menos él everyone except him
■ **5 menos 2 son tres** 5 minus 2 is three
■ **a menos que** unless

el **mensaje** NOUN
message
■ **un mensaje de texto** a text message
■ **el envío de mensajes con foto** picture messaging

el **mensajero**, la **mensajera** NOUN
messenger

**mensual** (FEM **mensual**) ADJECTIVE
monthly
■ **50 dólares mensuales** 50 dollars a month

la **menta** NOUN
mint
▫ un caramelo de menta a mint sweet

la **mentalidad** NOUN
mentality (PL mentalities)
▫ Tiene mentalidad de burócrata. He has a bureaucratic mentality.
■ **Tiene una mentalidad muy abierta.** He has a very open mind.

la **mente** NOUN
mind
▫ No me lo puedo quitar de la mente. I can't get it out of my mind.
■ **tener en mente hacer algo** to be thinking of doing something ▫ Tiene en mente cambiar de empleo. He's thinking of changing jobs.

**mentir*** VERB [51]
to lie
▫ No me mientas. Don't lie to me.

la **mentira** NOUN
lie
▫ No digas mentiras. Don't tell lies.
■ **Parece mentira que aún no te haya pagado.** It's incredible that he still hasn't paid you.
■ **una pistola de mentira** a toy pistol

el **mentiroso**, la **mentirosa** NOUN
liar

el **menú** (PL los **menús**) NOUN
menu
■ **el menú del día** the set meal

**menudo** (FEM **menuda**) ADJECTIVE
slight
▫ Es una chica muy menuda. She's a very slight girl.
■ **¡Menudo lío!** What a mess!
■ **a menudo** often

el **meñique** NOUN
little finger

el **mercado** NOUN
market

la **mercancía** NOUN
commodity (PL commodities)

la **mercería** NOUN

haberdasher's (PL haberdashers' shops)

**merecer\*** VERB [12]
to deserve
  □ Mereces que te castiguen. You deserve to be punished.
  ■ **merece la pena** it's worthwhile

**merendar\*** VERB [39]
to have tea

el **merengue** NOUN
meringue

la **merienda** NOUN
tea

el **mérito** NOUN
merit
  □ una obra de gran mérito artístico a work of great artistic merit
  ■ **Eso tiene mucho mérito.** That's very commendable.
  ■ **El mérito es todo suyo.** The credit is all his.

la **merluza** NOUN
hake

la **mermelada** NOUN
jam

**mero** ADVERB (Mexico)
almost
  □ Ya mero no vengo. I almost didn't come.

el **mes** (PL los **meses**) NOUN
month
  □ el mes que viene next month  □ a final de mes at the end of the month

la **mesa** NOUN
table
  ■ **poner la mesa** to lay the table
  ■ **quitar la mesa** to clear the table

la **mesera** NOUN (Latin America)
waitress (PL waitresses)

el **mesero** NOUN (Latin America)
waiter

la **mesilla** NOUN
  ■ **una mesilla de noche** a bedside table

la **meta** NOUN
1 aim
2 finishing line
3 goal

el **metal** NOUN
metal

**metálico** (FEM **metálica**) ADJECTIVE
metal
  □ un objeto metálico a metal object
  ■ **en metálico** in cash
  ⟨ **LANGUAGE TIP** Word for word, **en metálico** means 'in metallic'.

**meter** VERB [8]
to put
  □ ¿Dónde has metido las llaves? Where have you put the keys?
  ■ **meterse en** to go into  □ Se metió en la

cueva. He went into the cave.
  ■ **meterse en política** to go into politics
  ■ **No te metas donde no te llaman.** Don't poke your nose in where it doesn't belong.
  ■ **meterse con alguien** to pick on somebody

el **método** NOUN
method

el **metro** NOUN
1 underground
  □ coger el metro to take the underground
2 metre
  □ Mide tres metros de largo. It's three metres long.

el **mexicano** (FEM la **mexicana**) ADJECTIVE, NOUN
Mexican

**México** MASC NOUN
Mexico

la **mezcla** NOUN
mixture

**mezclar** VERB
to mix
  □ Hay que mezclar el azúcar y la harina. You have to mix the sugar and the flour.
  ■ **mezclarse en algo** to get mixed up in something

**mezquino** (FEM **mezquina**) ADJECTIVE
mean

la **mezquita** NOUN
mosque

**mi** (FEM **mi**, PL **mis**) ADJECTIVE
my
  □ mis hermanas my sisters

**mí** PRONOUN
me
  □ para mí for me
  ■ **Para mí que ...** I think that ...
  ■ **Por mí no hay problema.** There's no problem as far as I'm concerned.

el **microbio** NOUN
microbe

el **micrófono** NOUN
microphone

el **microondas** (PL los **microondas**) NOUN
microwave
  □ un horno microondas a microwave oven

el **microscopio** NOUN
microscope

**midiendo** VERB ▷ see **medir**

el **miedo** NOUN
fear
  □ el miedo a la oscuridad fear of the dark
  ■ **tener miedo** to be afraid  □ Le tenía miedo a su padre. He was afraid of his father.
  □ Tengo miedo a morir. I'm afraid of dying.
  □ Tenemos miedo de que nos ataquen. We're afraid that they may attack us.

m

■ **dar miedo a** to scare □ Me daba miedo hacerlo. I was scared of doing it.

■ **pasarlo de miedo** to have a fantastic time *(colloquial)*

**miedoso** (FEM **miedosa**) ADJECTIVE

■ **¡No seas tan miedoso!** Don't be such a coward!

■ **Mi hijo es muy miedoso.** My son gets frightened very easily.

la **miel** NOUN
honey

el **miembro** NOUN
limb

el/la **miembro** NOUN
member

**mientras** ADVERB, CONJUNCTION
while

□ Lava tú mientras yo seco. You wash while I dry.

■ **Seguiré conduciendo mientras pueda.** I'll carry on driving for as long as I can.

■ **mientras que** while

■ **mientras tanto** meanwhile

el **miércoles** (PL los **miércoles**) NOUN
Wednesday

□ La vi el miércoles. I saw her on Wednesday. □ todos los miércoles every Wednesday □ el miércoles pasado last Wednesday □ el miércoles que viene next Wednesday □ Jugamos los miércoles. We play on Wednesdays.

la **mierda** NOUN
shit

■ **Esta película es una mierda.** *(vulgar)* This film's a load of crap.

■ **¡Vete a la mierda!** *(colloquial)* Go to hell!

la **miga** NOUN
crumb

■ **hacer buenas migas** *(colloquial)* to hit it off

LANGUAGE TIP Word for word, **hacer buenas migas** means 'to make good breadcrumbs'.

**mil** (FEM **mil**) ADJECTIVE, PRONOUN
thousand

□ miles de personas thousands of people
□ dos mil euros two thousand euros

■ **miles de veces** hundreds of times

el **milagro** NOUN
miracle

□ No nos hemos matado de milagro. It was a miracle we weren't killed.

la **mili** NOUN
military service

□ hacer la mili to do one's military service

el **milímetro** NOUN
millimetre

el/la **militar** NOUN
soldier

■ **los militares** the military

**militar** (FEM **militar**) ADJECTIVE
military

la **milla** NOUN
mile

el **millón** (PL los **millones**) NOUN
million

□ millones de personas millions of people

■ **mil millones** a billion

el **millonario**, la **millonaria** NOUN
millionaire

**mimado** (FEM **mimada**) ADJECTIVE
spoiled

la **mina** NOUN
mine

el **mineral** ADJECTIVE, NOUN
mineral

el **minero**, la **minera** NOUN
miner

la **miniatura** NOUN
miniature

■ **una casa en miniatura** a miniature house

el **minidisco** NOUN
Minidisc®

la **minifalda** NOUN
miniskirt

**mínimo** (FEM **mínima**) ADJECTIVE
minimum

□ el salario mínimo the minimum wage

■ **No tienes ni la más mínima idea.** You haven't the faintest idea.

el **mínimo** NOUN
minimum

□ un mínimo de 10 euros a minimum of 10 euros

■ **lo mínimo que puede hacer** the least he can do

■ **Como mínimo podrías haber llamado.** You could at least have called.

el **ministerio** NOUN
ministry (PL ministries)

el **ministro**, la **ministra** NOUN
minister

la **minoría** NOUN
minority (PL minorities)

□ las minorías étnicas ethnic minorities

**minucioso** (FEM **minuciosa**) ADJECTIVE
thorough

la **minúscula** NOUN
small letter

la **minusválida** NOUN
disabled woman (PL disabled women)

el **minusválido** NOUN
disabled man (PL disabled men)

■ **los minusválidos** the disabled

el **minuto** NOUN
minute

**m**

201

□ Espera un minuto. Wait a minute.

**mío** (FEM **mía**) ADJECTIVE, PRONOUN
mine
□ Estos caballos son míos. Those horses are mine. □ ¿De quién es esta bufanda? — Es mía. Whose scarf is this? — It's mine. □ El mío está en el armario. Mine's in the cupboard. □ Éste es el mío. This one's mine.
■ **un amigo mío** a friend of mine

**miope** (FEM **miope**) ADJECTIVE
short-sighted

la **mirada** NOUN
look
□ con una mirada de odio with a look of hatred
■ **echar una mirada a algo** to have a look at something □ ¿Le has echado una mirada a mi informe? Have you had a look at my report?

**mirar** VERB [25]
to look
□ ¡Mira! Un ratón. Look! A mouse. □ Mira a ver si está ahí. Look and see if he is there.
■ **mirar algo** to look at something □ Mira esta foto. Look at this photo.
■ **mirar por la ventana** to look out of the window
■ **mirar algo fijamente** to stare at something
■ **¡Mira que es tonto!** What an idiot!
■ **mirarse al espejo** to look at oneself in the mirror
■ **Se miraron asombrados.** They looked at each other in amazement.

la **misa** NOUN
mass (PL masses)
□ la misa del gallo midnight mass □ ir a misa to go to mass

la **miseria** NOUN
1 poverty
□ estar en la miseria to be living in poverty
2 pittance
□ Gano una miseria. I earn a pittance.

la **misión** (PL las **misiones**) NOUN
mission

el **misionero**, la **misionera** NOUN
missionary (PL missionaries)

**mismo** (FEM **misma**) ADJECTIVE
▷ see also **mismo** ADVERB, PRONOUN
same
□ Nos gustan los mismos libros. We like the same books. □ Vivo en su misma calle. I live in the same street as him.
■ **yo mismo** myself □ Lo hice yo mismo. I did it myself.

**mismo** ADVERB
▷ see also **mismo** ADJECTIVE, PRONOUN
■ **Hoy mismo le escribiré.** I'll write to him

today.
■ **Nos podemos encontrar aquí mismo.** We can meet right here.
■ **enfrente mismo del colegio** right opposite the school

**mismo** PRONOUN
▷ see also **mismo** ADJECTIVE, ADVERB
■ **lo mismo** the same □ Yo tomaré lo mismo. I'll have the same.
■ **Da lo mismo.** It doesn't matter.
■ **No ha llamado pero lo mismo viene.** He hasn't phoned but he may well come.

el **misterio** NOUN
mystery (PL mysteries)

**misterioso** (FEM **misteriosa**) ADJECTIVE
mysterious

la **mitad** NOUN
half (PL halves)
□ Se comió la mitad del pastel. He ate half the cake. □ más de la mitad de los trabajadores more than half the workers
■ **La mitad son chicas.** Half of them are girls.
■ **a mitad de precio** half-price
■ **a mitad de camino** halfway there
■ **Corta el pan por la mitad.** Cut the loaf in half.

el **mito** NOUN
myth

**mixto** (FEM **mixta**) ADJECTIVE
mixed
□ una escuela mixta a mixed school

el **mobiliario** NOUN
furniture

la **mochila** NOUN
rucksack

el **moco** NOUN
■ **Límpiate los mocos.** Wipe your nose.
■ **tener mocos** to have a runny nose

la **moda** NOUN
fashion
■ **estar de moda** to be in fashion
■ **pasado de moda** old-fashioned

los **modales** NOUN
manners
□ buenos modales good manners

el/la **modelo** ADJECTIVE, NOUN
model
□ una niña modelo a model child □ Quiero ser modelo. I want to be a model.

**moderado** (FEM **moderada**) ADJECTIVE
moderate

**modernizar*** VERB
to modernize
■ **modernizarse** to get up to date

**moderno** (FEM **moderna**) ADJECTIVE
modern

la **modestia** NOUN

modesty

**modesto** (FEM **modesta**) ADJECTIVE
modest

**modificar*** VERB [48]
to modify

el **modisto**, la **modista** NOUN
dressmaker
□ Es modista. She's a dressmaker.

el **modo** NOUN
way
□ Le gusta hacerlo todo a su modo. She likes to do everything her own way.
■ **de todos modos** anyway
■ **de modo que 1** so □ No has hecho los deberes, de modo que no puedes salir. You haven't done your homework so you can't go out. **2** so that □ Mueve la tele de modo que todos la podamos ver. Move the TV so that we can all see it.
■ **los buenos modos** good manners
■ **los malos modos** bad manners
■ **'modo de empleo'** 'instructions for use'

el **moho** NOUN
**1** mould
**2** rust

**mojado** (FEM **mojada**) ADJECTIVE
wet

**mojar** VERB [25]
to get...wet
□ ¡No mojes la alfombra! Don't get the carpet wet! □ Me he mojado las mangas. I got my sleeves wet.
■ **Moja el pan en la salsa.** Dip the bread into the sauce.
■ **mojarse** to get wet

el **molde** NOUN
mould

**moler*** VERB [33]
to grind
■ **Estoy molido.** (colloquial) I'm knackered.

**molestar** VERB
**1** to bother
□ ¿Te molesta la radio? Is the radio bothering you? □ Siento molestarle. I'm sorry to bother you.
**2** to disturb
□ No me molestes, que estoy trabajando. Don't disturb me, I'm working.
■ **molestarse** to get upset □ Se molestó por algo que dije. She got upset because of something I said.
■ **molestarse en hacer algo** to bother to do something

la **molestia** NOUN
■ **tomarse la molestia de hacer algo** to take the trouble to do something
■ **'perdonen las molestias'** 'we apologize for any inconvenience'

■ **Aún tengo molestias en el hombro.** My shoulder still bothers me.

**molesto** (FEM **molesta**) ADJECTIVE
annoying
■ **estar molesto** to be annoyed

el **molinillo** NOUN
■ **un molinillo de café** a coffee grinder

el **molino** NOUN
mill
□ un molino de viento a windmill

el **momento** NOUN
moment
□ Espera un momento. Wait a moment.
□ en un momento in a moment
■ **en este momento** at the moment
□ Tenemos mucho trabajo en este momento. We've got a lot of work at the moment.
■ **de un momento a otro** any moment now
□ Llegarán de un momento a otro. They'll be here any moment now.
■ **por el momento** for the moment
■ **Llegó el momento de irnos.** The time came for us to go.

la **momia** NOUN
mummy (PL mummies)

el/la **monarca** NOUN
monarch

la **monarquía** NOUN
monarchy (PL monarchies)

el **monasterio** NOUN
monastery (PL monasteries)

la **moneda** NOUN
coin
□ una moneda de dos euros a two-euro coin
■ **la moneda extranjera** foreign currency

el **monedero** NOUN
purse

el **monitor**, la **monitora** NOUN
instructor
□ un monitor de esquí a skiing instructor

el **monitor** NOUN
monitor

la **monja** NOUN
nun

el **monje** NOUN
monk

**mono** (FEM **mona**) ADJECTIVE
pretty
□ ¡Qué piso tan mono! What a pretty flat!
■ **¡Qué niña tan mona!** What a sweet little girl!

el **mono** NOUN
**1** monkey
**2** overalls pl
**3** dungarees pl

el **monopatín** (PL los **monopatines**) NOUN
skateboard

**monótono** (FEM **monótona**) ADJECTIVE
monotonous

el **monstruo** NOUN
monster

la **montaña** NOUN
mountain
□ Fuimos de vacaciones a la montaña.
We went to the mountains on holiday.
■ **la montaña rusa** the roller coaster

> LANGUAGE TIP Word for word,
> **montaña rusa** means 'Russian
> mountain'.

**montañoso** (FEM **montañosa**) ADJECTIVE
mountainous

**montar** VERB [25]
1 to assemble
2 to set up
■ **montar una tienda** to put up a tent
■ **montar a caballo** to ride a horse
■ **montar en bici** to ride a bike
■ **montarse** to get on □ Se montó en el
autobús. He got on the bus.

el **monte** NOUN
mountain

el **montón** (PL los **montones**) NOUN
pile
□ Puso el montón de libros sobre la mesa.
He put the pile of books on the table.
■ **un montón de ...** loads of ...
□ un montón de gente loads of people □ un
montón de dinero loads of money

el **monumento** NOUN
monument

el **moño** NOUN
bun
□ Mi abuela siempre lleva moño. My
grandmother always wears her hair in a bun.

la **moqueta** NOUN
carpet

la **mora** NOUN
1 blackberry (PL blackberries)
2 mulberry (PL mulberries)

**morado** (FEM **morada**) ADJECTIVE
purple
□ un vestido morado a purple dress

**moral** (FEM **moral**) ADJECTIVE
moral

la **moral** NOUN
1 morale
■ **levantar la moral a alguien** to cheer
somebody up
■ **estar bajo de moral** to be down
2 morals pl
□ No tienen moral. They have no morals.

la **moraleja** NOUN
moral

la **morcilla** NOUN
black pudding

**morder*** VERB [33]
to bite
■ **morderse las uñas** to bite one's nails

el **mordisco** NOUN
bite
□ Dame un mordisco de tu bocadillo. Let
me have a bite of your sandwich.
■ **dar un mordisco** to bite □ Me dio un
mordisco. He bit me.

**moreno** (FEM **morena**) ADJECTIVE
1 dark
■ **Es moreno. 1** He has dark hair. **2** He is
dark-skinned.
■ **ponerse moreno** to get brown
2 brown

**morir*** VERB [32]
to die
□ Murió de cáncer. He died of cancer.
■ **morirse de hambre** to starve □ ¡Me
muero de hambre! I'm starving!
■ **morirse de vergüenza** to die of shame
■ **Me muero de ganas de ir a nadar.** I'm
dying to go for a swim.

la **mortadela** NOUN
mortadella

**mortal** (FEM **mortal**) ADJECTIVE
1 fatal
2 mortal

la **mosca** NOUN
fly (PL flies)
■ **por si las moscas** just in case

> LANGUAGE TIP Word for word, **por si
> las moscas** means 'for if the flies'.

el **mosquito** NOUN
mosquito (PL mosquitoes)

la **mostaza** NOUN
mustard

el **mostrador** NOUN
counter

**mostrar*** VERB [11]
to show
□ Nos mostró el camino. He showed us the
way.
■ **mostrarse amable** to be kind

el **mote** NOUN
nickname

el **motivo** NOUN
1 reason
□ Dejó el trabajo por motivos personales.
He left the job for personal reasons.
■ **sin motivo** for no reason
2 motive
□ ¿Cuál fue el motivo del crimen? What was
the motive for the crime?

la **moto** NOUN
motorbike

la **motocicleta** NOUN
motorbike

el **motor** NOUN
motor

el/la **motorista** NOUN
motorcyclist

**mover\*** VERB [33]
to move
□ Mueve un poco las cajas para que podamos pasar. Move the boxes a bit so that we can get past.
■ **moverse** to move □ ¡No te muevas! Don't move!

**móvil** (FEM **móvil**) ADJECTIVE
mobile

el **móvil** NOUN
1 mobile
2 motive

el **movimiento** NOUN
movement

la **moza** NOUN
girl

el **mozo** NOUN
1 youth
2 waiter
■ **un mozo de estación** a porter

el **MP3** NOUN
MP3
□ un reproductor de MP3 an MP3 player

la **muchacha** NOUN
1 girl
2 maid

el **muchacho** NOUN
boy

la **muchedumbre** NOUN
crowd

**mucho** (FEM **mucha**) ADJECTIVE
▷ see also **mucho** PRONOUN, ADVERB
1 a lot of
□ Había mucha gente. There were a lot of people. □ Tiene muchas plantas. He has got a lot of plants.
2 much (PL many)
□ No tenemos mucho tiempo. We haven't got much time. □ ¿Conoces a mucha gente? Do you know many people? □ Muchas personas creen que ... Many people think that ...
■ **no hace mucho tiempo** not long ago
■ **Hace mucho calor.** It's very hot.
■ **Tengo mucho frío.** I'm very cold.
■ **Tengo mucha hambre.** I'm very hungry.
■ **Tengo mucha sed.** I'm very thirsty.

**mucho** PRONOUN
▷ see also **mucho** ADJECTIVE, ADVERB
1 a lot
□ Tengo mucho que hacer. I've got a lot to do. □ ¿Cuántos había? — Muchos. How many were there? — A lot.
2 much (PL many)

□ No tengo mucho que hacer. I haven't got much to do. □ ¿Hay manzanas? — Sí, pero no muchas. Are there any apples? — Yes, but not many.
■ **¿Vinieron muchos?** Did many people come?
■ **Muchos dicen que ...** Many people say that ...

**mucho** ADVERB
▷ see also **mucho** ADJECTIVE, PRONOUN
1 very much
□ Te quiero mucho. I love you very much. □ No me gusta mucho la carne. I don't like meat very much. □ Me gusta mucho el jazz. I really like jazz.
2 a lot
□ Come mucho. He eats a lot.
■ **mucho más** a lot more
■ **mucho antes** long before
■ **No tardes mucho.** Don't be long.
■ **Como mucho leo un libro al mes.** At most I read one book a month.
■ **Fue, con mucho, el mejor.** He was by far the best.
■ **Por mucho que lo quieras no debes mimarlo.** No matter how much you love him, you shouldn't spoil him.

la **mudanza** NOUN
move

**mudarse** VERB [25]
to move
■ **mudarse de casa** to move house

**mudo** (FEM **muda**) ADJECTIVE
dumb
■ **quedarse mudo de asombro** to be dumbfounded

el **mueble** NOUN
■ **un mueble** a piece of furniture
■ **los muebles** furniture *sing*
■ **seis muebles** six pieces of furniture

la **muela** NOUN
tooth (PL teeth)
■ **una muela del juicio** a wisdom tooth

el **muelle** NOUN
1 spring
2 quay

**muelo** VERB ▷ see **moler**

**muerdo** VERB ▷ see **morder**

la **muerta** NOUN
dead woman (PL dead women)

la **muerte** NOUN
death
□ Lo condenaron a muerte. He was sentenced to death.
■ **Nos dio un susto de muerte.** He nearly frightened us to death.
■ **un hotel de mala muerte** a grotty hotel

**muerto** VERB ▷ see **morir**

**muerto** (FEM **muerta**) ADJECTIVE
dead
- **Está muerto de cansancio.** *(colloquial)* He's dead tired.

el **muerto** NOUN
dead man (PL dead men)
- **los muertos** the dead
- **Hubo tres muertos.** Three people were killed.
- **hacer el muerto** to float

la **muestra** NOUN
1 sample
□ una muestra gratuita a free sample
2 sign
□ dar muestras de to show signs of
3 token
□ Me lo regaló como muestra de afecto. She gave it to me as a token of affection.

**muestro** VERB ▷ *see* **mostrar**

**muevo** VERB ▷ *see* **mover**

la **mujer** NOUN
1 woman (PL women)
□ Vino a verte una mujer. A woman came to see you.
2 wife (PL wives)
□ la mujer del médico the doctor's wife

la **muleta** NOUN
crutch (PL crutches)

> **DID YOU KNOW...?**
> In bullfighting, the **muleta** is a special stick with a red cloth attached to it that the matador uses.

la **multa** NOUN
fine
□ una multa de 50 euros a 50-euro fine
- **poner una multa a alguien** to fine somebody

**múltiple** (FEM **múltiple**) ADJECTIVE
- **múltiples** many □ un sistema con múltiples inconvenientes a system with many drawbacks

**multiplicar\*** VERB [48]
to multiply
□ Hay que multiplicarlo por cinco. You have to multiply it by five.
- **la tabla de multiplicar** the multiplication tables *pl*

la **multitud** NOUN
crowd
- **multitud de** lots of

**mundial** (FEM **mundial**) ADJECTIVE
1 world
2 worldwide

el **mundial** NOUN
world championship

el **mundo** NOUN
world

- **todo el mundo** everybody □ Se lo ha dicho a todo el mundo. He has told everybody.
- **No lo cambiaría por nada del mundo.** I wouldn't change it for anything in the world.

**municipal** (FEM **municipal**) ADJECTIVE
1 council
2 local
3 public

el **municipio** NOUN
1 municipality (PL municipalities)
2 town council

la **muñeca** NOUN
1 wrist
2 doll

el **muñeco** NOUN
1 doll
- **un muñeco de peluche** a soft toy
2 figure

la **muralla** NOUN
city wall

el **murciélago** NOUN
bat

el **murmullo** NOUN
murmur

la **murmuración** (PL las **murmuraciones**)
NOUN
gossip *sing*

el **muro** NOUN
wall

el **músculo** NOUN
muscle

el **museo** NOUN
museum
- **un mueso de arte** an art gallery

la **música** NOUN
1 music
□ la música pop pop music
2 musician

el **músico** NOUN
musician

el **muslo** NOUN
thigh

el **musulmán** (FEM la **musulmana**, MASC PL
los **musulmanes**) ADJECTIVE, NOUN
Moslem

**mutuo** (FEM **mutua**) ADJECTIVE
mutual
□ de mutuo acuerdo by mutual agreement

**muy** ADVERB
very
□ muy bonito very pretty
- **Eso es muy español.** That's typically Spanish.
- **No me gusta por muy guapa que sea.** However pretty she is, I still don't like her.

# Nn

el **nabo** NOUN
turnip

**nacer\*** VERB
to be born
  □ Nació en 1964. He was born in 1964.

el **nacimiento** NOUN
1 birth
2 crib

la **nación** (PL las **naciones**) NOUN
nation
  ■ **las Naciones Unidas** the United Nations

**nacional** (FEM **nacional**) ADJECTIVE
1 national
2 home
  ■ **vuelos nacionales** domestic flights

la **nacionalidad** NOUN
nationality (PL nationalities)

el **nacionalismo** NOUN
nationalism

el/la **nacionalista** ADJECTIVE, NOUN
nationalist

**nada** PRONOUN
  ▷ see also **nada** ADVERB
1 nothing
  □ ¿Qué has comprado? — Nada. What have
  you bought? — Nothing. □ No dijo nada.
  He said nothing.
2 anything
  □ No quiero nada. I don't want anything.
  ■ **No dijo nada más.** He didn't say anything
  else.
  ■ **Quiero uno nada más.** I only want one,
  that's all.
  ■ **Encendió la tele nada más llegar.** He
  turned on the TV as soon as he came in.
  ■ **¡Gracias! — De nada.** Thanks! — Don't
  mention it.
  ■ **Se lo advertí, pero como si nada.** I
  warned him but he paid no attention.
  ■ **No sabe nada de español.** He knows no
  Spanish at all.
  ■ **No me dio nada de nada.** He gave me
  absolutely nothing.

**nada** ADVERB
  ▷ see also **nada** PRONOUN
at all

  □ Esto no me gusta nada. I don't like this at
  all. □ No está nada triste. He isn't sad at all.

**nadar** VERB [25]
to swim

**nadie** PRONOUN
1 nobody
  □ Nadie habló. Nobody spoke. □ No había
  nadie. There was nobody there.
2 anybody
  □ No quiere ver a nadie. He doesn't want to
  see anybody.

la **nafta** NOUN (River Plate)
petrol

el **naipe** NOUN
playing card

las **nalgas** NOUN
buttocks

la **nana** NOUN
lullaby (PL lullabies)

**naranja** ADJECTIVE
orange
  □ un anorak naranja an orange anorak

el **naranja** NOUN
orange

la **naranja** NOUN
orange

el **narcotráfico** NOUN
drug trafficking

la **nariz** (PL las **narices**) NOUN
nose
  ■ **No metas las narices en mis asuntos.**
  Don't poke your nose into my business.
  ■ **estar hasta las narices de algo** to be
  totally fed up with something

la **narración** (PL las **narraciones**) NOUN
story (PL stories)

**narrar** VERB [25]
to tell

la **narrativa** NOUN
fiction

la **nata** NOUN
1 cream
2 skin
  ■ **la nata líquida** single cream
  ■ **la nata montada** whipped cream

la **natación** NOUN

swimming
**natal** (FEM **natal**) ADJECTIVE
home
□ su pueblo natal his home town
las **natillas** NOUN
custard *sing*
**nato** (FEM **nata**) ADJECTIVE
■ un actor nato a born actor
**natural** (FEM **natural**) ADJECTIVE
natural
□ con ingredientes naturales with natural
ingredients □ Comes mucho y es natural
que estés gordo. You eat a lot, so it's only
natural you're fat.
■ **Es natural de Alicante.** He's from
Alicante.
la **naturaleza** NOUN
nature
■ **Es despistado por naturaleza.** He's
naturally absent-minded.
el **naufragio** NOUN
shipwreck
las **náuseas** NOUN
■ **tener náuseas** to feel sick
**náutico** (FEM **náutica**) ADJECTIVE
■ **club náutico** yacht club
la **navaja** NOUN
clasp knife (PL clasp knives)
■ **una navaja de afeitar** a razor
**Navarra** FEM NOUN
Navarre
la **nave** NOUN
ship
■ **una nave espacial** a spaceship
el **navegador** NOUN
browser
■ **un navegador de Web** a web browser
**navegar\*** VERB [37]
to sail
■ **navegar por Internet** to surf the Net
la **Navidad** NOUN
Christmas
■ **¡Feliz Navidad!** Happy Christmas!
la **neblina** NOUN
mist
**necesario** (FEM **necesaria**) ADJECTIVE
necessary
□ No estudié más de lo necesario. I didn't
study any more than necessary.
■ **Ya tengo el dinero necesario para el
billete.** I've now got the money I need for
the ticket.
■ **Llamaré al médico si es necesario.** I'll
call the doctor if need be.
■ **No es necesario que vengas.** You don't
have to come.
la **necesidad** NOUN
1 need

□ No hay necesidad de hacerlo. There is no
need to do it.
2 necessity (PL necessities)
□ Comer bien es una necesidad, no un lujo.
Eating well is a necessity, not a luxury.
■ **Hizo sus necesidades.** He did his
business.
**necesitar** VERB [25]
to need
□ Necesito cien euros. I need a hundred
euros. □ Necesito sacar un notable en el
examen. I need to get a good mark in the
exam. □ Necesito que me ayudes. I need
you to help me.
■ **'Se necesita camarero'** 'Waiter wanted'
**negar\*** VERB [34]
1 to deny
□ Decían que era el ladrón, pero él lo
negaba. They said that he was the thief, but
he denied it.
■ **negar con la cabeza** to shake one's head
2 to refuse
□ Me negaron el permiso para entrar en el
bar. They refused me permission to go into
the bar.
■ **Se negó a pagar la multa.** He refused to
pay the fine.
**negativo** (FEM **negativa**) ADJECTIVE
negative
el **negativo** NOUN
negative
la **negociación** NOUN
negotiation
**negociar** VERB [25]
■ **Su empresa negocia con armas.** His
company deals in arms.
■ **Los dos gobiernos están negociando un
acuerdo.** The two governments are
negotiating an agreement.
el **negocio** NOUN
business (PL businesses)
□ Hemos montado un negocio de
videojuegos. We set up a video games
business.
■ **el mundo de los negocios** the business
world
la **negra** NOUN
black woman (PL black women)
■ **tener la negra** to be out of luck
**negro** (FEM **negra**) ADJECTIVE
black
el **negro** NOUN
1 black
2 black man (PL black men)
■ **los negros** Blacks
el **nervio** NOUN
nerve
■ **Me pone de los nervios.** He gets on my

nerves.

el **nerviosismo** NOUN
■ **Me entra nerviosismo cuando la veo.** I get nervous when I see her.

**nervioso** (FEM **nerviosa**) ADJECTIVE
nervous
□ Me pongo muy nervioso en los exámenes. I get very nervous during exams.
■ **¡Me pone nervioso!** He gets on my nerves!

el **neumático** NOUN
tyre

**neutral** (FEM **neutral**) ADJECTIVE
neutral

la **nevada** NOUN
snowfall

**nevar*** VERB [39]
to snow

la **nevera** NOUN
refrigerator

**ni** CONJUNCTION
**1** or
□ No bebe ni fuma. He doesn't drink or smoke.
**2** neither
□ Ella no fue, ni yo tampoco. She didn't go and neither did I.
■ **ni ... ni** neither ... nor □ No vinieron ni Carlos ni Sofía. Neither Carlos nor Sofía came.
■ **No me gustan ni el bacalao ni el hígado.** I don't like either cod or liver.
■ **No compré ni uno ni otro.** I didn't buy either of them.
■ **Ni siquiera me saludó.** He didn't even say hello.

**Nicaragua** FEM NOUN
Nicaragua

el/la **nicaragüense** ADJECTIVE, NOUN
Nicaraguan

la **nicotina** NOUN
nicotine

el **nido** NOUN
nest

la **niebla** NOUN
fog
■ **Hay niebla.** It's foggy.

**niego** VERB ▷ see **negar**

la **nieta** NOUN
granddaughter

el **nieto** NOUN
grandson
■ **los nietos** grandchildren

**nieva** VERB ▷ see **nevar**

la **nieve** NOUN
snow

**NIF** ABBREVIATION (= *número de identificación fiscal*)

**ningún** PRONOUN ▷ see **ninguno**

**ninguno** (FEM **ninguna**) ADJECTIVE, PRONOUN
**1** no
□ No tengo ningún interés en ir. I have no interest in going.
**2** any
□ No vimos ninguna serpiente en el río. We didn't see any snakes in the river.
**3** none
□ ¿Cuál eliges? — Ninguno. Which do you want? — None of them. □ No me queda ninguno. I have none left. □ Ninguno de nosotros va a ir a la fiesta. None of us are going to the party.
■ **No lo encuentro por ningún sitio.** I can't find it anywhere.
■ **ninguno de los dos 1** neither of them □ A ninguna de las dos les gusta el café. Neither of them likes coffee. **2** either of them □ No me gusta ninguno de los dos. I don't like either of them.

la **niña** NOUN
girl

la **niñera** NOUN
nursemaid

la **niñez** NOUN
childhood

**niño** (FEM **niña**) ADJECTIVE
young
□ Es todavía muy niño. He's still very young.

el **niño** NOUN
boy
■ **de niño** as a child
■ **los niños** the children

el **nitrógeno** NOUN
nitrogen

el **nivel** NOUN
**1** level
□ el nivel del agua the water level
**2** standard
□ Pretenden aumentar el nivel educativo. They are trying to raise the standard of education.
■ **el nivel de vida** the standard of living

**no** ADVERB
no
□ ¿Quieres venir? — No. Do you want to come? — No.
■ **¿Te gusta? — No mucho.** Do you like it? — Not really. □ No me gusta. I don't like it. □ María no habla inglés. María doesn't speak English. □ No puedo venir esta noche. I can't come tonight. □ No tengo tiempo. I haven't got time. □ No debes preocuparte. You mustn't worry. □ No hace

**n**

209

frío. It isn't cold. □ No conozco a nadie. I don't know anyone. □ Esto es tuyo, ¿no? This is yours, isn't it? □ Fueron al cine, ¿no? They went to the cinema, didn't they?
■ ¿Puedo salir esta noche? — ¡Que no! Can I go out tonight? — I said no!
■ **los no fumadores** non-smokers

**noble** (FEM **noble**) ADJECTIVE
noble

la **noche** NOUN
night
□ Pasó la noche sin dormir. He had a sleepless night.
■ **¡Buenas noches! 1** Good evening!
**2** Goodnight!
■ **esta noche** tonight
■ **hoy por la noche** tonight
■ **por la noche** at night □ Estudia por la noche. He studies at night. □ el sábado por la noche on Saturday night
■ **Era de noche cuando llegamos a casa.** It was night time when we got back home.
■ **No me gusta conducir de noche.** I don't like driving at night.

la **Nochebuena** NOUN
Christmas Eve

la **Nochevieja** NOUN
New Year's Eve

las **nociones** NOUN
■ **Tengo nociones de informática.** I know a little about computers.

**nocturno** (FEM **nocturna**) ADJECTIVE
**1** night
**2** evening

**nomás** ADVERB (Latin America)
just
□ Está ahí nomás. It's just there.
■ **así nomás** just like that

**nombrar** VERB [25]
**1** to appoint
□ Lo han nombrado director del colegio. He was appointed Head of the school.
**2** to mention
□ Me nombró en su discurso. He mentioned me in his speech.

el **nombre** NOUN
**1** name
■ **nombre de pila** first name
■ **nombre y apellidos** full name
**2** noun

la **nómina** NOUN
pay slip
■ **estar en nómina** to be on the payroll

el **nordeste** NOUN
northeast

el **noreste** NOUN
northeast

la **noria** NOUN

big wheel

la **norma** NOUN
rule

**normal** (FEM **normal**) ADJECTIVE
**1** normal
□ una persona normal a normal person
□ Es normal que quiera divertirse. It's only normal that he wants to enjoy himself.
**2** ordinary
□ ¿Es guapo? — No, normal. Is he handsome? — No, just ordinary.

**normalmente** ADVERB
normally

el **noroeste** NOUN
northwest

el **norte** NOUN
north

el **norteamericano** (FEM la **norteamericana**) ADJECTIVE, NOUN
American

**Noruega** FEM NOUN
Norway

el **noruego** (FEM la **noruega**) ADJECTIVE, NOUN
Norwegian

el **noruego** NOUN
Norwegian

**nos** PRONOUN
**1** us
□ Nos vinieron a ver. They came to see us.
□ Nos dio un consejo. He gave us some advice.
■ **Nos lo dio.** He gave it to us.
■ **Nos tienen que arreglar el ordenador.** They have to fix the computer for us.
**2** ourselves
□ Tenemos que defendernos. We must defend ourselves.
■ **Nos levantamos a las ocho.** We got up at eight o'clock.
**3** each other
□ No nos hablamos desde hace tiempo. We haven't spoken to each other for a long time. □ Nos dolían los pies. Our feet were hurting. □ Nos pusimos los abrigos. We put our coats on.

**nosotros** (FEM **nosotras**) PRONOUN
**1** we
□ Nosotros no somos italianos. We are not Italian.
**2** us
□ ¿Quién es? — Somos nosotros. Who is it? — It's us. □ Tu hermano vino con nosotros. Your brother came with us. □ Llegaron antes que nosotros. They arrived before us.
■ **nosotros mismos** ourselves

la **nota** NOUN
**1** mark
□ Saca muy malas notas. He gets very bad

marks.

**2** note

□ Tomó muchas notas en la conferencia. He took a lot of notes during the lecture. □ Te he dejado una nota en la nevera. I've left you a note on the fridge.

**notar** VERB [25]

**1** to notice

□ Notó que le seguían. He noticed they were following him.

**2** to feel

□ Con este abrigo no noto el frío. I don't feel the cold with this coat on.

■ **Se nota que has estudiado mucho este trimestre.** You can tell that you've studied a lot this term.

el **notario**, la **notaria** NOUN

notary (PL notaries)

la **noticia** NOUN

news *sing*

□ Tengo una buena noticia que darte. I've got some good news for you.

■ **Fue una noticia excelente para la economía.** It was an excellent piece of news for the economy.

■ **Vi las noticias de las nueve.** I watched the nine o'clock news.

■ **No tengo noticias de Juan.** I haven't heard from Juan.

⸚ **LANGUAGE TIP** Be careful! **noticia** does not mean **notice**.

**notificar\*** VERB [48]

to notify

el **novato**, la **novata** NOUN

beginner

**novecientos** (FEM **novecientas**) ADJECTIVE, PRONOUN

nine hundred

la **novedad** NOUN

■ **Las últimas novedades en moda infantil.** The latest in children's fashions.

■ **¿Cómo sigue tu hijo? — Sin novedad.** How's your son? — There's no change.

la **novela** NOUN

novel

■ **una novela policíaca** a detective story

**noveno** (FEM **novena**) ADJECTIVE, PRONOUN

ninth

■ **Vivo en el noveno.** I live on the ninth floor.

**noventa** (FEM **noventa**) ADJECTIVE, PRONOUN

ninety

■ **el noventa aniversario** the ninetieth anniversary

la **novia** NOUN

**1** girlfriend

**2** fiancée

**3** bride

el **noviazgo** NOUN

relationship

□ Su noviazgo duró muy poco. Their relationship didn't last very long.

**noviembre** MASC NOUN

November

□ en noviembre in November □ Llegará el 30 de noviembre. He'll arrive on 30 November.

los **novillos** NOUN

■ **hacer novillos** to play truant

el **novio** NOUN

**1** boyfriend

**2** fiancé

**3** bridegroom

■ **los novios** the bride and groom

la **nube** NOUN

cloud

**nublado** (FEM **nublada**) ADJECTIVE

cloudy

**nublarse** VERB [25]

to cloud over

**nuboso** (FEM **nubosa**) ADJECTIVE

cloudy

la **nuca** NOUN

nape

**nuclear** ADJECTIVE

nuclear

■ **una central nuclear** a nuclear power station

el **núcleo** NOUN

■ **el núcleo urbano** the city centre

el **nudo** NOUN

knot

■ **atar con un nudo** to tie in a knot

la **nuera** NOUN

daughter-in-law (PL daughters-in-law)

**nuestro** (FEM **nuestra**) ADJECTIVE, PRONOUN

**1** our

□ nuestro perro our dog □ nuestras bicicletas our bicycles

**2** ours

□ ¿De quién es esto? — Es nuestro. Whose is this? — It's ours. □ Esta casa es la nuestra. This house is ours.

■ **un amigo nuestro** a friend of ours

**nueve** (FEM **nueve**) ADJECTIVE, PRONOUN

nine

■ **Son las nueve.** It's nine o'clock.

■ **el nueve de marzo** the ninth of March

**nuevo** (FEM **nueva**) ADJECTIVE

new

□ Necesito un ordenador nuevo. I need a new computer. □ Soy nuevo en el colegio. I'm new at the school.

■ **El mecánico me dejó el coche como nuevo.** The mechanic left my car like new.

■ **Tuve que leer el libro de nuevo.** I had to read the book again.

la **nuez** (PL las **nueces**) NOUN
1 nut
   ■ **la nuez moscada** nutmeg
2 Adam's apple

el **número** NOUN
1 number
2 size
3 issue
   ■ **Calle Aribau, sin número.** Aribau street, no number.
   ■ **número de teléfono** telephone number
   ■ **montar un número** to make a scene

**nunca** ADVERB
1 never
   □ No viene nunca. He never comes.
   ■ **No le veré nunca más.** I'll never see him again.
2 ever
   □ Ninguno de nosotros había esquiado nunca. Neither of us had ever skied before.
   □ Casi nunca me escribe. He hardly ever writes to me.

la **nutria** NOUN
   otter

el **nylon** NOUN
   nylon

# Ññ

**ñoño** (FEM **ñoña**) ADJETIVO
soppy

el **ñu** SUSTANTIVO
gnu (PL gnus)

# Oo

**O** CONJUNCTION

or

□ ¿Quieres té o café? Would you like tea or coffee? □ ¿Vas a ayudarme o no? Are you going to help me or not?

■ **o ... o ...** either ... or ... □ O ha salido o no coge el teléfono. Either he's out or he's not answering the phone.

■ **O te callas o no sigo hablando.** If you're not quiet I won't go on.

**obedecer\*** VERB [12]

to obey

■ **obedecer a alguien** to obey someone

**obediente** (FEM **obediente**) ADJECTIVE

obedient

**obeso** (FEM **obesa**) ADJECTIVE

obese

el **obispo** NOUN

bishop

la **objeción** (PL las **objeciones**) NOUN

objection

■ **No puso ninguna objeción.** He didn't object.

el **objetivo** NOUN

objective

□ un objetivo militar a military objective

■ **Nuestro principal objetivo es ganar las elecciones.** Our main aim is to win the elections.

el **objeto** NOUN

object

□ un objeto metálico a metal object

■ **¿Cuál es el objeto de su visita?** What's the reason for your visit?

■ **con objeto de hacer algo** in order to do something

■ **los objetos de valor** valuables

la **obligación** (PL **obligaciones**) NOUN

obligation

■ **Obedecer a tus padres es tu obligación.** It's your duty to obey your parents.

**obligado** (FEM **obligada**) ADJECTIVE

■ **verse obligado a hacer algo** to be forced to do something □ Se vieron obligados a vender su casa. They were forced to sell their house.

■ **No estás obligado a venir si no quieres.** You don't have to come if you don't want to.

**obligar\*** VERB [37]

1 to force

□ Nadie te obliga a aceptar este empleo. Nobody's forcing you to accept this job.

2 to make

□ No puedes obligarme a ir. You can't make me go.

**obligatorio** (FEM **obligatoria**) ADJECTIVE

compulsory

la **obra** NOUN

1 work

■ **una obra de arte** a work of art

■ **la obra completa de Neruda** the complete works of Neruda

■ **una obra de teatro** a play

■ **una obra maestra** a masterpiece

2 building site

■ **'obras'** 'roadworks'

el **obrero**, la **obrera** NOUN

worker

□ Mi primo es obrero de la construcción. My cousin works on a building site.

el **obsequio** NOUN

gift

□ como obsequio as a gift

la **observación** (PL las **observaciones**) NOUN

1 observation

□ El paciente está en observación. The patient is under observation.

2 comment

□ hacer una observación to make a comment

**observador** (FEM **observadora**) ADJECTIVE

observant

**observar** VERB [25]

1 to observe

2 to remark

la **obsesión** (PL las **obsesiones**) NOUN

obsession

□ su obsesión por la limpieza his obsession with cleanliness

**obsesionar** VERB [25]

■ **Es un tema que le obsesiona.**

He's obsessed by the subject.

el **obstáculo** NOUN
obstacle
□ Nos puso muchos obstáculos. He put many obstacles in our way.

**obstante** ADVERB
■ **no obstante** nevertheless

**obstinado** (FEM **obstinada**) ADJECTIVE
obstinate

**obstinarse** VERB [25]
to insist
□ ¿Por qué te obstinas en hacerlo? Why do you insist on doing it?

**obtener\*** VERB [53]
to obtain

**obvio** (FEM **obvia**) ADJECTIVE
obvious

la **oca** NOUN
goose (PL geese)

la **ocasión** (PL las **ocasiones**) NOUN
1 opportunity (PL opportunities)
□ Ésta es la ocasión que esperábamos. This is the opportunity we've been waiting for.
2 occasion
□ en varias ocasiones on several occasions
■ **un libro de ocasión** a secondhand book

**ocasionar** VERB [25]
to cause

**occidental** (FEM **occidental**) ADJECTIVE
western
■ **los países occidentales** the West

el **occidente** NOUN
■ **el Occidente** the West

el **océano** NOUN
ocean
□ el océano Atlantico the Atlantic Ocean

**ochenta** (FEM **ochenta**) ADJECTIVE, PRONOUN
eighty
□ Tiene ochenta años. He's eighty.
■ **el ochenta aniversario** the eightieth anniversary

**ocho** (FEM **ocho**) ADJECTIVE, PRONOUN
eight
■ **Son las ocho.** It's eight o'clock.
■ **el ocho de agosto** the eighth of August

**ochocientos** (FEM **ochocientas**) ADJECTIVE, PRONOUN
eight hundred

el **ocio** NOUN
■ **en mis ratos de ocio** in my spare time

**octavo** (FEM **octava**) ADJECTIVE, PRONOUN
eighth
■ **Vivo en el octavo.** I live on the eighth floor.

**octubre** MASC NOUN
October
□ en octubre in October □ Llegaré el 3 de octubre. I'll arrive on 3 October.

el/la **oculista** NOUN
eye specialist
□ Es oculista. He's an eye specialist.

**ocultar** VERB [25]
to conceal
□ Nos ocultó su edad. He concealed his age from us.
■ **No nos ocultes la verdad.** Don't try to hide the truth from us.
■ **ocultarse** to hide

la **ocupación** (PL las **ocupaciones**) NOUN
1 activity (PL activities)
□ Tiene muchas ocupaciones. He's involved in many activities.
2 occupation
□ ¿Qué ocupación tiene? What's his occupation? □ la ocupación de la embajada por parte de los guerrilleros the occupation of the embassy by the guerrillas

**ocupado** (FEM **ocupada**) ADJECTIVE
1 busy
□ Estoy muy ocupado. I'm very busy.
2 engaged
□ La línea está ocupada. The line's engaged.
■ **'ocupado'** 'engaged'
■ **¿Está ocupado este asiento?** Is this seat taken?

**ocupar** VERB [25]
1 to occupy
□ Los obreros han ocupado la fábrica. The workers have occupied the factory. □ El edifico ocupa todo el solar. The building occupies the whole site.
2 to take up
□ Ocupa casi todo mi tiempo. It takes up almost all my time.
■ **Los espectadores ocuparon sus asientos.** The spectators took their seats.
■ **ocuparse de algo** to look after something
■ **Yo me ocuparé de decírselo.** I'll tell him.

la **ocurrencia** NOUN
■ **Juan tuvo la ocurrencia de decírselo a la cara.** Juan had the bright idea to tell her to her face.
■ **¡Qué ocurrencia!** Him and his crazy ideas!

**ocurrir** VERB [58]
to happen
□ Lo que ocurrió podría haberse evitado. What happened could have been avoided.
■ **¿Qué te ocurre?** What's the matter?
■ **Se nos ocurrió una idea brillante.** We had a brilliant idea.

**odiar** VERB [25]
to hate
□ Odio tener que levantarme pronto. I hate having to get up early.

el **odio** NOUN

hate

el **oeste** NOUN, ADJECTIVE
west
□ el oeste del país  the west of the country
□ en la costa oeste  on the west coast
■ **al oeste de la ciudad**  west of the city
■ **Viajábamos hacia el oeste.**  We were travelling west.
■ **una película del oeste**  a western
■ **vientos del oeste**  westerly winds

**ofender** VERB [8]
offend
■ **ofenderse**  to take offence

la **ofensa** NOUN
insult

la **oferta** NOUN
offer
■ **una oferta especial**  a special offer
■ **estar de oferta**  to be on special offer
■ **'ofertas de trabajo'**  'situations vacant'

**oficial** (FEM **oficial**) ADJECTIVE
official

el/la **oficial** NOUN
officer
□ Es oficial de marina.  He's an officer in the navy.

la **oficina** NOUN
office
■ **la oficina de turismo**  the tourist office
■ **la oficina de empleo**  the job centre
■ **la oficina de correos**  the post office
■ **la oficina de objetos perdidos**  the lost property office

el **oficio** NOUN
trade
□ Es carpintero de oficio.  He's a carpenter by trade.

**ofrecer*** VERB [12]
to offer
□ Nos ofrecieron tabaco.  They offered us cigarettes.
■ **ofrecerse para hacer algo**  to offer to do something
■ **¿Qué se le ofrece?**  What can I get you?

el **ofrecimiento** NOUN
offer

el **oído** NOUN
1  hearing
2  ear
■ **tener buen oído**  to have a good ear

**oír*** VERB [35]
1  to hear
□ He oído un ruido.  I heard a noise.  □ ¿Me oyes bien desde ahí?  Can you hear me all right from there?
2  to listen to
□ Óyeme bien, no vuelvas a hacerlo.  Now listen to what I'm telling you, don't do it

again.
■ **oír la radio**  to listen to the radio
■ **¡Oye!**  Hey!
■ **¡Oiga, por favor!**  Excuse me!

el **ojal** NOUN
buttonhole

**ojalá** EXCLAMATION
1  I hope
□ ¡Ojalá Toni venga hoy!  I hope Toni comes today!
2  if only
■ **¡Ojalá pudiera!**  If only I could!

las **ojeras** NOUN
■ **tener ojeras**  to have bags under one's eyes

el **ojo** NOUN
eye
□ Tengo algo en el ojo.  I've got something in my eye.
■ **ir con ojo**  to keep one's eyes open for trouble
■ **costar un ojo de la cara**  to cost an arm and a leg
■ **¡Ojo! Es muy mentiroso.**  Be careful! He's an awful liar.

la **ola** NOUN
wave

**oler*** VERB [36]
to smell
□ Me gusta oler las flores.  I like smelling the flowers.
■ **Huele a tabaco.**  It smells of cigarette smoke.
■ **oler bien**  to smell nice  □ Esta salsa huele muy bien.  This sauce smells very good.
■ **oler mal**  to smell awful  □ ¡Qué mal huelen estos zapatos!  These shoes smell awful!

el **olfato** NOUN
sense of smell

las **Olimpiadas** NOUN
the Olympics

**olímpico** (FEM **olímpica**) ADJECTIVE
Olympic
■ **los Juegos Olímpicos**  the Olympic Games

la **oliva** NOUN
olive
■ **el aceite de oliva**  olive oil

el **olivo** NOUN
olive tree

la **olla** NOUN
pot
■ **una olla a presión**  a pressure cooker

el **olor** NOUN
smell
□ un olor a tabaco  a smell of cigarette smoke

■ **¡Qué mal olor!** What a horrible smell!

**olvidar** VERB [25]
1 to forget
□ No olvides comprar el pan. Don't forget to buy the bread.
■ **olvidarse de hacer algo** to forget to do something
■ **Se me olvidó por completo.** I completely forgot.
2 to leave
□ Olvidé las llaves en la mesa. I left the keys on the table.

el **olvido** NOUN
■ **Ha sido un olvido imperdonable.** It was an unforgivable oversight.

el **ombligo** NOUN
navel

**omitir** VERB [58]
to leave out
□ Han omitido varios nombres de la lista. They've left several names out of the list.

**once** (FEM **once**) ADJECTIVE, PRONOUN
eleven
□ Tengo once años. I'm eleven.
■ **Son las once.** It's eleven o'clock.
■ **el once de agosto** the eleventh of August

la **onda** NOUN
wave
■ **onda corta** short wave

**ondear** VERB [25]
to fly

**ondulado** (FEM **ondulada**) ADJECTIVE
wavy
□ un chico con el pelo ondulado a boy with wavy hair

**ONG** ABBREVIATION (= *Organización no gubernamental*)
NGO (= *non-governmental organization*)

la **ONU** NOUN (= *Organización de las Naciones Unidas*)
UN (= *United Nations*)

**opaco** (FEM **opaca**) ADJECTIVE
1 opaque
2 dull

la **opción** (PL las **opciones**) NOUN
option
□ No tienes otra opción. You have no option.

la **ópera** NOUN
opera

la **operación** (PL **operaciones**) NOUN
operation
□ una operación de cataratas a cataract operation

**operar** VERB [25]
to operate on
□ Lo tienen que operar. They have to operate on him.

■ **Me van a operar del corazón.** I'm going to have a heart operation.
■ **operarse** to have an operation □ Me tengo que operar de la rodilla. I have to have a knee operation.

**opinar** VERB [25]
to think
□ ¿Y tú qué opinas de la propuesta? So what do you think about the proposal?

la **opinión** (PL las **opiniones**) NOUN
opinion
■ **en mi opinión** in my opinion

**oponerse**\* VERB [41]
to oppose
□ Se opuso al proyecto. He opposed the project.
■ **No me opongo.** I don't object.

la **oportunidad** NOUN
chance
□ No tuvo la oportunidad de hacerlo. He didn't have a chance to do it.
■ **dar otra oportunidad a alguien** to give someone another chance

**oportuno** (FEM **oportuna**) ADJECTIVE
■ **en el momento oportuno** at the right time

la **oposición** (PL las **oposiciones**) NOUN
opposition
■ **las oposiciones** public examinations

**optar** VERB [25]
■ **optar por hacer algo** to choose to do something □ Al final, optó por ir. In the end, she chose to go.

**optativo** (FEM **optativa**) ADJECTIVE
optional
□ las asignaturas optativas optional subjects

la **óptica** NOUN
optician's
□ Me he comprado unas gafas de sol en la óptica. I bought a pair of sunglasses at the optician's.

el **optimismo** NOUN
optimism

**optimista** (FEM **optimista**) ADJECTIVE
optimistic

el/la **optimista** NOUN
optimist

**óptimo** (FEM **óptima**) ADJECTIVE
optimum

**opuesto** (FEM **opuesta**) ADJECTIVE
1 conflicting
2 opposite

**opuse** VERB ▷ *see* **oponer**

la **oración** (PL las **oraciones**) NOUN
1 prayer
2 sentence

el **orador**, la **oradora** NOUN

**o**

speaker

**oral** (FEM **oral**) ADJECTIVE
oral
- **por vía oral** orally
- **un examen oral** an oral exam

la **órbita** NOUN
1 orbit
2 eye socket

el **orden** NOUN
order
- **por orden alfabético** in alphabetical order
- **La casa está en orden.** The house is tidy.

la **orden** (PL las **órdenes**) NOUN
order
- **¡Deja de darme órdenes!** Stop bossing me about!

**ordenado** (FEM **ordenada**) ADJECTIVE
tidy
□ Siempre tiene la habitación muy ordenada. He always keeps his room very tidy.

el **ordenador** NOUN
computer
- **un ordenador portátil** a laptop

**ordenar** VERB [25]
1 to tidy up
□ ¿Por qué no ordenas tu habitación? Why don't you tidy your room up?
2 to order
□ El policía nos ordenó que saliéramos del edificio. The policeman ordered us to get out of the building.

**ordeñar** VERB [25]
to milk

**ordinario** (FEM **ordinaria**) ADJECTIVE
1 common
□ Es una mujer muy ordinaria. She's a very common woman.
2 ordinary
□ los acontecimientos ordinarios ordinary events
- **de ordinario** usually □ De ordinario coge el autobús para ir a trabajar. He usually takes the bus to work.

la **oreja** NOUN
ear

**orgánico** (FEM **orgánica**) ADJECTIVE
organic

el **organismo** NOUN
organization
□ un organismo internacional an international organization

la **organización** (PL las **organizaciones**) NOUN
organization

**organizar\*** VERB [13]
to organize

- **organizarse** to organize oneself □ Te tienes que organizar mejor. You need to organize yourself better.

el **órgano** NOUN
organ

el **orgullo** NOUN
pride

**orgulloso** (FEM **orgullosa**) ADJECTIVE
proud

la **orientación** (PL las **orientaciones**) NOUN
- **tener sentido de la orientación** to have a good sense of direction
- **la orientación profesional** careers advice

el **oriente** NOUN
- **el Oriente** the East

el **origen** (PL los **orígenes**) NOUN
origin

**original** (FEM **original**) ADJECTIVE
original

la **originalidad** NOUN
originality

la **orilla** NOUN
1 shore
2 bank
- **a orillas de 1** on the shores of **2** on the banks of
- **un paseo a la orilla del mar** a walk along the seashore

la **orina** NOUN
urine

**orinar** VERB [25]
to urinate

el **oro** NOUN
gold
□ un collar de oro a gold necklace
- **oros**

> **DID YOU KNOW…?**
> Oros are 'golden coins', one of the suits in the Spanish card deck.

la **orquesta** NOUN
orchestra
- **una orquesta de jazz** a jazz band

**ortodoxo** (FEM **ortodoxa**) ADJECTIVE
orthodox

la **ortografía** NOUN
spelling

la **oruga** NOUN
caterpillar

**os** PRONOUN
1 you
□ No os oigo. I can't hear you. □ Os he comprado un libro a cada uno. I've bought each of you a book.
- **Os lo doy.** I'll give it to you.
- **¿Os han arreglado ya el ordenador?** Have they fixed the computer for you yet?
2 yourselves

□ ¿Os habéis hecho daño? Did you hurt yourselves?
■ **Os tenéis que levantar antes de las ocho.** You have to get up before eight.
**3** each other
□ Quiero que os pidáis perdón. I want you to say sorry to each other. □ No hace falta que os quitéis el abrigo. You don't need to take your coats off. □ Lavaos las manos. Wash your hands.

**oscilar** VERB [25]
to range
□ Las máximas han oscilado entre los 15 y los 20 grados. Maximum temperatures have ranged from 15 to 20 degrees.

**oscurecer\*** VERB [12]
to get dark

la **oscuridad** NOUN
darkness
■ **Estaban hablando en la oscuridad.** They were talking in the dark.

**oscuro** (FEM **oscura**) ADJECTIVE
dark
□ una habitación muy oscura a very dark room
■ **azul oscuro** dark blue
■ **a oscuras** in darkness

el **oso**, la **osa** NOUN
bear
■ **un oso de peluche** a teddy bear

el **ostión** (PL los **ostiones**) NOUN
oyster (Mexico)

la **ostra** NOUN
oyster
■ **¡Ostras!** Good grief!

la **OTAN** NOUN (= Organización del Tratado del Atlántico Norte)
NATO (= North Atlantic Treaty Organization)

el **otoño** NOUN
autumn
□ en otoño in autumn □ el otoño pasado last autumn

**otro** (FEM **otra**) ADJECTIVE, PRONOUN
**1** another
□ otro coche another car □ ¿Me das otra manzana, por favor? Can you give me another apple, please?
■ **¿Has perdido el lápiz? — No importa, tengo otro.** Have you lost your pencil? — It doesn't matter, I've got another one.
■ **¿Hay alguna otra manera de hacerlo?** Is there any other way of doing it?
■ **No quiero éste, quiero el otro.** I don't want this one, I want the other one.
**2** other
□ Tengo otros planes. I have other plans.
■ **Quiero otra cosa.** I want something else.
■ **otra vez** again
■ **otros tres libros** another three books
■ **Que lo haga otro.** Let someone else do it.
■ **Están enamorados el uno del otro.** They're in love with each other.

**ovalado** (FEM **ovalada**) ADJECTIVE
oval

la **oveja** NOUN
sheep (PL sheep)

el **ovillo** NOUN
ball
□ un ovillo de lana a ball of wool

el **OVNI** NOUN (= objeto volador no identificado)
UFO (= unidentified flying object)

**oxidado** (FEM **oxidada**) ADJECTIVE
rusty

**oxidarse** VERB [25]
to rust
□ Se ha oxidado la barandilla. The rail has rusted.

el **oxígeno** NOUN
oxygen

**oyendo** VERB ▷ see oír

el/la **oyente** NOUN
**1** listener
**2** occasional student

# Pp

la **paciencia** NOUN
patience
□ No tengo paciencia. I have very little patience. □ Perdí la paciencia y le grité. I lost my patience and I shouted at him.
■ ¡Ten paciencia! Be patient!

el/la **paciente** ADJECTIVE, NOUN
patient

el **Pacífico** NOUN
the Pacific

**pacífico** (FEM **pacífica**) ADJECTIVE
peaceful

el/la **pacifista** ADJECTIVE, NOUN
pacifist
■ el movimiento pacifista the peace movement

el **pacto** NOUN
agreement
□ hacer un pacto to make an agreement

**padecer*** VERB [12]
1 to suffer from
□ Padece de una enfermedad grave. He suffers from a serious illness.
■ Padece del corazón. He has heart trouble.
2 to suffer
□ El pobrecito ha padecido mucho. The poor man has suffered a lot.

el **padrastro** NOUN
stepfather

el **padre** NOUN
father
■ Es padre de familia. He's a family man.
■ mis padres my parents
■ rezar el Padre Nuestro to say the Lord's Prayer

el **padrino** NOUN
godfather
■ mis padrinos my godparents

DID YOU KNOW...?
At a wedding, the **padrino** is the person who escorts the bride down the aisle and gives her away, usually her father.

la **paella** NOUN
paella

la **paga** NOUN
1 pocket money
□ Me dan la paga los domingos. I get my pocket money on Sundays.
2 pay
■ la paga extra

DID YOU KNOW...?
In Spain, most employees receive two extra payments **pagas extras** a year, each equivalent to a month's salary.

**pagar*** VERB [37]
1 to pay
□ No han pagado el alquiler. They haven't paid the rent. □ Me pagan muy poco. I get paid very little.
■ Se puede pagar con tarjeta de crédito. You can pay by credit card.
2 to pay for
□ Tengo que pagar las entradas. I have to pay for the tickets.

la **página** NOUN
page
□ Está en la página 17. It's on page 17.
■ una página web a Web page
■ las páginas amarillas the yellow pages

el **pago** NOUN
payment

el **país** (PL los **países**) NOUN
country (PL countries)
■ el País Vasco the Basque Country
■ los Países Bajos the Netherlands

el **paisaje** NOUN
1 landscape
□ el paisaje de Castilla the Castilian landscape □ pintar un paisaje to paint a landscape
2 scenery
□ Estaba contemplando el paisaje. I was looking at the scenery.

la **paja** NOUN
1 straw
□ un sombrero de paja a straw hat
2 padding
□ El resto del texto es sólo paja. The rest of the text is just padding.

la **pajarita** NOUN

bow tie

el **pájaro** NOUN
bird

la **pajita** NOUN
drinking straw

la **pala** NOUN
1 spade
2 shovel
3 bat
4 blade

la **palabra** NOUN
word
▫ un título de dos palabras a two-word title
▫ Cumplió su palabra. He was true to his word. ▫ sin decir palabra without a word
■ **No me dirige la palabra.** He doesn't speak to me.

la **palabrota** NOUN
swearword
■ **soltar palabrotas** to swear

el **palacio** NOUN
palace

el **paladar** NOUN
palate

la **palanca** NOUN
lever
■ **la palanca de cambio** gear lever

la **palangana** NOUN
washbasin

el **palco** NOUN
box (PL boxes)

**Palestina** FEM NOUN
Palestine

el **palestino** (FEM la **palestina**) ADJECTIVE, NOUN
Palestinian

la **paleta** NOUN
1 trowel
2 palette

**pálido** (FEM **pálida**) ADJECTIVE
pale
▫ Se puso pálida. She turned pale.

el **palillo** NOUN
1 toothpick
2 chopstick

la **paliza** NOUN
1 beating
▫ Los ladrones le dieron una paliza. The burglars gave him a beating.
2 thrashing
▫ Si mi padre se entera me va a dar una paliza. If my father finds out he'll give me a thrashing.
■ **Sus clases son una paliza.** His classes are a real pain.
■ **¡No me des la paliza!** Don't be such a pain!

la **palma** NOUN

palm
■ **dar palmas** to clap

la **palmera** NOUN
palm tree

el **palmo** NOUN
■ **Mide un palmo.** It's several inches long.
■ **Se conoce el lugar de palmo a palmo.** He knows every inch of the place.

el **palo** NOUN
1 stick
▫ Le pegó con un palo. He hit him with a stick.
2 club (golf)
3 suit (cards)
■ **una cuchara de palo** a wooden spoon

la **paloma** NOUN
pigeon
▫ una paloma mensajera a carrier pigeon
▫ la paloma de la paz the dove of peace

las **palomitas** NOUN
■ **las palomitas de maíz** popcorn sing
LANGUAGE TIP Word for word, **palomitas de maíz** means 'little pigeons of corn'.

**palpar** VERB [25]
to feel

la **palpitación** (PL las **palpitaciones**) NOUN
palpitation

**palpitar** VERB [25]
1 to pound
▫ El corazón me palpitaba de miedo. My heart was pounding with fear.
2 to beat
▫ Su corazón dejó de palpitar. His heart stopped beating.

la **palta** NOUN (Chile, River Plate)
avocado (PL avocados)

el **pan** NOUN
1 bread
▫ pan con mantequilla bread and butter
▫ pan integral wholemeal bread ▫ pan de molde sliced bread ▫ una barra de pan a loaf of bread
■ **pan rallado** breadcrumbs pl
■ **pan tostado** toast
2 loaf (PL loaves)
▫ Compré dos panes. I bought two loaves.

la **pana** NOUN
corduroy

la **panadera** NOUN
baker
▫ Es panadera. She's a baker.

la **panadería** NOUN
bakery (PL bakeries)

el **panadero** NOUN
baker
▫ Es panadero. He's a baker.

**Panamá** MASC NOUN

P

Panama
el **panameño** (FEM la **panameña**) ADJECTIVE,
NOUN
Panamanian
la **pancarta** NOUN
banner
el **pancito** NOUN (*Latin America*)
bread roll
el **panda** NOUN (PL pandas)
panda
la **pandereta** NOUN
tambourine
la **pandilla** NOUN
gang
el **panfleto** NOUN
pamphlet
el **pánico** NOUN
panic
□ en un momento de pánico in a moment
of panic
■ **Me entró pánico.** I panicked.
■ **Les tengo pánico a las arañas.** I'm
terrified of spiders.
las **pantaletas** NOUN (*Mexico*)
panties
□ unas pantaletas a pair of panties
la **pantalla** NOUN
1 screen
■ **una pantalla plana** a flat screen
2 lampshade
los **pantalones** NOUN
trousers
■ **unos pantalones** a pair of trousers
■ **pantalones cortos** shorts
■ **pantalones vaqueros** jeans
el **pantano** NOUN
reservoir
la **pantera** NOUN
panther
las **pantimedias** NOUN (*Mexico*)
tights
□ unas pantimedias a pair of tights
los **pantis** NOUN
tights
□ unos pantis a pair of tights
la **pantorrilla** NOUN
calf (PL calves)
los **pants** NOUN (*Mexico*)
tracksuit *sing*
el **pañal** NOUN
nappy (PL nappies)
el **paño** NOUN
cloth
■ **un paño de cocina** a dishcloth
el **pañuelo** NOUN
1 handkerchief (PL handkerchiefs)
2 scarf (PL scarves)
222   3 headscarf (PL headscarves)

el **papa** NOUN
pope
■ **el Papa** the Pope
la **papa** NOUN (*Latin America*)
potato (PL potatoes)
■ **pescado frito con papas fritas** fish and
chips
■ **un paquete de papas fritas** a packet of
crisps
el **papá** (PL los **papás**) NOUN
dad
■ **mis papás** my mum and dad
■ **Papá Noel** Father Christmas
el **papalote** NOUN (*Mexico*)
kite
□ volar un papalote to fly a kite
el **papel** NOUN
1 paper
□ una bolsa de papel a paper bag
2 piece of paper
□ Lo escribí en un papel. I wrote it on a
piece of paper.
■ **papel de aluminio** tinfoil
■ **papel higiénico** toilet paper
   LANGUAGE TIP Word for word, **papel
   higiénico** means 'hygienic paper'.
■ **papel pintado** wallpaper
   LANGUAGE TIP Word for word, **papel
   pintado** means 'painted paper'.
3 role
□ Le han dado el papel principal. They gave
her the leading role. □ Jugó un papel muy
importante en las negociaciones. He played
a very important part in the negotiations.
■ **¿Qué papeles te piden para sacar el
pasaporte?** What documents do you need
to get a passport?
el **papeleo** NOUN
paperwork
la **papelera** NOUN
1 wastepaper bin
2 litter bin
la **papelería** NOUN
stationer's (PL stationers' shops)
la **papeleta** NOUN
1 results slip
2 ballot paper
3 raffle ticket
las **paperas** NOUN
mumps
□ tener paperas to have the mumps
la **papilla** NOUN
1 baby food
2 pap
el **paquete** NOUN
1 packet
2 parcel
□ Me mandaron un paquete por correo.

I got a parcel in the post.

**Paquistán** MASC NOUN
Pakistan

el/la **paquistaní** (PL los/las **paquistaníes**)
ADJECTIVE, NOUN
Pakistani

**par** (FEM **par**) ADJECTIVE
■ **número par** even number

el **par** NOUN
1 couple
□ un par de horas al día a couple of hours a day
2 pair
□ un par de calcetines a pair of socks
■ **Abrió la ventana de par en par.** He opened the window wide.

**para** PREPOSITION
1 for
□ Es para ti. It's for you. □ Tengo muchos deberes para mañana. I have a lot of homework to do for tomorrow. □ el autobús para Marbella the bus for Marbella
■ **¿Para qué lo quieres?** What do you want it for?
■ **¿Para qué sirve?** What's it for?
■ **para siempre** forever
■ **Para entonces ya era tarde.** It was already too late by then.
2 to
□ Estoy ahorrando para comprarme una moto. I'm saving up to buy a motorbike. □ Tengo bastante para vivir. I have enough to live on. □ Son cinco para las ocho. (Latin America) It's five to eight.
■ **Entré despacito para no despertarla.** I went in slowly so as not to wake her.
■ **para que te acuerdes de mí** so that you remember me

la **parabólica** NOUN
satellite dish

el **parabrisas** (PL los **parabrisas**) NOUN
windscreen

el **paracaídas** (PL los **paracaídas**) NOUN
parachute

el/la **paracaidista** NOUN
1 paratrooper
2 parachutist

el **parachoques** (PL los **parachoques**)
NOUN
bumper

la **parada** NOUN
stop
□ Hicimos una parada corta para descansar. We made a short stop to rest.
■ **una parada de autobús** a bus stop
■ **una parada de taxis** a taxi rank

el **paradero** NOUN (Latin America)
bus stop

**parado** (FEM **parada**) ADJECTIVE
unemployed
□ Hace seis meses que está parada. She's been unemployed for six months.
■ **No te quedes ahí parado.** Don't just stand there.
■ **Estuve toda la mañana parado.** (Latin America) I was standing all morning.

el **parador** NOUN

> **DID YOU KNOW...?**
> The **paradores** are a group of luxury Spanish hotels occupying castles, monasteries and other historical buildings and sited in scenic areas.

el **paraguas** (PL los **paraguas**) NOUN
umbrella

**Paraguay** MASC NOUN
Paraguay

el **paraguayo** (FEM la **paraguaya**) ADJECTIVE,
NOUN
Paraguayan

el **paraíso** NOUN
paradise

el **paralelo** ADJECTIVE, NOUN
parallel

la **parálisis** (PL las **parálisis**) NOUN
paralysis (PL paralyses)
■ **parálisis cerebral** cerebral palsy

**paralítico** (FEM **paralítica**) ADJECTIVE
■ **Está paralítico.** He's paralyzed.

el **parapente** NOUN
1 paragliding
2 paraglider

**parar** VERB [25]
to stop
□ Paramos a poner gasolina. We stopped to get some petrol. □ No paró de llover en toda la noche. It didn't stop raining all night.
■ **Nos equivocamos de tren y fuimos a parar a Manchester.** We got on the wrong train and ended up in Manchester.
■ **pararse 1** to stop □ El reloj se ha parado. The clock has stopped. **2** (Latin America) to stand up
■ **hablar sin parar** to talk non-stop

el **pararrayos** (PL los **pararrayos**) NOUN
lightning conductor

la **parcela** NOUN
plot of land

el **parche** NOUN
patch (PL patches)

el **parchís** NOUN
Spanish version of ludo

**parcial** (FEM **parcial**) ADJECTIVE
1 partial
□ un eclipse parcial a partial eclipse
■ **a tiempo parcial** part time
2 biased

el **parcial** NOUN
mid-term exam

**pareado** (FEM **pareada**) ADJECTIVE
■ **un chalet pareado** a semi-detached house

**parecer\*** VERB [12]
1 to seem
□ Parece muy simpática. She seems very nice. □ Todo parecía indicar que estaba muy interesado. It all seemed to indicate that he was interested.
■ **Parece mentira que ya haya pasado tanto tiempo.** I can't believe it has been so long.
2 to look
□ Parece más joven. He looks younger.
■ **Parece una modelo.** She looks like a model.
■ **Parece que va a llover.** It looks as if it's going to rain.
3 to think
■ **¿Qué te pareció la película?** What did you think of the film? □ Me parece bien que los multen. I think it's right that they should be fined.
■ **Me parece que sí.** I think so.
■ **Me parece que no.** I don't think so.
■ **si te parece bien** if that's all right with you
■ **parecerse** to look alike □ María y Ana se parecen mucho. María and Ana look very much alike.
■ **parecerse a** to look like □ Te pareces mucho a tu madre. You look very much like your mother.

**parecido** (FEM **parecida**) ADJECTIVE
similar
□ Las casas son todas parecidas. The houses are all similar. □ Tu blusa es parecida a la mía. Your blouse is similar to mine.
■ **o algo parecido** or something like that

la **pared** NOUN
wall

la **pareja** NOUN
1 couple
□ Había varias parejas bailando. There were several couples dancing.
2 pair
□ En este juego hay que formar parejas. For this game you have to get into pairs.
3 partner
□ Vino con su pareja. He came with his partner.

**parejo** (FEM **pareja**) ADJECTIVE (Latin America)
even

el **paréntesis** (PL los **paréntesis**) NOUN
bracket

□ entre paréntesis in brackets

el/la **pariente** NOUN
relative
□ Es pariente mío. He's a relative of mine.
◯ **LANGUAGE TIP** Be careful! **pariente** does not mean **parent**.

**París** MASC NOUN
Paris

el/la **parisiense** ADJECTIVE, NOUN
Parisian

el **parisino** (FEM la **parisina**) ADJECTIVE, NOUN
Parisian

el **parking** (PL los **parkings**) NOUN
car park

el **parlamento** NOUN
parliament

**parlanchín** (FEM **parlanchina**, MASC PL **parlanchines**) ADJECTIVE
chatty

el **parlante** NOUN (Latin America)
loudspeaker

el **paro** NOUN
1 unemployment
□ Ha bajado el paro. Unemployment has come down.
■ **Mi hermano está en paro.** My brother is on the dole.
■ **cobrar el paro** to get the dole
2 strike
□ un paro de tres días a three-day strike

**parpadear** VERB [25]
to blink

el **párpado** NOUN
eyelid

el **parque** NOUN
park
□ un parque nacional a national park
■ **un parque de atracciones** an amusement park
■ **un parque infantil** a children's playground
■ **un parque temático** a theme park
■ **un parque zoológico** a zoo

el **parquímetro** NOUN
parking meter

la **parra** NOUN
vine

el **párrafo** NOUN
paragraph

la **parrilla** NOUN
grill
■ **carne a la parrilla** grilled meat

la **parrillada** NOUN
grill

el **párroco** NOUN
parish priest

la **parroquia** NOUN
parish (PL parishes)

**P**

la **parte** NOUN
1 part
  □ El examen consta de dos partes. The exam consists of two parts. □ ¿De qué parte de Inglaterra eres? What part of England are you from?
2 share
  □ mi parte de la herencia my share of the inheritance □ Tengo que haberlo dejado en alguna parte. I must have left it somewhere. □ por todas partes everywhere
  ■ **en parte** partly □ Se debe en parte a su falta de experiencia. It's partly due to his lack of experience.
  ■ **la mayor parte de los españoles** most Spanish people
  ■ **la parte delantera** the front
  ■ **la parte de atrás** the back
  ■ **la parte de arriba** the top
  ■ **la parte de abajo** the bottom
  ■ **por una parte ..., por otra ...** on the one hand ..., on the other hand ...
  ■ **Llamo de parte de Juan.** I'm calling on behalf of Juan.
  ■ **¿De parte de quién?** Who's calling please?
  ■ **Estoy de tu parte.** I'm on your side.
**participar** VERB [25]
  to take part
  ■ **participar en un concurso** to take part in a competition
el **participio** NOUN
  participle
**particular** (FEM **particular**) ADJECTIVE
  private
  □ clases particulares private classes
  ■ **El vestido no tiene nada de particular.** The dress is nothing special.
  ■ **en particular** in particular
la **partida** NOUN
1 game
  □ echar una partida de cartas to have a game of cards
2 certificate
  □ partida de nacimiento birth certificate
**partidario** (FEM **partidaria**) ADJECTIVE
  ■ **ser partidario de algo** to be in favour of something
el **partidario**, la **partidaria** NOUN
  supporter
el **partido** NOUN
1 party (PL parties) *(political)*
2 match (PL matches) *(football, tennis)*
3 game *(Latin America)*
  □ un partido de ajedrez a game of chess
  ■ **Sabe sacarle partido a todo.** He knows how to make the most out of everything.
**partir** VERB [58]

1 to cut
2 to crack
3 to break off
4 to leave
  □ La expedición partirá mañana de París. The expedition is to leave from Paris tomorrow.
  ■ **a partir de enero** from January □ a partir de ahora from now on
  ■ **partirse** to break □ El remo se partió en dos. The oar broke in two.
  ■ **partirse de risa** to split one's sides laughing
la **partitura** NOUN
  score
el **parto** NOUN
  birth
  ■ **estar de parto** to be in labour
la **pasa** NOUN
  raisin
la **pasada** NOUN
  ■ **¡Ese coche es una pasada!** This car is amazing!
  ■ **¿Has visto cómo ha saltado? ¡Qué pasada!** Did you see him jump? Amazing!
**pasado** (FEM **pasada**) ADJECTIVE
1 last
  □ el verano pasado last summer
2 after
  □ Pasado el semáforo, verás un cine. After the traffic lights you'll see a cinema.
  □ Volvió pasadas las tres de la mañana. He returned after three in the morning.
  ■ **pasado mañana** the day after tomorrow
  ■ **un sombrero pasado de moda** an old-fashioned hat
el **pasado** NOUN
  past
  □ en el pasado in the past
el **pasador** NOUN
1 hair slide
2 tiepin
el **pasaje** NOUN
1 ticket
  ■ **un pasaje electrónico** an e-ticket
2 passage
**pasajero** (FEM **pasajera**) ADJECTIVE
1 temporary
2 passing
el **pasajero**, la **pasajera** NOUN
  passenger
el **pasamanos** (PL los **pasamanos**) NOUN
  banister
el **pasaporte** NOUN
  passport
**pasar** VERB [25]
1 to pass
  □ ¿Me pasas la sal, por favor? Can you pass

me the salt, please?

■ **Cuando termines pásasela a Isabel.**
When you've finished pass it on to Isabel.

■ **La foto fue pasando de mano en mano.**
The photo was passed around.

■ **Cuando muera la empresa pasará al hijo.** When he dies the company will go to his son.

■ **Un momento, te paso con Pedro.** Just a moment, I'll put you on to Pedro.

2 to go past
□ Pasaron varios coches. A number of cars went past. □ El autobús pasó de largo. The bus went past.

■ **¡Pase, por favor!** Please come in.

■ **El tiempo pasa deprisa.** Time goes so quickly.

■ **Pasaron cinco años.** Five years went by.

■ **Ya ha pasado una hora.** It's been an hour already.

3 to spend
□ Voy a pasar unos días con ella. I'm going to spend a few days with her. □ Me pasé el fin de semana estudiando. I spent the weekend studying.

4 to happen
□ Por suerte no le pasó nada. Luckily nothing happened to him. □ pase lo que pase whatever happens

■ **¿Qué pasa?** 1 What's the matter?
2 What's happening?

■ **¿Qué le pasa a Juan?** What's the matter with Juan?

■ **pasar la aspiradora** to do the vacuuming

■ **pasarlo bien** to have a good time

■ **pasarlo mal** to have a bad time

■ **Hemos pasado mucho frío.** We were very cold.

■ **Están pasando hambre.** They are starving.

■ **pasar algo a máquina** to type something

■ **¡Paso de todo!** I couldn't care less!

■ **pasar por 1** to go though □ Pasamos por un túnel muy largo. We went through a very long tunnel. □ No creo que el sofá pase por esa puerta. I don't think the settee will go through the door. □ pasar por la aduana to go through customs □ Está pasando por un mal momento. He's going through a bad patch. □ No pasamos por la ciudad. We don't go through the city. 2 to go past □ Ese autobús pasa por mi colegio. That bus goes past my school.

■ **Podrían perfectamente pasar por gemelos.** They could easily pass for twins.

■ **No puedo pasar sin teléfono.** I can't get by without a telephone.

■ **Está bien hacer ejercicio pero no hay**

que pasarse. It's OK to exercise but there's no point in overdoing it.

■ **pasarse de moda** to go out of fashion

el **pasatiempo** NOUN
hobby (PL hobbies)

la **Pascua** NOUN
Easter

■ **¡Felices Pascuas!** Happy Christmas!

el **pase** NOUN
pass (PL passes)
□ un pase gratis a free pass

■ **un pase de modelos** a fashion show

**pasear** VERB [25]
to walk

■ **ir a pasear** to go for a walk

el **paseo** NOUN
walk
□ Salimos a dar un paseo. We went out for a walk.

■ **ir de paseo** to go for a walk

■ **un paseo en barco** a boat trip

■ **un paseo en bicicleta** a bike ride

■ **el paseo marítimo** the promenade

LANGUAGE TIP Word for word, **paseo marítimo** means 'maritime walk'.

el **pasillo** NOUN
1 corridor
2 aisle

la **pasión** (PL las **pasiones**) NOUN
passion

**pasivo** (FEM **pasiva**) ADJECTIVE
passive

**pasmado** (FEM **pasmada**) ADJECTIVE
amazed
□ Cuando me enteré, me quedé pasmado. I was amazed when I found out.

el **paso** NOUN
1 step
□ Dio un paso hacia atrás. He took a step backwards. □ paso a paso step by step

■ **He oído pasos.** I heard footsteps.

■ **Vive a un paso de aquí.** He lives right near here.

■ **A ese paso no terminarán nunca.** At this rate they'll never finish.

2 way
□ Han cerrado el paso. They've blocked the way. □ La policía le abría paso. The police made way for him.

■ **'Ceda el paso'** 'Give way'

■ **'Prohibido el paso'** 'No entry'

■ **El banco me pilla de paso.** The bank is on my way.

■ **Están de paso por Barcelona.** They're just passing through Barcelona.

■ **un paso de peatones** a pedestrian crossing

■ **un paso de cebra** a zebra crossing

■ **un paso a nivel** a level crossing

la **pasta** NOUN
1  pasta
2  dosh
    ■ **pastas de té** biscuits
    ■ **pasta de dientes** toothpaste

**pastar** VERB [25]
    to graze

el **pastel** NOUN
    cake

la **pastelería** NOUN
    patisserie

la **pastilla** NOUN
1  pill
    ■ **pastillas para la tos** cough sweets
2  bar
3  piece
    ■ **pastillas de caldo** stock cubes

el **pasto** NOUN *(Latin America)*
    grass

el **pastor** NOUN
    shepherd
    ■ **un pastor alemán** an Alsatian
    ■ **un perro pastor** a sheepdog

la **pastora** NOUN
    shepherdess

la **pata** NOUN
    leg
    □ **las patas de la silla** the chair legs
    ■ **saltar a la pata coja** to hop
    ■ **Encontramos la casa patas arriba.** We
    found the house in a right mess.
    ■ **¡He vuelto a meter la pata!** I've gone
    and put my foot in it again!
    ■ **Me parece que he metido la pata en el
    examen de física.** I think I messed up my
    physics exam.

la **patada** NOUN
    ■ **Me dio una patada.** He kicked me.

**Patagonia** FEM NOUN
    Patagonia

la **patata** NOUN
    potato (PL potatoes)
    ■ **un filete con patatas fritas** steak and
    chips
    ■ **una bolsa de patatas fritas** a bag of
    crisps

el **paté** (PL los **patés**) NOUN
    pâté

la **patera** NOUN
    small boat

**paterno** (FEM **paterna**) ADJECTIVE
    paternal

la **patilla** NOUN
1  sideburn
    □ **dejarse patillas** to grow sideburns
2  arm *(of glasses)*

el **patín** (PL los **patines**) NOUN

1  roller skate
2  skate
3  pedal boat

el **patinaje** NOUN
1  roller skating
2  ice skating
    ■ **patinaje artístico** figure skating

**patinar** VERB [25]
1  to roller-skate
2  to skate
3  to skid

el **patinete** NOUN
    scooter

el **patio** NOUN
1  playground
2  courtyard
    ■ **el patio de butacas** the stalls *pl*

el **pato** NOUN
    duck

**patoso** (FEM **patosa**) ADJECTIVE
    clumsy

la **patria** NOUN
    homeland

**patriota** (FEM **patriota**) ADJECTIVE
    patriotic

el **patrocinador**, la **patrocinadora**
    NOUN
    sponsor

**patrocinar** VERB [25]
    to sponsor

el **patrón** (PL los **patrones**) NOUN
1  patron saint
2  boss (PL bosses)

la **patrona** NOUN
1  patron saint
2  landlady (PL landladies)

la **patrulla** NOUN
    patrol
    □ **estar de patrulla** to be on patrol

la **pausa** NOUN
1  pause
2  break

el **pavimento** NOUN
1  paving
2  surface

el **pavo** NOUN
    turkey
    ■ **un pavo real** a peacock

el **payaso**, la **payasa** NOUN
    clown
    ■ **Deja de hacer el payaso.** Stop clowning
    around.

la **paz** (PL las **paces**) NOUN
    peace
    ■ **¡Déjame en paz!** Leave me alone!
    ■ **Ha hecho las paces con su novio.** She's
    made it up with her boyfriend.

el **PC** ABBREVIATION

**Spanish-English**

PC (PL PCs)

**P.D.** ABBREVIATION (= *posdata*)
P.S.

el **peaje** NOUN
toll

el **peatón** (PL los **peatones**) NOUN
pedestrian

la **peca** NOUN
freckle

el **pecado** NOUN
sin

**pecar\*** VERB [48]
to sin

el **pecho** NOUN
1 chest
2 breast

■ **dar el pecho a un niño** to breastfeed a baby

■ **¡No te lo tomes a pecho! Era una broma.** Don't take it to heart. I was only joking.

la **pechuga** NOUN
breast

el **pedal** NOUN
pedal

□ el pedal del freno the brake pedal

**pedalear** VERB [25]
to pedal

**pedante** (FEM **pedante**) ADJECTIVE
pedantic

el **pedazo** NOUN
piece

□ un pedazo de pan a piece of bread

■ **hacer pedazos 1** to smash **2** to tear up

el/la **pediatra** NOUN
paediatrician

el **pedido** NOUN
order

□ hacer un pedido to place an order

**pedir\*** VERB [38]
1 to ask for

□ Le pedí dinero a mi padre. I asked my father for some money. □ He pedido hora para el médico. I've asked for a doctor's appointment.

2 to ask

□ ¿Te puedo pedir un favor? Can I ask you a favour? □ ¿Cuánto pide por el coche? How much is he asking for the car?

■ **Pedí que me enviaran la información por correo.** I asked them to mail me the information.

3 to order

□ Yo pedí paella. I ordered paella.

■ **Le pedí disculpas.** I apologized to him.

■ **Tuve que pedir dinero prestado.** I had to borrow some money.

el **pedo** NOUN
fart *(vulgar)*

■ **tirarse un pedo** *(vulgar)* to fart

la **pega** NOUN
snag

□ La única pega es que la oficina me queda lejos. The only snag is that the office is a long way away.

■ **Me pusieron muchas pegas.** They made things very difficult for me.

**pegadizo** (FEM **pegadiza**) ADJECTIVE
catchy

**pegajoso** (FEM **pegajosa**) ADJECTIVE
1 sticky
2 catchy *(Latin America)*

el **pegamento** NOUN
glue

**pegar\*** VERB [37]
1 to hit

□ Andrés me ha pegado. Andrés hit me. □ La pelota pegó en el árbol. The ball hit the tree.

2 to stick

□ Lo puedes pegar con celo. You can stick it on with sellotape. □ Tengo que pegar las fotos en el álbum. I have to stick the photos in the album.

■ **Se te va a pegar el arroz.** Be careful or the rice will stick.

3 to give

□ Le pegaron un tremendo empujón. They gave him a great push. □ Le pegó una bofetada. He gave him a slap. □ Me has pegado la gripe. You've given me the flu. □ ¡Qué susto me has pegado! What a fright you gave me!

■ **Pegó un grito.** He shouted.

■ **Le pegaron un tiro.** They shot him.

4 to look right

□ Ese jarrón no pega aquí. This vase doesn't look right here.

■ **Esta camisa no pega con el traje.** This shirt doesn't look right with the suit.

■ **El niño se pegó a su madre.** The boy clung to his mother.

la **pegatina** NOUN
sticker

el **peinado** NOUN
hairstyle

**peinar** VERB [25]
1 to comb

□ Péinate antes de salir. Comb your hair before you go out.

2 to brush

□ Su madre la estaba peinando. Her mother was brushing her hair.

■ **Mañana voy a peinarme.** I'm going to have my hair done tomorrow.

el **peine** NOUN
comb

**P**

**p.ej.** ABBREVIATION (= *por ejemplo*)
e.g.

**pelar** VERB [25]
1 to peel
2 to shell
  ■ **Se me está pelando la espalda.** My back is peeling.
  ■ **Hace un frío que pela.** It's bitterly cold.

el **peldaño** NOUN
1 step
2 rung

la **pelea** NOUN
1 fight
  □ Hubo una pelea en la discoteca. There was a fight at the disco.
2 argument
  □ Tuvo una pelea con su novio. She had an argument with her boyfriend.

**peleado** (FEM **peleada**) ADJECTIVE
  ■ **Están peleados.** They've fallen out.

**pelear** VERB [25]
1 to fight
  □ ¡Deja de pelear con tu hermano! Stop fighting with your brother! □ Dos niños se están peleando en el patio. There are two children fighting in the playground.
2 to argue
  □ Pelean por cualquier tontería. They argue over the slightest thing.

el **pelícano** NOUN
pelican

la **película** NOUN
film
  □ A las ocho ponen una película. There's a film on at eight.
  ■ **una película de dibujos animados** a cartoon
  ■ **una película del oeste** a western
  ■ **una película de suspense** a thriller

el **peligro** NOUN
danger
  □ Está fuera de peligro. He's out of danger.

**peligroso** (FEM **peligrosa**) ADJECTIVE
dangerous

**pelirrojo** (FEM **pelirroja**) ADJECTIVE
  ■ **es pelirrojo** he has red hair

el **pellejo** NOUN
skin
  ■ **No me gustaría estar en su pellejo.** I wouldn't like to be in his shoes.
  ■ **arriesgar el pellejo** to risk one's neck

**pellizcar*** VERB [48]
to pinch
  □ Me pellizcó el brazo. He pinched my arm.

el **pellizco** NOUN
pinch
  □ un pellizco de sal a pinch of salt

el **pelmazo**, la **pelmaza** NOUN

bore

el **pelo** NOUN
hair
  □ Tiene el pelo rizado. He has curly hair.
  ■ **No perdí el avión por un pelo.** I only just caught the plane.
  ■ **Se me pusieron los pelos de punta.** It made my hair stand on end.
  ■ **Me estás tomando el pelo.** You're pulling my leg.

la **pelota** NOUN
ball
  □ jugar a la pelota to play ball
  ■ **hacer la pelota a alguien** to suck up to someone

el/la **pelota** NOUN
creep (colloquial)

la **peluca** NOUN
wig

**peludo** (FEM **peluda**) ADJECTIVE
hairy

la **peluquera** NOUN
hairdresser

la **peluquería** NOUN
hairdresser's

el **peluquero** NOUN
hairdresser

la **pena** NOUN
shame
  □ Es una pena que no puedas venir. It's a shame you can't come. □ ¡Qué pena! What a shame!
  ■ **Me dio tanta pena el pobre animal.** I felt so sorry for the poor animal.
  ■ **Me da pena tener que marcharme.** I'm so sad to have to go away.
  ■ **No tengas pena.** (Latin America) Don't be embarrassed.
  ■ **Vale la pena.** It's worth it.
  ■ **No vale la pena gastarse tanto dinero.** It's not worth spending so much money.
  ■ **la pena de muerte** the death penalty

el **penalty** (PL los **penaltys**) NOUN
penalty (PL penalties)
  □ pitar penalty to award a penalty

el **pendejo**, la **pendeja** NOUN (Latin America)
nerd

**pendiente** (FEM **pendiente**) ADJECTIVE
  ■ **Tenemos un par de asuntos pendientes.** We have a couple of matters to sort out.
  ■ **Tiene una asignatura pendiente.** He has to resit one subject.
  ■ **Estaban pendientes de ella.** They were watching her intently.

el **pendiente** NOUN
earring

la **pendiente** NOUN
slope

el **pene** NOUN
penis (PL penises)

**penetrar** VERB [25]
■ **penetrar en** to find one's way into □ La luz apenas penetra en la cueva. The light hardly finds its way into the cave.

la **penicilina** NOUN
penicillin

la **península** NOUN
peninsula
■ **la Península Ibérica** the Iberian Peninsula

el **penique** NOUN
penny (PL pence)

el **pensamiento** NOUN
1 thought
2 pansy (PL pansies)

**pensar*** VERB [39]
1 to think
□ Piénsalo bien antes de contestar. Think carefully before you answer. □ ¿Piensas que vale la pena? Do you think it's worth it? □ ¿Qué piensas de Manolo? What do you think of Manolo?
■ **¿Qué piensas del aborto?** What do you think about abortion?
2 to think about
□ Tengo que pensarlo. I'll have to think about it.
■ **Sólo piensa en pasarlo bien.** All he thinks about is having a good time.
■ **Estaba pensando en ir al cine esta tarde.** I was thinking of going to the cinema this evening.
■ **¡Ni pensarlo!** (colloquial) No way!
■ **pensándolo bien ...** on second thoughts ...
■ **Piénsatelo.** Think it over.

**pensativo** (FEM **pensativa**) ADJECTIVE
thoughtful

la **pensión** (PL las **pensiones**) NOUN
1 pension
2 guest house
■ **pensión completa** full board
■ **media pensión** half board

el/la **pensionista** NOUN
pensioner

**penúltimo** (FEM **penúltima**) ADJECTIVE
■ **la penúltima estación** the last station but one

el **penúltimo**, la **penúltima** NOUN
■ **Soy el penúltimo.** I'm second to last.

el **peñón** (PL los **peñones**) NOUN
■ **el Peñón de Gibraltar** the Rock of Gibraltar

230  el **peón** (PL los **peones**) NOUN

1 labourer
2 pawn

la **peonza** NOUN
spinning top

**peor** (FEM **peor**) ADJECTIVE, ADVERB
1 worse
□ Su caso es peor que el nuestro. His case is worse than ours. □ Hoy me siento peor. I feel worse today.
2 worst
□ el peor día de mi vida the worst day of my life □ Sacó la peor nota de toda la clase. He got the worst mark in the whole class.
■ **el restaurante donde peor se come** the restaurant with the worst food
■ **y lo peor es que ...** and the worst thing is that ...
■ **Si no viene, peor para ella.** If she doesn't come, too bad for her.

el **pepinillo** NOUN
gherkin

el **pepino** NOUN
cucumber
■ **Me importa un pepino lo que piense.** I couldn't care less what he thinks.

la **pepita** NOUN
1 pip
2 nugget

**pequeño** (FEM **pequeña**) ADJECTIVE
small
□ Prefiero los coches pequeños. I prefer small cars. □ Estos zapatos me quedan pequeños. These shoes are too small for me.
■ **¿Cuál prefieres? — El pequeño.** Which one do you prefer? — The small one.
■ **mi hermana pequeña** my younger sister
■ **La pequeña estudia medicina.** The youngest is studying medicine.
■ **Tuvimos un pequeño problema.** We had a slight problem.

el **pequinés** NOUN
Pekinese

la **pera** NOUN
pear

**percatarse** VERB
■ **percatarse de algo** to notice something

la **percha** NOUN
1 coat hanger
2 coat hook

el **perchero** NOUN
1 coat rack
2 coat stand

**percibir** VERB [58]
1 to notice
2 to see
3 to sense

la **percusión** NOUN

percussion

**perdedor** (FEM **perdedora**) ADJECTIVE
losing
□ la pareja perdedora  the losing pair
el **perdedor**, la **perdedora** NOUN
loser
□ Eres mal perdedor.  You're a bad loser.
**perder\*** VERB [20]
1  to lose
□ He perdido el monedero.  I've lost my
purse. □ Está intentando perder peso.  He's
trying to lose weight. □ perder el
conocimiento  to lose consciousness
□ Perdimos dos a cero.  We lost two nil.
■ **Se le perdieron las llaves.**  He lost his
keys.
2  to miss
□ Date prisa o perderás el tren.  Hurry up or
you'll miss the train. □ No quiero perder
esta oportunidad.  I don't want to miss this
opportunity.
■ **¡No te lo pierdas!**  Don't miss it!
■ **¡Me estás haciendo perder el tiempo!**
You're wasting my time!
■ **Has echado a perder la sorpresa.**  You've
ruined the surprise.
■ **Ana es la que saldrá perdiendo.**  Ana is
the one who will lose out.
■ **Tenía miedo de perderme.**  I was afraid
of getting lost.
la **perdición** NOUN
ruin
la **pérdida** NOUN
1  loss (PL losses)
2  leak
■ **Fue una pérdida de tiempo.**  It was a
waste of time.
**perdido** (FEM **perdida**) ADJECTIVE
1  lost
□ la oficina de objetos perdidos  the lost
property office
2  remote
□ un pueblecito perdido en la montaña  a
remote little village in the mountains
■ **Es tonto perdido.**  He's a complete idiot.
el **perdigón** (PL los **perdigones**) NOUN
pellet
la **perdiz** (PL las **perdices**) NOUN
partridge
el **perdón** NOUN
■ **Le pedí perdón.**  I apologized to him.
■ **¡Perdón! 1** Sorry! **2** Excuse me!
**perdonar** VERB [25]
to forgive
□ ¿Me perdonas?  Do you forgive me?
□ No perdona que me haya olvidara de su
cumpleaños.  He hasn't forgiven me for
forgetting his birthday.

■ **¡Perdona! ¿Tienes hora?**  Excuse me, do
you have the time?
■ **¡Perdona! ¿Te he hecho daño?**  I'm so
sorry. Did I hurt you?
el **peregrino**, la **peregrina** NOUN
pilgrim
el **perejil** NOUN
parsley
la **pereza** NOUN
laziness
■ **¡Qué pereza tengo!**  I feel so lazy!
■ **Me da pereza levantarme.**  I can't be
bothered to get up.
**perezoso** (FEM **perezosa**) ADJECTIVE
lazy
**perfeccionar** VERB [25]
to improve
□ Fue a Inglaterra para perfeccionar el
inglés.  He went to England to improve his
English.
**perfectamente** ADVERB
perfectly
**perfecto** (FEM **perfecta**) ADJECTIVE
perfect
el **perfil** NOUN
profile
□ un retrato de perfil  a profile portrait
■ **ponerse de perfil**  to stand side on
el **perfume** NOUN
perfume
la **perfumería** NOUN
perfume shop
**periódico** (FEM **periódica**) ADJECTIVE
periodic
el **periódico** NOUN
newspaper
el **periodismo** NOUN
journalism
el/la **periodista** NOUN
journalist
□ Mi tío es periodista.  My uncle is a
journalist.
el **periodo** NOUN
period
□ un periodo de tres meses  a three-month
period
■ **Tiene el periodo.**  She has her period.
el **periquito** NOUN
budgerigar
**perjudicar\*** VERB [48]
1  to damage
2  to be harmful to
□ Esta ley puede perjudicarnos.  This law
could be harmful to our interests.
■ **El cambio ha perjudicado sus estudios.**
The change has had an adverse effect on his
studies.
**perjudicial** (FEM **perjudicial**) ADJECTIVE

P

231

damaging
■ **El tabaco es perjudicial para la salud.** Smoking damages your health.

la **perla** NOUN
pearl

**permanecer\*** VERB [12]
to remain

**permanente** (FEM **permanente**) ADJECTIVE
permanent

la **permanente** NOUN
perm
■ **hacerse la permanente** to have a perm

el **permiso** NOUN
1 permission
□ Tengo que pedirles permiso a mis padres. I have to ask my parents' permission.
■ **¡Con permiso!** Excuse me.
2 leave
□ Pidió cinco días de permiso. He requested five days' leave. □ Mi hermano está de permiso. My brother is on leave.
3 permit
□ Necesitas un permiso de trabajo. You need a work permit.
■ **un permiso de conducir** a driving licence

**permitir** VERB [58]
to allow
□ No nos permiten fumar aquí. We're not allowed to smoke here.
■ **No me lo puedo permitir.** I can't afford it.
■ **¿Me permite?** May I?

**pero** CONJUNCTION
but
□ Me gustaría, pero no puedo. I'd like to, but I can't.

**perpendicular** (FEM **perpendicular**) ADJECTIVE
at right angles
□ una pared perpendicular a otra one wall at right angles to another

**perplejo** (FEM **perpleja**) ADJECTIVE
puzzled

la **perra** NOUN
dog
□ Es una perra muy buena. She's a very good dog.
■ **¿Es perra o perro?** Is it a bitch or a dog?

la **perrera** NOUN
dog's home

el **perrito** NOUN
■ **un perrito caliente** a hot dog

el **perro** NOUN
dog
■ **un perro callejero** a stray dog
■ **un perro guardián** a guard dog
■ **un perro pastor** a sheepdog
■ **un perro policía** a police dog
■ **un perro salchicha** a dachshund

el/la **persa** ADJECTIVE, NOUN
Persian

**perseguir\*** VERB [50]
1 to chase
□ Me persigue la policía. The police are chasing me.
2 to persecute
□ Se siente perseguido por su ideología. He feels persecuted for his ideology.

la **persiana** NOUN
blind

**persiguiendo** VERB ▷ see **perseguir**

la **persona** NOUN
person
□ Es una persona encantadora. He's a charming person.
■ **en persona** in person
■ **personas** people □ Había unas diez personas en la sala. There were about ten people in the hall.

el **personaje** NOUN
1 character
□ los personajes de la novela the characters in the novel
2 figure
□ un personaje público a public figure

**personal** (FEM **personal**) ADJECTIVE
personal

el **personal** NOUN
staff

la **personalidad** NOUN
personality (PL personalities)

**personalmente** ADVERB
personally

la **perspectiva** NOUN
perspective
□ en perspectiva in perspective
■ **perspectivas** prospects □ buenas perspectivas económicas good economic prospects

**persuadir** VERB [58]
to persuade
□ Me persuadió para que la acompañara. She persuaded me to go with her.

**pertenecer\*** VERB [12]
■ **pertenecer a** to belong to □ Este reloj perteneció a su abuelo. This watch belonged to his grandfather. □ No pertenezco a ningún partido político. I don't belong to any political party.

las **pertenencias** NOUN
belongings

la **pértiga** NOUN
pole
■ **el salto con pértiga** the pole vault

**Perú** MASC NOUN
Peru

el **peruano** (FEM la **peruana**) ADJECTIVE, NOUN
Peruvian

**perverso** (FEM **perversa**) ADJECTIVE
wicked

el **pervertido**, la **pervertida** NOUN
pervert

la **pesa** NOUN
weight
■ **hacer pesas** to do weight training

la **pesadez** NOUN
■ **Es una pesadez tener que madrugar.**
(colloquial) It's such a pain having to get up
early.
■ **¡Qué pesadez de película!** What a boring
film!

la **pesadilla** NOUN
nightmare

**pesado** (FEM **pesada**) ADJECTIVE
1 heavy
2 tiring
3 boring
■ **¡No seas pesado!** Don't be a pain in the
neck!

el **pesado**, la **pesada** NOUN
■ **Mi primo es un pesado.** My cousin is a
pain in the neck.

el **pésame** NOUN
condolences pl
□ Fuimos a darle el pésame. We went to
offer our condolences.

**pesar** VERB [25]
1 to weigh
□ El paquete pesaba 2 kilos. The package
weighed 2 kilos. □ ¿Cuánto pesas? How
much do you weigh? □ Tengo que pesarme.
I must weigh myself.
2 to be heavy
□ Esta maleta pesa mucho. This suitcase is
very heavy. □ ¡No pesa nada! It's not heavy
at all!
■ **pesar poco** to be very light
■ **Me pesa haberlo hecho.** I regret having
done it.
■ **a pesar del mal tiempo** in spite of the
bad weather
■ **a pesar de que la quiero** even though I
love her

la **pesca** NOUN
fishing
□ ir de pesca to go fishing

la **pescadería** NOUN
fishmonger's (PL fishmongers' shops)

la **pescadilla** NOUN
whiting (PL whiting)

el **pescado** NOUN
fish (PL fish)
□ Quiero comprar pescado. I want to buy
some fish.

el **pescador** NOUN
fisherman (PL fishermen)
□ Mi tío es pescador. My uncle is a
fisherman.

**pescar*** VERB [48]
1 to fish
□ Los domingos íbamos a pescar. On
Sundays we used to go fishing.
2 to catch
□ Pescamos varias truchas. We caught
several trout. □ Me pescaron fumando.
I got caught smoking.

el **pesero** NOUN (Mexico)
minibus (PL minibuses)

la **peseta** NOUN
peseta

**pesimista** (FEM **pesimista**) ADJECTIVE
pessimistic
□ una visión pesimista a pessimistic view
■ **No seas pesimista.** Don't be a pessimist.

el/la **pesimista** NOUN
pessimist

**pésimo** (FEM **pésima**) ADJECTIVE
terrible
□ La comida era pésima. The food was
terrible.

el **peso** NOUN
1 weight
□ ganar peso to gain weight □ Ha perdido
mucho peso. He's lost a lot of weight.
■ **La fruta se vende a peso.** Fruit is sold by
weight.
2 scales pl
3 peso

**pesquero** (FEM **pesquera**) ADJECTIVE
fishing
□ un pueblecito pesquero a fishing village

la **pestaña** NOUN
eyelash (PL eyelashes)

**pestañear** VERB [25]
to blink

la **peste** NOUN
1 plague
2 stink
□ ¡Qué peste hay aquí! There's a real stink in
here!

el **pesticida** NOUN
pesticide

el **pestillo** NOUN
1 bolt
2 latch (PL latches)

la **petaca** NOUN
hip flask

el **pétalo** NOUN
petal

el **petardo** NOUN
firecracker

la **petición** (PL las **peticiones**) NOUN

**1** request

□ Hicieron una petición al gobierno. They made a request to the government. □ a petición de la pareja at the request of the couple

**2** petition

□ firmar una petición to sign a petition

el **petirrojo** NOUN
robin

el **petróleo** NOUN
oil

el **petrolero** NOUN
oil tanker

el **pez** (PL los **peces**) NOUN
fish (PL fish)

□ Cogimos tres peces. We caught three fish.

■ un pez de colores a goldfish

LANGUAGE TIP Word for word, **pez de colores** means 'fish of colours'.

■ Se sentía como el pez en el agua. He felt in his element.

la **pezuña** NOUN
hoof (PL hooves)

el/la **pianista** NOUN
pianist

□ Soy pianista. I'm a pianist.

el **piano** NOUN
piano

■ un piano de cola a grand piano

**piar*** VERB [21]
to chirp

el **pibe**, la **piba** NOUN (River Plate)
kid (colloquial)

la **picada** NOUN (Latin America)

■ El avión cayó en picada. The plane nose-dived.

**picado** (FEM **picada**) ADJECTIVE

**1** bad

**2** choppy

■ El avión cayó en picado. The plane nose-dived.

la **picadura** NOUN

**1** bite

**2** sting

**picante** (FEM **picante**) ADJECTIVE
hot

el **picaporte** NOUN
door handle

**picar*** VERB [48]

**1** to bite

□ Me han picado los mosquitos. I've been bitten by mosquitoes.

**2** to sting

**3** to chop up

□ Luego picas un poquito de jamón. Then you chop up a bit of ham.

**4** to mince

■ La salsa pica bastante. The sauce is

quite hot.

■ Saqué algunas cosas para picar. I put out some nibbles.

■ Me pica la espalda. I've got an itchy back.

■ Me pica la garganta. My throat tickles.

el **pichi** NOUN
pinafore

el **picnic** (PL los **picnics**) NOUN
picnic

el **pico** NOUN

**1** beak

**2** peak

**3** pick

■ Eran las tres y pico. It was just after three.

■ doscientos y pico euros just over two hundred euros

■ cuello de pico V-neck

■ la hora pico (Latin America) the rush hour

**picoso** (FEM **picosa**) ADJECTIVE (Mexico)
hot (food)

**pidiendo** VERB ▷ see pedir

el **pie** NOUN
foot (PL feet)

□ Fuimos a pie. We went on foot. □ Al pie de la página hay una explicación. There's an explanation at the foot of the page.

■ Estaba de pie junto a mi cama. He was standing next to my bed.

■ ponerse de pie to stand up

■ de pies a cabeza from head to foot

la **piedad** NOUN
mercy

□ tener piedad de alguien to have mercy on someone

la **piedra** NOUN
stone

□ Nos tiraban piedras. They were throwing stones at us.

■ una piedra preciosa a precious stone

■ Cuando me lo dijeron me quedé de piedra. I was stunned when they told me.

la **piel** NOUN

**1** skin

□ Tengo la piel grasa. I have greasy skin.

**2** fur

□ un abrigo de pieles a fur coat

**3** leather

□ un bolso de piel a leather bag

**4** peel

**pienso** VERB ▷ see pensar

**pierdo** VERB ▷ see perder

la **pierna** NOUN
leg

■ una pierna de cordero a leg of lamb

la **pieza** NOUN
piece

□ una pieza del rompecabezas  a piece of the jigsaw puzzle □ una pieza de recambio  a spare part

**el pijama** NOUN
pyjamas *pl*

**pijo** (FEM **pija**) ADJECTIVE
posh

**la pila** NOUN
1 battery (PL batteries)
  □ Funciona con pilas.  It goes on batteries.
2 pile
  □ una pila de revistas  a pile of magazines
3 sink

**el pilar** NOUN
pillar

**la píldora** NOUN
pill
  □ ¿Tomas la píldora?  Are you on the pill?

**la pileta** NOUN (*River Plate*)
sink

**pillar** VERB [25]
1 to catch
  □ pillar a un ladrón  to catch a thief □ ¡Vaya catarro que has pillado!  That's a nasty cold you've caught. □ Lo pillé fumando.  I caught him smoking.
  ■ Se pilló los dedos en la puerta.  He caught his fingers in the door.
2 to hit
  □ La pilló una moto.  She was hit by a motorbike.
  ■ La estación nos pilla cerca de casa.  The station is pretty close to our house.

**pillo** (FEM **pilla**) ADJECTIVE
1 crafty
2 naughty

**el/la piloto** NOUN
1 pilot
2 driver
  ■ piloto de carreras  racing driver

**el pimentón** NOUN
paprika

**la pimienta** NOUN
pepper
  □ pimienta negra  black pepper

**el pimiento** NOUN
pepper
  □ un pimiento morrón  a red pepper

**el pin** (PL los **pins**) NOUN
badge

**el pincel** NOUN
paintbrush (PL paintbrushes)

**el/la pinchadiscos** (PL los/las **pinchadiscos**) NOUN
disc jockey (PL disc jockeys)

**pinchar** VERB [25]
1 to prick
  □ Me pinché con un alfiler.  I pricked myself

on a pin.
2 to burst
  □ El clavo pinchó la pelota.  The nail burst the ball.
  ■ Me pincharon en el brazo.  They gave me an injection in the arm.
  ■ Se me pinchó una rueda.  I had a puncture.
  ■ Los cactus pinchan.  Cactuses are prickly.

**el pinchazo** NOUN
1 puncture
  □ Tuve un pinchazo en la autopista.  I got a puncture on the motorway.
2 sharp pain

**el pincho** NOUN
1 thorn
2 snack
  □ Tomamos unos pinchos en el bar.  We had some snacks in the bar.
  ■ un pincho moruno  a kebab

**el ping-pong** NOUN
table tennis
  □ jugar al ping-pong  to play table tennis

**el pingüino** NOUN
penguin

**el pino** NOUN
pine tree
  ■ hacer el pino  to do a headstand
  💭 LANGUAGE TIP Word for word, **hacer el pino** means 'to do the pine tree'.

**la pinta** NOUN
  ■ tener buena pinta  to look good □ La paella tiene muy buena pinta.  The paella looks delicious.
  ■ Con esas gafas tienes pinta de maestra.  You look like a teacher with those glasses on.

**las pintadas** NOUN
graffiti

**el pintalabios** NOUN (PL los **pintalabios**)
lipstick

**pintar** VERB [25]
1 to paint
  □ Quiero pintar la habitación de azul.  I want to paint the room blue.
2 to colour in
  □ Dibujó un árbol y lo pintó.  He drew a tree and coloured it in.
  ■ Nunca me pinto.  I never wear makeup.
  ■ pintarse los labios  to put on lipstick
  ■ pintarse las uñas  to paint one's nails

**el pintor**, **la pintora** NOUN
painter
  □ Soy pintor.  I'm a painter.

**pintoresco** (FEM **pintoresca**) ADJECTIVE
picturesque

**la pintura** NOUN
1 paint

P

235

□ Tengo que comprar más pintura. I've got to buy some more paint.

2  painting

□ Me gusta la pintura abstracta. I like abstract painting. □ varias pinturas al óleo several oil paintings

la **pinza** NOUN
1  clothes peg
2  hairgrip
3  pincer

■ **unas pinzas** a pair of tweezers

la **piña** NOUN
1  pine cone
2  pineapple

el **piñón** (PL los **piñones**) NOUN
1  pine nut
2  sprocket

el **piojo** NOUN
louse (PL lice)

la **pipa** NOUN
1  pipe
□ Fuma en pipa. He smokes a pipe.
2  seed

■ **comer pipas** to eat sunflower seeds

el **pipí** NOUN
wee
□ hacer pipí to have a wee

la **piragua** NOUN
canoe (PL canoes)

el **piragüismo** NOUN
canoeing

la **pirámide** NOUN
pyramid

**pirata** (FEM **pirata**) ADJECTIVE
pirate

el/la **pirata** NOUN
pirate

■ **un pirata informático** a hacker

**piratear** VERB
to hack into a system

los **Pirineos** NOUN
the Pyrenees

el **piropo** NOUN
compliment
□ echar piropos a alguien to make compliments to someone

el **pirulí** (PL los **pirulís**) NOUN
lollipop

la **pisada** NOUN
1  footprint
2  footstep

el **pisapapeles** (PL los **pisapapeles**) NOUN
paperweight

**pisar** VERB [25]
1  to walk on
■ ¿Se puede pisar el suelo de la cocina? Can I walk on the kitchen floor?
2  to tread on

□ Perdona, te he pisado. Sorry, I trod on your foot.

■ **Pisé el acelerador a fondo.** I put my foot down.

la **piscina** NOUN
swimming pool

**Piscis** MASC NOUN
Pisces

■ **Soy piscis.** I'm Pisces.

el **piso** NOUN
1  flat
□ Vivimos en un piso céntrico. We live in a flat in the town centre.
2  floor
□ Su oficina está en el segundo piso. His office is on the second floor. □ El piso estaba lleno de papeles. The floor was covered in pieces of paper.

la **pista** NOUN
1  clue
□ ¿Te doy una pista? Shall I give you a clue?
2  track
□ Los cazadores siguen las pistas del animal. The hunters follow the animal's tracks.
3  court (sport)
■ **la pista de aterrizaje** the runway
■ **la pista de baile** the dance floor
■ **la pista de carreras** the racetrack
■ **la pista de esquí** the ski slope
■ **la pista de patinaje** the ice rink

la **pistola** NOUN
pistol

**pitar** VERB [25]
1  to blow one's whistle
□ El policía nos pitó. The policeman blew his whistle at us.
2  to hoot
□ No sé por qué me pita. I don't know why he's hooting at me.
■ **Salió pitando.** He was off like a shot.

**pitear** VERB [25] (Latin America)
to whistle

el **pito** NOUN
whistle
■ **Me importa un pito.** I don't care a hoot.

el **piyama** NOUN (Latin America)
pyjamas pl

la **pizarra** NOUN
1  blackboard
2  slate

la **pizca** NOUN
pinch
□ una pizca de sal a pinch of salt

la **pizza** NOUN
pizza

la **placa** NOUN
1  plaque
□ una placa conmemorativa a

commemorative plaque

**2** badge

**3** hotplate

■ **una placa de matrícula** a number plate

el **placer** NOUN

pleasure

la **plaga** NOUN

**1** pest

□ una plaga que estropea los cultivos a pest that damages the crops

**2** plague

□ las plagas de Egipto the plagues of Egypt

■ **la plaga del terrorismo** the scourge of terrorism

el **plan** NOUN

plan

□ ¿Qué planes tienes para este verano? What are your plans for the summer?

■ **viajar en plan económico** to travel cheap

■ **Lo dije en plan de broma.** I said it as a joke.

■ **el plan de estudios** the syllabus

la **plancha** NOUN

iron

■ **pescado a la plancha** grilled fish

**planchar** VERB [25]

**1** to iron

□ Tengo que planchar esta camisa. I've got to iron this shirt.

**2** to do the ironing

□ ¿Quieres que planche? Do you want me to do the ironing?

el **planeador** NOUN

glider

**planear** VERB [25]

**1** to plan

**2** to glide

el **planeta** NOUN

planet

la **planificación** NOUN

planning

■ **planificación familiar** family planning

**planificar*** VERB [48]

to plan

**plano** (FEM **plana**) ADJECTIVE

flat

el **plano** NOUN

**1** street plan

**2** plan

■ **en primer plano** in close-up

la **planta** NOUN

**1** plant

□ regar las plantas to water the plants

**2** floor

□ El edificio tiene tres plantas. The building has three floors. □ la planta baja the ground floor

■ **la planta del pie** the sole of the foot

**plantado** (FEM **plantada**) ADJECTIVE

■ **dejar a alguien plantado** to stand someone up

**plantar** VERB [25]

to plant

**plantear** VERB

to bring up

□ Se lo plantearé al jefe. I'll bring it up with the boss.

■ **Incluso me planteé dejar los estudios.** I even thought of giving up my studies.

la **plantilla** NOUN

**1** insole

**2** staff

el **plástico** NOUN

plastic

□ cubiertos de plástico plastic cutlery

la **Plastilina®** NOUN

Plasticine®

la **plata** NOUN

**1** silver

**2** money (*Latin America*)

la **plataforma** NOUN

platform

□ zapatos de plataforma platform shoes

■ **una plataforma petrolífera** an oil rig

el **plátano** NOUN

banana

**platicar*** VERB [48] (*Mexico*)

**1** to talk

□ Estuve platicando con Manuel. I was talking to Manuel.

**2** to tell

□ ¿Qué te platicaron? What did they tell you?

el **platillo** NOUN

■ **un platillo volante** a flying saucer

■ **los platillos** the cymbals

el **platino** NOUN

platinum

el **plato** NOUN

**1** plate

□ ¿Me pasas un plato? Could you pass me a plate?

**2** dish (PL dishes)

□ un plato típico de Galicia a typical Galician dish

■ **el plato del día** the dish of the day

**3** course

□ ¿Qué hay de segundo plato? What's for the main course?

■ **un plato combinado** a main course with vegetables included

**4** saucer

la **playa** NOUN

**1** beach (PL beaches)

□ Los niños jugaban en la playa. The

children were playing on the beach.
**2** seaside

□ Prefiero la playa a la montaña. I prefer the seaside to the mountains.

la **playera** NOUN
**1** canvas shoe
**2** T-shirt *(Mexico)*

la **plaza** NOUN
**1** square
□ la plaza del pueblo the town square
■ **la plaza mayor** the main square
**2** market
□ No había pescado en la plaza. There was no fish at the market.
**3** place
□ Todavía quedan plazas. There are still some places left.
■ **una plaza de toros** a bullring

el **plazo** NOUN
**1** period
□ en un plazo de diez días within a period of ten days
■ **El viernes se cumple el plazo.** Friday is the deadline.
**2** instalment
□ pagar a plazos to pay in instalments
□ comprar a plazos to buy on instalments
■ **una solución a corto plazo** a short-term solution

**plegable** (FEM **plegable**) ADJECTIVE
folding

**plegar*** VERB [34]
to fold

**pleno** (FEM **plena**) ADJECTIVE
■ **en pleno verano** in the middle of summer
■ **a plena luz del día** in broad daylight

la **pletina** NOUN
tape deck

**pliegue** VERB ▷ see **plegar**

el **pliegue** NOUN
**1** fold
**2** pleat

el **plomero**, la **plomera** NOUN *(Latin America)*
plumber

el **plomo** NOUN
lead
■ **gasolina sin plomo** unleaded petrol
■ **Se han fundido los plomos.** The fuses have blown.

la **pluma** NOUN
**1** feather
**2** pen
■ **una pluma atómica** *(Latin America)* a ballpoint pen
■ **una pluma estilográfica** a fountain pen

el **plural** ADJECTIVE, NOUN

plural

la **población** (PL las **poblaciones**) NOUN
**1** population
**2** town

**pobre** (FEM **pobre**) ADJECTIVE
poor
□ Somos pobres. We're poor.
■ **¡Pobre Pedro!** Poor Pedro!
■ **los pobres** the poor

la **pobreza** NOUN
poverty

**poco** (FEM **poca**) ADJECTIVE, ADVERB, PRONOUN
not much
□ Hay poca leche. There isn't much milk.
□ Tenemos muy poco tiempo. We have very little time.
■ **Sus libros son poco conocidos aquí.** His books are not very well known here.
■ **un poco** a bit □ ¿Tienes frío? — Un poco. Are you cold? — A bit. □ ¿Me das un poco? Can I have a bit? □ He bebido un poco, pero no estoy borracho. I had a bit to drink, but I'm not drunk.
■ **Tomé un poco de vino.** I had a little wine.
■ **pocos** not many □ Tiene pocos amigos. He hasn't got many friends.
■ **unos pocos** a few □ Me llevé unos pocos. I took a few with me.
■ **poco a poco** little by little
■ **poco después** shortly after
■ **dentro de poco** in a short time
■ **hace poco** not long ago
■ **por poco** nearly □ Por poco me caigo. I nearly fell.

**podar** VERB [25]
to prune

el **poder** NOUN
power
□ estar en el poder to be in power

**poder*** VERB [40]
**1** can
□ Yo puedo ayudarte. I can help you. □ ¡No puede ser! That can't be true! □ ¿Puedo usar tu teléfono? Can I use your phone? □ Pudiste haberte hecho daño. You could have hurt yourself. □ ¡Me lo podías haber dicho! You could have told me! □ Aquí no se puede fumar. You can't smoke here.
**2** to be able to
□ Creo que mañana no voy a poder ir. I don't think I'll be able to come tomorrow.
■ **¿Se puede?** May I?
■ **Puede que llegue mañana.** He might arrive tomorrow.
■ **Puede ser.** It's possible.
■ **No puedo con tanto trabajo.** I can't cope with so much work.

**poderoso** (FEM **poderosa**) ADJECTIVE

powerful

el **podólogo**, la **podóloga** NOUN
chiropodist

**podrido** (FEM **podrida**) ADJECTIVE
rotten

**podrirse** VERB = **pudrirse**

el **poema** NOUN
poem

la **poesía** NOUN
1 poetry
□ Me gusta la poesía. I like poetry.
2 poem
□ una poesía de Machado a poem by
Machado

el/la **poeta** NOUN
poet

el **póker** NOUN
poker

**polaco** (FEM **polaca**) ADJECTIVE
Polish

el **polaco**, la **polaca** NOUN
Pole
■ **los polacos** the Poles

el **polaco** NOUN
Polish

la **polémica** NOUN
controversy (PL controversies)

**polémico** (FEM **polémica**) ADJECTIVE
controversial

el **polen** NOUN
pollen
■ **alergia al polen** hay fever

el **policía** NOUN
policeman (PL policemen)
□ Es policía. He's a policeman.

la **policía** NOUN
1 police
□ Llamamos a la policía. We called the
police.
2 policewoman (PL policewomen)
□ Soy policía. I'm a policewoman.

**policíaco** (FEM **policíaca**) ADJECTIVE
■ **una novela policíaca** a detective novel

el **polideportivo** NOUN
sports centre

la **polilla** NOUN
moth (PL moths)

la **polio** NOUN
polio

la **política** NOUN
1 politics *sing*
□ Hablaban de política. They were talking
about politics.
2 policy (PL policies)
□ política exterior foreign policy
3 politician
□ Soy política. I'm a politician.

**político** (FEM **política**) ADJECTIVE

political

el **político** NOUN
politician

el **pollo** NOUN
chicken
■ **pollo asado** roast chicken

el **polluelo** NOUN
chick

el **polo** NOUN
1 ice lolly (PL ice lollies)
2 polo shirt
■ **el Polo Norte** the North Pole
■ **el Polo Sur** the South Pole

**Polonia** FEM NOUN
Poland

el **polvo** NOUN
dust
■ **limpiar el polvo** to dust
■ **quitar el polvo** to do the dusting
■ **quitar el polvo a algo** to dust something
■ **en polvo** powdered □ leche en polvo
powdered milk
■ **polvos de talco** talcum powder
■ **Estoy hecho polvo.** I'm shattered.
■ **echar un polvo** *(vulgar)* to have a shag

la **pólvora** NOUN
gunpowder

la **pomada** NOUN
ointment

el **pomelo** NOUN
grapefruit (PL grapefruit)

el **pomo** NOUN
handle

la **pompa** NOUN
1 bubble
□ pompas de jabón soap bubbles
2 pomp

el **pómulo** NOUN
cheekbone

**ponchar** VERB [25] *(Mexico)*
■ **Se nos ponchó una llanta.** We had a
puncture.

el **ponche** NOUN
punch (PL punches)

el **poncho** NOUN
poncho (PL ponchos)

**pondrá** VERB ▷ see **poner**

**poner\*** VERB [41]
1 to put
□ ¿Dónde pongo mis cosas? Where shall I
put my things?
2 to put on
□ Me puse el abrigo. I put on my coat. □ Voy
a poner las patatas. I'm going to put the
potatoes on. □ ¿Pongo música? Shall I put
some music on? □ Pon el radiador. Put the
heater on.
■ **No sé que ponerme.** I don't know what

P

239

to wear.

■ **Ponlo más alto.** Turn it up.

■ **¿Ponen alguna película esta noche?** Is there a film on tonight?

**3** to set

□ La maestra nos puso un examen. Our teacher set us an exam. □ Puse el despertador para las siete. I set the alarm for seven o'clock. □ poner la mesa to set the table

**4** to put in

□ Queremos poner calefacción. We want to put in central heating.

■ **¿Me pone con el Sr. García, por favor?** Could you put me through to Mr. Garcia, please?

■ **Le pusieron Mónica.** They called her Monica.

■ **¿Qué te pongo?** What can I get you?

■ **Cuando se lo dije se puso muy triste.** He was very sad when I told him.

■ **¡Qué guapa te has puesto!** You look beautiful!

■ **Se puso a mi lado en clase.** He sat down beside me in class.

■ **ponerse a hacer algo** to start doing something

el **poney** (PL los **poneys**) NOUN
pony (PL ponies)

**pongo** VERB ▷ see poner

**pop** (FEM **pop**, PL **pop**) ADJECTIVE
pop
□ música pop pop music

el **popote** NOUN (Mexico)
straw

**popular** (FEM **popular**) ADJECTIVE
popular

**por** PREPOSITION
**1** for
□ Lo hice por mis padres. I did it for my parents. □ Lo vendió por 100 euros. He sold it for 100 euros. □ Me castigaron por mentir. I was punished for lying.

**2** through
□ La conozco por mi hermano. I know her through my brother. □ por la ventana through the window □ Pasamos por Valencia. We went through Valencia.

**3** by
□ Fueron apresados por la policía. They were captured by the police. □ por correo by post □ Me agarró por el brazo. He grabbed me by the arm.

**4** along
□ Paseábamos por la playa. We were walking along the beach.

**5** around

240 □ viajar por el mundo to travel around the

world □ Viven por esta zona. They live around this area.

**6** because of
□ Tuvo que suspenderse por el mal tiempo. It had to be cancelled because of bad weather.

**7** per
□ 100 kilómetros por hora 100 kilometres per hour □ diez euros por persona ten euros per person

■ **por aquí cerca** near here

■ **por escrito** in writing

■ **por la mañana** in the morning

■ **por la noche** at night

■ **por mí ...** as far as I'm concerned ...

■ **¿Por qué?** Why?

la **porcelana** NOUN
porcelain

el **porcentaje** NOUN
percentage

el **porche** NOUN
porch (PL porches)

la **porción** (PL las **porciones**) NOUN
portion

**porno** (FEM **porno**, PL **porno**) ADJECTIVE
porn
□ una película porno a porn film

la **pornografía** NOUN
pornography

**pornográfico** (FEM **pornográfica**) ADJECTIVE
pornographic

el **poro** NOUN
**1** pore
**2** leek (Mexico)

el **poroto** NOUN (Chile, River Plate)
bean

**porque** CONJUNCTION
because
□ No fuimos porque llovía. We didn't go because it was raining.

la **porquería** NOUN
■ **Este CD es una porquería.** This CD's rubbish.

la **porra** NOUN
truncheon
■ **mandar a alguien a la porra** to send someone packing

el **porrazo** NOUN
■ **Me di un porrazo en la rodilla.** I banged my knee.
■ **Daba porrazos en la puerta.** He was banging on the door.

el **porro** NOUN
joint (colloquial)

la **portada** NOUN
**1** front page
**2** cover

el **portal** NOUN

**1** hallway
□ Los buzones están en el portal. The letterboxes are in the hallway.

**2** portal
■ **el portal de Belén** the nativity scene

**portarse** VERB [25]
■ **portarse bien** to behave well
■ **portarse mal** to behave badly
■ **Se portó muy bien conmigo.** He treated me very well.

**portátil** (FEM **portátil**) ADJECTIVE
portable

el **portavoz** (PL los **portavoces**) NOUN
spokesman (PL spokesmen)

la **portavoz** (PL las **portavoces**) NOUN
spokeswoman (PL spokeswomen)

el **portazo** NOUN
■ **Dio un portazo.** He slammed the door.

la **portera** NOUN
**1** caretaker
**2** goalkeeper

la **portería** NOUN
goal
□ El balón entró en la portería. The ball went into the goal.

el **portero** NOUN
**1** caretaker
**2** goalkeeper
■ **un portero automático** an entryphone
   **LANGUAGE TIP** Word for word, **portero automático** means 'automatic doorman'.

el **portorriqueño** (FEM la **portorriqueña**)
ADJECTIVE, NOUN
Puerto Rican

**Portugal** MASC NOUN
Portugal

el **portugués** (FEM la **portuguesa**, MASC PL
los **portugueses**) ADJECTIVE, NOUN
Portuguese

el **portugués** NOUN
Portuguese

el **porvenir** NOUN
future

**posar** VERB [25]
to pose
□ Posó para los fotógrafos. He posed for photographs.
■ **posarse** to land □ El pájaro se posó en la rama. The bird landed on the brach.

la **posdata** NOUN
postscript

**poseer\*** VERB [30]
to possess

la **posguerra** NOUN
■ **durante la posguerra** during the postwar period
■ **los años de posguerra** the years after the war

la **posibilidad** NOUN
**1** possibility (PL possibilities)
□ Es una posibilidad. It's a possibility.
**2** chance
□ Tendrás la posibilidad de viajar. You'll have the chance to travel.
■ **Tiene muchas posibilidades de ganar.** He has a good chance of winning.

**posible** (FEM **posible**) ADJECTIVE
possible
□ Es posible. It's possible.
■ **hacer todo lo posible** to do everything possible
■ **Es posible que ganen.** They might win.

la **posición** (PL las **posiciones**) NOUN
position
□ una posición estratégica a strategic position
■ **Está en primera posición.** He's in first place.

**positivo** (FEM **positiva**) ADJECTIVE
positive
■ **El test dio positivo.** The test was positive.

**posponer\*** VERB [41]
to postpone

**posta**
■ **a posta** ADVERB on purpose

la **postal** NOUN
postcard

el **poste** NOUN
**1** post
**2** pole

el **póster** (PL los **pósters**) NOUN
poster

**posterior** (FEM **posterior**) ADJECTIVE
rear
□ los asientos posteriores the rear seats
■ **la parte posterior** the rear

**postizo** (FEM **postiza**) ADJECTIVE
false

el **postizo** NOUN
hairpiece

el **postre** NOUN
dessert
□ De postre tomé un helado. I had ice cream for dessert. □ ¿Qué hay de postre? What's for dessert?

la **postura** NOUN
position

**potable** (FEM **potable**) ADJECTIVE
■ **agua potable** drinking water

el **potaje** NOUN
stew
□ potaje de garbanzos chickpea stew

la **potencia** NOUN
power
□ la potencia del motor the power of the

engine
■ **Es un artista en potencia.** He has the makings of an artist.

**potencial** (FEM **potencial**) ADJECTIVE
potential

**potente** (FEM **potente**) ADJECTIVE
powerful

el **potro** NOUN
1 colt
2 horse

el **pozo** NOUN
well

la **práctica** NOUN
practice
▢ No tengo mucha práctica. I haven't had much practice.
■ **en la práctica** in practice
■ **poner algo en práctica** to put something into practice

**prácticamente** ADVERB
practically

**practicante** (FEM **practicante**) ADJECTIVE
practising
▢ Es una católica practicante. She is a practising Catholic.

el/la **practicante** NOUN
nurse

**practicar*** VERB [48]
to practise
▢ Tengo que practicar un poco más. I need to practise a bit more.
■ **No practico ningún deporte.** I don't do any sports.

**práctico** (FEM **práctica**) ADJECTIVE
practical
▢ Es una mujer muy práctica. She is a very practical woman.

el **prado** NOUN
meadow

la **precaución** (PL las **precauciones**) NOUN
precaution
▢ tomar precauciones to take precautions
■ **con precaución** with caution

**precavido** (FEM **precavida**) ADJECTIVE
■ **Es muy precavida.** She's always very well-prepared.

el **precinto** NOUN
seal

el **precio** NOUN
price
▢ Han subido los precios. Prices have gone up.
■ **¿Qué precio tiene?** How much is it?

la **preciosidad** NOUN
■ **La casa es una preciosidad.** The house is beautiful.

**precioso** (FEM **preciosa**) ADJECTIVE
beautiful

▢ ¡Es precioso! It's beautiful!

el **precipicio** NOUN
precipice

**precipitarse** VERB [25]
■ **No hay que precipitarse.** There's no need to rush into anything.
■ **Reconozco que me precipité al tomar esa decisión.** I admit I rushed into the decision.

**precisamente** ADVERB
precisely

**precisar** VERB [25]
■ **¿Puedes precisar un poco más?** Can you be a little more specific?
■ **Precisó que no se trataba de un virus.** He said specifically that it was not a virus.

**preciso** (FEM **precisa**) ADJECTIVE
1 precise
▢ Recibió instrucciones precisas. He received precise instructions. ▢ en ese preciso momento at that precise moment
2 accurate
▢ un reloj muy preciso a very accurate watch
■ **si es preciso** if necessary
■ **No es preciso que vengas.** There's no need for you to come.

**precoz** (FEM **precoz**, PL **precoces**) ADJECTIVE
precocious

**predecir*** VERB [15]
to predict

**predicar*** VERB [48]
to preach

la **predicción** (PL las **predicciones**) NOUN
prediction

**predicho** VERB ▷ see **predecir**

**preescolar** (FEM **preescolar**) ADJECTIVE
pre-school

**prefabricado** (FEM **prefabricada**) ADJECTIVE
prefabricated

la **preferencia** NOUN
1 preference
▢ No tengo ninguna preferencia. I have no preference.
2 priority
▢ Tienen preferencia los coches que vienen por la derecha. Cars coming from the right have priority.

**preferido** (FEM **preferida**) ADJECTIVE
favourite

**preferir*** VERB [51]
to prefer
▢ Prefiero un buen libro a una película. I prefer a good book to a film.
■ **Prefiero ir mañana.** I'd rather go tomorrow.

**prefiero** VERB ▷ see **preferir**

el **prefijo** NOUN

P

code

□ ¿Cuál es el prefijo de Andorra? What is the code for Andorra?

la **pregunta** NOUN
question

□ hacer una pregunta to ask a question

**preguntar** VERB [25]
to ask

□ Siempre me preguntas lo mismo. You're always asking me the same question.

■ **Me preguntó por ti.** He asked after you.

■ **Me pregunto si estará enterado.** I wonder if he's heard yet.

**prehistórico** (FEM **prehistórica**) ADJECTIVE
prehistoric

el **prejuicio** NOUN
prejudice

■ **Yo no tengo prejuicios.** I'm not prejudiced.

**prematuro** (FEM **prematura**) ADJECTIVE
premature

**premiar** VERB [25]
1 to award a prize to

□ Han premiado su película. His film has been awarded a prize.

■ **el director premiado** the award-winning director

2 to reward

□ premiar los esfuerzos de un niño to reward a child's efforts

el **premio** NOUN
1 prize

□ llevarse un premio to get a prize

2 reward

□ como premio a tu sacrificio as a reward for your sacrifice

■ **el premio gordo** the jackpot

la **prenda** NOUN
garment

**prender** VERB [8]
1 to light
2 to switch on (Latin America)

■ **prender fuego a algo** to set fire to something

la **prensa** NOUN
press

□ una rueda de prensa a press conference

la **preocupación** (PL las **preocupaciones**) NOUN
worry (PL worries)

**preocupado** (FEM **preocupada**) ADJECTIVE
worried

■ **estar preocupado por algo** to be worried about something

**preocupar** VERB [25]
to worry

□ No te preocupes. Don't worry. □ Me preocupa su salud. I'm worried about his

health.

■ **preocuparse por algo** to worry about something

■ **Si llego un poco tarde se preocupa.** If I arrive a bit late he gets worried.

■ **Yo me preocupo de comprar las entradas.** I'll see to buying the tickets.

**preparar** VERB [25]
1 to prepare

□ No he preparado el discurso. I haven't prepared my speech.

2 to prepare for

□ ¿Te has preparado el examen? Have you prepared for the exam?

3 to cook

□ Mi madre estaba preparando la cena. My mother was cooking dinner.

■ **Me estaba preparando para salir.** I was getting ready to go out.

los **preparativos** NOUN
preparations

la **presa** NOUN
1 dam
2 prey
3 prisoner

**prescindir** VERB [58]

■ **prescindir de** to do without □ No puede prescindir de su secretaria. He can't do without his secretary.

la **presencia** NOUN
presence

□ en presencia de un sacerdote in the presence of a priest

■ **El puesto requiere buena presencia.** A smart appearance is required for the position.

**presenciar** VERB [25]
to witness

el **presentador**, la **presentadora** NOUN
1 presenter
2 newsreader

**presentar** VERB [25]
1 to introduce

□ Me presentó a sus padres. He introduced me to his parents.

2 to hand in

□ Mañana tengo que presentar un trabajo. I have to hand in an essay tomorrow. □ Presentó la dimisión. He handed in his resignation.

3 to present

□ J. Pérez presenta el programa. The programme is presented by J. Pérez.

■ **presentarse 1** to turn up □ Se presentó en mi casa sin avisar. He turned up at my house without warning. **2** to introduce oneself □ Me voy a presentar. Let me

**P**

introduce myself.

■ **presentarse a un examen** to sit an exam

el **presente** ADJECTIVE, NOUN
present
□ Juan no estaba presente en la reunión. Juan was not present at the meeting.
■ **el presente** the present
■ **los presentes** those present
■ **¡Presente!** Present!

el **presentimiento** NOUN
premonition

el **preservativo** NOUN
condom

la **presidenta** NOUN
1 president
2 chairperson

el **presidente** NOUN
1 president
2 chairman (PL chairmen)

la **presión** (PL las **presiones**) NOUN
pressure
■ **la presión sanguínea** blood pressure

**presionar** VERB [25]
1 to put pressure on
□ El casero lo está presionando para que se mude. The landlord is putting pressure on him to move.
2 to press

**preso** (FEM **presa**) ADJECTIVE
■ **Estuvo tres años preso.** He was in prison for three years.
■ **llevarse a alguien preso** to take someone prisoner

el **preso** NOUN
prisoner

**prestado** (FEM **prestada**) ADJECTIVE
■ **La cinta no es mía, es prestada.** It's not my tape, someone lent it to me.
■ **Le pedí prestada la bicicleta.** I asked if I could borrow his bicycle.
■ **Me dejó el coche prestado.** He lent me his car.

el **préstamo** NOUN
loan
□ Pidieron un préstamo al banco. They asked the bank for a loan.

**prestar** VERB [25]
to lend
□ Un amigo me prestó el traje. A friend lent me the suit.
■ **¿Me prestas el boli?** Can I borrow your pen?
■ **Tienes que prestar atención.** You must pay attention.
■ **Se negó a prestar ayuda.** He refused to help.

el **prestigio** NOUN
prestige

■ **una marca de prestigio** a prestigious brand

**presumido** (FEM **presumida**) ADJECTIVE
vain

**presumir** VERB [58]
to show off
□ Lleva ropa cara para presumir. He dresses expensively just to show off.
■ **Luis presume de guapo.** Luis thinks he's really handsome.

el **presupuesto** NOUN
1 budget
□ No puedo salirme del presupuesto. I can't go over the budget.
2 estimate
□ Le he pedido un presupuesto al carpintero. I've asked the joiner for an estimate.

**pretender** VERB [8]
1 to intend
□ Pretendo sacar al menos un notable. I intend to get at least a B.
■ **¿Qué pretendes decir con eso?** What do you mean by that?
2 to expect
□ ¡No pretenderás que te pague la comida! You're not expecting me to pay for your meal, are you?

LANGUAGE TIP Be careful! **pretender** does not mean **to pretend**.

el **pretexto** NOUN
excuse
□ Era sólo un pretexto. It was only an excuse.
■ **Vino con el pretexto de ver al abuelo.** He came in order to see Granddad, or so he said.

la **prevención** NOUN
prevention
□ prevención de incendios fire prevention
■ **las medidas de prevención** preventive measures

**prevenir*** VERB [56]
1 to prevent
□ prevenir un accidente to prevent an accident
2 to warn
□ Mi madre ya me había prevenido. My mother had already warned me.

**prever*** VERB [57]
1 to foresee
□ Nadie había previsto esta tragedia. Nobody had foreseen this tragedy.
■ **Han previsto nevadas en el norte.** Snow is forecast for the north.
2 to plan
■ **Tienen previsto acabar el metro para el 2003.** They plan to finish the metro by the

year 2003.

**previo** (FEM **previa**) ADJECTIVE
previous
□ No tengo experiencia previa en ese campo. I have no previous experience in the field.

**previsible** (FEM **previsible**) ADJECTIVE
foreseeable

**previsto** VERB
▷ see also **previsto** ADJECTIVE ▷ see **prever**

**previsto** (FEM **prevista**) ADJECTIVE
▷ see also **previsto** VERB
■ **Tengo previsto volver mañana.** I plan to return tomorrow.
■ **El avión tiene prevista su llegada a las dos.** The plane is due in at two o'clock.
■ **Como estaba previsto, ganó él.** As expected, he was the winner.

la **prima** NOUN
1 cousin
2 bonus

**primario** (FEM **primaria**) ADJECTIVE
primary
□ la educación primaria primary education

la **primavera** NOUN
spring
□ en primavera in spring

**primer** ▷ see **primero**

**primero** (FEM **primera**) ADJECTIVE, PRONOUN
first
□ el primer día the first day □ Primer plato: sopa. First course: soup. □ Primero vamos a comer. Let's eat first.
■ **en primera fila** in the front row
■ **En primer lugar, veamos los datos.** Firstly, let's look at the facts.
■ **primer ministro** prime minister
■ **Vivo en el primero.** I live on the first floor.
■ **Fui la primera en llegar.** I was the first to arrive.
■ **Juan es el primero de la clase.** Juan is top of the class.
■ **Lo primero es la salud.** The most important thing is your health.
■ **El examen será a primeros de mayo.** The exam will be at the beginning of May.

**primitivo** (FEM **primitiva**) ADJECTIVE
primitive

el **primo** NOUN
cousin
■ **primo segundo** second cousin

la **princesa** NOUN
princess (PL princesses)

**principal** (FEM **principal**) ADJECTIVE
main
□ el personaje principal the main character
■ **Lo principal es estar sano.** The main

thing is to stay healthy.

**principalmente** ADVERB
mainly

el **príncipe** NOUN
prince

el/la **principiante** NOUN
beginner

el **principio** NOUN
1 beginning
□ El principio me gustó. I liked the beginning.
■ **Al principio parecía fácil.** It seemed easy at first.
■ **a principios de año** at the beginning of the year
2 principle
□ No tiene principios. He has no principles.
■ **En principio me parece una buena idea.** On the face of it, it's a good idea.

la **prioridad** NOUN
priority (PL priorities)

la **prisa** NOUN
rush
■ **Con las prisas me olvidé el paraguas.** In the rush I forgot my umbrella.
■ **¡Date prisa!** Hurry up!
■ **Tengo prisa.** I'm in a hurry.

la **prisión** (PL las **prisiones**) NOUN
prison
□ Lo condenaron a seis años de prisión. He was sentenced to six years in prison.

el **prisionero**, la **prisionera** NOUN
prisoner

los **prismáticos** NOUN
binoculars

**privado** (FEM **privada**) ADJECTIVE
private
□ un colegio privado a private school

**privarse** VERB [25]
■ **En vacaciones no me privo de nada.** When I'm on holiday I really spoil myself.

**privatizar\*** VERB
to privatize

el **privilegio** NOUN
privilege

el **pro** NOUN
■ **los pros y contras** the pros and cons

las **probabilidades** NOUN
■ **Tiene muchas probabilidades de ganar.** He has a very good chance of winning.
■ **No tengo muchas probabilidades de aprobar.** I don't have much chance of passing.

**probable** (FEM **probable**) ADJECTIVE
likely
□ Es muy probable. It's very likely.
■ **Es probable que llegue tarde.** He'll probably arrive late.

P

245

**probablemente** ADVERB
probably

el **probador** NOUN
changing room

**probar\*** VERB [11]
1 to prove
  □ La policía no pudo probarlo. The police could not prove it.
2 to taste
  □ Probé la sopa para ver si le faltaba sal. I tasted the soup to see if it needed more salt.
3 to try
  □ Prueba estas patatas a ver si te gustan. Try these potatoes and see if you like them.
  □ Pruébalo antes para ver si funciona bien. Try it first and see if it works properly.
  ■ **Me probé un vestido.** I tried on a dress.

la **probeta** NOUN
test tube
  ■ **un niño probeta** a test-tube baby

el **problema** NOUN
problem
  □ Tengo que resolver este problema. I have to solve this problem.
  ■ **Este coche nunca me ha dado problemas.** This car has never given me any trouble.
  ■ **tener problemas de estómago** to have stomach trouble

**procedente** (FEM **procedente**) ADJECTIVE
  ■ **procedente de** from □ el tren procedente de Barcelona the train from Barcelona

el **procesador** NOUN
processor
  ■ **un procesador de textos** a word processor

el **procesamiento** NOUN
  ■ **el procesamiento de textos** word processing

la **procesión** (PL las **procesiones**) NOUN
procession

el **proceso** NOUN
process (PL processes)
  □ Será un proceso muy largo. It will be a long process.
  ■ **el proceso de datos** data processing

**proclamar** VERB [25]
to proclaim

**procurar** VERB [25]
to try
  ■ **Procura terminarlo mañana.** Try to finish it tomorrow.

la **producción** (PL las **producciones**) NOUN
production
  ■ **la producción en serie** mass production

**producir\*** VERB [9]
1 to produce

□ La película fue producida por Juan Pérez. The film was produced by Juan Pérez. □ No producimos lo suficiente. We are not producing enough.
2 to cause
  □ Puede producir efectos secundarios. It can cause side-effects.
  ■ **¿Cómo se produjo el accidente?** How did the accident happen?

**productivo** (FEM **productiva**) ADJECTIVE
productive

el **producto** NOUN
product
  □ productos de limpieza cleaning products
  □ productos lácteos dairy products
  ■ **los productos del campo** farm produce

el **productor**, la **productora** NOUN
producer

la **profesión** (PL las **profesiones**) NOUN
profession

el/la **profesional** ADJECTIVE, NOUN
professional

el **profesor**, la **profesora** NOUN
teacher
  □ Amelia es profesora de inglés. Amelia is an English teacher.
  ■ **mi profesor particular** my private tutor
  ■ **un profesor universitario** a university lecturer

  **LANGUAGE TIP** Be careful! The Spanish word **profesor** does not mean **professor**.

**profundamente** ADVERB
1 deeply
2 soundly

la **profundidad** NOUN
depth (PL depths)
  □ la profundidad de la piscina the depth of the pool □ analizar un texto en profundidad to analyze a text in depth
  ■ **Tiene dos metros de profundidad.** It's two metres deep.

**profundo** (FEM **profunda**) ADJECTIVE
deep
  ■ **una piscina poco profunda** a shallow pool

el **programa** NOUN
1 programme
  □ un programa de televisión a television programme
  ■ **un programa-concurso** a quiz show
  ■ **el programa de estudios** the syllabus
2 program

la **programación** NOUN
1 programmes *pl*
2 programming

el **programador**, la **programadora**
NOUN

programmer

□ Balbino es programador. Balbino is a programmer.

**programar** VERB [25]
to programme

□ Programé el vídeo para grabar el partido. I programmed the video to tape the match.

**progresar** VERB [25]
to progress

el **progreso** NOUN
progress

□ progreso tecnológico technological progress

■ **Carmen ha hecho muchos progresos este trimestre.** Carmen has made great progress this term.

**prohibir\*** VERB [42]
to ban

□ Le prohibieron la entrada en el edificio. He was banned from entering the building. □ Han prohibido las armas de fuego. Firearms have been banned.

■ **queda terminantemente prohibido** it is strictly forbidden

■ **Te prohíbo que toques mi ordenador.** I won't allow you to touch my computer.

■ **'prohibido fumar'** 'no smoking'

**prolijo** (FEM **prolija**) ADJECTIVE (River Plate)
neat

el **prólogo** NOUN
prologue

**prolongar\*** VERB [37]
to extend

el **promedio** NOUN
average

la **promesa** NOUN
promise

**prometer** VERB [8]
to promise

□ Prometió llevarnos al cine. He promised to take us to the cinema.

■ **¡Te lo prometo!** I promise!

la **promoción** (PL **promociones**) NOUN
promotion

■ **Está en promoción.** It's on offer.

el **pronombre** NOUN
pronoun

**pronosticar\*** VERB [48]
to forecast

el **pronóstico** NOUN

■ **el pronóstico del tiempo** the weather forecast

**pronto** ADVERB
1 soon

□ Los invitados llegarán pronto. The guests will be here soon.

■ **lo más pronto posible** as soon as possible

■ **¡Hasta pronto!** See you soon!

2 early

□ ¿Por qué has llegado tan pronto? Why have you arrived so early? □ Hoy me he levantado muy pronto. I got up very early today.

■ **De pronto, empezó a nevar.** All of a sudden it began to snow.

**pronunciar** VERB [25]
to pronounce

□ ¿Cómo se pronuncia esta palabra? How do you pronounce that word?

la **propaganda** NOUN
1 advertising

□ Las revistas están llenas de propaganda. Magazines are full of advertising.

■ **Han hecho mucha propaganda del concierto.** The concert has been well-advertised.

2 junk mail

□ Los buzones están llenos de propaganda. The letterboxes are full of junk mail.

**propagarse\*** VERB [37]
to spread

la **propiedad** NOUN
property (PL properties)

el **propietario**, la **propietaria** NOUN
owner

la **propina** NOUN
tip

□ ¿Vamos a dejar propina? Shall we leave a tip?

■ **Siempre doy propina a los camareros.** I always tip waiters.

**propio** (FEM **propia**) ADJECTIVE
1 own

□ Tengo mi propia habitación. I have my own room.

2 himself (FEM herself)

□ Lo anunció el propio ministro. It was announced by the minister himself.

3 typical

□ Eso es muy propio de los países mediterráneos. That's very typical of the Mediterranean countries.

■ **un nombre propio** a proper noun

**proponer\*** VERB [41]
1 to suggest

□ Nos propuso pagar la cena a medias. He suggested that we should share the cost of the meal.

■ **Me propuso un trato.** He made me a proposition.

2 to nominate

□ Propusieron a Manuel para alcalde. Manuel was nominated for mayor.

■ **Se ha propuesto adelgazar.** He's decided to lose some weight.

P

247

**Spanish-English**

la **proporción** (PL las **proporciones**) NOUN
proportion

**proporcional** (FEM **proporcional**) ADJECTIVE
proportional

**proporcionar** VERB [25]
to provide
□ Ellos me proporcionaron la información.
They provided me with the information.

el **propósito** NOUN
purpose
□ ¿Cuál es el propósito de su visita? What is
the purpose of your visit?
■ **A propósito, ya tengo los billetes.** By
the way, I've got the tickets.
■ **Lo hizo a propósito.** He did it
deliberately.

la **propuesta** NOUN
proposal

**propuesto** VERB ▷ see **proponer**

la **prórroga** NOUN
1 extension
2 extra time

el **prospecto** NOUN
leaflet

**prosperar** VERB [25]
to do well

**próspero** (FEM **próspera**) ADJECTIVE
■ **¡Próspero Año Nuevo!** A prosperous
New year!

la **prostituta** NOUN
prostitute

el/la **protagonista** NOUN
main character
□ El protagonista no muere en la película.
The main character doesn't die in the film.
■ **El protagonista es Tom Cruise.** Tom
Cruise plays the lead.

la **protección** NOUN
protection

**protector** (FEM **protectora**) ADJECTIVE
protective
□ una funda protectora a protective cover

**proteger\*** VERB [7]
to protect
□ El muro le protegió de las balas. The wall
protected him from the bullets.
■ **Nos protegimos de la lluvia en la
cabaña.** We sheltered from the rain in the
hut.

la **proteína** NOUN
protein

la **protesta** NOUN
protest
□ como protesta por los despidos as a
protest against redundancies

el/la **protestante** ADJECTIVE, NOUN
Protestant

**protestar** VERB [25]

1 to protest
□ Protestaron contra la subida de la
gasolina. They protested against the rise in
the price of petrol.
2 to complain
□ Cómete la verdura y no protestes. Eat
your vegetables and don't complain.

el **provecho** NOUN
■ **¡Buen provecho!** Enjoy your meal!
■ **Sacó mucho provecho del curso.** He got
a lot out of the course.

el **proverbio** NOUN
proverb

la **provincia** NOUN
province

**provisional** (FEM **provisional**) ADJECTIVE
provisional

las **provisiones** NOUN
provisions

**provocar\*** VERB [48]
1 to provoke
□ No quería pegarle pero me provocó. I
didn't mean to hit him but he provoked me.
2 to cause
□ La lluvia ha provocado graves
inundaciones. The rain caused serious
flooding.
■ **El incendio fue provocado.** The fire was
started deliberately.

**provocativo** (FEM **provocativa**) ADJECTIVE
provocative

**próximo** (FEM **próxima**) ADJECTIVE
next
□ Lo haremos la próxima semana. We'll do
it next week. □ la próxima vez next time
□ la próxima calle a la izquierda the next
street on the left

**proyectar** VERB
1 to show
2 to cast
■ **la imagen que un país proyecta al
extranjero** the image a country projects
abroad

el **proyectil** NOUN
missile

el **proyecto** NOUN
1 plan
□ ¿Tienes algún proyecto a la vista? Have
you got any plans?
2 project
□ el proyecto en el que estamos trabajando
the project we are working on
■ **un proyecto de ley** a bill

el **proyector** NOUN
projector

**prudente** (FEM **prudente**) ADJECTIVE
wise
□ Lo más prudente sería esperar. It would

**P**

be wisest to wait.

■ **Debería ser más prudente.** He should be more careful.

**prueba** VERB ▷ see **probar**

la **prueba** NOUN

1 test

□ El médico me hizo más pruebas. The doctor did some more tests.

■ **pruebas nucleares** nuclear tests

2 proof

□ Eso es la prueba de que lo hizo él. This is the proof that he did it.

■ **El fiscal presentó nuevas pruebas.** The prosecutor presented new evidence.

3 heat

□ la prueba de los cien metros valla the hundred metres hurdles heat

■ **a prueba de balas** bullet-proof

**pruebo** VERB ▷ see **probar**

la **psicóloga** NOUN

psychologist

la **psicología** NOUN

psychology

**psicológico** (FEM **psicológica**) ADJECTIVE

psychological

el **psicólogo** NOUN

psychologist

el/la **psiquiatra** NOUN

psychiatrist

**psiquiátrico** (FEM **psiquiátrica**) ADJECTIVE

psychiatric

**ptas.** ABBREVIATION (= pesetas)

pesetas

la **púa** NOUN

1 plectrum

2 tooth (PL teeth) (of comb)

el **pub** (PL los **pubs**) NOUN

bar

**publicar*** VERB [48]

to publish

la **publicidad** NOUN

1 advertising

□ una campaña de publicidad an advertising campaign

2 publicity

□ La conferencia tuvo poca publicidad. The conference received little publicity.

**público** (FEM **pública**) ADJECTIVE

public

el **público** NOUN

1 public

□ cerrado al público closed to the public

2 audience

3 spectators pl

**pude** VERB ▷ see **poder**

**pudrirse** VERB

to rot

el **pueblo** NOUN

1 village

2 town

3 people pl

□ El pueblo está a favor de la democracia. The people are in favour of democracy.

**puedo** VERB ▷ see **poder**

el **puente** NOUN

bridge

■ **el puente aéreo** the shuttle service

○ LANGUAGE TIP Word for word, **puente aéreo** means 'air bridge'.

■ **hacer puente** to make a long weekend of it

○ DID YOU KNOW...?

When a public holiday falls on a Tuesday or Thursday people often take off Monday or Friday as well to give themselves a long weekend.

el **puerco** NOUN

1 pig

2 pork (Mexico)

el **puerro** NOUN

leek

la **puerta** NOUN

1 door

■ **un coche de cuatro puertas** a four-door car

2 gate

■ **Llaman a la puerta.** Somebody's at the door.

■ **Susana me acompañó a la puerta.** Susana saw me out.

■ **la puerta de embarque** boarding gate

el **puerto** NOUN

port

□ un puerto pesquero a fishing port

■ **un puerto deportivo** a marina

■ **un puerto de montaña** a mountain pass

**Puerto Rico** MASC NOUN

Puerto Rico

el **puertorriqueño** (FEM la **puertorriqueña**) ADJECTIVE, NOUN

Puerto Rican

**pues** CONJUNCTION

1 then

□ Tengo sueño. — ¡Pues vete a la cama! I'm tired. — Then go to bed!

2 well

□ Pues, como te iba contando ... Well, as I was saying ... □ ¡Pues no lo sabía! Well I didn't know!

■ **¡Pues claro!** Yes, of course!

la **puesta** NOUN

■ **la puesta de sol** sunset

■ **la puesta en libertad de dos presos** the release of two prisoners

**puesto** VERB ▷ see **poner**

el **puesto** NOUN

## pulga – puñado

**1** place
□ Acabé la carrera en primer puesto.
I finished in first place.
**2** stall
□ un puesto de verduras a vegetable stall
■ **un puesto de trabajo** a job
■ **un puesto de socorro** a first aid station
■ **puesto que** since □ Puesto que no lo
querías, se lo di a Pedro. Since you didn't
want it, I gave it to Pedro.

la **pulga** NOUN
flea

la **pulgada** NOUN
inch (PL inches)

el **pulgar** NOUN
thumb

**pulir** VERB [58]
to polish

el **pulmón** (PL los **pulmones**) NOUN
lung

la **pulpería** NOUN (Latin America)
shop

el **púlpito** NOUN
pulpit

el **pulpo** NOUN
octopus (PL octopuses)
□ Me gusta el pulpo. I like octopus.

**pulsar** VERB [25]
to press

la **pulsera** NOUN
bracelet
■ **un reloj de pulsera** a wrist watch

el **pulso** NOUN
pulse
□ El doctor le tomó el pulso. The doctor
took his pulse.
■ **Tengo muy mal pulso.** My hand is very
unsteady.
■ **Echamos un pulso y le gané.** We had an
arm-wrestling match and I won.
■ **Lo levantó a pulso.** He lifted it with his
bare hands.

el **pulverizador** NOUN
spray

el/la **punk** ADJECTIVE, NOUN
punk

la **punta** NOUN
**1** nail (of metal)
**2** tip (of finger, tongue)
**3** point (of pen, knife)
■ **Sácale punta al lápiz.** Sharpen your
pencil.
■ **Vivo en la otra punta del pueblo.** I live
at the other end of the town.
■ **la hora punta** the rush hour

el **puntapié** (PL los **puntapiés**) NOUN
■ **Le dio un puntapié a la piedra.** He
kicked the stone.

la **puntería** NOUN
■ **tener buena puntería** to be a good shot

**puntiagudo** (FEM **puntiaguda**) ADJECTIVE
pointed

la **puntilla** NOUN
lace edging
■ **andar de puntillas** to tiptoe
■ **ponerse de puntillas** to stand on tiptoe

el **punto** NOUN
**1** point
□ Perdieron por tres puntos. They lost by
three points. □ Ése es un punto importante.
That's an important point. □ desde ese
punto de vista from that point of view
**2** stitch (PL stitches)
**3** dot
**4** full stop
■ **punto y seguido** full stop, new sentence
■ **punto y aparte** full stop, new paragraph
■ **punto y coma** semi-colon
■ **dos puntos** colon
■ **puntos suspensivos** dot, dot, dot
■ **Estábamos a punto de salir cuando
llamaste.** We were about to go out when
you phoned.
■ **Mila estaba a punto de llorar.** Mila was
on the verge of tears.
■ **Estuve a punto de perder el tren.** I very
nearly missed the train.
■ **a la una en punto** at one o'clock sharp
■ **Me gusta hacer punto.** I like knitting.

la **puntuación** (PL las **puntuaciones**) NOUN
**1** punctuation
□ los signos de puntuación punctuation
marks
**2** score
□ Recibió una alta puntuación. He got a
high score.

**puntual** (FEM **puntual**) ADJECTIVE
**1** punctual
□ Sé puntual. Be punctual.
■ **Jamás llega puntual.** He never arrives on
time.
**2** specific
□ Sólo trató aspectos puntuales del tema.
He only dealt with specific aspects of the
subject.

la **puntualidad** NOUN
punctuality

**puntuar*** VERB
■ **Este trabajo no puntúa para la nota
final.** This essay doesn't count towards the
final mark.
■ **un profesor que puntúa muy bajo** a
teacher who gives very low marks

el **puñado** NOUN
handful
□ un puñado de arena a handful of sand

P

el **puñal** NOUN
dagger

la **puñalada** NOUN
■ **Le dieron una puñalada.** He was
stabbed.

el **puñetazo** NOUN
punch (PL punches)
□ un puñetazo en la cara  a punch in the
face
■ **Le pegó un puñetazo.** He punched him.

el **puño** NOUN
1 fist
2 cuff

la **pupa** NOUN
■ **¿Te has hecho pupa?** Did you hurt
yourself?

el **pupitre** NOUN
desk

el **puré** (PL los **purés**) NOUN
■ **puré de verduras** puréed vegetables
■ **puré de patatas** mashed potato

**puro** (FEM **pura**) ADJECTIVE
pure
□ pura lana  pure wool □ por pura
casualidad  by pure chance
■ **Es la pura verdad.** That's the absolute
truth.
■ **Son puras mentiras.** (Latin America)
It's all lies.

el **puro** NOUN
cigar

el **pus** NOUN
pus

**puse** VERB ▷ see **poner**

# Qq

**que** CONJUNCTION
▷ *see also* **que** PRONOUN
1 than
□ Es más alto que tú. He's taller than you.
■ **Yo que tú, iría.** I'd go if I were you.
2 that
□ José sabe que estás aquí. José knows that you're here. □ Dijo que vendría. He said he'd come.
■ **Dile a Rosa que me llame.** Ask Rosa to call me.
■ **¡Que te mejores!** Get well soon!
■ **¿De verdad que te gusta? — ¡Que sí!** Do you really like it? — Of course I do!

**que** PRONOUN
▷ *see also* **que** CONJUNCTION
1 which
□ la película que ganó el premio the film which won the award □ el sombrero que te compraste the hat you bought □ el libro del que te hablé the book I spoke to you about
2 who
□ el hombre que vino ayer the man who came yesterday □ la chica que conocí the girl I met

**qué** ADJECTIVE, ADVERB, PRONOUN
1 what
□ ¿Qué fecha es hoy? What's today's date?
□ No sabe qué es. He doesn't know what it is. □ No sé qué hacer. I don't know what to do.
■ **¿qué?** what?
2 which
□ ¿Qué película quieres ver? Which film do you want to see?
■ **¡Qué asco!** How revolting!
■ **¡Qué día más bonito!** What a glorious day!
■ **¿Qué tal?** How are things?
■ **¿Qué tal está tu madre?** How's your mother?
■ **No lo he hecho. ¿Y qué?** I haven't done it. So what?

el **quebrado** NOUN
fraction

**quebrar\*** VERB [39]
to go bankrupt
■ **quebrarse** *(Latin America)* to break
□ Alberto se quebró una pierna. Alberto broke his leg.

**quedar** VERB [25]
1 to be left
□ No queda ninguno. There are none left.
■ **Me quedan quince euros.** I've got 15 euros left.
2 to be
□ Eso queda muy lejos de aquí. That's a long way from here.
3 to arrange to meet
□ He quedado con ella en el cine. I've arranged to meet her at the cinema.
■ **¿Quedamos en la parada?** Shall we meet at the bus stop?
4 to suit
□ No te queda bien ese vestido. That dress doesn't suit you.
■ **quedarse** to stay □ Ve tú, yo me quedo. You go, I'll stay.
■ **quedarse atrás** to fall behind
■ **quedarse sordo** to go deaf
■ **quedarse con algo** to keep something
□ Quédate con el cambio. Keep the change.

los **quehaceres** NOUN
■ **los quehaceres de la casa** the household chores

la **queja** NOUN
complaint

**quejarse** VERB [25]
to complain
■ **quejarse de algo** to complain about something
■ **quejarse de que ...** to complain that ...
□ Pablo se quejó de que nadie lo escuchaba. Pablo complained that nobody listened to him.

el **quejido** NOUN
1 moan
2 whine

**quemado** (FEM **quemada**) ADJECTIVE
burnt

la **quemadura** NOUN
burn

■ **quemaduras de sol** sunburn *sing*
**quemar** VERB [25]
1 to burn
□ Un incendio quemó todo el bosque. A fire burned the entire forest.
2 to be burning hot
□ Esta sopa quema. This soup's burning hot.
■ **quemarse** to burn oneself □ Me quemé con una cerilla. I burned myself with a match.
**quepa** VERB ▷*see* **caber**
**querer\*** VERB [43]
1 to want
□ No quiero ir. I don't want to go.
■ **Quiero que vayas.** I want you to go.
■ **¿Quieres un café?** Would you like some coffee?
2 to love
□ Ana quiere mucho a sus hijos. Ana loves her children dearly.
3 to mean
□ No quería hacerte daño. I didn't mean to hurt you. □ Lo hice sin querer. I didn't mean to do it.
■ **querer decir** to mean □ ¿Qué quieres decir? What do you mean?
**querido** (FEM **querida**) ADJECTIVE
dear
**querré** VERB ▷*see* **querer**
el **queso** NOUN
cheese
el **quicio** NOUN
■ **sacar a alguien de quicio** to drive somebody up the wall
la **quiebra** NOUN
■ **ir a la quiebra** to go bankrupt
**quien** PRONOUN
who
□ Fue Juan quien nos lo dijo. It was Juan who told us. □ Vi al chico con quien sales. I saw the boy you're going out with.
**quién** PRONOUN
who
□ ¿Quién es ésa? Who's that? □ ¿A quién viste? Who did you see? □ No sé quién es. I don't know who he is.
■ **¿De quién es ...?** Whose is ...? □ ¿De quién es este libro? Whose is this book?
■ **¿Quién es?** 1 Who's there? 2 Who's calling?
**quiero** VERB ▷*see* **querer**
**quieto** (FEM **quieta**) ADJECTIVE
still
■ **¡Estáte quieto!** Keep still!
la **química** NOUN
1 chemistry
□ clase de química chemistry class

2 chemist
□ Es química. She's a chemist.
el **químico** NOUN
chemist
□ Es químico. He's a chemist.
**quince** (FEM **quince**) ADJECTIVE, PRONOUN
fifteen
■ **el quince de enero** the fifteenth of January
■ **quince días** a fortnight
el **quinceañero**, la **quinceañera** NOUN
teenager
la **quincena** NOUN
fortnight
**quincenal** (FEM **quincenal**) ADJECTIVE
fortnightly
la **quiniela** NOUN
football pools *pl*
**quinientos** (FEM **quinientas**) ADJECTIVE, PRONOUN
five hundred
**quinto** (FEM **quinta**) ADJECTIVE, PRONOUN
fifth
■ **Vivo en el quinto.** I live on the fifth floor.
el **quiosco** NOUN
1 news stand
2 drinks stand
3 flower stall
4 bandstand
el **quirófano** NOUN
operating theatre
**quirúrgico** (FEM **quirúrgica**) ADJECTIVE
surgical
■ **una intervención quirúrgica** an operation
**quise** VERB ▷*see* **querer**
**quisquilloso** (FEM **quisquillosa**) ADJECTIVE
1 fussy
□ No soy quisquillosa con la comida. I'm not fussy about what I eat.
2 touchy
□ Está muy quisquilloso últimamente. He's been very touchy lately.
el **quitaesmalte** NOUN
nail polish remover
el **quitamanchas** (PL los **quitamanchas**) NOUN
stain remover
la **quitanieves** (PL las **quitanieves**) NOUN
snowplough
**quitar** VERB [25]
1 to remove
□ Tardaron dos días en quitar los escombros. It took two days to remove the rubble. □ Este producto quita todo tipo de manchas. This product removes all types of stain.
2 to take away

253

## quizá - quizás

□ Su hermana le quitó la pelota. His sister took the ball away from him.
■ **Me han quitado la cartera.** I've had my wallet stolen.
■ **Esto te quitará el dolor.** This will relieve the pain.

■ **quitarse** to take off □ Juan se quitó la chaqueta. Juan took his jacket off.
■ **¡Quítate de en medio!** Get out of the way!

**quizá** ADVERB = **quizás**

**quizás** ADVERB
perhaps

# Rr

el **rábano** NOUN
radish (PL radishes)
■ **¡Me importa un rábano!** I don't give a monkey's!

la **rabia** NOUN
1 rage
□ Lo hizo por rabia. He did it out of rage.
■ **Me da mucha rabia.** It's really annoying.
2 rabies *sing*
□ Vacunamos al perro contra la rabia. We had the dog vaccinated against rabies.

la **rabieta** NOUN
tantrum
■ **agarrarse una rabieta** to throw a tantrum

el **rabo** NOUN
tail

la **racha** NOUN
■ **una racha de buen tiempo** a spell of good weather
■ **una racha de viento** a gust of wind
■ **pasar una mala racha** to go through a bad patch

**racial** (FEM **racial**) ADJECTIVE
racial

el **racimo** NOUN
bunch (PL bunches)

la **ración** (PL las **raciones**) NOUN
portion

el **racismo** NOUN
racism

el/la **racista** ADJECTIVE, NOUN
racist

el **radar** NOUN
radar
■ **'velocidad controlada por radar'** 'radar speed checks in operation'

la **radiación** NOUN
radiation

la **radiactividad** NOUN
radioactivity

**radiactivo** (FEM **radiactiva**) ADJECTIVE
radioactive

el **radiador** NOUN
radiator

la **radio** NOUN
radio
□ Por la mañana escucho la radio. In the morning I listen to the radio.
■ **Lo oí por la radio.** I heard it on the radio.

el **radio** NOUN
1 radius (PL radii *o* radiuses)
□ La explosión se oyó en un radio de 50 kilómetros. The explosion could be heard within a 50-kilometre radius.
2 radio (*Latin America*)
3 spoke

el **radiocasete** NOUN
radio cassette player

la **radiografía** NOUN
X-ray
■ **Tengo que hacerme una radiografía.** I've got to have an X-ray.

el **radiotaxi** NOUN
radio taxi

el **raíl** NOUN
rail

la **raíz** (PL las **raíces**) NOUN
root
■ **La planta está echando raíces.** The plant's taking root.
■ **a raíz de** as a result of

la **raja** NOUN
1 crack
2 tear (*in fabric*)
3 slice

**rajarse** VERB [25]
1 to crack
2 to split

**rallar** VERB [25]
to grate

el **rally** (PL los **rallys**) NOUN
rally (PL rallies)

la **rama** NOUN
branch (PL branches)

el **ramo** NOUN
bunch (PL bunches)
□ un ramo de claveles a bunch of carnations
■ **el ramo textil** the textile industry

la **rampa** NOUN
ramp

la **rana** NOUN

frog
la **ranchera** NOUN
1 Mexican folk song
2 estate car
el **rancho** NOUN
ranch (PL ranches)
**rancio** (FEM **rancia**) ADJECTIVE
rancid
el **rango** NOUN
rank
■ **políticos de alto rango** high-ranking politicians
la **ranura** NOUN
slot
□ Introduzca la moneda en la ranura. Put the coin in the slot.
**rapar** VERB [25]
1 to crop
2 to shave
el **rape** NOUN
monkfish (PL monkfish)
**rápidamente** ADVERB
quickly
la **rapidez** NOUN
speed
■ **con rapidez** quickly
**rápido** (FEM **rápida**) ADJECTIVE
▷ see also **rápido** ADVERB
1 fast
□ un coche muy rápido a very fast car
2 quick
□ Fue una visita muy rápida. It was a very quick visit.
**rápido** ADVERB
▷ see also **rápido** ADJECTIVE
fast
□ Conduces demasiado rápido. You drive too fast.
■ **Lo hice tan rápido como pude.** I did it as quickly as I could.
■ **¡Rápido!** Hurry up!
**raptar** VERB [25]
to kidnap
el **rapto** NOUN
kidnapping
la **raqueta** NOUN
1 racket
2 bat
**raramente** ADVERB
rarely
**raro** (FEM **rara**) ADJECTIVE
1 strange
□ Tiene unas costumbres muy raras. He has some very strange habits.
■ **¡Qué raro!** How strange!
■ **Sabe un poco raro.** It tastes a bit funny.
2 rare
□ una especie muy rara a very rare species

256

■ **Es raro que haga tan buen tiempo.** It's unusual to have such good weather.
■ **rara vez** seldom
el **rascacielos** (PL los **rascacielos**) NOUN
skyscraper
**rascar\*** VERB [48]
1 to scratch
□ ¿Me rascas la espalda? Could you scratch my back for me?
2 to scrape
□ Tuvimos que rascar la pintura de la puerta. We had to scrape the paint off the door.
■ **rascarse** to scratch □ No deja de rascarse. He can't stop scratching.
**rasgar\*** VERB [37]
to rip
el **rasgo** NOUN
feature
□ Tiene unos rasgos muy delicados. He has very fine features.
el **rasguño** NOUN
scratch (PL scratches)
■ **Me he hecho un rasguño.** I've scratched myself.
el **rastrillo** NOUN
1 rake
2 razor (Mexico)
el **rastro** NOUN
1 trail
□ seguir el rastro de alguien to follow somebody's trail
2 trace
□ Desaparecieron sin dejar rastro. They vanished without trace.
3 fleamarket
**rasurarse** VERB [25] (Latin America)
to shave
la **rata** NOUN
rat
el **rato** NOUN
while
□ después de un rato after a while
■ **Estaba aquí hace un rato.** He was here a few minutes ago.
■ **al poco rato** shortly after
■ **pasar el rato** to while away the time
■ **pasar un buen rato** to have a good time
■ **Pasamos un mal rato.** We had a dreadful time.
■ **en mis ratos libres** in my free time
■ **Tengo para rato con esta redacción.** I've got a way to go yet with this essay.
■ **Tenemos para rato; el avión tiene retraso.** We'll be here for a while yet; the plane has been delayed.
el **ratón** (PL los **ratones**) NOUN
mouse (PL mice)
la **raya** NOUN

**1** line
- □ **trazar una raya** to draw a line
- ■ **pasarse de la raya** to overstep the mark

**2** stripe
- ■ **un jersey a rayas** a striped jumper

**3** parting
- □ **Me hago la raya en medio.** I have my parting in the middle.

**4** crease (PL creases)

**5** dash (PL dashes)

**rayar** VERB [25]
to scratch

el **rayo** NOUN

**1** lightning
- □ **Cayó un rayo en la torre de la iglesia.** The church tower was struck by lightning.

**2** ray
- □ **un rayo de luz** a ray of light □ **los rayos del sol** the sun's rays
- ■ **los rayos X** X-rays
- ■ **los rayos láser** laser beams

la **raza** NOUN

**1** race
- □ **la raza humana** the human race

**2** breed
- □ **¿De qué raza es tu gato?** What breed's your cat?
- ■ **un perro de raza** a pedigree dog

la **razón** (PL las **razones**) NOUN
reason
- □ **¿Cuál era la razón de su visita?** What was the reason for his visit?
- ■ **tener razón** to be right
- ■ **dar la razón a alguien** to agree that somebody is right
- ■ **no tener razón** to be wrong

**razonable** (FEM **razonable**) ADJECTIVE
reasonable

la **reacción** (PL las **reacciones**) NOUN
reaction

**reaccionar** VERB [25]
to react

el **reactor** NOUN

**1** jet plane

**2** jet engine
- ■ **un reactor nuclear** a nuclear reactor

**real** (FEM **real**) ADJECTIVE

**1** real
- □ **Esta vez el dolor era real.** This time the pain was real.
- ■ **La película está basada en hechos reales.** The film is based on actual events.

**2** royal
- □ **la familia real** the royal family

la **realidad** NOUN
reality (PL realities)
- ■ **en la realidad** in real life
- ■ **en realidad** actually □ **Parece mayor,**

pero en realidad es más joven que yo. He looks older but actually he's younger than I am.
- ■ **Mi sueño se hizo realidad.** My dream came true.
- ■ **realidad virtual** virtual reality

**realista** (FEM **realista**) ADJECTIVE
realistic

el **reality** (PL los **realitys**) NOUN
reality show

**realizar\*** VERB [13]

**1** to carry out
- □ **realizar una investigación** to carry out an investigation
- ■ **Has realizado un buen trabajo.** You've done a good job.

**2** to realize
- □ **Nunca realizó su sueño de dar la vuelta al mundo.** He never realized his dream of going round the world.
- ■ **realizarse** to come true □ **Su sueño nunca llegó a realizarse.** His dream never came true.

**realmente** ADVERB

**1** really
- □ **Fue una época realmente difícil.** It was a really difficult period.

**2** actually
- □ **No creí que realmente ganara.** I didn't think he would actually win.

la **rebaja** NOUN

**1** discount
- □ **Me hizo una rebaja por pagar al contado.** He gave me a discount for paying cash.

**2** reduction
- □ **La blusa tenía una mancha y pedí una rebaja.** There was a mark on the blouse so I asked for a reduction.
- ■ **las rebajas** the sales □ **las rebajas de enero** the January sales
- ■ **Todos los grandes almacenes están de rebajas.** There are sales on in all the department stores.

**rebajar** VERB [25]
to reduce
- □ **Han rebajado los abrigos.** Coats have been reduced. □ **Cada fin de temporada rebajan los precios.** Prices are reduced at the end of every season.
- ■ **rebajarse** to demean oneself □ **No quiere rebajarse a pedirme perdón.** He won't demean himself by apologizing to me.

la **rebanada** NOUN
slice
- □ **Cortó el pan en rebanadas.** He cut the bread into slices.

el **rebaño** NOUN
flock

□ un rebaño de ovejas  a flock of sheep

la **rebeca**  NOUN
cardigan

**rebelarse**  VERB [25]
to rebel
□ rebelarse contra alguien  to rebel against somebody

**rebelde**  (FEM **rebelde**)  ADJECTIVE
rebellious

el/la **rebelde**  NOUN
rebel

la **rebelión**  (PL las **rebeliones**)  NOUN
rebellion

**rebobinar**  VERB [25]
to rewind

**rebotar**  VERB [25]
to bounce
■ **La pelota rebotó en el poste.**  The ball bounced off the post.

**rebozado**  (FEM **rebozada**)  ADJECTIVE
1  breaded
2  battered

el **recado**  NOUN
1  message
□ Dejé recado de que me llamara.  I left a message for him to call me.
2  errand
□ Fui a hacer unos recados.  I went to do some errands.

la **recaída**  NOUN
relapse
□ sufrir una recaída  to have a relapse

**recalcar***  VERB [48]
to stress
□ Me gustaría recalcar que …  I'd like to stress that …

la **recámara**  NOUN  (Mexico)
bedroom

el **recambio**  NOUN
1  spare
□ la rueda de recambio  the spare wheel
■ **una pieza de recambio**  a spare part
2  refill

**recargar***  VERB [37]
1  to recharge
2  to fill up

el **recargo**  NOUN
■ **El taxista me cobró un recargo por el equipaje.**  The taxi driver charged me extra for my luggage.

**recaudar**  VERB [25]
to collect
□ Recaudó dinero para una ONG.  He collected money for an NGO.

la **recepción**  (PL las **recepciones**)  NOUN
reception

el/la **recepcionista**  NOUN
receptionist

el **receptor**  NOUN
receiver

la **recesión**  (PL las **recesiones**)  NOUN
recession

la **receta**  NOUN
1  recipe
□ Me dio la receta de los raviolis.  He gave me the recipe for the ravioli.
2  prescription
□ Los antibióticos sólo se venden con receta.  Antibiotics are only available on prescription.
 **LANGUAGE TIP** Be careful! **receta** does not mean **receipt**.

**recetar**  VERB [25]
to prescribe
□ Las enfermeras no pueden recetar medicamentos.  Nurses can't prescribe drugs.
■ **El médico me recetó un jarabe.**  The doctor gave me a prescription for cough syrup.

**rechazar***  VERB [13]
1  to reject
□ El director rechazó mi propuesta.  The manager rejected my proposal.
2  to turn down
□ Tuve que rechazar su oferta.  I had to turn down his offer.

**rechoncho**  (FEM **rechoncha**)  ADJECTIVE
stocky

el **recibidor**  NOUN
entrance hall

**recibir**  VERB [58]
1  to receive
□ No he recibido tu carta.  I haven't received your letter.
■ **Recibí muchos regalos.**  I got a lot of presents.
2  to meet
□ Vinieron a recibirnos al aeropuerto.  They came and met us at the airport.
■ **El director me recibió en su despacho.**  The manager saw me in his office.

el **recibo**  NOUN
1  receipt
□ No se admiten devoluciones sin recibo.  No refunds will be given without a receipt.
2  bill
□ pagar el recibo del teléfono  to pay the telephone bill

el **reciclaje**  NOUN
recycling

**reciclar**  VERB [25]
to recycle

**recién**  ADVERB
just
□ El comedor está recién pintado.  The

r

dining room has just been painted.
- **Recién se fueron.** *(Latin America)* They've just left.
- **los recién casados** the newly-weds
- **un recién nacido** a newborn baby
- **'recién pintado'** 'wet paint'

**reciente** (FEM **reciente**) ADJECTIVE
recent
- **pan reciente** fresh bread

**recientemente** ADVERB
recently

el **recipiente** NOUN
container

el **recital** NOUN
recital
□ dar un recital de piano to give a piano recital

**recitar** VERB [25]
to recite

la **reclamación** (PL las **reclamaciones**) NOUN
complaint
□ presentar una reclamación to make a complaint
- **el libro de reclamaciones** the complaints' book

**reclamar** VERB [25]
1 to complain
□ Fui a reclamar al director. I went and complained to the manager.
2 to demand
□ Reclaman mejores condiciones de trabajo. They're demanding better working conditions.

el **reclamo** NOUN *(Latin America)*
complaint

el/la **recluta** NOUN
recruit

el **recogedor** NOUN
dustpan

**recoger*** VERB [7]
1 to pick up
□ Se agachó para recoger la cuchara. He bent down to pick up the spoon. □ Recogí el papel del suelo. I picked the paper up off the floor. □ Me recogieron en la estación. They picked me up at the station.
- **recoger fruta** to pick fruit
2 to collect
□ A las diez recogen la basura. The rubbish gets collected at ten o'clock.
3 to clear up
□ Recógelo todo antes de marcharte. Clear up everything before you leave.
- **Recogí los platos y los puse en el fregadero.** I cleared away the plates and put them in the sink.
- **recoger la mesa** to clear the table

la **recogida** NOUN
collection
□ la recogida de basuras the refuse collection □ el horario de recogida del correo the mail collection times
- **recogida de equipajes** baggage reclaim

la **recomendación** (PL las **recomendaciones**) NOUN
1 recommendation
□ Fuimos a ese restaurante por recomendación de un amigo. We went to that restaurant on the recommendation of a friend.
- **una carta de recomendación** a letter of recommendation
2 advice
□ Hago régimen por recomendación del médico. I'm on a diet on my doctor's advice.

**recomendar*** VERB [39]
to recommend

la **recompensa** NOUN
reward
□ Ofrecen una recompensa de mil euros. They're offering a thousand-euro reward.

**reconciliarse** VERB [25]
- **reconciliarse con alguien** to make it up with somebody □ Riñeron, pero ya se han reconciliado. They had a row but they've made it up again.

**reconocer*** VERB [12]
1 to recognize
□ No te había reconocido con ese sombrero. I didn't recognize you in that hat.
2 to admit
□ Reconócelo, ha sido culpa tuya. Admit it, it was your fault.

el **reconocimiento** NOUN
checkup
□ hacerse un reconocimiento médico to have a checkup

la **reconquista** NOUN
reconquest

**reconstruir*** VERB [10]
to rebuild

el **récord** (PL los **récords**) NOUN
record
□ Posee el récord mundial de salto de altura. He holds the world record in the high jump.
- **batir el récord** to break the record
- **establecer un récord** to set a record

**recordar*** VERB [25]
1 to remember
□ No recuerdo dónde lo puse. I can't remember where I put it.
2 to remind
□ Recuérdame que hable con Daniel. Remind me to speak to Daniel. □ Me

recuerda a su padre. He reminds me of his father.

*LANGUAGE TIP* Be careful! **recordar** does not mean **to record**.

**recorrer** VERB [8]
**1** to travel around
□ Recorrimos Francia en moto. We travelled around France on a motorbike.
**2** to do
□ Ese día recorrimos 100 kilómetros. We did 100 kilometres that day.

el **recorrido** NOUN
■ **¿Qué recorrido hace este autobús?** Which route does this bus take?
■ **un recorrido turístico** a tour
■ **un tren de largo recorrido** an inter-city train

**recortar** VERB [25]
to cut out
□ Recorté el artículo para enseñárselo a Pedro. I cut the article out to show it to Pedro.
■ **recortar gastos** to cut costs

el **recorte** NOUN
■ **recortes de prensa** press cuttings
■ **recortes de personal** staff cutbacks

**recostarse*** VERB [11]
to lie down
□ Se recostó en el sofá. He lay down on the settee.

el **recreo** NOUN
break
□ Tenemos 20 minutos de recreo. We have a 20-minute break.
■ **Salimos al recreo a las 11.** We have a break at 11 o'clock.
■ **la hora del recreo** playtime

la **recta** NOUN
straight line
■ **la recta final** the home straight

**rectangular** (FEM **rectangular**) ADJECTIVE
rectangular

el **rectángulo** NOUN
rectangle

**recto** (FEM **recta**) ADJECTIVE, ADVERB
straight
□ una línea recta a straight line □ Mantén la espalda recta. Keep your back straight.
■ **todo recto** straight on □ Siga todo recto. Go straight on.

el **recuadro** NOUN
box (PL boxes)

**recuerdo** VERB ▷ see **recordar**

el **recuerdo** NOUN
**1** memory (PL memories)
□ Me trae buenos recuerdos. It brings back happy memories.
**2** souvenir

□ una tienda de recuerdos a souvenir shop
■ **un recuerdo de familia** a family heirloom
■ **¡Recuerdos a tu madre!** Give my regards to your mother!
■ **Dale recuerdos de mi parte.** Give him my regards.

la **recuperación** (PL las **recuperaciones**)
NOUN
**1** recovery
**2** resit

**recuperar** VERB [25]
to get back
□ Tardé unos minutos en recuperar el aliento. It took me a few minutes to get my breath back.
■ **recuperar fuerzas** to get one's strength back
■ **recuperarse de 1** to get over □ Tardé una semana en recuperarme de la gripe. It took me a week to get over my flu. **2** to recover from □ Se está recuperando de la operación. He's recovering from the operation.
■ **recuperar el tiempo perdido** to make up for lost time

**recurrir** VERB [58]
■ **recurrir a algo** to resort to something
□ Hay que evitar recurrir a la violencia. We must avoid resorting to violence.
■ **recurrir a alguien** to turn to somebody
□ ¿A quién puedo recurrir? Who can I turn to?

el **recurso** NOUN
■ **como último recurso** as a last resort
■ **recursos** resources □ recursos naturales natural resources

la **red** NOUN
**1** net
□ una red de pesca a fishing net □ La pelota dio contra la red. The ball went into the net.
**2** network
□ una red informática a computer network
■ **la Red** the Net
■ **una red de tiendas** a chain of shops

la **redacción** (PL las **redacciones**) NOUN
essay (PL essays)
■ **hacer una redacción sobre algo** to do an essay on something
■ **el equipo de redacción** the editorial staff

**redactar** VERB [25]
to write
□ redactar un artículo de periódico to write a newspaper article

el **redactor**, la **redactora** NOUN
editor
□ el redactor deportivo the sports editor
□ la redactora jefe the editor in chief

la **redada** NOUN
  raid
  □ Fue detenido en una redada policial. He was arrested during a police raid.
  ■ **La policía hizo una redada en el club.** The police raided the club.

**redondo** (FEM **redonda**) ADJECTIVE
  round
  □ una mesa redonda  a round table
  ■ **Todo salió redondo.** Everything worked out perfectly.

la **reducción** (PL las **reducciones**) NOUN
  reduction

**reducir*** VERB [9]
1 to reduce
  □ Reduzca la velocidad.  Reduce speed.
2 to cut
  □ Van a reducir personal.  They're going to cut staff.

**reembolsar** VERB [25]
  to refund

el **reembolso** NOUN
  refund
  □ Cancelaron la excursión y nos hicieron un reembolso. They cancelled the trip and gave us a refund.
  ■ **enviar algo contra reembolso** to send something cash on delivery

**reemplazar*** VERB [13]
  to replace

la **referencia** NOUN
  reference
  □ un punto de referencia  a point of reference
  ■ **con referencia a** with reference to
  ■ **hacer referencia a** to refer to
  ■ **referencias** references  □ La niñera traía muy buenas referencias. The nanny had very good references.

el **referéndum** (PL los **referéndums**) NOUN
  referendum (PL referenda *o* referendums)

**referente** (FEM **referente**) ADJECTIVE
  ■ **referente a** concerning  □ el párrafo referente al uniforme escolar  the paragraph concerning school uniform

**referirse*** VERB [51]
  ■ **referirse a** to refer to  □ ¿Te refieres a mí? Are you referring to me?
  ■ **¿A qué te refieres? 1** What exactly do you mean? **2** What are you referring to?

la **refinería** NOUN
  refinery (PL refineries)

**refiriendo** VERB ▷ *see* referir

**reflejar** VERB [25]
  to reflect

el **reflejo** NOUN
  reflection
  □ el reflejo de la luna en el lago  the reflection of the moon in the lake
  ■ **reflejos** reflexes  □ Estás bien de reflejos. You have good reflexes.

la **reflexión** (PL las **reflexiones**) NOUN
  reflection

**reflexionar** VERB [25]
  to think
  □ Hace las cosas sin reflexionar. He does things without thinking.  □ reflexionar sobre algo  to think about something
  ■ **Reflexiona bien antes de tomar una decisión.** Think it over carefully before taking a decision.

**reflexivo** (FEM **reflexiva**) ADJECTIVE
  reflexive

la **reforma** NOUN
1 reform
  □ la reforma educativa  the education reforms *pl*
2 alteration
  □ Estamos haciendo reformas en el piso. We're having alterations made to the flat.
  ■ **'Cerrado por reformas'** 'Closed for refurbishment'

**reformar** VERB [25]
1 to reform
2 to do up

el **refrán** (PL los **refranes**) NOUN
  saying

**refrescante** (FEM **refrescante**) ADJECTIVE
  refreshing

**refrescar*** VERB [48]
  to get cooler
  ■ **refrescarse** to freshen up

el **refresco** NOUN
  soft drink

el **refrigerador** NOUN
  fridge

el **refugiado**, la **refugiada** NOUN
  refugee

**refugiarse** VERB [25]
1 to shelter
  □ Nos refugiamos de la lluvia en un portal. We sheltered from the rain in a doorway.
2 to take refuge
  □ La gente se refugiaba en los sótanos. People took refuge in the cellars.

el **refugio** NOUN
  refuge
  □ un refugio de montaña  a mountain refuge
  ■ **Los montañeros buscaron refugio en una cueva.** The climbers sheltered in a cave.
  ■ **un refugio antiaéreo** an air-raid shelter

la **regadera** NOUN
1 watering can
2 shower (*Mexico*)
  ■ **estar como una regadera** to be as mad

r

as a hatter
**regalar** VERB [25]
**1** to give
□ ¿Y si le regalamos un libro? What about giving him a book?
■ **Ayer fue mi cumpleaños. — ¿Qué te regalaron?** It was my birthday yesterday. — What did you get?
**2** to give away
□ La tele vieja la vamos a regalar. We're going to give the old TV away.
el **regaliz** NOUN
liquorice
el **regalo** NOUN
present
□ hacer un regalo a alguien to give somebody a present
■ **una tienda de regalos** a gift shop
■ **papel de regalo** wrapping paper
■ **de regalo** free □ Te dan un CD de regalo. They give you a free CD.
**regañadientes**
■ **a regañadientes** ADVERB reluctantly
**regañar** VERB [25]
to tell off
□ La maestra me regañó por llegar tarde. The teacher told me off for being late.
**regar\*** VERB [34]
to water
la **regata** NOUN
yacht race
**regatear** VERB [25]
**1** to haggle
□ Regateaban por el precio de la alfombra. They were haggling over the price of the carpet.
**2** to dodge past
□ Regateó a varios defensas. He dodged past several defenders.
el **régimen** (PL los **regímenes**) NOUN
**1** diet
■ **estar a régimen** to be on a diet
■ **ponerse a régimen** to go on a diet
**2** regime
□ un régimen comunista a communist regime
el **regimiento** NOUN
regiment
la **región** (PL las **regiones**) NOUN
region
**regional** (FEM **regional**) ADJECTIVE
regional
**registrar** VERB [25]
**1** to search
□ Estuvieron registrando la casa. They were searching the house. □ Me registraron. They searched me.
**2** to register

□ Tienes que registrarte en el consulado. You have to register at the consulate.
**3** to check in
□ Fui a recepción a registrarme. I went to reception to check in.
■ **Me registré en el hotel.** I checked into the hotel.
el **registro** NOUN
**1** search (PL searches)
■ **realizar un registro en un lugar** to carry out a search of a place
**2** register
■ **el registro civil** the registry office
la **regla** NOUN
**1** rule
□ saltarse las reglas to break the rules
**2** period
□ Estoy con la regla. I've got my period.
**3** ruler
□ Trazó la línea con una regla. He drew the line with a ruler.
■ **por regla general** generally
■ **tener todo en regla** to have everything in order
el **reglamento** NOUN
regulations pl
□ El reglamento no lo permite. The regulations don't allow it.
**regresar** VERB [25]
**1** to go back
□ Paco regresó a casa por el paraguas. Paco went back home for his umbrella.
**2** to come back
□ Regresaré sobre las ocho. I'll come back at about eight.
■ **Regresamos tarde.** We got back late.
**3** to give back (Latin America)
■ **regresarse 1** (Latin America) to go back **2** (Latin America) to come back
el **regreso** NOUN
return
■ **a nuestro regreso** on our return
■ **de regreso** on the way back □ De regreso paramos a comer en Ávila. On the way back we stopped to have lunch in Ávila.
**regulable** (FEM **regulable**) ADJECTIVE
adjustable
**regular** (FEM **regular**) ADJECTIVE
▷ see also **regular** ADVERB
regular
□ un verbo regular a regular verb □ a intervalos regulares at regular intervals
■ **La obra estuvo regular.** The play was pretty ordinary.
**regular** ADVERB
▷ see also **regular** ADJECTIVE
■ **El examen me fue regular.** My exam didn't go brilliantly.

■ **¿Cómo te encuentras?** — **Regular.**
How are you? — Not too bad.
**rehacer\*** VERB [26]
to redo
el/la **rehén** (PL los/las **rehenes**) NOUN
hostage
la **reina** NOUN
queen
el **reinado** NOUN
reign
el **reino** NOUN
kingdom
el **Reino Unido** NOUN
the United Kingdom
**reír\*** VERB [44]
to laugh
□ No te rías. Don't laugh.
■ **echarse a reír** to burst out laughing
■ **Siempre nos reímos con él.** We always
have a good laugh with him.
■ **reírse** to laugh
■ **reírse de** to laugh at □ ¿De qué te ríes?
What are you laughing at?
la **reivindicación** (PL las
**reivindicaciones**) NOUN
claim
□ reivindicaciones salariales wage claims
la **reja** NOUN
grille
□ La puerta de la joyería está protegida con
una reja. The door to the jeweller's is
protected with a grille.
■ **estar entre rejas** to be behind bars
la **relación** (PL las **relaciones**) NOUN
1 link
□ la relación entre el tabaco y el cáncer the
link between smoking and cancer
2 relationship
□ Tenemos una relación de amistad. We
have a friendly relationship.
■ **las relaciones entre empresarios y
trabajadores** the relationship between
employers and workers
■ **con relación a** in relation to
■ **relaciones públicas** public relations
■ **relaciones sexuales** sexual relations
**relacionar** VERB [25]
to link
□ Los expertos relacionan el tabaco con el
cáncer. The experts link smoking with
cancer.
■ **Le gusta relacionarse con niños
mayores que él.** He likes mixing with older
children.
■ **No se relaciona mucho con la gente.**
He doesn't mix much.
**relajado** (FEM **relajada**) ADJECTIVE
1 relaxed

□ ¿Estás relajado? Are you feeling relaxed?
2 laid-back
□ Es un tipo muy relajado. He's a very laid-
back guy.
**relajante** (FEM **relajante**) ADJECTIVE
relaxing
**relajar** VERB [25]
to relax
□ Relaja los músculos. Relax your muscles.
□ ¡Relájate! Relax!
■ **La música clásica me relaja mucho.** I
find classical music really relaxing.
el **relámpago** NOUN
flash of lightning (PL flashes of lightning)
□ Vimos varios relámpagos. We saw several
flashes of lightning.
■ **No me gustan los relámpagos.** I don't
like lightning.
**relativamente** ADVERB
relatively
**relativo** (FEM **relativa**) ADJECTIVE
relative
□ un pronombre relativo a relative pronoun
□ Eso es muy relativo. That's all relative.
■ **en lo relativo a** concerning
el **relato** NOUN
story
el **relevo** NOUN
■ **una carrera de relevos** a relay race
■ **tomar el relevo a alguien** to take over
from somebody
la **religión** (PL las **religiones**) NOUN
religion
**religioso** (FEM **religiosa**) ADJECTIVE
religious
el **rellano** NOUN
landing
**rellenar** VERB [25]
1 to stuff
□ Rellene los pimientos con el arroz. Stuff
the peppers with the rice.
2 to fill in
□ Rellene este impreso, por favor. Can you
fill in this form please.
**relleno** (FEM **rellena**) ADJECTIVE
stuffed
□ aceitunas rellenas stuffed olives
■ **relleno de algo** filled with something
el **reloj** NOUN
1 clock
□ El reloj de la cocina va atrasado. The
kitchen clock's slow.
■ **un reloj despertador** an alarm clock
■ **un reloj de cuco** a cuckoo clock
■ **contra reloj** against the clock
2 watch (PL watches)
□ Se me ha parado el reloj. My watch has
stopped.

r

- **un reloj digital** a digital watch
- **un reloj sumergible** a waterproof watch
- **El horno tiene un reloj automático.** The cooker has an automatic timer.
- **un reloj de sol** a sundial

la **relojera** NOUN
watchmaker

la **relojería** NOUN
watchmaker's (PL watchmakers' shops)

el **relojero** NOUN
watchmaker

**relucir\*** VERB
to shine

**remar** VERB [25]
1 to paddle
2 to row

**remediar** VERB [25]
to solve
□ Con llorar no vas a remediar nada. You're not going to solve anything by crying.
- **Me eché a reír, no lo pude remediar.** I began to laugh, I couldn't help it.

el **remedio** NOUN
remedy (PL remedies)
□ un remedio contra la tos  a cough remedy
□ un remedio casero  a household remedy
- **No tuve más remedio que hacerlo.** I had no choice but to do it.

el **remite** NOUN
name and address of sender

el/la **remitente** NOUN
sender

el **remo** NOUN
1 oar
2 rowing

**remojar** VERB [25]
to soak

el **remojo** NOUN
- **poner algo en remojo** to leave something to soak

la **remolacha** NOUN
beetroot

**remolcar\*** VERB [48]
to tow

el **remolque** NOUN
trailer

el **remordimiento** NOUN
remorse *sing*
□ No siente remordimientos por lo que ha hecho. He feels no remorse for what he has done.

**remoto** (FEM **remota**) ADJECTIVE
remote

**remover\*** VERB [33]
1 to stir
2 to toss
3 to turn over

264  el **renacuajo** NOUN

tadpole

el **rencor** NOUN
ill-feeling
□ Existe mucho rencor entre los dos. There's a lot of ill-feeling between the two of them.
- **guardar rencor a alguien** to bear a grudge against somebody □ No le guardo rencor. I don't bear him a grudge.

**rencoroso** (FEM **rencorosa**) ADJECTIVE
- **No soy rencoroso.** I don't bear grudges.

**rendido** (FEM **rendida**) ADJECTIVE
worn out
□ Estaba rendido de tanto andar.  I was worn out after so much walking.

la **rendija** NOUN
1 crack
2 gap

el **rendimiento** NOUN
performance

**rendir\*** VERB [38]
- **Este negocio no rinde.** This business doesn't pay.
- **El dinero rinde poco en una cuenta corriente.** You don't get much interest on your money in a current account.
- **rendirse 1** to give up □ No sé la respuesta; me rindo. I don't know the answer; I give up. **2** to surrender □ El enemigo se rindió. The enemy surrendered.

el **renglón** (PL los **renglones**) NOUN
line

el **reno** NOUN
reindeer (PL reindeer o reindeers)

**renovable** (FEM **renovable**) ADJECTIVE
renewable

**renovar\*** VERB [11]
1 to renew
□ Tengo que renovarme el pasaporte. I must renew my passport.
2 to renovate
□ Van a renovar la fachada del edificio. They're going to renovate the front of the building.
3 to change
□ Han renovado el mobiliario de la casa. They've changed the furniture in the house.

la **renta** NOUN
1 income
2 rent

**rentable** (FEM **rentable**) ADJECTIVE
profitable
□ No es rentable hacer el viaje en coche. It isn't profitable to make the journey by car.
- **una fábrica poco rentable** an uneconomic factory

**rentar** VERB [25] *(Mexico)*

r

**reñido** (FEM **reñida**) ADJECTIVE
hard-fought

**reñir\*** VERB [45]
1 to tell somebody off
□ No le riñas, la culpa no es suya. Don't tell her off, it's not her fault.
2 to quarrel
□ Mi hermana y yo siempre estábamos riñendo. My sister and I were always quarrelling.
3 to fall out
□ Ángeles y Manolo han reñido. Ángeles and Manolo have fallen out. □ Ha reñido con su novio. She has fallen out with her boyfriend.

la **reparación** (PL las **reparaciones**) NOUN
repair

■ 'reparaciones en el acto' 'repairs while you wait'

**reparar** VERB [25]
to repair

**repartir** VERB [58]
1 to hand out
□ El profesor repartió los exámenes. The teacher handed out the examination papers.
2 to share out
□ Nos repartimos el dinero. We shared out the money.
3 to deliver
□ Repartimos pizzas a domicilio. We deliver pizzas.
4 to deal

el **reparto** NOUN
1 delivery (PL deliveries)
■ reparto a domicilio home delivery service
2 cast
□ un reparto estelar a star cast

**repasar** VERB [25]
1 to check
□ Repasé la declaración antes de firmarla. I checked the statement before signing it.
2 to revise
■ repasar para un examen to revise for an exam

el **repaso** NOUN
revision
■ Tengo que darles un repaso a los apuntes. I must revise my notes.

el **repelente** NOUN
repellent

el/la **repelente** NOUN
know-all

**repente** ADVERB
■ de repente suddenly

**repentino** (FEM **repentina**) ADJECTIVE
sudden

el **repertorio** NOUN
repertoire

la **repetición** (PL las **repeticiones**) NOUN
repetition

**repetidamente** ADVERB
repeatedly

**repetir\*** VERB [38]
1 to repeat
□ ¿Podría repetirlo, por favor? Could you repeat that, please?
2 to have a second helping
□ El arroz está tan bueno que voy a repetir. The rice is so good that I'm going to have a second helping.

**repetitivo** (FEM **repetitiva**) ADJECTIVE
repetitive

la **repisa** NOUN
shelf (PL shelves)
■ la repisa de la chimenea the mantelpiece

LANGUAGE TIP Word for word, **repisa de la chimenea** means 'shelf of the chimney'.

**repitiendo** VERB ▷ see **repetir**

el **repollo** NOUN
cabbage

el **reportaje** NOUN
1 documentary (PL documentaries)
2 article

el **reposacabezas** (PL los **reposacabezas**) NOUN
headrest

la **reposición** (PL las **reposiciones**) NOUN
1 repeat (in television)
2 revival (in theatre)

**repostar** VERB [25]
to refuel

la **repostería** NOUN
confectionery

la **representación** (PL las **representaciones**) NOUN
performance

el/la **representante** NOUN
1 representative
2 agent

**representar** VERB [25]
1 to represent
□ La representaba su abogado. Her lawyer was representing her.
2 to put on
□ Los niños van a representar una obra de teatro. The children are going to put on a play.
3 to play
□ Representa el papel de Don Juan. He's playing the part of Don Juan.
■ Tiene cuarenta años pero no los

**representa.** He's forty but he doesn't look it.

**representativo** (FEM **representativa**) ADJECTIVE
representative

el **reprimido** (FEM la **reprimida**) ADJECTIVE, NOUN
■ **Es una reprimida.** She's repressed.

**reprobar\*** VERB [11] (Latin America)
to fail
□ Le reprobaron en matemáticas. He failed maths.

**reprochar** VERB [25]
■ **Me reprochó que no la hubiera invitado.** He reproached me for not having invited her.

la **reproducción** (PL las **reproducciones**) NOUN
reproduction

**reproducirse\*** VERB [9]
to reproduce

el **reproductor** NOUN
■ **un reproductor de CD** a CD player

el **reptil** NOUN
reptile

la **república** NOUN
republic

la **República Dominicana** NOUN
the Dominican Republic

el **republicano** (FEM la **republicana**) ADJECTIVE, NOUN
republican

el **repuesto** NOUN
spare part
■ **de repuesto** spare □ la rueda de repuesto the spare wheel

**repugnante** (FEM **repugnante**) ADJECTIVE
revolting

la **reputación** (PL las **reputaciones**) NOUN
reputation
■ **tener buena reputación** to have a good reputation

el **requesón** NOUN
cottage cheese

el **requisito** NOUN
requirement
□ Cumple todos los requisitos para el puesto. He satisfies all the requirements for the job.

la **resaca** NOUN
hangover
■ **tener resaca** to have a hangover

**resaltar** VERB [25]
1  to stand out
□ Lo escribí en mayúsculas para que resaltara. I wrote it in capitals to make it stand out.
2  to highlight

□ El conferenciante resaltó el problema del paro. The speaker highlighted the problem of unemployment.

**resbaladizo** (FEM **resbaladiza**) ADJECTIVE
slippery

**resbalar** VERB [25]
1  to be slippery
□ Ten cuidado que este suelo resbala. Be careful, this floor's slippery.
2  to skid
□ El coche resbaló y casi nos estrellamos. The car skidded and we almost crashed.
■ **resbalarse** to slip □ Me resbalé con el hielo de la acera. I slipped on the icy pavement.

**rescatar** VERB [25]
to rescue

el **rescate** NOUN
1  rescue
□ un equipo de rescate a rescue team
2  ransom
■ **pedir un rescate por alguien** to hold somebody to ransom

el/la **reserva** NOUN
reserve

la **reserva** NOUN
1  reservation
□ He hecho una reserva en el Hilton para dos noches. I've made a reservation at the Hilton for two nights.
■ **Tengo mis reservas al respecto.** I've got reservations about it.
2  reserve
□ una reserva natural a nature reserve
□ El país tiene abundantes reservas de trigo. The country has got plentiful reserves of wheat.

**reservado** (FEM **reservada**) ADJECTIVE
reserved

**reservar** VERB [25]
to reserve

**resfriado** (FEM **resfriada**) ADJECTIVE
■ **estar resfriado** to have a cold □ No fui porque estaba muy resfriado. I didn't go because I had a bad cold.

el **resfriado** NOUN
cold
■ **agarrarse un resfriado** to catch a cold

**resfriarse\*** VERB [21]
to catch a cold

el **resguardo** NOUN
1  ticket
2  receipt

la **residencia** NOUN
residence
□ un permiso de residencia a residence permit □ La reunión tuvo lugar en la residencia del primer ministro. The

meeting took place at the prime minister's residence.

■ **una residencia de ancianos** an old people's home

■ **una residencia de estudiantes** a hall of residence

■ **una residencia sanitaria** a hospital

**residencial** (FEM **residencial**) ADJECTIVE
residential

□ una zona residencial a residential area

los **residuos** NOUN
waste *sing*

□ residuos radiactivos radioactive waste

la **resistencia** NOUN
resistance

□ Los manifestantes no ofrecieron resistencia. The demonstrators didn't offer any resistance.

■ **resistencia física** stamina

**resistente** (FEM **resistente**) ADJECTIVE
tough

□ El diamante es una piedra muy resistente. Diamond is a very tough stone.

■ **resistente al calor** heat-resistant

**resistir** VERB [58]

1 to resist
□ No pude resistir la tentación. I couldn't resist the temptation.

2 to take
□ Esta caja no va a resistir tanto peso. This box won't take so much weight.

3 to stand
□ No puedo resistir este frío. I can't stand this cold.

■ **Se resisten a cooperar.** They are refusing to cooperate.

**resolver\*** VERB [33]
to solve

**respaldar** VERB [25]
to back up

□ Mis hermanos me respaldaron. My brothers and sisters backed me up.

el **respaldo** NOUN
back

**respectivamente** ADVERB
respectively

**respecto** NOUN

■ **con respecto a** with regard to

**respetable** (FEM **respetable**) ADJECTIVE
respectable

**respetar** VERB [25]

1 to respect

2 to obey
□ No se respetan las normas de seguridad. The safety regulations aren't being obeyed.

el **respeto** NOUN
respect

□ el respeto a los animales respect for animals

■ **tener respeto a alguien** to respect somebody

■ **No le faltes al respeto.** Don't be disrespectful to him.

la **respiración** NOUN
breathing

□ Tenía la respiración irregular. His breathing was irregular.

■ **quedarse sin respiración** to be out of breath

■ **la respiración boca a boca** the kiss of life
□ Le hicieron la respiración boca a boca. They gave him the kiss of life.

■ **la respiración artificial** artificial respiration

**respirar** VERB [25]
to breathe

**responder** VERB [8]

1 to answer
□ Eso no responde a mi pregunta. That doesn't answer my question.

2 to reply
□ No han respondido a mi carta. They haven't replied to my letter. □ Respondió que ya habían salido. He replied that they had already gone out.

3 to respond
□ No responde al tratamiento. He's not responding to the treatment.

la **responsabilidad** NOUN
responsibility (PL responsibilities)

**responsable** (FEM **responsable**) ADJECTIVE
responsible

□ Cada cual es responsable de sus acciones. Everybody is responsible for their own actions.

el/la **responsable** NOUN

■ **Tú eres la responsable de lo ocurrido.** You're responsible for what happened.

■ **Los responsables serán castigados.** Those responsible will be punished.

■ **Juan es el responsable de la cocina.** Juan is in charge of the kitchen.

la **respuesta** NOUN
answer

**resquebrajarse** VERB [25]
to crack

la **resta** NOUN
subtraction

**restante** (FEM **restante**) ADJECTIVE
remaining

**restar** VERB [25]
to subtract

□ Está aprendiendo a restar. He's learning to subtract.

■ **Tienes que restar 16 de 36.** You have to take 16 away from 36.

r

la **restauración** (PL las **restauraciones**)
NOUN
restoration

el **restaurante** NOUN
restaurant

**restaurar** VERB [25]
to restore

el **resto** NOUN
rest
□ Yo haré el resto. I'll do the rest.
■ **los restos 1** the leftovers **2** the wreckage
*sing*

**restregar*** VERB [37]
to rub
□ Cuando tiene sueño se restriega los ojos.
He rubs his eyes when he's sleepy.

la **restricción** (PL las **restricciones**) NOUN
restriction

**resuelto** VERB ▷ *see* **resolver**

**resuelvo** VERB ▷ *see* **resolver**

el **resultado** NOUN
**1** result
**2** score
■ **dar resultado** to work □ Nuestro plan no
dio resultado. Our plan didn't work.

**resultar** VERB [25]
to turn out
□ Al final resultó que él tenía razón. In the
end it turned out that he was right.
■ **Me resultó violento decírselo.** I found it
embarrassing to tell him.

el **resumen** (PL los **resúmenes**) NOUN
summary (PL summaries)
□ un resumen de las noticias a news
summary
■ **hacer un resumen de algo** to
summarize something
■ **en resumen** in short

**resumir** VERB [58]
to summarize
■ **Dijo, resumiendo, que el viaje había
sido un desastre.** He said, in short, that the
trip had been a disaster.

**retar** VERB [25]
**1** to challenge
**2** to tell off (*Chile, River Plate*)

**retirar** VERB [25]
**1** to take away
□ La camarera retiró las copas. The waitress
took the glasses away. □ Le han retirado el
permiso de conducir. He's had his driving
licence taken away.
**2** to withdraw
□ Fui a retirar dinero de la cuenta. I went to
withdraw some money from my account.
□ Se retiraron del torneo. They withdrew
from the tournament.
■ **retirarse** to retire □ Mi padre se retira el

año que viene. My father will be retiring
next year.

el **reto** NOUN
challenge

**retorcer*** VERB
to twist
□ Me retorció el brazo. He twisted my arm.
■ **retorcerse de risa** to double up with
laughter

la **retransmisión** (PL las **retransmisiones**)
NOUN
broadcast
□ una retransmisión en directo a live
broadcast

**retransmitir** VERB [58]
to broadcast

**retrasado** (FEM **retrasada**) ADJECTIVE
**1** behind
□ Voy retrasado con este trabajo. I'm
behind with this work.
**2** slow
□ Este reloj va retrasado veinte minutos.
This clock is twenty minutes slow.
■ **Tienen un hijo un poco retrasado.**
They've got a son with learning difficulties.

**retrasar** VERB [25]
**1** to postpone
□ Retrasaron la boda al quince. They
postponed the wedding until the fifteenth.
**2** to delay
□ El mal tiempo retrasó nuestro vuelo. Our
flight was delayed due to bad weather.
**3** to put back
□ A las dos hay que retrasar los relojes una
hora. At two o'clock the clocks have to be
put back one hour.
■ **retrasarse** to be late □ El tren de las
nueve se retrasó. The nine o'clock train was
late.
■ **Tu reloj se retrasa.** Your watch is slow.

el **retraso** NOUN
delay (PL delays)
□ La niebla causó algunos retrasos. The fog
caused some delays.
■ **Perdonad por el retraso.** Sorry I'm late.
■ **ir con retraso** to be running late
■ **llegar con retraso** to be late □ El vuelo
llegó con una hora de retraso. The flight was
an hour late.

el **retrato** NOUN
portrait
■ **hacer un retrato a alguien** to paint
somebody's portrait

el **retrete** NOUN
toilet

**retroceder** VERB [8]
to go back

el **retrovisor** NOUN

r

rear-view mirror
**retuerzo** VERB ▷ *see* **retorcer**
el **reúma** NOUN
rheumatism
la **reunión** (PL las **reuniones**) NOUN
1 meeting
□ Mañana tenemos una reunión. We've got a meeting tomorrow.
2 gathering
□ una reunión familiar a family gathering
**reunir*** VERB [46]
1 to gather together
□ La maestra reunió a los niños en el patio. The teacher gathered the children together in the playground.
2 to satisfy
□ Paula reúne los requisitos para el puesto. Paula satisfies all the requirements for the job.
3 to raise
□ Estamos reuniendo dinero para el viaje. We're raising money for the trip.
■ **reunirse 1** to gather □ Miles de personas se reunieron en la plaza. Thousands of people gathered in the square. **2** to get together □ En Navidad nos reunimos toda la familia. The whole family gets together at Christmas. **3** to meet □ El comité se reúne una vez al mes. The committee meets once a month.
**revelar** VERB [25]
1 to develop
□ Luis revela sus propias fotos. Luis develops his own photos.
■ **Todavía no hemos revelado las fotos.** We haven't had the photos developed yet.
■ **Llevé los carretes a revelar.** I took the films to be developed.
2 to reveal
□ No quería revelar su identidad. He didn't want to reveal his identity.
**reventar*** VERB [39]
to burst
■ **Me revienta tener que ponerme corbata.** I hate having to wear a tie.
el **revés** (PL los **reveses**) NOUN
backhand
■ **al revés 1** the other way round □ ¿Tres, tres, dos? — No, al revés: dos, dos, tres. Three, three, two? — No, the other way round: two, two, three. **2** inside out □ Te has puesto los calcetines al revés. You've put your socks on inside out. **3** back to front □ Miré el cuello y vi que llevaba el jersey al revés. I looked at the collar and realized that I had my jumper on back to front. **4** upside down □ El dibujo está al revés. The picture's upside down.

**reviento** VERB ▷ *see* **reventar**
**revisar** VERB [25]
1 to check
□ Un electricista me revisó la instalación. An electrician checked the wiring for me.
■ **Tengo que ir a que me revisen el coche.** I must take my car for a service.
2 to search *(Latin America)*
la **revisión** (PL las **revisiones**) NOUN
service
□ He llevado el coche a revisión. I've taken the car for a service.
■ **una revisión médica** a checkup
el **revisor**, la **revisora** NOUN
ticket inspector
la **revista** NOUN
magazine
■ **una revista electrónica** a webzine
**revoltoso** (FEM **revoltosa**) ADJECTIVE
naughty
la **revolución** (PL las **revoluciones**) NOUN
revolution
el **revolucionario**, la **revolucionaria** NOUN
revolutionary (PL revolutionaries)
**revolver*** VERB [59]
1 to mess up
□ Los niños han revuelto la habitación otra vez. The children have messed the room up again.
■ **No revuelvas mis papeles.** Don't muddle my papers up.
2 to turn upside down
□ Los ladrones revolvieron toda la casa. The burglars turned the whole house upside down.
3 to rummage in
□ No me gusta que me revuelvas el bolso. I don't like you rummaging in my bag.
el **revólver** (PL los **revólveres**) NOUN
revolver
**revuelto** VERB
▷ *see also* **revuelto** ADJECTIVE ▷ *see* **revolver**
**revuelto** (FEM **revuelta**) ADJECTIVE
▷ *see also* **revuelto** VERB
in a mess
□ Todo estaba revuelto. Everything was in a mess.
■ **Las fotos están revueltas.** The photos are muddled up.
■ **El tiempo está muy revuelto.** The weather's very unsettled.
■ **Tengo el estómago revuelto.** I've got an upset stomach.
el **rey** (PL los **reyes**) NOUN
king
■ **Los reyes visitaron China.** The King and Queen visited China.

r

■ **los Reyes Magos** the Three Wise Men

> **DID YOU KNOW...?**
> As part of the Christmas festivities, the Spanish celebrate **el día de Reyes** (Epiphany) on 6th of January, when the Three Wise Men bring presents to children.

> **LANGUAGE TIP** Word for word, **Reyes Magos** means 'Magician Kings'.

**rezar\*** VERB [13]
to pray

□ rezar por algo to pray for something

■ **rezar el Padrenuestro** to say the Lord's Prayer

la **ría** NOUN
estuary (PL estuaries)

el **riachuelo** NOUN
stream

la **ribera** NOUN
bank

la **rica** NOUN
rich woman (PL rich women)

el **rico** NOUN
rich man (PL rich men)

■ **los ricos** the rich

**rico** (FEM **rica**) ADJECTIVE
1 rich

□ Son muy ricos. They're very rich.
2 delicious

□ ¡Qué rico! How delicious!

**ridiculizar\*** VERB [13]
to ridicule

**ridículo** (FEM **ridícula**) ADJECTIVE
ridiculous

□ ¿A que suena ridículo? Doesn't it sound ridiculous?

■ **hacer el ridículo** to make a fool of oneself

■ **poner a alguien en ridículo** to make a fool of somebody

el **riel** NOUN
rail

las **riendas** NOUN
reins

**riendo** VERB ▷ see reír

el **riesgo** NOUN
risk

■ **correr riesgos** to take risks □ No quiero correr ese riesgo. I'd rather not take that risk.

■ **Corres el riesgo de que te despidan.** You run the risk of being dismissed.

■ **un seguro a todo riesgo** a fully comprehensive insurance policy

la **rifa** NOUN
raffle

el **rifle** NOUN
rifle

**rígido** (FEM **rígida**) ADJECTIVE
1 stiff
2 strict

**riguroso** (FEM **rigurosa**) ADJECTIVE
1 strict
2 severe

la **rima** NOUN
rhyme

el **rímel** NOUN
mascara

□ No me he puesto rímel. I haven't put any mascara on.

el **rincón** (PL los **rincones**) NOUN
corner

el **rinoceronte** NOUN
rhinoceros (PL rhinoceroses o rhinoceros)

la **riña** NOUN
1 row
2 brawl

**riñendo** VERB ▷ see reñir

el **riñón** (PL los **riñones**) NOUN
kidney (PL kidneys)

□ un transplante de riñón a kidney transplant

■ **Me duelen los riñones.** I've got a pain in my lower back.

la **riñonera** NOUN
bum bag

**río** VERB ▷ see reír

el **río** NOUN
river

□ el río Támesis the River Thames

la **riqueza** NOUN
1 wealth

□ la distribución de la riqueza the distribution of wealth
2 richness

□ la riqueza de su lenguaje the richness of his language

la **risa** NOUN
laugh

□ una risa contagiosa an infectious laugh

■ **Me da risa.** It makes me laugh.

■ **Daba risa la manera en que lo explicaba.** It was so funny the way he told it.

■ **¡Qué risa!** What a laugh!

■ **partirse de risa** to split one's sides laughing

el **ritmo** NOUN
1 rhythm

□ No tiene sentido del ritmo. He has no sense of rhythm.

■ **Daban palmas al ritmo de la música.** They were clapping in time to the music.
2 pace

□ el ritmo de vida the pace of life

el **ritual** NOUN

r

ritual

el/la **rival** ADJECTIVE, NOUN
rival

la **rivalidad** NOUN
rivalry (PL rivalries)

**rizado** (FEM **rizada**) ADJECTIVE
curly
□ Tiene el pelo rizado. He has curly hair.

**rizar*** VERB [13]
1 to curl
□ Me rizo las pestañas. I curl my eyelashes.
2 to perm
■ **Se ha rizado el pelo.** She has had her hair permed.

el **rizo** NOUN
curl

**robar** VERB [25]
1 to steal
□ Me han robado la cartera. My wallet has been stolen. □ Les robaba dinero a sus compañeros de clase. He was stealing money from his classmates.
2 to rob
□ ¡Nos han robado! We've been robbed!
3 to break into
□ Entraron a robar en mi casa. They broke into my house.

el **roble** NOUN
oak

el **robo** NOUN
1 theft
2 robbery (PL robberies)
3 burglary (PL burglaries)
■ **¡Estos precios son un robo!** This is daylight robbery!

el **robot** (PL los **robots**) NOUN
robot
■ **el robot de cocina** the food processor

**robusto** (FEM **robusta**) ADJECTIVE
strong

la **roca** NOUN
rock

**rociar*** VERB [21]
to spray

el **rocío** NOUN
dew

la **rodaja** NOUN
slice
□ cortar algo en rodajas to cut something into slices

el **rodaje** NOUN
shooting
■ **El coche está en rodaje.** The car's running in.

**rodar*** VERB [11]
1 to roll
□ La pelota bajó rodando por la cuesta. The ball rolled down the slope.
2 to shoot
□ rodar una película to shoot a film

**rodear** VERB [25]
to surround
□ el bosque que rodea el palacio the forest that surrounds the palace
■ **rodeado de** surrounded by

la **rodilla** NOUN
knee
■ **ponerse de rodillas** to kneel down

el **rodillo** NOUN
1 rolling pin
2 roller

**rogar*** VERB
1 to beg
□ Me rogó que le perdonara. He begged me to forgive him.
2 to pray
□ Le rogué a Dios que se curara. I prayed to God to make him better.
■ **'Se ruega no fumar'** 'Please do not smoke'

el **rojo** ADJECTIVE, NOUN
red
□ Va vestida de rojo. She's wearing red.
■ **ponerse rojo** to go red □ Se puso rojo de vergüenza. He went red with embarrassment.

el **rollo** NOUN
roll
□ un rollo de papel higiénico a roll of toilet paper
■ **La conferencia fue un rollo.** The lecture was really boring.
■ **¡Qué rollo de película!** What a boring film.
■ **Nos soltó el rollo de siempre.** He gave us the same old lecture.

**Roma** FEM NOUN
Rome

el **romano** (FEM la **romana**) ADJECTIVE, NOUN
Roman
□ los números romanos Roman numerals
■ **Es romano.** He's from Rome.
■ **los romanos** 1 the Romans 2 Romans

el **romántico** (FEM la **romántica**) ADJECTIVE, NOUN
romantic

el **rombo** NOUN
rhombus (PL rhombuses o rhombi)

el **rompecabezas** (PL los **rompecabezas**) NOUN
1 jigsaw
2 puzzle

**romper*** VERB [0]
1 to break
□ Me rompí el brazo. I broke my arm. □ Se ha roto una taza. A cup has got broken.

r

□ romper una promesa to break a promise
2 to tear up
□ Rompí la foto de mi novia. I tore up the
photo of my girlfriend. □ Rompió la carta a
pedazos. He tore the letter up.
■ **Se ha roto una sábana.** A sheet has got
torn.
■ **Se me han roto los pantalones.** I've torn
my trousers.
■ **romper con alguien** to finish with
somebody □ Ha roto con el novio. She has
finished with her boyfriend.

el **ron** NOUN
rum

**roncar*** VERB [48]
to snore

**ronco** (FEM **ronca**) ADJECTIVE
hoarse
■ **quedarse ronco** to go hoarse

la **ronda** NOUN
round
□ Esta ronda la pago yo. I'll get this round.
■ **hacer la ronda** to be on patrol

el **ronquido** NOUN
snore

**ronronear** VERB [25]
to purr

la **ropa** NOUN
clothes *pl*
□ Voy a cambiarme de ropa. I'm going to
change my clothes.
■ **la ropa interior** underwear

> LANGUAGE TIP Word for word, **ropa
interior** means 'interior clothes'.

■ **ropa de deporte** sportswear
■ **la ropa de cama** bed linen
■ **la ropa lavada** the washing
■ **la ropa sucia** the dirty washing

el **rosa** ADJECTIVE, NOUN
pink
□ Va vestida de rosa. She's wearing pink.
■ **Llevaba unos calcetines rosa.** He was
wearing pink socks.

la **rosa** NOUN
rose

**rosado** (FEM **rosada**) ADJECTIVE
rosé

el **rosal** NOUN
rosebush (PL rosebushes)

el **rostro** NOUN
face

**roto** VERB ▷ see **romper**
**roto** (FEM **rota**) ADJECTIVE
1 broken
2 torn
3 worn out

el **roto** NOUN
hole

la **rotonda** NOUN
roundabout

el **rotulador** NOUN
1 felt-tip pen
2 highlighter pen

el **rótulo** NOUN
sign

**rozar*** VERB [13]
to rub against
□ El sofá roza la pared. The sofa's rubbing
against the wall. □ Las botas me rozan el
tobillo. My boots are rubbing against my
ankle.
■ **La rocé al pasar.** I brushed past her.

**rubio** (FEM **rubia**) ADJECTIVE
fair
□ Luis tiene el pelo rubio. Luis has got fair
hair. □ Yo soy morena pero mi hermana es
rubia. I'm dark but my sister is fair.
■ **Es rubia con los ojos azules.** She has got
fair hair and blue eyes. □ Quiero teñirme el
pelo de rubio. I want to dye my hair blond.

**ruborizarse*** VERB [13]
to blush

**rudimentario** (FEM **rudimentaria**)
ADJECTIVE
basic

la **rueda** NOUN
wheel
□ la rueda delantera the front wheel □ la
rueda trasera the back wheel
■ **Se te ha pinchado la rueda.** You've got a
puncture.
■ **una rueda de prensa** a press conference

**ruedo** VERB ▷ see **rodar**
**ruego** VERB ▷ see **rogar**

el **rugby** NOUN
rugby
□ jugar al rugby to play rugby

**rugir*** VERB [16]
to roar

el **ruido** NOUN
noise
□ ¿Has oído ese ruido? Did you hear that
noise? □ No hagáis tanto ruido. Don't make
so much noise.

**ruidoso** (FEM **ruidosa**) ADJECTIVE
noisy

la **ruina** NOUN
■ **Su socio lo llevó a la ruina.** His business
partner ruined him financially.
■ **las ruinas** the ruins □ El castillo está en
ruinas. The castle is in ruins.

el **rulo** NOUN
roller

la **rulot** (PL las **rulots**) NOUN
caravan

la **rumana** NOUN

Romanian

**Rumanía** FEM NOUN
Romania

el **rumano** ADJECTIVE, NOUN
Romanian

la **rumba** NOUN
rumba

el **rumor** NOUN

1 rumour
▫ Corre el rumor de que se retira. There's a rumour going round that he's retiring.

2 murmur
▫ el rumor de las olas the murmur of the waves

**rural** (FEM **rural**) ADJECTIVE
rural

la **rusa** NOUN
Russian

**Rusia** FEM NOUN
Russia

el **ruso** ADJECTIVE, NOUN
Russian

la **ruta** NOUN
route

la **rutina** NOUN
routine
▫ la rutina diaria the daily routine
■ **un chequeo de rutina** a routine check-up

# Ss

el **sábado** NOUN
Saturday
□ La vi el sábado. I saw her on Saturday.
□ todos los sábados every Saturday □ el sábado pasado last Saturday □ el sábado que viene next Saturday □ Jugamos los sábados. We play on Saturdays.

la **sábana** NOUN
sheet

**saber*** VERB [47]
1 to know
□ No lo sé. I don't know. □ Sabe mucho de ordenadores. He knows a lot about computers.
■ **Lo dudo, pero nunca se sabe.** I doubt it, but you never know. □ ¡Y yo que sé! How should I know?
2 to find out
□ En cuanto lo supimos fuimos a ayudarle. As soon as we found out, we went to help him.
■ **No sé nada de ella.** I haven't heard from her.
■ **que yo sepa** as far as I know
3 can
□ No sabe nadar. She can't swim. □ ¿Sabes inglés? Can you speak English?
4 to taste
□ Sabe a pescado. It tastes of fish.
■ **saberse** to know □ Se sabe la lista de memoria. He knows the list off by heart.

**sabio** (FEM **sabia**) ADJECTIVE
wise

el **sabor** NOUN
1 taste
□ Tiene un sabor muy raro. It's got a very strange taste.
2 flavour
□ ¿De qué sabor lo quieres? What flavour do you want?

el **sabotaje** NOUN
sabotage

**sabré** VERB ▷ see **saber**

**sabroso** (FEM **sabrosa**) ADJECTIVE
tasty

el **sacacorchos** (PL los **sacacorchos**) NOUN

corkscrew

el **sacapuntas** (PL los **sacapuntas**) NOUN
pencil sharpener

**sacar*** VERB [48]
1 to take out
□ Voy a sacar dinero del cajero. I'm going to take some money out of the machine. □ Se sacó las llaves del bolsillo. He took the keys out of his pocket. □ sacar la basura to take the rubbish out
■ **Me han sacado una muela.** I've had a tooth taken out.
■ **sacar a pasear al perro** to take the dog out for a walk
■ **sacar a alguien a bailar** to get somebody up for a dance
2 to get
□ Yo sacaré las entradas. I'll get the tickets.
□ sacar buenas notas to get good marks
3 to release
□ Han sacado un nuevo disco. They've released a new record.
■ **sacar algo adelante** to conclude
■ **sacar una foto a alguien** to take a photo of somebody
■ **sacar la lengua a alguien** to stick your tongue out at somebody
■ **sacarse el carnet de conducir** to pass one's driving test
■ **sacarse el título de abogado** to qualify as a lawyer
■ **sacarse las botas** to take off one's boots

la **sacarina** NOUN
saccharin

el **sacerdote** NOUN
priest

el **saco** NOUN
1 sack
□ un saco de harina a sack of flour
■ **un saco de dormir** a sleeping bag
2 jacket *(Latin America)*

el **sacrificio** NOUN
sacrifice

**sacudir** VERB [58]
to shake
□ Hay que sacudir la alfombra. The carpet

needs shaking. □ Un terremoto sacudió la ciudad. An earthquake shook the city.

**Sagitario** MASC NOUN
Sagittarius

■ **Soy sagitario.** I'm Sagittarius.

**sagrado** (FEM **sagrada**) ADJECTIVE
1 sacred
2 holy

la **sal** NOUN
salt

la **sala** NOUN
1 room
2 ward
3 hall

■ **sala de embarque** departure lounge
■ **sala de espera** waiting room
■ **sala de estar** living room
■ **sala de fiestas** nightclub
■ **sala de juegos recreativos** amusement arcade
■ **sala de profesores** staffroom

**salado** (FEM **salada**) ADJECTIVE
1 salty
□ La carne está muy salada. The meat's very salty.
2 savoury
□ ¿Es dulce o salado? Is it sweet or savoury?

el **salario** NOUN
pay

■ **el salario mínimo** the minimum wage

la **salchicha** NOUN
sausage

el **salchichón** (PL los **salchichones**) NOUN
spiced salami sausage

el **saldo** NOUN
balance

■ **saldos** sales

**saldré** VERB ▷ see **salir**

el **salero** NOUN
salt cellar

**salgo** VERB ▷ see **salir**

la **salida** NOUN
1 exit
□ salida de emergencia emergency exit
□ salida de incendios fire exit
■ **a la salida del teatro** on the way out of the theatre
2 departure
□ la terminal de salidas nacionales the domestic departures terminal
■ **El tren de Londres efectuará su salida por el andén número dos.** The London train will depart from platform two.
3 start
■ **El juez dio la salida a la carrera.** The referee started the race.
■ **la salida del sol** sunrise

**salir\*** VERB [49]

1 to come out
□ cuando salimos del cine when we came out of the cinema □ Acaba de salir un disco suyo. A record of his has just come out. □ Nos levantamos antes de que saliera el sol. We got up before the sun came out.
2 to go out
□ ¿Vas a salir esta noche? Are you going out tonight?
■ **Ha salido.** She's out.
■ **salir con alguien** to go out with somebody □ Está saliendo con un compañero de clase. She's going out with one of her classmates.
3 to get out
□ ¡Sal de ahí ahora mismo! Get out of here right now!
4 to leave
□ El autocar sale a las ocho. The coach leaves at eight. □ Quiere salir del país. She wants to leave the country.
5 to appear
□ Su foto salió en todos los periódicos. Her picture appeared in all the newspapers.
■ **Sale a 15 euros por persona.** It works out at 15 euros each.
■ **Me está saliendo una muela del juicio.** One of my wisdom teeth is coming through.
■ **No sé cómo vamos a salir adelante.** I don't know how we're going to go on.
■ **salir bien** to work out well □ El plan salió bien. The plan worked out well.
■ **Espero que todo salga bien.** I hope everything works out all right.
■ **Les salió mal el proyecto.** Their plan didn't work out.
■ **¡Qué mal me ha salido el dibujo!** My drawing hasn't come out very well, has it!
■ **salirse 1** to boil over □ Se ha salido la leche. The milk's boiled over. **2** to leak □ Se salía el aceite del motor. Oil was leaking out of the engine. **3** to come off □ Nos salimos de la carretera. We came off the road. **4** to come out □ Se ha salido el enchufe. The plug has come out.

la **saliva** NOUN
saliva

el **salmón** (PL los **salmones**) NOUN
salmon

■ **rosa salmón** salmon pink

el **salón** (PL los **salones**) NOUN
1 living room
■ **salón de actos** meeting hall
■ **salón de belleza** beauty salon
■ **salón de juegos recreativos** amusement arcade

S

## salpicadera – santo

**2** classroom *(Mexico)*

la **salpicadera** NOUN
mudguard *(Mexico)*

el **salpicadero** NOUN
dashboard

**salpicar*** VERB [48]
to splash

la **salsa** NOUN
**1** sauce
□ salsa de tomate  tomato sauce
**2** salsa

el **saltamontes** (PL los **saltamontes**) NOUN
grasshopper

**saltar** VERB [25]
to jump
□ El caballo saltó la valla.  The horse jumped
over the wall.  □ saltar por la ventana  to
jump out of the window
■ **hacer saltar algo por los aires** to blow
something up
■ **saltarse** to skip  □ Te has saltado una
página.  You've skipped a page.
■ **saltarse un semáforo en rojo** to go
through a red light

el **salto** NOUN
**1** jump
**2** dive
■ **dar un salto** to jump
■ **salto de altura** high jump
■ **salto de longitud** long jump
■ **salto mortal** somersault
○ **LANGUAGE TIP** Word for word, **salto
mortal** means 'mortal jump'.
■ **salto con pértiga** pole vault
■ **salto de trampolín** springboard diving

la **salud** NOUN
health

**salud** EXCLAMATION
**1** cheers!
**2** bless you!

**saludable** (FEM **saludable**) ADJECTIVE
healthy

**saludar** VERB [25]
**1** to say hello
□ Entré a saludarla.  I went in to say hello to
her.
**2** to greet
□ Me saludó dándome un beso.  He greeted
me with a kiss.
■ **Lo saludé desde la otra acera.** I waved
to him from the other side of the street.
**3** to salute

el **saludo** NOUN
**1** greeting
□ No contestó a mi saludo.  He didn't
respond to my greeting.
**2** regards
□ Carolina te manda un saludo.  Carolina

sends her regards.  □ Saludos cordiales.
Kind regards.
■ **¡Saludos a Teresa de mi parte!** Say hello
to Teresa for me!

**salvaje** (FEM **salvaje**) ADJECTIVE
wild

el **salvapantallas** NOUN
screensaver

**salvar** VERB [25]
to save
□ Pocos se salvaron del naufragio.  Few were
saved from the shipwreck.

el **salvavidas** (PL los **salvavidas**) NOUN
lifebelt

**salvo** PREPOSITION
except
□ todos salvo yo  everyone except me
■ **salvo que** unless
■ **estar a salvo** to be safe
■ **Consiguieron ponerse a salvo.** They
managed to reach safety.

**San** ADJECTIVE
Saint
□ San Pedro  Saint Peter

la **sandalia** NOUN
sandal
■ **unas sandalias** a pair of sandals

la **sandía** NOUN
watermelon

el **sandwich** (PL los **sandwiches**) NOUN
**1** sandwich (PL sandwiches)
**2** toasted sandwich

**sangrar** VERB [25]
to bleed
□ Me sangra la nariz.  My nose is bleeding.

la **sangre** NOUN
blood
■ **echar sangre** to bleed

la **sangría** NOUN
sangria

la **sanidad** NOUN
public health
□ una reforma de la sanidad pública  a
reform in public health

**sano** (FEM **sana**) ADJECTIVE
healthy
□ una dieta sana  a healthy diet
■ **sano y salvo** safe and sound
○ **LANGUAGE TIP** Be careful! **sano** does
not mean **sane**.

la **santa** NOUN
saint
□ Santa Clara  Saint Clara

**santo** (FEM **santa**) ADJECTIVE
holy

el **santo** NOUN
**1** saint
□ Santo Domingo  Saint Dominic

**2** name day

> **DID YOU KNOW...?**
> Besides birthdays, some Spaniards also celebrate the feast day of the saint they are named after.

el **sapo** NOUN
toad

el **saque** NOUN
service

■ **saque de esquina** corner
■ **saque inicial** kick-off

el **sarampión** (PL los **sarampiones**) NOUN
measles *sing*

**sarcástico** (FEM **sarcástica**) ADJECTIVE
sarcastic

la **sardina** NOUN
sardine

el/la **sargento** NOUN
sergeant

el **sarpullido** NOUN
rash (PL rashes)
□ Le ha salido un sarpullido en la cara. His face has come out in a rash.

el **sarro** NOUN
tartar

la **sarta** NOUN
■ **Nos contó una sarta de mentiras.** He told us a pack of lies.

la **sartén** (PL las **sartenes**) NOUN
frying pan

el **sartén** (PL los **sartenes**) NOUN *(Latin America)*
frying pan

el **sastre** NOUN
tailor

el **satélite** NOUN
satellite
□ la televisión vía satélite satellite television

la **satisfacción** (PL las **satisfacciones**) NOUN
satisfaction
□ Expresó su satisfacción por la victoria. She expressed her satisfaction at the victory.
■ **Recibió la noticia con satisfacción.** He was pleased to hear the news.

**satisfacer*** VERB [26]
to satisfy

**satisfactorio** (FEM **satisfactoria**) ADJECTIVE
satisfactory

**satisfecho** (FEM **satisfecha**) ADJECTIVE
satisfied
□ No estoy satisfecho con el resultado. I'm not satisfied with the result.

la **sauna** NOUN
sauna

el **saxofón** (PL los **saxofones**) NOUN
saxophone

**sazonar** VERB [25]
to season

**se** PRONOUN
□ Pedro necesitaba la calculadora y se la dejé. Pedro needed the calculator and I lent it to him. □ No quiero que Rosa lo sepa. No se lo digas. I don't want Rosa to know. Don't tell her. □ He hablado con mis padres y se lo he explicado. I've talked to my parents and explained it to them. □ Aquí tiene el libro. ¿Se lo envuelvo, señor? Here's your book. Shall I wrap it for you, sir? □ Dáselo a Enrique. Give it to Enrique. □ No se lo digas a Susana. Don't tell Susana. □ ¿Se lo has preguntado a tus padres? Have you asked your parents about it? □ Marcos se ha cortado con un cristal. Marcos cut himself on a piece of broken glass. □ Margarita se estaba preparando para salir. Margarita was getting herself ready to go out. □ La calefacción se apaga sola. The heating turns itself off automatically. □ ¿Se ha hecho usted daño? Have you hurt yourself?
■ **Se está afeitando.** He's shaving.
■ **Mi hermana nunca se queja.** My sister never complains. □ Pablo se lavó los dientes. Pablo brushed his teeth. □ Carmen no podía abrocharse el vestido. Carmen couldn't do up her dress. □ Se dieron un beso. They gave each other a kiss. □ Se cree que el tabaco produce cáncer. It is believed that smoking causes cancer. □ Es lo que pasa cuando se come tan deprisa. That's what happens when you eat so fast.
■ **'se vende'** 'for sale'

**sé** VERB ▷ *see* saber

**sea** VERB ▷ *see* ser

el **secador** NOUN
hair dryer

la **secadora** NOUN
**1** tumble dryer
**2** hair dryer *(Mexico)*

**secar*** VERB [48]
to dry
□ Voy a secarme el pelo. I'm going to dry my hair.
■ **secarse** to dry □ Sécate con la toalla. Dry yourself with the towel.
■ **¿Se ha secado ya la ropa?** Is the washing dry yet?
■ **Se han secado las plantas.** The plants have dried up.

la **sección** (PL las **secciones**) NOUN
**1** section
□ la sección de deportes del periódico the sports section of the newspaper
**2** department
□ la sección de perfumería the perfumery department

**seco** (FEM **seca**) ADJECTIVE
1 dry
 □ El suelo ya está seco. The floor's dry now.
 □ Tiene una tos muy seca. He's got a very dry cough.
2 dried
 □ flores secas dried flowers

el **secretario**, la **secretaria** NOUN
secretary (PL secretaries)
 ■ una secretaria de dirección a PA (= personal assistant)

el **secreto** NOUN
secret
 □ Te voy a contar un secreto. I'm going to tell you a secret.
 ■ en secreto in secret

**secreto** (FEM **secreta**) ADJECTIVE
secret

la **secta** NOUN
sect

el **sector** NOUN
sector
 □ el sector de la minería the mining sector

la **secuencia** NOUN
sequence

el **secuestrador**, la **secuestradora** NOUN
1 kidnapper
2 hijacker

**secuestrar** VERB [25]
1 to kidnap
2 to hijack

el **secuestro** NOUN
1 kidnapping
2 hijack

**secundario** (FEM **secundaria**) ADJECTIVE
secondary

la **sed** NOUN
thirst
 ■ tener sed to be thirsty

la **seda** NOUN
silk
 □ una camisa de seda a silk shirt

el **sedal** NOUN
fishing line

el **sedante** NOUN
sedative

la **sede** NOUN
1 headquarters pl
 □ la sede de la ONU the UN headquarters
2 venue
 □ Barcelona fue la sede de los Juegos Olímpicos del 92. Barcelona was the venue for the 1992 Olympics.

**sediento** (FEM **sedienta**) ADJECTIVE
thirsty

**segar\*** VERB
1 to reap

2 to mow

**seguido** (FEM **seguida**) ADJECTIVE
in a row
 □ La he visto tres días seguidos. I've seen her three days in a row.
 ■ en seguida straight away □ En seguida estoy con usted. I'll be with you straight away.
 ■ En seguida termino. I'm just about to finish.
 ■ todo seguido straight on □ Vaya todo seguido hasta la plaza y luego ... Go straight on until the square and then ...

**seguir\*** VERB [50]
1 to carry on
 □ ¡Sigue, por favor! Carry on, please! □ El ordenador seguía funcionando. The computer carried on working.
 ■ El ascensor sigue estropeado. The lift's still not working.
 ■ Sigo sin comprender. I still don't understand.
 ■ Sigue lloviendo. It's still raining.
2 to follow
 □ Tú ve primero que yo te sigo. You go first and I'll follow you.
 ■ seguir adelante to go ahead □ Los Juegos Olímpicos siguieron adelante a pesar del atentado. The Olympics went ahead despite the attack.

**según** PREPOSITION
1 according to
 □ Según tú, no habrá problemas de entradas. According to you there won't be any problems with the tickets.
2 depending on
 □ Iremos o no, según esté el tiempo. We might go, depending on the weather.

**segundo** (FEM **segunda**) ADJECTIVE, PRONOUN
second
 ■ el segundo plato the second course
 ■ Vive en el segundo. He lives on the second floor.

el **segundo** NOUN
second
 □ Es un segundo nada más. It'll only take a second.

**seguramente** ADVERB
probably
 □ Seguramente llegarán mañana. They'll probably arrive tomorrow.
 ■ ¿Lo va a comprar? — Seguramente. Are you going to buy it? — Almost certainly.

la **seguridad** NOUN
1 safety
 □ Hay que mejorar la seguridad en los autocares. Safety on coaches must be improved.

**2** security
□ Las medidas de seguridad son muy estrictas. The security measures are very strict.

**3** certainty
□ con toda seguridad with complete certainty
■ **seguridad en uno mismo** self-confidence □ Le falta seguridad en sí mismo. He lacks self-confidence.
■ **la seguridad social** social security

**seguro** (FEM **segura**) ADJECTIVE

**1** safe
□ Este avión es muy seguro. This plane is very safe. □ Aquí estaremos seguros. We'll be safe here.

**2** sure
□ Estoy segura de que ganaremos. I'm sure we'll win. □ Está muy seguro de sí mismo. He's very sure of himself.

**3** certain
□ No es seguro que vayan a venir. It's not certain that they're going to come.

el **seguro** NOUN
insurance
□ el seguro del coche car insurance
■ **seguro de vida** life assurance

**seis** (FEM **seis**) ADJECTIVE, PRONOUN
six
■ **Son las seis.** It's six o'clock.
■ **el seis de enero** the sixth of January

**seiscientos** (FEM **seiscientas**) ADJECTIVE, PRONOUN
six hundred

la **selección** (PL las **selecciones**) NOUN

**1** selection
□ una selección de los mejores vídeos a selection of the finest videos

**2** team
□ la selección nacional the national team

**seleccionar** VERB [25]
to pick
□ Lo seleccionaron para jugar en su equipo. He was picked to play in the team.

la **selectividad** NOUN
university entrance exam

**sellar** VERB [25]

**1** to seal

**2** to stamp

**3** to sign on

el **sello** NOUN

**1** stamp
□ Colecciona sellos. He collects stamps.

**2** seal
□ El producto lleva un sello de calidad. The product bears a seal of quality.

la **selva** NOUN
jungle

■ **la selva tropical** the rainforest

el **semáforo** NOUN
traffic lights pl
■ **un semáforo en rojo** a red light

la **semana** NOUN
week
□ dentro de una semana in a week's time
□ una vez a la semana once a week
■ **entre semana** during the week
■ **Semana Santa** Holy Week

**semanal** (FEM **semanal**) ADJECTIVE
weekly

**sembrar*** VERB [39]

**1** to plant

**2** to sow

**semejante** (FEM **semejante**) ADJECTIVE

**1** similar
□ Tenemos unos rasgos muy semejantes. We have very similar features.

**2** such
□ Nunca he dicho semejante cosa. I've never said such a thing.

el **semicírculo** NOUN
semicircle

la **semifinal** NOUN
semi-final

la **semilla** NOUN
seed

el **senado** NOUN
senate

el **senador**, la **senadora** NOUN
senator

**sencillamente** ADVERB
simply
□ Es sencillamente imposible. It's simply impossible.

**sencillo** (FEM **sencilla**) ADJECTIVE

**1** simple
□ Es muy sencillo. It's really simple. □ un vestido sencillo a simple dress

**2** modest
□ Es muy sencillo en el trato. He has a very modest manner.

el **sencillo** NOUN

**1** single (record)

**2** small change (Latin America)

el **senderismo** NOUN
trekking

el **sendero** NOUN
path

la **sensación** (PL las **sensaciones**) NOUN
feeling
□ Tengo la sensación de que mienten. I get the feeling they're lying. □ una sensación de escozor a burning feeling

**sensacional** (FEM **sensacional**) ADJECTIVE
sensational

**sensato** (FEM **sensata**) ADJECTIVE

279

**sensible**
□ Lo sensato sería no moverse de aquí. The sensible thing would be not to move from here.

**sensible** (FEM **sensible**) ADJECTIVE
sensitive
□ Es un chico muy sensible. He's a very sensitive boy. □ Tengo los ojos muy sensibles. My eyes are very sensitive.

> **LANGUAGE TIP** Be careful! The Spanish word **sensible** does not mean **sensible**.

**sensual** (FEM **sensual**) ADJECTIVE
sensuous

**sentado** (FEM **sentada**) ADJECTIVE
■ **estar sentado** to be sitting down

**sentar*** VERB [39]
1 to suit
□ Ese vestido te sienta muy bien. That dress really suits you.
2 to agree with
□ No me sienta bien cenar tanto. Having so much dinner doesn't agree with me.
■ **Le ha sentado mal que no lo invitaras a la boda.** He was put out that you didn't invite him to the wedding.
■ **sentarse** to sit down □ Por favor, siéntese. Please sit down.

**la sentencia** NOUN
sentence

**el sentido** NOUN
1 sense
□ No tiene sentido. It doesn't make sense.
2 meaning
□ palabras con doble sentido words with a double meaning
■ **sentido común** common sense
■ **sentido del humor** sense of humour
■ **una calle de sentido único** a one-way street
■ **en algún sentido** in some respects
■ **en cierto sentido** in a certain sense

**sentimental** (FEM **sentimental**) ADJECTIVE
sentimental

**el sentimiento** NOUN
feeling

**sentir*** VERB [51]
1 to feel
□ Sentí un dolor en la pierna. I felt a pain in my leg.
■ **De pronto sentí un poco de frío.** Suddenly I felt a bit cold.
2 to hear
□ No la sentí entrar. I didn't hear her come in.
3 to be sorry
□ Lo siento mucho. I'm very sorry. □ Siento llegar tarde. I'm sorry I'm late.

■ **sentirse** to feel □ No me siento nada bien. I don't feel at all well.

**la seña** NOUN
sign
□ Les hice una seña. I made a sign to them.
□ Nos comunicábamos por señas. We communicated by signs.
■ **señas** address

**la señal** NOUN
1 sign
■ **señal de tráfico** road sign
■ **señal indicadora** signpost
■ **señal de llamada** dialling tone
2 signal
□ Yo daré la señal. I'll give the signal.
■ **Les hice una señal para que se fueran.** I signalled to them to go.
3 deposit
□ Dimos una señal de 30 euros. We paid a deposit of 30 euros.

**señalar** VERB [25]
to mark
□ Señálalo con un bolígrafo rojo. Mark it with a red pen.
■ **señalar con el dedo** to point

**señalizar*** VERB [13]
1 to indicate
2 to signpost

**el señor** NOUN
1 man (PL men)
□ Este señor ha llegado antes que yo. This man was before me.
■ **¿Le ocurre algo, señor?** Is there something the matter?
■ **¿Qué le pongo, señor?** What would you like, sir?
2 Mr
□ el señor Delgado Mr Delgado
3 lord
□ un señor feudal a feudal lord
■ **Muy señor mío ...** Dear Sir ...
■ **el señor alcalde** the mayor

**la señora** NOUN
1 lady (PL ladies)
□ Deja pasar a esta señora. Let the lady past.
■ **¿Le ocurre algo, señora?** Is there something the matter?
■ **¿Qué le pongo, señora?** What would you like, madam?
2 Mrs
□ la señora Delgado Mrs Delgado
3 wife
□ Vino con su señora. He came with his wife.

**la señorita** NOUN
young lady
□ Deja pasar a esta señorita. Let the young

lady past. □ la señorita Delgado  Miss Delgado

**sepa** VERB ▷ *see* **saber**

la **separación** (PL las **separaciones**) NOUN
**1** separation
**2** gap
□ Había una gran separación entre el andén y la vía. There was a large gap between the platform and the rails.

**separado** (FEM **separada**) ADJECTIVE
**1** separate
□ Duermen en camas separadas. They sleep in separate beds.
■ **por separado** separately
**2** separated
□ Está separado de su mujer. He's separated from his wife.

**separar** VERB [25]
to separate
■ **separarse 1** to separate **2** to split up

**septiembre** MASC NOUN
September
□ en septiembre  in September □ Ella nació el 11 de septiembre. She was born on 11 September.

**séptimo** (FEM **séptima**) ADJECTIVE, PRONOUN
seventh
■ **Vivo en el séptimo.** I live on the seventh floor.

la **sequía** NOUN
drought

**ser\*** VERB [52]
to be
□ Es muy alto. He's very tall. □ Es médico. He's a doctor. □ La fiesta va a ser en su casa. The party's going to be in her house. □ Fue construido en 1960. It was built in 1960. □ Era de noche. It was night.
■ **Soy Lucía.** It's Lucía.
■ **Son las seis y media.** It's half past six.
■ **Éramos cinco en el coche.** There were five of us in the car.
■ **¡Es cierto!** That's right!
■ **Me es imposible asistir.** It's impossible for me to attend.
■ **ser de 1**
■ **Es de Joaquín.** It's Joaquín's. **2** to be from □ ¿De dónde eres? Where are you from? **3** to be made of □ Es de piedra. It's made of stone.
■ **a no ser que ...** unless ... □ a no ser que salgamos mañana  unless we leave tomorrow
■ **O sea, que no vienes.** So you're not coming.
■ **mis hijos, o sea, Juan y Pedro** my children, that is, Juan and Pedro

el **ser** NOUN

being
■ **un ser humano** a human being
■ **un ser vivo** a living being

la **serie** NOUN
series
□ Tuvimos una serie de reuniones.  We had a series of meetings. □ una serie policíaca  a police series

**serio** (FEM **seria**) ADJECTIVE
serious
■ **en serio** seriously □ No hablaba en serio. I wasn't speaking seriously.
■ **¿Lo dices en serio?** Do you really mean it?

el **sermón** (PL los **sermones**) NOUN
sermon

la **serpiente** NOUN
snake
■ **una serpiente de cascabel** a rattlesnake

**serrar\*** VERB [39]
to saw

el **serrucho** NOUN
saw

**servicial** (FEM **servicial**) ADJECTIVE
helpful

el **servicio** NOUN
**1** service
□ el servicio militar  national service □ El servicio no va incluido.  Service is not included.
■ **Tenemos servicio a domicilio.** We have a home delivery service.
■ **estar de servicio** to be on duty
■ **estar fuera de servicio 1** to be out of service **2** to be off duty
**2** toilet
□ Está en el servicio. He's in the toilet.
■ **el servicio de caballeros** the gents'
■ **el servicio de señoras** the ladies'
■ **Al servicio, Costa.** Costa to serve.

el **servidor** NOUN
server

la **servilleta** NOUN
napkin

**servir\*** VERB [38]
**1** to be useful for
□ Estas bolsas sirven para guardar alimentos. These bags are useful for storing food.
■ **¿Para qué sirve esto?** What's this for?
■ **Esta radio aún sirve.** This radio still works.
**2** to serve
□ Yo serviré la cena. I'll serve supper.
■ **Sírveme un poco más de vino.** Give me a little bit more wine.
■ **Trabaja sirviendo mesas.** She works as a waitress.

■ **no servir para nada** to be useless
■ **¿En qué puedo servirlo?** How can I help you?

**sesenta** (FEM **sesenta**) ADJECTIVE, PRONOUN
sixty
□ Tiene sesenta años. He's sixty.
■ **el sesenta aniversario** the sixtieth anniversary

la **sesión** (PL las **sesiones**) NOUN
1 session
□ una sesión parlamentaria a parliamentary session
2 showing
□ Fuimos a la última sesión del sábado. We went to the last showing on Saturday night.

la **seta** NOUN
mushroom
■ **seta venenosa** toadstool

**setecientos** (FEM **setecientas**) ADJECTIVE, PRONOUN
seven hundred

**setenta** (FEM **setenta**) ADJECTIVE, PRONOUN
seventy
□ Tiene setenta años. He's seventy.
■ **el setenta aniversario** the seventieth anniversary

el **seto** NOUN
hedge

el **seudónimo** NOUN
pseudonym

**severo** (FEM **severa**) ADJECTIVE
1 strict
2 harsh

**Sevilla** FEM NOUN
Seville

el/la **sexista** ADJECTIVE, NOUN
sexist

el **sexo** NOUN
sex

**sexto** (FEM **sexta**) ADJECTIVE, PRONOUN
sixth
■ **Vivo en el sexto.** I live on the sixth floor.

**sexual** (FEM **sexual**) ADJECTIVE
sexual
□ acoso sexual sexual harassment
■ **educación sexual** sex education

la **sexualidad** NOUN
sexuality

**si** CONJUNCTION
1 if
□ Si quieres, te dejo el coche. I'll lend you the car if you like. □ ¿Sabes si hemos cobrado ya? Do you know if we've been paid yet?
■ **¿Y si llueve?** And what if it rains?
■ **Si me hubiera tocado la lotería ...** If only I had won the lottery ...
2 whether

□ No sé si ir o no. I don't know whether to go or not.
■ **si no 1** otherwise □ Ponte crema. Si no, te quemarás. Put some cream on, otherwise you'll get sunburned. **2** if...not
□ Avisadme si no podéis venir. Let me know if you can't come.

**sí** ADVERB
▷ *see also* **sí** PRONOUN
yes
□ ¿Te apetece un café? — Sí, gracias. Do you fancy a coffee? — Yes, please.
■ **¿Te gusta? — Sí.** Do you like it? — Yes, I do.
■ **Creo que sí.** I think so.
■ **Él no quiere pero yo sí.** He doesn't want to but I do.

**sí** PRONOUN
▷ *see also* **sí** ADVERB
□ Sólo habla de sí mismo. He only talks about himself. □ Se perjudica a sí misma. She's harming herself. □ Pregúntese a sí mismo el motivo. Ask yourself the reason.
□ La pregunta en sí no era difícil. The question itself wasn't difficult. □ Hablaban entre sí. They were talking among themselves.
■ **La Tierra gira sobre sí misma.** The Earth turns on its own axis. □ Es mejor aprender las cosas por sí mismo. It's better to learn things by yourself.

**Sicilia** FEM NOUN
Sicily

el **sida** NOUN
AIDS

la **sidra** NOUN
cider

**siego** VERB ▷ *see* segar

**siembro** VERB ▷ *see* sembrar

**siempre** ADVERB
always
□ Siempre llega tarde. She always arrives late.
■ **como siempre** as usual
■ **para siempre** forever
■ **siempre y cuando** provided □ siempre y cuando acepte nuestras condiciones provided he accepts our conditions

**siendo** VERB ▷ *see* ser

**siento** VERB ▷ *see* sentir

la **sierra** NOUN
1 saw
2 mountain range
■ **Tenemos una casa en la sierra.** We have a house in the mountains.

la **siesta** NOUN
nap
■ **echarse la siesta** to have a nap

■ **la hora de la siesta** siesta time

**siete** (FEM **siete**) ADJECTIVE, PRONOUN
seven

■ **Son las siete.** It's seven o'clock.

■ **el siete de marzo** the seventh of March

las **siglas** NOUN
abbreviation *sing*

el **siglo** NOUN
century (PL centuries)

□ el siglo XX the 20th century

el **significado** NOUN
meaning

**significar\*** VERB [48]

1 to mean

□ ¿Qué significa 'wild'? What does 'wild' mean? □ No sé lo que significa. I don't know what it means.

2 to stand for

□ 'B.C.' significa 'before Christ'. 'B.C.' stands for 'before Christ'.

**significativo** (FEM **significativa**) ADJECTIVE
significant

el **signo** NOUN
sign

□ Ese apetito es signo de buena salud. Such an appetite is a sign of good health.

■ **¿De qué signo del zodíaco eres?** What star sign are you?

■ **signo de admiración** exclamation mark

■ **signo de interrogación** question mark

**siguiendo** VERB ▷ *see* **seguir**

**siguiente** (FEM **siguiente**) ADJECTIVE
next

□ el siguiente vuelo the next flight □ Al día siguiente visitamos Toledo. The next day we visited Toledo.

■ **¡Que pase el siguiente, por favor!** Next please!

la **sílaba** NOUN
syllable

**silbar** VERB [25]
to whistle

el **silbato** NOUN
whistle

el **silbido** NOUN
whistle

el **silencio** NOUN
silence

■ **guardar silencio** to keep quiet

■ **¡Silencio!** Quiet!

**silencioso** (FEM **silenciosa**) ADJECTIVE
silent

la **silla** NOUN
chair

■ **silla de montar** saddle

■ **silla de paseo** pushchair

■ **silla de ruedas** wheelchair

el **sillín** (PL los **sillines**) NOUN
saddle

el **sillón** (PL los **sillones**) NOUN
armchair

la **silueta** NOUN
outline

■ **Tiene una silueta perfecta.** She has a perfect figure.

el **símbolo** NOUN
symbol

la **simpatía** NOUN

1 kindness

2 friendly nature

■ **Les tengo simpatía.** I like them.

**simpático** (FEM **simpática**) ADJECTIVE
nice

□ Estuvo muy simpática con todos. She was very nice to everybody. □ Los cubanos son muy simpáticos. Cubans are very nice people.

■ **Me cae simpático.** I think he's really nice.

⸬ **LANGUAGE TIP** Be careful! **simpático** does not mean **sympathetic**.

**simple** (FEM **simple**) ADJECTIVE
simple

**simplemente** ADVERB
simply

**simultáneo** (FEM **simultánea**) ADJECTIVE
simultaneous

**sin** PREPOSITION
without

□ Es peligroso ir en moto sin casco. It's dangerous to ride a motorbike without a helmet. □ Salió sin hacer ruido. She went out without making a noise. □ sin que él se diera cuenta without him realising

■ **He dejado el crucigrama sin terminar.** I left the crossword unfinished.

■ **Me quedé sin habla.** I was speechless.

■ **la gente sin hogar** the homeless

**sincero** (FEM **sincera**) ADJECTIVE
honest

□ Fui sincera con él. I was honest with him.

el/la **sindicalista** NOUN
trade unionist

el **sindicato** NOUN
trade union

la **sinfonía** NOUN
symphony (PL symphonies)

el **singular** ADJECTIVE, NOUN
singular

■ **en singular** in the singular

**siniestro** (FEM **siniestra**) ADJECTIVE
sinister

**sino** CONJUNCTION
but

□ No son ingleses sino galeses. They're not English, but Welsh.

S

■ **No hace sino pedirnos dinero.** All he does is ask us for money.

■ **No solo nos ayudó, sino que también nos invitó a cenar.** He didn't just help us, he also bought us dinner.

**sintético** (FEM **sintética**) ADJECTIVE
synthetic

**sintiendo** VERB ▷ see **sentir**

el **síntoma** NOUN
symptom

el/la **sinvergüenza** NOUN
crook

■ **Es una sinvergüenza.** She's shameless.

**siquiera** ADVERB

■ **ni siquiera** not even □ Ni siquiera me dirigió la palabra. She didn't even acknowledge me.

la **sirena** NOUN
1 siren
2 mermaid

**sirviendo** VERB ▷ see **servir**

la **sirvienta** NOUN
maid

el **sirviente** NOUN
servant

el **sistema** NOUN
system

el **sitio** NOUN
1 place
□ un sitio tranquilo a peaceful place

■ **cambiar algo de sitio** to move something around

■ **en cualquier sitio** anywhere

■ **en algún sitio** somewhere

■ **en ningún sitio** nowhere

2 room
□ Hay sitio de sobra. There's room to spare.

■ **Hemos hecho sitio para ti en el coche.** We've made room for you in the car.

■ **un sitio web** website

la **situación** (PL las **situaciones**) NOUN
situation

**situado** (FEM **situada**) ADJECTIVE

■ **está situado en ...** it's situated in ...

el **SMS** (PL los **SMS**) NOUN
text message

el **sobaco** NOUN
armpit

el **soborno** NOUN
1 bribery
2 bribe

■ **Denunció un intento de soborno.** He reported an attempted bribe.

**sobra** FEM NOUN

■ **Tenemos comida de sobra.** We've got more than enough food.

■ **Sabes de sobra que yo no he sido.** You know full well that it wasn't me.

■ **las sobras** the leftovers

**sobrar** VERB [25]
1 to be left over
□ Ha sobrado mucha comida. There's plenty of food left over.
2 to be spare
□ Esta pieza sobra. This piece is spare.

■ **Este ejemplo sobra.** This example is unnecessary.

■ **Con este dinero sobrará.** This money will be more than enough.

**sobre** PREPOSITION
1 on
□ Dejó el dinero sobre la mesa. He left the money on the table.
2 about
□ información sobre vuelos information about flights

■ **sobre las seis** at about six o'clock

■ **sobre todo** above all

el **sobre** NOUN
envelope

la **sobredosis** (PL las **sobredosis**) NOUN
overdose

**sobrenatural** (FEM **sobrenatural**) ADJECTIVE
supernatural

el **sobresaliente** NOUN
distinction

**sobrevivir** VERB [58]
to survive

la **sobrina** NOUN
niece

el **sobrino** NOUN
nephew

■ **mis sobrinos** **1** my nephews **2** my nieces and nephews

**sobrio** (FEM **sobria**) ADJECTIVE
sober

la **socia** NOUN
1 partner
2 member

**social** (FEM **social**) ADJECTIVE
social

el **socialismo** NOUN
socialism

el/la **socialista** ADJECTIVE, NOUN
socialist

la **sociedad** NOUN
society (PL societies)

■ **una sociedad anónima** a limited company

el **socio** NOUN
1 partner
2 member

la **sociología** NOUN
sociology

el/la **socorrista** NOUN
lifeguard

el **socorro** NOUN
help
- **pedir socorro** to ask for help
- **Acudió en su socorro.** She went to his aid.

**socorro** EXCLAMATION
help!

la **soda** NOUN
soda

el **sofá** (PL los **sofás**) NOUN
sofa
- **un sofá-cama** a sofa bed

**sofisticado** (FEM **sofisticada**) ADJECTIVE
sophisticated

el **software** NOUN
software

**sois** VERB ▷ see ser

la **soja** NOUN
soya

el **sol** NOUN
sun
- **estar al sol** to be in the sun
- **Hace sol.** It's sunny.
- **tomar el sol** to sunbathe

**solamente** ADVERB
only

el **soldado** NOUN
soldier

**soleado** (FEM **soleada**) ADJECTIVE
sunny

la **soledad** NOUN
loneliness

**soler*** VERB [33]
□ Suele salir a las ocho. **He usually leaves at eight.** □ Solíamos ir todos los años a la playa. **We used to go to the beach every year.**

**solicitar** VERB [25]
1 to ask for
2 to apply for

la **solicitud** NOUN
1 application
- **presentar una solicitud** to submit an application
2 request

**sólido** (FEM **sólida**) ADJECTIVE
solid

**solitario** (FEM **solitaria**) ADJECTIVE
solitary

**sollozar*** VERB [13]
to sob

**solo** (FEM **sola**) ADJECTIVE
1 alone
□ ¡Déjame solo! **Leave me alone!** □ Me quedé solo. **I was left alone.**
- **¿Estás solo?** Are you on your own?
- **Lo hice solo.** I did it on my own.
2 lonely

□ A veces me siento solo. **Sometimes I feel lonely.**
3 single
□ No hubo una sola queja. **There wasn't a single complaint.**
- **Había un solo problema.** There was just one problem.
- **Habla solo.** He talks to himself.
- **un café solo** a black coffee

el **solo** NOUN
solo
□ un solo de guitarra **a guitar solo**

**sólo** ADVERB
only
□ Sólo cuesta diez libras. **It only costs ten pounds.** □ Era sólo una idea. **It was only an idea.** □ Yo también fumo, sólo que en pipa. **I smoke as well, only a pipe.**
- **no sólo ... sino ...** not only ... but ... □ No sólo es barato, sino también de buena calidad. **It's not only cheap, but it's good quality too.**

el **solomillo** NOUN
sirloin

**soltar*** VERB [11]
1 to let go of
□ No sueltes la cuerda. **Don't let go of the rope.**
- **¡Suéltame!** Let me go!
2 to put down
□ Soltó la bolsa de la compra en un banco. **She put her shopping bag down on a bench.**
3 to release
□ Han soltado a los rehenes. **They've released the hostages.**
4 to let out
□ Solté un suspiro de alivio. **I let out a sigh of relief.**

la **soltera** NOUN
single woman

**soltero** (FEM **soltera**) ADJECTIVE
single
□ Es soltero. **He's single.**

el **soltero** NOUN
bachelor

la **solución** (PL las **soluciones**) NOUN
1 solution
2 answer

**solucionar** VERB [25]
to solve
- **un problema sin solucionar** an unsolved problem

la **sombra** NOUN
1 shade
□ Prefiero quedarme a la sombra. **I prefer to stay in the shade.**
2 shadow
□ Sólo vi una sombra. **I only saw a shadow.**

■ sombra de ojos eye shadow
el **sombrero** NOUN
hat
la **sombrilla** NOUN
1 parasol
2 sunshade
el **somier** NOUN
mattress base
el **somnífero** NOUN
sleeping pill
el **sonajero** NOUN
rattle
**sonar*** VERB [11]
1 to sound
□ Sonabas un poco triste por teléfono. You
sounded a bit sad on the phone.
■ Escríbelo tal y como suena. Write it
down just the way it sounds.
2 to play
□ Sonaba una canción de Madonna por la
radio. They were playing a Madonna song
on the radio.
3 to ring
4 to go off
■ Me suena esa cara. That face rings a bell.
■ sonarse la nariz to blow one's nose
el **sondeo** NOUN
■ un sondeo de opinión an opinion poll
el **sonido** NOUN
sound
**sonreír*** VERB [44]
to smile
□ Me sonrió. She smiled at me.
la **sonrisa** NOUN
smile
**sonrojarse** VERB [25]
to blush
**soñar*** VERB [11]
to dream
□ Ayer soñé con él. I dreamed about him
yesterday.
la **sopa** NOUN
soup
□ sopa de pescado fish soup
**soplar** VERB [25]
to blow
□ ¡Sopla con fuerza! Blow hard! □ Soplaba
un viento fuerte. A strong wind was
blowing.
**soportar** VERB [25]
to stand
□ No lo soporto. I can't stand him. □ No
soporta que la critiquen. She can't stand
being criticised.

⸛ **LANGUAGE TIP** Be careful! soportar
does not mean **to support**.

la **soprano** NOUN
soprano

**sorber** VERB [8]
to sip
**sordo** (FEM **sorda**) ADJECTIVE
deaf
■ quedarse sordo to go deaf
**sordomudo** (FEM **sordomuda**) ADJECTIVE
deaf and dumb
**sorprendente** (FEM sorprendente)
ADJECTIVE
surprising
**sorprender** VERB [8]
to surprise
□ No me sorprende. It doesn't surprise me.
■ Me sorprendí al verlo allí. I was
surprised to see him there.
la **sorpresa** NOUN
surprise
□ ¡Qué sorpresa! What a surprise!
■ coger a alguien de sorpresa to take
somebody by surprise
el **sorteo** NOUN
draw
la **sortija** NOUN
ring
**soso** (FEM **sosa**) ADJECTIVE
1 dull
2 bland
■ Estas patatas fritas están sosas. These
chips need more salt.
la **sospecha** NOUN
suspicion
**sospechar** VERB [25]
to suspect
■ Sospechan de él. They suspect him.
el **sospechoso**, la **sospechosa** NOUN
suspect
**sospechoso** (FEM **sospechosa**) ADJECTIVE
suspicious
el **sostén** (PL los **sostenes**) NOUN
bra
**sostener*** VERB [53]
1 to support
□ Está sostenido por cuatro columnas. It is
supported by four columns.
2 to hold
□ Sostuvieron la caja entre los dos. They
held the box between the two of them.
■ ¿Puedes sostener la puerta un
momento? Can you hold the door open for
a moment?
■ La sombrilla no se sostiene con el
viento. The sunshade won't stay up in the
wind.
la **sota** NOUN
jack
el **sótano** NOUN
1 basement
2 cellar

**soy** VERB ▷see **ser**
el **spot** NOUN
■ un spot publicitario a commercial
**Sr.** ABBREVIATION
Mr
**Sra.** ABBREVIATION
Mrs
**Sres.** ABBREVIATION
Messrs
**Srta.** ABBREVIATION
Miss
**su** ADJECTIVE
1 his
□ su máquina de afeitar his razor □ sus padres his parents
2 her
□ su falda her skirt □ sus amigas her friends
3 its
□ un oso y su cachorro a bear and its cub □ el coche y sus accesorios the car and its fittings
4 their
□ su equipo favorito their favourite team □ sus amigos their friends
5 your
□ Su abrigo, señora. Your coat, madam. □ No olviden sus paraguas. Don't forget your umbrellas.
**suave** (FEM **suave**) ADJECTIVE
1 smooth
2 soft
3 gentle
4 mild
el **suavizante** NOUN
1 conditioner
2 fabric conditioner
la **subasta** NOUN
auction
el **subcampeón**, la **subcampeona**
(MASC PL los **subcampeones**) NOUN
runner-up (PL runners-up)
**subdesarrollado** (FEM **subdesarrollada**)
ADJECTIVE
underdeveloped
el **subdirector**, la **subdirectora** NOUN
1 deputy head
2 deputy director
3 deputy manager deputy manageress)
la **subida** NOUN
1 rise
□ una subida de los precios a rise in prices
2 ascent
□ una subida muy empinada a very steep ascent
**subir** VERB [58]
1 to go up
□ Subimos la cuesta. We went up the hill.

□ La gasolina ha vuelto a subir. Petrol's gone up again.
2 to come up
□ Sube, que te voy a enseñar unos discos. Come up, I've got some records to show you.
3 to climb
□ subir una montaña to climb a mountain
4 to take up
□ ¿Me puedes ayudar a subir las maletas? Can you help me to take up the cases?
5 to put up
□ Los taxistas han subido sus tarifas. Taxi drivers have put their fares up.
6 to raise
□ Sube los brazos. Raise your arms.
7 to turn up
□ Sube la radio, que no se oye. Turn the radio up, I can't hear it.
■ subirse a 1 to get into 2 to get onto 3 to get on
■ subirse a un árbol to climb a tree
el **subjuntivo** NOUN
subjunctive
el **submarino** NOUN
submarine
**subrayar** VERB [25]
to underline
el **subsidio** NOUN
subsidy (PL subsidies)
□ subsidio de paro unemployment benefit
el **subte** NOUN (River Plate)
underground
**subterráneo** (FEM **subterránea**) ADJECTIVE
underground
**subtitulado** (FEM **subtitulada**) ADJECTIVE
subtitled
los **subtítulos** NOUN
subtitles
el **suburbio** NOUN
slum area
la **subvención** (PL las **subvenciones**) NOUN
subsidy (PL subsidies)
**subvencionar** VERB [25]
to subsidize
**suceder** VERB [8]
to happen
□ ¿Les ha sucedido algo? Has something happened to them?
el **suceso** NOUN
1 event
□ los sucesos de la última decada the events of the last decade □ sucesos históricos historical events
2 incident
□ El suceso ocurrió sobre las tres de la tarde. The incident happened at around three in the afternoon.

■ **Acudieron rápidamente al lugar del suceso.** They rushed to the scene.

○ **LANGUAGE TIP** Be careful! **suceso** does not mean **success**.

la **suciedad** NOUN
dirt

**sucio** (FEM **sucia**) ADJECTIVE
dirty
□ Tienes las manos sucias. You've got dirty hands.

la **sucursal** NOUN
branch (PL branches)

la **sudadera** NOUN
sweatshirt

**Sudáfrica** FEM NOUN
South Africa

**Sudamérica** FEM NOUN
South America

el **sudamericano** (FEM la **sudamericana**) ADJECTIVE, NOUN
South American

**sudar** VERB [25]
to sweat

el **sudeste** NOUN
southeast

el **sudoeste** NOUN
southwest

el **sudor** NOUN
sweat

**sudoroso** (FEM **sudorosa**) ADJECTIVE
sweaty

la **sueca** NOUN
Swede

**Suecia** FEM NOUN
Sweden

**sueco** (FEM **sueca**) ADJECTIVE
Swedish

el **sueco** NOUN
1 Swede
2 Swedish

la **suegra** NOUN
mother-in-law (PL mothers-in-law)

el **suegro** NOUN
father-in-law (PL fathers-in-law)

los **suegros** NOUN
in-laws

la **suela** NOUN
sole

el **sueldo** NOUN
1 salary (PL salaries)
2 wages pl

el **suelo** NOUN
1 floor
□ un suelo de mármol a marble floor
2 ground
■ **Me caí al suelo.** I fell over.

**suelo** VERB ▷ see **soler**

**suelto** VERB

▷ see also **suelto** ADJECTIVE, NOUN ▷ see **soltar**

**suelto** (FEM **suelta**) ADJECTIVE
▷ see also **suelto** VERB, NOUN
loose
□ Tiene varias hojas sueltas. Some of the pages are loose. □ Lleva el pelo suelto. She wears her hair loose. □ No dejes al perro suelto. Don't let the dog loose.

el **suelto** NOUN
▷ see also **suelto** VERB, ADJECTIVE
change

**sueno** VERB ▷ see **sonar**

**sueño** VERB ▷ see **soñar**

el **sueño** NOUN
1 dream
□ Anoche tuve un mal sueño. I had a bad dream last night.
2 sleep
□ un sueño profundo a deep sleep
■ **Tengo sueño.** I'm sleepy.

la **suerte** NOUN
luck
□ No ha tenido mucha suerte. She hasn't had much luck.
■ **por suerte** luckily
■ **Tuvo suerte.** She was lucky.
■ **¡Qué suerte!** How lucky!
■ **¡Qué mala suerte!** What bad luck!

el **suéter** NOUN
sweater

**suficiente** (FEM **suficiente**) ADJECTIVE
enough
□ No tenía dinero suficiente. I didn't have enough money.

**suficientemente** ADVERB
sufficiently

**sufrir** VERB [58]
1 to have
□ Sufrió un ataque al corazón. He had a heart attack.
2 to suffer
□ Sufre de artritis. He suffers from arthritis.
■ **sufrir un colapso** to collapse

la **sugerencia** NOUN
suggestion
■ **hacer una sugerencia** to make a suggestion

**sugerir*** VERB [51]
to suggest
□ Sugirió que fuéramos al cinea. She suggested going to the cinema.

**sugiero** VERB ▷ see **sugerir**

el **suicidio** NOUN
suicide

**Suiza** FEM NOUN
Switzerland

el **suizo** (FEM la **suiza**) ADJECTIVE, NOUN
Swiss

■ **los suizos** the Swiss

el **sujetador** NOUN
bra

**sujetar** VERB [25]
1 to hold
□ Sujétame estos libros un momento. Hold these books for me a moment.
2 to fasten
□ Lo sujetó con un clip. He fastened it with a paper clip.
■ **Sujeta al perro, que no se escape.** Hold on to the dog so it doesn't get away.

el **sujeto** NOUN
subject

la **suma** NOUN
sum
□ una suma de dinero a sum of money
■ **¿Cuánto es la suma de todos los gastos?** What are the total expenses?
■ **hacer una suma** to do a sum

**sumar** VERB [25]
to add up

**suministrar** VERB [25]
to supply

el **suministro** NOUN
supply (PL supplies)

**supe** VERB ▷ see **saber**

**súper** (FEM **súper**) ADJECTIVE
■ **gasolina súper** four-star petrol

**superar** VERB [25]
1 to get over (illness, crisis)
2 to beat (record)
3 to pass (test)
■ **Las ventas han superado nuestras expectativas.** Sales have exceeded our expectations.

la **superficie** NOUN
1 surface
□ en la superficie terrestre on the Earth's surface
2 area
□ una superficie de 100 metros cuadrados an area of 100 square metres

**superior** (FEM **superior**) ADJECTIVE
1 upper
■ **el labio superior** the upper lip
2 top
□ el piso superior the top floor
■ **superior a** superior to
■ **Su inteligencia es superior a la media.** He has above-average intelligence.
■ **un curso de inglés de nivel superior** an advanced level English course

el **supermercado** NOUN
supermarket

el/la **superviviente** NOUN
survivor

el **suplemento** NOUN
supplement
□ el suplemento dominical the Sunday supplement

el/la **suplente** NOUN
1 reserve
2 supply teacher
3 locum

**suplicar*** VERB [48]
to beg

**suponer*** VERB [41]
1 to suppose
□ Supongo que vendrá. I suppose she'll come.
■ **Supongo que sí.** I suppose so.
2 to think
□ Te suponía más alto. I thought you'd be taller. □ Supusimos que no vendrías. We didn't think you would be coming.
3 to involve
□ Tener un coche supone más gastos. Having a car involves more expenses.

el **supositorio** NOUN
suppository

**suprimir** VERB [58]
to delete

**supuesto** VERB ▷ see **suponer**

el **supuesto** NOUN
■ **¿Y en el supuesto de que no venga?** And supposing he doesn't come?
■ **por supuesto** of course
■ **¡Por supuesto que no!** Of course not!

**supuse** VERB ▷ see **suponer**

el **sur** NOUN, ADJECTIVE
south
□ el sur del país the south of the country
□ en la costa sur on the south coast
■ **vientos del sur** southerly winds

**sureño** (FEM **sureña**) ADJECTIVE
southern

el **sureste** NOUN
southeast

el **surf** NOUN
surfing
■ **surf a vela** windsurfing
■ **practicar el surf** to surf

**surgir*** VERB [16]
to come up
□ Ha surgido un problema. A problem has come up.

el **suroeste** NOUN
southwest

**surtido** (FEM **surtida**) ADJECTIVE
assorted
□ pasteles surtidos assorted cakes
■ **estar bien surtido** to have a good selection

el **surtido** NOUN
selection

el **surtidor** NOUN
petrol pump

**susceptible** (FEM **susceptible**) ADJECTIVE
touchy

la **suscripción** (PL las **suscripciones**) NOUN
subscription

**suspender** VERB [8]
1 to call off
□ Han suspendido la boda. They've called the wedding off.
2 to postpone
□ Ha suspendido su visita hasta la semana que viene. He's postponed his visit until next week.
■ El partido se suspendió a causa de la lluvia. The game was rained off.
3 to fail
□ He suspendido Matemáticas. I've failed maths.

el **suspense** NOUN
suspense
□ una película de suspense a thriller

el **suspenso** NOUN
suspense (Latin America)
□ una película de suspenso a thriller
■ Tengo un suspenso en inglés. I failed English.

**suspicaz** (FEM **suspicaz**, PL **suspicaces**)
ADJECTIVE
suspicious

**suspirar** VERB [25]
to sigh

el **suspiro** NOUN
sigh

la **sustancia** NOUN
substance
■ una sustancia química a chemical

el **sustantivo** NOUN
noun

**sustituir*** VERB [10]
1 to replace
□ Lo sustituí como secretario del club. I replaced him as club secretary.
2 to stand in for

□ ¿Me puedes sustituir un par de semanas? Can you stand in for me for a couple of weeks?

el **sustituto**, la **sustituta** NOUN
1 replacement
2 substitute
■ Soy el sustituto del profesor de inglés. I'm standing in for the English teacher.

**sustituyendo** VERB ▷ see sustituir

el **susto** NOUN
fright
□ ¡Qué susto! What a fright!
■ dar un susto a alguien to give somebody a fright

**susurrar** VERB [25]
to whisper
□ Me susurró su nombre al oído. He whispered his name in my ear.

**sutil** (FEM **sutil**) ADJECTIVE
subtle

**suyo** (FEM **suya**) PRONOUN, ADJECTIVE
1 his
□ Todas estas tierras son suyas. All this land is his. □ ¿Es éste su cuarto? — No, el suyo está abajo. Is this his room? — No, his is downstairs.
■ un amigo suyo a friend of his
2 hers
□ Es suyo. It's hers. □ ¿Es éste su abrigo? — No, el suyo es marrón. Is this her coat? — No, hers is brown.
■ un amigo suyo a friend of hers
3 theirs
□ Es suyo. It's theirs. □ ¿Es ésta su casa? — No, la suya está más adelante. Is this their house? — No, theirs is further on.
■ un amigo suyo a friend of theirs
4 yours
□ Todos estos libros son suyos. All these books are yours. □ ¿Es ésta nuestra habitación? — No, la suya está arriba. Is this our room? — No, yours is upstairs.
■ un amigo suyo a friend of yours

# Tt

el **tabaco** NOUN
1 tobacco
   ■ tabaco negro dark tobacco
   ■ tabaco rubio Virginia tobacco
2 cigarettes *pl*

la **taberna** NOUN
   bar

el **tabique** NOUN
   partition

la **tabla** NOUN
   plank
   □ El agujero estaba cubierto con tablas. The hole was covered with planks.
   ■ la tabla de multiplicar the multiplication table
   ■ una tabla de cocina a chopping board
   ■ la tabla de planchar the ironing board
   ■ la tabla de surf the surfboard
   ■ quedar en tablas to draw

el **tablero** NOUN
   board
   ■ el tablero de ajedrez the chessboard
   ■ el tablero de mandos the dashboard

la **tableta** NOUN
1 bar
2 tablet

el **tablón** (PL los **tablones**) NOUN
   plank
   □ los tablones del andamio the scaffolding planks
   ■ el tablón de anuncios the notice board

el **tabú** (PL los **tabúes**) NOUN
   taboo (PL taboos)

el **taburete** NOUN
   stool

**tacaño** (FEM **tacaña**) ADJECTIVE
   mean

el **tacaño**, la **tacaña** NOUN
   skinflint

**tachar** VERB [25]
   to cross out
   □ No lo taches, bórralo. Don't cross it out, erase it.
   ■ La tacharon de mentirosa. They accused her of being a liar.

el **taco** NOUN
1 rawlplug
2 stud
3 cube
4 cue
5 swearword
   ■ soltar tacos to swear
6 heel *(Chile, River Plate)*

el **tacón** (PL los **tacones**) NOUN
   heel
   ■ zapatos de tacón high-heeled shoes

la **táctica** NOUN
   tactics *pl*
   □ El equipo cambió de táctica. The team changed tactics.

el **tacto** NOUN
1 touch
   □ suave al tacto smooth to the touch
2 tact
   ■ Lo dijo con mucho tacto. He said it very tactfully.

la **tajada** NOUN
   slice

**tajante** (FEM **tajante**) ADJECTIVE
1 emphatic
2 sharp
   □ Lo dijo de manera tajante. He said it sharply.

**tal** (FEM **tal**) ADJECTIVE, PRONOUN
   such
   □ En tales casos es mejor consultar con un médico. In such cases it's better to see a doctor. □ ¡En el aeropuerto había tal confusión! There was such confusion at the airport!
   ■ Lo dejé tal como estaba. I left it just as it was.
   ■ con tal de que as long as □ con tal de que regreséis antes de las once as long as you get back before eleven
   ■ ¿Qué tal? How are things?
   ■ ¿Qué tal has dormido? How did you sleep?
   ■ tal vez perhaps

la **taladradora** NOUN
1 pneumatic drill
2 punch (PL punches)

**taladrar** VERB [25]
to drill

el **taladro** NOUN
drill

el **talento** NOUN
talent
▫ Sus hijos tienen talento para la música.
Their children have a talent for music.

la **talla** NOUN
size
▫ ¿Tienen esta camisa en la talla cuatro?
Do you have this shirt in a size four?

**tallar** VERB [25]
1 to carve
2 to sculpt
3 to scrub (Chile, River Plate)

los **tallarines** NOUN
noodles

el **taller** NOUN
1 garage
▫ Tengo el coche en el taller. My car is in the garage.
2 workshop
■ un taller de teatro a theatre workshop

el **tallo** NOUN
stem

el **talón** (PL los **talones**) NOUN
1 heel
2 cheque
▫ cobrar un talón to cash a cheque

el **talonario** NOUN
1 chequebook
2 book of tickets
3 receipt book

el **tamaño** NOUN
size
■ ¿Qué tamaño tiene? What size is it?

**tambalearse** VERB [25]
1 to wobble
2 to stagger

**también** ADVERB
also
▫ Canta flamenco y también baila. He sings flamenco and also dances.
■ Tengo hambre. — Yo también. I'm hungry. — So am I.
■ Yo estoy de acuerdo. — Nosotros también. I agree. — So do we.

el **tambor** NOUN
drum

el **Támesis** NOUN
the Thames

el **tamiz** (PL los **tamices**) NOUN
sieve

**tampoco** ADVERB
1 either
▫ Yo tampoco lo compré. I didn't buy it either.

2 neither
▫ Yo no la vi. — Yo tampoco. I didn't see her. — Neither did I. ▫ Nunca he estado en París. — Yo tampoco. I've never been to Paris. — Neither have I.

el **tampón** (PL los **tampones**) NOUN
tampon

**tan** ADVERB
1 so
▫ No creí que fueras a venir tan pronto. I didn't think you'd come so soon. ▫ ¡No es tan difícil! It's not so difficult!
■ ¡Qué hombre tan amable! What a kind man!
■ tan ... que ... so ... that ... ▫ Habla tan deprisa que no la entiendo. She talks so fast that I can't understand her.
2 such
▫ No era una idea tan buena. It wasn't such a good idea. ▫ ¡Tiene unos amigos tan simpáticos! He has such nice friends!
■ tan ... como ... as ... as ... ▫ No es tan guapa como su madre. She's not as pretty as her mother. ▫ Vine tan pronto como pude. I came as soon as I could.

el **tanque** NOUN
tank

**tantear** VERB [25]
to weigh up

**tanto** (FEM **tanta**) ADJECTIVE, ADVERB, PRONOUN
1 so much (PL so many)
▫ Ahora no bebo tanta leche. I don't drink so much milk now. ▫ Se preocupa tanto que no puede dormir. He worries so much that he can't sleep. ▫ ¡Tengo tantas cosas que hacer hoy! I have so many things to do today! ▫ No necesitamos tantas. We don't need so many.
■ Vinieron tantos que no cabían en la sala. So many people came that they couldn't fit into the room.
■ No recibe tantas llamadas como yo. He doesn't get as many calls as I do.
■ Gano tanto como tú. I earn as much as you.
2 so often
▫ Ahora no la veo tanto. Now I don't see her so often.
■ ¡No corras tanto! Don't run so fast!
■ tanto tú como yo both you and I
■ tanto si viene como si no whether he comes or not
■ ¡Tanto gusto! How do you do?
■ entre tanto meanwhile
■ por lo tanto therefore

el **tanto** NOUN
1 goal
▫ Juárez marcó el segundo tanto. Juárez

t

scored the second goal.

**2** amount

□ Me paga un tanto fijo cada semana. He pays me a fixed amount each week.

■ **un tanto por ciento** a percentage

■ **Había cuarenta y tantos invitados.** There were forty-odd guests.

■ **Manténme al tanto.** Keep me informed.

la **tapa** NOUN

**1** lid

**2** top

**3** cover

**4** tapa

□ Pedimos unas tapas en el bar. We ordered some tapas in the bar.

la **tapadera** NOUN
lid

el **tapado** NOUN (River Plate)
coat

**tapar** VERB [25]
to cover

□ La tapé con una manta. I covered her with a blanket.

■ **Tapa la olla.** Put the lid on the pan.

■ **Me estás tapando el sol.** You're keeping the sun off me.

■ **Tápate bien que hace frío.** Wrap up well as it's cold.

el **tapete** NOUN

**1** embroidered tablecloth

**2** rug (Mexico)

la **tapia** NOUN
wall

□ la tapia del jardín the garden wall

la **tapicería** NOUN

**1** upholstery

**2** upholsterer's

el **tapiz** (PL los **tapices**) NOUN
tapestry (PL tapestries)

**tapizar*** VERB [13]
to upholster

el **tapón** (PL los **tapones**) NOUN

**1** plug

**2** top

**3** cork

■ **tapón de rosca** screw top

la **taquigrafía** NOUN
shorthand

la **taquilla** NOUN

**1** box office

**2** ticket office

**3** locker

**tararear** VERB [25]
to hum

**tardar** VERB [25]
to be late

□ Te espero a las ocho. No tardes. I expect you at eight. Don't be late.

■ **Tardaron una semana en contestar.** They took a week to reply. □ El arroz tarda media hora en hacerse. Rice takes half an hour to cook.

■ **En avión se tarda dos horas.** The plane takes two hours.

la **tarde** NOUN

**1** afternoon

□ a las tres de la tarde at three in the afternoon □ ¡Buenas tardes! Good afternoon! □ por la tarde in the afternoon □ hoy por la tarde this afternoon

**2** evening

□ a las ocho de la tarde at eight in the evening □ ¡Buenas tardes! Good evening! □ por la tarde in the evening □ hoy por la tarde this evening

**tarde** ADVERB
late

□ Se está haciendo tarde. It's getting late.

■ **más tarde** later

■ **tarde o temprano** sooner or later

■ **Llegaré a las nueve como muy tarde.** I'll arrive at nine at the latest.

la **tarea** NOUN
task

□ Una de sus tareas es repartir la correspondencia. One of his tasks is to hand out the mail.

■ **las tareas domésticas** the chores

■ **las tareas** (Latin America) homework

la **tarifa** NOUN

**1** rate

□ tarifa plana flat rate

**2** fare

■ **tarifa de precios** price list

la **tarima** NOUN
platform

la **tarjeta** NOUN
card

□ Me mandó una tarjeta de Navidad. He sent me a Christmas card.

■ **una tarjeta de cajero automático** a cash card

■ **una tarjeta de crédito** a credit card

■ **una tarjeta de visita** a visiting card

■ **una tarjeta telefónica** a phonecard

■ **una tarjeta de embarque** a boarding pass

el **tarro** NOUN

**1** jar

**2** mug (Mexico)

la **tarta** NOUN

**1** cake

□ una tarta de cumpleaños a birthday cake

**2** tart

**tartamudear** VERB [25]
to stammer

**tartamudo** (FEM **tartamuda**) ADJECTIVE
■ **ser tartamudo** to stutter

la **tasa** NOUN
rate
▫ la tasa de natalidad the birth rate

**tasar** VERB [25]
to value

la **tasca** NOUN
tavern

el **tata** NOUN (Latin America)
1 daddy
2 grandpa

el **tatuaje** NOUN
tattoo (PL tattoos)

**tatuar\*** VERB [1]
to tattoo

**Tauro** MASC NOUN
Taurus
■ **Soy tauro.** I'm Taurus.

el **taxi** NOUN
taxi
▫ tomar un taxi to take a taxi

el **taxímetro** NOUN
taximeter

el/la **taxista** NOUN
taxi driver

la **taza** NOUN
1 cup
▫ Tomamos una taza de café. We had a cup of coffee.
2 cupful
▫ una taza de arroz a cupful of rice
3 bowl

el **tazón** (PL los **tazones**) NOUN
bowl

**TDT** ABBREVIATION (= televisión digital terrestre)
DTT (= digital terrestrial television)

**te** PRONOUN
1 you
▫ Te quiero. I love you. ▫ Te voy a dar un consejo. I'm going to give you some advice.
■ **Me gustaría comprártelo.** I'd like to buy it for you.
2 yourself
▫ ¿Te has hecho daño? Have you hurt yourself? ▫ ¿Te duelen los pies? Do your feet hurt? ▫ Te tienes que poner el abrigo. You should put your coat on.

el **té** (PL los **tés**) NOUN
tea
■ **Me hice un té.** I made myself a cup of tea.

el **teatro** NOUN
theatre
▫ Por la noche fuimos al teatro. At night we went to the theatre.
■ **una obra de teatro** a play

el **tebeo** NOUN
comic

el **techo** NOUN
1 ceiling
▫ El techo está pintado de blanco. The ceiling is painted white.
2 roof (Latin America)

la **tecla** NOUN
key (PL keys)
■ **pulsar una tecla** to press a key

el **teclado** NOUN
keyboard

**teclear** VERB [25]
to type

la **técnica** NOUN
1 technique
2 technology (PL technologies)
3 technician
▫ Mi hermana es técnica de laboratorio. My sister is a laboratory technician.

**técnico** (FEM **técnica**) ADJECTIVE
technical

el **técnico** NOUN
1 technician
▫ un técnico de laboratorio a laboratory technician
2 repairman (PL repairmen)
▫ El técnico me arregló la lavadora. The repairman fixed my washing machine.

el **tecno** NOUN
techno

la **tecnología** NOUN
technology (PL technologies)
■ **tecnología punta** state-of-the-art technology

**tecnológico** (FEM **tecnológica**) ADJECTIVE
technological

la **teja** NOUN
tile

el **tejado** NOUN
roof (PL roofs)

los **tejanos** NOUN
jeans

**tejer** VERB [8]
1 to weave
2 to knit

el **tejido** NOUN
1 fabric
2 tissue

**tel.** ABBREVIATION (= teléfono)
tel.

la **tela** NOUN
fabric
■ **tela metálica** wire netting

la **telaraña** NOUN
cobweb

la **tele** NOUN
TV
▫ Estábamos viendo la tele. We were

watching TV.

las **telecomunicaciones** NOUN
telecommunications

el **telediario** NOUN
news *sing*
□ el telediario de las nueve the nine o'clock news

**teledirigido** (FEM **teledirigida**) ADJECTIVE
remote-controlled

el **teleférico** NOUN
cable car

**telefonear** VERB [25]
to phone
□ Tengo que telefonear a mis padres. I have to phone my parents.

**telefónico** (FEM **telefónica**) ADJECTIVE
telephone
■ **la guía telefónica** the telephone directory

el/la **telefonista** NOUN
telephonist

el **teléfono** NOUN
telephone
■ **No tengo teléfono.** I don't have a telephone.
■ **Hablamos por teléfono.** We spoke on the phone.
■ **Está hablando por teléfono.** He's on the phone.
■ **colgar el teléfono a alguien** to hang up the phone on somebody
■ **un teléfono de tarjeta** a card phone
■ **un teléfono con cámara** a camera phone
■ **un teléfono fijo** a landline (phone)
■ **un teléfono móvil** a mobile phone

el **telegrama** NOUN
telegram

la **telenovela** NOUN
soap opera (PL soap operas)

la **telepatía** NOUN
telepathy

la **telerrealidad** NOUN
reality TV

el **telescopio** NOUN
telescope

el **telesilla** NOUN
chairlift

el **telespectador**, la **telespectadora**
NOUN
viewer

el **telesquí** (PL los **telesquís**) NOUN
ski-lift

el **teletexto** NOUN
Teletext®

las **televentas** NOUN
telesales

**televisar** VERB [25]

to televise

la **televisión** (PL las **televisiones**) NOUN
television
■ **Dieron la noticia por la televisión.** They gave the news on the television.
■ **¿Qué ponen en la televisión esta noche?** What's on the television tonight?
■ **la televisión por cable** cable television
■ **la televisión digital** digital TV

el **televisor** NOUN
television set

el **telón** (PL los **telones**) NOUN
curtain
□ Subió el telón. The curtain rose.

el **tema** NOUN
1 topic
□ El tema de la redacción era 'Las vacaciones'. The topic of the essay was 'The holidays'.
2 subject
□ Luego hablaremos de ese tema. We'll talk about that subject later.
■ **cambiar de tema** to change the subject
■ **temas de actualidad** current affairs
■ **el tema de conversación** the talking point

**temblar*** VERB [39]
to tremble
□ Me temblaban las manos. My hands were trembling.
■ **temblar de miedo** to tremble with fear
■ **temblar de frío** to shiver

el **temblor de tierra** NOUN
earthquake

**tembloroso** (FEM **temblorosa**) ADJECTIVE
trembling

**temer** VERB [8]
1 to be afraid
□ No temas. Don't be afraid.
2 to be afraid of
□ Le teme al profesor. He's afraid of the teacher. □ Temo ofenderles. I'm afraid of offending them.

**temible** (FEM **temible**) ADJECTIVE
fearsome

el **temor** NOUN
fear
□ el temor a la oscuridad fear of the dark
□ por temor a equivocarme for fear of making a mistake

**temperamental** (FEM **temperamental**)
ADJECTIVE
temperamental

el **temperamento** NOUN
temperament

la **temperatura** NOUN
temperature
□ El médico le tomó la temperatura.

t

The doctor took his temperature.

la **tempestad** NOUN
storm

**templado** (FEM **templada**) ADJECTIVE
1 lukewarm
2 mild

el **templo** NOUN
temple

la **temporada** NOUN
season
□ la temporada de esquí the ski season □ la temporada alta the high season □ la temporada baja the low season

**temporal** (FEM **temporal**) ADJECTIVE
temporary

el **temporal** NOUN
storm

**temporario** (FEM **temporaria**) ADJECTIVE
(Latin America)
temporary

**temprano** ADVERB
early
■ **por la mañana temprano** early in the morning

**ten** VERB ▷ see **tener**

**tenaz** (FEM **tenaz**, PL **tenaces**) ADJECTIVE
tenacious

las **tenazas** NOUN
pliers

el **tendedero** NOUN
1 clothes line
2 clothes horse

la **tendencia** NOUN
tendency (PL tendencies)
■ **Tengo tendencia a engordar.** I tend to put on weight.

**tender*** VERB [20]
1 to hang out
□ Marta estaba tendiendo la ropa. Marta was hanging out the washing.
2 to lay out
□ Tendí la toalla sobre la arena. I laid the towel out on the sand.
■ **Me tendió la mano.** He stretched out his hand to me.
■ **tender a hacer algo** to tend to do something
■ **tender una trampa** to set a trap
■ **tenderse en el sofá** to lie down on the sofa
■ **tender la cama** (Latin America) to make the bed
■ **tender la mesa** (Latin America) to lay the table

el **tendero**, la **tendera** NOUN
shopkeeper

**tendido** (FEM **tendida**) ADJECTIVE
■ **La ropa estaba tendida.** The washing was hanging out.
■ **Lo encontré tendido en el suelo.** I found him lying on the floor.

el **tendón** (PL los **tendones**) NOUN
tendon

**tendrá** VERB ▷ see **tener**

el **tenedor** NOUN
fork

**tener*** VERB [53]
1 to have
□ Tengo dos hermanas. I have two sisters.
□ ¿Tienes dinero? Do you have any money?
□ Tiene el pelo rubio. He has blond hair.
□ Va a tener un niño. She's going to have a baby. □ Luis tiene la gripe. Luis has the flu.
■ **¿Cuántos años tienes?** How old are you?
■ **Tiene cinco metros de largo.** It's five metres long.
■ **Ten cuidado.** Be careful.
■ **No tengas miedo.** Don't be afraid.
■ **Tenía el pelo mojado.** His hair was wet.
2 to hold
□ Tenía el pasaporte en la mano. He was holding his passport in his hand.
■ **tener que hacer algo** to have to do something
■ **Tendrías que comer más.** You should eat more.
■ **No tienes por qué ir.** There's no reason why you should go.
■ **Eso no tiene nada que ver.** That's got nothing to do with it.
■ **¡Tenga!** Here you are!
■ **tenerse en pie** to stand

**tenga** VERB ▷ see **tener**

el/la **teniente** NOUN
lieutenant

el **tenis** NOUN
tennis
■ **¿Juegas al tenis?** Do you play tennis?
■ **tenis de mesa** table tennis

el/la **tenista** NOUN
tennis player

el **tenor** NOUN
tenor

**tensar** VERB [25]
to tighten

la **tensión** (PL las **tensiones**) NOUN
1 tension
□ Hubo mucha tensión durante la reunión. There was a lot of tension during the meeting.
2 blood pressure
□ El médico me tomó la tensión. The doctor took my blood pressure.
■ **un cable de alta tensión** a high-voltage cable

**tenso** (FEM **tensa**) ADJECTIVE

**1** tense
**2** taut

la **tentación** (PL las **tentaciones**) NOUN
temptation
■ **caer en la tentación** to give in to
temptation

**tentador** (FEM **tentadora**) ADJECTIVE
tempting

**tentar\*** VERB [39]
to tempt
□ Estuve tentado de marcharme. I was
tempted to leave.
■ **No me tienta la idea.** The idea isn't very
tempting.

la **tentativa** NOUN
attempt

el **tentempié** (PL los **tentempiés**) NOUN
snack

**tenue** (FEM **tenue**) ADJECTIVE
faint

**teñir\*** VERB [45]
to dye
□ Se ha teñido el pelo. He's dyed his hair.

la **teología** NOUN
theology

la **teoría** NOUN
theory (PL theories)
□ En teoría es fácil. In theory it's easy.

**teórico** (FEM **teórica**) ADJECTIVE
theoretical
□ Ése es un caso teórico. It's a theoretical
case.
■ **un examen teórico** a theory exam

**terapéutico** (FEM **terapéutica**) ADJECTIVE
therapeutic

la **terapia** NOUN
therapy (PL therapies)

**tercer** ▷ see **tercero**

**tercero** (FEM **tercera**) ADJECTIVE, PRONOUN
third
□ la tercera vez the third time □ Llegué el
tercero. I arrived third.
■ **una tercera parte de la población** a
third of the population
■ **Vivo en el tercero.** I live on the third
floor.
■ **el Tercer Mundo** the Third World

el **tercio** NOUN
third

el **terciopelo** NOUN
velvet

**terco** (FEM **terca**) ADJECTIVE
obstinate

**tergiversar** VERB [25]
to distort

el **terminal** NOUN
terminal

la **terminal** NOUN
terminal

**terminante** (FEM **terminante**) ADJECTIVE
**1** categorical
**2** strict

**terminantemente** ADVERB
strictly

**terminar** VERB [25]
**1** to finish
□ He terminado el libro. I've finished the
book.
■ **cuando terminó de hablar** when he
finished talking
**2** to end
□ ¿A qué hora termina la clase? At what
time does the class end?
■ **Terminé rendido.** I ended up exhausted.
■ **Terminaron peleándose.** They ended up
fighting.
■ **Se nos ha terminado el café.** We've run
out of coffee.
■ **He terminado con Andrés.** I've broken
up with Andrés.

el **término** NOUN
term
□ un término médico a medical term
■ **por término medio** on average

la **termita** NOUN
termite

el **termo**® NOUN
Thermos flask®

el **termómetro** NOUN
thermometer
■ **Le puse el termómetro.** I took his
temperature.

el **termostato** NOUN
thermostat

la **ternera** NOUN
**1** calf (PL calves) (animal)
**2** veal

el **ternero** NOUN
calf (PL calves) (animal)

la **ternura** NOUN
tenderness
■ **con ternura** tenderly

el/la **terrateniente** NOUN
landowner

la **terraza** NOUN
**1** balcony (PL balconies)
**2** roof terrace
■ **Salimos a la terraza del bar a tomar
algo.** We went out to the beer garden for a
drink.

el **terremoto** NOUN
earthquake

el **terreno** NOUN
**1** land
□ una granja con mucho terreno a farm
with a lot of land

■ **un terreno** a piece of land □ Hemos comprado un terreno. **We've bought a piece of land.**
2 field
□ terrenos plantados de naranjos fields planted with orange trees □ en el terreno de la informática in the field of computing science
■ **el terreno de juego** the pitch
■ **Lo decidiremos sobre el terreno.** We'll decide as we go along.

**terrestre** (FEM **terrestre**) ADJECTIVE
land

**terrible** (FEM **terrible**) ADJECTIVE
terrible
□ Fue una experiencia terrible. It was a terrible experience.
■ **Tenía un cansancio terrible.** I was awfully tired.

el **terrier** (PL los **terriers**) NOUN
terrier

el **territorio** NOUN
territory (PL territories)

el **terrón** (PL los **terrones**) NOUN
lump

el **terror** NOUN
terror
□ Fuimos víctimas de una campaña de terror. We were the victims of a terror campaign.
■ **Les tiene terror a los perros.** He's terrified of dogs.
■ **una película de terror** a horror film

el **terrorismo** NOUN
terrorism

el/la **terrorista** ADJECTIVE, NOUN
terrorist
■ **un terrorista suicida** a suicide bomber

la **tesis** (PL las **tesis**) NOUN
thesis (PL theses)

el **tesón** NOUN
determination

el **tesorero**, la **tesorera** NOUN
treasurer

el **tesoro** NOUN
treasure
■ **Ven aquí, tesoro.** Come here, darling.

el **test** (PL los **tests**) NOUN
test
□ Hoy nos han hecho un test. We had a test today.

el **testamento** NOUN
will
■ **hacer testamento** to make one's will
■ **el Antiguo Testamento** the Old Testament
■ **el Nuevo Testamento** the New Testament

**testarudo** (FEM **testaruda**) ADJECTIVE
stubborn

el/la **testigo** NOUN
witness (PL witnesses)
■ **un Testigo de Jehová** a Jehovah's Witness
■ **Fui testigo del accidente.** I witnessed the accident.

el **testimonio** NOUN
evidence

el **tétanos** NOUN
tetanus

la **tetera** NOUN
1 teapot
2 kettle (Chile, Mexico)
3 baby's bottle (Mexico)

la **tetina** NOUN
teat

el **textil** (FEM el **textil**) ADJECTIVE, NOUN
textile

el **texto** NOUN
text
■ **un libro de texto** a textbook

la **textura** NOUN
texture

la **tez** NOUN
complexion

**ti** PRONOUN
you
□ una llamada para ti a call for you
■ **Sólo piensas en ti mismo.** You only think of yourself.

la **tía** NOUN
1 aunt
□ mi tía my aunt
2 girl
□ Es una tía majísima. She's a really nice girl.

**tibio** (FEM **tibia**) ADJECTIVE
lukewarm

el **tiburón** (PL los **tiburones**) NOUN
shark

el **tic** NOUN
tic
□ un tic nervioso a nervous tic

el **tictac** NOUN
tick-tock

**tiemblo** VERB ▷ see **temblar**

el **tiempo** NOUN
1 time
□ No tengo tiempo. I don't have time.
□ ¿Qué haces en tu tiempo libre? What do you do in your spare time? □ Me llevó bastante tiempo. It took me quite a long time.
■ **¿Cuánto tiempo hace que vives aquí?** How long have you been living here?
■ **Hace mucho tiempo que no la veo.**

I haven't seen her for a long time.
- **al mismo tiempo** at the same time
- **perder el tiempo** to waste time
- **al poco tiempo** soon after
- **a tiempo** in time □ Llegamos a tiempo de ver la película. We got there in time to see the film.
- **¿Qué tiempo tiene el niño?** How old is the baby?

2 weather
- **¿Qué tiempo hace ahí?** What's the weather like there?
- **hizo buen tiempo** the weather was fine
- **Hace mal tiempo.** The weather's bad.

3 half
- **Metieron el gol durante el segundo tiempo.** They scored the goal during the second half.

la **tienda** NOUN
shop
- **una tienda de comestibles** a grocer's shop (PL grocers' shops)
- **una tienda de discos** a record shop
- **ir de tiendas** to go shopping
- **una tienda de campaña** a tent

**tiendo** VERB ▷ see tender
**tiene** VERB ▷ see tener
**tiento** VERB ▷ see tentar
**tierno** (FEM tierna) ADJECTIVE
1 tender
2 fresh

la **tierra** NOUN
1 land
□ Trabajan la tierra. They work the land.
- **la Tierra Santa** the Holy Land
- **tierra adentro** inland
2 soil
- **echar algo por tierra** to ruin something
□ Echó por tierra todos nuestros planes. It ruined all our plans.
- **la Tierra** the Earth

**tieso** (FEM tiesa) ADJECTIVE
1 stiff
- **quedarse tieso de frío** to be frozen stiff
2 straight
□ Ponte tiesa. Stand up straight.

el **tiesto** NOUN
flowerpot

el **tigre** NOUN
tiger

las **tijeras** NOUN
scissors
□ Es más fácil cortarlo con las tijeras. It's easier to cut with scissors.
- **¿Tienes unas tijeras?** Do you have a pair of scissors?
- **unas tijeras de podar** a pair of secateurs

**timar** VERB [25]

1 to con
2 to rip off
□ Te han timado con ese coche. They've ripped you off with that car.

el **timbrazo** NOUN
ring

el **timbre** NOUN
1 bell
□ Ya ha sonado el timbre. The bell has already gone.
- **llamar al timbre** to ring the bell
2 stamp (Mexico)

la **timidez** NOUN
shyness

**tímido** (FEM tímida) ADJECTIVE
shy

el **timo** NOUN
1 con
2 rip off
- **¡Vaya timo!** What a rip-off!

la **tinaja** NOUN
large earthenware vat

la **tinta** NOUN
ink
□ escrito con tinta written in ink
- **tinta China** Indian ink

 **LANGUAGE TIP** Word for word, tinta china means 'Chinese ink'.

- **sudar tinta** to sweat blood

el **tinte** NOUN
dye

el **tintero** NOUN
inkwell

el **tinto** NOUN
red wine

la **tintorería** NOUN
dry cleaner's

**tiñendo** VERB ▷ see teñir

el **tío** NOUN
1 uncle
- **mis tíos** my uncle and aunt
2 guy
□ Es un tío muy simpático. He's a really nice guy.
- **Oye, tío, me alegro de verte.** Hey, man, nice to see you.

el **tiovivo** NOUN
merry-go-round (PL merry-go-rounds)

**típicamente** ADVERB
typically

**típico** (FEM típica) ADJECTIVE
typical
- **Eso es muy típico de ella.** That's very typical of her.

el **tipo** NOUN
1 kind
□ No me gusta este tipo de fiestas. I don't like this kind of party.

■ **todo tipo de ...** all sorts of ...

2 figure
□ Marisa tiene un tipo muy bonito. **Marisa has a lovely figure.**

3 bloke
□ un tipo de aspecto sospechoso a suspicious-looking bloke

el **tíquet** (PL los **tíquets**) NOUN
1 ticket
2 receipt

la **tira** NOUN
strip
□ una tira de papel a strip of paper □ una tira cómica a comic strip
■ **Tiene la tira de libros.** He has lots of books.
■ **Hace la tira de tiempo que no la veo.** I haven't seen her for ages.

la **tirada** NOUN
1 print run
□ La tirada inicial fue de 50.000 ejemplares. The initial print run was 50,000 copies.
2 circulation
□ La revista tiene una tirada semanal de 200.000 ejemplares. The magazine has a weekly circulation of 200,000 copies.
■ **de una tirada** in one go

**tirado** (FEM **tirada**) ADJECTIVE
1 dirt-cheap
2 dead easy

el **tirador** NOUN
handle

la **tirana** NOUN
tyrant

**tiránico** (FEM **tiránica**) ADJECTIVE
tyrannical

el **tirano** NOUN
tyrant

**tirante** (FEM **tirante**) ADJECTIVE
1 tight
2 tense

el **tirante** NOUN
strap
■ **tirantes** braces

**tirar** VERB [25]
1 to throw
□ Tírame la pelota. Throw me the ball.
□ Les tiraban piedras a los soldados. They were throwing stones at the soldiers. □ Se tiró al suelo. He threw himself to the ground.
2 to throw away
□ No tires la comida. Don't throw away the food.
■ **tirar algo a la basura** to throw something out
■ **tirar al suelo** to knock over □ La moto la tiró al suelo. The motorbike knocked her

over.
■ **Tropezó con la maceta y la tiró al suelo.** He tripped on the flowerpot and knocked it to the ground.
3 to knock down
□ Queremos tirar esta pared. We want to knock this wall down.
4 to drop
■ **tirar a la derecha** to turn right
■ **tirar de algo** to pull something
■ **tirar la cadena** (Latin America) to pull the chain
■ **Vamos tirando.** We're getting by.
■ **tirarse al agua** to plunge into the water
■ **tirarse de cabeza** to dive in head first
■ **tirarse en el sofá** (Latin America) to lie down on the sofa
■ **Se tiró toda la mañana estudiando.** He spent the whole morning studying.

la **tirita** NOUN
plaster

**tiritar** VERB [25]
to shiver
■ **tiritar de frío** to shiver with cold

el **tiro** NOUN
shot
□ Oímos un tiro. We heard a shot.
■ **Lo mataron de un tiro.** They shot him dead.
■ **Me salió el tiro por la culata.** It backfired on me.
■ **tiro al blanco** target practice
■ **un tiro libre** a free kick

el **tiroteo** NOUN
shoot-out

el **títere** NOUN
puppet

**titubear** VERB [25]
to hesitate
□ Respondí sin titubear. I answered without hesitating.

**titulado** (FEM **titulada**) ADJECTIVE
qualified
□ una enfermera titulada a qualified nurse

el **titular** NOUN
headline

el/la **titular** NOUN
1 holder
2 owner

**titular** VERB [25]
to call
□ La novela se titula 'Marcianos'. The novel is called 'Marcianos'.
■ **¿Cómo vas a titular el trabajo?** What title are you going to give the essay?

el **título** NOUN
1 title
□ Necesito un título para el poema. I need a

title for the poem.
**2** qualification
□ Tiene el título de enfermera. She has a nursing qualification.
**3** certificate
□ Tenía los títulos colgados en la pared. His certificates were hanging on the wall.

la **tiza** NOUN
chalk
■ una tiza a piece of chalk

la **toalla** NOUN
towel
□ una toalla de baño a bath towel

el **tobillo** NOUN
ankle
□ Me he torcido el tobillo. I've twisted my ankle.

el **tobogán** (PL los **toboganes**) NOUN
**1** slide
**2** toboggan

el **tocadiscos** (PL los **tocadiscos**) NOUN
record player

el **tocador** NOUN
dressing table

**tocar\*** VERB [48]
**1** to touch
□ Si lo tocas te quemarás. If you touch it you'll burn yourself.
**2** to play
□ Toca el violín. He plays the violin.
**3** to ring
**4** to blow
■ tocar a la puerta (*Latin America*) to knock on the door
■ Te toca fregar los platos. It's your turn to do the dishes.
■ Le tocó la lotería. He won the lottery.

el **tocino** NOUN
pork fat

**todavía** ADVERB
**1** still
□ ¿Todavía estás en la cama? Are you still in bed? □ ¡Y todavía se queja! And he still complains!
**2** yet
□ Todavía no han llegado. They haven't arrived yet. □ ¿Todavía no has comido? Have you not eaten yet? □ Todavía no. Not yet.

**todo** (FEM **toda**) ADJECTIVE, PRONOUN
**1** all
□ todos los niños all the children □ Todos son caros. They're all expensive. □ el más bonito de todos the prettiest of all
■ toda la noche all night
■ todos vosotros all of you
■ todos los que quieran venir all those who want to come

**2** every
□ todos los días every day
**3** the whole
□ He limpiado toda la casa. I've cleaned the whole house.
■ Ha viajado por todo el mundo. He has travelled throughout the world.
■ Todo el mundo lo sabe. Everybody knows.
**4** everything
□ Lo sabemos todo. We know everything.
□ todo lo que me dijeron everything they told me
**5** everybody
□ Todos estaban de acuerdo. Everybody agreed.
■ Vaya todo seguido. Keep straight on.
■ todo lo contrario quite the opposite

el **toldo** NOUN
**1** sun blind
**2** awning
**3** sunshade

**tolerante** (FEM **tolerante**) ADJECTIVE
tolerant

**tolerar** VERB [25]
to tolerate
□ No voy a tolerar ese comportamiento. I won't tolerate that behaviour.
■ Sus padres le toleran demasiado. His parents let him get away with too much.

**tomar** VERB [25]
**1** to take
□ En clase tomamos apuntes. We take notes in class. □ Se lo ha tomado muy en serio. He's taken it very seriously. □ Se tomó la molestia de acompañarnos. He took the trouble to accompany us.
■ tomar a alguien de la mano to take somebody by the hand
■ tomarse algo a mal to take something badly
**2** to have
□ ¿Qué quieres tomar? What are you going to have? □ De postre tomé un helado. I had an ice cream for dessert.
■ Toma, esto es tuyo. Here, this is yours.
■ tomar cariño a alguien to become fond of somebody
■ tomar el pelo a alguien to pull somebody's leg
■ tomar el aire to get some fresh air
■ tomar el sol to sunbathe
■ tomar nota de algo to note something down

el **tomate** NOUN
tomato (PL tomatoes)
■ ponerse como un tomate to turn as red as a beetroot

el **tomillo** NOUN
thyme

el **tomo** NOUN
volume

el **tonel** NOUN
barrel

la **tonelada** NOUN
ton

la **tónica** NOUN
tonic

el **tono** NOUN
1 tone
□ Lo dijo en tono cariñoso. He said it in an affectionate tone.
■ **un tono de llamada** a ringtone
2 shade
□ un tono un poco más oscuro a slightly darker shade

la **tonta** NOUN
fool
■ **hacerse la tonta** to act dumb

la **tontería** NOUN
silly thing
□ Se pelearon por una tontería. They fell out over a silly thing.
■ **tonterías** nonsense □ ¡Eso son tonterías! That's nonsense! □ ¡No digas tonterías! Don't talk nonsense!

**tonto** (FEM **tonta**) ADJECTIVE
silly
□ ¡Qué error más tonto! What a silly mistake!

el **tonto** NOUN
fool
■ **hacer el tonto** to act the fool
■ **hacerse el tonto** to act dumb

**toparse** VERB [25]
■ **toparse con alguien** to bump into somebody

los **topes** NOUN
■ **El autobús iba hasta los topes.** The bus was packed.

el **tópico** NOUN
cliché (PL clichés)

**topless** (FEM + PL **topless**) ADJECTIVE
topless

el **topo** NOUN
mole

el **toque** NOUN
■ **dar los últimos toques a algo** to put the finishing touches to something
■ **el toque de queda** the curfew

el **tórax** NOUN
thorax

la **torcedura** NOUN
■ **una torcedura de tobillo** a sprained ankle

**torcer*** VERB

1 to twist
□ ¡Me estás torciendo el brazo! You're twisting my arm!
■ **torcerse el tobillo** to sprain one's ankle
2 to turn
□ torcer a la derecha to turn right □ torcer la esquina to turn the corner

**torcido** (FEM **torcida**) ADJECTIVE
1 crooked
□ Tiene la boca un poco torcida. His mouth's a bit crooked.
2 bent
□ El tronco está torcido. The trunk is bent.
■ **Ese cuadro está torcido.** That picture isn't straight.

**torear** VERB [25]
to fight
□ No volverá a torear. He will never fight again.

el **toreo** NOUN
bullfighting

el **torero**, la **torera** NOUN
bullfighter

la **tormenta** NOUN
storm
■ **Hubo tormenta.** There was a storm.
■ **un día de tormenta** a stormy day

el **torneo** NOUN
tournament

el **tornillo** NOUN
1 screw
■ **A tu hermana le falta un tornillo.** Your sister's got a screw loose.
2 bolt

el **toro** NOUN
bull
■ **los toros** bullfighting
■ **ir a los toros** to go to a bullfight

la **toronja** NOUN (Latin America)
grapefruit (PL grapefruit)

**torpe** (FEM **torpe**) ADJECTIVE
1 clumsy
2 dim

la **torre** NOUN
1 tower
□ la torre de control the control tower
2 pylon
3 rook

la **torta** NOUN
1 small flat cake
2 pie (Latin America)
3 filled roll (Mexico)
■ **pegar una torta a alguien** to give somebody a slap
■ **No entiendo ni torta.** I don't understand a thing.
■ **No ve ni torta.** He's as blind as a bat.

t

la **tortilla** NOUN
1 omelette
 ■ **una tortilla de patatas** a Spanish
 omelette
2 tortilla
la **tortuga** NOUN
1 tortoise
2 turtle
la **tortura** NOUN
 torture
**torturar** VERB [25]
 to torture
la **tos** (PL las **toses**) NOUN
 cough (PL coughs)
 ■ **Tengo mucha tos.** I have a bad cough.
**toser** VERB [8]
 to cough
la **tostada** NOUN
1 piece of toast
 □ ¿Quieres una tostada? Do you want a
 piece of toast?
 ■ **tostadas** toast □ Tomé café con
 tostadas. I had coffee and toast.
2 fried corn tortilla (Mexico)
**tostado** (FEM **tostada**) ADJECTIVE
1 toasted
2 roasted
3 tanned
el **tostador** NOUN
 toaster
**tostar\*** VERB [11]
1 to toast
2 to roast
el **total** (FEM el **total**) ADJECTIVE, NOUN
 total
 □ Fue un fracaso total. It was a total failure.
 □ El total son 45,75 euros. The total is 45.75
 euros.
 ■ **un cambio total** a complete change
 ■ **En total éramos catorce.** There were
 fourteen of us altogether.
**total** ADVERB
 ■ **Total, que perdí mi trabajo.** So, in the
 end, I lost my job.
**totalitario** (FEM **totalitaria**) ADJECTIVE
 totalitarian
**totalmente** ADVERB
1 totally
 □ Mario es totalmente distinto a Luis. Mario
 is totally different from Luis.
2 completely
 □ Estoy totalmente de acuerdo. I completely
 agree.
 ■ **¿Estás seguro? — Totalmente.** Are you
 sure? — Absolutely.
**tóxico** (FEM **tóxica**) ADJECTIVE
 toxic
el **toxicómano**, la **toxicómana** NOUN

drug addict (PL drug addicts)
la **toxina** NOUN
 toxin
**tozudo** (FEM **tozuda**) ADJECTIVE
 obstinate
**trabajador** (FEM **trabajadora**) ADJECTIVE
 hard-working
 □ un chico muy trabajador a very hard-
 working boy
el **trabajador**, la **trabajadora** NOUN
 worker
 □ trabajadores no cualificados unskilled
 workers
**trabajar** VERB [25]
 to work
 □ No trabajes tanto. Don't work so hard.
 ■ **¿En qué trabajas?** What's your job?
 ■ **Trabajo de camarero.** I work as a waiter.
 ■ **trabajar jornada completa** to work full-
 time
 ■ **trabajar media jornada** to work part-
 time
el **trabajo** NOUN
1 work
 □ Tengo mucho trabajo. I have a lot of work.
 □ Me puedes llamar al trabajo. You can call
 me at work.
 ■ **estar sin trabajo** to be unemployed
 ■ **trabajo en equipo** teamwork
 ■ **el trabajo de la casa** the housework
 ■ **trabajos manuales** handicrafts
2 job
 □ Le han ofrecido un trabajo en el banco.
 He's been offered a job in the bank. □ No
 encuentro trabajo. I can't find a job.
 ■ **quedarse sin trabajo** to find oneself out
 of work
3 essay (PL essays)
 □ Tengo que entregar dos trabajos mañana.
 I have to hand in two essays tomorrow.
el **tractor** NOUN
 tractor
la **tradición** (PL las **tradiciones**) NOUN
 tradition
**tradicional** (FEM **tradicional**) ADJECTIVE
 traditional
la **traducción** (PL las **traducciones**) NOUN
 translation
 □ Una traducción del italiano al inglés.
 A translation from Italian into English.
**traducir\*** VERB [9]
 to translate
 □ traducir del inglés al francés to translate
 from English into French
el **traductor**, la **traductora** NOUN
 translator
**traer\*** VERB [54]
1 to bring

303

□ He traído el paraguas por si acaso. I've brought the umbrella just in case.

**2** to carry

□ El periódico trae un artículo sobre eso. The newspaper carries an article on this.

**3** to wear

□ Traía un vestido nuevo. She was wearing a new dress.

el/la **traficante** NOUN
dealer

□ traficantes de armas arms dealers

el **tráfico** NOUN
traffic

■ un accidente de tráfico a road accident

■ tráfico de drogas drug-trafficking

**tragar\*** VERB [37]
to swallow

■ Nadie se va a tragar esa historia. Nobody is going to swallow that story.

■ No la trago. I can't stand her.

la **tragedia** NOUN
tragedy (PL tragedies)

**trágico** (FEM **trágica**) ADJECTIVE
tragic

el **trago** NOUN
drink

□ ¿Te apetece un trago? Do you fancy a drink?

■ de un trago in one gulp

la **traición** (PL las **traiciones**) NOUN

**1** betrayal

**2** treason

**traicionar** VERB [25]
to betray

**traicionero** (FEM **traicionera**) ADJECTIVE
treacherous

el **traidor**, la **traidora** NOUN
traitor

**traigo** VERB ▷ see traer

el **tráiler** (PL los **tráilers**) NOUN

**1** trailer

**2** articulated lorry

el **traje** NOUN

**1** suit

□ Luis llevaba un traje negro. Luis was wearing a black suit.

■ un traje de chaqueta a suit

■ un traje de buzo a diving suit

**2** dress (PL dresses)

□ un traje de noche an evening dress

■ el traje de novia the bridal gown

■ un traje de baño **1** a pair of swimming trunks **2** a swimsuit

la **trama** NOUN
plot

**tramitar** VERB [25]

■ Estoy tramitando un préstamo con el banco. I'm negotiating a loan with the bank.

■ Estamos tramitando el divorcio. We are going through the divorce proceedings.

el **tramo** NOUN

**1** section (of road)

**2** flight (of stairs)

la **trampa** NOUN
trap

□ caer en la trampa to fall into the trap

■ Les tendió una trampa. He set a trap for them.

■ hacer trampa to cheat

el **trampolín** (PL los **trampolines**) NOUN

**1** diving board

□ Se tiró desde el trampolín. He plunged from the diving board.

**2** trampoline

el **tramposo**, la **tramposa** NOUN
cheat

**tranquilamente** ADVERB
calmly

□ Háblale tranquilamente. Speak to him calmly.

■ Yo estaba sentado tranquilamente viendo la tele. I was sitting peacefully watching TV.

la **tranquilidad** NOUN
peace and quiet

□ Necesito un poco de tranquilidad. I need a little peace and quiet.

■ Respondió con tranquilidad. He answered calmly.

■ Llévatelo a casa y léelo con tranquilidad. Take it home with you and read it at your leisure.

■ ¡Qué tranquilidad! ¡Ya se han acabado los exámenes! What a relief! The exams are over at last!

**tranquilizar\*** VERB [13]
to calm down

□ ¡Tranquilízate! Calm down!

■ Las palabras del médico me tranquilizaron. The doctor's words reassured me.

**tranquilo** (FEM **tranquila**) ADJECTIVE

**1** calm

□ El día del examen estaba bastante tranquilo. On the day of the exam I was quite calm.

**2** peaceful

el **transatlántico** NOUN
ocean liner

el **transbordador** NOUN
ferry (PL ferries)

■ el transbordador espacial the space shuttle

el **transbordo** NOUN

■ Hay que hacer transbordo en París.

t

You have to change trains in Paris.

**transcurrir** VERB
to pass
□ Transcurrieron dos años. Two years passed.

el/la **transeúnte** NOUN
passer-by (PL passers-by)

la **transferencia** NOUN
transfer
□ transferencia bancaria bank transfer

la **transformación** (PL las transformaciones) NOUN
transformation

**transformar** VERB [25]
to transform
□ La cirugía estética lo ha transformado completamente. Plastic surgery has completely transformed him.
■ Hemos transformado el garaje en sala de estar. We've converted the garage into a living room.
■ El príncipe se transformó en un monstruo. The prince turned into a monster.

la **transfusión** (PL las transfusiones) NOUN
■ Me hicieron una transfusión de sangre. They gave me a blood transfusion.

**transgénico** (FEM transgénica) ADJECTIVE
genetically modified

la **transición** NOUN
transition

el **transistor** NOUN
transistor

**transitivo** (FEM transitiva) ADJECTIVE
transitive

el **tránsito** NOUN
traffic
■ los pasajeros en tránsito para Moscú transfer passengers to Moscow

la **transmisión** (PL las transmisiones) NOUN
broadcast
□ una transmisión en directo a live broadcast

**transmitir** VERB [58]
1 to transmit
2 to broadcast

**transparente** (FEM transparente) ADJECTIVE
transparent

la **transpiración** NOUN
perspiration

**transportar** VERB [25]
to carry
□ El camión transportaba medicamentos. The lorry was carrying medicines.

el **transporte** NOUN
transport

■ el transporte público public transport

el/la **transportista** NOUN
carrier

el **tranvía** NOUN
tram

el **trapo** NOUN
cloth
□ Lo limpié con un trapo. I wiped it with a cloth.
■ un trapo de cocina a dishcloth
■ Pásale un trapo al espejo. Give the mirror a wipe over.
■ el trapo del polvo the duster

la **tráquea** NOUN
windpipe

**tras** PREPOSITION
after
□ Salimos corriendo tras ella. We ran out after her. □ semana tras semana week after week

**trasero** (FEM trasera) ADJECTIVE
back
□ la rueda trasera de la bici the back wheel of the bike

el **trasero** NOUN
bottom

**trasladar** VERB [25]
1 to move
□ Mañana nos trasladamos al piso. We're moving to the flat tomorrow.
2 to transfer
□ Me quieren trasladar a otra sucursal. They want to transfer me to another branch.

el **traslado** NOUN
move
■ He pedido traslado a Barcelona. I've asked for a transfer to Barcelona.
■ los gastos de traslado de la oficina the office's relocation expenses

el **trasluz** NOUN
■ al trasluz against the light

**trasnochar** VERB [25]
to stay up late

**traspapelarse** VERB
to get mislaid

**traspasar** VERB
1 to go through
□ La bala traspasó el sofá. The bullet went through the sofa.
2 to transfer
3 to sell

el **traspié** (PL los traspiés) NOUN
■ dar un traspié to trip

**trasplantar** VERB
to transplant

el **trasplante** NOUN
transplant

el **trastero** NOUN

storage room

los **trastes** NOUN *(Mexico)*
pots and pans
∎ **lavar los trastes** to do the dishes

el **trasto** NOUN
piece of junk
▢ El coche es un trasto. The car's a piece of junk.
∎ **El desván está lleno de trastos.** The loft is full of junk.

**trastornado** (FEM **trastornada**) ADJECTIVE
disturbed

el **trastorno** NOUN
disruption
▢ La huelga ha causado muchos trastornos. The strike has caused a lot of disruption.
∎ **trastornos mentales** mental disorders

el **tratado** NOUN
treaty (PL treaties)

el **tratamiento** NOUN
treatment
∎ **Está en tratamiento médico.** He's having medical treatment.
∎ **tratamiento de datos** data processing
∎ **tratamiento de textos** word processing

**tratar** VERB [25]
1 to treat
▢ Su novio la trata muy mal. Her boyfriend treats her very badly.
2 to deal with
▢ Trataremos este tema en la reunión. We'll deal with this subject in the meeting.
∎ **Trato con todo tipo de gente.** I deal with all sorts of people.
∎ **tratar de hacer algo** to try to do something
∎ **¿De qué se trata?** What's it about?
∎ **La película trata de un adolescente en Nueva York.** The film is about a teenager in New York.

el **trato** NOUN
deal
▢ hacer un trato to make a deal
∎ **¡Trato hecho!** It's a deal!
∎ **No tengo mucho trato con él.** I don't have much to do with him.
∎ **recibir malos tratos de alguien** to be treated badly by somebody

el **trauma** NOUN
trauma

**través** PREPOSITION
∎ **a través de 1** across ▢ Nadó a través del río. He swam across the river. **2** through ▢ Se enteraron a través de un amigo. They found out through a friend.

la **travesía** NOUN
1 crossing
2 side-street

la **travesura** NOUN
prank
∎ **hacer travesuras** to get up to mischief

**travieso** (FEM **traviesa**) ADJECTIVE
naughty

el **trayecto** NOUN
1 journey (PL journeys)
2 way (PL ways)
∎ **¿Qué trayecto hace el 34?** What way does the 34 go?

**trazar\*** VERB [13]
1 to draw
2 to draw up

el **trébol** NOUN
clover
∎ **tréboles** clubs

**trece** (FEM **trece**) ADJECTIVE, PRONOUN
thirteen
▢ Tengo trece años. I'm thirteen.
∎ **el trece de enero** the thirteenth of January

**treinta** (FEM **treinta**) ADJECTIVE, PRONOUN
thirty
▢ Tiene treinta años. He's thirty.
∎ **el treinta aniversario** the thirtieth anniversary

**tremendo** (FEM **tremenda**) ADJECTIVE
1 terrible
▢ Tenía un tremendo dolor de cabeza. I had a terrible headache.
∎ **Hacía un frío tremendo.** It was terribly cold.
2 tremendous
▢ La película tuvo un éxito tremendo. The film was a tremendous success.

el **tren** NOUN
train
∎ **viajar en tren** to travel by train
∎ **Tomé un tren directo.** I took a through train.
∎ **con este tren de vida** with such a hectic life

la **trenza** NOUN
plait
∎ **Le hice una trenza.** I plaited her hair.

la **trepadora** NOUN
climber

**trepar** VERB [25]
to climb
∎ **trepar a un árbol** to climb a tree

**tres** (FEM **tres**) ADJECTIVE, PRONOUN
three
∎ **Son las tres.** It's three o'clock.
∎ **el tres de febrero** the third of February

**trescientos** (FEM **trescientas**) ADJECTIVE, PRONOUN
three hundred

el **tresillo** NOUN

t

three-seater sofa

el **triángulo** NOUN
triangle

la **tribu** NOUN
tribe

la **tribuna** NOUN
1 platform
2 stand

el **tribunal** NOUN
1 court
2 board of examiners

el **triciclo** NOUN
tricycle

**tridimensional** (FEM **tridimensional**)
ADJECTIVE
three-dimensional

el **trigo** NOUN
wheat

**trillar** VERB
to thresh

los **trillizos**, las **trillizas** NOUN
triplets

**trimestral** (FEM **trimestral**) ADJECTIVE
quarterly
■ **los exámenes trimestrales** the end-of-term exams

el **trimestre** NOUN
term

**trinchar** VERB [25]
to carve

la **trinchera** NOUN
trench

el **trineo** NOUN
1 sledge
2 sleigh

la **Trinidad** NOUN
the Trinity

el **trío** NOUN
trio

la **tripa** NOUN
gut

el **triple** NOUN
■ **Esta habitación es el triple de grande.**
This room is three times as big.
■ **Gastan el triple que nosotros.** They
spend three times as much as we do.

**triplicar\*** VERB [48]
to treble

la **tripulación** (PL las **tripulaciones**) NOUN
crew

**triste** (FEM **triste**) ADJECTIVE
1 sad
□ Me puse muy triste cuando me enteré.
I was very sad when I heard.
■ **El invierno me pone triste.** Winter
makes me miserable.
2 gloomy

la **tristeza** NOUN

sadness

**triturar** VERB [25]
1 to crush
2 to grind

**triunfar** VERB [25]
to triumph
□ Los socialistas triunfaron en las
elecciones. The socialists triumphed in the
elections.
■ **triunfar en la vida** to succeed in life

el **triunfo** NOUN
triumph

**trivial** (FEM **trivial**) ADJECTIVE
trivial

las **trizas** NOUN
■ **hacer algo trizas** to tear something to
shreds

**trocear** VERB [25]
to cut up
□ trocear las zanahorias to cut up the
carrots

el **trofeo** NOUN
trophy (PL trophies)

el **trombón** (PL los **trombones**) NOUN
trombone

la **trompa** NOUN
1 trunk *(of elephant)*
2 horn *(musical instrument)*
■ **coger una trompa** to get plastered

la **trompeta** NOUN
trumpet

**tronar\*** VERB [11]
to thunder
□ Ha estado tronando toda la noche. It has
been thundering all night.

**troncharse** VERB [25]
■ **Yo me tronchaba de risa.** I was killing
myself laughing.

el **tronco** NOUN
1 trunk
2 log
■ **dormir como un tronco** to sleep like a
log

el **trono** NOUN
throne

las **tropas** NOUN
troops

**tropezar\*** VERB [19]
to trip
□ Tropecé y me caí. I tripped and fell.
■ **tropezar con una piedra** to trip on a stone
■ **tropezar contra un árbol** to bump into
a tree
■ **Me tropecé con Juan en el banco.**
I bumped into Juan in the bank.

el **tropezón** (PL los **tropezones**) NOUN
trip
■ **dar un tropezón** to trip

**t**

**tropical** (FEM **tropical**) ADJECTIVE
tropical

el **trópico** NOUN
tropic

**tropiece** VERB ▷ see **tropezar**

**trotar** VERB [25]
to trot

el **trote** NOUN
■ **El abuelo ya no está para estos trotes.** Grandad is not up to that sort of thing any more.

el **trozo** NOUN
piece
□ un trozo de madera a piece of wood □ Dame un trocito sólo. Just give me a small piece.
■ **Vi la película a trozos.** I saw bits of the film.

la **trucha** NOUN
trout

el **truco** NOUN
trick
■ **Ya le he cogido el truco.** I've got the hang of it already.

**truena** VERB ▷ see **tronar**

el **trueno** NOUN
■ **Oímos un trueno.** We heard a clap of thunder.
■ **Me despertaron los truenos.** The thunder woke me up.

la **trufa** NOUN
truffle

**tu** ADJECTIVE
your
□ tu coche your car □ tus familiares your relations

**tú** PRONOUN
you
□ Cuando tú quieras. Whenever you like.
□ Llegamos antes que tú. We arrived before you.

la **tuberculosis** NOUN
tuberculosis

la **tubería** NOUN
pipe
□ Ha reventado una tubería. A pipe has burst.

el **tubo** NOUN
1 pipe
□ el tubo de escape the exhaust pipe
■ **el tubo de desagüe** the drainpipe
2 tube
□ un tubo de crema para las manos a tube of hand cream

la **tuerca** NOUN
nut

**tuerto** (FEM **tuerta**) ADJECTIVE
■ **Es tuerto.** He's blind in one eye.

**tuerzo** VERB ▷ see **torcer**

el **tuétano** NOUN
marrow

el **tufo** NOUN
stench

el **tulipán** (PL los **tulipanes**) NOUN
tulip

la **tumba** NOUN
1 grave
2 tomb
□ una tumba egipcia an Egyptian tomb

**tumbar** VERB [25]
to knock down
□ El perro me tumbó. The dog knocked me down.
■ **tumbarse** to lie down □ Me tumbé en el sofá. I lay down on the sofa.

el **tumbo** NOUN
■ **El borracho iba dando tumbos.** The drunk staggered along.

la **tumbona** NOUN
deck chair

el **tumor** NOUN
tumour

el **túnel** NOUN
tunnel
■ **un túnel de lavado** a car wash
⚬ **LANGUAGE TIP** Word for word, **túnel de lavado** means 'washing tunnel'.

**Túnez** MASC NOUN
1 Tunisia
2 Tunis

**tupido** (FEM **tupida**) ADJECTIVE
1 dense
2 close-woven
3 bushy

el **turbante** NOUN
turban

la **turbina** NOUN
turbine

**turbio** (FEM **turbia**) ADJECTIVE
cloudy

**turbulento** (FEM **turbulenta**) ADJECTIVE
turbulent

**turco** (FEM **turca**) ADJECTIVE
Turkish

el **turco**, la **turca** NOUN
Turk

el **turco** NOUN
Turkish

el **turismo** NOUN
1 tourism
□ El turismo es importante para nuestra economía. Tourism is important for our economy.
■ **turismo rural** tourism in rural areas
■ **casas de turismo rural** holiday cottages
■ **la oficina de turismo** the tourist office

**2** tourists *pl*
  □ En verano hay mucho turismo.
  In summer there are a lot of tourists.
**3** car
el/la **turista** NOUN
  tourist
**turístico** (FEM **turística**) ADJECTIVE
  tourist
**turnarse** VERB [25]
  to take it in turns
  □ Nos turnamos para fregar los platos.
  We take it in turns to do the washing-up.
el **turno** NOUN
**1** turn
  □ cuando me tocó el turno when it was my
  turn
**2** shift
  □ Hago el turno de tarde. I do the afternoon
  shift.
la **turquesa** ADJECTIVE, NOUN
  turquoise
  □ un anorak turquesa a turquoise anorak

**Turquía** FEM NOUN
  Turkey
el **turrón** (PL los **turrones**) NOUN
  nougat
**tutear** VERB [25]

> **DID YOU KNOW...?**
> to address somebody using the
> familiar **tú** form rather than the more
> formal **usted** form.

  □ Se tutean con el jefe. They address the
  boss in familiar terms.
el **tutor**, la **tutora** NOUN
**1** tutor
**2** guardian
**tuve** VERB ▷ *see* **tener**
**tuyo** (FEM **tuya**) ADJECTIVE, PRONOUN
  yours
  □ ¿Es tuyo este abrigo? Is this coat yours?
  □ La tuya está en el armario. Yours is in the
  cupboard. □ mis amigos y los tuyos my
  friends and yours
  ■ **un amigo tuyo** a friend of yours

# Uu

**u** CONJUNCTION

or

□ ¿Minutos u horas? Minutes or hours?

**ubicado** (FEM **ubicada**) ADJECTIVE

situated

□ bien ubicado well situated

**Ud.** ABBREVIATION = **usted**

**Uds.** ABBREVIATION = **ustedes**

la **UE** ABBREVIATION (= *Unión Europea*)

EU

**uf** INTERJECTION

1 phew!

2 ugh!

la **úlcera** NOUN

ulcer

**últimamente** ADVERB

recently

el **ultimátum** (PL los **ultimátums**) NOUN

ultimatum (PL ultimatums)

**último** (FEM **última**) ADJECTIVE

1 last

□ la última vez que hablé con ella the last time I spoke to her

2 top

□ No llego al último estante. I can't reach the top shelf.

3 back

□ Nos sentamos en la última fila. We sat in the back row.

■ **la última moda** the latest fashion

■ **a última hora** at the last minute □ A última hora decidió acompañarme. He decided to come with me at the last minute.

■ **llegar en último lugar** to arrive last

el **último**, la **última** NOUN

the last one

■ **a últimos de mes** towards the end of the month

■ **por último** lastly

el/la **ultra** NOUN

right-wing extremist

**ultrasónico** (FEM **ultrasónica**) ADJECTIVE

ultrasonic

**ultravioleta** (FEM **ultravioleta**) ADJECTIVE

ultraviolet

**un**, **una** ARTICLE

1 a

□ una silla a chair

2 an

□ un paraguas an umbrella

3 some

□ Fui con unos amigos. I went with some friends.

■ **Tiene unas uñas muy largas.** He has very long nails.

■ **Había unas 20 personas.** There were about 20 people.

■ **Me he comprado unos zapatos de tacón.** I have bought a pair of high-heels.

**unánime** (FEM **unánime**) ADJECTIVE

unanimous

**undécimo** (FEM **undécima**) ADJECTIVE, PRONOUN

eleventh

□ Vivo en el undécimo piso. I live on the eleventh floor.

**únicamente** ADVERB

only

□ Me encargo únicamente del teléfono. I'm only in charge of the telephone.

el **único** (FEM la **única**) ADJECTIVE, NOUN

only

□ el único día que tengo libre the only day I have free

■ **Soy hija única.** I'm an only child.

■ **el único que me queda** the only one I've got left

■ **Lo único que no me gusta ...** The only thing I don't like ...

■ **una colección de sellos única** a unique stamp collection

la **unidad** NOUN

1 unit

□ una unidad de peso a unit of weight

■ **unidad de cuidados intensivos** intensive care unit

2 unity

□ falta de unidad en la familia lack of family unity

**unido** (FEM **unida**) ADJECTIVE

close

□ una familia muy unida a very close family

u

**uniforme** (FEM **uniforme**) ADJECTIVE
even
  □ una superficie uniforme an even surface
el **uniforme** NOUN
uniform
  □ Llevaba el uniforme del colegio. He was wearing his school uniform.
la **unión** (PL las **uniones**) NOUN
union
  ■ la Unión Europea the European Union
**unir** VERB [58]
1 to link
  □ Este pasaje une los dos edificios. This passage links the two buildings.
2 to join
  □ Unió los dos extremos con una cuerda. He joined the two ends with some string.
3 to unite
  □ Los unió en matrimonio. He united them in marriage.
4 to bring together
  □ La enfermedad de la madre ha unido a los hijos. The mother's illness has brought the children together.
  ■ unirse a algo to join something □ Andrés se unió a la expedición. Andrés joined the expedition.
  ■ Más adelante los dos caminos se unen. The two paths join further on.
  ■ Los dos bancos se han unido. The two banks have merged.
**universal** (FEM **universal**) ADJECTIVE
universal
la **universidad** NOUN
university (PL universities)
  □ El año que viene voy a la universidad. I'm going to university next year.
  ■ Universidad a Distancia Open University

> **DID YOU KNOW...?**
> La **Open University** imparte cursos a distancia con el apoyo de programas de radio y televisión emitidos por la BBC.

**universitario** (FEM **universitaria**) ADJECTIVE
university
  □ estudiantes universitarios university students
el **universitario**, la **universitaria** NOUN
1 university student
2 graduate
el **universo** NOUN
universe
**uno** (FEM **una**) ADJECTIVE, PRONOUN
one
  □ Vivo en el número uno. I live at number one. □ Uno de ellos era mío. One of them

was mine.
  ■ unos pocos a few
  ■ uno mismo oneself
  ■ Entraron uno a uno. They came in one by one.
  ■ unas diez personas about ten people
  ■ el uno de abril the first of April
  ■ Es la una. It's one o'clock.
  ■ Unos querían ir, otros no. Some of them wanted to go, others didn't.
  ■ Se miraron uno al otro. They looked at each other.
**untar** VERB [25]
  ■ untar algo con algo to spread something on something □ Primero hay que untar el pan con mantequilla. First you have to spread the butter on the bread.
  ■ Te has untado las manos de chocolate. You've got chocolate all over your hands.
  ■ unta el molde con aceite grease the baking dish with oil
la **uña** NOUN
1 nail
2 claw
el **uranio** NOUN
uranium
la **urbanización** (PL las **urbanizaciones**) NOUN
housing estate
la **urgencia** NOUN
emergency (PL emergencies)
  □ en caso de urgencia in an emergency
  □ los servicios de urgencia the emergency services
  ■ urgencias accident and emergency
  ■ Tuvimos que ir a urgencias. We had to go to casualty.
  ■ con urgencia urgently
**urgente** (FEM **urgente**) ADJECTIVE
urgent
  ■ Lo mandé por correo urgente. I sent it express.
la **urna** NOUN
ballot box
**Uruguay** MASC NOUN
Uruguay
el **uruguayo** (FEM la **uruguaya**) ADJECTIVE, NOUN
Uruguayan
**usado** (FEM **usada**) ADJECTIVE
1 secondhand
  □ una tienda de ropa usada a secondhand clothes shop
2 worn
  □ Estas zapatillas están ya muy usadas. These slippers are very worn now.
**usar** VERB [25]
1 to use

□ Uso una maquinilla eléctrica. I use an electric razor.

**2** to wear

□ ¿Qué número de zapato usas? What size shoe do you take?

el **uso** NOUN

use

□ instrucciones de uso instructions for use

**usted** PRONOUN

you

□ Quisiera hablar con usted en privado. I'd like to speak to you in private.

**ustedes** PL PRONOUN

you

□ Quisiera hablar con ustedes en privado. I'd like to speak to you in private.

**usual** (FEM **usual**) ADJECTIVE

usual

el **usuario**, la **usuaria** NOUN

user

el **utensilio** NOUN

utensil

□ utensilios de cocina kitchen utensils

el **útero** NOUN

uterus

**útil** (FEM **útil**) ADJECTIVE

useful

**utilizar*** VERB [13]

to use

la **uva** NOUN

grape

■ **estar de mala uva** to be in a bad mood

# Vv

**va** VERB ▷ see **ir**

la **vaca** NOUN
1 cow
2 beef
　□ No como carne de vaca. I don't eat beef.

las **vacaciones** NOUN
　holidays
　■ **las vacaciones de Navidad** the Christmas holidays
　■ **La secretaria está de vacaciones.** The secretary is on holiday.
　■ **En agosto me voy de vacaciones.** I'm going on holiday in August.

**vacante** (FEM **vacante**) ADJECTIVE
1 vacant
2 unoccupied

la **vacante** NOUN
　vacancy (PL vacancies)

**vaciar\*** VERB [21]
　to empty
　□ Vacié la nevera para limpiarla. I emptied the fridge to clean it.

**vacilar** VERB [25]
　to hesitate
　□ Vaciló unos instantes antes de responder. He hesitated for a moment or two before answering.
　■ **sin vacilar** without hesitating

**vacío** (FEM **vacía**) ADJECTIVE
　empty

el **vacío** NOUN
　void
　□ Se arrojó al vacío. He hurled himself into the void.
　■ **envasado al vacío** vacuum-packed

la **vacuna** NOUN
　vaccine
　□ la vacuna de la hepatitis the hepatitis vaccine
　■ **¿Te has puesto la vacuna?** Have they given you the vaccination?

**vacunar** VERB [25]
　to vaccinate
　■ **Mi abuelo se vacuna contra la gripe.** My grandfather has flu vaccinations.

el **vado** NOUN

　■ **'vado permanente'** 'no parking – in constant use'

la **vaga** NOUN
　layabout

la **vagabunda** NOUN
　tramp

**vagabundo** (FEM **vagabunda**) ADJECTIVE
　stray

el **vagabundo** NOUN
　tramp

**vagar\*** VERB [37]
　to wander

la **vagina** NOUN
　vagina

**vago** (FEM **vaga**) ADJECTIVE
1 lazy
2 vague

el **vago** NOUN
　layabout
　■ **hacer el vago** to laze around

el **vagón** (PL los **vagones**) NOUN
　carriage
　■ **vagón cama** sleeper
　■ **vagón restaurante** restaurant car

el **vaho** NOUN
　steam

la **vainilla** NOUN
　vanilla
　□ un helado de vainilla a vanilla ice cream

la **vajilla** NOUN
　dishes pl
　□ La vajilla está en el lavaplatos. The dishes are in the dishwasher.
　■ **Me regaló una vajilla de porcelana.** She gave me a china dinner service.

el **vale** NOUN
1 voucher
　□ un vale de regalo a gift voucher
　■ **un vale de descuento** a money-off coupon
2 credit note

la **valenciana** NOUN
　Valencian

el **valenciano** ADJECTIVE, NOUN
　Valencian
　■ **Hablan valenciano.** They speak

**v**

Valencian.

**la valentía** NOUN
bravery
- **con valentía** bravely

**valer\*** VERB [55]
1 to cost
  - □ ¿Cuánto vale? How much does it cost?
2 to be worth
  - □ El terreno vale más que la casa. The land is worth more than the house.
  - **No vale mirar.** You're not allowed to look.
  - **¡Eso no vale!** That's not fair!
  - **vale la pena** it's worth it
  - **Vale la pena hacer el esfuerzo.** It's worth the effort.
  - **no vale la pena** it's not worth it
  - **No vale la pena gastar tanto dinero.** It's not worth spending that much money.
  - **Este cuchillo no vale para nada.** This knife is useless.
  - **Yo no valdría para enfermera.** I'd make a hopeless nurse.
  - **¿Vale?** OK?
  - **¿Vamos a tomar algo? — ¡Vale!** Shall we go for a drink? — OK!
  - **Más vale que te lleves el abrigo.** You'd better take your coat.
  - **No puede valerse por sí mismo.** He can't look after himself.

**válido** (FEM **válida**) ADJECTIVE
valid

**valiente** (FEM **valiente**) ADJECTIVE
brave

**la valija** NOUN
suitcase *(River Plate)*
- **valija diplomática** diplomatic bag

**valioso** (FEM **valiosa**) ADJECTIVE
valuable

**la valla** NOUN
fence
- **valla publicitaria** hoarding
- **los cien metros vallas** the hundred metre hurdles

**el valle** NOUN
valley (PL valleys)

**el valor** NOUN
1 value
  - □ valor sentimental sentimental value
  - **una pulsera de gran valor** an extremely valuable bracelet
2 courage
  - □ armarse de valor to pluck up courage
  - **objetos de valor** valuables
  - **valor adquisitivo** purchasing power

**valorar** VERB [25]
to value

**el vals** NOUN
waltz

- **bailar un vals** to waltz

**la válvula** NOUN
valve

**el vampiro**, la **vampira** NOUN
vampire

**el vandalismo** NOUN
vandalism

**la vanguardia** NOUN
avant-garde
- **de vanguardia** avant-garde

**la vanidad** NOUN
vanity

**vanidoso** (FEM **vanidosa**) ADJECTIVE
vain

**vano** (FEM **vana**) ADJECTIVE
vain
- □ un intento vano a vain attempt
- **en vano** in vain

**el vapor** NOUN
steam
- **plancha de vapor** steam iron
- **al vapor** steamed

**vaquero** (FEM **vaquera**) ADJECTIVE
denim
- □ una falda vaquera a denim skirt

**el vaquero** NOUN
cowboy (PL cowboys)
- **una película de vaqueros** a western
- **vaqueros** jeans □ Llevaba unos vaqueros negros. He was wearing black jeans.

**variable** (FEM **variable**) ADJECTIVE
variable
- **El tiempo es muy variable.** The weather is very changeable.

**variado** (FEM **variada**) ADJECTIVE
varied
- □ Prefiero un trabajo más variado. I prefer a more varied job.

**variar\*** VERB [21]
to vary
- □ Los precios varían según las tallas. Prices vary according to size.
- **Decidí ir en tren, para variar.** I decided to go by train for a change.

**la varicela** NOUN
chickenpox
- □ Yo no he pasado la varicela. I've never had chickenpox.

**la variedad** NOUN
variety (PL varieties)
- □ una nueva variedad de clavel a new variety of carnation

**la varilla** NOUN
rod
- **la varilla del aceite** the dipstick

**varios** (FEM **varias**) ADJECTIVE, PRONOUN
several
- □ Estuve enfermo varios días. I was ill for

several days. □ Le hicimos un regalo entre varios. Several of us clubbed together to get him a present.

la **variz** (PL las **varices**) NOUN
varicose vein

**varón** (PL **varones**) ADJECTIVE
male
□ los herederos varones the male heirs

el **varón** (PL los **varones**) NOUN
□ Tiene dos hembras y un varón. She has two girls and a boy.
■ **Sexo: varón.** Sex: male.

**Varsovia** FEM NOUN
Warsaw

la **vasca** NOUN
Basque

el **vasco** ADJECTIVE, NOUN
Basque
■ **Hablamos vasco.** We speak Basque.
■ **el País Vasco** the Basque Country

la **vasija** NOUN
vessel
□ una vasija fenicia a Phoenician vessel

el **vaso** NOUN
glass (PL glasses)
□ Bebí un vaso de leche. I drank a glass of milk.
■ **un vaso de plástico** a plastic cup
■ **un vaso sanguíneo** a blood vessel

el **váter** NOUN
loo (colloquial)

el **Vaticano** NOUN
Vatican

el **vatio** NOUN
watt

**vaya** VERB ▷see ir

**Vd.** ABBREVIATION = usted

**Vds.** ABBREVIATION = ustedes

**ve** VERB ▷see ir, ver

la **vecina** NOUN
1 neighbour
2 inhabitant

el **vecindario** NOUN
neighbourhood

**vecino** (FEM **vecina**) ADJECTIVE
neighbouring
□ las ciudades vecinas the neighbouring towns

el **vecino** NOUN
1 neighbour
□ los vecinos de al lado the next door neighbours
2 inhabitant
□ todos los vecinos de Torrevieja all the inhabitants of Torrevieja

la **vegetación** (PL las **vegetaciones**) NOUN
vegetation
■ **vegetaciones** adenoids

el **vegetal** ADJECTIVE, NOUN
vegetable
□ aceite vegetal vegetable oil

el **vegetariano** (FEM la **vegetariana**)
ADJECTIVE, NOUN
vegetarian
□ Es vegetariano. He's vegetarian.

el **vehículo** NOUN
vehicle

**veinte** (FEM **veinte**) ADJECTIVE, PRONOUN
twenty
□ Tiene veinte años. He's twenty.
■ **el veinte de enero** the twentieth of January
■ **el siglo veinte** the twentieth century

la **vejez** NOUN
old age

la **vejiga** NOUN
bladder

la **vela** NOUN
1 candle
□ Encendimos una vela. We lit a candle.
2 sail
3 sailing
■ **un barco de vela** a yacht
■ **Pasé la noche en vela.** I had a sleepless night.
■ **estar a dos velas** to be broke

**velarse** VERB [25]
■ **Se han velado las fotos.** The photos got exposed by accident.

el **velero** NOUN
yacht

el **vello** NOUN
1 hair
□ Tiene mucho vello. He's very hairy.
2 down

el **velo** NOUN
veil

la **velocidad** NOUN
1 speed
□ Pasó una moto a toda velocidad. A motorbike went past at full speed.
■ **¿A qué velocidad ibas?** How fast were you going?
2 gear
□ cambiar de velocidad to change gear

el **velocímetro** NOUN
speedometer

el/la **velocista** NOUN
sprinter

el **velódromo** NOUN
cycle track

**veloz** (FEM **veloz**, PL **veloces**) ADJECTIVE
swift

**ven** VERB ▷see ir, ver

la **vena** NOUN
vein

315

**vencedor** (FEM **vencedora**) ADJECTIVE
winning
□ el equipo vencedor the winning team
el **vencedor**, la **vencedora** NOUN
winner
**vencer\*** VERB
1 to defeat
2 to overcome
3 to expire
□ El pasaporte me vence mañana. My passport expires tomorrow.
**vencido** (FEM **vencida**) ADJECTIVE
■ darse por vencido to give up
la **venda** NOUN
1 bandage
■ Me pusieron una venda en el brazo. They bandaged my arm.
2 blindfold
■ poner una venda en los ojos a alguien to blindfold someone
**vendar** VERB [25]
to bandage
□ Me vendaron el codo. They bandaged my elbow.
■ vendar los ojos a alguien to blindfold someone
el **vendedor** NOUN
salesman (PL salesmen)
■ vendedor ambulante pedlar
■ vendedor de periódicos newspaper seller
la **vendedora** NOUN
saleswoman (PL saleswomen)
**vender** VERB [8]
to sell
□ He vendido el coche. I've sold the car.
■ Venden la oficina de arriba. The office upstairs is for sale.
■ 'se vende' 'for sale'
■ venderse por to sell for □ El cuadro se vendió por treinta mil euros. The painting sold for thirty thousand euros.
la **vendimia** NOUN
grape harvest
**vendré** VERB ▷ see venir
el **veneno** NOUN
1 poison
2 venom
**venenoso** (FEM **venenosa**) ADJECTIVE
poisonous
el **venezolano** (FEM la **venezolana**) ADJECTIVE, NOUN
Venezuelan
**Venezuela** FEM NOUN
Venezuela
la **venganza** NOUN
revenge
**vengarse\*** VERB

to take revenge
■ vengarse de alguien to take revenge on someone
■ vengarse de algo to avenge something
**vengo** VERB ▷ see venir
la **venida** NOUN
arrival
■ La venida la hicimos en autobús. We came by bus on the way here.
**venir\*** VERB [56]
1 to come
□ Vino en taxi. He came by taxi. □ Vinieron a verme al hospital. They came to see me in hospital. □ Viene en varios colores. It comes in several colours. □ ¡Ven aquí! Come here!
■ Enseguida vengo. I'll be back in a minute.
2 to be
□ La noticia venía en el periódico. The news was in the paper.
■ ¡Venga, vámonos! Come on, let's go!
■ La casa se está viniendo abajo. The house is falling apart.
■ Mañana me viene mal. Tomorrow isn't good for me.
■ ¿Te viene bien el sábado? Is Saturday alright for you?
■ el año que viene next year
■ ¡Venga ya! Come off it!
la **venta** NOUN
sale
■ estar en venta to be for sale
la **ventaja** NOUN
advantage
□ Tiene la ventaja de que está cerca de casa. It has the advantage of being close to home.
■ llevar ventaja a alguien to have an advantage over someone
■ jugar con ventaja to be at an advantage
la **ventana** NOUN
window
la **ventanilla** NOUN
1 window
□ Baja la ventanilla. Open the window.
2 box office
la **ventilación** NOUN
ventilation
■ El sótano tiene poca ventilación. The basement is poorly ventilated.
**ventilar** VERB [25]
to air
la **ventisca** NOUN
1 gale force winds
2 blizzard
**ver\*** VERB [57]
1 to see
□ Te vi en el parque. I saw you in the park.

□ ¡Cuánto tiempo sin verte! I haven't seen you for ages! □ No he visto esa película. I haven't seen that film. □ El médico todavía no la ha visto. The doctor hasn't seen her yet. □ ¿Ves? Ya te lo dije. See? I told you so.
■ **Voy a ver si está en su despacho.** I'll see if he's in his office.
■ **Quedamos en vernos en la estación.** We arranged to meet at the station.
■ **¡Luego nos vemos!** See you later!
■ **Eso no tiene nada que ver.** That has nothing to do with it.
■ **¡No la puede ver!** He can't stand her!
■ **A ver ...** Let's see ...
■ **Se ve que no tiene idea de informática.** It's clear he's got no idea about computers.
2 to watch

**veranear** VERB [25]
to spend the summer holidays
□ Veraneamos en Calpe. We spend our summer holidays in Calpe.

el **veraneo** NOUN
■ **lugar de veraneo** summer resort
■ **No pudimos ir de veraneo el año pasado.** We couldn't go on holiday last summer.

el **verano** NOUN
summer
□ En verano hace mucho calor. It's very hot in summer. □ las vacaciones de verano the summer holidays

**veras** FEM PL NOUN
■ **de veras** really

**veraz** (FEM **veraz**, PL **veraces**) ADJECTIVE
truthful

la **verbena** NOUN
open-air dance
■ **la verbena de San Roque** the festival of San Roque

el **verbo** NOUN
verb

la **verdad** NOUN
truth
□ Les dije la verdad. I told them the truth.
■ **¡Es verdad!** It's true!
■ **La verdad es que no tengo ganas.** I don't really feel like it.
■ **¿De verdad?** Really?
■ **De verdad que yo no dije eso.** I didn't say that, honestly.
■ **No era un policía de verdad.** He wasn't a real policeman.
■ **Es bonito, ¿verdad?** It's pretty, isn't it?
■ **No te gusta, ¿verdad?** You don't like it, do you?

**verdadero** (FEM **verdadera**) ADJECTIVE
real
□ Su apellido verdadero es Rodríguez. His

real surname is Rodríguez. □ Es un verdadero caballero. He's a real gentleman.

el **verde** ADJECTIVE, NOUN
1 green
□ Tiene los ojos verdes. She has green eyes.
□ Estos plátanos están todavía verdes. These bananas are still green.
2 dirty
□ un chiste verde a dirty joke
■ **los verdes** the Green Party

el **verdugo** NOUN
1 executioner
2 hangman

la **verdulería** NOUN
greengrocer's (PL greengrocers' shops)

la **verdura** NOUN
vegetables pl
□ Comemos mucha verdura. We eat a lot of vegetables.

la **vereda** NOUN
1 path
2 pavement (Chile, River Plate)

**vergonzoso** (FEM **vergonzosa**) ADJECTIVE
1 shy
□ Es muy vergonzosa. She is very shy.
2 disgraceful
□ Es vergonzoso cómo los trataron. It's disgraceful the way they were treated.

la **vergüenza** NOUN
1 embarrassment
□ Casi me muero de vergüenza. I almost died of embarrassment.
2 shame
□ No tienen vergüenza. They have no shame.
■ **¡Qué vergüenza!** How embarrassing!
■ **Le da vergüenza pedírselo.** He's embarrassed to ask her.
■ **¡Es una vergüenza!** It's disgraceful!

**verídico** (FEM **verídica**) ADJECTIVE
true

**verificar\*** VERB [48]
to check

la **verja** NOUN
1 railings pl
2 gate

el **vermut** NOUN
vermouth

la **verruga** NOUN
1 wart
2 verruca

la **versión** (PL las **versiones**) NOUN
version
■ **una película francesa en versión original** a film in the original French version

el **verso** NOUN
1 line
2 verse

V

317

la **vértebra** NOUN
vertebra (PL vertebrae)

el **vertedero** NOUN
rubbish tip

**verter*** VERB [20]
1 to pour
□ Vertió un poco de leche en el cazo. He poured a little milk into the saucepan.
2 to dump

**vertical** (FEM **vertical**) ADJECTIVE
vertical
■ **Ponlo vertical.** Put it upright.

el **vértigo** NOUN
vertigo
■ **Me da vértigo.** It makes me dizzy.

la **Vespa**® NOUN
scooter

**vespertino** (FEM **vespertina**) ADJECTIVE
evening
□ un diario vespertino an evening paper

el **vestíbulo** NOUN
1 hall
2 foyer

**vestido** (FEM **vestida**) ADJECTIVE
■ **Iba vestida de negro.** She was dressed in black.
■ **Yo iba vestido de payaso.** I was dressed as a clown.
■ **un hombre bien vestido** a well-dressed man

el **vestido** NOUN
dress (PL dresses)
■ **el vestido de novia** the bridal gown

**vestir*** VERB [38]
to wear
□ Vestía pantalones vaqueros y una camiseta. He was wearing jeans and a T-shirt.
■ **vestir a alguien** to dress someone
□ Estaba vistiendo a los niños. I was dressing the children.
■ **vestir bien** to dress well
■ **vestirse** to get dressed □ Se está vistiendo. He's getting dressed.
■ **Se vistió de princesa.** She dressed up as a princess.
■ **ropa de vestir** smart clothes *pl*

el **vestón** (PL los **vestones**) NOUN
jacket (Chile, River Plate)

el **vestuario** NOUN
1 changing room
2 wardrobe

el **veterinario**, la **veterinaria** NOUN
vet

la **vez** (PL las **veces**) NOUN
time
□ la próxima vez next time □ ¿Cuántas veces al año? How many times a year?
■ **a la vez** at the same time
■ **a veces** sometimes
■ **algunas veces** sometimes
■ **muchas veces** often
■ **cada vez más** more and more
■ **cada vez menos** less and less
■ **de una vez** once and for all
■ **de vez en cuando** from time to time
■ **en vez de** instead of
■ **¿La has visto alguna vez?** Have you ever seen her?
■ **otra vez** again
■ **tal vez** maybe
■ **una vez** once □ La veo una vez a la semana. I see her once a week.
■ **dos veces** twice
■ **una y otra vez** again and again

**vi** VERB ▷ see **ver**

la **vía** NOUN
1 track
2 platform
□ Nuestro tren sale por la vía dos. Our train leaves from platform two.
■ **por vía aérea** by airmail
■ **Madrid-Berlín vía París** Madrid-Berlin via Paris

**viajar** VERB [25]
to travel
□ viajar en autocar to travel by coach

el **viaje** NOUN
1 trip
■ **¡Buen viaje!** Have a good trip!
■ **un viaje de negocios** a business trip
2 journey
□ Es un viaje muy largo. It's a very long journey.
■ **estar de viaje** to be away
■ **salir de viaje** to go away
■ **una agencia de viajes** a travel agency
■ **el viaje de novios** honeymoon

el **viajero**, la **viajera** NOUN
passenger

la **víbora** NOUN
viper

la **vibración** (PL las **vibraciones**) NOUN
vibration

**vibrar** VERB [25]
to vibrate

la **vicepresidenta** NOUN
1 vice president
2 chairwoman (PL chairwomen)

el **vicepresidente** NOUN
1 vice president
2 chairman (PL chairmen)

**viceversa** ADVERB
vice versa

**viciarse** VERB [25]
to deteriorate

■ **viciarse con las drogas** to become addicted to drugs

el **vicio** NOUN
vice
□ El tabaco es mi único vicio. Smoking is my only vice.
■ **Tengo el vicio de morderme las uñas.** I bite my nails; I know it's a bad habit.

la **víctima** NOUN
victim

la **victoria** NOUN
victory (PL victories)
□ la victoria del partido conservador the conservative party victory
■ **su primera victoria fuera de casa** their first away win

la **vid** NOUN
vine

la **vida** NOUN
life (PL lives)
□ He vivido aquí toda mi vida. I've lived here all my life. □ Llevan una vida muy tranquila. They lead a very quiet life. □ ¡Esto sí que es vida! This is the life!
■ **la media de vida de un televisor** the average life span of a television set
■ **vida nocturna** nightlife
■ **estar con vida** to be alive
■ **salir con vida** to escape alive
■ **Se gana la vida haciendo traducciones.** He earns his living by translating.
■ **¡Vida mía!** My darling!

el **video** NOUN *(Latin America)*
video

el **vídeo** NOUN
video
□ Tengo la película en vídeo. I've got the film on video.
■ **cinta de vídeo** videotape

la **videocámara** NOUN
video camera

el **videojuego** NOUN
video game

la **videollamada** NOUN
video call

el **videoteléfono** NOUN
videophone

la **vidriera** NOUN
1 stained glass window
2 shop window *(Latin America)*

el **vidrio** NOUN
1 glass
□ botellas de vidrio glass bottles
■ **Me corté el dedo con un vidrio.** I cut my finger on a piece of glass.
2 windowpane

la **vieja** NOUN
old woman (PL old women)

□ Había una viejecita sentada a mi lado. There was an old woman sitting next to me.

**viejo** (FEM **vieja**) ADJECTIVE
old
□ un viejo amigo mío an old friend of mine □ Estos zapatos ya están muy viejos. These shoes are very old now.
■ **hacerse viejo** to get old

el **viejo** NOUN
old man (PL old men)
■ **los viejos** old people
■ **llegar a viejo** to reach old age

**viene** VERB ▷ *see* venir

el **viento** NOUN
wind
■ **Hace mucho viento.** It's very windy.

el **vientre** NOUN
stomach
■ **hacer de vientre** to go to the toilet

el **viernes** (PL los **viernes**) NOUN
Friday
□ La vi el viernes. I saw her on Friday. □ todos los viernes every Friday □ el viernes pasado last Friday □ el viernes que viene next Friday □ Jugamos los viernes. We play on Fridays.
■ **Viernes Santo** Good Friday

> **LANGUAGE TIP** Word for word, **Viernes Santo** means 'Holy Friday'.

**vierta** VERB ▷ *see* verter

el/la **vietnamita** ADJECTIVE, NOUN
Vietnamese
■ **los vietnamitas** the Vietnamese

la **viga** NOUN
1 beam
2 girder

la **vigilancia** NOUN
1 surveillance
□ bajo vigilancia policial under police surveillance
2 vigilance
□ El paciente necesita vigilancia constante. The patient needs constant vigilance.
■ **patrulla de vigilancia** security patrol

el/la **vigilante** NOUN
1 security guard
2 store detective
■ **vigilante jurado** security guard
■ **vigilante nocturno** night watchman (PL night watchmen)

**vigilar** VERB [25]
1 to guard
□ Un policía vigilaba al preso. A policeman was guarding the prisoner.
2 to watch
□ Nos vigilan. They're watching us.
3 to keep an eye on
□ ¿Me vigilas el bolso un momento? Can

you keep an eye on my bag for a minute?

**VIH** ABBREVIATION (= *virus de inmunodeficiencia humana*)
  HIV

la **villa** NOUN
1  town
2  villa

el **villancico** NOUN
  carol

el **vinagre** NOUN
  vinegar

el **vínculo** NOUN
  bond

**vine** VERB ▷ *see* venir

**viniendo** VERB ▷ *see* venir

el **vino** NOUN
  wine
  ■ **vino blanco**  white wine
  ■ **vino tinto**  red wine
  ■ **vino de la casa**  house wine

la **viña** NOUN
  vineyard

el **viñedo** NOUN
  vineyard

la **violación** (PL las **violaciones**) NOUN
1  rape
2  violation

el **violador**, la **violadora** NOUN
  rapist

**violar** VERB [25]
1  to rape
2  to violate

la **violencia** NOUN
  violence

**violento** (FEM **violenta**) ADJECTIVE
1  violent
  □ La película contiene algunas escenas violentas.  The film contains some violent scenes.
2  embarrassing
  □ Era una situación violenta.  It was an embarrassing situation.
  ■ **Me resulta violento decírselo.**  I'm embarrassed to tell him.

el **violeta** ADJECTIVE, NOUN
  purple
  □ unas cortinas violeta  purple curtains

la **violeta** NOUN
  violet

el **violín** (PL los **violines**) NOUN
  violin

el/la **violinista** NOUN
  violinist

el **violón** (PL los **violones**) NOUN
  double bass (PL double basses)

el/la **violonchelista** NOUN
  cellist

el **violonchelo** NOUN

cello (PL cellos)

**virgen** (FEM **virgen**, PL **vírgenes**) ADJECTIVE
1  virgin
  ■ **ser virgen**  to be a virgin
2  blank *(tape)*

la **virgen** (PL las **vírgenes**) NOUN
  virgin
  ■ **la Virgen**  the Virgin

**Virgo** MASC NOUN
  Virgo
  ■ **Soy virgo.**  I'm Virgo.

**viril** (FEM **viril**) ADJECTIVE
  virile

la **virilidad** NOUN
  virility

**virtual** ADJECTIVE
  virtual

la **virtud** NOUN
  virtue

la **viruela** NOUN
  smallpox
  □ Tiene la viruela.  He has smallpox.

el **virus** (PL los **virus**) NOUN
  virus (PL viruses)

la **visa** NOUN *(Latin America)*
  visa

el **visado** NOUN
  visa

la **visera** NOUN
1  peak
2  visor

la **visibilidad** NOUN
  visibility
  □ Había muy poca visibilidad.  Visibility was very poor.

**visible** (FEM **visible**) ADJECTIVE
  visible

el **visillo** NOUN
  net curtain

la **visión** (PL las **visiones**) NOUN
1  vision
  □ la visión nocturna  night vision
2  view
  □ una visión pesimista de la vida  a pessimistic view of life
  ■ **Tú estás viendo visiones.**  You're seeing things.

la **visita** NOUN
1  visit
  ■ **hacer una visita a alguien**  to visit someone
2  visitor
  □ Tienes visita.  You've got visitors.
  ■ **horario de visita**  visiting hours *pl*
  ■ **tarjeta de visita**  business card

el/la **visitante** NOUN
  visitor

**visitar** VERB [25]

**v**

to visit
□ 5.000 personas han visitado ya la exposición. 5000 people have already visited the exhibition.

el **viso** NOUN
slip *(clothes)*
■ **visos** signs □ La situación no tiene visos de mejorar. The situation shows no signs of improving.
■ **esta tela hace visos** this material is two-tone

el **visón** (PL los **visones**) NOUN
mink
■ **un abrigo de visón** a mink coat

la **víspera** NOUN
the day before
□ la víspera de la boda the day before the wedding
■ **la víspera de Navidad** Christmas Eve

la **vista** NOUN
1 sight
2 view
□ una habitación con vistas al mar a room with a sea view
■ **a primera vista** at first glance
■ **alzar la vista** to look up
■ **bajar la vista** to look down
■ **perder la vista** to lose one's sight
■ **volver la vista** to look back
■ **conocer a alguien de vista** to know someone by sight
■ **hacer la vista gorda** to turn a blind eye
■ **¡Hasta la vista!** See you!

el **vistazo** NOUN
■ **echar un vistazo a algo** to have a look at something

**vistiendo** VERB ▷ *see* vestir

**visto** VERB
▷ *see also* **visto** ADJECTIVE ▷ *see* ver

**visto** (FEM **vista**) ADJECTIVE
▷ *see also* **visto** VERB
■ **Está visto que ...** It's clear that ...
■ **Hurgarse la nariz está mal visto.** Picking your nose is frowned upon.
■ **por lo visto** apparently
■ **dar el visto bueno a algo** to give something one's approval

**vistoso** (FEM **vistosa**) ADJECTIVE
showy

**vital** (FEM **vital**) ADJECTIVE
vital

la **vitalidad** NOUN
vitality

la **vitamina** NOUN
vitamin

**vitorear** VERB [25]
to cheer

la **vitrina** NOUN

1 glass cabinet
2 shop window *(Latin America)*

**viuda** ADJECTIVE
■ **Es viuda.** She's a widow.
■ **quedarse viuda** to be widowed

la **viuda** NOUN
widow

**viudo** ADJECTIVE
■ **Es viudo.** He's a widower.
■ **Se quedó viudo a los 50 años.** He was widowed at 50.

el **viudo** NOUN
widower

**vivaracho** (FEM **vivaracha**) ADJECTIVE
lively

los **víveres** NOUN
provisions *pl*

el **vivero** NOUN
nursery (PL nurseries)

la **vivienda** NOUN
1 house
2 flat
3 housing
□ la escasez de la vivienda the housing shortage

**vivir** VERB [58]
1 to live
□ ¿Dónde vives? Where do you live?
2 to be alive
□ ¿Todavía vive? Is he still alive?
■ **vivir de algo** to live on something
□ Viven de su pensión. They live on his pension.
■ **¡Viva!** Hurray!

**vivo** (FEM **viva**) ADJECTIVE
1 alive
□ Estaba vivo. He was alive.
2 bright
■ **en vivo** live □ una retransmisión en vivo a live broadcast

el **vocabulario** NOUN
vocabulary

la **vocación** (PL las **vocaciones**) NOUN
vocation

la **vocal** NOUN
vowel

el **vodka** NOUN
vodka

el **volante** NOUN
1 steering wheel
2 shuttlecock
3 referral note
■ **volantes** flounce *sing*

**volar*** VERB [11]
1 to fly
□ El helicóptero volaba muy bajo. The helicopter was flying very low. □ Se me pasó la semana volando. The week just flew by.

**2** to blow up

□ Volaron el puente. They blew up the bridge.

■ **Tuvimos que ir volando al hospital.** We had to rush to the hospital.

el **volcán** (PL los **volcanes**) NOUN
volcano (PL volcanoes)

**volcar*** VERB

**1** to knock over

□ El perro volcó el cubo de la basura. The dog knocked the dustbin over.

**2** to capsize

**3** to overturn

el **voleibol** NOUN
volleyball

el **voltaje** NOUN
voltage

la **voltereta** NOUN

**1** forward roll

■ **dar una voltereta** to do a forward roll

**2** somersault

el **voltio** NOUN
volt

el **volumen** (PL los **volúmenes**) NOUN
volume

■ **bajar el volumen** to turn the volume down

■ **subir el volumen** to turn the volume up

la **voluntad** NOUN

**1** will

□ Lo hizo contra mi voluntad. He did it against my will.

**2** willpower

□ Le cuesta, pero tiene mucha voluntad. It's difficult for him, but he has a lot of willpower.

la **voluntaria** NOUN
volunteer

**voluntario** (FEM **voluntaria**) ADJECTIVE
voluntary

■ **ofrecerse voluntario para algo** to volunteer for something

el **voluntario** NOUN
volunteer

**volver*** VERB [59]

**1** to come back

**2** to go back

**3** to turn

□ Me volvió la espalda. He turned away from me.

■ **Me volví para ver quién era.** I turned round to see who it was.

**4** to become

■ **Se ha vuelto muy cariñoso.** He's become very affectionate.

■ **volver a hacer algo** to do something again

■ **volver en sí** to come round

**vomitar** VERB [25]
to be sick

□ Ha vomitado dos veces. He's been sick twice.

■ **Vomitó todo lo que había comido.** He threw up everything he'd eaten.

**vos** PRONOUN *(River Plate)*
you

**vosotros** (FEM **vosotras**) PL PRONOUN
you

□ Vosotros vendréis conmigo. You'll come with me.

■ **Hacedlo vosotros mismos.** Do it yourselves.

la **votación** (PL las **votaciones**) NOUN

■ **Hicimos una votación.** We took a vote.

■ **Salió elegida por votación.** She was voted in.

**votar** VERB [25]
to vote

□ Voté por Alcántara. I voted for Alcántara.

■ **Votaron a los socialistas.** They voted for the Socialists.

**voy** VERB ▷ *see* **ir**

la **voz** (PL las **voces**) NOUN
voice

□ No tengo buena voz. I don't have a very good voice.

■ **hablar en voz alta** to speak loudly

■ **dar voces** to shout

**vuelco** VERB ▷ *see* **volcar**

el **vuelco** NOUN

■ **dar un vuelco** to overturn
to capsize

■ **Me dio un vuelco el corazón.** My heart missed a beat.

**vuelo** VERB ▷ *see* **volar**

el **vuelo** NOUN
flight

■ **vuelo de bajo coste** low cost flight

■ **vuelo chárter** charter flight

■ **vuelo regular** scheduled flight

■ **Las gaviotas levantaron el vuelo.** The seagulls flew away.

la **vuelta** NOUN

**1** return

□ un billete de ida y vuelta a return ticket

**2** lap

□ Di tres vueltas a la pista. I did three laps of the track.

**3** change

□ Quédese con la vuelta. Keep the change.

■ **a vuelta de correo** by return of post

■ **Vive a la vuelta de la esquina.** He lives round the corner.

■ **El coche dio la vuelta.** The car turned round.

■ **Dimos una vuelta de campana.** We

overturned completely.

■ **dar la vuelta a la página** to turn the page
■ **dar la vuelta al mundo** to go round the world
■ **No le des más vueltas a lo que dijo.** Stop worrying about what he said.
■ **dar una vuelta 1** to go for a walk **2** to go for a drive
■ **dar media vuelta** to turn round
■ **estar de vuelta** to be back
■ **vuelta ciclista** cycle race

**vuelto** VERB ▷ *see* **volver**

el **vuelto** NOUN *(Latin America)*
change

**vuelvo** VERB ▷ *see* **volver**

**vuestro** (FEM **vuestra**) ADJECTIVE, PRONOUN
**1** your
□ vuestra casa your house □ vuestros amigos your friends
■ **un amigo vuestro** a friend of yours
**2** yours
□ ¿Son vuestros? Are they yours?
■ **¿Es ésta la vuestra?** Is this one yours?
■ **¿Y los bocadillos? — Los vuestros están aquí.** Where are the sandwiches? — Yours are over here.

**vulgar** (FEM **vulgar**) ADJECTIVE
vulgar

V

el **walkie-talkie** (PL los **walkie-talkies**)
NOUN
walkie-talkie

el **walkman**® (PL los **walkmans**) NOUN
Walkman®

el **wáter** NOUN
loo

la **web** NOUN
1  website

2  (World Wide) Web

el **western** (PL los **westerns**) NOUN
western

el **whisky** (PL los **whiskys**) NOUN
whisky (PL whiskies)

el **windsurf** NOUN
1  windsurfing
2  windsurf

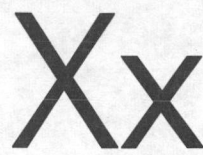

**xenófobo** (FEM **xenófoba**) ADJECTIVE
xenophobic

el **xilófono** NOUN
xylophone

# Yy

**y** CONJUNCTION
and
□ Andrés y su novia. Andrés and his girlfriend.
■ **Yo quiero una ensalada. ¿Y tú?** I'd like a salad. What about you?
■ **¡Y yo!** Me too!
■ **¿Y qué?** So what?
■ **Son las tres y cinco.** It's five minutes past three.

**ya** ADVERB
already
□ Ya se han ido. They've already left.
□ ¿Ya has terminado? Have you finished already?
■ **ya no** any more □ Ya no salimos juntos. We're not going out any more.
■ **Estos zapatos ya me están pequeños.** These shoes are too small for me now.
■ **ya que** since
■ **Ya lo sé.** I know.
■ **Ya veremos.** We'll see.
■ **Rellena el impreso y ya está.** Fill in the form and that's it.
■ **¡Ya voy!** I'm coming!

**el yacimiento** NOUN
site
■ **un yacimiento petrolífero** an oilfield

**el/la yanqui** (PL los/las **yanquis**) ADJECTIVE, NOUN
Yank

**el yate** NOUN
1 pleasure cruiser
2 yacht

**la yedra** NOUN
ivy

**la yegua** NOUN
mare

**la yema** NOUN
1 yolk
2 fingertip

**yendo** VERB ▷ see ir

**el yerno** NOUN
son-in-law (PL sons-in-law)

**el yeso** NOUN
plaster

**yo** PRONOUN
1 I
□ Carlos y yo no fuimos. Carlos and I didn't go.
2 me
□ ¿Quién ha visto la película? — Ana y yo. Who's seen the film? — Ana and me.
□ Es más alta que yo. She's taller than me.
□ Soy yo, María. It's me, María.
■ **¡Yo también!** Me too!
■ **yo mismo** myself □ Lo hice yo misma. I did it myself.
■ **yo que tú** if I were you

**el yoga** NOUN
yoga

**el yogur** NOUN
yoghurt

**el yudo** NOUN
judo

**Yugoslavia** FEM NOUN
Yugoslavia
□ en la antigua Yugoslavia in the former Yugoslavia

# Zz

el **zafiro** NOUN
sapphire

**zambullirse**\* VERB
to dive underwater

**zamparse** VERB [25]
to wolf down (colloquial)
□ Se zampó todas las galletas. He wolfed down all the biscuits.

la **zanahoria** NOUN
carrot

la **zancadilla** NOUN
■ **poner la zancadilla a alguien** to trip someone up

el **zancudo** NOUN (Latin America)
mosquito (PL mosquitos)

la **zanja** NOUN
ditch (PL ditches)

**zanjar** VERB [25]
to settle

la **zapatera** NOUN
shoemaker

la **zapatería** NOUN
1 shoe shop
2 shoe repairer's

el **zapatero** NOUN
shoemaker

la **zapatilla** NOUN
slipper
■ **zapatillas de ballet** ballet shoes
■ **zapatillas de deporte** training shoes

el **zapato** NOUN
shoe
■ **zapatos de tacón** high-heeled shoes
■ **zapatos planos** flat shoes

la **zarpa** NOUN
paw

**zarpar** VERB [25]
to set sail

la **zarza** NOUN
bramble

la **zarzamora** NOUN
blackberry bush

el **zigzag** NOUN
zigzag
■ **una carretera en zigzag** a winding road

**Zimbabue** MASC NOUN
Zimbabwe

el **zinc** NOUN
zinc

el **zíper** (PL los zípers) NOUN (Latin America)
zip

el **zócalo** NOUN
1 skirting board
2 main square (Latin America)

el **zodíaco** NOUN
zodiac
□ los signos del zodíaco the signs of the zodiac

la **zona** NOUN
area
□ Viven en una zona muy tranquila. They live in a very quiet area.
■ **Fue declarada zona neutral.** It was declared a neutral zone.
■ **una zona azul** a pay-and-display area
■ **una zona industrial** an industrial park
■ **una zona peatonal** a pedestrian precinct
■ **una zona verde** a green space

el **zoo** NOUN
zoo

la **zoóloga** NOUN
zoologist

la **zoología** NOUN
zoology

el **zoológico** NOUN
zoo

el **zoólogo** NOUN
zoologist

el **zoom** (PL los zooms) NOUN
zoom lens (PL zoom lenses)

**zoquete** (FEM zoquete) ADJECTIVE
dim (colloquial)

el/la **zoquete** NOUN
blockhead

el **zorro** NOUN
fox (PL foxes)
□ piel de zorro fox fur

el **zueco** NOUN
clog

**zumbar** VERB [25]
to buzz

Spanish-English

▫ Me zumban los oídos. **My ears are buzzing.**
■ **salir zumbando** *(colloquial)* to whizz off
el **zumo** NOUN
juice

▫ zumo de naranja orange juice
**zurcir\*** VERB

to darn
**zurdo** (FEM **zurda**) ADJECTIVE
1 left-handed
2 left-footed
**zurrar** VERB [25]
to thrash

# Spanish in Action

Océano Atlántico

FRANCIA

Mar Cantábrico

Santander

GALICIA  ASTURIAS  Oviedo  CANTABRIA  PAÍS VASCO  ANDORRA

Santiago de Compostela  *Cordillera Cantábrica*  Vitoria-Gasteiz  *Pirineos*

Logroño  Pamplona

NAVARRA

CASTILLA Y LEÓN  LA RIOJA

Valladolid  *Ebro*  Zaragoza  CATALUÑA

*Duero*  ARAGÓN  Barcelona

MADRID  Menorca

PORTUGAL  *Tajo*  Madrid  Palma de Mallorca  *Mallorca*

Toledo  VALENCIA

EXTREMADURA  CASTILLA-LA MANCHA  Valencia

Mérida  Ibiza  ISLAS BALEARES

*Guadiana*  Formentera

*Sierra Morena*

*Guadalquivir*  MURCIA

Sevilla  ANDALUCÍA  Murcia

*Sistemas Béticos*

*Mar Mediterráneo*

Ceuta

Melilla  ARGELIA

MARRUECOS  ©Collins Bartholomew Ltd 2007

- Spain is the second biggest country by area in Western Europe, covering 504 800 km² (well over twice the size of the UK).

- The River Ebro is around 910 km long, rising in the Cantabrian Mountains and flowing into the Mediterranean.

- Spain's highest mountain is in the Canary Islands: Teide (3 718m), in Tenerife.

- 40.8 million people live in Spain. The population is one of the slowest-growing in the world.

## Some useful phrases

| | |
|---|---|
| *Esta es mi hermana, Elena.* | This is my sister, Elena. |
| *Ella se casa el verano que viene.* | She's getting married next summer. |
| *Tengo un hermano gemelo.* | I have a twin brother. |
| *Tengo una hermana gemela.* | I have a twin sister. |
| *Tengo un hermanastro.* | I have a half-brother. |
| *Yo soy hijo único.* | I'm an only child. (boy) |
| *Yo soy hija única.* | I'm an only child. (girl) |
| *Mis padres están separados/divorciados.* | My parents are separated/divorced. |
| *Mi abuelo murió el año pasado.* | My grandfather died last year. |
| *Mi madre se ha vuelto a casar.* | My mother has got married again. |

| *Las relaciones* | Relationships |
|---|---|
| *Me llevo bien con mi hermana.* | I get on well with my sister. |
| *No me llevo nada bien con mi hermano.* | I don't get on at all with my brother. |
| *Mi mejor amigo se llama Tamir.* | My best friend is called Tamir. |
| *Tengo tres mejores amigas.* | I've got three best friends. |
| *Somos inseparables.* | We're always together. |
| *Me he peleado con Rachida.* | I've had a quarrel with Rachida. |
| *Ya no me hablo con Jessica.* | I'm not talking to Jessica any more. |

| *Los miembros de la familia* | Members of the family |
|---|---|
| *mi padre* | my father, my dad |
| *mi madre* | my mother, my mum |
| *mi hermano* | my brother |
| *mi hermana* | my sister |
| *mi tío* | my uncle |
| *mi tía* | my aunt |
| *mi primo* | my cousin (male) |
| *mi prima* | my cousin (female) |
| *mi abuelo* | my grandfather, my granddad |
| *mi abuela* | my grandmother, my gran |
| *mis abuelos* | my grandparents |
| *mi hermano mayor* | my big brother |
| *mi hermana pequeña* | my little sister |
| *el novio de mi hermana* | my sister's boyfriend |
| *la novia de mi hermano* | my brother's girlfriend |
| *el novio de mi hermana* | my sister's fiancé |
| *la novia de mi hermano* | my brother's fiancée |

| *Las emociones* | Emotions |
|---|---|
| *estar ...* | to be ... |
| *triste* | sad |
| *contento/contenta* | pleased |
| *feliz* | happy |
| *enfadado/enfadada* | angry |
| *enamorado/enamorada* | in love |
| *dolido/dolida* | hurt |

| | |
|---|---|
| *Estoy enamorada de Ruth.* | I'm in love with Ruth. |
| *Bruno y yo nos hemos separado.* | Bruno and I have split up. |
| *Estoy contenta de que vengas.* | I'm pleased you're coming. |
| *Estoy triste por irme.* | I'm sad to be leaving. |
| *Espero que no estés demasiado enfadado.* | I hope you're not too angry. |
| *Ella se molestó por no haber sido invitada.* | She was hurt that she wasn't invited. |

| ¿Dónde vives? | Where do you live? |
|---|---|
| *Vivo ...* | I live ... |
| en un pueblo | in a village |
| en una ciudad pequeña | in a small town |
| en el centro | in the town centre |
| en las afueras de Londres | in the suburbs of London |
| en el campo | in the countryside |
| en la playa | at the seaside |
| al lado de un riachuelo | beside a small river |
| a 100 km de Manchester | 100 km from Manchester |
| al norte de Birmingham | north of Birmingham |
| en una casa individual | in a detached house |
| en una casa adosada | in a semi-detached house |
| en una casa de dos plantas | in a two-storey house |
| en un bloque de pisos | in a block of flats |
| en un piso | in a flat |
| en una urbanización | on a housing estate |

| *Vivo en un piso ...* | I live in a flat ... |
|---|---|
| en la planta baja | on the ground floor |
| en la primera planta | on the first floor |
| en la segunda planta | on the second floor |
| en la última planta | on the top floor |

| *Vivo ...* | I live ... |
|---|---|
| en una casa moderna | in a modern house |
| en una casa nueva | in a new house |
| en una vieja casa eduardina | in an old Edwardian house |

| De casa al colegio | From home to school |
|---|---|
| El colegio está bastante lejos de mi casa. | School is quite a long way from my house. |
| Vivo a cinco minutos andando del colegio. | I live five minutes' walk from school. |
| Mi padre me lleva al colegio en coche. | My father takes me to school in the car. |
| Voy al colegio en autobús. | I go to school by bus. |

| En casa | At home |
|---|---|
| *En la planta baja está ...* | On the ground floor there is ... |
| la cocina | the kitchen |
| la sala de estar | the living room |
| el comedor | the dining room |
| el salón | the lounge |
| *En la primera planta, está ...* | Upstairs there is ... |
| mi habitación | my bedroom |
| la habitación de mi hermano | my brother's bedroom |
| la habitación de mis padres | my parents' room |
| la habitación de invitados | the spare bedroom |
| el cuarto de baño | the bathroom |
| un despacho | a study |
| un jardín | a garden |
| un campo de fútbol | a football pitch |
| una pista de tenis | a tennis court |
| un vecino | a neighbour |
| los vecinos de enfrente | the people opposite |
| los vecinos de al lado | the next-door neighbours |

## Some useful phrases

| | |
|---|---|
| Mi casa es muy pequeña. | My house is very small. |
| Mi habitación está ordenada. | My room is tidy. |
| Comparto mi habitación con mi hermano. | I share my bedroom with my brother. |
| Mi mejor amigo vive en la misma calle que yo. | My best friend lives in the same street as me. |
| Hay una pista de tenis al lado de mi casa. | There's a tennis court next to my house. |
| Nos mudamos el mes que viene. | We're moving next month. |

| Algunos sitios importantes | A few landmarks |
|---|---|
| un cine | a cinema |
| un teatro | a theatre |
| un museo | a museum |
| una plaza | public gardens |
| un cajero automático | a cash dispenser |
| la oficina de turismo | the tourist office |
| una catedral | a cathedral |
| una iglesia | a church |
| una mezquita | a mosque |
| una calle peatonal | a pedestrian street |
| un banco | a bank |
| la piscina | the swimming pool |
| la pista de patinaje sobre hielo | the ice rink |
| la biblioteca | the library |
| el ayuntamiento | the town hall |
| el mercado | the market square |

| Los medios de transporte | Means of transport |
|---|---|
| un autobús | a bus |
| un autocar | a coach |
| el metro | the underground |
| el tranvía | the tram |
| el tren | the train |
| la estación | the station |
| la estación de autobuses | the bus station |
| una estación de metro | an underground station |
| ¿A qué hora es el próximo tren para Madrid? | What time is the next train to Madrid? |
| Querría un billete de ida para Sevilla. | I'd like a single to Seville. |
| Un billete de ida y vuelta para Valencia, por favour. | A return to Valencia, please. |
| ¿Dónde está el andén 10? | Where is platform 10? |
| ¿Dónde está la estación de metro más cercana? | Where is the nearest underground station? |

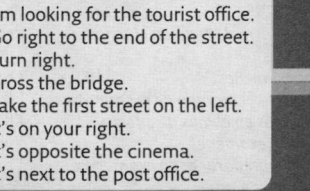

| Las direcciones | Directions |
|---|---|
| enfrente de | opposite |
| al lado de | next to |
| cerca de | near |
| entre ... y ... | between ... and ... |
| ¿Dónde se encuentra la estación de autobuses? | Where's the bus station? |
| Estoy buscando la oficina de turismo. | I'm looking for the tourist office. |
| Vaya hasta el final de la calle. | Go right to the end of the street. |
| Gire a la derecha. | Turn right. |
| Cruce el puente. | Cross the bridge. |
| Tome la primera calle a la izquierda. | Take the first street on the left. |
| Está a su derecha. | It's on your right. |
| Está enfrente del cine. | It's opposite the cinema. |
| Está al lado de correos. | It's next to the post office. |

# My plans for the future

| El trabajo | Work |
|---|---|
| **Me gustaría estudiar ...** | **I'd like to study ...** |
| medicina | medicine |
| ingeniería | engineering |
| derecho | law |
| sociología | sociology |
| psicología | psychology |
| idiomas | languages |
| arquitectura | architecture |
| **Me gustaría ...** | **I'd like to ...** |
| ganar mucho dinero | earn lots of money |
| trabajar en una tienda | work in a shop |
| trabajar en un banco | work in a bank |
| trabajar en el turismo | work in tourism |
| hacer prácticas | do an apprenticeship |
| conseguir un título | do a qualification |
| **Me gustaría ser ...** | **I'd like to be ...** |
| abogado | a solicitor |
| profesor | a teacher |
| dentista | a dentist |
| actriz | an actress |
| cantante | a singer |
| peluquero | a hairdresser |
| periodista | a journalist |
| actor | an actor |
| jugador de fútbol profesional | a professional footballer |
| músico | a musician |
| político | a politician |
| **Pienso que es ...** | **I think it's ...** |
| interesante | interesting |
| cansado | tiring |
| gratificante | rewarding |
| estresante | stressful |
| **Pienso que está ...** | **I think it's ...** |
| bien pagado | well paid |
| mal pagado | badly paid |

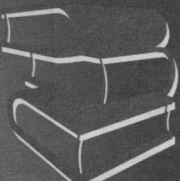

| Las ambiciones | Ambitions |
|---|---|
| Tengo la intención de ir a la universidad. | I'm planning to go to university. |
| Después me gustaría irme al extranjero. | Afterwards I'd like to go abroad. |
| Me gustaría casarme y tener muchos hijos. | I'd like to get married and have lots of children. |
| No sé todavía lo que quiero hacer. | I don't know yet what I want to do. |

| Los exámenes | Exams |
|---|---|
| un examen | an exam |
| un simulacro de examen | a mock exam |
| las notas | the results |
| Este año preparo el GCSE. | I'm doing my GCSEs this year. |
| Hago mi primer simulacro de examen el lunes que viene. | I'm going to do my first mock exam next Monday. |
| Espero aprobar los exámenes. | I hope I'll pass my exams. |
| Creo que he suspendido el examen de matemáticas. | I think I've failed my maths exam. |
| Me darán los resultados en el mes de agosto. | I'll get the results in August. |
| Me han salido bien los exámenes. | I've done well in my exams. |
| El año que viene voy a preparar ocho exámenes. | I'm going to do eight exams next year. |

# Jobs and hobbies

| Los deportes | Sports |
| --- | --- |
| **Juego ...** | **I play ...** |
| al fútbol | football |
| al baloncesto | basketball |
| al rugby | rugby |
| al tennis | tennis |
| al ping-pong | table tennis |
| | |
| **Hago ...** | **I ...** |
| esquí | ski |
| kayak | canoe |
| gimnasia | do gymnastics |
| natación | swim |
| equitación | go horse riding |
| vela | go sailing |
| | |
| Este verano voy a hacer un cursillo de vela. | I'm going to do a sailing course this summer. |
| Nunca he hecho esquí. | I've never been skiing. |
| Voy a aprender a hacer kayak. | I'm going to learn how to canoe. |

| Trabajo | Jobs |
| --- | --- |
| un currículum o CV | a CV |
| una entrevista | an interview |
| | |
| **Yo trabajo ...** | **I work ...** |
| en la farmacia el sábado | at the chemist's on Saturdays |
| en el supermercado en vacaciones | at the supermarket in the holidays |
| en una tienda de ropa el fin de semana | in a clothes shop at the weekend |
| | |
| Soy canguro. | I do baby-sitting. |
| Hago la compra para una señora mayor. | I do an old lady's shopping for her. |
| Reparto los periódicos. | I deliver papers. |
| Gano 7,50 euros por hora. | I earn 7.50 euros an hour. |
| Nunca he trabajado. | I've never had a job. |
| Voy a buscar un trabajo para este verano. | I'm going to look for a job for this summer. |

**Jobs and hobbies**

| Los instrumentos musicales | Musical instruments |
| --- | --- |
| **Yo toco ...** | **I play the ...** |
| el violín | violin |
| el piano | piano |
| la guitarra | guitar |
| la flauta | flute |
| | |
| Toco el violín desde hace ocho años. | I've been playing the violin since I was eight. |
| Toco en la orquesta del colegio. | I play in the school orchestra. |
| Me gustaría aprender a tocar la guitarra. | I'd like to learn to play the guitar. |

| Cocinar en casa | Cooking at home |
| --- | --- |
| Me gusta cocinar. | I like cooking |
| No sé cocinar. | I can't cook. |
| Hago muy bien los pasteles. | I'm very good at making cakes. |

| Mis pasatiempos preferidos | My favourite hobbies |
| --- | --- |
| Me gusta leer libros. | I like reading novels. |
| Me encanta escuchar música en mi habitación. | I love listening to music in my room. |
| Me gusta mucho ir a la ciudad con mis amigas. | I love going into town with my friends. |
| Mi pasatiempo preferido es la equitación. | My favourite hobby is riding. |
| Prefiero salir con mis amigos. | I'd rather go out with my friends. |

# Describing someone

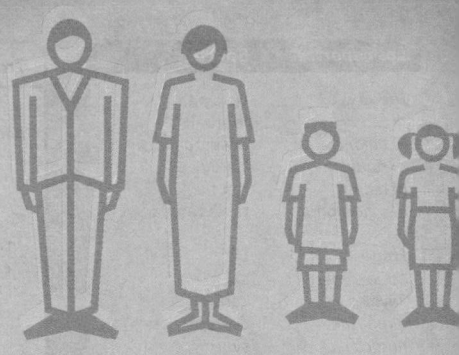

| La personalidad | Personality |
|---|---|
| *Él/Ella es ...* | **He/She is ...** |
| *divertido/divertida* | funny |
| *simpático/simpática* | nice |
| *tímido/tímida* | shy |
| *reservado/reservada* | quiet |
| *exasperante* | annoying |
| *generoso/generosa* | generous |
| *hablador/habladora* | talkative |
| *inteligente* | intelligent |
| *tonto/tonta* | stupid |
| *avaro* | stingy |
| *raro* | strange |

| Los colores | | Colours |
|---|---|---|
| *amarillo, amarilla* | | yellow |
| *naranja* | | orange |
| *rojo, roja* | | red |
| *rosa* | | pink |
| *violeta* | | purple |
| *azul* | | blue |
| *verde* | | green |
| *marrón* | | brown |
| *gris* | | grey |
| *negro, negra* | | black |
| *blanco, blanca* | | white |
| *burdeos* (masc, fem, pl) | | maroon |
| *azul marino* (masc, fem, pl) | | navy (blue) |
| *turquesa* (masc, fem, pl) | | turquoise |
| *beige* | | beige |
| *crema* (masc, fem, pl) | | cream |

**también para los ojos:** / **For eyes:**
*avellana* (masc, fem, pl) — hazel

**también para el pelo:** / **For hair:**

| | |
|---|---|
| *caoba* | auburn |
| *rubio, rubia* | blonde |
| *castaño* | brown |
| *castaño claro* | light brown |
| *moreno, morena* | dark brown |
| *pelirrojo, pelirroja* | red |

| | |
|---|---|
| *Tengo los ojos color avellana.* | I've got hazel eyes. |
| *Tiene el pelo castaño.* | He's got brown hair. |
| *Tiene el pelo corto y gris.* | She's got short grey hair. |
| *Ella es pelirroja.* | She's got red hair. |
| *Él es calvo.* | He's bald. |
| *Ella tiene el pelo rubio, largo y rizado.* | She's got long curly blonde hair. |

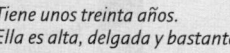

| Las características | Characteristics |
|---|---|
| **Él/Ella es ...** | **He/She is ...** |
| alto/alta | tall |
| bajo/baja | small |
| delgado/delgada | slim |
| gordo/gorda | fat |
| guapo/guapa | good-looking |
| joven | young |
| viejo/vieja | old |
| | |
| Tiene unos treinta años. | He's about thirty. |
| Ella es alta, delgada y bastante guapa. | She's tall, slim and quite nice-looking. |
| Se parece a Cameron Diaz. | She looks like Cameron Diaz. |

| La ropa | Clothes |
|---|---|
| un jersey | a jumper |
| un pantalón | trousers |
| una blusa | a blouse |
| una camiseta | a T-shirt |
| un abrigo | a coat |
| una chaqueta | a jacket |
| un chaleco | a cardigan |
| | |
| un vestido | a dress |
| une falda | a skirt |
| une corbata | a tie |
| una chaqueta | a jacket |
| una camisa | a shirt |
| | |
| zapatos | shoes |
| zapatillas de deporte | trainers |
| botas | boots |
| | |
| Ella lleva una camiseta azul claro. | She's wearing a light blue T-shirt. |
| Él lleva un traje gris oscuro. | He's wearing a dark grey suit. |
| Mi uniforme se compone de una falda azul marino, una blusa blanca, una corbata a rayas burdeos y gris, calcetines grises, una americana burdeos y zapatos negros. | My uniform consists of a navy blue skirt, a white blouse, a tie with maroon and grey stripes, grey socks, a maroon blazer and black shoes. |

| Las comidas | Meals |
|---|---|
| el desayuno | breakfast |
| el almuerzo | lunch |
| la merienda | afternoon snack |
| la cena | dinner |
| **Me encanta ...** | **I love ...** |
| el chocolate | chocolate |
| la ensalada | salad |
| **Me encantan ...** | **I love ...** |
| las fresas | strawberries |
| **Me gusta ...** | **I like ...** |
| el pescado | fish |
| la limonada | lemonade |
| **Me gustan ...** | **I like ...** |
| las verduras | vegetables |
| **No me gusta ...** | **I don't like ...** |
| el zumo de naranja | orange juice |
| el agua gaseosa | sparkling water |
| **No me gustan ...** | **I don't like ...** |
| los plátanos | bananas |
| No como cerdo. | I don't eat pork. |
| Como mucha fruta. | I eat a lot of fruit. |
| No como guarrerías entre comidas. | I don't eat junk food between meals. |
| Evito las bebidas gaseosas. | I avoid fizzy drinks. |
| Soy vegetariano/a. | I'm a vegetarian. |
| Soy alérgico/a a los cacahuetes. | I'm allergic to peanuts. |

| Las enfermedades | Ailments |
|---|---|
| **Me duele ...** | **I have a sore ...** |
| la barriga | stomach |
| la espalda | back |
| la rodilla | knee |
| el pie | foot |
| el cuello | neck |
| la cabeza | head |
| la garganta | throat |
| la pierna | leg |
| Me duelen los dientes. | I've got toothache. |
| Me duelen las orejas. | I've got earache. |
| Me duelen los ojos. | My eyes are hurting. |
| Estoy resfriado. | I've got a cold. |
| Tengo la gripe. | I've got flu. |
| Tengo ganas de vomitar. | I feel sick. |
| Estoy cansado. | I'm tired. |
| Estoy enfermo. | I'm ill. |
| **tener ...** | **to be ...** |
| frío | cold |
| calor | hot |
| miedo | scared |
| sed | thirsty |
| hambre | hungry |

Me temo que voy a suspender el examen.
I'm afraid that I'm going to fail the exam.

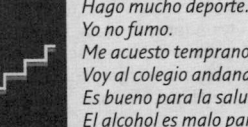

| Para estar en forma ... | To be fit ... |
|---|---|
| Hago mucho deporte. | I do a lot of sport. |
| Yo no fumo. | I don't smoke. |
| Me acuesto temprano. | I go to bed early. |
| Voy al colegio andando. | I walk to school. |
| Es bueno para la salud. | It's good for your health. |
| El alcohol es malo para la salud. | Alcohol is bad for your health. |

## When your number answers

| | |
|---|---|
| *Hola, ¿está Susana?* | Hello! Could I speak to Susana, please? |
| *Le puede decir que me llame, por favor?* | Would you ask him/her to call me back, please? |
| *Le vuelvo a llamar dentro de media hora.* | I'll call back in half an hour. |

## Answering the telephone

| | |
|---|---|
| *¿Diga? Soy Marcos.* | Hello! It's Marcos speaking. |
| *Sí, soy yo.* | Speaking. |
| *¿Con quién hablo?* | Who's speaking? |

## When the switchboard answers

| | |
|---|---|
| *¿De parte de quién?* | Who shall I say is calling? |
| *Le paso.* | I'm putting you through. |
| *No cuelgue.* | Please hold. |
| *¿Quiere dejar un mensaje?* | Would you like to leave a message? |

## Difficulties

| | |
|---|---|
| *No hay línea.* | I can't get through. |
| *Perdone, me he equivocado de número.* | I'm sorry, I've got the wrong number. |
| *Se oye muy mal.* | This is a very bad line. |
| *No les funciona el teléfono.* | Their phone is out of order. |

# Letter

## Writing a letter

**Date**

Valencia, 5 de junio de 2007

**Note colon**

Querido abuelos:

Muchas gracias a los dos por la preciosa pulsera que me mandásteis por mi cumpleaños, que me ha gustado muchísimo. Voy a disfrutar de verdad poniéndomela para mi fiesta del sábado, y estoy segura de que a Cristina le va a dar una envidia tremenda.

En realidad no hay demasiadas cosas nuevas que contaros, ya que últimamente parece que no hago otra cosa que estudiar para los exámenes, que ya están a la vuelta de la esquina. No sabéis las ganas que tengo de terminarlos todos y poder empezar a pensar en las vacaciones.

Paloma me encarga que os dé recuerdos de su parte.

Muchos besos de

Ana

**Writing a personal letter**
Just the name of the town/city you are writing from, and the date

**Alternatively**
Un abrazo (a un amigo o un familiar)
Con cariño

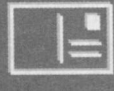

### Starting a personal letter

| | |
|---|---|
| *Gracias por tu carta.* | Thank you for your letter. |
| *Me alegró mucho tener noticias tuyas.* | It was lovely to hear from you. |
| *Perdona que no te haya escrito antes.* | I'm sorry I didn't write earlier. |

### Ending a personal letter

| | |
|---|---|
| *¡Escríbeme pronto!* | Write soon! |
| *Dale un beso a Vanesa de mi parte.* | Give my love to Vanesa. |
| *Samuel te manda recuerdos.* | Samuel sends his best wishes. |

## Writing an email

| Archivo | Edición | Ver | Herramientas | Correo | Ayuda | Enviar |
|---------|---------|-----|--------------|--------|-------|--------|

| | | Nuevo mensaje |
|---|---|---|
| A: | belen.huertas@glnet.es | Responder al autor |
| Cc: | | Responder a todos |
| Copia oculta: | | Reenviar |
| Asunto: | Concierto | Archivo adjunto |

Hola, ¿qué tal el fin de semana?

Me sobran dos entradas para el concierto de mañana, de unos amigos que no pueden venir. Si te interesa, o conoces a alguien que quiera ir, avísame en cuanto puedas.

Un beso,

E.

**Saying your email address**
To give your email address to someone in Spanish, say:
*"belen punto huertas arroba globanet punto es"*

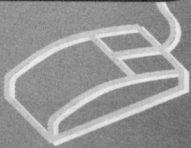

| Abbrev. | Spanish | English |
|---------|---------|---------|
| +trd | *más tarde* | later |
| 2 | *tú* | you |
| a2 | *adiós* | goodbye |
| bboo | *besos* | love (from) |
| find | *fin de semana* | weekend |
| gnl | *genial* | wonderful |
| h lgo HL | *hasta luego* | see you later |
| LAP | *lo antes posible* | asap (as soon as possible) |
| msj | *mensaje* | message |
| NLS | *no lo sé* | I don't know |
| q acc? q hcs? | *¿qué haces?* | what are you doing? |
| QT1BD | *¡que tengas un buen día!* | have a good day! |
| q tl? | *¿qué tal?* | how are you? |
| salu2 | *saludos* | best wishes |
| tq | *te quiero* | I love you |
| x | *por* | for, by etc |
| xdon | *perdón* | sorry |
| xq | *porque* | because |
| xq? | *¿por qué?* | why? |

| Spanish | English |
|---------|---------|
| *nuevo mensaje* (m) | new message |
| *A* | to |
| *de* | from |
| *asunto* | subject |
| *CC* | cc (carbon copy) |
| *copia oculta* | bcc (blind carbon copy) |
| *archivo adjunto* | attachment |
| *enviar* | send |
| *archivo* | file |
| *edición* (f) | edit |
| *ver* | view |
| *herramientas* (fpl) | tools |
| *correo* | mail |
| *ayuda* | help |
| *responder al autor* | reply to sender |
| *responder a todos* | reply to all |
| *reenviar* | forward |
| *fecha* | sent |

| Días de la semana | Days of the week |
| --- | --- |
| lunes | Monday |
| martes | Tuesday |
| miércoles | Wednesday |
| jueves | Thursday |
| viernes | Friday |
| sábado | Saturday |
| domingo | Sunday |
| | |
| el lunes | on Monday |
| los lunes | on Mondays |
| todos los lunes | every Monday |
| el martes pasado | last Tuesday |
| el próximo viernes | next Friday |
| el sábado de la semana que viene | a week on Saturday |
| el sábado de dentro de dos semanas | two weeks on Saturday |

| Los meses del año | Months of the year |
| --- | --- |
| enero | January |
| febrero | February |
| marzo | March |
| abril | April |
| mayo | May |
| junio | June |
| julio | July |
| agosto | August |
| septiembre | September |
| octubre | October |
| noviembre | November |
| diciembre | December |

| | |
| --- | --- |
| ¿A qué fecha estamos hoy? | What date is it today? |
| Estamos a 16 de junio. | It's 16th of June. |
| ¿Cuál es la fecha de tu cumpleaños? | What date is your birthday? |
| Es el 22 de mayo. | It's the 22nd of May. |

| Las fiestas | Festivals |
| --- | --- |
| Navidad (fem) | Christmas |
| el día de Navidad | Christmas Day |
| Nochebuena | Christmas Eve |
| la cena de Nochebuena | Christmas Eve celebrations |
| el día después de Navidad | Boxing Day |
| la Nochevieja | New Year's Eve |
| Año Nuevo | New Year's Day |
| San Valentín | Valentine's Day |
| martes de ceniza | Pancake Day |
| el día de los Santos Inocentes (28 de diciembre) | April Fool's Day |
| Semana Santa (fem) | Easter |
| el día de la madre | Mother's Day |
| el día del padre | Father's Day |
| el día de todos los santos | All Saints' Day |
| el 11 de noviembre | Remembrance Day |
| el Ramadán | Ramadan |
| | |
| ¡Feliz navidad! | Happy Christmas! |
| ¡Inocente! | April fool! |
| en Semana Santa | at Easter |
| celebrar Año Nuevo | to celebrate New Year |
| ¿Qué haces el día de Navidad? | What do you do on Christmas Day? |
| Pasamos el día después de Navidad en casa. | We spend Boxing Day at home. |
| Vamos a casa de mis primos el día de Año Nuevo. | We go to my cousins' for New Year. |

| Las vacaciones | Holidays |
| --- | --- |
| las vacaciones de verano | the summer holidays |
| el puente de todos los santos | the autumn half-term |
| las vacaciones de Navidad | the Christmas holidays |
| la semana blanca | the spring half-term |
| las vacaciones de Semana Santa | the Easter holidays |
| la playa | the seaside |
| la montaña | the mountains |
| | |
| ¿Qué vas a hacer durante las vacaciones? | What are you going to do in the holidays? |
| Este verano nos vamos una semana a Italia. | We're going to Italy for a week this summer. |
| Este año no nos vamos de vacaciones. | We're not going on holiday this year. |
| Siempre vamos a esquiar en febrero. | We always go skiing in February. |
| El verano que viene voy a pasar una semana en casa de mi correspondiente en Francia. | I'm going to stay with my pen-friend in France for a week next year. |
| El verano pasado fui a Estados Unidos. | Last summer I went to the United States. |

## ¿Qué hora es?                    What time is it?  It's...

es la una

es la una y diez

es la una y cuarto

es la una y media

son las dos menos veinte

son las dos menos cuarto

## ¿A qué hora?                    At what time?

a medianoche

al mediodía

a la una (de la tarde)

a las once (de la noche)

las 11:15 or las once quince

las 20:45 or las veinte cuarenta y cinco

In Spanish times are often given in the twenty-four hour clock.

# Numbers

## Numbers

| | |
|---|---|
| 1 | uno |
| 2 | dos |
| 3 | tres |
| 4 | cuatro |
| 5 | cinco |
| 6 | seis |
| 7 | siete |
| 8 | ocho |
| 9 | nueve |
| 10 | diez |
| 11 | once |
| 12 | doce |
| 13 | trece |
| 14 | catorce |
| 15 | quince |
| 16 | dieciséis |
| 17 | diecisiete |
| 18 | dieciocho |
| 19 | diecinueve |
| 20 | veinte |
| 21 | veintiuno |
| 30 | treinta |
| 31 | treinta y uno |
| 40 | cuarenta |
| 41 | cuarenta y uno |
| 50 | cincuenta |
| 60 | sesenta |
| 70 | setenta |
| 80 | ochenta |
| 90 | noventa |
| 100 | cien |
| 101 | ciento uno |
| 200 | doscientos |
| 201 | doscientos uno |
| 1000 | mil |
| 1001 | mil uno |
| 1,000,000 | un millón |

### Examples

*en la página diecinueve* – on page nineteen
*en el capítulo siete* – in chapter seven
*en una escala del uno al quince* – on a scale of one to fifteen

## Fractions etc

| | |
|---|---|
| 1/2 | un medio |
| 1/3 | un tercio |
| 1/4 | un cuarto |
| 1/5 | un quinto |
| 0,5 | cero coma cinco |
| 3,4 | tres coma cuatro |
| 6,89 | seis coma ochenta y nueve |
| 10% | diez por ciento |
| 100% | cien por cien |

| | |
|---|---|
| 1º | primero |
| 2º | segundo |
| 3º | tercero |
| 4º | cuarto |
| 5º | quinto |
| 6º | sexto |
| 7º | séptimo |
| 8º | octavo |
| 9º | noveno |
| 10º | décimo |
| 11º | decimoprimero |
| 12º | decimosegundo |
| 13º | decimotercero |
| 14º | decimocuarto |
| 15º | decimoquinto |
| 16º | decimosexto |
| 17º | decimoséptimo |
| 18º | decimoctavo |
| 19º | decimonoveno |
| 20º | vigésimo |
| 21º | vigésimo primero |
| 30º | trigésimo |
| 100º | centésimo |
| 101º | centésimo primero |
| 1000º | milésimo |

### Examples

*vive en el quinto piso* – he lives on the fifth floor
*llegó el tercero* – he came in third
*un cuarto del pastel* – a quarter of the cake

# Contents

# Spanish verb tables

This section is designed to help you find all the verb forms you need in Spanish. From pages 19–23 you will find a list of 59 regular and irregular verbs with a summary of their main forms, followed on pages 24-30 by 7 very common regular and irregular verbs shown in full, with example phrases.

## How to find the verb you need

All the verbs on the **Spanish – English** side of the dictionary are followed by a number in square brackets. Each of these numbers corresponds to a verb in this section.

> **limpiar** VERBO [25]
> **1** to clean

In this example, the number [25] after the verb **limpiar** means that **limpiar** follows the same pattern as verb number [25] in the list, which is **hablar**. In this instance, **hablar** is given in full on page 24.

> **introducir\*** VERBO [9]
> **1** to insert

For other verbs, a summary of the main forms is given. In the example above, **introducir** follows the same pattern as verb number [9] in the list, which is **conducir**. On page 19 of this section, you can see that the main forms of **conducir** are given to show you how this verb (and others like it) works.

In the full verb tables, you will find examples of regular verbs: a regular **-ar** verb (**hablar**), a regular **-er** verb (**comer**) and a regular **-ir** verb (**vivir**). Regular verbs follow one of three set patterns. When you have learnt these patterns, you will be able to form any regular verb.

You will also find **tener** (to have), **ser** (to be) and **estar** (to be) in the full verb tables. These are the most important irregular verbs and should be learnt. You use them when you want to say 'I have' *etc* or 'I am' *etc*. However, to form the **perfect tense** of any Spanish verb you use the present tense of **haber** (to have) + the past participle. **Haber** is verb number 24 in the list.

Finally, for more information on the various tenses of Spanish verbs, as well as additional verb tables, remember to visit **www.collinsdictionaries.com/easyresources**

# Spanish verb forms

| INFINITIVE | PRESENT | PERFECT | IMPERFECT | FUTURE | PRESENT SUBJUNCTIVE |
|---|---|---|---|---|---|
| 1 **actuar** | yo actúo<br>tú actúas<br>él/ella/usted actúa<br>nosotros/as actuamos<br>vosotros/as actuáis<br>ellos/ellas/ustedes actúan | yo he actuado | yo actuaba | yo actuaré | yo actúe |
| 2 **adquirir**<br>-ir verb with<br>a spelling<br>change | yo adquiero<br>tú adquieres<br>él/ella/usted adquiere<br>nosotros/as adquirimos<br>vosotros/as adquirís<br>ellos/ellas/ustedes adquieren | yo he adquirido | yo adquiría | yo adquiriré | yo adquiera<br>nosotros/as<br>adquiramos<br>vosotros/as<br>adquiráis |
| 3 **almorzar**<br>-ar verb with<br>a spelling<br>change | yo almuerzo<br>tú almuerzas<br>él/ella/usted almuerza<br>nosotros/as almorzamos<br>vosotros/as almorzáis<br>ellos/ellas/ustedes almuerzan | yo he almorzado | yo almorzaba | yo almorzaré | yo almuerce<br>nosotros/as<br>almorcemos<br>vosotros/as<br>almorcéis |
| 4 **andar**<br>-ar verb with<br>a spelling<br>change<br>(preterite<br>anduve) | yo ando<br>tú andas<br>él/ella/usted anda<br>nosotros/as andamos<br>vosotros/as andáis<br>ellos/ellas/ustedes andan | yo he andado | yo andaba | yo andaré | yo ande |
| 5 **caer**<br>-er verb with<br>a spelling<br>change | yo caigo<br>tú caes<br>él/ella/usted cae<br>nosotros/as caemos<br>vosotros/as caéis<br>ellos/ellas/ustedes caen | yo he caído | yo caía | yo caeré | yo caiga |
| 6 **cocer**<br>-er verb with<br>a spelling<br>change | yo cuezo<br>tú cueces<br>él/ella/usted cuece<br>nosotros/as cocemos<br>vosotros/as cocéis<br>ellos/ellas/ustedes cuecen | yo he cocido | yo cocía | yo coceré | yo cueza<br>nosotros/as<br>cozamos<br>vosotros/as<br>cozáis |
| 7 **coger**<br>-er verb with<br>a spelling<br>change | yo cojo<br>tú coges<br>él/ella/usted coge<br>nosotros/as cogemos<br>vosotros/as cogéis<br>ellos/ellas/ustedes cogen | yo he cogido | yo cogía | yo cogeré | yo coja |
| 8 **comer** | see full verb table page 25 | | | | |
| 9 **conducir**<br>-ir verb with<br>a spelling<br>change<br>(preterite<br>conduje) | yo conduzco<br>tú conduces<br>él/ella/usted conduce<br>nosotros/as conducimos<br>vosotros/as conducís<br>ellos/ellas/ustedes conducen | yo he conducido | yo conducía | yo conduciré | yo conduzca |
| 10 **construir**<br>-ir verb with<br>a spelling<br>change | yo construyo<br>tú construyes<br>él/ella/usted construye<br>nosotros/as construimos<br>vosotros/as construís<br>ellos/ellas/ustedes construyen | yo he construido | yo construía | yo construiré | yo construya |
| 11 **contar**<br>-ar verb with<br>a spelling<br>change | yo cuento<br>tú cuentas<br>él/ella/usted cuenta<br>nosotros/as contamos<br>vosotros/as contáis<br>ellos/ellas/ustedes cuentan | yo he contado | yo contaba | yo contaré | yo cuente<br>nosotros/as<br>contemos<br>vosotros/as<br>contéis |

| INFINITIVE | PRESENT | PERFECT | IMPERFECT | FUTURE | PRESENT SUBJUNCTIVE |
|---|---|---|---|---|---|
| 12 **crecer**<br>similar to<br>**cocer** [6] | yo crezco<br>tú creces | yo he crecido | yo crecía | yo creceré | yo crezca |
| 13 **cruzar**<br>**-ar** verb with<br>a spelling<br>change | yo cruce<br>tú cruces<br>él/ella/usted cruce<br>nosotros/as crucemos<br>vosotros/as crucéis<br>ellos/ellas/ustedes crucen | yo he cruzado | yo cruzaba | yo cruzaré | yo cruce |
| 14 **dar** | yo doy<br>tú das<br>él/ella/usted da<br>nosotros/as damos<br>vosotros/as dais<br>ellos/ellas/ustedes dan | yo he dado | yo daba | yo daré | yo dé |
| 15 **decir** | yo digo<br>tú dices<br>él/ella/usted dice<br>nosotros/as decimos<br>vosotros/as decís<br>ellos/ellas/ustedes dicen | yo he dicho | yo decía | yo diré | yo diga |
| 16 **dirigir**<br>**-ir** verb with<br>a spelling<br>change | yo dirijo<br>tú diriges<br>él/ella/usted dirige<br>nosotros/as dirigimos<br>vosotros/as dirigís<br>ellos/ellas/ustedes dirigen | yo he dirigido | yo dirigía | yo dirigiré | yo dirija |
| 17 **dormir**<br>**-ir** verb with<br>a spelling<br>change | yo duermo<br>tú duermes<br>él/ella/usted duerme<br>nosotros/as dormimos<br>vosotros/as dormís<br>ellos/ellas/ustedes duermen | yo he dormido | yo dormía | yo dormiré | yo duerma<br>nosotros/as<br>durmamos<br>vosotros/as<br>durmáis |
| 18 **elegir**<br>similar to<br>**dirigir** [16] | yo elijo | yo he elegido | yo elegía | yo elegiré | yo elija |
| 19 **empezar**<br>similar to<br>**almorzar** [3] | yo empiezo<br>nosotros/as empezamos<br>vosotros/as empezáis | yo he empezado | yo empezaba | yo empezaré | yo empiece<br>nosotros/as<br>empecemos<br>vosotros/as<br>empecéis |
| 20 **entender**<br>**-er** verb with<br>a spelling<br>change | yo entiendo<br>tú entiendes<br>él/ella/usted entiende<br>nosotros/as entendemos<br>vosotros/as entendéis<br>ellos/ellas/ustedes entienden | yo he entendido | yo entendía | yo entenderé | yo entienda<br>nosotros/as<br>entendamos<br>vosotros/as<br>entendáis |
| 21 **enviar**<br>similar to<br>**actuar** [1] | yo envío<br>tú envías | yo he enviado | yo enviaba | yo enviaré | yo envié |
| 22 **estar** | see full verb table page 27 | | | | |
| 23 **freír**<br>**-ir** verb with<br>a spelling<br>change | yo frío<br>tú fríes<br>él/ella/usted fríe<br>nosotros/as freímos<br>vosotros/as freís<br>ellos/ellas/ustedes fríen | yo he frito | yo freía | yo freiré | yo fría |
| 24 **haber** | yo he<br>tú has<br>él/ella/usted ha<br>nosotros/as hemos<br>vosotros/as habéis<br>ellos/ellas/ustedes han | yo he habido | yo había | yo habré | yo haya |

| INFINITIVE | PRESENT | PERFECT | IMPERFECT | FUTURE | PRESENT SUBJUNCTIVE |
|---|---|---|---|---|---|
| **25 hablar** | see full verb table page 24 | | | | |
| **26 hacer** | yo hago<br>tú haces<br>él/ella/usted hace<br>nosotros/as hacemos<br>vosotros/as hacéis<br>ellos/ellas/ustedes hacen | yo he hecho | yo hacía | yo haré | yo haga |
| **27 ir** | see full verb table page 28 | | | | |
| **28 jugar**<br>-ir verb with<br>a spelling<br>change | yo juego<br>tú juegas<br>él/ella/usted juega<br>nosotros/as jugamos<br>vosotros/as jugáis<br>ellos/ellas/ustedes juegan | yo he jugado | yo jugaba | yo jugaré | yo juegue<br>nosotros/as<br>juguemos<br>vosotros/as<br>juguéis |
| **29 lavarse** | yo me lavo<br>tú te lavas<br>él/ella/usted se lava<br>nosotros/as nos lavamos<br>vosotros/as os laváis<br>ellos/ellas/ustedes se lavan | yo me ha lavado | yo me lavaba | yo me lavaré | yo me lave |
| **30 leer**<br>-er verb with<br>a spelling<br>change | yo leo<br>tú lees<br>él/ella/usted lee<br>nosotros/as leemos<br>vosotros/as leéis<br>ellos/ellas/ustedes leen | yo he leído | yo leía | yo leeré | yo lea |
| **31 llover**<br>impersonal verb | llueve | ha llovido | llovía | lloverá | llueva |
| **32 morir**<br>-ir verb with<br>a spelling<br>change | yo muero<br>tú mueres<br>él/ella/usted muere<br>nosotros/as morimos<br>vosotros/as morís<br>ellos/ellas/ustedes mueren | yo he muerto | yo moría | yo moriré | yo muera<br>nosotros/as<br>muramos<br>vosotros/as<br>muráis |
| **33 mover**<br>-er verb with<br>a spelling<br>change | yo muevo<br>tú mueves<br>él/ella/usted mueve<br>nosotros/as movemos<br>vosotros/as movéis<br>ellos/ellas/ustedes mueven | yo he movido | yo movía | yo moveré | yo mueva<br>nosotros/as<br>movamos<br>vosotros/as<br>mováis |
| **34 negar**<br>-ar verb with<br>a spelling<br>change | yo niego<br>tú niegas<br>él/ella/usted niega<br>nosotros/as negamos<br>vosotros/as negáis<br>ellos/ellas/ustedes niegan | yo he negado | yo negaba | yo negaré | yo niegue<br>nosotros/as<br>neguemos<br>vosotros/as<br>neguéis |
| **35 oír**<br>-ir verb with<br>a spelling<br>change | yo oigo<br>tú oyes<br>él/ella/usted oye<br>nosotros/as oímos<br>vosotros/as oís<br>ellos/ellas/ustedes oyen | yo he oído | yo oía | yo oiré | yo oiga |
| **36 oler**<br>-er verb with<br>a spelling<br>change | yo huelo<br>tú hueles<br>él/ella/usted huele<br>nosotros/as olemos<br>vosotros/as oléis<br>ellos/ellas/ustedes huelen | yo he olido | yo olía | yo oleré | yo huela<br>nosotros/as<br>olamos<br>vosotros/as<br>oláis |

| INFINITIVE | PRESENT | PERFECT | IMPERFECT | FUTURE | PRESENT SUBJUNCTIVE |
|---|---|---|---|---|---|
| **37 pagar**<br>-ar verb with<br>a spelling<br>change | yo pago<br>tú pagas<br>él/ella/usted paga<br>nosotros/as pagamos<br>vosotros/as pagáis<br>ellos/ellas/ustedes pagan | yo he pagado | yo pagaba | yo pagaré | yo pague |
| **38 pedir**<br>-ir verb with<br>a spelling<br>change | yo pido<br>tú pides<br>él/ella/usted pide<br>nosotros/as pedimos<br>vosotros/as pedís<br>ellos/ellas/ustedes piden | yo he pedido | yo pedía | yo pediré | yo pida |
| **39 pensar**<br>-ar verb with<br>a spelling<br>change | yo pienso<br>tú piensas<br>él/ella/usted piensa<br>nosotros/as pensamos<br>vosotros/as pensáis<br>ellos/ellas/ustedes piensan | yo he pensado | yo pensaba | yo pensaré | yo piense<br>nosotros/as<br>pensemos<br>vosotros/as<br>penséis |
| **40 poder**<br>-er verb with<br>a spelling<br>change | yo puedo<br>tú puedes<br>él/ella/usted puede<br>nosotros/as podemos<br>vosotros/as podéis<br>ellos/ellas/ustedes pueden | yo he podido | yo podía | yo podré | yo pueda<br>nosotros/as<br>podamos<br>vosotros/as<br>podáis |
| **41 poner** | yo pongo<br>tú pones<br>él/ella/usted pone<br>nosotros/as ponemos<br>vosotros/as ponéis<br>ellos/ellas/ustedes ponen | yo he puesto | yo ponía | yo pondré | yo ponga<br>tú pongas<br>nosotros/as<br>pongamos<br>vosotros/as<br>pongáis |
| **42 prohibir**<br>similar to<br>**adquirir [2]** | yo prohíbo<br>tú prohíbes<br>él/ella/usted prohíbe<br>ellos/ellas/ustedes prohíben | yo he prohibido | yo prohibía | yo prohibiré | yo prohíba |
| **43 querer** | yo quiero<br>tú quieres<br>él/ella/usted quiere<br>nosotros/as queremos<br>vosotros/as queréis<br>ellos/ellas/ustedes quieren | yo he querido | yo quería | yo querré | yo quiera |
| **44 reír**<br>similar to<br>freír [23],<br>apart from the<br>perfect tense | yo río | yo he reído | yo reía | yo reiré | yo ría |
| **45 reñir**<br>-ir verb with<br>a spelling<br>change | yo riño<br>tú riñes<br>él/ella/usted riñe<br>nosotros/as reñimos<br>vosotros/as reñís<br>ellos/ellas/ustedes riñen | yo he reñido | yo reñía | yo reñiré | yo riña |
| **46 reunir**<br>-ir verb with<br>a spelling<br>change | yo reúno<br>tú reúnes<br>él/ella/usted reúne<br>nosotros/as reunimos<br>vosotros/as reunís<br>ellos/ellas/ustedes reúnen | yo he reunido | yo reunía | yo reuniré | yo reúna |
| **47 saber** | yo sé<br>tú sabes<br>él/ella/usted sabe<br>nosotros/as sabemos<br>vosotros/as sabéis<br>ellos/ellas/ustedes saben | yo he sabido | yo sabía | yo sabré | yo sepa |

| INFINITIVE | PRESENT | PERFECT | IMPERFECT | FUTURE | PRESENT SUBJUNCTIVE |
|---|---|---|---|---|---|
| **48 sacar**<br>-ar verb with<br>a spelling<br>change | yo saco<br>tú sacas<br>él/ella/usted saca<br>nosotros/as sacamos<br>vosotros/as sacáis<br>ellos/ellas/ustedes sacan | yo he sacado | yo sacaba | yo sacaré | yo saque |
| **49 salir**<br>similar to<br>decir [15]<br>apart from the<br>perfect and<br>future tenses | yo salgo | yo he salido | yo salía | yo saldré | yo salga |
| **50 seguir**<br>-ir verb with<br>a spelling<br>change | yo sigo<br>tú sigues<br>él/ella/usted sigue<br>nosotros/as seguimos<br>vosotros/as seguís<br>ellos/ellas/ustedes siguen | yo he seguido | yo seguía | yo seguiré | yo siga |
| **51 sentir**<br>-ir verb with<br>a spelling<br>change | yo siento<br>tú sientes<br>él/ella/usted siente<br>nosotros/as sentimos<br>vosotros/as sentís<br>ellos/ellas/ustedes sienten | yo he sentido | yo sentía | yo sentiré | yo sienta<br>nosotros/as<br>sintamos<br>vosotros/as<br>sintáis |
| **52 ser** | see full verb table page 29 | | | | |
| **53 tener** | see full verb table page 30 | | | | |
| **54 traer**<br>-er verb with<br>a spelling<br>change<br>(**preterite** traje) | yo traigo<br>tú traes<br>él/ella/usted trae<br>nosotros/as traemos<br>vosotros/as traéis<br>ellos/ellas/ustedes traen | yo he traído | yo traía | yo traeré | yo traiga |
| **55 valer**<br>-er verb with<br>a spelling<br>change | yo valgo<br>tú vales<br>él/ella/usted vale<br>nosotros/as valemos<br>vosotros/as valéis<br>ellos/ellas/ustedes valen | yo he valido | yo valía | yo valdré | yo valga |
| **56 venir** | yo vengo<br>tú vienes<br>él/ella/usted viene<br>nosotros/as venimos<br>vosotros/as venís<br>ellos/ellas/ustedes vienen | yo he venido | yo venía | yo vendré | yo venga |
| **57 ver**<br>similar to<br>comer [8]<br>apart from the<br>perfect tense | yo veo | yo he visto | yo veía | yo veré | yo vea |
| **58 vivir** | see full verb table page 26 | | | | |
| **59 volver**<br>-er verb with<br>a spelling<br>change | yo vuelvo<br>tú vuelves<br>él/ella/usted vuelve<br>nosotros/as volvemos<br>vosotros/as volvéis<br>ellos/ellas/ustedes vuelven | yo he vuelto | yo volví | yo volveré | yo vuelva<br>nosotros/as<br>volvamos<br>vosotros/as<br>volváis |

# hablar (to speak, to talk)

| | PRESENT | | PRESENT SUBJUNCTIVE |
|---|---|---|---|
| yo | hablo | yo | hable |
| tú | hablas | tú | hables |
| él/ella/usted | habla | él/ella/usted | hable |
| nosotros/as | hablamos | nosotros/as | hablemos |
| vosotros/as | habláis | vosotros/as | habléis |
| ellos/ellas/ustedes | hablan | ellos/ellas/ustedes | hablen |

| | PRETERITE | | IMPERFECT |
|---|---|---|---|
| yo | hablé | yo | hablaba |
| tú | hablaste | tú | hablabas |
| él/ella/usted | habló | él/ella/usted | hablaba |
| nosotros/as | hablamos | nosotros/as | hablábamos |
| vosotros/as | hablasteis | vosotros/as | hablabais |
| ellos/ellas/ustedes | hablaron | ellos/ellas/ustedes | hablaban |

| | FUTURE | | CONDITIONAL |
|---|---|---|---|
| yo | hablaré | yo | hablaría |
| tú | hablarás | tú | hablarías |
| él/ella/usted | hablará | él/ella/usted | hablaría |
| nosotros/as | hablaremos | nosotros/as | hablaríamos |
| vosotros/as | hablaréis | vosotros/as | hablaríais |
| ellos/ellas/ustedes | hablarán | ellos/ellas/ustedes | hablarían |

| IMPERATIVE | PAST PARTICIPLE |
|---|---|
| habla / hablad | hablado |

**GERUND**

hablando

---

**EXAMPLE PHRASES**

Hoy **he hablado** con mi hermana. I've spoken to my sister today.
No **hables** tan alto. Don't talk so loud.
No **se hablan**. They don't talk to each other.

**Remember that subject pronouns are not used very often in Spanish.**

# comer (to eat)

| | PRESENT | | PRESENT SUBJUNCTIVE |
|---|---|---|---|
| yo | como | yo | coma |
| tú | comes | tú | comas |
| él/ella/usted | come | él/ella/usted | coma |
| nosotros/as | comemos | nosotros/as | comamos |
| vosotros/as | coméis | vosotros/as | comáis |
| ellos/ellas/ustedes | comen | ellos/ellas/ustedes | coman |

| | PRETERITE | | IMPERFECT |
|---|---|---|---|
| yo | comí | yo | comía |
| tú | comiste | tú | comías |
| él/ella/usted | comió | él/ella/usted | comía |
| nosotros/as | comimos | nosotros/as | comíamos |
| vosotros/as | comisteis | vosotros/as | comíais |
| ellos/ellas/ustedes | comieron | ellos/ellas/ustedes | comían |

| | FUTURE | | CONDITIONAL |
|---|---|---|---|
| yo | comeré | yo | comería |
| tú | comerás | tú | comerías |
| él/ella/usted | comerá | él/ella/usted | comería |
| nosotros/as | comeremos | nosotros/as | comeríamos |
| vosotros/as | comeréis | vosotros/as | comeríais |
| ellos/ellas/ustedes | comerán | ellos/ellas/ustedes | comerían |

**IMPERATIVE**

come / comed

**PAST PARTICIPLE**

comido

**GERUND**

comiendo

**EXAMPLE PHRASES**

No **come** carne. He doesn't eat meat.
No **comas** tan deprisa. Don't eat so fast.
**Se lo ha comido** todo. He's eaten it all.

Remember that subject pronouns are not used very often in Spanish.

# vivir (to live)

| | PRESENT | | PRESENT SUBJUNCTIVE |
|---|---|---|---|
| yo | vivo | yo | viva |
| tú | vives | tú | vivas |
| él/ella/usted | vive | él/ella/usted | viva |
| nosotros/as | vivimos | nosotros/as | vivamos |
| vosotros/as | vivís | vosotros/as | viváis |
| ellos/ellas/ustedes | viven | ellos/ellas/ustedes | vivan |

| | PRETERITE | | IMPERFECT |
|---|---|---|---|
| yo | viví | yo | vivía |
| tú | viviste | tú | vivías |
| él/ella/usted | vivió | él/ella/usted | vivía |
| nosotros/as | vivimos | nosotros/as | vivíamos |
| vosotros/as | vivisteis | vosotros/as | vivíais |
| ellos/ellas/ustedes | vivieron | ellos/ellas/ustedes | vivían |

| | FUTURE | | CONDITIONAL |
|---|---|---|---|
| yo | viviré | yo | viviría |
| tú | vivirás | tú | vivirías |
| él/ella/usted | vivirá | él/ella/usted | viviría |
| nosotros/as | viviremos | nosotros/as | viviríamos |
| vosotros/as | viviréis | vosotros/as | viviríais |
| ellos/ellas/ustedes | vivirán | ellos/ellas/ustedes | vivirían |

| IMPERATIVE | PAST PARTICIPLE |
|---|---|
| vive / vivid | vivido |

**GERUND**

viviendo

---

**EXAMPLE PHRASES**

**Vivo** en Valencia. I live in Valencia.
**Vivieron** juntos dos años. They lived together for two years.
**Hemos vivido** momentos difíciles. We've had some difficult times.

**Remember that subject pronouns are not used very often in Spanish.**

# estar (to be)

| | PRESENT | | PRESENT SUBJUNCTIVE |
|---|---|---|---|
| yo | **estoy** | yo | **esté** |
| tú | **estás** | tú | **estés** |
| él/ella/usted | **está** | él/ella/usted | **esté** |
| nosotros/as | **estamos** | nosotros/as | **estemos** |
| vosotros/as | **estáis** | vosotros/as | **estéis** |
| ellos/ellas/ustedes | **están** | ellos/ellas/ustedes | **estén** |

| | PRETERITE | | IMPERFECT |
|---|---|---|---|
| yo | **estuve** | yo | **estaba** |
| tú | **estuviste** | tú | **estabas** |
| él/ella/usted | **estuvo** | él/ella/usted | **estaba** |
| nosotros/as | **estuvimos** | nosotros/as | **estábamos** |
| vosotros/as | **estuvisteis** | vosotros/as | **estabais** |
| ellos/ellas/ustedes | **estuvieron** | ellos/ellas/ustedes | **estaban** |

| | FUTURE | | CONDITIONAL |
|---|---|---|---|
| yo | **estaré** | yo | **estaría** |
| tú | **estarás** | tú | **estarías** |
| él/ella/usted | **estará** | él/ella/usted | **estaría** |
| nosotros/as | **estaremos** | nosotros/as | **estaríamos** |
| vosotros/as | **estaréis** | vosotros/as | **estaríais** |
| ellos/ellas/ustedes | **estarán** | ellos/ellas/ustedes | **estarían** |

| IMPERATIVE | PAST PARTICIPLE |
|---|---|
| **está / estad** | **estado** |

**GERUND**

**estando**

---

**EXAMPLE PHRASES**

**Estoy** cansado. I'm tired.
**Estuvimos** en casa de mis padres. We went to my parents.
¿A qué hora **estarás** en casa? What time will you be home?

**Remember that subject pronouns are not used very often in Spanish.**

# ir (to go)

| | PRESENT | | PRESENT SUBJUNCTIVE |
|---|---|---|---|
| yo | **voy** | yo | **vaya** |
| tú | **vas** | tú | **vayas** |
| él/ella/usted | **va** | él/ella/usted | **vaya** |
| nosotros/as | **vamos** | nosotros/as | **vayamos** |
| vosotros/as | **vais** | vosotros/as | **vayáis** |
| ellos/ellas/ustedes | **van** | ellos/ellas/ustedes | **vayan** |

| | PRETERITE | | IMPERFECT |
|---|---|---|---|
| yo | **fui** | yo | **iba** |
| tú | **fuiste** | tú | **ibas** |
| él/ella/usted | **fue** | él/ella/usted | **iba** |
| nosotros/as | **fuimos** | nosotros/as | **íbamos** |
| vosotros/as | **fuisteis** | vosotros/as | **ibais** |
| ellos/ellas/ustedes | **fueron** | ellos/ellas/ustedes | **iban** |

| | FUTURE | | CONDITIONAL |
|---|---|---|---|
| yo | **iré** | yo | **iría** |
| tú | **irás** | tú | **irías** |
| él/ella/usted | **irá** | él/ella/usted | **iría** |
| nosotros/as | **iremos** | nosotros/as | **iríamos** |
| vosotros/as | **iréis** | vosotros/as | **iríais** |
| ellos/ellas/ustedes | **irán** | ellos/ellas/ustedes | **irían** |

| IMPERATIVE | PAST PARTICIPLE |
|---|---|
| **ve / id** | **ido** |

**GERUND**

**yendo**

---

**EXAMPLE PHRASES**

¿**Vamos** a comer al campo? Shall we have a picnic in the country?
El domingo **iré** a Edimburgo. I'll go to Edinburgh on Sunday.
Yo no **voy** con ellos. I'm not going with them.

**Remember that subject pronouns are not used very often in Spanish.**

# ser (to be)

| | PRESENT | | PRESENT SUBJUNCTIVE |
|---|---|---|---|
| yo | soy | yo | sea |
| tú | eres | tú | seas |
| él/ella/usted | es | él/ella/usted | sea |
| nosotros/as | somos | nosotros/as | seamos |
| vosotros/as | sois | vosotros/as | seáis |
| ellos/ellas/ustedes | son | ellos/ellas/ustedes | sean |

| | PRETERITE | | IMPERFECT |
|---|---|---|---|
| yo | fui | yo | era |
| tú | fuiste | tú | eras |
| él/ella/usted | fue | él/ella/usted | era |
| nosotros/as | fuimos | nosotros/as | éramos |
| vosotros/as | fuisteis | vosotros/as | erais |
| ellos/ellas/ustedes | fueron | ellos/ellas/ustedes | eran |

| | FUTURE | | CONDITIONAL |
|---|---|---|---|
| yo | seré | yo | sería |
| tú | serás | tú | serías |
| él/ella/usted | será | él/ella/usted | sería |
| nosotros/as | seremos | nosotros/as | seríamos |
| vosotros/as | seréis | vosotros/as | seríais |
| ellos/ellas/ustedes | serán | ellos/ellas/ustedes | serían |

| IMPERATIVE | PAST PARTICIPLE |
|---|---|
| sé / sed | sido |

**GERUND**

siendo

---

**EXAMPLE PHRASES**

**Soy** español. I'm Spanish.
¿**Fuiste** tú el que llamó? Was it you who phoned?
**Era** de noche. It was dark.

**Remember that subject pronouns are not used very often in Spanish.**

# **tener** (to have)

| | PRESENT | | PRESENT SUBJUNCTIVE |
|---|---|---|---|
| yo | **tengo** | yo | **tenga** |
| tú | **tienes** | tú | **tengas** |
| él/ella/usted | **tiene** | él/ella/usted | **tenga** |
| nosotros/as | **tenemos** | nosotros/as | **tengamos** |
| vosotros/as | **tenéis** | vosotros/as | **tengáis** |
| ellos/ellas/ustedes | **tienen** | ellos/ellas/ustedes | **tengan** |

| | PRETERITE | | IMPERFECT |
|---|---|---|---|
| yo | **tuve** | yo | **tenía** |
| tú | **tuviste** | tú | **tenías** |
| él/ella/usted | **tuvo** | él/ella/usted | **tenía** |
| nosotros/as | **tuvimos** | nosotros/as | **teníamos** |
| vosotros/as | **tuvisteis** | vosotros/as | **teníais** |
| ellos/ellas/ustedes | **tuvieron** | ellos/ellas/ustedes | **tenían** |

| | FUTURE | | CONDITIONAL |
|---|---|---|---|
| yo | **tendré** | yo | **tendría** |
| tú | **tendrás** | tú | **tendrías** |
| él/ella/usted | **tendrá** | él/ella/usted | **tendría** |
| nosotros/as | **tendremos** | nosotros/as | **tendríamos** |
| vosotros/as | **tendréis** | vosotros/as | **tendríais** |
| ellos/ellas/ustedes | **tendrán** | ellos/ellas/ustedes | **tendrían** |

| IMPERATIVE | PAST PARTICIPLE |
|---|---|
| **ten / tened** | **tenido** |

**GERUND**

**teniendo**

---

**EXAMPLE PHRASES**

**Tengo** sed. I'm thirsty.
No **tenía** suficiente dinero. She didn't have enough money.
**Tuvimos** que irnos. We had to leave.

**Remember that subject pronouns are not used very often in Spanish.**

# Aa

**a** INDEFINITE ARTICLE

> **LANGUAGE TIP** Use **un** for masculine nouns, **una** for feminine nouns.

**1** un *masc*
> □ a book un libro

**2** una *fem*
> □ an apple una manzana

> **LANGUAGE TIP** Sometimes 'a' is not translated, particularly if referring to professions.

> □ He's a butcher. Es carnicero. □ I haven't got a car. No tengo coche. □ a year ago hace un año
- **a hundred pounds** cien libras
- **once a week** una vez a la semana
- **70 kilometres an hour** 70 kilómetros por hora
- **30 pence a kilo** 30 peniques el kilo

to **abandon** VERB
> abandonar

**abbey** NOUN
> la abadía

**abbreviation** NOUN
> la abreviatura

**ability** NOUN
> la capacidad
- **to have the ability to do something** tener la capacidad de hacer algo

**able** ADJECTIVE
- **to be able to do something** poder hacer algo □ Will you be able to come on Saturday? ¿Puedes venir el sábado?

to **abolish** VERB
> abolir∗

**abortion** NOUN
> el aborto
- **to have an abortion** abortar

**about** PREPOSITION, ADVERB

**1** sobre
> □ a book about London un libro sobre Londres □ I don't know anything about it. No sé nada sobre eso.
- **I'm phoning you about tomorrow's meeting.** Te llamo por lo de la reunión de mañana.
- **What's it about?** ¿De qué trata?

**2** unos (FEM unas) *(approximately)*
> □ It takes about 10 hours. Se tarda unas 10 horas.
- **at about 11 o'clock** sobre las 11

**3** por
> □ to walk about the town caminar por la ciudad
- **What about me?** ¿Y yo?
- **to be about to do something** estar a punto de hacer algo □ I was about to go out. Estaba a punto de salir.
- **How about going to the cinema?** ¿Qué tal si vamos al cine?

**above** PREPOSITION, ADVERB

> **LANGUAGE TIP** When something is located above something, use **encima de**. When there is movement involved, use **por encima de**.

**1** encima de
> □ There was a picture above the fireplace. Había un cuadro encima de la chimenea.

**2** por encima de
> □ He put his hands above his head. Puso las manos por encima de la cabeza.
- **the flat above** el piso de arriba
- **above all** sobre todo

**3** más de *(more than)*
> □ above 40 degrees más de 40 grados

**abroad** ADVERB
- **to go abroad** ir al extranjero
- **to live abroad** vivir en el extranjero

**abrupt** ADJECTIVE

**1** brusco (FEM brusca)
> □ He was a bit abrupt with me. Fue un poco brusco conmigo.

**2** repentino (FEM repentina)
> □ His abrupt departure aroused suspicion. Su repentina marcha levantó sospechas.

**abruptly** ADVERB
> de repente
> □ He got up abruptly. Se levantó de repente.

**absence** NOUN

**1** la ausencia *(of people)*

**2** la falta *(of things)*
- **absence from school** la falta de asistencia a clase

**absent** ADJECTIVE
ausente (FEM ausente)

**absent-minded** ADJECTIVE
distraído (FEM distraída)

**absolutely** ADVERB
totalmente
□ I absolutely refuse to do it. Me niego totalmente a hacerlo.
■ **Jill's absolutely right.** Jill tiene toda la razón.
■ **It's absolutely delicious!** ¡Está riquísimo!
■ **They did absolutely nothing to help him.** No hicieron absolutamente nada para ayudarle.
■ **Do you think it's a good idea? — Absolutely!** ¿Te parece una buena idea? — ¡Desde luego!

**absorbed** ADJECTIVE
■ **to be absorbed in something** estar absorto en algo

**absurd** ADJECTIVE
absurdo (FEM absurda)

**abuse** NOUN
▷ see also **abuse** VERB
el abuso (of power)
■ **to shout abuse at somebody** insultar a alguien

to **abuse** VERB
▷ see also **abuse** NOUN
maltratar
□ abused children niños maltratados

**abusive** ADJECTIVE
■ **He became abusive.** Se puso a insultar.

**academic** ADJECTIVE
académico (FEM académica)
□ the academic year el año académico

**academy** NOUN
la academia
□ a military academy una academia militar
■ **an academy of music** un conservatorio

to **accelerate** VERB
acelerar

**accelerator** NOUN
el acelerador

**accent** NOUN
el acento
□ He's got a Spanish accent. Tiene acento español.

to **accept** VERB
aceptar
□ She accepted the offer. Aceptó la oferta.
■ **to accept responsibility for something** asumir la responsabilidad de algo
■ **This telephone accepts 20 pence coins only.** Este teléfono sólo admite monedas de 20 peniques.

**acceptable** ADJECTIVE
aceptable (FEM aceptable)

**access** NOUN
el acceso
□ He has access to confidential information. Tiene acceso a información reservada.
■ **Her ex-husband has access to the children.** Su ex marido puede ver a los niños.

**accessible** ADJECTIVE
accesible (FEM accesible)

**accessory** NOUN
el accesorio
□ fashion accessories los accesorios de moda

**accident** NOUN
el accidente
□ to have an accident sufrir un accidente
■ **by accident 1** por casualidad □ They made the discovery by accident. Lo descubrieron por casualidad. **2** sin querer
□ The burglar killed him by accident. El ladrón lo mató sin querer.

**accidental** ADJECTIVE
■ **I didn't do it deliberately, it was accidental.** No lo hice adrede, fue sin querer.
■ **accidental death** la muerte por accidente

to **accommodate** VERB
alojar

**accommodation** NOUN
el alojamiento

to **accompany** VERB
acompañar

**accord** NOUN
■ **of his own accord** por su cuenta

**accordingly** ADVERB
en consecuencia (consequently)

**according to** PREPOSITION
según
□ According to him, everyone had gone. Según él, todos se habían ido.

**account** NOUN
**1** la cuenta
□ a bank account una cuenta bancaria
■ **to do the accounts** llevar la contabilidad
**2** el informe
□ He gave a detailed account of what happened. Dio un informe detallado de lo ocurrido.
■ **to take something into account** tener algo en cuenta
■ **by all accounts** a decir de todos
■ **on account of** a causa de □ We couldn't go out on account of the bad weather. No pudimos salir a causa del mal tiempo.

**accountable** ADJECTIVE
■ **to be accountable to someone** responder ante alguien

**accountancy** NOUN
la contabilidad

**accountant** NOUN
el/la contable (el contador, la contadora
*Latin America*)
▫ She's an accountant. Es contable.

to **account for** VERB
explicar*
▫ If she was ill, that would account for her
poor results. Si estuviera enferma, se
explicarían sus malos resultados.

**accuracy** NOUN
la exactitud

**accurate** ADJECTIVE
exacto (FEM exacta)

**accurately** ADVERB
con exactitud

**accusation** NOUN
la acusación (PL las acusaciones)

to **accuse** VERB
■ to accuse somebody of something
acusar a alguien de algo ▫ The police are
accusing her of murder. La policía la acusa
de asesinato.

**ace** NOUN
el as
▫ the ace of hearts el as de corazones

**ache** NOUN
▷ *see also* ache VERB
el dolor
▫ stomach ache dolor de estómago

to **ache** VERB
▷ *see also* ache NOUN
■ My leg's aching. Me duele la pierna.

to **achieve** VERB
conseguir*

**achievement** NOUN
el logro
▫ That was quite an achievement. Aquello
fue todo un logro.

**acid** NOUN
el ácido

**acid rain** NOUN
la lluvia ácida

**acne** NOUN
el acné

**acre** NOUN
el acre

**acrobat** NOUN
el/la acróbata

**across** PREPOSITION, ADVERB
1 al otro lado de
▫ He lives across the river. Vive al otro lado
del río.
2 a través de
▫ an expedition across the Sahara una
expedición a través del Sahara
■ the shop across the road la tienda en la
acera de enfrente
■ to run across the road cruzar la calle
corriendo
■ across from frente a ▫ He sat down
across from her. Se sentó frente a ella.

to **act** VERB
▷ *see also* act NOUN
actuar*
▫ The police acted quickly. La policía actuó
con rapidez. ▫ He acts really well. Actúa
muy bien.
■ She's acting the part of Juliet.
Interpreta el papel de Julieta.
■ She acts as his interpreter. Ella le hace
de intérprete.

**act** NOUN
▷ *see also* act VERB
el acto
▫ in the first act en el primer acto
■ It was all an act. Era todo un cuento.
■ an Act of Parliament una ley
parlamentaria

**action** NOUN
la acción (PL las acciones)
▫ The film was full of action. Era una
película con mucha acción.
■ to take firm action against tomar
severas medidas contra

**active** ADJECTIVE
activo (FEM activa)
▫ He's a very active person. Es una persona
muy activa.
■ an active volcano un volcán en actividad

**activity** NOUN
la actividad
▫ outdoor activities actividades al aire libre

**actor** NOUN
el actor

**actress** NOUN
la actriz (PL las actrices)

**actual** ADJECTIVE
real (FEM real)
▫ The film is based on actual events.
La película está basada en hechos reales.
⸂ LANGUAGE TIP Be careful not to
translate **actual** by the Spanish word
actual.

**actually** ADVERB
1 realmente
▫ Did it actually happen? ¿Ocurrió
realmente?
■ You only pay for the electricity you
actually use. Sólo pagas la electricidad que
consumes.
2 de hecho
▫ I was so bored I actually fell asleep!
¡Me aburría tanto que de hecho me quedé
dormido!

■ **Fiona's awful, isn't she? — Actually,
I quite like her.** Fiona es una antipática,
¿verdad? — Pues a mí me cae bien.

■ **Actually, I don't know him at all.**
La verdad es que no lo conozco de nada.

**acupuncture** NOUN
la acupuntura

**AD** ABBREVIATION (= Anno Domini)
d.C. (= después de Cristo)
□ in 800 AD en el año 800 d.C.

**ad** NOUN
el anuncio

to **adapt** VERB
adaptar
□ His novel was adapted for television.
Su novela fue adaptada para la televisión.
■ **to adapt to something** adaptarse a algo
□ He adapted to his new school very quickly.
Se adaptó a su nuevo colegio muy
rápidamente.

**adaptor** NOUN
1 el ladrón (PL los ladrones) (for several plugs)
2 el adaptador (for different types of plugs)

to **add** VERB
añadir
□ Add more flour to the dough. Añada más
harina a la masa.

to **add up** VERB
sumar
□ Add up the figures. Suma las cifras.

**addict** NOUN
el adicto
la adicta
■ **a drug addict** un drogadicto □ She's a
drug addict. Es drogadicta.
■ **Martin's a football addict.** Martin es un
fanático del fútbol.

**addicted** ADJECTIVE
■ **to be addicted to drugs** ser drogadicto
■ **She's addicted to heroin.** Es
heroinómana.
■ **She's addicted to soaps.** Es una
apasionada de las telenovelas.

**addition** NOUN
■ **in addition** además □ He's bought a new
car and, in addition, a motorbike. Se ha
comprado un coche nuevo y además una
moto.
■ **in addition to** además de □ There's a
postage fee in addition to the repair charge
Hay que pagar el envío, además de los
gastos de reparación.

**address** NOUN
la dirección (PL las direcciones)

**adjective** NOUN
el adjetivo

to **adjust** VERB
1 regular (temperature, height)

□ You can adjust the height of the chair.
Se puede regular la altura de la silla.
2 ajustar (mechanism)
□ It can be easily adjusted using a
screwdriver. Se ajusta fácilmente con un
destornillador.
■ **to adjust to something** adaptarse a algo
□ He adjusted to his new school very
quickly. Se adaptó a su nuevo colegio muy
rápidamente.

**adjustable** ADJECTIVE
regulable (FEM regulable)

**administration** NOUN
la administración

**admiral** NOUN
el almirante

to **admire** VERB
admirar

**admission** NOUN
la entrada
■ **'admission free'** 'entrada gratuita'

to **admit** VERB
reconocer*
□ I must admit that I've never heard of him.
Tengo que reconocer que nunca he oído
hablar de él. □ He admitted that he'd done
it. Reconoció que lo había hecho.

**adolescent** NOUN
el/la adolescente

to **adopt** VERB
adoptar

**adopted** ADJECTIVE
adoptivo (FEM adoptiva)

**adoption** NOUN
la adopción (PL las adopciones)

to **adore** VERB
adorar

**adult** NOUN
el adulto
la adulta
■ **adult education** la educación de adultos

to **advance** VERB
▷ see also **advance** NOUN
avanzar*
□ The troops are advancing. Las tropas
avanzan. □ Technology has advanced a lot.
La tecnología ha avanzado mucho.

**advance** NOUN
▷ see also **advance** VERB
■ **in advance** con antelación □ They
bought the tickets a month in advance.
Compraron los billetes con un mes de
antelación.

**advance booking** NOUN
■ **Advance booking is essential.** Es
indispensable reservar con antelación.

**advanced** ADJECTIVE
avanzado (FEM avanzada)

**advantage** NOUN
la ventaja
□ Going to university has many advantages. Ir a la universidad tiene muchas ventajas.
■ **to take advantage of something**
aprovechar algo □ He took advantage of his day off to have a rest. Aprovechó su día libre para descansar.
■ **to take advantage of somebody**
aprovecharse de alguien □ The company was taking advantage of its employees. La compañía se aprovechaba de sus empleados.

**adventure** NOUN
la aventura

**adverb** NOUN
el adverbio

**to advertise** VERB
anunciar
□ Jobs are advertised in the papers. Las ofertas de empleo se anuncian en los periódicos.

**advertising** NOUN
la publicidad

**advice** NOUN
el consejo
□ to ask for advice pedir consejo □ I'd like to ask your advice. Quería pedirte consejo.
■ **to give somebody advice** aconsejar a alguien
■ **a piece of advice** un consejo □ He gave me a good piece of advice. Me ha dado un buen consejo.

**to advise** VERB
aconsejar
　LANGUAGE TIP **aconsejar que** has to be followed by a verb in the subjunctive.
□ He advised me to wait. Me aconsejó que esperara. □ He advised me not to go there. Me aconsejó que no fuera.

**aerial** NOUN
la antena

**aerobics** NOUN
aerobic *masc*
□ I do aerobics. Hago aerobic.

**aeroplane** NOUN
el avión (PL los aviones)

**aerosol** NOUN
el aerosol

**affair** NOUN
1 la aventura
□ to have an affair with somebody tener una aventura con alguien
2 el asunto
□ The government has mishandled the affair. El gobierno ha llevado mal el asunto.

**to affect** VERB
afectar

**affectionate** ADJECTIVE
cariñoso (FEM cariñosa)

**to afford** VERB
permitirse
□ I can't afford a new pair of jeans. No puedo permitirme comprar otros vaqueros.
■ **We can't afford to go on holiday.** No podemos permitirnos el lujo de ir de vacaciones.

**afraid** ADJECTIVE
■ **to be afraid of something** tener miedo de algo □ I'm afraid of spiders. Tengo miedo de las arañas.
■ **I'm afraid I can't come.** Me temo que no puedo ir.
■ **I'm afraid so.** Me temo que sí.
■ **I'm afraid not.** Me temo que no.

**Africa** NOUN
África *fem*

**African** ADJECTIVE
▷ see also **African** NOUN
africano (FEM africana)

**African** NOUN
▷ see also **African** ADJECTIVE
el africano
la africana

**after** PREPOSITION, CONJUNCTION, ADVERB
1 después de
□ after the match después del partido
□ After watching television I went to bed. Después de ver la televisión me fui a la cama. □ After I'd had a rest I went for a walk. Después de descansar me fui a dar un paseo.
2 después de que
　LANGUAGE TIP When there's a change of subject in an 'after' clause, use **después de que** with a verb in an appropriate tense instead of **después de** + infinitive.
□ I met her after she had left the company. La conocí después de que dejó la empresa.
　LANGUAGE TIP **después de que** has to be followed by a verb in the subjunctive when referring to an event in the future.
□ I'll help you after we've finished this. Te ayudaré después de que terminemos esto.
□ She said she'd phone after her mother had gone out. Dijo que me llamaría después de que se marchara su madre.
■ **after dinner** después de cenar
■ **He ran after me.** Corrió detrás de mí.
■ **after all** después de todo
■ **soon after** poco después

**afternoon** NOUN
la tarde
□ in the afternoon por la tarde □ 3 o'clock

in the afternoon las 3 de la tarde □ on Saturday afternoon el sábado por la tarde

**afters** NOUN
el postre
□ What's for afters? ¿Qué hay de postre?

**aftershave** NOUN
el after shave

**afterwards** ADVERB
después
□ She left not long afterwards. Se marchó poco después.

**again** ADVERB
otra vez
□ They're friends again. Ya son amigos otra vez. □ I'd like to hear it again. Me gustaría escucharlo otra vez.

> **LANGUAGE TIP** In Spanish you often use the verb **volver a** and an infinitive to talk about doing something 'again'.

□ I'd like to hear it again. Me gustaría volver a escucharlo. □ I won't tell you again! ¡No te lo vuelvo a repetir!
■ **Can you tell me again?** ¿Me lo puedes repetir?
■ **not...again** no...más □ I won't go there again. No volveré más por allí.
■ **Do it again!** ¡Vuelve a hacerlo!
■ **again and again** una y otra vez

**against** PREPOSITION
1 contra
□ He leant against the wall. Se apoyó contra la pared.
2 en contra de
□ I'm against nuclear testing. Estoy en contra de las pruebas nucleares.

**age** NOUN
la edad
□ an age limit un límite de edad
■ **at the age of sixteen** a los dieciséis años
■ **I haven't been to the cinema for ages.** Hace siglos que no voy al cine.

**aged** ADJECTIVE
■ **aged 10** de 10 años

**agenda** NOUN
el orden del día

> **LANGUAGE TIP** Be careful not to translate **agenda** by the Spanish word **agenda**.

**agent** NOUN
el/la agente
□ an estate agent un agente inmobiliario
■ **She's a travel agent.** Es empleada de una agencia de viajes.

**aggressive** ADJECTIVE
agresivo (FEM agresiva)

**ago** ADVERB
■ **two days ago** hace dos días
■ **not long ago** no hace mucho

■ **How long ago did it happen?** ¿Cuánto hace que ocurrió?

**agony** NOUN
■ **to be in agony** sufrir mucho dolor
■ **It was agony!** ¡Fue un suplicio!

to **agree** VERB
estar* de acuerdo
□ I don't agree! ¡No estoy de acuerdo!
□ I agree with Carol. Estoy de acuerdo con Carol.
■ **to agree to do something 1** (when someone requests) aceptar hacer algo □ He agreed to go with her. Aceptó acompañarla. **2** (arrange) acordar hacer algo □ They agreed to meet again next week. Acordaron volver a reunirse la semana próxima.
■ **to agree that...** reconocer que... □ I agree it's difficult. Reconozco que es difícil.
■ **Garlic doesn't agree with me.** El ajo no me sienta bien.

**agreed** ADJECTIVE
acordado (FEM acordada)
□ at the agreed time a la hora acordada

**agreement** NOUN
el acuerdo
■ **to be in agreement** estar de acuerdo

**agricultural** ADJECTIVE
agrícola (FEM agrícola)

**agriculture** NOUN
la agricultura

**ahead** ADVERB
delante
□ She looked straight ahead. Miró hacia delante.
■ **ahead of time** con antelación
■ **to plan ahead** hacer planes con antelación
■ **The Spanish are five points ahead.** Los españoles llevan cinco puntos de ventaja.
■ **Go ahead! Help yourself!** ¡Venga! ¡Sírvete!

**aid** NOUN
la ayuda
■ **in aid of sick children** a beneficio de los niños enfermos

**AIDS** NOUN
el sida

to **aim** VERB
▷ see also **aim** NOUN
■ **to aim at** apuntar a □ He aimed a gun at me. Me apuntó con una pistola.
■ **The film is aimed at children.** La película está dirigida a los niños.
■ **to aim to do something** pretender hacer algo

**aim** NOUN
▷ see also **aim** VERB
el propósito

**air** NOUN
el aire
□ to get some fresh air tomar un poco el aire
■ **by air** en avión

**air-conditioned** ADJECTIVE
con aire acondicionado

**air conditioning** NOUN
el aire acondicionado

**Air Force** NOUN
el ejército del aire

**air hostess** NOUN
la azafata
□ She's an air hostess. Es azafata.

**airline** NOUN
la línea aérea

**airmail** NOUN
■ **by airmail** por correo aéreo

**airplane** NOUN (US)
el avión (PL los aviones)

**airport** NOUN
el aeropuerto

**aisle** NOUN
el pasillo (in plane, cinema)

**alarm** NOUN
la alarma
■ **a fire alarm** una alarma contra incendios

**alarm clock** NOUN
el despertador

**album** NOUN
el álbum

**alcohol** NOUN
el alcohol

**alcoholic** NOUN
▷ see also **alcoholic** ADJECTIVE
el alcohólico
la alcohólica

**alcoholic** ADJECTIVE
▷ see also **alcoholic** NOUN
alcohólico (FEM alcohólica)
□ alcoholic drinks bebidas alcohólicas

**alert** ADJECTIVE
1 despierto (FEM despierta)
□ He's a very alert baby. Es un bebé muy despierto.
2 atento (FEM atenta)
□ We must stay alert. Hay que estar atentos.

**A levels** PL NOUN

> **DID YOU KNOW...?**
> Under the reformed Spanish Educational System, if students stay on at school after the age of 16, they can do a two-year course – **bachillerato**. In order to get in to university, they sit an entrance exam – **la selectividad** – in the subjects they have been studying for the **bachillerato**.

**Algeria** NOUN
Argelia fem

**alike** ADVERB
■ **to look alike** parecerse □ The two sisters look alike. Las dos hermanas se parecen.

**alive** ADJECTIVE
vivo (FEM viva)

**all** ADJECTIVE, PRONOUN, ADVERB
todo (FEM toda)
□ That's all I can remember. Eso es todo lo que recuerdo. □ I ate all of it. Me lo comí todo. □ all day todo el día □ all the apples todas las manzanas
■ **All of us went.** Fuimos todos.
■ **all alone** completamente solo
■ **not at all** en absoluto □ I'm not at all tired. No estoy en absoluto cansado.
■ **Thank you. — Not at all.** Gracias. — De nada.
■ **She talks all the time.** No para de hablar.
■ **The score is five all.** El marcador es de empate a cinco.

**allergic** ADJECTIVE
alérgico (FEM alérgica)
□ to be allergic to something ser alérgico a algo

**alley** NOUN
la callejuela

**to allow** VERB
■ **to allow somebody to do something** dejar a alguien hacer algo □ His mum allowed him to go out. Su madre le dejó salir. □ He's not allowed to go out at night. No le dejan salir por la noche.
■ **Smoking is not allowed.** Está prohibido fumar.

**all right** ADVERB, ADJECTIVE
bien
□ Everything turned out all right. Todo salió bien. □ Are you all right? ¿Estás bien?
■ **Is that all right with you?** ¿Te parece bien?
■ **The film was all right.** La película no estuvo mal.
■ **We'll talk about it later. — All right.** Lo hablamos después. — Vale.

**almond** NOUN
la almendra

**almost** ADVERB
casi
□ I've almost finished. Ya casi he terminado.

**alone** ADJECTIVE, ADVERB
solo (FEM sola)
□ She lives alone. Vive sola.
■ **to leave somebody alone** dejar en paz a alguien □ Leave her alone! ¡Déjala en paz!
■ **to leave something alone** no tocar algo □ Leave my things alone! ¡No toques mis cosas!

**a**

**along** PREPOSITION, ADVERB
por
▫ Chris was walking along the beach. Chris paseaba por la playa.
■ **all along 1** a lo largo de ▫ There were bars all along the street. Había bares a lo largo de toda la calle. **2** desde el principio ▫ He was lying to me all along. Me había mentido desde el principio.

**aloud** ADVERB
en voz alta

**alphabet** NOUN
el alfabeto

**Alps** PL NOUN
los Alpes

**already** ADVERB
ya
▫ Liz had already gone. Liz ya se había ido.

**also** ADVERB
también

**altar** NOUN
el altar

to **alter** VERB
cambiar

**alternate** ADJECTIVE
■ **on alternate days** en días alternos

**alternative** NOUN
▷ see also **alternative** ADJECTIVE
la alternativa
▫ You have no alternative. No tienes otra alternativa.
■ **Fruit is a healthy alternative to chocolate.** La fruta es una opción más sana que el chocolate.
■ **There are several alternatives.** Hay varias posibilidades.

**alternatively** ADVERB
■ **Alternatively, we could just stay at home.** Si no, podemos simplemente quedarnos en casa.

**although** CONJUNCTION
aunque
▫ Although she was tired, she stayed up late. Aunque estaba cansada, se quedó levantada hasta tarde.

**altogether** ADVERB
**1** en total (in total)
▫ You owe me £20 altogether. En total me debes 20 libras.
**2** del todo (completely)
▫ I'm not altogether happy with your work. No estoy del todo satisfecho con tu trabajo.

**aluminium** (US **aluminum**) NOUN
el aluminio

**always** ADVERB
siempre
▫ He's always moaning. Siempre está quejándose.

**am** VERB ▷ see **be**

**a.m.** ABBREVIATION
de la mañana
▫ at 4 a.m. a las 4 de la mañana

**amateur** NOUN
el/la amateur (PL los/las amateurs)

**amazed** ADJECTIVE
asombrado (FEM asombrada)
▫ I was amazed that I managed to do it. Estaba asombrado de haberlo conseguido.

**amazing** ADJECTIVE
**1** asombroso (FEM asombrosa)
▫ That's amazing news! ¡Es una noticia asombrosa!
**2** extraordinario (FEM extraordinaria)
▫ Vivian's an amazing cook. Vivian es una cocinera extraordinaria.

**ambassador** NOUN
el embajador
la embajadora

**amber** ADJECTIVE
■ **an amber light** (when driving) un semáforo en ámbar

**ambition** NOUN
la ambición (PL las ambiciones)

**ambitious** ADJECTIVE
ambicioso (FEM ambiciosa)

**ambulance** NOUN
la ambulancia

**amenities** PL NOUN
■ **The hotel has very good amenities.** El hotel tiene excelentes servicios e instalaciones.
■ **The town has many amenities.** La ciudad ofrece gran variedad de servicios.

**America** NOUN
**1** los Estados Unidos masc pl (United States)
**2** América fem (continent)

**American** ADJECTIVE
▷ see also **American** NOUN
norteamericano (FEM norteamericana)

**American** NOUN
▷ see also **American** ADJECTIVE
el norteamericano
la norteamericana
▫ the Americans los norteamericanos

**among** PREPOSITION
entre

**amount** NOUN
la cantidad
▫ a huge amount of rice una cantidad enorme de arroz
■ **a large amount of money** una alta suma de dinero

**amp** NOUN
**1** el amplificador (amplifier)
**2** el amperio (ampere)

**amplifier** NOUN
el amplificador

to **amuse** VERB (make laugh)
divertir*
□ The thought seemed to amuse him. La idea parecía divertirle.

**amusement arcade** NOUN
el salón de juegos

**an** INDEFINITE ARTICLE ▷ see a

to **analyse** VERB
analizar*

**analysis** NOUN
el análisis (PL los análisis)

to **analyze** VERB (US)
analizar*

**ancestor** NOUN
el antepasado

**anchor** NOUN
el ancla *fem*

> **LANGUAGE TIP** Although it's a feminine noun, remember that you use **el** and **un** with **ancla**.

**ancient** ADJECTIVE
antiguo (FEM antigua)
□ ancient Greece la antigua Grecia
■ **an ancient monument** un monumento histórico

**and** CONJUNCTION
y
□ Mary and Jane Mary y Jane

> **LANGUAGE TIP** Use **e** to translate 'and' before words beginning with **i** or **hi** but not **hie**.

□ Miguel and Ignacio Miguel e Ignacio

> **LANGUAGE TIP** 'and' is not translated when linking numbers.

□ two hundred and fifty doscientos cincuenta
■ **Please try and come!** ¡Procura venir!
■ **He talked and talked.** No paraba de hablar.
■ **better and better** cada vez mejor

**angel** NOUN
el ángel

**anger** NOUN
el enfado (el enojo *Latin America*)

**angle** NOUN
el ángulo

**angler** NOUN
el pescador
la pescadora

**angling** NOUN
■ **His hobby is angling.** Su hobby es la pesca.

**angry** ADJECTIVE
enfadado (FEM enfadada) (enojado *Latin America*)
□ to be angry with somebody estar enfadado con alguien □ Your father looks very angry. Tu padre parece estar muy enfadado.
■ **to get angry** enfadarse (enojarse *Latin America*)

**animal** NOUN
el animal

**ankle** NOUN
el tobillo
□ I've twisted my ankle. Me he torcido el tobillo.

**anniversary** NOUN
el aniversario
□ wedding anniversary aniversario de bodas

to **announce** VERB
anunciar

**announcement** NOUN
el anuncio

to **annoy** VERB
molestar
□ Make a note of the things that annoy you. Haz una lista de las cosas que te molestan.
■ **He's really annoying me.** Me está fastidiando de verdad.
■ **to be annoyed with somebody** estar molesto con alguien
■ **to get annoyed** enfadarse (enojarse *Latin America*)
□ Don't get annoyed! ¡No te enfades!

**annoying** ADJECTIVE
molesto (FEM molesta)
□ the most annoying problem el problema más molesto
■ **I find it very annoying.** Me molesta mucho.

**annual** ADJECTIVE
anual (FEM anual)

**anorak** NOUN
el anorak (PL los anoraks)

**another** ADJECTIVE, PRONOUN
otro (FEM otra)
□ Have you got another skirt? ¿Tienes otra falda?
■ **another two kilometres** dos kilómetros más

to **answer** VERB
▷ see also **answer** NOUN
responder
□ Can you answer my question? ¿Puedes responder a mi pregunta?
■ **to answer the phone** contestar al teléfono
■ **to answer the door** abrir la puerta □ Can you answer the door please? ¿Puedes ir a abrir la puerta?

**answer** NOUN
▷ see also **answer** VERB
**1** la respuesta (to question)

**2** la solución (PL las soluciones) *(to problem)*

**answering machine** NOUN
el contestador automático

**ant** NOUN
la hormiga

**Antarctic** NOUN
■ **the Antarctic** el Antártico

**anthem** NOUN
■ **the national anthem** el himno nacional

**antibiotic** NOUN
el antibiótico

**antidepressant** NOUN
el antidepresivo

**antique** NOUN
la antigüedad

**antique shop** NOUN
la tienda de antigüedades

**antiseptic** NOUN
el antiséptico

**any** ADJECTIVE, ADVERB
▷ *see also* **any** PRONOUN

**LANGUAGE TIP** In questions and negative sentences 'any' is usually not translated.
□ Have you got any change? ¿Tienes cambio? □ Are there any beans left? ¿Quedan alubias? □ He hasn't got any friends. No tiene amigos.

**LANGUAGE TIP** Use **algún/alguna** + singular noun in questions and **ningún/ninguna** + singular noun in negatives where 'any' is used with plural nouns and the number of items is important.
□ Do you speak any foreign languages? ¿Hablas algún idioma extranjero? □ I haven't got any books by Cervantes. No tengo ningún libro de Cervantes.

**LANGUAGE TIP** Use **cualquier** in affirmative sentences.
□ Any teacher will tell you. Cualquier profesor te lo dirá.
■ **Come any time you like.** Ven cuando quieras.
■ **Would you like any more coffee?** ¿Quieres más café?
■ **I don't love him any more.** Ya no le quiero.

**any** PRONOUN
▷ *see also* **any** ADJECTIVE, ADVERB
**1** alguno (FEM alguna) *(in questions)*
□ I need a stamp. Have you got any left? Necesito un sello. ¿Te queda alguno?

**LANGUAGE TIP** Only use **alguno/alguna** if 'any' refers to a countable noun. Otherwise don't translate it.
□ I fancy some soup. Have we got any? Me apetece sopa. ¿Tenemos?

**2** ninguno (FEM ninguna) *(in negatives)*
□ I don't like any of them. No me gusta ninguno.

**LANGUAGE TIP** Only use **ninguno/ninguna** if 'any' refers to a countable noun. Otherwise don't translate it.
□ Did you buy the oranges? — No, there weren't any. ¿Compraste las naranjas? — No, no había.

**anybody** PRONOUN
**1** alguien
**LANGUAGE TIP** Use **alguien** in questions.
□ Has anybody got a pen? ¿Tiene alguien un bolígrafo?

**2** nadie
**LANGUAGE TIP** Use **nadie** in negative sentences.
□ I can't see anybody. No veo a nadie.

**3** cualquiera
**LANGUAGE TIP** Use **cualquiera** in affirmative sentences.
□ Anybody can learn to swim. Cualquiera puede aprender a nadar.

**anyhow** ADVERB
de todas maneras
□ He doesn't want to go out and anyhow he's not allowed. No quiere salir y de todas maneras no le dejan.

**anyone** PRONOUN
**1** alguien
**LANGUAGE TIP** Use **alguien** in questions.
□ Has anyone got a pen? ¿Tiene alguien un bolígrafo?

**2** nadie
**LANGUAGE TIP** Use **nadie** in negative sentences.
□ I can't see anyone. No veo a nadie.

**3** cualquiera
**LANGUAGE TIP** Use **cualquiera** in affirmative sentences.
□ Anyone can learn to swim. Cualquiera puede aprender a nadar.

**anything** PRONOUN
**1** algo
**LANGUAGE TIP** Use **algo** in questions.
□ Do you need anything? ¿Necesitas algo? □ Would you like anything to eat? ¿Quieres algo de comer?

**2** nada
**LANGUAGE TIP** Use **nada** in negative sentences.
□ I can't hear anything. No oigo nada.

**3** cualquier cosa
**LANGUAGE TIP** Use **cualquier cosa** in affirmative sentences.

▢ Anything could happen. Puede pasar cualquier cosa.

**anyway** ADVERB
de todas maneras

▢ He doesn't want to go out and anyway he's not allowed. No quiere salir y de todas maneras no le dejan.

**anywhere** ADVERB
1 en algún sitio

◌ **LANGUAGE TIP** Use **en** or **a algún sitio** in questions.

▢ Have you seen my coat anywhere? ¿Has visto mi abrigo en algún sitio? ▢ Are we going anywhere? ¿Vamos a algún sitio?
2 en ningún sitio

◌ **LANGUAGE TIP** Use **en** or **a ningún sitio** in negative sentences.

▢ I can't find it anywhere. No lo encuentro en ningún sitio. ▢ I can't go anywhere. No puedo ir a ningún sitio.
3 en cualquier sitio

◌ **LANGUAGE TIP** Use **en cualquier sitio** in affirmative sentences.

▢ You can buy stamps almost anywhere. Se pueden comprar sellos casi en cualquier sitio.

■ **You can sit anywhere you like.** Siéntate donde quieras.

**apart** ADVERB
■ **The two towns are 10 kilometres apart.** Los dos pueblos están a 10 kilómetros el uno del otro.

■ **It was the first time we had been apart.** Era la primera vez que estábamos separados.

■ **apart from** aparte de ▢ Apart from that, everything's fine. Aparte de eso, todo va bien.

**apartment** NOUN
el piso (el apartamento *Latin America*)

to **apologize** VERB
disculparse

▢ He apologized for being late. Se disculpó por llegar tarde.

■ **I apologize!** ¡Lo siento!

**apology** NOUN
la disculpa

▢ I owe you an apology. Te debo una disculpa.

**apostrophe** NOUN
el apóstrofo

**apparatus** NOUN
los aparatos

**apparent** ADJECTIVE
1 aparente (FEM aparente)

▢ for no apparent reason sin razón aparente
2 claro (FEM clara)

▢ It was apparent that he disliked me.

Estaba claro que no le caigo bien.

**apparently** ADVERB
por lo visto (dizque *Latin America*)

▢ Apparently he was abroad when it happened. Por lo visto estaba en el extranjero cuando ocurrió.

to **appeal** VERB
▷ *see also* **appeal** NOUN
1 hacer* un llamamiento

▢ They appealed for help. Hicieron un llamamiento de ayuda.
2 atraer*

▢ Greece doesn't appeal to me. Grecia no me atrae.

**appeal** NOUN
▷ *see also* **appeal** VERB
el llamamiento

▢ They have launched an appeal for unity. Han hecho un llamamiento a la unidad.

to **appear** VERB
1 aparecer*

▢ The bus appeared around the corner. El autobús apareció por la esquina.

■ **to appear on TV** salir en la tele
2 parecer*

▢ She appeared to be asleep. Parecía estar dormida.

**appearance** NOUN
el aspecto

▢ She takes great care over her appearance. Cuida mucho su aspecto.

■ **to make an appearance** aparecer

**appendicitis** NOUN
la apendicitis

▢ She's got appendicitis. Tiene apendicitis.

**appetite** NOUN
el apetito

to **applaud** VERB
aplaudir

**applause** NOUN
los aplausos

**apple** NOUN
la manzana

■ **an apple tree** un manzano

**applicant** NOUN
el candidato
la candidata

**application** NOUN
■ **a job application** una solicitud de empleo

**application form** NOUN
el impreso de solicitud

to **apply** VERB
■ **to apply for a job** solicitar un empleo
■ **to apply to** afectar a ▢ This rule doesn't apply to us. Esta norma no nos afecta.

**appointment** NOUN
la cita

□ to make an appointment with someone concertar una cita con alguien
■ **I've got a dental appointment.** Tengo hora con el dentista.

to **appreciate** VERB
agradecer*
□ I really appreciate your help. Agradezco de veras tu ayuda.

**apprentice** NOUN
el aprendiz (PL los aprendices)
la aprendiza

to **approach** VERB
1 acercarse* a
□ He approached the house. Se acercó a la casa.
2 abordar
□ to approach a problem abordar un problema

**appropriate** ADJECTIVE
apropiado (FEM apropiada)
□ That dress isn't very appropriate for an interview. Ese vestido no es muy apropiado para una entrevista.
■ **Tick the appropriate box.** Marque la casilla que corresponda.

**approval** NOUN
la aprobación

to **approve** VERB
■ **I don't approve of his choice.** No me parece bien su elección.
■ **They didn't approve of his girlfriend.** No veían con buenos ojos a su novia.

**approximate** ADJECTIVE
aproximado (FEM aproximada)

**apricot** NOUN
el albaricoque

**April** NOUN
abril masc
□ in April en abril □ on 4 April el 4 de abril
■ **April Fool's Day** el día de los Santos Inocentes (1 de abril)

> **DID YOU KNOW...?**
> In Spanish-speaking countries **el día de los Santos Inocentes** falls on the 28th of December. People play practical jokes in the same way as they do on April Fool's Day.

**apron** NOUN
el delantal

**Aquarius** NOUN
el Acuario (sign)
■ **I'm Aquarius.** Soy acuario.

**Arab** ADJECTIVE
▷ see also **Arab** NOUN
árabe (FEM árabe)

**Arab** NOUN
▷ see also **Arab** ADJECTIVE
el/la árabe
□ the Arabs los árabes

**Arabic** ADJECTIVE
árabe (FEM árabe)

**arch** NOUN
el arco

**archaeologist** NOUN
el arqueólogo
la arqueóloga
□ He's an archaeologist. Es arqueólogo.

**archaeology** NOUN
la arqueología

**archbishop** NOUN
el arzobispo

**archeologist** NOUN (US)
el arqueólogo
la arqueóloga

**archeology** NOUN (US)
la arqueología

**architect** NOUN
el arquitecto
la arquitecta
□ She's an architect. Es arquitecta.

**architecture** NOUN
la arquitectura

**Arctic** NOUN
■ **the Arctic** el Ártico

**are** VERB ▷ see **be**

**area** NOUN
1 la zona
□ a mountainous area of Spain una zona montañosa de España
2 la superficie
□ The field has an area of 1500 m². El terreno tiene una superficie de 1500 m².
3 el área fem (in football)

> **LANGUAGE TIP** Although it's a feminine noun, remember that you use **el** and **un** with **área**.

**Argentina** NOUN
Argentina fem

**Argentinian** ADJECTIVE
▷ see also **Argentinian** NOUN
argentino (FEM argentina)

**Argentinian** NOUN
▷ see also **Argentinian** ADJECTIVE
el argentino
la argentina

to **argue** VERB
discutir
□ They never stop arguing. Siempre están discutiendo.

**argument** NOUN
la discusión (PL las discusiones)
□ to have an argument discutir

**Aries** NOUN
el Aries (sign)
■ **I'm Aries.** Soy aries.

**arm** NOUN
el brazo

□ I burnt my arm.  Me quemé el brazo.

**armchair** NOUN
el sillón (PL los sillones)

**armour** (US armor) NOUN
la armadura

**army** NOUN
el ejército

**around** PREPOSITION, ADVERB
1 alrededor de
□ She wore a scarf around her neck.  Llevaba una bufanda alrededor del cuello.  □ It costs around £100.  Cuesta alrededor de 100 libras.
■ **She ignored the people around her.** Ignoró a la gente que estaba a su alrededor.
■ **Shall we meet at around 8 o'clock?** ¿Quedamos sobre las 8?
2 por
□ I've been walking around the town.  He estado paseando por la ciudad.
■ **We walked around for a while.** Paseamos por ahí durante un rato.
■ **around here** por aquí □ Is there a chemist's around here? ¿Hay alguna farmacia por aquí?

to **arrange** VERB
organizar*
□ to arrange a party  organizar una fiesta
■ **to arrange to do something** quedar en hacer algo □ They arranged to go out together on Friday.  Quedaron en salir juntos el viernes.

**arrangement** NOUN
■ **to make an arrangement to do something** quedar en hacer algo
■ **a flower arrangement** un arreglo floral
■ **arrangements** los preparativos
□ Pamela is in charge of the travel arrangements.  Pamela se encarga de los preparativos para el viaje.
■ **They made arrangements to go out on Friday night.** Hicieron planes de salir el viernes por la noche.

to **arrest** VERB
▷ see also **arrest** NOUN
detener*

**arrest** NOUN
▷ see also **arrest** VERB
la detención (PL las detenciones)
■ **You're under arrest!** ¡Queda detenido!

**arrival** NOUN
la llegada
□ the airport arrivals hall  la sala de llegadas del aeropuerto

to **arrive** VERB
llegar*
□ I arrived at 5 o'clock.  Llegué a las 5.

**arrow** NOUN
la flecha

**art** NOUN
el arte
■ **works of art** las obras de arte
■ **art school** la escuela de Bellas Artes

**artery** NOUN
la arteria

**art gallery** NOUN
1 el museo (state-owned)
2 la galería de arte (private)

**article** NOUN
el artículo

**artificial** ADJECTIVE
artificial (FEM artificial)

**artist** NOUN
el/la artista
□ She's an artist.  Es artista.

**artistic** ADJECTIVE
artístico (FEM artística)

**as** CONJUNCTION, ADVERB
1 cuando
□ He came in as I was leaving.  Entró cuando yo me iba.
2 mientras
□ Everyone looked at him as he stood up. Todos lo miraron mientras se levantaba.
3 como
□ As it's Sunday, you can have a lie-in. Como es domingo, puedes quedarte en la cama hasta tarde.
4 de
□ He works as a waiter in the holidays.  En vacaciones trabaja de camarero.
■ **as...as** tan...como □ Peter's as tall as Michael.  Peter es tan alto como Michael.
■ **as much...as** tanto...como □ I haven't got as much energy as you.  No tengo tanta energía como tú.
■ **Her coat cost twice as much as mine.** Su abrigo costó el doble que el mío.
■ **as soon as possible** cuanto antes
■ **as from tomorrow** a partir de mañana
■ **as if** como si

 ☼ LANGUAGE TIP **como si** has to be followed by a verb in the subjunctive.
□ She acted as if she hadn't seen me.  Hizo como si no me hubiese visto.
■ **as though** como si □ She acted as though she hadn't seen me.  Hizo como si no me hubiese visto.

**asap** ABBREVIATION (= as soon as possible)
cuanto antes

**ashamed** ADJECTIVE
■ **to be ashamed** estar avergonzado □ I'm ashamed of myself for shouting at you. Estoy avergonzado de gritarte.
■ **You should be ashamed of yourself!** ¡Debería darte vergüenza!

**ashtray** NOUN
el cenicero

**Asia** NOUN
Ásia *fem*

**Asian** ADJECTIVE
▷ *see also* **Asian** NOUN
asiático (FEM asiática)

**Asian** NOUN
▷ *see also* **Asian** ADJECTIVE
el asiático
la asiática

to **ask** VERB
1 preguntar
□ 'Have you finished?' she asked. '¿Has terminado?' preguntó.
■ **to ask somebody something** preguntar algo a alguien
■ **to ask about something** preguntar por algo □ I asked about train times to Leeds. Pregunté por el horario de trenes a Leeds.
■ **to ask somebody a question** hacer una pregunta a alguien
2 pedir*
LANGUAGE TIP **pedir que** has to be followed by a verb in the subjunctive.
□ She asked him to do the shopping. Le pidió que hiciera la compra.
■ **to ask for something** pedir algo □ He asked for a cup of tea. Pidió una taza de té.
■ **Peter asked her out.** Peter le pidió que saliera con él.
3 invitar
□ Have you asked Matthew to the party? ¿Has invitado a Matthew a la fiesta?

**asleep** ADJECTIVE
■ **to be asleep** estar dormido
■ **to fall asleep** quedarse dormido

**asparagus** NOUN
los espárragos

**aspect** NOUN
el aspecto

**aspirin** NOUN
la aspirina

**asset** NOUN
la ventaja
□ Her experience will be an asset to the firm. Su experiencia supondrá una ventaja para la empresa.

**assignment** NOUN
la tarea *(at school)*

**assistance** NOUN
la ayuda

**assistant** NOUN
1 el dependiente
la dependienta *(in shop)*
2 el/la ayudante *(helper)*

**association** NOUN
la asociación (PL las asociaciones)

**assortment** NOUN
el surtido

to **assume** VERB
suponer*
□ I assume she won't be coming. Supongo que no vendrá.

to **assure** VERB
asegurar
□ He assured me he was coming. Me aseguró que venía.

**asthma** NOUN
el asma *fem*
□ He's got asthma. Tiene asma.
LANGUAGE TIP Although it's a feminine noun, remember that you use **el** with **asma**.

to **astonish** VERB
pasmar

**astrology** NOUN
la astrología

**astronaut** NOUN
el/la astronauta

**astronomy** NOUN
la astronomía

**asylum seeker** NOUN
el/la solicitante de asilo

**at** PREPOSITION
1 en
□ at home en casa □ at school en la escuela □ at the office en la oficina □ at work en el trabajo
2 a
□ at 50 km/h a 50 km/h
■ **two at a time** de dos en dos
■ **at 4 o'clock** a las 4
■ **at night** por la noche
■ **at Christmas** en Navidad
■ **What are you doing at the weekend?** ¿Qué haces este fin de semana?

**ate** VERB ▷ *see* eat

**Athens** NOUN
Atenas *fem*

**athlete** NOUN
el/la atleta

**athletic** ADJECTIVE
atlético (FEM atlética)

**athletics** NOUN
el atletismo
□ I enjoy watching the athletics on television. Me gusta ver el atletismo en la televisión.

**Atlantic** NOUN
el Atlántico

**atlas** NOUN
el atlas (PL los atlas)

**atmosphere** NOUN
la atmósfera

**atom** NOUN

el átomo
**atomic** ADJECTIVE
atómico (FEM atómica)
to **attach** VERB
atar
▫ They attached a rope to the car. Ataron una cuerda al coche.
■ **Please find attached a cheque for £10.** Se adjunta cheque de 10 libras.
**attached** ADJECTIVE
■ **to be attached to somebody** tener cariño a alguien
**attachment** NOUN
el documento adjunto (to email)
to **attack** VERB
▷ see also **attack** NOUN
atacar*
**attack** NOUN
▷ see also **attack** VERB
el ataque
■ **to be under attack** ser atacado
**attempt** NOUN
▷ see also **attempt** VERB
el intento
to **attempt** VERB
▷ see also **attempt** NOUN
■ **to attempt to do something** intentar hacer algo ▫ I attempted to write a song. Intenté escribir una canción.
to **attend** VERB
asistir a
▫ to attend a meeting asistir a una reunión
**attention** NOUN
la atención
■ **to pay attention to** prestar atención a ▫ He didn't pay attention to what I was saying. No prestó atención a lo que estaba diciendo.
■ **Don't pay any attention to him!** ¡No le hagas caso!
■ **Pay attention, please!** ¡Atención por favor!
**attic** NOUN
el desván (PL los desvanes) (el altillo Latin America)
**attitude** NOUN
la actitud
**attorney** NOUN (US)
el abogado
la abogada
to **attract** VERB
atraer*
▫ The Lake District attracts lots of tourists. La Región de los Lagos atrae a muchos turistas.
**attraction** NOUN
la atracción (PL las atracciones)
▫ a tourist attraction una atracción turística

**attractive** ADJECTIVE
atractivo (FEM atractiva)
**aubergine** NOUN
la berenjena
**auction** NOUN
la subasta
**audience** NOUN
el público
**audition** NOUN
la prueba
**August** NOUN
agosto masc
▫ in August en agosto ▫ on 13 August el 13 agosto
**au pair** NOUN
la au pair (PL las au pairs)
**Australia** NOUN
Australia fem
**Australian** ADJECTIVE
▷ see also **Australian** NOUN
australiano (FEM australiana)
**Australian** NOUN
▷ see also **Australian** ADJECTIVE
el australiano
la australiana
▫ the Australians los australianos
**Austria** NOUN
Austria fem
**Austrian** ADJECTIVE
▷ see also **Austrian** NOUN
austríaco (FEM austríaca)
**Austrian** NOUN
▷ see also **Austrian** ADJECTIVE
el austríaco
la austríaca
▫ the Austrians los austríacos
**author** NOUN
el autor
la autora
▫ the author of the book el autor del libro
■ **a famous author** un escritor famoso
**autobiography** NOUN
la autobiografía
**autograph** NOUN
el autógrafo
**automatic** ADJECTIVE
automático (FEM automática)
**automatically** ADVERB
automáticamente
**autumn** NOUN
el otoño
▫ in autumn en el otoño
**availability** NOUN
la disponibilidad
**available** ADJECTIVE
disponible (FEM disponible)
▫ There is very little available information. Hay muy poca información disponible.

15

■ **Free brochures are available on request.** Disponemos de folletos gratuitos para quien los solicite.

■ **Is Mr Cooke available today?** ¿Está libre el señor Cooke hoy?

**avalanche** NOUN
el alud

**avenue** NOUN
la avenida

**average** NOUN
▷ see also **average** ADJECTIVE
la media

□ on average  de media

**average** ADJECTIVE
▷ see also **average** NOUN
medio (FEM media)

□ the average price  el precio medio

**avocado** NOUN
el aguacate

to **avoid** VERB
evitar

□ Avoid going out on your own at night. Evite salir solo por la noche.

**awake** ADJECTIVE
■ **to be awake**  estar despierto

**award** NOUN
el premio

□ the award for the best actor  el premio al mejor actor

**away** ADJECTIVE, ADVERB
■ **It's two kilometres away.**  Está a dos kilómetros de distancia.

■ **The coast is two hours away by car.** La costa está a dos horas en coche.

■ **The holiday was two weeks away.** Faltaban dos semanas para las vacaciones.

■ **to be away**  estar fuera  □ Jason was away on a business trip.  Jason estaba fuera en viaje de negocios.

■ **He's away for a week.**  Se ha ido una semana.

■ **Go away!** ¡Vete!

■ **away from**  lejos de  □ away from family and friends  lejos de la familia y los amigos

■ **It's 30 miles away from town.**  Está a 30 millas de la ciudad.

■ **He was still working away in the library.**  Seguía trabajando sin parar en la biblioteca.

**away match** NOUN
■ **It is their last away match.**  Es el último partido que juegan fuera.

**awful** ADJECTIVE
horrible (FEM horrible)

□ The weather's awful.  Hace un tiempo horrible.

■ **I feel awful.**  Me siento fatal.

■ **We met and I thought he was awful.** Nos conocimos y me cayó fatal.

■ **an awful lot of work**  un montón de trabajo

**awfully** ADVERB
■ **I'm awfully sorry.**  Lo siento muchísimo.

**awkward** ADJECTIVE
1  incómodo (FEM incómoda)

□ It was awkward to carry.  Era incómodo de llevar.  □ an awkward situation  una situación incómoda

■ **Mike's being awkward about letting me have the car.**  Mike no hace más que ponerme pegas para dejarme el coche.

■ **It's a bit awkward for me to come and see you.**  Me viene un poco mal pasar a verte.

2  torpe (FEM torpe)

□ an awkward gesture  un gesto torpe

**axe** NOUN
el hacha *fem*

> **LANGUAGE TIP** Although it's a feminine noun, remember that you use **el** and **un** with **hacha**.

# Bb

**BA** ABBREVIATION (= *Bachelor of Arts*)
la licenciatura en Letras
- ■ **a BA in French** una licenciatura en Filología Francesa
- ■ **She's got a BA in History.** Es licenciada en Historia.

**baby** NOUN
el/la bebé (PL los/las bebés)

**baby carriage** NOUN (US)
el cochecito de niño

to **babysit** VERB
hacer* de canguro

**babysitter** NOUN
el/la canguro

**babysitting** NOUN
- ■ **I don't like babysitting.** No me gusta hacer de canguro.

**bachelor** NOUN
el soltero

**back** NOUN
▷ *see also* **back** ADJECTIVE, ADVERB, VERB
1 la espalda *(of person)*
  □ He's got a bad back. Tiene problemas de espalda.
2 el lomo *(of animal)*
  - ■ **the back of a chair** el respaldo de una silla
  - ■ **on the back of the cheque** al dorso del cheque
  - ■ **at the back of the house** en la parte de atrás de la casa
  - ■ **in the back of the car** en la parte trasera del coche
  - ■ **at the back of the class** al fondo de la clase

**back** ADJECTIVE, ADVERB
▷ *see also* **back** NOUN, VERB
trasero (FEM trasera)
  □ the back seat el asiento trasero
  - ■ **the back door** la puerta de atrás
  - ■ **He's not back yet.** Todavía no ha vuelto.
  - ■ **to get back** volver □ What time did you get back? ¿A qué hora volviste? □ We went there by bus and walked back. Fuimos allí en autobús y volvimos a pie.
  - ■ **to call somebody back** volver a llamar a alguien

- ■ **I'll call back later.** Volveré a llamar más tarde.

to **back** VERB
▷ *see also* **back** NOUN, ADJECTIVE
respaldar
  □ The union is backing his claim for compensation. El sindicato respalda su demanda de compensación.
  - ■ **to back a horse** apostar por un caballo
  - ■ **She backed into the parking space.** Aparcó dando marcha atrás.

to **back out** VERB
echarse para atrás
  □ They promised to help us and then backed out. Prometieron ayudarnos y luego se echaron para atrás.

to **back up** VERB
respaldar
  □ She complained, and her colleagues backed her up. Presentó una queja y sus colegas la respaldaron.

**backache** NOUN
el dolor de espalda
  □ to have backache tener dolor de espalda

**backbone** NOUN
la columna vertebral

to **backfire** VERB
tener* el efecto contrario *(go wrong)*

**background** NOUN
el fondo *(of picture)*
  □ a house in the background una casa en el fondo
  - ■ **background noise** ruido de fondo
  - ■ **his family background** su historial familiar

**backhand** NOUN
el revés (PL los reveses)

**backing** NOUN
el apoyo
  □ They promised their backing. Prometieron su apoyo.

**backpack** NOUN
la mochila

**backpacker** NOUN
el mochilero
la mochilera

**backside** NOUN
el trasero

**backstroke** NOUN
la espalda

**backup** NOUN
el apoyo
▢ We have extensive computer backup. Tenemos amplio apoyo informático.
▪ They've got a generator as an emergency backup. Tienen un generador de reserva para emergencias.
▪ a backup file una copia de seguridad

**backwards** ADVERB
hacia atrás
▢ to take a step backwards dar un paso hacia atrás
▪ to fall backwards caerse de espaldas

**back yard** NOUN
el patio trasero

**bacon** NOUN
el bacon (el tocino *Latin America*)
▢ bacon and eggs los huevos fritos con bacon

**bad** ADJECTIVE
1 malo (FEM mala)
▢ You bad boy! ¡Malo!

> **LANGUAGE TIP** Use **mal** before a masculine singular noun.

▢ bad weather mal tiempo

**WORD POWER**
You can use a number of other words instead of **bad** to mean 'terrible':
**awful** horrible
▢ awful weather un tiempo horrible
**dreadful** terrible
▢ a dreadful mistake un terrible error
**terrible** espantoso
▢ a terrible book un libro espantoso

▪ to be in a bad mood estar de mal humor
▪ to be bad at something ser malo para algo ▢ I'm really bad at maths. Soy muy malo para las matemáticas.
2 grave (FEM grave) *(serious)*
▢ a bad accident un accidente grave
▪ to go bad *(food)* echarse a perder
▪ I feel bad about it. *(guilty)* Me siento un poco culpable.
▪ How are you? — Not bad. ¿Cómo estás? — Bien.
▪ That's not bad at all. No está nada mal.
▪ bad language las palabrotas

**badge** NOUN
1 la chapa *(metal, plastic)*
2 el escudo *(cloth)*

**badly** ADVERB
mal
▢ badly paid mal pagado
▪ badly wounded gravemente herido
▪ He badly needs a rest. Le hace muchísima falta un descanso.

**badminton** NOUN
el bádminton
▢ to play badminton jugar al bádminton

**bad-tempered** ADJECTIVE
▪ to be bad-tempered 1 *(by nature)* tener mal genio ▢ He's a really bad-tempered person. Es una persona con muy mal genio.
2 *(temporarily)* estar de mal humor ▢ He was really bad-tempered yesterday. Ayer estaba de muy mal humor.

**bag** NOUN
la bolsa

**baggage** NOUN
el equipaje

**baggage reclaim** NOUN
la recogida de equipajes

**baggy** ADJECTIVE
ancho (FEM ancha) *(trousers)*

**bagpipes** PL NOUN
la gaita

to **bake** VERB
▪ to bake bread hacer pan
▪ She loves to bake. Le gusta cocinar al horno.

**baked beans** PL NOUN
las alubias blancas en salsa de tomate

**baker** NOUN
el panadero
la panadera
▢ He's a baker. Es panadero.
▪ at the baker's en la panadería

**bakery** NOUN
la panadería

**baking** ADJECTIVE
▪ It's baking in here! ¡Aquí hace un calor insoportable!

**balance** NOUN
▷ *see also* **balance** VERB
el equilibrio
▢ to lose one's balance perder el equilibrio

**balanced** ADJECTIVE
equilibrado (FEM equilibrada)

**balcony** NOUN
el balcón (PL los balcones)

**bald** ADJECTIVE
calvo (FEM calva)

**ball** NOUN
1 la pelota *(for tennis, basketball, rugby)*
2 el balón (PL los balones) *(for football)*
▢ a golf ball una pelota de golf

**ballet** NOUN
el ballet (PL los ballets)
▢ We went to a ballet. Fuimos a ver un ballet.
▪ ballet lessons las clases de ballet

**ballet dancer** NOUN
el bailarín (PL los bailarines)
la bailarina
**ballet shoes** PL NOUN
las zapatillas de ballet
**balloon** NOUN
el globo
■ **a hot-air balloon** un globo aerostático
**ballpoint pen** NOUN
el bolígrafo
**ballroom dancing** NOUN
el baile de salón
**ban** NOUN
▷ see also **ban** VERB
la prohibición (PL las prohibiciones)
to **ban** VERB
▷ see also **ban** NOUN
prohibir*
**banana** NOUN
el plátano
□ a banana skin una piel de plátano
**band** NOUN
1 el grupo (pop, rock)
2 la banda (military)
3 la orquesta (at a dance)
**bandage** NOUN
▷ see also **bandage** VERB
la venda
to **bandage** VERB
▷ see also **bandage** NOUN
vendar
□ The nurse bandaged his arm.
La enfermera le vendó el brazo.
**Band-Aid®** NOUN (US)
la tirita
**bandit** NOUN
el bandido
**bang** NOUN
▷ see also **bang** VERB
1 el estallido (noise)
□ I heard a loud bang. Oí un fuerte estallido.
2 el golpe (blow)
□ a bang on the head un golpe en la cabeza
to **bang** VERB
▷ see also **bang** NOUN
golpear
□ I banged my head. Me golpeé la cabeza.
■ **to bang on the door** aporrear la puerta
■ **to bang the door** dar un portazo
**banger** NOUN
la salchicha (informal)
□ bangers and mash las salchichas con
puré de patatas
**bank** NOUN
1 el banco (financial)
2 la orilla (of river, lake)
**bank account** NOUN
la cuenta bancaria

**banker** NOUN
el banquero
la banquera
□ He's a banker. Es banquero.
**bank holiday** NOUN
el día festivo
**banknote** NOUN
el billete de banco
**bar** NOUN
1 el bar (pub)
2 la barra (counter)
■ **a bar of chocolate 1** (large) una tableta
de chocolate **2** (small) una chocolatina
■ **a bar of soap** una pastilla de jabón
**barbaric** ADJECTIVE
bárbaro (FEM bárbara)
**barbecue** NOUN
la barbacoa
□ to have a barbecue hacer una barbacoa
**barber** NOUN
el barbero
□ He's a barber. Es barbero.
■ **at the barber's** en la barbería
**bare** ADJECTIVE
desnudo (FEM desnuda)
**barefoot** ADJECTIVE, ADVERB
descalzo (FEM descalza)
□ The children go around barefoot. Los
niños van descalzos.
**barely** ADVERB
apenas
□ I could barely hear what she was saying.
Apenas oía lo que estaba diciendo.
**bargain** NOUN
la ganga
□ It was a bargain! ¡Era una ganga!
**barge** NOUN
la barcaza
to **bark** VERB
ladrar
**barmaid** NOUN
la camarera
□ She's a barmaid. Es camarera.
**barman** NOUN
el barman (PL los barmans)
□ He's a barman. Es barman.
**barn** NOUN
el granero
**barrel** NOUN
1 el barril (container)
2 el cañón (PL los cañones) (of gun)
**barrier** NOUN
la barrera
**bartender** NOUN (US)
el barman (PL los barmans)
□ He's a bartender. Es barman.
**base** NOUN
la base

**English-Spanish**

**b**

**baseball** NOUN
el béisbol
◽ to play baseball jugar al béisbol
▪ **a baseball cap** una gorra de béisbol

**based** ADJECTIVE
▪ **based on** basado en

**basement** NOUN
el sótano
◽ a basement flat un apartamento en el sótano

to **bash** VERB
▷ see also **bash** NOUN
golpear con fuerza

**bash** NOUN
▷ see also **bash** VERB
▪ **I'll have a bash at it.** Lo intentaré.

**basic** ADJECTIVE
básico (FEM básica)
◽ It's a basic model. Es un modelo básico.
▪ **The accommodation was pretty basic.**
El alojamiento tenía sólo lo imprescindible.

**basically** ADVERB
básicamente
◽ They are basically the same thing. Son básicamente lo mismo.
▪ **Basically, I just don't like him.**
Simplemente, no me gusta.

**basics** PL NOUN
los principios básicos

**basil** NOUN
la albahaca

**basin** NOUN
1 el lavabo (washbasin)
2 el cuenco (for cooking, mixing food)

**basis** NOUN
la base
◽ On the basis of what you've said. En base a lo que has dicho.
▪ **on a daily basis** diariamente
▪ **on a regular basis** regularmente

**basket** NOUN
el cesto

**basketball** NOUN
el baloncesto
◽ to play basketball jugar al baloncesto

**bass** NOUN
el bajo (voice)
▪ **a bass guitar** un bajo
▪ **a double bass** un contrabajo

**bass drum** NOUN
el bombo

**bassoon** NOUN
el fagot (PL los fagots)

**bat** NOUN
1 el bate (for baseball, cricket)
2 la raqueta (for table tennis)
3 el murciélago (animal)

**bath** NOUN

1 el baño
◽ a hot bath un baño caliente
▪ **to have a bath** bañarse
2 la bañera (bathtub)

to **bathe** VERB
bañarse

**bathing suit** NOUN (US)
el traje de baño

**bathroom** NOUN
el cuarto de baño

**baths** PL NOUN
▪ **swimming baths** la piscina
▪ **Turkish baths** los baños turcos

**bath towel** NOUN
la toalla de baño

**batter** NOUN
la masa para rebozar

**battery** NOUN
1 la pila (for torch, toy)
2 la batería (for car)

**battle** NOUN
la batalla
◽ the Battle of Hastings la batalla de Hastings
▪ **It was a battle, but we managed in the end.** Fue muy difícil, pero al final lo conseguimos.

**battleship** NOUN
el acorazado

**bay** NOUN
la bahía

**BC** ABBREVIATION (= before Christ)
a.C. (= antes de Cristo)

to **be** VERB

> LANGUAGE TIP There are two basic verbs to translate 'be' into Spanish: **estar** and **ser**. **estar** is used to form continuous tenses; to talk about where something is; and with adjectives describing a temporary state. It is also used with past participles used adjectivally even if these describe a permanent state.

1 estar*
◽ What are you doing? ¿Qué estás haciendo? ◽ Edinburgh is in Scotland. Edimburgo está en Escocia. ◽ I've never been to Madrid. No he estado nunca en Madrid. ◽ I'm very happy. Estoy muy contento. ◽ The window is broken. La ventana está rota. ◽ Is he hurt? ¿Está herido? ◽ He's dead. Está muerto.
▪ **You're late.** Llegas tarde.

> LANGUAGE TIP **ser** is used to talk about the time and date; with adjectives describing permanent or inherent states such as nationality and colour; with nouns to say what somebody or something is; and to form the passive.

**2** <u>ser</u>*

▫ It's four o'clock. Son las cuatro. ▫ It's the 28th of October today. Hoy es 28 de octubre. ▫ She's English. Es inglesa. ▫ He's a doctor. Es médico. ▫ Paris is the capital of France. París es la capital de Francia. ▫ He's very tall. Es muy alto. ▫ The house was destroyed by an earthquake. La casa fue destruida por un terremoto.

> **LANGUAGE TIP** Passive constructions are not as common in Spanish as in English. Either the active or a reflexive construction are preferred.

▫ He was killed by a terrorist. Lo mató un terrorista. ▫ These cars are produced in Spain. Estos coches se fabrican en España.

> **LANGUAGE TIP** When referring to the weather, use **hacer**.

▫ It's a nice day, isn't it? Hace buen día, ¿verdad? ▫ It's cold. Hace frío. ▫ It's too hot. Hace demasiado calor.

> **LANGUAGE TIP** With certain adjectives, such as 'cold', 'hot', 'hungry', and 'thirsty', use **tener**\* with a noun.

▫ I'm cold. Tengo frío. ▫ I'm hungry. Tengo hambre.

> **LANGUAGE TIP** When saying how old somebody is, use **tener**\*.

▫ I'm fourteen. Tengo catorce años. ▫ How old are you? ¿Cuántos años tienes?

**beach** NOUN
la <u>playa</u>

**bead** NOUN
la <u>cuenta</u>

**beak** NOUN
el <u>pico</u>

**beam** NOUN
el <u>rayo</u> *(of light)*

**beans** PL NOUN
las <u>alubias</u>

■ **beans on toast** las alubias blancas en salsa de tomate sobre una tostada

**bear** NOUN
▷ *see also* **bear** VERB
el <u>oso</u>

to **bear** VERB
▷ *see also* **bear** NOUN
<u>aguantar</u>

▫ I can't bear it! ¡No lo aguanto!

**beard** NOUN
la <u>barba</u>

▫ a man with a beard un hombre con barba
■ **He's got a beard.** Lleva barba.

**bearded** ADJECTIVE
con <u>barba</u> (FEM con barba)

**beat** NOUN
▷ *see also* **beat** VERB
el <u>ritmo</u>

to **beat** VERB
▷ *see also* **beat** NOUN
<u>ganar</u>

▫ We beat them three-nil. Les ganamos tres a cero.

■ **Beat it!** ¡Lárgate! *(informal)*

**beautiful** ADJECTIVE
<u>precioso</u> (FEM preciosa)

**beauty** NOUN
la <u>belleza</u>

**beauty spot** NOUN
el <u>lugar pintoresco</u> *(place)*

**became** VERB ▷ *see* **become**

**because** CONJUNCTION
<u>porque</u>

■ **because of** a causa de ▫ because of the weather por culpa del mal tiempo

to **become** VERB
<u>llegar</u>* a ser

**bed** NOUN
la <u>cama</u>

■ **to go to bed** acostarse
■ **to go to bed with somebody** irse a la cama con alguien

**bed and breakfast** NOUN
la <u>pensión</u> (PL las pensiones)

▫ We stayed in a bed and breakfast. Nos quedamos en una pensión.

■ **How much is it for bed and breakfast?** ¿Cuánto es la habitación con desayuno?

**bedclothes** PL NOUN
la <u>ropa de cama</u>

**bedding** NOUN
la <u>ropa de cama</u>

**bedroom** NOUN
el <u>dormitorio</u>

■ **a three-bedroom house** una casa de tres dormitorios

**bedsit** NOUN
el <u>cuarto de alquiler</u>

**bedspread** NOUN
la <u>colcha</u>

**bedtime** NOUN
■ **Ten o'clock is my usual bedtime.** Normalmente me voy a la cama a las diez.
■ **Bedtime!** ¡A la cama!

**bee** NOUN
la <u>abeja</u>

**beef** NOUN
la <u>carne de vaca</u>

■ **roast beef** el rosbif

**beefburger** NOUN
la <u>hamburguesa</u>

**been** VERB ▷ *see* **be**

**beer** NOUN
la <u>cerveza</u>

**beetle** NOUN
el <u>escarabajo</u>

**beetroot** NOUN
la remolacha

**before** PREPOSITION, CONJUNCTION, ADVERB
1 antes de
□ before Tuesday antes del martes □ Before opening the packet, read the instructions. Antes de abrir el paquete, lea las instrucciones. □ I'll phone before I leave. Llamaré antes de salir.
2 antes de que

⚬ **LANGUAGE TIP** antes de que has to be followed by a verb in the subjunctive.
□ I'll call her before she leaves. La llamaré antes de que se vaya.
■ **I've seen this film before.** Esta película ya la he visto.
■ **the week before** la semana anterior

**beforehand** ADVERB
con antelación

to **beg** VERB
1 mendigar* *(for money, food)*
2 suplicar*

⚬ **LANGUAGE TIP** suplicar que has to be followed by a verb in the subjunctive.
□ He begged me to stop. Me suplicó que parara.

**began** VERB ▷see **begin**

**beggar** NOUN
el mendigo
la mendiga

to **begin** VERB
empezar*
■ **to begin doing something** empezar a hacer algo

**beginner** NOUN
el/la principiante

**beginning** NOUN
el comienzo
■ **in the beginning** al principio

**begun** VERB ▷see **begin**

**behalf** NOUN
■ **on behalf of somebody** de parte de alguien

to **behave** VERB
comportarse
□ He behaved like an idiot. Se comportó como un idiota.
■ **to behave oneself** portarse bien □ Did the children behave themselves? ¿Se portaron bien los niños?
■ **Behave!** ¡Compórtate!

**behaviour** (US **behavior**) NOUN
el comportamiento

**behind** PREPOSITION, ADVERB
▷see also **behind** NOUN
detrás de
□ behind the television detrás de la televisión

■ **to be behind** *(late)* ir atrasado □ I'm behind with my work. Voy atrasado con mi trabajo.

**behind** NOUN
▷see also **behind** PREPOSITION, ADVERB
el trasero

**beige** ADJECTIVE
beige (FEM + PL beige)

⚬ **LANGUAGE TIP** Pronounce this word like the English word 'base'.

**Belgian** ADJECTIVE
▷see also **Belgian** NOUN
belga (FEM belga)
□ He's Belgian. Es belga.

**Belgian** NOUN
▷see also **Belgian** ADJECTIVE
el/la belga
□ the Belgians los belgas

**Belgium** NOUN
Bélgica *fem*

to **believe** VERB
creer*
□ I don't believe you. No te creo.
■ **I don't believe it!** ¡No me lo creo!
■ **to believe in something** creer en algo
□ Do you believe in ghosts? ¿Crees en los fantasmas?

**bell** NOUN
1 el timbre *(of door, in school)*
□ The bell goes at half past three. El timbre suena a las tres y media.
2 la campana *(of church)*
□ the church bell la campana de la iglesia
3 el cascabel *(of toy, on animal)*
□ Our cat has a bell on its collar. Nuestro gato lleva un cascabel en el collar.

**belly** NOUN
la barriga

to **belong** VERB
■ **to belong to somebody** pertenecer a alguien □ This ring belonged to my grandmother. Este anillo pertenecía a mi abuela.
■ **Who does it belong to?** ¿De quién es?
■ **That belongs to me.** Eso es mío.
■ **Do you belong to any clubs?** ¿Eres miembro de algún club?
■ **Where does this belong?** ¿Dónde va esto?

**belongings** PL NOUN
■ **I collected my belongings.** Recogí mis cosas.
■ **personal belongings** los efectos personales

**below** PREPOSITION, ADVERB
1 debajo de
□ the apartment directly below ours el apartamento que está justo debajo del nuestro

**2** abajo

□ seen from below visto desde abajo □ on the floor below en el piso de abajo

■ **ten degrees below freezing** diez grados bajo cero

**belt** NOUN
el cinturón (PL los cinturones)

**beltway** NOUN (US)
la carretera de circunvalación

**bench** NOUN
el banco

**bend** NOUN
▷ see also **bend** VERB
la curva

to **bend** VERB
▷ see also **bend** NOUN
**1** doblar
□ I can't bend my arm. No puedo doblar el brazo.
**2** torcerse*
□ It bends easily. Se tuerce fácilmente.

to **bend down** VERB
agacharse

to **bend over** VERB
inclinarse

**beneath** PREPOSITION
bajo

**benefit** NOUN
▷ see also **benefit** VERB
el beneficio

■ **state benefits** los subsidios estatales

to **benefit** VERB
▷ see also **benefit** NOUN
beneficiar
□ This will benefit us all. Esto nos beneficiará a todos.

■ **He'll benefit from the change.** Se beneficiará con el cambio.

**bent** VERB ▷ see **bend**

**bent** ADJECTIVE
torcido (FEM torcida)
□ a bent fork un tenedor torcido

■ **to be bent on doing something** estar empeñado en hacer algo

**beret** NOUN
la boina

**berserk** ADJECTIVE

■ **to go berserk** ponerse hecho una fiera

**berth** NOUN
la litera (bunk)

**beside** PREPOSITION
al lado de
□ beside the television al lado de la televisión

■ **He was beside himself.** Estaba fuera de sí.

■ **That's beside the point.** Eso no viene al caso.

**besides** ADVERB
además
□ Besides, it's too expensive. Además, es demasiado caro.

■ **... and much more besides.** ... y mucho más todavía.

**best** ADJECTIVE, ADVERB
mejor (FEM mejora)
□ He's the best player in the team. Es el mejor jugador del equipo. □ Janet's the best at maths. Janet es la mejor en matemáticas. □ Emma sings best. Emma es la que canta mejor.

■ **That's the best I can do.** No puedo hacer más.

■ **to do one's best** hacer todo lo posible
□ It's not perfect, but I did my best. No es perfecto, pero he hecho todo lo posible.

■ **You'll just have to make the best of it.** Tendrás que arreglártelas con lo que hay.

**best man** NOUN
el padrino de boda

**bet** NOUN
▷ see also **bet** VERB
la apuesta

to **bet** VERB
▷ see also **bet** NOUN
apostar*
□ I bet you he won't come. Te apuesto a que no viene.

to **betray** VERB
traicionar

**better** ADJECTIVE, ADVERB
mejor (FEM mejora)
□ This one's better than that one. Éste es mejor que aquél. □ Are you feeling better now? ¿Te sientes mejor ahora?

■ **That's better!** ¡Así está mejor!

■ **better still** mejor todavía

■ **to get better 1** (improve) mejorar □ I hope the weather gets better soon. Espero que el tiempo mejore pronto. **2** (from illness) mejorarse □ I hope you get better soon. Espero que te mejores pronto.

■ **You'd better do it straight away.** Más vale hacerlo enseguida.

■ **I'd better go home.** Tengo que irme a casa.

**betting shop** NOUN
la casa de apuestas

**between** PREPOSITION
entre
□ between 15 and 20 minutes entre 15 y 20 minutos

**bewildered** ADJECTIVE
desconcertado (FEM desconcertada)

**beyond** PREPOSITION, ADVERB
al otro lado de

23

**b**

□ There is a lake beyond the mountains. Hay un lago al otro lado de las montañas.

■ **We have no plans beyond the year 2009.** No tenemos planes para después del año 2009.

■ **the wheat fields and the mountains beyond** los campos de trigo y las montañas al fondo

■ **It's beyond me.** No lo entiendo.

■ **beyond belief** increíble

■ **beyond repair** irreparable

**biased** ADJECTIVE
parcial (FEM parcial)

**Bible** NOUN
la Biblia

**bicycle** NOUN
la bicicleta

**bifocals** PL NOUN
las gafas bifocales

**big** ADJECTIVE
grande (FEM grande)

□ a big house una casa grande □ a big car un coche grande

> LANGUAGE TIP Use **gran** before a singular noun.

□ It's a big business. Es un gran negocio.

**WORD POWER**
You can use a number of other words instead of **big** to mean 'large':
**enormous** enorme
□ an enormous cake un pastel enorme
**gigantic** gigantesco
□ a gigantic house una casa gigantesca
**huge** enorme
□ a huge garden un jardín enorme
**immense** inmenso
□ an immense room una habitación inmensa

■ **my big brother** mi hermano mayor

■ **He's a big guy.** Es un tipo grandote.

■ **Big deal!** ¡Vaya cosa!

**bigheaded** ADJECTIVE

■ **to be bigheaded** ser engreído

**bike** NOUN
1 la bici (bicycle)
□ by bike en bici
2 la moto (motorbike)

> LANGUAGE TIP Although **moto** ends in -o, it is actually a feminine noun.

**bikini** NOUN
el bikini

**bilingual** ADJECTIVE
bilingüe (FEM bilingüe)

**bill** NOUN
1 la cuenta (in restaurant)
□ Can we have the bill, please? ¿Nos trae la cuenta, por favor?

2 la factura (for gas, electricity, telephone)
□ the gas bill la factura del gas
3 el billete (US)
□ a five-dollar bill un billete de cinco dólares

**billiards** NOUN
el billar
□ to play billiards jugar al billar

**billion** NOUN
los mil millones
□ two billion dollars dos mil millones de dólares

**bin** NOUN
1 el cubo de la basura (in kitchen)
2 la papelera (for paper)

**bingo** NOUN
el bingo

**binoculars** PL NOUN
los prismáticos
□ a pair of binoculars unos prismáticos

**biochemistry** NOUN
la bioquímica

**biography** NOUN
la biografía

**biology** NOUN
la biología

**bird** NOUN
el pájaro

**birdwatching** NOUN

■ **He likes to go birdwatching on Sundays.** Los domingos le gusta ir a ver pájaros.

**Biro®** NOUN
el bolígrafo

**birth** NOUN
el nacimiento
□ date of birth la fecha de nacimiento

**birth certificate** NOUN
la partida de nacimiento

**birth control** NOUN
el control de natalidad

**birthday** NOUN
el cumpleaños (PL los cumpleaños)
□ a birthday cake un pastel de cumpleaños
□ a birthday card una tarjeta de cumpleaños
□ a birthday party una fiesta de cumpleaños
□ When's your birthday? ¿Cuándo es tu cumpleaños?

**biscuit** NOUN
la galleta

**bishop** NOUN
el obispo

**bit** VERB ▷ see bite

**bit** NOUN
el trozo
□ Would you like another bit? ¿Quieres otro trozo?

■ **a bit** un poco □ He's a bit mad. Está un poco loco. □ Wait a bit! ¡Espera un poco!

■ **a bit of 1** un trozo de □ a bit of cake un trozo de pastel **2** un poco de □ a bit of music un poco de música

■ **It's a bit of a nuisance.** Es un poco fastidioso.

■ **to fall to bits** caerse a pedazos

■ **to take something to bits** desmontar algo

■ **bit by bit** poco a poco

**bitch** NOUN
1 la perra (female dog)
2 la bruja (rude: woman)

to **bite** VERB
▷ see also **bite** NOUN
1 morder* (person, dog)
□ My dog's never bitten anyone. Mi perro nunca ha mordido a nadie.
2 picar* (insect)
□ I got bitten by mosquitoes. Me picaron los mosquitos.

■ **to bite one's nails** morderse las uñas

**bite** NOUN
▷ see also **bite** VERB
1 la picadura (insect bite)
2 el mordisco (animal bite)

■ **to have a bite to eat** comer alguna cosa

**bitter** ADJECTIVE
1 amargo (FEM amarga)
□ It tastes bitter. Sabe amargo.
2 glacial (FEM glacial)
□ It's bitter today. Hoy hace un frío glacial.

**black** ADJECTIVE
negro (FEM negra)
□ a black jacket una chaqueta negra
□ She's black. Es negra.

■ **black and white** blanco y negro

**blackberry** NOUN
la mora

**blackbird** NOUN
el mirlo

**blackboard** NOUN
la pizarra

**black coffee** NOUN
el café solo

**blackcurrant** NOUN
la grosella negra

**blackmail** NOUN
▷ see also **blackmail** VERB
el chantaje

to **blackmail** VERB
▷ see also **blackmail** NOUN
chantajear

**blackout** NOUN
el apagón (PL los apagones) (power cut)

■ **to have a blackout** (faint) sufrir un desvanecimiento

**black pudding** NOUN
la morcilla

**blade** NOUN
la hoja

to **blame** VERB
echar la culpa a
□ Don't blame me! ¡No me eches la culpa a mí! □ He blamed it on my sister. Le echó la culpa a mi hermana.

**blank** ADJECTIVE
▷ see also **blank** NOUN
en blanco (sheet of paper)

■ **My mind went blank.** Me quedé en blanco.

**blank cheque** NOUN
el cheque en blanco

**blanket** NOUN
la manta

**blast** NOUN
■ **a bomb blast** una explosión

**blatant** ADJECTIVE
flagrante (FEM flagrante)

**blaze** NOUN
el incendio

**blazer** NOUN
el blazer (PL los blazers)

**bleach** NOUN
la lejía

**bleak** ADJECTIVE
poco prometedor (FEM poco prometedora)
□ The future looks bleak. Se presenta un futuro poco prometedor.

to **bleed** VERB
sangrar

■ **to bleed to death** morir desangrado

■ **My nose is bleeding.** Me sangra la nariz.

**bleeper** NOUN
el busca

⦂ **LANGUAGE TIP** Although **busca** ends in -**a**, it is actually a masculine noun.

**blender** NOUN
la licuadora

to **bless** VERB
bendecir*

■ **Bless you!** (after sneezing) ¡Jesús! (¡Salud! Latin America)

**blew** VERB ▷ see **blow**

**blind** ADJECTIVE
▷ see also **blind** NOUN
ciego (FEM ciega)

**blind** NOUN
▷ see also **blind** ADJECTIVE
la persiana (for window)

**blindfold** NOUN
▷ see also **blindfold** VERB
la venda

to **blindfold** VERB
▷ see also **blindfold** NOUN
■ **to blindfold somebody** vendar los ojos a alguien

**b**

to **blink** VERB
parpadear

**bliss** NOUN
■ **It was bliss!** ¡Era la gloria!

**blister** NOUN
la ampolla

**blizzard** NOUN
la ventisca de nieve

**blob** NOUN
la gota
□ a blob of glue una gota de pegamento

**block** NOUN
▷ see also **block** VERB
el bloque
□ He lives in our block. Vive en nuestro bloque. □ a block of flats un bloque de apartamentos

to **block** VERB
▷ see also **block** NOUN
bloquear

**blockage** NOUN
la obstrucción (PL las obstrucciones)

**bloke** NOUN
el tío (informal)

**blonde** ADJECTIVE
rubio (FEM rubia)
□ She's got blonde hair. Tiene el pelo rubio.

**blood** NOUN
la sangre

**blood pressure** NOUN
la presión sanguínea
■ **to have high blood pressure** tener la tensión alta

**blood sports** PL NOUN
los deportes sangrientos

**blood test** NOUN
el análisis de sangre (PL los análisis de sangre)

**bloody** ADJECTIVE
■ **that bloody television** esa maldita televisión
■ **Bloody hell!** ¡Me cago en la mar!
■ **The exam was bloody difficult.** El examen fue difícil con ganas.

**blouse** NOUN
la blusa

**blow** NOUN
▷ see also **blow** VERB
el golpe

to **blow** VERB
▷ see also **blow** NOUN
soplar
□ A cold wind was blowing. Soplaba un viento frío. □ He blew on his fingers. Se sopló los dedos.
■ **They were one-all when the whistle blew.** Iban uno a uno cuando sonó el pito.
■ **to blow one's nose** sonarse la nariz

to **blow up** VERB
1 volar*
□ They blew up a plane. Volaron un avión.
2 inflar
□ We've blown up the balloons. Hemos inflado los globos.
3 saltar por los aires
□ The house blew up. La casa saltó por los aires.

**blow-dry** NOUN
el secado con secador de mano
■ **A cut and blow-dry, please.** Un corte y un secado a mano, por favor.

**blue** ADJECTIVE
azul (FEM azul)
□ a blue dress un vestido azul
■ **a blue movie** una película porno
■ **out of the blue** en el momento menos pensado

**blues** PL NOUN
el blues (PL los blues) (music)

to **bluff** VERB
▷ see also **bluff** NOUN
farolear

**bluff** NOUN
▷ see also **bluff** VERB
el farol

**blunder** NOUN
la metedura de pata

**blunt** ADJECTIVE
1 directo (FEM directa) (person)
2 desafilado (FEM desafilada) (knife)

to **blush** VERB
ruborizarse*

**board** NOUN
1 la tabla (plank)
2 la pizarra (blackboard)
3 el tablón de anuncios (PL los tablones de anuncios) (noticeboard)
4 el trampolín (PL los trampolines) (for diving)
5 el tablero (for games)
■ **on board** a bordo
■ **'full board'** 'pensión completa'

**boarder** NOUN
el interno
la interna

**board game** NOUN
el juego de mesa

**boarding card** NOUN
la tarjeta de embarque

**boarding school** NOUN
el internado

to **boast** VERB
alardear
□ to boast about something alardear de algo
■ **Stop boasting!** ¡Deja ya de presumir!

**boat** NOUN
el barco

**body** NOUN
1 el cuerpo
   □ the human body el cuerpo humano
2 el cadáver (*corpse*)
**bodybuilding** NOUN
   el culturismo
**bodyguard** NOUN
   el guardaespaldas (PL los guardaespaldas)
   □ He's a bodyguard. Es guardaespaldas.
**bog** NOUN
   la ciénaga (*marsh*)
**boil** NOUN
   ▷ *see also* **boil** VERB
   el furúnculo
to **boil** VERB
   ▷ *see also* **boil** NOUN
   hervir*
   □ to boil some water hervir un poco de agua
   □ The water's boiling. El agua está hirviendo.
   ■ **to boil an egg** cocer un huevo
to **boil over** VERB
   salirse*
**boiled** ADJECTIVE
   hervido (FEM hervida)
   ■ **a boiled egg** un huevo pasado por agua
**boiling** ADJECTIVE
   ■ **It's boiling in here!** ¡Aquí dentro se asa uno!
   ■ **a boiling hot day** un día asfixiante de calor
**bolt** NOUN
1 el cerrojo (*on door, window*)
2 el tornillo (*type of screw*)
**bomb** NOUN
   ▷ *see also* **bomb** VERB
   la bomba
to **bomb** VERB
   ▷ *see also* **bomb** NOUN
   bombardear
**bomber** NOUN
   el bombardero (*plane*)
**bombing** NOUN
   el bombardeo
**bond** NOUN
   el vínculo
   □ the bond between mother and child el vínculo entre la madre y el hijo
**bone** NOUN
1 el hueso (*of human, animal*)
2 la espina (*of fish*)
**bone dry** ADJECTIVE
   completamente seco (FEM completamente seca)
**bonfire** NOUN
   la hoguera
**bonnet** NOUN
   el capó (*of car*)
**bonus** NOUN

1 el plus (*extra payment*)
2 la ventaja (*added advantage*)
**book** NOUN
   ▷ *see also* **book** VERB
   el libro
to **book** VERB
   ▷ *see also* **book** NOUN
   reservar
   ■ **We haven't booked.** No hemos hecho reserva.
**bookcase** NOUN
   la librería
**booklet** NOUN
   el folleto
**bookmark** NOUN
   el marcador (*book, computer*)
**bookshelf** NOUN
   la estantería
**bookshop** NOUN
   la librería
to **boost** VERB
   ■ **The win boosted the team's morale.** La victoria levantó la moral del equipo.
   ■ **They're trying to boost the economy.** Intentan dar un empuje a la economía.
**boot** NOUN
1 el maletero (*of car*)
2 la bota (*fashion boots*)
3 el borceguí (PL los borceguíes) (*for hiking*)
**booze** NOUN
   la bebida
**border** NOUN
   la frontera
**bore** VERB ▷ *see* **bear**
**bored** ADJECTIVE
   aburrido (FEM aburrida)
   □ to be bored estar aburrido
   ■ **to get bored** aburrirse
**boredom** NOUN
   el aburrimiento
**boring** ADJECTIVE
   aburrido (FEM aburrida)
   □ It's boring. Es aburrido.
**born** ADJECTIVE
   ■ **to be born** nacer □ I was born in 1992. Nací en 1992.
to **borrow** VERB
   pedir* prestado
   ■ **to borrow something from somebody** pedir algo prestado a alguien □ I borrowed some money from a friend. Le pedí dinero prestado a un amigo.
   ■ **Can I borrow your pen?** ¿Me prestas el bolígrafo?
**Bosnia** NOUN
   la Bosnia
**Bosnian** ADJECTIVE
   bosnio (FEM bosnia)

**boss** NOUN
el jefe
la jefa

to **boss around** VERB
■ **to boss somebody around** mandonear a
alguien

**bossy** ADJECTIVE
mandón (FEM mandona, PL mandones)

**both** ADJECTIVE, PRONOUN, ADVERB
los dos (FEM los dosa)
□ We both went. Fuimos los dos. □ Both of
your answers are wrong. Tus respuestas
están las dos mal. □ Both of them play the
piano. Los dos tocan el piano.
■ **Both Emma and Jane went.** Fueron
Emma y Jane.
■ **He has houses in both France and in
Spain.** Tiene casas tanto en Francia como
en España.

to **bother** VERB
▷ *see also* **bother** NOUN
1 preocupar (*worry*)
□ What's bothering you? ¿Qué es lo que te
preocupa?
2 molestar (*disturb*)
□ I'm sorry to bother you. Siento molestarle.
■ **Don't bother!** ¡No te preocupes!
■ **to bother to do something** tomarse la
molestia de hacer algo □ He didn't bother to
tell me about it. Ni se tomó la molestia de
decírmelo.

**bottle** NOUN
la botella

**bottle bank** NOUN
el contenedor del vidrio

**bottle-opener** NOUN
el abrebotellas (PL los abrebotellas)

**bottom** NOUN
▷ *see also* **bottom** ADJECTIVE
1 el fondo (*of container, bag, sea*)
■ **at the bottom of the page** al final de la
página
■ **He was always bottom of the class.**
Siempre era el último de la clase.
2 el trasero (*buttocks*)

**bottom** ADJECTIVE
▷ *see also* **bottom** NOUN
de abajo
□ the bottom shelf el estante de abajo

**bought** VERB ▷ *see* **buy**

to **bounce** VERB
rebotar

**bouncer** NOUN
el gorila
LANGUAGE TIP Although **gorila** ends in
-a, it is actually a masculine noun.

**bound** ADJECTIVE
■ **He's bound to fail.** Seguro que suspende.

■ **She's bound to come.** Es seguro que
vendrá.

**boundary** NOUN
el límite

**bow** NOUN
▷ *see also* **bow** VERB
1 el lazo (*knot*)
□ to tie a bow hacer un lazo
2 el arco
□ a bow and arrow un arco y flecha

to **bow** VERB
▷ *see also* **bow** NOUN
hacer* una reverencia

**bowels** PL NOUN
los intestinos

**bowl** NOUN
▷ *see also* **bowl** VERB
1 el tazón (PL los tazones) (*for soup, cereals*)
2 el cuenco (*for cooking, mixing food*)

to **bowl** VERB
▷ *see also* **bowl** NOUN
lanzar* la pelota

**bowler** NOUN
el lanzador
la lanzadora

**bowling** NOUN
los bolos
■ **to go bowling** jugar a los bolos
■ **a bowling alley** una bolera

**bowls** PL NOUN
los bolos

**bow tie** NOUN
la pajarita

**box** NOUN
1 la caja
□ a box of matches una caja de cerillas
■ **a cardboard box** una caja de cartón
2 la casilla (*on form*)

**boxer** NOUN
el boxeador

**boxer shorts** PL NOUN
los bóxers
□ a pair of boxer shorts unos bóxers

**boxing** NOUN
el boxeo

**Boxing Day** NOUN
el 26 de diciembre

**boy** NOUN
1 el muchacho (*young man*)
□ a boy of fifteen un muchacho de quince
años
2 el niño (*child*)
□ a boy of seven un niño de siete años
■ **She has two boys and a girl.** Tiene dos
niños y una niña.
■ **a baby boy** un niño

**boyfriend** NOUN
el novio

□ Have you got a boyfriend? ¿Tienes novio?

**bra** NOUN
el sostén (PL los sostenes)

**brace** NOUN
el aparato (on teeth)
□ Richard wears a brace. Richard lleva un aparato.

**bracelet** NOUN
la pulsera

**brackets** PL NOUN
■ in brackets entre paréntesis

**brain** NOUN
el cerebro

**brainy** ADJECTIVE
inteligente (FEM inteligente)

**brake** NOUN
▷ see also **brake** VERB
el freno

to **brake** VERB
▷ see also **brake** NOUN
frenar

**branch** NOUN
1 la rama (of tree)
2 la sucursal (of bank)

**brand** NOUN
la marca
□ a well-known brand of coffee una marca de café muy conocida

**brand name** NOUN
la marca

**brand-new** ADJECTIVE
flamante (FEM flamante)

**brandy** NOUN
el coñac (PL los coñacs)

**brass** NOUN
el latón (metal)
■ the brass section los bronces

**brass band** NOUN
la banda de música

**brat** NOUN
el mocoso
la mocosa
□ He's a spoiled brat. Es un mocoso consentido.

**brave** ADJECTIVE
valiente (FEM valiente)

**Brazil** NOUN
el Brasil

**bread** NOUN
el pan
□ bread and butter el pan con mantequilla

**break** NOUN
▷ see also **break** VERB
1 la pausa (rest)
□ to take a break hacer una pausa
2 el recreo (at school)
■ the Christmas break las vacaciones de Navidad

■ Give me a break! ¡Déjame en paz!

to **break** VERB
▷ see also **break** NOUN
1 romper*
□ Careful, you'll break something! ¡Cuidado, que vas a romper algo!
■ I broke my leg. Me rompí la pierna.
2 romperse*
□ Careful, it'll break! ¡Ten cuidado, que se va a romper!
■ to break a promise faltar a una promesa
■ to break a record batir un récord

to **break down** VERB
averiarse*
■ The car broke down. El coche se averió.

to **break in** VERB
■ The thief had broken in through a window. El ladrón había entrado por una ventana.

to **break off** VERB
desprenderse (come free)

to **break out** VERB
1 estallar (war)
2 desencadenarse (fire, fighting)
3 escaparse (prisoner)
■ He broke out in a rash. Le salió un sarpullido.

to **break up** VERB
1 disolver*
□ Police broke up the demonstration. La policía disolvió la demostración.
2 dispersarse (crowd)
3 fracasar (marriage)
□ More and more marriages break up. Cada día fracasan más matrimonios.
4 romper* (two lovers)
□ Richard and Marie have broken up. Richard y Marie han roto.
■ to break up a fight poner fin a una pelea
■ We break up next Wednesday. El miércoles que viene empezamos las vacaciones.
■ You're breaking up. (mobile phone) No hay cobertura.

**breakdown** NOUN
1 la crisis nerviosa (PL las crisis nerviosas)
□ He had a breakdown because of the stress. Sufrió una crisis nerviosa debida al estrés.
2 la avería (in vehicle)
□ to have a breakdown tener una avería

**breakdown van** NOUN
la grúa

**breakfast** NOUN
el desayuno
■ to have breakfast desayunar

**break-in** NOUN
■ There have been a lot of break-ins in

**b**

**my area.** Han entrado a robar en muchas casas de mi barrio.

**breast** NOUN
el pecho
■ **chicken breast** la pechuga de pollo

to **breast-feed** VERB
amamantar

**breaststroke** NOUN
la braza

**breath** NOUN
el aliento
□ He's got bad breath. Tiene mal aliento.
■ **I'm out of breath.** Estoy sin aliento.
■ **to get one's breath back** recobrar el aliento

to **breathe** VERB
respirar

to **breathe in** VERB
aspirar

to **breathe out** VERB
espirar

to **breed** VERB
▷ see also **breed** NOUN
reproducirse* (reproduce)
■ **to breed dogs** criar perros

**breed** NOUN
▷ see also **breed** VERB
la raza

**breeze** NOUN
la brisa

**brewery** NOUN
la fábrica de cerveza

to **bribe** VERB
▷ see also **bribe** NOUN
sobornar

**brick** NOUN
el ladrillo

**bricklayer** NOUN
el albañil
□ He's a bricklayer. Es albañil.

**bride** NOUN
la novia

**bridegroom** NOUN
el novio

**bridesmaid** NOUN
la dama de honor

**bridge** NOUN
1 el puente
2 el bridge (card game)
□ to play bridge jugar al bridge

**brief** ADJECTIVE
breve (FEM breve)

**briefcase** NOUN
el maletín (PL los maletines)

**briefly** ADVERB
brevemente

**briefs** PL NOUN
los calzoncillos

□ a pair of briefs unos calzoncillos

**bright** ADJECTIVE
1 vivo (FEM viva)
□ a bright colour un color vivo □ bright red rojo vivo
2 brillante (FEM brillante) (light)
3 listo (FEM lista)
□ He's not very bright. No es muy listo.

**brilliant** ADJECTIVE
1 estupendo (FEM estupenda)
■ **We had a brilliant time!** ¡Lo pasamos estupendo!
2 genial (FEM genial)
□ a brilliant scientist un científico genial

to **bring** VERB
traer*
□ Bring warm clothes. Trae ropa de abrigo.
□ Can I bring a friend? ¿Puedo traer a un amigo?

to **bring back** VERB
devolver* (book)
■ **That song brings back memories.** Esa canción me trae recuerdos.

to **bring forward** VERB
adelantar
□ The meeting was brought forward. La reunión se adelantó.

to **bring up** VERB
criar*
□ She brought up five children on her own. Crió a cinco hijos ella sola.

**Britain** NOUN
la Gran Bretaña

**British** ADJECTIVE
británico (FEM británica)
■ **the British** los británicos
■ **the British Isles** las Islas Británicas
■ **She's British.** Es británica.

**broad** ADJECTIVE
ancho (FEM ancha)
■ **in broad daylight** a plena luz del día

**broadband** NOUN
la banda ancha

**broadcast** NOUN
▷ see also **broadcast** VERB
la emisión (PL las emisiones)

to **broadcast** VERB
▷ see also **broadcast** NOUN
emitir
□ The interview was broadcast all over the world. La entrevista se emitió a todo el mundo.
■ **to broadcast live** emitir en directo

**broad-minded** ADJECTIVE
■ **He's very broad-minded.** Tiene una mentalidad muy abierta.

**broccoli** NOUN
el brécol

**brochure** NOUN
el folleto

to **broil** VERB (US)
1 hacer* al grill (in cooker)
2 asar a la parrilla (barbecue)

**broke** VERB ▷ see **break**

**broke** ADJECTIVE
■ **to be broke** estar sin blanca (informal)

**broken** ADJECTIVE
roto (FEM rota)
□ It's broken. Está roto. □ He's got a broken arm. Tiene un brazo roto.

**bronchitis** NOUN
la bronquitis

**bronze** NOUN
el bronce
□ the bronze medal la medalla de bronce

**brooch** NOUN
el broche

**broom** NOUN
la escoba

**brother** NOUN
el hermano

**brother-in-law** NOUN
el cuñado

**brought** VERB ▷ see **bring**

**brown** ADJECTIVE
1 marrón (FEM marrón, PL marrones) (clothes)
2 castaño (FEM castaña) (hair, eyes)
3 moreno (FEM morena) (tanned)
■ **brown bread** el pan integral

**Brownie** NOUN
la guía

to **browse** VERB
navegar (on internet)

**browser** NOUN
el navegador

**bruise** NOUN
el moretón (PL los moretones)

**brush** NOUN
▷ see also **brush** VERB
1 el cepillo (for hair, teeth)
2 el pincel (paintbrush)

to **brush** VERB
▷ see also **brush** NOUN
cepillar
■ **to brush one's hair** cepillarse el pelo
■ **to brush one's teeth** cepillarse los dientes □ I brush my teeth every night. Me cepillo los dientes todas las noches.

**Brussels** NOUN
la Bruselas

**Brussels sprouts** PL NOUN
las coles de Bruselas

**brutal** ADJECTIVE
brutal (FEM brutal)

**BSc** ABBREVIATION (= Bachelor of Science)
la licenciatura en Ciencias

■ **a BSc in Mathematics** una licenciatura en Matemáticas
■ **She's got a BSc in Chemistry.** Es licenciada en Química.

**bubble** NOUN
1 la pompa (of soap)
2 la burbuja (of air, gas)

**bubble bath** NOUN
el baño de espuma

**bubble gum** NOUN
el chicle

**bucket** NOUN
el cubo

**buckle** NOUN
la hebilla (on belt, watch, shoe)

**Buddhism** NOUN
el budismo

**Buddhist** ADJECTIVE
budista (FEM budista)

**buddy** NOUN (US)
el amiguete
la amigueta

**budget** NOUN
▷ see also **budget** VERB
el presupuesto

**budgie** NOUN
el periquito

**buffet** NOUN
el buffet

**buffet car** NOUN
el coche restaurante

**bug** NOUN
1 el insecto (insect)
2 el virus (PL los virus) (illness, in computer)
□ There's a bug going round. Hay un virus en el ambiente.
■ **a stomach bug** una gastroenteritis

**bugged** ADJECTIVE
■ **The phone was bugged.** El teléfono estaba pinchado.

to **build** VERB
construir*
□ They're going to build houses here. Van a construir viviendas aquí.

to **build up** VERB
1 acumular
□ He has built up a huge collection of stamps. Ha ido acumulando una gran colección de sellos.
2 acumularse
□ Our debts are building up. Nuestras deudas se están acumulando.

**builder** NOUN
1 el/la contratista (contractor)
2 el albañil (worker)

**building** NOUN
el edificio

**built** VERB ▷ see **build**

**bulb** NOUN
1 la bombilla *(electric)*
2 el bulbo *(of flower)*

**bull** NOUN
el toro

**bullet** NOUN
la bala

**bulletin board** NOUN
el tablón de noticias

**bullfighting** NOUN
■ **Do you like bullfighting?** ¿Te gustan los toros?

**bully** NOUN
▷ *see also* **bully** VERB
el matón (PL los matones)
□ He's a bully. Es un matón.

to **bully** VERB
▷ *see also* **bully** NOUN
intimidar

**bum** NOUN
el culo *(informal)*

**bum bag** NOUN
la riñonera

**bump** NOUN
▷ *see also* **bump** VERB
1 el chichón (PL los chichones) *(on head)*
2 el bulto *(on surface)*
3 el bache *(on road)*
4 el golpe *(minor accident)*
□ We had a bump. Nos dimos un golpe.

to **bump** VERB
▷ *see also* **bump** NOUN
□ I bumped my head on the wall. Me di con la cabeza en la pared.

**bumper** NOUN
el parachoques (PL los parachoques)

**bumpy** ADJECTIVE
lleno de baches (FEM llena de baches) *(road)*

**bun** NOUN
el bollo *(bread)*

**bunch** NOUN
■ **a bunch of flowers** un ramo de flores
■ **a bunch of grapes** un racimo de uvas
■ **a bunch of keys** un manojo de llaves

**bunches** PL NOUN
las coletas
□ She has her hair in bunches. Lleva coletas.

**bungalow** NOUN
el bungalow

**bunk** NOUN
la litera

**burger** NOUN
la hamburguesa

**burglar** NOUN
el ladrón (PL los ladrones)
la ladrona

to **burglarize** VERB (US)
entrar a robar en

**burglary** NOUN
el robo *(con allanamiento de morada)*

to **burgle** VERB
entrar a robar en
□ Her house was burgled. Le entraron a robar en casa.

**burn** NOUN
▷ *see also* **burn** VERB
la quemadura

to **burn** VERB
▷ *see also* **burn** NOUN
quemar *(rubbish, documents)*
□ I burned the rubbish. Quemé la basura.
■ I burned the cake. Se me quemó el pastel.
■ **to burn oneself** quemarse
■ I've burned my hand. Me quemé la mano.

to **burn down** VERB
quedar reducido a cenizas
□ The factory burned down. La fábrica quedó reducida a cenizas.

to **burst** VERB
reventarse*
□ The balloon burst. El globo se reventó.
■ **to burst a balloon** reventar un globo
■ **to burst out laughing** echarse a reír
■ **to burst into tears** romper a llorar
■ **to burst into flames** incendiarse

to **bury** VERB
enterrar*

**bus** NOUN
el autobús (PL los autobuses)
□ by bus en autobús
■ **the school bus** el autocar escolar
■ **a bus ticket** un billete de autobús

**bush** NOUN
el arbusto

**business** NOUN
1 el negocio *(firm)*
□ He's got his own business. Tiene su propio negocio.
2 los negocios
□ He's away on business. Está en un viaje de negocios.
■ **a business trip** un viaje de negocios
■ **It's none of my business.** No es asunto mío.

**businessman** NOUN
el hombre de negocios

**businesswoman** NOUN
la mujer de negocios

**busker** NOUN
el músico callejero
la música callejera

**bust** NOUN
el busto

**busy** ADJECTIVE

**1** <u>ocupado</u> (FEM ocupada) *(person, telephone line)*

□ She's a very busy woman.  Es una mujer muy ocupada.

**2** <u>ajetreado</u> (FEM ajetreada) *(day, week)*

□ It's been a very busy day.  Ha sido un día muy ajetreado.

**3** <u>concurrido</u> (FEM concurrida) *(street, shop)*

**busy signal** NOUN (US)

la <u>señal de comunicando</u>

**but** PREPOSITION, CONJUNCTION

**1** <u>pero</u>

□ I'd like to come, but I'm busy.  Me gustaría venir, pero tengo trabajo.

**2** <u>sino</u>

**LANGUAGE TIP** Use **sino** when you want to correct a previous negative statement.

□ He's not English but French.  No es inglés sino francés.

**3** <u>menos</u>

□ They won all but two of their matches.  Ganaron todos los partidos menos dos.

■ **the last but one**  el penúltimo

**butcher** NOUN

el <u>carnicero</u>

la <u>carnicera</u>

□ He's a butcher.  Es carnicero.

■ **at the butcher's**  en la carnicería

**butter** NOUN

la <u>mantequilla</u>

**butterfly** NOUN

la <u>mariposa</u> *(insect, swimming)*

□ Her favourite stroke is the butterfly.  Su estilo favorito es mariposa.

**buttocks** PL NOUN

las <u>nalgas</u>

**button** NOUN

**1** el <u>botón</u> (PL los botones)

**2** la <u>chapa</u> (US: *metal, plastic*)

to **buy** VERB

▷ *see also* **buy** NOUN

<u>comprar</u>

□ He bought me an ice cream.  Me compró un helado.

■ **to buy something from somebody**

comprar algo a alguien  □ I bought a watch from him.  Le compré un reloj.

**buy** NOUN

▷ *see also* **buy** VERB

■ **It was a good buy.**  Fue una buena compra.

**by** PREPOSITION

**1** <u>por</u>

□ The thieves were caught by the police.  Los ladrones fueron capturados por la policía.

**2** <u>de</u>

□ a painting by Picasso  un cuadro de Picasso

**3** <u>en</u>

□ by car  en coche

■ **by train**  en tren

■ **by bus**  en autobús

**4** <u>junto a</u>

□ Where's the bank? — It's by the post office.  ¿Dónde está el banco? — Está junto a la oficina de correos.

**5** <u>para</u>

□ We have to be there by 4 o'clock.  Tenemos que estar allí para las cuatro.

■ **by the time...**  cuando  □ By the time I got there it was too late.  Cuando llegué allí ya era demasiado tarde.  □ It'll be ready by the time you get back.  Estará listo para cuando regreses.

■ **That's fine by me.**  Por mí no hay problema.

■ **all by himself**  él solo

■ **I did it all by myself.**  Lo hice yo solo.

■ **by the way**  a propósito

**bye** EXCLAMATION

¡adiós!

**bypass** NOUN

la <u>carretera de circunvalación</u> *(road)*

# Cc

**cab** NOUN
el taxi
□ I'll go by cab. Iré en taxi.

**cabbage** NOUN
la berza

**cabin** NOUN
1 el camarote (on ship)
2 la cabina (on aeroplane)

**cabinet** NOUN
■ **a bathroom cabinet** un armario de cuarto de baño
■ **a drinks cabinet** un mueble-bar

**cable** NOUN
el cable

**cable car** NOUN
el teleférico

**cable television** NOUN
la televisión por cable

**cadet** NOUN
el/la cadete
□ a police cadet un cadete de policía

**café** NOUN
la cafetería

**cage** NOUN
la jaula

**cagoule** NOUN
el canguro (chubasquero)

**cake** NOUN
el pastel

to **calculate** VERB
calcular

**calculation** NOUN
el cálculo

**calculator** NOUN
la calculadora

**calendar** NOUN
el calendario

**calf** NOUN
1 el ternero (of cow)
2 la pantorrilla (of leg)

**call** NOUN
▷ see also **call** VERB
la llamada
□ Thanks for your call. Gracias por su llamada. □ a phone call una llamada telefónica

■ **to be on call** (doctor) estar de guardia

to **call** VERB
▷ see also **call** NOUN
llamar
□ We called the police. Llamamos a la policía. □ I'll tell him you called. Le diré que has llamado.

■ **to be called** llamarse □ He's called Fluffy. Se llama Fluffy. □ What's she called? ¿Cómo se llama?

to **call back** VERB
volver* a llamar
□ I'll call back later. Volveré a llamar más tarde.

■ **Can I call you back later?** ¿Puedo llamarte más tarde?

to **call for** VERB
1 pasar a recoger
□ Shall I call for you at seven thirty? ¿Paso a recogerte a las siete y media?
2 requerir*
□ This calls for strong nerves. Esto require unos nervios de acero.

■ **This calls for a drink!** ¡Esto hay que celebrarlo!

to **call off** VERB
suspender
□ The match was called off. El partido se suspendió.

**call box** NOUN
la cabina telefónica

**call centre** NOUN
el centro de atención al cliente

**calm** ADJECTIVE
tranquilo (FEM tranquila)

to **calm down** VERB
calmarse
□ Calm down! ¡Cálmate!

**Calor gas®** NOUN
el butano

**calorie** NOUN
la caloría

**calves** PL NOUN ▷ see **calf**

**camcorder** NOUN
la videocámara

**came** VERB ▷ see **come**

**camel** NOUN
el camello

**camera** NOUN
la cámara

**cameraman** NOUN
el cámara

**camera phone** NOUN
el teléfono con cámara

to **camp** VERB
▷ see also **camp** NOUN
acampar

**camp** NOUN
▷ see also **camp** VERB
el campamento
□ a summer camp un campamento de verano
■ **a refugee camp** un campo de refugiados

**campaign** NOUN
▷ see also **campaign** VERB
la campaña

**camper** NOUN
el/la campista
■ **a camper van** una caravana

**camping** NOUN
■ **to go camping** ir de camping

**camping gas®** NOUN
el camping gas®

**campsite** NOUN
el camping (PL los campings)

**campus** NOUN
el campus (PL los campus)

**can** NOUN
▷ see also **can** VERB
la lata
□ a can of peas una lata de guisantes
□ a can of beer una lata de cerveza
■ **a can of petrol** un bidón de gasolina

**can** VERB
▷ see also **can** NOUN
1 poder* (be able to, be allowed to)
□ Can I use your phone? ¿Puedo usar el teléfono? □ I can't do that. No puedo hacer eso. □ I'll do it as soon as I can. Lo haré tan pronto como pueda. □ That can't be true! ¡No puede ser cierto! □ You could hire a bike. Podrías alquilar una bici. □ He couldn't concentrate because of the noise. No se podía concentrar a causa del ruido.
2 saber* (know how to)
□ I can swim. Sé nadar. □ He can't drive. No sabe conducir.
⚬ **LANGUAGE TIP** 'can' is sometimes not translated.
□ I can't hear you. No te oigo. □ I can't remember. No me acuerdo. □ Can you speak French? ¿Hablas francés?
■ **You could be right.** Es posible que tengas razón.

**Canada** NOUN
el Canadá

**Canadian** ADJECTIVE
▷ see also **Canadian** NOUN
canadiense (FEM canadiense)

**Canadian** NOUN
▷ see also **Canadian** ADJECTIVE
el/la canadiense

**canal** NOUN
el canal

**Canaries** NOUN
■ **the Canaries** las Canarias

**canary** NOUN
el canario
■ **the Canary Islands** las islas Canarias

to **cancel** VERB
cancelar
□ I had to cancel my appointment. Tuve que cancelar la cita. □ Our flight was cancelled. Cancelaron nuestro vuelo.

**cancellation** NOUN
la cancelación (PL las cancelaciones)

**Cancer** NOUN
el Cáncer (sign)
■ I'm Cancer. Soy cáncer.

**cancer** NOUN
el cáncer
□ He's got cancer. Tiene cáncer.

**candidate** NOUN
el candidato
la candidata

**candle** NOUN
1 la vela
2 el cirio (in church)

**candy** NOUN (US)
los dulces
□ I love candy. Me encantan los dulces.
■ **a candy** un caramelo

**candyfloss** NOUN
el algodón de azúcar

**cannabis** NOUN
el canabis

**canned** ADJECTIVE
en lata (food)

**cannot** VERB = **can not**

**canoe** NOUN
la canoa

**canoeing** NOUN
■ **to go canoeing** hacer piragüismo □ We went canoeing. Fuimos a hacer piragüismo.

**can-opener** NOUN
el abrelatas (PL los abrelatas)

**can't** VERB = **can not**

**canteen** NOUN
la cantina

**canvas** NOUN
la lona

**cap** NOUN

**c**

**1** el tapón (PL los tapones) *(of bottle, tube)*
**2** la gorra *(hat)*
**capable** ADJECTIVE
capaz (FEM capaz)
■ **to be capable of doing something** ser capaz de hacer algo □ She's capable of doing much more. Es capaz de hacer mucho más.
**capacity** NOUN
la capacidad
□ The tank has a 40-litre capacity. El depósito tiene una capacidad de 40 litros. □ He has a capacity for hard work. Tiene mucha capacidad de trabajo.
**capital** NOUN
**1** la capital
□ Cardiff is the capital of Wales. Cardiff es la capital del país de Gales.
**2** la mayúscula *(letter)*
□ in capitals en mayúsculas
**capitalism** NOUN
el capitalismo
**capital punishment** NOUN
la pena capital
**Capricorn** NOUN
el Capricornio *(sign)*
■ **I'm Capricorn.** Soy capricornio.
to **capsize** VERB
volcar*
**captain** NOUN
el capitán (PL los capitanes)
la capitana
**caption** NOUN
la leyenda
to **capture** VERB
capturar
**car** NOUN
el coche
■ **to go by car** ir en coche □ We went by car. Fuimos en coche.
■ **a car crash** un accidente de coche
**caramel** NOUN
el caramelo
□ a box of caramels una caja de caramelos
**caravan** NOUN
la caravana
□ a caravan site un cámping de caravanas
**card** NOUN
**1** la tarjeta
□ I got lots of cards and presents on my birthday. Recibí muchas tarjetas y regalos para mi cumpleaños.
**2** la carta
■ **a card game** un juego de cartas
**cardboard** NOUN
el cartón
□ a cardboard box una caja de cartón
**cardigan** NOUN

la chaqueta de punto
**cardphone** NOUN
el teléfono de tarjeta
**care** NOUN
▷ *see also* **care** VERB
el cuidado
□ with care con cuidado
■ **to take care of** cuidar a □ I take care of the children on Saturdays. Yo cuido a los niños los sábados.
■ **Take care! 1** *(be careful!)* ¡Ten cuidado!
**2** *(look after yourself!)* ¡Cuídate!
to **care** VERB
▷ *see also* **care** NOUN
■ **to care about** preocuparse por □ a company that cares about the environment una empresa que se preocupa por el medio ambiente □ They don't care about their image. No se preocupan por su imagen.
■ **I don't care!** ¡No me importa!
■ **Who cares?** ¿Y a quién le importa?
**career** NOUN
la carrera
**careful** ADJECTIVE
■ **Be careful!** ¡Ten cuidado!
**carefully** ADVERB
con cuidado *(cautiously)*
□ Drive carefully! ¡Conduce con cuidado!
■ **Think carefully!** ¡Piénsalo bien!
■ **She carefully avoided talking about it.** Tuvo mucho cuidado de no hablar del tema.
**careless** ADJECTIVE
**1** poco cuidado (FEM poco cuidada) *(work)*
■ **a careless mistake** un error de descuido
**2** poco cuidadoso (FEM poco cuidadosa) *(person)*
□ She's very careless. Es muy poco cuidadosa.
■ **a careless driver** un conductor imprudente
**caretaker** NOUN
el/la conserje
■ **school caretaker** el bedel
**cargo** NOUN
el cargamento
**car hire** NOUN
el alquiler de coches
**Caribbean** ADJECTIVE
▷ *see also* **Caribbean** NOUN
caribeño (FEM caribeña)
**Caribbean** NOUN
▷ *see also* **Caribbean** ADJECTIVE
■ **We're going to the Caribbean.** Vamos al Caribe.
■ **the Caribbean** *(sea)* el mar Caribe
**caring** ADJECTIVE
bondadoso (FEM bondadosa)
■ **the caring professions** las profesiones

de vocación social

**carnation** NOUN
el clavel

**carnival** NOUN
el carnaval

**carol** NOUN
■ **a Christmas carol** un villancico

**car park** NOUN
el aparcamiento

**carpenter** NOUN
el carpintero
la carpintera
□ He's a carpenter. Es carpintero.

**carpet** NOUN
1 la moqueta *(fitted)*
2 la alfombra
□ a Persian carpet una alfombra persa

**car rental** NOUN (US)
el alquiler de coches

**carriage** NOUN
el vagón (PL los vagones) *(of train)*

**carrier bag** NOUN
la bolsa de plástico

**carrot** NOUN
la zanahoria

to **carry** VERB
1 llevar
□ I'll carry your bag. Te llevo la bolsa.
2 transportar
□ a plane carrying 100 passengers un avión que transporta 100 pasajeros

to **carry on** VERB
seguir*
□ She carried on talking. Siguió hablando.
■ **Carry on!** ¡Sigue! □ Am I boring you? — No, carry on! ¿Te estoy aburriendo? — ¡No, sigue!

to **carry out** VERB
1 cumplir *(orders)*
2 llevar a cabo *(threat, task, instructions)*

**carrycot** NOUN
el moisés (PL los moisés)

**cart** NOUN
el carro

**carton** NOUN
el cartón (PL los cartones) *(of milk, fruit juice)*

**cartoon** NOUN
1 los dibujos animados *(film)*
2 el chiste *(in newspaper)*
■ **a strip cartoon** una tira cómica

**cartridge** NOUN
el cartucho

to **carve** VERB
trinchar
□ Dad carved the roast. Papá trinchó el asado.
■ **a carved oak chair** una silla de roble tallado

**case** NOUN
1 la maleta
□ I've packed my case. He hecho mi maleta.
2 el caso
□ in some cases en algunos casos □ The police are investigating the case. La policía está investigando el caso.
■ **in case it rains** por si llueve
■ **just in case** por si acaso □ Take some money with you, just in case. Llévate algo de dinero por si acaso.

**cash** NOUN
▷ see also **cash** VERB
el dinero
□ I'm a bit short of cash. Ando un poco justo de dinero.
■ **in cash** en efectivo □ £200 in cash 200 libras esterlinas en efectivo
■ **to pay cash** pagar al contado

**cashier** NOUN
el cajero
la cajera

**cashmere** NOUN
el cachemir
□ a cashmere sweater un suéter de cachemir

**casino** NOUN
el casino

**casserole** NOUN
el guiso
□ to make a casserole hacer un guiso
■ **a casserole dish** una cazuela

**cast** NOUN
el reparto
□ There is a very famous actor in the cast. Hay un actor muy famoso en el reparto.
■ **After the play, we met the cast.** Cuando terminó la obra charlamos con los actores.

**castle** NOUN
el castillo

**casual** ADJECTIVE
1 informal (FEM informal)
□ I prefer casual clothes. Prefiero la ropa informal.
2 despreocupado (FEM despreocupada)
□ a casual attitude una actitud despreocupada
3 eventual (FEM eventual)
□ It's just a casual job. Es sólo un trabajo eventual.
■ **a casual remark** un comentario hecho de pasada

**casually** ADVERB
■ **to dress casually** vestir informal

**casualty** NOUN
1 urgencias *fem pl (hospital department)*
□ He was taken to casualty after the accident. Lo llevaron a urgencias después del accidente.

37

**2** la víctima
□ The casualties include a young boy. Entre las víctimas se encuentra un niño.

**cat** NOUN
el gato
la gata

**catalogue** NOUN
el catálogo

**catalytic converter** NOUN
el catalizador

**catarrh** NOUN
el catarro

**catastrophe** NOUN
la catástrofe

to **catch** VERB
**1** coger* *(Spain)* (agarrar *Latin America*)

> **LANGUAGE TIP** Be very careful with the verb **coger**: in most of Latin America this is an extremely rude word that should be avoided. However, in Spain this verb is common and not rude at all.

□ They caught the thief. Cogieron al ladrón.
□ We caught the last train. Cogimos el último tren.
■ **My cat catches birds.** Mi gato caza pájaros.
**2** agarrar
□ He caught her arm. La agarró del brazo.
■ **to catch a cold** resfriarse
■ **I didn't catch his name.** No me enteré de su nombre.
■ **He caught her stealing.** La pilló robando.
■ **If they catch you smoking you'll be in trouble.** Si te pillan fumando te la vas a cargar.

to **catch up** VERB
**1** ponerse* al día
□ I've got to catch up on my work. Tengo que ponerme al día con el trabajo.
**2** alcanzar*
□ She caught me up. Me alcanzó.

**catching** ADJECTIVE
contagioso (FEM contagiosa)
□ Don't worry, it's not catching! ¡No te preocupes, no es contagioso!

**catering** NOUN
■ **The hotel did all the catering for the wedding.** El hotel se encargó de organizar el banquete de bodas.

**cathedral** NOUN
la catedral

**Catholic** ADJECTIVE
> *see also* **Catholic** NOUN
católico (FEM católica)

**Catholic** NOUN
> *see also* **Catholic** ADJECTIVE

el católico
la católica
□ I'm a Catholic. Soy católico.

**cattle** PL NOUN
el ganado

**caught** VERB ▷ *see* **catch**

**cauliflower** NOUN
la coliflor

**cause** NOUN
> *see also* **cause** VERB
la causa

to **cause** VERB
> *see also* **cause** NOUN
causar

**cautious** ADJECTIVE
prudente (FEM prudente)

**cautiously** ADVERB
con cautela

**cave** NOUN
la cueva

**CCTV** NOUN (= *closed-circuit television*)
el circuito cerrado de televisión

**CD** NOUN
el CD (PL los CDs)

**CD player** NOUN
el reproductor de CD

**CD-ROM** NOUN
el CD-ROM

**ceasefire** NOUN
el alto el fuego

**ceiling** NOUN
el techo

to **celebrate** VERB
celebrar

**celebration** NOUN
la celebración

**celebrity** NOUN
la celebridad

**celery** NOUN
el apio

**cell** NOUN
**1** la celda
□ Prisoners spend many hours in their cells. Los prisioneros pasan muchas horas en sus celdas.
**2** la célula *(in biology)*

**cellar** NOUN
el sótano

**cello** NOUN
el violonchelo

**cell phone** NOUN
el móvil

**cement** NOUN
el cemento

**cemetery** NOUN
el cementerio

**cent** NOUN
**1** el centavo *(division of dollar)*

**2** el céntimo *(division of euro)*

**centenary** NOUN
el centenario

**center** NOUN (US)
el centro

**centigrade** ADJECTIVE
centígrado (FEM centígrada)
□ 20 degrees centigrade 20 grados centígrados

**centimetre** (US **centimeter**) NOUN
el centímetro

**central** ADJECTIVE
central (FEM central)

**central heating** NOUN
la calefacción central

**centre** NOUN
el centro

**century** NOUN
el siglo
□ the twentieth century el siglo veinte

**cereal** NOUN
los cereales
□ I have cereal for breakfast. Desayuno cereales.

**ceremony** NOUN
la ceremonia

**certain** ADJECTIVE
**1** cierto (FEM cierta) *(particular)*
□ a certain person cierta persona
**2** seguro (FEM segura) *(definite)*
□ I am certain he's not coming. Estoy seguro de que no viene.
■ **for certain** con certeza
■ **to make certain** cerciorarse □ I made certain the door was locked. Me cercioré de que la puerta estaba cerrada con llave.

**certainly** ADVERB
por supuesto
□ I shall certainly be there. Por supuesto que estaré allí. □ Certainly not! ¡Por supuesto que no!
■ **So it was a surprise? — It certainly was!** ¿Así que fue una sorpresa? — ¡Ya lo creo!

**certificate** NOUN
el certificado

**chain** NOUN
la cadena
□ a gold chain una cadena de oro

**chair** NOUN
**1** la silla
□ a table and four chairs una mesa y cuatro sillas
**2** el sillón (PL los sillones) *(armchair)*

**chairlift** NOUN
el telesilla

⸰⸰ **LANGUAGE TIP** Although **telesilla** ends in -a, it is actually a masculine noun.

**chairman** NOUN

el presidente
la presidenta

**chalet** NOUN
el chalet (PL los chalets)

**chalk** NOUN
la tiza
■ **a piece of chalk** una tiza

**challenge** NOUN
▷ see also **challenge** VERB
el reto

to **challenge** VERB
▷ see also **challenge** NOUN
retar
□ She challenged me to a race. Me retó a echar una carrera.

**challenging** ADJECTIVE
estimulante (FEM estimulante)
□ a challenging job un trabajo estimulante

**chambermaid** NOUN
la camarera

**champagne** NOUN
el champán

**champion** NOUN
el campeón (PL los campeones)
la campeona

**championship** NOUN
el campeonato

**chance** NOUN
**1** la posibilidad
□ The team's chances of winning are very good. El equipo tiene muchas posibilidades de ganar.
**2** la oportunidad
□ I had the chance of working in Brazil. Tuve la oportunidad de trabajar en Brasil.
■ **I'll write when I get the chance.** Te escribiré cuando tenga un momento.
■ **by chance** por casualidad
■ **No chance!** ¡Ni en broma!
■ **to take a chance** arriesgarse □ I'm taking no chances! ¡No me quiero arriesgar!

**Chancellor of the Exchequer** NOUN
el Ministro de Economía y Hacienda
la Ministra de Economía y Hacienda

to **change** VERB
▷ see also **change** NOUN
**1** cambiar
□ The town has changed a lot. La ciudad ha cambiado mucho. □ I'd like to change £50. Quisiera cambiar 50 libras esterlinas. □ I'd like to change this jumper, it's too small. Me gustaría cambiar este jersey, es demasiado pequeño.
**2** cambiar de
□ He wants to change his job. Quiere cambiar de trabajo. □ I'm going to change my shoes. Voy a cambiarme de zapatos.
■ **to get changed** cambiarse

C

■ **to change one's mind** cambiar de idea

**change** NOUN

▷ *see also* **change** VERB

1 el cambio

□ There's been a change of plan. Ha habido un cambio de planes.

■ **a change of clothes** una muda

■ **for a change** para variar

2 el dinero suelto

□ I haven't got any change. No tengo dinero suelto.

■ **Can you give me change for a pound?** ¿Me puede cambiar una libra?

■ **There's your change.** Aquí tiene el cambio.

**changeable** ADJECTIVE

variable (FEM variable)

**changing room** NOUN

1 el probador *(in shop)*

2 el vestuario *(for sport)*

**channel** NOUN

el canal *(TV)*

■ **the English Channel** el Canal de la Mancha

■ **the Channel Islands** las islas del Canal de la Mancha

■ **the Channel Tunnel** el túnel del Canal de la Mancha

**chaos** NOUN

el caos

**chap** NOUN

el tipo *(informal)*

**chapel** NOUN

la capilla

**chapter** NOUN

el capítulo

**character** NOUN

1 el carácter (PL los caracteres)

□ Can you describe his character? ¿Puede describirme cómo es su carácter?

2 el personaje *(in film, book)*

■ **She's quite a character.** Es todo un personaje.

**characteristic** NOUN

la característica

**charcoal** NOUN

1 el carbón vegetal *(for barbecue)*

2 el carboncillo *(for drawing)*

**charge** NOUN

▷ *see also* **charge** VERB

■ **Is there a charge for delivery?** ¿Cobran por el envío?

■ **an extra charge** un suplemento

■ **free of charge** gratuito

■ **I'd like to reverse the charges.** Quisiera llamar a cobro revertido.

■ **to be in charge** ser el responsable □ She was in charge of the group. Ella era la

responsable del grupo.

to **charge** VERB

▷ *see also* **charge** NOUN

1 cobrar

□ How much did he charge you? ¿Cuánto te cobró?

2 acusar *(with crime)*

□ The police have charged him with murder. La policía lo ha acusado de asesinato.

**charity** NOUN

la organización benéfica (PL las organizaciones benéficas) *(organization)*

□ He gave the money to charity. Donó el dinero a una organización benéfica.

■ **to collect for charity** recaudar dinero para obras benéficas

**charm** NOUN

el encanto

**charming** ADJECTIVE

encantador (FEM encantadora)

**chart** NOUN

el gráfico

□ The chart shows the rise of unemployment. El gráfico muestra el aumento del desempleo.

■ **the charts** la lista de éxitos □ The album is still in the charts. El disco está todavía en la lista de éxitos.

**charter flight** NOUN

el vuelo chárter

to **chase** VERB

▷ *see also* **chase** NOUN

1 perseguir*

□ The policeman chased the thief along the road. El policía persiguió al ladrón a lo largo de la calle.

2 ir* detrás de

□ He's always chasing the girls. Siempre va detrás de las chicas.

**chase** NOUN

▷ *see also* **chase** VERB

la persecución (PL las persecuciones)

□ a car chase una persecución en coche

**chat** NOUN

la charla

■ **to have a chat** charlar

**chatroom** NOUN

el chat

**chat show** NOUN

el programa de entrevistas

> **LANGUAGE TIP** Although **programa** ends in -a, it is actually a masculine noun.

**cheap** ADJECTIVE

barato (FEM barata)

□ a cheap T-shirt una camiseta barata □ It's cheaper by bus. Es más barato en autobús.

■ **a cheap flight** un vuelo económico

to **cheat** VERB
▷ *see also* **cheat** NOUN
1 hacer* trampa *(at cards)*
  □ You're cheating! ¡Estás haciendo trampa!
2 copiar *(in exam)*
**cheat** NOUN
  ▷ *see also* **cheat** VERB
  el tramposo
  la tramposa
**check** NOUN
  ▷ *see also* **check** VERB
1 el control
  □ a security check  un control de seguridad
2 el cheque (US)
  □ to write a check  extender un cheque
3 la cuenta (US)
  □ The waiter brought us the check.  El
  camarero nos trajo la cuenta.
to **check** VERB
  ▷ *see also* **check** NOUN
  comprobar*
  □ Could you check the oil, please? ¿Podría
  comprobar el aceite, por favor?
  ■ **to check with somebody** preguntarle
  a alguien  □ I'll check with the driver what
  time the bus leaves. Le preguntaré al
  conductor a qué hora sale el autobús.
to **check in** VERB
1 facturar *(at airport)*
2 registrarse *(in hotel)*
to **check out** VERB
  dejar el hotel
**checked** ADJECTIVE
  a cuadros
**checkers** NOUN (US)
  las damas
  □ to play checkers  jugar a las damas
**check-in** NOUN
  la facturación de equipajes
**checking account** NOUN (US)
  la cuenta corriente
**checkout** NOUN
  la caja
**check-up** NOUN
  el reconocimiento
**cheek** NOUN
  la mejilla
  □ He kissed her on the cheek. La besó en la
  mejilla.
  ■ **What a cheek!** ¡Qué cara!
**cheeky** ADJECTIVE
  descarado (FEM descarada)
  □ Don't be cheeky! ¡No seas descarado!
  ■ **a cheeky smile** una sonrisilla maliciosa
**cheer** NOUN
  ▷ *see also* **cheer** VERB
  ■ **Three cheers for the winner!** ¡Viva el
  ganador!

■ **Cheers!** 1 *(when drinking)* ¡Salud! 2 *(thank
you)* ¡Gracias!
to **cheer** VERB
  ▷ *see also* **cheer** NOUN
  vitorear
  ■ **to cheer somebody up** levantar el ánimo
  a alguien  □ I was trying to cheer him up.
  Estaba intentando levantarle el ánimo.
  ■ **Cheer up!** ¡Anímate!
**cheerful** ADJECTIVE
  alegre (FEM alegre)
**cheerio** EXCLAMATION
  ¡hasta luego!
**cheese** NOUN
  el queso
**chef** NOUN
  el/la chef (PL los/las chefs)
**chemical** NOUN
  la sustancia química
**chemist** NOUN
1 el farmacéutico
  la farmacéutica *(dispenser)*
  □ She's a chemist. Es farmacéutica
2 la farmacia *(shop)*
  □ You get it from the chemist.  Se compra en
  la farmacia.

  **DID YOU KNOW...?**
  Chemist's shops in Spain are
  identified by a green cross outside the
  shop.
3 el químico
  la química *(scientist)*
**chemistry** NOUN
  la química
  □ the chemistry lab  el laboratorio de
  química
**cheque** NOUN
  el cheque
  □ to write a cheque  extender un cheque
  □ to pay by cheque  pagar con cheque
**chequebook** NOUN
  el talonario de cheques
**cherry** NOUN
  la cereza
**chess** NOUN
  el ajedrez
  □ He likes playing chess.  Le gusta jugar al
  ajedrez.
**chessboard** NOUN
  el tablero de ajedrez
**chest** NOUN
  el pecho
  □ I've got a pain in my chest.  Tengo un dolor
  en el pecho.
**chestnut** NOUN
  la castaña
to **chew** VERB
  masticar*

**chewing gum** NOUN
el chicle

■ **a piece of chewing gum** un chicle

**chick** NOUN
el polluelo

□ a hen and her chicks una gallina y sus polluelos

**chicken** NOUN
1 la gallina *(animal)*
2 el pollo *(food)*

**chickenpox** NOUN
la varicela

□ I've got chickenpox. Tengo la varicela.

**chickpeas** PL NOUN
los garbanzos

**chief** NOUN
▷ *see also* **chief** ADJECTIVE
el jefe
la jefa

□ the chief of security el jefe de seguridad

**chief** ADJECTIVE
▷ *see also* **chief** NOUN
principal (FEM principal)

□ His chief reason for resigning was the low pay. El motivo principal de su dimisión fue el sueldo bajo.

**child** NOUN
1 el niño
la niña

□ a child of six un niño de seis años
2 el hijo
la hija

□ Susan is our eldest child. Susan es nuestra hija mayor. □ They've got three children. Tienen tres hijos.

**childish** ADJECTIVE
infantil (FEM infantil)

**child minder** NOUN
la niñera

**children** PL NOUN ▷ *see* **child**

**Chile** NOUN
Chile *masc*

**to chill** VERB
▷ *see also* **chill** NOUN
poner* a enfriar *(drink, food)*

■ **Serve chilled.** Sírvase bien frío.

**chilli** NOUN
el chile

■ **chilli con carne** el chile con carne

**chilly** ADJECTIVE
frío (FEM fría)

**chimney** NOUN
la chimenea

**chin** NOUN
la barbilla

■ **Keep your chin up!** ¡No pierdas el ánimo!

**china** NOUN
la porcelana

□ a china plate un plato de porcelana

**China** NOUN
China *fem*

**Chinese** ADJECTIVE
▷ *see also* **Chinese** NOUN
chino (FEM china)

■ **a Chinese man** un chino
■ **a Chinese woman** una china

**Chinese** NOUN
▷ *see also* **Chinese** ADJECTIVE
el chino *(language)*

■ **the Chinese** los chinos

**chip** NOUN
1 la patata frita (la papa frita *Latin America*) *(food)*
2 el chip (PL los chips) *(in computer)*

**chiropodist** NOUN
el podólogo
la podóloga

□ He's a chiropodist. Es podólogo.

**chives** PL NOUN
los cebollinos

**chocolate** NOUN
1 el chocolate

□ a chocolate cake un pastel de chocolate
2 el bombón (PL los bombones)

□ a box of chocolates una caja de bombones

**choice** NOUN
la elección (PL las elecciones)

■ **I had no choice.** No tenía otro remedio.

**choir** NOUN
el coro

**to choke** VERB
atragantarse *(on food)*

**to choose** VERB
elegir*

**to chop** VERB
▷ *see also* **chop** NOUN
1 picar* *(onion, herbs)*
2 cortar en trozos pequeños *(meat)*

**chop** NOUN
▷ *see also* **chop** VERB
la chuleta

□ a pork chop una chuleta de cerdo

**chopsticks** PL NOUN
los palillos

**chose, chosen** VERB ▷ *see* **choose**

**Christ** NOUN
Cristo *masc*

**christening** NOUN
el bautismo

**Christian** NOUN
▷ *see also* **Christian** ADJECTIVE
el cristiano
la cristiana

**Christian** ADJECTIVE
▷ *see also* **Christian** NOUN

cristiano (FEM cristiana)

**Christian name** NOUN
el nombre de pila

**Christmas** NOUN
la Navidad
□ Happy Christmas! ¡Feliz Navidad!
■ **Christmas Day** el día de Navidad
■ **on Christmas Day** el día de Navidad
■ **Christmas Eve** Nochebuena
■ **a Christmas tree** un árbol de Navidad
■ **Christmas dinner** la comida de Navidad

> DID YOU KNOW...?
> As well as lunch on Christmas Day,
> Spaniards also have a special supper
> on Christmas Eve.

■ **a Christmas present** un regalo de
Navidad

> DID YOU KNOW...?
> In Spain Christmas presents are
> traditionally given on 6th January
> although more and more people are
> exchanging gifts on Christmas Eve.

■ **Christmas pudding** el pudin de Navidad
■ **Christmas card** la tarjeta de Navidad
■ **at Christmas** en Navidad

**chunk** NOUN
el pedazo
□ Cut the meat into chunks. Córtese la
carne en pedazos.

**church** NOUN
la iglesia
■ **the Church of England** la Iglesia
Anglicana

**cider** NOUN
la sidra

**cigar** NOUN
el puro

**cigarette** NOUN
el cigarrillo

**cigarette lighter** NOUN
el mechero

**cinema** NOUN
el cine

**cinnamon** NOUN
la canela

**circle** NOUN
el círculo

**circular** ADJECTIVE
circular

**circulation** NOUN
1 la circulación
□ She has poor circulation. Tiene mala
circulación.
2 la tirada
□ The newspaper has a circulation of around
8000. El periódico tiene una tirada de unos
8.000 ejemplares.

**circumstances** PL NOUN
las circunstancias
□ in the circumstances dadas las
circunstancias
■ **under no circumstances** bajo ningún
concepto

**circus** NOUN
el circo

**citizen** NOUN
el ciudadano
la ciudadana

**City** NOUN
■ **the City** la City de Londres

**city** NOUN
la ciudad
□ the city centre el centro de la ciudad

**city technology college** NOUN
el centro de formación profesional

**civilization** NOUN
la civilización (PL las civilizaciones)

**civil servant** NOUN
el funcionario
la funcionaria
□ He's a civil servant. Es funcionario.

**civil war** NOUN
la guerra civil

to **claim** VERB
▷ see also **claim** NOUN
1 asegurar
□ He claims he found the money. Asegura
haber encontrado el dinero.
2 reclamar
□ He's claiming compensation from the
company. Reclama una indemnización por
parte de la empresa.
3 cobrar
□ She's claiming unemployment benefit.
Cobra subsidio de desempleo.
■ **We claimed on our insurance.**
Reclamamos al seguro.

**claim** NOUN
▷ see also **claim** VERB
1 la reclamación (PL las reclamaciones) (on
insurance policy)
■ **to make a claim** reclamar al seguro
2 la afirmación (PL las afirmaciones)
□ The manufacturer's claims are obviously
untrue. Las afirmaciones del fabricante son
obviamente falsas.

to **clap** VERB
aplaudir
■ **to clap one's hands** dar palmadas

**clarinet** NOUN
el clarinete

to **clash** VERB
1 desentonar (colours)
□ Red clashes with orange. El rojo
desentona con el naranja.
2 coincidir (events)

□ The party clashes with the meeting. La fiesta coincide con la reunión.

**clasp** NOUN
el cierre *(of necklace, handbag)*

**class** NOUN
la clase
□ We're in the same class. Estamos en la misma clase. □ I go to dancing classes. Voy a clases de baile.

**classic** ADJECTIVE
▷ *see also* **classic** NOUN
clásico (FEM clásica)
□ a classic example un ejemplo clásico

**classic** NOUN
▷ *see also* **classic** ADJECTIVE
el clásico

**classical** ADJECTIVE
clásico (FEM clásica)
□ classical music la música clásica

**classmate** NOUN
el compañero de clase
la compañera de clase

**classroom** NOUN
la clase

**claw** NOUN
1 la garra *(of lion, eagle)*
2 la uña *(of cat, parrot)*
3 la pinza *(of crab, lobster)*

**clean** ADJECTIVE
▷ *see also* **clean** VERB
limpio (FEM limpia)

to **clean** VERB
▷ *see also* **clean** ADJECTIVE
limpiar

**cleaner** NOUN
1 el hombre de la limpieza
la mujer de la limpieza *(person)*
2 el producto de limpieza *(substance)*

**cleaner's** NOUN
la tintorería
□ He took his coat to the cleaner's. Llevó el abrigo a la tintorería.

**cleaning lady** NOUN
la mujer de la limpieza

**cleansing lotion** NOUN
la leche limpiadora

**clear** ADJECTIVE
▷ *see also* **clear** VERB
1 claro (FEM clara)
□ a clear explanation una explicación clara
□ It's clear you don't believe me. Está claro que no me crees.
■ **Have I made myself clear?** ¿Me explico?
2 despejado (FEM despejada)
□ Wait till the road is clear. Espera hasta que la carretera esté despejada. □ a clear day un día despejado
3 transparente (FEM transparente)

□ It comes in a clear plastic bottle. Viene en una botella de plástico transparente.

to **clear** VERB
▷ *see also* **clear** ADJECTIVE
1 despejar
□ They are clearing the road. Están despejando la carretera.
■ **She was cleared of murder.** La absolvieron del cargo de asesinato.
■ **to clear the table** quitar la mesa
2 despejarse *(fog, mist)*

to **clear off** VERB
largarse*
□ Clear off and leave me alone! ¡Lárgate y déjame en paz!

to **clear up** VERB
1 ordenar
□ Who's going to clear all this up? ¿Quién va a ordenar todo esto?
2 resolver*
□ Let's try to clear up this problem. Intentemos resolver este problema.
■ **I think it's going to clear up.** *(weather)* Creo que va a despejar.

**clearly** ADVERB
claramente
□ to speak clearly hablar claramente
■ **Clearly this project will cost money.** Evidentemente este proyecto costará dinero.

**clementine** NOUN
la clementina

**clever** ADJECTIVE
1 listo (FEM lista)
□ She's very clever. Es muy lista.
2 ingenioso (FEM ingeniosa)
□ a clever system un sistema ingenioso
■ **What a clever idea!** ¡Qué idea más genial!

to **click on** VERB
hacer* clic en *(computing)*
□ to click on an icon hacer clic en un icono
■ **to click on the mouse** hacer clic con el ratón

**client** NOUN
el cliente
la clienta

**cliff** NOUN
el acantilado

**climate** NOUN
el clima
　　LANGUAGE TIP Although **clima** ends in -a, it is actually a masculine noun.

to **climb** VERB
1 escalar
□ Her ambition is to climb Mount Everest. Su ambición es escalar el Monte Everest.
2 trepar a

□ They climbed a tree. Treparon a un árbol.
■ **to climb the stairs** subir las escaleras

**climber** NOUN
el escalador
la escaladora

**climbing** NOUN
el montañismo
■ **to go climbing** hacer montañismo
□ We're going climbing in Scotland. Vamos a hacer montañismo en Escocia.

**clinic** NOUN
1 el consultorio (in NHS hospital)
2 la clínica (private hospital)

**clip** NOUN
1 la horquilla (for hair)
2 la secuencia
□ some clips from Scarlett Johansson's latest film unas secuencias de la última película de Scarlett Johansson

**clippers** PL NOUN
■ **nail clippers** el cortauñas (PL los cortauñas)

**cloakroom** NOUN
1 el guardarropa (for coats)

    LANGUAGE TIP Although **guardarropa** ends in -a, it is actually a masculine noun.

2 los servicios (toilet)

**clock** NOUN
el reloj
■ **an alarm clock** un despertador
■ **a clock radio** un radio-despertador

**clockwork** NOUN
■ **to go like clockwork** ir sobre ruedas

**clone** NOUN
▷ see also **clone** VERB
el clon

to **clone** VERB
▷ see also **clone** NOUN
clonar
□ to clone a sheep clonar una oveja
■ **a cloned sheep** una oveja clónica

**close** ADJECTIVE, ADVERB
▷ see also **close** VERB
1 cerca (FEM cerca)
□ The shops are very close. Las tiendas están muy cerca. □ The hotel is close to the station. El hotel está cerca de la estación.
■ **Come closer.** Acércate más.
■ **She was close to tears.** Estaba a punto de llorar.
2 cercano (FEM cercana)
□ We have only invited close relations. Sólo hemos invitado a parientes cercanos.
3 íntimo (FEM íntima)
□ She's a close friend of mine. Es amiga íntima mía.
■ **I'm very close to my sister.** Estoy muy

unida a mi hermana.
4 reñido (FEM reñida)
□ It was a very close contest. Fue un concurso muy reñido.
■ **It's close this afternoon.** Hace bochorno esta tarde.

to **close** VERB
▷ see also **close** ADJECTIVE
1 cerrar*
□ The shops close at five thirty. Las tiendas cierran a las cinco y media. □ Please close the door. Cierra la puerta, por favor.
2 cerrarse*
□ The doors close automatically. Las puertas se cierran automáticamente.

**closed** ADJECTIVE
cerrado (FEM cerrada)

**closely** ADVERB
de cerca (look, examine)
■ **This will be a closely fought race.** Será una carrera muy reñida.

**cloth** NOUN
la tela
□ I would like five metres of this cloth, please. Quisiera cinco metros de esta tela, por favor.
■ **a cloth** un trapo □ Wipe it with a damp cloth. Límpialo con un trapo húmedo.

**clothes** PL NOUN
la ropa
■ **clothes horse** el tendedero plegable
■ **clothes line** la cuerda de tender
■ **clothes peg** la pinza para tender la ropa

**cloud** NOUN
la nube

**cloudy** ADJECTIVE
nublado (FEM nublada)

**clove** NOUN
■ **a clove of garlic** un diente de ajo

**clown** NOUN
el payaso

**club** NOUN
1 el club
□ a golf club un club de golf □ the youth club el club juvenil
2 la discoteca
□ We had dinner and went on to a club. Cenamos y fuimos a una discoteca.
■ **clubs** (at cards) los tréboles □ the ace of clubs el as de tréboles

**clubbing** NOUN
■ **to go clubbing** ir de discotecas

to **club together** VERB
hacer* una colecta
□ We clubbed together to buy her a present. Hicimos una colecta para comprarle un regalo.

**clue** NOUN

la pista
□ an important clue una pista clave
■ **I haven't a clue.** No tengo ni idea.

**clumsy** ADJECTIVE
torpe (FEM torpe)

**clutch** NOUN
▷ *see also* **clutch** VERB
el embrague *(of car)*

**coach** NOUN
1 el autobús
□ by coach en autobús □ the coach station
la estación de autobuses □ a coach trip una
excursión en autobús
2 el entrenador
la entrenadora *(trainer)*
■ **the Spanish coach** el entrenador del
equipo español

**coal** NOUN
el carbón
■ **a coal mine** una mina de carbón
■ **a coal miner** un minero de carbón

**coarse** ADJECTIVE
1 basto (FEM basta)
□ The bag was made of coarse black cloth.
La bolsa estaba hecha de una tela basta de
color negro.
2 grueso (FEM gruesa)
□ The sand is very coarse on that beach. La
arena es muy gruesa en esa playa.

**coast** NOUN
la costa
□ It's on the west coast of Scotland. Está en
la costa oeste de Escocia.

**coastguard** NOUN
el guardacostas (PL los guardacostas)

**coat** NOUN
el abrigo
□ a woollen coat un abrigo de lana
■ **a coat of paint** una mano de pintura

**coat hanger** NOUN
la percha

**cobweb** NOUN
la telaraña

**cocaine** NOUN
la cocaína

**cockerel** NOUN
el gallo

**cocoa** NOUN
el cacao
■ **a cup of cocoa** una taza de chocolate

**coconut** NOUN
el coco

**cod** NOUN
el bacalao

**code** NOUN
1 la clave
□ It's written in code. Está escrito en clave.
2 el prefijo *(for telephone)*

□ What is the code for London? ¿Cuál es el
prefijo de Londres?

**coffee** NOUN
el café (PL los cafés)
□ a cup of coffee una taza de café
■ **A cup of coffee, please.** Un café, por
favor.

**coffeepot** NOUN
la cafetera

**coffee table** NOUN
la mesa de centro

**coffin** NOUN
el ataúd

**coin** NOUN
la moneda
□ a 20p coin una moneda de 20 peniques

**coincidence** NOUN
la coincidencia

**Coke**® NOUN
la Coca-Cola®

**colander** NOUN
el colador

**cold** ADJECTIVE
▷ *see also* **cold** NOUN
frío (FEM fría)
□ The water's cold. El agua está fría.
□ It's cold. Hace frío. □ Are you cold?
¿Tienes frío?

**cold** NOUN
▷ *see also* **cold** ADJECTIVE
1 el frío
□ I can't stand the cold. No soporto el frío.
2 el resfriado *(illness)*
■ **to catch a cold** resfriarse
■ **to have a cold** estar resfriado

**coleslaw** NOUN
la ensalada de col

to **collapse** VERB
1 venirse* abajo
□ The bridge collapsed during the storm.
El puente se vino abajo en medio de la
tormenta.
2 sufrir un colapso
□ He collapsed while playing tennis. Sufrió
un colapso mientras jugaba al tenis.

**collar** NOUN
1 el cuello *(of coat, shirt)*
2 el collar *(for animal)*

**collarbone** NOUN
la clavícula

**colleague** NOUN
el/la colega

to **collect** VERB
1 recoger*
□ The teacher collected the exercise books.
El maestro recogió los cuadernos. □ Their
mother collects them from school. Su
madre los recoge del colegio.

**2** coleccionar

□ He collects stamps. Colecciona sellos.

**3** hacer\* una colecta

□ I'm collecting for UNICEF. Estoy haciendo una colecta para la UNICEF.

**collect call** NOUN (US)
la llamada a cobro revertido

**collection** NOUN

**1** la colección (PL las colecciones)

□ my CD collection mi colección de CDs

**2** la colecta

□ a collection for charity una colecta para obras benéficas

**collector** NOUN
el/la coleccionista

**college** NOUN
la universidad (university)

to **collide** VERB
chocar\*

**collision** NOUN
la colisión (PL las colisiones)

**colon** NOUN
dos puntos (punctuation mark)

**colonel** NOUN
el/la coronel

**colour** (US **color**) NOUN
el color

□ What colour is it? ¿De qué color es?

■ **a colour TV** una televisión en color

**colourful** (US **colorful**) ADJECTIVE
de colores muy vistosos

**colouring** (US **coloring**) NOUN
el colorante (for food)

**comb** NOUN
▷ see also **comb** VERB
el peine

to **comb** VERB
▷ see also **comb** NOUN

■ **You haven't combed your hair.** No te has peinado.

**combination** NOUN
la combinación (PL las combinaciones)

to **combine** VERB

**1** combinar

□ The film combines humour with suspense. La película combina el humor con el suspense.

**2** compaginar

□ It's difficult to combine a career with a family. Es difícil compaginar la profesión con la vida familiar.

to **come** VERB

**1** venir\*

□ Helen came with me. Helen vino conmigo. □ Come home. Ven a casa. □ Come and see us soon. Ven a vernos pronto.

■ **Where do you come from?** ¿De dónde eres?

**2** llegar\*

□ They came late. Llegaron tarde. □ The letter came this morning. La carta llegó esta mañana.

■ **I'm coming!** ¡Ya voy!

to **come back** VERB
volver\*

□ My brother is coming back tomorrow. Mi hermano vuelve mañana.

to **come down** VERB
bajar

to **come in** VERB
entrar

□ Come in! ¡Entra!

to **come out** VERB

**1** salir\*

□ We came out of the cinema at 10. Salimos del cine a las 10. □ Her book comes out in May. Su libro sale en mayo.

■ **None of my photos came out.** No salió ninguna de mis fotos.

**2** irse\*

□ I don't think this stain will come out. No creo que esta mancha se vaya a quitar.

to **come round** VERB
volver\* en sí (after faint, operation)

□ He came round after about 10 minutes. Volvió en sí después de unos 10 minutos.

to **come up** VERB

**1** subir

□ Come up here! ¡Sube aquí!

**2** surgir\*

□ Something's come up so I'll be late home. Ha surgido algo, así es que llegaré tarde a casa.

■ **to come up to somebody** acercarse a alguien □ She came up to me and kissed me. Se me acercó y me besó.

**comedian** NOUN
el cómico
la cómica

**comedy** NOUN
la comedia

**comfortable** ADJECTIVE

**1** cómodo (FEM cómoda)

□ comfortable shoes zapatos cómodos
□ Make yourself comfortable! ¡Ponte cómodo!

**2** confortable (FEM confortable) (house, room)

□ Their house is small but comfortable. Su casa es pequeña pero confortable.

**comic** NOUN
el comic (PL los comics)

**comic strip** NOUN
la tira cómica

**coming** ADJECTIVE
próximo (FEM próxima)

## comma – compensation

□ In the coming weeks, we will all have to work hard. En las próximas semanas todos tendremos que trabajar duro.

**comma** NOUN
la coma

**command** NOUN
la orden (PL las órdenes)

**comment** NOUN
▷ see also **comment** VERB
el comentario
□ He made no comment. No hizo ningún comentario.
■ **No comment!** ¡Sin comentarios!

to **comment** VERB
▷ see also **comment** NOUN
hacer* comentarios
□ The police have not commented on these rumours. La policía no ha hecho comentarios sobre estos rumores.

**commentary** NOUN
la crónica

**commentator** NOUN
el/la comentarista

**commercial** ADJECTIVE
▷ see also **commercial** NOUN
comercial (FEM comercial)

**commission** NOUN
la comisión (PL las comisiones)
□ The bank charges 1% commission. El banco cobra un 1% de comisión. □ to work on commission trabajar a comisión

to **commit** VERB
■ **to commit a crime** cometer un crimen
■ **to commit suicide** suicidarse
■ **I don't want to commit myself.** No quiero comprometerme.

**committee** NOUN
el comité

**common** ADJECTIVE
▷ see also **common** NOUN
común (FEM común, PL comunes)
□ 'Smith' is a very common surname. 'Smith' es un apellido muy común.
■ **in common** en común □ We've got a lot in common. Tenemos mucho en común.

**common** NOUN
▷ see also **common** ADJECTIVE
el campo comunal
□ We went for a walk on the common. un paseo por el campo comunal

**Commons** PL NOUN
■ **the House of Commons** la Cámara de los Comunes

**common sense** NOUN
el sentido común

to **communicate** VERB
comunicar*

**communication** NOUN

la comunicación (PL las comunicaciones)

**communion** NOUN
la comunión (PL las comuniones)

**communism** NOUN
el comunismo

**communist** NOUN
▷ see also **communist** ADJECTIVE
el/la comunista

**communist** ADJECTIVE
▷ see also **communist** NOUN
comunista (FEM comunista)

**community** NOUN
la comunidad
■ **the local community** el vecindario
■ **community service** el trabajo comunitario

to **commute** VERB
□ She commutes between Oxford and London. Para ir al trabajo se desplaza diariamente de Oxford a Londres.

**compact disc** NOUN
el disco compacto
■ **compact disc player** el lector de discos compactos

**companion** NOUN
el compañero
la compañera

**company** NOUN
1 la empresa
□ He works for a big company. Trabaja para una empresa grande.
2 la compañía
□ an insurance company una compañía de seguros □ a theatre company una compañía de teatro
■ **to keep somebody company** hacerle compañía a alguien

**comparatively** ADVERB
relativamente

to **compare** VERB
comparar
□ They compared his work to that of Joyce. Compararon su obra a la de Joyce. □ People always compare him with his brother. La gente siempre lo compara con su hermano.
■ **compared with** en comparación a
□ Oxford is small compared with London. Oxford es pequeño en comparación a Londres.

**comparison** NOUN
la comparación (PL las comparaciones)

**compartment** NOUN
el compartimento

**compass** NOUN
la brújula

**compensation** NOUN
la indemnización
□ They got £2000 compensation.

Recibieron 2.000 libras esterlinas de indemnización.

**compere** NOUN
el presentador
la presentadora

to **compete** VERB
■ **to compete in** competir en □ I'm competing in the marathon. Compito en el maratón.
■ **to compete for something** competir por algo □ There are 50 students competing for 6 places. Hay 50 estudiantes compitiendo por 6 puestos.

**competent** ADJECTIVE
competente (FEM competente)

**competition** NOUN
1 el concurso
□ a singing competition un concurso de canto
2 la competencia
□ Competition in the computer sector is fierce. La competencia en el sector de la informática es muy intensa.

**competitive** ADJECTIVE
competitivo (FEM competitiva)

**competitor** NOUN
1 el/la concursante (contestant)
2 el/la rival

to **complain** VERB
1 reclamar
□ We're going to complain to the manager. Vamos a reclamar al director.
2 quejarse
□ She's always complaining about her husband. Siempre se está quejando de su marido.

**complaint** NOUN
la queja

**complete** ADJECTIVE
completo (FEM completa)

**completely** ADVERB
completamente

**complexion** NOUN
el cutis (PL los cutis)

**complicated** ADJECTIVE
complicado (FEM complicada)

**compliment** NOUN
▷ see also **compliment** VERB
el cumplido
□ to pay somebody a compliment hacerle un cumplido a alguien

to **compliment** VERB
▷ see also **compliment** NOUN
felicitar
■ They complimented me on my Spanish. Me felicitaron por mi español.

**complimentary** ADJECTIVE
■ **complimentary ticket** entrada de regalo

**composer** NOUN
el compositor
la compositora

**comprehension** NOUN
el ejercicio de comprensión (school exercise)

**comprehensive school** NOUN
el instituto

**compromise** NOUN
▷ see also **compromise** VERB
el arreglo
□ We reached a compromise. Llegamos a un arreglo.

to **compromise** VERB
▷ see also **compromise** NOUN
llegar* a un acuerdo

**compulsory** ADJECTIVE
obligatorio (FEM obligatoria)

**computer** NOUN
el ordenador (el computador, la computadora Latin America)

**computer game** NOUN
el juego de ordenador

**computer programmer** NOUN
el programador
la programadora

**computer science** NOUN
la informática

**computing** NOUN
la informática

to **concentrate** VERB
concentrarse
□ I couldn't concentrate. No me podía concentrar. □ I was concentrating on my homework. Me estaba concentrando en los deberes.

**concentration** NOUN
la concentración

**concerned** ADJECTIVE
preocupado (FEM preocupada)
□ His mother is concerned about him. Su madre está preocupada por él.
■ As far as the new project is concerned … En lo que respecta al nuevo proyecto …
■ As far as I'm concerned, you can come any time you like. Por mí, puedes venir cuando quieras.
■ It's a stressful situation for everyone concerned. Es una situación estresante para todos los involucrados.

**concert** NOUN
el concierto

**concrete** NOUN
el hormigón

to **condemn** VERB
condenar

**condition** NOUN
la condición (PL las condiciones)
□ I'll do it, on one condition. Lo haré, con

49

una condición.

■ **in good condition** en buen estado

**conditional** NOUN
el condicional

**conditioner** NOUN
el suavizante (el enjuague *Latin America*)
*(for hair)*

**condom** NOUN
el preservativo

to **conduct** VERB
dirigir* *(orchestra)*

**conductor** NOUN
1 el director de orquesta
la directora de orquesta *(of orchestra)*
2 el cobrador
la cobradora *(on bus)*

**cone** NOUN
1 el cucurucho
□ an ice cream cone un cucurucho
2 el cono *(geometric shape)*
■ **a traffic cone** un cono para señalizar el tráfico

**conference** NOUN
la conferencia

to **confess** VERB
confesar*
□ He confessed to the murder. Confesó haber cometido el asesinato.

**confession** NOUN
la confesión (PL las confesiones)

**confidence** NOUN
1 la confianza
□ I've got a lot of confidence in him. Tengo mucha confianza en él.
2 la confianza en sí mismo
□ She lacks confidence. Le falta confianza en sí misma.
■ **I told you that story in confidence.** Te conté esa historia de manera confidencial.

**confident** ADJECTIVE
1 seguro (FEM segura) *(sure of something)*
□ I'm confident everything will be okay. Estoy seguro de que todo saldrá bien.
2 seguro de sí mismo (FEM segura de sí misma) *(self-assured)*
□ She seems quite confident. Parece muy segura de sí misma.

**confidential** ADJECTIVE
confidencial (FEM confidencial)

to **confirm** VERB
confirmar

**confirmation** NOUN
la confirmación (PL las confirmaciones)

**conflict** NOUN
el conflicto

to **confuse** VERB
confundir

**confused** ADJECTIVE

confuso (FEM confusa) *(person)*

**confusing** ADJECTIVE
poco claro (FEM poco clara)
□ The traffic signs are confusing. Las señales de tráfico están poco claras.

**confusion** NOUN
la confusión

to **congratulate** VERB
felicitar
□ My friends congratulated me on passing my test. Mis amigos me felicitaron por aprobar el examen.

**congratulations** PL NOUN
la enhorabuena
□ Congratulations on your new job! ¡Enhorabuena por tu nuevo empleo!

**conjunction** NOUN
la conjunción

**conjurer** NOUN
el prestidigitador
la prestidigitadora

**connection** NOUN
1 la conexión (PL las conexiones)
□ There's no connection between the two events. No hay ninguna conexión entre los dos sucesos.
2 el enlace
□ We missed our connection. Perdimos el enlace.
■ **There's a loose connection.** Hay un hilo suelto.

to **conquer** VERB
1 conquistar *(country)*
2 vencer* *(enemy, fear)*

**conscience** NOUN
la conciencia
■ **to have a guilty conscience** tener remordimientos de conciencia

**conscious** ADJECTIVE
consciente (FEM consciente)
□ He was still conscious when the doctor arrived. Estaba todavía consciente cuando llegó el médico. □ She was conscious of Max looking at her. Era consciente de que Max la miraba.
■ **He made a conscious decision to tell nobody.** Tomó la firme decisión de no decírselo a nadie.

**consciousness** NOUN
el conocimiento
□ I lost consciousness. Perdí el conocimiento.

**consequence** NOUN
la consecuencia

**consequently** ADVERB
por consiguiente

**conservation** NOUN
la conservación

■ **energy conservation** la conservación de la energía

**conservative** ADJECTIVE
▷ *see also* **conservative** NOUN
conservador (FEM conservadora)
■ **the Conservative Party** el partido Conservador

**Conservative** NOUN
▷ *see also* **conservative** ADJECTIVE
el conservador
la conservadora
■ **to vote Conservative** votar a favor del partido Conservador

**conservatory** NOUN
el invernadero

to **consider** VERB
1 considerar
□ He considers it a waste of time. Lo considera una pérdida de tiempo.
2 pensar* en
■ **We considered cancelling our holiday.** Pensamos en cancelar nuestras vacaciones.

**considerate** ADJECTIVE
considerado (FEM considerada)

**considering** PREPOSITION
1 teniendo en cuenta
□ Considering he was ill, he ate well. Teniendo en cuenta que estaba enfermo, comío bien.
2 después de todo
□ I got a good mark, considering. Saqué buena nota, después de todo.

to **consist** VERB
■ **to consist of** consistir en

**consonant** NOUN
la consonante

**constant** ADJECTIVE
constante (FEM constante)

**constantly** ADVERB
constantemente

**constipated** ADJECTIVE
estreñido (FEM estreñida)
□ I'm constipated. Estoy estreñido.
LANGUAGE TIP Be careful not to translate **constipated** by **constipado**.

to **construct** VERB
construir*

**construction** NOUN
la construcción (PL las construcciones)

to **consult** VERB
consultar

**consumer** NOUN
el consumidor
la consumidora

**contact** NOUN
▷ *see also* **contact** VERB
el contacto

□ I'm in contact with her. Estoy en contacto con ella.

to **contact** VERB
▷ *see also* **contact** NOUN
ponerse* en contacto con
□ Where can we contact you? ¿Dónde podemos ponernos en contacto contigo?

**contact lenses** PL NOUN
las lentillas (los lentes de contacto *Latin America*)

to **contain** VERB
contener*

**container** NOUN
el recipiente

**contempt** NOUN
el desprecio

**contents** PL NOUN
el contenido

**contest** NOUN
la competición (PL las competiciones)
□ a fishing contest una competición de pesca
■ **a beauty contest** un concurso de belleza

**contestant** NOUN
el/la concursante

**context** NOUN
el contexto

**continent** NOUN
el continente
■ **the Continent** el continente europeo

**continental breakfast** NOUN
el desayuno continental

to **continue** VERB
continuar*
□ She continued talking to her friend. Continuó hablando con su amiga. □ We continued working after lunch. Continuamos trabajando después de la comida.

**continuous** ADJECTIVE
continuo (FEM continua)
■ **continuous assessment** la evaluación continua

**contraceptive** NOUN
el anticonceptivo

**contract** NOUN
el contrato

to **contradict** VERB
contradecir*

**contrary** NOUN
■ **on the contrary** al contrario

**contrast** NOUN
el contraste

to **contribute** VERB
■ **to contribute to** contribuir a □ Everyone contributed to the success of the play. Todos contribuyeron al éxito de la obra.
□ She contributed £10 to the collection. Contribuyó 10 libras esterlinas a la colecta.

C

**contribution** NOUN
la contribución (PL las contribuciones)

**control** NOUN
▷ *see also* **control** VERB
el control

■ **to lose control** *(of vehicle)* perder el control

■ **the controls** *(of machine)* los mandos

■ **He always seems to be in control.** Parece que siempre está en control la situación.

■ **She can't keep control of the class.** No sabe controlar a la clase.

■ **out of control** fuera de control ▢ That boy is out of control. Ese muchacho está fuera de control.

to **control** VERB
▷ *see also* **control** NOUN
controlar

▢ He can't control the class. No sabe controlar a la clase. ▢ I couldn't control the horse. No pude controlar al caballo.

▢ Please control yourself, everyone's looking at us. Por favor contrólate, todos nos están mirando.

**controversial** ADJECTIVE
polémico (FEM polémica)

▢ Euthanasia is a controversial subject. La eutanasia es un tema polémico.

**convenient** ADJECTIVE
bien situado (FEM bien situada) *(place)*

▢ The hotel's convenient for the airport. El hotel está bien situado con respecto al aeropuerto.

■ **It's not a convenient time for me.** A esa hora no me va bien.

■ **Would Monday be convenient for you?** ¿Te iría bien el lunes?

**conventional** ADJECTIVE
convencional (FEM convencional)

**convent school** NOUN
el colegio de monjas

**conversation** NOUN
las conversación (PL las conversaciones)

▢ We had a long conversation. Tuvimos una larga conversación.

to **convert** VERB
convertir*

▢ We've converted the loft into a bedroom. Hemos convertido el desván en un dormitorio.

to **convict** VERB
▷ *see also* **convict** NOUN
declarar culpable

▢ He was convicted of the murder. Fue declarado culpable del asesinato.

to **convince** VERB
convencer*

▢ I'm not convinced. No me convence.

to **cook** VERB
▷ *see also* **cook** NOUN
1 cocinar

▢ I can't cook. No sé cocinar.

■ **The chicken isn't cooked.** El pollo no está hecho.

2 preparar

▢ She's cooking lunch. Está preparando el almuerzo.

**cook** NOUN
▷ *see also* **cook** VERB
el cocinero
la cocinera

▢ She is a cook in a hotel. Es cocinera en un hotel. ▢ Maria's an excellent cook. María es una cocinera excelente.

**cookbook** NOUN
el libro de cocina

**cooker** NOUN
la cocina *(aparato)*

▢ a gas cooker una cocina de gas

**cookery** NOUN
la cocina *(gastronomía)*

**cookie** NOUN (US)
la galleta

**cooking** NOUN
la cocina *(gastronomía)*

▢ French cooking la cocina francesa

■ **I like cooking.** Me gusta cocinar.

**cool** ADJECTIVE
fresco (FEM fresca)

▢ a cool place un lugar fresco

■ **to stay cool** *(keep calm)* mantenerse en calma ▢ He stayed cool throughout the crisis. Se mantuvo en calma durante toda la crisis.

**cooperation** NOUN
la cooperación

**cop** NOUN
el/la poli *(informal)*

to **cope** VERB
arreglárselas

▢ It was hard, but we coped. Fue difícil, pero nos las arreglamos.

■ **She's got a lot of problems to cope with.** Tiene muchos problemas a los que hacer frente.

**copper** NOUN
1 el cobre

▢ a copper bracelet un brazalete de cobre

2 el/la poli *(informal: policeman)*

**copy** NOUN
▷ *see also* **copy** VERB
1 la copia *(of letter, document)*

2 el ejemplar *(of book)*

to **copy** VERB
▷ *see also* **copy** NOUN
copiar

■ **to copy and paste** *(computing)* copiar y pegar

**core** NOUN
el corazón (PL los corazones) *(of fruit)*

**cork** NOUN
el corcho

**corkscrew** NOUN
el sacacorchos (PL los sacacorchos)

**corn** NOUN
1 el trigo *(wheat)*
2 el maíz *(sweetcorn)*
■ **corn on the cob** la mazorca de maíz

**corner** NOUN
1 la esquina
□ the shop on the corner la tienda de la esquina □ He lives just round the corner. Vive a la vuelta de la esquina.
2 el rincón (PL los rincones)
□ in a corner of the room en un rincón de la habitación
3 el saque de esquina *(in football)*

**cornet** NOUN
1 la corneta *(instrument)*
2 el cucurucho *(ice cream)*

**cornflakes** PL NOUN
los copos de maíz

**cornstarch** NOUN (US)
la harina de maíz

**Cornwall** NOUN
el Cornualles

**corporal** NOUN
el cabo

**corporal punishment** NOUN
el castigo corporal

**corpse** NOUN
el cadáver

**correct** ADJECTIVE
▷ *see also* **correct** VERB
correcto (FEM correcta)
□ That's correct! ¡Correcto! □ the correct answer la respuesta correcta
■ **You're absolutely correct.** Tienes toda la razón.

to **correct** VERB
▷ *see also* **correct** ADJECTIVE
corregir*

**correction** NOUN
la corrección (PL las correcciones)

**correctly** ADVERB
correctamente

**correspondent** NOUN
el/la corresponsal

**corridor** NOUN
el pasillo

**corruption** NOUN
la corrupción

**cosmetics** PL NOUN
los productos de belleza

to **cost** VERB
▷ *see also* **cost** NOUN
costar*
□ The meal cost £20. La comida costó 20 libras esterlinas. □ How much does it cost? ¿Cuánto cuesta?

**cost** NOUN
▷ *see also* **cost** VERB
el coste (el costo *Latin America*)
□ the cost of living el coste de vida
■ **at all costs** a toda costa

**costume** NOUN
el traje

**cosy** ADJECTIVE
acogedor (FEM acogedora)
□ a cosy room una habitación acogedora

**cot** NOUN
la cuna

**cottage** NOUN
el chalet (PL los chalets)

**cottage cheese** NOUN
el requesón

**cotton** NOUN
el algodón
□ a cotton shirt una camisa de algodón

**couch** NOUN
el sofá (PL los sofás)

**couchette** NOUN
la litera

to **cough** VERB
▷ *see also* **cough** NOUN
toser

**cough** NOUN
▷ *see also* **cough** VERB
la tos
□ I've got a cough. Tengo tos.
■ **cough mixture** el jarabe para la tos

**could** VERB ▷ *see* **can**

**council** NOUN
el ayuntamiento *(in town)*
□ He's on the council. Es concejal del ayuntamiento.
■ **a council estate** un barrio de viviendas de protección oficial
■ **a council house** una casa de protección oficial

**councillor** NOUN
el concejal
la concejala

to **count** VERB
contar*

to **count on** VERB
contar* con
□ You can count on me. Puedes contar conmigo.

**counter** NOUN
1 el mostrador *(in shop)*

**2** la ventanilla *(in bank, post office)*
**3** la ficha *(in game)*
**country** NOUN
**1** el país
□ the border between the two countries
la frontera entre los dos países
**2** el campo
□ I live in the country. Vivo en el campo.
■ **country dancing** la danza folklórica
**countryside** NOUN
el campo
**county** NOUN
el condado

> **DID YOU KNOW...?**
> The nearest Spanish equivalent of a
> county would be a **provincia**.

■ **county council** una corporación
administrativa que gobierna un condado

> **DID YOU KNOW...?**
> The nearest Spanish equivalent of a
> county council would be a
> **diputación provincial**.

**couple** NOUN
**1** la pareja
□ the couple who live next door la pareja
que vive al lado
**2** el par
□ a couple of hours un par de horas
**courage** NOUN
el valor
**courgette** NOUN
el calabacín (PL los calabacines)
**courier** NOUN
**1** el/la guía *(for tourists)*
**2** el servicio de mensajero *(delivery service)*
□ They sent it by courier. Lo enviaron por
servicio de mensajero.
**course** NOUN
**1** el curso
□ a Spanish course un curso de español
□ to go on a course hacer un curso
**2** el plato
□ the main course el segundo plato □ the
first course el primer plato
**3** el campo
□ a golf course un campo de golf
■ **of course** por supuesto □ Do you love
me? — Of course I do! ¿Me quieres? — ¡Por
supuesto que te quiero!
**court** NOUN
el tribunal *(of law)*
■ **a tennis court** una pista de tenis (una
cancha de tenis *Latin America*)
**courtyard** NOUN
el patio
**cousin** NOUN
el primo
la prima

**cover** NOUN
▷ *see also* **cover** VERB
**1** la tapa *(of book)*
**2** la funda *(of duvet)*
to **cover** VERB
▷ *see also* **cover** NOUN
cubrir*
□ My face was covered with mosquito bites.
Tenía la cara cubierta de picaduras de
mosquito. □ Our insurance didn't cover it.
Nuestro seguro no lo cubría.
**cow** NOUN
la vaca
**coward** NOUN
el/la cobarde
**cowardly** ADJECTIVE
cobarde (FEM cobarde)
**cowboy** NOUN
el vaquero
**crab** NOUN
el cangrejo
**crack** NOUN
▷ *see also* **crack** VERB
**1** la grieta *(in wall)*
**2** la raja *(in cup, window)*
**3** el crack *(drug)*
■ **He opened the door a crack.** Abrió la
puerta un poquito.
■ **I'll have a crack at it.** Lo intentaré.
to **crack** VERB
▷ *see also* **crack** NOUN
cascar* *(nut, egg)*
■ **He cracked his head on the pavement.**
Se dio con la cabeza en la acera.
■ **I think we've cracked it!** ¡Creo que lo
hemos resuelto!
■ **to crack a joke** contar un chiste
to **crack down on** VERB
tomar medidas severas contra
□ The police are cracking down on drink-
drivers. La policía está tomando medidas
severas contra los conductores que beben.
**cracked** ADJECTIVE
**1** rajado (FEM rajada) *(cup, window)*
**2** resquebrajado (FEM resquebrajada) *(wall)*
**cracker** NOUN
la galleta salada *(biscuit)*
■ **Christmas cracker** el petardo sorpresa
**cradle** NOUN
la cuna
**craft** NOUN
la artesanía
■ **a craft shop** una tienda de objetos de
artesanía
**craftsman** NOUN
el artesano
to **cram** VERB
■ **We crammed our stuff into the boot.**

Apretamos nuestras cosas dentro del maletero.
- **She crammed her bag with books.** Abarrotó su bolso de libros.
- **to cram for an exam** empollar a última hora para un examen *(informal)*

**crane** NOUN
la grúa *(machine)*

to **crash** VERB
▷ *see also* **crash** NOUN
chocar*
□ The two cars crashed. Los dos coches chocaron.
- **to crash into something** chocar con algo
- **He's crashed his car.** Ha tenido un accidente con el coche.
- **The plane crashed.** El avión se estrelló.

**crash** NOUN
▷ *see also* **crash** VERB
el accidente
- **a crash helmet** un casco protector
- **a crash course** un curso intensivo

to **crawl** VERB
▷ *see also* **crawl** NOUN
gatear *(baby)*

**crawl** NOUN
▷ *see also* **crawl** VERB
el crol
- **to do the crawl** nadar estilo crol

**crazy** ADJECTIVE
loco (FEM loca)

**cream** ADJECTIVE
▷ *see also* **cream** NOUN
de color crema (FEM + PL de color crema)
□ a cream silk blouse una blusa de seda de color crema

**cream** NOUN
▷ *see also* **cream** ADJECTIVE
1 la nata (la crema de leche *Latin America*)
□ strawberries and cream fresas con nata
□ a cream cake un pastel de nata
- **cream cheese** el queso cremoso
2 la crema *(for skin)*

**crease** NOUN
1 la arruga *(in clothes, paper)*
2 la raya *(in trousers)*

**creased** ADJECTIVE
arrugado (FEM arrugada)

to **create** VERB
crear

**creation** NOUN
la creación (PL las creaciones)

**creative** ADJECTIVE
creativo (FEM creativa)

**creature** NOUN
la criatura

**crèche** NOUN
la guardería infantil

**credit** NOUN
el crédito
□ on credit a crédito
- **He's a credit to his family.** Hace honor a su familia.

**credit card** NOUN
la tarjeta de crédito

to **creep up** VERB
- **to creep up on somebody** acercarse sigilosamente a alguien

**crept** VERB ▷ *see* **creep up**

**cress** NOUN
el berro

**crew** NOUN
la tripulación (PL las tripulaciones) *(of plane, boat)*
- **a film crew** un equipo de rodaje

**crew cut** NOUN
el pelo cortado al rape

**cricket** NOUN
1 el críquet
□ I play cricket. Juego al críquet.
2 el grillo *(insect)*

**crime** NOUN
1 el delito *(offence)*
□ He committed a crime. Cometió un delito. □ the scene of the crime el lugar del delito
2 el crimen (PL los crímenes) *(very serious)*
□ a crime against humanity un crimen contra la humanidad
3 la delincuencia *(activity)*
□ Crime is rising. La delincuencia va en aumento.

**criminal** NOUN
▷ *see also* **criminal** ADJECTIVE
el/la delincuente

**criminal** ADJECTIVE
▷ *see also* **criminal** NOUN
- **It's a criminal offence.** Constituye un delito.
- **to have a criminal record** tener antecedentes penales

**crisis** NOUN
la crisis (PL las crisis)

**crisp** ADJECTIVE
crujiente (FEM crujiente) *(food)*

**crisps** PL NOUN
las patatas fritas (las papas fritas *Latin America*)
□ a bag of crisps una bolsa de patatas fritas

**criterion** NOUN
el criterio
□ the selection criteria los criterios de selección
- **Only one candidate met all the criteria.** Sólo uno de los candidatos cumplía todos los requisitos.

**critic** NOUN
el crítico
la crítica

**critical** ADJECTIVE
crítico (FEM crítica)

**criticism** NOUN
la crítica

to **criticize** VERB
criticar*

**Croatia** NOUN
Croacia fem

to **crochet** VERB
1 hacer* ganchillo
□ She enjoys crocheting. Le gusta hacer ganchillo.
2 a ganchillo
□ I crocheted a hat. Un gorro a ganchillo.

**crocodile** NOUN
el cocodrilo

**crook** NOUN
el/la sinvergüenza

**crop** NOUN
la cosecha
□ a good crop of apples una buena cosecha de manzanas

**cross** NOUN
▷ see also **cross** ADJECTIVE, VERB
la cruz (PL las cruces)

**cross** ADJECTIVE
▷ see also **cross** NOUN, VERB
enfadado (FEM enfadada) (enojado Latin America)
□ He was cross about something. Estaba enfadado por algo.

to **cross** VERB
▷ see also **cross** NOUN, ADJECTIVE
cruzar* (road, river)

to **cross out** VERB
tachar

**cross-country** NOUN
■ a cross-country race un cross
■ cross-country skiing el esquí de fondo

**crossing** NOUN
1 la travesía
□ a 10-hour crossing una travesía de 10 horas
2 el paso de peatones (for pedestrians)

**crossroads** NOUN
el cruce

**crossword** NOUN
el crucigrama

> LANGUAGE TIP Although **crucigrama** ends in -**a**, it is actually a masculine noun.

to **crouch down** VERB
agacharse

**crow** NOUN
el cuervo

**crowd** NOUN
1 la muchedumbre
2 el público (at sports match)

**crowded** ADJECTIVE
abarrotado de gente (FEM abarrotada de gente)

**crown** NOUN
la corona

**crucifix** NOUN
el crucifijo

**crude** ADJECTIVE
vulgar (FEM vulgara)
□ crude language lenguaje vulgar
■ crude oil el petróleo en crudo

**cruel** ADJECTIVE
cruel (FEM cruel)

**cruise** NOUN
el crucero

**crumb** NOUN
la miga

to **crush** VERB
1 aplastar (box, fingers)
2 machacar*
□ Crush two cloves of garlic. Machacar dos dientes de ajo.

**crutch** NOUN
la muleta

**cry** NOUN
▷ see also **cry** VERB
el grito
□ He gave a cry of pain. Dio un grito de dolor.
■ She had a good cry. Se dio una buena de llorar.

to **cry** VERB
▷ see also **cry** NOUN
1 llorar
□ The baby's crying. El bebé está llorando.
2 gritar
□ 'You're wrong', he cried. 'No es cierto', gritó.

**crystal** NOUN
el cristal

**CTC** NOUN (= city technology college)
el centro de formación profesional

**cub** NOUN
1 el cachorro (animal)
2 el lobato (scout)

**cube** NOUN
1 el cubo (geometric shape)
2 el dado
□ Cut the meat into cubes. Cortar la carne en dados.
3 el terrón (PL los terrones) (of sugar)

**cubic** ADJECTIVE
■ a cubic metre un metro cúbico

**cucumber** NOUN
el pepino

to **cuddle** VERB
abrazar*

**cue** NOUN
el taco *(for snooker, pool)*

**culottes** PL NOUN
la falda pantalón *(PL las faldas pantalón)*

**culture** NOUN
la cultura

**cunning** ADJECTIVE
1 astuto *(FEM astuta) (person)*
2 ingenioso *(FEM ingeniosa)*
  □ a cunning plan  un plan ingenioso

**cup** NOUN
1 la taza
  □ a china cup  una taza de porcelana
  ■ **a cup of coffee** un café
2 la copa *(trophy)*

**cupboard** NOUN
el armario

to **cure** VERB
  ▷ see also **cure** NOUN
  curar

**cure** NOUN
  ▷ see also **cure** VERB
  la cura
  □ There is no simple cure for the common cold.  No hay una cura sencilla para el catarro común.

**curious** ADJECTIVE
  curioso *(FEM curiosa)*
  ■ **to be curious about something** sentir curiosidad por algo

**curl** NOUN
el rizo

**curly** ADJECTIVE
rizado *(FEM rizada)*

**currant** NOUN
la pasa

**currency** NOUN
la moneda
  □ foreign currency  la moneda extranjera

**current** NOUN
  ▷ see also **current** ADJECTIVE
  la corriente
  □ The current is very strong.  La corriente es muy fuerte.

**current** ADJECTIVE
  ▷ see also **current** NOUN
1 actual *(FEM actual)*
  □ the current situation  la situación actual
2 presente *(FEM presente)*
  □ the current financial year  el presente año financiero

**current account** NOUN
la cuenta corriente

**current affairs** PL NOUN
los temas de actualidad

**curriculum** NOUN
el plan de estudios

**curriculum vitae** NOUN
el currículum vitae

**curry** NOUN
el curry *(PL los curries)*

**curse** NOUN
la maldición *(PL las maldiciones)*

**curtain** NOUN
la cortina

**cushion** NOUN
el cojín *(PL los cojines)*

**custard** NOUN
las natillas

**custody** NOUN
la custodia
  □ The mother has custody of the children.  La madre tiene la custodia de los hijos.
  ■ **to be remanded in custody** estar detenido

**custom** NOUN
la costumbre
  □ It's an old custom.  Es una vieja costumbre.

**customer** NOUN
el cliente
la clienta

**customs** PL NOUN
la aduana
  ■ **to go through customs** pasar por la aduana

**customs officer** NOUN
el oficial de aduanas
la oficial de aduanas

**cut** NOUN
  ▷ see also **cut** VERB
1 el corte
  □ He's got a cut on his forehead.  Tiene un corte en la frente.
2 la reducción *(PL las reducciones) (in price, spending)*

to **cut** VERB
  ▷ see also **cut** NOUN
1 cortar
  □ I'll cut some bread.  Voy a cortar pan.
  □ I cut my foot on a piece of glass.  Me corté el pie con un cristal.
  ■ **to cut oneself** cortarse
2 reducir* *(price, spending)*

to **cut down** VERB
cortar
  ■ **She cut down the elm tree.** Cortó el olmo.

to **cut off** VERB
cortar
  □ The electricity has been cut off.  Han cortado la electricidad.  □ We've been cut off.  Se ha cortado la comunicación.

to **cut up** VERB
picar* *(vegetables, meat)*

**cutback** NOUN
el recorte
□ There have been cutbacks in public services.  Ha habido recortes en los servicios públicos.

**cute** ADJECTIVE
mono (FEM mona) *(baby, pet)*
□ Isn't he cute!  ¡Qué mono es!

**cutlery** NOUN
la cubertería

**CV** NOUN
el currículum vitae

**cybercafé** NOUN
el cibercafé

to **cycle** VERB
▷ *see also* **cycle** NOUN
ir* en bicicleta
□ I cycle to school.  Voy al colegio en bicicleta.

**cycle** NOUN
▷ *see also* **cycle** VERB

la bicicleta
□ a cycle ride  un paseo en bicicleta

**cycling** NOUN
el ciclismo
■ **The roads round here are ideal for cycling.** Las carreteras de por aquí son ideales para ir en bicicleta.

**cyclist** NOUN
el/la ciclista

**cylinder** NOUN
el cilindro

**Cyprus** NOUN
Chipre *fem*

**Czech** NOUN
▷ *see also* **Czech** ADJECTIVE
1 el checo
la checa *(person)*
□ the Czechs  los checos
2 el checo *(language)*

**Czech** ADJECTIVE
▷ *see also* **Czech** NOUN
checo (FEM checa)
■ **the Czech Republic** la República Checa

# Dd

**dad** NOUN
1 el padre
   □ my dad mi padre
2 papá
   □ I'll ask Dad. Se lo preguntaré a papá.

**daddy** NOUN
papá

**daffodil** NOUN
el narciso

**daft** ADJECTIVE
estúpido (FEM estúpida)

**daily** ADJECTIVE, ADVERB
1 diario
   □ daily life la vida diaria □ It's part of my daily routine. Forma parte de mi rutina diaria.
   ■ **a daily paper** un periódico
2 todos los días
   □ The pool is open daily. La piscina abre todos los días.

**dairy** NOUN
la lechería

**dairy products** PL NOUN
los productos lácteos

**daisy** NOUN
la margarita

**dam** NOUN
la presa

**damage** NOUN
▷ see also **damage** VERB
los daños
   □ The storm did a lot of damage. La tormenta provocó muchos daños.

to **damage** VERB
▷ see also **damage** NOUN
dañar

**damn** NOUN
▷ see also **damn** ADJECTIVE
   ■ **I don't give a damn!** (informal) ¡Me importa un rábano!
   ■ **Damn!** (informal) ¡Maldita sea!

**damn** ADJECTIVE
▷ see also **damn** NOUN
   ■ **It's a damn nuisance!** (informal) ¡Es una verdadera lata!

**damp** ADJECTIVE
húmedo (FEM húmeda)

**dance** NOUN
▷ see also **dance** VERB
el baile

to **dance** VERB
▷ see also **dance** NOUN
bailar

**dancer** NOUN
1 el bailador
   la bailadora
   ■ **He is not a very good dancer.** No baila muy bien.
2 el bailarín (PL los bailarines)
   la bailarina (professional)

**dandruff** NOUN
la caspa

**Dane** NOUN
el danés (PL los daneses)
la danesa
   □ the Danes los daneses

**danger** NOUN
el peligro
   ■ **in danger** en peligro
   ■ **We were in danger of missing the plane.** Corríamos el riesgo de perder el avión.

**dangerous** ADJECTIVE
peligroso (FEM peligrosa)

**Danish** ADJECTIVE
▷ see also **Danish** NOUN
danés (FEM danesa)

**Danish** NOUN
▷ see also **Danish** ADJECTIVE
el danés (language)

to **dare** VERB
atreverse
   □ I didn't dare to tell my parents. No me atrevía a decírselo a mis padres.
   ■ **I dare say it'll be okay.** Yo diría que va a salir bien.
   ■ **Don't you dare!** ¡Ni se te ocurra!
   ■ **I dare you!** ¡A que no te atreves!

**daring** ADJECTIVE
atrevido (FEM atrevida)

**dark** ADJECTIVE
▷ see also **dark** NOUN
oscuro (FEM oscura)
   □ a dark green sweater un jersey verde oscuro

**d**

□ It's dark in here. Está oscuro aquí dentro.
■ **She's got dark hair.** Tiene el pelo oscuro.
■ **He's got dark skin.** Tiene la piel morena.
■ **It's getting dark.** Está oscureciendo.

**dark** NOUN
▷ see also **dark** ADJECTIVE
la oscuridad
□ I'm afraid of the dark. Me da miedo la oscuridad.
■ **after dark** después del anochecer

**darkness** NOUN
la oscuridad
□ in the darkness en la oscuridad
■ **The room was in darkness.** La habitación estaba a oscuras.

**darling** NOUN
cariño
□ Thank you, darling. Gracias, cariño.

**dart** NOUN
el dardo
□ to play darts jugar a los dardos

to **dash** VERB
▷ see also **dash** NOUN
ir* corriendo
□ Everyone dashed to the window. Todos fueron corriendo a la ventana.
■ **I've got to dash!** ¡Tengo que salir pitando!

**dash** NOUN
▷ see also **dash** VERB
1 el chorrito
□ a dash of vinegar un chorrito de vinagre
2 la raya (punctuation mark)

**data** PL NOUN
los datos

**database** NOUN
la base de datos

**date** NOUN
1 la fecha
□ my date of birth mi fecha de nacimiento
■ **What's the date today?** ¿A qué estamos hoy?
■ **He's got a date with his girlfriend.** Ha quedado con su novia.
■ **out of date 1** (document) caducado □ My passport's out of date. Tengo el pasaporte caducado. **2** (technology, idea) anticuado
2 el dátil (fruit)

**daughter** NOUN
la hija

**daughter-in-law** NOUN
la nuera

**dawn** NOUN
el amanecer
□ at dawn al amanecer

**day** NOUN
el día

LANGUAGE TIP Although **día** ends in -a, it is actually a masculine noun.

□ during the day por el día □ It's a lovely day. Hace un día precioso. □ every day todos los días
■ **the day after tomorrow** pasado mañana
■ **the day before yesterday** anteayer
■ **a day off** un día libre
■ **a day return** un billete de ida y vuelta para el día

**dead** ADJECTIVE
▷ see also **dead** ADVERB
muerto (FEM muerta)
□ He was dead. Estaba muerto.
■ **He was shot dead.** Lo mataron de un tiro.

**dead** ADVERB
▷ see also **dead** ADJECTIVE
■ **You're dead right!** ¡Tienes toda la razón!
■ **It was dead easy.** Fue facilísimo.
■ **dead centre** justo en el centro
■ **dead on time** a la hora exacta

**dead end** NOUN
el callejón sin salida

**deadline** NOUN
■ **October is the deadline for applications.** El plazo para presentar las solicitudes se acaba en octubre.
■ **We're going to miss the deadline.** No vamos a poder cumplir con el plazo.

**deaf** ADJECTIVE
sordo (FEM sorda)

**deafening** ADJECTIVE
ensordecedor (FEM ensordecedora)

**deal** NOUN
▷ see also **deal** VERB
el trato
□ It's a good deal. Es un buen trato. □ He made a deal with the kidnappers. Hizo un trato con los secuestradores.
■ **It's a deal!** ¡Trato hecho!
■ **Big deal!** ¡Vaya cosa!
■ **It's no big deal.** No pasa nada.
■ **a great deal** mucho □ a great deal of money mucho dinero

to **deal** VERB
▷ see also **deal** NOUN
dar* cartas
□ It's your turn to deal. Te toca dar cartas.

**dealer** NOUN
■ **a drug dealer** un traficante de drogas (FEM una traficante de drogas)
■ **an antique dealer** un anticuario (FEM una anticuaria)

**dealt** VERB ▷ see **deal**

**dear** ADJECTIVE
1 querido (FEM querida)
□ Dear Paul Querido Paul
■ **Dear Mrs Smith** Estimada señora Smith
■ **Dear Sir** Muy señor mío
■ **Dear Madam** Estimada señora

■ **Dear Sir/Madam** *(in a circular)*
Estimados Sres.
■ **Oh dear! I've spilled my coffee.** ¡Oh, no!
He derramado el café.
2 caro (FEM cara) *(expensive)*
□ These shoes are too dear. Estos zapatos
son demasiado caros.

**death** NOUN
la muerte
□ after his death después de su muerte
■ **I was bored to death.** Estaba aburrido
como una ostra.

**debate** NOUN
▷ *see also* **debate** VERB
el debate

to **debate** VERB
▷ *see also* **debate** NOUN
discutir

**debt** NOUN
la deuda
□ heavy debts grandes deudas
■ **to be in debt** estar endeudado

**decade** NOUN
la década

**decaffeinated** ADJECTIVE
descafeinado (FEM descafeinada)

to **deceive** VERB
engañar

**December** NOUN
diciembre *masc*
■ **in December** en diciembre
■ **on 22 December** el 22 de diciembre

**decent** ADJECTIVE
decente (FEM decente)

to **decide** VERB
1 decidir
□ I decided to write to her. Decidí escribirle.
□ I decided not to go. Decidí no ir.
2 decidirse
□ Haven't you decided yet? ¿Aún no te has
decidido?

**decimal** ADJECTIVE
decimal (FEM decimal)
□ the decimal system el sistema decimal
■ **decimal point** la coma decimal

**decision** NOUN
la decisión (PL las decisiones)
■ **to make a decision** tomar una decisión

**decisive** ADJECTIVE
decidido (FEM decidida) *(person)*

**deck** NOUN
1 la cubierta *(of ship)*
■ **on deck** en cubierta
2 el piso *(of bus)*
■ **a deck of cards** una baraja

**deckchair** NOUN
la tumbona

to **declare** VERB

declarar

to **decorate** VERB
1 decorar
□ I decorated the cake with glacé cherries.
Decoré el pastel con guindas confitadas.
2 pintar *(paint)*
3 empapelar *(wallpaper)*

**decrease** NOUN
▷ *see also* **decrease** VERB
la disminución (PL las disminuciones)
□ There has been a decrease in the school
roll. Ha habido una disminución en el
número de alumnos.

to **decrease** VERB
▷ *see also* **decrease** NOUN
disminuir*

**dedicated** ADJECTIVE
■ **a very dedicated teacher** un maestro
totalmente entregado a su trabajo
■ **dedicated followers of classical music**
devotos seguidores de la música clásica

to **deduct** VERB
descontar*

**deep** ADJECTIVE
1 profundo (FEM profunda)
■ **a hole four metres deep** un agujero de
cuatro metros de profundidad
■ **How deep is the lake?** ¿Qué profundidad
tiene el lago?
2 espeso (FEM espesa)
□ a deep layer of snow una espesa capa de
nieve
3 grave (FEM grave)
□ He's got a deep voice. Tiene la voz grave.
■ **to take a deep breath** respirar hondo
■ **to be deep in debt** estar hasta el cuello
de deudas

**deeply** ADVERB
profundamente
□ deeply grateful profundamente
agradecido

**deer** NOUN
el ciervo

**defeat** NOUN
▷ *see also* **defeat** VERB
la derrota

to **defeat** VERB
▷ *see also* **defeat** NOUN
derrotar

**defect** NOUN
el defecto

**defence** NOUN
la defensa

to **defend** VERB
defender*

**defender** NOUN
1 el defensor
la defensora *(of person, ideas)*

**d**

2 el/la defensa *(in sports)*

to **define** VERB
definir

**definite** ADJECTIVE
1 concreto (FEM concreta)
□ I haven't got any definite plans. No tengo planes concretos.
2 definitivo (FEM definitiva)
□ It's too soon to give a definite answer. Es pronto aún para dar una respuesta definitiva.
3 seguro (FEM segura)
□ Maybe we'll go to Spain, but it's not definite. Quizá vayamos a España, pero no es seguro.
■ **He was definite about it.** Fue rotundo acerca de esto.
4 claro (FEM clara)
□ It's a definite improvement. Es una clara mejoría.

**definitely** ADVERB
sin duda
□ He's definitely the best player. Es sin duda el mejor jugador.
■ **He's the best player. — Definitely!** Es el mejor jugador. — ¡Desde luego!
■ **Are you going out with him? — Definitely not!** ¿Vas a salir con él? — ¡En absoluto!

**definition** NOUN
la definición (PL las definiciones)

**degree** NOUN
1 el grado
□ a temperature of 30 degrees una temperatura de 30 grados
2 la licenciatura
□ a degree in English una licenciatura en filología inglesa
■ **She's got a degree in English.** Es licenciada en filología inglesa.

to **delay** VERB
▷ *see also* **delay** NOUN
retrasar
□ We decided to delay our departure. Decidimos retrasar la salida.
■ **Don't delay!** ¡No pierdas tiempo!
■ **to be delayed** retrasarse □ Our flight was delayed. Nuestro vuelo se retrasó.

**delay** NOUN
▷ *see also* **delay** VERB
el retraso
□ The tests have caused some delay. Las pruebas han ocasionado algún retraso.
■ **without delay** enseguida

to **delete** VERB
suprimir

**deliberate** ADJECTIVE
intencionado (FEM intencionada)

**deliberately** ADVERB
a propósito

**delicate** ADJECTIVE
delicado (FEM delicada)

**delicatessen** NOUN
la charcutería

**delicious** ADJECTIVE
delicioso (FEM deliciosa)

**delight** NOUN
el placer

**delighted** ADJECTIVE
encantado (FEM encantada)
□ He'll be delighted to see you. Estará encantado de verte.

**delightful** ADJECTIVE
encantador (FEM encantadora)

to **deliver** VERB
1 repartir
□ I deliver newspapers. Reparto periódicos.
2 entregar*
□ The package was delivered in the morning. Entregaron el paquete por la mañana.
■ **Doctor Hamilton delivered the twins.** El Doctor Hamilton asistió en el parto de los gemelos.

**delivery** NOUN
1 la entrega
□ Allow 28 days for delivery. La entrega se realizará en un plazo de 28 días.
2 el parto *(of baby)*

to **demand** VERB
▷ *see also* **demand** NOUN
exigir*
□ I demand an explanation. Exijo una explicación.

**demand** NOUN
▷ *see also* **demand** VERB
1 la petición (PL las peticiones) *(firm request)*
□ His demand for compensation was rejected. Rechazaron su petición de indemnización.
2 la reivindicación (PL las reivindicaciones) *(of trade union)*
□ They met to discuss the union's demands. Se reunieron para discutir las reivindicaciones del sindicato.
3 la demanda
□ Demand for coal is down. Ha bajado la demanda de carbón.

**demanding** ADJECTIVE
■ **It's a very demanding job.** Es un trabajo que exige mucho.
■ **a demanding child** un niño exigente

**demo** NOUN
la manifestación (PL las manifestaciones)

**democracy** NOUN
la democracia

**democratic** ADJECTIVE
democrático (FEM democrática)

to **demolish** VERB
derribar

to **demonstrate** VERB
1 demostrar*
▢ You have to demonstrate that you are reliable. Tienes que demostrar que se puede confiar en ti.
▪ **She demonstrated the technique.** Hizo una demostración de la técnica.
2 manifestarse*
▢ They demonstrated outside the court. Se manifestaron a las puertas del tribunal.

**demonstration** NOUN
1 la demostración (PL las demostraciones) (of method, product)
2 la manifestación (PL las manifestaciones) (protest)

**demonstrator** NOUN
el/la manifestante

**denim** NOUN
▪ **a denim jacket** una cazadora vaquera

**denims** PL NOUN
los vaqueros

**Denmark** NOUN
Dinamarca fem

**dense** ADJECTIVE
1 denso (FEM densa) (smoke, fog)
2 espeso (FEM espesa) (vegetation)
▪ **He's so dense!** ¡Mira que es corto! (informal)

**dent** NOUN
▷ see also **dent** VERB
la abolladura

to **dent** VERB
▷ see also **dent** NOUN
abollar

**dental** ADJECTIVE
dental (FEM dental)
▢ dental treatment el tratamiento dental
▪ **a dental appointment** una cita con el dentista
▪ **dental floss** la seda dental

**dentist** NOUN
el/la dentista
▢ Catherine is a dentist. Catherine es dentista. ▢ at the dentist's en el dentista

to **deny** VERB
negar*
▢ She denied everything. Lo negó todo.

**deodorant** NOUN
el desodorante

to **depart** VERB
1 partir* (person)
▢ He departed at three o'clock precisely. Partió a las tres en punto.
2 salir*

▢ Trains depart for the airport every half hour. Los trenes salen para el aeropuerto cada media hora.

**department** NOUN
1 la sección (PL las secciones)
▢ the toy department la sección de juguetes
2 el departamento
▢ the English department el departamento de inglés

**department store** NOUN
los grandes almacenes

**departure** NOUN
la salida
▢ The departure of this flight has been delayed. Se ha retrasado la salida de este vuelo.
▪ **His sudden departure worried us.** Su marcha repentina nos dejó preocupados.

**departure lounge** NOUN
la sala de embarque

to **depend** VERB
▪ **to depend on** depender de ▢ The price depends on the quality. El precio depende de la calidad.
▪ **You can depend on him.** Puedes confiar en él.
▪ **depending on** según
   LANGUAGE TIP **según** has to be followed by a verb in the subjunctive.
▢ depending on the weather según el tiempo que haga
▪ **It depends.** Depende.

to **deport** VERB
deportar

**deposit** NOUN
1 el depósito (on hired goods)
▢ You get the deposit back when you return the bike. Al devolver la bici te devuelven el depósito.
2 la señal (advance payment)
▢ You have to pay a deposit when you book. Se paga una señal al hacer la reserva.
3 la entrada (in house buying)
▢ He paid a £2000 deposit on the house. Dio una entrada de 2.000 libras para la casa.

**depressed** ADJECTIVE
deprimido (FEM deprimida)
▢ I'm feeling depressed. Estoy deprimido.

**depressing** ADJECTIVE
deprimente (FEM deprimente)

**depth** NOUN
la profundidad
▢ 14 feet in depth 14 pies de profundidad
▪ **to deal with a subject in depth** tratar un tema a fondo

**deputy head** NOUN
el subdirector
la subdirectora

**English-Spanish**

**d**

to **descend** VERB
descender*
□ They descended from the roof slowly.
Descendieron con cuidado del tejado.
to **describe** VERB
describir*
**description** NOUN
la descripción (PL las descripciones)
**desert** NOUN
el desierto
**desert island** NOUN
la isla desierta
to **deserve** VERB
merecer*
**design** NOUN
▷ *see also* **design** VERB
1 el diseño
□ The design of the plane makes it safer.
El diseño del avión lo hace más seguro.
□ a design fault  un fallo en el diseño
2 el motivo
□ a geometric design  un motivo geométrico
■ **fashion design**  diseño de modas
to **design** VERB
▷ *see also* **design** NOUN
1 diseñar
□ She designed the dress herself.  Ella
misma diseñó el vestido.
2 elaborar
□ We will design an exercise plan specially
for you.  Elaboraremos un programa de
ejercicios especial para ti.
**designer** NOUN
el/la modista (*of clothes*)
■ **designer clothes**  la ropa de diseño
**desire** NOUN
▷ *see also* **desire** VERB
el deseo
to **desire** VERB
▷ *see also* **desire** NOUN
desear
**desk** NOUN
1 el escritorio (*in office*)
2 el pupitre (*for pupil*)
3 el mostrador (*in hotel, at airport*)
**despair** NOUN
la desesperación
□ a feeling of despair  un sentimiento de
desesperación
■ **to be in despair**  estar desesperado
**desperate** ADJECTIVE
desesperado (FEM desesperada)
□ a desperate situation  una situación
desesperada
■ **I was starting to get desperate.**  Estaba
empezando a desesperarme.
**desperately** ADVERB
1 tremendamente

□ We're desperately worried.  Estamos
tremendamente preocupados.
2 desesperadamente
□ He was desperately trying to persuade her.
Intentaba desesperadamente convencerla.
to **despise** VERB
despreciar
**despite** PREPOSITION
a pesar de
**dessert** NOUN
el postre
□ for dessert  de postre
**destination** NOUN
el destino
to **destroy** VERB
destruir*
**destruction** NOUN
la destrucción
**detached house** NOUN
la casa no adosada
**detail** NOUN
el detalle
□ I can't remember the details.  No recuerdo
los detalles.
■ **in detail**  detalladamente
**detailed** ADJECTIVE
detallado (FEM detallada)
**detective** NOUN
el/la detective
□ He's a detective.  Es detective.  □ a private
detective  un detective privado
■ **a detective story**  una novela policíaca
**detention** NOUN
■ **to get a detention**  quedarse castigado
después de clase
**detergent** NOUN
el detergente
**determined** ADJECTIVE
decidido (FEM decidida)
□ She's determined to succeed.  Está
decidida a triunfar.
**detour** NOUN
el desvío
**devaluation** NOUN
la devaluación
**devastated** ADJECTIVE
deshecho (FEM deshecha)
□ I was devastated when they told me.
Cuando me lo dijeron me quedé deshecho.
**devastating** ADJECTIVE
devastador (FEM devastadora) (*flood, storm*)
□ Unemployment has a devastating effect
on people.  El desempleo tiene efectos
devastadores en la gente.
■ **She received some devastating news.**
Recibió unas noticias desoladoras.
to **develop** VERB
1 desarrollar (*idea, quality*)

□ I developed his original idea. Yo desarrollé su idea original.

2 desarrollarse

□ Girls develop faster than boys. Las chicas se desarrollan más rápido que los chicos.

3 revelar

□ to get a film developed revelar un carrete

■ **to develop into** convertirse en □ The argument developed into a fight. La discusión se convirtió en una pelea.

**development** NOUN
el desarrollo

□ economic development in Pakistan el desarrollo económico de Pakistán

■ **the latest developments** los últimos acontecimientos

**device** NOUN
el dispositivo

**devil** NOUN
el diablo

to **devise** VERB
idear

**devoted** ADJECTIVE
leal (FEM leal) (friend)

■ **a devoted wife** una abnegada esposa
■ **He's completely devoted to her.** Está totalmente entregado a ella.

**diabetes** NOUN
la diabetes

**diabetic** ADJECTIVE
diabético (FEM diabética)

□ I'm diabetic. Soy diabético.

■ **diabetic chocolate** el chocolate para diabéticos

**diagonal** ADJECTIVE
diagonal (FEM diagonal)

**diagram** NOUN
el diagrama

> **LANGUAGE TIP** Although **diagrama** ends in **-a**, it is actually a masculine noun.

to **dial** VERB
marcar* (discar* Latin America)

**dialling tone** NOUN
la señal de marcar

**dialogue** NOUN
el diálogo

**diamond** NOUN
el diamante

□ a diamond ring un anillo de diamantes

■ **diamonds** (at cards) los diamantes □ the ace of diamonds el as de diamantes

**diaper** NOUN (US)
el pañal

**diarrhoea** NOUN
la diarrea

□ to have diarrhoea tener diarrea

**diary** NOUN

1 la agenda

□ I've got her phone number in my diary. Tengo su número de teléfono en la agenda.

2 el diario

□ I keep a diary. Estoy escribiendo un diario.

**dice** NOUN
el dado

**dictation** NOUN
el dictado

**dictionary** NOUN
el diccionario

**did** VERB ▷ see **do**

to **die** VERB
morir*

□ He died last year. Murió el año pasado.
□ She's dying. Se está muriendo.

■ **to be dying to do something** morirse de ganas de hacer algo

**diesel** NOUN

1 el gasoil (fuel)

2 el coche diesel (car)

**diet** NOUN
▷ see also **diet** VERB

1 la dieta

□ a healthy diet una dieta sana

2 el régimen (PL los regímenes)

□ I'm on a diet. Estoy a régimen.

■ **a diet Coke®** una Coca-Cola® light

to **diet** VERB
▷ see also **diet** NOUN
hacer* régimen

□ I've been dieting for two months. Llevo dos meses haciendo régimen.

**difference** NOUN
la diferencia

□ There's not much difference in age between us. No hay mucha diferencia de edad entre nosotros.

■ **Good weather makes all the difference.** Con buen tiempo la cosa cambia mucho.

■ **It makes no difference.** Da lo mismo.

**different** ADJECTIVE
distinto (FEM distinta)

**difficult** ADJECTIVE
difícil (FEM difícil)

□ It was difficult to choose. Era difícil escoger. □ It was a difficult decision to make. Era una decisión difícil de tomar.

**difficulty** NOUN
la dificultad

□ What's the difficulty? ¿Cuál es la dificultad?

■ **to have difficulty doing something** tener dificultades para hacer algo

to **dig** VERB

1 cavar

□ They're digging a hole in the road. Están cavando un hoyo en la calle. □ Dad's out digging the garden. Papá está fuera cavando en el jardín.

**2** <u>escarbar</u>

□ The dog dug a hole in the sand. El perro escarbó un agujero en la arena.

**digestion** NOUN
la <u>digestión</u>

**digger** NOUN
la <u>excavadora</u>

**digital camera** NOUN
la <u>cámara digital</u>

**digital radio** NOUN
la radio <u>digital</u>

**digital television** NOUN
la <u>televisión digital</u>

**digital watch** NOUN
el <u>reloj digital</u> (PL los relojes <u>digitales</u>)

**dim** ADJECTIVE

**1** <u>tenue</u> (FEM tenue) (light)

**2** <u>lerdo</u> (FEM lerda) (person)

**dimension** NOUN
la <u>dimensión</u> (PL las dimensiones)

to **diminish** VERB
<u>disminuir</u>*

**din** NOUN

**1** el <u>estruendo</u> (of traffic, machinery)

**2** el <u>jaleo</u> (of crowd, voices)

**diner** NOUN (US)
el <u>restaurante barato</u>

**dinghy** NOUN

■ **a rubber dinghy** una lancha neumática

■ **a sailing dinghy** una embarcación de vela ligera

**dining car** NOUN
el <u>vagón restaurante</u> (PL los vagones restaurante)

**dining room** NOUN
el <u>comedor</u>

**dinner** NOUN

**1** la <u>comida</u> (at midday)

**2** la <u>cena</u> (la <u>comida</u> Latin America) (in the evening)

■ **The children have dinner at school.** Los niños comen en la escuela.

**dinner jacket** NOUN
el <u>esmoquin</u> (PL los esmóquines)

**dinner party** NOUN
la <u>cena</u>

**dinner time** NOUN

**1** la <u>hora de la comida</u> (at midday)

**2** la <u>hora de la cena</u> (in the evening)

**dinosaur** NOUN
el <u>dinosaurio</u>

**dip**

▷ see also **dip** VERB NOUN
la <u>salsa</u>

□ a spicy dip una salsa picante

■ **to go for a dip** ir a darse un chapuzón

to **dip** VERB

▷ see also **dip** NOUN
<u>mojar</u>

□ He dipped a biscuit into his tea. Mojó una galleta en el té.

**diploma** NOUN
el <u>diploma</u>

⚬ **LANGUAGE TIP** Although **diploma** ends in **-a**, it is actually a masculine noun.

**diplomat** NOUN
el <u>diplomático</u>
la <u>diplomática</u>

**diplomatic** ADJECTIVE
<u>diplomático</u> (FEM diplomática)

**direct** ADJECTIVE, ADVERB

▷ see also **direct** VERB
<u>directo</u> (FEM directa)

□ the most direct route el camino más directo

■ **You can't fly to Manchester direct from Seville.** No hay vuelos directos a Manchester desde Sevilla.

to **direct** VERB

▷ see also **direct** ADJECTIVE
<u>dirigir</u>*

**direction** NOUN
la <u>dirección</u> (PL las direcciones)

□ We're going in the wrong direction. Vamos en la dirección equivocada.

■ **to ask somebody for directions** preguntar el camino a alguien

**director** NOUN
el <u>director</u>
la <u>directora</u>

**directory** NOUN

**1** la <u>guía telefónica</u> (telephone)

■ **directory enquiries** información telefónica

**2** el <u>directorio</u> (in computing)

**dirt** NOUN
la <u>suciedad</u>

**dirty** ADJECTIVE
<u>sucio</u> (FEM sucia)

□ It's dirty. Está sucio.

■ **to get dirty** ensuciarse

■ **to get something dirty** ensuciarse algo

□ He got his hands dirty. Se ensució las manos.

■ **a dirty joke** un chiste verde (un chiste colorado Latin America)

**disabled** ADJECTIVE, NOUN
<u>minusválido</u> (FEM minusválida)

■ **disabled people** los minusválidos

**disadvantage** NOUN
la <u>desventaja</u>

■ **to be at a disadvantage** estar en desventaja

to **disagree** VERB

■ **We always disagree.** Nunca estamos de acuerdo.

■ **He disagrees with me.** No está de acuerdo conmigo.

**disagreement** NOUN
el desacuerdo

to **disappear** VERB
desaparecer*

**disappearance** NOUN
la desaparición (PL las desapariciones)

**disappointed** ADJECTIVE
decepcionado (FEM decepcionada)
▢ I'm disappointed. Estoy decepcionado.

**disappointing** ADJECTIVE
decepcionante (FEM decepcionante)
▢ It's disappointing. Es decepcionante.

**disappointment** NOUN
la decepción (PL las decepciones)

**disaster** NOUN
el desastre

**disastrous** ADJECTIVE
desastroso (FEM desastrosa)

**disc** NOUN
el disco

**discipline** NOUN
la disciplina

**disc jockey** NOUN
el/la discjockey (PL los/las discjockeys)
▢ He's a disc jockey. Es discjockey.

**disco** NOUN
1 la discoteca (place)
2 el baile
▢ There's a disco at school tonight. Esta noche hay baile en la escuela.

to **disconnect** VERB
desconectar (appliance)

■ **to disconnect the water supply** cortar el agua

**discount** NOUN
el descuento
▢ a 20% discount un descuento del 20 por ciento

to **discourage** VERB
desanimar

■ **to get discouraged** desanimarse

to **discover** VERB
descubrir*

**discrimination** NOUN
la discriminación
▢ racial discrimination la discriminación racial

to **discuss** VERB
1 discutir
▢ I'll discuss it with my parents. Lo discutiré con mis padres.
2 discutir sobre (topic)
▢ We discussed the topic at length. Discutimos sobre el tema largo y tendido.

**discussion** NOUN
la discusión (PL las discusiones)

**disease** NOUN
la enfermedad

**disgraceful** ADJECTIVE
vergonzoso (FEM vergonzosa)

**disgusted** ADJECTIVE
indignado (FEM indignada)
▢ I was completely disgusted. Estaba totalmente indignado.

⊙ **LANGUAGE TIP** Be careful not to translate **disgusted** by **disgustado**.

**disgusting** ADJECTIVE
1 asqueroso (FEM asquerosa) (food, smell)
▢ It looks disgusting. Tiene un aspecto asqueroso.
2 indignante (FEM indignante) (disgraceful)
▢ That's disgusting! ¡Es indignante!

**dish** NOUN
el plato
▢ a china dish un plato de porcelana
▢ a vegetarian dish un plato vegetariano
■ **to do the dishes** fregar los platos
■ **a satellite dish** una antena parabólica

**dishonest** ADJECTIVE
poco honrado (FEM poco honrada)

**dish soap** NOUN (US)
el lavavajillas (PL los lavavajillas)

**dish towel** NOUN (US)
el paño de cocina

**dishwasher** NOUN
el lavaplatos (PL los lavaplatos)

**disinfectant** NOUN
el desinfectante

**disk** NOUN
el disco
■ **the hard disk** el disco duro
■ **disk drive** la unidad de disco

**diskette** NOUN
el disquete

to **dislike** VERB
▷ see also **dislike** NOUN
■ **I dislike it.** No me gusta.

**dislike** NOUN
▷ see also **dislike** VERB
■ **to take a dislike to somebody** coger antipatía a alguien (agarrar antipatía a alguien Latin America)

⊙ **LANGUAGE TIP** Be very careful with the verb **coger**: in most of Latin America this is an extremely rude word that should be avoided. However, in Spain this verb is common and not rude at all.

■ **my likes and dislikes** lo que me gusta y lo que no

to **dismiss** VERB
despedir* (employee)

**disobedient** ADJECTIVE
desobediente (FEM desobediente)
**display** NOUN
▷ see also **display** VERB
■ **The assistant took the watch out of the display.** El dependiente sacó el reloj de la vitrina.
■ **There was a lovely display of fruit in the window.** Había un estupendo surtido de fruta en el escaparate.
■ **to be on display** estar expuesto
■ **a firework display** fuegos artificiales
to **display** VERB
▷ see also **display** NOUN
1 mostrar*
□ She proudly displayed her medal. Mostró con orgullo su medalla.
2 exponer* (in shop window)
**disposable** ADJECTIVE
desechable (FEM desechable)
■ **a disposable razor** una maquinilla desechable
to **disqualify** VERB
descalificar*
■ **to be disqualified** ser descalificado
□ They were disqualified from the competition. Fueron descalificados del campeonato.
■ **He was disqualified from driving.** Le retiraron el carnet de conducir.
to **disrupt** VERB
interrumpir
□ The meeting was disrupted by protesters. La reunión fue interrumpida por unos manifestantes.
■ **Train services are being disrupted by the strike.** El servicio ferroviario se está viendo alterado por la huelga.
**dissatisfied** ADJECTIVE
insatisfecho (FEM insatisfecha)
□ We were dissatisfied with the service. Estábamos insatisfechos con el servicio.
to **dissolve** VERB
disolver*
**distance** NOUN
la distancia
□ a distance of forty kilometres una distancia de cuarenta kilómetros
■ **It's within walking distance.** Se puede ir andando.
■ **in the distance** a lo lejos
**distant** ADJECTIVE
lejano (FEM lejana)
□ in the distant future en un futuro lejano
**distinction** NOUN
1 la distinción (PL las distinciones)
□ to make a distinction between two things hacer una distinción entre dos cosas

2 la matrícula de honor
□ I got a distinction in Spanish. Saqué una matrícula de honor en lengua española.
**distinctive** ADJECTIVE
característico (FEM característica)
to **distract** VERB
distraer*
to **distribute** VERB
distribuir*
**district** NOUN
1 el barrio (of town)
2 la región (PL las regiones) (of country)
to **disturb** VERB
molestar
□ I'm sorry to disturb you. Siento molestarte.
**ditch** NOUN
▷ see also **ditch** VERB
la zanja
to **ditch** VERB
▷ see also **ditch** NOUN
dejar
□ She's just ditched her boyfriend. Acaba de dejar al novio.
**dive** NOUN
▷ see also **dive** VERB
1 el salto de cabeza (into water)
2 el buceo (under water)
to **dive** VERB
▷ see also **dive** NOUN
1 tirarse de cabeza (into water)
2 bucear (under water)
**diver** NOUN
el/la buzo
**diversion** NOUN
el desvío (for traffic)
○ **LANGUAGE TIP** Be careful not to translate **diversion** by diversión.
to **divide** VERB
1 dividir
□ Divide the pastry in half. Divide la masa en dos.
■ **12 divided by 3 is 4.** 12 dividido entre 3 es 4.
2 dividirse
□ We divided into two groups. Nos dividimos en dos grupos.
**diving** NOUN
1 el buceo
□ diving equipment equipo de buceo
2 el salto de trampolín
□ a diving competition una competición de saltos de trampolín
**division** NOUN
la división (PL las divisiones)
**divorce** NOUN
el divorcio
**divorced** ADJECTIVE

divorciado (FEM divorciada)

□ My parents are divorced. Mis padres están divorciados.

■ **to get divorced** divorciarse

**DIY** NOUN

el bricolaje

□ to do DIY hacer bricolaje □ a DIY shop una tienda de bricolaje

**dizzy** ADJECTIVE

■ **I feel dizzy.** Estoy mareado.

**DJ** NOUN

el/la discjockey (PL los/las discjockeys)

□ He's a DJ. Es discjockey.

to **do** VERB

1 hacer*

□ What are you doing this evening? ¿Qué vas a hacer esta noche? □ She did it by herself. Lo hizo ella sola. □ I'll do my best. Haré todo lo que pueda. □ I want to do physics at university. Quiero hacer física en la universidad.

■ **What does your father do?** ¿A qué se dedica tu padre?

2 ir*

□ She's doing well at school. Va bien en el colegio.

■ **How are you doing?** ¿Qué tal?

■ **How do you do?** Mucho gusto.

3 valer*

□ It's not very good, but it'll do. No es muy bueno, pero valdrá. □ Will £10 do? ¿Valdrá con diez libras?

■ **That'll do, thanks.** Así está bien, gracias.

◌ **LANGUAGE TIP** 'do' is not translated when used to form questions.

□ Do you speak English? ¿Hablas inglés?

□ Do you like reading? ¿Te gusta leer?

□ Where does he live? ¿Dónde vive?

□ Where did you go for your holidays? ¿Dónde te fuiste de vacaciones?

◌ **LANGUAGE TIP** Use 'no' in negative sentences for 'don't'.

□ I don't understand. No entiendo. □ You didn't tell me anything. No me dijiste nada. □ He didn't come. No vino. □ Why didn't you come? ¿Por qué no viniste?

◌ **LANGUAGE TIP** 'do' is not translated when it is used in place of another verb.

□ I hate maths. — So do I. Odio las matemáticas. — Yo también. □ I didn't like the film. — Neither did I. No me gustó la película. — A mí tampoco. □ Do you speak English? — Yes, I do. ¿Hablas inglés? — Sí. □ Do you like horses? — No, I don't. ¿Te gustan los caballos? — No.

◌ **LANGUAGE TIP** Use ¿no? or ¿verdad? to check information.

□ You go swimming on Fridays, don't you? Los viernes vas a nadar, ¿no? □ It doesn't matter, does it? No importa, ¿verdad?

to **do up** VERB

1 atarse (shoes)

□ Do up your shoes! ¡Átate los zapatos!

2 abrocharse (shirt, cardigan, coat)

□ Do your coat up. Abróchate el abrigo.

■ **Do up your zip!** ¡Súbete la cremallera!

3 reformar (house, room)

to **do without** VERB

pasar sin

□ I can't do without my computer. Yo no puedo pasar sin el ordenador.

**dock** NOUN

el muelle

**doctor** NOUN

el médico

la médica

□ He's a doctor. Es médico. □ at the doctor's en el médico

**document** NOUN

el documento

**documentary** NOUN

el documental

to **dodge** VERB

esquivar (attacker, blow)

**dodgems** PL NOUN

los coches de choque

**does** VERB ▷ see do

**doesn't** = does not

**dog** NOUN

el perro

□ Have you got a dog? ¿Tienes perro?

**do-it-yourself** NOUN

el bricolaje

**dole** NOUN

el subsidio de paro

■ **He's on the dole.** Está parado.

■ **to go on the dole** quedarse parado

**doll** NOUN

la muñeca

**dollar** NOUN

el dólar

**dolphin** NOUN

el delfín (PL los delfines)

**domestic** ADJECTIVE

■ **a domestic flight** un vuelo nacional

**dominoes** PL NOUN

■ **to have a game of dominoes** echar una partida al dominó

to **donate** VERB

donar

**done** ADJECTIVE

listo (FEM lista)

□ Is the pasta done? ¿Está lista la pasta?

■ **How do you like your steak? — Well done.** ¿Cómo quieres el filete? — Muy hecho.

**donkey** NOUN
el burro

**donor** NOUN
el/la donante

**don't** = do not

**door** NOUN
la puerta

**doorbell** NOUN
el timbre

**doorman** NOUN
el portero

**doorstep** NOUN
el peldaño de la puerta
■ **on my doorstep** en mi puerta

**dormitory** NOUN
el dormitorio

**dose** NOUN
la dosis (PL las dosis)

**dosh** NOUN
la pasta (la lana *Latin America*) (*informal*)

**dot** NOUN
el punto
■ **on the dot** en punto □ He arrived at nine on the dot. Llegó a las nueve en punto.

to **double** VERB
▷ *see also* **double** ADJECTIVE, ADVERB
1 doblar
□ They doubled their prices. Doblaron los precios.
2 doblarse
□ The number of attacks has doubled. El número de agresiones se ha doblado.

**double** ADJECTIVE, ADVERB
▷ *see also* **double** VERB
doble (FEM doble)
□ a double helping una ración doble
□ to cost double costar el doble
■ **double bed** la cama de matrimonio
■ **a double room** una habitación doble

**double bass** NOUN
el contrabajo

to **double-click** VERB
hacer* doble clic
□ to double-click on an icon hacer doble clic en un icono

**double glazing** NOUN
el doble acristalamiento

**doubles** PL NOUN
dobles *masc pl* (*in tennis*)
□ to play mixed doubles jugar un partido de dobles mixtos

**doubt** NOUN
▷ *see also* **doubt** VERB
la duda
□ I have my doubts. Tengo mis dudas.
■ **no doubt** sin duda □ as you no doubt know como sin duda sabrá

to **doubt** VERB

▷ *see also* **doubt** NOUN
dudar
□ I doubt it. Lo dudo.

LANGUAGE TIP Use the subjunctive after **dudar que**.

□ I doubt that he'll agree. Dudo que vaya a estar de acuerdo.

**doubtful** ADJECTIVE
dudoso (FEM dudosa)
□ It's doubtful. Es dudoso.
■ **to be doubtful about doing something** no estar seguro de hacer algo □ I'm doubtful about going by myself. No estoy seguro de ir solo.
■ **You sound doubtful.** No pareces muy convencido.

**dough** NOUN
la masa

**doughnut** NOUN
el buñuelo
□ a jam doughnut un buñuelo de mermelada

**down** ADJECTIVE, ADVERB, PREPOSITION
1 abajo
□ His office is down on the first floor. Su despacho está abajo en el primer piso.
□ It's down there. Está allí abajo.
2 al suelo
□ He threw down his racket. Tiró la raqueta al suelo.
■ **They live just down the road.** Viven más adelante en esta calle.
■ **to feel down** estar desanimado
■ **The computer's down.** El ordenador no funciona.

to **download** VERB
bajarse
□ to download sth from the Internet bajarse algo de Internet

**downpour** NOUN
el chaparrón (PL los chaparrones)

**downstairs** ADVERB, ADJECTIVE
1 abajo
□ The bathroom's downstairs. El baño está abajo.
■ **to go downstairs** bajar
2 de abajo
□ the downstairs bathroom el baño de abajo
■ **the neighbours downstairs** los vecinos de abajo

**downtown** ADVERB (US)
1 al centro de la ciudad (*go, come*)
2 en el centro de la ciudad (*live, be*)

to **doze** VERB
dormitar

to **doze off** VERB
quedarse dormido

**dozen** NOUN
la docena
□ a dozen eggs una docena de huevos
□ two dozen dos docenas
■ **I've told you that dozens of times.** Te lo he dicho cientos de veces.

**drab** ADJECTIVE
triste (FEM triste) *(clothes)*

**draft** NOUN (US)
la corriente de aire

to **drag** VERB
▷ *see also* **drag** NOUN
arrastrar *(thing, person)*
■ **to drag and drop** arrastrar y soltar

**drag** NOUN
▷ *see also* **drag** VERB
■ **It's a real drag!** ¡Es una verdadera lata! *(informal)*

**dragon** NOUN
el dragón (PL los dragones)

**drain** NOUN
▷ *see also* **drain** VERB
1 el desagüe *(of house)*
2 la alcantarilla *(in street)*

to **drain** VERB
▷ *see also* **drain** NOUN
escurrir *(vegetables, pasta)*

**draining board** NOUN
el escurridero

**drainpipe** NOUN
el tubo de desagüe

**drama** NOUN
1 el drama
> LANGUAGE TIP Although **drama** ends in -a, it is actually a masculine noun.
□ a TV drama un drama para televisión
2 el teatro
□ Greek drama el teatro griego □ Drama is my favourite subject. Mi asignatura favorita es teatro.
■ **drama school** la escuela de arte dramático

**dramatic** ADJECTIVE
espectacular (FEM espectacular)
□ a dramatic improvement una espectacular mejoría
■ **dramatic news** noticias sensacionales

**drank** VERB ▷ *see* **drink**

**drapes** PL NOUN (US)
las cortinas

**drastic** ADJECTIVE
drástico (FEM drástica)
□ to take drastic action tomar medidas drásticas

**draught** NOUN
la corriente de aire
□ There's a draught from the window. Entra corriente por la ventana.
■ **draught beer** la cerveza de barril

**draughts** NOUN
las damas
□ to play draughts jugar a las damas

**draw** NOUN
▷ *see also* **draw** VERB
1 el empate
□ The game ended in a draw. El partido terminó en empate.
2 el sorteo
□ The draw takes place on Saturday. El sorteo es el sábado.

to **draw** VERB
▷ *see also* **draw** NOUN
1 dibujar *(a scene, a person)*
■ **to draw a picture** hacer un dibujo
■ **to draw a picture of somebody** hacer un retrato de alguien
■ **to draw a line** trazar una línea
2 empatar
□ We drew two all. Empatamos a dos.
■ **to draw the curtains 1** *(open)* descorrer las cortinas **2** *(close)* correr las cortinas

**drawback** NOUN
el inconveniente

**drawer** NOUN
el cajón (PL los cajones)

**drawing** NOUN
el dibujo
■ **He's good at drawing.** Se le da bien dibujar.

**drawing pin** NOUN
la chincheta

**drawn** VERB ▷ *see* **draw**

**dreadful** ADJECTIVE
1 terrible (FEM terrible)
□ a dreadful mistake un terrible error
2 horrible (FEM horrible)
□ The weather was dreadful. Hizo un tiempo horrible.
■ **You look dreadful.** Tienes muy mal aspecto.
■ **I feel dreadful about not having phoned.** Me siento muy mal por no haber llamado.

to **dream** VERB
▷ *see also* **dream** NOUN
soñar*
□ Do you dream every night? ¿Sueñas todas las noches? □ She dreamt about her baby. Soñó con su bebé.

**dream** NOUN
▷ *see also* **dream** VERB
el sueño

to **drench** VERB
■ **I got drenched.** Me puse empapado.

**dress** NOUN
▷ *see also* **dress** VERB
el vestido

d

71

**to dress** VERB
▷ *see also* **dress** NOUN
vestirse*
□ I got up, dressed, and went downstairs.
Me levanté, me vestí y bajé.
■ **to dress somebody** vestir a alguien
■ **to get dressed** vestirse
**to dress up** VERB
disfrazarse*
□ I dressed up as a ghost. Me disfracé de
fantasma.
**dressed** ADJECTIVE
vestido (FEM vestida)
□ I'm not dressed yet. Aún no estoy vestido.
□ How was she dressed? ¿Cómo iba vestida?
□ She was dressed in white. Iba vestida de
blanco.
■ **She was dressed in a green sweater
and jeans.** Llevaba un jersey verde y
vaqueros.
**dresser** NOUN
el aparador *(furniture)*
**dressing gown** NOUN
la bata
**dressing table** NOUN
el tocador
**drew** VERB ▷ *see* **draw**
**dried** ADJECTIVE
seco (FEM seca)
■ **dried milk** la leche en polvo
■ **dried fruits** las frutas pasas
**drier** = **dryer**
**drift** NOUN
▷ *see also* **drift** VERB
■ **a snow drift** el ventisquero
**to drift** VERB
▷ *see also* **drift** NOUN
1 ir* a la deriva *(boat)*
2 amontonarse *(snow)*
**drill** NOUN
▷ *see also* **drill** VERB
la taladradora
**to drill** VERB
▷ *see also* **drill** NOUN
taladrar
■ **He drilled a hole in the wall.** Hizo un
agujero en la pared.
**to drink** VERB
▷ *see also* **drink** NOUN
beber (tomar *Latin America*)
□ What would you like to drink? ¿Qué te
apetece beber? □ She drank three cups of
tea. Se bebió tres tazas de té. □ He had
been drinking. Había bebido.
**drink** NOUN
▷ *see also* **drink** VERB
1 la bebida
□ a cold drink una bebida fría

2 la copa *(alcoholic)*
□ They've gone out for a drink. Han salido a
tomar una copa.
■ **to have a drink** tomar algo □ Would you
like a drink? ¿Quieres tomar algo?
**drinking water** NOUN
el agua potable *fem*

> **LANGUAGE TIP** Although it's a feminine
> noun, remember that you use **el** with
> **agua.**

**drive** NOUN
▷ *see also* **drive** VERB
1 el paseo en coche
□ to go for a drive ir a dar un paseo en coche
■ **We've got a long drive tomorrow.**
Mañana nos espera un largo viaje en coche.
2 el camino de entrada a la casa
□ He parked his car in the drive. Aparcó el
coche en el camino de entrada a la casa.
**to drive** VERB
▷ *see also* **drive** NOUN
1 conducir* (manejar *Latin America*) *(a car)*
□ Can you drive? ¿Sabes conducir?
2 ir* en coche *(go by car)*
□ We never drive into the town centre.
Nunca vamos en coche al centro.
3 llevar en coche *(transport)*
□ My mother drives me to school. Mi madre
me lleva al colegio en coche.
■ **to drive somebody home** acercar a
alguien a su casa en coche
■ **to drive somebody mad** volver loco a
alguien □He drives her mad. La vuelve loca.
**driver** NOUN
el conductor
la conductora
□ He's a bus driver. Es conductor de
autobús.
■ **She's an excellent driver.** Conduce muy
bien.
**driver's license** NOUN (US)
el permiso de conducir
**driving instructor** NOUN
el profesor de autoescuela
la profesora de autoescuela
□ He's a driving instructor. Es profesor de
autoescuela.
**driving lesson** NOUN
la clase de conducir
**driving licence** NOUN
el permiso de conducir
**driving test** NOUN
■ **to take one's driving test** hacer el
examen de conducir
■ **She's just passed her driving test.**
Acaba de sacarse el carnet de conducir.
**drizzle** NOUN
la llovizna

**drop** NOUN
▷ *see also* **drop** VERB
1 la gota *(of liquid)*
□ Would you like some milk? — Just a drop.
¿Quieres leche? — Una gota nada más.
2 la bajada
□ a drop in temperature una bajada de las
temperaturas

to **drop** VERB
▷ *see also* **drop** NOUN
1 bajar
□ The temperature will drop tonight.
La temperatura bajará esta noche.
2 soltar*
□ The cat dropped the mouse at my feet.
El gato soltó al ratón junto a mis pies.
■ **I dropped the glass.** Se me cayó el vaso.
3 dejar
□ Could you drop me at the station? ¿Me
puedes dejar en la estación?
■ **I'm going to drop chemistry.** No voy a
dar más química.

**drought** NOUN
la sequía

**drove** VERB ▷ *see* **drive**

to **drown** VERB
ahogarse*
□ A boy drowned here yesterday. Un chico
se ahogó ayer aquí.

**drug** NOUN
1 el medicamento
□ They need food and drugs. Necesitan
comida y medicamentos.
2 la droga
□ hard drugs drogas duras □ soft drugs
drogas blandas
■ **to take drugs** drogarse
■ **a drug addict** un drogadicto
■ **a drug pusher** un camello *(informal)*
■ **a drug smuggler** un narcotraficante
■ **the drugs squad** la brigada antidroga

**drugstore** NOUN (US)
la farmacia

**drum** NOUN
el tambor
□ an African drum un tambor africano
■ **a drum kit** una batería
■ **to play the drums** tocar la batería

**drummer** NOUN
el/la batería *(in rock group)*

**drunk** VERB ▷ *see* **drink**

**drunk** ADJECTIVE
▷ *see also* **drunk** NOUN
borracho (FEM borracha)
□ He was drunk. Estaba borracho.
■ **to get drunk** emborracharse

**drunk** NOUN
▷ *see also* **drunk** ADJECTIVE

el borracho
la borracha

**dry** ADJECTIVE
▷ *see also* **dry** VERB
seco (FEM seca)
□ The paint isn't dry yet. Aún no está seca la
pintura. □ It's been exceptionally dry this
spring. Esta primavera ha sido
extraordinariamente seca.
■ **a long dry period** un largo periodo sin
lluvia

to **dry** VERB
▷ *see also* **dry** ADJECTIVE
1 secar*
□ to dry the dishes secar los platos
□ There's nowhere to dry clothes here. Aquí
no hay un sitio para poner a secar la ropa.
2 secarse*
□ The washing will dry quickly in the sun.
La colada se secará rápido al sol.
■ **to dry one's hair** secarse el pelo

**dry-cleaner's** NOUN
la tintorería

**dryer** NOUN
■ **a tumble dryer** una secadora
■ **a hair dryer** un secador

**DTP** NOUN (= *desktop publishing*)
la autoedición

**dubbed** ADJECTIVE
doblado (FEM doblada)
□ The film was dubbed into Spanish. La
película estaba doblada al español.

**dubious** ADJECTIVE
■ **My parents were a bit dubious about it.**
Mis padres tenían sus dudas sobre el tema.

**duck** NOUN
el pato

**due** ADJECTIVE, ADVERB
■ **He's due to arrive tomorrow.** Debe
llegar mañana.
■ **The plane's due in half an hour.** El avión
llegará en media hora.
■ **When's the baby due?** ¿Para cuándo
nacerá el niño?
■ **due to** debido a □ The trip was cancelled
due to bad weather. El viaje se suspendió
debido al mal tiempo.

**dug** VERB ▷ *see* **dig**

**dull** ADJECTIVE
1 soso (FEM sosa)
□ He's nice, but a bit dull. Es simpático,
pero un poco soso.
2 gris (FEM grisa)
□ It's always dull and wet. El tiempo está
siempre gris y lluvioso.

**dumb** ADJECTIVE
1 mudo (FEM muda)
2 bobo (FEM boba)

□ Don't be so dumb! ¡No seas bobo!
■ **That was a really dumb thing I did!**
¡Lo que hice fue una verdadera bobada!

**dummy** NOUN
el chupete *(for baby)*

**dump** NOUN
▷ *see also* **dump** VERB
■ **It's a real dump!** ¡Es una auténtica
pocilga!
■ **a rubbish dump** un vertedero

to **dump** VERB
▷ *see also* **dump** NOUN
verter* *(waste)*
□ 'No dumping.' 'Prohibido verter basuras.'

**dungarees** PL NOUN
el mono (el overol *Latin America*)

**dungeon** NOUN
la mazmorra

**duration** NOUN
la duración
□ Courses are of two years' duration. Los
cursos tienen una duración de dos años.
■ **for the duration of the trial** durante
todo el juicio

**during** PREPOSITION
durante

**dusk** NOUN
el anochecer
■ **at dusk** al anochecer

**dust** NOUN
▷ *see also* **dust** VERB
el polvo

to **dust** VERB
▷ *see also* **dust** NOUN
limpiar el polvo de
□ I dusted the shelves. Limpié el polvo de
las estanterías.

**dustbin** NOUN

el cubo de la basura (el balde *Latin America*)

**dustman** NOUN
el basurero

**dusty** ADJECTIVE
polvoriento (FEM polvorienta)

**Dutch** ADJECTIVE
▷ *see also* **Dutch** NOUN
holandés (FEM holandesa)
□ She's Dutch. Es holandesa.

**Dutch** NOUN
▷ *see also* **Dutch** ADJECTIVE
el holandés *(language)*
■ **the Dutch** los holandeses

**Dutchman** NOUN
el holandés

**Dutchwoman** NOUN
la holandesa

**duty** NOUN
el deber
□ It was his duty to tell the police. Su deber
era decírselo a la policía.
■ **to be on duty 1** *(policeman)* estar de
servicio **2** *(doctor, nurse)* estar de guardia

**duty-free** ADJECTIVE
libre de impuestos (FEM libre de impuestos)

**duvet** NOUN
el edredón (PL los edredones)

**DVD** NOUN
el DVD
■ **a DVD player** un lector de DVD

**dwarf** NOUN
el enano
la enana

**dying** VERB ▷ *see* **die**

**dynamic** ADJECTIVE
dinámico (FEM dinámica)

**dyslexia** NOUN
la dislexia

# Ee

**each** ADJECTIVE, PRONOUN
1 cada (FEM cada)
□ each day cada día
■ **Each house has its own garden.** Todas las casas tienen jardín.
2 cada uno (FEM cada una)
□ They have 10 points each. Tienen 10 puntos cada uno. □ The plates cost £5 each. Los platos cuestan 5 libras cada uno. □ He gave each of us £10. Nos dio 10 libras a cada uno.

   **LANGUAGE TIP** Use a reflexive verb to translate 'each other'.

□ They hate each other. Se odian. □ We write to each other. Nos escribimos. □ They don't know each other. No se conocen.

**eager** ADJECTIVE
■ **He was eager to tell us about his experiences.** Estaba impaciente por contarnos sus experiencias.

**ear** NOUN
la oreja

**earache** NOUN
■ **to have earache** tener dolor de oídos

**earlier** ADVERB
1 antes
□ I saw him earlier. Lo vi antes.
2 más temprano (in the morning)
□ I ought to get up earlier. Debería levantarme más temprano.

**early** ADVERB, ADJECTIVE
1 temprano
□ I have to get up early. Tengo que levantarme temprano.
■ **to have an early night** irse a la cama temprano
2 pronto (ahead of time)
□ I came early to avoid the heavy traffic. Vine pronto para evitar el tráfico denso.

**to earn** VERB
ganar
□ She earns £5 an hour. Gana 5 libras esterlinas a la hora.

**earnings** PL NOUN
los ingresos
□ Her earnings exceed £100,000 per year.

Sus ingresos superan las 100.000 libras anuales.

**earring** NOUN
el pendiente (el arete Latin America)

**earth** NOUN
la tierra
■ **What on earth are you doing here?** ¿Qué diablos haces aquí?

**earthquake** NOUN
el terremoto

**easily** ADVERB
fácilmente

**east** ADJECTIVE, ADVERB
▷ see also **east** NOUN
■ **an east wind** un viento del este
■ **the east coast** la costa oriental
■ **east of** al este de □ It's east of London. Está al este de Londres.
hacia el este
□ We were travelling east. Viajábamos hacia el este.

**east** NOUN
▷ see also **east** ADJECTIVE, ADVERB
el este (direction, region)
□ in the east of the country al este del país

**Easter** NOUN
la Pascua
■ **Easter egg** el huevo de Pascua
■ **the Easter holidays** las vacaciones de Semana Santa

**eastern** ADJECTIVE
oriental (FEM oriental)
□ the eastern part of the island la parte oriental de la isla
■ **Eastern Europe** la Europa del Este

**easy** ADJECTIVE
fácil (FEM fácil)

**easy chair** NOUN
el sillón (PL los sillones)

**easy-going** ADJECTIVE
■ **to be easy-going** ser una persona de trato fácil □ She's very easy-going. Es una persona de trato fácil.

**to eat** VERB
comer
□ Would you like something to eat?

¿Quieres comer algo?

**EC** NOUN (= European Community)
la CE (= la Comunidad Europea)

**eccentric** ADJECTIVE
excéntrico (FEM excéntrica)

**echo** NOUN
el eco

**ecology** NOUN
la ecología

**e-commerce** NOUN
el comercio electrónico

**economic** ADJECTIVE
1 económico (FEM económica) (growth, development, policy)
2 rentable (FEM rentable) (profitable)

**economical** ADJECTIVE
económico (FEM económica)
□ My car is very economical to run. Mi coche me sale muy económico.

**economics** NOUN
la economía
□ the economics of the third world countries la economía de los países tercermundistas
■ **He's doing economics at university.** Estudia económicas en la universidad.

to **economize** VERB
economizar*
■ **to economize on something** economizar en algo

**economy** NOUN
la economía

**ecstasy** NOUN
el éxtasis (drug)
■ **to be in ecstasy** estar en éxtasis

**eczema** NOUN
el eczema
⚬ LANGUAGE TIP Although **eczema** ends in -a, it is actually a masculine noun.
□ She's got eczema. Tiene eczema.

**edge** NOUN
1 el borde
□ on the edge of the desk en el borde del escritorio
■ **They live on the edge of the town.** Viven en los límites de la ciudad.
2 la orilla (of lake)
■ **to be on the edge of tears** estar a punto de llorar

**edgy** ADJECTIVE
nervioso (FEM nerviosa)

**Edinburgh** NOUN
Edimburgo masc

**editor** NOUN
1 el director
la directora (of newspaper, magazine)
2 el redactor
la redactora

□ the sports editor el redactor de la sección de deportes

**educated** ADJECTIVE
culto (FEM culta)

**education** NOUN
1 la educación
□ There should be more investment in education. Debería invertirse más dinero en educación.
2 la enseñanza (teaching)
□ She works in education. Trabaja en la enseñanza.

**educational** ADJECTIVE
1 educativo (FEM educativa) (toy)
2 instructivo (FEM instructiva) (experience, film)

**effect** NOUN
el efecto
□ special effects los efectos especiales

**effective** ADJECTIVE
eficaz (PL eficaces)

**efficient** ADJECTIVE
1 eficiente (FEM eficiente)
□ His secretary is very efficient. Su secretaria es muy eficiente.
2 eficaz (FEM eficaz, PL eficaces)
□ It's a very efficient system. Es un sistema muy eficaz.

**effort** NOUN
el esfuerzo
■ **to make an effort to do something** esforzarse en hacer algo

**e.g.** ABBREVIATION
p.ej.

**egg** NOUN
el huevo
□ a hard-boiled egg un huevo duro □ a soft-boiled egg un huevo pasado por agua □ a fried egg un huevo frito □ scrambled eggs los huevos revueltos

**egg cup** NOUN
la huevera

**eggplant** NOUN (US)
la berenjena

**Egypt** NOUN
Egipto masc

**eight** NUMERAL
ocho
□ She's eight. Tiene ocho años.

**eighteen** NUMERAL
dieciocho
□ She's eighteen. Tiene dieciocho años.

**eighteenth** ADJECTIVE
decimoctavo (FEM decimoctava)
■ **the eighteenth floor** la planta dieciocho
■ **the eighteenth of August** el dieciocho de agosto

**eighth** ADJECTIVE
octavo (FEM octava)

□ the eighth floor el octavo piso
■ **the eighth of August** el ocho de agosto

**eighty** NUMERAL
ochenta
□ He's eighty. Tiene ochenta años.

**Eire** NOUN
Eire *masc*

**either** ADJECTIVE, CONJUNCTION, PRONOUN, ADVERB
tampoco
□ I don't like milk, and I don't like eggs either. No me gusta la leche, y tampoco me gustan los huevos. □ I've never been to Spain. — I haven't either. No he estado nunca en España. — Yo tampoco.
■ **either...or...** o...o... □ You can have either ice cream or yoghurt. Puedes tomar o helado o yogur.
■ **either of them** uno u otro □ Choose either of them. Tienes que elegir entre uno u otro.
■ **I don't like either of them.** No me gusta cualquiera de los dos.
■ **on either side of the road** a ambos lados de la carretera

**elastic** NOUN
el elástico

**elastic band** NOUN
la goma elástica

**elbow** NOUN
el codo

**elder** ADJECTIVE
mayor (FEM mayor)
□ my elder sister mi hermana mayor

**elderly** ADJECTIVE
anciano (FEM anciana)
■ **an elderly man** un anciano
■ **the elderly** los ancianos

**eldest** ADJECTIVE, NOUN
mayor (FEM mayor)
□ my eldest sister mi hermana mayor
■ **He's the eldest.** Él es el mayor.

to **elect** VERB
elegir*

**election** NOUN
la elección (PL las elecciones)

**electric** ADJECTIVE
eléctrico (FEM eléctrica)
□ an electric fire una estufa eléctrica
□ an electric guitar una guitarra eléctrica
□ an electric blanket una manta eléctrica

**electrical** ADJECTIVE
eléctrico (FEM eléctrica)
□ electrical engineering la ingeniería eléctrica
■ **an electrical engineer** un ingeniero en electrónica

**electrician** NOUN
el/la electricista
□ He's an electrician. Es electricista.

**electricity** NOUN
la electricidad

**electronic** ADJECTIVE
electrónico (FEM electrónica)

**electronics** NOUN
la electrónica

**elegant** ADJECTIVE
elegante (FEM elegante)

**elementary school** NOUN (US)
la escuela primaria

**elephant** NOUN
el elefante

**elevator** NOUN (US)
el ascensor

**eleven** NUMERAL
once
□ She's eleven. Tiene once años.

**eleventh** ADJECTIVE
undécimo (FEM undécima)
■ **the eleventh floor** el piso once
■ **the eleventh of August** el once de agosto

**else** ADVERB
■ **somebody else** otra persona
■ **nobody else** nadie más
■ **something else** otra cosa
■ **nothing else** nada más
■ **somewhere else** en algún otro sitio
■ **Did you look anywhere else?** ¿Miraste en otro sitio?
■ **I would be happy anywhere else.** Estaría contento en cualquier otro sitio.
■ **I didn't look anywhere else.** No miré en ningún otro sitio.
■ **Would you like anything else?** ¿Desea alguna otra cosa?
■ **I don't want anything else.** No quiero nada más.
■ **Arrive on time or else!** ¡Llega a tiempo o si no...!

**email** NOUN
▷ *see also* **email** VERB
el e-mail

to **email** VERB
▷ *see also* **email** NOUN
■ **to email somebody** enviar un e-mail a alguien
■ **I'll email you the details.** Te mandaré la información por e-mail.

**email address** NOUN
la dirección de e-mail
□ My email address is jones at collins dot uk. Mi dirección de e-mail es jones arroba collins punto uk.

**embankment** NOUN
el terraplén (PL los terraplenes) *(of railway)*

**embarrassed** ADJECTIVE
■ **I was really embarrassed.** Me dio mucha vergüenza.

e

**LANGUAGE TIP** Be careful not to translate **embarrassed** by **embarazada**.

**embarrassing** ADJECTIVE
embarazoso (FEM embarazosa) *(mistake, situation)*
- **It was so embarrassing.** Fue una situación muy violenta.
- **How embarrassing!** ¡Qué vergüenza!

**embassy** NOUN
la embajada

to **embroider** VERB
bordar

**embroidery** NOUN
el bordado
- **I do embroidery in the afternoon.** Bordo por las tardes.

**emergency** NOUN
la emergencia
- ▢ This is an emergency! ¡Es una emergencia!
- **in an emergency** en caso de emergencia
- **an emergency exit** una salida de emergencia
- **an emergency landing** un aterrizaje forzoso
- **the emergency services** los servicios de urgencia

to **emigrate** VERB
emigrar

**emotion** NOUN
la emoción (PL las emociones)

**emotional** ADJECTIVE
emotivo (FEM emotiva)
- ▢ She's very emotional. Es una persona muy emotiva.
- **He got very emotional at the farewell party.** Se emocionó mucho en la fiesta de despedida.

**emperor** NOUN
el emperador

to **emphasize** VERB
recalcar*
- ▢ He emphasized the importance of the issue. Recalcó la importancia de la cuestión.
- **to emphasize that** subrayar que

**empire** NOUN
el imperio

to **employ** VERB
emplear
- ▢ The factory employs 600 people. La fábrica emplea a 600 trabajadores.
- **Thousands of people are employed in tourism.** Miles de personas trabajan en el sector de turismo.

**employee** NOUN
el empleado
la empleada

**employer** NOUN
el empresario
la empresaria

**employment** NOUN
el empleo

**empty** ADJECTIVE
▷ *see also* **empty** VERB
vacío (FEM vacía)

to **empty** VERB
▷ *see also* **empty** ADJECTIVE
vaciar*
- **to empty something out** vaciar algo

to **encourage** VERB
animar
- ▢ to encourage somebody to do something animar a alguien a hacer algo

**encouragement** NOUN
el estímulo

**encyclopedia** NOUN
la enciclopedia

**end** NOUN
▷ *see also* **end** VERB
1 el final
- ▢ the end of the film el final de la película
- ▢ the end of the holidays el final de las vacaciones
- **in the end** al final ▢ In the end I decided to stay at home. Al final decidí quedarme en casa. ▢ It turned out all right in the end. Al final resultó bien.
2 el extremo
- ▢ at the other end of the table al otro extremo de la mesa
- **at the end of the street** al final de la calle
- **for hours on end** durante horas enteras

to **end** VERB
▷ *see also* **end** NOUN
terminar
- ▢ What time does the film end? ¿A qué hora termina la película?
- **to end up doing something** terminar haciendo algo ▢ I ended up walking home. Terminé yendo a casa andando.

**ending** NOUN
el final
- ▢ a happy ending un final feliz

**endless** ADJECTIVE
interminable (FEM interminable)
- ▢ The journey seemed endless. El viaje parecía interminable.

**enemy** NOUN
el enemigo
la enemiga

**energetic** ADJECTIVE
activo (FEM activa)
- ▢ She's very energetic. Es muy activa.

**energy** NOUN
la energía

**engaged** ADJECTIVE
**1** ocupado (FEM ocupada) *(telephone, toilet)*
**2** prometido (FEM prometida)
　□ Brian and Mary are engaged. Brian y Mary están prometidos.
　■ **to get engaged** prometerse
**engaged tone** NOUN
la señal de comunicando
**engagement** NOUN
compromiso
　□ They announced their engagement yesterday. Anunciaron su compromiso ayer.
　■ **The engagement lasted 10 months.** El noviazgo duró 10 meses.
　■ **engagement ring** anillo de compromiso
**engine** NOUN
**1** el motor *(of vehicle)*
**2** la locomotora *(of train)*
**engineer** NOUN
el ingeniero
la ingeniera
　□ He's an engineer. Es ingeniero.
　■ **service engineer** el técnico
**engineering** NOUN
la ingeniería
**England** NOUN
Inglaterra *fem*
**English** ADJECTIVE
　▷ *see also* **English** NOUN
inglés (FEM inglesa, PL ingleses)
**English** NOUN
　▷ *see also* **English** ADJECTIVE
el inglés *(language)*
　□ the English teacher el profesor de inglés
　■ **the English** *(people)* los ingleses
**Englishman** NOUN
el inglés (PL los ingleses)
**Englishwoman** NOUN
la inglesa
**to enjoy** VERB
　■ **Did you enjoy the film?** ¿Te gustó la película?
　■ **to enjoy oneself** divertirse □ Did you enjoy yourselves at the party? ¿Os divertisteis en la fiesta?
**enjoyable** ADJECTIVE
agradable (FEM agradable)
**enlargement** NOUN
la ampliación (PL las ampliaciones) *(of photo)*
**enormous** ADJECTIVE
enorme (FEM enorme)
**enough** ADJECTIVE, PRONOUN, ADVERB
bastante (FEM bastante)
　□ I didn't have enough money. No tenía bastante dinero. □ Have you got enough? ¿Tienes bastante?
　■ **big enough** suficientemente grande
　■ **I've had enough!** ¡Ya estoy harto!

　■ **That's enough!** ¡Ya basta!
**to enquire** VERB
　■ **to enquire about something** informarse acerca de algo
**enquiry** NOUN
la investigación (PL las investigaciones) *(official investigation)*
**to enter** VERB
entrar en
　□ He entered the room and sat down. Entró en la habitación y se sentó.
　■ **to enter a competition** presentarse a un concurso
**to entertain** VERB
recibir *(guests)*
**entertainer** NOUN
el animador
la animadora
**entertaining** ADJECTIVE
entretenido (FEM entretenida) *(book, movie)*
**enthusiasm** NOUN
el entusiasmo
**enthusiast** NOUN
el/la entusiasta
　□ She's a DIY enthusiast. Es una entusiasta del bricolaje.
**enthusiastic** ADJECTIVE
entusiasta (FEM entusiasta) *(response, welcome)*
　■ **She didn't seem very enthusiastic about your idea.** No pareció muy entusiasmada con tu idea.
**entire** ADJECTIVE
entero (FEM entera)
　□ the entire world el mundo entero
**entirely** ADVERB
completamente
　□ an entirely new approach un enfoque completamente nuevo
　■ **I agree entirely.** Estoy totalmente de acuerdo.
**entrance** NOUN
la entrada
　■ **an entrance exam** un examen de ingreso
　■ **entrance fee** la cuota de entrada
**entry** NOUN
la entrada
　■ **'no entry' 1** *(on door)* 'prohibido el paso'
　**2** *(on road sign)* 'dirección prohibida'
　■ **an entry form** un impreso de inscripción
**entry phone** NOUN
el portero automático
**envelope** NOUN
el sobre
**envious** ADJECTIVE
envidioso (FEM envidiosa)
**environment** NOUN
el entorno *(surroundings)*

□ She adjusted quickly to her new environment. Se adaptó rápidamente a su nuevo entorno.

■ **the environment** el medio ambiente
□ We are committed to protecting the environment. Estamos comprometidos con la protección del medio ambiente.

**environmental** ADJECTIVE
medioambiental (FEM medioambiental)
□ environmental pollution  contaminación ambiental

■ **environmental groups** grupos ecologistas

**environment-friendly** ADJECTIVE
ecológico (FEM ecológica)

**envy** NOUN
▷ see also **envy** VERB
la envidia

to **envy** VERB
▷ see also **envy** NOUN
envidiar

**epileptic** NOUN
el epiléptico
la epiléptica

**episode** NOUN
el episodio

**equal** ADJECTIVE
igual (FEM igual)
□ The cake was divided into 12 equal parts. El pastel se dividió en 12 partes iguales.

■ **Women demand equal rights at work.** Las mujeres exigen igualdad de derechos en el trabajo.

**equality** NOUN
la igualdad

to **equalize** VERB
empatar (in sport)

**equator** NOUN
el ecuador

**equipment** NOUN
el equipo
□ skiing equipment  el equipo de esquí

**equipped** ADJECTIVE
equipado (FEM equipada)
□ This caravan is equipped for four people. Esta caravana está equipada para cuatro personas.

■ **equipped with** provisto de  □ All rooms are equipped with phones, computers and faxes. Todas las habitaciones están provistas de teléfonos, ordenadores y fax.

■ **He was well equipped for the job.** Estaba bien preparado para el puesto.

**equivalent** NOUN
▷ see also **equivalent** ADJECTIVE
el equivalente

**error** NOUN
el error

**escalator** NOUN
la escalera mecánica

**escape** NOUN
▷ see also **escape** VERB
la fuga (from prison)

■ **We had a narrow escape.** Nos salvamos por muy poco.

to **escape** VERB
▷ see also **escape** NOUN
escaparse
□ A lion has escaped.  Se ha escapado un león.

■ **The passengers escaped unhurt.** Los pasajeros salieron ilesos.

■ **to escape from prison** fugarse de la cárcel

**escort** NOUN
la escolta
□ a police escort  una escolta policial

**especially** ADVERB
especialmente
□ It's very hot there, especially in the summer. Allí hace mucho calor, especialmente en verano.

**essay** NOUN
el trabajo
□ a history essay  un trabajo de historia

**essential** ADJECTIVE
esencial (FEM esencial)
□ It's essential to bring warm clothes. Es esencial traer ropa de abrigo.

**estate** NOUN
1 la urbanización (PL las urbanizaciones)
□ I live on an estate.  Vivo en una urbanización.
2 la finca
□ He's got a large estate in the country. Tiene una finca grande en el campo.

**estate agent** NOUN
el agente inmobiliario
la agente inmobiliaria
□ She's an estate agent.  Es agente inmobiliaria.

**estate car** NOUN
la ranchera

to **estimate** VERB
calcular
□ They estimated it would take three weeks. Calcularon que llevaría tres semanas.

**etc** ABBREVIATION (= et cetera)
etc.

**Ethiopia** NOUN
Etiopía fem

**ethnic** ADJECTIVE
1 étnico (FEM étnica)
□ an ethnic minority  una minoría étnica
■ **ethnic cleansing** la limpieza étnica
2 exótico (FEM exótica) (restaurant, food)

**e-ticket** NOUN
el billete electrónico (el boleto electrónico
*Latin America*)

**EU** NOUN *(= European Union)*
la UE

**euro** NOUN
el euro

**Europe** NOUN
Europa *fem*

**European** ADJECTIVE
▷ *see also* **European** NOUN
europeo (FEM europea)

**European** NOUN
▷ *see also* **European** ADJECTIVE
el europeo
la europea

to **evacuate** VERB
evacuar*

**eve** NOUN
■ **Christmas Eve** la Nochebuena
■ **New Year's Eve** la Nochevieja

**even** ADVERB
▷ *see also* **even** ADJECTIVE
incluso
□ I like all animals, even snakes. Me gustan
todos los animales, incluso las serpientes.
■ **not even** ni siquiera □ He didn't even say
hello. Ni siquiera saludó.
■ **even if** aunque

LANGUAGE TIP Use the subjunctive
after **aunque** when translating 'even
if'.

□ I'd never do that, even if you asked me.
Nunca haría eso, aunque me lo pidieras.
■ **even though** aunque □ She's a
successful writer, even though she's still
only 25. Es una escritora de éxito, aunque
todavía tiene sólo 25 años.
■ **even more** aún más □ I liked Granada
even more than Seville. Me gustó Granada
aún más que Sevilla.

**even** ADJECTIVE
▷ *see also* **even** ADVERB
uniforme (FEM uniforme)
□ an even layer of snow una capa de nieve
uniforme
■ **an even surface** una superficie lisa
■ **an even number** un número par
■ **to get even with somebody** vengarse en
alguien

**evening** NOUN
1 la tarde *(before dark)*
2 la noche *(after dark)*
□ in the evening por la tarde/noche
■ **Good evening!** ¡Buenas tardes/noches!
■ **evening class** la clase nocturna

**event** NOUN
1 el acontecimiento

□ It was one of the most important events in
his life. Fue uno de los acontecimientos
más importantes de su vida.
■ **a sporting event** un acontecimiento
deportivo
2 la prueba
□ She took part in two events at the last
Olympic Games. Participó en dos pruebas
en los últimos Juegos Olímpicos.
■ **in the event of** en caso de □ in the event
of an accident en caso de accidente

**eventful** ADJECTIVE
lleno de incidentes (FEM llena de incidentes)
*(race, journey)*

**eventually** ADVERB
finalmente

**ever** ADVERB
■ **Have you ever been to Portugal?** ¿Has
estado alguna vez en Portugal?
■ **Have you ever seen her?** ¿La has visto
alguna vez?
■ **the best I've ever seen** el mejor que he
visto
■ **I haven't ever done that.** Jamás he
hecho eso.
■ **It will become ever more complex.** Irá
siendo cada vez más complicado.
■ **for the first time ever** por primera vez
■ **ever since** desde que □ ever since I met
him desde que lo conozco
■ **ever since then** desde entonces
■ **It's ever so kind of you.** Es muy amable
de su parte.

**every** ADJECTIVE
cada (FEM cada)
□ every pupil cada alumno □ every time
cada vez
■ **every day** todos los días
■ **every now and then** de vez en cuando

**everybody** PRONOUN
todo el mundo
□ Everybody makes mistakes. Todo el
mundo se equivoca.
■ **Everybody had a good time.** Todos se lo
pasaron bien.

**everyone** PRONOUN
todo el mundo
□ Everyone makes mistakes. Todo el mundo
se equivoca.
■ **Everyone had a good time.** Todos se lo
pasaron bien.

**everything** PRONOUN
todo
□ You've thought of everything! ¡Has
pensado en todo! □ Money isn't everything.
El dinero no lo es todo.

**everywhere** ADVERB
en todas partes

## evil – expect

□ I looked everywhere, but I couldn't find it. Miré en todas partes, pero no lo encontré.

○ **LANGUAGE TIP dondequiera** has to be followed by a verb in the subjunctive.

■ **I see him everywhere I go.** Lo veo dondequiera que vaya.

**evil** ADJECTIVE
1 malvado (FEM malvada) (person)
2 maligno (FEM maligna) (plan, spirit)

**ex-** PREFIX
ex-
□ his ex-wife su ex-esposa

**exact** ADJECTIVE
exacto (FEM exacta)

**exactly** ADVERB
exactamente
□ exactly the same exactamente igual
■ **It's exactly 10 o'clock.** Son las 10 en punto.

to **exaggerate** VERB
exagerar

**exaggeration** NOUN
la exageración (PL las exageraciones)

**exam** NOUN
el examen (PL los exámenes)
□ a French exam un examen de francés
□ the exam results los resultados de los exámenes

**examination** NOUN
el examen (PL los exámenes)

to **examine** VERB
examinar
□ He examined her passport. Le examinó el pasaporte. □ The doctor examined him. El médico lo examinó.

**examiner** NOUN
el examinador
la examinadora

**example** NOUN
el ejemplo
□ for example por ejemplo

**excellent** ADJECTIVE
excelente (FEM excelente)

**except** PREPOSITION
excepto
□ everyone except me todos excepto yo
■ **except for** excepto

○ **LANGUAGE TIP salvo que** may be followed by a verb in subjunctive.

■ **except that** salvo que □ The weather was great, except that it was a bit cold. El tiempo fue estupendo, salvo que hizo un poco de frío.

**exception** NOUN
la excepción (PL las excepciones)
□ to make an exception hacer una excepción

**exceptional** ADJECTIVE
excepcional (FEM excepcional)

**excess baggage** NOUN
el exceso de equipaje

to **exchange** VERB
▷ see also **exchange** NOUN
cambiar
□ I exchanged the book for a CD. Cambié el libro por un CD.

**exchange rate** NOUN
el tipo de cambio

**excited** ADJECTIVE
entusiasmado (FEM entusiasmada)

**exciting** ADJECTIVE
emocionante (FEM emocionante)

**exclamation mark** NOUN
el signo de admiración

**excuse** NOUN
▷ see also **excuse** VERB
la excusa

to **excuse** VERB
▷ see also **excuse** NOUN
■ **Excuse me! 1** (to attract attention, apologize) ¡Perdón! **2** (when you want to get past) ¡Con permiso!

**ex-directory** ADJECTIVE
■ **She's ex-directory.** Su nombre no aparece en la guía.

to **execute** VERB
ejecutar

**execution** NOUN
la ejecución (PL las ejecuciones)

**executive** NOUN
el ejecutivo
la ejecutiva
□ He's an executive. Es ejecutivo.

**exercise** NOUN
el ejercicio
□ page ten, exercise three página diez, ejercicio tres □ to take some exercise hacer un poco de ejercicio
■ **exercise book** el cuaderno
■ **an exercise bike** una bicicleta estática

**exhausted** ADJECTIVE
agotado (FEM agotada)

**exhaust fumes** PL NOUN
los gases de escape

**exhaust pipe** NOUN
el tubo de escape

**exhibition** NOUN
la exposición (PL las exposiciones)

to **exist** VERB
existir

**exit** NOUN
la salida

○ **LANGUAGE TIP** Be careful not to translate **exit** by **éxito**.

**exotic** ADJECTIVE
exótico (FEM exótica)

to **expect** VERB

**1** esperar
□ I'm expecting him for dinner. Lo espero para cenar. □ She's expecting a baby. Está esperando un bebé. □ I didn't expect that from him. No me esperaba eso de él.
**2** imaginarse
□ I expect he'll be late. Me imagino que llegará tarde.
■ **I expect so.** Me imagino que sí.

**expedition** NOUN
la expedición (PL las expediciones)

to **expel** VERB
■ **to get expelled** (from school) ser expulsado

**expenses** PL NOUN
los gastos

**expensive** ADJECTIVE
caro (FEM cara)

**experience** NOUN
la experiencia

**experienced** ADJECTIVE
■ **an experienced teacher** un maestro con experiencia
■ **She's very experienced in looking after children.** Tiene mucha experiencia en cuidar niños.

**experiment** NOUN
el experimento

**expert** ADJECTIVE
▷ see also **expert** NOUN
experto (FEM experta)
■ **He's an expert cook.** Es un experto cocinero.

to **expire** VERB
caducar
□ My passport has expired. Mi pasaporte ha caducado.

to **explain** VERB
explicar*

**explanation** NOUN
la explicación (PL las explicaciones)

to **explode** VERB
estallar

to **exploit** VERB
explotar

**exploitation** NOUN
la explotación

to **explore** VERB
explorar (place)

**explorer** NOUN
el explorador
la exploradora

**explosion** NOUN
la explosión (PL las explosiones)

**explosive** ADJECTIVE
▷ see also **explosive** NOUN
explosivo (FEM explosiva)

**explosive** NOUN

▷ see also **explosive** ADJECTIVE
el explosivo

to **express** VERB
expresar
■ **to express oneself** expresarse □ It's not easy to express oneself in a foreign language. No es fácil expresarse en un idioma extranjero.

**expression** NOUN
la expresión (PL las expresiones)
□ It's an English expression. Es una expresión inglesa.

**expressway** NOUN (US)
la autopista

**extension** NOUN
**1** la ampliación (PL las ampliaciones) (of building)
**2** la extensión (PL las extensiones) (telephone)
□ Extension three one three seven, please. Con la extensión tres uno tres siete, por favor.

**extensive** ADJECTIVE
**1** extenso (FEM extensa)
□ The hotel is situated in extensive grounds. El hotel está situado en medio de extensos jardines.
**2** amplio (FEM amplia)
□ My brother has an extensive knowledge of this subject. Mi hermano tiene amplio conocimiento sobre esta materia.
■ **extensive damage** daños de consideración

**extent** NOUN
■ **to some extent** hasta cierto punto

**exterior** ADJECTIVE
exterior (FEM exteriora)

**extinct** ADJECTIVE
extinto (FEM extinta)
□ to be extinct estar extinto □ Dinosaurs are extinct. Los dinosaurios están extintos.
■ **to become extinct** extinguirse

**extinguisher** NOUN
el extintor (el extinguidor Latin America)

**extortionate** ADJECTIVE
exorbitante (FEM exorbitante)

**extra** ADJECTIVE, ADVERB
■ **He gave me an extra blanket.** Me dio una manta más.
■ **to pay extra** pagar un suplemento
■ **Breakfast is extra.** El desayuno no está incluido.
■ **Be extra careful!** ¡Ten muchísimo cuidado!

**extraordinary** ADJECTIVE
extraordinario (FEM extraordinaria)

**extravagant** ADJECTIVE
derrochador (FEM derrochadora) (person)

**extreme** ADJECTIVE
extremo (FEM extrema)

83

■ **with extreme caution** con sumo cuidado

**extremely** ADVERB
sumamente

**extremist** NOUN
el/la extremista

**eye** NOUN
el ojo
□ I've got green eyes. Tengo los ojos verdes.
■ **to keep an eye on something** vigilar algo

**eyebrow** NOUN
la ceja

**eyelash** NOUN
la pestaña

**eyelid** NOUN
el párpado

**eyeliner** NOUN
el lápiz de ojos (PL los lápices de ojos)

**eye shadow** NOUN
la sombra de ojos

**eyesight** NOUN
la vista
□ to have good eyesight tener buena vista

**e**

# Ff

**fabric** NOUN
la tela

> **LANGUAGE TIP** Be careful not to translate **fabric** by **fábrica**.

**fabulous** ADJECTIVE
fabuloso (FEM fabulosa)

**face** NOUN
▷ see also **face** VERB
1 la cara
□ He was red in the face. Tenía la cara colorada. □ the north face of the mountain la cara norte de la montaña
■ **face to face** cara a cara
2 la esfera (of clock)
■ **on the face of it** a primera vista
■ **in the face of these difficulties** en vista de estas dificultades

to **face** VERB
▷ see also **face** NOUN
1 estar* frente a
□ They stood facing each other. Estaban de pie el uno frente al otro.
■ **The garden faces south.** El jardín da al sur.
2 enfrentarse a
□ They face serious problems. Se enfrentan a graves problemas.
■ **Let's face it, we're lost.** Tenemos que admitirlo, estamos perdidos.

**face cloth** NOUN
la toallita para lavarse

**facilities** PL NOUN
las instalaciones
□ This school has excellent facilities. Esta escuela tiene unas instalaciones magníficas.
■ **The youth hostel has cooking facilities.** El albergue juvenil dispone de cocina.

**fact** NOUN

> **LANGUAGE TIP** Use the subjunctive after **el hecho de que**.

■ **the fact that ...** el hecho de que ... □ The fact that you are very busy is of no interest to me. El hecho de que estés muy ocupado no me interesa.
■ **facts and figures** datos y cifras
■ **in fact** de hecho

**factory** NOUN
la fábrica

to **fade** VERB
1 desteñirse*
□ My jeans have faded. Se me han desteñido los vaqueros.
2 apagarse*
□ The light was fading fast. La luz se apagaba con rapidez. □ The noise gradually faded. El ruido se fue apagando.

**fag** NOUN
el cigarro

to **fail** VERB
▷ see also **fail** NOUN
1 suspender
□ He failed his driving test. Suspendió el examen de conducir.
2 fallar
□ The lorry's brakes failed. Al camión le fallaron los frenos.
3 fracasar
□ The plan failed. El plan fracasó.
■ **to fail to do something** no lograr hacer algo □ They failed to reach the quarter finals. No lograron llegar a los cuartos de final.
■ **The bomb failed to explode.** La bomba no llegó a estallar.

**fail** NOUN
▷ see also **fail** VERB
el suspenso
□ D is a pass, E is a fail. D es un aprobado, E es un suspenso.
■ **without fail** sin falta

**failure** NOUN
1 el fracaso
□ The attempt was a complete failure. El intento fue un completo fracaso.
2 el fallo
□ a mechanical failure un fallo mecánico
■ **I feel a failure.** Me siento un fracasado.

**faint** ADJECTIVE
▷ see also **faint** VERB
débil (FEM débil)
□ His voice was very faint. Tenía la voz muy débil.
■ **to feel faint** sentirse mareado

**English-Spanish**

to **faint** VERB
 ▷ *see also* **faint** ADJECTIVE
 desmayarse
**fair** ADJECTIVE
 ▷ *see also* **fair** NOUN
1 justo (FEM justa)
 □ That's not fair. Eso no es justo.
 ■ **I paid more than my fair share.** Pagué más de lo que me correspondía.
2 rubio (FEM rubia)
 □ He's got fair hair. Tiene el pelo rubio.
3 blanco (FEM blanca)
 □ people with fair skin la gente con la piel blanca
4 considerable (FEM considerable)
 □ That's a fair distance. Esa es una distancia considerable.
 ■ **I have a fair chance of winning.** Tengo bastantes posibilidades de ganar.
5 bueno (FEM buena) *(weather)*
 □ The weather was fair. El tiempo era bueno.

  ⌣ **LANGUAGE TIP** Use **buen** before a masculine singular noun.

**fair** NOUN
 ▷ *see also* **fair** ADJECTIVE
1 la feria *(travelling funfair)*
2 el parque de atracciones *(on permanent site)*
 ■ **a trade fair** una feria de muestras
**fair-haired** ADJECTIVE
 rubio (FEM rubia)
**fairly** ADVERB
1 equitativamente
 □ The cake was divided fairly. La tarta se repartió equitativamente.
2 bastante
 □ My car is fairly new. Mi coche es bastante nuevo. □ The weather was fairly good. El tiempo fue bastante bueno.
**fairy** NOUN
 el hada *fem*

  ⌣ **LANGUAGE TIP** Although it's a feminine noun, remember that you use **el** and **un** with **hada**.

**fairy tale** NOUN
 el cuento de hadas
**faith** NOUN
1 la confianza
 □ People have lost faith in the government. La gente ha perdido la confianza en el gobierno.
2 la fe
 □ the Catholic faith la fe católica
**faithful** ADJECTIVE
 fiel (FEM fiel)
**faithfully** ADVERB
 ■ **Yours faithfully...** *(in letter)* Le saluda atentamente...

**fake** NOUN
 ▷ *see also* **fake** ADJECTIVE
 la falsificación (PL las falsificaciones)
 □ The painting was a fake. El cuadro era una falsificación.
**fake** ADJECTIVE
 ▷ *see also* **fake** NOUN
 falso (FEM falsa)
 □ a fake banknote un billete falso
 ■ **a fake fur coat** un abrigo de piel sintética
**fall** NOUN
 ▷ *see also* **fall** VERB
1 la caída
 □ She had a nasty fall. Tuvo una mala caída.
 ■ **a fall of snow** una nevada
 ■ **Niagara Falls** las cataratas del Niágara
2 el otoño *(*US: autumn*)*
to **fall** VERB
 ▷ *see also* **fall** NOUN
1 caer*
 □ Bombs fell on the town. Las bombas caían sobre la ciudad.

  ⌣ **LANGUAGE TIP** When the action of falling is not deliberate, use **caerse**.

 □ He tripped and fell. Tropezó y se cayó.
 □ The book fell off the shelf. El libro se cayó de la estantería.
 ■ **to fall in love with someone** enamorarse de alguien
2 bajar
 □ Prices are falling. Están bajando los precios.
to **fall down** VERB
 caerse*
 □ She's fallen down. Se ha caído. □ The house is slowly falling down. La casa se está cayendo poco a poco.
to **fall for** VERB
1 tragarse*
 □ They fell for it! ¡Se lo tragaron!
2 enamorarse de
 □ She fell for him immediately. Se enamoró de él en el acto.
to **fall out** VERB
 reñir*
 □ Sarah's fallen out with her boyfriend. Sarah ha reñido con su novio.
to **fall through** VERB
 fracasar
 □ Our plans have fallen through. Nuestros planes han fracasado.
**false** ADJECTIVE
 falso (FEM falsa)
 ■ **a false alarm** una falsa alarma
 ■ **false teeth** la dentadura postiza
**fame** NOUN
 la fama
**familiar** ADJECTIVE
 familiar (FEM familiar)

**f**

□ The name sounded familiar to me. El nombre me sonaba familiar.

■ **a familiar face** un rostro conocido

■ **to be familiar with something** conocer bien algo □ I'm familiar with his work. Conozco bien su obra.

**family** NOUN
la familia

□ the Cooke family la familia Cooke

■ **family planning** la planificación familiar

**famine** NOUN
la hambruna

**famous** ADJECTIVE
famoso (FEM famosa)

**fan** NOUN
1 el/la hincha

□ the England fans los hinchas ingleses
2 el/la fan (PL los/las fans)

□ the Oasis fan club el club de fans de Oasis

■ **I'm one of his greatest fans.** Soy uno de sus mayores admiradores.
3 el aficionado
la aficionada

□ a rap music fan un aficionado al rap
4 el abanico

□ a silk fan un abanico de seda

■ **an electric fan** un ventilador

**fanatic** NOUN
el fanático
la fanática

to **fancy** VERB
apetecer*

□ I fancy an ice cream. Me apetece un helado. □ What do you fancy doing? ¿Qué te apetece hacer?

◌ LANGUAGE TIP apetecer que has to be followed by a verb in the subjunctive.

□ Do you fancy going to the cinema sometime? ¿Te apetece que vayamos al cine algún día?

■ **He fancies her.** Le gusta ella.

**fancy dress** NOUN
el disfraz (PL los disfraces)

■ **a fancy dress ball** un baile de disfraces

**fantastic** ADJECTIVE
fantástico (FEM fantástica)

**far** ADJECTIVE, ADVERB
lejos

□ Is it far? ¿Está lejos? □ It's not far from London. No está lejos de Londres.

■ **How far is it to Madrid?** ¿A qué distancia está Madrid?

■ **It's far from easy.** No es nada fácil.

■ **How far have you got?** ¿Hasta dónde has llegado?

■ **at the far end of the swimming pool** al otro extremo de la piscina

■ **far better** mucho mejor

■ **as far as I know** por lo que yo sé

■ **so far** hasta ahora

**fare** NOUN
la tarifa

□ Rail fares are very high in Britain. Las tarifas de tren son muy altas en Gran Bretaña. □ The air fare was very reasonable. La tarifa del vuelo fue bastante razonable.

■ **He didn't have the bus fare, so he had to walk.** No tenía dinero para el autobús, así que tuvo que ir andando.

■ **full fare** el precio del billete completo

■ **Children pay half fare on the bus.** Los niños pagan la mitad en el autobús.

**Far East** NOUN

■ **the Far East** el Extremo Oriente

**farm** NOUN
la granja (la estancia Latin America)

**farmer** NOUN
el granjero
la granjera (el estanciero, la estanciera Latin America)

□ He's a farmer. Es granjero.

**farmhouse** NOUN
el caserío

**farming** NOUN
la agricultura

□ organic farming agricultura biológica

■ **dairy farming** la ganadería (especializada en la producción de leche)

**fascinating** ADJECTIVE
fascinante (FEM fascinante)

**fashion** NOUN
la moda

■ **to be in fashion** estar de moda

■ **to go out of fashion** pasar de moda

**fashionable** ADJECTIVE
de moda

□ That colour is very fashionable. Ese color está muy de moda.

■ **Jane wears fashionable clothes.** Jane viste a la moda.

**fast** ADJECTIVE, ADVERB
rápido (FEM rápida)

□ a fast car un coche rápido □ They work very fast. Trabajan muy rápido.

■ **That clock's fast.** Ese reloj va adelantado.

■ **He's fast asleep.** Está profundamente dormido.

**fat** ADJECTIVE
▷ see also **fat** NOUN
gordo (FEM gorda)

□ She thinks she's too fat. Piensa que está demasiado gorda.

**fat** NOUN
▷ see also **fat** ADJECTIVE
1 la grasa (on meat, in food)

□ It's very high in fat. Es muy rico en grasas.

87

**2** la manteca *(used for cooking)*
**fatal** ADJECTIVE
**1** mortal (FEM mortal)
□ a fatal accident un accidente mortal
**2** fatal (FEM fatal)
□ a fatal mistake un error fatal
**father** NOUN
el padre
■ **my father and mother** mis padres
■ **Father Christmas** Papá Noel
**father-in-law** NOUN
el suegro
**faucet** NOUN (US)
el grifo
**fault** NOUN
**1** la culpa
□ It wasn't my fault. No fue culpa mía.
**2** el defecto
□ He has his faults, but I still like him. Tiene sus defectos, pero aun así me gusta.
■ **a mechanical fault** un fallo mecánico
**faulty** ADJECTIVE
defectuoso (FEM defectuosa)
**favour** (US **favor**) NOUN
el favor (PL los favores)
□ Could you do me a favour? ¿Me harías un favor?
■ **to be in favour of something** estar a favor de algo
**favourite** (US **favorite**) ADJECTIVE
▷ *see also* **favourite** NOUN
favorito (FEM favorita)
□ Blue's my favourite colour. El azul es mi color favorito.
**favourite** (US **favorite**) NOUN
▷ *see also* **favourite** ADJECTIVE
el favorito
la favorita
□ Liverpool are favourites to win the Cup. El Liverpool es el favorito para ganar la Copa.
**fax** NOUN
▷ *see also* **fax** VERB
el fax (PL los faxes)
to **fax** VERB
▷ *see also* **fax** NOUN
mandar por fax
□ I'll fax you the details. Te mandaré la información por fax.
**fear** NOUN
▷ *see also* **fear** VERB
el miedo
to **fear** VERB
▷ *see also* **fear** NOUN
temer
□ You have nothing to fear. No tienes nada que temer.
**feather** NOUN
la pluma

**feature** NOUN
la característica
□ an important feature una característica importante
**February** NOUN
febrero *masc*
□ in February en febrero  □ on 18 February el 18 de febrero
**fed** VERB ▷ *see* **feed**
**fed up** ADJECTIVE
■ **to be fed up with something** estar harto de algo
to **feed** VERB
dar* de comer a
□ Have you fed the cat? ¿Le has dado de comer al gato? □ He worked hard to feed his family. Trabajaba mucho para dar de comer a su familia.
to **feel** VERB
**1** sentir*
□ I didn't feel much pain. No sentí mucho dolor.
**2** sentirse*
□ I don't feel well. No me siento bien.
□ I felt lonely. Me sentía solo.
■ **I was feeling hungry.** Tenía hambre.
■ **I was feeling cold, so I went inside.** Tenía frío, así que entré.
**3** tocar*
□ The doctor felt his forehead. El médico le tocó la frente.
■ **to feel like doing something** tener ganas de hacer algo  □ I don't feel like going out tonight. No tengo ganas de salir esta noche.
■ **Do you feel like an ice cream?** ¿Te apetece un helado?
**feeling** NOUN
**1** la sensación (PL las sensaciones)
□ a burning feeling una sensación de escozor
**2** el sentimiento
□ He was afraid of hurting my feelings. Tenía miedo de herir mis sentimientos.
■ **What are your feelings about it?** ¿Tú qué opinas de ello?
**feet** PL NOUN ▷ *see* **foot**
**fell** VERB ▷ *see* **fall**
**felt** VERB ▷ *see* **feel**
**felt-tip pen** NOUN
el rotulador
**female** ADJECTIVE
▷ *see also* **female** NOUN
**1** hembra (FEM + PL hembra)
□ a female bat un murciélago hembra
**2** femenino (FEM femenina)
□ the female sex el sexo femenino
**female** NOUN
▷ *see also* **female** ADJECTIVE
la hembra *(animal)*

f

**feminine** ADJECTIVE
femenino (FEM femenina)

**feminist** NOUN
el/la feminista

**fence** NOUN
la valla

**fern** NOUN
el helecho

**ferry** NOUN
el ferry

**fertile** ADJECTIVE
fértil (FEM fértil)

**fertilizer** NOUN
el abono

**festival** NOUN
el festival
□ a jazz festival un festival de jazz

to **fetch** VERB
1 ir* a por
□ Fetch the bucket. Ve a por el cubo.
■ **to fetch something for someone** traer algo a alguien □ Fetch me a glass of water. Tráeme un vaso de agua.
2 venderse por
□ His painting fetched £5000. Su cuadro se vendió por 5.000 libras esterlinas.

**fever** NOUN
la fiebre

**few** ADJECTIVE, PRONOUN
1 pocos (FEM pocas)
□ He has few friends. Tiene pocos amigos.
■ **a few** unos □ She was silent for a few seconds. Se quedó callada unos segundos.
2 algunos (FEM algunas)
□ a few of them algunos de ellos
■ **quite a few people** bastante gente

**fewer** ADJECTIVE
menos
□ There were fewer people than yesterday. Había menos gente que ayer.

**fiancé** NOUN
el novio *(prometido)*

**fiancée** NOUN
la novia *(prometida)*

**fiction** NOUN
la narrativa *(novels)*

**field** NOUN
el campo
□ a field of wheat un campo de trigo □ a football field un campo de fútbol (una cancha de fútbol *Latin America*)
□ He's an expert in his field. Es un experto en su campo.

**fierce** ADJECTIVE
1 feroz (FEM feroz, PL feroces)
□ a fierce Alsatian un pastor alemán feroz
2 encarnizado (FEM encarnizada)
□ There's fierce competition between the companies. Existe una encarnizada competencia entre las empresas.
3 violento (FEM violenta)
□ a fierce attack un violento ataque

**fifteen** NUMERAL
quince
□ I'm fifteen. Tengo quince años.

**fifteenth** ADJECTIVE
decimoquinto (FEM decimoquinta)
■ **the fifteenth floor** la planta quince
■ **the fifteenth of August** el quince de agosto

**fifth** ADJECTIVE
quinto (FEM quinta)
□ the fifth floor el quinto piso
■ **the fifth of August** el cinco de agosto

**fifty** NUMERAL
cincuenta
□ He's fifty. Tiene cincuenta años.

**fifty-fifty** ADJECTIVE, ADVERB
a medias
□ They split the prize money fifty-fifty. Se repartieron a medias el dinero del premio.
■ **a fifty-fifty chance** un cincuenta por ciento de posibilidades

**fight** NOUN
▷ *see also* **fight** VERB
1 la pelea
□ There was a fight in the pub. Hubo una pelea en el pub.
■ **She had a fight with her best friend.** Se peleó con su mejor amiga.
2 la lucha
□ the fight against cancer la lucha contra el cáncer

to **fight** VERB
▷ *see also* **fight** NOUN
1 pelearse
□ The fans started fighting. Los hinchas empezaron a pelearse.
2 luchar
□ She has fought against racism all her life. Ha luchado toda su vida contra el racismo.
□ The demonstrators fought with the police. Los manifestantes lucharon con la policía.
■ **The doctors tried to fight the disease.** Los médicos intentaron combatir la enfermedad.

**fighting** NOUN
1 la pelea
□ Fighting broke out outside the pub. Se desató una pelea a las puertas del pub.
2 los combates
□ Many people have died in the fighting. Ha muerto mucha gente en los combates.

**figure** NOUN
1 la cifra
□ Can you give me the exact figures? ¿Me puedes dar las cifras exactas?

2 la silueta
  □ Helen saw the figure of a man on the bridge. Helen vio la silueta de un hombre en el puente.
  ■ **She's got a good figure.** Tiene buen tipo.
  ■ **I have to watch my figure.** Tengo que mantener la línea.
3 la figura
  □ She's an important political figure. Es una importante figura política.

to **figure out** VERB
1 calcular
  □ I'll try to figure out how much it'll cost. Intentaré calcular lo que va a costar.
2 llegar* a comprender
  □ I couldn't figure out what it meant. No llegué a comprender lo que significaba.

**file** NOUN
  ▷ see also **file** VERB
1 el expediente
  □ There was stuff in that file that was private. Había cosas privadas en ese expediente.
  ■ **The police have a file on him.** Está fichado por la policía.
2 la carpeta
  □ She put the photocopy into her file. Metió la fotocopia en su carpeta.
3 la lima
  □ a nail file una lima de uñas
4 el fichero (on computer)

to **file** VERB
  ▷ see also **file** NOUN
1 archivar
  □ You have to file all these documents. Tienes que archivar todos estos documentos.
2 limarse
  □ She was filing her nails. Se estaba limando las uñas.

to **fill** VERB
  llenar
  □ She filled the glass with water. Llenó el vaso de agua.

to **fill in** VERB
1 rellenar
  □ Can you fill in this form, please? Rellene este impreso, por favor.
2 llenar
  □ He filled the hole in with soil. Llenó el agujero de tierra.

to **fill up** VERB
  llenar
  □ He filled the cup up to the brim. Llenó la taza hasta el borde.
  ■ **Fill it up, please.** (at petrol station) Lleno, por favor.

**film** NOUN
1 la película (movie)

2 el carrete
  □ I need a 36 exposure film. Quería un carrete de 36.

**film star** NOUN
  la estrella de cine

**filthy** ADJECTIVE
  mugriento (FEM mugrienta)

**final** ADJECTIVE
  ▷ see also **final** NOUN
1 último (FEM última)
  □ a final attempt un último intento
2 definitivo (FEM definitiva)
  □ a final decision una decisión definitiva
  ■ **I'm not going and that's final.** He dicho que no voy y se acabó.

**final** NOUN
  ▷ see also **final** ADJECTIVE
  la final
  □ Andy Murray is in the final. Andy Murray ha llegado a la final.

**finally** ADVERB
1 por último
  □ Finally, I would like to say thank you to all of you. Por último me gustaría darles las gracias a todos.
2 al final
  □ They finally decided to leave on Saturday. Al final decidieron salir el sábado.

to **find** VERB
  encontrar*
  □ I can't find the exit. No encuentro la salida.

to **find out** VERB
  averiguar*
  □ I found out what happened. Averigüé lo que ocurrió.
  ■ **to find out about** enterarse de □ Try to find out about the cost of a hotel. Intenta enterarte de lo que costaría un hotel. □ Find out as much as possible about the town. Entérate de todo lo que puedas sobre la ciudad.

**fine** ADJECTIVE, ADVERB
  ▷ see also **fine** NOUN
1 estupendo (FEM estupenda)
  □ He's a fine musician. Es un músico estupendo.
  ■ **How are you? — I'm fine.** ¿Qué tal estás? — Bien.
  ■ **I feel fine.** Me siento bien.
  ■ **It'll be ready tomorrow. — That's fine, thanks.** Mañana estará listo. — Muy bien, gracias.
  ■ **The weather is fine today.** Hoy hace muy buen tiempo.
2 fino (FEM fina)
  □ She's got very fine hair. Tiene el pelo muy fino.

**fine** NOUN
  ▷ see also **fine** ADJECTIVE

la multa
□ I got a fine for driving through a red light.
Me pusieron una multa por saltarme un
semáforo en rojo.

**finger** NOUN
el dedo
■ **my little finger** el meñique □ I hurt my
little finger. Me hice daño en el meñique.

**fingernail** NOUN
la uña

**finish** NOUN
▷ see also **finish** VERB
1 el fin
□ from start to finish de principio a fin
2 la llegada
□ We saw the finish of the London Marathon.
Vimos la llegada del maratón de Londres.

to **finish** VERB
▷ see also **finish** NOUN
terminar
□ I've finished! ¡Ya he terminado!
■ **to finish doing something** terminar de
hacer algo □ Have you finished eating?
¿Has terminado de comer?

**Finland** NOUN
Finlandia *fem*

**Finn** NOUN
el finlandés (PL los finlandeses)
la finlandesa
□ the Finns los finlandeses

**Finnish** ADJECTIVE
▷ see also **Finnish** NOUN
finlandés (FEM finlandesa, PL finlandeses)

**Finnish** NOUN
▷ see also **Finnish** ADJECTIVE
el finlandés *(language)*

**fire** NOUN
▷ see also **fire** VERB
1 el fuego *(flames)*
□ The fire spread quickly. El fuego se
extendió rápidamente.
2 el incendio *(blaze)*
□ The house was destroyed by a fire. La casa
fue destruida por un incendio.
3 la hoguera
□ He made a fire to warm himself up.
Encendió una hoguera para calentarse.
4 la estufa
□ an electric fire una estufa eléctrica
■ **to be on fire** estar ardiendo

to **fire** VERB
▷ see also **fire** NOUN
disparar
□ She fired at him. Le disparó.
■ **to fire a gun** disparar
■ **to fire somebody** despedir a alguien
□ He was fired from his job. Le despidieron
del trabajo.

**fire alarm** NOUN
la alarma contra incendios

**fire brigade** NOUN
el cuerpo de bomberos

**fire escape** NOUN
la escalera de incendios

**fireman** NOUN
el bombero
□ He's a fireman. Es bombero.

**fireplace** NOUN
la chimenea

**fireworks** PL NOUN
los fuegos artificiales

**firm** ADJECTIVE
▷ see also **firm** NOUN
1 firme (FEM firme)
□ to be firm with somebody mostrarse
firme con alguien
2 duro (FEM dura)
□ a firm mattress un colchón duro

**firm** NOUN
▷ see also **firm** ADJECTIVE
la empresa

**first** ADJECTIVE, NOUN, ADVERB
1 primero (FEM primera)
□ for the first time por primera vez □ Rachel
came first in the race. Rachel quedó
primera en la carrera. □ She was the first to
arrive. Fue la primera en llegar.

 LANGUAGE TIP Use **primer** before a
 masculine singular noun.
□ my first job mi primer trabajo
■ **the first of September** el uno de
septiembre
■ **at first** al principio
2 antes
□ I want to get a job, but first I have to
graduate. Quiero encontrar un trabajo, pero
antes tengo que acabar la carrera.
■ **first of all** ante todo

**first aid** NOUN
los primeros auxilios
■ **a first aid kit** un botiquín

**first-class** ADJECTIVE, ADVERB
1 de primera clase
□ a first-class ticket un billete de primera
clase
2 de primera
□ a first-class meal una comida de primera
■ **to travel first class** viajar en primera
■ **a first-class stamp** un sello para correo
urgente

 DID YOU KNOW...?
 In Spain there is no first-class or
 second-class postage. If you want
 your mail to arrive fast, you must have
 it sent express – **urgente** – from a
 post office.

**English-Spanish**

**firstly** ADVERB
en primer lugar

**fish** NOUN
▷ see also **fish** VERB
1 el pez (PL los peces) (animal)
□ I caught three fish. Pesqué tres peces.
2 el pescado (food)
□ I don't like fish. No me gusta el pescado.
□ fish and chips pescado rebozado con patatas fritas

to **fish** VERB
▷ see also **fish** NOUN
pescar*
■ **to go fishing** ir a pescar

**fisherman** NOUN
el pescador
□ He's a fisherman. Es pescador.

**fish fingers** PL NOUN
los palitos de pescado

**fishing** NOUN
la pesca
□ I enjoy fishing. Me gusta la pesca.
■ **a fishing boat** un barco pesquero
■ **fishing rod** la caña de pescar

**fishing tackle** NOUN
los aparejos de pesca

**fish sticks** PL NOUN (US)
los palitos de pescado

**fist** NOUN
el puño

**fit** ADJECTIVE
▷ see also **fit** VERB, NOUN
en forma
□ He felt relaxed and fit after his holiday. Se sentía relajado y en forma tras las vacaciones.
■ **Will he be fit to play next Saturday?** ¿Estará en condiciones de jugar el próximo sábado?

**fit** NOUN
▷ see also **fit** ADJECTIVE, VERB
■ **to have a fit 1** (epileptic) sufrir un ataque de epilepsia **2** (be angry) ponerse hecho una furia □ My Mum will have a fit when she sees the carpet! ¡Mi madre se va a poner hecha una furia cuando vea la moqueta!

to **fit** VERB
▷ see also **fit** ADJECTIVE, NOUN
1 caber* (go into a space)
□ It's small enough to fit into your pocket. Es lo bastante pequeño como para que caber en el bolsillo.
2 encajar
□ Make sure the cork fits well into the bottle. Asegúrese de que el corcho encaja bien en la botella.
3 instalar (install)
□ He fitted an alarm in his car. Instaló una alarma en el coche.

4 poner* (attach)
□ She fitted a plug to the hair dryer. Le puso un enchufe al secador.
■ **to fit somebody** estar bien a alguien
□ These trousers don't fit me. Estos pantalones no me están bien.
■ **Does it fit?** ¿Te está bien?

to **fit in** VERB
1 encajar
□ That story doesn't fit in with what he told us. Esa historia no encaja con lo que él nos contó.
2 adaptarse
□ She fitted in well at her new school. Se adaptó bien al nuevo colegio.

**fitted carpet** NOUN
la moqueta

**fitted kitchen** NOUN
la cocina amueblada

**fitting room** NOUN
el probador (PL los probadores)

**five** NUMERAL
cinco
□ He's five. Tiene cinco años.

to **fix** VERB
1 arreglar
□ Can you fix my bike? ¿Me puedes arreglar la bici?
2 fijar
□ Let's fix a date for the party. Vamos a fijar una fecha para la fiesta.

**fixed** ADJECTIVE
fijo (FEM fija)
□ at a fixed time a una hora fija
■ **My parents have very fixed ideas.** Mis padres son de ideas fijas.

**fizzy** ADJECTIVE
gaseoso (FEM gaseosa)

**flabby** ADJECTIVE
fofo (FEM fofa)

**flag** NOUN
la bandera

**flame** NOUN
la llama

**flamingo** NOUN
el flamenco

**flan** NOUN
1 la tarta (sweet)
□ a raspberry flan una tarta de frambuesa
2 el pastel (savoury)
□ a cheese and onion flan un pastel de queso y cebolla

**flannel** NOUN
la toallita para lavarse (for face)

to **flap** VERB
■ **The bird flapped its wings.** El pájaro batió las alas.

**flash** NOUN
▷ see also **flash** VERB

el flash (of camera)
■ **a flash of lightning** un relámpago
■ **in a flash** en un abrir y cerrar de ojos
to **flash** VERB
▷ see also **flash** NOUN
■ **A lorry driver flashed him.** Un camionero le hizo señales con los faros.
■ **They flashed a torch in his face.** Le enfocaron con una linterna en la cara.

**flask** NOUN
el termo (vacuum flask)

**flat** ADJECTIVE
▷ see also **flat** NOUN
llano (FEM llana)
□ a flat surface una superficie llana
■ **flat shoes** zapatos bajos
■ **I've got a flat tyre.** Tengo una rueda desinflada.

**flat** NOUN
▷ see also **flat** ADJECTIVE
el piso (el apartamento Latin America)

**flattered** ADJECTIVE
halagado (FEM halagada)

**flavour** (US **flavor**) NOUN
el sabor (PL los sabores)
□ a very strong flavour un sabor muy fuerte
□ Which flavour of ice cream would you like? ¿De qué sabor quieres el helado?

**flavouring** (US **flavoring**) NOUN
el condimento

**flew** VERB ▷ see **fly**

**flexible** ADJECTIVE
flexible (FEM flexible)
□ flexible working hours un horario de trabajo flexible

to **flick** VERB
■ **She flicked the switch to turn the light on.** Le dio al interruptor para encender la luz.
■ **to flick through a book** hojear un libro

to **flicker** VERB
parpadear (light)

**flight** NOUN
el vuelo
□ What time is the flight to Paris? ¿A qué hora es el vuelo para París?
■ **a flight of stairs** un tramo de escaleras

**flight attendant** NOUN
el/la auxiliar de vuelo

to **fling** VERB
arrojar
□ He flung the dictionary onto the floor. Arrojó el diccionario al suelo.

to **float** VERB
flotar

**flock** NOUN
■ **a flock of sheep** un rebaño de ovejas
■ **a flock of birds** una bandada de pájaros

**flood** NOUN
▷ see also **flood** VERB
la inundación (PL las inundaciones)
□ The rain has caused many floods. La lluvia ha provocado muchas inundaciones.
■ **He received a flood of letters.** Recibió un aluvión de cartas.

to **flood** VERB
▷ see also **flood** NOUN
inundar
□ The river has flooded the village. El río ha inundado el pueblo.

**flooding** NOUN
la inundación

**floor** NOUN
1 el suelo (el piso Latin America)
□ a tiled floor un suelo embaldosado
■ **the dance floor** la pista de baile
2 el piso
□ the first floor el primer piso □ on the first floor en el primer piso

**flop** NOUN
el fracaso
□ The film was a flop. La película fue un fracaso.

**floppy disk** NOUN
el disquete

**florist** NOUN
el/la florista

**flour** NOUN
la harina

to **flow** VERB
fluir*
□ The river flows through the valley. El río fluye por el valle. □ Traffic is now flowing normally. El tráfico ya fluye con normalidad.
■ **Water was flowing from the pipe.** El agua brotaba de la tubería.

**flower** NOUN
▷ see also **flower** VERB
la flor (PL las flores)

to **flower** VERB
▷ see also **flower** NOUN
florecer*

**flown** VERB ▷ see **fly**

**flu** NOUN
la gripe
□ I've got flu. Tengo gripe.

**fluent** ADJECTIVE
■ **He speaks fluent Spanish.** Habla español con fluidez.

**flung** VERB ▷ see **fling**

to **flush** VERB
■ **to flush the toilet** tirar de la cadena

**flute** NOUN
la flauta

**fly** NOUN
▷ see also **fly** VERB
la mosca

93

to **fly** VERB
  ▷ *see also* **fly** NOUN
  volar*
  □ He flew from London to Glasgow. Voló de Londres a Glasgow. □ The bird flew away. El pájaro salió volando.
**foal** NOUN
  el potro
**focus** NOUN
  ▷ *see also* **focus** VERB
  el centro
  □ He was the focus of attention. Era el centro de atención.
  ■ **to be out of focus** estar desenfocado
to **focus** VERB
  ▷ *see also* **focus** NOUN
  enfocar*
  □ Try to focus the binoculars. Intenta enfocar los prismáticos.
  ■ **to focus on something 1** *(with camera, telescope)* enfocar algo □ The cameraman focused on the bird. El cámara enfocó al pájaro. **2** *(concentrate on)* centrarse en algo
**fog** NOUN
  la niebla
**foggy** ADJECTIVE
  ■ **It's foggy.** Hay niebla.
  ■ **a foggy day** un día de niebla
**foil** NOUN
  el papel de aluminio *(kitchen foil)*
**fold** NOUN
  ▷ *see also* **fold** VERB
  el pliegue
to **fold** VERB
  ▷ *see also* **fold** NOUN
  doblar
  □ He folded the newspaper in half. Dobló el periódico por la mitad.
  ■ **to fold one's arms** cruzarse de brazos
**folder** NOUN
  la carpeta
**folding** ADJECTIVE
  plegable ‹FEM plegable› *(bed, chair)*
to **follow** VERB
  seguir*
  □ You go first and I'll follow. Ve tú primero y yo te sigo. □ He followed my advice. Siguió mi consejo.
**following** ADJECTIVE
  siguiente ‹FEM siguiente›
  □ the following day al día siguiente
**fond** ADJECTIVE
  ■ **to be fond of somebody** tener cariño a alguien □ I'm very fond of her. Le tengo mucho cariño.
**food** NOUN
  la comida
  □ cat food comida para gatos □ We need to

buy some food. Hay que comprar comida.
**food processor** NOUN
  el robot de cocina ‹PL los robots de cocina›
**fool** NOUN
  el/la idiota
**foot** NOUN
  **1** el pie *(of person)*
  □ My feet are aching. Me duelen los pies.
  ■ **on foot** a pie

  > **DID YOU KNOW...?**
  > In Spain measurements are in metres and centimetres rather than feet and inches. A foot is about 30 centimetres.

  □ Dave is six foot tall. Dave mide un metro ochenta.
  **2** la pata *(of animal)*
**football** NOUN
  **1** el fútbol
  □ I like playing football. Me gusta jugar al fútbol.
  ■ **football boots** las botas de fútbol
  **2** el balón ‹PL los balones›
  □ Paul threw the football over the fence. Paul lanzó el balón por encima de la valla.
**footballer** NOUN
  el/la futbolista
**football player** NOUN
  el/la futbolista
**footpath** NOUN
  el sendero
**footprint** NOUN
  la pisada
  □ He saw some footprints in the sand. Vio algunas pisadas en la arena.
**footstep** NOUN
  el paso
  □ I can hear footsteps on the stairs. Oigo pasos en la escalera.
**for** PREPOSITION

  > **LANGUAGE TIP** There are three basic ways of translating 'for' into Spanish: **para**, **por** and **durante**. Check the boxes at the beginning of each translation to find the meaning or example you need. If you can't find it look at the phrases at the end of the entry.

  **1** para

  > **LANGUAGE TIP para** is used to indicate destination, employment, intention and purpose.

  □ a present for me un regalo para mí □ the train for London el tren para Londres □ He works for the government. Trabaja para el gobierno. □ What for? ¿Para qué? □ What's it for? ¿Para qué es?
  **2** por

**LANGUAGE TIP** **por** is used to indicate reason or cause. Use it also when talking about amounts of money.

□ for fear of being criticized por temor a ser criticado □ Oxford is famous for its university. Oxford es famoso por su universidad. □ I'll do it for you. Lo haré por ti. □ I'm sorry for Steve, but it's his own fault. Lo siento por Steve, pero es culpa suya. □ I sold it for £5. Lo vendí por 5 libras. □ What did he do that for? ¿Por qué ha hecho eso?

**3** durante

**LANGUAGE TIP** When referring to periods of time, use **durante** to refer to the future and completed actions in the past. Note that it can often be omitted, as in the next two examples.

□ She will be away for a month. Estará fuera (durante) un mes. □ He worked in Spain for two years. Trabajó (durante) dos años en España.

**LANGUAGE TIP** Use **hace...que** and the present to describe actions and states that started in the past and are still going on. Alternatively use the present and **desde hace**. Another option is **llevar** and an **-ando/-iendo** form.

□ He has been learning French for two years. Hace dos años que estudia francés. □ I haven't seen her for two years. No la veo desde hace dos años. □ She's been learning German for four years. Lleva cuatro años estudiando alemán.

**LANGUAGE TIP** See how the tenses change when talking about something that 'had' happened or 'had been' happening 'for' a time.

□ He had been learning French for two years. Hacía dos años que estudiaba francés. □ I hadn't seen her for two years. No la veía desde hacía dos años. □ She had been learning German for four years. Llevaba cuatro años estudiando alemán.

■ **There are road works for three kilometres.** Hay obras en tres kilómetros.

■ **What's the English for 'león'?** ¿Cómo se dice 'león' en inglés?

■ **It's time for lunch.** Es la hora de comer.

■ **Can you do it for tomorrow?** ¿Puedes hacerlo para mañana?

■ **Are you for or against the idea?** ¿Estás a favor o en contra de la idea?

to **forbid** VERB
prohibir*

■ **to forbid somebody to do something** prohibir a alguien que haga algo

**force** NOUN
▷ see also **force** VERB
la fuerza
□ the force of the explosion la fuerza de la explosión

■ **UN forces** las fuerzas de la ONU

■ **in force** (law, rules) en vigor

to **force** VERB
▷ see also **force** NOUN
obligar*
□ They forced him to open the safe. Le obligaron a abrir la caja fuerte.

**forecast** NOUN
■ **the weather forecast** el pronóstico del tiempo

**foreground** NOUN
el primer plano
□ in the foreground en primer plano

**forehead** NOUN
la frente

**foreign** ADJECTIVE
**1** extranjero (FEM extranjera)
□ a foreign language una lengua extranjera
**2** exterior (FEM exterior)
□ US foreign policy la política exterior estadounidense

**foreigner** NOUN
el extranjero
la extranjera

to **foresee** VERB
prever*

**forest** NOUN
el bosque

**forever** ADVERB
**1** para siempre
□ He's gone forever. Se ha ido para siempre.
**2** siempre
□ She's forever complaining. Siempre se está quejando.

**forgave** VERB ▷ see **forgive**

to **forge** VERB
falsificar*
□ She forged his signature. Falsificó su firma.

to **forget** VERB
olvidar
□ I've forgotten his name. He olvidado su nombre.

■ **to forget to do something** olvidarse de hacer algo □ I forgot to close the window. Me olvidé de cerrar la ventana.

■ **I'm sorry, I had completely forgotten!** ¡Lo siento, se me había olvidado por completo!

■ **Forget it!** ¡No importa!

to **forgive** VERB
perdonar
□ I forgive you. Te perdono.

■ **to forgive somebody for doing something** perdonar a alguien que haya hecho algo

**forgot, forgotten** VERB ▷ see **forget**

**fork** NOUN
1 el tenedor (for eating)
2 la horca
□ He was piling up hay with a fork. Apilaba heno con una horca.
3 la bifurcación (PL las bifurcaciones) (in road)

**form** NOUN
1 el impreso (la planilla Latin America)
■ **to fill in a form** rellenar un impreso
2 la forma
□ I'm against hunting in any form. Estoy en contra de cualquier forma de caza.
■ **in top form** en plena forma
■ **She's in the first form.** Está haciendo primero de secundaria.

**formal** ADJECTIVE
1 oficial (FEM oficial)
□ a formal occasion un acto oficial
■ **a formal dinner** una cena de gala
■ **formal clothes** la ropa de etiqueta
2 formal (FEM formal)
□ In English, 'residence' is a formal term. En inglés, 'residence' es un término formal.
■ **He's got no formal education.** No tiene formación académica.

**former** ADJECTIVE
antiguo (FEM antigua)

   **LANGUAGE TIP** Put **antiguo** before the noun when translating 'former'.

□ a former pupil un antiguo alumno

**formerly** ADVERB
antiguamente

**fort** NOUN
el fuerte

**forth** ADVERB
■ **to go back and forth** ir de acá para allá
■ **and so forth** y demás

**fortnight** NOUN
■ **a fortnight** quince días □ I'm going on holiday for a fortnight. Me voy quince días de vacaciones.

**fortunate** ADJECTIVE
■ **He was extremely fortunate to survive.** Tuvo la gran suerte de salir vivo.
■ **It's fortunate that I remembered the map.** Menos mal que me acordé de traer el mapa.

**fortunately** ADVERB
afortunadamente

**fortune** NOUN
la fortuna
□ He made his fortune in car sales. Consiguió su fortuna con la venta de coches.
■ **Kate earns a fortune!** ¡Kate gana un dineral!

■ **to tell somebody's fortune** decir la buenaventura a alguien

**forty** NUMERAL
cuarenta
□ He's forty. Tiene cuarenta años.

**forward** ADVERB
   ▷ see also **forward** VERB
hacia delante
□ to look forward mirar hacia delante
■ **to move forward** avanzar

to **forward** VERB
   ▷ see also **forward** ADVERB
remitir (letter)

to **foster** VERB
acoger*
□ She has fostered more than fifteen children. Ha acogido a más de quince niños.

**foster child** NOUN
el niño acogido en una familia

**fought** VERB ▷ see **fight**

**foul** ADJECTIVE
   ▷ see also **foul** NOUN
1 horrible (FEM horrible)
□ The weather was foul. El tiempo era horrible.
2 asqueroso (FEM asquerosa)
□ It smells foul. Huele asqueroso.
■ **Brenda is in a foul mood.** Brenda está de muy mal humor.

**foul** NOUN
   ▷ see also **foul** ADJECTIVE
la falta (in sports)

**found** VERB ▷ see **find**

to **found** VERB
fundar

**foundations** PL NOUN
los cimientos

**fountain** NOUN
la fuente

**fountain pen** NOUN
la pluma estilográfica (la plumafuente Latin America)

**four** NUMERAL
cuatro
□ She's four. Tiene cuatro años.

**fourteen** NUMERAL
catorce
□ I'm fourteen. Tengo catorce años.

**fourteenth** ADJECTIVE
decimocuarto (FEM decimocuarta)
■ **the fourteenth floor** la planta catorce
■ **the fourteenth of July** el catorce de julio

**fourth** ADJECTIVE
cuarto (FEM cuarta)
□ the fourth floor el cuarto piso
■ **the fourth of July** el cuatro de julio

**fox** NOUN
el zorro

**fragile** ADJECTIVE
frágil (FEM frágil)

**frame** NOUN
el marco
□ a silver frame un marco de plata
■ **glasses with plastic frames** gafas con montura de plástico

**France** NOUN
Francia fem

**frantic** ADJECTIVE
frenético (FEM frenética)
□ There was frantic activity before the party started. Había una actividad frenética antes de empezar la fiesta. □ I was going frantic. Me estaba poniendo frenético.
■ **to be frantic with worry** estar muerto de preocupación

**fraud** NOUN
1 el fraude
□ He was jailed for fraud. Lo encarcelaron por fraude.
2 el impostor
la impostora
□ You're a fraud! ¡Eres un impostor!

**freckles** PL NOUN
las pecas

**free** ADJECTIVE
▷ see also **free** VERB
1 gratuito (FEM gratuita)
□ a free brochure un folleto gratuito
■ **You can get it for free.** Se puede conseguir gratis.
2 libre (FEM libre)
□ Is this seat free? ¿Está libre este asiento?
□ Are you free after school? ¿Estás libre después de clase?

to **free** VERB
▷ see also **free** ADJECTIVE
liberar

**freedom** NOUN
la libertad

**freeway** NOUN (US)
la autopista

to **freeze** VERB
1 congelar
□ She froze the rest of the raspberries. Congeló el resto de las frambuesas.
2 helarse*
□ The water had frozen. El agua se había helado.

**freezer** NOUN
el congelador

**freezing** ADJECTIVE
■ **It's freezing!** ¡Hace un frío que pela! (informal)
■ **I'm freezing!** ¡Me estoy congelando!
■ **three degrees below freezing** tres grados bajo cero

**freight** NOUN
las mercancías (goods)
■ **a freight train** un tren de mercancías

**French** ADJECTIVE
▷ see also **French** NOUN
francés (FEM francesa, PL franceses)

**French** NOUN
▷ see also **French** ADJECTIVE
el francés (language)
□ the French teacher el profesor de francés
■ **the French** los franceses

**French beans** PL NOUN
las judías verdes

**French fries** PL NOUN
las patatas fritas (las papas fritas Latin America)

**French horn** NOUN
la trompa de llaves

**French loaf** NOUN
la barra de pan

**Frenchman** NOUN
el francés (PL los franceses)

**French windows** PL NOUN
la puerta ventana

**Frenchwoman** NOUN
la francesa

**frequent** ADJECTIVE
frecuente (FEM frecuente)

**fresh** ADJECTIVE
fresco (FEM fresca)
□ I always buy fresh fish. Siempre compro pescado fresco.
■ **I need some fresh air.** Necesito tomar el aire.

to **freshen up** VERB
refrescarse*

to **fret** VERB
preocuparse

**Friday** NOUN
el viernes (PL los viernes)
□ I saw her on Friday. La vi el viernes.
□ every Friday todos los viernes □ last Friday el viernes pasado □ next Friday el viernes que viene □ on Fridays los viernes

**fridge** NOUN
la nevera (la refrigeradora Latin America)

**fried** ADJECTIVE
frito (FEM frita)
□ a fried egg un huevo frito

**friend** NOUN
el amigo
la amiga

**friendly** ADJECTIVE
simpático (FEM simpática)
□ She's really friendly. Es muy simpática.
■ **Liverpool is a friendly city.** Liverpool es una ciudad acogedora.
■ **a friendly match** un partido amistoso

**friendship** NOUN
la amistad

**fright** NOUN
el susto
□ She gave us a fright. Nos dio un susto.
□ to get a fright llevarse un susto

to **frighten** VERB
asustar
□ She was trying to frighten him. Intentaba asustarlo.
■ Horror films frighten him. Le dan miedo las películas de terror.

**frightened** ADJECTIVE
■ to be frightened tener miedo □ I'm frightened! ¡Tengo miedo!
■ Anna's frightened of spiders. A Anna le dan miedo las arañas.

**frightening** ADJECTIVE
aterrador (FEM aterradora)

**fringe** NOUN
el flequillo
□ She's got a fringe. Lleva flequillo.

**Frisbee**® NOUN
el disco volador

**fro** ADVERB
■ to go to and fro ir de acá para allá

**frog** NOUN
la rana

**from** PREPOSITION
1 de
□ Where do you come from? ¿De dónde eres? □ a letter from my sister una carta de mi hermana □ The hotel is one kilometre from the beach. El hotel está a un kilómetro de la playa. □ The price was reduced from £10 to £5. Rebajaron el precio de 10 a 5 libras esterlinas.
2 desde
□ Breakfast is available from 6 a.m. Se puede desayunar desde las 6 de la mañana. □ I can't see anything from here. Desde aquí no veo nada.

LANGUAGE TIP In the following phrases **de** and **desde** are interchangeable. Use **a** to translate 'to' if you have chosen **de** and **hasta** if you have opted for **desde**.

■ He flew from London to Bilbao. Voló de Londres a Bilbao.
■ from one o'clock to three desde la una hasta las tres
■ She works from nine to five. Trabaja de nueve a cinco.
■ from...onwards a partir de... □ We'll be at home from seven o'clock onwards. Estaremos en casa a partir de las siete.

**front** NOUN
▷ see also **front** ADJECTIVE
la parte delantera
□ The switch is at the front of the vacuum cleaner. El interruptor está en la parte delantera de la aspiradora.
■ the front of the dress el delantero del vestido
■ the front of the house la fachada de la casa
■ I was sitting in the front. (of car) Yo iba sentado delante.
■ at the front of the train al principio del tren
■ in front delante □ the car in front el coche de delante
■ in front of delante de □ Irene sits in front of me in class. Irene se sienta delante de mí en clase.

**front** ADJECTIVE
▷ see also **front** NOUN
1 primero (FEM primera)
□ the front row la primera fila
LANGUAGE TIP Use **primer** before a masculine singular noun.
2 delantero (FEM delantera)
□ the front seats of the car los asientos delanteros del coche
■ the front door la puerta principal

**frontier** NOUN
la frontera

**frost** NOUN
la helada
□ There was a frost last night. Anoche cayó una helada.

**frosting** NOUN (US)
el glaseado (on cake)

**frosty** ADJECTIVE
■ It's frosty today. Hoy ha helado.

to **frown** VERB
fruncir* el ceño

**frozen** ADJECTIVE
congelado (FEM congelada)

**fruit** NOUN
la fruta
■ fruit juice el zumo de fruta (el jugo de fruta Latin America)
■ fruit salad la macedonia (la ensalada de frutas Latin America)

**fruit machine** NOUN
la máquina tragaperras (PL las máquinas tragaperras)

**frustrated** ADJECTIVE
frustrado (FEM frustrada)

to **fry** VERB
freír*

**frying pan** NOUN
la sartén (PL las sartenes)

**fuel** NOUN
el combustible

□ We've run out of fuel. Nos hemos quedado sin combustible.

to **fulfil** VERB
realizar*
□ He fulfilled his dream to visit China. Realizó su sueño de viajar a China.
■ **to fulfil a promise** cumplir una promesa

**full** ADJECTIVE
1 lleno (FEM llena)
□ The tank's full. El depósito está lleno.
■ **I'm full.** Estoy lleno.
■ **There was a full moon.** Había luna llena.
2 completo (FEM completa)
□ He asked for full information on the job. Solicitó información completa sobre el trabajo. □ My full name is Ian John Marr. Mi nombre completo es Ian John Marr.
■ **full board** la pensión completa
■ **at full speed** a toda velocidad

**full stop** NOUN
el punto (signo de puntuación)

**full-time** ADJECTIVE, ADVERB
■ **She's got a full-time job.** Tiene un trabajo de jornada completa.
■ **She works full-time.** Trabaja la jornada completa.

**fully** ADVERB
completamente
□ He hasn't fully recovered from his illness. No se ha recuperado completamente de su enfermedad.

**fumes** PL NOUN
el humo

**fun** ADJECTIVE
▷ see also **fun** NOUN
divertido (FEM divertida)
□ She's a fun person. Es una persona divertida.

**fun** NOUN
▷ see also **fun** ADJECTIVE
■ **to have fun** divertirse
■ **It's fun!** ¡Es divertido!
■ **Have fun!** ¡Que te diviertas!
■ **for fun** por gusto
■ **to make fun of somebody** reírse de alguien

**funds** PL NOUN
los fondos
□ to raise funds recaudar fondos

**funeral** NOUN
el funeral

**funfair** NOUN
1 la feria (travelling fair)

2 el parque de atracciones (fair on permanent site)

**funny** ADJECTIVE
1 gracioso (FEM graciosa)
□ a funny joke un chiste gracioso
2 raro (FEM rara)
□ There's something funny about him. Hay algo raro en él.

**fur** NOUN
1 la piel
■ **a fur coat** un abrigo de pieles
2 el pelaje
□ the cat's fur el pelaje del gato

**furious** ADJECTIVE
furioso (FEM furiosa)

**furniture** NOUN
los muebles
■ **a piece of furniture** un mueble

**further** ADVERB, ADJECTIVE
1 más lejos
□ London is further from here than Paris. Londres está más lejos de aquí que París.
■ **I can't walk any further.** No puedo andar más.
■ **How much further is it?** ¿Cuánto queda todavía?
2 más
□ Please write to us if you need any further information. No dude en escribirnos si necesita más información.

**further education** NOUN
la educación superior

**fuse** NOUN
el fusible
□ The fuse has blown. Se ha fundido el fusible.

**fuss** NOUN
el jaleo
□ What's all the fuss about? ¿A qué viene tanto jaleo?
■ **He's always making a fuss about nothing.** Siempre monta el número por cualquier tontería. (informal)

**fussy** ADJECTIVE
quisquilloso (FEM quisquillosa)
□ She is very fussy about her food. Es muy quisquillosa con la comida.

**future** NOUN
el futuro
□ What are your plans for the future? ¿Qué planes tienes para el futuro?
■ **in future** de ahora en adelante □ Be more careful in future. De ahora en adelante ten más cuidado.

# Gg

to **gain** VERB
ganar
□ What do you hope to gain from this? ¿Qué esperas ganar con esto?
■ **to gain speed** adquirir velocidad
■ **to gain weight** engordar

**gallery** NOUN
1 el museo de arte (state-owned)
2 una galería de arte (private)

to **gamble** VERB
jugarse*
□ He gambled £100 at the casino. Se jugó 100 libras en el casino.

**gambler** NOUN
el jugador
la jugadora

**gambling** NOUN
el juego (de azar)

**game** NOUN
1 el juego
□ The children were playing a game. Los niños jugaban a un juego.
2 el partido
□ a game of football un partido de fútbol
■ **a game of cards** una partida de cartas
■ **We have games on Thursdays.** Tenemos deporte los jueves.

**gang** NOUN
1 la banda (of thieves, troublemakers)
2 la pandilla (of friends)

**gangster** NOUN
el gángster

**gap** NOUN
1 el hueco
□ There's a gap in the hedge. Hay un hueco en el seto.
2 el intervalo
□ a gap of four years un intervalo de cuatro años

**garage** NOUN
1 el garaje (for keeping the car)
2 el taller (for car repairs)

**garbage** NOUN
la basura
□ the garbage can el cubo de la basura
■ **That's garbage!** ¡Eso son tonterías!

**garden** NOUN
el jardín (PL los jardines)

**gardener** NOUN
el jardinero
la jardinera
□ He's a gardener. Es jardinero.

**gardening** NOUN
la jardinería
□ Margaret loves gardening. A Margaret le encanta la jardinería.

**gardens** PL NOUN
el parque

**garlic** NOUN
el ajo

**garment** NOUN
la prenda de vestir

**gas** NOUN
1 el gas
■ **a gas cooker** una cocina de gas
■ **a gas cylinder** una bombona de gas
■ **a gas fire** una estufa de gas
■ **a gas leak** un escape de gas
2 la gasolina (US: petrol)

**gasoline** NOUN (US)
la gasolina

**gate** NOUN
1 la puerta (made of wood)
2 la verja (made of metal)
■ **Please go to gate seven.** Diríjanse a la puerta siete.

**gateau** NOUN
la tarta

to **gather** VERB
1 reunirse*
□ We gathered around the fireplace. Nos reunimos en torno a la chimenea.
2 reunir*
□ We gathered enough firewood to last the night. Reunimos leña suficiente para toda la noche. □ to gather information reunir información
■ **to gather speed** adquirir velocidad □ The train gathered speed. El tren adquirió velocidad.

**gave** VERB ▷ see **give**

**gay** ADJECTIVE

gay (FEM + PL gay)

to **gaze** VERB
- ■ **to gaze at** mirar fijamente □ He was gazing at her. La miraba fijamente.

**GCSE** NOUN (= General Certificate of Secondary Education)

> **DID YOU KNOW...?**
> In Spain, under the reformed educational system, if you leave school at the age of 16, you get a **Título de Graduado en Educación Secundaria**.

**gear** NOUN
1 la marcha
  - □ to change gear cambiar de marcha
  - □ He left the car in gear. Dejó el coche con una marcha metida.
  - ■ **in first gear** en primera
2 el equipo
  - □ camping gear el equipo de acampada
  - ■ **sports gear** la ropa de deporte

**gear lever** NOUN
la palanca de cambio

**gearshift** NOUN (US)
la palanca de cambio

**geese** PL NOUN ▷ see **goose**

**gel** NOUN
el gel
- ■ **hair gel** el fijador

**gem** NOUN
la gema

**Gemini** NOUN
el Géminis (sign)
- ■ **I'm Gemini.** Soy géminis.

**gender** NOUN
el género (of noun)

**general** NOUN
▷ see also **general** ADJECTIVE
el general

**general** ADJECTIVE
▷ see also **general** NOUN
general (FEM general)
- ■ **in general** en general

**general election** NOUN
las elecciones generales

**general knowledge** NOUN
la cultura general

**generally** ADVERB
generalmente
- □ I generally go shopping on Saturdays. Generalmente voy de compras los sábados.

**generation** NOUN
la generación (PL las generaciones)
- □ the younger generation la nueva generación

**generator** NOUN
el generador

**generous** ADJECTIVE
generoso (FEM generosa)
- □ That's very generous of you. Es muy generoso de tu parte.

**Geneva** NOUN
Ginebra fem

**genius** NOUN
el genio
- □ She's a genius. Es un genio.

**gentle** ADJECTIVE
1 dulce (FEM dulce) (person, voice)
2 suave (FEM suave) (wind, touch)

**gentleman** NOUN
el caballero

**gently** ADVERB
1 dulcemente (to say, smile)
2 suavemente (to touch)

**gents** NOUN
el servicio de caballeros
- □ Can you tell me where the gents is, please? ¿El servicio de caballeros, por favor?
- ■ **'gents'** (on sign) 'caballeros'

**genuine** ADJECTIVE
1 auténtico (FEM auténtica)
  - □ These are genuine diamonds. Estos son diamantes auténticos.
2 sincero (FEM sincera)
  - □ She's a very genuine person. Es una persona muy sincera.

**geography** NOUN
la geografía

**gerbil** NOUN
el gerbo

**germ** NOUN
el microbio

**German** ADJECTIVE
▷ see also **German** NOUN
alemán (FEM alemana, PL alemanes)

**German** NOUN
▷ see also **German** ADJECTIVE
1 el alemán (PL los alemanes)
  la alemana (person)
  - □ the Germans los alemanes
2 el alemán (language)
  - □ our German teacher nuestro profesor de alemán

**German measles** NOUN
la rubéola
- □ to have German measles tener rubéola

**Germany** NOUN
Alemania fem

**gesture** NOUN
el gesto

to **get** VERB
> **LANGUAGE TIP** There are several ways of translating 'get'. Scan the examples to find one that is similar to what you want to say.
1 recibir (have, receive)
  - □ I got a letter from him. Recibí una carta de él.

g

■ **I got lots of presents.** Me hicieron muchos regalos.

2 conseguir* *(obtain)*

□ He had trouble getting a hotel room. Tuvo dificultades para conseguir una habitación de hotel.

■ **to get something for somebody** conseguir algo a alguien □ The librarian got the book for me. El bibliotecario me consiguió el libro.

■ **Jackie got good exam results.** Jackie sacó buenas notas en los exámenes.

3 ir* a buscar *(fetch)*

□ Quick, get help! ¡Rápido, ve a buscar ayuda!

4 coger* *(catch, take)*

> **LANGUAGE TIP** Be very careful with the verb **coger**: in most of Latin America this is an extremely rude word that should be avoided. However, in Spain this verb is common and not rude at all.

□ They've got the thief. Han cogido al ladrón. (Han atrapado al ladrón. *Latin America*) □ I'm getting the bus into town. Voy a coger el autobús al centro. (Voy a tomar el autobús al centro. *Latin America*)

5 entender* *(understand)*

□ I don't get the joke. No entiendo el chiste.

6 llegar* *(arrive)*

□ He should get here soon. Debería llegar pronto. □ How do you get to the cinema? ¿Cómo se llega al cine?

■ **to get angry** enfadarse (enojarse *Latin America*)

■ **to get tired** cansarse

> **LANGUAGE TIP** For other phrases with 'get' and an adjective, such as 'to get old, to get drunk', you should look under the word 'old', 'drunk', etc.

■ **to get something done** mandar hacer algo □ I'm getting my car fixed. He mandado arreglar el coche.

■ **I got my hair cut.** Me corté el pelo.

■ **I'll get it! 1** *(telephone)* ¡Yo contesto! **2** *(door)* ¡Ya voy yo!

to **get away** VERB

escapar

□ One of the burglars got away. Uno de los ladrones escapó.

to **get back** VERB

1 volver*

□ What time did you get back? ¿A qué hora volvisteis?

2 recuperar

□ He got his money back. Recuperó su dinero.

to **get in** VERB

llegar*

□ What time did you get in last night? ¿A qué hora llegaste anoche?

to **get into** VERB

entrar en

□ How did you get into the house? ¿Cómo entraste en la casa?

■ **Sharon got into the car.** Sharon subió al coche.

■ **Get into bed!** ¡Métete en la cama!

to **get off** VERB

1 bajarse de

□ Isobel got off the train. Isobel se bajó del tren.

2 salir*

□ He managed to get off early from work yesterday. Logró salir de trabajar pronto ayer.

to **get on** VERB

1 subirse a

□ Phyllis got on the bus. Phyllis se subió al autobús.

2 llevarse bien

□ We got on really well. Nos llevábamos muy bien. □ He doesn't get on with his parents. No se lleva bien con sus padres.

■ **How are you getting on?** ¿Cómo te va?

to **get out** VERB

1 salir*

□ Get out! ¡Sal!

■ **She got out of the car.** Se bajó del coche.

2 sacar*

□ She got the map out. Sacó el mapa.

to **get over** VERB

1 recuperarse de

□ It took her a long time to get over the illness. Tardó mucho tiempo en recuperarse de la enfermedad.

2 superar

□ He managed to get over the problem. Logró superar el problema.

to **get together** VERB

reunirse*

□ Could we get together this evening? ¿Podemos reunirnos esta tarde?

to **get up** VERB

levantarse

□ What time do you get up? ¿A qué hora te levantas?

**ghost** NOUN

el fantasma

> **LANGUAGE TIP** Although **fantasma** ends in **-a**, it is actually a masculine noun.

**giant** ADJECTIVE

▷ *see also* **giant** NOUN

enorme (FEM enorme)

**giant** NOUN
▷ see also **giant** ADJECTIVE
1 el gigante
2 la giganta
**gift** NOUN
el regalo
■ **to have a gift for something** tener dotes para algo □ Dave's got a gift for painting. Dave tiene dotes para la pintura.
**gifted** ADJECTIVE
de talento
□ Janice is a gifted dancer. Janice es una bailarina de talento.
■ **He's one of this country's most gifted artists.** Es uno de los artistas con más dotes de este país.
**gift shop** NOUN
la tienda de regalos
**gigantic** ADJECTIVE
gigantesco (FEM gigantesca)
**gin** NOUN
la ginebra
**ginger** NOUN
▷ see also **ginger** ADJECTIVE
el jengibre
**ginger** ADJECTIVE
▷ see also **ginger** NOUN
■ **She's got ginger hair.** Es pelirroja.
**giraffe** NOUN
la jirafa
**girl** NOUN
1 la niña (young)
□ a five-year old girl una niña de cinco años
□ They've got a girl and two boys. Tienen una niña y dos niños.
2 la chica (older)
□ a sixteen-year old girl una chica de dieciséis años
**girlfriend** NOUN
1 la novia
□ Paul's girlfriend is called Janice. La novia de Paul se llama Janice.
2 la amiga
□ She often went out with her girlfriends. Solía salir con sus amigas.
to **give** VERB
dar*
■ **to give something to somebody** dar algo a alguien □ He gave me £10. Me dio 10 libras.
■ **to give somebody a present** hacer un regalo a alguien
■ **to give way** (in car) ceder el paso
to **give in** VERB
rendirse*
□ I give in! ¡Me rindo!
to **give out** VERB
repartir
□ He gave out the exam papers. Repartió las

hojas de examen.
to **give up** VERB
darse* por vencido
□ I couldn't do it, so I gave up. No podía hacerlo, así que me di por vencido.
■ **to give oneself up** entregarse □ She gave herself up. Se entregó.
■ **to give up doing something** dejar de hacer algo □ He gave up smoking. Dejó de fumar.
**glad** ADJECTIVE
contento (FEM contenta)
□ She's glad she's done it. Está contenta de haberlo hecho.
> LANGUAGE TIP **alegrarse de que** has to be followed by a verb in the subjunctive.
■ **I'm glad you're here.** Me alegro de que estés aquí.
**glamorous** ADJECTIVE
atractivo (FEM atractiva)
to **glance** VERB
▷ see also **glance** NOUN
■ **to glance at something** echar una mirada a algo □ Peter glanced at his watch. Peter echó una mirada al reloj.
**glance** NOUN
▷ see also **glance** VERB
la mirada
□ We exchanged a glance. Intercambiamos una mirada.
■ **at first glance** a primera vista
to **glare** VERB
■ **to glare at somebody** lanzar una mirada de odio a alguien □ She glared at him. Le lanzó una mirada de odio.
**glaring** ADJECTIVE
■ **a glaring mistake** un error patente
**glass** NOUN
1 el vaso (without stem)
□ a glass of milk un vaso de leche
2 la copa (with stem)
□ a glass of champagne una copa de champán
3 el vidrio (substance)
□ a glass door una puerta de vidrio
**glasses** PL NOUN
las gafas (los anteojos Latin America)
**glider** NOUN
el planeador
**global** ADJECTIVE
mundial (FEM mundial)
□ on a global scale a escala mundial
■ **a global view** una visión global
**global warming** NOUN
el calentamiento del planeta
**globe** NOUN
el globo terráqueo

## gloomy ADJECTIVE
oscuro (FEM oscura)
□ He lives in a small gloomy flat. Vive en un piso pequeño y oscuro.
■ **She's been feeling very gloomy recently.** Últimamente está muy desanimada.

## glorious ADJECTIVE
espléndido (FEM espléndida)

## glove NOUN
el guante

## glove compartment NOUN
la guantera

## glue NOUN
▷ see also **glue** VERB
el pegamento

## to glue VERB
▷ see also **glue** NOUN
pegar*
■ **to glue something together** pegar algo

## GM ADJECTIVE (= genetically-modified)
■ **GM foods** los alimentos transgénicos

## GMO NOUN (= genetically-modified organism)
el organismo transgénico

## go NOUN
▷ see also **go** VERB
■ **to have a go at doing something** probar a hacer algo □ He had a go at making a cake. Probó a hacer una tarta.
■ **Whose go is it?** ¿A quién le toca?
■ **It's your go.** Te toca a ti.

## to go VERB
▷ see also **go** NOUN
1 ir*
□ Where are you going? ¿Adónde vas? □ I'm going to the cinema tonight. Voy al cine esta noche.
2 irse* (leave, go away)
□ Where's Judy? — She's gone. ¿Dónde está Judy? — Se ha ido. □ I'm going now. Yo me voy ya. □ We went home. Nos fuimos a casa.
3 funcionar (work)
□ My car won't go. El coche no funciona.
■ **to go home** irse a casa
■ **to go into** entrar en □ She went into the kitchen. Entró en la cocina.
■ **to go for a walk** ir a dar un paseo
■ **How did the exam go?** ¿Cómo te fue en el examen?
■ **I'm going to do it tomorrow.** Lo voy a hacer mañana.
■ **It's going to be difficult.** Va a ser difícil.

## to go after VERB
perseguir*
□ Quick, go after them! ¡Rápido, persíguelos!

## to go ahead VERB

seguir* adelante
□ We'll go ahead with your suggestion. Seguiremos adelante con su propuesta.

## to go away VERB
irse*
□ Go away! ¡Vete!

## to go back VERB
volver*
□ We went back to the same place. Volvimos al mismo sitio. □ He's gone back home. Ha vuelto a casa.

## to go by VERB
pasar
□ Two policemen went by. Pasaron dos policías.

## to go down VERB
1 bajar
□ He went down the stairs. Bajó las escaleras. □ The price of computers has gone down. Ha bajado el precio de los ordenadores.
2 desinflarse
□ My airbed's gone down. Mi colchoneta se ha desinflado.
■ **My brother's gone down with flu.** Mi hermano ha pillado la gripe.

## to go for VERB
ir* a por
□ Suddenly the dog went for me. De pronto el perro fue a por mí.
■ **Go for it!** ¡Adelante!

## to go in VERB
entrar
□ He knocked on the door and went in. Llamó a la puerta y entró.

## to go off VERB
1 marcharse
□ They went off after lunch. Se marcharon después de comer.
2 estallar
□ The bomb went off at 10 o'clock. La bomba estalló a las 10.
■ **The gun went off by accident.** El arma se disparó accidentalmente.
3 sonar*
□ My alarm goes off at seven. Mi despertador suena a las siete.
4 echarse a perder*
□ This milk has gone off. Esta leche se ha echado a perder.
5 apagarse*
□ All the lights went off. Se apagaron todas las luces.
■ **I've gone off that idea.** Ya no me gusta la idea.

## to go on VERB
1 pasar
□ What's going on? ¿Qué pasa?

**2** seguir*
- ■ **to go on doing** seguir haciendo □ He went on reading. Siguió leyendo.

**3** durar
- □ The concert went on until 11 o'clock at night. El concierto duró hasta las 11 de la noche.
- ■ **to go on at somebody** dar la lata a alguien □ They're always going on at me. Están siempre dándome la lata.
- ■ **Go on!** ¡Venga! □ Go on, tell me what the problem is! ¡Venga, dime cuál es el problema!

to **go out** VERB
**1** salir*
- □ Are you going out tonight? ¿Vas a salir esta noche? □ I went out with Steven last night. Ayer por la noche salí con Steven. □ They went out for a meal. Salieron a comer.
- ■ **Are you going out with him?** ¿Estás saliendo con él?

**2** apagarse*
- □ Suddenly the lights went out. De pronto se apagaron las luces.

to **go past** VERB
- ■ **to go past something** pasar por delante de algo □ He went past the shop. Pasó por delante de la tienda.

to **go round** VERB
visitar
- □ We want to go round the museum today. Hoy queremos visitar el museo.
- ■ **I love going round the shops.** Me encanta ir de tiendas.
- ■ **to go round to somebody's house** ir a casa de alguien □ We're all going round to Linda's house tonight. Esta noche vamos todos a casa de Linda.
- ■ **There's a bug going round.** Hay un virus por ahí rondando.
- ■ **Is there enough food to go round?** ¿Hay comida suficiente para todos?

to **go through** VERB
**1** atravesar*
- □ We went through London to get to Brighton. Atravesamos Londres para llegar a Brighton.

**2** pasar por
- □ I know what you're going through. Sé por lo que estás pasando.

**3** repasar
- □ They went through the plan again. Repasaron de nuevo el plan.

**4** registrar
- □ Someone had gone through her things. Alguien había registrado sus cosas.

to **go up** VERB

subir
- □ She went up the stairs. Subió las escaleras. □ The price has gone up. El precio ha subido.
- ■ **to go up in flames** arder en llamas

to **go with** VERB
pegar* con
- □ Does this blouse go with that skirt? ¿Pega esta blusa con la falda?

**goal** NOUN
**1** el gol
- □ He scored the first goal. Él metió el primer gol.

**2** el objetivo
- □ His goal is to become the world champion. Su objetivo es ser campeón del mundo.

**goalkeeper** NOUN
el portero

**goat** NOUN
la cabra
- ■ **goat's cheese** el queso de cabra

**god** NOUN
el dios
- □ I believe in God. Creo en Dios.

**goddaughter** NOUN
la ahijada

**godfather** NOUN
el padrino

**godmother** NOUN
la madrina

**godson** NOUN
el ahijado

**goggles** PL NOUN
las gafas protectoras (los anteojos protectores *Latin America*)

**gold** NOUN
el oro
- □ a gold necklace un collar de oro □ the gold medal la medalla de oro

**goldfish** NOUN
el pez de colores (PL los peces de colores)

**gold-plated** ADJECTIVE
chapado en oro (FEM chapada en oro)

**golf** NOUN
el golf
- ■ **a golf club 1** (*stick*) un palo de golf **2** (*place*) un club de golf
- ■ **a golf course** un campo de golf

**gone** VERB ▷ see **go**

**good** ADJECTIVE
**1** bueno (FEM buena)
- ⚬ **LANGUAGE TIP** Use **buen** before a masculine singular noun.
- □ It's a very good film. Es una película muy buena. □ a good day un buen día □ Be good! ¡Sé bueno! □ The soup is very good here. Aquí la sopa es muy buena.

**WORD POWER**

You can use a number of other words instead of **good** to mean 'great':

**excellent** excelente
□ an excellent book  un libro excelente

**fabulous** fabuloso
□ a fabulous idea  una idea fabulosa

**fantastic** fantástico
□ fantastic weather  un tiempo fantástico

**great** estupendo
□ a great film  una película estupenda

**2** amable (FEM amable) *(kind)*
□ That's very good of you.  Es muy amable de tu parte.

■ **They were very good to me.** Se portaron muy bien conmigo.

■ **Have a good journey!** ¡Buen viaje!

■ **Good!** ¡Bien!

■ **Good morning!** ¡Buenos días!

■ **Good afternoon!** ¡Buenas tardes!

■ **Good evening!** ¡Buenas noches!

■ **Good night!** ¡Buenas noches!

■ **I'm feeling really good today.** Hoy me siento realmente bien.

■ **to be good for somebody** hacer bien a alguien  □ Vegetables are good for you. La verdura te hace bien.

■ **Jane's very good at maths.** A Jane se le dan muy bien las matemáticas.

■ **for good** definitivamente  □ One day he left for good.  Un día se marchó definitivamente.

■ **It's no good complaining.** De nada sirve quejarse.

**goodbye** EXCLAMATION
¡adiós!

**Good Friday** NOUN
el Viernes Santo

**good-looking** ADJECTIVE
guapo (FEM guapa)

**good-natured** ADJECTIVE
bueno (FEM buena)

**LANGUAGE TIP** Use **buen** before a masculine singular noun.

**goods** PL NOUN
los productos
□ They sell a wide range of goods.  Venden una amplia gama de productos.

■ **a goods train** un tren de mercancías

**goose** NOUN
la oca

**gooseberry** NOUN
la grosella espinosa

**gorgeous** ADJECTIVE
**1** guapísimo (FEM guapísima)
□ She's gorgeous!  ¡Es guapísima!
**2** estupendo (FEM estupenda)

□ The weather was gorgeous.  El tiempo fue estupendo.

**gorilla** NOUN
el gorila

**LANGUAGE TIP** Although **gorila** ends in **-a**, it is actually a masculine noun.

**gospel** NOUN
el evangelio

**gossip** NOUN
▷ *see also* **gossip** VERB
**1** el cotilleo
□ Tell me the gossip!  ¡Cuéntame el cotilleo!
**2** el/la cotilla
□ What a gossip!  ¡Menudo cotilla!

to **gossip** VERB
▷ *see also* **gossip** NOUN
cotillear (comadrear *Latin America*)
□ They were always gossiping.  Siempre estaban cotilleando.

**got** VERB
■ **to have got** *(own)* tener  □ How many have you got?  ¿Cuántos tienes?
■ **to have got to do something** tener que hacer algo  □ I've got to tell him.  Tengo que decírselo.

**government** NOUN
el gobierno

**GP** NOUN (= *General Practitioner*)
el médico de cabecera
la médica de cabecera

to **grab** VERB
agarrar
□ He grabbed my arm.  Me agarró el brazo.

**graceful** ADJECTIVE
elegante (FEM elegante)

**grade** NOUN
la nota
□ He got good grades in his exams.  Sacó buenas notas en los exámenes.

**grade school** NOUN (US)
la escuela primaria

**gradual** ADJECTIVE
gradual (FEM gradual)

**gradually** ADVERB
gradualmente

**graduate** NOUN
**1** el licenciado (el egresado *Latin America*)
la licenciada (la egresada *Latin America*)
*(from university)*
**2** el/la bachiller *(from US high school)*

**graffiti** PL NOUN
las pintadas

**grain** NOUN
**1** el grano
□ a grain of rice  un grano de arroz
**2** los cereales
□ She only eats grain and pulses.  Sólo come cereales y legumbres.

**gram** NOUN
el gramo

**grammar** NOUN
la gramática
□ a grammar exercise un ejercicio de gramática

**grammar school** NOUN

> **DID YOU KNOW...?**
> The equivalent to a grammar school in Spain is **el instituto de segunda enseñanza**.

**grammatical** ADJECTIVE
gramatical (FEM gramatical)

**gramme** NOUN
el gramo

**grand** ADJECTIVE
grandioso (FEM grandiosa)
□ Her house is very grand. Su casa es grandiosa.

**granddad** NOUN
el abuelo

**granddaughter** NOUN
la nieta

**grandfather** NOUN
el abuelo

**grandma** NOUN
la abuela

**grandmother** NOUN
la abuela

**grandpa** NOUN
el abuelo

**grandparents** PL NOUN
los abuelos

**grandson** NOUN
el nieto

**granny** NOUN
la abuelita

**grant** NOUN
1 la beca (for study)
2 la subvención (PL las subvenciones) (for industry, organization)

**grape** NOUN
la uva

**grapefruit** NOUN
el pomelo

**graph** NOUN
el gráfico

to **grasp** VERB
agarrar

**grass** NOUN
1 la hierba
□ The grass is long. La hierba está alta.
2 el césped (lawn)
■ 'Keep off the grass' 'Prohibido pisar el césped'
■ to cut the grass cortar el césped

**grasshopper** NOUN
el saltamontes (PL los saltamontes)

to **grate** VERB
rallar
□ grated cheese el queso rallado

**grateful** ADJECTIVE
agradecido (FEM agradecida)

**grave** NOUN
la tumba

**gravel** NOUN
la grava

**graveyard** NOUN
el cementerio

**gravy** NOUN
el jugo de carne

**grease** NOUN
1 la grasa (in hair, on skin)
2 el aceite (for cars, machines)

**greasy** ADJECTIVE
1 aceitoso (FEM aceitosa)
□ The food was very greasy. La comida estaba muy aceitosa.
2 graso (FEM grasa)
□ He has greasy hair. Tiene el pelo graso.

**great** ADJECTIVE
1 estupendo (FEM estupenda) (chévere Latin America)
□ That's great! ¡Estupendo!

**WORD POWER**
You can use a number of other words instead of **great** to mean 'good':
**amazing** increíble
□ amazing news una noticia increíble
**marvellous** estupendo
□ a marvellous idea una idea estupenda
**superb** magnífico
□ a superb meal una comida magnífica
**wonderful** maravilloso
□ a wonderful opportunity una oportunidad maravillosa

2 grande (FEM grande)

> **LANGUAGE TIP** Use gran before a singular noun.

□ a great oak tree un gran roble □ a greatest hits album un disco de grandes éxitos

**Great Britain** NOUN
Gran Bretaña fem

**great-grandfather** NOUN
el bisabuelo

**great-grandmother** NOUN
la bisabuela

**Greece** NOUN
Grecia fem

**greedy** ADJECTIVE
1 glotón (FEM glotona, PL glotones)
□ Don't be greedy, you've already had three doughnuts. No seas glotón, ya te has comido tres donuts.

**g**

**2** codicioso (FEM codiciosa)
  □ She is greedy and selfish. Es codiciosa y egoísta.

**Greek** ADJECTIVE
  ▷ see also **Greek** NOUN
  griego (FEM griega)

**Greek** NOUN
  ▷ see also **Greek** ADJECTIVE
**1** el griego
  la griega (person)
  □ the Greeks los griegos
**2** el griego (language)
  □ our Greek teacher nuestro profesor de griego

**green** ADJECTIVE
  ▷ see also **green** NOUN
  verde (FEM verde)
  □ a green car un coche verde □ a green light (at traffic lights) un semáforo en verde
  ■ **green beans** las judías verdes
  ■ **the Green Party** el Partido Verde

**green** NOUN
  ▷ see also **green** ADJECTIVE
  el verde
  □ a dark green un verde oscuro
  ■ **greens** (vegetables) la verdura
  ■ **the Greens** (party) los verdes

**greengrocer's** NOUN
  la verdulería

**greenhouse** NOUN
  el invernadero
  ■ **the greenhouse effect** el efecto invernadero

**to greet** VERB
  saludar
  □ He greeted me with a kiss. Me saludó con un beso.

**greetings card** NOUN
  la tarjeta de felicitación

**grew** VERB ▷ see **grow**

**grey** ADJECTIVE
  gris (FEM grisa)
  □ They wore grey suits. Llevaban trajes grises.
  ■ **He's going grey.** Le están saliendo canas.
  ■ **grey hair** las canas

**grey-haired** ADJECTIVE
  canoso (FEM canosa)

**grid** NOUN
**1** la cuadrícula (in road, on map)
**2** la red (of electricity)

**grief** NOUN
  la pena

**grill** NOUN
  ▷ see also **grill** VERB
**1** el grill (of cooker)
**2** la parrilla (for barbecue)
  ■ **a mixed grill** una parrillada mixta

**to grill** VERB

  ▷ see also **grill** NOUN
**1** hacer* al grill (in cooker)
**2** asar a la parrilla (barbecue)

**grim** ADJECTIVE
  deprimente (FEM deprimente)
  □ The outskirts of the city are very grim. Las afueras de la ciudad son muy deprimentes.

**to grin** VERB
  ▷ see also **grin** NOUN
  sonreír* ampliamente
  □ Dave grinned at me. Dave me sonrió ampliamente.

**grin** NOUN
  ▷ see also **grin** VERB
  la amplia sonrisa

**to grind** VERB
**1** moler* (coffee, pepper)
**2** picar (US: meat)

**to grip** VERB
  agarrar

**grit** NOUN
  la gravilla

**to groan** VERB
  ▷ see also **groan** NOUN
  gemir*
  □ He groaned with pain. Gimió de dolor.

**groan** NOUN
  ▷ see also **groan** VERB
  el gemido

**grocer** NOUN
**1** el tendero
**2** la tendera

**groceries** PL NOUN
  los comestibles
  ■ **I'll get some groceries.** Traeré algunas provisiones.

**grocer's** NOUN
  la tienda de ultramarinos

**grocery store** NOUN (US)
  la tienda de ultramarinos

**groom** NOUN
  el novio
  □ the groom and his best man el novio y su padrino de boda

**to grope** VERB
  ■ **to grope for something** buscar algo a tientas □ He groped for the light switch. Buscó a tientas el interruptor.

**gross** ADJECTIVE
**1** horrible (FEM horrible) (revolting)
  ■ **That's gross!** ¡Qué asco!
**2** bruto (FEM bruta)
  □ gross income ingresos brutos

**grossly** ADVERB
  enormemente
  □ It's grossly unfair. Es enormemente injusto.
  ■ **We're grossly underpaid.** Estamos tremendamente mal pagados.

**g**

**ground** NOUN
▷ *see also* **ground** VERB
1 el suelo
□ The ground's wet. El suelo está húmedo.
2 el campo (la cancha *Latin America*)
□ a football ground un campo de fútbol
3 el motivo
□ We've got grounds for complaint.
Tenemos motivos para quejarnos.
■ **on the ground** en el suelo □ We sat on
the ground. Nos sentamos en el suelo.

**ground** VERB ▷ *see* **grind**
▷ *see also* **ground** NOUN

**ground floor** NOUN
la planta baja

**group** NOUN
el grupo

**to grow** VERB
1 crecer*
□ Haven't you grown! ¡Cómo has crecido!
2 aumentar
□ The number of unemployed has grown.
Ha aumentado el número de desempleados.
3 cultivar
□ He grew vegetables in his garden.
Cultivaba hortalizas en su jardín.
■ **He's grown out of his jacket.** La
chaqueta se le ha quedado pequeña.
■ **to grow a beard** dejarse barba □ I'm
growing a beard. Me estoy dejando barba.
■ **He grew a moustache.** Se dejó bigote.

**to grow up** VERB
criarse*
□ I grew up in Rome. Me crié en Roma.
■ **Oh, grow up!** ¡No seas crío!

**to growl** VERB
gruñir*

**grown** VERB ▷ *see* **grow**

**growth** NOUN
el crecimiento
□ economic growth crecimiento económico

**grub** NOUN
la manduca (*informal*)

**grudge** NOUN
■ **to have a grudge against somebody**
guardar rencor a alguien □ He's always had
a grudge against me. Siempre me ha
guardado rencor.

**gruesome** ADJECTIVE
horroroso (FEM horrorosa)

**guarantee** NOUN
▷ *see also* **guarantee** VERB
la garantía
□ a five-year guarantee una garantía de
cinco años □ It's still under guarantee.
Todavía tiene garantía.

**to guarantee** VERB
▷ *see also* **guarantee** NOUN

garantizar*
□ I can't guarantee he'll come. No puedo
garantizar que venga.

**to guard** VERB
▷ *see also* **guard** NOUN
vigilar
□ The police were guarding the entrance.
La policía vigilaba la entrada.

**guard** NOUN
▷ *see also* **guard** VERB
1 el/la guardia (*person*)
2 el jefe de tren (*on train*)
■ **a security guard** un guarda jurado

**to guess** VERB
▷ *see also* **guess** NOUN
adivinar
□ Can you guess what it is? A ver si adivinas
qué es.
■ **to guess wrong** equivocarse
■ **Guess what!** ¿Sabes qué?

**guess** NOUN
▷ *see also* **guess** VERB
la suposición (PL las suposiciones)
□ It's just a guess. Sólo es una suposición.
■ **Have a guess!** ¡Adivina!

**guest** NOUN
1 el invitado
la invitada
□ We have guests staying with us. Tenemos
invitados en casa.
2 el/la huésped (*in hotel*)

**guesthouse** NOUN
la pensión (PL las pensiones)

**guide** NOUN
1 la guía
□ We bought a guide to Granada.
Compramos una guía de Granada.
2 el/la guía
□ The guide showed us around the castle.
El guía nos enseñó el castillo.
3 la exploradora (*girl guide*)

**guidebook** NOUN
la guía

**guide dog** NOUN
el perro lazarillo

**guilty** ADJECTIVE
culpable (FEM culpable)
□ She was found guilty. Fue declarada
culpable. □ He felt guilty about lying to her.
Se sentía culpable por haberle mentido.
■ **He has a guilty conscience.** Tiene
remordimientos de conciencia.

**guinea pig** NOUN
el cobayo
□ She's got a guinea pig. Tiene un cobayo.

**guitar** NOUN
la guitarra

**gum** NOUN

## gun – gypsy

el <u>chicle</u> *(chewing gum)*
- **a piece of gum** un chicle
- **gums** *(in mouth)* las encías

**gun** NOUN
1 la <u>pistola</u> *(small)*
2 el <u>fusil</u> *(rifle)*

**gunpoint** NOUN
- **at gunpoint** a punta de pistola

**gust** NOUN
- **a gust of wind** una ráfaga de viento

**guy** NOUN
el <u>tío</u> *(informal)*

> **LANGUAGE TIP** The word **tío** in this sense is confined to Spain. In Latin America, the equivalent is **tipo**.

□ Who's that guy? ¿Quién es ese tío?
□ He's a nice guy. Es un tío simpático.

**gym** NOUN
el <u>gimnasio</u>
□ I go to the gym every day. Voy al gimnasio todos los días.
- **gym classes** las clases de gimnasia

**gymnast** NOUN
el/la <u>gimnasta</u>

**gymnastics** NOUN
la <u>gimnasia</u>

**gypsy** NOUN
el <u>gitano</u>
la <u>gitana</u>

# Hh

**habit** NOUN
la costumbre

to **hack** VERB
■ **to hack into a system** piratear un sistema

**hacker** NOUN
el pirata informático
la pirata informática

**had** VERB ▷ see **have**

**haddock** NOUN
el abadejo

**hadn't** = had not

**hail** NOUN
▷ see also **hail** VERB
el granizo

to **hail** VERB
▷ see also **hail** NOUN
granizar*

**hair** NOUN
el pelo
□ She's got long hair. Tiene el pelo largo.
□ I'm allergic to cat hair. Soy alérgico al pelo de los gatos.
■ **to have one's hair cut** cortarse el pelo
■ **grey hair** las canas
■ **to brush one's hair** cepillarse el pelo
■ **to wash one's hair** lavarse la cabeza

**hairbrush** NOUN
el cepillo (para el pelo)

**haircut** NOUN
el corte de pelo
□ You need a haircut. Necesitas un corte de pelo.
■ **to have a haircut** cortarse el pelo

**hairdresser** NOUN
el peluquero
la peluquera
□ He's a hairdresser. Es peluquero.
■ **at the hairdresser's** en la peluquería

**hair dryer** NOUN
el secador de pelo

**hair gel** NOUN
el fijador

**hairgrip** NOUN
la horquilla

**hair spray** NOUN
la laca

**hairstyle** NOUN
el peinado

**hairy** ADJECTIVE
peludo (FEM peluda)
□ He's very hairy. Es muy peludo.
■ **He's got hairy legs.** Tiene mucho pelo en las piernas.

**half** NOUN
▷ see also **half** ADJECTIVE
1 la mitad
□ half of the cake la mitad de la tarta
■ **to cut something in half** cortar algo por la mitad
2 el billete para niños (ticket)
□ One and two halves, please. Un billete normal y dos para niños, por favor.
■ **two and a half** dos y medio
■ **half a kilo** medio kilo
■ **half an hour** media hora
■ **half past ten** las diez y media

**half** ADJECTIVE, ADVERB
▷ see also **half** NOUN
medio (FEM media)
□ a half chicken medio pollo

> **LANGUAGE TIP** When you use **medio** before an adjective, it does not change.

□ She was half asleep. Estaba medio dormida. □ They were half drunk. Estaban medio borrachos.

**half-price** ADJECTIVE, ADVERB
a mitad de precio
□ I bought it half-price. Lo compré a mitad de precio.

**half-term** NOUN
las vacaciones de mitad de trimestre

**half-time** NOUN
el descanso (del partido)

**halfway** ADVERB
1 a medio camino
□ Reading is halfway between Oxford and London. Reading está a medio camino entre Oxford y Londres.
2 a la mitad
□ halfway through the film a la mitad de la película

h

## hall – hang-gliding

**hall** NOUN
1 el vestíbulo *(in house)*
2 la sala
  □ a lecture hall una sala de conferencias
  ■ **a concert hall** un auditorio
  ■ **a sports hall** un gimnasio
  ■ **village hall** el salón de actos municipal

**Hallowe'en** NOUN
la víspera de Todos los Santos

**hallway** NOUN
el vestíbulo

**halt** NOUN
  ■ **to come to a halt** pararse

**ham** NOUN
el jamón (PL los jamones)

> **DID YOU KNOW...?**
> In Spain there are two basic kinds of
> ham in the shops: **jamón serrano**,
> which is cured and similar to Parma
> ham, and **jamón de York** or **jamón
> dulce**, which is boiled and similar to
> British ham.

**hamburger** NOUN
la hamburguesa

**hammer** NOUN
el martillo

**hamster** NOUN
el hámster

**hand** NOUN
  ▷ *see also* **hand** VERB
1 la mano *(of person)*

> **LANGUAGE TIP** Although **mano** ends in
> **-o** it is actually a feminine noun.

2 la manecilla *(of clock)*
  ■ **to give someone a hand** echar una
  mano a alguien □ Can you give me a hand?
  ¿Me echas una mano?
  ■ **on the one hand ..., on the other
  hand ...** por un lado ..., por otro ...

**to hand** VERB
  ▷ *see also* **hand** NOUN
pasar
  □ He handed me the book. Me pasó el libro.

**handbag** NOUN
el bolso (la cartera *Latin America*)

**handball** NOUN
el balonmano

**handbook** NOUN
el manual

**handcuffs** PL NOUN
las esposas

**handkerchief** NOUN
el pañuelo

**handle** NOUN
  ▷ *see also* **handle** VERB
1 el picaporte *(of door)*
2 la asa *(of cup, briefcase)*
3 el mango *(of knife, saucepan)*

**to handle** VERB
  ▷ *see also* **handle** NOUN
1 encargarse* de
  □ Kath handled the travel arrangements.
  Kath se encargó de organizar el viaje.
2 manejar
  □ It was a difficult situation, but he handled
  it well. Era una situación difícil, pero él supo
  manejarla bien.
3 tratar
  □ She's good at handling children. Sabe
  tratar a los niños.
  ■ **'handle with care'** 'frágil'

**handlebars** PL NOUN
el manillar

**handmade** ADJECTIVE
hecho a mano (FEM hecha a mano)

**handsome** ADJECTIVE
guapo (FEM guapa)
  □ My father's very handsome. Mi padre es
  muy guapo.

**handwriting** NOUN
la letra
  □ His handwriting is terrible. Tiene una letra
  horrible.

**handy** ADJECTIVE
1 práctico (FEM práctica)
  □ This knife's very handy. Este cuchillo es
  muy práctico.
2 a mano
  □ Have you got a pen handy? ¿Tienes un
  bolígrafo a mano?

**to hang** VERB
1 colgar*
  □ Mike hung the painting on the wall. Mike
  colgó el cuadro en la pared. □ There was a
  bulb hanging from the ceiling. Una bombilla
  colgaba del techo.
2 ahorcar*
  □ In the past criminals were hanged.
  Antiguamente se ahorcaba a los criminales.

**to hang around** VERB
pasar el rato
  □ On Saturdays we hang around in the
  park. Los sábados pasamos el rato en el
  parque.

**to hang on** VERB
esperar
  □ Hang on a minute please. Espera un
  momento, por favor.

**to hang up** VERB
colgar* *(clothes, phone)*
  □ Don't hang up! ¡No cuelgues! □ He hung
  up on me. Me colgó.

**hanger** NOUN
la percha

**hang-gliding** NOUN
el ala delta

**LANGUAGE TIP** Although it's a feminine noun, remember that you use **el** and **un** with **ala**.

■ **to go hang-gliding** hacer ala delta

**hangover** NOUN
la resaca
□ I woke up with a hangover. Me desperté con resaca.

to **happen** VERB
pasar
□ What happened? ¿Qué pasó?
■ **As it happens, I do know him.** Da la casualidad de que lo conozco.
■ **Do you happen to know if she's at home?** ¿Por casualidad sabes si está en casa?

**happily** ADVERB
1 alegremente
□ 'Don't worry!', he said happily. '¡No te preocupes!' dijo alegremente.
2 felizmente
□ He's happily married. Está felizmente casado.
■ **And they lived happily ever after.** Y vivieron felices y comieron perdices.
3 afortunadamente
□ Happily, everything went well. Afortunadamente todo fue bien.

**happiness** NOUN
la felicidad

**happy** ADJECTIVE
feliz (FEM feliz, PL felices)
□ Janet looks happy. Janet parece feliz.

**WORD POWER**
You can use a number of other words instead of **happy** to mean 'glad':
**cheerful** alegre
□ a cheerful song una canción alegre
**glad** contento
□ to be glad estar contento
**satisfied** satisfecho
□ a satisfied customer un cliente satisfecho

■ **to be happy with something** estar contento con algo □ I'm very happy with your work. Estoy muy contento con tu trabajo.
■ **Happy birthday!** ¡Feliz cumpleaños!
■ **a happy ending** un final feliz

**harbour** (US **harbor**) NOUN
el puerto

**hard** ADJECTIVE, ADVERB
1 duro (FEM dura)
□ This cheese is very hard. Este queso está muy duro. □ to work hard trabajar duro
2 difícil (FEM difícil)
□ The exam was very hard. El examen fue muy difícil.

**hard disk** NOUN
el disco duro

**hardly** ADVERB
apenas
□ I hardly know you. Apenas te conozco.
■ **I've got hardly any money.** Casi no tengo dinero.
■ **hardly ever** casi nunca
■ **hardly anything** casi nada

**hard up** ADJECTIVE
■ **to be hard up** estar sin un duro (estar sin plata *Latin America*) (*informal*)

**hardware** NOUN
el hardware

**hare** NOUN
la liebre

to **harm** VERB
■ **to harm somebody** hacer daño a alguien
□ I didn't mean to harm you. No quería hacerte daño.
■ **to harm something** dañar algo
□ Chemicals harm the environment. Los productos químicos dañan el medio ambiente.

**harmful** ADJECTIVE
perjudicial (FEM perjudicial)
□ harmful to the environment perjudicial para el medio ambiente

**harmless** ADJECTIVE
inofensivo (FEM inofensiva)

**harsh** ADJECTIVE
1 severo (FEM severa)
□ He deserves a harsh punishment for what he did. Merece un severo castigo por lo que ha hecho.
2 áspero (FEM áspera)
□ She's got a very harsh voice. Tiene una voz muy áspera.

**has** VERB ▷ *see* **have**

**hasn't** = **has not**

**hat** NOUN
el sombrero

to **hate** VERB
odiar

**hatred** NOUN
el odio

**haunted** ADJECTIVE
■ **a haunted house** una casa embrujada

to **have** VERB
**LANGUAGE TIP** Use the verb **haber** to form the perfect tenses.
1 haber*
□ I've already seen that film. Ya he visto esa película. □ Has he gone? ¿Se ha ido?
□ If you had phoned me I would have come around. Si me hubieras llamado habría venido.

**LANGUAGE TIP** If you are using 'have' in question tags to confirm a statement use ¿no? or ¿verdad?.
□ You've done it, haven't you? Lo has hecho, ¿verdad? □ They've arrived, haven't they? Ya han llegado, ¿no?

**LANGUAGE TIP** 'have' is not translated when giving simple negative or positive answers to questions.
□ Have you read that book? — Yes, I have. ¿Has leído el libro? — Sí. □ Has he told you? — No, he hasn't. ¿Te lo ha dicho? — No.

2 tener*
□ I have a terrible cold. Tengo un resfriado horrible. □ She had a baby last year. Tuvo un niño el año pasado. □ Do you have any brothers or sisters? ¿Tienes hermanos?
■ **to have to do something.** tener que hacer algo.

3 tomar
□ I'll have a coffee. Tomaré un café. □ Shall we have a drink? ¿Tomamos algo de beber?
■ **to have a shower** ducharse
■ **to have one's hair cut** cortarse el pelo

**haven't** = have not

**hay** NOUN
el heno

**hay fever** NOUN
la alergia al polen

**hazelnut** NOUN
la avellana

**he** PRONOUN
él

**LANGUAGE TIP** 'he' generally isn't translated unless it is emphatic.
□ He is very tall. Es muy alto.

**LANGUAGE TIP** Use él for emphasis.
□ He did it but she didn't. Él lo hizo, pero ella no.

**head** NOUN
▷ see also **head** VERB

1 la cabeza
□ Mind your head! ¡Cuidado con la cabeza! □ The wine went to my head. El vino se me subió a la cabeza. □ He lost his head and started screaming. Perdió la cabeza y empezó a gritar.

2 el director
la directora (of school)

3 el jefe
la jefa (leader)
□ a head of state un jefe de Estado
■ **I've got no head for figures.** No se me dan bien los números.
■ **Heads or tails? — Heads.** ¿Cara o cruz? — Cara.

to **head** VERB
▷ see also **head** NOUN

■ **to head for** dirigirse a □ They headed for the church. Se dirigieron a la iglesia.

**headache** NOUN
el dolor de cabeza
□ I've got a headache. Tengo dolor de cabeza.

**headlight** NOUN
el faro (de coche)

**headline** NOUN
el titular

**headmaster** NOUN
el director

**headmistress** NOUN
la directora

**headphones** PL NOUN
los auriculares

**headquarters** PL NOUN
el cuartel general (of army)
■ **The bank's headquarters are in London.** La oficina central del banco está en Londres.

**headteacher** NOUN
el director
la directora

to **heal** VERB
curar

**health** NOUN
la salud
□ She's in good health. Tiene buena salud.

**healthy** ADJECTIVE
sano (FEM sana)
□ She's very healthy. Es muy sana.
□ a healthy diet una dieta sana

**heap** NOUN
el montón (PL los montones)

to **hear** VERB
oír*
□ We heard the dog bark. Oímos ladrar al perro. □ She can't hear very well. No oye bien.
■ **I heard she was ill.** Me han dicho que estaba enferma.
■ **to hear about something** enterarse de algo □ I've heard about your new job. Me he enterado de que tienes un nuevo trabajo. □ Did you hear the good news? ¿Te has enterado de la buena noticia?
■ **to hear from somebody** tener noticias de alguien □ I haven't heard from him recently. Últimamente no tengo noticias de él.

**heart** NOUN
el corazón (PL los corazones)
■ **hearts** (at cards) los corazones □ the ace of hearts el as de corazones
■ **to learn something by heart** aprenderse algo de memoria

**heart attack** NOUN
el infarto

**heartbroken** ADJECTIVE
- ■ **to be heartbroken** tener el corazón partido

**heat** NOUN
▷ *see also* **heat** VERB
el calor

to **heat** VERB
▷ *see also* **heat** NOUN
calentar*
□ Heat gently for five minutes. Caliente a fuego lento durante cinco minutos.

to **heat up** VERB
1 calentar*
□ He heated the soup up. Calentó la sopa.
2 calentarse* (water, oven)
□ The water is heating up. El agua se está calentando.

**heater** NOUN
el calentador
□ a water heater un calentador de agua
■ **an electric heater** una estufa eléctrica
■ **Could you put on the heater?** (in car) ¿Puedes poner la calefacción?

**heather** NOUN
el brezo

**heating** NOUN
la calefacción

**heaven** NOUN
el cielo
■ **to go to heaven** ir al cielo

**heavily** ADVERB
■ **It rained heavily in the night.** Llovió con fuerza por la noche.
■ **He's a heavily built man.** Es un hombre corpulento.
■ **He drinks heavily.** Bebe demasiado.

**heavy** ADJECTIVE
pesado (FEM pesada)
□ a heavy load una carga pesada
■ **This bag's very heavy.** Esta bolsa pesa mucho.
■ **heavy rain** fuerte lluvia
■ **He's a heavy drinker.** Es un bebedor empedernido.

**he'd** = he would; he had

**hedge** NOUN
el seto

**hedgehog** NOUN
el erizo

**heel** NOUN
1 el tacón (PL los tacones) (of shoe)
2 el talón (PL los talones) (of foot)

**height** NOUN
1 la estatura (of person)
2 la altura (of object, mountain)

**heir** NOUN
el heredero

**heiress** NOUN
la heredera

**held** VERB ▷ *see* **hold**

**helicopter** NOUN
el helicóptero

**hell** NOUN
el infierno
■ **Hell!** ¡Maldita sea!

**he'll** = he will; he shall

**hello** EXCLAMATION
1 ¡hola! (when you see somebody)
2 ¡dígame! (¡aló! *Latin America*) (on the phone)

**helmet** NOUN
el casco

to **help** VERB
▷ *see also* **help** NOUN
ayudar
□ Can you help me? ¿Puedes ayudarme?
■ **Help!** ¡Socorro!
■ **Help yourself!** ¡Sírvete!
■ **I couldn't help laughing.** No pude evitar reírme.

**help** NOUN
▷ *see also* **help** VERB
la ayuda
□ Do you need any help? ¿Necesitas ayuda?

**helpful** ADJECTIVE
útil (FEM útil)
□ He gave me some helpful advice. Me dio algunos consejos útiles.
■ **You've been very helpful!** ¡Muchas gracias por su ayuda!

**hen** NOUN
la gallina

**her** ADJECTIVE
▷ *see also* **her** PRONOUN
su (FEM SU, PL SUS)
□ her father su padre □ her house su casa
□ her two best friends sus dos mejores amigos □ her sisters sus hermanas

> LANGUAGE TIP 'her' is usually translated by the definite article el/los or la/las when it's clear from the sentence who the possessor is or when referring to clothing or parts of the body.

□ They stole her car. Le robaron el coche.
□ She took off her coat. Se quitó el abrigo.
□ She's washing her hair. Se está lavando la cabeza.

**her** PRONOUN
▷ *see also* **her** ADJECTIVE
1 la

> LANGUAGE TIP Use la when 'her' is the direct object of the verb in the sentence.

□ I saw her. La vi. □ Look at her! ¡Mírala!
2 le

> LANGUAGE TIP Use le when 'her' means 'to her'.

**h**

115

□ I gave her a book. Le di un libro. □ You have to tell her the truth. Tienes que decirle la verdad.

**3** se

> **LANGUAGE TIP** Use **se** not **le** when 'her' is used in combination with a direct-object pronoun.

□ Give it to her. Dáselo.

**4** ella

> **LANGUAGE TIP** Use **ella** after prepositions, in comparisons, and with the verb 'to be'.

□ I'm going with her. Voy con ella. □ I'm older than her. Soy mayor que ella. □ It must be her. Debe de ser ella.

■ **She was carrying it on her.** Lo llevaba consigo.

**herb** NOUN
la hierba (medicinal o aromática)

**here** ADVERB
aquí

□ I live here. Vivo aquí. □ Here he is! ¡Aquí está! □ Here are the books. Aquí están los libros.

■ **Here's your coffee.** Aquí tienes el café.
■ **Have you got my pen? — Here you are.** ¿Tienes mi boli? — Aquí tienes.
■ **Here are the papers you asked for.** Aquí tienes los papeles que pediste.

**hero** NOUN
el héroe

**heroin** NOUN
la heroína

■ **a heroin addict** un heroinómano

**heroine** NOUN
la heroína

**hers** PRONOUN
**1** el suyo masc (PL los suyos)
□ Is this her coat? — No, hers is black. ¿Es éste su abrigo? — No, el suyo es negro. □ my parents and hers mis padres y los suyos
**2** la suya fem (PL las suyas)
□ Is this her scarf? — No, hers is red. ¿Es ésta su bufanda? — No, la suya es roja. □ my sisters and hers mis hermanas y las suyas
**3** suyo masc (PL suyos)
□ Is that car hers? ¿Es suyo ese coche?
**4** suya fem (PL suyas)
□ Is that wallet hers? ¿Es suya esa cartera?
■ **Isobel is a friend of hers.** Isobel es amiga suya.

> **LANGUAGE TIP** Use **de ella** instead of **suyo** if you want to avoid confusion with 'his', 'theirs', etc.

□ Whose is this? — It's hers. ¿De quién es esto? — Es de ella.

**herself** PRONOUN
**1** se (reflexive)
□ She's hurt herself. Se ha hecho daño.
**2** sí misma (after preposition)
□ She talked mainly about herself. Habló principalmente de sí misma.
**3** ella misma (for emphasis)
□ She did it herself. Lo hizo ella misma.
■ **by herself** (alone) sola □ She came by herself. Vino sola.

**he's** = he is; he has

to **hesitate** VERB
dudar
□ Don't hesitate to ask. No dudes en preguntar.

**heterosexual** ADJECTIVE
heterosexual (FEM heterosexual)

**hi** EXCLAMATION
¡hola!

to **hide** VERB
**1** esconder
□ Paula hid the present. Paula escondió el regalo.
**2** esconderse
□ He hid behind a bush. Se escondió detrás de un arbusto.

**hide-and-seek** NOUN
■ **to play hide-and-seek** jugar al escondite

**hideous** ADJECTIVE
horroroso (FEM horrorosa)

**hi-fi** NOUN
el equipo de alta fidelidad

**high** ADJECTIVE, ADVERB
**1** alto (FEM alta)
□ The gate's too high. La verja es demasiado alta. □ Prices are higher in Germany. Los precios están más altos en Alemania. □ It's very high in fat. Tiene un alto contenido en grasas. □ The plane flew high over the mountains. El avión volaba alto sobre las montañas.
■ **How high is the wall?** ¿Cómo es de alto el muro?
■ **The wall's two metres high.** El muro tiene dos metros de altura.
**2** agudo (FEM aguda)
□ She's got a very high voice. Tiene la voz muy aguda.
■ **at high speed** a gran velocidad
■ **to be high** (on drugs) estar colocado (informal)
■ **to get high** (on drugs) colocarse (informal)

**higher education** NOUN
la enseñanza superior

**high-heeled** ADJECTIVE
■ **high-heeled shoes** los zapatos de tacón alto

**high jump** NOUN
el salto de altura

**highlight** NOUN
▷ see also **highlight** VERB
el punto culminante
◻ the highlight of the evening el punto culminante de la velada

to **highlight** VERB
▷ see also **highlight** NOUN
poner* de relieve

**highlighter** NOUN
el rotulador

**high-rise** NOUN
la torre de pisos

**high school** NOUN
el instituto (el liceo *Latin America*)

to **hijack** VERB
secuestrar

**hijacker** NOUN
el secuestrador
la secuestradora

**hike** NOUN
la caminata *(por el campo)*

**hiking** NOUN
■ to go hiking ir de excursión al campo

**hilarious** ADJECTIVE
graciosísimo (FEM graciosísima)

**hill** NOUN
1 la colina
◻ a house at the top of a hill una casa en lo alto de una colina
2 la cuesta
◻ I climbed the hill up to the office. Subí la cuesta hasta la oficina.

**hill-walking** NOUN
el senderismo
◻ to go hill-walking hacer senderismo

**him** PRONOUN
1 lo
○ LANGUAGE TIP Use **lo** when 'him' is the direct object of the verb in the sentence.
◻ I saw him. Lo vi. ◻ Look at him! ¡Míralo!
2 le
○ LANGUAGE TIP Use **le** when 'him' means 'to him'.
◻ I gave him a book. Le di un libro. ◻ You have to tell him the truth. Tienes que decirle la verdad.
3 se
○ LANGUAGE TIP Use **se** not **le** when 'him' is used in combination with a direct-object pronoun.
◻ Give it to him. Dáselo.
4 él
○ LANGUAGE TIP Use **él** after prepositions, in comparisons and with the verb 'to be'.
◻ I'm going with him. Voy con él. ◻ I'm older than him. Soy mayor que él. ◻ It must be him. Debe de ser él.

■ He was carrying it on him. Lo llevaba consigo.

**himself** PRONOUN
1 se *(reflexive)*
◻ He's hurt himself. Se ha hecho daño.
2 sí mismo *(after preposition)*
◻ He talked mainly about himself. Habló principalmente de sí mismo.
3 él mismo *(for emphasis)*
◻ He did it himself. Lo hizo él mismo.
■ by himself *(alone)* solo ◻ He came by himself. Vino solo.

**Hindu** ADJECTIVE
hindú (PL hindúes)

**hint** NOUN
▷ see also **hint** VERB
la indirecta
■ to drop a hint soltar una indirecta
■ to take a hint captar una indirecta

to **hint** VERB
▷ see also **hint** NOUN
insinuar*
◻ He hinted that something was going on. Insinuó que estaba pasando algo.

**hip** NOUN
la cadera
◻ She put her hands on her hips. Se puso las manos en las caderas.

**hippie** NOUN
el/la hippy (PL los hippies)

**hippo** NOUN
el hipopótamo

to **hire** VERB
▷ see also **hire** NOUN
1 alquilar
◻ We hired a car. Alquilamos un coche.
2 contratar
◻ They hired a lawyer. Contrataron a un abogado.

**hire** NOUN
▷ see also **hire** VERB
el alquiler
◻ car hire el alquiler de coches
■ 'for hire' 'se alquila'

**hire car** NOUN
el coche de alquiler

**his** ADJECTIVE
▷ see also **his** PRONOUN
su (FEM SU, PL SUS)
◻ his father su padre ◻ his house su casa ◻ his two best friends sus dos mejores amigos ◻ his sisters sus hermanas
○ LANGUAGE TIP 'his' is usually translated by the definite article **el/los** or **la/las** when it's clear from the sentence who the possessor is or when referring to clothing or parts of the body.

□ They stole his car. Le robaron el coche.
□ He took off his coat. Se quitó el abrigo.
□ He's washing his hair. Se está lavando la cabeza.

**his** PRONOUN
▷ *see also* **his** ADJECTIVE
1 el suyo *masc* (PL los suyos)
□ Is this his coat? — No, his is black. ¿Es éste su abrigo? — No, el suyo es negro.
□ my parents and his mis padres y los suyos
2 la suya *fem* (PL las suyas)
□ Is this his scarf? — No, his is red. ¿Es ésta su bufanda? — No, la suya es roja. □ my sisters and his mis hermanas y las suyas
3 suyo *masc* (PL suyos)
□ Is that car his? ¿Es suyo ese coche?
4 suya *fem* (PL suyas)
□ Is that wallet his? ¿Es suya esa cartera?
■ **Isobel is a friend of his.** Isobel es amiga suya.

LANGUAGE TIP Use **de él** instead of **suyo** if you want to avoid confusion with 'hers', 'theirs', etc.

□ Whose is this? — It's his. ¿De quién es esto? — Es de él.

**history** NOUN
la historia

to **hit** VERB
▷ *see also* **hit** NOUN
1 pegar*
□ He hit the ball. Le pegó a la bola.
□ Andrew hit him. Andrew le pegó.
2 chocar* con
□ The car hit a road sign. El coche chocó con una señal de tráfico.
■ **He was hit by a car.** Le pilló un coche.
■ **to hit the target** dar en el blanco
■ **to hit it off with somebody** hacer buenas migas con alguien

**hit** NOUN
▷ *see also* **hit** VERB
el éxito
□ Coldplay's latest hit el último éxito de Coldplay □ The film was a massive hit. La película fue un éxito enorme.

**hitch** NOUN
el contratiempo
□ There's been a slight hitch. Ha habido un pequeño contratiempo.

to **hitchhike** VERB
hacer* autoestop

**hitchhiker** NOUN
el/la autoestopista

**hitchhiking** NOUN
el autoestop

**hit man** NOUN
el asesino a sueldo

118 **HIV-positive** ADJECTIVE

seropositivo (FEM seropositiva)

**hobby** NOUN
la afición (PL las aficiones)

**hockey** NOUN
el hockey
□ I like playing hockey. Me gusta jugar al hockey.

to **hold** VERB
1 tener*
□ He was holding her in his arms. La tenía entre sus brazos.
2 sujetar
□ Hold the ladder. Sujeta la escalera.
3 contener*
□ This bottle holds one litre. Esta botella contiene un litro.
■ **to hold a meeting** celebrar una reunión
■ **Hold the line!** (on telephone) ¡No cuelgue!
■ **Hold it!** ¡Espera!
■ **to get hold of something** hacerse con algo

to **hold on** VERB
1 agarrarse (keep hold)
□ The cliff was slippery but he managed to hold on. El acantilado se escurría, pero logró agarrarse.
■ **to hold on to something** agarrarse a algo
2 esperar (wait)
□ Hold on, I'm coming! ¡Espera que ya voy!
■ **Hold on!** (on telephone) ¡No cuelgue!

to **hold up** VERB
1 levantar
□ Peter held up his hand. Peter levantó la mano.
2 retrasar
□ We were held up by the traffic. Nos retrasamos por culpa del tráfico.
3 atracar*
□ to hold up a bank atracar un banco
■ **I was held up at the office.** Me entretuvieron en la oficina.

**hold-up** NOUN
1 el atraco
□ A bank clerk was injured in the hold-up. Un empleado del banco resultó herido en el atraco.
2 el retraso
□ No-one explained the reason for the hold-up. Nadie explicó el motivo del retraso.
3 el embotellamiento
□ a hold-up on the motorway un embotellamiento en la autopista

**hole** NOUN
1 el agujero (in general)
□ a hole in the wall un agujero en la pared
2 el hoyo (in the ground, in golf)
□ to dig a hole cavar un hoyo

**holiday** NOUN

**1** las vacaciones
  □ the school holidays las vacaciones escolares  □ on holiday de vacaciones  □ to go on holiday irse de vacaciones  □ to be on holiday estar de vacaciones
**2** el día festivo  (el día feriado *Latin America*)
  □ Next Monday is a holiday. El lunes que viene es día festivo.
  ■ **He took a day's holiday.** Se tomó un día libre.

**Holland** NOUN
  Holanda *fem*

**hollow** ADJECTIVE
  hueco (FEM hueca)

**holly** NOUN
  el acebo

**holy** ADJECTIVE
**1** santo (FEM santa)
  □ the Holy Spirit el Espíritu Santo
**2** sagrado (FEM sagrada)
  □ a holy place un lugar sagrado

**home** NOUN
  ▷ *see also* **home** ADVERB
  la casa
  □ at home en casa
  ■ **Make yourself at home.** Estás en tu casa.
  ■ **an old people's home** una residencia de ancianos

**home** ADVERB
  ▷ *see also* **home** NOUN
**1** en casa
  □ I'll be home at five o'clock. Estaré en casa a las cinco.
**2** a casa
  □ to get home llegar a casa

**home address** NOUN
  el domicilio

**homeless** ADJECTIVE, NOUN
  sin hogar
  ■ **homeless people** los sin techo

**home match** NOUN
  el partido en casa

**homeopathy** NOUN
  la homeopatía

**home page** NOUN
  la página principal

**homesick** ADJECTIVE
  ■ **to be homesick** tener morriña

**homework** NOUN
  los deberes
  □ Have you done your homework? ¿Has hecho los deberes?  □ my geography homework mis deberes de geografía

**homosexual** ADJECTIVE
  homosexual (FEM homosexual)

**honest** ADJECTIVE
**1** honrado (FEM honrada)

  □ She's a very honest person. Es una persona muy honrada.
**2** sincero (FEM sincera)
  □ Tell me your honest opinion. Dame tu sincera opinión.
  ■ **To be honest, I don't like the idea.** La verdad es que no me gusta la idea.

**honestly** ADVERB
  francamente
  □ I honestly don't know. Francamente no lo sé.

**honesty** NOUN
  la honradez

**honey** NOUN
  la miel

**honeymoon** NOUN
  la luna de miel
  ■ **to go on honeymoon** irse de luna de miel

**honour** (US **honor**) NOUN
  el honor

**hood** NOUN
**1** la capucha (*on coat*)
**2** el capó (US: *bonnet of car*)

**hook** NOUN
**1** el gancho
  □ The jacket hung from a hook. La chaqueta estaba colgada de un gancho.
**2** la alcayata
  □ He hung the painting on the hook. Colgó el cuadro de la alcayata.
**3** el anzuelo
  □ He felt a fish pull at his hook. Notó que un pez tiraba del anzuelo.
  ■ **to take the phone off the hook** descolgar el teléfono

**hooligan** NOUN
  el gamberro
  la gamberra

**hooray** EXCLAMATION
  ¡hurra!

**Hoover®** NOUN
  la aspiradora

to **hoover** VERB
  pasar la aspiradora por
  □ He hoovered the lounge. Pasó la aspiradora por el salón.

to **hope** VERB
  ▷ *see also* **hope** NOUN
  esperar

  ◯ LANGUAGE TIP Use the subjunctive after esperar que.

  □ I hope he comes. Espero que venga.
  ■ **I hope so.** Espero que sí.
  ■ **I hope not.** Espero que no.

**hope** NOUN
  ▷ *see also* **hope** VERB
  la esperanza
  □ to give up hope perder la esperanza

**h**

119

English-Spanish

h

**hopeful** ADJECTIVE
prometedor (FEM prometedora)
□ The prospects look hopeful. Las
perspectivas parecen prometedoras.
■ He's hopeful of winning. Tiene
esperanzas de ganar.
■ How did the interview go? — I'm
hopeful. ¿Cómo fue la entrevista? — Tengo
esperanzas.
■ We're hopeful everything will go okay.
Confiamos en que todo irá bien.

**hopefully** ADVERB
LANGUAGE TIP Use the subjunctive
after esperar que.
■ Hopefully, he'll make it in time.
Esperemos que llegue a tiempo.

**hopeless** ADJECTIVE
■ She's hopeless at maths. Es una negada
para las matemáticas.

**horizon** NOUN
el horizonte

**horizontal** ADJECTIVE
horizontal (FEM horizontal)

**horn** NOUN
1 el claxon
□ He sounded the horn. Tocó el claxon.
2 la trompa
□ He plays the horn. Toca la trompa.
3 el cuerno (el cacho Latin America)
□ a bull's horns los cuernos de un toro

**horoscope** NOUN
el horóscopo

**horrible** ADJECTIVE
horrible (FEM horrible)
□ What a horrible dress! ¡Qué vestido tan
horrible!

**horror** NOUN
el horror
□ To my horror I discovered I was locked out.
Descubrí con horror que me había dejado
las llaves dentro.

**horror film** NOUN
la película de terror

**horse** NOUN
el caballo

**horse-racing** NOUN
las carreras de caballos

**horseshoe** NOUN
la herradura

**hose** NOUN
la manguera

**hosepipe** NOUN
la manguera

**hospital** NOUN
el hospital
□ to go into hospital ingresar en el hospital

**hospitality** NOUN
la hospitalidad

**host** NOUN
el anfitrión (PL los anfitriones)
la anfitriona

**hostage** NOUN
el rehén (PL los rehenes)
■ to take somebody hostage tomar como
rehén a alguien

**hostile** ADJECTIVE
hostil (FEM hostil)

**hot** ADJECTIVE
1 caliente (FEM caliente)
□ a hot bath un baño caliente
2 caluroso (FEM calurosa)
□ a hot country un país caluroso
■ a cup of hot chocolate una taza de
chocolate
LANGUAGE TIP When you are talking
about a person being hot, you use
tener calor.
□ I'm hot. Tengo calor.
LANGUAGE TIP When you talk about
the weather being hot, you use hacer
calor.
□ It's hot today. Hoy hace calor.
3 picante (FEM picante)
□ Mexican food's too hot. La comida
mejicana es demasiado picante.

**hot dog** NOUN
el perrito caliente

**hotel** NOUN
el hotel

**hour** NOUN
la hora
□ She always takes hours to get ready.
Siempre se tira horas para arreglarse.
■ a quarter of an hour un cuarto de hora
■ two and a half hours dos horas y media
■ half an hour media hora

**hourly** ADJECTIVE, ADVERB
■ There are hourly buses. Hay autobuses
cada hora.
■ She's paid hourly. Le pagan por horas.

**house** NOUN
la casa
□ at his house en su casa

**housewife** NOUN
el ama de casa (PL las amas de casa)
□ She's a housewife. Es ama de casa.

**housework** NOUN
las tareas de la casa

**hovercraft** NOUN
el aerodeslizador

**how** ADVERB
1 cómo
□ How are you? ¿Cómo estás?
2 qué
□ How strange! ¡Qué raro!
■ He told them how happy he was.

Les dijo lo feliz que era.
- **How many?** ¿Cuántos?
- **How much?** ¿Cuánto? □ How much is it? ¿Cuánto es? □ How much sugar do you want? ¿Cuánto azúcar quieres?
- **How old are you?** ¿Cuántos años tienes?
- **How far is it to Edinburgh?** ¿Qué distancia hay de aquí a Edimburgo?
- **How long have you been here?** ¿Cuánto tiempo llevas aquí?
- **How long does it take?** ¿Cuánto se tarda?

> **LANGUAGE TIP** Remember the accents on question and exclamation words **cómo**, **qué** and **cuánto**.

**however** CONJUNCTION
sin embargo
□ This, however, isn't true. Esto, sin embargo, no es cierto.

to **howl** VERB
aullar*
□ The dog howled all night. El perro estuvo aullando toda la noche. □ He howled with pain. Aullaba de dolor.

**HTML** NOUN
el HTML

to **hug** VERB
> see also **hug** NOUN
abrazar*
□ He hugged his daughter. Abrazó a su hija. □ They hugged each other. Se abrazaron.

**hug** NOUN
> see also **hug** VERB
el abrazo
□ to give somebody a hug dar un abrazo a alguien

**huge** ADJECTIVE
enorme (FEM enorme)

to **hum** VERB
tararear

**human** ADJECTIVE
humano (FEM humana)
□ the human body el cuerpo humano □ the human race el género humano

**human being** NOUN
el ser humano

**humble** ADJECTIVE
humilde (FEM humilde)

**humour** (US humor) NOUN
el humor
- **to have a sense of humour** tener sentido del humor

**hundred** NUMERAL

> **LANGUAGE TIP** Use **cien** before nouns or before another number that is being multiplied by a hundred.

- **a hundred** cien □ a hundred people cien personas □ a hundred thousand cien mil

> **LANGUAGE TIP** Use **ciento** before a number that is not multiplied but simply added to a hundred.

□ a hundred and one ciento uno

> **LANGUAGE TIP** When 'hundred' follows another number, use the compound forms, which must agreee with the noun.

□ three hundred trescientos □ five hundred people quinientas personas □ five hundred and one quinientos uno
- **hundreds of people** cientos de personas

**hung** VERB > see **hang**

**Hungary** NOUN
Hungría fem

**hunger** NOUN
el hambre fem

> **LANGUAGE TIP** Although it's a feminine noun, remember that you use **el** and **un** with **hambre**.

**hungry** ADJECTIVE
- **to be hungry** tener hambre □ I'm very hungry. Tengo mucha hambre.

to **hunt** VERB
1 cazar*
□ They hunt foxes. Cazan zorros.
2 buscar*
□ The police are hunting the killer. La policía está buscando al asesino.
- **to go hunting** ir de caza
- **to hunt for something** buscar algo □ I've hunted everywhere for that book. He buscado ese libro por todas partes.

**hunting** NOUN
la caza
□ fox-hunting la caza del zorro

**hurricane** NOUN
el huracán (PL los huracanes)

to **hurry** VERB
> see also **hurry** NOUN
darse* prisa (apurarse Latin America)
□ Hurry up! ¡Date prisa!
- **Sharon hurried back home.** Sharon volvió a casa a toda prisa.

**hurry** NOUN
> see also **hurry** VERB
- **to be in a hurry** tener prisa (tener apuro Latin America)
- **to do something in a hurry** hacer algo a toda prisa
- **There's no hurry.** No hay prisa.

to **hurt** VERB
> see also **hurt** ADJECTIVE
1 hacer* daño a
□ You're hurting me! ¡Me haces daño!
□ Have you hurt yourself? ¿Te has hecho daño?
2 doler*
□ My leg hurts. Me duele la pierna.

**h**

121

■ **Hey! That hurts!** ¡Hey! ¡Que me haces daño!

3 herir*

□ His remarks really hurt me. Sus comentarios me hirieron mucho.

**hurt** ADJECTIVE

▷ see also **hurt** VERB

herido (FEM herida)

□ Is he badly hurt? ¿Está herido de gravedad? □ Luckily, nobody got hurt.

Por suerte, nadie salió herido.

■ **I was hurt by what he said.** Me hirió lo que dijo.

**husband** NOUN

el marido

**hut** NOUN

la cabaña

**hymn** NOUN

el himno *(religioso)*

**hypermarket** NOUN

el hipermercado

**hyphen** NOUN

el guión (PL los guiones)

# I i

**I** PRONOUN

yo

□ Ann and I Ann y yo

　**LANGUAGE TIP** 'I' generally isn't translated unless it is emphatic.

□ I speak Spanish. Hablo español.

　**LANGUAGE TIP** Use **yo** for emphasis.

□ He was frightened but I wasn't. Él estaba asustado, pero yo no.

**ice** NOUN

el hielo

**iceberg** NOUN

el iceberg (PL los icebergs)

**icebox** NOUN (US)

la nevera

**ice cream** NOUN

el helado

□ vanilla ice cream el helado de vainilla

**ice cube** NOUN

el cubito de hielo

**ice hockey** NOUN

el hockey sobre hielo

□ I like playing ice hockey. Me gusta jugar al hockey sobre hielo.

**Iceland** NOUN

Islandia *fem*

**ice lolly** NOUN

el polo

**ice rink** NOUN

la pista de patinaje sobre hielo

**ice-skating** NOUN

el patinaje sobre hielo

■ **Yesterday we went ice-skating.** Ayer fuimos a patinar sobre hielo.

**icing** NOUN

el glaseado *(on cake)*

■ **icing sugar** el azúcar glas

**icon** NOUN

el icono

**ICT** NOUN (= *Information and Communications Technology*)

la informática

**icy** ADJECTIVE

helado (FEM helada)

□ an icy wind un viento helado □ The roads are icy. Las carreteras están heladas.

**I'd** = I had; I would

**idea** NOUN

la idea

□ Good idea! ¡Buena idea!

**ideal** ADJECTIVE

ideal (FEM ideal)

**identical** ADJECTIVE

idéntico (FEM idéntica)

**identification** NOUN

la identificación (PL las identificaciones)

**to identify** VERB

identificar*

**identity card** NOUN

el carnet de identidad

**idiot** NOUN

el/la idiota

**idiotic** ADJECTIVE

idiota (FEM idiota)

**idle** ADJECTIVE

■ **It's just idle gossip.** No es más que cotilleo.

■ **I asked out of idle curiosity.** Lo pregunté por pura curiosidad.

■ **to be idle** *(worker)* estar sin trabajo

**i.e.** ABBREVIATION

es decir

**if** CONJUNCTION

si

□ You can go if you like. Puedes ir si quieres. □ He asked me if I had eaten. Me preguntó si había comido. □ If it's fine we'll go swimming. Si hace bueno, iremos a nadar.

　**LANGUAGE TIP** Use **si** with a past subjunctive to translate 'if' followed by a past tense when talking about conditions.

□ If you studied harder you would pass your exams. Si estudiaras más aprobarías los exámenes.

■ **if only** ojalá

　**LANGUAGE TIP** **ojalá** has to be followed by a verb in the subjunctive.

□ If only I had more money! ¡Ojalá tuviera más dinero!

■ **if not** si no □ Are you coming? If not, I'll go with Mark. ¿Vienes? Si no, iré con Mark.

■ **if so** si es así □ Are you coming? If so, I'll wait. ¿Vienes? Si es así te espero.

■ **If I were you I would go to Spain.** Yo que tú iría a España.

**ignorant** ADJECTIVE
ignorante (FEM ignorante)

to **ignore** VERB
■ **to ignore something** hacer caso omiso de algo □ She ignored my advice. Hizo caso omiso de mi consejo.
■ **to ignore somebody** ignorar a alguien □ She saw me, but she ignored me. Me vió, pero me ignoró completamente.
■ **Just ignore him!** ¡No le hagas caso!

**ill** ADJECTIVE
enfermo (FEM enferma)
□ She was taken ill. Se puso enferma.

**I'll** = I will

**illegal** ADJECTIVE
ilegal (FEM ilegal)

**illegible** ADJECTIVE
ilegible (FEM ilegible)

**illness** NOUN
la enfermedad

**illusion** NOUN
la ilusión (PL las ilusiones)
□ an optical illusion una ilusión óptica
■ **He was under the illusion that he would win.** Se creía que iba a ganar.

**illustration** NOUN
la ilustración (PL las ilustraciones)

**image** NOUN
la imagen (PL las imágenes)
□ The company has changed its image. La empresa ha cambiado de imagen.

**imagination** NOUN
la imaginación (PL las imaginaciones)
□ She lets her imagination run away with her. Se deja llevar por su imaginación. □ It's only your imagination. Son imaginaciones tuyas.

to **imagine** VERB
imaginarse
□ You can imagine how I felt! ¡Imagínate cómo me sentí! □ Is he angry? — I imagine so! ¿Está enfadado? — ¡Me imagino que sí!

to **imitate** VERB
imitar

**imitation** NOUN
la imitación (PL las imitaciones)
■ **imitation leather** el cuero de imitación

**immediate** ADJECTIVE
inmediato (FEM inmediata)
□ We need an immediate answer. Necesitamos una respuesta inmediata.

**immediately** ADVERB
inmediatamente

**immigrant** NOUN
el/la inmigrante

**immigration** NOUN
la inmigración (PL las inmigraciones)

**immoral** ADJECTIVE
inmoral (FEM inmoral)

**impartial** ADJECTIVE
imparcial (FEM imparcial)

**impatience** NOUN
la impaciencia

**impatient** ADJECTIVE
impaciente (FEM impaciente)
■ **to get impatient** impacientarse
□ People are getting impatient. La gente se está impacientando.

**impatiently** ADVERB
con impaciencia

**impersonal** ADJECTIVE
impersonal (FEM impersonal)

**importance** NOUN
la importancia

**important** ADJECTIVE
importante (FEM importante)

**impossible** ADJECTIVE
imposible (FEM imposible)

to **impress** VERB
impresionar
□ She's trying to impress you. Está tratando de impresionarte.

**impressed** ADJECTIVE
impresionado (FEM impresionada)
■ **I'm very impressed!** ¡Estoy impresionado!

**impression** NOUN
la impresión (PL las impresiones)
□ I was under the impression that you were going out. Tenía la impresión de que te ibas.

**impressive** ADJECTIVE
impresionante (FEM impresionante)

to **improve** VERB
mejorar
□ They have improved the service. Han mejorado el servicio. □ The weather is improving. El tiempo está mejorando.

**improvement** NOUN
1 la mejora (in situation, design)
■ **There's been an improvement in his French.** Su francés ha mejorado.
2 la mejoría (in health)

**in** PREPOSITION, ADVERB

> **LANGUAGE TIP** There are several ways of translating 'in'. Scan the examples to find one that is similar to what you want to say. For other expressions with 'in', see the verbs 'go', 'come', 'get', 'give', etc.

1 en
□ in the house en casa □ in my bag en mi bolsa □ in the country en el campo □ in town en la ciudad □ in Spain en España

□ **in school** en el colegio □ **in hospital** en el hospital □ **in London** en Londres □ **in spring** en primavera □ **in May** en Mayo □ **in 1996** en mil novecientos noventa y seis □ **I did it in three hours.** Lo hice en tres horas. □ **in French** en francés □ **in a loud voice** en voz alta □ **in good condition** en buen estado

**2** de

□ **the best pupil in the class** el mejor alumno de la clase □ **at two o'clock in the afternoon** a las dos de la tarde □ **at six in the morning** a las seis de la mañana □ **the boy in the blue shirt** el muchacho de la camisa azul

**3** dentro de

□ **I'll see you in three weeks.** Te veré dentro de tres semanas. □ **I'll be back in one hour.** Volveré dentro de una hora.

**4** por

□ **I've got an exam in the morning.** Tengo un examen por la mañana. □ **I always feel sleepy in the afternoon.** Siempre tengo sueño por la tarde.
- **in the sun** al sol
- **in the rain** bajo la lluvia
- **It was written in pencil.** Estaba escrito a lápiz.
- **in here** aquí dentro □ **It's hot in here.** Aquí dentro hace calor.
- **one person in ten** una persona de cada diez
- **to be in** *(at home, work)* estar □ **He wasn't in.** No estaba.
- **in writing** por escrito

**inaccurate** ADJECTIVE
inexacto (FEM inexacta)

**incentive** NOUN
el incentivo
□ **There's no incentive to work.** No hay incentivo para trabajar.

**inch** NOUN
la pulgada

> **DID YOU KNOW...?**
> In Spain measurements are in metres and centimetres rather than feet and inches. An inch is about 2.5 centimetres.

□ **6 inches** 15 centímetros

**incident** NOUN
el incidente

**inclined** ADJECTIVE
- **to be inclined to do something** tener tendencia a hacer algo □ **He's inclined to arrive late.** Tiene tendencia a llegar tarde.

to **include** VERB
incluir*
□ **Service is not included.** El servicio no está incluido.

**including** PREPOSITION
- **It will be two hundred pounds, including tax.** Son doscientas libras esterlinas con impuestos incluidos.

**inclusive** ADJECTIVE
- **The inclusive price is two hundred pounds.** Son doscientas libras esterlinas con todo incluido.
- **inclusive of VAT** con el IVA incluido

**income** NOUN
los ingresos
□ **his main source of income** su principal fuente de ingresos

**income tax** NOUN
el impuesto sobre la renta

**incompetent** ADJECTIVE
incompetente (FEM incompetente)

**incomplete** ADJECTIVE
incompleto (FEM incompleta)

**inconvenience** NOUN
la molestia
□ **I don't want to cause any inconvenience.** No quiero causar molestia.

**inconvenient** ADJECTIVE
- **It's a bit inconvenient at the moment.** Me viene un poco mal en este momento.

**incorrect** ADJECTIVE
incorrecto (FEM incorrecta)

**increase** NOUN
▷ *see also* **increase** VERB
el aumento
□ **an increase in road accidents** un aumento de accidentes de tráfico

to **increase** VERB
▷ *see also* **increase** NOUN
aumentar
□ **Traffic on motorways has increased.** El tráfico en las autopistas ha aumentado. □ **They have increased his salary.** Le han aumentado el sueldo.
- **to increase in size** aumentar de tamaño

**incredible** ADJECTIVE
increíble (FEM increíble)

**indecisive** ADJECTIVE
indeciso (FEM indecisa) *(person)*

**indeed** ADVERB
realmente
□ **It's very hard indeed.** Es realmente difícil.
- **Know what I mean? — Indeed I do.** ¿Me comprendes? — Por supuesto que sí.
- **Thank you very much indeed!** ¡Muchísimas gracias!

**independence** NOUN
la independencia

**independent** ADJECTIVE
independiente (FEM independiente)
- **an independent school** un colegio privado

**English-Spanish**

**index** NOUN
el índice alfabético (in book)
**index finger** NOUN
el dedo índice
**India** NOUN
la India
**Indian** ADJECTIVE
▷ see also **Indian** NOUN
indio (FEM india)
**Indian** NOUN
▷ see also **Indian** ADJECTIVE
el indio
la india
□ the Indians los indios
■ **American Indian** el indio americano
(FEM la india americana)
to **indicate** VERB
1 indicar*
□ The report indicates that changes are needed. El informe indica que se necesitan cambios.
2 señalizar* (when driving)
□ He indicated right and turned into the Gran Vía. Señalizó hacia la derecha y torció a la Gran Vía.
**indicator** NOUN
el intermitente (in car)
**indigestion** NOUN
la indigestión (PL las indigestiones)
□ I've got indigestion. Tengo indigestión.
**individual** NOUN
▷ see also **individual** ADJECTIVE
el individuo
**indoor** ADJECTIVE
■ **an indoor swimming pool** una piscina cubierta
**indoors** ADVERB
dentro
□ They're indoors. Están dentro.
■ **We'd better go indoors.** Es mejor que entremos.
**industrial** ADJECTIVE
industrial (FEM industrial)
**industrial estate** NOUN
la zona industrial
**industry** NOUN
la industria
□ the oil industry la industria petrolífera
□ I'd like to work in industry. Me gustaría trabajar en la industria.
■ **the tourist industry** el turismo
**inefficient** ADJECTIVE
ineficiente (FEM ineficiente)
**inevitable** ADJECTIVE
inevitable (FEM inevitable)
**inexpensive** ADJECTIVE
económico (FEM económica)
**inexperienced** ADJECTIVE

inexperto (FEM inexperta)
**infant school** NOUN
el colegio
**infection** NOUN
la infección (PL las infecciones)
□ an ear infection una infección de oído
**infectious** ADJECTIVE
contagioso (FEM contagiosa)
**infinitive** NOUN
el infinitivo
**infirmary** NOUN
el hospital
**inflatable** ADJECTIVE
inflable (FEM inflable) (mattress, dinghy)
**inflation** NOUN
la inflación (PL las inflaciones)
**influence** NOUN
▷ see also **influence** VERB
la influencia
□ He's a bad influence on her. Ejerce mala influencia sobre ella.
to **influence** VERB
▷ see also **influence** NOUN
influenciar
**influenza** NOUN
la gripe
□ to have influenza tener gripe
to **inform** VERB
informar
□ Nobody informed me of the change of plan. Nadie me informó del cambio de planes.
**informal** ADJECTIVE
■ **informal language** el lenguaje coloquial
■ **an informal visit** una visita informal
■ **'informal dress'** 'no se requiere traje de etiqueta'
**information** NOUN
la información (PL las informaciones)
□ Could you give me some information about trains to Barcelona? ¿Podría darme información sobre trenes a Barcelona?
■ **a piece of information** un dato
**information office** NOUN
la oficina de información
**infuriating** ADJECTIVE
exasperante (FEM exasperante)
**ingredient** NOUN
el ingrediente
**inhabitant** NOUN
el/la habitante
to **inherit** VERB
heredar
□ She inherited her father's house. Heredó la casa de su padre.
**initials** PL NOUN
las iniciales
□ Her initials are CDT. Sus iniciales son CDT.

**initiative** NOUN
la iniciativa

to **inject** VERB
inyectar
□ They injected me with antibiotics.
Me inyectaron antibióticos.

**injection** NOUN
la inyección (PL las inyecciones)
□ The doctor gave me an injection.
El médico me puso una inyección.

to **injure** VERB
herir*
□ He injured his leg. Se hirió la pierna.

**injured** ADJECTIVE
herido (FEM herida)

**injury** NOUN
la lesión (PL las lesiones)

**injury time** NOUN
el tiempo de descuento

**injustice** NOUN
la injusticia

**ink** NOUN
la tinta

**in-laws** PL NOUN
los suegros

**inn** NOUN
el hostal

**inner** ADJECTIVE
interior (FEM interior)
■ the inner city los núcleos urbanos
deprimidos

**inner tube** NOUN
la cámara de aire

**innocent** ADJECTIVE
inocente (FEM inocente)

**inquest** NOUN
la investigación judicial (PL las
investigaciones judiciales)

to **inquire** VERB
■ to inquire about something informarse
acerca de algo

**inquiry** NOUN
la investigación (PL las investigaciones)
(official investigation)

**inquisitive** ADJECTIVE
curioso (FEM curiosa)

**insane** ADJECTIVE
loco (FEM loca)

**inscription** NOUN
la inscripción (PL las inscripciones)

**insect** NOUN
el insecto

**insect repellent** NOUN
la loción anti-insectos (PL las lociones anti-
insectos)

**insensitive** ADJECTIVE
insensible (FEM insensible)

**inside** NOUN
▷ see also **inside** PREPOSITION, ADVERB
el interior

**inside** PREPOSITION, ADVERB
▷ see also **inside** NOUN
dentro
□ inside the house dentro de la casa □ He
opened the envelope and read what was inside.
Abrió el sobre y leyó lo que había dentro.
■ Come inside! ¡Entra!
■ Let's go inside, it's starting to rain.
Entremos, está empezando a llover.
■ inside out al revés □ He put his jumper
on inside out. Se puso el jersey al revés.

**insincere** ADJECTIVE
falso (FEM falsa)

to **insist** VERB
insistir
□ I didn't want to, but he insisted. Yo no
quería, pero él insistió. □ He insisted he was
innocent. Insistía en que era inocente.
■ to insist on doing something insistir en
hacer algo □ She insisted on paying. Insistió
en pagar.

**inspector** NOUN
el inspector
la inspectora

**instalment** NOUN
1 el plazo (of payment)
□ to pay in instalments pagar a plazos
2 el episodio (of TV, radio serial)
3 el fascículo (of publication)

**instance** NOUN
■ for instance por ejemplo

**instant** NOUN
▷ see also **instant** ADJECTIVE
el instante

**instantly** ADVERB
al instante

**instead** PREPOSITION, ADVERB
■ instead of en lugar de □ We played
tennis instead of going swimming. Jugamos
al tenis en lugar de ir a nadar. □ She went
instead of Peter. En lugar de ir Peter, fue
ella.
■ The pool was closed, so we played
tennis instead. La piscina estaba cerrada,
así que jugamos al tenis.

**instinct** NOUN
el instinto

**institute** NOUN
el instituto

**institution** NOUN
la institución (PL las instituciones)

to **instruct** VERB
■ to instruct somebody to do something
ordenar a alguien que haga algo
LANGUAGE TIP ordenar que has to be
followed by a verb in the subjunctive.

□ She instructed us to wait outside. Nos ordenó que esperáramos fuera.

**instructions** PL NOUN
las instrucciones

**instructor** NOUN
el instructor
la instructora
□ skiing instructor el instructor de esquí
□ driving instructor el instructor de autoescuela

**instrument** NOUN
el instrumento
□ Do you play an instrument? ¿Tocas algún instrumento?

**insufficient** ADJECTIVE
insuficiente (FEM insuficiente)

**insulin** NOUN
la insulina

**insult** NOUN
▷ see also **insult** VERB
el insulto

to **insult** VERB
▷ see also **insult** NOUN
insultar

**insurance** NOUN
el seguro
□ his car insurance su seguro de automóvil
■ an insurance policy una póliza de seguros

**intelligent** ADJECTIVE
inteligente (FEM inteligente)

to **intend** VERB
■ to intend to do something tener la intención de hacer algo □ I intend to do languages at university. Tengo la intención de estudiar idiomas en la universidad.

**intense** ADJECTIVE
intenso (FEM intensa)

**intensive** ADJECTIVE
intensivo (FEM intensiva)

**intention** NOUN
la intención (PL las intenciones)

**intercom** NOUN
el interfono

**interest** NOUN
▷ see also **interest** VERB
1 el interés (PL los intereses)
□ to show an interest in something mostrar interés en algo
2 la afición (PL las aficiones)
□ My main interest is music. Mi mayor afición es la música.
■ It's in your own interest to study hard. Te conviene estudiar mucho.

to **interest** VERB
▷ see also **interest** NOUN
interesar
□ It doesn't interest me. No me interesa.

■ to be interested in something estar interesado en algo □ I'm very interested in what you're telling me. Estoy muy interesado en lo que me dices.
■ Are you interested in politics? ¿Te interesa la política?

**interesting** ADJECTIVE
interesante (FEM interesante)

**interior** NOUN
el interior

**interior designer** NOUN
el diseñador de interiores
la diseñadora de interiores

**intermediate** ADJECTIVE
intermedio (FEM intermedia)

**internal** ADJECTIVE
interno (FEM interna)

**international** ADJECTIVE
internacional (FEM internacional)

**internet** NOUN
el/la Internet
□ on the internet en Internet

**internet café** NOUN
el cibercafé

**internet user** NOUN
el/la internauta

to **interpret** VERB
hacer* de intérprete
□ Steve couldn't speak Spanish so his friend interpreted. Steve no hablaba español, así que su amigo hizo de intérprete.

**interpreter** NOUN
el/la intérprete

to **interrupt** VERB
interrumpir

**interruption** NOUN
la interrupción (PL las interrupciones)

**interval** NOUN
el intervalo

**interview** NOUN
▷ see also **interview** VERB
la entrevista

to **interview** VERB
▷ see also **interview** NOUN
entrevistar
□ I was interviewed on the radio. Me entrevistaron en la radio.

**interviewer** NOUN
el entrevistador
la entrevistadora

**intimate** ADJECTIVE
íntimo (FEM íntima)

**into** PREPOSITION
1 a
□ I'm going into town. Voy a la ciudad.
□ Translate it into Spanish. Tradúcelo al español. □ He got into the car. Subió al coche.

**2** en
  □ to get into bed meterse en la cama □ I
  poured the milk into a cup. Vertí la leche en
  una taza. □ They divided into two groups.
  Se dividieron en dos grupos.
  ■ **to walk into a lamppost** tropezar con
  una farola
**intranet** NOUN
  la intranet
to **introduce** VERB
  presentar
  □ He introduced me to his parents.
  Me presentó a sus padres.
**introduction** NOUN
  la introducción (PL las introducciones)
  (in book)
**intruder** NOUN
  el intruso
  la intrusa
**intuition** NOUN
  la intuición (PL las intuiciones)
to **invade** VERB
  invadir
**invalid** NOUN
  el inválido
  la inválida
to **invent** VERB
  inventar
**invention** NOUN
  el invento
**inventor** NOUN
  el inventor
  la inventora
**investigation** NOUN
  la investigación (PL las investigaciones)
**investment** NOUN
  la inversión (PL las inversiones)
**invisible** ADJECTIVE
  invisible (FEM invisible)
**invitation** NOUN
  la invitación (PL las invitaciones)
to **invite** VERB
  invitar
  □ Michael's not invited. Michael no está
  invitado. □ You're invited to a party at
  Claire's house. Estás invitado a una fiesta en
  casa de Claire.
to **involve** VERB
  suponer*
  □ It involves a lot of work. Supone mucho
  trabajo.
  ■ **He wasn't involved in the robbery.**
  No estuvo implicado en el robo.
  ■ **She was involved in politics.** Estaba
  metida en política.
  ■ **to be involved with somebody** tener
  una relación con alguien □ She was
  involved with a married man. Tenía una

relación con un hombre casado.
  ■ **I don't want to get involved in the
  argument.** No quiero meterme en la
  discusión.
**IQ** ABBREVIATION (= intelligence quotient)
  el CI (= el coeficiente intelectual)
**Iran** NOUN
  Irán masc
**Iraq** NOUN
  Iraq masc
**Ireland** NOUN
  Irlanda fem
**Irish** NOUN
  ▷ see also **Irish** ADJECTIVE
  el irlandés (language)
  ■ **the Irish** (people) los irlandeses
**Irish** ADJECTIVE
  ▷ see also **Irish** NOUN
  irlandés (FEM irlandesa, PL irlandeses)
**Irishman** NOUN
  el irlandés (PL los irlandeses)
**Irishwoman** NOUN
  la irlandesa
**iron** NOUN
  ▷ see also **iron** VERB
**1** la plancha (for clothes)
**2** el hierro (metal)
to **iron** VERB
  ▷ see also **iron** NOUN
  planchar
**ironic** ADJECTIVE
  irónico (FEM irónica)
**ironing** NOUN
  ■ **to do the ironing** planchar
  ■ **I hate ironing.** No me gusta nada
  planchar.
**ironing board** NOUN
  la tabla de planchar
**ironmonger's** NOUN
  la ferretería
**irrelevant** ADJECTIVE
  irrelevante (FEM irrelevante)
  □ That's irrelevant. Eso es irrelevante.
**irresponsible** ADJECTIVE
  irresponsable (FEM irresponsable)
  □ That was irresponsible of him. Eso fue
  irresponsable por su parte.
**irritating** ADJECTIVE
  irritante (FEM irritante)
**is** VERB ▷ see be
**Islam** NOUN
  el Islam
**Islamic** ADJECTIVE
  islámico (FEM islámica)
  □ Islamic law la ley islámica
**island** NOUN
  la isla
**isle** NOUN

i

■ **the Isle of Man** la Isla de Man
■ **the Isle of Wight** la Isla de Wight
**isolated** ADJECTIVE
aislado ⟨FEM aislada⟩
**ISP** NOUN (= Internet Service Provider)
el proveedor de servicios de Internet
**Israel** NOUN
Israel masc
**issue** NOUN
▷ see also **issue** VERB
1 el tema

> **LANGUAGE TIP** Although **tema** ends in
> **-a**, it is actually a masculine noun.

□ a controversial issue un tema polémico
2 el número (magazine)
□ a back issue un número atrasado
to **issue** VERB
▷ see also **issue** NOUN
1 hacer* público
□ The minister issued a statement
yesterday. El ministro hizo pública una
declaración ayer.
2 proporcionar (equipment, supplies)
**it** PRONOUN

> **LANGUAGE TIP** When 'it' is the subject
> of a sentence it is practically never
> translated.

□ Where's my book? — It's on the table.
¿Dónde está mi libro? — Está sobre la mesa.
□ It's raining. Está lloviendo. □ It's six
o'clock. Son las seis. □ It's Friday tomorrow.
Mañana es viernes. □ It's expensive. Es
caro. □ Who is it? — It's me. ¿Quién es? —
Soy yo.

> **LANGUAGE TIP** When 'it' is the direct
> object of the verb in a sentence, use
> **lo** if it stands for a masculine noun or
> **la** if it stands for a feminine noun.

□ There's a croissant left. Do you want it?
Queda un croissant. ¿Lo quieres? □ I doubt
it. Lo dudo. □ It's a good film. Have you
seen it? Es una buena película. ¿La has
visto?

> **LANGUAGE TIP** Use **le** when 'it' is the
> indirect object of the verb in the
> sentence.

□ Give it another coat of paint. Dale otra
mano de pintura.

> **LANGUAGE TIP** For general concepts
> use the word **ello**.

□ I spoke to him about it. Hablé con él sobre
ello. □ I'm against it. Estoy en contra de
ello.
**Italian** ADJECTIVE
▷ see also **Italian** NOUN
italiano ⟨FEM italiana⟩

**Italian** NOUN
▷ see also **Italian** ADJECTIVE
1 el italiano
la italiana (person)
□ the Italians los italianos
2 el italiano (language)
**Italy** NOUN
Italia fem
to **itch** VERB
picar*
□ It itches. Me pica. □ My head is itching.
Me pica la cabeza.
**itchy** ADJECTIVE
■ **My head's itchy.** Me pica la cabeza.
■ **I've got an itchy nose.** Me pica la nariz.
**it'd** = it had; it would
**item** NOUN
1 la pieza
□ a collector's item una pieza de colección
2 el artículo
□ The first item he bought was an alarm
clock. El primer artículo que compró fue un
despertador.
3 la partida
□ He checked the items on his bill.
Comprobó las partidas de su factura.
4 el punto
□ The next item on the agenda is...
El siguiente punto del orden del día es...
■ **an item of news** una noticia
**itinerary** NOUN
el itinerario
**it'll** = it will
**its** ADJECTIVE
su ⟨FEM su, PL sus⟩
□ Everything in its place. Cada cosa en su sitio.
□ It has its advantages. Tiene sus ventajas.

> **LANGUAGE TIP** 'its' is usually translated
> by the definite article **el/los** or **la/las**
> when it's clear from the sentence
> who the possessor is or when
> referring to clothing or parts of the
> body.

□ The dog is losing its hair. El perro está
perdiendo el pelo. □ The bird was in its
cage. El pájaro estaba en la jaula.
**it's** = it is; it has
**itself** PRONOUN
se (reflexive)
□ The heating switches itself off. La
calefacción se apaga sola. □ The dog
scratched itself. El perro se rascó.
■ **The meal itself was tasty, though**
**expensive.** La comida en sí estaba rica,
aunque era cara.
**I've** = I have

# Jj

**jab** NOUN
la inyección (PL las inyecciones)
**jack** NOUN
1 el gato
□ The jack's in the boot. El gato está en el maletero.
2 la jota (in ordinary pack of cards)
3 la sota (in Spanish pack of cards)
**jacket** NOUN
la chaqueta
■ **jacket potatoes** las patatas asadas con piel (las papas asadas con cáscara *Latin America*)
**jackpot** NOUN
el premio gordo
□ to win the jackpot sacarse el premio gordo
**jail** NOUN
▷ *see also* **jail** VERB
la cárcel
□ to go to jail ir a la cárcel
to **jail** VERB
▷ *see also* **jail** NOUN
■ **He was jailed for ten years.** Lo condenaron a diez años de cárcel.
**jam** NOUN
la mermelada
□ strawberry jam la mermelada de fresas
■ **a traffic jam** un atasco
**jammed** ADJECTIVE
atascado (FEM atascada)
□ The window's jammed. La ventana está atascada.
**jam-packed** ADJECTIVE
atestado (FEM atestada)
□ The room was jam-packed. La habitación estaba atestada.
**janitor** NOUN
el/la conserje
□ He's a janitor. Es conserje.
**January** NOUN
enero *masc*
□ in January en enero □ the January sales las rebajas de enero
**Japan** NOUN
el Japón *masc*

**Japanese** ADJECTIVE
▷ *see also* **Japanese** NOUN
japonés (FEM japonesa, PL japoneses)
**Japanese** NOUN
▷ *see also* **Japanese** ADJECTIVE
1 el japonés
la japonesa (person)
■ **the Japanese** los japoneses
2 el japonés (language)
**jar** NOUN
el tarro
□ a jar of honey un tarro de miel
**jaundice** NOUN
la ictericia
□ He's got jaundice. Tiene ictericia.
**javelin** NOUN
la jabalina
**jaw** NOUN
la mandíbula
**jazz** NOUN
el jazz
**jealous** ADJECTIVE
celoso (FEM celosa)
□ to be jealous estar celoso
**jeans** PL NOUN
los vaqueros
□ a pair of jeans unos vaqueros
**Jehovah's Witness** NOUN
el/la testigo de Jehová
□ She's a Jehovah's Witness. Es testigo de Jehová.
**Jello**® NOUN (US)
la gelatina
**jelly** NOUN
la gelatina
**jellyfish** NOUN
la medusa
**jersey** NOUN
el jersey (PL los jerseys)
**Jesus** NOUN
Jesús *masc*
**jet** NOUN
el reactor
**jetty** NOUN
el embarcadero
**Jew** NOUN

el judío
la judía

**jewel** NOUN
la joya

**jeweller** (US **jeweler**) NOUN
el joyero
la joyera
□ She's a jeweller. Es joyera.

**jeweller's shop** (US **jeweler's shop**) NOUN
la joyería

**jewellery** (US **jewelry**) NOUN
las joyas

**Jewish** ADJECTIVE
judío (FEM judía)

**jigsaw** NOUN
el rompecabezas (PL los rompecabezas)

**job** NOUN
el trabajo
□ a part-time job un trabajo de media jornada
■ You've done a good job. Lo has hecho muy bien.

**job centre** NOUN
la oficina de empleo

**jobless** ADJECTIVE
desempleado (FEM desempleada)

**jockey** NOUN
el/la jockey (PL los/las jockeys)

**to jog** VERB
hacer* footing

**jogging** NOUN
el footing
□ to go jogging hacer footing

**john** NOUN (US)
el wáter

**to join** VERB
hacerse* socio de
□ I'm going to join the ski club. Voy a hacerme socio del club de esquí.
■ I'll join you later if I can. Yo iré luego si puedo.
■ If you're going for a walk, do you mind if I join you? Si vais a dar un paseo, ¿os importa que os acompañe?

**to join in** VERB
■ He doesn't join in with what we do. No participa en lo que hacemos.
■ She started singing, and the audience joined in. Empezó a cantar, y el público se unió a ella.

**joiner** NOUN
el carpintero
la carpintera
□ He's a joiner. Es carpintero.

**joint** NOUN
1 la articulación (PL las articulaciones)
□ I've got pains in my joints. Me duelen las articulaciones.

2 el porro (drugs: informal)
■ We had a joint of lamb for lunch. Comimos asado de cordero.

**joke** NOUN
▷ see also **joke** VERB
1 la broma
□ Don't get upset, it was only a joke. No te enfades, era sólo una broma.
■ to play a joke on somebody gastarle una broma a alguien
2 el chiste
□ to tell a joke contar un chiste

**to joke** VERB
▷ see also **joke** NOUN
bromear
■ You must be joking! ¡Estás de broma!

**jolly** ADJECTIVE
alegre (FEM alegre)

**Jordan** NOUN
Jordania fem

**to jot down** VERB
apuntar

**jotter** NOUN
el bloc (PL los blocs)

**journalism** NOUN
el periodismo

**journalist** NOUN
el/la periodista
□ I'm a journalist. Soy periodista.

**journey** NOUN
el viaje
□ to go on a journey hacer un viaje
■ The journey to school takes about half an hour. Se tarda una media hora en ir al colegio.

**joy** NOUN
la alegría

**joystick** NOUN
el mando (for computer games)

**judge** NOUN
▷ see also **judge** VERB
el/la juez (PL los/las jueces)

**to judge** VERB
▷ see also **judge** NOUN
juzgar*

**judo** NOUN
el judo
□ My favourite sport is judo. Mi deporte favorito es el judo.

**jug** NOUN
la jarra

**juggler** NOUN
el/la malabarista

**juice** NOUN
el zumo
□ orange juice el zumo de naranja

**July** NOUN
julio masc
□ in July en julio

**jumble sale** NOUN
la venta de objetos usados

to **jump** VERB
saltar
□ They jumped over the wall. Saltaron el muro. □ He jumped out of the window. Saltó por la ventana. □ He jumped off the roof. Saltó del tejado.
■ **You made me jump!** ¡Qué susto me has dado!

**jumper** NOUN
el jersey (PL los jerseys)

**junction** NOUN
el cruce (of roads)

**June** NOUN
junio masc
□ in June en junio

**jungle** NOUN
la selva

**junior school** NOUN
el colegio

**junk** NOUN
los trastos viejos
□ The attic's full of junk. El desván está lleno de trastos viejos.
■ **to eat junk food** comer porquerías
■ **junk shop** la tienda de objetos usados

**jury** NOUN
el jurado

**just** ADVERB
**1** justo
□ just in time justo a tiempo □ just after Christmas justo después de Navidad □ We had just enough money. Teníamos el dinero justo.
■ **He's just arrived.** Acaba de llegar.
■ **I did it just now.** Lo acabo de hacer.
■ **I'm rather busy just now.** Ahora mismo estoy bastante ocupada.
■ **I'm just coming!** ¡Ya voy!
■ **just here** aquí mismo
**2** sólo
□ It's just a suggestion. Es sólo una sugerencia.
■ **I just thought that you would like it.** Yo pensé que te gustaría.
■ **Just a minute!** ¡Un momento!
■ **just about** casi □ It's just about finished. Está casi terminado.

**justice** NOUN
la justicia

to **justify** VERB
justificar*

j

# Kk

**kangaroo** NOUN
el canguro

**karate** NOUN
el kárate
□ My favourite sport is karate. Mi deporte favorito es el kárate.

**kebab** NOUN
el pincho moruno

**keen** ADJECTIVE
entusiasta (FEM entusiasta)
□ a keen supporter un hincha entusiasta
■ **He doesn't seem very keen.** No parece muy entusiasmado.
■ **She's a keen student.** Es una alumna aplicada.
■ **I'm not very keen on maths.** No me gustan mucho las matemáticas.
■ **He's keen on her.** Ella le gusta.
■ **to be keen on doing something** tener ganas de hacer algo □ I'm not very keen on going. No tengo muchas ganas de ir.

to **keep** VERB
1 quedarse con
□ You can keep the watch. Puedes quedarte con el reloj.
■ **You can keep it.** Puedes quedártelo.
2 mantenerse* (remain)
□ to keep fit mantenerse en forma
■ **Keep still!** ¡Estáte quieto!
■ **Keep quiet!** ¡Cállate!
3 seguir*
□ Keep straight on. Siga recto.
■ **I keep forgetting my keys.** Siempre me olvido las llaves.
■ **'keep out'** 'prohibida la entrada'
■ **'keep off the grass'** 'prohibido pisar el césped'

to **keep on** VERB
continuar*
□ He kept on reading. Continuó leyendo.
■ **The car keeps on breaking down.** El coche no deja de averiarse.

to **keep up** VERB
■ **Matthew walks so fast I can't keep up.** Matthew camina tan rápido que no puedo seguirle el ritmo.

**keep-fit** NOUN
la gimnasia
□ I go to keep-fit classes. Voy a clases de gimnasia.

**kennel** NOUN
la caseta del perro (in garden)
■ **a kennels** una residencia canina

**kept** VERB ▷ see **keep**

**kerosene** NOUN (US)
el queroseno

**kettle** NOUN
el hervidor

**key** NOUN
la llave

**keyboard** NOUN
el teclado

**keyring** NOUN
el llavero

**kick** NOUN
▷ see also **kick** VERB
la patada

to **kick** VERB
▷ see also **kick** NOUN
■ **to kick somebody** dar una patada a alguien □ He kicked me. Me dio una patada.
■ **He kicked the ball hard.** Le dio un puntapié fuerte al balón.
■ **to kick off** (in football) hacer el saque inicial

**kick-off** NOUN
el saque inicial
■ **The kick-off is at 10 o'clock.** El partido empieza a las diez.

**kid** NOUN
▷ see also **kid** VERB
el crío
la cría (informal)
□ the kids los críos

to **kid** VERB
▷ see also **kid** NOUN
bromear
□ I'm not kidding, it's snowing. No estoy bromeando, está nevando.
■ **I'm just kidding.** Es una broma.

to **kidnap** VERB
secuestrar

**kidney** NOUN
el riñón (PL los riñones)
□ He's got kidney trouble. Tiene problemas de riñón. □ I don't like kidneys. No me gustan los riñones.

to **kill** VERB
matar
□ She killed her husband. Mató a su marido.
■ **to be killed** morir □ He was killed in a car accident. Murió en un accidente de coche.
■ **to kill oneself** suicidarse □ He killed himself. Se suicidó.

**killer** NOUN
1 el asesino
la asesina *(murderer)*
□ The police are searching for the killer. La policía está buscando al asesino.
2 el asesino a sueldo
la asesina a sueldo *(hired killer)*
■ **Meningitis can be a killer.** La meningitis puede ser mortal.

**kilo** NOUN
el kilo
□ at £5 a kilo a 5 libras esterlinas el kilo

**kilometre** (US **kilometer**) NOUN
el kilómetro

**kilt** NOUN
la falda escocesa

**kind** ADJECTIVE
▷ *see also* **kind** NOUN
amable (FEM amable)
□ to be kind to somebody ser amable con alguien
■ **Thank you for being so kind.** Gracias por su amabilidad.

**kind** NOUN
▷ *see also* **kind** ADJECTIVE
el tipo
□ It's a kind of sausage. Es un tipo de salchicha.

**kindergarten** NOUN
el jardín de infancia (PL los jardines de infancia)

**kindly** ADVERB
amablemente

**kindness** NOUN
la amabilidad

**king** NOUN
el rey
■ **the King and Queen** los reyes

**kingdom** NOUN
el reino

**kiosk** NOUN
el quiosco *(stall)*
■ **a telephone kiosk** una cabina telefónica

**kipper** NOUN
el arenque ahumado

**kiss** NOUN

▷ *see also* **kiss** VERB
el beso

to **kiss** VERB
▷ *see also* **kiss** NOUN
1 besar
□ He kissed her passionately. La besó apasionadamente.
2 besarse
□ They kissed. Se besaron.

**kit** NOUN
el equipo
□ I've forgotten my gym kit. Me he olvidado el equipo de gimnasia.
■ **a tool kit** un juego de herramientas
■ **a sewing kit** un costurero
■ **a first-aid kit** un botiquín
■ **a puncture repair kit** un juego de reparación de pinchazos
■ **a drum kit** una batería

**kitchen** NOUN
la cocina
□ a fitted kitchen una cocina amueblada
□ a kitchen knife un cuchillo de cocina
■ **the kitchen units** los armarios de cocina

**kite** NOUN
la cometa

**kitten** NOUN
el gatito
la gatita

**knee** NOUN
la rodilla
□ to be on one's knees estar de rodillas

to **kneel** VERB
arrodillarse

to **kneel down** VERB
arrodillarse

**knew** VERB ▷ *see* **know**

**knickers** PL NOUN
las bragas (los calzones *Latin America*)
□ a pair of knickers unas bragas (unos calzones *Latin America*)

**knife** NOUN
el cuchillo
□ a kitchen knife un cuchillo de cocina
□ a sheath knife un cuchillo de monte
■ **a penknife** una navaja

to **knit** VERB
hacer* punto (tejer *Latin America*)
□ I like knitting. Me gusta hacer punto.
■ **She is knitting a jumper.** Está haciendo un jersey a punto.

**knives** PL NOUN ▷ *see* **knife**

**knob** NOUN
1 el pomo *(on door)*
2 el dial *(on radio, TV)*

to **knock** VERB
▷ *see also* **knock** NOUN
llamar

□ Someone's knocking at the door. Alguien llama a la puerta.
■ **to knock somebody down** atropellar a alguien □ She was knocked down by a car. La atropelló un coche.
■ **to knock somebody out** 1 *(defeat)* eliminar a alguien □ They were knocked out early in the tournament. Fueron eliminados al poco de iniciarse el torneo. **2** *(stun)* dejar sin sentido a alguien □ They knocked out the watchman. Dejaron al vigilante sin sentido.

**knock** NOUN
▷ *see also* **knock** VERB
el golpe

**knot** NOUN
el nudo
□ to tie a knot in something hacer un nudo en algo

**to know** VERB

> **LANGUAGE TIP** Use **saber** for knowing facts, **conocer** for knowing people and places.

**1** saber*
□ Yes, I know. Sí, ya lo sé. □ I don't know. No sé. □ I don't know any German. No sé nada de alemán.
■ **to know that** saber que □ I didn't know that your Dad was a policeman. No sabía que tu padre era policía.
**2** conocer*
□ I know her. La conozco. □ I know Paris well. Conozco bien París.

■ **to know about something** 1 *(be aware of)* estar enterado de algo □ Do you know about the meeting this afternoon? ¿Estás enterado de la reunión de esta tarde? **2** *(be knowledgeable about)* saber de algo □ He knows a lot about cars. Sabe mucho de coches. □ I don't know much about computers. No sé mucho de ordenadores.
■ **to get to know somebody** llegar a conocer a alguien
■ **How should I know?** ¿Y yo qué sé?
■ **You never know!** ¡Nunca se sabe!

**know-all** NOUN
el/la sabelotodo
□ He's such a know-all! ¡Es un sabelotodo!

**know-how** NOUN
la pericia

**knowledge** NOUN
el conocimiento
□ scientific knowledge el conocimiento científico
■ **my knowledge of French** mis conocimientos de francés

**knowledgeable** ADJECTIVE
■ **to be knowledgeable about something** saber mucho de algo

**known** VERB ▷ *see* **know**

**Koran** NOUN
el Corán

**Korea** NOUN
Corea *fem*

**kosher** ADJECTIVE
kosher (FEM + PL kosher)

# Ll

**lab** NOUN
el laboratorio
□ a lab technician un técnico de laboratorio

**label** NOUN
la etiqueta

**labor** NOUN (US)
■ **to be in labor** estar de parto
■ **the labor market** el mercado de trabajo
■ **labor union** el sindicato

**laboratory** NOUN
el laboratorio

**Labour** NOUN
los laboristas
□ My parents vote Labour. Mis padres votan a los laboristas.
■ **the Labour Party** el Partido Laborista

**labour** NOUN
■ **to be in labour** estar de parto
■ **the labour market** el mercado de trabajo

**labourer** NOUN
el peón (PL los peones)
■ **farm labourer** el jornalero

**lace** NOUN
1 el cordón (PL los cordones) (of shoe)
2 el encaje
□ a lace collar un cuello de encaje

**lack** NOUN
la falta
□ He got the job, despite his lack of experience. Consiguió el empleo, a pesar de su falta de experiencia.

**lacquer** NOUN
la laca

**lad** NOUN
el muchacho

**ladder** NOUN
la escalera (de mano)

**lady** NOUN
la señora
■ **Ladies and gentlemen...** Damas y caballeros...
■ **the ladies'** los servicios de señoras
■ **a young lady** una señorita

**ladybird** NOUN
la mariquita

**to lag behind** VERB
quedarse atrás

**lager** NOUN
la cerveza rubia

**laid** VERB ▷ see **lay**

**laid-back** ADJECTIVE
relajado (FEM relajada) (informal)

**lain** VERB ▷ see **lie**

**lake** NOUN
el lago
□ Lake Michigan el Lago Michigan

**lamb** NOUN
el cordero
□ a lamb chop una chuleta de cordero

**lame** ADJECTIVE
cojo (FEM coja)
□ to be lame estar cojo □ The accident left her lame. Se quedó coja después del accidente.
■ **My pony is lame.** Mi pony cojea.

**lamp** NOUN
la lámpara

**lamppost** NOUN
la farola

**lampshade** NOUN
la pantalla

**land** NOUN
▷ see also **land** VERB
la tierra
□ We have a lot of land. Tenemos mucha tierra.
■ **to work on the land** trabajar la tierra
■ **a piece of land** un terreno

**to land** VERB
▷ see also **land** NOUN
aterrizar*
□ The plane landed at five o'clock. El avión aterrizó a las cinco.

**landing** NOUN
1 el aterrizaje (of plane)
2 el rellano (of staircase)

**landlady** NOUN
1 la casera (of rented property)
2 la patrona (of pub)

**landlord** NOUN
1 el casero (of rented property)
2 el patrón (PL los patrones) (of pub)

**l**

**landmark** NOUN
el punto de referencia
□ Big Ben is one of London's landmarks.
El Big Ben es uno de los puntos de referencia de Londres.

**landowner** NOUN
el/la terrateniente

**landscape** NOUN
el paisaje

**lane** NOUN
1 el camino
□ a country lane un camino rural
2 el carril
□ the outside lane (in the UK) el carril de la derecha □ the outside lane (on the Continent) el carril de la izquierda

**language** NOUN
el idioma

> LANGUAGE TIP Although **idioma** ends in -**a**, it is actually a masculine noun.

□ Greek is a difficult language. El griego es un idioma difícil.
■ **to use bad language** decir palabrotas

**language laboratory** NOUN
el laboratorio de idiomas

**lap** NOUN
la vuelta
□ I ran 10 laps. Corrí 10 vueltas.
■ **Andrew was sitting on his mother's lap.** Andrew estaba sentado en el regazo de su madre.

**laptop** NOUN
el (ordenador) portátil

**larder** NOUN
la despensa

**large** ADJECTIVE
grande (FEM grande)
□ a large house una casa grande □ a large dog un perro grande

> LANGUAGE TIP Use **gran** before a singular noun.

□ a large number of people un gran número de personas

> LANGUAGE TIP Be careful not to translate **large** by **largo**.

**largely** ADVERB
en gran parte

**laser** NOUN
el láser

**lass** NOUN
la muchacha

**last** ADJECTIVE, ADVERB
> see also **last** VERB
1 pasado (FEM pasada)
□ last Friday el viernes pasado
2 último (FEM última)
□ the last time la última vez
3 por última vez

□ I've lost my bag. — When did you last see it? He perdido el bolso. — ¿Cuándo lo viste por última vez?
4 en último lugar
□ the team which finished last el equipo que quedó en último lugar
■ **He arrived last.** Llegó el último.
■ **last night** anoche □ I got home at midnight last night. Anoche llegué a casa a medianoche. □ I couldn't sleep last night. Anoche no pude dormir.
■ **at last** por fin

**to last** VERB
> see also **last** ADJECTIVE, ADVERB
durar
□ The concert lasts two hours. El concierto dura dos horas.

**lastly** ADVERB
por último

**late** ADJECTIVE, ADVERB
tarde (FEM tarde)
□ Hurry up or you'll be late! ¡Date prisa o llegarás tarde! □ I'm often late for school. A menudo llego tarde al colegio. □ I went to bed late. Me fui a la cama tarde. □ to arrive late llegar tarde
■ **The flight will be one hour late.** El vuelo llegará con una hora de retraso.
■ **in the late afternoon** al final de la tarde
■ **in late May** a finales de mayo
■ **the late Mr Philips** el difunto Sr. Philips

**lately** ADVERB
últimamente
□ I haven't seen him lately. No lo he visto últimamente.

**later** ADVERB
más tarde
□ I'll do it later. Lo haré más tarde.
■ **See you later!** ¡Hasta luego!

**latest** ADJECTIVE
último (FEM última)
□ their latest album su último álbum
■ **at the latest** como muy tarde □ by 10 o'clock at the latest a las 10 como muy tarde

**Latin** NOUN
el latín
□ I do Latin. Estudio latín.

**Latin America** NOUN
América Latina fem

**Latin American** ADJECTIVE
> see also **Latin American** NOUN
latinoamericano (FEM latinoamericana)

**Latin American** NOUN
> see also **Latin American** ADJECTIVE
el latinoamericano
la latinoamericana

**laugh** NOUN

▷ *see also* **laugh** VERB
la risa
■ **It was a good laugh.** Fue muy divertido.
to **laugh** VERB
▷ *see also* **laugh** NOUN
reírse*
■ **to laugh at something** reírse de algo
□ He laughed at my accent. Se rió de mi acento.
■ **to laugh at somebody** reírse de alguien
□ They laughed at her. Se rieron de ella.
to **launch** VERB
lanzar* *(product, rocket)*
**Launderette**® NOUN
la lavandería automática
**Laundromat**® NOUN (US)
la lavandería automática
**laundry** NOUN
la colada
□ She does my laundry. Me hace la colada.
**lavatory** NOUN
el servicio
**lavender** NOUN
la lavanda
**law** NOUN
1 la ley
□ strict laws leyes severas
■ **It's against the law.** Es ilegal.
2 el derecho
□ My sister's studying law. Mi hermana estudia derecho.
**lawn** NOUN
el césped
**lawnmower** NOUN
el cortacésped
**law school** NOUN (US)
la facultad de derecho
**lawyer** NOUN
el abogado
la abogada
□ My mother's a lawyer. Mi madre es abogada.
to **lay** VERB
poner*
□ She laid the baby in his cot. Puso al bebé en la cuna. □ to lay the table poner la mesa
to **lay off** VERB
despedir*
□ My father's been laid off. Han despedido a mi padre.
**lay-by** NOUN
el área de descanso
> **LANGUAGE TIP** Although it's a feminine noun, remember that you use **el** and **un** with **área**.
**layer** NOUN
la capa
**lazy** ADJECTIVE

perezoso (FEM perezosa)
**lead (1)** NOUN
▷ *see also* **lead** VERB
el plomo *(metal)*
□ a lead pipe una tubería de plomo
**lead (2)** NOUN
▷ *see also* **lead** VERB
1 el cable *(cable)*
2 la correa
□ Dogs must be kept on a lead. Los perros deben llevarse siempre sujetos con una correa.
■ **to be in the lead (2)** ir en cabeza
to **lead** VERB
▷ *see also* **lead (2)** NOUN
llevar
□ the street that leads to the station la calle que lleva a la estación □ It could lead to a civil war. Podría llevar a una guerra civil.
■ **to lead the way** ir delante
**leader** NOUN
el/la líder
**lead singer** NOUN
el/la cantante principal
**leaf** NOUN
la hoja
**leaflet** NOUN
el folleto
**league** NOUN
la liga
□ They are at the top of the league. Están a la cabeza de la liga.
■ **the Premier League** la primera división
**leak** NOUN
▷ *see also* **leak** VERB
1 el escape
□ a gas leak un escape de gas □ a leak in the pipe un escape en la tubería
2 la gotera
□ a leak in the roof una gotera en el tejado
to **leak** VERB
▷ *see also* **leak** NOUN
1 tener* un agujero *(bucket, pipe)*
2 tener* goteras *(roof)*
3 salirse* *(water, gas)*
to **lean** VERB
apoyar
□ to lean something against the wall apoyar algo contra la pared
■ **to lean on something** apoyarse en algo
□ He leant on the table. Se apoyó en la mesa.
■ **to be leaning against something** estar apoyado contra algo □ The ladder was leaning against the wall. La escalera estaba apoyada contra la pared.
to **lean forward** VERB
inclinarse hacia adelante

to **lean out** VERB
asomarse
▢ She leant out of the window. Se asomó a la ventana.

to **lean over** VERB
inclinarse
▢ Don't lean over too far. No te inclines demasiado.

to **leap** VERB
saltar
■ **He leapt out of his chair when his team scored.** Dio un salto de la silla cuando su equipo marcó.

**leap year** NOUN
el año bisiesto

to **learn** VERB
aprender
▢ I'm learning to ski. Estoy aprendiendo a esquiar.

**learner** NOUN
■ **She's a quick learner.** Aprende con mucha rapidez.
■ **Spanish learners** los estudiantes de español

**learner driver** NOUN
el conductor en prácticas
la conductora en prácticas

**learnt** VERB ▷ see **learn**

**least** ADJECTIVE, PRONOUN, ADVERB
1 menor (FEM menor )
▢ I haven't the least idea. No tengo la menor idea.
2 menos
▢ Go for the ones with least fat. Escoge los que tengan menos grasa. ▢ the least expensive hotel el hotel menos caro ▢ It takes the least time. Es lo que menos tiempo lleva. ▢ It's the least I can do. Es lo menos que puedo hacer. ▢ Maths is the subject I like the least. Las matemáticas es la asignatura que menos me gusta. ▢ That's the least of my worries. Eso es lo que menos me preocupa.
■ **at least 1** por lo menos ▢ It'll cost at least £200. Costará por lo menos 200 libras esterlinas. **2** al menos ▢ There was a lot of damage but at least nobody was hurt. Hubo muchos daños pero al menos nadie resultó herido. ▢ It's very unfair, at least that's my opinion. Es muy injusto, al menos eso pienso yo.

**leather** NOUN
el cuero
▢ a black leather jacket una chaqueta de cuero negra

**leave** NOUN
▷ see also **leave** VERB
el permiso (from job, army)
▢ My brother is on leave for a week. Mi hermano está de permiso durante una semana.

to **leave** VERB
▷ see also **leave** NOUN
1 dejar
▢ Don't leave your camera in the car. No dejes la cámara en el coche.
2 salir*
▢ The bus leaves at eight. El autobús sale a las ocho.
3 salir* de
▢ We leave London at six o'clock. Salimos de Londres a las seis.
4 irse*
▢ They left yesterday. Se fueron ayer. ▢ She left home when she was sixteen. Se fue de casa a los dieciséis años.
■ **to leave somebody alone** dejar a alguien en paz ▢ Leave me alone! ¡Déjame en paz!

to **leave out** VERB
excluir*
▢ Not knowing the language I felt really left out. Al no saber el idioma me sentía muy excluido.

**leaves** PL NOUN ▷ see **leaf**

**Lebanon** NOUN
Líbano masc

**lecture** NOUN
▷ see also **lecture** VERB
1 la clase (at university)
2 la conferencia (public)

to **lecture** VERB
▷ see also **lecture** NOUN
1 dar* clases
▢ She lectures at the technical college. Da clases en la escuela politécnica.
2 sermonear
▢ He's always lecturing us. Siempre nos está sermoneando.

**lecturer** NOUN
el profesor universitario
la profesora universitaria
■ **She's a lecturer in German.** Es profesora de alemán en la universidad.

**led** VERB ▷ see **lead**

**leek** NOUN
el puerro

**left** VERB ▷ see **leave**

**left** ADJECTIVE, ADVERB
▷ see also **left** NOUN
1 izquierdo (FEM izquierda )
▢ my left hand mi mano izquierda
2 a la izquierda
▢ Turn left at the traffic lights. Doble a la izquierda al llegar al semáforo.
■ **I haven't got any money left.** No me queda nada de dinero.

■ **Is there any ice cream left?** ¿Queda algo de helado?

**left** NOUN
▷ *see also* **left** ADJECTIVE
la izquierda
□ **on the left** a la izquierda

**left-hand** ADJECTIVE
■ **the left-hand side** la izquierda □ It's on the left-hand side. Está a la izquierda.

**left-handed** ADJECTIVE
zurdo (FEM zurda )

**left-luggage office** NOUN
la consigna

**leg** NOUN
la pierna
□ She's broken her leg. Se ha roto la pierna.
■ **a chicken leg** un muslo de pollo
■ **a leg of lamb** una pierna de cordero

**legal** ADJECTIVE
legal (FEM legal )

**leggings** NOUN
las mallas

**leisure** NOUN
el tiempo libre
□ What do you do in your leisure time?
¿Qué haces en tu tiempo libre?

**leisure centre** NOUN
el centro recreativo

**lemon** NOUN
el limón (PL los limones )

**lemonade** NOUN
la gaseosa

to **lend** VERB
prestar
□ I can lend you some money. Te puedo prestar algo de dinero.

**length** NOUN
la longitud
■ **It's about a metre in length.** Mide aproximadamente un metro de largo.

**lens** NOUN
1 la lentilla él lente de contacto *Latin America) (contact lens)*
2 el cristal *(of spectacles)*
3 el objetivo *(of camera)*

**Lent** NOUN
la Cuaresma

**lent** VERB ▷ *see* **lend**

**lentil** NOUN
la lenteja

**Leo** NOUN
el Leo *(sign)*
■ **I'm Leo.** Soy leo.

**leotard** NOUN
el leotardo

**lesbian** NOUN
la lesbiana

**less** ADJECTIVE, PRONOUN, ADVERB

menos
□ A bit less, please. Un poco menos, por favor. □ It's less than a kilometre from here. Está a menos de un kilómetro de aquí.
□ less than half menos de la mitad □ I've got less than you. Tengo menos que tú. □ It cost less than we thought. Costó menos de lo que pensábamos.
■ **less and less** cada vez menos

**lesson** NOUN
1 la clase
□ an English lesson una clase de inglés
□ The lessons last forty minutes. Las clases duran cuarenta minutos.
2 la lección (PL las lecciones ) *(in textbook)*

to **let** VERB
1 dejar
■ **to let somebody do something** dejar a alguien hacer algo □ Let me have a look. Déjame ver.
■ **Let me go!** ¡Suéltame!
■ **to let somebody know something** informar a alguien de algo □ We must let him know that we are coming to stay. Tenemos que informarle de que venimos a quedarnos.
■ **When can you come to dinner? — I'll let you know.** ¿Cuándo puedes venir a cenar? — Ya te lo diré.
■ **to let in** dejar entrar □ They wouldn't let me in because I was under 18. No me dejaron entrar porque tenía menos de 18 años.

LANGUAGE TIP To make suggestions using 'let's', you can ask questions using **por qué no** .

□ Let's go to the cinema! ¿Por qué no vamos al cine?
■ **Let's have a break! — Yes, let's.** Vamos a descansar un poco. — ¡Buena idea!
2 alquilar
□ 'to let' 'se alquila'

to **let down** VERB
defraudar
□ I won't let you down. No te defraudaré.

**letter** NOUN
1 la carta
□ She wrote me a long letter. Me escribió una carta larga.
2 la letra
□ 'A' is the first letter of the alphabet. La 'a' es la primera letra del alfabeto.

**letterbox** NOUN
el buzón (PL los buzones )

**lettuce** NOUN
la lechuga

**leukaemia** NOUN
la leucemia

□ He suffers from leukaemia. Tiene leucemia.

**level** ADJECTIVE
▷ *see also* **level** NOUN
llano (FEM llana)
□ a level surface una superficie llana

**level** NOUN
▷ *see also* **level** ADJECTIVE
el nivel
□ The level of the river is rising. El nivel del río está subiendo.
■ 'A' levels

DID YOU KNOW...?
Under the reformed Spanish educational system, if students stay on at school after the age of 16, they can do a two-year course – **bachillerato**. In order to get in to university, they sit an entrance exam – **la selectividad** – in the subjects they have been studying for the **bachillerato**.

**level crossing** NOUN
el paso a nivel

**lever** NOUN
la palanca

**liable** ADJECTIVE
■ He's liable to panic. Tiene tendencia a dejarse llevar por el pánico.

**liar** NOUN
el mentiroso
la mentirosa

**liberal** ADJECTIVE
liberal (FEM liberal) *(view, system)*
■ the Liberal Democrats los demócratas liberales

**liberation** NOUN
la liberación

**Libra** NOUN
la Libra *(sign)*
■ I'm Libra. Soy libra.

**librarian** NOUN
el bibliotecario
la bibliotecaria
□ I'm a librarian. Soy bibliotecaria.

**library** NOUN
la biblioteca

LANGUAGE TIP Be careful not to translate **library** by **librería**.

**Libya** NOUN
Libia *fem*

**licence** (US **license**) NOUN
el permiso
■ a driving licence un carnet de conducir

**to lick** VERB
lamer

**lid** NOUN
la tapa

**lie** NOUN
▷ *see also* **lie** VERB
la mentira
■ to tell a lie mentir

**to lie** VERB
▷ *see also* **lie** NOUN
1 mentir*
□ I know she's lying. Sé que está mintiendo.
□ You lied to me! ¡Me mentiste!
2 tumbarse
□ I lay on the floor. Me tumbé en el suelo.
■ He was lying on the sofa. Estaba tumbado en el sofá.

**lie-in** NOUN
■ to have a lie-in quedarse en la cama hasta tarde

**lieutenant** NOUN
el/la teniente

**life** NOUN
la vida

**lifebelt** NOUN
el salvavidas (PL los salvavidas)

**lifeboat** NOUN
el bote salvavidas (PL los botes salvavidas)

**lifeguard** NOUN
el/la socorrista

**life jacket** NOUN
el chaleco salvavidas (PL los chalecos salvavidas)

**life-saving** NOUN
el socorrismo
□ I've done a course in life-saving. He hecho un curso de socorrismo.

**lifestyle** NOUN
el estilo de vida

**to lift** VERB
▷ *see also* **lift** NOUN
levantar
□ It's too heavy, I can't lift it. Pesa mucho, no lo puedo levantar.

**lift** NOUN
▷ *see also* **lift** VERB
el ascensor
□ The lift isn't working. El ascensor no funciona.
■ He gave me a lift to the cinema. Me acercó al cine en coche.
■ Would you like a lift? ¿Quieres que te lleve en coche?

**light** ADJECTIVE
▷ *see also* **light** NOUN, VERB
1 ligero (FEM ligera) *(not heavy)*
□ a light jacket una chaqueta ligera
□ a light meal una comida ligera
2 claro (FEM clara) *(colour)*
□ a light blue sweater un jersey azul claro

**light** NOUN
▷ *see also* **light** ADJECTIVE, VERB

**I**

la luz (PL las luces)
- □ He switched on the light. Encendió la luz.
- □ He switched off the light. Apagó la luz.
- ■ **the traffic lights** el semáforo
- ■ **Have you got a light?** ¿Tienes fuego?

to **light** VERB
> ▷ *see also* **light** ADJECTIVE, NOUN
encender*

**light bulb** NOUN
la bombilla

**lighter** NOUN
el mechero

**lighthouse** NOUN
el faro

**lightning** NOUN
el relámpago
- □ thunder and lightning truenos y relámpagos
- □ a flash of lightning un relámpago

to **like** VERB
> ▷ *see also* **like** PREPOSITION

> **LANGUAGE TIP** The most common translation for 'to like' when talking about things and activities is **gustar**. Remember that the construction is the opposite of English, with the thing you like being the subject of the sentence.

- □ I don't like mustard. No me gusta la mostaza. □ Do you like apples? ¿Te gustan las manzanas? □ I like riding. Me gusta montar a caballo.
- ■ **I like him.** Me cae bien.
- ■ **I'd like...** Quería... □ I'd like this blouse in size 10, please. Quería esta blusa en la talla 10, por favor.
- ■ **I'd like an orange juice, please.** Un zumo de naranja, por favor.
- ■ **I'd like to...** Me gustaría... □ I'd like to go to China. Me gustaría ir a China.

> **LANGUAGE TIP** To ask someone if they would like something, or like to do something, use **querer**.

- □ Would you like some coffee? ¿Quieres café? □ Would you like to go for a walk? ¿Quieres ir a dar un paseo?
- ■ **... if you like** ... si quieres

**like** PREPOSITION
> ▷ *see also* **like** VERB
como
- □ a city like Paris una ciudad como París

> **LANGUAGE TIP** When asking questions, use **cómo** instead of **como**.

- □ What was his house like? ¿Cómo era su casa?
- ■ **What's the weather like?** ¿Qué tiempo hace?
- ■ **It's a bit like salmon.** Se parece un poco al salmón.

- ■ **It's fine like that.** Así está bien.
- ■ **Do it like this.** Hazlo así.
- ■ **something like that** algo así

**likely** ADJECTIVE
probable (FEM probable)
- □ That's not very likely. Es poco probable.

> **LANGUAGE TIP** **es probable que** has to be followed by a verb in the subjunctive.

- □ She's likely to come. Es probable que venga. □ She's not likely to come. Es probable que no venga.

**lime** NOUN
la lima *(fruit)*

**limit** NOUN
el límite
- ■ **the speed limit** el límite de velocidad

**limousine** NOUN
la limusina

to **limp** VERB
cojear

**line** NOUN
1 la línea
- □ a straight line una línea recta □ He wrote a few lines. Escribió unas cuantas líneas.
- □ to draw a line trazar una línea
2 la fila
- □ a line of people una fila de gente
- ■ **railway line** la vía férrea
- ■ **Hold the line, please.** No cuelgue, por favor.
- ■ **It's a very bad line.** Se oye muy mal.

**linen** NOUN
el lino
- □ a linen jacket una chaqueta de lino

**liner** NOUN
el transatlántico

**link** NOUN
> ▷ *see also* **link** VERB
1 la relación (PL las relaciones)
- □ the link between smoking and cancer la relación entre el tabaco y el cáncer
- ■ **cultural links** los lazos culturales
2 el enlace *(computing)*

to **link** VERB
> ▷ *see also* **link** NOUN
1 asociar *(facts)*
2 conectar *(towns, terminals)*

**lino** NOUN
el linóleo

**lion** NOUN
el león (PL los leones)

**lioness** NOUN
la leona

**lip** NOUN
el labio

to **lip-read** VERB
leer* los labios

**lip salve** NOUN
la crema protectora para los labios

**lipstick** NOUN
el lápiz de labios (PL los lápices de labios )

**liqueur** NOUN
el licor

**liquid** NOUN
el líquido

**liquidizer** NOUN
la licuadora

**list** NOUN
▷ see also list VERB
la lista

to **list** VERB
▷ see also list NOUN
1 hacer* una lista de (in writing)
2 enumerar (verbally)

to **listen** VERB
escuchar
□ Listen to this! ¡Escucha esto! □ Listen to
me! ¡Escúchame!

**listener** NOUN
el/la oyente

**lit** VERB ▷ see light

**liter** NOUN (US)
el litro

**literally** ADVERB
literalmente
□ It was literally impossible to find a seat.
Era literalmente imposible encontrar un
asiento. □ to translate literally traducir
literalmente

**literature** NOUN
la literatura

**litre** NOUN
el litro

**litter** NOUN
la basura

**litter bin** NOUN
el cubo de la basura

**little** ADJECTIVE, PRONOUN
pequeño (FEM pequeña )
□ a little girl una niña pequeña

**WORD POWER**
You can use a number of other words
instead of **little** to mean 'small':
**miniature** en miniatura
□ a miniature doll una muñeca en
miniatura
**minute** minúsculo
□ a minute plant una planta minúscula
**tiny** enano
□ a tiny garden un jardín enano

■ **a little** un poco □ How much would you
like? — Just a little. ¿Cuánto quiere? — Sólo
un poco.

■ **very little** muy poco □ We've got very
little time. Tenemos muy poco tiempo.
■ **little by little** poco a poco

**live** ADJECTIVE
▷ see also live VERB
vivo (FEM viva )
□ I'm against tests on live animals. Estoy en
contra de los experimentos en animales
vivos.
■ **a live broadcast** una emisión en directo
■ **a live concert** un concierto en vivo

to **live** VERB
▷ see also live ADJECTIVE
vivir
□ I live with my grandmother. Vivo con mi
abuela. □ Where do you live? ¿Dónde vives?
□ I live in Edinburgh. Vivo en Edimburgo.

to **live together** VERB
vivir juntos

**lively** ADJECTIVE
■ **She's got a lively personality.** Tiene un
carácter muy alegre.

**liver** NOUN
el hígado

**lives** PL NOUN ▷ see life

**living** NOUN
■ **to make a living** ganarse la vida
■ **What does she do for a living?** ¿A qué se
dedica?

**living room** NOUN
la sala de estar

**lizard** NOUN
1 la lagartija (small)
2 el lagarto (big)

**load** NOUN
▷ see also load VERB
■ **loads of** (informal) un montón de
□ They've got loads of money. Tienen un
montón de dinero.
■ **You're talking a load of rubbish!** ¡Lo que
dices es una estupidez!

to **load** VERB
▷ see also load NOUN
cargar*
□ a trolley loaded with luggage un carrito
cargado de equipaje

**loaf** NOUN
el pan
■ **a loaf of bread 1** (French bread) una barra
de pan **2** (baked in tin) un pan de molde

**loan** NOUN
▷ see also loan VERB
el préstamo

to **loan** VERB
▷ see also loan NOUN
prestar

to **loathe** VERB
detestar

□ I loathe her. La detesto.
**loaves** PL NOUN ▷see **loaf**
**lobster** NOUN
la langosta
**local** ADJECTIVE
local (FEM local)
□ the local paper el periódico local
■ **a local call** una llamada urbana
**loch** NOUN
el lago
**lock** NOUN
▷see also **lock** VERB
la cerradura
to **lock** VERB
▷see also **lock** NOUN
cerrar* con llave
□ Make sure you lock your door. No te
olvides de cerrar tu puerta con llave.
to **lock out** VERB
■ **The door slammed and I was locked
out.** La puerta se cerró de golpe y me quedé
fuera sin llaves.
**locker** NOUN
la taquilla
□ left-luggage lockers las taquillas de
consigna
■ **locker room** el vestuario
**locket** NOUN
el relicario
**lodger** NOUN
el inquilino
la inquilina
**loft** NOUN
el desván (PL los desvanes)
**log** NOUN
el leño
**logical** ADJECTIVE
lógico (FEM lógica)
to **log in** VERB
entrar en el sistema
to **log off** VERB
salir* del sistema
to **log on** VERB
entrar en el sistema
to **log out** VERB
salir* del sistema
**lollipop** NOUN
el pirulí (PL los pirulís)
**lolly** NOUN
■ **ice lolly** el polo (la paleta helada
Latin America)
**London** NOUN
Londres masc
**Londoner** NOUN
el/la londinense
**loneliness** NOUN
la soledad
**lonely** ADJECTIVE

solo (FEM sola)
□ I sometimes feel lonely. A veces me
siento solo.
■ **a lonely cottage** una casita aislada
**long** ADJECTIVE, ADVERB
▷see also **long** VERB
largo (FEM larga)
□ She's got long hair. Tiene el pelo largo.
□ The room is six metres long. La habitación
tiene seis metros de largo.
■ **a long time** mucho tiempo □ It takes a
long time. Lleva mucho tiempo. □ I've been
waiting a long time. Llevo esperando
mucho tiempo.
■ **How long?** (time) ¿Cuánto tiempo?
□ How long have you been here? ¿Cuánto
tiempo llevas aquí? □ How long will it take?
¿Cuánto tiempo llevará?
■ **How long is the flight?** ¿Cuánto dura el
vuelo?
■ **as long as** siempre que
  LANGUAGE TIP **siempre que** has to be
  followed by a verb in the subjunctive.
□ I'll come as long as it's not too expensive.
Iré siempre que no sea demasiado caro.
to **long** VERB
▷see also **long** ADJECTIVE
■ **to long to do something** estar deseando
hacer algo
**long-distance** ADJECTIVE
■ **a long-distance call** una llamada de
larga distancia
**longer** ADVERB
▷see also **long** ADJECTIVE
■ **They're no longer going out together.**
Ya no salen juntos.
■ **I can't stand it any longer.** Ya no lo
aguanto más.
**long jump** NOUN
el salto de longitud
**loo** NOUN
el wáter (el baño Latin America)
**look** NOUN
▷see also **look** VERB
■ **Have a look at this!** ¡Échale una ojeada a
esto!
■ **I don't like the look of it.** No me gusta
nada.
to **look** VERB
▷see also **look** NOUN
1 mirar
□ Look! ¡Mira!
■ **to look at something** mirar algo □ Look
at the picture. Mira la foto.
■ **Look out!** ¡Cuidado!
2 parecer*
□ She looks surprised. Parece sorprendida.
■ **That cake looks nice.** Ese pastel tiene

145

buena pinta.

■ **to look like somebody** parecerse a alguien ▢ He looks like his brother. Se parece a su hermano.

■ **What does she look like?** ¿Cómo es físicamente?

to **look after** VERB

cuidar
▢ I look after my little sister. Cuido a mi hermana pequeña.

to **look for** VERB

buscar*
▢ I'm looking for my passport. Estoy buscando mi pasaporte.

to **look forward to** VERB

tener* muchas ganas de
▢ to look forward to doing something tener muchas ganas de hacer algo  ▢ I'm looking forward to meeting you. Tengo muchas ganas de conocerte.

■ **I'm really looking forward to the holidays.** Estoy deseando que lleguen las vacaciones.

■ **Looking forward to hearing from you...** A la espera de sus noticias...

to **look round** VERB

**1** volverse*
▢ I called him and he looked round. Lo llamé y se volvió.

**2** mirar
▢ I'm just looking round. Sólo estoy mirando.

■ **to look round an exhibition** visitar una exposición

■ **I like looking round the shops.** Me gusta ir a ver tiendas.

to **look up** VERB

buscar*
▢ If you don't know a word, look it up in the dictionary. Si no conoces una palabra, búscala en el diccionario.

**loose** ADJECTIVE

holgado (FEM holgada )
▢ a loose shirt una camisa holgada

■ **a loose screw** un tornillo flojo

■ **loose change** dinero suelto

**lord** NOUN

el señor (feudal)

■ **the House of Lords** la Cámara de los Lores

■ **the Lord** (God) el Señor

■ **Good Lord!** ¡Dios mío!

**lorry** NOUN

el camión (PL los camiones )

**lorry driver** NOUN

el camionero
la camionera
▢ He's a lorry driver. Es camionero.

to **lose** VERB

perder*
▢ I've lost my purse. He perdido el monedero.

■ **to get lost** perderse  ▢ I was afraid of getting lost. Tenía miedo de perderme.

**loss** NOUN

la pérdida

**lost** VERB ▷ see lose

**lost** ADJECTIVE

perdido (FEM perdida )

**lost-and-found** NOUN (US)

la oficina de objetos perdidos

**lost property office** NOUN

la oficina de objetos perdidos

**lot** NOUN

■ **a lot** mucho  ▢ She talks a lot. Habla mucho.  ▢ Do you like football? — Not a lot. ¿Te gusta el fútbol? — No mucho.

■ **a lot of** mucho  ▢ I drink a lot of coffee. Bebo mucho café.  ▢ We saw a lot of interesting things. Vimos muchas cosas interesantes.  ▢ He's got lots of friends. Tiene muchos amigos.  ▢ She's got lots of self-confidence. Tiene mucha confianza en sí misma.

■ **That's the lot.** Eso es todo.

**lottery** NOUN

la lotería
▢ to win the lottery ganar la lotería

**loud** ADJECTIVE

fuerte (FEM fuerte )
▢ The television is too loud. La televisión está muy fuerte.

**loudly** ADVERB

fuerte

**loudspeaker** NOUN

el altavoz (PL los altavoces )

**lounge** NOUN

la sala de estar

**lousy** ADJECTIVE

asqueroso (FEM asquerosa ) (informal)
▢ It was a lousy meal. Fue una comida asquerosa.

■ **I feel lousy.** Me siento fatal.

**love** NOUN

▷ see also **love** VERB

el amor

■ **to be in love** estar enamorado  ▢ She's in love with Paul. Está enamorada de Paul.

■ **to make love** hacer el amor

■ **Give Gloria my love.** Dale recuerdos a Gloria de mi parte.

■ **Love, Rosemary.** Un abrazo, Rosemary.

to **love** VERB

▷ see also **love** NOUN

querer*
▢ Everybody loves her. Todos la quieren.

□ I love you. Te quiero.

■ **I love chocolate.** Me encanta el chocolate.

■ **Would you like to come? — Yes, I'd love to.** ¿Te gustaría venir? — Sí, me encantaría.

**lovely** ADJECTIVE

1 encantador (FEM encantadora) *(person)*
□ She's a lovely person. Es una persona encantadora.

2 precioso (FEM preciosa)
□ They've got a lovely house. Tienen una casa preciosa.

■ **What a lovely surprise!** ¡Qué sorpresa tan agradable!

■ **It's a lovely day.** Hace un tiempo estupendo.

■ **Is your meal okay? — Yes, it's lovely.** ¿Está bueno? — Sí, buenísimo.

■ **Have a lovely time!** ¡Que lo paséis bien!

**lover** NOUN
el/la amante

**low** ADJECTIVE, ADVERB
bajo (FEM baja)
□ low prices los bajos precios □ That plane is flying very low. Ese avión vuela muy bajo.
□ in the low season en temporada baja

to **lower** VERB
▷ *see also* **lower** ADJECTIVE
bajar
□ He was so tall that the dentist had to lower the chair. Era tan alto que el dentista tuvo que bajar la silla.

**lower** ADJECTIVE
▷ *see also* **lower** VERB
inferior (FEM inferior)

**low-fat** ADJECTIVE

1 de bajo contenido graso *(margarine, cheese)*
2 desnatado (FEM desnatada) *(milk, yoghurt)*

**loyalty** NOUN
la lealtad

**loyalty card** NOUN
la tarjeta de cliente

**luck** NOUN
la suerte
□ She hasn't had much luck. No ha tenido mucha suerte.

■ **Bad luck!** ¡Mala suerte!

■ **Good luck!** ¡Suerte!

**luckily** ADVERB
afortunadamente

**lucky** ADJECTIVE
afortunado (FEM afortunada)
□ I consider myself lucky. Me considero afortunado.

■ **to be lucky** *(fortunate)* tener suerte
□ He's lucky, he's got a job. Tiene suerte de tener trabajo.

■ **That was lucky!** ¡Qué suerte!

■ **Black cats are lucky in Britain.** En Gran Bretaña los gatos negros traen buena suerte.

■ **a lucky horseshoe** una herradura de la suerte

**luggage** NOUN
el equipaje

**lukewarm** ADJECTIVE
tibio (FEM tibia)

**lump** NOUN

1 el trozo
□ a lump of butter un trozo de mantequilla
2 el chichón (PL los chichones) *(swelling)*
□ He's got a lump on his forehead. Tiene un chichón en la frente.

**lunatic** NOUN
el loco
la loca
□ He's an absolute lunatic. Está loco perdido.

**lunch** NOUN
el almuerzo
■ **to have lunch** almorzar □ We have lunch at half past twelve. Almorzamos a las doce y media.

**luncheon voucher** NOUN
el tíquet restaurante (PL los tíquets restaurante)

**lung** NOUN
el pulmón (PL los pulmones)
□ lung cancer el cáncer de pulmón

**luscious** ADJECTIVE
exquisito (FEM exquisita)

**lush** ADJECTIVE
exuberante (FEM exuberante)

**lust** NOUN
la lujuria

**Luxembourg** NOUN
Luxemburgo *masc*

**luxurious** ADJECTIVE
lujoso (FEM lujosa)

**luxury** NOUN
el lujo
□ It was luxury! ¡Era un lujo! □ a luxury hotel un hotel de lujo

**lying** VERB ▷ *see* **lie**

**lyrics** PL NOUN
la letra

# Mm

**mac** NOUN
el impermeable

**macaroni** NOUN
los macarrones

**machine** NOUN
la máquina
◻ It's a complicated machine. Es una
máquina complicada.
▪ **I put my clothes in the machine.**
Puse mi ropa en la lavadora.

**machine gun** NOUN
la ametralladora

**machinery** NOUN
la maquinaria

**mackerel** NOUN
la caballa

**mad** ADJECTIVE
1 loco (FEM loca)
◻ You're mad! ¡Estás loco! ◻ Have you gone
mad? ¿Te has vuelto loco?
2 furioso (FEM furiosa)
◻ She'll be mad when she finds out. Se
pondrá furiosa cuando se entere.
▪ **He's mad about football.** Está loco por
el fútbol.
▪ **She's mad about horses.** Le encantan
los caballos.

**madam** NOUN
la señora
◻ How may I help you, Madam? ¿Qué desea
la señora?

**made** VERB ▷ see **make**

**madly** ADVERB
▪ **They're madly in love.** Están locamente
enamorados.

**madman** NOUN
el loco

**madness** NOUN
la locura
◻ It's absolute madness. Es una locura.

**magazine** NOUN
la revista

**magic** NOUN
▷ see also **magic** ADJECTIVE
la magia
◻ My hobby is magic. Mi hobby es la magia.

**magic** ADJECTIVE
▷ see also **magic** NOUN
mágico (FEM mágica)
◻ a magic wand una varita mágica
▪ **It was magic!** (brilliant) ¡Fue fantástico!

**magician** NOUN
el mago
la maga
◻ There was a magician at the party. Había
un mago en la fiesta.

**magnet** NOUN
el imán (PL los imanes)

**magnificent** ADJECTIVE
espléndido (FEM espléndida)
◻ a magnificent view una vista espléndida
▪ **It was a magnificent effort on their
part.** Fue un esfuerzo extraordinario por su
parte.

**magnifying glass** NOUN
la lupa

**maid** NOUN
1 la sirvienta (servant)
2 la camarera (in hotel)
▪ **an old maid** (spinster) una solterona

**maiden name** NOUN
el apellido de soltera

> **DID YOU KNOW...?**
> When women marry in Spain they
> don't usually take the name of their
> husband but keep their own instead.
> If the couple have children they take
> both their father's and mother's
> surnames.

**mail** NOUN
1 el correo
▪ **by mail** por correo
2 la correspondencia (letters)
◻ We receive a lot of mail. Recibimos
mucha correspondencia.

**mailbox** NOUN (US)
el buzón (PL los buzones)

**mailing list** NOUN
la lista de correo

**mailman** NOUN (US)
el cartero

**main** ADJECTIVE

principal (FEM principal)
□ the main suspect el principal sospechoso
■ **The main thing is to get it finished.** Lo principal es terminarlo.

**mainly** ADVERB
principalmente

**main road** NOUN
la carretera principal

to **maintain** VERB
mantener*
□ Teachers try hard to maintain standards. Los maestros se esfuerzan por mantener el nivel educativo. □ Old houses are expensive to maintain. Las casas viejas son costosas de mantener.

**maintenance** NOUN
1 el mantenimiento
□ car maintenance el mantenimiento del coche
2 la pensión alimenticia
□ £30 a week in maintenance 30 libras esterlinas a la semana en concepto de pensión alimenticia

**maize** NOUN
el maíz

**majesty** NOUN
la majestad
■ **Your Majesty** su Majestad

**major** ADJECTIVE
muy importante (FEM muy importante)
□ a major factor un factor muy importante
■ **Drugs are a major problem.** La droga es un grave problema.
■ **in C major** en do mayor

**Majorca** NOUN
Mallorca *fem*

**majority** NOUN
la mayoría

**make** NOUN
▷ *see also* **make** VERB
la marca
□ What make is it? ¿De qué marca es?

to **make** VERB
▷ *see also* **make** NOUN
1 hacer*
□ I'm going to make a cake. Voy a hacer un pastel. □ I'd like to make a phone call. Quisiera hacer una llamada. □ I make my bed every morning. Me hago la cama cada mañana. □ It's well made. Está bien hecho.
■ **She's making lunch.** Está preparando el almuerzo.
■ **Two and two make four.** Dos y dos son cuatro.
2 fabricar*
□ 'made in Spain' 'fabricado en España'
3 ganar
□ He makes a lot of money. Gana mucho

dinero.
■ **to make somebody do something** hacer a alguien hacer algo □ My mother makes me eat vegetables. Mi madre me hace comer verduras.
■ **You'll have to make do with a cheaper car.** Tendrás que conformarte con un coche más barato.
■ **What time do you make it?** ¿Qué hora tienes?

to **make out** VERB
1 descifrar
□ I can't make out the address on the label. No consigo descifrar la dirección que viene en la etiqueta.
2 dar* a entender
□ They're making out it was my fault. Están dando a entender que fue culpa mía.
■ **to make a cheque out to somebody** hacer un cheque a favor de alguien

to **make up** VERB
1 componer*
□ Women make up thirty per cent of the police force. Las mujeres componen el treinta por ciento del cuerpo de policía.
2 inventarse
□ He made up the whole story. Se inventó toda la historia.
3 hacer* las paces
□ They had a quarrel, but soon made up. Riñeron, pero poco después hicieron las paces.
4 maquillarse
□ She spends hours making herself up. Pasa horas maquillándose.

**maker** NOUN
el/la fabricante
□ Spain's biggest car maker el mayor fabricante de automóviles de España

**make-up** NOUN
el maquillaje
■ **She put on her make-up.** Se maquilló.

**male** ADJECTIVE
▷ *see also* **male** NOUN
1 macho *(animal, plant)*
□ a male kitten un gatito macho
2 varón (PL varones) *(person)*
□ Sex: Male Sexo: Varón
■ **Most football players are male.** La mayoría de los futbolistas son hombres.
■ **a male nurse** un enfermero
■ **a male chauvinist** un machista

**male** NOUN
▷ *see also* **male** ADJECTIVE
el macho *(animal)*

**mall** NOUN
el centro comercial

**mammoth** ADJECTIVE

**m**

colosal (FEMcolosal) *(project, building)*
■ **a mammoth task** una obra de titanes
**man** NOUN
el hombre
to **manage** VERB
1 arreglárselas
□ We haven't got much money, but we manage. No tenemos mucho dinero, pero nos las arreglamos.
2 dirigir*
□ She manages a big store. Dirige una tienda grande. □ He manages our football team. Dirige nuestro equipo de fútbol.
■ **to manage to do something** conseguir hacer algo □ Luckily I managed to pass the exam. Por suerte, conseguí aprobar el examen.
■ **Can you manage a bit more?** *(food)*
¿Te pongo un poco más?
■ **Can you manage with that suitcase?**
¿Puedes con la maleta?
**manageable** ADJECTIVE
factible (FEMfactible) *(task, goal)*
**management** NOUN
la dirección
□ He's responsible for the management of the project. Es responsable de la dirección del proyecto. □ management and workers la dirección y los trabajadores
**manager** NOUN
1 el director
la directora *(of company, department, performer)*
□ I complained to the manager. Fui a reclamar al director.
2 el/la gerente *(of restaurant, store)*
3 el entrenador
la entrenadora *(of team)*
□ the England manager el entrenador de la selección inglesa
**manageress** NOUN
la gerente *(of restaurant, store)*
**mandarin** NOUN
la mandarina
**mango** NOUN
el mango
**maniac** NOUN
el maníaco
la maníaca
■ **He drives like a maniac.** Conduce como un loco.
to **manipulate** VERB
manipular
**man-made** ADJECTIVE
sintético (FEMsintética) *(fibre)*
**manner** NOUN
la manera
□ She was behaving in an odd manner.

Se comportaba de una manera extraña.
■ **He has a confident manner.** Se muestra seguro de sí mismo.
**manners** PL NOUN
los modales
□ Her manners are appalling. Tiene muy malos modales.
■ **good manners** la buena educación
■ **It's bad manners to speak with your mouth full.** Es de mala educación hablar con la boca llena.
**manpower** NOUN
la mano de obra
LANGUAGE TIP Although **mano** ends in-o , **mano de obra** is actually a feminine noun.
**mansion** NOUN
la mansión (PLlas mansiones)
**mantelpiece** NOUN
la repisa de la chimenea
**manual** NOUN
el manual
to **manufacture** VERB
fabricar*
**manufacturer** NOUN
el/la fabricante
**manure** NOUN
el estiércol
**manuscript** NOUN
el manuscrito
**many** ADJECTIVE, PRONOUN
muchos (FEMmuchas)
□ He hasn't got many friends. No tiene muchos amigos. □ Were there many people at the concert? — Not many. ¿Había mucha gente en el concierto? — No mucha.
■ **very many** muchos (FEMmuchas)
□ I haven't got very many CDs. No tengo muchos CDs.
■ **how many?** ¿cuántos? (FEM¿cuántas?)
□ How many hours a week do you work?
¿Cuántas horas trabajas a la semana?
■ **too many** demasiados (FEMdemasiadas)
□ Sixteen people? That's too many.
¿Dieciséis personas? Son demasiadas.
■ **so many** tantos (FEMtantas)
□ He told so many lies! ¡Dijo tantas mentiras!
**map** NOUN
1 el mapa *(of country, region)*
LANGUAGE TIP Although **mapa** ends in-a , it is actually a masculine noun.
2 el plano *(of town, city)*
**marathon** NOUN
el maratón (PLlos maratones)
**marble** NOUN
el mármol

□ a marble statue una estatua de mármol
■ **a marble** una canica
**March** NOUN
marzo *masc*
□ in March en marzo □ on 9 March el 9 de marzo
to **march** VERB
▷ *see also* **march** NOUN
desfilar
□ The troops marched past the King. Las tropas desfilaron delante del Rey.
**march** NOUN
▷ *see also* **march** VERB
la marcha
□ a peace march una marcha por la paz
**mare** NOUN
la yegua
**margarine** NOUN
la margarina
**margin** NOUN
el margen (PLlos márgenes)
□ She wrote a note in the margin. Escribió una nota al margen.
**marijuana** NOUN
la marihuana
**marital status** NOUN
el estado civil
**mark** NOUN
▷ *see also* **mark** VERB
1 la nota
□ I get good marks for French. Saco buenas notas en francés.
2 la mancha
□ There were red marks all over his back. Tenía manchas rojas por toda la espalda.
□ You've got a mark on your shirt. Tienes una mancha en la camisa.
3 el marco *(former German currency)*
□ 30 million marks 30 millones de marcos
to **mark** VERB
▷ *see also* **mark** NOUN
1 corregir*
□ The teacher hasn't marked my homework yet. El maestro no me ha corregido los deberes todavía.
2 señalar
□ Mark its position on the map. Señala su posición en el mapa.
**market** NOUN
el mercado
**marketing** NOUN
el márketing
**marmalade** NOUN
la mermelada de naranja
**maroon** ADJECTIVE
granate (FEM + PLgranate)
**marriage** NOUN
el matrimonio

**married** ADJECTIVE
casado (FEMcasada)
□ They are not married. No están casados.
■ **a married couple** un matrimonio
■ **to get married** casarse
**marrow** NOUN
el calabacín grande (PLlos calabacines grandes) *(vegetable)*
■ **bone marrow** la médula
to **marry** VERB
1 casarse
□ They married in June. Se casaron en junio.
2 casarse con
□ He wants to marry her. Quiere casarse con ella.
■ **to get married** casarse □ My brother's getting married in March. Mi hermano se casa en marzo.
**marvellous** (US **marvelous**) ADJECTIVE
estupendo (FEMestupenda)
□ The weather was marvellous. Hacía un tiempo estupendo. □ That's a marvellous idea! ¡Es una idea estupenda!
**marzipan** NOUN
el mazapán
**mascara** NOUN
el rímel
**masculine** ADJECTIVE
masculino (FEMmasculina)
**mashed potatoes** PL NOUN
el puré de patatas (el puré de papas *Latin America*)
**mask** NOUN
la máscara
**masked** ADJECTIVE
encapuchado (FEMencapuchada) *(terrorist, attacker)*
**mass** NOUN
1 el montón (PLlos montones)
□ a mass of books and papers un montón de libros y papeles
2 la misa
□ We go to mass on Sunday. Vamos a misa los domingos.
■ **the mass media** los medios de comunicación de masas
**massage** NOUN
el masaje
**massive** ADJECTIVE
enorme (FEMenorme)
to **master** VERB
▷ *see also* **master** NOUN
dominar
□ Students need to master a second language. Los estudiantes tienen que dominar un segundo idioma.
**masterpiece** NOUN
la obra maestra (PLlas obras maestras)

## mat - me

**mat** NOUN
el felpudo (*doormat*)
■ **a table mat** un mantel individual

**match** NOUN
▷ *see also* **match** VERB
1 el partido
□ a football match un partido de fútbol
2 la cerilla
□ a box of matches una caja de cerillas

to **match** VERB
▷ *see also* **match** NOUN
1 hacer\* juego con
□ The jacket matches the trousers. La chaqueta hace juego con los pantalones.
2 hacer\* juego
□ These colours don't match. Estos colores no hacen juego.

**matching** ADJECTIVE
a juego
□ My bedroom has matching wallpaper and curtains. Mi habitación tiene el papel y las cortinas a juego.

**mate** NOUN
el amigo
la amiga
□ He always goes on holiday with his mates. Siempre va de vacaciones con sus amigos.

**material** NOUN
1 el tejido
□ The curtains are made of a thin material. Las cortinas están hechas de un tejido fino.
2 el material
□ I'm collecting material for my project. Estoy recogiendo material para mi proyecto.

**mathematics** NOUN
las matemáticas

**maths** NOUN
las matemáticas

**matron** NOUN
la enfermera jefe (*in hospital*)

**matter** NOUN
▷ *see also* **matter** VERB
el asunto
□ It's a matter of life and death. Es un asunto de vida o muerte.
■ **What's the matter?** ¿Qué pasa?
■ **as a matter of fact** de hecho

to **matter** VERB
▷ *see also* **matter** NOUN
importar
□ I can't give you the money today. — It doesn't matter. No te puedo dar el dinero hoy. — No importa.
■ **Shall I phone today or tomorrow? — Whenever, it doesn't matter.** ¿Telefoneo hoy o mañana? — Cuando quieras, da igual.
■ **It matters a lot to me.** Significa mucho para mí.

**mattress** NOUN
el colchón (PL los colchones)

**mature** ADJECTIVE
maduro (FEM madura)

**maximum** NOUN
▷ *see also* **maximum** ADJECTIVE
el máximo
□ a maximum of two years in prison un máximo de dos años de cárcel

**maximum** ADJECTIVE
▷ *see also* **maximum** NOUN
máximo (FEM máxima)
□ The maximum speed is 100 km/h. La velocidad máxima permitida es 100km/h.

**May** NOUN
mayo *masc*
□ in May en mayo □ on 7 May el 7 de mayo
■ **May Day** el Primero de Mayo

**may** VERB
poder\*
□ The police may come and catch us here. La policía puede venir y pillarnos aquí.
□ May I smoke? ¿Puedo fumar?

   **LANGUAGE TIP** **Puede que** has to be followed by a verb in the subjunctive.

□ I may go. Puede que vaya. □ It may rain. Puede que llueva.

   **LANGUAGE TIP** **A lo mejor** can also be used but it is a more colloquial alternative.

□ Are you going to the party? — I don't know, I may. ¿Vas a ir a la fiesta? — No sé, a lo mejor.

**maybe** ADVERB
a lo mejor
□ Maybe she's at home. A lo mejor está en casa. □ Maybe he'll change his mind. A lo mejor cambia de idea.

**mayonnaise** NOUN
la mayonesa

**mayor** NOUN
el alcalde
la alcaldesa

**maze** NOUN
el laberinto

**me** PRONOUN

   **LANGUAGE TIP** Use **me** to translate 'me' when it is the direct object of the verb in the sentence, or when it means 'to me'.

me
□ Look at me! ¡Mírame! □ Could you lend me your pen? ¿Me prestas tu bolígrafo?

   **LANGUAGE TIP** Use **yo** after the verb 'to be' and in comparisons.

□ It's me. Soy yo. □ He's older than me. Es mayor que yo.

○ **LANGUAGE TIP** Use **mí** after prepositions.
□ without me sin mí

○ **LANGUAGE TIP** Remember that 'with me' translates as **conmigo**.
□ He was with me. Estaba conmigo.

**meal** NOUN
la comida
■ **Enjoy your meal!** ¡Que aproveche!

**mealtime** NOUN
■ **at mealtimes** a las horas de comer

to **mean** VERB
▷ see also **mean** ADJECTIVE
1 significar*
□ What does 'alcalde' mean? ¿Qué significa 'alcalde'? □ I don't know what it means. No sé lo que significa.
2 querer* decir
□ That's not what I meant. Eso no es lo que quería decir.
3 referirse* a
□ Which one did he mean? ¿A cuál se refería? □ Do you mean me? ¿Te refieres a mí?
■ **to mean to do something** querer hacer algo □ I didn't mean to hurt you. No quería hacerte daño.
■ **Do you really mean it?** ¿Lo dices en serio?
■ **He means what he says.** Habla en serio.

**mean** ADJECTIVE
▷ see also **mean** VERB
1 tacaño (FEM tacaña)
□ He's too mean to buy presents. Es demasiado tacaño para comprar regalos.
2 mezquino (FEM mezquina)
□ You're being mean to me. Estás siendo mezquino conmigo.
■ **That's a really mean thing to say!** ¡Parece mentira que digas eso!

**meaning** NOUN
el significado

**means** NOUN
el medio
□ a means of transport un medio de transporte □ He'll do it by any possible means. Lo hará por todos los medios.
■ **by means of** por medio de □ They identified him by means of a photograph. Lo identificaron por medio de una clave.
■ **Can I come in? — By all means!** ¿Puedo entrar? — ¡Claro que sí!

**meant** VERB ▷ see **mean**

**meanwhile** ADVERB
mientras tanto

**measles** NOUN
el sarampión
□ I've got measles. Tengo el sarampión.

to **measure** VERB
medir*

**meat** NOUN
la carne

**Mecca** NOUN
La Meca

**mechanic** NOUN
el mecánico
la mecánica
□ He's a mechanic. Es mecánico.

**mechanical** ADJECTIVE
mecánico (FEM mecánica)

**medal** NOUN
la medalla

**media** PL NOUN
■ **the media** los medios de comunicación

**median strip** NOUN (US)
la mediana

**medical** ADJECTIVE
▷ see also **medical** NOUN
médico (FEM médica)
□ medical treatment el tratamiento médico
■ **medical insurance** el seguro médico
■ **to have medical problems** tener problemas de salud
■ **She's a medical student.** Es una estudiante de medicina.

**medical** NOUN
▷ see also **medical** ADJECTIVE
■ **He had a medical last week.** Se hizo un chequeo la semana pasada.

**medicine** NOUN
1 la medicina (science)
□ I want to study medicine. Quiero estudiar medicina.
■ **alternative medicine** la medicina alternativa
2 el medicamento (medication)
□ I need some medicine. Necesito un medicamento.

**Mediterranean** NOUN
▷ see also **Mediterranean** ADJECTIVE
■ **the Mediterranean** el Mediterráneo

**medium** ADJECTIVE
mediano (FEM mediana)
□ a man of medium height un hombre de estatura mediana

**medium-sized** ADJECTIVE
■ **a medium-sized town** una ciudad de tamaño mediano

to **meet** VERB
1 encontrarse* con (by chance)
□ I met Paul in town. Me encontré con Paul en el centro.
■ **We met by chance in the supermarket.** Nos encontramos por casualidad en el supermercado.
2 reunirse* (by arrangement)

**m**

153

□ The committee met at two o'clock. El comité se reunió a las dos.

■ **Where shall we meet?** ¿Dónde quedamos?

■ **I'm going to meet my friends at the swimming pool.** He quedado con mis amigos en la piscina.

■ **I'll meet you at the station.** Te voy a buscar a la estación.

3 conocer* *(get to know)*

□ He met Tim at a party. Conoció a Tim en una fiesta.

■ **Have you met her before?** ¿La conoces?

**meeting** NOUN

1 el encuentro *(socially)*

□ their first meeting su primer encuentro

2 la reunión (PLlas reuniones ) *(for work)*

□ a business meeting una reunión de trabajo

**mega** ADJECTIVE

■ **He's mega rich.** *(informal)* Es super rico.

**melody** NOUN
la melodía

**melon** NOUN
el melón (PLlos melones )

to **melt** VERB

1 derretir*

□ Melt 100 grams of butter in a saucepan. Derrita 100 gramos de mantequilla en una sartén.

2 derretirse*

□ The snow is melting. La nieve se está derritiendo.

**member** NOUN
el/la miembro

■ **'members only'** 'reservado para los socios'

■ **a Member of Parliament** un diputado (FEMuna diputada )

**membership** NOUN
la afiliación (PLlas afiliaciones ) *(of party, union)*

■ **I'm going to apply for membership of the club.** Voy a solicitar el ingreso al club.

**membership card** NOUN
el carnet de socio (PLlos carnets de socio )

**memento** NOUN
el recuerdo

**memorial** NOUN
memorial

to **memorize** VERB
memorizar*

**memory** NOUN

1 la memoria *(also for computer)*

□ I've got a terrible memory. Tengo una memoria espantosa.

2 el recuerdo

□ happy memories los recuerdos felices

**men** PL NOUN ▷see **man**

to **mend** VERB
arreglar

**meningitis** NOUN
la meningitis

□ Her daughter's got meningitis. Su hija tiene meningitis.

**mental** ADJECTIVE
mental (FEMmental )

□ mental illness la enfermedad mental

■ **mental hospital** el hospital psiquiátrico

to **mention** VERB
mencionar

□ He didn't mention it to me. No me lo mencionó.

■ **I mentioned she might come later.** Dije que a lo mejor vendría más tarde.

■ **Thank you! — Don't mention it!** ¡Gracias! — ¡No hay de qué!

**menu** NOUN

1 la carta

□ Could I have the menu please? ¿Me trae la carta por favor?

2 el menú (PLlos menús ) *(on computer)*

**merchant** NOUN
el/la comerciante

■ **a wine merchant** un vinatero

**mercy** NOUN
la compasión

**mere** ADJECTIVE

■ **a mere five percent** sólo un cinco por ciento

■ **It's a mere formality.** No es más que una formalidad.

**meringue** NOUN
el merengue

**merry** ADJECTIVE

■ **Merry Christmas!** ¡Feliz Navidad!

**merry-go-round** NOUN
el tiovivo

**mess** NOUN
el desorden

■ **My hair's a mess today.** Hoy tengo el pelo hecho un desastre.

■ **I'll be in a mess if I fail the exam.** Voy a tener problemas si suspendo el examen.

to **mess about** VERB

■ **Yesterday I just messed about with some friends.** Ayer estuve sin hacer nada con unos amigos.

■ **Stop messing about with my computer!** ¡Deja de toquetear mi ordenador!

**message** NOUN
el mensaje

□ a secret message un mensaje secreto

■ **Would you like to leave him a message?** ¿Quiere dejarle un recado?

to **mess up** VERB

estropear

□ You've messed up my CDs! ¡Me has estropeado los CDs!

■ **I messed up my chemistry exam.** Metí la pata en el examen de química.

**messenger** NOUN
el mensajero
la mensajera

**messy** ADJECTIVE
desordenado (FEM desordenada)

□ Your room is really messy. Tu habitación está muy desordenada. □ She's so messy! ¡Es más desordenada!

■ **a really messy job** un trabajo muy sucio

■ **Her writing is very messy.** Tiene muy mala letra.

**met** VERB ▷ see **meet**

**metal** NOUN
el metal

**meter** NOUN
1 el contador (for gas, electricity)
2 el taxímetro (for taxi)
3 el parquímetro (parking meter)
4 el metro (US: unit of measurement)

**method** NOUN
el método

**Methodist** NOUN
el/la metodista

□ He's a Methodist. Es metodista.

**metre** (US **meter**) NOUN
el metro

**metric** ADJECTIVE
métrico (FEM métrica)

**Mexico** NOUN
Méjico masc

to **miaow** VERB
maullar*

**mice** PL NOUN ▷ see **mouse**

**microchip** NOUN
el microchip (PL los microchips)

**microphone** NOUN
el micrófono

**microscope** NOUN
el microscopio

**mid** ADJECTIVE
■ **in mid May** a mediados de mayo

■ **He's in his mid twenties.** Tiene unos veinticinco años.

**midday** NOUN
el mediodía

□ at midday al mediodía

**middle** ADJECTIVE
▷ see also **middle** NOUN
del medio

□ the middle seat el asiento del medio

**middle-aged** ADJECTIVE
de mediana edad

**Middle Ages** PL NOUN

■ **the Middle Ages** la Edad Media

**middle-class** ADJECTIVE
de clase media

**Middle East** NOUN
■ **the Middle East** el Oriente Medio

**middle name** NOUN
el segundo nombre

**midge** NOUN
el mosquito

**midnight** NOUN
la medianoche

□ at midnight a medianoche

**midwife** NOUN
la comadrona

□ She's a midwife. Es comadrona.

**might** VERB
poder*

□ The teacher might come at any moment. El profesor podría venir en cualquier momento.

> **LANGUAGE TIP** **Puede que** has to be followed by a verb in the subjunctive.

□ He might come later. Puede que venga más tarde. □ She might not have understood. Puede que no haya entendido.

> **LANGUAGE TIP** **A lo mejor** can also be used but it is a more colloquial alternative.

□ We might go to Spain next year. A lo mejor vamos a España el año que viene.

**migraine** NOUN
la jaqueca

□ I've got a migraine. Tengo jaqueca.

**mike** NOUN
el micro

**mild** ADJECTIVE
suave (FEM suave)

□ a mild flavour un sabor suave □ The winters are quite mild. Los inviernos son bastante suaves. □ mild soap el jabón suave

**mile** NOUN
la milla

> **DID YOU KNOW...?**
> In Spain distances are expressed in kilometres. A mile is about 1.6 kilometres.

□ It's five miles from here. Está a unas cinco millas de aquí. □ at 50 miles per hour a 50 millas por hora

■ **We walked for miles!** ¡Caminamos kilómetros y kilómetros!

**military** ADJECTIVE
militar (FEM militara)

**milk** NOUN
▷ see also **milk** VERB
la leche

to **milk** VERB

155

▷ *see also* **milk** NOUN
ordeñar

**milk chocolate** NOUN
el chocolate con leche

**milkman** NOUN
el lechero

> **DID YOU KNOW...?**
> In Spain milk is not delivered to
> people's homes.

**milk shake** NOUN
el batido

**mill** NOUN
el molino *(for grain)*

**millennium** NOUN
el milenio

**millimetre** (US **millimeter**) NOUN
el milímetro

**million** NOUN
el millón  (PL los millones)
□ two million pounds dos millones de libras esterlinas

**millionaire** NOUN
el millonario
la millonaria

to **mimic** VERB
imitar

**mince** NOUN
la carne picada  (la carne molida *Latin America*)

**mince pie** NOUN
la empanadilla rellena de fruta picada

to **mind** VERB
▷ *see also* **mind** NOUN
1 cuidar *(look after)*
□ Could you mind the baby this afternoon? ¿Podrías cuidar al niño esta tarde? □ Could you mind my bags for a few minutes? ¿Me cuidas las bolsas un momento?
2 importar *(matter)*
□ Do you mind if I open the window? — No, I don't mind. ¿Le importa que abra la ventana? — No, no me importa.
■ **I don't mind the noise.** No me molesta el ruido.
■ **Never mind! 1** *(don't worry)* ¡No te preocupes! **2** *(it's not important)* ¡No importa!
■ **Mind you don't fall.** Ten cuidado, no te vayas a caer.
■ **Mind the step!** ¡Cuidado con el escalón!

**mind** NOUN
▷ *see also* **mind** VERB
la mente
□ What have you got in mind? ¿Qué tienes en mente?
■ **I haven't made up my mind yet.** No me he decidido todavía.
■ **He's changed his mind.** Ha cambiado de idea.

■ **Are you out of your mind?** ¿Estás loco?

**mine** PRONOUN
▷ *see also* **mine** NOUN
1 el mío *masc* (PL los míos)
□ Is this your coat? — No, mine is black. ¿Es éste tu abrigo? — No, el mío es negro.
□ your parents and mine tus padres y los míos
2 la mía *fem* (PL las mías)
□ Is this your scarf? — No, mine is red. ¿Es ésta tu bufanda? — No, la mía es roja.
□ her sisters and mine sus hermanas y las mías
3 mío *masc* (PL míos)
□ That car is mine. Ese coche es mío.
4 mía *fem* (PL mías)
□ Sorry, that beer is mine. Disculpa, esa cerveza es mía. □ Isabel is a friend of mine. Isabel es amiga mía.

**mine** NOUN
▷ *see also* **mine** PRONOUN
la mina
□ a coal mine una mina de carbón □ a land mine una mina

**miner** NOUN
el minero
la minera
□ My father was a miner. Mi padre era minero.

**mineral water** NOUN
el agua mineral *fem*

> **LANGUAGE TIP** Although it's a feminine noun, remember that you use **el** and **un** with **agua mineral**.

**miniature** ADJECTIVE
en miniatura

**minibus** NOUN
el microbús (PL los microbuses)

**minicab** NOUN
el taxi

**Minidisc®** NOUN
el minidisco

**minimum** NOUN
▷ *see also* **minimum** ADJECTIVE
el mínimo

**minimum** ADJECTIVE
▷ *see also* **minimum** NOUN
mínimo (FEM mínima)
□ The minimum age for driving is 17. La edad mínima para poder conducir es 17 años. □ minimum wage salario mínimo

**miniskirt** NOUN
la minifalda

**minister** NOUN
1 el ministro
la ministra
□ the Minister for Education el Ministro de Educación

**2** el pastor
la pastora *(of church)*
**ministry** NOUN
el ministerio *(in politics)*
**minor** ADJECTIVE
secundario (FEMsecundaria)
□ a minor problem un problema secundario
■ **a minor operation** una operación de
poca importancia
■ **in D minor** en re menor
**minority** NOUN
la minoría
**mint** NOUN
**1** el caramelo de menta *(sweet)*
**2** la menta *(plant)*
□ mint sauce salsa de menta
**minus** PREPOSITION
menos
□ sixteen minus three dieciséis menos tres
■ **I got a B minus for my French.** Me
pusieron un notable bajo en francés.
■ **minus two degrees** dos grados bajo cero
**minute** NOUN
▷ see also **minute** ADJECTIVE
el minuto
□ Wait a minute! ¡Espera un minuto!
**minute** ADJECTIVE
▷ see also **minute** NOUN
minúsculo (FEMminúscula)
□ Her flat is minute. Su apartamento es
minúsculo.
**miracle** NOUN
el milagro
**mirror** NOUN
**1** el espejo
□ She looked at herself in the mirror. Se miró
en el espejo.
**2** el retrovisor
□ She got in the car and adjusted the mirror.
Entró en el coche y ajustó el retrovisor.
to **misbehave** VERB
portarse mal
**mischief** NOUN
■ **She's always up to mischief.** Siempre
está haciendo travesuras.
■ **full of mischief** travieso
**mischievous** ADJECTIVE
travieso (FEMtraviesa)
**miser** NOUN
el avaro
la avara
**miserable** ADJECTIVE
infeliz (FEMinfeliz, PLinfelices)
□ a miserable life una vida infeliz
■ **I'm feeling miserable.** Me siento
deprimido.
■ **miserable weather** un tiempo deprimente
**misfortune** NOUN

la desgracia
**mishap** NOUN
el contratiempo
□ without mishap sin contratiempos
to **misjudge** VERB
juzgar* mal
□ I may have misjudged him. A lo mejor lo
juzgué mal.
■ **The driver misjudged the bend.** El
conductor no calculó bien la curva.
to **mislay** VERB
■ **I've mislaid my glasses.** No sé dónde he
puesto las gafas.
**misleading** ADJECTIVE
engañoso (FEMengañosa)
**Miss** NOUN
**1** señorita *fem*
□ Miss Peters wants to see you. La señorita
Peters quiere verte.
**2** Srta. *(in address)*
to **miss** VERB
perder*
□ Hurry or you'll miss the bus. Date prisa o
perderás el autobús.
■ **It's too good an opportunity to miss.**
Es una oportunidad demasiado buena para
dejarla pasar.
■ **He missed the target.** No dio en el blanco.
■ **I miss my family.** Echo de menos a mi
familia.
■ **You've missed a page.** Te has saltado
una página.
**missing** ADJECTIVE
perdido (FEMperdida)
□ the missing link el eslabón perdido
■ **to be missing** faltar □ Two members of
the group are missing. Faltan dos miembros
del grupo.
■ **a missing person** una persona
desaparecida
**missionary** NOUN
el misionero
la misionera
**mist** NOUN
la neblina
**mistake** NOUN
▷ see also **mistake** VERB
el error
□ There must be some mistake. Debe de
haber algún error.
■ **a spelling mistake** una falta de ortografía
■ **to make a mistake 1** *(in speaking)*
cometer un error □ He makes a lot of
mistakes when he speaks English. Comete
muchos errores cuando habla inglés. **2** *(get
mixed up)* equivocarse □ I'm sorry, I made a
mistake. Lo siento, me equivoqué.
■ **by mistake** por error

**m**

157

to **mistake** VERB
▷ *see also* **mistake** NOUN
confundir
□ He mistook me for my sister. Me confundió con mi hermana.

**mistaken** ADJECTIVE
■ **to be mistaken** estar equivocado □ If you think I'm going to pay, you're mistaken. Estás equivocado si piensas que voy a pagar.

**mistletoe** NOUN
el muérdago

**mistook** VERB ▷ *see* **mistake**

**mistress** NOUN
1 la maestra (*in primary school*)
2 la profesora (*in secondary school*)
□ our English mistress nuestra profesora de inglés
3 la amante
□ He's got a mistress. Tiene una amante.

**misty** ADJECTIVE
neblinoso (FEM neblinosa)
□ a misty morning una mañana neblinosa

to **misunderstand** VERB
entender* mal
□ Sorry, I misunderstood you. Lo siento, te entendí mal.

**misunderstanding** NOUN
el malentendido

**misunderstood** VERB ▷ *see* **misunderstand**

**mix** NOUN
▷ *see also* **mix** VERB
la mezcla
□ The film is a mix of science fiction and comedy. La película es una mezcla de ciencia ficción y comedia.
■ **a cake mix** un preparado para pastel

to **mix** VERB
▷ *see also* **mix** NOUN
mezclar
□ Mix the flour with the sugar. Mezcle la harina con el azúcar. □ He's mixing business with pleasure. Está mezclando los negocios con el placer.
■ **I like mixing with all sorts of people.** Me gusta tratar con todo tipo de gente.
■ **He doesn't mix much.** No se relaciona mucho.

to **mix up** VERB
confundir
□ He mixed up their names. Confundió sus nombres. □ The travel agent mixed up the bookings. La agencia de viajes confundió las reservas.
■ **I'm getting mixed up.** Me estoy confundiendo.

**mixed** ADJECTIVE
mixto (FEM mixta)

□ a mixed salad una ensalada mixta □ a mixed school un colegio mixto
■ **I've got mixed feelings about it.** No sé qué pensar de ello.

**mixer** NOUN
la batidora (*for food*)

**mixture** NOUN
la mezcla
□ a mixture of spices una mezcla de especias

**mix-up** NOUN
la confusión (PL las confusiones)

**MMS** ABBREVIATION (= *multimedia message service*)
el MMS

to **moan** VERB
quejarse
□ She's always moaning about something. Siempre se está quejando de algo.

**mobile** NOUN
el móvil (*phone*)

**mobile home** NOUN
la caravana fija (el trailer *Latin America*)

**mobile phone** NOUN
el móvil

to **mock** VERB
▷ *see also* **mock** ADJECTIVE
ridiculizar*

**mock** ADJECTIVE
▷ *see also* **mock** VERB
■ **a mock exam** un examen de práctica

**mod cons** PL NOUN
■ **with all mod cons** con todas las comodidades

**model** NOUN
▷ *see also* **model** ADJECTIVE
1 el modelo
□ His car is the latest model. Su coche es el último modelo.
2 la maqueta
□ a model of the castle una maqueta del castillo
3 el/la modelo
□ She's a famous model. Es una modelo famosa.

**model** ADJECTIVE
▷ *see also* **model** NOUN
■ **a model railway** una vía férrea en miniatura
■ **a model plane** una maqueta de avión
■ **He's a model pupil.** Es un alumno modelo.

**modem** NOUN
el módem (PL los módems)

**moderate** ADJECTIVE
moderado (FEM moderada)
□ His views are quite moderate. Tiene opiniones bastante moderadas.
■ **I do a moderate amount of exercise.** Hago un poco de gimnasia.

**modern** ADJECTIVE
moderno (FEMmoderna)

to **modernize** VERB
modernizar*

**modest** ADJECTIVE
modesto (FEMmodesta)

to **modify** VERB
modificar*

**moist** ADJECTIVE
húmedo (FEMhúmeda)
□ Sow the seeds in moist compost. Plantar las semillas en abono húmedo.

**moisture** NOUN
la humedad

**moisturizer** NOUN
la crema hidratante

**moldy** ADJECTIVE (US)
mohoso (FEMmohosa)

**mole** NOUN
1 el lunar
□ I've got a mole on my back. Tengo un lunar en la espalda.
2 el topo (animal)

**moment** NOUN
el momento
□ Just a moment! ¡Un momento! □ at the moment en este momento □ any moment now de un momento a otro

**monarch** NOUN
el/la monarca

**monarchy** NOUN
la monarquía

**monastery** NOUN
el monasterio

**Monday** NOUN
el lunes (PLlos lunes)
□ I saw her on Monday. La vi el lunes.
□ every Monday todos los lunes □ last Monday el lunes pasado □ next Monday el lunes que viene □ on Mondays los lunes

**money** NOUN
el dinero
□ I need to change some money. Tengo que cambiar dinero. □ to make money ganar dinero

**mongrel** NOUN
el perro mestizo
■ My dog's a mongrel. Mi perro es mestizo.

**monitor** NOUN
el monitor (on computer)

**monk** NOUN
el monje

**monkey** NOUN
el mono
la mona

**monster** NOUN
el monstruo

**month** NOUN
el mes
□ this month este mes □ next month el mes que viene □ last month el mes pasado □ at the end of the month a fin de mes

**monthly** ADJECTIVE
mensual (FEMmensual)

**monument** NOUN
el monumento

**mood** NOUN
el humor
□ to be in a good mood estar de buen humor □ to be in a bad mood estar de mal humor

**moody** ADJECTIVE
malhumorado (FEMmalhumorada) (in a bad mood)
■ to be moody (temperamental) tener un humor cambiante

**moon** NOUN
la luna
□ There's a full moon tonight. Esta noche hay luna llena.
■ She's over the moon about it. Está en el séptimo cielo de contenta.

**moor** NOUN
▷ see also **moor** VERB
el páramo

to **moor** VERB
▷ see also **moor** NOUN
amarrar

**mop** NOUN
la fregona (el trapeador Latin America)

**moped** NOUN
el ciclomotor

**moral** NOUN
la moraleja
□ The moral of the story is… La moraleja de la historia es…
■ morals la moral

**morale** NOUN
la moral
□ Morale was at an all-time low. La moral estaba más baja que nunca.

**more** ADJECTIVE, PRONOUN, ADVERB
más
□ It costs a lot more. Cuesta mucho más.
□ There isn't any more. Ya no hay más.
□ A bit more? ¿Un poco más? □ Is there any more? ¿Hay más? □ It'll take a few more days. Llevará unos cuantos días más.
■ more than más que

LANGUAGE TIP Use más que when comparing two things or people and más de when talking about quantities.

□ He's more intelligent than me. Es más inteligente que yo. □ I spent more than £10.

Yo gasté más de 10 libras esterlinas.
□ **more than 20 people** más de 20 personas
■ **more or less** más o menos
■ **more than ever** más que nunca
■ **more and more** cada vez más
**moreover** ADVERB
además
**morning** NOUN
la mañana
□ **in the morning** por la mañana □ **at 7 o'clock in the morning** a las 7 de la mañana □ **on Saturday morning** el sábado por la mañana □ **tomorrow morning** mañana por la mañana
■ **the morning papers** los periódicos de la mañana
**Morocco** NOUN
Marruecos *masc*
**Moscow** NOUN
Moscú *masc*
**Moslem** NOUN
el musulmán (PL los musulmanes)
la musulmana
□ **He's a Moslem.** Es musulmán.
**mosque** NOUN
la mezquita
**mosquito** NOUN
el mosquito
■ **a mosquito bite** una picadura de mosquito
**most** ADJECTIVE, PRONOUN, ADVERB
más
□ **the thing she feared most** lo que más temía □ **He's the one who talks the most.** Es el que más habla. □ **the most expensive restaurant** el restaurante más caro
■ **most of** la mayor parte de □ **most of the time** la mayor parte del tiempo □ **I did most of the work alone.** Hice la mayor parte del trabajo solo.
■ **most of them** la mayoría □ **Most of them have cars.** La mayoría tienen coches.
□ **Most people go out on Friday nights.** La mayoría de la gente sale los viernes por la noche.
■ **He won the most votes.** Fue el que sacó más votos.
■ **at the most** como mucho □ **two hours at the most** dos horas como mucho
■ **to make the most of something** aprovechar algo al máximo □ **He made the most of his holiday.** Aprovechó sus vacaciones al máximo.
**mostly** ADVERB
■ **The teachers are mostly quite nice.** La mayoría de los profesores son bastante simpáticos.
**MOT** NOUN

la ITV
□ **My car has failed its MOT.** El coche no me ha pasado la ITV.
**motel** NOUN
el motel
**moth** NOUN
**1** la mariposa nocturna
**2** la polilla *(clothes moth)*
**mother** NOUN
la madre
■ **my mother and father** mis padres
■ **mother tongue** la lengua materna
**mother-in-law** NOUN
la suegra
**Mother's Day** NOUN
el Día de la Madre
**motionless** ADJECTIVE
inmóvil (FEM inmóvil)
**motivated** ADJECTIVE
■ **He is highly motivated.** Está muy motivado.
**motivation** NOUN
la motivación (PL las motivaciones)
**motive** NOUN
**1** el motivo
□ **the motive for the killing** el motivo del homicidio
**2** la intención (PL las intenciones)
□ **for the best of motives** con la mejor de las intenciones
**motor** NOUN
el motor
**motorbike** NOUN
la moto
**LANGUAGE TIP** Although **moto** ends in **-o**, it is actually a feminine noun.
**motorboat** NOUN
la lancha motora
**motorcycle** NOUN
la motocicleta
**motorcyclist** NOUN
el/la motociclista
**motorist** NOUN
el conductor
la conductora
**motor mechanic** NOUN
el mecánico
la mecánica
**motor racing** NOUN
las carreras de coches
**motorway** NOUN
la autopista
□ **I had an accident on the motorway.** Tuve un accidente en la autopista.
**mouldy** ADJECTIVE
mohoso (FEM mohosa)
**mountain** NOUN
la montaña

◻ in the mountains en la montaña
■ **a mountain bike** una bicicleta de
montaña
**mountaineer** NOUN
el/la alpinista
**mountaineering** NOUN
el alpinismo
◻ I go mountaineering. Hago alpinismo.
**mountainous** ADJECTIVE
montañoso (FEM montañosa)
**mouse** NOUN
el ratón (PL los ratones) (also for computer)
**mouse mat** NOUN
la alfombrilla del ratón
**mousse** NOUN
1 la mousse
◻ chocolate mousse la mousse de
chocolate
2 la espuma (for hair)
**moustache** NOUN
el bigote
◻ He's got a moustache. Tiene bigote.
**mouth** NOUN
la boca
**mouthful** NOUN
1 el bocado (of food)
2 el trago (of drink)
**mouth organ** NOUN
la armónica
**mouthwash** NOUN
el elixir bucal
**move** NOUN
▷ see also **move** VERB
1 el paso
◻ That was a good move! ¡Ese fue un paso
bien dado!
■ **It's your move.** Te toca jugar.
2 la mudanza
◻ our move from Oxford to Luton nuestra
mudanza de Oxford a Luton
■ **Get a move on!** ¡Date prisa!
to **move** VERB
▷ see also **move** NOUN
1 moverse*
◻ Don't move! ¡No te muevas!
2 mover*
◻ He can't move his arm. No puede mover
el brazo.
■ **Could you move your stuff please?**
¿Podrías quitar tus cosas de aquí, por favor?
3 avanzar*
◻ The car was moving very slowly. El coche
avanzaba muy lentamente.
4 conmover*
◻ I was very moved by the film. La película
me conmovió mucho.
■ **to move house** mudarse de casa ◻ We're
moving in July. Nos mudamos en julio.

to **move in** VERB
■ **When are the new tenants moving in?**
¿Cuándo vienen los nuevos inquilinos?
to **move over** VERB
correrse
◻ Could you move over a bit, please? ¿Te
podrías correr un poco, por favor?
**movement** NOUN
el movimiento
**movie** NOUN
la película
■ **the movies** el cine
**moving** ADJECTIVE
1 en movimiento
◻ a moving bus un autobús en movimiento
2 conmovedor (FEM conmovedora)
◻ a moving story una historia conmovedora
to **mow** VERB
cortar
◻ I sometimes mow the lawn. A veces corto
el césped.
**mower** NOUN
el cortacésped
**mown** VERB ▷ see **mow**
**MP** ABBREVIATION
el diputado
la diputada
**MP3 player** NOUN
el reproductor de MP3
**Mr** ABBREVIATION
1 señor masc
◻ Mr Jones wants to see you. El señor Jones
quiere verte.
2 Sr. (in address)
**Mrs** ABBREVIATION
1 señora fem
◻ Mrs Philips wants to see you. La señora
Philips quiere verte.
2 Sra. (in address)
**Ms** ABBREVIATION
1 señora fem
◻ Ms Brown wants to see you. La señora
Brown quiere verte.
2 Sra. (in address)

**DID YOU KNOW...?**
There isn't a direct equivalent of Ms in
Spanish. If you are writing to a woman
and don't know whether she is
married, use **Señora**.

**much** ADJECTIVE, PRONOUN, ADVERB
mucho (FEM mucha)
◻ I feel much better now. Ahora me siento
mucho mejor. ◻ I haven't got much money.
No tengo mucho dinero. ◻ Have you got a
lot of luggage? — No, not much. ¿Tienes
mucho equipaje? — No, no mucho.
■ **very much** mucho ◻ I enjoyed myself
very much. Me divertí mucho.

■ **Thank you very much.** Muchas gracias.
■ **how much?** ¿cuánto? □ How much time have you got? ¿Cuánto tiempo tienes?
□ How much is it? ¿Cuánto es?
■ **too much** demasiado □ That's too much! ¡Eso es demasiado! □ They give us too much homework. Nos ponen demasiados deberes.
■ **so much** tanto □ I didn't think it would cost so much. No pensé que costaría tanto.
□ I've never seen so much rain. Nunca había visto tanta lluvia.
■ **What's on TV? — Not much.** ¿Qué ponen en la tele? — Nada especial.

**mud** NOUN
el barro

**muddle** NOUN
■ **to be in a muddle** estar todo revuelto
□ The photos are in a muddle. Las fotos están todas revueltas.

to **muddle up** VERB
confundir
□ He muddles me up with my sister. Me confunde con mi hermana.
■ **to get muddled up** hacerse un lío
*(informal)* □ I'm getting muddled up. Me estoy haciendo un lío.

**muddy** ADJECTIVE
lleno de barro (FEMllena de barro)

**muesli** NOUN
el muesli

**muffler** NOUN (US)
el silenciador

**mug** NOUN
▷ *see also* **mug** VERB
la taza alta
□ Do you want a cup or a mug? ¿Quieres una taza normal o una taza alta?
■ **a beer mug** una jarra de cerveza

to **mug** VERB
▷ *see also* **mug** NOUN
atracar*
□ He was mugged in the city centre. Lo atracaron en el centro de la ciudad.

**mugger** NOUN
el atracador
la atracadora

**mugging** NOUN
el atraco

**muggy** ADJECTIVE
■ **It's muggy today.** Hoy hace bochorno.

**multiple choice test** NOUN
el examen tipo test

**multiple sclerosis** NOUN
la esclerosis múltiple
□ She's got multiple sclerosis. Tiene esclerosis múltiple.

**multiplication** NOUN
la multiplicación

to **multiply** VERB
multiplicar*
□ to multiply six by three multiplicar seis por tres

**multi-storey car park** NOUN
el aparcamiento de varias plantas

**mum** NOUN
mamá *fem*
□ I'll ask Mum. Le preguntaré a mamá.
□ my mum mi mamá

**mummy** NOUN
1 mamá *fem*
□ Mummy says I can go. Mamá dice que puedo ir.
2 la momia *(Egyptian)*

**mumps** NOUN
las paperas
□ My brother's got mumps. Mi hermano tiene paperas.

**murder** NOUN
▷ *see also* **murder** VERB
el asesinato

to **murder** VERB
▷ *see also* **murder** NOUN
asesinar
□ He was murdered. Fue asesinado.

**murderer** NOUN
el asesino
la asesina

**muscle** NOUN
el músculo

**muscular** ADJECTIVE
musculoso (FEMmusculosa)
□ He's got muscular legs. Tiene piernas musculosas.

**museum** NOUN
el museo

**mushroom** NOUN
el champiñón (PLlos champiñones)

**music** NOUN
la música

**musical** ADJECTIVE
▷ *see also* **musical** NOUN
musical (FEMmusical)
■ **I'm not musical.** No tengo aptitudes para la música.

**musical** NOUN
▷ *see also* **musical** ADJECTIVE
el musical

**music centre** NOUN
el equipo de música

**musician** NOUN
el músico
la música
□ He's a musician. Es músico.

**Muslim** NOUN
el musulmán (PLmusulmanes)
la musulmana

□ She's a Muslim. Es musulmana.

**mussel** NOUN

el mejillón (PLlos mejillones)

**must** VERB

1 tener* que *(it's necessary)*

□ I must do it. Tengo que hacerlo. □ I must buy some presents. Tengo que comprar unos regalos. □ I really must go now. De verdad que me tengo que ir ya. □ You must come again next year. Tienes que volver el año que viene.

■ **You mustn't forget to send her a card.** No te vayas a olvidar de mandarle una tarjeta.

2 deber de *(I suppose)*

□ There must be some problem. Debe de haber algún problema. □ You must be tired. Debes de estar cansada.

**mustard** NOUN

la mostaza

**mustn't** VERB = must not

to **mutter** VERB

mascullar

**mutton** NOUN

la carne de cordero

**my** ADJECTIVE

mi (PLmis)

□ my father mi padre □ my house mi casa □ my two best friends mis dos mejores amigos □ my sisters mis hermanas

> **LANGUAGE TIP** 'my' is usually translated by the definite article **el/los** or **la/las** when it's clear from the sentence who the possessor is or when referring to clothing or parts of the body.

□ They stole my car. Me robaron el coche. □ I took off my coat. Me quité el abrigo. □ I'm washing my hair. Me estoy lavando la cabeza.

**myself** PRONOUN

1 me *(reflexive)*

□ I've hurt myself. Me he hecho daño.

2 mí mismo (FEMmí misma) *(after preposition)*

□ I talked mainly about myself. Hablé principalmente de mí mismo.

■ **a beginner like myself** un principiante como yo

3 yo mismo (FEMyo misma) *(for emphasis)*

□ I made it myself. Lo hice yo misma.

■ **by myself** solo (FEMsola)

□ I don't like travelling by myself. No me gusta viajar solo.

**mysterious** ADJECTIVE

misterioso (FEMmisteriosa)

**mystery** NOUN

el misterio

■ **a murder mystery** una novela policíaca

**myth** NOUN

el mito

□ a Greek myth un mito griego □ That's a myth. *(untrue story)* Eso es un mito.

**mythology** NOUN

la mitología

# Nn

**naff** ADJECTIVE
hortera (FEM hortera)

to **nag** VERB
dar* la lata
□ She's always nagging me. Siempre me está dando la lata.

**nail** NOUN
1 la uña
□ She bites her nails. Se muerde las uñas.
2 el clavo *(made of metal)*

**nailbrush** NOUN
el cepillo de uñas

**nailfile** NOUN
la lima para las uñas

**nail scissors** PL NOUN
las tijeras para las uñas

**nail varnish** NOUN
el esmalte de uñas
■ nail varnish remover el quitaesmaltes

**naked** ADJECTIVE
desnudo (FEM desnuda)

**name** NOUN
el nombre
■ What's your name? ¿Cómo te llamas?

**nanny** NOUN
la niñera *(nursemaid)*

**nap** NOUN
la siesta
□ She likes to have a nap in the afternoon. Le gusta echarse una siesta por la tarde.

**napkin** NOUN
la servilleta

**nappy** NOUN
el pañal

**narrow** ADJECTIVE
estrecho (FEM estrecha)

**narrow-minded** ADJECTIVE
estrecho de miras (FEM estrecho de miras)

**nasty** ADJECTIVE
1 malo (FEM mala)
□ Don't be nasty. No seas malo. □ What nasty weather! ¡Qué tiempo más malo!
　LANGUAGE TIP Use **mal** before a masculine singular noun.
2 desagradable (FEM desagradable)
□ a nasty smell un olor desagradable

■ He gave me a nasty look. Me miró de mala manera.

**nation** NOUN
la nación (PL las naciones)

**national** ADJECTIVE
nacional (FEM nacional)

**national anthem** NOUN
el himno nacional

**National Health Service** NOUN
el servicio sanitario de la Seguridad Social

**nationalism** NOUN
el nacionalismo

**nationalist** NOUN
el/la nacionalista

**nationality** NOUN
la nacionalidad

**national park** NOUN
el parque nacional

**native** ADJECTIVE
natal (FEM natal)
□ my native country mi país natal
■ his native language su lengua materna

**natural** ADJECTIVE
natural (FEM natural)
□ Helping him seemed the natural thing to do. Ayudarlo parecía lo más natural.

**naturalist** NOUN
el/la naturalista

**naturally** ADVERB
naturalmente
□ Naturally, we were very disappointed. Naturalmente, estábamos muy decepcionados.

**nature** NOUN
la naturaleza
□ the wonders of nature las maravillas de la naturaleza
■ It's not in his nature to behave like that. Comportarse así no es propio de él.

**naughty** ADJECTIVE
travieso (FEM traviesa)
□ Naughty girl! ¡Qué traviesa!

**navy** NOUN
la armada
□ He's in the navy. Está en la armada.

**navy-blue** ADJECTIVE

azul marino (FEM + PL azul marino)
▫ a navy-blue skirt una falda azul marino

**near** ADJECTIVE
  ▷ *see also* **near** PREPOSITION, ADVERB
1 cerca (FEM cerca)
  ▫ It's fairly near. Está bastante cerca. ▫ My house is near enough to walk. Mi casa está muy cerca, se puede ir andando.
2 cercano (FEM cercana)
  ▫ Where's the nearest service station? ¿Dónde está la gasolinera más cercana?
  ■ in the near future en un futuro cercano

**near** PREPOSITION, ADVERB
  ▷ *see also* **near** ADJECTIVE
1 cerca
  ▫ Is there a bank near here? ¿Hay algún banco por aquí cerca?
2 cerca de
  ▫ I live near Liverpool. Vivo cerca de Liverpool.
  ■ near to cerca de ▫ It's very near to the school. Está muy cerca del colegio.

**nearby** ADJECTIVE
  ▷ *see also* **nearby** ADVERB
  cercano (FEM cercana)
  ▫ a nearby village un pueblo cercano

**nearby** ADVERB
  ▷ *see also* **nearby** ADJECTIVE
  cerca
  ▫ There's a supermarket nearby. Hay un supermercado cerca.

**nearly** ADVERB
  casi
  ▫ Dinner's nearly ready. La cena está casi lista. ▫ I'm nearly fifteen. Tengo casi quince años.
  ■ I nearly missed the train. Por poco pierdo el tren.

**neat** ADJECTIVE
  ordenado (FEM ordenada)
  ▫ My brother's not very neat. Mi hermano no es muy ordenado.
  ■ He always looks very neat. Siempre está muy pulcro.

**neatly** ADVERB
  ■ neatly folded cuidadosamente doblado
  ■ neatly dressed bien vestido

**necessarily** ADVERB
  ■ not necessarily no necesariamente

**necessary** ADJECTIVE
  necesario (FEM necesaria)

**necessity** NOUN
  la necesidad
  ▫ A car is a necessity, not a luxury. Un coche es una necesidad, no un lujo.

**neck** NOUN
  el cuello
  ▫ a V-neck sweater un jersey de cuello en pico

■ She had a stiff neck. Tenía tortícolis.
■ the back of your neck la nuca

**necklace** NOUN
  el collar

to **need** VERB
  ▷ *see also* **need** NOUN
  necesitar
  ▫ I need a bigger size. Necesito una talla más grande. ▫ I need to change some money. Necesito cambiar dinero.
  ■ You don't need to go. No tienes por qué ir.

**need** NOUN
  ▷ *see also* **need** VERB
  ■ There's no need to book. No hace falta hacer reserva.
  ⓘ LANGUAGE TIP hace falta que has to be followed by a verb in the subjunctive.
  ▫ There's no need for you to do that. No hace falta que hagas eso.

**needle** NOUN
  la aguja

**negative** NOUN
  ▷ *see also* **negative** ADJECTIVE
  el negativo *(photo)*

**negative** ADJECTIVE
  ▷ *see also* **negative** NOUN
  negativo (FEM negativa)
  ▫ He's got a very negative attitude. Tiene una actitud muy negativa.

**neglected** ADJECTIVE
  abandonado (FEM abandonada)
  ▫ The garden is neglected. El jardín está abandonado.

to **negotiate** VERB
  negociar

**negotiations** PL NOUN
  las negociaciones

**neighbour** (US **neighbor**) NOUN
  el vecino
  la vecina

**neighbourhood** (US **neighborhood**) NOUN
  el barrio

**neither** ADJECTIVE, CONJUNCTION, PRONOUN
1 ninguno de los dos (FEM ninguna de las dos)
  ▫ Carrots or peas? — Neither, thanks. ¿Zanahorias o guisantes? — Ninguno de los dos, gracias. ▫ Neither of them is coming. No viene ninguno de los dos. ▫ Neither woman looked happy. Ninguna de las dos parecía contenta.
2 tampoco
  ▫ I don't like him. — Neither do I! No me cae bien. — ¡A mí tampoco! ▫ I've never been to Spain. — Neither have we. No he estado nunca en España. — Nosotros tampoco.

**n**

■ **neither...nor...** ni...ni... □ Neither Sarah nor Tamsin is coming to the party. No vienen ni Sarah ni Tamsin a la fiesta.

**neon** NOUN
el neón
□ a neon light una lámpara de neón

**nephew** NOUN
el sobrino

**nerve** NOUN
el nervio
□ That noise really gets on my nerves. Ese ruido me pone los nervios de punta.
■ **He's got a nerve!** ¡Qué cara tiene!
■ **I wouldn't have the nerve to do that!** ¡Yo no me atrevería a hacer eso!

**nerve-racking** ADJECTIVE
angustioso (FEMangustiosa)

**nervous** ADJECTIVE
nervioso (FEMnerviosa)
□ I bite my nails when I'm nervous. Cuando estoy nervioso me muerdo las uñas. □ I'm a bit nervous about the exams. Estoy un poco nervioso por los exámenes.

**nest** NOUN
el nido

**Net** NOUN
la Red
■ **to surf the Net** navegar por la Red

**net** NOUN
la red
□ a fishing net una red de pesca

**netball** NOUN

DID YOU KNOW...?
Netball is not played in Spain.

**Netherlands** PL NOUN
■ **the Netherlands** los Países Bajos

**network** NOUN
la red

**neurotic** ADJECTIVE
neurótico (FEMneurótica)

**never** ADVERB
nunca
□ Have you ever been to Argentina? — No, never. ¿Has estado alguna vez en Argentina? — No, nunca. □ Never leave valuables in your car. No dejen nunca objetos de valor en el coche.

LANGUAGE TIP When **nunca** comes before the verb in Spanish it is not necessary to use **no** as well.

□ I never believed him. Yo nunca le creí.
■ **Never again!** ¡Nunca más!
■ **Never, ever do that again!** ¡No vuelvas a hacer eso nunca jamás!
■ **Never mind.** No importa.

**new** ADJECTIVE
nuevo (FEMnueva)
□ her new boyfriend su nuevo novio

**newborn** ADJECTIVE
■ **a newborn baby** un bebé recién nacido

**newcomer** NOUN
■ **They were newcomers to the area.** Eran nuevos en la zona.

**news** NOUN
1 las noticias
□ good news buenas noticias □ I watch the news every evening. Veo las noticias todas las noches.
■ **It was nice to have your news.** Me dio alegría saber de ti.
2 la noticia
□ That's wonderful news! ¡Qué buena noticia!
■ **an interesting piece of news** una noticia interesante

**newsagent** NOUN
la tienda de periódicos

**newspaper** NOUN
el periódico

**newsreader** NOUN
1 el presentador
la presentadora (on TV)
2 el locutor
la locutora (on radio)

**New Year** NOUN
el Año Nuevo
□ to celebrate New Year celebrar el Año Nuevo
■ **Happy New Year!** ¡Feliz Año Nuevo!
■ **New Year's Day** el día de Año Nuevo
■ **New Year's Eve** Nochevieja (la noche de Fin de Año Latin America)
■ **a New Year's Eve party** una fiesta de Fin de Año

**New Zealand** NOUN
Nueva Zelanda fem

**New Zealander** NOUN
el neozelandés (PLlos neozelandeses)
la neozelandesa

**next** ADJECTIVE, ADVERB, PREPOSITION
1 próximo (FEMpróxima)
□ next Saturday el próximo sábado □ the next time I see you la próxima vez que te vea
2 siguiente (FEMsiguiente)
□ Next please! ¡El siguiente, por favor!
□ The next day we visited Gerona. Al día siguiente visitamos Gerona.
3 luego
□ What did you do next? ¿Qué hiciste luego?
■ **next to** al lado de □ next to the bank al lado del banco
■ **next door** al lado □ They live next door. Viven al lado.
■ **the next-door neighbours** los vecinos de al lado
■ **the next room** la habitación de al lado

**NHS** ABBREVIATION (= *National Health Service*)
el servicio sanitario de la Seguridad Social

**nice** ADJECTIVE

**1** simpático (FEM simpática ) *(friendly)*
□ Your parents are very nice. Tus padres son muy simpáticos.

**2** amable (FEM amable ) *(kind)*
□ She was always very nice to me. Siempre fue muy amable conmigo. □ It was nice of you to remember my birthday. Fue muy amable de tu parte que te acordaras de mi cumpleaños.

**3** bonito (FEM bonita ) *(pretty)*
□ That's a nice dress! ¡Qué vestido más bonito! □ Segovia is a nice town. Segovia es una ciudad bonita.

> **WORD POWER**
> You can use a number of other words instead of **nice** to mean 'pretty':
> **attractive** atractivo
> □ an attractive girl una chica atractiva
> **beautiful** precioso
> □ a beautiful painting un cuadro precioso
> **gorgeous** magnífico
> □ a gorgeous scarf un pañuelo magnífico
> **lovely** precioso
> □ a lovely dress un vestido precioso

**4** bueno (FEM buena ) *(good)*
□ This paella is very nice. Esta paella está muy buena. □ a nice cup of coffee una buena taza de café

> **LANGUAGE TIP** Use **buen** before a masculine singular noun.

□ nice weather buen tiempo □ It's a nice day. Hace buen día.
■ **Have a nice time!** ¡Que te diviertas!

**nickname** NOUN
el apodo

**niece** NOUN
la sobrina

**night** NOUN
la noche
□ I want a single room for two nights. Quiero una habitación individual para dos noches.
■ **at night** por la noche
■ **Good night!** ¡Buenas noches!
■ **last night** anoche □ We went to a party last night. Anoche fuimos a una fiesta.

**night club** NOUN
la sala de fiestas

**nightdress** NOUN
el camisón (PL los camisones )

**nightie** NOUN
el camisón (PL los camisones )

**nightlife** NOUN

la vida nocturna
□ There's plenty of nightlife in Madrid. Hay mucha vida nocturna en Madrid.

**nightmare** NOUN
la pesadilla
□ to have nightmares tener pesadillas
□ The whole trip was a nightmare. El viaje entero fue una pesadilla.

**nil** NOUN
el cero
□ We won one-nil. Ganamos uno a cero.

**nine** NUMERAL
nueve
■ She's nine. Tiene nueve años.

**nineteen** NUMERAL
diecinueve
■ She's nineteen. Tiene diecinueve años.

**nineteenth** ADJECTIVE
decimonoveno (FEM decimonovena )
■ the nineteenth floor la planta diecinueve
■ the nineteenth of March el diecinueve de marzo

**ninety** NUMERAL
noventa
□ He's ninety. Tiene noventa años.

**ninth** ADJECTIVE
noveno (FEM novena )
■ on the ninth floor en el noveno piso
■ on 9th August el 9 de agosto

**no** ADVERB, ADJECTIVE
no
□ Are you coming? — No. ¿Vienes? — No. □ Would you like some more? — No thank you. ¿Quieres un poco más? — No, gracias. □ There's no hot water. No hay agua caliente.
■ I've got no idea. No tengo ni idea.
■ I have no questions. No tengo ninguna pregunta.
■ No way! ¡Ni hablar!
■ 'no smoking' 'prohibido fumar'

**nobody** PRONOUN
nadie
□ Who's going with you? — Nobody. ¿Quién va contigo? — Nadie. □ There was nobody in the office. No había nadie en la oficina.
■ I've got nobody to play with. No tengo a nadie con quien jugar.

> **LANGUAGE TIP** When 'nobody' goes before a verb in English it can be translated by either **nadie ...** or **no ... nadie** .

□ Nobody saw me. Nadie me vio. □ Nobody likes him. No le cae bien a nadie.

**to nod** VERB

**1** asentir* con la cabeza *(in agreement)*
**2** saludar con la cabeza *(as greeting)*

**noise** NOUN
el ruido
■ **to make a noise** hacer ruido

**noisy** ADJECTIVE
ruidoso (FEM ruidosa)
□ the noisiest city in the world la ciudad más ruidosa del mundo
■ **It's very noisy here.** Hay mucho ruido aquí.

to **nominate** VERB
nombrar*
□ She was nominated for the post. La nombraron para el cargo.
■ **He was nominated for an Oscar.** Le nominaron para un Oscar.

**none** PRONOUN

> LANGUAGE TIP When 'none' refers to something you can count, such as sisters or friends, Spanish uses **ninguno** with a singular verb. When it refers to something you cannot count, such as wine, Spanish uses **nada**.

1 ninguno (FEM ninguna)
□ How many sisters have you got? — None. ¿Cuántas hermanas tienes? — Ninguna.
□ None of my friends wanted to come. Ninguno de mis amigos quiso venir.
□ There are none left. No queda ninguno.
2 nada
□ There's none left. No queda nada.

**nonsense** NOUN
las tonterías
□ She talks a lot of nonsense. Dice muchas tonterías.
■ **Nonsense!** ¡Tonterías!

**non-smoker** NOUN
el no fumador
la no fumadora
■ **He's a non-smoker.** No fuma.

**non-smoking** ADJECTIVE
■ **a non-smoking area** un área reservada para no fumadores

> LANGUAGE TIP Although it's a feminine noun, remember that you use **el** and **un** with **área**.

■ **a non-smoking carriage** un vagón para no fumadores

**non-stop** ADJECTIVE, ADVERB
1 directo (FEM directa)
□ a non-stop flight un vuelo directo
■ **We flew non-stop.** Tomamos un vuelo directo.
2 sin parar
□ He talks non-stop. Habla sin parar.

**noodles** PL NOUN
los fideos

**noon** NOUN
las doce del mediodía

■ **at noon** a las doce del mediodía

**no one** PRONOUN
nadie
□ Who's going with you? — No one. ¿Quién va contigo? — Nadie. □ There was no one in the office. No había nadie en la oficina.
■ **I've got no one to play with.** No tengo a nadie con quien jugar.

> LANGUAGE TIP When 'no one' goes before a verb in English it can be translated by either **nadie ...** or **no ... nadie**.

□ No one saw me. Nadie me vio. □ No one likes him. No le cae bien a nadie.

**nor** CONJUNCTION
tampoco
□ I didn't like the film. — Nor did I. No me gustó la película. — A mí tampoco. □ We haven't seen him. — Nor have we. No lo hemos visto. — Nosotros tampoco.
■ **neither...nor** ni...ni □ neither the cinema nor the swimming pool ni el cine ni la piscina

**normal** ADJECTIVE
normal (FEM normal)

**normally** ADVERB
1 normalmente (usually)
□ I normally arrive at nine o'clock. Normalmente llego a las nueve.
2 con normalidad (as normal)
□ Airports are working normally over Christmas. Durante las Navidades los aeropuertos funcionan con normalidad.

**north** NOUN
▷ see also **north** ADJECTIVE, ADVERB
el norte
□ in the north of Spain en el norte de España

**north** ADJECTIVE, ADVERB
▷ see also **north** NOUN
hacia el norte
□ We were travelling north. Viajábamos hacia el norte.
■ **North London** el norte de Londres
■ **north of** al norte de □ It's north of London. Está al norte de Londres.
■ **the north coast** la costa septentrional

**North America** NOUN
América del Norte fem

**northbound** ADJECTIVE
■ **Northbound traffic is moving very slowly.** El tráfico que se dirige hacia el norte avanza muy despacio.

**northeast** NOUN
el noreste
■ **in the northeast** al noreste

**northern** ADJECTIVE
del norte

□ Northern Europe Europa del Norte
■ **the northern part of the island** la zona norte de la isla

**Northern Ireland** NOUN
Irlanda del Norte *fem*

**North Pole** NOUN
■ **the North Pole** el Polo Norte

**North Sea** NOUN
■ **the North Sea** el Mar del Norte

**northwest** NOUN
el noroeste
■ **in the northwest** al noroeste

**Norway** NOUN
Noruega *fem*

**Norwegian** ADJECTIVE
▷ *see also* **Norwegian** NOUN
noruego (FEM noruega )

**Norwegian** NOUN
▷ *see also* **Norwegian** ADJECTIVE
1 el noruego
la noruega *(person)*
□ the Norwegians los noruegos
2 el noruego *(language)*

**nose** NOUN
la nariz (PL las narices )

**nosebleed** NOUN
■ **I often get nosebleeds.** Me sangra la nariz a menudo.

**nosy** ADJECTIVE
fisgón (FEM fisgona )

**not** ADVERB
no
□ I'm not sure. No estoy seguro. □ Are you coming or not? ¿Vienes o no? □ Did you like it? — Not really. ¿Te gustó? — No mucho.
■ **Thank you very much. — Not at all.** Muchas gracias. — De nada.
■ **not yet** todavía no □ They haven't arrived yet. Todavía no han llegado.

**note** NOUN
1 la nota
□ I'll drop her a note. Le dejaré una nota.
■ **Remember to take notes.** Acuérdate de tomar apuntes.
■ **to make a note of something** tomar nota de algo
2 el billete
□ a five pound note un billete de cinco libras

to **note down** VERB
anotar

**notebook** NOUN
el cuaderno

**notepad** NOUN
el bloc de notas (PL los blocs de notas )

**notepaper** NOUN
el papel de cartas

**nothing** NOUN
nada

□ What's wrong? — Nothing. ¿Qué pasa? — Nada. □ What are you doing tonight? — Nothing special. ¿Qué haces esta noche? — Nada especial. □ He does nothing. No hace nada.
■ **He does nothing but sleep.** No hace nada más que dormir.
■ **There's nothing to do.** No hay nada que hacer.

> LANGUAGE TIP When 'nothing' goes before a verb in English it can be translated by either **nada ...** or **no ... nada** .

□ Nothing frightens him. Nada lo asusta. □ Nothing will happen. No pasará nada.

**notice** NOUN
▷ *see also* **notice** VERB
1 el letrero *(physical object)*
□ There was a notice outside the house. Había un letrero fuera de la casa.
2 el aviso *(information)*
□ There's a notice on the board about the trip. Hay un aviso en el tablón sobre el viaje.
■ **a warning notice** un aviso
■ **He was transferred without notice.** Lo trasladaron sin previo aviso.
■ **until further notice** hasta nuevo aviso
■ **Don't take any notice of him!** ¡No le hagas caso!

> LANGUAGE TIP Be careful not to translate **notice** by **noticia** .

to **notice** VERB
▷ *see also* **notice** NOUN
■ **to notice something** darse cuenta de algo □ Don't worry. He won't notice the mistake. No te preocupes. No se dará cuenta del error.

**notice board** NOUN
el tablón de anuncios (PL los tablones de anuncios )

**nought** NOUN
cero *masc*

**noun** NOUN
el nombre

**novel** NOUN
la novela

**novelist** NOUN
el/la novelista

**November** NOUN
noviembre *masc*
□ in November en noviembre □ on 7th November el 7 de noviembre

**now** ADVERB
ahora
□ What are you doing now? ¿Qué haces ahora?
■ **just now** en este momento □ I'm rather busy just now. En este momento estoy muy

n

ocupado.
■ **I did it just now.** Lo acabo de hacer.
■ **It should be ready by now.** Ya debería estar listo.
■ **from now on** de ahora en adelante
■ **now and then** de vez en cuando
**nowhere** ADVERB
a ninguna parte
▫ Where are you going for your holidays? — Nowhere. ¿Adónde vas en vacaciones? — A ninguna parte.
■ **nowhere else** a ninguna otra parte
▫ You can go to the shops but nowhere else. Puedes ir a las tiendas pero a ninguna otra parte.
■ **The children were nowhere to be seen.** No se podía ver a los niños por ninguna parte.
■ **There was nowhere to play.** No se podía jugar en ninguna parte.
**nuclear** ADJECTIVE
nuclear (FEM nuclear)
▫ nuclear power la energía nuclear
**nude** NOUN
▷ see also **nude** ADJECTIVE
■ **in the nude** desnudo
**nude** ADJECTIVE
▷ see also **nude** NOUN
desnudo (FEM desnuda)
**nudist** NOUN
el/la nudista
**nuisance** NOUN
fastidio
▫ It's a nuisance having to clean the car. Es un fastidio tener que limpiar el coche.
■ **Sorry to be a nuisance.** Siento molestarle.
■ **You're a nuisance!** ¡Eres un pesado!
**numb** ADJECTIVE
■ **numb with cold** helado de frío
**number** NOUN
el número

▫ I can't read the second number. No puedo leer el segundo número. ▫ They live at number five. Viven en el número cinco. ▫ a large number of people un gran número de gente
■ **You've got the wrong number.** Se ha equivocado de número.
■ **What's your number?** (telephone) ¿Cuál es tu teléfono?
**number plate** NOUN
la matrícula (la placa Latin America)
**nun** NOUN
la monja
**nurse** NOUN
el enfermero
la enfermera
■ **She's a nurse.** Es enfermera.
**nursery** NOUN
**1** la guardería infantil (for children)
**2** el vivero (for plants)
**nursery school** NOUN
el preescolar (guardería Latin America)
**nursery slope** NOUN
la pista para principiantes
**nut** NOUN
**1** la almendra (almond)
**2** el cacahuete (peanut)
**3** la avellana (hazelnut)
**4** la nuez (PL las nueces) (walnut)
■ **I don't like nuts.** No me gustan los frutos secos.
**5** la tuerca (made of metal)
**nutmeg** NOUN
la nuez moscada
**nutritious** ADJECTIVE
nutritivo (FEM nutritiva)
**nuts** ADJECTIVE
■ **He's nuts.** (informal) Está chiflado.
**nutter** NOUN
■ **He's a nutter.** (informal) Es un chiflado.
**nylon** NOUN
nylon

n

# Oo

**oak** NOUN
el roble
□ an oak barrel un barril de roble

**oar** NOUN
el remo

**oats** PL NOUN
la avena

**obedient** ADJECTIVE
obediente (FEM obediente)

to **obey** VERB
obedecer*
■ **to obey the rules** (in game) atenerse a las reglas del juego

**object** NOUN
el objeto

**objection** NOUN
la objeción (PL las objeciones)
□ There were no objections to the plan. No hubo objeciones al plan.

**objective** ADJECTIVE
▷ see also **objective** NOUN
objetivo (FEM objetiva)

**oblong** ADJECTIVE
rectangular (FEM rectangular)

**oboe** NOUN
el oboe

**obscene** ADJECTIVE
obsceno (FEM obscena)

**observant** ADJECTIVE
observador (FEM observadora)

to **observe** VERB
observar

**obsessed** ADJECTIVE
obsesionado (FEM obsesionada)
□ He's obsessed with trains. Está obsesionado con los trenes.

**obsession** NOUN
la obsesión (PL las obsesiones)
□ Football's an obsession of mine. El fútbol es una obsesión mía.

**obsolete** ADJECTIVE
obsoleto (FEM obsoleta)

**obstacle** NOUN
el obstáculo

**obstinate** ADJECTIVE
terco (FEM terca)

to **obstruct** VERB
bloquear
□ A lorry was obstructing the traffic. Un camión bloqueaba el tráfico.

to **obtain** VERB
obtener*

**obvious** ADJECTIVE
obvio (FEM obvia)

**obviously** ADVERB
claro
□ Do you want to pass the exam? — Obviously! ¿Quieres aprobar el examen? — ¡Claro! □ It was obviously impossible. Estaba claro que era imposible.
■ **Obviously not!** ¡Claro que no!

**occasion** NOUN
la ocasión (PL las ocasiones)
□ a special occasion una ocasión especial
■ **on several occasions** en varias ocasiones

**occasionally** ADVERB
de vez en cuando

**occupation** NOUN
el empleo

to **occupy** VERB
ocupar
□ The toilet was occupied. El lavabo estaba ocupado.

to **occur** VERB
ocurrir
□ The accident occurred yesterday. El accidente ocurrió ayer.
■ **It suddenly occurred to me that...** De repente se me ocurrió que...

**ocean** NOUN
el océano

**o'clock** ADVERB
■ **at four o'clock** a las cuatro
■ **It's one o'clock.** Es la una.
■ **It's five o'clock.** Son las cinco.

**October** NOUN
octubre masc
□ in October en octubre □ on 12 October el 12 de octubre

**octopus** NOUN
el pulpo

**odd** ADJECTIVE

**1** raro (FEM rara )
□ That's odd! ¡Qué raro!
**2** impar (FEM impara )
□ an odd number un número impar
■ **odd socks** calcetines desparejados

**of** PREPOSITION
de
□ a boy of 10 un niño de 10 años □ a kilo of oranges un kilo de naranjas □ It's made of wood. Es de madera. □ a glass of wine un vaso de vino

⌁ **LANGUAGE TIP** de +el changes to del .
□ the wheels of the car las ruedas del coche
■ **There were three of us.** Éramos tres.
■ **a friend of mine** un amigo mío
■ **That's very kind of you.** Es muy amable de su parte.

**off** ADJECTIVE, ADVERB, PREPOSITION

⌁ **LANGUAGE TIP** For other expressions with 'off', see the verbs 'get', 'take', 'turn' etc.

**1** apagado (FEM apagada ) (heater, light, TV)
□ All the lights are off. Todas las luces están apagadas.
**2** cerrado (FEM cerrada ) (tap, gas)
□ Are you sure the tap is off? ¿Seguro que el grifo está cerrado?
**3** cortado (FEM cortada ) (milk)
**4** estropeado (FEM estropeada ) (meat)
■ **to be off sick** estar ausente por enfermedad
■ **a day off** un día libre □ She took a day off work to go to the wedding. Se tomó un día libre para ir a la boda.
■ **I've got tomorrow off.** Mañana tengo el día libre.
■ **She's off school today.** Hoy no ha ido al colegio.
■ **I must be off now.** Me tengo que ir ahora.
■ **I'm off.** Me voy.
■ **The match is off.** El partido se ha suspendido.

**offence** (US **offense**) NOUN
el delito (crime)

**offensive** ADJECTIVE
ofensivo (FEM ofensiva )

**offer** NOUN
▷ see also **offer** VERB
**1** la oferta (of money, job)
**2** el ofrecimiento (of help)
■ **There was a special offer on CDs.** Los CDs estaban de oferta.

**to offer** VERB
▷ see also **offer** NOUN
ofrecer*
□ He offered me a cigarette. Me ofreció un cigarrillo.

■ **He offered to help me.** Se ofreció a ayudarme.

**office** NOUN
la oficina
■ **during office hours** en horas de oficina

**officer** NOUN
el/la oficial (in the army)

**official** ADJECTIVE
oficial (FEM oficial )

**off-licence** NOUN
la tienda de bebidas alcohólicas

**off-peak** ADJECTIVE
■ **off-peak calls** llamadas de tarifa reducida

**offside** ADJECTIVE
fuera de juego

**often** ADVERB
a menudo
□ It often rains. Llueve a menudo.
■ **How often do you go to the gym?** ¿Cada cuánto vas al gimnasio?

**oil** NOUN
▷ see also **oil** VERB
**1** el aceite (for lubrication, cooking)
**2** el petróleo (crude oil)
■ **an oil painting** una pintura al óleo

**to oil** VERB
▷ see also **oil** NOUN
engrasar

**oil rig** NOUN
la plataforma petrolífera

**oil slick** NOUN
la marea negra

**oil well** NOUN
el pozo de petróleo

**ointment** NOUN
la pomada

**okay** EXCLAMATION, ADVERB
**1** de acuerdo (more formally)
□ Your appointment's at six o'clock. — Okay. Su cita es a las seis. — De acuerdo.
**2** vale (less formally)
□ I'll meet you at six o'clock, okay? Te veré a las seis, ¿vale?
■ **Are you okay?** ¿Estás bien?
■ **I'll do it tomorrow, if that's okay with you.** Lo haré mañana, si te parece bien.
■ **The film was okay.** La película no estuvo mal.

**old** ADJECTIVE
**1** viejo (FEM vieja )
□ an old house una casa vieja
■ **an old man** un viejo

⌁ **LANGUAGE TIP** When talking about people it is more polite to use anciano instead of viejo .
■ **old people** los ancianos
**2** antiguo (FEM antigua ) (former)

o

□ my old English teacher mi antiguo profesor de inglés
- **How old are you?** ¿Cuántos años tienes?
- **How old is the baby?** ¿Cuánto tiempo tiene el bebé?
- **a twenty-year-old woman** una mujer de veinte años
- **He's ten years old.** Tiene diez años.
- **older** mayor □ my older brother mi hermano mayor □ my older sister mi hermana mayor □ She's two years older than me. Es dos años mayor que yo.
- **I'm the oldest in the family.** Soy el mayor de la familia.

**old age pensioner** NOUN
el/la pensionista

**old-fashioned** ADJECTIVE
anticuado (FEM anticuada )
□ My parents are rather old-fashioned. Mis padres son bastante anticuados.

**olive** NOUN
la aceituna

**olive oil** NOUN
el aceite de oliva

**olive tree** NOUN
el olivo

**Olympic** ADJECTIVE
olímpico (FEM olímpica )
- **the Olympics** las Olimpiadas

**omelette** NOUN
la tortilla francesa

**on** PREPOSITION, ADVERB
▷ see also **on** ADJECTIVE

> **LANGUAGE TIP** There are several ways of translating 'on'. Scan the examples to find one that is similar to what you want to say. For other expressions with 'on', see the verbs 'go', 'put', 'turn' etc.

**1** en
□ on an island en una isla □ on the wall en la pared □ It's on Channel four. Lo dan en el Canal cuatro. □ on TV en la tele □ on the 2nd floor en el segundo piso □ I go to school on my bike. Voy al colegio en bicicleta. □ We went on the train. Fuimos en tren.

**2** sobre (on top of, about)
□ on the table sobre la mesa □ a book on Ghandi un libro sobre Ghandi

> **LANGUAGE TIP** With days and dates, the definite article – **el, los** – is used in Spanish instead of a preposition.

□ on Friday el viernes □ on Fridays los viernes □ on 20 June el 20 de junio
- **on the left** a la izquierda
- **on holiday** de vacaciones
- **It's about 10 minutes on foot.** Está a

unos 10 minutos andando.
- **She was on antibiotics for a week.** Estuvo una semana tomando antibióticos.
- **The coffee is on the house.** Al café invita la casa.
- **The drinks are on me.** Invito yo.
- **What is he on about?** ¿De qué está hablando?

**on** ADJECTIVE
▷ see also **on** PREPOSITION, ADVERB
**1** encendido (FEM encendida ) (heater, light, TV)
□ I think I left the light on. Me parece que he dejado la luz encendida.
**2** abierto (FEM abierta ) (tap, gas)
□ Leave the tap on. Deja el grifo abierto.
**3** en marcha
□ Is the dishwasher on? ¿Está en marcha el lavavajillas?
- **What's on at the cinema?** ¿Qué echan en el cine?
- **Is the party still on?** ¿Todavía se va a hacer la fiesta?
- **I've got a lot on this weekend.** Tengo mucho que hacer este fin de semana.

**once** ADVERB
una vez
□ once a week una vez a la semana □ once more una vez más □ I've been to Italy once before. Ya he estado una vez en Italia.
- **Once upon a time...** Érase una vez...
- **once in a while** de vez en cuando
- **once and for all** de una vez por todas
- **at once** enseguida

**one** NUMERAL, PRONOUN
uno (FEM una )
□ I need a smaller one. Necesito uno más pequeño.
- **one by one** uno a uno

> **LANGUAGE TIP** Use **un** before a masculine noun.

□ I've got one brother and one sister. Tengo un hermano y una hermana.
- **One never knows.** Nunca se sabe.
- **one another** unos a otros □ They all looked at one another. Se miraron todos unos a otros.

**oneself** PRONOUN
**1** se (reflexive)
□ to hurt oneself hacerse daño □ to wash oneself lavarse
**2** uno mismo (FEM una misma ) (after preposition, for emphasis)
□ It's quicker to do it oneself. Es más rápido si lo hace uno mismo.

**one-way** ADJECTIVE
- **a one-way street** una calle de sentido único
- **a one-way ticket** un billete de ida

**onion** NOUN
la cebolla
**online** ADJECTIVE
en línea
**only** ADVERB
▷ *see also* **only** ADJECTIVE, CONJUNCTION
sólo
□ How much was it? — Only £10. ¿Cuánto valía? — Sólo 10 libras. □ We only want to stay for one night. Sólo queremos quedarnos una noche. □ It's only a game! ¡Es sólo un juego!
**only** ADJECTIVE
▷ *see also* **only** ADVERB, CONJUNCTION
único (FEM única)
□ She's an only child. Es hija única.
□ Monday is the only day I'm free. El lunes es el único día que tengo libre.
**only** CONJUNCTION
▷ *see also* **only** ADJECTIVE, ADVERB
pero
□ I'd like the same sweater, only in black. Quería el mismo jersey, pero en negro.
**onwards** ADVERB
en adelante
□ from July onwards de julio en adelante
**open** ADJECTIVE
▷ *see also* **open** VERB
abierto (FEM abierta)
□ The shop's open on Sunday mornings. La tienda está abierta los domingos por la mañana.
■ **Are you open tomorrow?** ¿Abre mañana?
■ **in the open air** al aire libre
to **open** VERB
▷ *see also* **open** ADJECTIVE
1 abrir*
□ What time do the shops open? ¿A qué hora abren las tiendas? □ Can I open the window? ¿Puedo abrir la ventana?
2 abrirse*
□ The door opens automatically. La puerta se abre automáticamente.
**opening hours** PL NOUN
el horario de apertura
**opera** NOUN
la ópera
to **operate** VERB
operar *(machine)*
■ **to operate on someone** operar a alguien
**operation** NOUN
la operación (PL las operaciones)
■ **I've never had an operation.** Nunca me han operado.
**operator** NOUN
el operador
la operadora

**opinion** NOUN
la opinión (PL las opiniones)
□ in my opinion en mi opinión
■ **What's your opinion?** ¿Tú qué opinas?
**opinion poll** NOUN
el sondeo de opinión
**opponent** NOUN
el adversario
la adversaria
**opportunity** NOUN
la oportunidad
□ I've never had the opportunity to go to Spain. No he tenido nunca la oportunidad de ir a España.
**opposed** ADJECTIVE
■ **to be opposed to something** oponerse a algo □ I've always been opposed to violence. Siempre me he opuesto a la violencia.
**opposing** ADJECTIVE
contrario (FEM contraria)
□ the opposing team el equipo contrario
**opposite** ADJECTIVE, ADVERB, PREPOSITION
1 contrario (FEM contraria)
□ It's in the opposite direction. Está en dirección contraria.
2 opuesto (FEM opuesta)
□ the opposite sex el sexo opuesto
3 enfrente
□ They live opposite. Viven enfrente.
4 frente a
□ the girl sitting opposite me la chica sentada frente a mí
**opposition** NOUN
la oposición
□ There is a lot of opposition to the new law. Hay una fuerte oposición a la nueva ley.
**optician** NOUN
el óptico
la óptica
■ **He's gone to the optician's.** Ha ido a la óptica.
**optimist** NOUN
el/la optimista
**optimistic** ADJECTIVE
optimista (FEM optimista)
**option** NOUN
1 la opción (PL las opciones)
□ I've got no option. No tengo otra opción.
2 la asignatura optativa *(at school)*
□ I'm doing geology as my option. Tengo geología como asignatura optativa.
**optional** ADJECTIVE
1 optativo (FEM optativa) *(subject)*
□ Biology was optional at my school. La biología era optativa en mi colegio.
2 opcional (FEM opcional) *(feature)*
□ Fog lights are available as optional extras. Los faros antiniebla son opcionales.

**or** CONJUNCTION
**1** o
□ Would you like tea or coffee? ¿Quieres té o café?

> LANGUAGE TIP Use **u** before words beginning with **o** or **ho**.

□ six or eight seis u ocho □ men or women mujeres u hombres
■ **Hurry up or you'll miss the bus.** Date prisa, que vas a perder el autobús.
**2** ni
□ I don't eat meat or fish. No como carne ni pescado. □ She can't dance or sing. No sabe bailar ni cantar.

**oral** ADJECTIVE
▷ *see also* **oral** NOUN
oral (FEM oral)
□ an oral exam un examen oral

**oral** NOUN
▷ *see also* **oral** ADJECTIVE
el examen oral (PL los exámenes orales)
□ I've got my Spanish oral soon. Tengo el examen oral de español pronto.

**orange** NOUN
▷ *see also* **orange** ADJECTIVE
la naranja
■ **orange juice** el zumo de naranja (el jugo de naranja *Latin America*)

**orange** ADJECTIVE
▷ *see also* **orange** NOUN
naranja (FEM + PL naranja)

**orchard** NOUN
el huerto

**orchestra** NOUN
la orquesta

**order** NOUN
▷ *see also* **order** VERB
**1** el orden (*arrangement*)
□ in alphabetical order por orden alfabético
**2** la orden (PL las órdenes) (*command*)
□ to obey an order obedecer una orden
■ **The waiter took our order.** El camarero tomó nota de lo que íbamos a comer.
■ **in order to** para □ He does it in order to earn money. Lo hace para ganar dinero.
■ '**out of order**' 'averiado'

**to order** VERB
▷ *see also* **order** NOUN
pedir*
□ We ordered steak and chips. Pedimos un filete con patatas fritas. □ Are you ready to order? ¿Han decidido qué van a pedir?

**ordinary** ADJECTIVE
normal y corriente (FEM normal y corriente)
□ He's an ordinary man. Es un hombre normal y corriente. □ an ordinary day un día normal y corriente

**organ** NOUN
el órgano (*instrument*)

**organic** ADJECTIVE
biológico (FEM biológica) (*fruit, vegetables*)

**organization** NOUN
la organización (PL las organizaciones)

**to organize** VERB
organizar*

**origin** NOUN
el origen (PL los orígenes)

**original** ADJECTIVE
original (FEM original)

**originally** ADVERB
al principio

**Orkneys** PL NOUN
■ **the Orkneys** las Islas Órcadas

**ornament** NOUN
el adorno

**orphan** NOUN
el huérfano
la huérfana

**ostrich** NOUN
el avestruz (PL los avestruces)

**other** ADJECTIVE, PRONOUN
otro (FEM otra)
□ Have you got these jeans in other colours? ¿Tienen estos vaqueros en otros colores?
□ on the other side of the street al otro lado de la calle
■ **the other one** el otro (FEM la otra)
□ This one? — No, the other one. ¿Éste? — No, el otro.
■ **the others** los demás (FEM las demás)
□ The others are going but I'm not. Los demás van, pero yo no.

**otherwise** ADVERB, CONJUNCTION
**1** si no (*if not*)
□ Note down the number, otherwise you'll forget it. Apúntate el número, si no se te olvidará.
**2** por lo demás (*in other ways*)
□ I'm tired, but otherwise I'm fine. Estoy cansado, pero por lo demás estoy bien.

**ought** VERB

> LANGUAGE TIP To translate 'ought to' use the conditional of **deber**.

□ I ought to phone my parents. Debería llamar a mis padres. □ You ought not to do that. No deberías hacer eso. □ He ought to win. Debería ganar.

> LANGUAGE TIP For 'ought to have' use the conditional of **deber** plus **haber** or the imperfect of **deber**.

□ You ought to have warned me. Me deberías haber avisado. □ He ought to have known. Debía saberlo.

**ounce** NOUN
la onza

**DID YOU KNOW...?**

In Spain measurements are in grams and kilograms. One ounce is about 28 grams.

**our** ADJECTIVE

nuestro (FEM nuestra )
  □ our house nuestra casa  □ Our neighbours are very nice. Nuestros vecinos son muy simpáticos.

**LANGUAGE TIP** 'Our' is usually translated by the definite article **el/los** or **la/las** when it's clear from the sentence who the possessor is or when referring to clothing or parts of the body.

  □ We took off our coats. Nos quitamos los abrigos.  □ They stole our car. Nos robaron el coche.

**ours** PRONOUN

1 el nuestro *masc* (PL los nuestros )
  □ Your car is much bigger than ours. Vuestro coche es mucho más grande que el nuestro.  □ Our teachers are strict. — Ours are too. Nuestros profesores son estrictos. — Los nuestros también.

2 la nuestra *fem* (PL las nuestras )
  □ Your house is very different from ours. Vuestra casa es muy distinta a la nuestra.

3 nuestro *masc* (PL nuestros )
  □ Is this ours? ¿Esto es nuestro?  □ a friend of ours un amigo nuestro

4 nuestra *fem* (PL nuestras )
  □ Sorry, that table is ours. Disculpen, esa mesa es nuestra.  □ Isabel is a close friend of ours. Isabel es muy amiga nuestra.

**ourselves** PRONOUN

1 nos *(reflexive)*
  □ We really enjoyed ourselves. Nos divertimos mucho.

2 nosotros mismos (FEM nosotras mismas )
*(after preposition, for emphasis)*
  □ Let's not talk about ourselves any more. No hablemos más de nosotros mismos.  □ We built our garage ourselves. Nos construimos el garaje nosotros mismos.
  ■ **by ourselves** solos (FEM solas )
  □ We prefer to be by ourselves. Preferimos estar solos.

**out** PREPOSITION, ADVERB
  ▷ *see also* **out** ADJECTIVE

**LANGUAGE TIP** There are several ways of translating 'out'. Scan the examples to find one that is similar to what you want to say. For other expressions with 'out', see the verbs 'go', 'put', 'turn' etc.

nuestro
  □ It's cold out. Fuera hace frío.  □ It's dark out there. Está oscuro ahí fuera.

■ **She's out.** Ha salido.
■ **She's out for the afternoon.** No estará en toda la tarde.
■ **to go out** salir  □ I'm going out tonight. Voy a salir esta noche.
■ **to go out with somebody** salir con alguien  □ I've been going out with him for two months. Llevo dos meses saliendo con él.
■ **a night out with my friends** una noche por ahí con mis amigos
■ **'way out'** 'salida'
■ **out of town** fuera de la ciudad  □ He lives out of town. Vive fuera de la ciudad.
■ **three kilometres out of town** a tres kilómetros de la ciudad
■ **to take something out of your pocket** sacar algo del bolsillo
■ **out of curiosity** por curiosidad
■ **We're out of milk.** Se nos ha acabado la leche.
■ **in nine cases out of ten** en nueve de cada diez casos

**out** ADJECTIVE
  ▷ *see also* **out** PREPOSITION, ADVERB

1 apagado (FEM apagada ) *(lights, fire)*
  □ All the lights are out. Todas las luces están apagadas.

2 eliminado (FEM eliminada ) *(eliminated)*
  ■ **That's it, Liverpool are out.** Ya está, Liverpool queda eliminado.
  ■ **The film is now out on DVD.** La película ya ha salido en DVD.

**outbreak** NOUN

1 la epidemia
  □ a salmonella outbreak una epidemia de salmonelosis

2 el comienzo
  □ the outbreak of war el comienzo de la guerra

**outcome** NOUN

el resultado

**outdoor** ADJECTIVE

al aire libre
  □ an outdoor swimming pool una piscina al aire libre

**outdoors** ADVERB

al aire libre

**outfit** NOUN

el traje
  □ a cowboy outfit un traje de vaquero

**outgoing** ADJECTIVE

extrovertido (FEM extrovertida )

**outing** NOUN

la excursión (PL las excursiones )
  □ to go on an outing ir de excursión

**outline** NOUN

1 el esquema *(summary)*

o

**LANGUAGE TIP** Although **esquema** ends in -**a**, it is actually a masculine noun.
□ This is an outline of the plan. Aquí tienen un esquema del plan.
2 el contorno *(shape)*
□ We could see the outline of the mountain. Veíamos el contorno de la montaña.

**outlook** NOUN
1 la actitud *(attitude)*
2 las perspectivas *(prospects)*

**outrageous** ADJECTIVE
1 escandaloso *(FEM escandalosa) (behaviour)*
2 exorbitante *(FEM exorbitante) (price)*
3 extravagante *(FEM extravagante) (clothes)*

**outset** NOUN
■ **at the outset** al principio

**outside** NOUN, ADJECTIVE
▷ *see also* **outside** PREPOSITION, ADVERB
1 el exterior
□ the outside of the house el exterior de la casa
2 exterior *(FEM exterior)*
□ the outside walls las paredes exteriores

**outside** PREPOSITION, ADVERB
▷ *see also* **outside** NOUN, ADJECTIVE
1 fuera
□ It's very cold outside. Hace mucho frío fuera.
2 fuera de
□ outside the school fuera del colegio
□ outside school hours fuera del horario escolar

**outsize** ADJECTIVE
■ **outsize clothes** ropa de tallas muy grandes

**outskirts** PL NOUN
las afueras
□ on the outskirts of town en las afueras de la ciudad

**outstanding** ADJECTIVE
excepcional *(FEM excepcional)*

**oval** ADJECTIVE
ovalado *(FEM ovalada)*

**oven** NOUN
el horno

**over** ADJECTIVE, ADVERB, PREPOSITION

**LANGUAGE TIP** When something is located over something, use **encima de**. When there is movement over something, use **por encima de**.
1 encima de
□ There's a mirror over the washbasin. Encima del lavabo hay un espejo.
2 por encima de
□ The ball went over the wall. La pelota pasó por encima de la pared.
■ **a bridge over the Thames** un puente sobre el Támesis
3 más de
□ It's over 20 kilos. Pesa más de 20 kilos.
■ **The temperature was over 30 degrees.** La temperatura superaba los 30 grados.
4 durante
□ over the holidays durante las vacaciones
□ over Christmas durante las Navidades
5 terminado *(FEM terminada)*
■ **I'll be happy when the exams are over.** Estaré feliz cuando se hayan terminado los exámenes.
■ **over here** aquí
■ **It's over there.** Está por allí.
■ **all over Scotland** en toda Escocia
■ **The shop is over the road.** La tienda está al otro lado de la calle.
■ **I spilled coffee over my shirt.** Me manché la camisa de café.

**overall** ADVERB
▷ *see also* **overall** ADJECTIVE
en general
□ Overall, we played very well. En general jugamos muy bien.

**overalls** PL NOUN
el mono *(el overol Latin America) (for work)*

**overcast** ADJECTIVE
cubierto *(FEM cubierta)*
□ The sky was overcast. El cielo estaba cubierto.

to **overcharge** VERB
cobrar de más
□ They overcharged us for the meal. Nos cobraron de más por la comida.

**overcoat** NOUN
el abrigo

**overdone** ADJECTIVE
1 recocido *(FEM recocida) (vegetables)*
2 demasiado hecho *(FEM demasiado hecha) (steak)*

**overdose** NOUN
la sobredosis *(PL las sobredosis)*

**overdraft** NOUN
el descubierto

to **overestimate** VERB
sobreestimar
□ We overestimated how long it would take. Sobreestimamos el tiempo que se tardaría.

**overhead projector** NOUN
el retroproyector

to **overlook** VERB
1 tener* vistas a
□ The hotel overlooked the beach. El hotel tenía vistas a la playa.
2 pasar por alto
□ He had overlooked one important problem. Había pasado por alto un problema importante.

**overseas** ADVERB
en el extranjero *(live, work)*
□ I'd like to work overseas. Me gustaría trabajar en el extranjero.

**oversight** NOUN
el descuido

to **oversleep** VERB
quedarse dormido
□ I overslept this morning. Me quedé dormido esta mañana.

to **overtake** VERB
adelantar (rebasar *Latin America*)

**overtime** NOUN
las horas extras
■ **to work overtime** trabajar horas extras

**overweight** ADJECTIVE
■ **to be overweight** tener exceso de peso

to **owe** VERB
deber
□ How much do I owe you? ¿Cuánto te debo?

**owing to** PREPOSITION
debido a
□ owing to bad weather debido al mal tiempo

**owl** NOUN
el búho

**own** ADJECTIVE, PRONOUN
▷ *see also* **own** VERB
propio (FEM propia)
□ This is my own recipe. Ésta es mi propia receta. □ I wish I had a room of my own. Me gustaría tener mi propia habitación.
■ **on his own** él solo □ **on her own** ella sola
□ **on our own** nosotros solos

to **own** VERB
▷ *see also* **own** ADJECTIVE
tener*

to **own up** VERB
confesarse* culpable
■ **to own up to something** confesar algo

**owner** NOUN
el proprietario
la propietaria

**oxygen** NOUN
el oxígeno

**oyster** NOUN
la ostra

**ozone layer** NOUN
la capa de ozono

# Pp

**PA** NOUN (= *personal assistant*)
el secretario de dirección
la secretaria de dirección
□ She's a PA. Es secretaria de dirección.
■ **the PA system** (*public address*) la
megafonía

**pace** NOUN
el ritmo
□ the frantic pace of life in London el
frenético ritmo de vida de Londres

**Pacific** NOUN
■ **the Pacific** el Pacífico

**pacifier** NOUN (US)
el chupete

to **pack** VERB
▷ *see also* **pack** NOUN
hacer* las maletas (empacar *Latin America*)
□ I'll help you pack. Te ayudaré a hacer las
maletas.
■ **I've already packed my case.** Ya he
hecho mi maleta.
■ **Pack it in!** ¡Vale ya!

**pack** NOUN
▷ *see also* **pack** VERB
el paquete
□ a pack of cigarettes un paquete de tabaco
■ **a pack of cards** una baraja

**package** NOUN
el paquete
■ **a package holiday** unas vacaciones
organizadas

**packed** ADJECTIVE
abarrotado (FEM abarrotada)
□ The cinema was packed. El cine estaba
abarrotado.

**packed lunch** NOUN
■ **I take a packed lunch to school.** Me
llevo la comida al colegio.

**packet** NOUN
el paquete
□ a packet of cigarettes un paquete de
tabaco
■ **a packet of crisps** una bolsa de patatas
fritas

**pad** NOUN
el bloc

to **paddle** VERB
▷ *see also* **paddle** NOUN
1 chapotear (*swim*)
2 remar
□ to paddle a canoe remar en canoa

**paddle** NOUN
▷ *see also* **paddle** VERB
la pala
■ **to go for a paddle** mojase los pies

**padlock** NOUN
el candado

**page** NOUN
▷ *see also* **page** VERB
la página
□ on page 13 en la página 13

to **page** VERB
▷ *see also* **page** NOUN
■ **to page somebody** llamar a alguien al
busca

**pager** NOUN
el busca

> **LANGUAGE TIP** Although **busca** ends in
> **-a**, it is actually a masculine noun.

**paid** VERB ▷ *see* **pay**

**paid** ADJECTIVE
1 remunerado (FEM remunerada)
□ to do paid work realizar trabajo remunerado
2 pagado (FEM pagada)
□ three weeks' paid holiday tres semanas
de vacaciones pagadas

**pail** NOUN
el cubo

**pain** NOUN
el dolor
□ a terrible pain un dolor tremendo
■ **I've got a pain in my stomach.** Me duele
el estómago.
■ **She's in a lot of pain.** Tiene muchos
dolores.
■ **He's a real pain.** (*informal*) Es un
auténtico pelmazo.

**painful** ADJECTIVE

> **LANGUAGE TIP** **doloroso** is used when
> talking about what causes pain, and
> **dolorido** for the person or thing that
> feels pain.

English-Spanish

1 doloroso (FEM dolorosa)
  □ a painful injury una herida dolorosa
2 dolorido (FEM dolorida)
  □ Her feet were swollen and painful. Tenía
  los pies hinchados y doloridos.
  ■ Is it painful? ¿Te duele?
**painkiller** NOUN
  el analgésico
**paint** NOUN
  ▷ see also **paint** VERB
  la pintura
to **paint** VERB
  ▷ see also **paint** NOUN
  pintar
  □ to paint something green pintar algo de
  verde
**paintbrush** NOUN
1 el pincel (for an artist)
2 la brocha (for decorating)
**painter** NOUN
  el pintor
  la pintora
  □ The painters made a real mess of the
  windows. Los pintores dejaron las ventanas
  hechas un desastre.
**painting** NOUN
1 el cuadro
  □ a painting by Picasso un cuadro de
  Picasso
2 la pintura
  □ My hobby is painting. Mi hobby es la
  pintura.
**pair** NOUN
  el par
  □ a pair of shoes un par de zapatos
  ■ a pair of scissors unas tijeras
  ■ a pair of trousers unos pantalones
  ■ in pairs por parejas
**pajamas** PL NOUN (US)
  el pijama (el piyama Latin America)
  □ my pajamas mi pijama
  ■ a pair of pajamas un pijama
  ⋯ LANGUAGE TIP Although **pijama** ends
  in -a, it is actually a masculine noun.
**Pakistan** NOUN
  Paquistán masc
**Pakistani** ADJECTIVE
  ▷ see also **Pakistani** NOUN
  paquistaní (PL paquistaníes)
**Pakistani** NOUN
  ▷ see also **Pakistani** ADJECTIVE
  el/la paquistaní (PL los paquistaníes)
**pal** NOUN
  el amiguete
  la amigueta
**palace** NOUN
  el palacio
**pale** ADJECTIVE

1 pálido (FEM pálida)
  □ She still looks very pale. Está todavía muy
  pálida.
  ■ to turn pale ponerse pálido
2 claro (FEM clara)
  □ pale green verde claro
  ■ pale pink rosa pálido
  ■ pale blue azul celeste
**Palestine** NOUN
  Palestina fem
**Palestinian** ADJECTIVE
  ▷ see also **Palestinian** NOUN
  palestino (FEM palestina)
**Palestinian** NOUN
  ▷ see also **Palestinian** ADJECTIVE
  el palestino
  la palestina
**palm** NOUN
  la palma
  □ the palm of your hand la palma de la
  mano
  ■ a palm tree una palmera
**pamphlet** NOUN
  el folleto
**pan** NOUN
1 la cacerola (saucepan)
2 la sartén (PL las sartenes) (frying pan)
**pancake** NOUN
  la crepe (el panqueque Latin America)
**panic** NOUN
  ▷ see also **panic** VERB
  el pánico
  □ The shouting caused quite a panic.
  El griterío provocó el pánico.
to **panic** VERB
  ▷ see also **panic** NOUN
  ■ He panicked as soon as he saw the
  blood. Le entró pánico en cuanto vio la
  sangre.
  ■ Don't panic! ¡Tranquilo!
**panther** NOUN
  la pantera
**panties** PL NOUN
  las bragas
**pantomime** NOUN
  la revista musical representada en Navidad
**pants** PL NOUN
1 las bragas (for women)
2 los calzoncillos (for men)
3 los pantalones (US)
**pantyhose** PL NOUN (US)
  las medias
**paper** NOUN
1 el papel
  □ a paper bag una bolsa de papel
  ■ a piece of paper un papel (una hoja Latin
  America)
  ■ an exam paper un examen

P

**2** el periódico
  □ I saw an advert in the paper. Vi un anuncio en el periódico.

**paperback** NOUN
  el libro de bolsillo

**paper boy** NOUN
  el repartidor de periódicos

**paper clip** NOUN
  el clip (PL los clips)

**paper girl** NOUN
  la repartidora de periódicos

**paper round** NOUN
  ■ **to do a paper round** repartir los periódicos a domicilio

**paperweight** NOUN
  el pisapapeles (PL los pisapapeles)

**paperwork** NOUN
  el papeleo
  □ I've got a lot of paperwork to do. Tengo un montón de papeleo que hacer.

**parachute** NOUN
  el paracaídas (PL los paracaídas)

**parade** NOUN
  el desfile

**paradise** NOUN
  el paraíso

**paraffin** NOUN
  el queroseno
  ■ **a paraffin lamp** una lámpara de petróleo

**paragraph** NOUN
  el párrafo

**parallel** ADJECTIVE
  paralelo (FEM paralela)

**paralysed** ADJECTIVE
  paralizado (FEM paralizada)

**paramedic** NOUN
  el auxiliar sanitario
  la auxiliar sanitaria

**parcel** NOUN
  el paquete

**pardon** NOUN
  ■ **Pardon?** ¿Cómo?

**parents** PL NOUN
  los padres (los papás *Latin America*)
  ⦂ **LANGUAGE TIP** Be careful not to translate **parents** by **parientes**.

**Paris** NOUN
  París *masc*

**park** NOUN
  ▷ *see also* **park** VERB
  el parque
  ■ **a national park** un parque nacional
  ■ **a theme park** un parque temático
  ■ **a car park** un aparcamiento (un estacionamiento *Latin America*)

to **park** VERB
  ▷ *see also* **park** NOUN
  aparcar*

□ Where can I park my car? ¿Dónde puedo aparcar el coche?
  ■ **'no parking'** 'prohibido aparcar'

**parking lot** NOUN (US)
  el aparcamiento

**parking meter** NOUN
  el parquímetro

**parking ticket** NOUN
  la multa de aparcamiento

**parliament** NOUN
  el parlamento
  ■ **the Spanish Parliament** las Cortes

**parole** NOUN
  ■ **on parole** en libertad condicional

**parrot** NOUN
  el loro

**parsley** NOUN
  el perejil

**part** NOUN
  ▷ *see also* **part** VERB
**1** la parte
  □ The first part of the play was boring. La primera parte de la obra fue aburrida.
**2** el papel
  □ She had a small part in the film. Tenía un pequeño papel en la película.
**3** la pieza
  □ spare parts piezas de repuesto
  ■ **to take part in something** participar en algo □ Thousands of people took part in the demonstration. Miles de personas participaron en la manifestación.

**particular** ADJECTIVE
**1** concreto (FEM concreta) *(definite)*
  □ I can't remember that particular film. No recuerdo esa película concreta.
**2** especial (FEM especial) *(special)*
  □ He showed a particular interest in the subject. Mostró un interés especial en el tema.
  ■ **in particular** en concreto □ Are you looking for anything in particular? ¿Busca algo en concreto? □ nothing in particular nada en concreto

**particularly** ADVERB
  especialmente
  □ a particularly boring lecture una clase especialmente aburrida

**parting** NOUN
  la raya

**partly** ADVERB
  en parte
  □ It was partly my own fault. En parte fue culpa mía.

**partner** NOUN
**1** el socio
  la socia
  □ He's a partner in a law firm. Es socio de un bufete de abogados.

P

**2** la pareja

□ That doesn't mean you don't love your partner. Eso no significa que no quieras a tu pareja. □ my dancing partner mi pareja de baile

**part-time** ADJECTIVE, ADVERB
a tiempo parcial

□ a part-time job un trabajo a tiempo parcial □ She works part-time. Trabaja a tiempo parcial.

**party** NOUN
**1** la fiesta

□ a birthday party una fiesta de cumpleaños
**2** el partido

□ the Conservative Party el partido conservador
**3** el grupo

□ a party of tourists un grupo de turistas

**pass** NOUN
▷ see also **pass** VERB
**1** el pase (in football)

□ a short pass un pase en corto
**2** el puerto

□ The pass was blocked with snow. El puerto estaba bloqueado por la nieve.
**3** el aprobado

□ She got a pass in her piano exam. Sacó un aprobado en el examen de piano.
■ a bus pass un abono para el autobús

to **pass** VERB
▷ see also **pass** NOUN
**1** pasar

□ Could you pass me the salt, please? ¿Me pasas la sal, por favor? □ The time has passed quickly. El tiempo ha pasado rápido.
**2** adelantar

□ We were passed by a huge lorry. Nos adelantó un camión enorme.
**3** pasar por delante de

□ I pass his house on my way to school. Paso por delante de su casa de camino al colegio.
**4** aprobar*

□ Did you pass? ¿Has aprobado? □ to pass an exam aprobar un examen

to **pass out** VERB
desmayarse

**passage** NOUN
**1** el pasaje

□ Read the passage carefully. Lea el pasaje con atención.
**2** el pasillo

□ a narrow passage un estrecho pasillo

**passenger** NOUN
el pasajero
la pasajera

**passion** NOUN
la pasión (PL las pasiones)

□ Football is a passion of his. El fútbol es una de sus pasiones.

**passive** ADJECTIVE
pasivo (FEM pasiva)

□ a passive smoker un fumador pasivo

**Passover** NOUN
la Pascua judía

**passport** NOUN
el pasaporte

□ passport control el control de pasaportes

**password** NOUN
la contraseña

**past** ADJECTIVE, ADVERB, PREPOSITION
▷ see also **past** NOUN
pasado (FEM pasada)

□ This past year has been very difficult. Este año pasado ha sido muy difícil.
■ The school is 100 metres past the traffic lights. El colegio está a unos 100 metros pasado el semáforo.
■ to go past pasar □ The bus went past without stopping. El autobús pasó sin parar.
■ It's half past ten. Son las diez y media.
■ It's a quarter past nine. Son las nueve y cuarto.
■ It's ten past eight. Son las ocho y diez.
■ It's past midnight. Es pasada la medianoche.

**past** NOUN
▷ see also **past** ADJECTIVE, ADVERB, PREPOSITION
el pasado

□ I try not to think of the past. Intento no pensar en el pasado.
■ This was common in the past. Antiguamente esto era normal.

**pasta** NOUN
la pasta

**paste** NOUN
el engrudo (glue)

**pasteurized** ADJECTIVE
pasteurizado (FEM pasteurizada)

**pastime** NOUN
el pasatiempo

**pastry** NOUN
**1** la masa (dough)
**2** el pastel (cake)

**patch** NOUN
el parche

□ a patch of material un parche de tela
■ He's got a bald patch. Tiene una calva incipiente.
■ They're going through a bad patch. Están pasando una mala racha.

**patched** ADJECTIVE
■ a pair of patched jeans unos vaqueros con remiendos

**pâté** NOUN
el paté

**path** NOUN
el sendero

**pathetic** ADJECTIVE
penoso (FEM penosa)
□ That was a pathetic excuse. Fue una excusa penosa.

**patience** NOUN
1 la paciencia
□ He hasn't got much patience. No tiene mucha paciencia.
2 el solitario (game)
□ She was playing patience. Estaba haciendo un solitario.

**patient** NOUN
▷ see also **patient** ADJECTIVE
el paciente
la paciente

**patient** ADJECTIVE
▷ see also **patient** NOUN
paciente (FEM paciente)

**patio** NOUN
el patio

**patriotic** ADJECTIVE
patriótico (FEM patriótica)

**patrol** NOUN
la patrulla
■ to be on patrol estar de patrulla

**patrol car** NOUN
el coche patrulla (PL los coches patrulla)

**pattern** NOUN
1 el motivo (design)
□ a geometric pattern un motivo geométrico
2 el patrón (for sewing)

**pause** NOUN
la pausa

**pavement** NOUN
la acera

**paw** NOUN
la pata

**pay** NOUN
▷ see also **pay** VERB
el sueldo
□ a pay rise un aumento de sueldo

to **pay** VERB
▷ see also **pay** NOUN
pagar*
□ They pay me more on Sundays. Me pagan más los domingos. □ Can I pay by cheque? ¿Puedo pagar con cheque?
■ to pay money into an account ingresar dinero en una cuenta
■ I'll pay you back tomorrow. Mañana te devuelvo el dinero.
■ to pay for something pagar algo □ I paid for my ticket. Pagué el billete.
■ I paid £50 for it. Me costó 50 libras.
■ Does your current account pay interest? ¿Le rinde intereses su cuenta corriente?
■ to pay somebody a visit ir a ver a alguien
□ Paul paid us a visit last night. Paul vino a vernos anoche.

**payable** ADJECTIVE
■ Who's the cheque payable to? ¿A nombre de quién extiendo el cheque?

**payment** NOUN
el pago
□ mortgage payments los pagos de la hipoteca

**payphone** NOUN
el teléfono público

**PC** NOUN (= personal computer)
el PC

**PE** NOUN (= physical education)
la educación física
□ We do PE twice a week. Tenemos educación física dos veces a la semana.

**pea** NOUN
el guisante

**peace** NOUN
la paz
■ peace talks conversaciones de paz
■ a peace treaty un tratado de paz

**peaceful** ADJECTIVE
1 pacífico (FEM pacífica) (non-violent)
□ a peaceful protest una manifestación pacífica
2 apacible (FEM apacible) (restful)
□ a peaceful afternoon una tarde apacible

**peach** NOUN
el melocotón (PL los melocotones)

**peacock** NOUN
el pavo real

**peak** NOUN
1 la cumbre
□ the snow-covered peaks las cumbres nevadas
2 el apogeo
□ She's at the peak of her career. Está en el apogeo de su carrera profesional.
■ in peak season en temporada alta

**peanut** NOUN
el cacahuete (el maní Latin America)

**peanut butter** NOUN
la crema de cacahuete

**pear** NOUN
la pera

**pearl** NOUN
la perla

**pebble** NOUN
el guijarro

**peckish** ADJECTIVE
■ to feel a bit peckish tener un poquito de hambre

**peculiar** ADJECTIVE

raro (FEM rara)
□ He's a peculiar person. Es una persona rara. □ It tastes peculiar. Sabe raro.

**pedal** NOUN
el pedal

**pedestrian** NOUN
el peatón (PL los peatones)

**pedestrian crossing** NOUN
el paso de peatones

**pedestrianized** ADJECTIVE
■ a pedestrianized street una calle peatonal

**pedestrian precinct** NOUN
la zona peatonal

**pedigree** ADJECTIVE
de raza
□ a pedigree dog un perro de raza □ a pedigree labrador un labrador de pura raza

**pee** NOUN
■ to have a pee hacer pis

**peek** NOUN
■ to have a peek at something echar una ojeada a algo □ I had a peek at your dress and it's lovely. Le eché una ojeada a tu vestido y es muy mono.

**peel** NOUN
▷ see also **peel** VERB
la piel

to **peel** VERB
▷ see also **peel** NOUN
pelar
□ Shall I peel the potatoes? ¿Pelo las patatas?
■ My nose is peeling. Se me está pelando la nariz.

**peg** NOUN
1 el gancho (for coats)
2 la pinza (clothes peg)
3 la estaca (tent peg)

**Pekinese** NOUN
el pequinés (PL los pequineses)

**pellet** NOUN
el perdigón (PL los perdigones) (for gun)

**pelvis** NOUN
la pelvis (PL las pelvis)

**pen** NOUN
1 el bolígrafo (ballpoint pen)
2 la pluma (fountain pen)
3 el rotulador (felt-tip pen)

**penalty** NOUN
1 la pena
□ The penalty for this offence is life imprisonment. La pena por este delito es cadena perpetua.
■ the death penalty la pena de muerte
2 el penalty (PL los penaltys) (in football)
3 el golpe de castigo (in rugby)
■ a penalty shoot-out una tanda de penaltys

**pence** PL NOUN
■ 24 pence 24 peniques

**pencil** NOUN
el lápiz (PL los lápices) (el lapicero Latin America)
■ to write in pencil escribir a lápiz

**pencil case** NOUN
el estuche

**pencil sharpener** NOUN
el sacapuntas (PL los sacapuntas)

**penfriend** NOUN
el amigo por correspondencia
la amiga por correspondencia

**penguin** NOUN
el pingüino

**penicillin** NOUN
la penicilina

**penis** NOUN
el pene

**penitentiary** NOUN (US)
la cárcel

**penknife** NOUN
la navaja

**penny** NOUN
el penique

**pension** NOUN
la pensión (PL las pensiones)

**pensioner** NOUN
el/la pensionista

**pentathlon** NOUN
el pentatlón

**people** PL NOUN
1 la gente
□ The people were nice. La gente era simpática. □ a lot of people mucha gente
2 las personas
□ six people seis personas □ several people varias personas
■ People say that... Dicen que...
■ How many people are there in your family? ¿Cuántos sois en tu familia?
■ Spanish people los españoles

**pepper** NOUN
1 la pimienta
□ Pass the pepper, please. ¿Me pasas la pimienta?
2 el pimiento (el chile Latin America)
□ a green pepper un pimiento verde

**peppermill** NOUN
el molinillo de pimienta

**peppermint** NOUN
el caramelo de menta
■ peppermint chewing gum el chicle de menta

**per** PREPOSITION
por
□ per person por persona □ 30 miles per hour 30 millas por hora

■ **per day** al día
■ **per week** a la semana
**per cent** ADVERB
por ciento
□ 50 per cent 50 por ciento
**percentage** NOUN
el porcentaje
**percolator** NOUN
la cafetera de filtro
**percussion** NOUN
la percusión
□ I play percussion. Toco la percusión.
**perfect** ADJECTIVE
perfecto (FEM perfecta)
□ Dave speaks perfect Spanish. Dave habla
un español perfecto.
**perfectly** ADVERB
■ You know perfectly well what happened.
Sabes perfectamente lo que ocurrió.
■ a perfectly normal child un niño
completamente normal
to **perform** VERB
representar *(a play)*
□ to perform Hamlet representar Hamlet
■ The team performed brilliantly.
El equipo tuvo una brillante actuación.
**performance** NOUN
1 el espectáculo
□ The performance lasts two hours.
El espectáculo dura dos horas.
2 la interpretación (PL las interpretaciones)
□ his performance as Hamlet su
interpretación de Hamlet
**perfume** NOUN
el perfume
**perhaps** ADVERB
quizás
□ Perhaps they were tired. Quizás estaban
cansados.
> LANGUAGE TIP Use the present
subjunctive after **quizás** to refer to
the future.
□ Perhaps he'll come tomorrow. Quizás
venga mañana.
■ perhaps not quizás no
**period** NOUN
1 el periodo
□ for a limited period por un periodo limitado
2 la clase
□ Each period lasts forty minutes. Cada
clase dura cuarenta minutos.
3 la época
□ the Victorian period la época victoriana
4 la regla
□ I'm having my period. Estoy con la regla.
**perm** NOUN
la permanente
□ She's got a perm. Lleva permanente.

**permanent** ADJECTIVE
1 permanente (FEM permanente)
□ a permanent state of tension un estado
permanente de tensión
2 fijo (FEM fija)
□ a permanent job un trabajo fijo
**permission** NOUN
el permiso
□ Could I have permission to leave early?
¿Tengo permiso para salir antes?
**permit** NOUN
el permiso
□ a work permit un permiso de trabajo
**Persian** ADJECTIVE
■ a Persian cat un gato persa
**persistent** ADJECTIVE
persistente (FEM persistente)
**person** NOUN
la persona
□ She's a very nice person. Es muy buena
persona.
■ in person en persona
**personal** ADJECTIVE
personal (FEM personal)
□ Those letters are personal. Son cartas
personales. □ He's a personal friend of
mine. Es amigo íntimo mío.
**personality** NOUN
la personalidad
**personally** ADVERB
personalmente
□ Personally I don't agree. Yo
personalmente no estoy de acuerdo.
■ I don't know him personally. No lo
conozco en persona.
■ Don't take it personally. No te lo tomes
como algo personal.
**personal stereo** NOUN
el walkman®
**personnel** NOUN
el personal
**perspiration** NOUN
la transpiración
to **persuade** VERB
convencer*
> LANGUAGE TIP Use the subjunctive
after **convencer de que** when
translating 'to persuade somebody
to do something'.
■ to persuade sb to do sth convencer a
alguien de que haga algo □ She persuaded
me to go with her. Me convenció de que
fuera con ella.
**Peru** NOUN
Perú *masc*
**Peruvian** ADJECTIVE
▷ *see also* **Peruvian** NOUN
peruano (FEM peruana)

**English-Spanish**

**Peruvian** NOUN
▷ see also **Peruvian** ADJECTIVE
el peruano
la peruana

**pessimist** NOUN
el/la pesimista

**pessimistic** ADJECTIVE
pesimista (FEM pesimista)
□ Don't be so pessimistic! ¡No seas tan
pesimista! □ a pessimistic forecast un
pronóstico pesimista

**pest** NOUN
el pesado
la pesada
□ He's a real pest! ¡Es un pesado!

to **pester** VERB
dar* la lata a
□ He's always pestering me. Siempre me
está dando la lata.

**pet** NOUN
el animal doméstico
■ Have you got a pet? ¿Tenéis algún
animal en casa?
■ She's the teacher's pet. Es la enchufada
del profesor.

**petition** NOUN
la petición (PL las peticiones)

**petrified** ADJECTIVE
■ She's petrified of spiders. Las arañas le
dan terror.

**petrol** NOUN
la gasolina
■ unleaded petrol gasolina sin plomo
■ 4-star petrol gasolina súper

**petrol station** NOUN
la gasolinera

**petrol tank** NOUN
el depósito de gasolina

**phantom** NOUN
el fantasma

**LANGUAGE TIP** Although **fantasma**
ends in **-a**, it is actually a masculine
noun.

**pharmacy** NOUN
la farmacia

**DID YOU KNOW...?**
Pharmacies in Spain are identified
by a green cross outside the shop.

**pheasant** NOUN
el faisán (PL los faisanes)

**philosophy** NOUN
la filosofía

**phobia** NOUN
la fobia

**phone** NOUN
▷ see also **phone** VERB
el teléfono
■ by phone por teléfono

■ to be on the phone 1 (talking) estar al
teléfono □ She's on the phone at the
moment. Ahora mismo está al teléfono.
2 (to have a phone) tener teléfono □ We're
not on the phone. No tenemos teléfono.
■ Can I use the phone, please? ¿Puedo
hacer una llamada?

to **phone** VERB
▷ see also **phone** NOUN
llamar
□ I'll phone you tomorrow. Mañana te
llamo. □ Could you phone for a taxi for me,
please? ¿Me puedes llamar a un taxi, por
favor?

**phone bill** NOUN
la factura del teléfono

**phone book** NOUN
la guía telefónica

**phone box** NOUN
la cabina telefónica

**phone call** NOUN
la llamada de teléfono
■ There's a phone call for you. Tienes una
llamada.
■ to make a phone call hacer una llamada

**phonecard** NOUN
la tarjeta telefónica

**phone number** NOUN
el número de teléfono

**photo** NOUN
la foto

**LANGUAGE TIP** Although **foto** ends in
**-o**, it is actually a feminine noun.

■ to take a photo hacer una foto □ I took a
photo of the bride and groom. Les hice una
foto a los novios.

**photocopier** NOUN
la fotocopiadora

**photocopy** NOUN
▷ see also **photocopy** VERB
la fotocopia

to **photocopy** VERB
▷ see also **photocopy** NOUN
fotocopiar

**photograph** NOUN
▷ see also **photograph** VERB
la fotografía
■ to take a photograph hacer una
fotografía □ I took a photograph of the bride
and groom. Les hice una fotografía a los
novios.

to **photograph** VERB
▷ see also **photograph** NOUN
fotografiar*

**photographer** NOUN
el fotógrafo
la fotógrafa
□ She's a photographer. Es fotógrafa.

P

**photography** NOUN
la fotografía
□ My hobby is photography. Mi hobby es la fotografía.

**phrase** NOUN
la frase

**phrase book** NOUN
el manual de conversación

**physical** ADJECTIVE
▷ see also **physical** NOUN
físico (FEM física)

**physical** NOUN (US)
▷ see also **physical** ADJECTIVE
el reconocimiento médico

**physicist** NOUN
el físico
la física
□ a nuclear physicist un físico nuclear

**physics** NOUN
la física
□ She teaches physics. Enseña física.

**physiotherapist** NOUN
el/la fisioterapeuta

**physiotherapy** NOUN
la fisioterapia

**pianist** NOUN
el/la pianista

**piano** NOUN
el piano
□ I play the piano. Toco el piano.

**pick** NOUN
▷ see also **pick** VERB
■ **Take your pick!** ¡Elige el que quieras!
LANGUAGE TIP Replace **el que** with **la que, los que** or **las que** as appropriate to agree with the thing or things you can take your pick of.

to **pick** VERB
▷ see also **pick** NOUN
1 elegir* (choose)
□ I picked the biggest piece. Elegí el trozo más grande.
2 seleccionar (for team)
□ I've been picked for the team. Me han seleccionado para el equipo.
3 recoger* (fruit, flowers)
■ **to pick on somebody** meterse con alguien □ She's always picking on me. Siempre se está metiendo conmigo.

to **pick out** VERB
escoger*
□ I like them all – it's difficult to pick one out. Todos me gustan, es difícil escoger uno.

to **pick up** VERB
1 recoger*
□ We'll come to the airport to pick you up. Iremos a recogerte al aeropuerto. □ Could

you help me pick up the toys? ¿Me ayudas a recoger los juguetes?
2 aprender
□ I picked up some Spanish during my holiday. Aprendí un poco de español en las vacaciones.

**pickpocket** NOUN
el/la carterista

**picnic** NOUN
el picnic (PL los picnics)
■ **to have a picnic** irse de picnic

**picture** NOUN
1 la ilustración (PL las ilustraciones)
□ Children's books have lots of pictures. Los libros para niños tienen muchas ilustraciones.
2 la foto
LANGUAGE TIP Although **foto** ends in **-o**, it is actually a feminine noun.
□ My picture was in the paper. Mi foto salió en el periódico.
3 el cuadro (painting)
□ a picture by Picasso un cuadro de Picasso
■ **a picture of his wife** un retrato de su mujer
4 el dibujo (drawing)
■ **to draw a picture of something** dibujar algo
■ **to paint a picture of something** pintar algo
■ **the pictures** el cine □ Shall we go to the pictures? ¿Vamos al cine?

**picturesque** ADJECTIVE
pintoresco (FEM pintoresca)

**pie** NOUN
1 la tarta (sweet)
□ an apple pie una tarta de manzana
2 el pastel (of meat)
□ a meat pie un pastel de carne

**piece** NOUN
1 el trozo
□ a piece of cake un trozo de tarta
■ **A small piece, please.** Un trocito, por favor.
2 pieza (individual)
□ a 500-piece jigsaw un puzzle de 500 piezas
3 pedazo (of something larger)
□ A piece of plaster fell from the roof. Un pedazo de yeso se cayó del tejado.
■ **a piece of furniture** un mueble
■ **a piece of advice** un consejo
■ **a 10p piece** una moneda de 10 peniques

**pier** NOUN
el muelle

**pierced** ADJECTIVE
■ **I've got pierced ears.** Tengo los agujeros hechos en las orejas.

P

187

**pig** NOUN
el cerdo

**pigeon** NOUN
la paloma

**piggyback** NOUN
■ **to give somebody a piggyback** llevar a alguien a cuestas

**piggy bank** NOUN
la hucha

**pigtail** NOUN
la trenza

**pile** NOUN
1 el montón (PL los montones) *(untidy heap)*
□ a pile of dirty laundry un montón de ropa sucia
2 la pila *(tidy stack)*
■ **Put your books in a pile on my desk.** Apilad vuestros cuadernos en mi mesa.

**piles** PL NOUN
las almorranas

**pile-up** NOUN
el accidente en cadena

**pill** NOUN
la píldora
■ **to be on the pill** tomar la píldora

**pillar** NOUN
1 el pilar

**pillar box** NOUN
2 el buzón (PL los buzones)

**pillow** NOUN
la almohada

**pilot** NOUN
el/la piloto
□ He's a pilot. Es piloto.

**pimple** NOUN
el grano

**pin** NOUN
el alfiler
■ **pins and needles** el hormigueo □ I've got pins and needles. Tengo hormigueo.

**PIN** NOUN *(= personal identification number)*
el número secreto

**pinafore** NOUN
el pichi

**pinball** NOUN
la máquina de bolas
■ **They're playing pinball.** Juegan a la máquina.

to **pinch** VERB
1 pellizcar*
□ He pinched me! ¡Me ha pellizcado!
2 birlar* *(informal)*
□ Who's pinched my pen? ¿Quién me ha birlado el bolígrafo?

**pine** NOUN
el pino
□ a pine table una mesa de pino

**pineapple** NOUN

la piña

**pink** ADJECTIVE
rosa (FEM + PL rosa)

**pint** NOUN
la pinta

> **DID YOU KNOW...?**
> In Spain measurements are in litres and centilitres. A pint is about 0.6 litres.

■ **to have a pint** tomarse una cerveza
□ He's gone out for a pint. Ha salido a tomarse una cerveza.

**pipe** NOUN
1 la tubería
□ The pipes froze. Se helaron las tuberías.
2 la pipa
□ He smokes a pipe. Fuma en pipa.
■ **the pipes** la gaita □ He plays the pipes. Toca la gaita.

**pirate** NOUN
el/la pirata

**pirated** ADJECTIVE
pirata (FEM + PL pirata)
□ a pirated video un vídeo pirata

**Pisces** NOUN
el Piscis *(sign)*
■ **I'm Pisces.** Soy piscis.

**pissed** ADJECTIVE
mamado (FEM mamada) *(rude)*

**pistol** NOUN
la pistola

**pitch** NOUN
▷ see also **pitch** VERB
el campo (la cancha *Latin America*)
□ a football pitch un campo de fútbol

to **pitch** VERB
▷ see also **pitch** NOUN
montar
□ We pitched our tent near the beach. Montamos la tienda cerca de la playa.

**pity** NOUN
▷ see also **pity** VERB
la compasión
□ They showed no pity. No demostraron ninguna compasión.
■ **What a pity!** ¡Qué pena!

to **pity** VERB
▷ see also **pity** NOUN
compadecer*
□ I don't hate him, I pity him. No lo odio, lo compadezco.

**pizza** NOUN
la pizza

**place** NOUN
▷ see also **place** VERB
1 el lugar
□ It's a quiet place. Es un lugar tranquilo.
2 la plaza

□ Book your place for the trip now. Reserve ya su plaza para el viaje. □ a university place una plaza en la universidad
**3** el puesto *(in sports)*
□ Britain won third place in the games. Gran Bretaña consiguió el tercer puesto en los juegos.
■ **a parking place** un sitio para aparcar
■ **to change places** cambiarse de sitio
■ **to take place** tener lugar □ Elections will take place on November 25th. Las elecciones tendrán lugar el 25 de noviembre.
■ **at your place** en tu casa □ Shall we meet at your place? ¿Nos vemos en tu casa?
■ **Do you want to come round to my place?** ¿Quieres venir a mi casa?
**to place** VERB
▷ *see also* **place** NOUN
colocar*
□ He placed his hand on hers. Colocó su mano sobre la de ella.
**plain** ADJECTIVE, ADVERB
▷ *see also* **plain** NOUN
**1** liso (FEM lisa) *(not patterned)*
□ a plain tie una corbata lisa
**2** sencillo (FEM sencilla) *(not fancy)*
□ a plain white blouse una blusa blanca sencilla
■ **It was plain to see.** Era obvio.
**plain** NOUN
▷ *see also* **plain** ADJECTIVE, ADVERB
la llanura
**plain chocolate** NOUN
el chocolate amargo
**plait** NOUN
la trenza
□ She wears her hair in plaits. Lleva trenzas.
**plan** NOUN
▷ *see also* **plan** VERB
**1** el plan
□ What are your plans for the holidays? ¿Qué planes tienes para las vacaciones?
■ **to make plans** hacer planes
■ **Everything went according to plan.** Todo fue según lo previsto.
**2** el plano
□ a plan of the campsite un plano del camping
■ **my essay plan** el esquema de mi trabajo
**to plan** VERB
▷ *see also* **plan** NOUN
**1** planear *(make plans for)*
□ We're planning a trip to France. Estamos planeando hacer un viaje a Francia.
**2** planificar* *(schedule)*
□ Plan your revision carefully. Tienes que planificar bien el repaso.

■ **to plan to do something** tener la intención de hacer algo □ I'm planning to get a job in the holidays. Tengo la intención de encontrar un trabajo para las vacaciones.
**plane** NOUN
el avión (PL los aviones)
□ by plane en avión
**planet** NOUN
el planeta
LANGUAGE TIP Although **planeta** ends in **-a**, it is actually a masculine noun.
**planning** NOUN
■ **The trip needs careful planning.** Hay que planear bien el viaje.
■ **family planning** la planificación familiar
**plant** NOUN
▷ *see also* **plant** VERB
la planta
□ I water my plants every week. Riego las plantas todas las semanas.
■ **a chemical plant** una planta química
**to plant** VERB
▷ *see also* **plant** NOUN
plantar
□ We planted fruit trees and vegetables. Plantamos árboles frutales y hortalizas.
**plant pot** NOUN
la maceta
**plaque** NOUN
**1** la placa conmemorativa *(to famous person, event)*
**2** el sarro *(on teeth)*
**plaster** NOUN
**1** la tirita
□ Have you got a plaster, by any chance? ¿No tendrás una tirita, por casualidad?
**2** la escayola
■ **Her leg's in plaster.** Lleva la pierna escayolada.
**plastic** NOUN
▷ *see also* **plastic** ADJECTIVE
el plástico
□ It's made of plastic. Es de plástico.
**plastic** ADJECTIVE
▷ *see also* **plastic** NOUN
de plástico
□ a plastic bag una bolsa de plástico
**plate** NOUN
el plato
**platform** NOUN
**1** el andén (PL los andenes)
**2** el estrado *(for speaker, performer)*
**play** NOUN
▷ *see also* **play** VERB
la obra de teatro
■ **a play by Shakespeare** una obra de Shakespeare
■ **to put on a play** montar una obra

P

189

to **play** VERB
▷ see also **play** NOUN
1 jugar*
□ He's playing with his friends. Está jugando con sus amigos.
2 jugar contra
□ Spain will play Scotland next month. España juega contra Escocia el mes que viene.
3 jugar a
□ Can you play pool? ¿Sabes jugar al billar americano?
4 tocar*
□ I play the guitar. Toco la guitarra. □ What sort of music do they play? ¿Qué clase de música tocan?
5 poner*
□ She's always playing that CD. Siempre está poniendo ese CD.
6 hacer* de
□ I would love to play Cleopatra. Me encantaría hacer de Cleopatra.

to **play down** VERB
quitar importancia a
□ He tried to play down his illness. Trató de quitarle importancia a su enfermedad.

**player** NOUN
1 el jugador
la jugadora
□ a game for four players un juego para cuatro jugadores
■ **a football player** un futbolista
2 el músico
la música (musician)
■ **a piano player** un pianista
■ **a saxophone player** un saxofonista

**playful** ADJECTIVE
juguetón (FEM juguetona)

**playground** NOUN
1 el patio de recreo (at school)
2 los columpios (in park)

**playgroup** NOUN
la guardería

**playing card** NOUN
el naipe

**playing field** NOUN
el campo de deportes (la cancha de deportes Latin America)

**playtime** NOUN
el recreo

**playwright** NOUN
el dramaturgo
la dramaturga

**pleasant** ADJECTIVE
agradable (FEM agradable)
□ We had a very pleasant evening. Pasamos una tarde muy agradable.

**please** EXCLAMATION
por favor

□ Two coffees, please. Dos cafés, por favor.

LANGUAGE TIP **por favor** is not as common as 'please' and can be omitted in many cases. Spanish speakers may show their politeness by their intonation, or by using **usted**.

■ **Can we have the bill please?** ¿Nos puede traer la cuenta?
■ **Please come in.** Pase.
■ **Would you please be quiet?** ¿Quieres hacer el favor de callarte?

**pleased** ADJECTIVE
■ **My mother's not going to be very pleased.** A mi madre no le va a hacer mucha gracia.
■ **It's beautiful: she'll be very pleased with it.** Es precioso: le va a gustar mucho.
■ **Pleased to meet you!** ¡Encantado!

**pleasure** NOUN
el placer
□ I read for pleasure. Leo por placer.

**plenty** PRONOUN
■ **Fifteen minutes is plenty.** Quince minutos es más que suficiente.
■ **I've got plenty.** Tengo de sobra.
■ **That's plenty, thanks.** Así está bien, gracias.
■ **I've got plenty to do.** Tengo un montón de cosas que hacer.
■ **plenty of 1** (lots of) mucho □ He's got plenty of energy. Tiene mucha energía.
2 (more than enough) de sobra □ We've got plenty of time. Tenemos tiempo de sobra.

**pliers** NOUN
los alicates

**plot** NOUN
▷ see also **plot** VERB
1 el argumento (of story, play)
2 el complot (PL los complots) (conspiracy)
□ a plot against the president un complot contra el presidente
3 el huerto (for vegetables)

to **plot** VERB
▷ see also **plot** NOUN
conspirar

**plough** NOUN
▷ see also **plough** VERB
el arado

to **plough** VERB
▷ see also **plough** NOUN
arar

**plug** NOUN
1 el enchufe (electrical)
2 el tapón (PL los tapones) (for sink)

to **plug in** VERB
enchufar
□ Is the iron plugged in? ¿Está enchufada la plancha?

**plum** NOUN
la ciruela

**plumber** NOUN
el fontanero
la fontanera
□ He's a plumber. Es fontanero.

**plump** ADJECTIVE
rechoncho (FEM rechoncha)

to **plunge** VERB
zambullirse*
□ He plunged into the water. Se zambulló
en el agua.

**plural** NOUN
el plural

**plus** PREPOSITION, ADJECTIVE
más (FEM mása)
□ 4 plus 3 equals 7. 4 más 3 son 7.
■ **three children plus a dog** tres niños y
un perro
■ **I got a B plus.** Saqué un notable alto.

**p.m.** ABBREVIATION

○ **LANGUAGE TIP** Use **de la tarde** if it's
light and **de la noche** if it's dark.

■ **at 2 p.m.** a las dos de la tarde
■ **at 9 p.m.** a las nueve de la noche

**pneumonia** NOUN
la pulmonía

**poached** ADJECTIVE
■ **a poached egg** un huevo escalfado

**pocket*** NOUN
el bolsillo
□ He had his hands in his pockets. Tenía las
manos en los bolsillos.

**poem** NOUN
el poema

○ **LANGUAGE TIP** Although **poema** ends
in -a, it is actually a masculine noun.

**poet** NOUN
el poeta
la poetisa

**poetry** NOUN
la poesía

**point** NOUN
▷ see also **point** VERB
1 el punto
□ a point on the horizon un punto en el
horizonte □ They scored five points.
Sacaron cinco puntos.
2 el momento
□ At that point, we decided to leave. En
aquel momento decidimos marcharnos.
3 la punta
□ a pencil with a sharp point un lápiz con la
punta afilada
4 el comentario
□ He made some interesting points. Hizo
algunos comentarios de interés.
■ **They were on the point of finding it.**

Estaban a punto de encontrarlo.
■ **Sorry, I don't get the point.** Perdona,
pero no lo entiendo.
■ **a point of view** un punto de vista
■ **That's a good point!** ¡Tiene razón!
■ **That's not the point.** Eso no tiene nada
que ver.
■ **There's no point.** No tiene sentido.
□ There's no point in waiting. No tiene
sentido esperar.
■ **What's the point?** ¿Para qué? □ What's
the point of leaving so early? ¿Para qué salir
tan pronto?
■ **Punctuality isn't my strong point.**
La puntualidad no es mi fuerte.
■ **two point five (2.5)** dos coma cinco (2,5)

to **point** VERB
▷ see also **point** NOUN
señalar con el dedo
□ Don't point! ¡No señales con el dedo!
■ **to point at somebody** señalar a alguien
con el dedo □ She pointed at Anne. Señaló
a Anne con el dedo.
■ **to point a gun at somebody** apuntar a
alguien con una pistola

to **point out** VERB
1 señalar
□ The guide pointed out the Alhambra to us.
El guía nos señaló la Alhambra.
2 indicar*
□ I should point out that... Me gustaría
indicar que...

**pointless** ADJECTIVE
inútil (FEM inútil)
□ It's pointless arguing. Es inútil discutir.

**poison** NOUN
▷ see also **poison** VERB
el veneno

to **poison** VERB
▷ see also **poison** NOUN
envenenar

**poisonous** ADJECTIVE
1 venenoso (FEM venenosa) (animal, plant)
2 tóxico (FEM tóxica) (chemical)
□ poisonous gases gases tóxicos

to **poke** VERB
■ **He poked me in the eye.** Me metió un
dedo en el ojo.

**poker** NOUN
el póker
□ I play poker. Juego al póker.

**Poland** NOUN
Polonia fem

**polar bear** NOUN
el oso polar

**Pole** NOUN
el polaco
la polaca

**pole** NOUN
el poste
□ a telegraph pole un poste de telégrafos
■ **a tent pole** un mástil de tienda
■ **a ski pole** un bastón de esquí
■ **the North Pole** el Polo Norte
■ **the South Pole** el Polo Sur

**pole vault** NOUN
■ **the pole vault** el salto con pértiga

**police** PL NOUN
la policía
□ We called the police. Llamamos a la policía.

**policeman** NOUN
el policía (el agente *Latin America*)

**police officer** NOUN
el/la agente de policía

**police station** NOUN
la comisaría

**policewoman** NOUN
la policía (la agente *Latin America*)

**polio** NOUN
la polio

> **LANGUAGE TIP** Although **polio** ends in -o, it is actually a feminine noun.

**Polish** ADJECTIVE
▷ *see also* **Polish** NOUN
polaco (FEM polaca)

**Polish** NOUN
▷ *see also* **Polish** ADJECTIVE
el polaco (*language*)

**polish** NOUN
▷ *see also* **polish** VERB
1 el betún (*for shoes*)
2 la cera (*for furniture*)

to **polish** VERB
▷ *see also* **polish** NOUN
limpiar (*shoes, glass*)
■ **to polish the furniture** sacar brillo a los muebles

**polite** ADJECTIVE
educado (FEM educada)
□ a polite child un niño educado
■ **It's not polite to point.** Es de mala educación señalar con el dedo.

**politeness** NOUN
la cortesía

**political** ADJECTIVE
político (FEM política)

**politician** NOUN
el político
la política

**politics** NOUN
la política
□ I'm not interested in politics. No me interesa la política.

**poll** NOUN
el sondeo de opinión

**pollen** NOUN
el polen

to **pollute** VERB
contaminar

**pollution** NOUN
la contaminación

**polo-necked sweater** NOUN
el suéter de cuello alto

**polo shirt** NOUN
el polo

**polythene bag** NOUN
la bolsa de plástico

**pond** NOUN
1 la charca (*natural*)
2 el estanque (*artificial*)

**pony** NOUN
el poney

**ponytail** NOUN
la coleta
□ He's got a ponytail. Lleva coleta.

**pony trekking** NOUN
■ **to go pony trekking** ir de excursión en poney

**poodle** NOUN
el caniche

**pool** NOUN
1 el estanque (*pond*)
2 la piscina (*swimming pool*)
3 el billar americano (*game*)
■ **a pool table** una mesa de billar
■ **the pools** las quinielas □ I do the pools every week. Juego a las quinielas todas las semanas.

**poor** ADJECTIVE
1 pobre (FEM pobre)

> **LANGUAGE TIP** **pobre** goes after the noun when it means that someone has not got very much money. It goes before the noun when you want to show that you feel sorry for someone.

□ a poor family una familia pobre □ Poor David, he's very unlucky! ¡Pobre David, tiene muy mala suerte!
■ **the poor** los pobres
2 malo (FEM mala)

> **LANGUAGE TIP** Use **mal** before a masculine singular noun.

□ He's a poor actor. Es un mal actor.
□ a poor mark una mala nota

**poorly** ADJECTIVE
□ She's feeling a bit poorly. No se siente muy bien.

**pop** ADJECTIVE
pop (FEM + PL pop)
□ pop music la música pop □ a pop star una estrella pop
■ **a pop group** un grupo de música pop

to **pop in** VERB

entrar un momento

**to pop out** VERB
salir\* un momento

**to pop round** VERB
■ **I'm just popping round to John's.** Voy a pasarme por casa de John.

**popcorn** NOUN
las palomitas de maíz

**poppy** NOUN
la amapola

**Popsicle®** NOUN (US)
el polo

**popular** ADJECTIVE
popular (FEM populara)
□ Football is the most popular game in this country. El fútbol es el deporte más popular de este país.
■ **She's a very popular girl.** Es una chica que cae bien a todo el mundo.
■ **This is a very popular style.** Este estilo está muy de moda.

**population** NOUN
la población (PL las poblaciones)

**porch** NOUN
el porche de entrada

**pork** NOUN
la carne de cerdo (la carne de puerco *Latin America*)
■ **a pork chop** una chuleta de cerdo

**porn** NOUN
▷ *see also* **porn** ADJECTIVE
el porno

**porn** ADJECTIVE
▷ *see also* **porn** NOUN
porno (FEM + PL porno)
□ a porn film una película porno

**pornographic** ADJECTIVE
pornográfico (FEM pornográfica)
□ a pornographic magazine una revista pornográfica

**pornography** NOUN
la pornografía

**porridge** NOUN
las gachas de avena

**port** NOUN
el puerto
□ a fishing port un puerto pesquero

**portable** NOUN
portátil
□ a portable TV un televisor portátil

**porter** NOUN
1 el portero
la portera *(in hotel)*
2 el mozo de equipajes
la moza de equipajes *(at station)*

**portion** NOUN
1 la porción (PL las porciones)
2 la ración (PL las raciones) *(of food)*

□ a large portion of chips una ración grande de patatas fritas

**portrait** NOUN
el retrato

**Portugal** NOUN
Portugal *masc*

**Portuguese** ADJECTIVE
▷ *see also* **Portuguese** NOUN
portugués (PL portugueses, FEM portuguesa)

**Portuguese** NOUN
▷ *see also* **Portuguese** ADJECTIVE
el portugués *(language)*
■ **the Portuguese** los portugueses

**posh** ADJECTIVE
de lujo
□ a posh car un coche de lujo

**position** NOUN
la posición (PL las posiciones)
□ an uncomfortable position una posición incómoda

**positive** ADJECTIVE
1 positivo (FEM positiva)
□ a positive attitude una actitud positiva
2 seguro (FEM segura) *(sure)*
□ I'm positive. Estoy completamente seguro.

**to possess** VERB
poseer\*
□ She lost everything she possessed. Perdió todo lo que poseía.

**possession** NOUN
■ **Have you got all your possessions?** ¿Tienes todas tus pertenencias?

**possibility** NOUN
la posibilidad
□ There were several possibilities. Había varias posibilidades.

**possible** ADJECTIVE
posible (FEM posible)
■ **as soon as possible** lo antes posible
⏺ **LANGUAGE TIP** **es posible que** has to be followed by a verb in the subjunctive.
■ **It's possible that he's gone away.** Es posible que se haya ido.

**possibly** ADVERB
tal vez
□ Are you coming to the party? — Possibly. ¿Vas a venir a la fiesta? — Tal vez.
■ **... if you possibly can.** ... si es que puedes.
■ **I can't possibly go.** Me es del todo imposible ir.

**post** NOUN
▷ *see also* **post** VERB
1 el correo
□ Has the post arrived yet? ¿Ha llegado ya el correo?

■ **by post** por correo

■ **Is there any post for me?** ¿Tengo alguna carta?

2 el poste

□ The ball hit the post. El balón dio en el poste.

to **post** VERB

▷ see also **post** NOUN

mandar por correo

□ You could post it. Puedes mandarlo por correo.

■ **I've got some cards to post.** Tengo que mandar algunas postales.

■ **Would you post this letter for me?** ¿Me echas esta carta al correo?

**postage** NOUN

el franqueo

**postbox** NOUN

el buzón (PL los buzones)

**postcard** NOUN

la postal

**postcode** NOUN

el código postal

**poster** NOUN

1 el cartel (public)

□ There are posters all over town. Hay carteles por toda la ciudad.

2 el póster (PL los pósters) (personal)

□ I've got posters on my bedrooms walls. Tengo pósters en las paredes de mi cuarto.

**postman** NOUN

el cartero

□ He's a postman. Es cartero.

**postmark** NOUN

el matasellos (PL los matasellos)

**post office** NOUN

la oficina de correos

□ Where's the post office, please? ¿Sabe dónde está la oficina de correos?

■ **She works for the post office.** Trabaja en correos.

to **postpone** VERB

aplazar*

□ The match has been postponed. El partido ha sido aplazado.

**postwoman** NOUN

la cartera

□ She's a postwoman. Es cartera.

**pot** NOUN

1 el tarro (el pote Latin America)

□ a pot of jam un tarro de mermelada

■ **a pot of paint** un bote de pintura

■ **the pots and pans** las cacerolas

2 la tetera (teapot)

■ **a coffeepot** una cafetera

3 la maría (informal)

□ to smoke pot fumar maría

**potato** NOUN

la patata (la papa Latin America)

■ **mashed potatoes** el puré de patatas ped

**potential** NOUN

▷ see also **potential** ADJECTIVE

■ **He has great potential.** Promete mucho.

**potential** ADJECTIVE

▷ see also **potential** NOUN

posible (FEM posible)

□ a potential problem un posible problema

**pothole** NOUN

el bache

**pot plant** NOUN

la planta de interior

**pottery** NOUN

la cerámica

**pound** NOUN

▷ see also **pound** VERB

1 la libra

> **DID YOU KNOW...?**
>
> In Spain measurements are in grams and kilograms. One pound is about 450 grams.

□ a pound of carrots una libra de zanahorias

2 la libra esterlina

■ **20 pounds** 20 libras

■ **a pound coin** una moneda de una libra

to **pound** VERB

▷ see also **pound** NOUN

latir con fuerza

□ My heart was pounding. El corazón me latía con fuerza.

to **pour** VERB

1 echar

□ She poured some water into the pan. Echó un poco de agua en la olla.

2 llover* a cántaros

□ It's pouring. Está lloviendo a cántaros.

■ **in the pouring rain** bajo una lluvia torrencial

**poverty** NOUN

la pobreza

**powder** NOUN

el polvo

■ **a fine white powder** un polvillo blanco

**power** NOUN

1 la corriente (electrical)

□ The power's off. Se ha ido la corriente.

2 la energía

□ nuclear power la energía nuclear □ solar power la energía solar

3 el poder

□ They were in power for 18 years. Estuvieron 18 años en el poder.

■ **a power point** un enchufe

**powerful** ADJECTIVE

1 poderoso (FEM poderosa) (person, organization)

□ the most powerful country in the world el país más poderoso del mundo

**2** potente (FEM potente) *(machine, substance)*

□ a powerful computer system un potente sistema informático

**practical** ADJECTIVE

práctico (FEM práctica)

□ a practical suggestion un consejo práctico

□ She's very practical. Es muy práctica.

**practically** ADVERB

prácticamente

□ It's practically impossible. Es prácticamente imposible.

**practice** NOUN

**1** la práctica

□ You'll get better with practice. Mejorarás con la práctica.

■ **in practice** en la práctica

■ **It's normal practice in our school.** Es lo normal en nuestro colegio.

**2** el entrenamiento

□ football practice entrenamiento de fútbol

■ **I'm out of practice.** Estoy desentrenado.

■ **I've got to do my piano practice.** Tengo que hacer los ejercicios de piano.

■ **a medical practice** una consulta médica

to **practise** (US **practice**) VERB

**1** practicar*

□ I ought to practise more. Debería practicar más.  □ I practise the flute every evening. Practico flauta todas las tardes.

□ I practised my Spanish when we were on holiday. Practiqué el español cuando estuvimos de vacaciones.

**2** entrenarse *(train)*

□ The team practises on Thursdays. El equipo se entrena los jueves.

**practising** ADJECTIVE

practicante (FEM practicante)

□ She's a practising Catholic. Es católica practicante.

to **praise** VERB

elogiar

□ Everyone praises her cooking. Todo el mundo elogia cómo cocina.

**pram** NOUN

el cochecito de niño

**prawn** NOUN

la gamba

**prawn cocktail** NOUN

el cóctel de gambas (el cóctel de camarón *Latin America*)

to **pray** VERB

rezar*

□ to pray for something rezar por algo

**prayer** NOUN

la oración (PL las oraciones)

**precaution** NOUN

la precaución (PL las precauciones)

■ **to take precautions** tomar precauciones

**preceding** ADJECTIVE

anterior (FEM anteriora)

**precinct** NOUN

■ **a shopping precinct** un centro comercial

**precious** ADJECTIVE

precioso (FEM preciosa)

□ a precious stone una piedra preciosa

**precise** ADJECTIVE

preciso (FEM precisa)

□ at that precise moment en aquel preciso instante

■ **to be precise** para ser exacto

**precisely** ADVERB

precisamente

□ That is precisely what it's meant for. Para eso precisamente está hecho.

■ **Precisely!** ¡Exactamente!

■ **at 10 a.m. precisely** a las diez en punto de la mañana

to **predict** VERB

predecir*

**predictable** ADJECTIVE

previsible (FEM previsible)

**prefect** NOUN

el monitor

la monitora *(in school)*

to **prefer** VERB

preferir*

□ Which would you prefer? ¿Tú cuál prefieres?  □ I prefer chemistry to maths. Prefiero la química a las matemáticas.

**preference** NOUN

la preferencia

**pregnant** ADJECTIVE

embarazada

□ She's six months pregnant. Está embarazada de seis meses.

**prehistoric** ADJECTIVE

prehistórico (FEM prehistórica)

**prejudice** NOUN

el prejuicio

□ That's just a prejudice. Eso no es más que un prejuicio.

■ **There's a lot of racial prejudice.** Hay muchos prejuicios raciales.

**prejudiced** ADJECTIVE

■ **to be prejudiced against somebody** tener prejuicios contra alguien

**premature** ADJECTIVE

prematuro (FEM prematura)

□ a premature baby un bebé prematuro

**Premier League** NOUN

la primera división

**premises** PL NOUN

el local

□ They're moving to new premises.

Se cambian de local.

**premonition** NOUN
el presentimiento

**preoccupied** ADJECTIVE
preocupado (FEM preocupada)

**prep** NOUN
los deberes
□ history prep  los deberes de historia

to **prepare** VERB
preparar
□ He was preparing dinner.  Estaba preparando la cena.
■ **to prepare for something**  hacer los preparativos para algo  □ We're preparing for our holiday.  Estamos haciendo los preparativos para las vacaciones.

**prepared** ADJECTIVE
■ **to be prepared to do something**  estar dispuesto a hacer algo  □ I'm prepared to help you.  Estoy dispuesto a ayudarte.

**prep school** NOUN
el colegio privado (de enseñanza primaria)

**Presbyterian** ADJECTIVE
▷ see also **Presbyterian** NOUN
presbiteriano (FEM presbiteriana)

**Presbyterian** NOUN
▷ see also **Presbyterian** ADJECTIVE
el presbiteriano
la presbiteriana

to **prescribe** VERB
recetar
□ The doctor prescribed a course of antibiotics for me.  El doctor me recetó antibióticos.

**prescription** NOUN
la receta
□ a prescription for penicillin  una receta de penicilina
■ **on prescription**  con receta médica

**presence** NOUN
la presencia
■ **presence of mind**  presencia de ánimo

**present** ADJECTIVE
▷ see also **present** NOUN, VERB
1 presente (FEM presente)
□ He wasn't present at the meeting.  No estuvo presente en la reunión.
2 actual (FEM actual)
□ the present situation  la situación actual
■ **the present tense**  el presente

**present** NOUN
▷ see also **present** ADJECTIVE, VERB
1 el regalo
■ **to give somebody a present**  hacer un regalo a alguien  □ He gave me a lovely present.  Me hizo un precioso regalo.
2 el presente
□ to live in the present  vivir el presente
■ **at present**  actualmente

■ **for the present**  por el momento
■ **up to the present**  hasta el momento presente

to **present** VERB
▷ see also **present** ADJECTIVE, NOUN
■ **to present somebody with something**  entregar algo a alguien  □ The Mayor presented the winner with a medal.  El alcalde le entregó una medalla al vencedor.
■ **He agreed to present the show.**  Aceptó presentar el espectáculo.

**presenter** NOUN
el presentador
la presentadora

**presently** ADVERB
1 enseguida
□ You'll feel better presently.  Enseguida te sentirás mejor.
2 actualmente
□ They're presently on tour.  Actualmente están de gira.

**president** NOUN
el presidente
la presidenta

**press** NOUN
▷ see also **press** VERB
la prensa
□ The story appeared in the press last week.  La historia salió en la prensa la semana pasada.

to **press** VERB
▷ see also **press** NOUN
apretar*
□ Don't press too hard!  ¡No aprietes muy fuerte!
■ **He pressed the accelerator.**  Pisó el acelerador.

**pressed** ADJECTIVE
■ **We are pressed for time.**  Andamos mal de tiempo.

**press-up** NOUN
■ **to do press-ups**  hacer flexiones

**pressure** NOUN
la presión (PL las presiones)
■ **a pressure group**  un grupo de presión
■ **to be under pressure**  estar presionado
□ She was under pressure from the management.  Estaba presionada por la dirección.
■ **He's been under a lot of pressure recently.**  Últimamente ha estado muy agobiado.

to **pressurize** VERB
■ **to pressurize somebody to do something**  presionar a alguien para que haga algo  □ My parents are pressurizing me to stay on at school.  Mis padres me están presionando para que siga estudiando.

**prestige** NOUN
el prestigio

**prestigious** ADJECTIVE
prestigioso (FEM prestigiosa)

**presumably** ADVERB
■ **Presumably she already knows what's happened.** Supongo que ya sabe lo que ha pasado.

to **presume** VERB
suponer*
□ I presume so. Supongo que sí. □ I presume he'll come. Supongo que vendrá.

to **pretend** VERB
■ **to pretend to do something** fingir hacer algo
■ **to pretend to be asleep** hacerse el dormido

⚆ **LANGUAGE TIP** Be careful not to translate **to pretend** by **pretender**.

**pretty** ADJECTIVE, ADVERB
1 bonito (FEM bonita)
□ She wore a pretty dress. Llevaba un vestido bonito.
2 guapo (FEM guapa)
□ She's very pretty. Es muy guapa.
3 bastante
□ That film was pretty bad. La película era bastante mala.
■ **The weather was pretty awful.** Hacía un tiempo horroroso.
■ **It's pretty much the same.** Es más o menos lo mismo.

to **prevent** VERB
evitar
□ Every effort had been made to prevent the accident. Se había hecho todo lo posible para evitar el accidente.

⚆ **LANGUAGE TIP** **evitar que** has to be followed by a verb in the subjunctive.

■ **to prevent something happening** evitar que pase algo □ I want to prevent this happening again. Quiero evitar que esto se repita.

⚆ **LANGUAGE TIP** **impedir a alguien que** has to be followed by a verb in the subjunctive.

■ **to prevent somebody from doing something** impedir a alguien que haga algo □ My only thought was to prevent him from speaking. Mi única idea era impedirle que hablara.

**previous** ADJECTIVE
anterior (FEM anterior)
□ the previous night la noche anterior
■ **He has no previous experience.** No tiene experiencia previa.

**previously** ADVERB
antes

**prey** NOUN
la presa
■ **a bird of prey** un ave rapaz

**price** NOUN
el precio
□ What price is this painting? ¿Qué precio tiene este cuadro?
■ **to go up in price** subir de precio
■ **to come down in price** bajar de precio

**price list** NOUN
la lista de precios

to **prick** VERB
pinchar
□ I've pricked my finger. Me he pinchado un dedo.

**pride** NOUN
el orgullo

**priest** NOUN
el sacerdote

**primary school** NOUN
la escuela primaria

**prime minister** NOUN
el primer ministro
la primera ministra

**primitive** ADJECTIVE
primitivo (FEM primitiva)

**prince** NOUN
el príncipe
□ the Prince of Wales el príncipe de Gales

**princess** NOUN
la princesa
□ Princess Victoria la princesa Victoria

**principal** ADJECTIVE
▷ see also **principal** NOUN
principal (FEM principal)

**principal** NOUN
▷ see also **principal** ADJECTIVE
el director
la directora

**principle** NOUN
el principio
□ the basic principles of physics los principios básicos de física
■ **in principle** en principio
■ **on principle** por principio

**print** NOUN
1 la foto

⚆ **LANGUAGE TIP** Although **foto** ends in **-o**, it is actually a feminine noun.

□ colour prints fotos a color
2 la letra
□ in small print en letra pequeña
3 la huella
□ The policeman took his prints. El policía le tomó las huellas.
4 el grabado
□ a framed print un grabado enmarcado

**printer** NOUN

P

la impresora
**printout** NOUN
la copia impresa
**priority** NOUN
la prioridad
□ My family takes priority over my work.
Mi familia tiene prioridad sobre mi trabajo.
**prison** NOUN
la cárcel
□ to send somebody to prison for 5 years
condenar a alguien a 5 años de cárcel
■ in prison en la cárcel
**prisoner** NOUN
1 el preso
la presa (in prison)
2 el prisionero
la prisionera (captive)
■ to take somebody prisoner hacer
prisionero a alguien
**prison officer** NOUN
el funcionario de prisiones
la funcionaria de prisiones
**privacy** NOUN
la intimidad
□ in privacy en la intimidad
**private** ADJECTIVE
1 privado (FEM privada)
□ a private school un colegio privado
■ private life la vida privada
■ private property la propiedad privada
2 particular (for one person only)
□ private lessons clases particulares
□ She has a private secretary. Tiene
secretaria particular.
■ a private bathroom un baño individual
■ 'private' (on envelope) 'confidencial'
■ in private en privado
to **privatize** VERB
privatizar*
**privilege** NOUN
el privilegio
**prize** NOUN
el premio
□ to win a prize ganar un premio
**prize-giving** NOUN
la entrega de premios
**prizewinner** NOUN
el premiado
la premiada
**pro** NOUN
■ the pros and cons los pros y los contras
**probable** ADJECTIVE
probable (FEM probable)
**probably** ADVERB
probablemente
□ He'll probably come tomorrow.
Probablemente vendrá mañana.
198 **problem** NOUN

el problema

LANGUAGE TIP Although **problema**
ends in -a, it is actually a masculine
noun.

□ the drug problem el problema de la droga
■ No problem! 1 ¡Por supuesto! □ Can you
repair it? — No problem! ¿Lo puedes
arreglar? — ¡Por supuesto! 2 ¡No importa!
□ I'm sorry about that — No problem! Lo
siento — ¡No importa!
■ What's the problem? ¿Qué pasa?
**proceeds** PL NOUN
la recaudación
□ All proceeds will go to charity. Toda la
recaudación se destinará a obras benéficas.
**process** NOUN
el proceso
□ the peace process el proceso de paz
■ We're in the process of painting the
kitchen. Ahora mismo estamos pintando la
cocina.
**procession** NOUN
la procesión (PL las procesiones)
to **produce** VERB
1 producir* (manufacture, create)
2 montar (on stage)
**producer** NOUN
1 el productor
la productora (of film, record, TV programme)
2 el director
la directora (of play, show)
**product** NOUN
el producto
**production** NOUN
1 la producción (PL las producciones)
□ They're increasing production of luxury
models. Están aumentando la producción
de modelos de lujo.
2 el montaje
□ a production of 'Hamlet' un montaje de
'Hamlet'
**profession** NOUN
la profesión (PL las profesiones)
**professional** NOUN
▷ see also **professional** ADJECTIVE
el/la profesional
**professional** ADJECTIVE
▷ see also **professional** NOUN
profesional (FEM profesional)
□ a professional musician un músico
profesional □ a very professional piece of
work un trabajo muy profesional
**professionally** ADVERB
■ She sings professionally. Es cantante
profesional.
**professor** NOUN
el catedrático
la catedrática

**LANGUAGE TIP** Be careful not to translate **professor** by the Spanish word **profesor**.

**profit** NOUN
los beneficios
□ to make a profit sacar beneficios
□ a profit of £10,000 unos beneficios de 10.000 libras

**profitable** ADJECTIVE
rentable (FEM rentable)

**program** NOUN
▷ see also **program** VERB
el programa

**LANGUAGE TIP** Although **programa** ends in -a, it is actually a masculine noun.

□ a computer program un programa informático
■ a TV program (US) un programa de televisión

to **program** VERB
▷ see also **program** NOUN
programar

**programme** NOUN
el programa

**LANGUAGE TIP** Although **programa** ends in -a, it is actually a masculine noun.

□ a TV programme un programa de televisión

**programmer** NOUN
el programador
la programadora
□ She's a programmer. Es programadora.

**programming** NOUN
la programación

**progress** NOUN
el progreso
□ You're making progress! ¡Estás haciendo progresos!

to **prohibit** VERB
prohibir*
□ Smoking is prohibited. Está prohibido fumar.

**project** NOUN
1 el proyecto
□ an international project un proyecto internacional
2 el trabajo (research)
□ I'm doing a project on the greenhouse effect. Estoy haciendo un trabajo sobre el efecto invernadero.

**projector** NOUN
el proyector

**promenade** NOUN
el paseo marítimo

**promise** NOUN
▷ see also **promise** VERB

la promesa
□ He made me a promise. Me hizo una promesa.
■ That's a promise! ¡Lo prometo!

to **promise** VERB
▷ see also **promise** NOUN
prometer
□ He didn't do what he promised. No hizo lo que prometió.
■ She promised to write. Prometió que escribiría.
■ I'll write, I promise! ¡Escribiré, lo prometo!

**promising** ADJECTIVE
prometedor (FEM prometedora)
□ a promising tennis player un tenista prometedor

to **promote** VERB
ascender* (employee, team)
□ She was promoted six months later. La ascendieron seis meses después.

**promotion** NOUN
el ascenso

**prompt** ADJECTIVE, ADVERB
1 rápido (FEM rápida)
□ a prompt reply una rápida respuesta
2 puntual (FEM puntual)
□ He's always very prompt. Siempre es muy puntual.
■ at eight o'clock prompt a las ocho en punto

**promptly** ADVERB
1 puntualmente (on time)
□ We left promptly at seven. Nos marchamos puntualmente a las siete.
2 enseguida (immediately)
□ He sat down and promptly fell asleep. Se sentó y se quedó dormido enseguida.

**pronoun** NOUN
el pronombre

to **pronounce** VERB
pronunciar
□ How do you pronounce that word? ¿Cómo se pronuncia esa palabra?

**pronunciation** NOUN
la pronunciación (PL las pronunciaciones)

**proof** NOUN
la prueba
■ I've got proof that he did it. Tengo pruebas de que lo hizo.

**proper** ADJECTIVE
1 de verdad (genuine)
□ It's difficult to get a proper job. Es difícil conseguir un trabajo de verdad.
2 adecuado (FEM adecuada) (suitable)
□ You have to have the proper equipment. Tienes que tener el equipo adecuado.
■ If you had come at the proper time... 199

Si hubieras llegado a tu hora...

**properly** ADVERB
correctamente

☐ You're not doing it properly. No lo estás haciendo correctamente. ☐ Dress properly for your interview. Vaya correctamente vestido a la entrevista.

**property** NOUN
la propiedad

■ **'private property'** 'propiedad privada'
■ **stolen property** objetos robados

**proportional** ADJECTIVE
proporcional (FEM proporcional)

☐ proportional representation la representación proporcional

**proposal** NOUN
la propuesta

to **propose** VERB
proponer*

☐ I propose a new plan. Propongo un cambio de planes. ☐ What do you propose to do? ¿Qué te propones hacer?

◯ LANGUAGE TIP proponer que has to be followed by a verb in the subjunctive.

☐ He proposed that we stay at home. Propuso que nos quedáramos en casa.
■ **to propose to somebody** (for marriage) declararse a alguien

to **prosecute** VERB
■ **They were prosecuted for murder.** Les procesaron por asesinato.

**prospect** NOUN
la perspectiva

☐ His future prospects are good. Tiene buenas perspectivas de futuro.

**prospectus** NOUN
el prospecto

**prostitute** NOUN
la prostituta

■ **a male prostitute** un prostituto

to **protect** VERB
proteger*

**protection** NOUN
la protección

**protein** NOUN
la proteína

**protest** NOUN
▷ see also **protest** VERB
la protesta

☐ He ignored their protests. Ignoró sus protestas.
■ **a protest march** una manifestación

to **protest** VERB
▷ see also **protest** NOUN
protestar

**Protestant** NOUN
▷ see also **Protestant** ADJECTIVE

el/la protestante

☐ I'm a Protestant. Soy protestante.

**Protestant** ADJECTIVE
▷ see also **Protestant** NOUN
protestante (FEM protestante)

**protester** NOUN
el/la manifestante

**proud** ADJECTIVE
orgulloso (FEM orgullosa)

☐ Her parents are proud of her. Sus padres están orgullosos de ella.

to **prove** VERB
probar*

☐ The police couldn't prove it. La policía no pudo probarlo.

**proverb** NOUN
el proverbio

☐ a Chinese proverb un proverbio chino

to **provide** VERB
proporcionar

■ **to provide somebody with something** proporcionar algo a alguien ☐ They provided us with maps. Nos proporcionaron mapas.

to **provide for** VERB
mantener*

☐ He can't provide for his family any more. Ya no puede mantener a su familia.

**provided** CONJUNCTION
siempre que

◯ LANGUAGE TIP siempre que has to be followed by a verb in the subjunctive.

☐ He'll play in the next match provided he's fit. Jugará el próximo partido siempre que esté en condiciones.

**prowler** NOUN
el merodeador
la merodeadora

**prune** NOUN
la ciruela pasa

to **pry** VERB
inmiscuirse*

☐ He's always prying into other people's affairs. Siempre está inmiscuyéndose en asuntos ajenos.

**pseudonym** NOUN
el seudónimo

**psychiatrist** NOUN
el/la psiquiatra

**psychoanalyst** NOUN
el/la psicoanalista

**psychological** ADJECTIVE
psicológico (FEM psicológica)

**psychologist** NOUN
el psicólogo
la psicóloga

**psychology** NOUN
la psicología

P

**PTO** ABBREVIATION (= *please turn over*)
sigue

**pub** NOUN
el bar

**public** NOUN
▷ *see also* **public** ADJECTIVE
■ **the public** el público □ open to the public abierto al público
■ **in public** en público

**public** ADJECTIVE
▷ *see also* **public** NOUN
público (FEM pública)
■ **a public holiday** un día festivo (un día feriado *Latin America*)
■ **public opinion** la opinión pública
■ **the public address system** la megafonía
■ **to be in the public eye** ser un personaje público

**publican** NOUN
■ He's a publican. Es dueño de un pub.

**publicity** NOUN
la publicidad

**public school** NOUN
el colegio privado

**public transport** NOUN
el transporte público

to **publish** VERB
publicar*

**publisher** NOUN
1 el editor
la editora (*person*)
2 la editorial (*company*)

**pudding** NOUN
el postre
□ What's for pudding? ¿Qué hay de postre?
■ **rice pudding** el arroz con leche
■ **black pudding** la morcilla

**puddle** NOUN
el charco

**puff pastry** NOUN
el hojaldre

to **pull** VERB
1 tirar (*to make something move*)
□ Pull as hard as you can. Tira con todas tus fuerzas.
2 tirar de (jalar *Latin America*) (*to tug at something*)
□ She pulled my hair. Me tiró del pelo.
■ **He pulled the trigger.** Apretó el gatillo.
■ **I pulled a muscle when I was training.** Me dio un tirón mientras entrenaba.
■ **You're pulling my leg!** ¡Me estás tomando el pelo!
■ **Pull yourself together!** ¡Tranquilízate!

to **pull down** VERB
echar abajo
□ The old school was pulled down last year. El año pasado echaron abajo la vieja escuela.

to **pull out** VERB
1 sacar* (*remove*)
□ to pull a tooth out sacar una muela
2 echarse a un lado (*car*)
□ The car pulled out to overtake. El coche se echó a un lado para adelantar.
3 retirarse (*from competition*)
□ She pulled out of the tournament. Se retiró del torneo.

to **pull through** VERB
recuperarse
□ They think he'll pull through. Creen que se recuperará.

to **pull up** VERB
parar (*car*)
□ A black car pulled up beside me. Un coche negro paró a mi lado.

**pullover** NOUN
el jersey (PL los jerseys)

**pulse** NOUN
el pulso
□ The nurse took his pulse. La enfermera le tomó el pulso.

**pulses** PL NOUN
las legumbres

**pump** NOUN
▷ *see also* **pump** VERB
1 la bomba
□ a bicycle pump una bomba de bicicleta
2 la zapatilla (*de deporte*)
□ She was wearing a black leotard and black pumps. Llevaba malla y zapatillas negras.

to **pump** VERB
▷ *see also* **pump** NOUN
bombear
■ **to pump up a tyre** inflar una rueda

**pumpkin** NOUN
la calabaza

**punch** NOUN
▷ *see also* **punch** VERB
1 el puñetazo (*blow*)
2 el ponche (*drink*)

to **punch** VERB
▷ *see also* **punch** NOUN
dar* un puñetazo a
□ He punched me! ¡Me ha dado un puñetazo!

**punch-up** NOUN
la pelea

**punctual** ADJECTIVE
puntual (FEM puntual)

**punctuation** NOUN
la puntuación

**puncture** NOUN
el pinchazo
□ I had a puncture on the motorway. Tuve un pinchazo en la autopista.

to **punish** VERB
castigar*

□ They were severely punished for their disobedience. Les castigaron severamente por su desobediencia.

■ **to punish somebody for doing something** castigar a alguien por haber hecho algo

**punishment** NOUN
el castigo

**punk** NOUN
el/la punki

■ **a punk rock band** un grupo punk

**pupil** NOUN
el alumno
la alumna

**puppet** NOUN
el títere

**puppy** NOUN
el cachorro

to **purchase** VERB
adquirir*

**pure** ADJECTIVE
puro (FEM pura)

□ He's doing pure maths. Estudia matemáticas puras.

**purple** ADJECTIVE
morado (FEM morada)

**purpose** NOUN
el objetivo

□ What is the purpose of these changes? ¿Cuál es el objetivo de estos cambios?

■ **his purpose in life** su meta en la vida

■ **It's being used for military purposes.** Se está usando con fines militares.

■ **on purpose** a propósito □ He did it on purpose. Lo hizo a propósito.

to **purr** VERB
ronronear

**purse** NOUN
1 el monedero (for money)
2 el bolso (US: handbag)

**pursuit** NOUN
la actividad

□ outdoor pursuits actividades al aire libre

**push** NOUN
▷ see also **push** VERB
el empujón (PL los empujones)

■ **to give somebody a push** dar un empujón a alguien

to **push** VERB
▷ see also **push** NOUN
empujar

□ Don't push! ¡No empujes!

■ **to push a button** pulsar un botón

■ **to push drugs** pasar droga

■ **I'm pushed for time today.** Hoy ando fatal de tiempo.

■ **Push off!** ¡Lárgate!

■ **Don't push your luck!** ¡No tientes a la suerte!

to **push around** VERB
dar* órdenes a

□ He likes pushing people around. Le gusta dar órdenes a la gente.

to **push through** VERB
■ **I pushed my way through.** Me abrí camino a empujones.

**pushchair** NOUN
la silla de paseo

**pusher** NOUN
el camello (of drugs)

to **put** VERB
poner*

□ Where shall I put my things? ¿Dónde pongo mis cosas? □ Don't forget to put your name on the paper. No te olvides de poner tu nombre en la hoja.

■ **She's putting the baby to bed.** Está acostando al niño.

to **put aside** VERB
apartar

□ Can you put this aside for me till tomorrow? ¿Me lo puede apartar hasta mañana?

to **put away** VERB
1 guardar

□ Can you put the dishes away, please? ¿Guardas los platos?

2 encerrar* (in prison)

□ I hope they put him away for a long time. Espero que lo encierren por muchos años.

to **put back** VERB
1 poner* en su sitio (in place)

□ Put it back when you've finished with it. Ponlo en su sitio cuando hayas terminado.

2 aplazar* (postpone)

□ The meeting has been put back till 2 o'clock. La reunión ha sido aplazada hasta las 2.

to **put down** VERB
1 soltar*

□ I'll put these bags down for a minute. Voy a soltar estas bolsas un momento.

2 apuntar (note)

□ I've put down a few ideas. He apuntado algunas ideas.

■ **to have an animal put down** sacrificar a un animal □ We had to have our dog put down. Tuvimos que sacrificar a nuestro perro.

■ **to put the phone down** colgar

to **put forward** VERB
adelantar (clock)

to **put in** VERB
poner* (install)

□ We're going to get central heating put in. Vamos a poner calefacción central.

■ **He has put in a lot of work on this**

**project**. Ha dedicado mucho trabajo a este proyecto.

■ **I've put in for a new job.** He solicitado otro empleo.

to **put off** VERB

1 apagar* *(light, TV)*
□ Shall I put the light off? ¿Apago la luz?

2 aplazar* *(delay)*
□ I keep putting it off. No hago más que aplazarlo.

3 distraer* *(distract)*
□ Stop putting me off! ¡Deja ya de distraerme!

4 desanimar *(discourage)*
□ He's not easily put off. No es de los que se desaniman fácilmente.

to **put on** VERB

1 ponerse* *(clothes, lipstick)*
□ I put my coat on. Me puse el abrigo.

2 poner* *(CD, DVD)*
□ Put on some music. Pon algo de música.

3 encender* *(light, TV)*
□ Shall I put the heater on? ¿Enciendo el radiador?

4 representar *(play, show)*
□ We're putting on 'Bugsy Malone'. Estamos representando 'Bugsy Malone'.

■ **I'll put the potatoes on.** Voy a poner a hacer las patatas.

■ **to put on weight** engordar □ He has put on a lot of weight. Ha engordado mucho.

■ **She's not ill: she's just putting it on.** No está enferma: es puro teatro.

to **put out** VERB

apagar*
□ It took them five hours to put out the fire. Tardaron cinco horas en apagar el incendio.

■ **He's a bit put out that nobody came.** Le sentó mal que no viniera nadie.

to **put through** VERB

poner* (comunicar* *Latin America*)
□ Can you put me through to the manager?

¿Me pone con el director? □ I'm putting you through. Le pongo.

to **put up** VERB

1 colgar* *(on wall)*
□ I'll put the poster up on my wall. Colgaré el póster en la pared.

2 montar
□ We put up our tent in a field. Montamos la tienda en un prado.

3 subir
□ They've put up the price. Han subido el precio.

■ **My friend will put me up for the night.** Me quedaré a dormir en casa de mi amigo.

■ **to put one's hand up** levantar la mano
□ If you have any questions, put your hand up. Quien tenga alguna pregunta que levante la mano.

■ **to put up with something** aguantar algo
□ I'm not going to put up with it any longer. No pienso aguantarlo más.

■ **to put something up for sale** poner algo en venta □ They're going to put their house up for sale. Van a poner la casa en venta.

**puzzle** NOUN
el rompecabezas (PL los rompecabezas)

**puzzled** ADJECTIVE
perplejo (FEM perpleja)
□ You look puzzled! ¡Te has quedado perplejo!

**puzzling** ADJECTIVE
desconcertante (FEM desconcertante)

**pyjamas** PL NOUN
el pijama (el piyama *Latin America*)
□ my pyjamas mi pijama
■ **a pair of pyjamas** un pijama

◌ **LANGUAGE TIP** Although **pijama** ends in **-a**, it is actually a masculine noun.

**pyramid** NOUN
la pirámide

**Pyrenees** PL NOUN
■ **the Pyrenees** los Pirineos

**P**

# Qq

**quaint** ADJECTIVE
pintoresco (FEM pintoresca) (house, village)

**qualification** NOUN
el título
□ He left school without any qualifications. Dejó la escuela sin sacarse ningún título. □ vocational qualifications los títulos de formación profesional □ a teaching qualification un título de profesor

**qualified** ADJECTIVE
1 cualificado (FEM cualificada)
□ a qualified driving instructor un profesor de autoescuela cualificado
2 titulado (FEM titulada)
□ a qualified teacher un profesor titulado
■ She was well qualified for the position. Estaba suficientemente capacitada para el puesto.

to **qualify** VERB
1 sacarse* el título (recibirse Latin America)
□ She qualified as a teacher last year. Se sacó el título de profesora el año pasado.
2 clasificarse*
□ Our team didn't qualify for the finals. Nuestro equipo no se clasificó para la final.

**quality** NOUN
1 la calidad
□ a good quality of life una buena calidad de vida □ good-quality paper el papel de calidad
2 la cualidad
□ She's got lots of good qualities. Tiene un montón de buenas cualidades.

**quantity** NOUN
la cantidad

**quarantine** NOUN
la cuarentena
□ in quarantine en cuarentena

**quarrel** NOUN
▷ see also **quarrel** VERB
la pelea (discusión)
■ We had a quarrel. Nos peleamos.

to **quarrel** VERB
▷ see also **quarrel** NOUN
pelearse (discutir)

**quarry** NOUN

la cantera (for stone)

**quarter** NOUN
el cuarto
■ three quarters tres cuartos
■ a quarter of an hour un cuarto de hora
■ a quarter past ten las diez y cuarto
■ a quarter to eleven las once menos cuarto

**quartet** NOUN
el cuarteto
□ a string quartet un cuarteto de cuerda

**quay** NOUN
el muelle (embarcadero)

**queasy** ADJECTIVE
■ I feel queasy. Tengo náuseas.

**queen** NOUN
1 la reina
□ Queen Elizabeth la reina Isabel
2 la dama
□ the queen of hearts la dama de corazones
■ the Queen Mother la reina madre

**query** NOUN
▷ see also **query** VERB
la pregunta

to **query** VERB
▷ see also **query** NOUN
poner* en duda
□ No one queried my decision. Nadie puso en duda mi decisión.
■ They queried the bill. Pidieron explicaciones sobre la factura.

**question** NOUN
▷ see also **question** VERB
1 la pregunta
□ Can I ask a question? ¿Puedo hacer una pregunta?
2 la cuestión (PL las cuestiones)
□ That's a difficult question. Ésa es una cuestión complicada. □ It's just a question of... Tan sólo es cuestión de...
■ It's out of the question. Es imposible.

to **question** VERB
▷ see also **question** NOUN
interrogar*
□ He was questioned by the police. Lo interrogó la policía.

**q**

**question mark** NOUN
el signo de interrogación

**questionnaire** NOUN
el cuestionario

**queue** NOUN
▷*see also* **queue** VERB
la cola
▫ People were standing in a queue outside the cinema. La gente hacía cola a las puertas del cine.

**to queue** VERB
▷*see also* **queue** NOUN
hacer* cola
▫ We had to queue for tickets. Tuvimos que hacer cola para comprar los billetes.

**quick** ADJECTIVE, ADVERB
rápido (FEM rápida)
▫ a quick lunch un almuerzo rápido ▫ It's quicker by train. Se va más rápido en tren.
■ **She's a quick learner.** Aprende rápido.
■ **Quick, phone the police!** ¡Rápido, llama a la policía!
■ **Be quick!** ¡Date prisa!

**quickly** ADVERB
rápidamente
▫ It was all over very quickly. Se acabó todo muy rápidamente.

**quiet** ADJECTIVE
1 callado (FEM callada)
▫ You're very quiet today. Estás muy callado hoy. ▫ She's a very quiet girl. Es una chica muy callada.
2 silencioso (FEM silenciosa)
▫ The engine's very quiet. El motor es muy silencioso.
3 tranquilo (FEM tranquila)
▫ a quiet little town un pueblecito tranquilo ▫ a quiet weekend un fin de semana tranquilo
■ **Be quiet!** ¡Cállate!
■ **Quiet!** ¡Silencio!

**quietly** ADVERB
1 en voz baja
▫ She's dead. — He said quietly. Está muerta. — Dijo en voz baja.
2 sin hacer ruido
▫ He quietly opened the door. Abrió la puerta sin hacer ruido.

**quilt** NOUN
el edredón (PL los edredones)

**to quit** VERB
1 dejar
▫ I quit my job last week. Dejé mi trabajo la semana pasada.

2 marcharse
▫ I've been given notice to quit. Me han dado el aviso para que me marche.

**quite** ADVERB
1 bastante
▫ It's quite warm today. Hoy hace bastante calor. ▫ It's quite a long way. Está bastante lejos. ▫ I quite liked the film. La película me gustó bastante.
■ **How was the film? — Quite good.** ¿Qué tal la película? — No está mal.
2 totalmente
▫ It's quite different. Es totalmente distinto. ▫ I quite agree with you. Estoy totalmente de acuerdo contigo.
■ **It's quite clear that this plan won't work.** Está clarísimo que este plan no va a funcionar.
■ **not quite...** no del todo... ▫ I'm not quite sure. No estoy del todo seguro.
■ **It's not quite the same.** No es exactamente lo mismo.
■ **quite a...** todo un ▫ It was quite a shock. Fue todo un susto.
■ **quite a lot** bastante ▫ I've been there quite a lot. He estado allí bastante. ▫ quite a lot of money bastante dinero ▫ It costs quite a lot to go abroad. Es bastante caro ir al extranjero.
■ **There were quite a few people there.** Había bastante gente allí.

**quiz** NOUN
el concurso *(de preguntas)*
▫ a quiz show un programa concurso

**quota** NOUN
el cupo

**quotation** NOUN
la cita
▫ a quotation from Shakespeare una cita de Shakespeare

**quote** NOUN
▷*see also* **quote** VERB
1 la cita
▫ a Shakespeare quote una cita de Shakespeare
2 el presupuesto
▫ Can you give me a quote for the work? ¿Puede darme un presupuesto por el trabajo?
■ **quotes** las comillas ▫ in quotes entre comillas

**to quote** VERB
▷*see also* **quote** NOUN
citar

**q**

# Rr

**rabbi** NOUN
el rabino
la rabina

**rabbit** NOUN
el conejo
■ **rabbit hutch** la conejera

**rabies** NOUN
la rabia
■ **a dog with rabies** un perro rabioso

**race** NOUN
▷ see also **race** VERB
1 la carrera
■ **a cycle race** una carrera ciclista
2 la raza
■ **race relations** las relaciones interraciales

to **race** VERB
▷ see also **race** NOUN
1 correr
□ We raced to get there on time. Corrimos
para llegar allí a tiempo.
2 echarle una carrera a
□ I'll race you! ¡Te echo una carrera!

**racecourse** NOUN
el hipódromo

**racehorse** NOUN
el caballo de carreras

**racer** NOUN
la bicicleta de carreras

**racetrack** NOUN
1 el circuito (for cars)
2 el velódromo (for cycles)

**racial** ADJECTIVE
racial (FEM racial)
□ racial discrimination la discriminación
racial

**racing car** NOUN
el coche de carreras

**racing driver** NOUN
el/la piloto de carreras

**racism** NOUN
el racismo

**racist** ADJECTIVE
▷ see also **racist** NOUN
racista (FEM racista)

**racist** NOUN
▷ see also **racist** ADJECTIVE

el/la racista
□ He's a racist. Es racista.

**rack** NOUN
el portaequipajes (PL los portaequipajes)
(for luggage)

**racket** NOUN
1 la raqueta (for sport)
□ my tennis racket mi raqueta de tenis
2 el jaleo (informal: noise)
□ They're making a terrible racket. Están
armando muchísimo jaleo.

**racquet** NOUN
la raqueta

**radar** NOUN
el radar

**radiation** NOUN
la radiación

**radiator** NOUN
el radiador

**radio** NOUN
la radio
**LANGUAGE TIP** Although **radio** ends in
-o, it is actually a feminine noun.
■ **on the radio** por la radio
■ **a radio station** una emisora de radio

**radioactive** ADJECTIVE
radiactivo (FEM radiactiva)

**radio-controlled** ADJECTIVE
teledirigido (FEM teledirigida)

**radish** NOUN
el rábano

**RAF** ABBREVIATION (= Royal Air Force)
las fuerzas aéreas británicas
□ He's in the RAF. Está en las fuerzas aéreas
británicas.

**raffle** NOUN
la rifa
□ a raffle ticket una papeleta de rifa

**raft** NOUN
la balsa

**rag** NOUN
el trapo
□ a piece of rag un trapo
■ **dressed in rags** cubierto de harapos

**rage** NOUN
rabia

□ mad with rage  loco de rabia
■ **to be in a rage**  estar furioso
■ **It's all the rage.**  Es el último grito.

**raid** NOUN
▷ *see also* **raid** VERB
1 el asalto
□ a bank raid  un asalto de banco
2 la redada
□ a police raid  una redada policial

to **raid** VERB
▷ *see also* **raid** NOUN
1 asaltar *(bank)*
2 hacer* una redada en
□ The police raided a club in Soho.  La policía hizo una redada en un club del Soho.

**rail** NOUN
1 la barandilla *(on stairs, bridge, balcony)*
2 el riel *(for curtains)*
■ **by rail**  por ferrocarril

**railcard** NOUN
la tarjeta de descuento para viajes en tren

**railroad** NOUN (US)
el ferrocarril
■ **railroad line**  la línea ferroviaria
■ **railroad station**  la estación de ferrocarril

**railway** NOUN
el ferrocarril
■ **railway line**  la línea ferroviaria
■ **railway station**  la estación de ferrocarril

**rain** NOUN
▷ *see also* **rain** VERB
la lluvia
□ in the rain  bajo la lluvia
■ **It looks like rain.**  Parece que va a llover.

to **rain** VERB
▷ *see also* **rain** NOUN
llover*
□ It rains a lot here.  Aquí llueve mucho.
■ **It's raining.**  Está lloviendo.

**rainbow** NOUN
el arco iris (PL los arco iris)

**raincoat** NOUN
el impermeable

**rainforest** NOUN
la selva tropical

**rainy** ADJECTIVE
lluvioso (FEM lluviosa)

to **raise** VERB
1 levantar
□ He raised his hand.  Levantó la mano.
2 mejorar
□ They want to raise standards in schools.  Quieren mejorar el nivel escolar.
3 aumentar
□ to raise interest rates  aumentar los tipos de interés
■ **to raise money**  recaudar fondos
□ The school is raising money for a new gym.

El colegio está recaudando fondos para un gimnasio nuevo.

**raisin** NOUN
la pasa

**rake** NOUN
el rastrillo

**rally** NOUN
1 la concentración (PL las concentraciones)
*(of people)*
□ There was rally in Trafalgar Square.  Hubo una concentración en Trafalgar Square.
2 el rally (PL los rallys) *(sport)*
□ a rally driver  un piloto de rally
3 el peloteo *(in tennis)*

to **ram** VERB
embestir* contra
□ The thieves rammed a police car.  Los ladrones embistieron contra un coche de la policía.

**ramble** NOUN
■ **to go for a ramble**  *(de marcha)* ir de excursión

**rambler** NOUN
el/la excursionista

**ramp** NOUN
la rampa

**ran** VERB ▷ *see* **run**

**ranch** NOUN
el rancho

**random** ADJECTIVE
■ **a random selection**  una selección hecha al azar
■ **at random**  al azar □ We picked the number at random.  Elegimos el número al azar.

**rang** VERB ▷ *see* **ring**

**range** NOUN
▷ *see also* **range** VERB
la variedad
□ There's a wide range of colours.  Hay una gran variedad de colores.
■ **It's out of my price range.**  Está fuera de mis posibilidades.
■ **a range of mountains**  una cadena montañosa

to **range** VERB
▷ *see also* **range** NOUN
■ **to range from...to...**  oscilar entre...y...
□ Temperatures in summer range from 20 to 35 degrees.  En verano las temperaturas oscilan entre los 20 y los 35 grados.
■ **Tickets range from £2 to £20.**  El precio de las entradas va de 2 a 20 libras esterlinas.

**rank** NOUN
▷ *see also* **rank** VERB
■ **a taxi rank**  una parada de taxis

to **rank** VERB
▷ *see also* **rank** NOUN

**English-Spanish**

■ **He's ranked third in the United States.**
Está clasificado tercero en los Estados Unidos.

**ransom** NOUN
el rescate

**rap** NOUN
el rap

**rape** NOUN
▷ *see also* **rape** VERB
la violación (PL las violaciones)

to **rape** VERB
▷ *see also* **rape** NOUN
violar

**rapist** NOUN
el violador

**rare** ADJECTIVE
1 raro (FEM rara) *(unusual)*
2 poco hecho (FEM poco hecha) *(steak)*

**rash** ADJECTIVE
▷ *see also* **rash** NOUN
precipitado (FEM precipitada)

**rasher** NOUN
■ **a rasher of bacon** una loncha de bacon

**raspberry** NOUN
la frambuesa

**rat** NOUN
la rata

**rate** NOUN
▷ *see also* **rate** VERB
1 la tarifa
□ There are reduced rates for students.
Hay tarifas reducidas para estudiantes.
2 el tipo
□ a high rate of interest un tipo de interés
elevado
■ **the divorce rate** el porcentaje de divorcios
■ **the birth rate** la tasa de natalidad

to **rate** VERB
▷ *see also* **rate** NOUN
considerar
□ He was rated the best. Era considerado el
mejor.

**rather** ADVERB
bastante
□ I was rather disappointed. Quedé
bastante decepcionado. □ £20! That's
rather a lot! ¡20 libras esterlinas! ¡Es
bastante caro!
■ **rather a lot of** mucho □ I've got rather
a lot of homework to do. Tengo muchos
deberes que hacer.
■ **I'd rather...** Preferiría... □ Would you like
a sweet? — I'd rather have an apple.
¿Quieres un caramelo? — Preferiría una
manzana. □ I'd rather stay in tonight.
Preferiría no salir esta noche.

> **LANGUAGE TIP preferiría que** has
> to be followed by a verb in the
> subjunctive.

□ I'd rather he didn't come to the party.
Preferiría que no viniera a la fiesta.
■ **rather than...** en lugar de... □ We
decided to camp, rather than stay at a hotel.
Decidimos acampar, en lugar de quedarnos
en un hotel.

**rattle** NOUN
el sonajero

to **rave** VERB
poner* por las nubes
□ They raved about the film. Pusieron la
película por las nubes.

**raven** NOUN
el cuervo

**raving** ADJECTIVE
■ **to be raving mad** estar loco como una
cabra

**raw** ADJECTIVE
crudo (FEM cruda) *(food)*
■ **raw material** la materia prima

**razor** NOUN
la maquinilla de afeitar
■ **razor blade** la hoja de afeitar

**RE** ABBREVIATION *(= Religious Education)*
la religión

**reach** NOUN
▷ *see also* **reach** VERB
■ **out of reach** fuera del alcance □ Keep
medicine out of reach of children.
Guárdense los medicamentos fuera del
alcance de los niños.
■ **within easy reach of** a poca distancia de
□ The hotel is within easy reach of the town
centre. El hotel está a poca distancia del
centro de la ciudad.

to **reach** VERB
▷ *see also* **reach** NOUN
1 llegar* a
□ We reached the hotel at seven o'clock.
Llegamos al hotel a las siete. □ We hope to
reach the final. Esperamos llegar a la final.
□ Eventually they reached a decision.
Finalmente llegaron a una decisión.
2 ponerse* en contacto con *(get in touch)*
□ How can I reach you? ¿Cómo puedo
ponerme en contacto contigo?

to **react** VERB
reaccionar

**reaction** NOUN
la reacción (PL las reacciones)

**reactor** NOUN
el reactor
□ a nuclear reactor un reactor nuclear

to **read** VERB
leer*
□ I don't read much. No leo mucho. □ Read
the text out loud. Lee el texto en voz alta.

to **read out** VERB

**r**

leer* *(en voz alta)*
□ I was reading it out to the children. Se lo estaba leyendo a los niños.

**reader** NOUN
el lector
la lectora *(person)*

**reading** NOUN
la lectura
□ Reading is one of my hobbies. La lectura es una de mis aficiones.
■ I like reading. Me gusta leer.

**ready** ADJECTIVE
preparado (FEM preparada)
□ The meal is ready. La comida está preparada.
■ She's nearly ready. Está casi lista.
■ He's always ready to help. Siempre está dispuesto a ayudar.
■ to get ready prepararse
■ to get something ready preparar algo
□ He's getting the dinner ready. Está preparando la cena.

**real** ADJECTIVE
1 verdadero (FEM verdadera)
□ the real reason el verdadero motivo
□ It was a real nightmare. Fue una verdadera pesadilla.
■ in real life en la vida real
2 auténtico (FEM auténtica)
□ It's real leather. Es piel auténtica.

**realistic** ADJECTIVE
realista (FEM realista)

**reality** NOUN
la realidad

**reality TV** NOUN
la telerrealidad
■ a reality TV show un reality (show)

**to realize** VERB
■ to realize that... darse cuenta de que...
□ We realized that something was wrong. Nos dimos cuenta de que algo iba mal.

**really** ADVERB
de verdad
□ I'm learning German. — Really? Estoy aprendiendo alemán. — ¿De verdad?
■ Do you really think so? ¿Tú crees?
■ She's really nice. Es muy simpática.
■ Do you want to go? — Not really. ¿Quieres ir? — La verdad es que no.

**realtor** NOUN (US)
el agente inmobiliario
la agente inmobiliaria

**rear** ADJECTIVE
▷ *see also* **rear** NOUN
trasero (FEM trasera)
□ the rear wheel la rueda trasera

**rear** NOUN
▷ *see also* **rear** ADJECTIVE
la parte trasera
□ at the rear of the train en la parte trasera del tren

**reason** NOUN
la razón (PL las razones)
□ There's no reason to think that he's dangerous. No hay razón para pensar que es peligroso.
■ for security reasons por motivos de seguridad
■ That was the main reason I went. Fui mayormente por eso.

**reasonable** ADJECTIVE
1 razonable (FEM razonable)
□ Be reasonable! ¡Sé razonable!
2 bastante aceptable (FEM bastante aceptable)
□ He wrote a reasonable essay. Escribió una redacción bastante aceptable.

**reasonably** ADVERB
bastante
□ The team played reasonably well. El equipo jugó bastante bien.
■ reasonably priced accommodation alojamiento a precios razonables

**to reassure** VERB
tranquilizar*

**reassuring** ADJECTIVE
tranquilizador (FEM tranquilizadora)

**rebellious** ADJECTIVE
rebelde (FEM rebelde)

**receipt** NOUN
1 el ticket *(for goods bought)*
2 el recibo *(for work done)*

LANGUAGE TIP Be careful not to translate **receipt** by **receta**.

**to receive** VERB
recibir

**receiver** NOUN
el auricular
■ to pick up the receiver descolgar

**recent** ADJECTIVE
reciente (FEM reciente)
□ recent scientific discoveries los recientes descubrimientos científicos
■ in recent weeks en las últimas semanas

**recently** ADVERB
últimamente
□ I haven't seen him recently. No lo he visto últimamente. □ I've been doing a lot of training recently. Últimamente he estado entrenando mucho.
■ until recently hasta hace poco

**reception** NOUN
la recepción (PL las recepciones)
□ Please leave your key at reception. Por favor dejen la llave en recepción. □ The reception will be at a big hotel. La recepción tendrá lugar en un gran hotel.

**English-Spanish**

**receptionist** NOUN
el/la recepcionista
□ She's a receptionist in a hotel.  Es recepcionista en un hotel.
**recession** NOUN
la recesión (PL las recesiones)
**recipe** NOUN
la receta
to **reckon** VERB
creer*
□ What do you reckon?  ¿Tú qué crees?
**reclining** ADJECTIVE
■ **a reclining seat** un asiento reclinable
**recognizable** ADJECTIVE
reconocible (FEM reconocible)
to **recognize** VERB
reconocer*
to **recommend** VERB
recomendar*
□ What do you recommend?  ¿Qué me recomienda?
to **reconsider** VERB
reconsiderar
**record** NOUN
▷ see also **record** VERB
1  el récord (PL los récords) (sport)
2  el disco (music)
□ the world record  el récord mundial
■ **in record time** en un tiempo récord
■ **criminal record** los antecedentes penales  □ He's got a criminal record. Tiene antecedentes penales.
■ **There is no record of your booking.** No tenemos constancia de su reserva.
■ **records** los archivos  □ I'll check in the records.  Miraré en los archivos.
to **record** VERB
▷ see also **record** NOUN
grabar
□ They've just recorded their new album.  Acaban de grabar su nuevo álbum.

⸻ **LANGUAGE TIP** Be careful not to translate **to record** by **recordar**.

**recorded delivery** NOUN
■ **to send something recorded delivery** enviar algo por correo certificado
**recorder** NOUN
la flauta dulce (musical instrument)
■ **video recorder** el vídeo
**recording** NOUN
la grabación (PL las grabaciones)
**record player** NOUN
el tocadiscos (PL los tocadiscos)
to **recover** VERB
recuperarse
□ He's recovering from a knee injury.  Se está recuperando de una lesión de rodilla.
**recovery** NOUN

la mejora
■ **Best wishes for a speedy recovery!** ¡Que te mejores pronto!
**rectangle** NOUN
el rectángulo
**rectangular** ADJECTIVE
rectangular
to **recycle** VERB
reciclar
**recycling** NOUN
el reciclaje
**red** ADJECTIVE
rojo (FEM roja)
□ a red rose  una rosa roja  □ red meat  la carne roja
■ **Gavin's got red hair.** Gavin es pelirrojo.
■ **to go through a red light** saltarse un semáforo en rojo
■ **red wine** vino tinto
**Red Cross** NOUN
la Cruz Roja
**redcurrant** NOUN
la grosella
to **redecorate** VERB
1  volver* a pintar (with paint)
2  volver* a empapelar (with wallpaper)
**red-haired** ADJECTIVE
pelirrojo (FEM pelirroja)
**red-handed** ADJECTIVE
■ **to catch somebody red-handed** coger a alguien con las manos en la masa (Spain) (agarrar a alguien con las manos en la masa Latin America)

⸻ **LANGUAGE TIP** Be very careful with the verb **coger**: in most of Latin America this is an extremely rude word that should be avoided. However, in Spain this verb is common and not rude at all.

**redhead** NOUN
el pelirrojo
la pelirroja
to **redo** VERB
rehacer*
to **reduce** VERB
reducir*
□ at a reduced price  a precio reducido
■ **'reduce speed now'** 'disminuya la velocidad'
**reduction** NOUN
la reducción (PL las reducciones)
■ **a five per cent reduction** un descuento del cinco por ciento
■ **'huge reductions!'** '¡grandes rebajas!'
**redundancy** NOUN
el despido
□ a redundancy payment  una indemnización por despido

**r**

**redundant** ADJECTIVE
■ **to be made redundant** ser despedido
**reed** NOUN
el junco
**reel** NOUN
el carrete *(of thread)*
to **refer** VERB
■ **to refer to** referirse a □ What are you referring to? ¿A qué te refieres?
**referee** NOUN
el árbitro
la árbitra
**reference** NOUN
1 la referencia
□ He made no reference to the murder. No hizo referencia al homicidio.
2 las referencias
□ Would you please give me a reference? ¿Me podría facilitar referencias?
■ **a reference book** un libro de consulta
to **refill** VERB
volver* a llenar
□ He refilled my glass. Volvió a llenarme el vaso.
**refinery** NOUN
la refinería
to **reflect** VERB
1 reflejar *(image)*
2 reflexionar *(think)*
**reflection** NOUN
el reflejo *(image)*
**reflex** NOUN
el reflejo
**reflexive** ADJECTIVE
reflexivo (FEM reflexiva)
□ a reflexive verb un verbo reflexivo
**refresher course** NOUN
el curso de reciclaje
**refreshing** ADJECTIVE
1 refrescante (FEM refrescante)
□ a refreshing drink una bebida refrescante
2 estimulante (FEM estimulante)
□ It was a refreshing change. Fue un cambio estimulante.
**refreshments** PL NOUN
el refrigerio
**refrigerator** NOUN
el frigorífico
to **refuel** VERB
repostar
□ The plane stops in Boston to refuel. El avión hace escala en Boston para repostar.
**refuge** NOUN
el refugio
**refugee** NOUN
el refugiado
la refugiada
**refund** NOUN

▷ *see also* **refund** VERB
el reembolso
to **refund** VERB
▷ *see also* **refund** NOUN
reembolsar
**refusal** NOUN
la negativa
□ her refusal to accept money su negativa a aceptar dinero
to **refuse** VERB
▷ *see also* **refuse** NOUN
negarse*
□ He refused to comment. Se negó a hacer comentarios.
**refuse** NOUN
▷ *see also* **refuse** VERB
la basura
■ **refuse collection** la recogida de basuras
to **regain** VERB
■ **to regain consciousness** recobrar el conocimiento
**regard** NOUN
▷ *see also* **regard** VERB
■ **with regard to** con respecto a
■ **Give my regards to Alice.** Dale recuerdos a Alice.
■ **'with kind regards'** 'un cordial saludo'
to **regard** VERB
▷ *see also* **regard** NOUN
■ **They regarded it as unfair.** Lo consideraron injusto.
■ **as regards...** en lo que se refiere a...
**regarding** PREPOSITION
referente a
□ the laws regarding the export of animals las leyes referentes a la exportación de animales
■ **Regarding John,...** En cuanto a John,...
**regardless** ADVERB
■ **to carry on regardless** continuar como si nada
**regiment** NOUN
el regimiento
**region** NOUN
la región (PL las regiones)
**regional** ADJECTIVE
regional (FEM regional)
**register** NOUN
▷ *see also* **register** VERB
el registro *(in hotel)*
■ **to call the register** pasar lista
to **register** VERB
▷ *see also* **register** NOUN
inscribirse* *(to enrol)*
■ **The car was registered in his wife's name.** El coche estaba matriculado a nombre de su esposa.
**registered** ADJECTIVE

■ **a registered letter** una carta certificada
**registration** NOUN
el número de matrícula
■ **Registration starts at 8.30.** La
inscripción empieza a las ocho y media.
**regret** NOUN
▷ see also **regret** VERB
■ **I've got no regrets.** No me arrepiento.
to **regret** VERB
▷ see also **regret** NOUN
arrepentirse*
□ Try it, you won't regret it! ¡Pruébalo! ¡No
te arrepentirás!
■ **to regret doing something** arrepentirse
de haber hecho algo □ I regret saying that.
Me arrepiento de haber dicho eso.
**regular** ADJECTIVE
1 regular (FEM regular)
□ at regular intervals a intervalos regulares
■ **to take regular exercise** hacer ejercicio
con regularidad
2 normal (FEM normal)
□ a regular portion of fries una porción
normal de patatas fritas
**regularly** ADVERB
con regularidad
**rehearsal** NOUN
el ensayo
■ **dress rehearsal** el ensayo general
to **rehearse** VERB
ensayar
**reindeer** NOUN
el reno
to **reject** VERB
1 rechazar* (proposal, invitation)
2 desechar (idea, advice)
■ **I applied but they rejected me.**
Presenté una solicitud, pero no me
aceptaron.
**relapse** NOUN
la recaída
□ to have a relapse tener una recaída
**related** ADJECTIVE
■ **We're related.** Somos parientes.
■ **Are you related to her?** ¿Eres pariente
suyo?
■ **The two events are not related.** Los dos
sucesos no están relacionados.
**relation** NOUN
1 el/la pariente
□ He's a distant relation. Es un pariente
lejano mío.
2 la relación (PL las relaciones)
□ It has no relation to reality. No guarda
ninguna relación con la realidad.
■ **in relation to** con relación a
**relationship** NOUN
la relación (PL las relaciones)

□ Their relationship is over. Su relación ha
acabado. □ We have a good relationship.
Tenemos una buena relación.
■ **I'm not in a relationship at the
moment.** No tengo relaciones
sentimentales con nadie en este momento.
**relative** NOUN
el/la pariente
**relatively** ADVERB
relativamente
to **relax** VERB
relajarse
□ I relax listening to music. Me relajo
escuchando música.
■ **Relax! Everything's fine.** ¡Tranquilo!
No pasa nada.
**relaxation** NOUN
el esparcimiento
□ I don't have much time for relaxation.
No tengo muchos momentos de
esparcimiento.
**relaxed** ADJECTIVE
relajado (FEM relajada)
**relaxing** ADJECTIVE
relajante (FEM relajante)
□ Having a bath is very relaxing. Darse un
baño es muy relajante.
■ **I find cooking relaxing.** Cocinar me
relaja.
**relay** NOUN
■ **a relay race** una carrera de relevos
to **release** VERB
▷ see also **release** NOUN
1 poner* en libertad (prisoner)
2 hacer* público (report, news)
3 sacar* a la venta (CD, DVD)
**release** NOUN
▷ see also **release** VERB
la puesta en libertad
□ the release of the prisoners la puesta en
libertad de los presos
■ **the band's latest release** el último
trabajo del grupo
**relegated** ADJECTIVE
■ **to be relegated** (sport) bajar de división
**relevant** ADJECTIVE
pertinente (FEM pertinente) (documents)
■ **That's not relevant.** Eso no viene al caso.
■ **to be relevant to something** guardar
relación con algo □ Education should be
relevant to real life. La educación debería
guardar relación con la vida real.
**reliable** ADJECTIVE
fiable (FEM fiable)
□ a reliable car un coche fiable □ He's not
very reliable. No es una persona muy fiable.
**relief** NOUN
el alivio

□ That's a relief! ¡Es un alivio! □ Much to my relief she made no objection. Para mi gran alivio, no hizo objeción alguna.

to **relieve** VERB
aliviar
□ This injection will relieve the pain. Esta inyección le aliviará el dolor.

**relieved** ADJECTIVE
■ **to be relieved** sentir un gran alivio
□ I was relieved to hear he was better. Sentí un gran alivio al saber que estaba mejor.

**religion** NOUN
la religión (PL las religiones)
□ What religion are you? ¿De qué religión eres?

**religious** ADJECTIVE
religioso (FEM religiosa)
□ I'm not religious. No soy religioso.

**reluctant** ADJECTIVE
reacio (FEM reacia)
■ **to be reluctant to do something** ser reacio a hacer algo □ They were reluctant to help us. Eran reacios a ayudarnos.

**reluctantly** ADVERB
de mala gana
□ She reluctantly accepted. Aceptó de mala gana.

to **rely on** VERB
confiar* en
□ I'm relying on you. Confío en ti.

to **remain** VERB
permanecer*
□ to remain silent permanecer callado

**remaining** ADJECTIVE
restante (FEM restante)
□ the remaining ingredients los ingredientes restantes

**remains** PL NOUN
los restos
□ the remains of the picnic los restos de la merienda □ human remains restos humanos
■ **Roman remains** los restos romanos

**remake** NOUN
la nueva versión

**remark** NOUN
el comentario

**remarkable** ADJECTIVE
extraordinario (FEM extraordinaria)

**remarkably** ADVERB
extraordinariamente

to **remarry** VERB
volver* a casarse
□ She remarried three years ago. Se volvió a casar hace tres años.

**remedy** NOUN
el remedio
□ a good remedy for a sore throat un buen remedio para el dolor de garganta

to **remember** VERB
1 acordarse*
□ I don't remember. No me acuerdo.
2 acordarse* de
□ I can't remember his name. No me acuerdo de su nombre. □ I don't remember saying that. No me acuerdo de haber dicho eso.

⌐ **LANGUAGE TIP** In Spanish you often say **no te olvides** – 'don't forget' – instead of 'remember'.

□ Remember your passport! ¡No te olvides del pasaporte! □ Remember to write your name on the form. No te olvides de escribir tu nombre en el impreso.

to **remind** VERB
recordar*
□ The scenery here reminds me of Scotland. Este paisaje me recuerda a Escocia.

⌐ **LANGUAGE TIP** When talking about reminding someone to do something, **recordar a alguien que** has to be followed by a verb in the subjunctive.

□ Remind me to speak to Daniel. Recuérdame que hable con Daniel.

**remorse** NOUN
el remordimiento
□ He showed no remorse. No tenía ningún remordimiento.

**remote** ADJECTIVE
remoto (FEM remota)
□ a remote village un pueblo remoto

**remote control** NOUN
el mando a distancia

**removable** ADJECTIVE
separable (FEM separable)

**removal** NOUN
la mudanza
■ **a removal van** un camión de mudanzas

to **remove** VERB
quitar
□ Please remove your bag from my seat. Por favor, quite su bolsa de mi asiento. □ Did you remove the stain? ¿Quitaste la mancha?

**rendezvous** NOUN
la cita

to **renew** VERB
renovar* (passport, licence)

**renewable** ADJECTIVE
renovable (FEM renovable)

to **renovate** VERB
renovar*
□ The building's been renovated. Han renovado el edificio.

**renowned** ADJECTIVE
renombrdo (FEM renombrda)

**rent** NOUN
▷ see also **rent** VERB
el alquiler

to **rent** VERB
  ▷ *see also* **rent** NOUN
  alquilar
  □ We rented a car. Alquilamos un coche.
**rental** NOUN
  el alquiler
  □ Car rental is included in the price.  El
  alquiler del coche está incluído en el precio.
**rental car** NOUN
  el coche de alquiler
to **reorganize** VERB
  reorganizar*
**rep** NOUN (= *representative*)
  el/la representante
**repaid** VERB ▷ *see* **repay**
to **repair** VERB
  ▷ *see also* **repair** NOUN
  reparar
  □ Can you repair this for me? ¿Me puede
  reparar esto?  □ I got the washing machine
  repaired.  Me repararon la lavadora.
**repair** NOUN
  ▷ *see also* **repair** VERB
  la reparación (PL las reparaciones)
to **repay** VERB
  devolver* (*money*)
  ■ I don't know how I can ever repay you.
  No sé cómo podré devolverle el favor.
**repayment** NOUN
  el pago
  □ mortgage repayments  los pagos de la
  hipoteca
to **repeat** VERB
  ▷ *see also* **repeat** NOUN
  repetir*
**repeat** NOUN
  ▷ *see also* **repeat** VERB
  la reposición (PL las reposiciones)
  □ There are too many repeats on TV.
  Hay demasiadas reposiciones en la tele.
**repeatedly** ADVERB
  repetidamente
**repellent** NOUN
  ■ insect repellent  la loción anti-insectos
**repetitive** ADJECTIVE
  repetitivo (FEM repetitiva)
to **replace** VERB
  1 sustituir*
  2 cambiar (*batteries*)
**replay** NOUN
  ▷ *see also* **replay** VERB
  ■ There will be a replay on Friday.
  El partido se volverá a jugar el viernes.
to **replay** VERB
  ▷ *see also* **replay** NOUN
  1 volver* a jugar (*match*)
  2 volver* a poner (*track*)
**replica** NOUN

la réplica
**reply** NOUN
  ▷ *see also* **reply** VERB
  la respuesta
to **reply** VERB
  ▷ *see also* **reply** NOUN
  responder
**report** NOUN
  ▷ *see also* **report** VERB
  1 el informe (*of event*)
  2 el reportaje (*news report*)
  □ a report in the paper  un reportaje en el
  periódico
  3 las notas (*at school*)
  ■ I got a good report this term.  He sacado
  buenas notas este trimestre.
to **report** VERB
  ▷ *see also* **report** NOUN
  1 dar* parte de
  □ I reported the theft to the police.  Di parte
  del robo a la policía.
  2 presentarse
  □ Report to reception when you arrive.
  Preséntese en recepción cuando llegue.
  ■ I'll report back as soon as I hear anything.
  En cuanto tenga noticias, te lo haré saber.
**reporter** NOUN
  el/la periodista
to **represent** VERB
  1 representar a (*client, country*)
  2 representar (*change, achievement*)
**representative** ADJECTIVE
  representativo (FEM representativa)
**reproduction** NOUN
  la reproducción (PL las reproducciones)
**reptile** NOUN
  el reptil
**republic** NOUN
  la república
**repulsive** ADJECTIVE
  repugnante (FEM repugnante)
**reputable** ADJECTIVE
  acreditado (FEM acreditada)
**reputation** NOUN
  la reputación (PL las reputaciones)
**request** NOUN
  ▷ *see also* **request** VERB
  la petición (PL las peticiones)
to **request** VERB
  ▷ *see also* **request** NOUN
  solicitar
to **require** VERB
  requerir*
  □ Her job requires a lot of patience.
  Su trabajo requiere mucha paciencia.
**requirement** NOUN
  el requisito
  □ What are the requirements for the job?

r

¿Cuáles son los requisitos para el puesto?
■ **entry requirements** (*for university*) los requisitos para el acceso

to **rescue** VERB
▷ *see also* **rescue** NOUN
rescatar

**rescue** NOUN
▷ *see also* **rescue** VERB
el rescate
□ a rescue operation una operación de rescate □ a mountain rescue team un equipo de rescate de montaña
■ **to come to somebody's rescue** ir en auxilio de alguien

**research** NOUN
la investigación (PL las investigaciones)
□ He's doing research. Realiza trabajos de investigación.
■ **She's doing some research in the library.** Está investigando en la biblioteca.

**resemblance** NOUN
el parecido

to **resent** VERB
■ **I resent being dependent on her.** Me molesta tener que depender de ella.

**reservation** NOUN
la reserva
□ I've got a reservation for two nights. Tengo una reserva para dos noches. □ I'd like to make a reservation for this evening. Quisiera hacer una reserva para esta tarde.
■ **I've got reservations about the idea.** Tengo mis reservas al respecto.

**reserve** NOUN
▷ *see also* **reserve** VERB
1 la reserva (*place*)
□ a nature reserve una reserva natural
2 el/la suplente (*person*)
□ I was reserve in the game last Saturday. Yo era suplente en el partido del sábado.

to **reserve** VERB
▷ *see also* **reserve** NOUN
reservar
□ I'd like to reserve a table for tomorrow evening. Quisiera reservar una mesa para mañana por la noche.

**reserved** ADJECTIVE
reservado (FEM reservada)
□ a reserved seat un asiento reservado
□ He's quite reserved. Es bastante reservado.

**reservoir** NOUN
el embalse

**resident** NOUN
el vecino
la vecina
□ local residents los vecinos del lugar

**residential** ADJECTIVE
residencial (FEM residencial)

□ a residential area una zona residencial

to **resign** VERB
dimitir

**resistance** NOUN
la resistencia

to **resit** VERB
volver* a presentarse a
□ I'm resitting the exam in December. Me vuelvo a presentar al examen en diciembre.

**resolution** NOUN
el propósito
□ Have you made any New Year's resolutions? ¿Has hecho algún buen propósito para el Año Nuevo?

**resort** NOUN
el centro turístico
□ a resort on the Costa del Sol un centro turístico en la Costa del Sol
■ **as a last resort** como último recurso

**resource** NOUN
el recurso

**respect** NOUN
▷ *see also* **respect** VERB
el respeto
■ **in some respects** en algunos aspectos

to **respect** VERB
▷ *see also* **respect** NOUN
respetar

**respectable** ADJECTIVE
1 respetable (FEM respetable)
□ a respectable family una familia respetable
2 decente (FEM decente)
□ My marks were quite respectable. Mis notas eran bastante decentes.

**respectively** ADVERB
respectivamente
□ Spain and France came third and fourth respectively. España y Francia llegaron en tercero y cuarto lugar respectivamente.

**responsibility** NOUN
la responsabilidad

**responsible** ADJECTIVE
responsable (FEM responsable)
□ You should be more responsible! ¡Deberías ser más responsable!
■ **to be responsible for something** ser responsable de algo □ He's responsible for booking the tickets. Es responsable de reservar las entradas.
■ **It's a responsible job.** Es un puesto de responsabilidad.

**rest** NOUN
▷ *see also* **rest** VERB
1 el descanso
□ five minutes' rest cinco minutos de descanso
■ **to have a rest** descansar □ We stopped to have a rest. Nos paramos a descansar.

**2** el resto

□ I'll do the rest. Yo haré el resto. □ the rest of the money el resto del dinero

■ **the rest of them** los demás □ The rest of them went swimming. Los demás fueron a nadar.

to **rest** VERB

▷ see also **rest** NOUN

**1** descansar

□ She's resting in her room. Está descansando en su habitación.

■ **He has to rest his knee.** Tiene que descansar la rodilla.

**2** apoyar

□ I rested my bike against the window. Apoyé la bicicleta en la ventana.

**restaurant** NOUN

el restaurante

□ We don't often go to restaurants. No solemos ir a restaurantes.

■ **restaurant car** el vagón restaurante

**restful** ADJECTIVE

plácido (FEM plácida)

**restless** ADJECTIVE

inquieto (FEM inquieta)

**restoration** NOUN

la restauración

to **restore** VERB

restaurar (building, painting)

to **restrict** VERB

limitar

**rest room** NOUN (US)

los servicios

**result** NOUN

el resultado

□ my exam results los resultados de mis exámenes □ The result was one-nil. El resultado fue uno a cero.

**résumé** NOUN (US)

el currículum vitae

to **retire** VERB

jubilarse

**retired** ADJECTIVE

jubilado (FEM jubilada)

□ She's retired. Está jubilada. □ a retired teacher un maestro jubilado

**retirement** NOUN

■ **since his retirement** desde que se jubiló

to **retrace** VERB

■ **I retraced my steps.** Volví sobre mis pasos.

**return** NOUN

▷ see also **return** VERB

**1** el regreso

□ his sudden return home su repentino regreso a casa

■ **the return journey** el viaje de vuelta

■ **a return match** un partido de vuelta

**2** el billete de ida y vuelta

□ A return to Bilbao, please. Un billete de ida y vuelta a Bilbao, por favor.

■ **in return** a cambio □ She helps me and I help her in return. Me ayuda y yo la ayudo a cambio.

■ **in return for** a cambio de

■ **Many happy returns!** ¡Que cumplas muchos más!

to **return** VERB

▷ see also **return** NOUN

**1** volver*

□ I've just returned from holiday. Acabo de volver de vacaciones. □ He returned to Spain the following year. Volvió a España al año siguiente.

**2** devolver*

□ She borrows my things and doesn't return them. Toma prestadas mis cosas y no las devuelve.

**reunion** NOUN

la reunión (PL las reuniones)

□ We had a big family reunion at Christmas. Tuvimos una gran reunión familiar en Navidad.

to **reuse** VERB

reutilizar*

to **reveal** VERB

revelar

**revenge** NOUN

la venganza

□ in revenge como venganza

■ **to take revenge** vengarse □ They planned to take revenge on him. Planearon vengarse de él.

to **reverse** VERB

▷ see also **reverse** ADJECTIVE

dar* marcha atrás (car)

□ He reversed without looking. Dio marcha atrás sin mirar.

■ **to reverse the charges** llamar a cobro revertido

**reverse** ADJECTIVE

▷ see also **reverse** VERB

inverso (FEM inversa)

□ in reverse order en orden inverso

■ **in reverse gear** en marcha atrás

■ **reverse charge call** llamada a cobro revertido

**review** NOUN

**1** la revisión (PL las revisiones) (of policy, salary)

**2** el repaso (of subject)

to **revise** VERB

estudiar para un examen

□ I haven't started revising yet. Todavía no he empezado a estudiar para el examen.

■ **I've revised my opinion.** He cambiado de opinión.

**revision** NOUN
■ **Have you done a lot of revision?** ¿Has estudiado mucho para el examen?

to **revive** VERB
resucitar
□ The nurses tried to revive him. Las enfermeras intentaron resucitarlo.

**revolting** ADJECTIVE
repugnante (FEM repugnante)

**revolution** NOUN
la revolución (PL las revoluciones)

**revolutionary** ADJECTIVE
revolucionario (FEM revolucionaria)

**revolver** NOUN
el revólver

**reward** NOUN
la recompensa

**rewarding** ADJECTIVE
gratificante (FEM gratificante)
□ a rewarding job un trabajo gratificante

to **rewind** VERB
rebobinar
□ to rewind a cassette rebobinar una cinta

**rheumatism** NOUN
el reumatismo
□ I've got rheumatism. Tengo reumatismo.

**rhinoceros** NOUN
el rinoceronte

**rhubarb** NOUN
el ruibarbo

**rhythm** NOUN
el ritmo

**rib** NOUN
la costilla

**ribbon** NOUN
la cinta

**rice** NOUN
el arroz
■ **rice pudding** el arroz con leche

**rich** ADJECTIVE
rico (FEM rica)
■ **the rich** los ricos

to **rid** VERB
■ **to get rid of** deshacerse de □ I want to get rid of some old clothes. Quiero deshacerme de algunas ropas viejas.

**ridden** VERB ▷ see **ride**

**ride** NOUN
▷ see also **ride** VERB
■ **to go for a ride 1** (on horse) montar a caballo **2** (on bike) dar un paseo en bicicleta □ We went for a bike ride. Fuimos a dar un paseo en bicicleta.
■ **It's a short bus ride to the town centre.** El centro de la ciudad queda cerca en autobús.

to **ride** VERB
▷ see also **ride** NOUN
montar a caballo

□ I'm learning to ride. Estoy aprendiendo a montar a caballo.
■ **to ride a bike** ir en bicicleta □ Can you ride a bike? ¿Sabes ir en bicicleta?

**rider** NOUN
**1** el jinete
□ She's a good rider. Ella monta muy bien a caballo.
**2** el/la ciclista (cyclist)

**ridiculous** ADJECTIVE
ridículo (FEM ridícula)

**riding** NOUN
la equitación (as sport)
□ a riding school una escuela de equitación
■ **to go riding** montar a caballo

**rifle** NOUN
el rifle

**rig** NOUN
■ **oil rig** la plataforma petrolífera

**right** ADJECTIVE, ADVERB
▷ see also **right** NOUN

**LANGUAGE TIP** There are several ways of translating 'right'. Scan the examples to find one that is similar to what you want to say.

**1** correcto (FEM correcta)
□ the right answer la respuesta correcta
**2** adecuado (FEM adecuada) (place, time)
□ We're on the right train. Estamos en el tren adecuado. □ It isn't the right size. Ésta no es la talla adecuada.
■ **Is this the right road for Ávila?** ¿Vamos bien por aquí para Ávila?
■ **to be right 1** (person) tener razón □ You were right! ¡Tenías razón! **2** (statement, opinion) ser verdad □ That's right! ¡Es verdad!
■ **Do you have the right time?** ¿Tienes hora?
**3** bien
□ It's not right to behave like that. No está bien comportarse así. □ Am I pronouncing it right? ¿Lo pronuncio bien?
■ **I think you did the right thing.** Creo que hiciste bien.
**4** derecho (FEM derecha) (not left)
□ my right hand mi mano derecha
**5** a la derecha (turn, look)
□ Turn right at the traffic lights. Cuando llegues al semáforo dobla a la derecha.
■ **Right! Let's get started!** ¡Bueno! ¡Empecemos!
■ **right away** enseguida □ I'll do it right away. Lo haré enseguida.

**right** NOUN
▷ see also **right** ADJECTIVE
**1** el derecho
□ You've got no right to do that. No tienes derecho de hacer eso.

**2** la derecha
- **on the right** a la derecha □ **on the right of Mr. Yates** a la derecha del Sr. Yates
- **right of way** la prioridad □ **We had right of way.** Teníamos prioridad.

**right-hand** ADJECTIVE
- **the right-hand side** la derecha □ **It's on the right-hand side.** Está a la derecha.

**right-handed** ADJECTIVE
diestro (FEM diestra)

**rim** NOUN
la montura
□ **glasses with metal rims** las gafas con montura metálica

**ring** NOUN
▷ *see also* **ring** VERB
**1** el anillo
□ **a gold ring** un anillo de oro
- **a wedding ring** una alianza

**2** el círculo
□ **to stand in a ring** formar un círculo

**3** el timbrazo *(at door)*
- **After three or four rings the door was opened.** Después de tres o cuatro timbrazos la puerta se abrió.
- **There was a ring at the door.** Se oyó el timbre de la puerta.
- **to give somebody a ring** llamar a alguien por teléfono

**to ring** VERB
▷ *see also* **ring** NOUN
**1** llamar
□ **Your mother rang this morning.** Tu madre llamó esta mañana.
- **to ring somebody** llamar a alguien

**2** sonar*
□ **The phone's ringing.** El teléfono está sonando.
- **to ring the bell** tocar el timbre

**to ring back** VERB
volver* a llamar
□ **I'll ring back later.** Volveré a llamar más tarde.

**to ring up** VERB
llamar por teléfono

**ring binder** NOUN
la carpeta de anillas (la carpeta de anillos *Latin America*)

**ring road** NOUN
la carretera de circunvalación

**ringtone** NOUN
el tono de llamada

**rink** NOUN
**1** la pista de hielo *(for ice-skating)*
**2** la pista de patinaje *(for roller-skating)*

**to rinse** VERB
enjuagar*

**riot** NOUN

▷ *see also* **riot** VERB
el disturbio

**to riot** VERB
▷ *see also* **riot** NOUN
causar disturbios

**to rip** VERB
rasgar*
□ **I've ripped my jeans.** Me he rasgado los vaqueros. □ **My shirt's ripped.** Mi camisa está rasgada.

**to rip off** VERB
timar *(informal)*
□ **The hotel ripped us off.** En el hotel nos timaron.

**to rip up** VERB
hacer* pedazos
□ **He read the note and then ripped it up.** Leyó la nota y la hizo pedazos.

**ripe** ADJECTIVE
maduro (FEM madura)

**rip-off** NOUN
- **It's a rip-off!** *(informal)* ¡Es un timo!

**rise** NOUN
▷ *see also* **rise** VERB
**1** la subida *(in prices, temperature)*
□ **a sudden rise in temperature** una repentina subida de las temperaturas
**2** el aumento *(pay rise)*

**to rise** VERB
▷ *see also* **rise** NOUN
**1** subir *(increase)*
□ **Prices are rising.** Los precios están subiendo.
**2** salir*
□ **The sun rises early in June.** En junio el sol sale temprano.

**riser** NOUN
- **to be an early riser** ser madrugador

**risk** NOUN
▷ *see also* **risk** VERB
el riesgo
- **to take risks** correr riesgos
- **It's at your own risk.** Es a tu propia cuenta y riesgo.

**to risk** VERB
▷ *see also* **risk** NOUN
arriesgarse*
□ **You risk getting a fine.** Te arriesgas a que te multen. □ **I wouldn't risk it if I were you.** Yo en tu lugar no me arriesgaría.

**risky** ADJECTIVE
arriesgado (FEM arriesgada)

**rival** NOUN
▷ *see also* **rival** ADJECTIVE
el/la rival

**rival** ADJECTIVE
▷ *see also* **rival** NOUN
**1** rival (FEM rival)

◻ a rival gang una banda rival
2 competidor (FEM competidora)
◻ a rival company una empresa competidora
**rivalry** NOUN
la rivalidad
**river** NOUN
el río
■ **the river Tagus** el río Tajo
**Riviera** NOUN
■ **the French Riviera** la Costa Azul
■ **the Italian Riviera** la Riviera
**road** NOUN
1 la carretera
◻ There's a lot of traffic on the roads. Hay mucho tráfico en las carreteras. ◻ a road accident un accidente de carretera
2 la calle
◻ They live across the road. Viven al otro lado de la calle.
**road map** NOUN
el mapa de carreteras

◌ **LANGUAGE TIP** Although **mapa** ends in -a, it is actually a masculine noun.

**road rage** NOUN
la conducta agresiva al volante
**road sign** NOUN
la señal de tráfico
**roadworks** PL NOUN
las obras
◻ There are roadworks on the motorway. Hay obras en la autopista.
**roast** ADJECTIVE
asado (FEM asada)
◻ roast chicken pollo asado
■ **roast pork** el asado de cerdo
■ **roast beef** el rosbif
to **rob** VERB
■ **to rob somebody** robar a alguien ◻ I've been robbed. Me han robado.
■ **to rob somebody of something** robar algo a alguien ◻ He was robbed of his wallet. Le robaron la cartera.
■ **to rob a bank** asaltar un banco
**robber** NOUN
el ladrón
la ladrona
■ **a bank-robber** un asaltante de bancos (FEM una asaltante de bancos)
**robbery** NOUN
el robo
■ **a bank robbery** un asalto a un banco
■ **an armed robbery** un asalto a mano armada
**robin** NOUN
el petirrojo
**robot** NOUN
el robot (PL los robots)

**rock** NOUN
▷ see also **rock** VERB
1 la roca
◻ They tunnelled through the rock. Abrieron un túnel a través de la roca. ◻ I sat on a rock. Me senté encima de una roca.
2 la piedra
◻ The crowd started to throw rocks. La multitud empezó a lanzar piedras.
3 el rock
◻ a rock concert un concierto de rock
■ **rock and roll** el rock and roll
■ **a stick of rock** una barra de caramelo
to **rock** VERB
▷ see also **rock** NOUN
1 mecer
■ **to rock a baby** (in one's arms) acunar a un bebé
2 sacudir
◻ The explosion rocked the building. La explosión sacudió el edificio.
**rocket** NOUN
el cohete (spacecraft, firework)
**rocking chair** NOUN
la mecedora
**rocking horse** NOUN
el caballo de balancín
**rod** NOUN
la caña de pescar (for fishing)
**rode** VERB ▷ see **ride**
**role** NOUN
el papel
◻ to play a role hacer un papel
**role play** NOUN
el juego de roles
◻ to do a role play hacer un juego de roles
**roll** NOUN
▷ see also **roll** VERB
1 el rollo
◻ a toilet roll un rollo de papel higiénico
■ **a roll of film** un carrete de fotos
2 el panecillo
◻ a cheese roll un panecillo de queso
■ **Roll call is at 8.30.** Pasan lista a las ocho y media.
to **roll** VERB
▷ see also **roll** NOUN
rodar* (ball, bottle)
**roller** NOUN
el rulo (for hair)
**rollercoaster** NOUN
la montaña rusa
**roller skates** PL NOUN
los patines de ruedas
**roller-skating** NOUN
el patinaje sobre ruedas
■ **to go roller-skating** (sobre ruedas) ir a patinar

**r**

219

**rolling pin** NOUN
el rodillo

**Roman** ADJECTIVE, NOUN
romano (FEM romana)
▫ the Roman empire el imperio romano
■ the Romans los romanos

**Roman Catholic** NOUN
el católico
la católica
▫ He's a Roman Catholic. Es católico.

**romance** NOUN
1 las novelas románticas (novels)
▫ I read a lot of romance. Leo muchas
novelas románticas.
2 el romanticismo
▫ the romance of Paris el romanticismo de
París
■ a holiday romance un romance de verano

**Romania** NOUN
Rumania fem

**Romanian** ADJECTIVE
rumano (FEM rumana)

**romantic** ADJECTIVE
romántico (FEM romántica)

**roof** NOUN
el techo

**roof rack** NOUN
la baca

**room** NOUN
1 la habitación (PL las habitaciones)
▫ She's in her room. Está en su habitación.
■ a single room una habitación individual
■ a double room una habitación doble
2 sala (in school)
▫ the music room la sala de música
3 el espacio
▫ There's no room for that box. No hay
espacio para esa caja.

**roommate** NOUN
el compañero de cuarto
la compañera de cuarto

**root** NOUN
la raíz (PL las raíces)

**rope** NOUN
la cuerda

**rose** VERB ▷ see rise

**rose** NOUN
la rosa (flower)

to **rot** VERB
pudrirse*
▫ The wood had started to rot. La madera
había empezado a pudrirse
■ Sugar rots your teeth. El azúcar pica los
dientes.

**rotten** ADJECTIVE
podrido (FEM podrida)
▫ a rotten apple una manzana podrida
■ rotten weather un tiempo asqueroso

■ That's a rotten thing to do! ¡Eso está fatal!
■ to feel rotten sentirse fatal

**rough** ADJECTIVE, ADVERB
1 áspero (FEM áspera)
▫ My hands are rough. Tengo las manos
ásperas.
2 violento (FEM violenta)
▫ Rugby's a rough sport. El rugby es un
deporte violento.
3 peligroso (FEM peligrosa)
▫ It's a rough area. Es una zona peligrosa.
4 agitado (FEM agitada)
▫ The sea was rough. El mar estaba agitado.
5 aproximado (FEM aproximada)
▫ I've got a rough idea. Tengo una idea
aproximada.
■ to feel rough sentirse mal
■ to sleep rough dormir en la calle ▫ A lot
of people sleep rough in London. Mucha
gente duerme en la calle en Londres.

**roughly** ADVERB
aproximadamente
■ It weighs roughly 20 kilos. Pesa
aproximadamente 20 kilos.

**round** ADJECTIVE, ADVERB, PREPOSITION
▷ see also **round** NOUN
1 redondo (FEM redonda)
▫ a round table una mesa redonda
2 alrededor de
▫ We were sitting round the table.
Estábamos sentados alrededor de la mesa.
▫ She wore a scarf round her neck. Llevaba
una bufanda alrededor del cuello.
■ It's just round the corner. Está a la
vuelta de la esquina.
■ to go round to somebody's house ir a
casa de alguien
■ to have a look round echar un vistazo
▫ We had a look round the shoe
department. Echamos un vistazo a la
sección de zapatos.
■ to go round a museum visitar un museo
■ round here por aquí cerca ▫ He lives
round here. Vive aquí cerca. ▫ Is there a
chemist's round here? ¿Hay alguna
farmacia por aquí cerca?
■ all round por todos lados ▫ There were
vineyards all round. Había viñedos por
todos lados.
■ all year round todo el año
■ round about alrededor de ▫ It costs
round about £100. Cuesta alrededor de
100 libras esterlinas.
■ round about eight o'clock hacia las ocho

**round** NOUN
▷ see also **round** ADJECTIVE, ADVERB, PREPOSITION
1 la vuelta (of tournament)
2 el round (PL los rounds) (of boxing match)

■ **a round of golf** una vuelta de golf

■ **a round of drinks** una ronda de bebidas

□ He bought them a round of drinks. Les invitó a una ronda de bebidas.

■ **I think it's my round.** Creo que me toca pagar.

**roundabout** NOUN

1 la rotonda *(at junction)*

2 el tiovivo *(at funfair)*

**rounders** SING NOUN

**DID YOU KNOW...?**
Rounders is not played in Spain.

**round trip** NOUN (US)
el viaje de ida y vuelta

■ **a round-trip ticket** un billete de ida y vuelta

**route** NOUN
el itinerario

□ We are planning our route. Estamos planeando el itinerario.

■ **bus route** el recorrido del autobús

**routine** NOUN
la rutina

□ my daily routine mi rutina diaria

**row (1)** NOUN
▷ *see also* **row** VERB

1 el jaleo

□ What's that terrible row? ¿Qué es ese jaleo tan tremendo?

2 la pelea

■ **to have a row** pelearse □ They've had a row. Se han peleado.

**row (2)** NOUN
▷ *see also* **row (2)** VERB

1 la hilera

□ a row of houses una hilera de casas

2 la fila *(of people, seats)*

□ in the front row en primera fila

■ **five times in a row** cinco veces seguidas

to **row** VERB
▷ *see also* **row (2)** NOUN
remar

**rowboat** NOUN (US)
la barca de remos

**rowing** NOUN
el remo

□ My hobby is rowing. My hobby es el remo.

■ **rowing boat** la barca de remos

**royal** ADJECTIVE
real *(FEM real)*

□ the royal family la familia real

to **rub** VERB

1 frotar *(stain)*

2 restregarse* *(part of body)*

□ Don't rub your eyes. No te restriegues los ojos.

**rubber** NOUN

1 la goma

□ rubber soles suelas de goma

2 la goma de borrar *(eraser)*

□ Can I borrow your rubber? ¿Me prestas la goma?

■ **a rubber band** una goma elástica

**rubbish** NOUN
▷ *see also* **rubbish** ADJECTIVE

1 la basura

□ When do they collect the rubbish? ¿Cuándo recogen la basura? □ They sell a lot of rubbish at the market. Venden mucha basura en el mercado.

■ **That magazine is rubbish!** *(informal)* ¡Esa revista es una porquería!

2 las estupideces

□ Don't talk rubbish! ¡No digas estupideces!

■ **That's a load of rubbish!** ¡Son puras tonterías!

■ **rubbish bin** el cubo de la basura

■ **rubbish dump** el vertedero

**rubbish** ADJECTIVE
▷ *see also* **rubbish** NOUN

■ **They're a rubbish team!** ¡Es un equipo que no vale nada!

**rucksack** NOUN
la mochila

**rude** ADJECTIVE
grosero *(FEM grosera)*

□ He was very rude to me. Fue muy grosero conmigo.

■ **It's rude to interrupt.** Es de mala educación interrumpir.

■ **a rude joke** un chiste verde

■ **a rude word** una palabrota

**rug** NOUN

1 la alfombra *(carpet)*

2 la manta de viaje *(travelling rug)*

**rugby** NOUN
el rugby

□ He enjoys playing rugby. Le gusta jugar al rugby.

**ruin** NOUN
▷ *see also* **ruin** VERB
la ruina

□ the ruins of the castle las ruinas del castillo

■ **in ruins** en ruinas

to **ruin** VERB
▷ *see also* **ruin** NOUN

1 estropear

□ You'll ruin your shoes. Te vas a estropear los zapatos. □ It ruined our holiday. Nos estropeó las vacaciones.

2 arruinar *(financially)*

**rule** NOUN
▷ *see also* **rule** VERB

1 la regla

□ the rules of grammar las reglas de la gramática

r

221

■ **as a rule** por regla general
**2** la norma
□ It's against the rules. Va en contra de las normas.

to **rule out** VERB
descartar (possibility)

**ruler** NOUN
la regla

**rum** NOUN
el ron

**rumour** (US **rumor**) NOUN
el rumor
□ It's just a rumour. Es sólo un rumor.

**run** NOUN
▷ see also **run** VERB
■ **to go for a run** salir a correr □ I go for a run every morning. Salgo a correr todas las mañanas.
■ **I did a 10-kilometre run.** Corrí 10 kilómetros.
■ **The criminals are still on the run.** Los delincuentes están todavía en fuga.
■ **in the long run** a la larga

to **run** VERB
▷ see also **run** NOUN
**1** correr
■ **I ran five kilometres.** Corrí cinco kilómetros.
■ **to run a marathon** correr un maratón
**2** dirigir*
□ He runs a large company. Dirige una gran empresa.
**3** organizar*
□ They run music courses in the holidays. Organizan cursos de música en las vacaciones.
**4** llevar (by car)
□ I can run you to the station. Te puedo llevar a la estación.
■ **Don't leave the tap running.** No dejen el grifo abierto. (No dejen la llave abierta. Latin America)
■ **to run a bath** llenar la bañera
■ **The buses stop running at midnight.** Los autobuses dejan de funcionar a medianoche.

to **run away** VERB
huir*
□ They ran away before the police came. Huyeron antes de que llegara la policía.

to **run out** VERB
■ **Time is running out.** Queda poco tiempo.
■ **to run out of something** quedarse sin algo □ We ran out of money. Nos quedamos sin dinero.

to **run over** VERB
atropellar
■ **to get run over** ser atropellado

**rung** VERB ▷ see **ring**

**runner** NOUN
el corredor
la corredora

**runner beans** PL NOUN
las judías verdes (las habichuelas verdes Latin America)

**runner-up** NOUN
el subcampeón (PL los subcampeones)
la subcampeona

**running** NOUN
el footing
■ **Running is my favourite sport.** El footing es mi deporte favorito. □ to go running hacer footing

**runway** NOUN
la pista de aterrizaje

**rural** ADJECTIVE
rural (FEM rural)

**rush** NOUN
▷ see also **rush** VERB
la prisa
□ I'm in a rush. Tengo prisa. □ There's no rush. No corre prisa.
■ **to do something in a rush** hacer algo deprisa

to **rush** VERB
▷ see also **rush** NOUN
**1** correr
□ Everyone rushed outside. Todos corrieron hacia fuera.
**2** precipitarse
□ There's no need to rush. No hay por qué precipitarse.

**rush hour** NOUN
la hora punta (la hora pico Latin America)

**rusk** NOUN
la galleta para bebés

**Russia** NOUN
la Rusia

**Russian** ADJECTIVE
▷ see also **Russian** NOUN
ruso (FEM rusa)

**Russian** NOUN
▷ see also **Russian** ADJECTIVE
**1** el ruso
la rusa (person)
□ the Russians los rusos
**2** el ruso (language)

**rust** NOUN
el óxido

**rusty** ADJECTIVE
oxidado (FEM oxidada)

**ruthless** ADJECTIVE
despiadado (FEM despiadada)

**rye** NOUN
el centeno
■ **rye bread** el pan de centeno

# Ss

**sack** NOUN
  ▷ *see also* **sack** VERB
  el saco
  ☐ a sack of potatoes  un saco de patatas
  ■ **to give somebody the sack**  despedir a
  alguien
  ■ **He got the sack.**  Lo despidieron.
to **sack** VERB
  ▷ *see also* **sack** NOUN
  ■ **to sack somebody**  despedir a alguien
  ☐ He was sacked.  Lo despidieron.
**sacred** ADJECTIVE
  sagrado (FEM sagrada)
  ☐ sacred places  lugares sagrados
  ■ **sacred music**  música sacra
**sacrifice** NOUN
  el sacrificio
**sad** ADJECTIVE
  triste (FEM triste)

**WORD POWER**
You can use a number of other words
instead of **sad** to mean 'unhappy':
**miserable** desgraciado
  ☐ a miserable face  una cara desgraciada
**unhappy** infeliz
  ☐ an unhappy child  un niño infeliz
**upset** disgustado
  ☐ to be upset  estar disgustado

**saddle** NOUN
  1 la silla de montar *(for horse)*
  2 el sillín *(on bike)*
**saddlebag** NOUN
  1 la cartera *(on bike)*
  2 la alforja *(for horse)*
**sadly** ADVERB
  1 con tristeza
    ☐ 'She's gone', he said sadly.  'Se ha ido' dijo
    con tristeza.
  2 desgraciadamente
    ☐ Sadly, it was too late.  Desgraciadamente,
    era ya demasiado tarde.
**safe** NOUN
  ▷ *see also* **safe** ADJECTIVE
  la caja fuerte (PL las cajas fuertes)

**safe** ADJECTIVE
  ▷ *see also* **safe** NOUN
  1 seguro (FEM segura)
    ☐ This car isn't safe.  Este coche no es seguro.
  2 a salvo
    ☐ You're safe now.  Ya estás a salvo.
    ■ **to feel safe**  sentirse protegido
    ■ **Is the water safe to drink?**  ¿Es agua
    potable?
    ■ **Don't worry, it's perfectly safe.**  No te
    preocupes, no tiene el menor peligro.
    ■ **safe sex**  el sexo sin riesgo
**safety** NOUN
  la seguridad
    ■ **safety belt**  el cinturón de seguridad
    ■ **safety pin**  el imperdible (el seguro *Latin
    America*)
**Sagittarius** NOUN
  el Sagitario *(sign)*
    ■ **I'm Sagittarius.**  Soy sagitario.
**Sahara** NOUN
    ■ **the Sahara Desert**  el Sáhara
**said** VERB  ▷ *see* say
**sail** NOUN
  ▷ *see also* **sail** VERB
  la vela
    ■ **to set sail**  zarpar
to **sail** VERB
  ▷ *see also* **sail** NOUN
  1 navegar*
    ☐ to sail around the world  dar la vuelta al
    mundo navegando
  2 zarpar
    ☐ The boat sails at eight o'clock.  El barco
    zarpa a las ocho.
**sailing** NOUN
  la vela *(sport)*
    ■ **to go sailing**  hacer vela
    ■ **sailing boat**  el barco de vela
    ■ **sailing ship**  el velero
**sailor** NOUN
  el marinero
    ☐ He's a sailor.  Es marinero.
**saint** NOUN
  el santo
  la santa

**S**

LANGUAGE TIP When used before a man's name, the word **Santo** is shortened to **San**, the exceptions being **Santo Tomás** and **Santo Domingo**.

□ Saint John San Juan

**sake** NOUN
■ **for the sake of argument** pongamos por caso
■ **for the sake of the children** por el bien de los niños
■ **For goodness sake!** ¡Por el amor de Dios!

**salad** NOUN
la ensalada
■ **salad cream** la mayonesa
■ **salad dressing** el aliño para la ensalada

**salami** NOUN
el salami

**salary** NOUN
el sueldo

**sale** NOUN
1 las rebajas
□ There's a sale on at Harrods. En Harrods están de rebajas. □ the January sales las rebajas de enero
2 la venta
□ Newspaper sales have fallen. Ha descendido la venta de periódicos.
■ **on sale** a la venta
■ **The house is for sale.** La casa está en venta.
■ **'for sale'** 'se vende'

**sales assistant** NOUN
el dependiente
la dependienta

**salesman** NOUN
1 el representante *(commercial)*
□ an insurance salesman un representante de seguros
2 el dependiente *(sales assistant)*
■ **a car salesman** un vendedor de coches

**sales rep** NOUN
el/la representante

**saleswoman** NOUN
1 la representante *(commercial)*
□ an insurance saleswoman una representante de seguros
2 la dependienta *(sales assistant)*

**salmon** NOUN
el salmón (PL los salmones)

**salon** NOUN
el salón (PL los salones)
□ hair salon salón de peluquería □ beauty salon salón de belleza

**saloon car** NOUN
el turismo

**salt** NOUN
la sal

**salty** ADJECTIVE
salado (FEM salada)

to **salute** VERB
saludar

**Salvation Army** NOUN
el Ejército de Salvación

**same** ADJECTIVE
mismo (FEM misma)
□ the same model el mismo modelo
■ **It's not the same.** No es lo mismo.
■ **They're exactly the same.** Son exactamente iguales.
■ **The house is still the same.** La casa sigue igual.

**sample** NOUN
la muestra
□ a free sample of perfume una muestra gratuita de perfume

**sand** NOUN
la arena

**sandal** NOUN
la sandalia
□ a pair of sandals unas sandalias

**sand castle** NOUN
el castillo de arena

**sandwich** NOUN
1 el sandwich (PL los sandwiches) *(with sliced bread)*
2 el bocadillo *(with French bread)*

**sang** VERB ▷ *see* **sing**

**sanitary towel** NOUN
la compresa

**sank** VERB ▷ *see* **sink**

**Santa Claus** NOUN
Papá Noel *masc*

**sarcastic** ADJECTIVE
sarcástico (FEM sarcástica)

**sardine** NOUN
la sardina

**sat** VERB ▷ *see* **sit**

**satchel** NOUN
la cartera

**satellite** NOUN
el satélite
□ by satellite vía satélite
■ **a satellite dish** una antena parabólica
■ **satellite television** la televisión vía satélite

**satisfactory** ADJECTIVE
satisfactorio (FEM satisfactoria)

**satisfied** ADJECTIVE
satisfecho (FEM satisfecha)

**Saturday** NOUN
el sábado (PL los sábados)
□ I saw her on Saturday. La vi el sábado.
□ every Saturday todos los sábados □ last Saturday el sábado pasado □ next Saturday el sábado que viene □ on Saturdays los sábados

■ **I've got a Saturday job.** Tengo un trabajo los sábados.

**sauce** NOUN
1 la salsa
   □ tomato sauce salsa de tomate
2 la crema
   □ chocolate sauce crema de chocolate

**saucepan** NOUN
   el cazo

**saucer** NOUN
   el platillo

**Saudi Arabia** NOUN
   Arabia Saudí *fem*

**sauna** NOUN
   la sauna

**sausage** NOUN
   la salchicha
   ■ **a sausage roll** un pastelito de salchicha

to **save** VERB
1 ahorrar
   □ I saved money by staying in youth hostels. Ahorré dinero yendo a albergues juveniles.
   □ I've saved £50 already. Ya llevo ahorradas 50 libras. □ It saved us time. Nos ahorró tiempo.
   ■ **We went in a taxi to save time.** Para ganar tiempo fuimos en taxi.
2 salvar
   □ Doctors saved her from cancer. Los médicos la salvaron del cáncer.
   ■ **Luckily, all the passengers were saved.** Afortunadamente, todos los pasajeros se salvaron.
3 guardar
   □ Don't forget to save your work regularly. No te olvides de guardar tu trabajo de vez en cuando.

to **save up** VERB
   ahorrar
   □ I'm saving up for a new bike. Estoy ahorrando para una bici nueva.

**savings** PL NOUN
   los ahorros
   □ She spent all her savings on a computer. Se gastó todos sus ahorros en un ordenador.

**savoury** ADJECTIVE
   salado (FEM salada)
   □ Is it sweet or savoury? ¿Es dulce o salado?

**saw** VERB ▷ see **see**

**saw** NOUN
   la sierra

**sax** NOUN
   el saxo

**saxophone** NOUN
   el saxofón (PL los saxofones)

to **say** VERB
   decir*
   □ to say yes decir que sí □ What did he say?

¿Qué dijo él?
   ■ **Could you say that again?** ¿Podrías repetir eso?
   ■ **The clock said four minutes past eleven.** El reloj marcaba las once y cuatro minutos.
   ■ **It goes without saying that...** Ni que decir tiene que...

**saying** NOUN
   el dicho

**scale** NOUN
   la escala
   □ a large-scale map un mapa a gran escala
   ■ **He underestimated the scale of the problem.** Ha subestimado la envergadura del problema.

**scales** PL NOUN
1 el peso *(in kitchen)*
2 la báscula *(in shop)*
   ■ **bathroom scales** la báscula de baño

**scampi** PL NOUN
   las gambas rebozadas

**scandal** NOUN
1 el escándalo *(outrage)*
   □ It caused a scandal. Causó escándalo.
2 las habladurías *(gossip)*
   □ It's just scandal. No son más que habladurías.

**scar** NOUN
   la cicatriz (PL las cicatrices)

**scarce** ADJECTIVE
   escaso (FEM escasa)
   □ scarce resources recursos escasos
   ■ **Jobs are scarce.** Escasean los trabajos.

**scarcely** ADVERB
   apenas
   □ I scarcely knew him. Apenas lo conocía.

**scare** NOUN
   ▷ see also **scare** VERB
   el susto
   □ We got a bit of a scare. Nos pegamos un susto.
   ■ **a bomb scare** una amenaza de bomba

to **scare** VERB
   ▷ see also **scare** NOUN
   asustar
   □ You scared me! ¡Me has asustado!

**scarecrow** NOUN
   el espantapájaros (PL los espantapájaros)

**scared** ADJECTIVE
   ■ **to be scared** tener miedo □ Are you scared of him? ¿Le tienes miedo?
   ■ **I was scared stiff.** Estaba muerto de miedo.

**scarf** NOUN
1 la bufanda *(woollen)*
2 el pañuelo *(light)*

**scary** ADJECTIVE

- **It was really scary.** Daba verdadero miedo.
- **a scary film** una película de miedo

**scene** NOUN
1 la escena
   □ love scenes las escenas de amor  □ It was an amazing scene. Era una escena asombrosa.
2 el lugar
   □ at the scene of the crime en el lugar del crimen  □ The police were soon on the scene. La policía no tardó en acudir al lugar de los hechos.
- **to make a scene** montar el número

**scenery** NOUN
el paisaje

**scent** NOUN
el perfume

**schedule** NOUN
el programa

> **LANGUAGE TIP** Although **programa** ends in **-a**, it is actually a masculine noun.

   □ a production schedule un programa de producción
- **There's a tight schedule for this project.** Este proyecto tiene un calendario muy justo.
- **a busy schedule** una agenda muy apretada
- **on schedule** sin retraso
- **to be behind schedule** ir con retraso

**scheduled flight** NOUN
el vuelo regular

**scheme** NOUN
el plan
   □ a road-widening scheme un plan de ensanchamiento de calzadas  □ a crazy scheme he dreamed up un plan descabellado que se le ocurrió

**scholarship** NOUN
la beca

**school** NOUN
1 el colegio (for children)
   □ at school en el colegio  □ to go to school ir al colegio
- **after school** después de clase
2 la facultad (at university)
   □ art school la facultad de bellas artes
- **school uniform** el uniforme de colegio

**schoolbook** NOUN
el libro de texto

**schoolboy** NOUN
el colegial

**schoolchildren** PL NOUN
los colegiales

**schoolgirl** NOUN
la colegiala

**science** NOUN
la ciencia

**science fiction** NOUN
la ciencia ficción

**scientific** ADJECTIVE
científico (FEM científica)

**scientist** NOUN
el científico
la científica

**scissors** PL NOUN
las tijeras
   □ a pair of scissors unas tijeras

**to scoff** VERB
1 mofarse
   □ My friends scoffed at the idea. Mis amigos se mofaron de la idea.
2 zamparse (informal)
   □ My brother scoffed all the sandwiches. Mi hermano se zampó todos los sandwiches.

**scone** NOUN
el pastel de pan

**scooter** NOUN
1 la Vespa® (motorcycle)
2 el patinete (child's toy)

**score** NOUN
▷ see also **score** VERB
1 la puntuación (PL las puntuaciones)
   □ the highest score by an English batsman la puntuación más alta de un bateador inglés
2 el resultado
   □ The score was three nil. El resultado fue de tres a cero.
- **What's the score?** ¿Cómo van?

**to score** VERB
▷ see also **score** NOUN
1 marcar*
   □ to score a goal marcar un gol
- **to score a point** anotar un punto
- **to score six out of ten** sacar una puntuación de seis sobre diez
2 llevar el tanteo
   □ Who's going to score? ¿Quién va a llevar el tanteo?

**Scorpio** NOUN
el Escorpio (sign)
- **I'm Scorpio.** Soy escorpio.

**Scot** NOUN
el escocés
la escocesa (person)

**Scotch tape®** NOUN (US)
el celo

**Scotland** NOUN
Escocia fem

**Scots** ADJECTIVE
escocés (FEM escocesa, PL escoceses)
   □ a Scots accent un acento escocés

**Scotsman** NOUN
el escocés (PL los escoceses)

**Scotswoman** NOUN
la escocesa

**Scottish** ADJECTIVE
escocés (FEM escocesa, PL escoceses)

□ a Scottish accent un acento escocés

**scout** NOUN
el boy scout
la girl scout

**scrambled eggs** PL NOUN
los huevos revueltos

**scrap** NOUN
▷ see also **scrap** VERB
1 el trocito
□ a scrap of paper un trocito de papel
2 la pelea
□ There was a scrap outside the pub. Hubo una pelea a la salida del pub.
■ **scrap iron** la chatarra

to **scrap** VERB
▷ see also **scrap** NOUN
desechar
□ In the end the plan was scrapped. Al final se desechó el plan.

**scrapbook** NOUN
el álbum de recortes (PL los álbumes de recortes)

to **scratch** VERB
▷ see also **scratch** NOUN
1 rascarse* (when itchy)
□ Stop scratching! ¡Deja de rascarte!
2 arañar (cut)
□ He scratched his arm on the bushes. Se arañó el brazo con las zarzas.
3 rayar (scrape)
□ You'll scratch the worktop with that knife. Vas a rayar la encimera con ese cuchillo.

**scratch** NOUN
▷ see also **scratch** VERB
el arañazo (on skin, floor)
■ **to start from scratch** partir de cero
■ **a scratch card** una tarjeta de 'rasque y gane'

**scream** NOUN
▷ see also **scream** VERB
el grito

to **scream** VERB
▷ see also **scream** NOUN
gritar

**screen** NOUN
la pantalla (television, cinema, computer)

**screw** NOUN
el tornillo

**screwdriver** NOUN
el destornillador

to **scribble** VERB
garabatear

to **scrub** VERB
fregar*

**sculpture** NOUN
la escultura

**sea** NOUN
el mar

□ by sea por mar □ a house by the sea una casa junto al mar
⬤ **LANGUAGE TIP** The word **mar** is masculine in most cases, but in some set expressions it is feminine.
□ The fishermen put out to sea. Los pescadores se hicieron a la mar.

**seafood** NOUN
el marisco
□ I don't like seafood. No me gusta el marisco.
■ **a seafood restaurant** una marisquería

**seagull** NOUN
la gaviota

**seal** NOUN
▷ see also **seal** VERB
1 la foca (animal)
2 el sello (on letter)

to **seal** VERB
▷ see also **seal** NOUN
sellar

**seaman** NOUN
el marinero

to **search** VERB
▷ see also **search** NOUN
1 buscar*
□ They're searching for the missing climbers. Están buscando a los alpinistas desaparecidos.
2 registrar
□ The police searched him for drugs. La policía lo registró en busca de drogas.
■ **They searched the woods for the little girl.** Rastrearon el bosque en busca de la niña.

**search** NOUN
▷ see also **search** VERB
1 la búsqueda
□ The search was abandoned. Se abandonó la búsqueda.
■ **to go in search of** ir en busca de
2 el registro
□ a search of the building un registro del edificio

**search engine** NOUN
el buscador

**search party** NOUN
el equipo de búsqueda

**seashore** NOUN
la orilla del mar
□ on the seashore a la orilla del mar

**seasick** ADJECTIVE
■ **to be seasick** marearse en barco

**seaside** NOUN
la playa
■ **a seaside resort** un lugar de veraneo en la playa

**season** NOUN
la estación (PL las estaciones)

□ What's your favourite season? ¿Cuál es tu estación preferida?
■ **out of season** fuera de temporada
■ **during the holiday season** en la temporada de vacaciones
■ **a season ticket** un abono

**seat** NOUN
1 el asiento
□ I was sitting in the back seat. Yo iba sentada en el asiento trasero.
■ **Are there any seats left?** ¿Quedan localidades?
2 el escaño
□ to win a seat at the election conseguir un escaño en las elecciones

**seat belt** NOUN
el cinturón de seguridad (PL los cinturones de seguridad)

**seaweed** NOUN
el alga marina *fem*

> LANGUAGE TIP Although it's a feminine noun, remember that you use el and un with alga.

**second** ADJECTIVE, ADVERB
▷ *see also* **second** NOUN
segundo (FEM segunda)
□ the second time la segunda vez
■ **to come second** llegar en segundo lugar
■ **the second of March** el dos de marzo

**second** NOUN
▷ *see also* **second** ADJECTIVE, ADVERB
el segundo
□ It'll only take a second. Es un segundo nada más.

**secondary school** NOUN
1 el instituto (*state*)
2 el colegio (*private*)

**second-class** ADJECTIVE, ADVERB
de segunda clase (*ticket, compartment*)
■ **to travel second class** viajar en segunda
■ **second-class postage**

> DID YOU KNOW...?
In Spain there is no first-class or second-class postage. If you want your mail to arive fast, you must have it sent express – **urgente** – from a post office.

**secondhand** ADJECTIVE
de segunda mano

**secondly** ADVERB
en segundo lugar

**secret** ADJECTIVE
▷ *see also* **secret** NOUN
secreto (FEM secreta)
□ a secret mission una misión secreta

**secret** NOUN
▷ *see also* **secret** ADJECTIVE
el secreto

□ Can you keep a secret? ¿Me guardas un secreto?
■ **in secret** en secreto

**secretary** NOUN
el secretario
la secretaria

**secretly** ADVERB
en secreto

**section** NOUN
la sección (PL las secciones)

**security** NOUN
la seguridad
□ They are trying to improve airport security. Intentan mejorar las medidas de seguridad en el aeropuerto. □ They have no job security. No tienen seguridad en el empleo.
■ **security guard** el/la guarda jurado

**sedan** NOUN (US)
el turismo

to **see** VERB
ver*
□ I can't see. No veo nada. □ I saw him yesterday. Lo vi ayer.
■ **You need to see a doctor.** Tienes que ir a ver a un médico.
■ **See you!** ¡Hasta luego!
■ **See you soon!** ¡Hasta pronto!

**seed** NOUN
la semilla
□ poppy seeds semillas de amapola

to **seem** VERB
parecer*
□ She seems tired. Parece cansada. □ That seems like a good idea. Me parece una buena idea.
■ **The shop seemed to be closed.** Parecía que la tienda estaba cerrada.
■ **It seems that...** Parece que... □ It seems you have no alternative. Parece que no tienes otra opción.
■ **It seems she's getting married.** Por lo visto se casa.
■ **There seems to be a problem.** Parece que hay un problema.

**seen** VERB ▷ *see* see

**seesaw** NOUN
el balancín (PL los balancines)

**see-through** ADJECTIVE
transparente (FEM transparente)

**seldom** ADVERB
rara vez

to **select** VERB
seleccionar

**selection** NOUN
1 la selección (PL las selecciones)
□ a selection test una prueba de selección
2 el surtido
□ the widest selection on the market el más

amplio surtido del mercado

**self-assured** ADJECTIVE
seguro de sí mismo (FEM segura de sí misma)

**self-catering** ADJECTIVE
■ **self-catering apartment** el apartamento

**self-centred** (US **self-centered**) ADJECTIVE
egocéntrico (FEM egocéntrica)

**self-confidence** NOUN
la confianza en uno mismo
◻ I lost all my self-confidence. Perdí toda la confianza en mí mismo.

**self-conscious** ADJECTIVE
1 cohibido (FEM cohibida)
◻ She was really self-conscious at first. Al principio estaba muy cohibida.
2 acomplejado (FEM acomplejada)
◻ She was self-conscious about her height. Estaba acomplejada por su estatura.

**self-contained** ADJECTIVE
independiente (FEM independiente)

**self-control** NOUN
el autocontrol

**self-defence** (US **self-defense**) NOUN
la defensa personal
◻ self-defence classes clases de defensa personal
■ She killed him in self-defence. Lo mató en defensa propia.

**self-discipline** NOUN
la autodisciplina

**self-employed** ADJECTIVE
autónomo (FEM autónoma)
■ to be self-employed ser autónomo
■ the self-employed los trabajadores autónomos

**selfish** ADJECTIVE
egoísta (FEM egoísta)

**self-respect** NOUN
el amor propio

**self-service** ADJECTIVE
de autoservicio

to **sell** VERB
vender
◻ He sold it to me. Me lo vendió.

to **sell off** VERB
liquidar

to **sell out** VERB
■ The tickets sold out in three hours. Las entradas se agotaron en tres horas.

**sell-by date** NOUN
la fecha de caducidad

**selling price** NOUN
el precio de venta

**Sellotape®** NOUN
el celo

**semi** NOUN
la casa adosada

**semicircle** NOUN

el semicírculo

**semicolon** NOUN
el punto y coma (PL los punto y coma)

**semi-detached house** NOUN
la casa adosada
◻ We live in a semi-detached house. Vivimos en una casa adosada.
■ a street of semi-detached houses una calle de casas pareadas

**semi-final** NOUN
la semifinal

**semi-skimmed milk** NOUN
la leche semidesnatada

to **send** VERB
mandar
◻ She sent me a birthday card. Me mandó una tarjeta de cumpleaños. ◻ He was sent to London. Lo mandaron a Londres.

to **send back** VERB
devolver*

to **send off** VERB
1 enviar* por correo
◻ We sent off your order yesterday. Le enviamos el pedido por correo ayer.
2 expulsar
◻ He was sent off. Lo expulsaron.

to **send out** VERB
enviar*

**sender** NOUN
el/la remitente

**senior** ADJECTIVE, NOUN
alto (FEM alta)
◻ senior officials in the British government altos cargos del gobierno británico ◻ senior management los altos directivos
■ She's five years my senior. Es cinco años mayor que yo.
■ senior school el instituto de enseñanza secundaria
■ senior pupils los alumnos más mayores

**senior citizen** NOUN
la persona de la tercera edad

**sensational** ADJECTIVE
sensacional (FEM sensacional)

**sense** NOUN
el sentido
◻ the five senses los cinco sentidos ◻ Use your common sense! ¡Usa el sentido común!
■ It makes sense. Tiene sentido.
■ It doesn't make sense. No tiene sentido.
■ a keen sense of smell un olfato finísimo
■ sense of humour sentido del humor

**senseless** ADJECTIVE
1 sin sentido
◻ senseless violence violencia sin sentido
◻ It is senseless to protest. No tiene sentido protestar.

**2** inconsciente (FEM inconsciente)
□ He was lying senseless on the floor. Yacía inconsciente en el suelo.

**sensible** ADJECTIVE
sensato (FEM sensata)
□ Be sensible! ¡Sé sensato! □ It would be sensible to check first. Lo más sensato sería comprobarlo antes.

> **LANGUAGE TIP** Be careful not to translate **sensible** by the Spanish word **sensible**.

**sensitive** ADJECTIVE
sensible (FEM sensible)

**sensuous** ADJECTIVE
sensual (FEM sensual)

**sent** VERB ▷ see **send**

**sentence** NOUN
▷ see also **sentence** VERB
**1** la oración (PL las oraciones)
□ What does this sentence mean? ¿Qué significa esta oración?
**2** la sentencia
□ to pass sentence dictar sentencia
**3** la condena
□ a sentence of 10 years una condena de 10 años
■ **the death sentence** la pena de muerte
■ **He got a life sentence.** Fue condenado a cadena perpetua.

to **sentence** VERB
▷ see also **sentence** NOUN
■ **to sentence somebody to life imprisonment** condenar a alguien a cadena perpetua
■ **to sentence somebody to death** condenar a muerte a alguien

**sentimental** ADJECTIVE
sentimental (FEM sentimental)

**separate** ADJECTIVE
▷ see also **separate** VERB
distinto (FEM distinta)
□ separate changing rooms vestuarios distintos
■ **The children have separate rooms.** Los niños tienen cada uno su habitación.
■ **I wrote it on a separate sheet.** Lo escribí en una hoja aparte.
■ **on separate occasions** en diversas ocasiones

to **separate** VERB
▷ see also **separate** ADJECTIVE
**1** separar
□ Police moved in to separate the two groups. La policía intervino para separar a los dos grupos.
**2** separarse
□ Her parents separated last year. Sus padres se separaron el año pasado.

**separately** ADVERB
por separado

**separation** NOUN
la separación (PL las separaciones)

**September** NOUN
septiembre masc
□ in September en septiembre □ on 23 September el 23 de septiembre

**sequel** NOUN
la continuación (PL las continuaciones)

**sequence** NOUN
**1** la serie
□ a sequence of events una serie de acontecimientos
**2** el orden (PL los órdenes)
□ in sequence en orden
**3** la secuencia
□ the best sequence in the film la mejor secuencia de la película

**sergeant** NOUN
**1** el/la sargento (army)
**2** el/la oficial de policía (police)

**serial** NOUN
**1** el serial (on TV, radio)
**2** la novela por entregas (in magazine)

**series** NOUN
la serie

**serious** ADJECTIVE
**1** serio (FEM seria)
□ You're looking very serious. Estás muy serio.
■ **Are you serious?** ¿Lo dices en serio?
**2** grave (FEM grave)
□ a serious illness una grave enfermedad

**seriously** ADVERB
en serio
□ No, but seriously... No, pero ya en serio...
□ to take somebody seriously tomar en serio a alguien
■ **seriously injured** gravemente herido
■ **Seriously?** ¿De verdad?

**sermon** NOUN
el sermón (PL los sermones)

**servant** NOUN
el criado
la criada

to **serve** VERB
▷ see also **serve** NOUN
**1** servir*
□ Dinner is served. La cena está servida.
■ **It's Murray's turn to serve.** Al servicio Murray.
■ **Are you being served?** ¿Le atienden ya?
**2** cumplir
□ to serve a life sentence cumplir cadena perpetua
■ **to serve time** cumplir condena
■ **It serves you right.** Te está bien empleado.

S

**serve** NOUN
▷ *see also* **serve** VERB
el servicio

**server** NOUN
el servidor

to **service** VERB
▷ *see also* **service** NOUN
revisar (*car, washing machine*)

**service** NOUN
▷ *see also* **service** VERB
1 el servicio
□ Service is included. El servicio está incluido. □ the postal service el servicio de correos
■ **a bus service** una línea de autobús
2 la revisión (PL las revisiones)
□ The car needs a service. Al coche le hace falta una revisión.
3 el oficio religioso
□ a memorial service un oficio religioso conmemorativo
■ **the armed services** las fuerzas armadas

**service area** NOUN
el área de servicios *fem*

> LANGUAGE TIP Although it's a feminine noun, remember that you use **el** and **un** with **área**.

**service charge** NOUN
el servicio
□ Service charge is included. El servicio va incluido.

**serviceman** NOUN
el militar

**service station** NOUN
la estación de servicio (PL las estaciones de servicio)

**serviette** NOUN
la servilleta

**session** NOUN
la sesión (PL las sesiones)

**set** NOUN
▷ *see also* **set** VERB
1 el juego (*of objects, tools*)
□ a set of keys un juego de llaves
■ **The sofa and chairs are only sold as a set.** El sofá y los sillones no se venden por separado.
2 el set (PL los sets) (*in tennis*)
□ She was leading 5–1 in the first set. Iba ganando 5 a 1 en el primer set.

to **set** VERB
▷ *see also* **set** NOUN
1 poner*
□ I set the alarm for seven o'clock. Puse el despertador a las siete.
2 establecer*
□ The world record was set last year. El récord mundial se estableció el año pasado.

3 ponerse*
□ The sun was setting. Se estaba poniendo el sol.
■ **The film is set in Morocco.** La película se desarrolla en Marruecos.
■ **to set something on fire** prender fuego a algo
■ **to set sail** zarpar
■ **to set the table** poner la mesa

to **set off** VERB
salir*
□ We set off for London at nine o'clock. Salimos para Londres a las nueve.

to **set out** VERB
salir*
□ We set out for London at nine o'clock. Salimos para Londres a las nueve.

**settee** NOUN
el sofá (PL los sofás)

to **settle** VERB
1 zanjar
□ That should settle the problem. Esto debería zanjar el problema.
2 pagar*
□ I'll settle the bill tomorrow. Mañana pagaré la cuenta.

to **settle down** VERB
calmarse

to **settle in** VERB
adaptarse

**seven** NUMERAL
siete
□ She's seven. Tiene siete años.

**seventeen** NUMERAL
diecisiete
□ He's seventeen. Tiene diecisiete años.

**seventeenth** ADJECTIVE
decimoséptimo (FEM decimoséptima)
■ **the seventeenth floor** la planta diecisiete
■ **the seventeenth of April** el diecisiete de abril

**seventh** ADJECTIVE
séptimo (FEM séptima)
□ the seventh floor el séptimo piso
■ **the seventh of August** el siete de agosto

**seventy** NUMERAL
setenta
□ She's seventy. Tiene setenta años.

**several** ADJECTIVE, PRONOUN
varios (FEM variosa)
□ several schools varios colegios □ several times varias veces

to **sew** VERB
coser

to **sew up** VERB
coser

**sewing** NOUN
la costura
□ I like sewing. Me gusta la costura.
■ **sewing machine** la máquina de coser
**sewn** VERB ▷ *see* sew
**sex** NOUN
el sexo
□ the opposite sex el sexo opuesto
■ **to have sex with somebody** tener
relaciones sexuales con alguien
■ **sex education** la educación sexual
**sexism** NOUN
el sexismo
**sexist** ADJECTIVE
sexista (FEM sexista)
**sexual** ADJECTIVE
sexual (FEM sexual)
□ sexual discrimination la discriminación
sexual □ sexual harassment el acoso sexual
**sexuality** NOUN
la sexualidad
**sexy** ADJECTIVE
sexy (PL sexy)
**shabby** ADJECTIVE
andrajoso (FEM andrajosa) *(person, clothes)*
**shade** NOUN
1 la sombra
□ It was 35 degrees in the shade. Hacía
35 grados a la sombra.
2 el tono
□ a beautiful shade of blue un tono de azul
muy bonito
**shadow** NOUN
la sombra
to **shake** VERB
1 sacudir
□ She shook the rug. Sacudió la alfombra.
■ **'Shake well before use'** 'Agítese bien
antes de usarse'
2 temblar*
□ He was shaking with cold. Temblaba de
frío.
■ **Donald shook his head.** Donald negó
con la cabeza.
■ **to shake hands with somebody** dar la
mano a alguien □ They shook hands. Se
dieron la mano.
**shaken** ADJECTIVE
afectado (FEM afectada)
□ I was feeling a bit shaken. Estaba un poco
afectado.
**shaky** ADJECTIVE
tembloroso (FEM temblorosa) *(hand, voice)*
■ **I was feeling a bit shaky.** Estaba un poco
débil.
**shall** VERB
■ **Shall I shut the window?** ¿Cierro la
ventana?

LANGUAGE TIP **pedir que** has to be
followed by a verb in the subjunctive.
■ **Shall we ask him to come with us?**
¿Le pedimos que venga con nosotros?
**shallow** ADJECTIVE
poco profundo (FEM poco profunda)
**shambles** NOUN
el desastre
□ It's a complete shambles. Es un desastre
total.
**shame** NOUN
la vergüenza
□ I'd die of shame! ¡Me moriría de
vergüenza!
■ **What a shame!** ¡Qué pena!

LANGUAGE TIP **es una pena que** has
to be followed by a verb in the
subjunctive.
■ **It's a shame that...** Es una pena que...
□ It's a shame he isn't here. Es una pena
que no esté aquí.
**shampoo** NOUN
el champú (PL los champús)
□ a bottle of shampoo un bote de champú
**shandy** NOUN
la clara *(de cerveza con gaseosa)*
**shan't** = shall not
**shape** NOUN
la forma
□ in the shape of a star en forma de estrella
■ **to be in good shape** estar en buena
forma
**share** NOUN
▷ *see also* **share** VERB
1 la acción (PL las acciones)
□ They've got shares in many companies.
Tienen acciones en muchas empresas.
2 la parte
□ He refused to pay his share of the bill.
Se negó a pagar su parte de la factura.
to **share** VERB
▷ *see also* **share** NOUN
compartir
□ to share a room with somebody compartir
habitación con alguien
to **share out** VERB
repartir
□ They shared the sweets out among the
children. Repartieron los caramelos entre
los niños.
**shark** NOUN
el tiburón (PL los tiburones)
**sharp** ADJECTIVE, ADVERB
1 afilado (FEM afilada)
□ Be careful, that knife's sharp! ¡Cuidado
con ese cuchillo que está afilado!
2 puntiagudo (FEM puntiaguda) *(point, spike)*
3 listo (FEM lista) *(intelligent)*

□ She's very sharp. Es muy lista.
■ **at two o'clock sharp** a las dos en punto
to **shave** VERB
afeitarse
□ He took a bath and shaved. Se dio un baño y se afeitó.
■ **to shave one's legs** depilarse las piernas
**shaver** NOUN
■ **electric shaver** la maquinilla de afeitar eléctrica
**shaving cream** NOUN
la crema de afeitar
**shaving foam** NOUN
la espuma de afeitar
**she** PRONOUN
ella

LANGUAGE TIP 'she' generally isn't translated unless it's emphatic.

□ She's very nice. Es muy maja.

LANGUAGE TIP Use **ella** for emphasis.

□ She did it but he didn't. Ella lo hizo, pero él no.
**shed** NOUN
el cobertizo
**she'd** = she had; she would
**sheep** NOUN
la oveja
**sheepdog** NOUN
el perro pastor (PL los perros pastores)
**sheer** ADJECTIVE
puro (FEM pura)
□ It's sheer greed. Es pura codicia.
**sheet** NOUN
la sábana
□ to change the sheets cambiar las sábanas
■ **a sheet of paper** una hoja de papel
**shelf** NOUN
1 el estante (on wall, in shop)
2 la parrilla (in oven)
**shell** NOUN
1 la concha (el caracol Latin America)
2 la cáscara (of egg, nut)
3 el obús (PL los obuses) (explosive)
**she'll** = she will
**shellfish** NOUN
el marisco
**shell suit** NOUN
el chándal de nylon (PL los chándals de nylon)
**shelter** NOUN
el refugio
□ a bomb shelter un refugio antiaéreo
■ **to take shelter** refugiarse
**shelves** PL NOUN ▷ see shelf
**shepherd** NOUN
el pastor
**sheriff** NOUN
el sheriff

**sherry** NOUN
el jerez
**she's** = she is; she has
**shield** NOUN
el escudo
**shift** NOUN
▷ see also shift VERB
el turno
□ the night shift el turno de noche
□ His shift starts at eight o'clock. Su turno empieza a las ocho.
■ **to do shift work** trabajar por turnos
to **shift** VERB
▷ see also shift NOUN
trasladar
□ I couldn't shift the wardrobe on my own. No podía trasladar el armario yo solo.
■ **Shift yourself!** (informal) ¡Quita de ahí!
**shifty** ADJECTIVE
sospechoso (FEM sospechosa)
□ He looked shifty. Tenía una pinta sospechosa.
■ **He has shifty eyes.** Tiene una mirada furtiva.
**shin** NOUN
la espinilla
to **shine** VERB
brillar
□ The sun was shining. Brillaba el sol.
**shiny** ADJECTIVE
brillante (FEM brillante)
**ship** NOUN
el barco
□ by ship en barco
■ **a merchant ship** un buque mercante
**shipbuilding** NOUN
la construcción naval
**shipwreck** NOUN
el naufragio
**shipwrecked** ADJECTIVE
■ **to be shipwrecked** naufragar
**shipyard** NOUN
el astillero
**shirt** NOUN
la camisa
**shit** EXCLAMATION
¡Mierda! (rude)
to **shiver** VERB
tiritar
□ to shiver with cold tiritar de frío
**shock** NOUN
▷ see also shock VERB
1 la conmoción (PL las conmociones)
□ The news came as a shock. La noticia causó conmoción.
2 el calambre
□ I got a shock when I touched the switch. Me dio calambre al tocar el interruptor.

233

to **shock** VERB
▷ see also **shock** NOUN
1 horrorizar∗ (upset)
□ They were shocked by the tragedy.
Quedaron horrorizados por la tragedia.
2 escandalizar∗ (scandalize)
□ Nothing shocks me any more. Ya nada
me escandaliza.

**shocking** ADJECTIVE
escandaloso (FEM escandalosa)
□ It's shocking! ¡Es escandaloso!

**shoe** NOUN
el zapato
□ a pair of shoes un par de zapatos

**shoelace** NOUN
el cordón (PL los cordones)

**shoe polish** NOUN
el betún

**shoe shop** NOUN
la zapatería

**shone** VERB ▷ see **shine**

**shook** VERB ▷ see **shake**

to **shoot** VERB
1 disparar (fire a shot)
□ Don't shoot! ¡No disparen!
■ to shoot at somebody disparar contra
alguien
■ He shot himself with a revolver.
Se pegó un tiro con un revólver.
■ He was shot dead by the police.
Murió de un disparo de la policía.
2 fusilar (execute)
□ He was shot at dawn. Lo fusilaron al
amanecer.
3 rodar∗
□ The film was shot in Prague. La película se
rodó en Praga.
4 chutar (in football)

**shooting** NOUN
1 los disparos
□ They heard shooting. Oyeron disparos.
■ a shooting un tiroteo
2 la caza
□ to go shooting ir de caza

**shop** NOUN
la tienda
□ a sports shop una tienda de deportes

**shop assistant** NOUN
el dependiente
la dependienta

**shopkeeper** NOUN
el/la comerciante (tendero)

**shoplifting** NOUN
el hurto en las tiendas

**shopping** NOUN
la compra
□ Can you get the shopping from the car?
¿Puedes sacar la compra del coche?

■ to go shopping 1 (for food) ir a hacer la
compra 2 (for pleasure) ir de compras
■ I love shopping. Me encanta ir de compras.
■ shopping bag la bolsa de la compra
■ shopping centre el centro comercial

**shop window** NOUN
el escaparate

**shore** NOUN
la orilla
□ on the shores of the lake a orillas del lago
■ on shore en tierra

**short** ADJECTIVE
1 corto (FEM corta)
□ a short skirt una falda corta □ short hair
pelo corto □ a short walk un paseo corto
□ It was a great holiday, but too short.
Fueron unas vacaciones estupendas, pero
demasiado cortas.
■ a short break un pequeño descanso
■ a short time ago hace poco
2 bajo (FEM baja)
□ She's quite short. Es bastante baja.
■ to be short of something andar escaso
de algo
■ at short notice con poco tiempo de
antelación
■ In short, the answer is no. En una
palabra, la respuesta es no.

**shortage** NOUN
la escasez
□ a water shortage escasez de agua

**short cut** NOUN
el atajo

**shorthand** NOUN
la taquigrafía

**shortly** ADVERB
dentro de poco
□ I'll be there shortly. Estaré allí dentro de
poco.
■ She arrived shortly after midnight.
Llegó poco después de la medianoche.

**shorts** PL NOUN
los pantalones cortos
□ a pair of shorts unos pantalones cortos

**short-sighted** ADJECTIVE
miope (FEM miope)

**short story** NOUN
el cuento

**shot** VERB ▷ see **shoot**

**shot** NOUN
1 el tiro
□ to fire a shot disparar un tiro □ a shot at
goal un tiro a puerta
2 la foto
**LANGUAGE TIP** Although **foto** ends in
-a, it is actually a feminine noun.
□ a shot of Edinburgh castle una foto del
castillo de Edimburgo

S

**3** la inyección (PL las inyecciones) *(vaccination)*

**shotgun** NOUN
la escopeta

**should** VERB

> LANGUAGE TIP When 'should' means 'ought to', use the conditional of **deber**.

deber
□ You should take more exercise. Deberías hacer más ejercicio. □ He should be there by now. Ya debería estar allí. □ That shouldn't be too hard. Eso no debería ser muy difícil.

> LANGUAGE TIP **tener\* que** is also a very common way to translate 'should'.

□ I should have told you before. Tendría que habértelo dicho antes.

> LANGUAGE TIP When 'should' means 'would', use the conditional.

■ I should go if I were you. Yo que tú, iría.
■ I should be so lucky! ¡Ojalá!

**shoulder** NOUN
el hombro
□ I looked over my shoulder. Miré por encima del hombro.
■ **shoulder bag** el bolso de bandolera

**shouldn't** = should not

**to shout** VERB
▷ see also **shout** NOUN
gritar
□ Don't shout! ¡No grites!

**shout** NOUN
▷ see also **shout** VERB
el grito

**shovel** NOUN
la pala

**show** NOUN
▷ see also **show** VERB
**1** el espectáculo
□ to stage a show montar un espectáculo
**2** el programa

> LANGUAGE TIP Although **programa** ends in -a, it is actually a masculine noun.

□ a radio show un programa de radio
■ **fashion show** el pase de modelos
■ **motor show** el salón del automóvil

**to show** VERB
▷ see also **show** NOUN
**1** enseñar
■ **to show somebody something** enseñar algo a alguien □ Have I shown you my hat? ¿Te he enseñado ya mi sombrero?
**2** demostrar\*
□ She showed great courage. Demostró gran valentía.
■ **It shows.** Se nota. □ I've never been

riding before. — It shows. Nunca había montado a caballo antes. — Se nota.

**to show off** VERB
presumir

**to show up** VERB
presentarse
□ He showed up late as usual. Se presentó tarde, como de costumbre.

**shower** NOUN
**1** la ducha
■ **to have a shower** ducharse
**2** el chubasco
□ scattered showers chubascos dispersos

**showerproof** ADJECTIVE
impermeable (FEM impermeable)

**showing** NOUN
el pase *(of a film)*
□ a private showing un pase privado

**shown** VERB ▷ see **show**

**show-off** NOUN
el fantasmón (PL los fantasmones)
la fantasmona

**shrank** VERB ▷ see **shrink**

**to shriek** VERB
chillar

**shrimps** PL NOUN
los camarones

**to shrink** VERB
encogerse\* *(clothes, fabric)*

**Shrove Tuesday** NOUN
el martes de carnaval

**to shrug** VERB
■ **to shrug one's shoulders** encogerse de hombros

**shrunk** VERB ▷ see **shrink**

**to shudder** VERB
estremecerse\*

**to shuffle** VERB
■ **to shuffle the cards** barajar las cartas

**to shut** VERB
cerrar\*
□ What time do you shut? ¿A qué hora cierran? □ What time do the shops shut? ¿A qué hora cierran las tiendas?

**to shut down** VERB
cerrar\*
□ The cinema shut down last year. El cine cerró el año pasado.

**to shut up** VERB
callarse
□ Shut up! ¡Cállate!

**shutters** PL NOUN
las contraventanas

**shuttle** NOUN
■ **I'll get the shuttle.** Tomaré el puente aéreo.

**shuttlecock** NOUN
el volante *(de bádminton)*

**shy** ADJECTIVE
tímido (FEM tímida)

**Sicily** NOUN
Sicilia fem

**sick** ADJECTIVE
1 enfermo (FEM enferma)
□ She looks after her sick mother. Cuida de su madre enferma.
2 de mal gusto
□ That's really sick! ¡Eso es de muy mal gusto!
■ **to be sick** devolver (arrojar Latin America)
□ I was sick twice last night. Anoche devolví dos veces.
■ **I feel sick.** Tengo ganas de devolver.
■ **to be sick of something** estar harto de algo □ I'm sick of your jokes. Estoy harto de tus bromas.

**sickening** ADJECTIVE
repugnante (FEM repugnante)

**sick leave** NOUN
la baja por enfermedad

**sickness** NOUN
la enfermedad

**sick note** NOUN
1 el justificante de ausencia (from parents)
2 la baja médica (from doctor)

**sick pay** NOUN
la prestación por enfermedad

**side** NOUN
1 el lado (of object, building, car)
□ He was driving on the wrong side of the road. Iba por el lado contrario de la carretera.
■ **a house on the side of a mountain** una casa en la ladera de una montaña
■ **We sat side by side.** Nos sentamos uno al lado del otro.
2 el borde (of pool, bed, road)
□ The car was abandoned at the side of the road. El coche estaba abandonado al borde de la carretera.
■ **by the side of the lake** a la orilla del lago
3 la cara (of paper, tape)
□ Play side A. Pon la cara A.
4 el equipo (team)
□ He's on my side. Está en mi equipo.
■ **I'm on your side.** Yo estoy de tu parte.
■ **to take somebody's side** ponerse de parte de alguien
■ **to take sides** tomar partido
■ **the side entrance** la entrada lateral

**sideboard** NOUN
el aparador

**side-effect** NOUN
el efecto secundario

**side street** NOUN
la calle lateral

**sidewalk** NOUN (US)
la acera

**sideways** ADVERB
■ **to look sideways** mirar de reojo
■ **to move sideways** moverse de lado
■ **sideways on** de perfil

**sieve** NOUN
1 el colador (for liquids)
2 la criba (for solids)

**sigh** NOUN
▷ see also **sigh** VERB
el suspiro

to **sigh** VERB
▷ see also **sigh** NOUN
suspirar

**sight** NOUN
1 la vista
□ I'm losing my sight. Estoy perdiendo la vista.
■ **at first sight** a primera vista
■ **to know somebody by sight** conocer a alguien de vista
■ **in sight** a la vista
2 el espectáculo
□ It was an amazing sight. Era un espectáculo asombroso.
■ **Keep out of sight!** ¡Que no te vean!
■ **the sights** las atracciones turísticas
■ **to see the sights of London** hacer turismo por Londres

**sightseeing** NOUN
■ **to go sightseeing** hacer turismo

**sign** NOUN
▷ see also **sign** VERB
1 el letrero
□ There was a big sign saying 'private'. Había un gran letrero que ponía 'privado'.
2 la señal
□ She made a sign to the waiter. Le hizo una señal al camarero. □ There's no sign of improvement. No hay señales de mejoría.
■ **road sign** la señal de tráfico
■ **What sign are you?** ¿De qué signo eres?

to **sign** VERB
▷ see also **sign** NOUN
firmar

to **sign on** VERB
apuntarse al paro

**signal** NOUN
▷ see also **signal** VERB
la señal

to **signal** VERB
▷ see also **signal** NOUN
■ **to signal to somebody** hacer señas a alguien

**signalman** NOUN
el guardavía

**LANGUAGE TIP** Although **guardavía** ends in **-a**, it is actually a masculine noun.

**signature** NOUN
la firma

**significance** NOUN
la importancia

**significant** ADJECTIVE
significativo (FEM significativa)

**sign language** NOUN
el lenguaje por señas

**signpost** NOUN
la señal

**silence** NOUN
el silencio

**silencer** NOUN
el silenciador

**silent** ADJECTIVE
1 silencioso (FEM silenciosa) *(place)*
  □ a silent room  una habitación silenciosa
2 callado (FEM callada) *(person)*

**silicon chip** NOUN
el chip de silicio (PL los chips de silicio)

**silk** NOUN
la seda
  □ a silk scarf  un pañuelo de seda

**silky** ADJECTIVE
sedoso (FEM sedosa)

**silly** ADJECTIVE
tonto (FEM tonta)

**silver** NOUN
la plata
  □ a silver medal  una medalla de plata

**similar** ADJECTIVE
parecido (FEM parecida)
  ■ **similar to**  parecido a

**simple** ADJECTIVE
1 sencillo (FEM sencilla)
  □ It's very simple.  Es muy sencillo.
2 simple (FEM simple)
  □ He's a bit simple.  Es un poco simple.

**simply** ADVERB
sencillamente

**simultaneous** ADJECTIVE
simultáneo (FEM simultánea)

**sin** NOUN
  ▷ see also **sin** VERB
el pecado

to **sin** VERB
  ▷ see also **sin** NOUN
pecar*

**since** PREPOSITION, ADVERB, CONJUNCTION
1 desde
  □ since Christmas  desde Navidad  □ since then  desde entonces
  ■ **I haven't seen him since.**  Desde entonces no lo he vuelto a ver.
2 desde que

  □ I haven't seen her since she left.  No la he visto desde que se fue.
  ■ **It's a few years since I've seen them.**  Hace varios años que no los veo.
3 como
  □ Since you're tired, let's stay at home.  Como estás cansado podemos quedarnos en casa.

**sincere** ADJECTIVE
sincero (FEM sincera)

**sincerely** ADVERB
  ■ **Yours sincerely...**  Atentamente...

to **sing** VERB
cantar

**singer** NOUN
el/la cantante

**singing** NOUN
el canto
  □ singing lessons  clases de canto
  ■ **flamenco singing**  el cante flamenco

**single** ADJECTIVE
  ▷ see also **single** NOUN
1 individual (FEM individual)
  □ a single room  una habitación individual
  □ a single bed  una cama individual
2 soltero (FEM soltera)
  □ a single mother  una madre soltera
3 solo (FEM sola)
  □ She hadn't said a single word.  No había dicho una sola palabra.
  ■ **not a single thing**  nada de nada

**single** NOUN
  ▷ see also **single** ADJECTIVE
1 el billete de ida
2 el single
  □ a CD single  un single en CD

**single parent** NOUN
  ■ **She's a single parent.**  Es madre soltera.
  ■ **a single parent family**  una familia monoparental

**singles** PL NOUN
los individuales *(in tennis)*
  □ the women's singles  los individuales femeninos

**singular** NOUN
singular
  □ in the singular  en singular

**sinister** ADJECTIVE
siniestro (FEM siniestra)

**sink** NOUN
  ▷ see also **sink** VERB
1 el fregadero *(in the kitchen)*
2 el lavabo *(in the bathroom)*

to **sink** VERB
  ▷ see also **sink** NOUN
1 hundir
  □ We sank the enemy's ship.  Hundimos el buque enemigo.

**2** hundirse
□ The boat was sinking fast. El barco se hundía rápidamente.

**sir** NOUN
el señor
□ Yes sir. Sí, señor.

**siren** NOUN
la sirena

**sister** NOUN
**1** la hermana
□ my little sister mi hermana pequeña
**2** la enfermera jefe (nurse)

**sister-in-law** NOUN
la cuñada

to **sit** VERB
sentarse*
□ He sat in front of the TV. Se sentó frente a la tele.
■ **to be sitting** estar sentado □ He was sitting in front of the TV. Estaba sentado frente a la tele.
■ **to sit an exam** presentarse a un examen

to **sit down** VERB
sentarse*
□ He sat down at his desk. Se sentó en su escritorio.

**sitcom** NOUN
la telecomedia

**site** NOUN
**1** el lugar
□ the site of the accident el lugar del accidente
**2** el camping (PL los campings) (campsite)

**sitting room** NOUN
la sala de estar (PL las salas de estar)

**situated** ADJECTIVE
■ **to be situated...** estar situado... (estar ubicado... Latin America)

**situation** NOUN
la situación (PL las situaciones)

**six** NUMERAL
seis
□ He's six. Tiene seis años.

**sixteen** NUMERAL
dieciséis
□ He's sixteen. Tiene dieciséis años.

**sixteenth** ADJECTIVE
decimosexto (FEM decimosexta)
■ **the sixteenth floor** la planta dieciséis
■ **the sixteenth of August** el dieciséis de agosto

**sixth** ADJECTIVE
sexto (FEM sexta)
□ the sixth floor el sexto piso
■ **the sixth of August** el seis de agosto

**sixty** NUMERAL
sesenta
□ She's sixty. Tiene sesenta años.

**size** NOUN

**1** el tamaño (of object, place)
□ plates of various sizes platos de varios tamaños

⌒ **DID YOU KNOW...?**
│ Spain uses the European system for
⌒ clothing and shoe sizes.

**2** la talla (of clothing)
□ What size do you take? ¿Qué talla usas?
**3** el número (of shoes)
■ **I take size five.** Calzo un treinta y ocho.

to **skate** VERB
patinar

**skateboard** NOUN
el monopatín (PL los monopatines)

**skateboarding** NOUN
■ **to go skateboarding** montar en monopatín

**skates** PL NOUN
los patines

**skating** NOUN
el patinaje
□ to go skating ir a patinar
■ **skating rink** la pista de patinaje

**skeleton** NOUN
el esqueleto

**sketch** NOUN
▷ see also **sketch** VERB
el boceto

to **sketch** VERB
▷ see also **sketch** NOUN
esbozar*

to **ski** VERB
▷ see also **ski** NOUN
esquiar*

**ski** NOUN
▷ see also **ski** VERB
el esquí
□ a pair of skis unos esquís
■ **ski boots** las botas de esquí
■ **ski lift** el telesilla

⌒ **LANGUAGE TIP** Although **telesilla** ends
│ in -a, it is actually a masculine noun.

■ **ski pants** los pantalones de esquí
■ **ski pole** el bastón de esquí (PL los bastones de esquí)
■ **ski resort** la estación de esquí
■ **ski slope** la pista de esquí
■ **ski suit** el traje de esquí

to **skid** VERB
patinar

**skier** NOUN
el esquiador
la esquiadora

**skiing** NOUN
el esquí
□ I love skiing. Me encanta el esquí.
■ **to go skiing** ir a esquiar
■ **to go on a skiing holiday** irse de vacaciones a esquiar

**skilful** ADJECTIVE
hábil (FEM hábil)

**skill** NOUN
la habilidad
□ It requires a lot of skill. Requiere mucha habilidad.

**skilled** ADJECTIVE
■ a skilled worker un trabajador cualificado

**skimmed milk** NOUN
la leche desnatada

**skimpy** ADJECTIVE
1 mínimo (FEM mínima) (clothes)
2 escaso (FEM escasa) (meal)

**skin** NOUN
la piel
■ skin cancer el cáncer de piel

**skinhead** NOUN
el/la cabeza rapada (PL los/las cabezas rapadas)

**skinny** ADJECTIVE
flaco (FEM flaca)

**skin-tight** ADJECTIVE
muy ajustado (FEM muy ajustada)

**skip** NOUN
▷ see also **skip** VERB
el contenedor de basuras

to **skip** VERB
▷ see also **skip** NOUN
saltarse
□ You should never skip breakfast. No debes saltarte nunca el desayuno.
■ to skip school hacer novillos

**skirt** NOUN
la falda

**skittles** PL NOUN
los bolos

to **skive** VERB
escaquearse (informal)
■ to skive off school hacer novillos

**skull** NOUN
1 la calavera (of corpse)
2 el cráneo (in anatomy)

**sky** NOUN
el cielo

**skyscraper** NOUN
el rascacielos (PL los rascacielos)

**slack** ADJECTIVE
1 flojo (FEM floja) (rope)
2 descuidado (FEM descuidada) (person)

to **slag off** VERB
poner* verde a (informal)

to **slam** VERB
cerrar* de un portazo
□ She slammed the door. Cerró la puerta de un portazo.
■ The door slammed. La puerta se cerró de un portazo.

**slang** NOUN
el argot

**slap** NOUN
▷ see also **slap** VERB
la bofetada

to **slap** VERB
▷ see also **slap** NOUN
dar* una bofetada a

**slate** NOUN
la teja de pizarra

**sledge** NOUN
el trineo

**sledging** NOUN
■ to go sledging ir en trineo

**sleep** NOUN
▷ see also **sleep** VERB
el sueño
□ lack of sleep falta de sueño
■ I need some sleep. Necesito dormir.
■ to go to sleep dormirse

to **sleep** VERB
▷ see also **sleep** NOUN
dormir*
□ I couldn't sleep last night. Anoche no podía dormir.

to **sleep around** VERB
irse* a la cama con cualquiera

to **sleep in** VERB
dormir* hasta tarde

to **sleep together** VERB
acostarse* juntos

**sleeping bag** NOUN
el saco de dormir

**sleeping car** NOUN
el coche cama (PL los coches cama)

**sleeping pill** NOUN
el somnífero

**sleepy** ADJECTIVE
■ to feel sleepy tener sueño
■ a sleepy little village un pueblecito tranquilo

**sleet** NOUN
▷ see also **sleet** VERB
la aguanieve

to **sleet** VERB
▷ see also **sleet** NOUN
■ It's sleeting. Está cayendo aguanieve.

**sleeve** NOUN
la manga (of shirt, coat)

**sleigh** NOUN
el trineo

**slept** VERB ▷ see **sleep**

**slice** NOUN
▷ see also **slice** VERB
1 la rebanada (of bread)
2 el trozo (of cake)
3 la rodaja (of lemon, pineapple)
4 la loncha (of ham, cheese)

to **slice** VERB
▷ see also **slice** NOUN
cortar

**slick** ADJECTIVE
▷ see also **slick** NOUN
impecable (FEM impecable)
□ a slick performance una actuación impecable

**slide** NOUN
▷ see also **slide** VERB
1 el tobogán (PL los toboganes) (in playground)
2 la diapositiva (photo)
3 el pasador (hair slide)

to **slide** VERB
▷ see also **slide** NOUN
deslizarse*
□ Tears were sliding down his cheeks. Las lágrimas se deslizaban por sus mejillas.
■ **She slid the door open.** Corrió la puerta.

**slight** ADJECTIVE
ligero (FEM ligera)
□ a slight improvement una ligera mejoría
■ **a slight problem** un pequeño problema

**slightly** ADVERB
ligeramente
□ They are slightly more expensive. Son ligeramente más caros.

**slim** ADJECTIVE
▷ see also **slim** VERB
delgado (FEM delgada)

to **slim** VERB
▷ see also **slim** ADJECTIVE
adelgazar*
□ I'm trying to slim. Estoy intentando adelgazar.
■ **I'm slimming.** Estoy a régimen.

**sling** NOUN
el cabestrillo
□ She had her arm in a sling. Llevaba el brazo en cabestrillo.

**slip** NOUN
▷ see also **slip** VERB
1 el desliz (PL los deslices) (mistake)
2 la combinación (PL las combinaciones) (underskirt)
■ **a slip of paper** un papelito
■ **a slip of the tongue** un lapsus

to **slip** VERB
▷ see also **slip** NOUN
resbalar
□ He slipped on the ice. Resbaló en el hielo.

to **slip up** VERB
equivocarse*

**slipper** NOUN
la zapatilla

**slippery** ADJECTIVE
resbaladizo (FEM resbaladiza)

**slip-up** NOUN

el desliz (PL los deslices)

**slope** NOUN
1 la cuesta (surface)
□ The street was on a slope. La calle era en cuesta.
2 la pendiente (angle)
□ a slope of 10 degrees una pendiente del 10 por ciento

**sloppy** ADJECTIVE
descuidado (FEM descuidada)

**slot** NOUN
la ranura

**slot machine** NOUN
1 la máquina tragaperras (PL las máquinas tragaperras) (for gambling)
2 la máquina expendedora (vending machine)

**slow** ADJECTIVE, ADVERB
lento (FEM lenta)
□ He's a bit slow. Es un poco lento. □ to go slow ir lento
■ **Drive slower!** ¡Conduce más despacio!
■ **My watch is slow.** Mi reloj se atrasa.

to **slow down** VERB
reducir* la velocidad
□ The car slowed down. El coche redujo la velocidad.

**slowly** ADVERB
lentamente

**slug** NOUN
la babosa

**slum** NOUN
el barrio bajo

**slush** NOUN
la nieve medio derretida

**sly** ADJECTIVE
astuto (FEM astuta)
□ She's very sly. Es muy astuta.
■ **a sly smile** una sonrisa maliciosa

**smack** NOUN
▷ see also **smack** VERB
el cachete

to **smack** VERB
▷ see also **smack** NOUN
dar* un cachete a

**small** ADJECTIVE
pequeño (FEM pequeña) (chico Latin America)
□ two small children dos niños pequeños

**WORD POWER**
You can use a number of other words instead of **small** to mean 'little':
**miniature** en miniatura
□ a miniature doll una muñeca en miniatura
**minute** minúsculo
□ a minute plant una planta minúscula
**tiny** enano
□ a tiny garden un jardín enano
■ **small change** el dinero suelto

**smart** ADJECTIVE
1 elegante (FEM elegante)
  □ a smart navy blue suit un elegante traje azul marino
2 listo (FEM lista)
  □ He thinks he's smarter than Sarah. Se cree más listo que Sarah.

**smash** NOUN
  ▷ see also **smash** VERB
  el accidente de coche

to **smash** VERB
  ▷ see also **smash** NOUN
1 romper*
  □ They smashed windows. Rompieron ventanas.
2 romperse*
  □ The glass smashed into tiny pieces. El vaso se rompió en pedazos.

**smashing** ADJECTIVE
  estupendo (FEM estupenda)
  □ That's a smashing idea. Me parece una idea estupenda.

**smell** NOUN
  ▷ see also **smell** VERB
  el olor
  □ a smell of lemon un olor a limón
  ■ the sense of smell el olfato

to **smell** VERB
  ▷ see also **smell** NOUN
  oler*
  □ That dog smells! ¡Cómo huele ese perro!
  □ I can't smell anything. No huelo nada.
  ■ I can smell gas. Me huele a gas.
  ■ to smell of something oler a algo □ It smells of petrol. Huele a gasolina.

**smelly** ADJECTIVE
  maloliente (FEM maloliente)
  □ The pub was dirty and smelly. El pub era sucio y maloliente.
  ■ He's got smelly feet. Le huelen los pies.

**smile** NOUN
  ▷ see also **smile** VERB
  la sonrisa

to **smile** VERB
  ▷ see also **smile** NOUN
  sonreír*

**smoke** NOUN
  ▷ see also **smoke** VERB
  el humo

to **smoke** VERB
  ▷ see also **smoke** NOUN
  fumar
  □ I don't smoke. No fumo.

**smoker** NOUN
  el fumador
  la fumadora

**smoking** NOUN
  ■ to stop smoking dejar de fumar

  ■ Smoking is bad for you. Fumar es malo para la salud.
  ■ 'no smoking' 'prohibido fumar'

**smooth** ADJECTIVE
  liso (FEM lisa)
  □ a smooth surface una superficie lisa

**SMS** ABBREVIATION (= short message service)
  el SMS

**smudge** NOUN
  el borrón (PL los borrones)

**smug** ADJECTIVE
  engreído (FEM engreída)

to **smuggle** VERB
  ■ to smuggle in meter de contrabando
  ■ to smuggle out sacar de contrabando

**smuggler** NOUN
  el/la contrabandista

**smuggling** NOUN
  el contrabando

**smutty** ADJECTIVE
  ■ smutty jokes chistes verdes

**snack** NOUN
  ■ to have a snack picar algo

**snack bar** NOUN
  la cafetería

**snail** NOUN
  el caracol

**snake** NOUN
  la serpiente

to **snap** VERB
  partirse
  □ The branch snapped. La rama se partió.
  ■ to snap one's fingers chasquear los dedos

**snapshot** NOUN
  la foto *fem*

  LANGUAGE TIP Although **foto** ends in **-o**, it is actually a feminine noun.

to **snarl** VERB
  gruñir*

to **snatch** VERB
  arrebatar
  ■ to snatch something from somebody arrebatar algo a alguien □ He snatched the keys from my hand. Me arrebató las llaves de la mano.
  ■ My bag was snatched. Me robaron el bolso.

to **sneak** VERB
  ■ to sneak in entrar a hurtadillas
  ■ to sneak out salir a hurtadillas
  ■ to sneak up on somebody acercarse sigilosamente a alguien

to **sneeze** VERB
  estornudar

to **sniff** VERB
1 sorberse la nariz
  □ Stop sniffing! ¡Deja de sorberte la nariz!

**English-Spanish**

**2** olfatear
- □ The dog sniffed my hand.  El perro me olfateó la mano.
- ■ **to sniff glue** esnifar pegamento

**snob** NOUN
el/la esnob (PL los/las esnobs)

**snooker** NOUN
el billar

**snooze** NOUN
la cabezadita *(informal)*
- □ to have a snooze  echar una cabezadita

to **snore** VERB
roncar*

**snow** NOUN
▷ *see also* **snow** VERB
la nieve

to **snow** VERB
▷ *see also* **snow** NOUN
nevar*
- □ It's snowing.  Está nevando.

**snowball** NOUN
la bola de nieve

**snowflake** NOUN
el copo de nieve

**snowman** NOUN
el muñeco de nieve
- □ to build a snowman  hacer un muñeco de nieve

**so** CONJUNCTION, ADVERB
**1** así que *(therefore)*
- □ The shop was closed, so I went home.  La tienda estaba cerrada, así que me fui a casa.  □ So, have you always lived in London?  Así que, ¿siempre has vivido en Londres?
- ■ **So what?** ¿Y qué?

**2** para que *(so that)*

> **LANGUAGE TIP** **para que** has to be followed by a verb in the subjunctive.

- □ He took her upstairs so they wouldn't be overheard.  La subió al piso de arriba para que nadie los oyera.

**3** tan *(very, as)*
- □ He was talking so fast I couldn't understand.  Hablaba tan rápido que no lo entendía.  □ He's like his sister but not so clever.  Es como su hermana pero no tan listo.
- ■ **It was so heavy!** ¡Pesaba tanto!
- ■ **How's your father? — Not so good.** ¿Cómo está tu padre? — No muy bien.
- ■ **so much** tanto  □ I love you so much.  Te quiero tanto.  □ She's got so much energy.  Tiene tanta energía.
- ■ **so many** tantos  □ I've got so many things to do today.  Tengo tantas cosas que hacer hoy.
- ■ **That's not so.** No es así.

**4** también *(also)*
- ■ **so do I** y yo también  □ I work a lot. — So do I.  Trabajo mucho. — Y yo también.
- ■ **I love horses. — So do I.** Me encantan los caballos. — A mí también.
- ■ **so have we** y nosotros también  □ I've been waiting for ages! — So have we.  ¡Llevo esperando un siglo! — Y nosotros también.
- ■ **I think so.** Creo que sí.
- ■ **... or so** ... o así  □ at five o'clock or so  a las cinco o así  □ ten or so people  diez personas o así

to **soak** VERB
**1** poner* en remojo
- □ Soak the beans for two hours.  Ponga las judías en remojo dos horas.

**2** empapar
- □ Water had soaked his jacket.  El agua le había empapado la chaqueta.

**soaked** ADJECTIVE
- ■ **to get soaked** empaparse

**soaking** ADJECTIVE
empapado (FEM empapada)
- □ By the time we got back we were soaking.  Cuando regresamos estábamos empapados.
- ■ **Your shoes are soaking wet.** Tienes los zapatos calados.

**soap** NOUN
el jabón

**soap opera** NOUN
la telenovela

**soap powder** NOUN
el detergente en polvo

to **sob** VERB
sollozar*

**sober** ADJECTIVE
sobrio (FEM sobria)

to **sober up** VERB
- ■ **He sobered up.** Se le pasó la borrachera.

**soccer** NOUN
el fútbol
- □ to play soccer  jugar al fútbol
- ■ **soccer player** el/la futbolista

**social** ADJECTIVE
social (FEM social)
- □ social problems  problemas sociales
- ■ **I have a good social life.** Tengo mucha vida social.

**socialism** NOUN
el socialismo

**socialist** ADJECTIVE, NOUN
socialista (FEM socialista)

**social security** NOUN
la seguridad social
- ■ **to be on social security** cobrar de la seguridad social

**social worker** NOUN
el asistente social

**S**

la asistenta social

**society** NOUN
1 la sociedad
□ a multi-cultural society una sociedad pluricultural
2 la asociación (PL las asociaciones)
□ a drama society una asociación de amigos del teatro

**sociology** NOUN
la sociología

**sock** NOUN
el calcetín (PL los calcetines) (la media *Latin America*)

**socket** NOUN
el enchufe

**soda** NOUN
la soda

**soda pop** NOUN (US)
el refresco

**sofa** NOUN
el sofá (PL los sofás)

**soft** ADJECTIVE
1 suave (FEM suave)
□ a soft towel una toalla suave
2 blando (FEM blanda)
□ The mattress is too soft. El colchón es demasiado blando.
■ **to be soft on somebody** ser blando con alguien
■ **soft cheeses** los quesos tiernos
■ **a soft drink** un refresco
■ **soft drugs** las drogas blandas
■ **soft option** la alternativa fácil

**software** NOUN
el software

**soggy** ADJECTIVE
1 revenido (FEM revenida) *(bread, biscuits)*
2 pasado (FEM pasada) *(salad)*

**soil** NOUN
la tierra

**solar power** NOUN
la energía solar

**sold** VERB ▷ *see* **sell**

**soldier** NOUN
el soldado

**solicitor** NOUN
1 el abogado
la abogada *(for lawsuits)*
2 el notario
la notaria *(for wills, property)*

**solid** ADJECTIVE
sólido (FEM sólida)
□ a solid wall un muro sólido
■ **solid gold** oro macizo
■ **for three solid hours** durante tres horas seguidas

**solo** NOUN
el solo

□ a guitar solo un solo de guitarra

**solution** NOUN
la solución (PL las soluciones)

**to solve** VERB
resolver*

**some** ADJECTIVE, PRONOUN

⌐ **LANGUAGE TIP** When 'some' refers to something you can't count, it usually isn't translated.

□ Would you like some bread? ¿Quieres pan? □ Have you got some mineral water? ¿Tiene agua mineral? □ Would you like some coffee? — No thanks, I've got some. ¿Quiere café? — No gracias, ya tengo.
■ **I only want some of it.** Sólo quiero un poco.

⌐ **LANGUAGE TIP** When 'some' refers to something you can count, use **alguno**, which is shortened to **algún** before a masculine singular noun.

□ some day algún día □ some books algunos libros □ You have to be careful with mushrooms: some are poisonous. Cuidado con las setas: algunas son venenosas.
■ **I'm going to buy some stamps. Do you want some too?** Voy a por sellos. ¿Quieres que te traiga?
■ **some day next week** un día de la semana que viene
■ **Some people say that...** Hay gente que dice que...
■ **some of them** algunos □ I only sold some of them. Sólo vendí algunos.

**somebody** PRONOUN
alguien
□ I need somebody to help me. Necesito que me ayude alguien.

**somehow** ADVERB
de alguna manera
■ **I'll do it somehow.** De alguna manera lo haré.
■ **Somehow I don't think he believed me.** Por alguna razón me parece que no me creyó.

**someone** PRONOUN
alguien
□ I need someone to help me. Necesito que me ayude alguien.

**something** PRONOUN
algo
□ something special algo especial □ Wear something warm. Ponte algo que abrigue.
■ **It cost £100, or something like that.** Costó 100 libras, o algo así.
■ **His name is Peter or something.** Se llama Peter o algo por el estilo.

**sometime** ADVERB
algún día

□ You must come and see us sometime.
Tienes que venir a vernos algún día.
■ **sometime last month** el mes pasado

**sometimes** ADVERB
a veces
□ Sometimes I drink beer. A veces bebo
cerveza.

**somewhere** ADVERB
en algún sitio
□ I left my keys somewhere. Me he dejado
las llaves en algún sitio.
■ **I'd like to go on holiday, somewhere
exotic.** Me gustaría irme de vacaciones,
a algún sitio exótico.

**son** NOUN
el hijo

**song** NOUN
la canción (PL las canciones)

**son-in-law** NOUN
el yerno

**soon** ADVERB
pronto
□ very soon muy pronto
■ **soon afterwards** poco después
■ **as soon as possible** cuanto antes

**sooner** ADVERB
antes
□ Can't you come a bit sooner? ¿No puedes
venir un poco antes?
■ **sooner or later** tarde o temprano
■ **the sooner the better** cuanto antes
mejor

**soot** NOUN
el hollín

**soppy** ADJECTIVE
sentimentaloide (FEM sentimentaloide)

**soprano** NOUN
la soprano

LANGUAGE TIP Although **soprano** ends
in -o, it is actually a feminine noun.

**sore** ADJECTIVE
▷ see also **sore** NOUN
■ **It's sore.** Me duele.
■ **I have a sore throat.** Me duele la garganta.
■ **That's a sore point.** Ése es un tema
delicado.

**sore** NOUN
▷ see also **sore** ADJECTIVE
la llaga

**sorry** ADJECTIVE
■ **I'm sorry.** Lo siento. □ I'm very sorry.
Lo siento mucho. □ I'm sorry, I haven't got
any change. Lo siento, no tengo cambio.
■ **I'm sorry I'm late.** Siento llegar tarde.
■ **Sorry!** ¡Perdón!
■ **Sorry?** ¿Cómo?
■ **I'm sorry about the noise.** Perdón por el
ruido.

■ **You'll be sorry!** ¡Te arrepentirás!
■ **to feel sorry for somebody** sentir pena
por alguien

**sort** NOUN
el tipo
□ What sort of bike have you got? ¿Qué tipo
de bicicleta tienes?
■ **all sorts of...** todo tipo de...

**to sort out** VERB
1 ordenar
□ Sort out all your books. Ordena todos tus
libros.
2 arreglar
□ They have sorted out their problems. Han
arreglado sus problemas.

**so-so** ADVERB
así así
□ How are you feeling? — So-so. ¿Cómo te
encuentras? — Así así.

**soul** NOUN
1 el alma *fem*

LANGUAGE TIP Although it's a feminine
noun, remember that you use **el** and
**un** with **alma**.

2 el soul
□ a soul singer una cantante de soul

**sound** NOUN
▷ see also **sound** VERB, ADJECTIVE
1 el ruido
□ Don't make a sound! ¡No hagas ruido!
□ the sound of footsteps el ruido de pasos
2 el sonido
□ at the speed of sound a la velocidad del
sonido
■ **Can I turn the sound down?** ¿Puedo
bajar el volumen?

**to sound** VERB
▷ see also **sound** NOUN, ADJECTIVE
sonar*
□ That sounds interesting. Eso suena
interesante.
■ **It sounds as if she's doing well at
school.** Parece que le va bien en el colegio.
■ **That sounds like a good idea.** Eso me
parece buena idea.

**sound** ADJECTIVE, ADVERB
▷ see also **sound** NOUN, VERB
válido (FEM válida)
□ His reasoning is perfectly sound. Su
argumentación es perfectamente válida.
■ **Julian gave me some sound advice.**
Julian me dio un buen consejo.
■ **sound asleep** profundamente dormido

**soundtrack** NOUN
la banda sonora

**soup** NOUN
la sopa

**sour** ADJECTIVE

agrio (FEM agria)

**south** ADJECTIVE, ADVERB
▷ *see also* **south** NOUN
1 del sur
□ a south wind un viento del sur
■ **the south coast** la costa meridional
2 hacia el sur
□ We were travelling south. Viajábamos hacia el sur.
■ **south of** al sur de □ It's south of London. Está al sur de Londres.

**south** NOUN
▷ *see also* **south** ADJECTIVE
el sur
□ the South of France el sur de Francia

**South Africa** NOUN
Sudáfrica *fem*

**South America** NOUN
Sudamérica *fem*

**South American** ADJECTIVE
▷ *see also* **South American** NOUN
sudamericano (FEM sudamericana)

**South American** NOUN
▷ *see also* **South American** ADJECTIVE
el sudamericano
la sudamericana
□ South Americans los sudamericanos

**southbound** ADJECTIVE
■ **Southbound traffic is moving very slowly.** El tráfico que se dirige hacia el sur avanza muy despacio.

**southeast** NOUN
el sudeste
■ **southeast England** el sudeste de Inglaterra

**southern** ADJECTIVE
■ **the southern hemisphere** el hemisferio sur
■ **Southern England** el sur de Inglaterra
■ **southern cuisine** la cocina sureña

**South Pole** NOUN
el Polo Sur

**South Wales** NOUN
Gales del Sur *masc*

**southwest** NOUN
el sudoeste

**souvenir** NOUN
el recuerdo
□ souvenir shop la tienda de recuerdos

**soya** NOUN
la soja

**soy sauce** NOUN
la salsa de soja

**space** NOUN
el espacio
□ There isn't enough space. No hay espacio suficiente. □ in space en el espacio
■ **a parking space** un sitio para aparcar

**spacecraft** NOUN
la nave espacial

**spade** NOUN
la pala
■ **spades** *(at cards)* las picas □ the ace of spades el as de picas
LANGUAGE TIP Be careful not to translate **spade** by **espada**.

**Spain** NOUN
España *fem*

**Spaniard** NOUN
el español
la española *(person)*

**spaniel** NOUN
el perro de aguas

**Spanish** ADJECTIVE
▷ *see also* **Spanish** NOUN
español (FEM española)

**Spanish** NOUN
▷ *see also* **Spanish** ADJECTIVE
el español
DID YOU KNOW...?
The official name for the Spanish language in Spain and Latin America is **el castellano** and is also the term many Spanish speakers prefer to use. Despite controversies, both **español** and **castellano** are perfectly acceptable.
□ Spanish lessons las clases de español
■ **the Spanish** los españoles

to **spank** VERB
zurrar

**spanner** NOUN
la llave inglesa

**spare** ADJECTIVE
▷ *see also* **spare** VERB, NOUN
1 de repuesto
□ Take a few spare batteries. Llévate unas pilas de repuesto. □ spare wheel la rueda de repuesto
2 de sobra
□ Have you got a spare pencil? ¿Tienes un lápiz de sobra?
■ **spare part** el repuesto
■ **spare room** el cuarto de los huéspedes
■ **spare time** el tiempo libre

to **spare** VERB
▷ *see also* **spare** ADJECTIVE, NOUN
■ **Can you spare a moment?** ¿Tienes un momento?
■ **I can't spare the time.** No tengo tiempo.
■ **They've got no money to spare.** No les sobra el dinero.
■ **We arrived with time to spare.** Llegamos con tiempo de sobra.

**spare** NOUN
▷ *see also* **spare** ADJECTIVE, VERB

**■ I've lost my key. — Have you got a spare?** He perdido la llave. — ¿Tienes una de sobra?

**sparkling** ADJECTIVE
con gas
□ a sparkling drink una bebida con gas
□ sparkling water agua con gas
**■ sparkling wine** vino espumoso

**sparrow** NOUN
el gorrión (PL los gorriones)

**spat** VERB ▷ see spit

to **speak** VERB
hablar

**■ Do you speak English?** ¿Hablas inglés?
□ Have you spoken to him? ¿Has hablado con él? □ She spoke to him about it. Habló de ello con él.
**■ Could I speak to Alison? — Speaking!** ¿Podría hablar con Alison? — ¡Soy yo!

to **speak up** VERB
hablar más alto
□ You'll need to speak up – we can't hear you. Habla más alto que no te oímos.

**speaker** NOUN
1 el altavoz (PL los altavoces) *(loudspeaker)*
2 el orador
la oradora *(at conference)*
**■ French speakers** los hablantes de francés

**special** ADJECTIVE
especial (FEM especial)

**specialist** NOUN
el/la especialista

**speciality** NOUN
la especialidad

to **specialize** VERB
especializarse*
□ She specialized in Russian. Se especializó en ruso.
**■ We specialize in skiing equipment.** Estamos especializados en material de esquí.

**specially** ADVERB
especialmente
□ It can be very cold here, specially in winter. Llega a hacer mucho frío aquí, especialmente en invierno. □ It's specially designed for teenagers. Está especialmente pensado para adolescentes. □ Do you like opera? — Not specially. ¿Te gusta la ópera? — No especialmente.

**species** NOUN
la especie

**specific** ADJECTIVE
1 específico (FEM específica)
□ certain specific issues ciertos temas específicos
2 concreto (FEM concreta)

□ Could you be more specific? ¿Podrías ser más concreto?

**specifically** ADVERB
1 específicamente
□ It's specifically designed for teenagers. Está específicamente pensado para adolescentes.
2 concretamente
□ in Britain, or more specifically in England en Gran Bretaña, o más concretamente en Inglaterra
**■ I specifically said that...** Especifiqué claramente que...

**specs, spectacles** PL NOUN
las gafas (los anteojos *Latin America*)

**spectacular** ADJECTIVE
espectacular (FEM espectacular)

**spectator** NOUN
el espectador
la espectadora

**speech** NOUN
el discurso
□ to make a speech dar un discurso

**speechless** ADJECTIVE
**■ I was speechless.** Me quedé sin habla.

**speed** NOUN
la velocidad
□ at top speed a toda velocidad
**■ a three-speed bike** una bicicleta de tres marchas

to **speed up** VERB
acelerar

**speedboat** NOUN
la lancha motora

**speeding** NOUN
el exceso de velocidad
□ He was fined for speeding. Lo multaron por exceso de velocidad.

**speed limit** NOUN
el límite de velocidad
**■ to break the speed limit** saltarse el límite de velocidad

**speedometer** NOUN
el velocímetro

to **spell** VERB
▷ see also **spell** NOUN
deletrear
□ Can you spell that please? ¿Me lo deletrea, por favor?
**■ How do you spell 'library'?** ¿Cómo se escribe 'library'?
**■ I can't spell.** Cometo faltas de ortografía.

**spell** NOUN
▷ see also **spell** VERB
el hechizo
□ to be under somebody's spell estar bajo el hechizo de alguien
**■ to cast a spell on somebody** hechizar a alguien

**spelling** NOUN
la ortografía
□ My spelling is terrible. Cometo muchas faltas de ortografía.
■ **a spelling mistake** una falta de ortografía
to **spend** VERB
1 gastar
□ They spend enormous amounts of money on advertising. Gastan cantidades enormes de dinero en publicidad.
2 dedicar*
□ He spends a lot of time and money on his hobbies. Dedica mucho tiempo y dinero a sus aficiones.
3 pasar
□ He spent a month in France. Pasó un mes en Francia.

**spice** NOUN
la especia

**spicy** ADJECTIVE
picante (FEM picante)

**spider** NOUN
la araña

to **spill** VERB
■ **You've spilled coffee on your shirt.** Se te ha caído café en la camisa.

**spinach** NOUN
las espinacas

**spin drier** NOUN
la centrifugadora

**spine** NOUN
la columna vertebral

**spinster** NOUN
la solterona

**spire** NOUN
la aguja

**spirit** NOUN
1 el espíritu
□ a youthful spirit un espíritu joven
2 el valor
□ Everyone admired her spirit. Todos admiraban su valor.
3 el brío
□ They played with great spirit. Jugaron con mucho brío.

**spirits** PL NOUN
los licores
□ I don't drink spirits. No bebo licores.
■ **to be in good spirits** estar de buen ánimo

**spiritual** ADJECTIVE
espiritual (FEM espiritual)

**spit** NOUN
▷ see also **spit** VERB
la saliva

to **spit** VERB
▷ see also **spit** NOUN
escupir

**spite** NOUN

▷ see also **spite** VERB
■ **in spite of** a pesar de
■ **out of spite** por despecho
to **spite** VERB
▷ see also **spite** NOUN
fastidiar
□ He just did it to spite me. Lo hizo sólo para fastidiarme.

**spiteful** ADJECTIVE
1 rencoroso (FEM rencorosa) (person)
2 malintencionado (FEM malintencionada) (action)

to **splash** VERB
▷ see also **splash** NOUN
salpicar*
□ Don't splash me! ¡No me salpiques!
■ **He splashed water on his face.** Se echó agua en la cara.

**splash** NOUN
▷ see also **splash** VERB
el chapoteo
□ I heard a splash. Oí un chapoteo.
■ **a splash of colour** una mancha de color

**splendid** ADJECTIVE
espléndido (FEM espléndida)

**splint** NOUN
la tablilla

**splinter** NOUN
la astilla

to **split** VERB
1 partir
□ He split the wood with an axe. Partió la madera con un hacha.
2 partirse
□ The ship hit a rock and split in two. El barco chocó con una roca y se partió en dos.
3 dividir
□ a decision that will split the party una decisión que dividirá al partido
■ **They decided to split the profits.** Decidieron repartir los beneficios.

to **split up** VERB
separarse

to **spoil** VERB
1 estropear
□ It spoiled our holiday. Nos estropeó las vacaciones.
2 mimar
□ Grandparents like to spoil their grandchildren. A los abuelos les encanta mimar a sus nietos.

**spoiled** ADJECTIVE
mimado (FEM mimada)
□ a spoiled child un niño mimado

**spoilsport** NOUN
el/la aguafiestas (PL los/las aguafiestas)

**spoke** VERB ▷ see **speak**

**spoke** NOUN
el radio

**spoken** VERB ▷ see **speak**

**spokesman** NOUN
el portavoz (PL los portavoces) (el vocero Latin America)

**spokeswoman** NOUN
la portavoz (PL las portavoces) (la vocera Latin America)

**sponge** NOUN
la esponja
■ **sponge bag** la bolsa de aseo
■ **sponge cake** el bizcocho

**sponsor** NOUN
▷ see also **sponsor** VERB
el patrocinador
la patrocinadora

to **sponsor** VERB
▷ see also **sponsor** NOUN
patrocinar
□ The tournament was sponsored by local firms. El torneo fue patrocinado por empresas locales.

**spontaneous** ADJECTIVE
espontáneo (FEM espontánea)

**spooky** ADJECTIVE
■ **The house is really spooky at night.** La casa te pone los pelos de punta de noche.

**spoon** NOUN
la cuchara

**spoonful** NOUN
■ **a spoonful** una cucharada

**sport** NOUN
el deporte
■ **sports bag** la bolsa de deporte
■ **sports car** el coche deportivo
■ **sports jacket** la chaqueta de sport

**sportsman** NOUN
el deportista

**sportswear** NOUN
la ropa de deporte

**sportswoman** NOUN
la deportista

**sporty** ADJECTIVE
deportista (FEM deportista)
□ I'm not very sporty. No soy muy deportista.

**spot** NOUN
▷ see also **spot** VERB
1 la mancha
□ There's a spot on your shirt. Tienes una mancha en la camisa.
2 el lunar
□ a red dress with white spots un vestido rojo con lunares blancos
3 el grano
□ He's covered in spots. Está lleno de granos.

4 el sitio
□ It's a lovely spot for a picnic. Es un sitio precioso para un picnic.
■ **on the spot 1** en el acto □ They gave her the job on the spot. Le dieron el trabajo en el acto. **2** en el mismo sitio □ Luckily they were able to mend the car on the spot. Afortunadamente consiguieron arreglar el coche en el mismo sitio.

to **spot** VERB
▷ see also **spot** NOUN
notar
□ I spotted a mistake. Noté un error.

**spotless** ADJECTIVE
inmaculado (FEM inmaculada)

**spotlight** NOUN
el foco

**spotty** ADJECTIVE
con granos

**spouse** NOUN
el/la cónyuge

to **sprain** VERB
▷ see also **sprain** NOUN
torcerse*
□ She's sprained her ankle. Se ha torcido el tobillo.

**sprain** NOUN
▷ see also **sprain** VERB
la torcedura

**spray** NOUN
▷ see also **spray** VERB
el spray (PL los sprays) (spray can)

to **spray** VERB
▷ see also **spray** NOUN
1 rociar*
□ She sprayed perfume on my hand. Me roció perfume en la mano.
2 fumigar*
□ to spray against insects fumigar contra los insectos
■ **There was graffiti sprayed on the wall.** Había pintadas de spray en la pared.

**spread** NOUN
▷ see also **spread** VERB
■ **cheese spread** el queso para untar
■ **chocolate spread** la crema de chocolate

to **spread** VERB
▷ see also **spread** NOUN
1 extender*
□ She spread a towel on the sand. Extendió una toalla sobre la arena.
2 untar
□ Spread the top of the cake with whipped cream. Unte la parte superior de la tarta con nata montada.
3 propagarse*
□ The news spread rapidly. La noticia se propagó rápidamente.

to **spread out** VERB
1 dispersarse
  □ The soldiers spread out across the field.
  Los soldados se dispersaron por el campo.
2 desplegar*
  □ He spread the map out on the table.
  Desplegó el mapa sobre la mesa.

**spreadsheet** NOUN
  la hoja de cálculo

**spring** NOUN
1 la primavera
  □ in spring en primavera
2 el muelle (metal)
3 el manantial (of water)

**spring-cleaning** NOUN
  la limpieza general

**springtime** NOUN
  la primavera

**sprinkler** NOUN
  el aspersor

**sprint** NOUN
  ▷ see also **sprint** VERB
  la carrera de velocidad
  ■ the women's 100 metres sprint los cien
  metros lisos femeninos

to **sprint** VERB
  ▷ see also **sprint** NOUN
  correr a toda velocidad
  □ She sprinted for the bus. Corrió a toda
  velocidad para coger el autobús.

  > LANGUAGE TIP Be very careful with the
  verb **coger**: in most of Latin America
  this is an extremely rude word that
  should be avoided. However, in Spain
  this verb is common and not rude at all.

**sprinter** NOUN
  el/la velocista

**sprouts** PL NOUN
  ■ Brussels sprouts las coles de Bruselas

**spy** NOUN
  el/la espía

**spying** NOUN
  el espionaje

to **squabble** VERB
  reñir*
  □ Stop squabbling! ¡Vale ya de reñir!

**square** NOUN
  ▷ see also **square** ADJECTIVE
1 el cuadrado
  □ a square and a triangle un cuadrado y un
  triángulo
2 la plaza
  □ the town square la plaza mayor

**square** ADJECTIVE
  ▷ see also **square** NOUN
  cuadrado (FEM cuadrada)
  □ two square metres dos metros cuadrados
  ■ It's two metres square. Mide dos por dos.

**squash** NOUN
  ▷ see also **squash** VERB
  el squash (sport)
  ■ squash court la cancha de squash
  ■ squash racket la raqueta de squash
  ■ orange squash la naranjada
  ■ lemon squash la limonada

to **squash** VERB
  ▷ see also **squash** NOUN
  aplastar
  □ You're squashing me. Me estás
  aplastando.

to **squeak** VERB
1 chillar (mouse, child)
2 chirriar* (door, wheel)
3 crujir (shoes)

to **squeeze** VERB
1 exprimir
  □ Squeeze two large lemons. Exprima dos
  limones grandes.
2 apretar*
  □ She squeezed my hand. Me apretó la
  mano.
  ■ The thieves squeezed through a tiny
  window. Los ladrones se colaron por una
  pequeña ventana.

to **squeeze in** VERB
  hacer* un hueco a
  □ I can squeeze you in at two o'clock.
  Te puedo hacer un hueco a las dos.

**squint** NOUN
  el estrabismo
  ■ He has a squint. Es estrábico.

**squirrel** NOUN
  la ardilla

to **stab** VERB
  apuñalar

**stable** NOUN
  ▷ see also **stable** ADJECTIVE
  la cuadra

**stable** ADJECTIVE
  ▷ see also **stable** NOUN
  estable (FEM estable)
  □ a stable relationship una relación estable

**stack** NOUN
  la pila
  □ There were stacks of books on the table.
  Había pilas de libros sobre la mesa.
  ■ They've got stacks of money. Tienen
  cantidad de dinero.

**stadium** NOUN
  el estadio

**staff** NOUN
1 el personal (in company)
2 el profesorado (in school)

**stage** NOUN
1 la etapa
  □ in stages por etapas

**S**

249

■ **at this stage in the negotiations** a estas alturas de las negociaciones
**2** el escenario
□ The band came on stage late. El grupo salió tarde al escenario.
■ **I always wanted to go on the stage.** Siempre quise dedicarme al teatro.

to **stagger** VERB
tambalearse

**stain** NOUN
▷ see also **stain** VERB
la mancha

to **stain** VERB
▷ see also **stain** NOUN
manchar

**stainless steel** NOUN
el acero inoxidable

**stain remover** NOUN
el quitamanchas (PL los quitamanchas)

**stair** NOUN
el escalón (PL los escalones)

**staircase** NOUN
la escalera

**stairs** PL NOUN
las escaleras

**stale** ADJECTIVE
■ **stale bread** el pan duro

**stalemate** NOUN
el punto muerto
□ to reach a stalemate llegar a un punto muerto
■ **The game ended in stalemate.** (in chess) La partida terminó en tablas.

**stall** NOUN
el puesto
□ He's got a market stall. Tiene un puesto en el mercado.
■ **the stalls** (in theatre) la platea

**stamina** NOUN
la resistencia física

**stammer** NOUN
el tartamudeo
■ **He's got a stammer.** Es tartamudo.

**stamp** NOUN
▷ see also **stamp** VERB
el sello (la estampilla Latin America)
□ My hobby is stamp collecting. Mi afición es coleccionar sellos.
■ **stamp album** el álbum de sellos (PL los álbumes de sellos)

to **stamp** VERB
▷ see also **stamp** NOUN
sellar
□ The file was stamped 'confidential'. El archivo iba sellado como 'confidencial'.
■ **The audience stamped their feet.** El público pateaba.

250   to **stand** VERB

**1** estar* de pie
□ He was standing by the door. Estaba de pie junto a la puerta.
■ **What are you standing there for?** ¿Qué haces ahí de pie?
■ **They all stood when I came in.** Se pusieron de pie cuando entré.
**2** soportar
□ I can't stand all this noise. No soporto todo este ruido.

to **stand for** VERB
**1** significar*
□ 'EU' stands for 'European Union'. 'EU' significa 'European Union'.
**2** consentir*
□ I won't stand for it any more! ¡No pienso consentirlo más!

to **stand out** VERB
destacar*

to **stand up** VERB
**1** ponerse* de pie
□ I stood up and walked out. Me puse de pie y me fui.
**2** estar* de pie
□ She has to stand up all day. Tiene que estar todo el día de pie.

**standard** ADJECTIVE
▷ see also **standard** NOUN
normal (FEM normal)
□ the standard procedure el procedimiento normal
■ **standard equipment** el equipamiento de serie

**standard** NOUN
▷ see also **standard** ADJECTIVE
el nivel
□ The standard is very high. El nivel es muy alto.
■ **She's got high standards.** Es muy exigente.
■ **standard of living** el nivel de vida

**stand-by ticket** NOUN
el billete en lista de espera

**standpoint** NOUN
el punto de vista

**stands** PL NOUN
la tribuna

**stank** VERB ▷ see **stink**

**staple** ADJECTIVE
▷ see also **staple** NOUN
básico (FEM básica)
□ their staple food su alimento básico

**stapler** NOUN
la grapadora

**star** NOUN
▷ see also **star** VERB
la estrella
□ a TV star una estrella de televisión

■ **the stars** el horóscopo

to **star** VERB
  ▷ see also **star** NOUN
  ■ **to star in a film** protagonizar una película
  ■ **The film stars Sharon Stone.** La protagonista de la película es Sharon Stone.
  ■ **...starring Johnny Depp** ...con Johnny Depp

to **stare** VERB
  mirar fijamente
  □ Andy stared at him. Andy lo miraba fijamente.

**stark** ADVERB
  ■ **stark naked** en cueros

**start** NOUN
  ▷ see also **start** VERB
1  el principio
  □ at the start of the film al principio de la película □ from the start desde el principio
  ■ **for a start** para empezar
  ■ **Shall we make a start on the washing-up?** ¿Nos ponemos a fregar los platos?
2  la salida (of race)

to **start** VERB
  ▷ see also **start** NOUN
1  empezar*
  □ What time does it start? ¿A qué hora empieza?
  ■ **to start doing something** empezar a hacer algo □ I started learning Spanish two years ago. Empecé a aprender español hace dos años.
2  montar (business, organization, campaign)
  □ He wants to start his own business. Quiere montar su propio negocio.
3  arrancar*
  □ He couldn't start the car. No conseguía arrancar el coche. □ The car wouldn't start. El coche no arrancaba.

to **start off** VERB
  ponerse* en camino
  □ We started off first thing in the morning. Nos pusimos en camino pronto por la mañana.

**starter** NOUN
  el primer plato (first course)

to **starve** VERB
  morirse* de hambre
  □ People are starving. La gente se muere de hambre.
  ■ **I'm starving!** ¡Me muero de hambre!

**state** NOUN
  ▷ see also **state** VERB
  el estado
  □ It's an independent state. Es un estado independiente. □ She was in a state of depression. Se encontraba en un estado de depresión.

■ **He wasn't in a fit state to drive.** No estaba en condiciones de conducir.
■ **Tim was in a real state.** Tim estaba de los nervios.
■ **the States** los Estados Unidos

to **state** VERB
  ▷ see also **state** NOUN
  declarar
  □ He stated his intention to resign. Declaró que tenía intención de dimitir.
  ■ **Please state your name and address.** Por favor indique su nombre y dirección.

**stately home** NOUN
  la casa señorial

**statement** NOUN
1  la declaración (PL las declaraciones)
  □ statements by witnesses las declaraciones de testigos
2  la afirmación (PL las afirmaciones)
  □ Andrew now disowns the statement he made. Ahora Andrew desmiente la afirmación que hizo.
  ■ **a bank statement** un extracto de cuenta

**station** NOUN
  la estación (PL las estaciones)
  ■ **bus station** la estación de autobuses
  ■ **police station** la comisaría
  ■ **radio station** la emisora de radio

**stationer's** NOUN
  la papelería

**station wagon** NOUN (US)
  la ranchera

**statue** NOUN
  la estatua

**stay** NOUN
  ▷ see also **stay** VERB
  la estancia
  □ my stay in Spain mi estancia en España

to **stay** VERB
  ▷ see also **stay** NOUN
  quedarse
  □ Stay here! ¡Quédate aquí! □ I'm going to be staying with friends. Me voy a quedar en casa de unos amigos.
  ■ **Where are you staying? In a hotel?** ¿Dónde estás? ¿En un hotel?
  ■ **to stay the night** pasar la noche
  ■ **We stayed in Belgium for a few days.** Pasamos unos días en Bélgica.

to **stay in** VERB
  quedarse en casa

to **stay up** VERB
  quedarse levantado
  □ We stayed up till midnight. Nos quedamos levantados hasta las doce.

**steady** ADJECTIVE
1  fijo (FEM fija)
  □ a steady job un trabajo fijo

■ **a steady boyfriend** un novio formal
2 firme (FEM firme)
▫ a steady hand un pulso firme
3 constante (FEM constante)
▫ a steady pace un ritmo constante
■ **Steady on!** ¡Calma!

**steak** NOUN
el filete

to **steal** VERB
robar

**steam** NOUN
el vapor
▫ a steam engine una máquina de vapor

**steel** NOUN
el acero

**steep** ADJECTIVE
empinado (FEM empinada)

**steeple** NOUN
la aguja

**steering wheel** NOUN
el volante

**step** NOUN
▷ see also **step** VERB
1 el paso
▫ He took a step forward. Dio un paso adelante.
2 el peldaño
▫ She tripped over the step. Tropezó con el peldaño.

to **step** VERB
▷ see also **step** NOUN
dar* un paso
▫ I tried to step forward. Traté de dar un paso adelante.
■ **Step this way, please.** Pase por aquí, por favor.

**stepbrother** NOUN
el hermanastro

**stepdaughter** NOUN
la hijastra

**stepfather** NOUN
el padrastro

**stepladder** NOUN
la escalera de tijera

**stepmother** NOUN
la madrastra

**stepsister** NOUN
la hermanastra

**stepson** NOUN
el hijastro

**stereo** NOUN
el equipo de música

**sterling** ADJECTIVE
■ **pound sterling** la libra esterlina
■ **one hundred pounds sterling** cien libras esterlinas

**stew** NOUN
el estofado (el guisado Latin America)

**steward** NOUN
1 el auxiliar de vuelo (on plane)
2 el camarero (on ship)

**stewardess** NOUN
1 la auxiliar de vuelo (on plane)
2 la camarera (on ship)

**stick** NOUN
▷ see also **stick** VERB
el palo
■ **a walking stick** un bastón (PL unos bastones)

to **stick** VERB
▷ see also **stick** NOUN
1 pegar*
▫ Stick the stamps on the envelope. Pegue los sellos en el sobre.
2 pegarse*
▫ The rice stuck to the pan. El arroz se pegó a la olla.
3 meter
▫ He picked up the papers and stuck them in his briefcase. Recogió los papeles y los metió en el maletín.
■ **I can't stick it any longer.** Ya no lo aguanto más.

to **stick out** VERB
sacar*
▫ The little girl stuck out her tongue. La niña sacó la lengua.

**sticker** NOUN
la pegatina

**stick insect** NOUN
el insecto palo

**sticky** ADJECTIVE
1 pegajoso (FEM pegajosa)
▫ to have sticky hands tener las manos pegajosas
2 adhesivo (FEM adhesiva)
▫ a sticky label una etiqueta adhesiva

**stiff** ADJECTIVE, ADVERB
rígido (FEM rígida)
■ **to have a stiff neck** tener tortícolis
■ **to feel stiff** estar agarrotado
■ **to be bored stiff** estar aburrido como una ostra
■ **to be frozen stiff** estar tieso de frío
■ **to be scared stiff** estar muerto de miedo

**still** ADVERB
▷ see also **still** ADJECTIVE
1 todavía
▫ I still haven't finished. No he terminado todavía. ▫ Are you still in bed? ¿Todavía estás en la cama?
■ **Do you still live in Glasgow?** ¿Sigues viviendo en Glasgow?
■ **better still** mejor aún
2 aun así (even so)
▫ She knows I don't like it, but she still does it.

Sabe que no me gusta, pero aun así lo hace.

**3** en fin *(after all)*
□ Still, it's the thought that counts. En fin, la intención es lo que cuenta.

**still** ADJECTIVE
▷ *see also* **still** ADVERB
quieto (FEM quieta)
□ He stood still. Se quedó quieto.
■ **Keep still!** ¡No te muevas!

**sting** NOUN
▷ *see also* **sting** VERB
la picadura
□ a bee sting una picadura de abeja

to **sting** VERB
▷ *see also* **sting** NOUN
picar*

**stingy** ADJECTIVE
tacaño (FEM tacaña)

to **stink** VERB
▷ *see also* **stink** NOUN
apestar
□ You stink of garlic! ¡Apestas al ajo!

**stink** NOUN
▷ *see also* **stink** VERB
el tufo
□ the stink of beer el tufo a cerveza

to **stir** VERB
agitar

to **stitch** VERB
▷ *see also* **stitch** NOUN
coser

**stitch** NOUN
▷ *see also* **stitch** VERB
**1** la puntada *(in sewing)*
**2** el punto *(in knitting, in wound)*
□ I had five stitches. Me pusieron cinco puntos.

**stock** NOUN
▷ *see also* **stock** VERB
**1** la reserva
□ stocks of ammunition reservas de munición
**2** las existencias
□ the shop's stock las existencias de la tienda
■ **Yes, we've got your size in stock.** Sí, nos quedan existencias de su número.
■ **out of stock** agotado □ I'm sorry, they're both out of stock. Lo siento, están los dos agotados.
**3** el caldo
□ chicken stock caldo de pollo

to **stock** VERB
▷ *see also* **stock** NOUN
vender
□ Do you stock camping stoves? ¿Venden infiernillos?

to **stock up** VERB

abastecerse*
□ to stock up with something abastecerse de algo

**stock cube** NOUN
la pastilla de caldo

**stocking** NOUN
la media

**stomach** NOUN
el estómago

**stone** NOUN
**1** la piedra
□ a stone wall un muro de piedra
**2** el hueso
□ an apricot stone un hueso de albaricoque

> **DID YOU KNOW...?**
> In Spain measurements are in grams and kilograms. One stone is about 6.3 kg.

■ **I weigh eight stone.** Peso unos cincuenta kilos.

**stood** VERB ▷ *see* **stand**

**stool** NOUN
el taburete

to **stop** VERB
▷ *see also* **stop** NOUN
**1** parar
□ The bus doesn't stop there. El autobús no para allí.
**2** pararse
□ The music stopped. Se paró la música.
■ **This has got to stop!** ¡Esto se tiene que acabar!
■ **I think the rain's going to stop.** Creo que va a dejar de llover.
■ **to stop doing something** dejar de hacer algo □ to stop smoking dejar de fumar
**3** acabar con
□ a campaign to stop whaling una campaña para acabar con la caza de ballenas

> **LANGUAGE TIP** impedir que has to be followed by a verb in the subjunctive.

■ **to stop somebody doing something** impedir que alguien haga algo □ She would have liked to stop us seeing each other. Le hubiera gustado impedir que nos siguiéramos viendo.
■ **Stop!** ¡Alto!

**stop** NOUN
▷ *see also* **stop** VERB
la parada
□ a bus stop una parada de autobús
■ **This is my stop.** Yo me bajo aquí.

**stopwatch** NOUN
el cronómetro

**store** NOUN
▷ *see also* **store** VERB
**1** la tienda
□ a furniture store una tienda de muebles

2 el almacén (PL los almacenes)
□ a grain store un almacén de grano

to **store** VERB
▷ see also **store** NOUN
1 guardar
□ They store potatoes in the cellar. Guardan patatas en el sótano.
2 almacenar
□ to store information almacenar información

**storey** NOUN
la planta
□ a three-storey building un edificio de tres plantas

**storm** NOUN
la tormenta

**stormy** ADJECTIVE
tormentoso (FEM tormentosa)

**story** NOUN
1 el cuento (tale)
2 la historia (account)

**stove** NOUN
1 la cocina (in kitchen)
2 el infiernillo (camping stove)

**straight** ADJECTIVE, ADVERB
1 recto (FEM recta)
□ a straight line una línea recta
2 liso (FEM lisa)
□ straight hair pelo liso
3 heterosexual (FEM heterosexual) (not gay)
■ He looked straight at me. Me miró directamente a los ojos.
■ straight away enseguida
■ I'll come straight back. Vuelvo enseguida.
■ Keep straight on. Siga todo recto.

**straightforward** ADJECTIVE
1 sencillo (FEM sencilla)
□ It's very straightforward. Es muy sencillo.
2 sincero (FEM sincera)
□ She's very straightforward. Es muy sincera.

**strain** NOUN
▷ see also **strain** VERB
la tensión (PL las tensiones)
■ It was a strain. Fue muy estresante.

to **strain** VERB
▷ see also **strain** NOUN
■ to strain one's eyes forzar la vista
■ I strained my back. Me dio un tirón en la espalda.
■ to strain a muscle sufrir un tirón muscular

**strained** ADJECTIVE
■ a strained muscle una distensión muscular

**stranded** ADJECTIVE
■ We were stranded on the motorway. Nos quedamos tirados en la autopista.

254 **strange** ADJECTIVE

raro (FEM rara)
□ That's strange! ¡Qué raro!
LANGUAGE TIP es raro que has to be followed by a verb in the subjunctive.
□ It's strange that she doesn't talk to us anymore. Es raro que ya no nos hable.

**stranger** NOUN
el desconocido
la desconocida
□ Don't talk to strangers. No hables con desconocidos.
■ I'm a stranger here. Yo no soy de aquí.

to **strangle** VERB
estrangular

**strap** NOUN
1 el tirante (of bra, dress)
2 la correa (of watch, camera, suitcase)
3 el asa fem (of bag)
LANGUAGE TIP Although it's a feminine noun, remember that you use **el** and **un** with asa.

**straw** NOUN
1 la paja
□ a straw hat un sombrero de paja
2 la pajita
□ He was drinking his lemonade through a straw. Se bebía la gaseosa con pajita.
■ That's the last straw! ¡Eso es la gota que colma el vaso!

**strawberry** NOUN
la fresa (la frutilla Latin America)

**stray** ADJECTIVE
extraviado (FEM extraviada)
□ a stray cat un gato extraviado

**stream** NOUN
el riachuelo

**street** NOUN
la calle

**streetcar** NOUN (US)
el tranvía
LANGUAGE TIP Although tranvía ends in -a, it is actually a masculine noun.

**streetlamp** NOUN
la farola

**street plan** NOUN
el plano de la ciudad

**streetwise** ADJECTIVE
■ to be streetwise sabérselas todas
■ a streetwise kid un pillo

**strength** NOUN
la fuerza
□ with all his strength con todas sus fuerzas

to **stress** VERB
▷ see also **stress** NOUN
recalcar*
□ I would like to stress that... Me gustaría recalcar que...

**stress** NOUN

▷ *see also* **stress** VERB
el estrés

□ She's under a lot of stress. Está pasando mucho estrés.

to **stretch** VERB

**1** estirarse

□ The dog woke up and stretched. El perro se despertó y se estiró.

■ **I went out to stretch my legs.** Salí a estirar las piernas.

■ **My jumper stretched after I washed it.** Se me dio de sí el jersey al lavarlo.

**2** tender*

□ They stretched a rope between two trees. Tendieron una cuerda entre dos árboles.

**stretcher** NOUN
la camilla

**stretchy** ADJECTIVE
elástico (FEM elástica)

**strict** ADJECTIVE
estricto (FEM estricta)

**strike** NOUN
▷ *see also* **strike** VERB
la huelga

■ **to be on strike** estar en huelga

■ **to go on strike** hacer huelga

to **strike** VERB
▷ *see also* **strike** NOUN
golpear

□ She struck him across the mouth. Le golpeó en la boca.

■ **The clock struck three.** El reloj dio las tres.

■ **to strike a match** encender una cerilla

**striker** NOUN

**1** el/la huelguista *(person on strike)*

**2** el delantero
la delantera *(footballer)*

**striking** ADJECTIVE

**1** asombroso (FEM asombrosa)

□ a striking resemblance un parecido asombroso

**2** en huelga

□ striking miners mineros en huelga

**string** NOUN
la cuerda

■ **a piece of string** una cuerda

to **strip** VERB
▷ *see also* **strip** NOUN
desnudarse

**strip** NOUN
▷ *see also* **strip** VERB
la tira

■ **strip cartoon** la tira cómica (la historieta *Latin America*)

**stripe** NOUN
la franja

**striped** ADJECTIVE
a rayas

■ **a striped skirt** una falda de rayas

**stripper** NOUN
el/la artista de striptease

**stripy** ADJECTIVE
de rayas

to **stroke** VERB
▷ *see also* **stroke** NOUN
acariciar

**stroke** NOUN
▷ *see also* **stroke** VERB
el derrame cerebral

□ to have a stroke sufrir un derrame cerebral

■ **a stroke of luck** un golpe de suerte

**stroll** NOUN

■ **to go for a stroll** ir a dar un paseo

**stroller** NOUN (US)
la silla de paseo

**strong** ADJECTIVE
fuerte (FEM fuerte)

**strongly** ADVERB

■ **We strongly advise you to…** Te aconsejamos encarecidamente que…

■ **He smelt strongly of tobacco.** Olía mucho a tabaco.

■ **strongly built** corpulento

■ **I don't feel strongly about it.** Me da un poco igual.

**struck** VERB ▷ *see* **strike**

to **struggle** VERB
▷ *see also* **struggle** NOUN
forcejear

□ He struggled, but he couldn't escape. Forcejeó, pero no pudo escapar.

■ **to struggle to do something 1** *(fight)* luchar por hacer algo □ He struggled to get custody of his daughter. Luchó por conseguir la custodia de su hija. **2** *(have difficulty)* pasar apuros para hacer algo □ They struggle to pay their bills. Pasan apuros para pagar las facturas.

**struggle** NOUN
▷ *see also* **struggle** VERB
la lucha

□ a struggle for survival una lucha por la supervivencia

■ **It was a struggle.** Nos costó mucho.

**stub** NOUN
la colilla

**stubborn** ADJECTIVE
terco (FEM terca)

to **stub out** VERB
apagar*

**stuck** VERB ▷ *see* **stick**

**stuck** ADJECTIVE
atascado (FEM atascada)

□ The lid is stuck. La tapadera está atascada.

■ **to get stuck** quedarse atascado

■ **We got stuck in a traffic jam.** Nos metimos en un atasco.

**stuck-up** ADJECTIVE
creído (FEM creída) (informal)

**stud** NOUN
1 el pendiente (earring)
2 el taco (on football boots)

**student** NOUN
el/la estudiante

**studio** NOUN
el estudio

□ a TV studio un estudio de televisión

■ **a studio flat** un estudio

to **study** VERB
estudiar

**stuff** NOUN
las cosas

□ Have you got all your stuff? ¿Tienes todas tus cosas? □ There's some stuff on the table for you. En la mesa hay unas cosas para ti.

■ **I need some stuff for hay fever.** Me hace falta algo para la alergia al polen.

**stuffy** ADJECTIVE

■ **a stuffy room** una habitación mal ventilada

■ **It's stuffy in here.** Hay un ambiente muy cargado aquí.

to **stumble** VERB
tropezar*

**stung** VERB ▷ see sting

**stunk** VERB ▷ see stink

**stunned** ADJECTIVE
pasmado (FEM pasmada)

□ I was stunned. Me quedé pasmado.

**stunning** ADJECTIVE
pasmoso (FEM pasmosa)

**stunt** NOUN

■ **It's a publicity stunt.** Es un truco publicitario.

**stuntman** NOUN
el especialista

**stupid** ADJECTIVE
estúpido (FEM estúpida)

to **stutter** VERB
▷ see also **stutter** NOUN
tartamudear

**stutter** NOUN
▷ see also **stutter** VERB
el tartamudeo

■ **He's got a stutter.** Es tartamudo.

**style** NOUN
el estilo

□ That's not his style. No es su estilo.

**subject** NOUN
1 el tema

LANGUAGE TIP Although **tema** ends in -a, it is actually a masculine noun.

□ The subject of my project is the internet. El tema de mi trabajo es Internet.

2 la asignatura

□ What's your favourite subject? ¿Cuál es tu asignatura preferida?

3 el sujeto

□ 'I' is the subject in 'I love you'. 'I' es el sujeto en 'I love you'.

**submarine** NOUN
el submarino

**subscription** NOUN
la suscripción (PL las suscripciones) (to paper, magazine)

■ **to take out a subscription to something** suscribirse a algo

**subsequently** ADVERB
posteriormente

to **subsidize** VERB
subvencionar

**subsidy** NOUN
la subvención (PL las subvenciones)

**substance** NOUN
la sustancia

**substitute** NOUN
▷ see also **substitute** VERB
1 el sustituto
la sustituta (replacement)
2 el/la suplente (in football, rugby)

to **substitute** VERB
▷ see also **substitute** NOUN
sustituir*

□ to substitute A for B sustituir a B por A

**subtitled** ADJECTIVE
subtitulado (FEM subtitulada)

**subtitles** PL NOUN
los subtítulos

□ a Spanish film with English subtitles una película española con subtítulos en inglés

**subtle** ADJECTIVE
sutil (FEM sutil)

to **subtract** VERB
restar

□ to subtract 3 from 5 restar 3 a 5

**suburb** NOUN
el barrio residencial

□ a London suburb un barrio residencial de Londres

■ **They live in the suburbs.** Viven en las afueras.

**suburban** ADJECTIVE

■ **a suburban train** un tren de cercanías

■ **a suburban shopping centre** un centro comercial de las afueras

**subway** NOUN
1 el metro (underground)
2 el paso subterráneo (underpass)

to **succeed** VERB
1 tener* éxito

□ to succeed in business  tener éxito en los negocios

**2** salir* bien

□ The plan did not succeed.  El plan no salió bien.

■ **to succeed in doing something**  lograr hacer algo

**success** NOUN
el éxito

> LANGUAGE TIP  Be careful not to translate **success** by **suceso**.

**successful** ADJECTIVE
de éxito (exitoso *Latin America*)

□ a successful lawyer  un abogado de éxito

■ **a successful attempt**  un intento fructífero

■ **to be successful**  tener éxito

■ **to be successful in doing something** lograr hacer algo

**successfully** ADVERB
con éxito

**successive** ADJECTIVE
consecutivo (FEM consecutiva)

□ He was the winner for a second successive year.  Fue el ganador por segundo año consecutivo.

**such** ADJECTIVE, ADVERB

**1** tan

□ such clever people  gente tan lista □ such a long journey  un viaje tan largo

**2** tal (FEM tal)

□ I wouldn't dream of doing such a thing. No se me ocurriría hacer tal cosa. □ The pain was such that...  El dolor era tal que...

■ **such a lot**  tanto □ such a lot of work tanto trabajo □ such a long time ago  hace tanto tiempo

■ **such as**  como □ a hot country, such as India...  un país caluroso, como la India...

■ **as such**  propiamente dicho □ She's not an expert as such, but...  No es una experta propiamente dicha, pero...

■ **There's no such thing.**  Eso no existe.

□ There's no such thing as the yeti.  El yeti no existe.

**such-and-such** ADJECTIVE
tal (FEM tal)

□ such-and-such a place  tal lugar

**to suck** VERB
chupar

■ **to suck one's thumb**  chuparse el pulgar

**sudden** ADJECTIVE
repentino (FEM repentina)

□ a sudden change  un cambio repentino

■ **all of a sudden**  de repente

**suddenly** ADVERB
de repente

**suede** NOUN
el ante (la gamuza *Latin America*)

□ a suede jacket  una chaqueta de ante

**to suffer** VERB
sufrir

□ She was really suffering.  Sufría de verdad.

■ **to suffer from something**  padecer de algo □ I suffer from hay fever.  Padezco de alergia al polen.

**to suffocate** VERB
ahogarse*

**sugar** NOUN
el azúcar

**to suggest** VERB

**1** sugerir*

> LANGUAGE TIP  Use the subjunctive after **sugerir que**.

□ She suggested going out for a pizza. Sugirió que saliéramos a tomar una pizza.

**2** aconsejar

> LANGUAGE TIP  Use the subjunctive after **aconsejar que**.

□ I suggested they set off early.  Yo les aconsejé que salieran pronto.

■ **What are you trying to suggest?**  ¿Qué insinúas?

**suggestion** NOUN
la sugerencia

□ to make a suggestion  hacer una sugerencia

**suicide** NOUN
el suicidio

■ **to commit suicide**  suicidarse

**suicide bomber** NOUN
el/la terrorista suicida

**suit** NOUN

▷ *see also* **suit** VERB

**1** el traje (man's)

**2** el traje de chaqueta (woman's)

**to suit** VERB

▷ *see also* **suit** NOUN

**1** venir* bien a

□ What time would suit you?  ¿Qué hora te vendría bien?

■ **That suits me fine.**  Eso me viene estupendamente.

**2** sentar* bien a

□ That dress really suits you.  Ese vestido te sienta la mar de bien.

■ **Suit yourself!**  ¡Haz lo que te parezca!

**suitable** ADJECTIVE

**1** conveniente (FEM conveniente)

□ a suitable time  una hora conveniente

**2** apropiado (FEM apropiada)

□ suitable clothing  ropa apropiada

**suitcase** NOUN
la maleta (la valija *Latin America*)

**suite** NOUN
la suite

□ a suite at the Paris Hilton  una suite en el Hilton de París

S

- **a bedroom suite** un dormitorio completo
- **three-piece suite** un tresillo

to **sulk** VERB
estar* de mal humor

**sulky** ADJECTIVE
malhumorado (FEM malhumorada)

**sultana** NOUN
la pasa de Esmirna

**sum** NOUN
la suma

□ to do sums hacer sumas □ a sum of money una suma de dinero

to **summarize** VERB
resumir

**summary** NOUN
el resumen (PL los resúmenes)

**summer** NOUN
el verano

□ summer clothes ropa de verano □ the summer holidays las vacaciones de verano □ a summer camp un campamento de verano

**summertime** NOUN
el verano

**summit** NOUN
la cumbre

□ the NATO summit la cumbre de la OTAN □ the summit of Mount Everest la cumbre del Everest

to **sum up** VERB
resumir

- **To sum up...** Resumiendo...

**sun** NOUN
el sol

□ in the sun al sol □ sun cream la crema solar

to **sunbathe** VERB
tomar el sol

**sunblock** NOUN
la crema solar de protección total

**sunburn** NOUN
la quemadura

**sunburnt** ADJECTIVE
quemado por el sol (FEM quemado por el sol)

- **Mind you don't get sunburnt!** ¡Cuidado de quemarte con el sol!

**Sunday** NOUN
el domingo (PL los domingos)

□ I saw her on Sunday. La vi el domingo. □ every Sunday todos los domingos □ last Sunday el domingo pasado □ next Sunday el domingo que viene □ on Sundays los domingos

**Sunday school** NOUN
la catequesis

**DID YOU KNOW...?**
The Spanish equivalent of Sunday school takes place during the week after school rather than on a Sunday.

**sunflower** NOUN
el girasol

□ sunflower seeds pipas de girasol

**sung** VERB ▷ see **sing**

**sunglasses** PL NOUN
las gafas de sol

**sunk** VERB ▷ see **sink**

**sunlight** NOUN
la luz del sol

**sunny** ADJECTIVE
soleado (FEM soleada)

□ a sunny morning una mañana soleada
- **It's sunny.** Hace sol.
- **a sunny day** un día de sol

**sunrise** NOUN
la salida del sol

**sunroof** NOUN
el techo corredizo

**sunscreen** NOUN
el protector solar

**sunset** NOUN
la puesta de sol

**sunshine** NOUN
el sol

□ in the sunshine al sol

**sunstroke** NOUN
la insolación (PL las insolaciones)

**suntan** NOUN
el bronceado

- **to get a suntan** broncearse
- **suntan lotion** la crema bronceadora
- **suntan oil** el aceite bronceador

**super** ADJECTIVE
estupendo (FEM estupenda)

**superb** ADJECTIVE
magnífico (FEM magnífica)

**supermarket** NOUN
el supermercado

**supernatural** ADJECTIVE
sobrenatural (FEM sobrenatural)

**superstitious** ADJECTIVE
supersticioso (FEM supersticiosa)

to **supervise** VERB
supervisar

**supervisor** NOUN
el supervisor
la supervisora

**supper** NOUN
la cena

**supplement** NOUN
el suplemento

**supplies** PL NOUN
las provisiones

- **medical supplies** material médico

to **supply** VERB
▷ see also **supply** NOUN
suministrar

- **to supply somebody with something**

suministrar algo a alguien □ The centre supplied us with all the equipment. El centro nos suministró todo el material.

**supply** NOUN
▷ see also **supply** VERB
el suministro
□ the water supply el suministro de agua
■ **a supply of paper** una remesa de papel

**supply teacher** NOUN
el profesor interino
la profesora interina

to **support** VERB
▷ see also **support** NOUN
1 apoyar
□ My mum has always supported me. Mi madre siempre me ha apoyado.
2 mantener*
□ She had to support five children on her own. Tenía que mantener a cinco niños ella sola.
■ **What team do you support?** ¿De qué equipo eres?

> **LANGUAGE TIP** Be careful not to translate **to support** by soportar.

**support** NOUN
▷ see also **support** VERB
el apoyo

**supporter** NOUN
1 el/la hincha
□ a Liverpool supporter un hincha del Liverpool
2 el partidario
la partidaria
□ a supporter of the Labour Party un partidario del partido laborista

to **suppose** VERB
suponer*
□ I suppose he'll be late. Supongo que llegará tarde. □ Suppose you win the lottery... Supón que te toca la lotería...
■ **I suppose so.** Supongo que sí.
■ **You're supposed to show your passport.** Tienes que enseñar el pasaporte.
■ **You're not supposed to smoke in the toilet.** No está permitido fumar en el servicio.
■ **It's supposed to be the best hotel in the city.** Dicen que es el mejor hotel de la ciudad.

**supposing** CONJUNCTION

> **LANGUAGE TIP** suponiendo que has to be followed by a verb in the subjunctive.

■ **Supposing you won the lottery...** Suponiendo que te tocara la lotería...

**surcharge** NOUN
el recargo

**sure** ADJECTIVE
seguro (FEM segura)

□ Are you sure? ¿Estás seguro?
■ **Sure!** ¡Claro!
■ **to make sure that...** asegurarse de que...
□ I'm going to make sure the door's locked. Voy a asegurarme de que la puerta está cerrada con llave.

**surely** ADVERB
■ **Surely you don't believe that?** ¿No te creerás eso, no?

**surf** NOUN
▷ see also **surf** VERB
la espuma de las olas

to **surf** VERB
▷ see also **surf** NOUN
hacer* surf

**surface** NOUN
la superficie

**surfboard** NOUN
la tabla de surf

**surfing** NOUN
el surf
□ to go surfing hacer surf

**surgeon** NOUN
el cirujano
la cirujana

**surgery** NOUN
1 el consultorio médico (room)
2 la cirugía (treatment)
■ **surgery hours** las horas de consulta

**surname** NOUN
el apellido

**surprise** NOUN
la sorpresa

**surprised** ADJECTIVE
■ **I was surprised to see him.** Me sorprendió verlo.
■ **I'm not surprised that ...** No me sorprende que...

**surprising** ADJECTIVE
sorprendente (FEM sorprendente)

to **surrender** VERB
rendirse*

to **surround** VERB
rodear
□ surrounded by trees rodeado de árboles

**surroundings** PL NOUN
el entorno
□ a hotel in beautiful surroundings un hotel en un hermoso entorno

**survey** NOUN
la encuesta
□ They did a survey of a thousand students. Hicieron una encuesta a mil estudiantes.

**surveyor** NOUN
1 el perito tasador
la perito tasadora (of buildings)
2 el agrimensor
la agrimensora (of land)

**survivor** NOUN
el/la superviviente
□ There were no survivors. No hubo supervivientes.

to **suspect** VERB
▷ see also **suspect** NOUN
sospechar

**suspect** NOUN
▷ see also **suspect** VERB
el sospechoso
la sospechosa

to **suspend** VERB
1 expulsar temporalmente (from school)
2 excluir* (from team)
3 suspender (from job)

**suspenders** PL NOUN (US: braces)
los tirantes

**suspense** NOUN
1 la incertidumbre
□ The suspense was terrible. La incertidumbre era terrible.
2 el suspense
□ a film with lots of suspense una película llena de suspense

**suspension** NOUN
1 la expulsión temporal (from school)
2 la exclusión (from team)
3 la suspensión (from job)
■ a suspension bridge un puente colgante

**suspicious** ADJECTIVE
1 receloso (FEM recelosa) (mistrustful)
□ He was suspicious at first. Al principio estaba receloso.
2 sospechoso (FEM sospechosa) (suspicious-looking)
□ a suspicious person un individuo sospechoso

to **swallow** VERB
tragar*

**swam** VERB ▷ see **swim**

**swan** NOUN
el cisne

to **swap** VERB
cambiar
□ to swap A for B cambiar A por B
■ Do you want to swap? ¿Quieres que cambiemos?

to **swat** VERB
aplastar

to **sway** VERB
balancearse

to **swear** VERB
1 jurar
□ to swear allegiance to jurar fidelidad a
2 decir* palabrotas
□ It's wrong to swear. No se deben decir palabrotas.

**swearword** NOUN
la palabrota

**sweat** NOUN
▷ see also **sweat** VERB
el sudor

to **sweat** VERB
▷ see also **sweat** NOUN
sudar

**sweater** NOUN
el jersey (PL los jerseys) (el suéter Latin America)

**sweaty** ADJECTIVE
1 sudoroso (FEM sudorosa) (hands, face)
2 sudado (FEM sudada) (clothes)

**Swede** NOUN
el sueco
la sueca (person)

**swede** NOUN
el nabo

**Sweden** NOUN
Suecia fem

**Swedish** ADJECTIVE, NOUN
sueco (FEM sueca)

to **sweep** VERB
barrer
□ to sweep the floor barrer el suelo

**sweet** NOUN
▷ see also **sweet** ADJECTIVE
1 el caramelo
□ a bag of sweets una bolsa de caramelos
2 el postre
□ Are you going to have a sweet? ¿Vas a tomar postre?

**sweet** ADJECTIVE
▷ see also **sweet** NOUN
1 dulce (FEM dulce)
□ a sweet wine un vino dulce
2 amable (FEM amable)
□ That was really sweet of you. Fue muy amable de tu parte.
■ sweet and sour pork el cerdo agridulce

**sweetcorn** NOUN
el maíz dulce

**sweltering** ADJECTIVE
■ It was sweltering. Hacía un calor asfixiante.

**swept** VERB ▷ see **sweep**

to **swerve** VERB
girar bruscamente
□ I swerved to avoid the cyclist. Giré bruscamente para esquivar al ciclista.

**swim** NOUN
▷ see also **swim** VERB
■ to go for a swim ir a nadar

to **swim** VERB
▷ see also **swim** NOUN
nadar
□ Can you swim? ¿Sabes nadar?

■ **She swam across the river.** Cruzó el río a
nado.

**swimmer** NOUN
el nadador
la nadadora

**swimming** NOUN
la natación
□ swimming lessons clases de natación
■ **Do you like swimming?** ¿Te gusta nadar?
■ **to go swimming** ir a nadar
■ **swimming cap** el gorro de baño
■ **swimming costume** el traje de baño
■ **swimming pool** la piscina
■ **swimming trunks** el bañador

**swimsuit** NOUN
el traje de baño

to **swing** VERB
▷ see also **swing** NOUN
1 columpiarse (on a swing)
2 balancearse
□ Her bag swung as she walked. El bolso
se balanceaba según iba andando.
■ **He was swinging on a rope.** Se
balanceaba colgado de una cuerda.
3 colgar*
□ A large key swung from his belt. Le
colgaba una gran llave del cinturón.
4 balancear
□ He was swinging his bag back and forth.
Balanceaba la bolsa de un lado al otro.
■ **Roy swung his legs off the couch.**
Con un movimiento rápido, Roy quitó las
piernas del sofá.
■ **The canoe suddenly swung round.**
De repente la canoa dio un viraje.

**swing** NOUN
▷ see also **swing** VERB
el columpio

**Swiss** ADJECTIVE, NOUN
suizo (FEM suiza)
■ **the Swiss** los suizos

**switch** NOUN
▷ see also **switch** VERB
el interruptor

to **switch** VERB
▷ see also **switch** NOUN
cambiar de
□ We switched partners. Cambiamos de
pareja.

to **switch off** VERB
apagar* (TV, machine, engine)

to **switch on** VERB
encender* (prender Latin America)

**Switzerland** NOUN
Suiza fem

**swollen** ADJECTIVE
hinchado (FEM hinchada)
□ My ankle is very swollen. Tengo el tobillo
muy hinchado.

to **swop** VERB
cambiar
□ to swop A for B cambiar A por B
■ **Do you want to swop?** ¿Quieres que
cambiemos?

**sword** NOUN
la espada

**swot** NOUN
▷ see also **swot** VERB
el empollón
la empollona

to **swot** VERB
▷ see also **swot** NOUN
empollar
□ I'll have to swot for the maths exam.
Para el examen de matemáticas me va a
tocar empollar.

**swum** VERB ▷ see **swim**

**swung** VERB ▷ see **swing**

**syllabus** NOUN
el programa de estudios
> LANGUAGE TIP Although **programa**
ends in -**a**, it is actually a masculine
noun.

**symbol** NOUN
el símbolo

**sympathetic** ADJECTIVE
comprensivo (FEM comprensiva)
> LANGUAGE TIP Be careful not to
translate **sympathetic** by **simpático**.

to **sympathize** VERB
■ **to sympathize with somebody**
1 (feel sorry for) compadecerse de alguien
2 (understand) comprender a alguien

**sympathy** NOUN
1 la compasión (sorrow)
2 la comprensión (understanding)

**symptom** NOUN
el síntoma
> LANGUAGE TIP Although **síntoma** ends
in -**a**, it is actually a masculine noun.

**syringe** NOUN
la jeringuilla

**system** NOUN
el sistema
> LANGUAGE TIP Although **sistema** ends
in -**a**, it is actually a masculine noun.

# Tt

**table** NOUN
la mesa
- **to lay the table** poner la mesa

**tablecloth** NOUN
el mantel

**tablespoon** NOUN
la cuchara de servir

**tablet** NOUN
la pastilla

**table tennis** NOUN
el tenis de mesa
□ to play table tennis jugar al tenis de mesa

**tabloid** NOUN
- **the tabloids** la prensa amarilla

**tackle** NOUN
▷ see also **tackle** VERB
1 la entrada (in football)
2 el placaje (in rugby)
- **fishing tackle** el equipo de pesca

to **tackle** VERB
▷ see also **tackle** NOUN
- **to tackle somebody 1** (in football) entrar a alguien **2** (in rugby) placar a alguien
- **to tackle a problem** abordar un problema

**tact** NOUN
el tacto

**tactful** ADJECTIVE
diplomático (FEM diplomática)

**tactics** PL NOUN
la táctica sing

**tactless** ADJECTIVE
poco diplomático (FEM poco diplomática)
□ He's so tactless! ¡Es tan poco diplomático!
- **a tactless remark** un comentario con poco tacto

**tadpole** NOUN
el renacuajo

**tag** NOUN
la etiqueta (label)

**tail** NOUN
1 la cola (of horse, bird, fish)
2 el rabo (of dog, bull, ox)
- **Heads or tails?** ¿Cara o cruz?

**tailor** NOUN
el sastre
□ He's a tailor. Es sastre.

to **take** VERB
1 tomar
□ Do you take sugar? ¿Tomas azúcar?
- **He took a plate out of the cupboard.** Sacó un plato del armario.
2 llevar
□ When will you take me to London? ¿Cuándo me llevarás a Londres? □ Don't forget to take your camera. No te olvides de llevarte la cámara. □ It takes about one hour. Se tarda más o menos una hora. □ It won't take long. No tardará mucho tiempo.
- **That takes a lot of courage.** Hace falta mucho valor para eso.
- **It takes a lot of money to do that.** Hace falta mucho dinero para hacer eso.
3 soportar
□ He can't take being criticized. No soporta que le critiquen.
4 hacer*
□ Have you taken your driving test yet? ¿Ya has hecho el examen de conducir? □ I decided to take French instead of German. Decidí hacer francés en vez de alemán.
5 aceptar
□ We take credit cards. Aceptamos tarjetas de crédito.

to **take after** VERB
parecerse* a
□ She takes after her mother. Se parece a su madre.

to **take apart** VERB
- **to take something apart** desmontar algo

to **take away** VERB
1 llevarse
□ They took away all his belongings. Se llevaron todas sus pertenencias.
2 quitar
□ She was afraid her children would be taken away from her. Tenía miedo de que le quitaran a los niños.
- **hot meals to take away** platos calientes para llevar

to **take back** VERB
devolver*

□ I took it back to the shop. Lo devolví a la tienda.

■ **I take it all back!** ¡Retiro lo dicho!

to **take down** VERB
quitar

□ She took down the painting. Quitó el cuadro.

to **take in** VERB
1 comprender

□ I didn't really take it in. La verdad es que no lo comprendí.

2 engañar

□ They were taken in by his story. Se dejaron engañar por la historia que les contó.

to **take off** VERB
1 despegar*

□ The plane took off 20 minutes late. El avión despegó con 20 minutos de retraso.

2 quitar

□ Take your coat off. Quítate el abrigo.

to **take out** VERB
sacar*

□ He opened his wallet and took out some money. Abrió la cartera y sacó dinero.

■ **He took her out to the theatre.** La invitó al teatro.

to **take over** VERB
hacerse* cargo de

□ He took over the running of the company last year. Se hizo cargo del control de la empresa el año pasado.

■ **to take over from somebody 1** (replace) sustituir a alguien **2** (in shift work) relevar a alguien

**takeaway** NOUN
la comida para llevar (meal)

**takeoff** NOUN
el despegue (of plane)

**talcum powder** NOUN
los polvos de talco

**tale** NOUN
el cuento

**talent** NOUN
el talento

□ He's got a lot of talent. Tiene mucho talento.

■ **to have a talent for something** tener talento para algo

■ **He's got a real talent for languages.** Tiene verdadera facilidad para los idiomas.

**talented** ADJECTIVE

■ **She's a talented pianist.** Es una pianista de talento.

**talk** NOUN
▷ see also **talk** VERB
1 la conversación (PL las conversaciones)

□ We had a long talk about her problems. Tuvimos una larga conversación acerca de

sus problemas.

■ **I had a talk with my Mum about it.** Hablé sobre eso con mi madre.

■ **to give a talk on something** dar una charla sobre algo □ She gave a talk on ancient Egypt. Dio una charla sobre el antiguo Egipto.

2 las habladurías (gossip)

□ It's just talk. Son sólo habladurías.

to **talk** VERB
▷ see also **talk** NOUN
hablar

□ What did you talk about? ¿De qué hablasteis?

■ **to talk to somebody** hablar con alguien

■ **to talk to oneself** hablar consigo mismo

■ **to talk something over with somebody** discutir algo con alguien

**talkative** ADJECTIVE
hablador (FEM habladora)

**tall** ADJECTIVE
alto (FEM alta)

■ **to be two metres tall** medir dos metros

**tame** ADJECTIVE
domesticado (FEM domesticada) (animal)

**tampon** NOUN
el tampón (PL los tampones)

**tan** NOUN
el bronceado

■ **to get a tan** broncearse

**tangerine** NOUN
la mandarina

**tank** NOUN
1 el depósito (for water, petrol)
2 la cisterna (on truck)
3 el tanque (military)

**tanker** NOUN
1 el petrolero (ship)
2 el camión cisterna (PL los camiones cisterna) (truck)

■ **an oil tanker** un petrolero

■ **a petrol tanker** un camión cisterna

**tap** NOUN
1 el grifo (la llave Latin America) (for water)

□ the hot tap el grifo de agua caliente

2 el golpecito (gentle knock)

□ I heard a tap on the window. Oí un golpecito en la ventana.

■ **There was a tap on the door.** Llamaron a la puerta.

**tap-dancing** NOUN
el claqué

□ I do tap-dancing. Bailo claqué.

to **tape** VERB
▷ see also **tape** NOUN
grabar

□ Did you tape that film last night? ¿Grabaste la película de anoche?

**tape** NOUN
▷ see also **tape** VERB
1 la cinta (music)
2 la cinta adhesiva (sticky tape)

**tape measure** NOUN
la cinta métrica

**tape recorder** NOUN
1 el casete (large)
2 la grabadora (hand-held)

**target** NOUN
1 la diana (board)
2 el objetivo (goal)

**tart** NOUN
la tarta
□ an apple tart una tarta de manzana

**tartan** ADJECTIVE
escocés (PL escoceses, FEM escocesa)
□ a tartan scarf una bufanda escocesa

**task** NOUN
la tarea

**taste** NOUN
▷ see also **taste** VERB
1 el sabor
□ It's got a really strange taste. Tiene un sabor muy extraño.
2 el gusto
□ His joke was in bad taste. Su broma fue de mal gusto.
■ **Would you like a taste?** ¿Quiere probarlo?

to **taste** VERB
▷ see also **taste** NOUN
probar*
□ Would you like to taste it? ¿Quiere probarlo?
■ **to taste of something** saber a algo
□ It tastes of fish. Sabe a pescado.
■ **You can taste the garlic in it.** Se le nota el sabor a ajo.

**tasteful** ADJECTIVE
de buen gusto

**tasteless** ADJECTIVE
1 soso (FEM sosa) (food)
2 de mal gusto (in bad taste)
□ a tasteless remark un comentario de mal gusto

**tasty** ADJECTIVE
sabroso (FEM sabrosa)

**tattoo** NOUN
el tatuaje

**taught** VERB ▷ see **teach**

**Taurus** NOUN
el Tauro (sign)
■ **I'm Taurus.** Soy tauro.

**tax** NOUN
el impuesto
■ **I pay a lot of tax.** Pago muchos impuestos.

■ **income tax** el impuesto sobre la renta

**taxi** NOUN
el taxi
■ **a taxi driver** un/una taxista

**taxi rank** NOUN
la parada de taxis

**TB** ABBREVIATION (= tuberculosis)
la tuberculosis
□ He's got TB. Tiene tuberculosis.

**tea** NOUN
1 té
□ Would you like some tea? ¿Te apetece un té?
■ **a cup of tea** una taza de té
2 la merienda (afternoon tea)
■ **to have tea** merendar □ We had tea at the Savoy. Merendamos en el Savoy.
3 la cena (evening meal)
■ **to have tea** cenar □ We're having sausages and beans for tea. Vamos a cenar salchichas con alubias.

to **teach** VERB
1 enseñar
□ My sister taught me to swim. Mi hermana me enseñó a nadar.
2 dar* clases de (subject)
□ She teaches physics. Da clases de física.
■ **That'll teach you!** ¡Así aprenderás!

**teacher** NOUN
1 el profesor
la profesora (in secondary school)
□ a maths teacher un profesor de matemáticas □ She's a teacher. Es profesora.
2 el maestro
la maestra (in primary school)
□ He's a primary school teacher. Es maestro.

**team** NOUN
el equipo
□ a football team un equipo de fútbol

**teapot** NOUN
la tetera

**tear** NOUN
▷ see also **tear** VERB
la lágrima
■ **She was in tears.** Estaba llorando.

to **tear** VERB
▷ see also **tear** NOUN
1 romper*
□ Be careful or you'll tear the page. Ten cuidado que vas a romper la página.
■ **He tore his jacket.** Se rasgó la chaqueta.
■ **Your shirt is torn.** Tu camisa está rota.
2 romperse*
□ It won't tear, it's very strong. No se rompe, es muy resistente.

to **tear up** VERB

hacer* pedazos
□ He tore up the letter. Hizo pedazos la carta.

**tear gas** NOUN
el gas lacrimógeno

to **tease** VERB
1 atormentar
□ Stop teasing that poor animal! ¡Deja de atormentar al pobre animal!
2 tomar el pelo a
□ He's teasing you. Te está tomando el pelo.
■ **I was only teasing.** Lo decía en broma.

**teaspoon** NOUN
la cucharita

**teatime** NOUN
la hora de cenar (in evening)
□ It was nearly teatime. Era casi la hora de cenar.
■ **Teatime!** ¡A la mesa!

**tea towel** NOUN
el paño de cocina

**technical** ADJECTIVE
técnico (FEM técnica)
■ **technical college** el centro de formación profesional (la escuela politécnica Latin America)

**technician** NOUN
el técnico
la técnica

**technique** NOUN
la técnica

**techno** NOUN
el tecno

**technological** ADJECTIVE
tecnológico (FEM tecnológica)

**technology** NOUN
la tecnología

**teddy bear** NOUN
el osito de peluche

**teenage** ADJECTIVE
■ **a teenage magazine** una revista para adolescentes
■ **She has two teenage daughters.** Tiene dos hijas adolescentes.

**teenager** NOUN
el/la adolescente

**teens** PL NOUN
■ **She's in her teens.** Es adolescente.

**tee-shirt** NOUN
la camiseta

**teeth** PL NOUN ▷ see **tooth**

to **teethe** VERB
echar los dientes

**teetotal** ADJECTIVE
abstemio (FEM abstemia)

**telecommunications** PL NOUN
las telecomunicaciones

**telephone** NOUN
el teléfono
□ on the telephone al teléfono
■ **a telephone box** una cabina telefónica
■ **a telephone call** una llamada telefónica
■ **a telephone directory** una guía telefónica
■ **a telephone number** un número de teléfono

**telesales** NOUN
las televentas

**telescope** NOUN
el telescopio

**television** NOUN
la televisión
□ The match is on television tonight. Ponen el partido en televisión esta noche.

to **tell** VERB
decir*
■ **to tell somebody something** decir algo a alguien □ Did you tell your mother? ¿Se lo has dicho a tu madre? □ I told him I was going on holiday. Le dije que me iba de vacaciones.

> **LANGUAGE TIP** Use the subjunctive after **decir a alguien que** when translating 'to tell somebody to do something'.

■ **to tell somebody to do something** decir a alguien que haga algo □ He told me to wait a moment. Me dijo que esperara un momento.
■ **to tell lies** decir mentiras
■ **to tell a story** contar un cuento
■ **I can't tell the difference between them.** No puedo distinguirlos.
■ **You can tell he's not serious.** Se nota que no se lo toma en serio.

to **tell off** VERB
regañar

**telly** NOUN (informal)
la tele
□ to watch telly ver la tele □ on telly en la tele

**temper** NOUN
el genio
□ He's got a terrible temper. Tiene muy mal genio.
■ **to be in a temper** estar de mal humor
■ **to lose one's temper** perder los estribos

**temperature** NOUN
la temperatura
■ **to have a temperature** tener fiebre

**temple** NOUN
1 el templo (building)
2 la sien (on head)

**temporary** ADJECTIVE
temporal (FEM temporal)

265

to **tempt** VERB
tentar*
□ I'm very tempted! ¡Tienta mucho!
■ **to tempt somebody to do something**
tentar a alguien a hacer algo
**temptation** NOUN
la tentación (PL las tentaciones)
**tempting** ADJECTIVE
tentador (FEM tentadora)
**ten** NUMERAL
diez
□ She's ten. Tiene diez años.
**tenant** NOUN
el inquilino
la inquilina
to **tend** VERB
■ **to tend to do something** tener tendencia
a hacer algo □ He tends to arrive late. Tiene
tendencia a llegar tarde.
**tender** ADJECTIVE
tierno (FEM tierna)
**tennis** NOUN
el tenis
□ to play tennis jugar al tenis
■ **a tennis ball** una pelota de tenis
■ **a tennis court** una pista de tenis
■ **a tennis racket** una raqueta de tenis
**tennis player** NOUN
el/la tenista
□ He's a tennis player. Es tenista.
**tenor** NOUN
el tenor
**tenpin bowling** NOUN
los bolos
□ to go tenpin bowling jugar a los bolos
**tense** ADJECTIVE
▷ see also **tense** NOUN
tenso (FEM tensa)
**tense** NOUN
▷ see also **tense** ADJECTIVE
el tiempo
■ **the present tense** el presente
■ **the future tense** el futuro
**tension** NOUN
la tensión (PL las tensiones)
**tent** NOUN
la tienda de campaña
■ **a tent peg** una estaquilla
■ **a tent pole** un mástil de tienda
**tenth** ADJECTIVE
décimo (FEM décima)
□ the tenth floor el décimo piso
■ **the tenth of August** el diez de agosto
**term** NOUN
1 el trimestre (at school)
□ It's nearly the end of term. Ya casi es final
de trimestre.
2 el plazo

□ in the long term a largo plazo
■ **to come to terms with something**
aceptar algo □ He hasn't yet come to terms
with his disability. Todavía no ha aceptado
su invalidez.
**terminal** ADJECTIVE
▷ see also **terminal** NOUN
terminal (FEM terminal) (illness, patient)
**terminal** NOUN
▷ see also **terminal** ADJECTIVE
el terminal (of computer)
■ **airport terminal** la terminal del
aeropuerto
■ **bus terminal** la terminal de autobuses
■ **oil terminal** la terminal petrolera
**terminally** ADVERB
■ **to be terminally ill** estar en fase terminal
**terrace** NOUN
1 la terraza (patio)
□ We were sitting on the terrace.
Estábamos sentados en la terraza.
2 la hilera de casas adosadas (row of houses)
■ **the terraces** (in stadium) las gradas
**terraced** ADJECTIVE
■ **a terraced house** una casa adosada
**terrible** ADJECTIVE
espantoso (FEM espantosa)
□ This coffee is terrible. Este café es
espantoso.
■ **I feel terrible.** Me siento fatal.
**terrier** NOUN
el/la terrier (PL los/las terriers)
**terrific** ADJECTIVE
estupendo (FEM estupenda) (wonderful)
□ That's terrific! ¡Estupendo!
■ **You look terrific!** ¡Estás guapísima!
**terrified** ADJECTIVE
aterrorizado (FEM aterrorizada)
□ I was terrified! ¡Estaba aterrorizado!
**terrorism** NOUN
el terrorismo
**terrorist** NOUN
el/la terrorista
■ **a terrorist attack** un atentado terrorista
**test** NOUN
▷ see also **test** VERB
1 la prueba
□ a spelling test una prueba de ortografía
□ nuclear tests pruebas nucleares
2 el análisis (PL los análisis) (of blood, urine)
□ a blood test un análisis de sangre
■ **an eye test** un examen de la vista
3 el examen de conducir (driving test)
□ He's just passed his test. Acaba de
aprobar el examen de conducir.
to **test** VERB
▷ see also **test** NOUN
probar*

■ **to test something out** probar algo

■ **He tested us on the new vocabulary.**
Nos hizo una prueba del vocabulario nuevo.

■ **She was tested for drugs.** Le hicieron la prueba antidoping.

**test match** NOUN
el partido internacional

**test tube** NOUN
la probeta

**tetanus** NOUN
el tétano

■ **a tetanus injection** una inyección contra el tétano

**text** NOUN
▷ see also **text** VERB
el SMS *(text message)*

to **text** VERB
▷ see also **text** NOUN
enviar* un SMS a

□ I'll text you when I get there. Te envío un SMS cuando llegue.

**textbook** NOUN
el libro de texto

□ a Spanish textbook un libro de texto de español

**text message** NOUN
el SMS

**Thames** NOUN
el Támesis

**than** CONJUNCTION
1 que

□ She's taller than me. Es más alta que yo.
□ I've got more CDs than tapes. Tengo más CDs que cintas.

2 de

□ more than once en más de una ocasión
□ more than 10 years más de 10 años

to **thank** VERB
dar* las gracias a

□ Don't forget to write and thank them.
Acuérdate de escribirles y darles las gracias.

■ **thank you** gracias

■ **thank you very much** muchas gracias

**thanks** EXCLAMATION
¡Gracias!

■ **thanks to** gracias a □ Thanks to him, everything went OK. Gracias a él, todo salió bien.

**that** ADJECTIVE
▷ see also **that** PRONOUN, CONJUNCTION, ADVERB
1 ese (FEM esa)

□ that man ese hombre □ that road esa carretera

◌ **LANGUAGE TIP** To refer to something more distant, use **aquel** and **aquella**.

2 aquel (FEM aquella)

□ Look at that car over there! ¡Mira aquel coche! □ THAT road there aquella carretera

■ **that one** ése (FEM ésa)

□ This man? — No, that one. ¿Este hombre?
— No, ése. □ Do you like this photo? — No, I prefer that one. ¿Te gusta esta foto? — No, prefiero ésa.

◌ **LANGUAGE TIP** To refer to something more distant, use **aquél** and **aquélla**.

3 aquél (FEM aquélla)

□ That one over there is cheaper. Aquél es más barato. □ Which woman? — That one over there. ¿Qué mujer? — Aquélla.

**that** PRONOUN
▷ see also **that** ADJECTIVE, CONJUNCTION, ADVERB
1 ése (FEM ésa, NEUTER eso)

□ That's impossible. Eso es imposible.
□ What's that? ¿Qué es eso?

■ **Who's that?** *(who is that man)* ¿Quién es ése?

■ **Who's that?** *(who is that woman)* ¿Quién es ésa?

■ **Who's that?** *(on the telephone)* ¿Con quién hablo?

◌ **LANGUAGE TIP** To refer to something more distant, use **aquél**, **aquélla** and **aquello**.

2 aquél (FEM aquélla, NEUTER aquello)

□ That's my French teacher over there.
Aquél es mi profesor de francés. □ That's my sister over by the window. Aquélla de la ventana es mi hermana. □ That was a silly thing to do. Aquello fue una tontería.

■ **Is that you?** ¿Eres tú?

3 que *(in relative clauses)*

□ the man that saw us el hombre que nos vio □ the dog that she bought el perro que ella compró □ the man that we saw el hombre que vimos

◌ **LANGUAGE TIP** After a preposition **que** becomes **el que**, **la que**, **los que**, **las que** to agree with the noun.

□ the man that we spoke to el hombre con el que hablamos □ the women that she was chatting to las mujeres con las que estaba hablando

**that** CONJUNCTION
▷ see also **that** ADJECTIVE, PRONOUN, ADVERB
que

□ He thought that Henry was ill. Creía que Henry estaba enfermo. □ I know that she likes chocolate. Sé que le gusta el chocolate.

**that** ADVERB
▷ see also **that** ADJECTIVE, PRONOUN, CONJUNCTION

■ **It was that big.** Era así de grande.

■ **It's about that high.** Es más o menos así de alto.

■ **It's not that difficult.** No es tan difícil.

**thatched** ADJECTIVE

■ **a thatched cottage** una casita con tejado de paja

**the** DEFINITE ARTICLE
1 el *masc* (PL los)
□ the boy el niño □ the cars los coches

> **LANGUAGE TIP** a + **el** changes to **al** and de + **el** changes to **del**.

□ They went to the theatre. Fueron al teatro. □ the soup of the day la sopa del día
2 la *fem* (PL las)
□ the woman la mujer □ the chairs las sillas

**theatre** (US **theater**) NOUN
el teatro

**theft** NOUN
el robo

**their** ADJECTIVE
su (PL sus)
□ their father su padre □ their house su casa □ their parents sus padres □ their sisters sus hermanas

> **LANGUAGE TIP** 'Their' is usually translated by the definite article **el/ los** or **la/las** when it's clear from the sentence who the possessor is, particularly when referring to clothing or parts of the body.

□ They took off their coats. Se quitaron los abrigos. □ after washing their hands después de lavarse las manos □ Someone stole their car. Alguien les robó el coche.

**theirs** PRONOUN
1 el suyo *masc* (PL los suyos)
□ Is this this car? — No, theirs is red. ¿Es éste su coche? — No, el suyo es rojo. □ my parents and theirs mis padres y los suyos
2 la suya *fem* (PL las suyas)
□ Is this their house? — No, theirs is white. ¿Es ésta su casa? — No, la suya es blanca. □ my sisters and theirs mis hermanas y las suyas

> **LANGUAGE TIP** Use **de ellos** (masculine) or **de ellas** (feminine) instead of **suyo** if you want to be specific about a masculine or feminine group.

□ It's not our car, it's theirs. No es nuestro coche, es suyo. □ The suitcase is theirs. La maleta es suya. □ Whose is this? — It's theirs. ¿De quién es esto? — Es de ellos.
■ **Isobel is a friend of theirs.** Isobel es amiga suya.

**them** PRONOUN
1 los (FEM las)

> **LANGUAGE TIP** Use **los** or **las** when 'them' is the direct object of the verb in the sentence.

□ I didn't know them. No los conocía.

□ Have you seen my slippers? I'd left them here. ¿Has visto mis zapatillas? Las había dejado aquí. □ Look at them! ¡Míralos! □ I had to give them to her. Tuve que dárselos.
2 les

> **LANGUAGE TIP** Use **les** when 'them' means 'to them'.

□ I gave them some brochures. Les di unos folletos. □ You have to tell them the truth. Tienes que decirles la verdad.
3 se

> **LANGUAGE TIP** Use **se** not **les** when 'them' is used in combination with a direct-object pronoun.

□ Give it to them. Dáselo.
4 ellos (FEM ellas)

> **LANGUAGE TIP** Use **ellos** or **ellas** after prepositions, in comparisons, and with the verb 'to be'.

□ It's for them. Es para ellos. □ My sisters didn't go. My mother stayed with them. Mis hermanas no fueron. Mi madre se quedó con ellas. □ We are older than them. Somos mayores que ellos. □ It must be them. Deben de ser ellos.
■ **They were carrying them on them.** Los llevaban consigo.

**theme** NOUN
el tema

> **LANGUAGE TIP** Although **tema** ends in -**a**, it is actually a masculine noun.

**theme park** NOUN
el parque temático

**themselves** PRONOUN
1 se *(reflexive)*
□ Did they hurt themselves? ¿Se hicieron daño?
2 sí mismos (FEM sí mismas) *(after preposition)*
□ They talked mainly about themselves. Hablaron sobre todo de sí mismos.
3 ellos mismos (FEM ellas mismas) *(for emphasis)*
□ They built it themselves. Lo construyeron ellos mismos.
■ **by themselves** por sí mismos (FEM por sí mismas)
□ The girls did it all by themselves. Las chicas lo hicieron todo por sí mismas.

**then** ADVERB, CONJUNCTION
1 después *(next)*
□ I get dressed. Then I have breakfast. Me visto. Después desayuno.
2 pues *(in that case)*
□ My pen's run out. — Use a pencil then! Se me ha acabado el bolígrafo. — ¡Pues usa un lápiz!
3 en aquella época *(in those days)*
□ There was no electricity then. En aquella época no había electricidad.

■ **now and then** de vez en cuando □ Do you play chess? — Now and then. ¿Juegas al ajedrez? — De vez en cuando.

■ **By then it was too late.** Para entonces ya era demasiado tarde.

**therapy** NOUN
la terapia

**there** ADVERB
ahí

□ Put it there, on the table. Ponlo ahí, en la mesa.

■ **over there** allí
■ **in there** ahí dentro
■ **on there** ahí encima
■ **up there** ahí arriba
■ **down there** ahí abajo
■ **There he is!** ¡Ahí está!
■ **there is** hay □ There's a factory near my house. Hay una fábrica cerca de mi casa.
■ **there are** hay □ There are 20 children in my class. Hay 20 niños en mi clase.
■ **There has been an accident.** Ha habido un accidente.

**therefore** ADVERB
por lo tanto

**there's** = there is; there has

**thermometer** NOUN
el termómetro

**Thermos®** NOUN
el termo

**these** ADJECTIVE
▷ see also **these** PRONOUN
estos (FEM estas)

□ these shoes estos zapatos □ THESE shoes estos zapatos de aquí □ these houses estas casas

**these** PRONOUN
▷ see also **these** ADJECTIVE
éstos (FEM éstas)

□ I want these! ¡Quiero éstos! □ I'm looking for some sandals. — Can I try these? Quiero unas sandalias. — ¿Puedo probarme éstas?

**they** PRONOUN
ellos (FEM ellas)

　　LANGUAGE TIP 'they' generally isn't translated unless it's emphatic.
□ They're fine, thank you. Están bien, gracias.

　　LANGUAGE TIP Use **ellos** or **ellas** as appropriate for emphasis.
□ We went to the cinema but they didn't. Nosotros fuimos al cine pero ellos no.
□ I spoke to my sisters. THEY agree with me. Hablé con mis hermanas. Ellas estaban de acuerdo conmigo.

■ **They say that…** Dicen que… □ They say that the house is haunted. Dicen que la casa está embrujada.

**they'd** = they had; they would
**they'll** = they will
**they're** = they are
**they've** = they have

**thick** ADJECTIVE
1 grueso (FEM gruesa) *(wall, slice)*
□ Give him a thick slice. Dále una rebanada gruesa.
■ **The walls are one metre thick.** Las paredes tienen un metro de grosor.
2 espeso (FEM espesa) *(soup)*
□ My soup turned out too thick. La sopa me quedó demasiado espesa.
3 corto (FEM corta) *(informal: stupid)*

**thief** NOUN
el ladrón (PL los ladrones)
la ladrona

**thigh** NOUN
el muslo

**thin** ADJECTIVE
1 fino (FEM fina)
□ a thin slice una rebanada fina
2 delgado (FEM delgada)
□ She's very thin. Está muy delgada.

**thing** NOUN
la cosa

□ beautiful things cosas bonitas □ Where shall I put my things? ¿Dónde pongo mis cosas?
■ **How's things?** ¿Qué tal?
■ **What's that thing called?** ¿Cómo se llama eso?
■ **You poor thing!** ¡Pobrecito!
■ **The best thing would be to leave it.** Lo mejor sería dejarlo.

to **think** VERB
1 pensar*
□ What do you think about it? ¿Qué piensas? □ Think carefully before you reply. Piénsalo bien antes de responder. □ What are you thinking about? ¿En qué estás pensando?
■ **I'll think it over.** Lo pensaré.
2 creer*
□ I think you're wrong. Creo que estás equivocado.
■ **I think so.** Creo que sí.
■ **I don't think so.** Creo que no.
3 imaginar
□ Think what life would be like without cars. Imagínate cómo sería la vida sin coches.

**third** ADJECTIVE, ADVERB
▷ see also **third** NOUN
tercero (FEM tercera)

　　LANGUAGE TIP Use **tercer** before a masculine singular noun.
□ the third prize el tercer premio □ the third time la tercera vez □ Rachel came third in

**t**

the race. Rachel quedó la tercera en la carrera.
■ **the third of March** el tres de marzo
**third** NOUN
▷ *see also* **third** ADJECTIVE, ADVERB
el tercio *(fraction)*
■ **a third of the population** una tercera parte de la población
**thirdly** ADVERB
en tercer lugar
**Third World** NOUN
el Tercer Mundo
**thirst** NOUN
la sed
**thirsty** ADJECTIVE
■ **to be thirsty** tener sed
**thirteen** NUMERAL
trece
□ I'm thirteen. Tengo trece años.
**thirteenth** ADJECTIVE
decimotercero (FEM decimotercera)
■ **the thirteenth floor** la planta trece
■ **the thirteenth of January** el trece de enero
**thirty** NUMERAL
treinta
□ He's thirty. Tiene treinta años.
**this** ADJECTIVE
▷ *see also* **this** PRONOUN
este (FEM esta)
□ this boy este niño □ this road esta carretera
■ **this one** éste (FEM ésta)
□ Pass me that pen. — This one? Acércame ese bolígrafo. — ¿Éste? □ This is my room and this one's my sister's. Ésta es mi habitación y ésta es la de mi hermana.
**this** PRONOUN
▷ *see also* **this** ADJECTIVE
éste (FEM ésta, NEUTER esto)
□ This is my office and this is the meeting room. Éste es mi despacho y ésta es la sala de reuniones. □ What's this? ¿Qué es esto?
■ **This is my mother.** *(introduction)* Te presento a mi madre.
■ **This is Gavin speaking.** *(on the phone)* Soy Gavin.
**thistle** NOUN
el cardo
**thorough** ADJECTIVE
minucioso (FEM minuciosa)
□ a thorough check un control minucioso
■ **She's very thorough.** Es muy meticulosa.
**thoroughly** ADVERB
minuciosamente
□ I checked the car thoroughly. Revisé el coche minuciosamente.
■ **Mix the ingredients thoroughly.** Mézclense bien los ingredientes.

■ **I thoroughly enjoyed myself.** Me divertí muchísimo.
**those** ADJECTIVE
▷ *see also* **those** PRONOUN
1 esos (FEM esas)
□ those shoes esos zapatos □ those girls esas chicas
> **LANGUAGE TIP** To refer to something more distant, use **aquellos** and **aquellas.**
2 aquellos (FEM aquellas)
□ THOSE shoes aquellos zapatos □ those houses over there aquellas casas
**those** PRONOUN
▷ *see also* **those** ADJECTIVE
1 ésos (FEM ésas)
□ I want those! ¡Quiero ésos!
> **LANGUAGE TIP** To refer to something more distant, use **aquéllos.**
2 aquéllos (FEM aquéllas)
□ Ask those children. — Those over there? Pregúntales a esos niños. — ¿A aquéllos?
**though** CONJUNCTION, ADVERB
aunque
□ Though she was tired she stayed up late. Aunque estaba cansada, se quedó levantada hasta muy tarde.
■ **It's difficult, though, to put into practice.** Pero es difícil llevarlo a la práctica.
**thought** VERB ▷ *see* think
**thought** NOUN
la idea
□ I've just had a thought. Se me ocurre una idea.
■ **He kept his thoughts to himself.** No le dijo a nadie lo que pensaba.
■ **It was a nice thought, thank you.** Fue muy amable de tu parte, gracias.
**thoughtful** ADJECTIVE
1 pensativo (FEM pensativa) *(deep in thought)*
□ You look thoughtful. Pareces pensativo.
2 considerado (FEM considerada) *(considerate)*
□ She's very thoughtful. Es muy considerada.
**thoughtless** ADJECTIVE
desconsiderado (FEM desconsiderada)
□ She's very thoughtless. Es muy desconsiderada.
■ **It was thoughtless of her to mention it.** Fue una falta de consideración por su parte mencionarlo.
**thousand** NUMERAL
■ **a thousand** mil □ a thousand euros mil euros
■ **two thousand pounds** dos mil libras
■ **thousands of people** miles de personas
**thread** NOUN
el hilo

**threat** NOUN
la amenaza

to **threaten** VERB
amenazar*
❑ He threatened me. Me amenazó.
■ **to threaten to do something** *(person)*
amenazar con hacer algo

**three** NUMERAL
tres
❑ She's three. Tiene tres años.

**three-dimensional** ADJECTIVE
tridimensional (FEM tridimensional)

**threw** VERB ▷ *see* **throw**

**thrifty** ADJECTIVE
ahorrativo (FEM ahorrativa)

**thrill** NOUN
la emoción (PL las emociones)
❑ I remember the thrill of Christmas as a child. Recuerdo la emoción que sentía de niño en Navidades.
■ **It was a great thrill to see my team win.**
Fue muy emocionante ver ganar a mi equipo.

**thrilled** ADJECTIVE
■ **I was thrilled.** Estaba emocionada.

**thriller** NOUN
1 la película de suspense (la película de misterio *Latin America*) *(film)*
2 la novela de suspense (la novela de misterio *Latin America*) *(novel)*

**thrilling** ADJECTIVE
emocionante (FEM emocionante)

**throat** NOUN
la garganta
❑ I have a sore throat. Me duele la garganta.

to **throb** VERB
■ **My arm's throbbing.** Tengo un dolor punzante en el brazo.
■ **a throbbing pain** un dolor punzante

**throne** NOUN
el trono

**through** ADJECTIVE, ADVERB, PREPOSITION
1 a través de
❑ to look through a telescope mirar a través de un telescopio ❑ I know her through my sister. La conozco a través de mi hermana.
■ **I saw him through the crowd.** Lo vi entre la multitud.
■ **The window was dirty and I couldn't see through.** La ventana estaba sucia y no podía ver nada.
2 por
❑ The thief got in through the kitchen window. El ladrón entró por la ventana de la cocina. ❑ to go through Birmingham pasar por Birmingham ❑ to walk through the woods pasear por el bosque
■ **to go through a tunnel** atravesar un túnel

■ He went straight through to the dining room. Pasó directamente al comedor.
■ **a through train** un tren directo
■ **'no through road'** 'calle sin salida'
■ **all through the night** durante toda la noche
■ **from May through to September** desde mayo hasta septiembre

**throughout** PREPOSITION
■ **throughout Britain** en toda Gran Bretaña
■ **throughout the year** durante todo el año

to **throw** VERB
tirar
❑ He threw the ball to me. Me tiró la pelota.
■ **to throw a party** dar una fiesta
■ **That really threw him.** Eso lo desconcertó por completo.

to **throw away** VERB
1 tirar *(rubbish)*
2 desperdiciar *(chance)*

to **throw out** VERB
1 tirar *(throw away)*
2 echar *(person)*
❑ I threw him out. Lo eché.

to **throw up** VERB
devolver*

**thug** NOUN
el matón (PL los matones)

**thumb** NOUN
el pulgar

**thumb tack** NOUN (US)
la chincheta

to **thump** VERB
■ **to thump somebody** pegar un puñetazo a alguien

**thunder** NOUN
los truenos

**thunderstorm** NOUN
la tormenta

**thundery** ADJECTIVE
tormentoso (FEM tormentosa)

**Thursday** NOUN
el jueves (PL los jueves)
❑ I saw her on Thursday. La vi el jueves.
❑ every Thursday todos los jueves ❑ last Thursday el jueves pasado ❑ next Thursday el jueves que viene ❑ on Thursdays los jueves

**thyme** NOUN
el tomillo

**tick** NOUN
▷ *see also* **tick** VERB
1 la señal
❑ Place a tick in the appropriate box. Marque con una señal la casilla correspondiente.
2 el tictac

□ The clock has a loud tick. El reloj tiene un tictac muy fuerte.

■ **in a tick** en un instante

**to tick** VERB
▷ *see also* **tick** NOUN

1 marcar*

□ Tick the appropriate box. Marque la casilla correspondiente.

2 hacer* tictac *(clock)*

**to tick off** VERB

1 marcar* *(on form, list)*

□ The teacher ticked the names off in the register. El profesor marcó los nombres de la lista con una señal.

2 regañar *(scold)*

□ He was ticked off for being late. Le regañaron por llegar tarde.

**ticket** NOUN

1 el billete (el boleto *Latin America) (for bus, train, tube)*

2 el billete (el pasaje *Latin America) (for plane)*

3 la entrada *(for cinema, theatre, concert, museum)*

4 el ticket (PL los tickets) *(for baggage, coat, parking)*

■ **a parking ticket** *(fine)* una multa de aparcamiento

**ticket inspector** NOUN
el revisor (FEM la revisora)

**ticket office** NOUN
la taquilla

**to tickle** VERB
hacer* cosquillas a

□ She enjoyed tickling the baby. Le gustaba hacer cosquillas al niño.

**ticklish** ADJECTIVE

■ **to be ticklish** tener cosquillas

**tide** NOUN
la marea

■ **high tide** la marea alta

■ **low tide** la marea baja

**tidy** ADJECTIVE
▷ *see also* **tidy** VERB
ordenado (FEM ordenada)

□ Your room is very tidy. Tu habitación está muy ordenada. □ She's very tidy. Es muy ordenada.

**to tidy** VERB
▷ *see also* **tidy** ADJECTIVE
ordenar *(room)*

**to tidy up** VERB
recoger* *(toys)*

□ Don't forget to tidy up afterwards. No os olvidéis de recoger las cosas después.

**tie** NOUN
▷ *see also* **tie** VERB

1 la corbata *(necktie)*

2 el empate *(in sport)*

**to tie** VERB
▷ *see also* **tie** NOUN

1 atar *(shoelaces, parcel)*

■ **to tie a knot in something** hacer un nudo en algo

2 empatar

□ They tied three all. Empataron a tres.

**to tie up** VERB

1 atar *(person, shoelaces, parcel)*

2 atracar* *(boat)*

**tiger** NOUN
el tigre

**tight** ADJECTIVE

1 ceñido (FEM ceñida) *(fitting)*

□ tight jeans vaqueros ceñidos

2 estrecho (FEM estrecha) *(too small)*

□ This dress is a bit tight. Este vestido es un poco estrecho.

**to tighten** VERB

1 tensar *(rope)*

2 apretar* *(screw)*

**tightly** ADVERB

■ **tightly closed** fuertemente cerrado

■ **She held his hand tightly.** Le agarró la mano con fuerza.

**tights** PL NOUN
las medias

□ a pair of tights unas medias

**tile** NOUN

1 la teja *(on roof)*

2 el azulejo *(for wall)*

3 la baldosa *(for floor)*

**tiled** ADJECTIVE

1 de tejas *(roof)*

2 alicatado (FEM alicatada) *(wall)*

3 de baldosas *(floor)*

**till** NOUN
▷ *see also* **till** PREPOSITION, CONJUNCTION
la caja

**till** PREPOSITION, CONJUNCTION
▷ *see also* **till** NOUN

1 hasta

□ I waited till 10 o'clock. Esperé hasta las 10.

■ **till now** hasta ahora

■ **till then** hasta entonces

■ **It won't be ready till next week.** No estará listo hasta la semana que viene.

2 hasta que

□ We stayed there till the doctor came. Nos quedamos allí hasta que vino el médico.

LANGUAGE TIP **hasta que** has to be followed by a verb in the subjunctive when referring to an event in the future.

□ Don't go till I arrive. No te vayas hasta que llegue yo. □ Wait till I come back. Espera hasta que yo vuelva.

**time** NOUN

**1** la hora
□ What time is it? ¿Qué hora es? □ What time do you get up? ¿A qué hora te levantas? □ It was two o'clock, Spanish time. Eran las dos, hora española.
■ **on time** a la hora □ He never arrives on time. Nunca llega a la hora.
**2** el tiempo
□ I'm sorry, I haven't got time. Lo siento, no tengo tiempo. □ We waited a long time. Esperamos mucho tiempo. □ Have you lived here for a long time? ¿Hace mucho tiempo que vives aquí?
■ **from time to time** de vez en cuando
■ **in time** a tiempo □ We arrived in time for lunch. Llegamos a tiempo para el almuerzo.
■ **just in time** justo a tiempo
**3** el momento
□ This isn't a good time to ask him. Éste no es buen momento para preguntarle.
■ **for the time being** por el momento
■ **in no time** en un momento □ It was ready in no time. Estuvo listo en un momento.
**4** la vez (PL las veces)
□ this time esta vez □ How many times? ¿Cuántas veces?
■ **at times** a veces
■ **two at a time** de dos en dos
■ **in a week's time** dentro de una semana
■ **Come and see us any time.** Ven a vernos cuando quieras.
■ **to have a good time** pasarlo bien □ Did you have a good time? ¿Lo pasaste bien?
■ **two times two is four** dos por dos son cuatro
**time bomb** NOUN
la bomba de relojería
**time off** NOUN
el tiempo libre
**timer** NOUN
el reloj automático (of video, oven)
■ **an egg timer** reloj de arena
**time-share** NOUN
■ **a time-share apartment** un apartamento en multipropiedad
**timetable** NOUN
**1** el horario (for train, bus, school)
**2** el programa (schedule of events)
LANGUAGE TIP Although **programa** ends in **-a**, it is actually a masculine noun.
**time zone** NOUN
el huso horario
**tin** NOUN
**1** la lata
□ a tin of beans una lata de alubias
□ a biscuit tin una lata de galletas

**2** el estaño (metal)
**tinned** ADJECTIVE
enlatado (FEM enlatada) (food)
□ tinned products productos enlatados
■ **tinned peaches** melocotones en lata
**tin opener** NOUN
el abrelatas (PL los abrelatas)
**tinsel** NOUN
el espumillón
**tinted** ADJECTIVE
ahumado (FEM ahumada) (glasses, window)
**tiny** ADJECTIVE
minúsculo (FEM minúscula)
**tip** NOUN
▷ see also **tip** VERB
**1** la propina (money)
□ to leave a tip dejar propina
**2** el consejo (advice)
□ a useful tip un consejo práctico
**3** la punta (end)
□ It's on the tip of my tongue. Lo tengo en la punta de la lengua.
■ **a rubbish tip** un vertedero de basuras
■ **This place is a complete tip!** ¡Esto es una pocilga!
to **tip** VERB
▷ see also **tip** NOUN
dar* una propina a
□ Don't forget to tip the waiter. No te olvides de darle una propina al camarero.
**tiptoe** NOUN
■ **on tiptoe** de puntillas
**tired** ADJECTIVE
cansado (FEM cansada)
□ I'm tired. Estoy cansado.
■ **to be tired of something** estar harto de algo
**tiring** ADJECTIVE
cansado (FEM cansada)
**tissue** NOUN
el Kleenex® (PL los Kleenex)
**title** NOUN
el título (of novel, film)
**title role** NOUN
el papel principal
**to** PREPOSITION
**1** a
LANGUAGE TIP a + el changes to al.
□ to go to school ir al colegio □ to go to the doctor's ir al médico □ Let's go to Anne's house. Vamos a casa de Anne. □ to go to Portugal ir a Portugal □ I sold it to a friend. Se lo vendí a un amigo. □ the answer to the question la respuesta a la pregunta □ the train to London el tren a Londres
■ **from...to...** de...a... □ from nine o'clock to half past three de las nueve a las tres y media

**2** de

□ It's easy to do. Es fácil de hacer.

□ something to drink algo de beber □ the key to the front door la llave de la puerta principal

■ It's difficult to say. Es difícil saberlo.

■ It's easy to criticize. Criticar es muy fácil.

■ I've never been to Valencia. Nunca he estado en Valencia.

■ ten to nine las nueve menos diez

**3** hasta

□ to count to ten contar hasta diez

**4** para *(in order to)*

□ I did it to help you. Lo hice para ayudarte.

□ She's too young to go to school. Es muy pequeña para ir al colegio. □ ready to go listo para irse □ ready to eat listo para comer

**5** con

□ to be kind to somebody ser amable con alguien □ They were very kind to me. Fueron muy amables conmigo.

■ Give it to her! ¡Dáselo!

■ That's what he said to me. Eso fue lo que me dijo.

■ I've got things to do. Tengo cosas que hacer.

**toad** NOUN
el sapo

**toadstool** NOUN
la seta venenosa

**toast** NOUN
**1** el pan tostado *(bread)*
■ a piece of toast una tostada
**2** el brindis (PL los brindis) *(speech)*
■ to drink a toast to somebody brindar por alguien

**toaster** NOUN
la tostadora

**tobacco** NOUN
el tabaco

**tobacconist's** NOUN
el estanco (la tabaquería *Latin America*)

**toboggan** NOUN
el trineo

**tobogganing** NOUN
■ to go tobogganing deslizarse en trineo

**today** ADVERB
hoy

**toddler** NOUN
el niño pequeño
la niña pequeña *(que empieza a caminar)*

**toe** NOUN
el dedo del pie (PL los dedos de los pies)
□ The dog bit my big toe. El perro me mordió el dedo gordo del pie.

**toffee** NOUN
el caramelo

**together** ADVERB
**1** juntos
□ Are they still together? ¿Todavía están juntos?
**2** a la vez *(at the same time)*
□ Don't all speak together! ¡No habléis todos a la vez!
■ together with junto con

**toilet** NOUN
**1** los servicios *(in public place)*
**2** el wáter *(in house)*

**toilet paper** NOUN
el papel higiénico

**toiletries** PL NOUN
los artículos de perfumería

**toilet roll** NOUN
el rollo de papel higiénico

**token** NOUN
■ a gift token un cheque-regalo (PL los cheques-regalo)

**told** VERB ▷ see **tell**

**tolerant** ADJECTIVE
tolerante (FEM tolerante)

**toll** NOUN
el peaje *(on bridge, motorway)*

**tomato** NOUN
el tomate
□ tomato soup sopa de tomate

**tomboy** NOUN
el marimacho

**tomorrow** ADVERB
mañana
□ tomorrow morning mañana por la mañana □ tomorrow night mañana por la noche
■ the day after tomorrow pasado mañana

**ton** NOUN
la tonelada
□ a ton of coal una tonelada de carbón
■ That old bike weighs a ton. Esa bici vieja pesa una tonelada.

**tongue** NOUN
la lengua
■ to say something tongue in cheek decir algo en plan de broma

**tonic** NOUN
la tónica
■ a gin and tonic un gin-tonic

**tonight** ADVERB
esta noche
□ Are you going out tonight? ¿Vas a salir esta noche? □ I'll sleep well tonight. Esta noche dormiré bien.

**tonsillitis** NOUN
la amigdalitis
□ She's got tonsillitis. Tiene amigdalitis.

**tonsils** PL NOUN
las amígdalas

**too** ADVERB
1 también *(as well)*
□ My sister came too. Mi hermana también vino.
2 demasiado *(excessively)*
□ The water's too hot. El agua está demasiado caliente. □ We arrived too late. Llegamos demasiado tarde.
■ **too much** demasiado (FEM demasiada)
□ too much noise demasiado ruido □ too much butter demasiada mantequilla □ At Christmas we always eat too much. En Navidades siempre comemos demasiado.
□ £50? — That's too much. ¿50 libras? — Eso es demasiado.
■ **too many** demasiados (FEM demasiadas)
□ too many problems demasiados problemas □ too many chairs demasiadas sillas
■ **Too bad!** *(what a pity)* ¡Qué pena!

**took** VERB ▷ see **take**

**tool** NOUN
la herramienta
■ **a tool box** una caja de herramientas

**tooth** NOUN
el diente

**toothache** NOUN
el dolor de muelas
□ These pills are good for toothache. Estas pastillas son buenas para el dolor de muelas.
■ **I've got toothache.** Me duele una muela.

**toothbrush** NOUN
el cepillo de dientes

**toothpaste** NOUN
el dentífrico

**top** NOUN
▷ see also **top** ADJECTIVE
1 la parte de arriba
□ at the top of the page en la parte de arriba de la página
2 la cima *(of mountain)*
3 la tapa *(of box, jar)*
4 el tapón (PL los tapones) *(of bottle)*
■ **a bikini top** la parte de arriba del bikini
■ **the top of the table** el tablero de la mesa
■ **on top of the cupboard** encima del armario
■ **There's a surcharge on top of that.** Hay un recargo, además.
■ **from top to bottom** de arriba abajo
□ I searched the house from top to bottom. Busqué en la casa de arriba abajo.

**top** ADJECTIVE
▷ see also **top** NOUN
1 de arriba *(shelf)*
□ It's on the top shelf. Está en la estantería de arriba.

■ **the top layer of skin** la capa superior de la piel
■ **the top floor** el último piso
2 eminente (FEM eminente)
□ a top surgeon un eminente cirujano
■ **a top model** una top model
■ **a top hotel** un hotel de primera
■ **He always gets top marks in French.** Siempre saca excelentes notas en francés.
■ **at top speed** a máxima velocidad

**topic** NOUN
el tema
**LANGUAGE TIP** Although **tema** ends in -a, it is actually a masculine noun.
□ The essay can be on any topic. La redacción puede ser sobre cualquier tema.

**topical** ADJECTIVE
de actualidad
□ a topical issue un tema de actualidad

**topless** ADJECTIVE
topless (FEM + PL topless)
■ **to go topless** ir en topless

**top-secret** ADJECTIVE
de alto secreto
□ top-secret documents documentos de alto secreto

**torch** NOUN
la linterna *(electric)*

**tore, torn** VERB ▷ see **tear**

**tortoise** NOUN
la tortuga

**torture** NOUN
▷ see also **torture** VERB
la tortura
□ It was pure torture. Fué una tortura.

to **torture** VERB
▷ see also **torture** NOUN
torturar
□ Stop torturing that poor animal! ¡Deja de torturar al pobre animal!

**Tory** ADJECTIVE
▷ see also **Tory** NOUN
conservador (FEM conservadora)
□ the Tory government el gobierno conservador

**Tory** NOUN
▷ see also **Tory** ADJECTIVE
el conservador
la conservadora
□ the Tories los conservadores

to **toss** VERB
■ **to toss pancakes** dar la vuelta a las crepes en el aire
■ **Shall we toss for it?** ¿Nos lo jugamos a cara o cruz?

**total** ADJECTIVE
▷ see also **total** NOUN
total (FEM total)

□ The total cost was very high. El coste total fue muy alto.

■ **the total amount** el total

**total** NOUN

▷ *see also* **total** ADJECTIVE

el total

■ **the grand total** la suma total

**totally** ADVERB

totalmente

**touch** NOUN

▷ *see also* **touch** VERB

■ **to get in touch with somebody** ponerse en contacto con alguien

■ **to keep in touch with somebody** mantenerse en contacto con alguien

■ **Keep in touch!** **1** *(write)* iEscribe de vez en cuando! **2** *(phone)* iLlama de vez en cuando!

■ **to lose touch** perder el contacto

■ **to lose touch with somebody** perder el contacto con alguien

to **touch** VERB

▷ *see also* **touch** NOUN

tocar*

□ Don't touch that! iNo toques eso!

**touchdown** NOUN

el aterrizaje *(of plane)*

**touched** ADJECTIVE

emocionado (FEM emocionada)

□ I was really touched. Estaba muy emocionada.

**touching** ADJECTIVE

conmovedor (FEM conmovedora)

**touchline** NOUN

la línea de banda

**touchy** ADJECTIVE

susceptible (FEM susceptible)

□ She's a bit touchy today. Hoy está un poco susceptible.

**tough** ADJECTIVE

**1** difícil (FEM difícil)

□ It was tough, but I managed okay. Fue difícil, pero me las arreglé.

■ **It's a tough job.** Es un trabajo duro.

**2** duro (FEM dura)

□ The meat is tough. La carne está dura.

**3** resistente (FEM resistente)

□ tough leather gloves guantes de cuero resistentes

■ **He thinks he's a tough guy.** Le gusta hacerse el duro.

■ **Tough luck!** iMala suerte!

**tour** NOUN

▷ *see also* **tour** VERB

**1** el recorrido turístico

□ We went on a tour of the city. Hicimos un recorrido turístico por la ciudad.

■ **a package tour** un viaje organizado

■ **a bus tour** un viaje en autobús

**2** la visita *(of building, exhibition)*

**3** la gira

■ **to go on tour** ir de gira

to **tour** VERB

▷ *see also* **tour** NOUN

■ **Robbie Williams is touring Europe.** Robbie Williams está haciendo una gira por Europa.

**tour guide** NOUN

el guía turístico

la guía turística

**tourism** NOUN

el turismo

**tourist** NOUN

el/la turista

■ **tourist information office** la oficina de información y turismo

**tournament** NOUN

el torneo

**tour operator** NOUN

el operador turístico (PL los operadores turísticos)

**towards** PREPOSITION

hacia

□ He came towards me. Vino hacia mí.

□ my feelings towards him mis sentimientos hacia él

**towel** NOUN

la toalla

**tower** NOUN

la torre

**town** NOUN

la ciudad

□ a town plan un plano de la ciudad

□ the town centre el centro de la ciudad

**tow truck** NOUN (US)

la grúa

**toy** NOUN

el juguete

■ **a toy shop** una juguetería

■ **a toy car** un coche de juguete

**trace** NOUN

▷ *see also* **trace** VERB

el rastro

□ There was no trace of the robbers. No había rastro de los ladrones.

to **trace** VERB

▷ *see also* **trace** NOUN

**1** trazar* *(draw)*

**2** encontrar* *(locate)*

**tracing paper** NOUN

el papel de calco

**track** NOUN

**1** el camino *(dirt road)*

□ a mountain track un camino de montaña

**2** la vía *(railway line)*

□ A woman fell onto the tracks. Una mujer

se cayó a la vía.

**3** la pista *(in sport)*

□ two laps of the track  dos vueltas a la pista

**4** la canción *(PL las canciones) (song)*

□ This is my favourite track.  Ésta es mi canción preferida.

**5** la huella *(trail)*

□ They followed the tracks for miles. Siguieron las huellas durante millas.

to **track down** VERB
encontrar*

□ The police never tracked down the killer. La policía nunca encontró al asesino.

**tracksuit** NOUN
el chándal *(PL los chándals)*

**tractor** NOUN
el tractor

**trade** NOUN
el oficio

□ to learn a trade  aprender un oficio

**trade union** NOUN
el sindicato

**trade unionist** NOUN
el/la sindicalista

**tradition** NOUN
la tradición *(PL las tradiciones)*

**traditional** ADJECTIVE
tradicional *(FEM tradicional)*

**traffic** NOUN
el tráfico

□ There was a lot of traffic.  Había mucho tráfico.

**traffic circle** NOUN *(US)*
la rotonda

**traffic jam** NOUN
el atasco

**traffic lights** PL NOUN
el semáforo

**traffic warden** NOUN
el/la guardia de tráfico

□ I'm a traffic warden.  Soy guardia de tráfico.

**tragedy** NOUN
la tragedia

**tragic** ADJECTIVE
trágico *(FEM trágica)*

**trailer** NOUN
**1** el remolque *(for luggage, boat)*
**2** el tráiler *(PL los tráilers) (of film)*

**train** NOUN
▷ *see also* **train** VERB
el tren

□ a train set  un tren eléctrico

to **train** VERB
▷ *see also* **train** NOUN
entrenar

□ to train for a race  entrenar para una carrera

■ to train as a teacher  estudiar magisterio

■ to train an animal to do something enseñar a un animal a hacer algo

**trained** ADJECTIVE
cualificado *(FEM cualificada) (calificado Latin America)*

□ highly trained workers  los trabajadores altamente cualificados

■ She's a trained nurse.  Es enfermera diplomada.

**trainee** NOUN
el aprendiz *(PL los aprendices)*
la aprendiza *(apprentice)*

□ He's a trainee plumber.  Es aprendiz de fontanero.

■ She's a trainee teacher.  Es profesora de prácticas.

**trainer** NOUN
**1** el entrenador
la entrenadora *(sports)*
**2** el amaestrador
la amaestradora *(of animals)*

**trainers** PL NOUN
las zapatillas de deporte

**training** NOUN
**1** la formación

□ a training course  un curso de formación
**2** el entrenamiento *(in sport)*

■ He strained a muscle in training. Se hizo un esguince entrenando.

**tram** NOUN
el tranvía

    **LANGUAGE TIP** Although tranvía ends in -a, it is actually a masculine noun.

**tramp** NOUN
el vagabundo
la vagabunda

**trampoline** NOUN
la cama elástica

**tranquillizer** NOUN
el sedante

□ She's on tranquillizers.  Está tomando sedantes.

**transfer** NOUN
**1** la transferencia

□ a bank transfer  una transferencia bancaria
**2** la calcomanía *(sticker)*

**transfusion** NOUN
la transfusión *(PL las transfusiones)*

**transistor** NOUN
el transistor

to **translate** VERB
traducir*

□ to translate something into English traducir algo al inglés

**translation** NOUN
la traducción *(PL las traducciones)*

**translator** NOUN
el traductor
la traductora
□ Anita's a translator. Anita es traductora.

**transparent** ADJECTIVE
transparente (FEM transparente)

**transplant** NOUN
el trasplante
□ a heart transplant un trasplante de corazón

**transport** NOUN
▷ see also **transport** VERB
el transporte
□ public transport el transporte público

to **transport** VERB
▷ see also **transport** NOUN
transportar

**trap** NOUN
la trampa

**trash** NOUN (US)
la basura
■ the trash can el cubo de la basura

**trashy** ADJECTIVE
malísimo (FEM malísima)
□ a trashy film una película malísima

**traumatic** ADJECTIVE
traumático (FEM traumática)
□ It was a traumatic experience. Fue una experiencia traumática.

**travel** NOUN
▷ see also **travel** VERB
■ Air travel is relatively cheap. Viajar en avión es relativamente barato.

to **travel** VERB
▷ see also **travel** NOUN
viajar
□ I prefer to travel by train. Prefiero viajar en tren.
■ I'd like to travel round the world. Me gustaría dar la vuelta al mundo.
■ We travelled over 800 kilometres. Hicimos más de 800 kilómetros.
■ News travels fast! ¡Las noticias vuelan!

**travel agency** NOUN
la agencia de viajes

**travel agent** NOUN
■ She's a travel agent. Es empleada de una agencia de viajes.

**traveller** (US **traveler**) NOUN
el viajero
la viajera

**traveller's cheque** (US **traveler's check**) NOUN
el cheque de viaje (PL los cheques de viaje)

**travelling** (US **traveling**) NOUN
■ I love travelling. Me encanta viajar.

**travel sickness** NOUN
el mareo

**tray** NOUN
la bandeja

to **tread** VERB
pisar
■ to tread on something pisar algo
□ He trod on her foot. Le pisó el pie.

**treasure** NOUN
el tesoro

**treat** NOUN
▷ see also **treat** VERB
■ As a birthday treat, I'll take you out to dinner. Como es tu cumpleaños, te invito a cenar.
■ She bought a special treat for the children. Les compró algo especial a los niños.
■ I'm going to give myself a treat. Me voy a dar un gusto.

to **treat** VERB
▷ see also **treat** NOUN
tratar
□ The hostages were well treated. Los rehenes fueron tratados bien.
■ She was treated for a minor head wound. La atendieron de una leve herida en la cabeza.
■ to treat somebody to something invitar a alguien a algo □ I'll treat you! ¡Te invito yo!

**treatment** NOUN
1 el tratamiento (medical)
□ an effective treatment for eczema un tratamiento efectivo contra el eccema
2 el trato (of person)
□ We don't want any special treatment. No queremos ningún trato especial.

to **treble** VERB
triplicarse*
□ The cost of living has trebled. El coste de la vida se ha triplicado.

**tree** NOUN
el árbol

to **tremble** VERB
temblar*

**trend** NOUN
1 la tendencia
□ There's a trend towards part-time employment. Existe una tendencia hacia el empleo a tiempo parcial.
2 la moda (fashion)
□ the latest trend la última moda

**trendy** ADJECTIVE
moderno (FEM moderna)

**trial** NOUN
el juicio (in law)

**triangle** NOUN
el triángulo

**tribe** NOUN
la tribu

**trick** NOUN
▷ *see also* **trick** VERB
1 la broma
□ to play a trick on somebody gastar una broma a alguien
2 el truco
□ It's not easy: there's a trick to it. No es fácil: tiene un truco.

to **trick** VERB
▷ *see also* **trick** NOUN
■ to trick somebody engañar a alguien

**tricky** ADJECTIVE
peliagudo (FEM peliaguda) *(problem)*

**tricycle** NOUN
el triciclo

**trifle** NOUN
el bizcocho borracho

to **trim** VERB
▷ *see also* **trim** NOUN
recortar

**trim** NOUN
▷ *see also* **trim** VERB
■ to have a trim cortarse las puntas

**trip** NOUN
▷ *see also* **trip** VERB
el viaje
□ to go on a trip ir de viaje □ Have a good trip! ¡Buen viaje!
■ a day trip una excursión de un día

to **trip** VERB
▷ *see also* **trip** NOUN
tropezarse* *(stumble)*
□ He tripped on the stairs. Se tropezó en las escaleras.

**triple** ADJECTIVE
triple (FEM triple)

**triplets** PL NOUN
los trillizos (FEM las trillizas)

**trivial** ADJECTIVE
insignificante (FEM insignificante)

**trod, trodden** VERB ▷ *see* tread

**trolley** NOUN
el carrito

**trombone** NOUN
el trombón (PL los trombones)

**troops** PL NOUN
las tropas

**trophy** NOUN
el trofeo

**tropical** ADJECTIVE
tropical (FEM tropical)

to **trot** VERB
trotar

**trouble** NOUN
el problema
> **LANGUAGE TIP** Although **problema** ends in **-a**, it is actually a masculine noun.

□ The trouble is, it's too expensive. El problema es que es demasiado caro.
■ What's the trouble? ¿Qué pasa?
■ to be in trouble tener problemas
■ stomach trouble problemas de estómago
■ to take a lot of trouble over something poner mucho cuidado en algo
■ Don't worry, it's no trouble. No te preocupes, no importa.

**troublemaker** NOUN
el alborotador
la alborotadora

**trousers** PL NOUN
los pantalones
□ a pair of trousers unos pantalones

**trout** NOUN
la trucha

**truant** NOUN
■ to play truant hacer novillos

**truck** NOUN
el camión (PL los camiones)

**trucker** NOUN
el camionero
la camionera

**true** ADJECTIVE
verdadero (FEM verdadera) *(love, courage)*
■ It's true. Es verdad.
■ to come true hacerse realidad □ I hope my dream will come true. Espero que mi sueño se haga realidad.

**trumpet** NOUN
la trompeta

**trunk** NOUN
1 el tronco *(of tree)*
2 la trompa *(of elephant)*
3 el baúl *(luggage)*
4 el maletero (US: *of car)*

**trunks** PL NOUN
■ swimming trunks el traje de baño

**trust** NOUN
▷ *see also* **trust** VERB
la confianza
□ to have trust in somebody tener confianza en alguien

to **trust** VERB
▷ *see also* **trust** NOUN
■ Don't you trust me? ¿No tienes confianza en mí?
■ Trust me! ¡Confía en mí!
■ I don't trust him. No me fío de él.

**trusting** ADJECTIVE
confiado (FEM confiada)

**truth** NOUN
la verdad

**truthful** ADJECTIVE
1 sincero (FEM sincera) *(person)*
□ She's a very truthful person. Es una

persona muy sincera.
**2** verídico (FEM verídica) *(account)*

**try** NOUN

▷ *see also* **try** VERB
el intento

□ his third try su tercer intento
■ **to give something a try** intentar algo
■ **It's worth a try.** Vale la pena intentarlo.
■ **Have a try!** ¡Inténtalo!

to **try** VERB

▷ *see also* **try** NOUN

**1** intentar
□ to try to do something intentar hacer algo
■ **to try again** volver a intentar

**2** probar*
□ Would you like to try some? ¿Quieres probar un poco?

to **try on** VERB
probarse* *(clothes)*

to **try out** VERB
probar* *(product, machine)*

**T-shirt** NOUN
la camiseta

**tube** NOUN
el tubo
■ **the Tube** *(underground)* el Metro

**tuberculosis** NOUN
la tuberculosis
□ He's got tuberculosis. Tiene tuberculosis.

**Tuesday** NOUN
el martes (PL los martes)
□ I saw her on Tuesday. La vi el martes.
□ every Tuesday todos los martes □ last Tuesday el martes pasado □ next Tuesday el martes que viene □ on Tuesdays los martes

**tug-of-war** NOUN
el juego de la cuerda

**tuition** NOUN
las clases
□ private tuition clases particulares

**tulip** NOUN
el tulipán (PL los tulipanes)

**tumble dryer** NOUN
la secadora

**tummy** NOUN
la tripa *(informal)*
■ **He has tummy ache.** Le duele la tripa.

**tuna** NOUN
el atún (PL los atunes)

**tune** NOUN
la melodía *(melody)*
■ **to play in tune** tocar bien
■ **to sing out of tune** desafinar

**Tunisia** NOUN
Túnez *masc*

**tunnel** NOUN
el túnel

□ the Channel Tunnel el túnel del Canal de la Mancha

**Turk** NOUN
el turco
la turca
□ the Turks los turcos

**turkey** NOUN
el pavo

**Turkey** NOUN
Turquía *fem*

**Turkish** ADJECTIVE

▷ *see also* **Turkish** NOUN
turco (FEM turca)

**Turkish** NOUN

▷ *see also* **Turkish** ADJECTIVE
el turco *(language)*

**turn** NOUN

▷ *see also* **turn** VERB
la curva *(bend in road)*
■ **'no left turn'** 'prohibido girar a la izquierda'
■ **to take turns** turnarse
■ **It's my turn!** ¡Me toca a mí!

to **turn** VERB

▷ *see also* **turn** NOUN

**1** girar
□ Turn right at the lights. Gira a la derecha al llegar al semáforo.

**2** ponerse*
□ When he's drunk he turns nasty. Cuando se emborracha se pone desagradable.
■ **The weather turned cold.** Empezó a hacer frío.
■ **to turn into something** convertirse en algo □ The holiday turned into a nightmare. Las vacaciones se convirtieron en una pesadilla.

to **turn back** VERB
volver* hacia atrás
□ We turned back. Volvimos hacia atrás.

to **turn down** VERB

**1** rechazar*
□ He turned down the offer. Rechazó la oferta.

**2** bajar
□ Shall I turn the heating down? ¿Bajo la calefacción?

to **turn off** VERB

**1** apagar* *(light, radio)*

**2** cerrar* *(tap)*

**3** parar *(engine)*

to **turn on** VERB

**1** encender* *(light, radio)*

**2** abrir* *(tap)*

**3** poner* en marcha *(engine)*

to **turn out** VERB
resultar
□ It turned out to be a mistake. Resultó ser

un error. ◻ It turned out that she was right. Resultó que ella tenía razón.

to **turn round** VERB
1 dar* la vuelta (car)
2 darse* la vuelta (person)

to **turn up** VERB
1 aparecer*
◻ She never turned up. No apareció.
◻ The lost dog turned up in the next village. El perro extraviado apareció en el pueblo vecino.
2 subir
◻ Could you turn up the radio? ¿Puedes subir la radio?

**turning** NOUN
■ We took the wrong turning. 1 (in the country) Nos equivocamos de carretera.
2 (in the city) Nos equivocamos de bocacalle.

**turnip** NOUN
el nabo

**turquoise** ADJECTIVE
turquesa (FEM + PL turquesa)

**turtle** NOUN
la tortuga de mar

**tutor** NOUN
el profesor particular
la profesora particular (private teacher)

**tuxedo** NOUN (US)
el esmoquin (PL los esmóquines)

**TV** NOUN
la tele

**tweezers** PL NOUN
las pinzas
◻ a pair of tweezers unas pinzas

**twelfth** ADJECTIVE
duodécimo (FEM duodécima)
◻ the twelfth floor el duodécimo piso
■ the twelfth of August el doce de agosto

**twelve** NUMERAL
doce
◻ She's twelve. Tiene doce años.
■ twelve o'clock las doce

**twentieth** ADJECTIVE
vigésimo (FEM vigésima)
■ the twentieth floor la planta veinte
■ the twentieth of May el veinte de mayo

**twenty** NUMERAL
veinte
◻ He's twenty. Tiene veinte años.

**twice** ADVERB
dos veces

◻ He had to repeat it twice. Tuvo que repetirlo dos veces.
■ twice as much el doble ◻ He gets twice as much pocket money as me. Le dan el doble de paga que a mí.

**twin** NOUN
el mellizo
la melliza
◻ my twin brother mi hermano mellizo
◻ her twin sister su hermana melliza
■ identical twins gemelos
■ a twin room una habitación con dos camas

**twinned** ADJECTIVE
hermanado (FEM hermanada)
◻ Nottingham is twinned with Minsk. Nottingham está hermanada con Minsk.

to **twist** VERB
1 torcer*
■ He's twisted his ankle. Se ha torcido el tobillo.
2 tergiversar*
◻ You're twisting my words. Estás tergiversando lo que he dicho.

**twit** NOUN
el/la imbécil (informal)

**two** NUMERAL
dos
◻ She's two. Tiene dos años.
■ The two of them can sing. Los dos saben cantar.

**type** NOUN
▷ see also **type** VERB
el tipo
◻ What type of camera have you got? ¿Qué tipo de cámara tienes?

to **type** VERB
▷ see also **type** NOUN
escribir* a máquina
◻ Can you type? ¿Sabes escribir a máquina?
◻ to type a letter escribir una carta a máquina

**typewriter** NOUN
la máquina de escribir

**typical** ADJECTIVE
típico (FEM típica)
◻ That's just typical! ¡Típico!

**tyre** (US **tire**) NOUN
el neumático
■ tyre pressure la presión de los neumáticos

# Uu

**UFO** ABBREVIATION (= *Unidentified Flying Object*)
el OVNI (= *el Objeto Volador No Identificado*)

**ugh** EXCLAMATION
¡puf!

**ugly** ADJECTIVE
feo (FEM fea)

**UK** ABBREVIATION (= *United Kingdom*)
el RU (= *el Reino Unido*)

**ulcer** NOUN
la úlcera
■ **a mouth ulcer** una llaga en la boca

**Ulster** NOUN
el Ulster

**ultimate** ADJECTIVE
máximo (FEM máxima)
□ the ultimate challenge el máximo desafío
■ **the ultimate in luxury** el no va más del lujo

**ultimately** ADVERB
a fin de cuentas
□ Ultimately, it's your decision. A fin de cuentas, es tu decisión.

**umbrella** NOUN
el paraguas (PL los paraguas)

**umpire** NOUN
el árbitro
la árbitra

**UN** ABBREVIATION (= *United Nations*)
la ONU (= *la Organización de las Naciones Unidas*)

**unable** ADJECTIVE
■ **to be unable to do something** no poder hacer algo □ He was unable to come. No ha podido venir.

**unacceptable** ADJECTIVE
inaceptable (FEM inaceptable)

**unanimous** ADJECTIVE
unánime (FEM unánime)

**unattended** ADJECTIVE
■ **Please do not leave your luggage unattended.** Por favor, no abandonen su equipaje.

**unavoidable** ADJECTIVE
inevitable (FEM inevitable)

**unaware** ADJECTIVE

■ **I was unaware of the regulations.** Ignoraba el reglamento.
■ **She was unaware that she was being filmed.** No se había dado cuenta de que la estaban filmando.

**unbearable** ADJECTIVE
insoportable (FEM insoportable)

**unbeatable** ADJECTIVE
inmejorable (FEM inmejorable) *(quality, price)*

**unbelievable** ADJECTIVE
increíble (FEM increíble)

**unborn** ADJECTIVE
■ **the unborn child** el feto

**unbreakable** ADJECTIVE
irrompible (FEM irrompible)

**uncanny** ADJECTIVE
extraño (FEM extraña)
□ That's uncanny! ¡Es extraño!
■ **an uncanny resemblance** un asombroso parecido

**uncertain** ADJECTIVE
incierto (FEM incierta)
□ The future is uncertain. El futuro es incierto.
■ **to be uncertain about something** no estar seguro de algo
■ **She was uncertain how to begin.** No sabía muy bien cómo empezar.

**uncivilized** ADJECTIVE
poco civilizado (FEM poco civilizada)

**uncle** NOUN
el tío
■ **my uncle and aunt** mis tíos

**uncomfortable** ADJECTIVE
incómodo (FEM incómoda)

**unconscious** ADJECTIVE
inconsciente (FEM inconsciente)

**unconventional** ADJECTIVE
poco convencional (FEM poco convencional)

**under** PREPOSITION

> LANGUAGE TIP When something is located under something, use **debajo de**. When there is movement involved, use **por debajo de**.

1 debajo de
□ The cat's under the table. El gato está debajo de la mesa. □ The tunnel goes under

the Channel. El túnel pasa por debajo del Canal.

■ **under there** ahí debajo □ What's under there? ¿Qué hay ahí debajo?

**2** menos de

□ **under 20 people** menos de 20 personas
■ **children under 10** niños menores de 10 años

**underage** ADJECTIVE
■ **He's underage.** Es menor de edad.

**undercover** ADJECTIVE, ADVERB
secreto (FEM secreta)

□ **an undercover agent** un agente secreto
□ **She was working undercover for the FBI.** Trabajaba como agente secreto para el FBI.

to **underestimate** VERB
subestimar

□ **You shouldn't underestimate her.** No la subestimes.

to **undergo** VERB
someterse a (operation)

**underground** ADVERB
▷ see also **underground** ADJECTIVE, NOUN
bajo tierra

□ **Moles live underground.** Los topos viven bajo tierra.

**underground** NOUN
▷ see also **underground** ADJECTIVE, ADVERB
el metro

□ **Is there an underground in Barcelona?** ¿Hay metro en Barcelona?

to **underline** VERB
subrayar

**underneath** PREPOSITION, ADVERB

⌐ **LANGUAGE TIP** When something is located underneath something, use **debajo de.** When there is movement involved, use **por debajo de.**

**1** debajo de

□ **underneath the carpet** debajo de la moqueta □ **I got out of the car and looked underneath.** Bajé del coche y miré debajo.

**2** por debajo de

□ **I walked underneath a ladder.** Pasé por debajo de una escalera.

**underpaid** ADJECTIVE
mal pagado (FEM mal pagada)

□ **Teachers are underpaid.** Los profesores están mal pagados.

**underpants** PL NOUN
los calzoncillos

□ **a pair of underpants** unos calzoncillos

**underpass** NOUN
el paso subterráneo

**undershirt** NOUN (US)
la camiseta

**underskirt** NOUN
las enaguas

to **understand** VERB
entender*

□ **Do you understand?** ¿Entiendes? □ **I don't understand the question.** No entiendo la pregunta.
■ **Is that understood?** ¿Está claro?

**understanding** ADJECTIVE
comprensivo (FEM comprensiva)

□ **She's very understanding.** Es muy comprensiva.

**understood** VERB ▷ see **understand**

**undertaker** NOUN
el empleado de una funeraria
la empleada de una funeraria

■ **the undertaker's** la funeraria

**underwater** ADJECTIVE, ADVERB
**1** subacuático (FEM subacuática)

□ **underwater photography** fotografía subacuática

**2** bajo el agua

□ **This sequence was filmed underwater.** Esta secuencia se filmó bajo el agua.

**underwear** NOUN
la ropa interior

**underwent** VERB ▷ see **undergo**

to **undo** VERB
**1** desabrochar (button, blouse)
**2** desatar (knot, parcel, shoe laces)
**3** abrir* (zipper)

to **undress** VERB
desnudarse (get undressed)

□ **The doctor told me to undress.** El médico me dijo que me desnudase.

**uneconomic** ADJECTIVE
■ **an uneconomic factory** una fábrica poco rentable
■ **It's uneconomic to put on courses for so few students.** No es rentable organizar cursos para tan pocos alumnos.

**unemployed** ADJECTIVE
parado (FEM parada) (desempleado Latin America)

■ **He's been unemployed for a year.** Lleva parado un año.
■ **the unemployed** los parados (los desempleados Latin America)

**unemployment** NOUN
el desempleo

**unexpected** ADJECTIVE
inesperado (FEM inesperada)

□ **an unexpected visitor** una visita inesperada

**unexpectedly** ADVERB
de improviso

**unfair** ADJECTIVE
injusto (FEM injusta)

□ **This law is unfair to women.** Esta ley es injusta para las mujeres.

**English-Spa**

**u**

283

**unfamiliar** ADJECTIVE
desconocido (FEM desconocida)
□ I heard an unfamiliar voice. Oí una voz desconocida.

**unfashionable** ADJECTIVE
pasado de moda (FEM pasado de moda)

**unfit** ADJECTIVE
■ I'm unfit at the moment. En este momento no estoy en forma.

to **unfold** VERB
desplegar*
□ She unfolded the map. Desplegó el mapa.

**unforgettable** ADJECTIVE
inolvidable (FEM inolvidable)

**unfortunately** ADVERB
desafortunadamente

**unfriendly** ADJECTIVE
antipático (FEM antipática)
□ The waiters are a bit unfriendly. Los camareros son un poco antipáticos.

**ungrateful** ADJECTIVE
desagradecido (FEM desagradecida)

**unhappy** ADJECTIVE
infeliz (FEM infeliz, PL infelices)
□ He was very unhappy as a child. De niño fue muy infeliz.
■ to look unhappy parecer triste

**unhealthy** ADJECTIVE
1 malo para la salud (FEM mala para la salud) (food)
2 con mala salud (ill)
3 malsano (FEM malsana) (atmosphere)

**uniform** NOUN
el uniforme
■ school uniform el uniforme de colegio

**uninhabited** ADJECTIVE
1 deshabitado (FEM deshabitada) (house)
2 despoblado (FEM despoblada) (island)

**union** NOUN
el sindicato (trade union)

**Union Jack** NOUN
la bandera del Reino Unido

**unique** ADJECTIVE
único (FEM única)

**unit** NOUN
la unidad
□ a unit of measurement una unidad de medida
■ a kitchen unit un módulo de cocina

**United Kingdom** NOUN
el Reino Unido

**United Nations** NOUN
las Naciones Unidas

**United States** NOUN
los Estados Unidos

**universe** NOUN
el universo

**university** NOUN

la universidad
□ She's at university. Está en la universidad.
□ Do you want to go to university? ¿Quieres ir a la universidad? □ Lancaster University la Universidad de Lancaster

**unleaded petrol** NOUN
la gasolina sin plomo

**unless** CONJUNCTION
a no ser que

LANGUAGE TIP **a no ser que** has to be followed by a verb in the subjunctive.

□ I won't come unless you phone me. No vendré a no ser que me llames.
■ Unless I am mistaken, we're lost. Si no me equivoco, estamos perdidos.

**unlike** PREPOSITION
a diferencia de
□ Unlike him, I really enjoy flying. A diferencia de él, a mí me encanta viajar en avión.

**unlikely** ADJECTIVE
poco probable (FEM poco probable)
□ That's possible, but unlikely. Es posible pero poco probable.

LANGUAGE TIP **es poco probable que** has to be followed by a verb in the subjunctive.

□ He's unlikely to come. Es poco probable que venga.

**unlisted** ADJECTIVE (US)
■ an unlisted number un número que no figura en la guía telefónica

to **unload** VERB
descargar*
□ We unloaded the furniture. Descargamos los muebles.

to **unlock** VERB
abrir*
□ He unlocked the door of the car. Abrió la puerta del coche.

**unlucky** ADJECTIVE
■ to be unlucky 1 (be unfortunate) tener mala suerte □ Did you win? — No, I was unlucky. ¿Ganaste? — No, tuve mala suerte.
2 (bring bad luck) traer mala suerte □ They say thirteen is an unlucky number. Dicen que el número trece trae mala suerte.

**unmarried** ADJECTIVE
soltero (FEM soltera)
□ an unmarried mother una madre soltera
■ an unmarried couple una pareja no casada

**unnatural** ADJECTIVE
poco natural (FEM poco natural)

**unnecessary** ADJECTIVE
innecesario (FEM innecesaria)

**unofficial** ADJECTIVE
no oficial (FEM no oficial)

u

to **unpack** VERB
deshacer*
□ I unpacked my suitcase. Deshice la
maleta. □ I took my case to my room to
unpack. Llevé mi maleta a mi habitación
para deshacerla.
■ **I haven't unpacked my clothes yet.**
Todavía no he sacado la ropa de la maleta.

**unpleasant** ADJECTIVE
desagradable (FEM desagradable)

to **unplug** VERB
desenchufar

**unpopular** ADJECTIVE
impopular (FEM impopulara)
□ It was an unpopular decision. Fue una
decisión impopular.
■ **She's an unpopular child.** Tiene muy
pocos amigos.

**unpredictable** ADJECTIVE
imprevisible (FEM imprevisible)

**unreal** ADJECTIVE
increíble (FEM increíble)
□ It was unreal! ¡Fue increíble!

**unrealistic** ADJECTIVE
poco realista (FEM poco realista)

**unreasonable** ADJECTIVE
poco razonable (FEM poco razonable)
□ I think her attitude is unreasonable. Creo
que su actitud es poco razonable.

**unreliable** ADJECTIVE
poco fiable (FEM poco fiable)
□ The car was slow and unreliable. El coche
era lento y poco fiable.
■ **He's completely unreliable.** Es muy
informal.

to **unroll** VERB
desenrollar

**unsatisfactory** ADJECTIVE
insatisfactorio (FEM insatisfactoria)

to **unscrew** VERB
1 destornillar (screw)
2 desenroscar* (lid)

**unshaven** ADJECTIVE
sin afeitar

**unskilled** ADJECTIVE
■ **an unskilled worker** un trabajador no
cualificado (un trabajador no calificado
Latin America)

**unstable** ADJECTIVE
inestable (FEM inestable)

**unsteady** ADJECTIVE
1 inestable (FEM inestable) (chair)
2 vacilante (FEM vacilante) (walk, voice)
■ **He was unsteady on his feet.** Caminaba
con paso vacilante.

**unsuccessful** ADJECTIVE
fallido (FEM fallida) (attempt)
■ **to be unsuccessful in doing something**

no conseguir hacer algo
■ **an unsuccessful artist** un artista sin
éxito

**unsuitable** ADJECTIVE
inapropiado (FEM inapropiada) (clothes,
equipment)

**untidy** ADJECTIVE
1 desordenado (FEM desordenada)
(disorganized)
□ Your bedroom is really untidy. Tu cuarto
está muy desordenado.
2 descuidado (FEM descuidada) (writing)
■ **She always looks so untidy.** Siempre va
tan desaliñada.

to **untie** VERB
1 deshacer* (knot, parcel)
2 desatar (shoelace, animal)

**until** PREPOSITION, CONJUNCTION
1 hasta
□ I waited until 10 o'clock. Esperé hasta las
10. □ It won't be ready until next week. No
estará listo hasta la semana que viene.
■ **until now** hasta ahora □ It's never been a
problem until now. Hasta ahora nunca ha
sido un problema.
■ **until then** hasta entonces □ Until then
I'd never been to Italy. Hasta entonces no
había estado nunca en Italia.
2 hasta que
□ We stayed there until the doctor came.
Nos quedamos allí hasta que vino el médico.

> LANGUAGE TIP **hasta que** has to be
followed by a verb in the subjunctive
when referring to a future event.

□ Don't go until I arrive. No te vayas hasta
que llegue yo. □ Wait until I come back.
Espera hasta que yo vuelva.

**unusual** ADJECTIVE
1 poco común (FEM poco común)
□ an unusual shape una forma poco común
2 raro (FEM rara)

> LANGUAGE TIP **es raro que** has to be
followed by a verb in the subjunctive.

□ It's unusual to get snow at this time of
year. Es raro que nieve en esta época del
año.

**unwilling** ADJECTIVE
■ **He was unwilling to help me.** No estaba
dispuesto a ayudarme.

to **unwind** VERB
relajarse (relax)

**unwise** ADJECTIVE
imprudente (FEM imprudente)
□ That was unwise of you. Lo que hiciste fue
imprudente.

**unwound** VERB ▷ see unwind

to **unwrap** VERB
abrir*

u

□ After the meal we unwrapped the presents. Después de comer abrimos los regalos.

**up** PREPOSITION, ADVERB

> LANGUAGE TIP For other expressions with 'up', see the verbs 'come', 'put', 'turn' etc.

arriba

□ up on the hill arriba de la colina □ up here aquí arriba □ up there allí arriba
■ **up north** en el norte
■ **They live up the road.** Viven en esta calle, un poco más allá.
■ **to be up** estar levantado □ We were up at six. A las seis estábamos levantados. □ He's not up yet. Todavía no se ha levantado.
■ **What's up?** ¿Qué hay?
■ **What's up with her?** ¿Qué le pasa?
■ **to go up** subir □ The bus went up the hill. El autobús subió la colina.
■ **to go up to somebody** acercarse a alguien □ She came up to me. Se me acercó.
■ **up to** hasta □ to count up to 50 contar hasta 50 □ up to three hours hasta tres horas □ up to now hasta ahora
■ **It's up to you.** Depende de ti.

**upbringing** NOUN
la educación

**uphill** ADJECTIVE
■ **It was an uphill struggle.** Fue una tarea muy difícil.

**upper** ADJECTIVE
superior (FEM superior)

**upright** ADJECTIVE
■ **to stand upright** tenerse derecho

**upset** NOUN
▷ see also **upset** ADJECTIVE, VERB
■ **I had a stomach upset.** Tenía mal el estómago.

**upset** ADJECTIVE
▷ see also **upset** NOUN, VERB
disgustado (FEM disgustada)
□ She's still a bit upset. Todavía está un poco disgustada.
■ **Don't get upset.** No te enfades.
■ **I had an upset stomach.** Tenía mal el estómago.

to **upset** VERB
▷ see also **upset** NOUN, ADJECTIVE
■ **to upset somebody** disgustar a alguien
■ **Don't upset yourself.** No te enfades.

**upside down** ADVERB
al revés
□ The painting was hung upside down. El cuadro estaba colgado al revés.

**upstairs** ADVERB
arriba
□ Where's your coat? — It's upstairs.

¿Dónde está tu abrigo? — Está arriba.
■ **the people upstairs** los de arriba
■ **He went upstairs to bed.** Subió para irse a la cama.

**uptight** ADJECTIVE
tenso (FEM tensa)
□ She's very uptight today. Está muy tensa hoy.

**up-to-date** ADJECTIVE
1 moderno (FEM moderna) (car, stereo)
2 actualizado (FEM actualizada)
□ an up-to-date timetable un horario actualizado
■ **to bring somebody up-to-date on something** poner a alguien al corriente de algo
■ **to bring something up-to-date** actualizar algo

**upwards** ADVERB
hacia arriba
□ to look upwards mirar hacia arriba

**urgent** ADJECTIVE
urgente (FEM urgente)

**urine** NOUN
la orina

**US** ABBREVIATION (= United States)
los EEUU (= los Estados Unidos)

**US** PRONOUN
1 nos

> LANGUAGE TIP Use nos to translate 'us' when it is the direct object of the verb in the sentence, or when it means 'to us'.

□ They helped us. Nos ayudaron. □ Look at us! ¡Míranos! □ They gave us some brochures. Nos dieron unos folletos.
2 nosotros (FEM nosotras)

> LANGUAGE TIP Use nosotros or nosotras after prepositions, in comparisons, and with the verb 'to be'.

□ Why don't you come with us? ¿Por qué no vienes con nosotras? □ They are older than us. Son mayores que nosotros. □ It's us. Somos nosotros.

**USA** ABBREVIATION (= United States of America)
los EEUU (= los Estados Unidos)

**use** NOUN
▷ see also **use** VERB
el uso
■ **'directions for use'** 'modo de empleo'
■ **It's no use shouting, she's deaf.** Es inútil gritar, es sorda.
■ **It's no use, I can't do it.** No hay manera, no puedo hacerlo.
■ **to make use of something** usar algo

to **use** VERB
▷ see also **use** NOUN
usar

□ Can I use your phone? ¿Puedo usar tu teléfono?

■ **I used to go camping as a child.** De pequeño solía ir de acampada.

■ **I didn't use to like maths, but now I love it.** Antes no me gustaban las matemáticas, pero ahora me encantan.

■ **to be used to something** estar acostumbrado a algo □ He wasn't used to driving on the right. No estaba acostumbrado a conducir por la derecha. □ Don't worry, I'm used to it. No te preocupes, estoy acostumbrado.

■ **a used car** un coche de segunda mano

to **use up** VERB

■ **We've used up all the paint.** Hemos acabado toda la pintura.

**useful** ADJECTIVE
útil (FEM útil)

**useless** ADJECTIVE
inútil (FEM inútil)

□ a piece of useless information una información inútil

■ **You're useless!** ¡Eres un inútil!

■ **This computer is useless.** Este ordenador no sirve para nada.

■ **It's useless asking her.** No sirve de nada preguntarle.

**user** NOUN
el usuario
la usuaria

**user-friendly** ADJECTIVE
fácil de usar (FEM fácil de usar)

**usual** ADJECTIVE
habitual (FEM habitual)

■ **as usual** como de costumbre

**usually** ADVERB
normalmente

□ I usually get to school at about half past eight. Normalmente llego al colegio sobre las ocho y media.

**U-turn** NOUN
el cambio de sentido

■ **to do a U-turn** cambiar de sentido

■ **'No U-turns'** 'Prohibido cambiar de sentido'

# Vv

**vacancy** NOUN
1 la vacante *(job)*
2 la habitación libre *(in hotel)*
■ **'no vacancies'** 'completo'
**vacant** ADJECTIVE
libre (FEM libre)
□ a vacant seat un asiento libre
**vacation** NOUN (US)
las vacaciones
□ to be on vacation estar de vacaciones
□ to take a vacation tomarse unas vacaciones
to **vaccinate** VERB
vacunar
to **vacuum** VERB
pasar la aspiradora
□ to vacuum the hall pasar la aspiradora por el vestíbulo
**vacuum cleaner** NOUN
la aspiradora
**vagina** NOUN
la vagina
**vague** ADJECTIVE
1 vago (FEM vaga)
□ I've only got a vague idea what he means.
Tengo sólo una vaga idea de lo que quiere decir.
2 distraído (FEM distraída)
□ He's getting a bit vague in his old age. Se está poniendo un poco distraído en su vejez.
**vain** ADJECTIVE
vanidoso (FEM vanidosa)
□ He's so vain! ¡Es más vanidoso!
■ **in vain** en vano
**Valentine card** NOUN
la tarjeta del día de los enamorados
**Valentine's Day** NOUN
el día de los enamorados *(el 14 de febrero, día de San Valentín)*
**valid** ADJECTIVE
válido (FEM válida)
□ a valid passport un pasaporte válido
■ **This ticket is valid for three months.**
Este billete tiene una validez de tres meses.
**valley** NOUN
el valle

**valuable** ADJECTIVE
1 de valor
□ a valuable painting un cuadro de valor
2 valioso (FEM valiosa)
□ valuable help una valiosa ayuda
**valuables** PL NOUN
los objetos de valor
**value** NOUN
el valor
**van** NOUN
la furgoneta
**vandal** NOUN
el vándalo
**vandalism** NOUN
el vandalismo
to **vandalize** VERB
destrozar*
**vanilla** NOUN
la vainilla
□ a vanilla ice cream un helado de vainilla
to **vanish** VERB
desaparecer*
■ **to vanish into thin air** esfumarse
**variable** ADJECTIVE
variable (FEM variable)
**variety** NOUN
la variedad
**various** ADJECTIVE
varios (FEM variosa)
□ We visited various villages in the area.
Visitamos varias aldeas de la zona.
to **vary** VERB
variar*
**vase** NOUN
el jarrón (PL los jarrones)
**VAT** NOUN
el IVA

　　　**LANGUAGE TIP** Although **IVA** ends in
　　　**-A**, it is actually a masculine noun.

**VCR** NOUN (= *video cassette recorder*)
el vídeo *(aparato)*
**veal** NOUN
la carne de ternera
**vegan** NOUN
el vegetariano estricto
la vegetariana estricta

**vegetable** NOUN
1 la verdura *(to be cooked)*
 □ vegetable soup sopa de verduras
2 la hortaliza *(for salads)*
 □ peppers, tomatoes and other vegetables pimientos, tomates y otras hortalizas
**vegetarian** NOUN
 ▷ *see also* **vegetarian** ADJECTIVE
 el vegetariano
 la vegetariana
 □ I'm a vegetarian. Soy vegetariano.
**vegetarian** ADJECTIVE
 ▷ *see also* **vegetarian** NOUN
 ■ **vegetarian lasagne** lasaña vegetariana
**vehicle** NOUN
 vehículo
**vein** NOUN
 la vena
**velvet** NOUN
 el terciopelo
**vending machine** NOUN
 la máquina expendedora
**Venetian blind** NOUN
 la persiana
**verb** NOUN
 el verbo
**verdict** NOUN
 el veredicto
**vertical** ADJECTIVE
 vertical (FEM vertical)
**vertigo** NOUN
 el vértigo
 □ I get vertigo. Tengo vértigo.
**very** ADVERB
 ▷ *see also* **very** ADJECTIVE
 muy
 □ very tall muy alto
 ■ **It's very cold.** Hace mucho frío.
 ■ **not very interesting** no demasiado interesante
 ■ **very much** muchísimo
 ■ **We were thinking the very same thing.** Estábamos pensando exactamente lo mismo.
**very** ADJECTIVE
 ▷ *see also* **very** ADVERBIO
 mismo (FEM misma)
 □ in this very house en esta misma casa
 □ That's the very book I was talking about. Ese es justamente el libro del que hablaba.
 ■ **The very idea!** ¡Cómo se te ocurre!
**vest** NOUN
1 la camiseta *(underclothing)*
2 el chaleco *(us: waistcoat)*
**vet** NOUN
 el veterinario
 la veterinaria
 □ She's a vet. Es veterinaria.

**via** PREPOSITION
1 por
 □ We drove to Lisbon via Salamanca. Fuimos a Lisboa por Salamanca.
2 vía
 □ a flight via Brussels un vuelo vía Bruselas
**vicar** NOUN
 el párroco
**vice** NOUN
 el tornillo de banco *(tool)*
**vice versa** ADVERB
 viceversa
**vicious** ADJECTIVE
1 brutal (FEM brutal)
 □ a vicious attack una brutal agresión
2 feroz (FEM feroz)
 □ a vicious dog un perro feroz
 ■ **He was a vicious man.** Era un hombre despiadado.
 ■ **a vicious circle** un círculo vicioso
**victim** NOUN
 la víctima
 □ He was the victim of a mugging. Fue víctima de un atraco.
**victory** NOUN
 la victoria
to **video** VERB
 ▷ *see also* **video** NOUN
 grabar en vídeo (grabar en video *Latin America*)
 □ They videoed the whole wedding. Grabaron en vídeo toda la boda.
**video** NOUN
 ▷ *see also* **video** VERB
 el vídeo (el video *Latin America*)
 □ to watch a video ver un vídeo
 ■ **a video camera** una videocámara
 ■ **a video game** un videojuego
 ■ **a video shop** un videoclub
**videophone** NOUN
 el videoteléfono
**view** NOUN
1 la vista
 □ There's an amazing view. La vista es magnífica.
2 la opinión (PL las opiniones)
 □ in my view en mi opinión
**viewer** NOUN
 el telespectador
 la telespectadora
**viewpoint** NOUN
 el punto de vista
**vile** ADJECTIVE
 repugnante (FEM repugnante)
**villa** NOUN
 el chalet
**village** NOUN
1 el pueblo *(large)*

V

**English-Spanish**

2 la aldea *(small)*
**villain** NOUN
1 el/la maleante *(criminal)*
2 el malo
la mala *(in film)*
**vine** NOUN
1 la vid *(trailing)*
2 la parra *(climbing)*
**vinegar** NOUN
el vinagre
**vineyard** NOUN
el viñedo
**viola** NOUN
la viola
**violence** NOUN
la violencia
**violent** ADJECTIVE
violento (FEM violenta)
**violin** NOUN
el violín (PL los violines)
**violinist** NOUN
el/la violinista
**virgin** NOUN
la virgen (PL las vírgenes)
□ to be a virgin ser virgen
**Virgo** NOUN
el Virgo *(sign)*
■ I'm Virgo. Soy virgo.
**virtual reality** NOUN
la realidad virtual
**virus** NOUN
el virus (PL los virus) *(also computing)*
**visa** NOUN
el visado (la visa *Latin America*)
**visible** ADJECTIVE
visible (FEM visible)
**visit** NOUN
▷ *see also* **visit** VERB
la visita
□ my last visit to my grandmother la última visita que le hice a mi abuela
■ I saw him on my latest visit to Spain. Lo vi la última vez que estuve en España.
to **visit** VERB
▷ *see also* **visit** NOUN
visitar
**visitor** NOUN
1 el/la visitante *(tourist)*
2 la visita *(guest)*
□ to have a visitor tener visita
**visual** ADJECTIVE
visual (FEM visual)
**vital** ADJECTIVE
vital (FEM vital)
**vitamin** NOUN
la vitamina

**vivid** ADJECTIVE
vivo (FEM viva)
□ vivid colours colores vivos
■ to have a vivid imagination tener una imaginación desbordante
**vocabulary** NOUN
el vocabulario
**vocational** ADJECTIVE
■ a vocational course un curso de formación profesional
**vodka** NOUN
el vodka

LANGUAGE TIP Although **vodka** ends in -a, it is actually a masculine noun.

**voice** NOUN
la voz (PL las voces)
**voicemail** NOUN
el buzón de voz
**volcano** NOUN
el volcán (PL los volcanes)
**volleyball** NOUN
el voleibol
**volt** NOUN
el voltio
**voltage** NOUN
el voltaje
**voluntary** ADJECTIVE
voluntario (FEM voluntaria)
■ to do voluntary work hacer voluntariado
**volunteer** NOUN
▷ *see also* **volunteer** VERB
el voluntario
la voluntaria
to **volunteer** VERB
▷ *see also* **volunteer** NOUN
■ to volunteer to do something ofrecerse a hacer algo
to **vomit** VERB
vomitar
to **vote** VERB
▷ *see also* **vote** NOUN
votar
□ Who did you vote for? ¿A quién votaste?
**vote** NOUN
▷ *see also* **vote** VERBO
el voto
**voucher** NOUN
el vale
□ a gift voucher un vale de regalo
**vowel** NOUN
la vocal
**vulgar** ADJECTIVE
vulgar (FEM vulgar)

V

# Ww

**wafer** NOUN
el barquillo

**wage** NOUN
la paga
  □ He collected his wages. Recogió la paga.

**waist** NOUN
la cintura

**waistcoat** NOUN
el chaleco

to **wait** VERB
esperar
  □ I'll wait for you. Te esperaré. □ Wait a minute! ¡Espera un momento!
  ■ **to keep somebody waiting** hacer esperar a alguien □ They kept us waiting for hours. Nos hicieron esperar durante horas.
  ■ **I can't wait for the holidays.** Estoy deseando que lleguen las vacaciones.
  ■ **I can't wait to see him again.** Me muero de ganas de verlo otra vez.

to **wait up** VERB
esperar levantado
  □ My mum always waits up till I get in. Mi madre siempre espera levantada hasta que llego.

**waiter** NOUN
el camarero

**waiting list** NOUN
la lista de espera

**waiting room** NOUN
la sala de espera

**waitress** NOUN
la camarera

to **wake up** VERB
despertarse*
  □ I woke up at six o'clock. Me desperté a las seis.
  ■ **to wake somebody up** despertar a alguien □ Please would you wake me up at seven o'clock? ¿Podría despertarme a las siete, por favor?

**Wales** NOUN
Gales *masc*
  ■ **the Prince of Wales** el Príncipe de Gales
  ■ **I'm from Wales.** Soy de Gales.

to **walk** VERB

▷ *see also* **walk** NOUN
1 andar*
  □ Don't walk so fast! ¡No andes tan deprisa!
  □ We walked 10 kilometres. Anduvimos 10 kilómetros.
2 ir* a pie *(go on foot)*
  □ Are you walking or going by bus? ¿Vas a ir a pie o en autobús?
3 pasear *(for fun)*
  □ I like walking through the park. Me gusta pasear por el parque.
  ■ **to walk the dog** pasear al perro

**walk** NOUN
▷ *see also* **walk** VERB
el paseo
  ■ **to go for a walk** ir a pasear
  ■ **It's 10 minutes' walk from here.** Está a 10 minutos de aquí a pie.

**walkie-talkie** NOUN
el walkie-talkie

**walking** NOUN
el senderismo
  □ I did some walking in the Alps last summer. El verano pasado hice senderismo por los Alpes.
  ■ **Walking is good for your health.** Andar es bueno para la salud.

**walking stick** NOUN
el bastón (PL los bastones)

**Walkman**® NOUN
el walkman®

**wall** NOUN
1 la pared *(of room, building)*
2 el muro *(freestanding)*
3 la muralla *(of castle, city)*

**wallet** NOUN
la cartera

**wallpaper** NOUN
el papel pintado

**walnut** NOUN
la nuez (PL las nueces)

to **want** VERB
querer*
  □ Do you want some cake? ¿Quieres un poco de pastel?
  ■ **to want to do something** querer hacer

**w**

algo □ What do you want to do tomorrow?
¿Qué quieres hacer mañana?

◌ **LANGUAGE TIP querer que** has to be
followed by a verb in the subjunctive.

■ **to want somebody to do something**
querer que alguien haga algo □ They want
us to wait here. Quieren que esperemos
aquí.

**war** NOUN
la guerra

■ **to be at war** estar en guerra
■ **a war memorial** un monumento a los
caídos

**ward** NOUN
la sala *(de un hospital)*

**warden** NOUN
el encargado
la encargada *(of youth hostel)*

**wardrobe** NOUN
el armario

**warehouse** NOUN
el almacén (PL los almacenes)

**warm** ADJECTIVE
1 caliente (FEM caliente)
□ warm water agua caliente
2 caluroso (FEM calurosa)
□ a warm day un día caluroso □ a warm
welcome una calurosa bienvenida
■ **warm clothing** ropa de abrigo
■ **This jumper is very warm.** Este jersey es
muy calentito.
■ **He's a very warm person.** Es una
persona muy afectuosa.
■ **It's warm in here.** Aquí dentro hace
calor.
■ **I'm too warm.** Tengo demasiado calor.

to **warn** VERB
advertir*
□ Well, I warned you! ¡Ya te lo había
advertido!

◌ **LANGUAGE TIP** Use the subjunctive
after **aconsejar a alguien que**.

■ **to warn somebody to do something**
aconsejar a alguien que haga algo

**warning** NOUN
la advertencia

**Warsaw** NOUN
Varsovia *fem*

**wart** NOUN
la verruga

**was** VERB ▷ *see* **be**

**wash** NOUN
▷ *see also* **wash** VERB
■ **to have a wash** lavarse
■ **to give something a wash** lavar algo
■ **The car needs a wash.** Al coche le hace
falta un lavado.

292  to **wash** VERB

▷ *see also* **wash** NOUN
1 lavar
□ to wash the car lavar el coche
2 lavarse *(have a wash)*
□ Every morning I get up, wash and get
dressed. Todas las mañanas me levanto,
me lavo y me visto.
■ **to wash one's hands** lavarse las manos
■ **to wash up** lavar los platos

**washbasin** NOUN
el lavabo

**washcloth** NOUN (US)
la toallita para lavarse

**washing** NOUN
la ropa lavada *(clean laundry)*
■ **to do the washing** lavar la ropa
■ **dirty washing** la ropa para lavar
■ **Have you got any washing?** ¿Tienes
ropa para lavar?

**washing machine** NOUN
la lavadora

**washing powder** NOUN
el detergente

**washing-up** NOUN
■ **to do the washing-up** lavar los platos

**washing-up liquid** NOUN
el lavavajillas (PL los lavavajillas)

**wasn't** = was not

**wasp** NOUN
la avispa

**waste** NOUN
▷ *see also* **waste** VERB
1 el desperdicio
□ It's such a waste! ¡Qué desperdicio!
■ **It's a waste of time.** Es una pérdida de
tiempo.
2 los residuos *pl*
□ nuclear waste residuos radioactivos

to **waste** VERB
▷ *see also* **waste** NOUN
desperdiciar *(food, space, opportunity)*
■ **to waste time** perder el tiempo
□ There's no time to waste. No hay tiempo
que perder.
■ **I don't like wasting money.** No me
gusta malgastar el dinero.

**wastepaper basket** NOUN
la papelera

**watch** NOUN
▷ *see also* **watch** VERB
el reloj

to **watch** VERB
▷ *see also* **watch** NOUN
1 mirar
■ **Watch me!** ¡Mírame!
2 ver*
□ to watch TV ver la tele
3 vigilar

□ The police were watching the house.
La policía vigilaba la casa.

to **watch out** VERB
tener* cuidado

■ **Watch out!** ¡Cuidado!

**water** NOUN
▷ *see also* **water** VERB
el agua *fem*

> ⊙ LANGUAGE TIP Although it's a feminine noun, remember that you use **el** with **agua**.

to **water** VERB
▷ *see also* **water** NOUN
regar*

□ He was watering his tulips. Estaba regando los tulipanes.

**waterfall** NOUN
la cascada

**watering can** NOUN
la regadera

**watermelon** NOUN
la sandía

**waterproof** ADJECTIVE
impermeable (FEM impermeable)

■ **a waterproof watch** un reloj sumergible

**water-skiing** NOUN
el esquí acuático

□ to go water-skiing hacer esquí acuático

**wave** NOUN
▷ *see also* **wave** VERB
la ola

to **wave** VERB
▷ *see also* **wave** NOUN

■ **to wave to somebody 1** *(say hello)* saludar a alguien con la mano **2** *(say goodbye)* hacer adiós con la mano

**wavy** ADJECTIVE
ondulado (FEM ondulada)

□ He's got wavy hair. Tiene el pelo ondulado.

**wax** NOUN
la cera

**way** NOUN
**1** la manera

□ She looked at me in a strange way. Me miró de manera extraña.

■ **This book tells you the right way to do it.** Este libro explica cómo hay que hacerlo.

■ **You're doing it the wrong way.** Lo estás haciendo mal.

■ **in a way...** en cierto sentido...

■ **a way of life** un estilo de vida

**2** el camino *(route)*

□ I don't know the way. No sé el camino.
□ We stopped for lunch on the way. Paramos a comer en el camino.

■ **Which way is it?** ¿Por dónde es?

■ **The supermarket is this way.** El supermercado es por aquí.

■ **Do you know the way to the hotel?** ¿Sabes cómo llegar al hotel?

■ **He's on his way.** Está de camino.

■ **It's a long way.** Está lejos. □ It's a long way from the hotel. Está lejos del hotel.

■ **'way in'** 'entrada'

■ **'way out'** 'salida'

■ **by the way...** a propósito...

**we** PRONOUN
nosotros (FEM nosotras)

> ⊙ LANGUAGE TIP 'we' generally isn't translated unless it is emphatic.

□ We were in a hurry. Teníamos prisa.

> ⊙ LANGUAGE TIP Use **nosotros** or **nosotras** as appropriate for emphasis.

□ They went but we didn't. Ellos fueron pero nosotros no.

**weak** ADJECTIVE
**1** débil (FEM débil)
**2** poco cargado (FEM poco cargada) *(tea, coffee)*

**wealthy** ADJECTIVE
rico (FEM rica)

**weapon** NOUN
el arma *fem*

> ⊙ LANGUAGE TIP Although it's a feminine noun, remember that you use **el** and **un** with **arma**.

to **wear** VERB
llevar

□ She was wearing a hat. Llevaba un sombrero.

■ **She was wearing black.** Iba vestida de negro.

**weather** NOUN
el tiempo

□ What's the weather like? ¿Qué tiempo hace?

**weather forecast** NOUN
el pronóstico del tiempo

**Web** NOUN
■ **the Web** la Web

**web browser** NOUN
el navegador de Internet

**webcam** NOUN
la webcam

**webmaster** NOUN
el administrador de Web
la administradora de Web

**web page** NOUN
la página web

**website** NOUN
el sitio web

**webzine** NOUN
la revista electrónica

**we'd** = we had; we would

**wedding** NOUN
la boda

**w**

293

■ **wedding anniversary** el aniversario de boda

■ **wedding dress** el vestido de novia

**Wednesday** NOUN
el miércoles (PL los miércoles)
□ I saw her on Wednesday. La vi el miércoles. □ every Wednesday todos los miércoles □ last Wednesday el miércoles pasado □ next Wednesday el miércoles que viene □ on Wednesdays los miércoles

**weed** NOUN
el hierbajo
□ The garden's full of weeds. El jardín está lleno de hierbajos.

**week** NOUN
la semana
□ in a week's time dentro de una semana
■ **a week on Friday** el viernes de la semana que viene
■ **during the week** durante la semana

**weekday** NOUN
el día entre semana

> LANGUAGE TIP Although **día** ends in **-a**, it is actually a masculine noun.

■ **on weekdays** los días entre semana

**weekend** NOUN
el fin de semana
■ **next weekend** el próximo fin de semana

to **weep** VERB
llorar

to **weigh** VERB
pesar
□ How much do you weigh? ¿Cuánto pesas?
■ **to weigh oneself** pesarse

**weight** NOUN
el peso
■ **to lose weight** adelgazar
■ **to put on weight** engordar

**weightlifter** NOUN
el levantador de pesas
la levantadora de pesas

**weightlifting** NOUN
el levantamiento de pesas

**weird** ADJECTIVE
raro (FEM rara)

**welcome** NOUN
▷ see also **welcome** VERB
la bienvenida
□ They gave her a warm welcome. Le dieron una calurosa bienvenida.
■ **Welcome!** ¡Bienvenido!

> LANGUAGE TIP If you're addressing a woman remember to use the feminine form: **¡Bienvenida!** If you're addressing more than one person use the plural form **¡Bienvenidos!** or **¡Bienvenidas!**.

to **welcome** VERB

▷ see also **welcome** NOUN
■ **to welcome somebody** dar la bienvenida a alguien
■ **Thank you! — You're welcome!** ¡Gracias! — ¡De nada!

**well** ADJECTIVE, ADVERB
▷ see also **well** NOUN
**1** bien
□ You did that really well. Lo hiciste realmente bien. □ She's doing really well at school. Le va muy bien en el colegio.
■ **to be well** estar bien □ I'm not very well at the moment. No estoy muy bien en este momento.
■ **Get well soon!** ¡Que te mejores!
■ **Well done!** ¡Muy bien!
**2** bueno
□ It's enormous! Well, quite big anyway. ¡Es enorme! Bueno, digamos que bastante grande.
■ **as well** también □ We worked hard, but we had some fun as well. Trabajamos mucho, pero también nos divertimos.
■ **as well as** además de □ We went to Gerona as well as Sitges. Fuimos a Gerona, además de Sitges.

**well** NOUN
▷ see also **well** ADJECTIVE, ADVERB
el pozo

**we'll** = we will

**well-behaved** ADJECTIVE
■ **to be well-behaved** portarse bien

**well-dressed** ADJECTIVE
bien vestido (FEM bien vestida)

**wellingtons** PL NOUN
las botas de agua

**well-known** ADJECTIVE
conocido (FEM conocida)
□ a well-known film star un conocido actor de cine

**well-off** ADJECTIVE
adinerado (FEM adinerada)

**Welsh** ADJECTIVE
▷ see also **Welsh** NOUN
galés (FEM galesa)

**Welsh** NOUN
▷ see also **Welsh** ADJECTIVE
el galés (language)
■ **the Welsh** los galeses

**Welshman** NOUN
el galés (PL los galeses)

**Welshwoman** NOUN
la galesa

**went** VERB ▷ see go
**were** VERB ▷ see be
**we're** = we are
**weren't** = were not
**west** NOUN

▷ *see also* **west** ADJECTIVE, ADVERB
el oeste

**west** ADJECTIVE, ADVERB
  ▷ *see also* **west** NOUN
1 occidental (FEM occidental)
  □ the west coast la costa occidental
  ■ **west of** al oeste de □ Stroud is west of
  Oxford. Stroud está al oeste de Oxford.
2 hacia el oeste
  □ We were travelling west. Viajábamos
  hacia el oeste.
  ■ **the West Country** el sudoeste de
  Inglaterra
**western** NOUN
  ▷ *see also* **western** ADJECTIVE
  el western
**western** ADJECTIVE
  ▷ *see also* **western** NOUN
  occidental (FEM occidental)
  □ the western part of the island la parte
  occidental de la isla
  ■ **Western Europe** Europa Occidental
**West Indian** ADJECTIVE
  ▷ *see also* **West Indian** NOUN
  antillano (FEM antillana)
  ■ **She's West Indian.** Es antillana.
**West Indian** NOUN
  ▷ *see also* **West Indian** ADJECTIVE
  el antillano
  la antillana
**West Indies** PL NOUN
  ■ **the West Indies** las Antillas
**wet** ADJECTIVE
  mojado (FEM mojada)
  □ wet clothes ropa mojada
  ■ **to get wet** mojarse
  ■ **dripping wet** chorreando
  ■ **wet weather** el tiempo lluvioso
  ■ **It was wet all week.** Llovió toda la semana.
**wetsuit** NOUN
  el traje de buzo
**we've** = we have
**whale** NOUN
  la ballena
**what** ADJECTIVE, PRONOUN
1 qué

  **LANGUAGE TIP** Use **qué** (with an
  accent) in direct and indirect
  questions and exclamations.

  □ What subjects are you studying? ¿Qué
  asignaturas estudias? □ What colour is it?
  ¿De qué color es? □ What's the matter?
  ¿Qué te pasa? □ What's it for? ¿Para qué es?
  □ I don't know what to do. No sé qué hacer.
  □ What a mess! ¡Qué desorden!

  **LANGUAGE TIP** Only translate 'what is'
  by **qué es** if asking for a definition or
  explanation.

□ What is it? ¿Qué es? □ What's a tractor,
Daddy? ¿Qué es un tractor, papá? □ I asked
him what DNA was. Le pregunté qué era el
ADN.
2 cuál (FEM cuál, PL cuáles)

  **LANGUAGE TIP** Translate 'what is'
  by **cuál es** when not asking for a
  definition or explanation.

  □ What's the capital of Finland? ¿Cuál es la
  capital de Finlandia? □ What's her
  telephone number? ¿Cuál es su número de
  teléfono?
3 lo que

  **LANGUAGE TIP** Use **lo que** (no accent)
  when 'what' isn't a question word.

  □ I saw what happened. Vi lo que pasó.
  □ I heard what he said. Oí lo que dijo.
  ■ **What?** 1 *(what did you say?)* ¿Cómo?
  **2** *(shocked)* ¿Qué?
  ■ **What's your name?** ¿Cómo te llamas?
**wheat** NOUN
  el trigo
**wheel** NOUN
  la rueda
  ■ **steering wheel** el volante
**wheelchair** NOUN
  la silla de ruedas
**when** ADVERB
  ▷ *see also* **when** CONJUNCTION
  cuándo

  **LANGUAGE TIP** Remember the accent
  on **cuándo** in direct and indirect
  questions.

  □ When did he go? ¿Cuándo se fue?
  □ I asked her when the next bus was. Le
  pregunté cuándo salía el próximo autobús.
**when** CONJUNCTION
  ▷ *see also* **when** ADVERB
  cuando
  □ She was reading when I came in. Cuando
  entré ella estaba leyendo.

  **LANGUAGE TIP** **cuando** has to be
  followed by a verb in the subjunctive
  when referring to an event in the
  future.

  □ Call me when you get there. Llámame
  cuando llegues.
**where** ADVERB
  ▷ *see also* **where** CONJUNCTION
  dónde

  **LANGUAGE TIP** Remember the accent
  on **dónde** in direct and indirect
  questions.

  □ Where do you live? ¿Dónde vives?
  □ Where are you from? ¿De dónde eres?
  □ She asked me where I had bought it.
  Me pregunté dónde lo había comprado.
  ■ **Where are you going?** ¿Adónde vas?

**English-Spanish**

**where** CONJUNCTION
▷ *see also* **where** ADVERB
donde
□ a shop where you can buy coffee  una tienda donde se puede comprar café
**whether** CONJUNCTION
si
□ I don't know whether to go or not.  No sé si ir o no.
**which** ADJECTIVE, PRONOUN
**1** cuál (FEM cuál, PL cuáles)

> LANGUAGE TIP  Remember the accent on **cuál** and **cuáles** in direct and indirect questions.

□ I know his sister. — Which one?  Conozco a su hermana. — ¿A cuál?  □ Which would you like? ¿Cuál quieres?  □ Of the five pairs, which were sold?  De los cinco pares, ¿cuáles se vendieron?
**2** qué

> LANGUAGE TIP  Use **qué** (with an accent) before nouns.

□ Which flavour do you want? ¿Qué sabor quieres?
**3** que
□ It's an illness which causes nerve damage.  Es una enfermedad que daña los nervios.  □ This is the skirt which Daphne gave me.  Ésta es la falda que me dio Daphne.  □ Our uniform, which is green, is quite nice.  Nuestro uniforme, que es verde, está bastante bien.

> LANGUAGE TIP  After a preposition **que** becomes **el que, la que, los que, las que** to agree with the noun.

□ That's the film which I was telling you about.  Ésa es la película de la que te hablaba.
**4** lo cual
□ The cooker isn't working, which is a nuisance.  La cocina no funciona, lo cual es un fastidio.
**while** CONJUNCTION
▷ *see also* **while** NOUN
**1** mientras
□ You hold the torch while I look inside.  Aguanta la linterna mientras yo miro por dentro.
**2** mientras que
□ Isobel is very dynamic, while Kay is more laid-back.  Isobel es muy dinámica, mientras que Kay es más tranquila.
**while** NOUN
▷ *see also* **while** CONJUNCTION
■ a while  un rato  □ after a while  después de un rato
■ a while ago  hace un momento  □ He was here a while ago.  Hace un momento estaba aquí.

■ for a while  durante un tiempo  □ I lived in London for a while.  Viví en Londres durante un tiempo.
■ quite a while  mucho tiempo  □ I haven't seen him for quite a while.  Hace mucho tiempo que no lo veo.
**whip** NOUN
▷ *see also* **whip** VERB
la fusta *(for horse)*
to **whip** VERB
▷ *see also* **whip** NOUN
**1** fustigar* *(animal)*
**2** azotar *(person)*
**3** batir *(eggs, cream)*
**whipped cream** NOUN
la nata montada
**whisk** NOUN
el batidor
**whiskers** PL NOUN
los bigotes *(of animal)*
**whisky** NOUN
el whisky (PL los whiskys)
to **whisper** VERB
susurrar
**whistle** NOUN
▷ *see also* **whistle** VERB
el silbato
□ The referee blew his whistle.  El árbitro tocó el silbato.
to **whistle** VERB
▷ *see also* **whistle** NOUN
**1** pitar *(with a whistle)*
**2** silbar *(with mouth)*
**white** ADJECTIVE
blanco (FEM blanca)
□ He's got white hair.  Tiene el cabello blanco.
■ white bread  el pan blanco
■ white coffee  el café con leche
■ a white man  un hombre blanco
■ white people  los blancos
■ white wine  el vino blanco
**Whitsun** NOUN
Pentecostés *masc*
**who** PRONOUN
**1** quién (PL quiénes)

> LANGUAGE TIP  Remember the accent on **quién** and **quiénes** in direct and indirect questions.

□ Who said that? ¿Quién dijo eso?  □ Who is it? ¿Quién es?  □ We don't know who broke the window.  No sabemos quién rompió la ventana.
**2** que
□ the people who know us  las personas que nos conocen

> LANGUAGE TIP  After a preposition **que** becomes **el que, la que, los que, las que** to agree with the noun.

**w**

□ the women who she was chatting with las mujeres con las que estaba hablando

LANGUAGE TIP Note that **a + el que** becomes **al que**.

□ the boy who I gave it to el chico al que se lo di

**whole** ADJECTIVE

▷ see also **whole** NOUN

entero (FEM entera)

□ the whole class la clase entera □ two whole days dos días enteros

■ **the whole afternoon** toda la tarde

■ **the whole world** todo el mundo

**whole** NOUN

▷ see also **whole** ADJECTIVE

■ **The whole of Wales was affected.** Todo Gales se vio afectado.

■ **on the whole** en general

**wholemeal** ADJECTIVE

integral (FEM integral)

□ wholemeal bread pan integral

**wholewheat** ADJECTIVE (US)

integral (FEM integral)

**whom** PRONOUN

**1** quién (PL quiénes)

LANGUAGE TIP Remember the accent on **quién** and **quiénes** in direct and indirect questions.

□ With whom did you go? ¿Con quién fuiste? □ Whom did you call? ¿A quién llamaste?

**2** quien

□ the man whom I saw el hombre a quien vi □ the woman to whom I spoke la mujer con quien hablé

**whose** ADJECTIVE

▷ see also **whose** PRONOUN

**1** de quién (PL de quiénes) (in questions)

LANGUAGE TIP Remember the accent on **quién** and **quiénes** in direct and indirect questions.

□ Whose books are these? ¿De quiénes son estos libros? □ Do you know whose jacket this is? ¿Sabes de quién es esta chaqueta?

**2** cuyo (FEM cuya) (relative)

□ the girl whose picture was in the paper la muchacha cuya foto venía en el periódico □ a neighbour whose sons go to that school un vecino cuyos hijos van a ese colegio

**whose** PRONOUN

▷ see also **whose** ADJECTIVE

de quién (PL de quiénes)

LANGUAGE TIP Remember the accent on **quién** and **quiénes** in direct and indirect questions.

□ Whose is this? ¿De quién es esto? □ I know whose they are. Yo sé de quiénes son.

**why** ADVERB

por qué

LANGUAGE TIP Remember to write **por qué** as two words with an accent on **qué** when translating 'why'.

□ Why did you do that? ¿Por qué hiciste eso?

■ **Why not?** ¿Por qué no?

■ **That's why he did it.** Por eso lo hizo.

**wicked** ADJECTIVE

**1** malvado (FEM malvada) (evil)

**2** sensacional (FEM sensacional) (really great)

**wicket** NOUN

los palos (stumps)

**wide** ADJECTIVE, ADVERB

ancho (FEM ancha)

□ a wide road una carretera ancha □ How wide is the room? — It's five metres wide. ¿Cómo es de ancha la habitación? — Tiene cinco metros de ancho.

■ **wide open** abierto de par en par □ The door was wide open. La puerta estaba abierta de par en par.

■ **wide awake** completamente despierto

**widow** NOUN

la viuda

□ She's a widow. Es viuda.

**widower** NOUN

el viudo

□ He's a widower. Es viudo.

**width** NOUN

la anchura

**wife** NOUN

la esposa

**wig** NOUN

la peluca

**wild** ADJECTIVE

**1** salvaje (FEM salvaje)

□ a wild animal un animal salvaje

**2** silvestre (FEM silvestre)

□ wild flowers flores silvestres

**3** loco (FEM loca)

□ She's a bit wild. Es un poco loca.

**wildlife** NOUN

la flora y fauna

**will** NOUN

▷ see also **will** VERB

el testamento (document)

**will** VERB

▷ see also **will** NOUN

LANGUAGE TIP 'will' can often be translated by the present tense, as in the following examples.

□ Come on, I'll help you. Venga, te ayudo. □ We'll talk about it later. Hablamos luego. □ Will you help me? ¿Me ayudas?

LANGUAGE TIP Use **voy a**, **va a**, and so on + the infinitive to talk about plans and intentions.

□ What will you do? ¿Qué vas a hacer?

W

□ We'll be having lunch late. Vamos a comer tarde.

> **LANGUAGE TIP** Use the future tense when guessing what will happen or when making a supposition.

□ It won't take long. No llevará mucho tiempo. □ We'll probably go out later. Seguramente saldremos luego. □ I'll always love you. Te querré siempre. □ That will be the postman. Será el cartero.

> **LANGUAGE TIP** Use **querer** for 'to be willing' in emphatic requests, and invitations.

□ Tom won't help me. Tom no me quiere ayudar. □ Will you be quiet! ¿Te quieres callar? □ Will you have some tea? ¿Quieres tomar un té?

**willing** ADJECTIVE
■ **to be willing to do something** estar dispuesto a hacer algo

to **win** VERB
▷ *see also* **win** NOUN
ganar
□ Did you win? ¿Ganaste? □ to win a prize ganar un premio

**win** NOUN
▷ *see also* **win** VERB
la victoria

to **wind** VERB
▷ *see also* **wind** NOUN
enrollar *(rope, wire)*

**wind** NOUN
▷ *see also* **wind** VERB
el viento
■ **a wind instrument** un instrumento de viento
■ **wind power** la energía eólica

**windmill** NOUN
el molino de viento

**window** NOUN
1 la ventana *(of building)*
2 la ventanilla *(in car, train)*
■ **a shop window** un escaparate
3 el cristal *(window pane)* (el vidrio *Latin America)*
□ to break a window romper un cristal

**windscreen** NOUN
el parabrisas (PL los parabrisas)

**windscreen wiper** NOUN
el limpiaparabrisas (PL los limpiaparabrisas)

**windshield** NOUN (US)
el parabrisas (PL los parabrisas)

**windshield wiper** NOUN (US)
el limpiaparabrisas (PL los limpiaparabrisas)

**windy** ADJECTIVE
■ **a windy day** un día de viento
■ **Edinburgh's a very windy city.** En Edimburgo hace mucho viento.

■ **It's windy.** Hace viento.

**wine** NOUN
el vino
□ white wine el vino blanco □ red wine el vino tinto
■ **a wine bar** un bar especializado en vinos
■ **a wine cellar** una bodega
■ **a wine glass** una copa de vino
■ **the wine list** la carta de vinos

**wing** NOUN
el ala *fem*

> **LANGUAGE TIP** Although it's a feminine noun, remember that you use **el** and **un** with **ala**.

to **wink** VERB
■ **to wink at somebody** guiñar el ojo a alguien

**winner** NOUN
el ganador
la ganadora

**winning** ADJECTIVE
vencedor (FEM vencedora)
□ the winning team el equipo vencedor
■ **the winning goal** el gol de la victoria

**winter** NOUN
el invierno

**winter sports** PL NOUN
los deportes de invierno

to **wipe** VERB
limpiar
■ **to wipe one's feet** limpiarse los zapatos
■ **to wipe one's nose** limpiarse la nariz
■ **Did you wipe up that water you spilled?** ¿Recogiste el agua que derramaste?

**wire** NOUN
el alambre
■ **copper wire** el hilo de cobre
■ **the telephone wire** el cable del teléfono

**wisdom tooth** NOUN
la muela del juicio

**wise** ADJECTIVE
sabio (FEM sabia)

to **wish** VERB
▷ *see also* **wish** NOUN
■ **to wish for something** desear algo
□ What more could you wish for? ¿Qué más podrías desear?
■ **to wish to do something** desear hacer algo □ I wish to make a complaint. Deseo hacer una reclamación.
■ **I wish you were here!** ¡Ojalá estuvieras aquí!
■ **I wish you'd told me!** ¡Me lo podrías haber dicho!
■ **to wish somebody happy birthday** desear a alguien un feliz cumpleaños

**wish** NOUN
▷ *see also* **wish** VERB

el deseo
□ to make a wish  pedir un deseo
■ 'best wishes' (on birthday card)
'felicidades'
■ 'with best wishes, Kathy'  'un abrazo,
Kathy'
**wit** NOUN
el ingenio
**with** PREPOSITION
1 con
□ He walks with a stick.  Camina con un
bastón.  □ Come with me.  Ven conmigo.
2 de
□ a woman with blue eyes  una mujer de
ojos azules  □ green with envy  muerto de
envidia  □ to shake with fear  temblar de
miedo  □ Fill the jug with water.  Llena la
jarra de agua.
■ We stayed with friends.  Nos quedamos
en casa de unos amigos.
**within** PREPOSITION
dentro de
□ I want it back within three days.  Quiero
que me lo devuelvas dentro de tres días.
■ The police arrived within minutes.
La policía llegó a los pocos minutos.
■ The shops are within easy reach.
Las tiendas están cerca.
**without** PREPOSITION
sin
□ without a coat  sin abrigo  □ without
speaking  sin hablar
**witness** NOUN
el/la testigo
□ There were no witnesses.  No había
testigos.
**witty** ADJECTIVE
ingenioso (FEM ingeniosa)
**wives** PL NOUN  ▷ see wife
**woke up** VERB  ▷ see wake up
**wolf** NOUN
el lobo
**woman** NOUN
la mujer
■ a woman doctor  una doctora
**won** VERB  ▷ see win
to **wonder** VERB
preguntarse
□ I wonder why she said that.  Me pregunto
por qué dijo eso.
■ I wonder where Caroline is.  ¿Dónde
estará Caroline?
**wonderful** ADJECTIVE
maravilloso (FEM maravillosa)
**won't** = will not
**wood** NOUN
1 la madera
□ It's made of wood.  Es de madera.

2 la leña (for fire)
3 el bosque
□ We went for a walk in the wood.  Fuimos
a pasear por el bosque.
**wooden** ADJECTIVE
de madera
□ a wooden chair  una silla de madera
**woodwork** NOUN
la carpintería
**wool** NOUN
la lana
□ It's made of wool.  Es de lana.
**word** NOUN
la palabra
■ What's the word for 'shop' in Spanish?
¿Cómo se dice 'shop' en español?
■ in other words  en otras palabras
■ to have a word with somebody  hablar
con alguien  □ Can I have a word with you?
¿Puedo hablar contigo?
■ the words (lyrics)  la letra
**word processing** NOUN
el procesamiento de textos
**word processor** NOUN
el procesador de textos
**wore** VERB  ▷ see wear
**work** NOUN
▷ see also **work** VERB
el trabajo
□ She's looking for work.  Está buscando
trabajo.
■ It's hard work.  Es duro.
■ at work  en el trabajo  □ He's at work until
five o'clock.  Está en el trabajo hasta las
cinco.
■ He's off work today.  Hoy tiene el día
libre.
■ to be out of work  estar sin trabajo
to **work** VERB
▷ see also **work** NOUN
1 trabajar
□ She works in a shop.  Trabaja en una
tienda.  □ to work hard  trabajar mucho
2 funcionar
□ The heating isn't working.  La calefacción
no funciona.  □ My plan worked perfectly.
Mi plan funcionó a la perfección.
to **work out** VERB
1 hacer* ejercicio (exercise)
□ I work out twice a week.  Hago ejercicio
dos veces a la semana.
2 salir* (turn out)
□ I hope it will work out well.  Espero que
salga bien.
3 calcular (calculate)
□ I worked it out in my head.  Lo calculé en
mi cabeza.
4 entender* (understand)

**w**

□ I just couldn't work it out. No lograba entenderlo.

■ **It works out at £10 each.** Sale a 10 libras esterlinas por persona.

**worker** NOUN
el trabajador
la trabajadora

□ She's a good worker. Trabaja bien.

**work experience** NOUN

■ **I'm going to do my work experience in a factory.** Voy a hacer las prácticas en una fábrica.

**working-class** ADJECTIVE
de clase obrera

□ a working-class family una familia de clase obrera

**workman** NOUN
el obrero

**works** NOUN
la fábrica

**worksheet** NOUN
la hoja de ejercicios

**workshop** NOUN
el taller

□ a drama workshop un taller de teatro

**workstation** NOUN
la terminal de trabajo

**world** NOUN
el mundo

■ **the world champion** el campeón mundial

■ **the World Cup** la Copa del Mundo

**worm** NOUN
el gusano

**worn** VERB ▷ see **wear**

**worn** ADJECTIVE
gastado (FEM gastada)

□ The carpet is a bit worn. La moqueta está un poco gastada.

■ **worn out** agotado □ We were worn out after the long walk. Estábamos agotados después de andar tanto.

**worried** ADJECTIVE
preocupado (FEM preocupada)

□ to be worried about something estar preocupado por algo □ to look worried parecer preocupado

to **worry** VERB
preocuparse

■ **Don't worry!** ¡No te preocupes!

**worse** ADJECTIVE, ADVERB
peor (FEM peora)

□ It was even worse than mine. Era incluso peor que el mío. □ I'm feeling worse. Me encuentro peor.

to **worship** VERB
adorar

**worst** ADJECTIVE

▷ see also **worst** NOUN
peor

□ the worst student in the class el peor alumno de la clase □ my worst enemy mi peor enemigo

■ **Maths is my worst subject.** Las matemáticas es la asignatura que peor se me da.

**worst** NOUN
▷ see also **worst** ADJECTIVE

■ **The worst of it is that...** Lo peor es que...

■ **at worst** en el peor de los casos

■ **if the worst comes to the worst** en el peor de los casos

**worth** ADJECTIVE

■ **to be worth** valer □ It's worth a lot of money. Vale mucho dinero. □ How much is it worth? ¿Cuánto vale?

■ **It's worth it.** Vale la pena.

**would** VERB

◌ **LANGUAGE TIP** The conditional is often used to translate 'would' + verb.

□ I said I would do it. Dije que lo haría. □ If you asked him he'd do it. Si se lo pidieras, lo haría. □ If you had asked him he would have done it. Si se lo hubieras pedido, lo habría hecho.

◌ **LANGUAGE TIP** When 'would you' is used to make requests, translate using **poder** in the present.

□ Would you close the door please? ¿Puedes cerrar la puerta, por favor?

■ **I'd like ...** 1 Me gustaría ... □ I'd like to go to China. Me gustaría ir a China. 2 Quería ... □ I'd like three tickets please. Quería tres entradas.

■ **Would you like a biscuit?** ¿Quieres una galleta?

◌ **LANGUAGE TIP** Use the subjunctive after **querer que**.

■ **Would you like me to iron your jeans for you?** ¿Quieres que te planche los pantalones?

■ **Would you like to go to the cinema?** ¿Quieres ir al cine?

**wouldn't** = would not

to **wound** VERB
▷ see also **wound** NOUN
herir*

□ He was wounded in the leg. Fue herido en la pierna.

**wound** NOUN
▷ see also **wound** VERB
la herida

to **wrap** VERB
envolver*

□ She's wrapping her Christmas presents. Está envolviendo los regalos de Navidad.

□ Can you wrap it for me please? ¿Me lo puede envolver en papel de regalo, por favor?

to **wrap up** VERB
1 envolver* *(parcel)*
2 abrigarse* *(put on warm clothes)*

**wrapping paper** NOUN
el papel de regalo

**wreck** NOUN
▷ *see also* **wreck** VERB
el cacharro
□ That car is a wreck! ¡Ese coche es un cacharro!
■ **After the exams I was a complete wreck.** Después de los exámenes estaba hecho polvo.

to **wreck** VERB
▷ *see also* **wreck** NOUN
1 destruir*
□ The explosion wrecked the whole house. La explosión destruyó toda la casa.
2 destrozar* *(car)*
3 echar por tierra
□ The bad weather wrecked our plans. El mal tiempo echó por tierra nuestros planes.

**wreckage** NOUN
1 los restos *(of vehicle)*
2 las ruinas *(of buildings)*

**wrestler** NOUN
el luchador
la luchadora

**wrestling** NOUN
la lucha libre

**wrinkled** ADJECTIVE
arrugado *(FEM arrugada)*

**wrist** NOUN
la muñeca

to **write** VERB
escribir*
□ to write a letter escribir una carta

to **write down** VERB
anotar
□ I wrote down her address. Anoté su dirección. □ Can you write it down for me, please? ¿Me lo puedes anotar, por favor?

**writer** NOUN
el escritor
la escritora

**writing** NOUN
la letra
□ I can't read your writing. No entiendo tu letra.
■ **in writing** por escrito

**written** VERB ▷ *see* **write**

**wrong** ADJECTIVE, ADVERB
1 incorrecto *(FEM incorrecta)*
□ The information they gave us was wrong. La información que nos dieron era incorrecta. □ the wrong answer la respuesta incorrecta
■ **You've got the wrong number.** Se ha equivocado de número.
2 mal
□ I think hunting is wrong. Opino que está mal cazar. □ You've done it wrong. Lo has hecho mal.
■ **to go wrong** *(plan)* ir mal □ The robbery went wrong and they got caught. El atraco fue mal y los pillaron.
■ **to be wrong** estar equivocado □ You're wrong about that. En eso estás equivocado.
■ **What's wrong?** ¿Qué pasa? □ What's wrong with her? ¿Qué le pasa?

**wrote** VERB ▷ *see* **write**

**W**

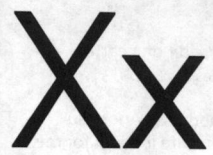

**Xmas** NOUN (= *Christmas*)
  la Navidad
to **X-ray** VERB
  ▷ *see also* **X-ray** NOUN
  hacer* una radiografía de
  □ They X-rayed my arm.  Me hicieron una

radiografía del brazo.
**X-ray** NOUN
  ▷ *see also* **X-ray** VERB
  la radiografía
  □ I had an X-ray taken.  Me hicieron una
  radiografía.

**yacht** NOUN
el yate

**yard** NOUN
1 la yarda

> **DID YOU KNOW...?**
> In Spain measurements are in metres and centimetres rather than feet and inches. A yard is about 90 cm.

2 el patio (of school, house)

to **yawn** VERB
bostezar*

**year** NOUN
el año
□ last year el año pasado
■ **to be 15 years old** tener 15 años
■ **an eight-year-old child** un niño de ocho años
■ **She's in the fifth year.** Está en quinto.

to **yell** VERB
gritar

**yellow** ADJECTIVE
amarillo (FEM amarilla)

**yes** ADVERB
sí
□ Do you like it? — Yes. ¿Te gusta? — Sí.

**yesterday** ADVERB
ayer
□ yesterday morning ayer por la mañana
□ all day yesterday todo el día de ayer

**yet** ADVERB
todavía
□ Have you eaten? — Not yet. ¿Ya has comido? — Todavía no. □ It's not finished yet. Todavía no está terminado. □ There's no news as yet. Todavía no se tienen noticias.
■ **Have you finished yet?** ¿Has terminado ya?

**yob** NOUN
el gamberro (el vándalo Latin America)

**yoghurt** NOUN
el yogur

**yolk** NOUN
la yema

**you** PRONOUN

> **LANGUAGE TIP** There are formal and informal ways of saying 'you' in Spanish. As you look down the entry, choose the informal options if talking to people your own age or that you know well. Otherwise use the formal options. Note that subject pronouns are used less in Spanish – for emphasis and in comparisons.

1 tú (informal: 1 person)
□ What do YOU think about it? ¿Y tú qué piensas? □ She's younger than you. Es más joven que tú.
■ **You don't understand me.** No me entiendes.

2 vosotros masc pl
vosotras fem pl (informal: 2 or more people)
□ You've got kids but we haven't. Vosotros tenéis hijos pero nosotros no. □ They're younger than you. Son más jóvenes que vosotros. □ I'd like to speak to you. (ie all female) Quiero hablar con vosotras.
■ **How are you?** ¿Qué tal estáis?

3 usted (formal: 1 person)
□ They're younger than you. Son más jóvenes que usted. □ This is for you. Esto es para usted.
■ **How are you?** ¿Cómo está?

4 ustedes (formal: 2 or more people)

> **LANGUAGE TIP** ustedes is always used in Latin America instead of vosotros.

□ They're younger than you. Son más jóvenes que ustedes. □ This is for you. Esto es para ustedes.
■ **How are you?** ¿Cómo están?

> **LANGUAGE TIP** When 'you' means 'one' or 'people' in general, the impersonal se is often used.

□ I doubt it, but you never know. Lo dudo, pero nunca se sabe.

> **LANGUAGE TIP** When 'you' is the object of the sentence, you have to use different forms from the ones above. See translations 5 to 10 below.

**y**

**5** te *(informal: 1 person)*
□ I love you. Te quiero. □ Shall I give it to you? ¿Te lo doy?
■ **This is for you.** Esto es para ti.
■ **Can I go with you?** ¿Puedo ir contigo?

**6** os *(informal: 2 or more people)*
□ I saw you. Os vi. □ I gave you the keys. Os di las llaves.
■ **I gave them to you.** Os los di.

**7** lo *masc sing*
la *fem sing (formal: 1 person – direct object)*
□ May I help you? ¿Puedo ayudarlo? □ I saw you, Mrs Jones. La vi, señora Jones.

**8** le *(formal: 1 person – indirect object)*
□ I gave you the keys. Le di las llaves.

> LANGUAGE TIP Change **le** to **se** before another object pronoun.

■ **I gave them to you.** Se las di.

**9** los *masc pl*
las *fem pl (formal: 2 or more people – direct object)*
□ May I help you? ¿Puedo ayudarlos?

**10** les *pl (formal: 2 or more people – indirect object)*

> LANGUAGE TIP Change **les** to **se** before another object pronoun.

□ I gave you the keys. Les di las llaves.
■ **I gave them to you.** Se las di.

**young** ADJECTIVE
joven (FEM joven, PL jóvenes)
■ **young people** los jóvenes
■ **He's younger than me.** Es menor que yo.
■ **my youngest brother** mi hermano pequeño

**your** ADJECTIVE

> LANGUAGE TIP Use **tu** and **vuestro/ vuestra** etc with people your own age or that you know well, and **su/sus** otherwise.

**1** tu (PL tus) *(informal: 1 person)*

> LANGUAGE TIP Remember there's no accent on **tu** meaning 'your'.

□ your house tu casa □ your books tus libros □ your sisters tus hermanas

**2** vuestro (FEM vuestra) *(informal: 2 or more people)*

> LANGUAGE TIP Remember to make **vuestro** agree with the person or thing it describes.

□ your dog vuestro perro □ These are your keys. Éstas son vuestras llaves.

**3** su (PL sus) *(formal)*

> LANGUAGE TIP Use **su** when talking to one person or to a group of people. **su** is used in Latin America instead of **vuestro**.

□ Can I see your passport, sir? ¿Me enseña su pasaporte, señor? □ your wife su mujer

□ your uncle and aunt sus tíos

> LANGUAGE TIP Use **el, la, los, las** as appropriate with parts of the body and to translate 'your' referring to people in general.

□ Have you washed your hair? ¿Te has lavado el pelo? □ Would you like to wash your hands? ¿Queréis lavaros las manos?
■ **It's bad for your health.** Es malo para la salud.

**yours** PRONOUN

> LANGUAGE TIP Use **tuyo/tuya** etc and **vuestro/vuestra** etc with people your own age or that you know well, and **su/sus** otherwise.

**1** tuyo (FEM tuya) *(informal: 1 person)*

> LANGUAGE TIP Remember to make **tuyo** agree with the person or thing it describes.

□ That's yours. Eso es tuyo. □ Is that box yours? ¿Ésa caja es tuya?

> LANGUAGE TIP Add the definite article when 'yours' means 'your one' or 'your ones'.

■ **I've lost my pen. Can I use yours?** He perdido el bolígrafo. ¿Puedo usar el tuyo?
■ **These are my keys and those are yours.** Éstas son mis llaves y ésas son las tuyas.

**2** vuestro (FEM vuestra) *(informal: 2 or more people)*

> LANGUAGE TIP Remember to make **vuestro** agree with the person or thing it describes.

□ That's yours. Eso es vuestro.

> LANGUAGE TIP Add the definite article when 'yours' means 'your one' or 'your ones'.

■ **These are my keys and those are yours.** Éstas son mis llaves y ésas son las vuestras.

**3** suyo (FEM suya) *(formal)*

> LANGUAGE TIP Use **suyo** in more formal situations with one person or a group of people, and remember to make it agree with the person or thing it describes. **suyo** is always used instead of **vuestro** in Latin America.

□ That's yours. Eso es suyo.

> LANGUAGE TIP Add the definite article when 'yours' means 'your one' or 'your ones'.

■ **I've lost my pen. Can I use yours?** He perdido el bolígrafo. ¿Puedo usar el suyo?
■ **These are my keys and those are yours.** Éstas son mis llaves y ésas son las suyas.
■ **Yours sincerely...** Le saluda atentamente...

y

**yourself** PRONOUN

> **LANGUAGE TIP** Use **te**, **tú mismo** and **ti mismo** when you are talking to someone of your own age or that you know well and **se** and **usted mismo** otherwise.

1 te *(reflexive)*
□ Have you hurt yourself? ¿Te has hecho daño?

2 tú mismo (FEM tú misma) *(for emphasis)*
□ Do it yourself! ¡Hazlo tú mismo!

3 ti mismo (FEM ti misma) *(after a preposition)*
□ You did it for yourself. Lo hiciste para ti mismo.

4 se *(reflexive)*
□ Have you hurt yourself? ¿Se ha hecho daño?

5 usted mismo (FEM usted misma) *(after a preposition, for emphasis)*
□ You did it for yourself. Lo hizo para usted mismo. □ Do it yourself! ¡Hágalo usted mismo!

**yourselves** PRONOUN

> **LANGUAGE TIP** In Spain use **os** and **vosotros mismos** when talking to people your own age or that you know well, and **se** or **ustedes mismos** otherwise. In Latin America **se** and **ustedes mismos** replace both **os** and **vosotros mismos**.

1 os *(reflexive)*
□ Did you enjoy yourselves? ¿Os divertisteis?

2 vosotros mismos (FEM vosotras mismas) *(after a preposition, for emphasis)*
□ Did you make it yourselves? ¿Lo habéis hecho vosotros mismos?

3 se *(reflexive)*
□ Did you enjoy yourselves? ¿Se divirtieron?

4 ustedes mismos (FEM ustedes mismas) *(after a preposition, for emphasis)*
□ Did you make it yourselves? ¿Lo han hecho ustedes mismos?

**youth club** NOUN
el club juvenil (PL los clubs juveniles)

**youth hostel** NOUN
el albergue juvenil

**Yugoslavia** NOUN
Yugoslavia *fem*
□ in the former Yugoslavia en la antigua Yugoslavia

# Zz

**zany** ADJECTIVE
estrafalario (FEM estrafalaria)

**zebra** NOUN
la cebra

**zebra crossing** NOUN
el paso de cebra

**zero** NOUN
el cero

**Zimbabwe** NOUN
Zimbabue *masc*

**Zimmer frame**® NOUN
el andador ortopédico

**zip** NOUN
la cremallera

**zip code** NOUN (US)
el código postal

**zipper** NOUN (US)
la cremallera

**zit** NOUN
el grano

**zodiac** NOUN
el zodíaco
▢ the signs of the zodiac  los signos del
zodíaco

**zone** NOUN
la zona

**zoo** NOUN
el zoo

**zoom lens** NOUN
el zoom

**zucchini** NOUN (US)
el calabacín (PL los calabacines)